A PICTURE HISTORY OF ART

WESTERN ART THROUGH THE AGES

Introductions by **Christopher Lloyd**

Compiled and edited by **Jenny Haviland**

Conceived and designed by **Elwyn Blacker**

Phaidon

PHAIDON PRESS LIMITED
Littlegate House, St Ebbe's Street, Oxford

Published in the United States of America by
E. P. DUTTON, New York

First published 1979 by Phaidon Press Limited

ISBN 7148 1910 7

Library of Congress Catalog Card Number: 78–20576

Photoset in England by Composing Operations Ltd.
Tunbridge Wells, Kent
Manufactured in Spain by Heraclio Fournier, S. A.
Vitoria

ACKNOWLEDGEMENTS

The publishers wish to thank museums, libraries, galleries, public and private foundations, and collectors who have kindly consented to the reproduction of works of art in their possession and acknowledge the copyrights held by SPADEM and ADAGP, Paris.

Part 4 Part 5 Part 6 Part 7 Part 8 Part 9 Part 10

ROMAN

SCAN

PERIOD

PTOLEMAIC

GOTHIC

BYZANTINE

EARLY CHRISTIAN

RENAISSANCE

NORMAN

MANNERISM
BAROQUE
ROCOCO
ROMANTICISM
NEO-CLASSICISM
PRE-RAPHAELITES
GOTHIC REVIVAL
SYMBOLISM
IMPRESSIONISM

ABSTRACT
FUTURISM
CONSTRUCTIVISM
BAUHAUS
DADA
SURREALISM
EXPRESSIONISM
OP ART
POP ART
PHOTO REALISM

BC AD

1,000

2,000

Alexander the Great

Pompeii destroyed

Christian Church established

Constantinople founded

Roman Empire falls

Viking invasions of Britain

Charlemagne first Holy Roman Emperor

First Crusade

Magna Carta

Ottomans take Constantinople

Columbus reaches America

Emperor Maximilian I

Declaration of Independence

French Revolution

First man on the Moon

1980

PHOTO-REALISM

POP ART

OP ART

ABSTRACT EXPRESSIONISM

SURREALISM

ABSTRACT

BAUHAUS

CONSTRUCTIVISM

FUTURISM

GOTHIC REVIVAL

PRE-RAPHAELITES

IMPRESSIONISM

SYMBOLISM

REALISM

CUBISM

DADA

NEO-CLASSICISM

REALISM

ROMANTICISM

1900

NEO-CLASSICISM

AMERICA

1800

1700

1600

1500

A PICTURE HISTORY OF

ART

WESTERN ART THROUGH THE AGES

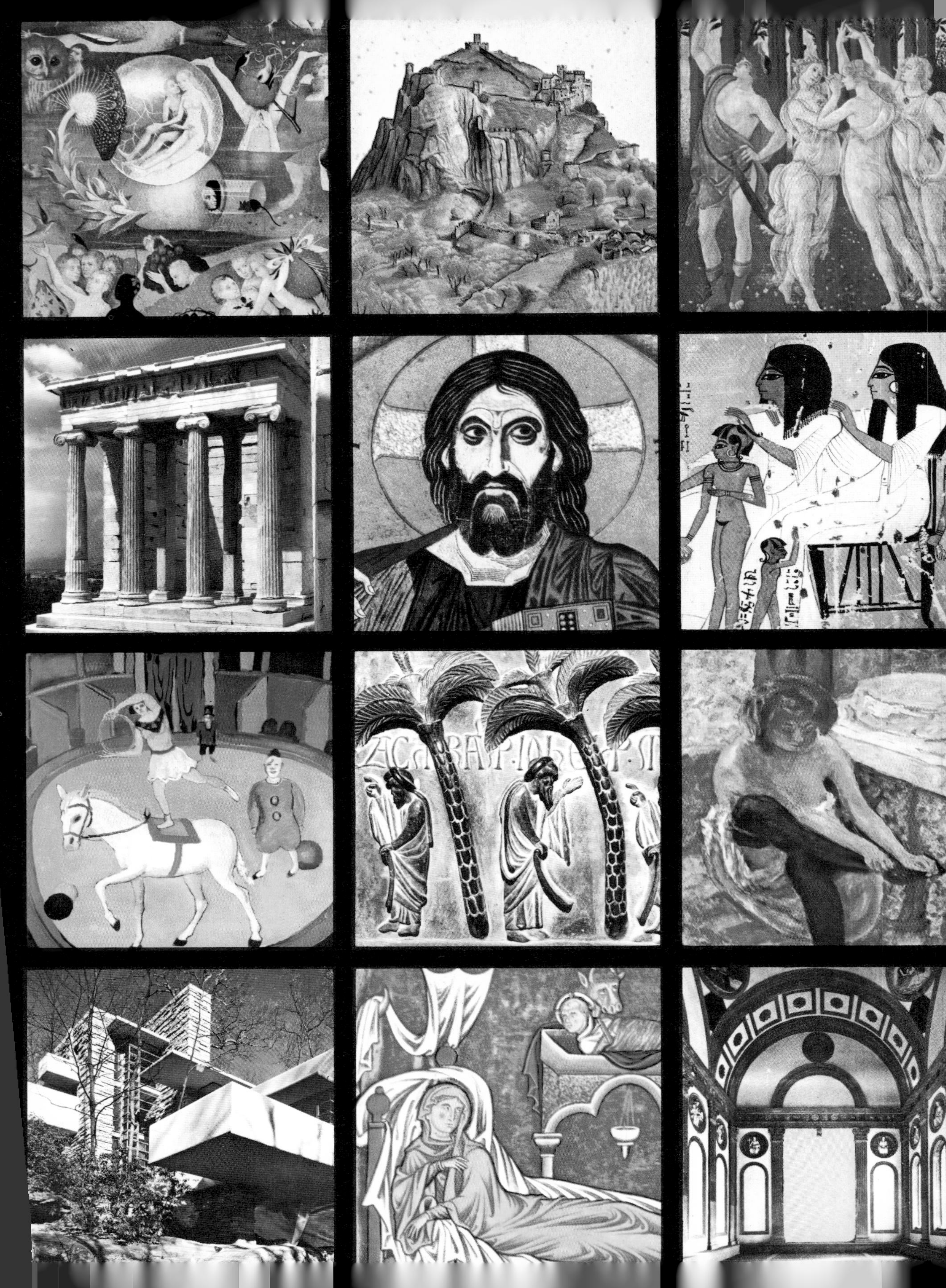

Contents

This illustrated handbook of art is, in essence, a personal museum of great works of Western painting, architecture and sculpture, from Palaeolithic times to the present. It is arranged chronologically and divided into ten periods, each with a brief introduction. The pages in any one period are identified by a coloured strip, enabling the reader to refer back to the relevant introduction.

At the end of the book there are Biographical notes (pages 307 to 315) on the artists illustrated and a Select bibliography (pages 316 and 317), which gives suggestions for further reading. A comprehensive view of the development of Western art through the ages is provided by the chart on the endpapers.

Introduction

nyone who looks at the pages of this visual lictionary in a purely perfunctory way will undoubtedly be impressed by the range of naterial. Here are illustrated buildings, pieces of sculpture, paintings, precious netals, tapestries, manuscripts: in short,

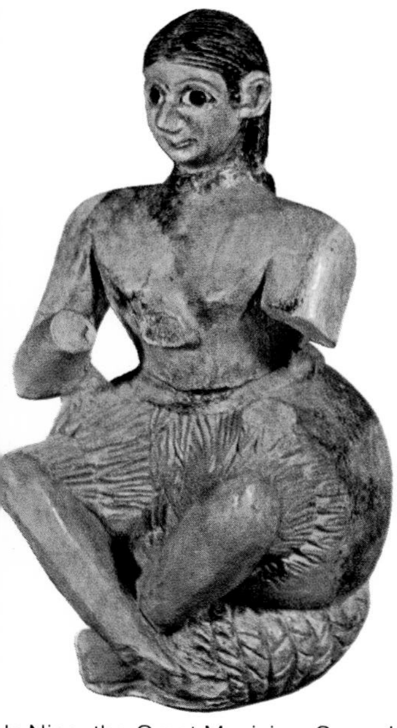

Jr-Nina, the Great Musician. Sumerian art, bout 3000–2500 BC. National Museum, Damascus

ne full panoply of Western art divided nto ten traditional sections. Some of the lustrations will be of objects or places well nown to the reader; others are perhaps ess celebrated. The panorama thus resented may be likened to one of ne great museums of the world, although

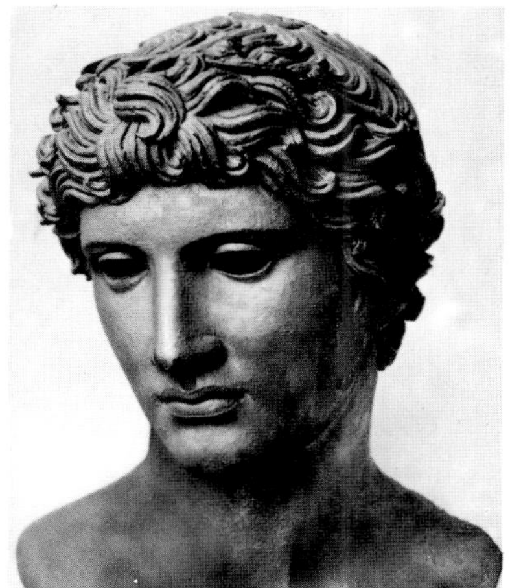

Head of an athlete. Bronze. Greek art, 450–400 BC. Louvre, Paris

of course no such museum could boast of the rich variety of material available here. André Malraux's concept of a 'museum without walls' is perhaps nowhere more applicable than it is in the present context, for the wide range of art provided in this book is an important part of the cultural heritage of the Western world to which we are all heirs and in which we should all be well versed. Although the selection of items illustrating the various epochs of Western art cannot be comprehensive, it is so arranged that anyone seeking information about a specific period will find those works of art that in one way or another typify it. In short, this visual dictionary aims for specificity of a general order rather than one of a particular kind. Its purpose is to provide information that is at once satisfying while

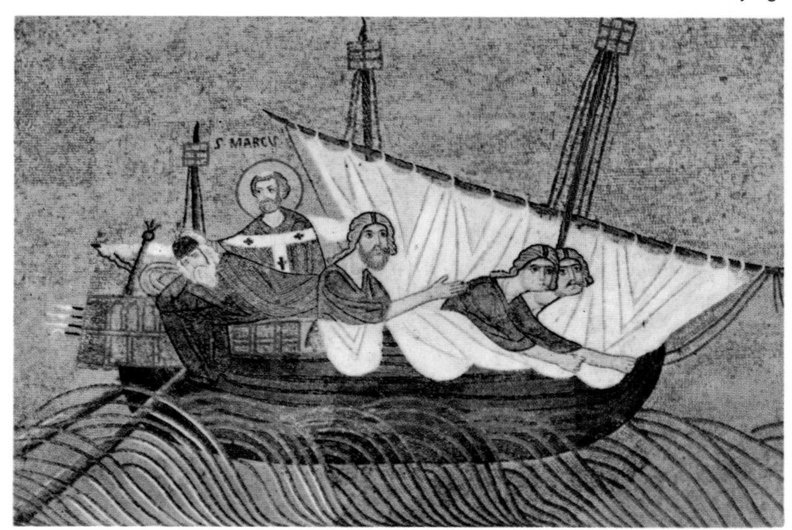

Above: *St Mark and the Boatman.* Mosaic. Byzantine art, 13th century. St Mark's, Venice

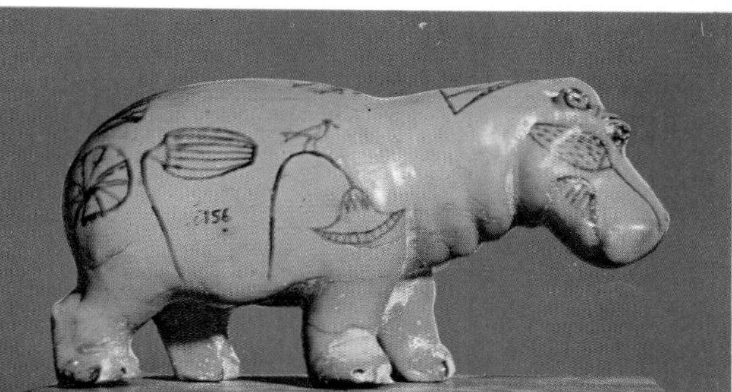

Left: Hippopotamus. Middle Kingdom. Egyptian Museum, Cairo

at the same time encouraging the reader to explore the subject in greater detail elsewhere.

A closer examination of this visual survey, however, does raise deeper issues. There is in the first place the interesting thought that, although these works of art may seem remarkably varied as finished images, their methods of preparation were severely limited. The physical properties of the available raw materials automatically reduce the number of possibilities open

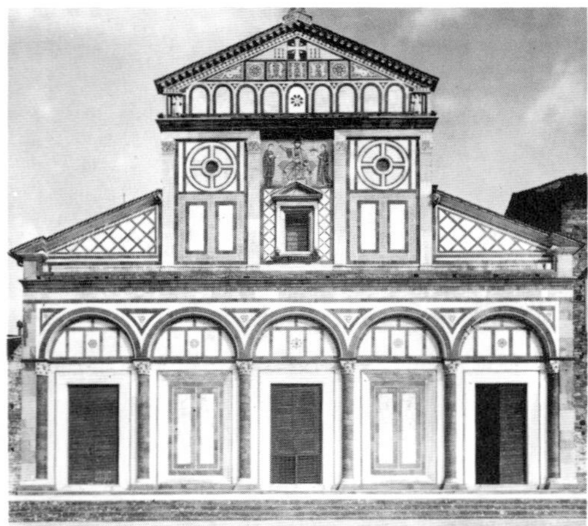

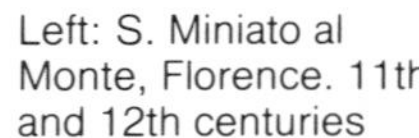

Left: S. Miniato al Monte, Florence. 11th and 12th centuries

Right: **Watteau:** *Meeting for the Hunt.* Detail. About 1720. Wallace Collection, London

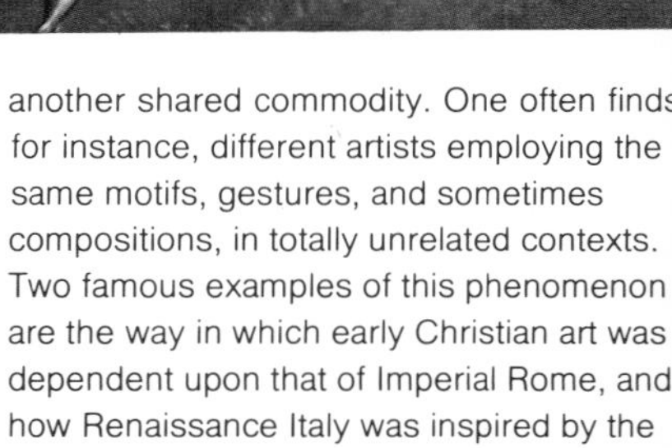

Below: *St Francis preaching to the Birds*. From the Chronicle of Matthew Paris. About 1255. Corpus Christi College, Cambridge

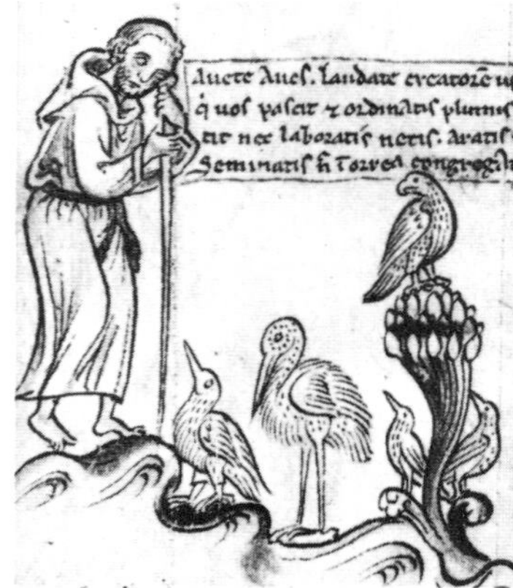

to the artist, and it is only with the development of new media that an artist can develop his work in fresh directions. Even with such materials to hand, though, the artists' control of line, colour, shape and mass is further limited by optical laws and psychological perception. Yet, regardless of these limitations, any number of combinations can be derived from them, and, indeed, it is for his creative ability in so manipulating them that an artist receives credit. The illustrations in this book do indeed attest the various levels of artistic creativity achieved by Western man, but even where one observes different forms of artistic expression in separate periods, iconography, or the heritage of images, emerges as another shared commodity. One often finds, for instance, different artists employing the same motifs, gestures, and sometimes compositions, in totally unrelated contexts. Two famous examples of this phenomenon are the way in which early Christian art was dependent upon that of Imperial Rome, and how Renaissance Italy was inspired by the classical past.

The acknowledgement of creative skills has always been a feature of Western society. Artists as individuals, or else their work, have always ultimately won acceptability whether official or otherwise. Yet, what binds the anonymous artist-craftsman of the earliest centuries to his much fêted counterpart in later periods, when greater emphasis was placed on the artist as an individual, is the influence his work had on his contemporaries. The work of the artist in primitive society was frequently associated with magic and often invested with similar properties. This has to some extent remained true even in more developed societies, so that when artists chose to depict the theme of the origin of painting, they illustrated the famous account – given amongst others by Pliny the Elder in his *Natural History* – of the painter tracing the outline of a figure from the shadow cast by the sunlight or by candlelight. Similarly, Leon Battista Alberti in fifteenth-century Italy identified the inventor of painting with Narcissus in that, like him, the artist attempted to capture the mirror image of real life. The same miraculous quality was thought to pertain to sculpture as well. Alberti, who enshrined so much of the classical tradition in his theoretical writings, again regarded Nature as the supreme sculptress because the clouds, the rocks and the action of water produce recognizable

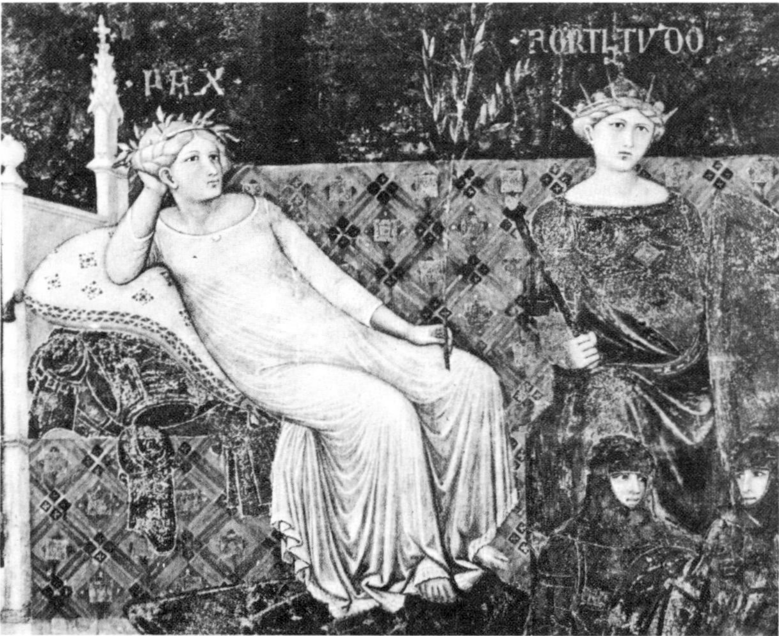

Ambrogio Lorenzetti: *Peace and Fortitude.* Detail from *Good Government.* About 1338–40. Palazzo Pubblico, Siena

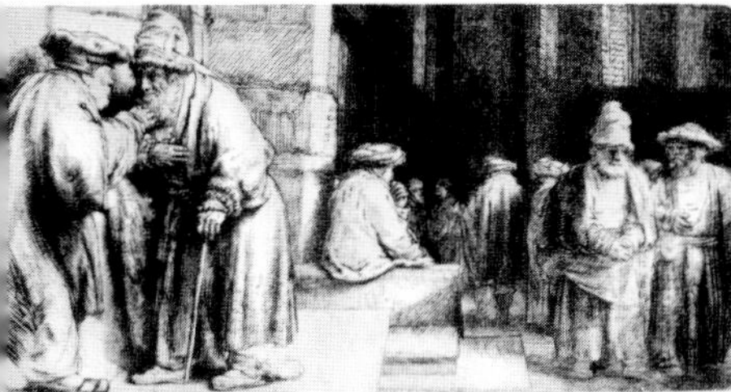

Above: **Rembrandt:** *The Synagogue.* Etching 1648. Rijksmuseum, Amsterdam

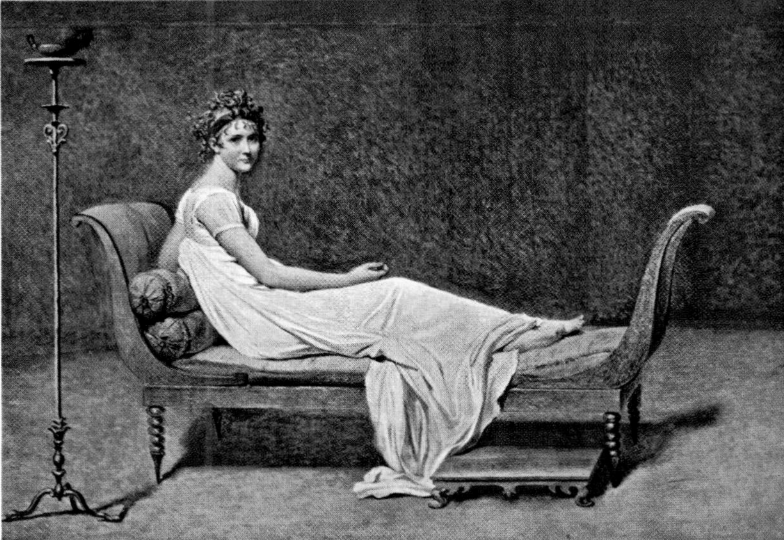

Right: **David:** *Madame Récamier.* 1800. Louvre, Paris

shapes. The skill of the artist lies in recognizing these shapes – 'images made by chance' – for what they are and in deploying his ability in imitating them, thus exercising both his imagination and his powers of imitation.

From such explanations for the origins of art it is only a short distance to the point where one can appreciate the power that the artist holds over the viewer by retaining the element of surprise, or of revelation, and by inspiring spontaneous and often intuitive responses. It is the chief characteristic of great art to evoke fresh and often totally divergent reactions from the viewer, but what is important is that before these comes the initial response. This may vary from sheer amazement at the precision with which the artist has been able to depict an object, to an acknowledgement of his prowess in transforming existing shapes or forms into others that are entirely new. The former category is well illustrated by the story, again recounted by Pliny the Elder, of a painting by the Greek painter Zeuxis of a bowl of fruit which was so faithfully rendered that the birds flew down and tried to settle on the grapes because they imagined they were real. How many of us have stood before a piece of statuary and imagined that it was living, or looked at a still life or flower painting with the impression that we could actually touch what we saw? The second category may be experienced when looking for instance at the work of Picasso, where we are forced to take a different view of the world about us, just as Stravinsky possessed the power to make us hear new sounds. Picasso's rendering of a bull's head using only the handle bars and seat of a bicycle is an admirable example of such a transformation.

It is perhaps because of the relationship between art and the numinous that works of art have been granted a talismanic quality. Today, unfortunately, this is all too readily translated into financial terms. Likewise, the concept of the museum has encouraged the viewer to contemplate works of art divorced from their original settings. Although this can only be beneficial for the survival of the works of art themselves, it tends to neuter them and to sap them of their visual potency. It should never be forgotten that artists reflect society and that to appreciate their work properly it has to be seen operating within a specific context. For prehistoric man art was a means of passing on information about methods of survival, but as he developed, so it gradually became a way of measuring improvements in his standard of living. Art also played an important role in the act of worship, whether in a pagan or a Christian society, whereas in secular terms art could be utilized as a political weapon, as a display of personal vanity, as a status symbol, or simply as an object of beauty in its own right. As the autonomy of the artist grew, however, so art came to be regarded as a vehicle of individual expression. Even if, overall, this narrowed down the scope of the artist's vision of society he, none the less, remained a reliable witness.

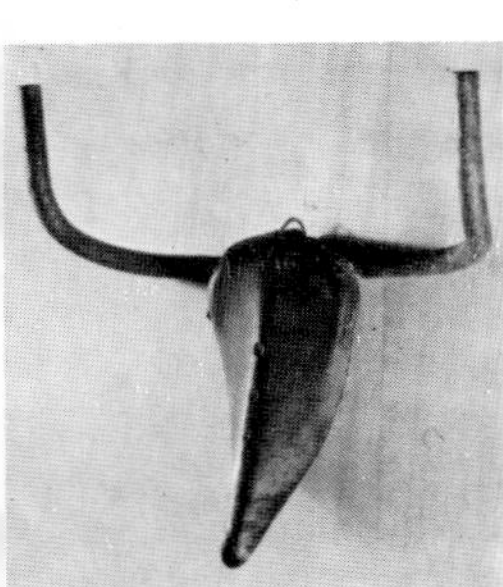

Left: **Picasso:** *Bull's Head.* Bronze. 1943

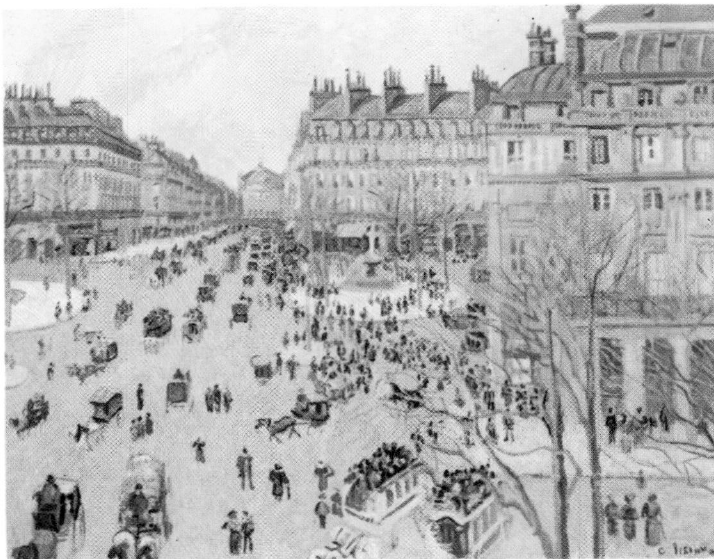

Right: **Pissarro:** *Avenue de l'Opéra.* 1898. National Museum, Belgrade

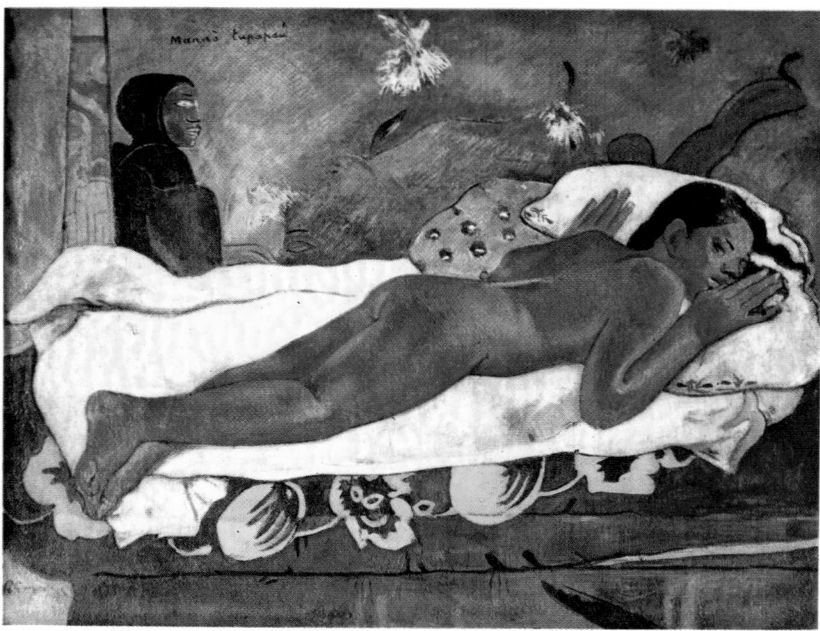

Gauguin: *Manao Tupapau.* 1892. Private Collection

Lastly, this visual dictionary attests the regenerative nature of art. For art it seems develops in an almost amoebic way, with each period seeking inspiration in those preceding it. The example of the Italian Renaissance constantly referring back to its classical forerunners, Greece and Rome, comes immediately to mind. The historicist inclinations of nineteenth-century artists are another occasion when pledges with earlier periods of art were renewed. Even the most revolutionary movements in art witnessed during our own century are not without their antecedents. The revival of interest in primitive art that began at the end of the nineteenth century and was sustained into the twentieth century was not simply an aesthetic exercise, but an attempt by artists to apply similar moral values, characterized by an implied innocence and simplicity, to their own work. Similarly, modern techniques in painting can be directly related to the theory propounded by Alberti and described as 'the spontaneous discovery of representational meanings in chance formations' already mentioned. A passage in Leonardo da Vinci's *Treatise on Painting* is perhaps a key to how we should approach modern art as a whole:

'I shall not fail to include among these precepts a new discovery, an aid to reflection which, although it seems a small thing and almost laughable, nevertheless is very useful in stimulating the mind to various discoveries. This is: look at a wall splashed with a number of stains or stones of various mixed colours. If you have to invent some scene, you can see there resemblances to a number of landscapes, adorned in various ways with mountains, rivers, rocks, trees, great plains, valleys, and hills. Moreover, you can see various battles, and rapid actions of figures, strange expressions on faces, costumes, and an infinite number of things, which you can reduce to good, integrated form. This happens thus on walls and varicoloured stones, as in the sound of bells, in whose pealing you can find every name and word you can imagine. Do not despise my opinion when I remind you that it should not be hard for you to stop sometimes and look into the stains of walls, or the ashes of a fire, or clouds, or mud, or like things, in which, if you consider them well, you will find really marvellous ideas.'

Thus are artistic expression and appreciation conjoined. The artist, by exercising his imagination, releases those who contemplate his work from the prison of their own mental straitjackets.

Malevich: *Suprematist Composition.* 1914–16. Stedelijk Museum, Amsterdam

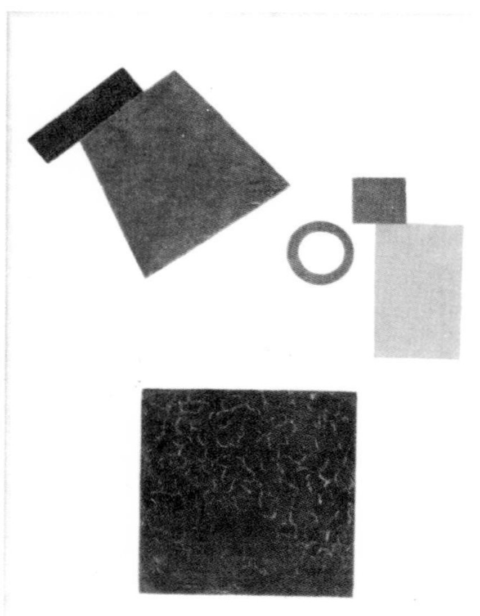

Nicholas de Staël: Agrigentum. 1954. Private Collection

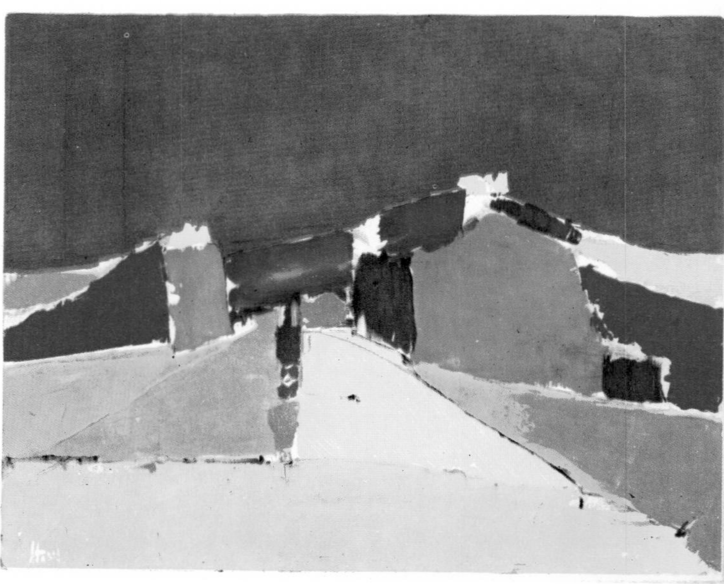

Part 1

Prehistoric Art

/ith the dawn of civilization, art finds its first xpression. The earliest paintings, like those n the walls of the caves at Lascaux, are of nimals. They are thus related specifically to ian's instinct for survival in the world, just as ie sculpted figurines of comparable date vere probably made to ensure fertility both of ie earth and of the body. It seems, therefore, iat at the outset the art of the Palaeolithic nd Mesolithic ages was associated with iagic, as, indeed, several centuries later it ecame linked with religion. Man immediately ecame aware that he was governed by forces ver which he could exercise little control, o that works of art, however primitive in esign, were created to serve as intercessors ith this as yet undefined power. Some tribal rt in Africa and Australia still retains these ame qualities today. With the end of the Ice ge, however, this kind of art disappeared, rimarily as a result of the spread of agriculture nd the establishment of permanent rchitecture. In the Neolithic Age new craft kills were evolved in relation to the evelopment of farming. Such works include veapons and tools made from stones, bones or wood. In Europe, especially in the south, fine examples of pottery have survived – mainly in the form of cult statuettes and models. Archaeology has shown that this is essentially the art of egalitarian societies maintaining basic skills in crafts flourishing in village communities.

During the Bronze and Iron Ages one encounters increasing sophistication. The products are the work of talented craftsmen capable of individual expression. Metal became the principal medium. Bronze was first of all used for fashioning weapons, but during the Iron Age it was reserved for finer objects, such as simple ornaments and jewellery. In this development there is a progression from art as a purely utilitarian exercise to art as decoration, in which changing styles, patterns and motifs can be observed. The Mediterranean appears to have been the most important source for the dissemination of motifs that were then adopted to form the basis of lively local styles of aristocratic ornament.

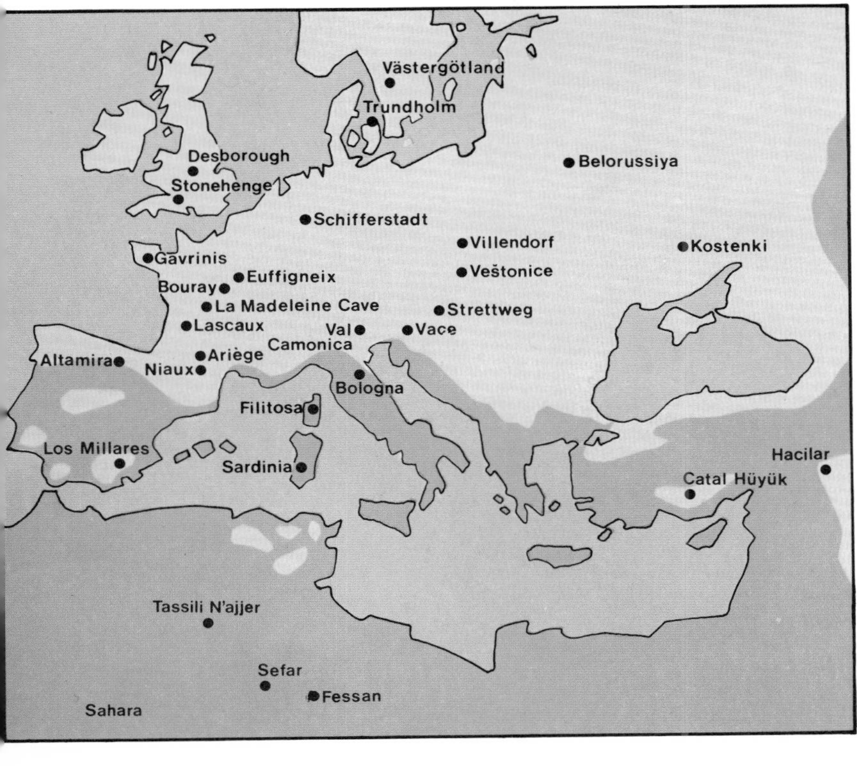

1. Silex hand tool. Middle Palaeolithic (Mousterian)
2. Frieze of horses. Lascaux cave, Dordogne, France. Palaeolithic (Perigordian)
3. Venus of Sireuil (Dordogne). Calcite. Palaeolithic (Gravettian). Musée des Antiquités Nationales, St-Germain-en-Laye
4. Deer. Lascaux cave, Dordogne, France. Palaeolithic (Perigordian)
5. Venus of Kostenki (Moravia). Mammoth ivory. Palaeolithic (Gravettian)
6. Venus of Veštonice (Moravia). Loess and powdered bone. Palaeolithic (Gravettian)
7. Venus of Willendorf (Austria). Limestone. Palaeolithic (end of Gravettian). Naturhistorisches Museum, Vienna
8. Cow. Lascaux cave, Dordogne, France. Palaeolithic (Perigordian)

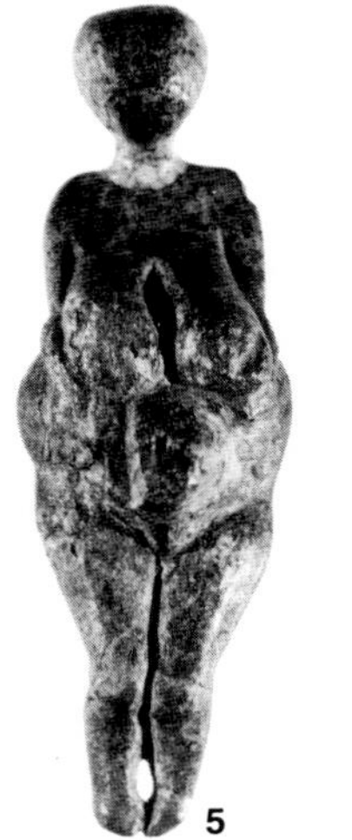
5

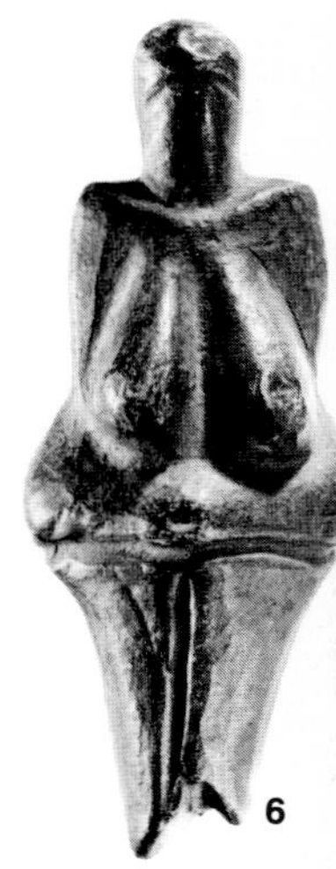
6

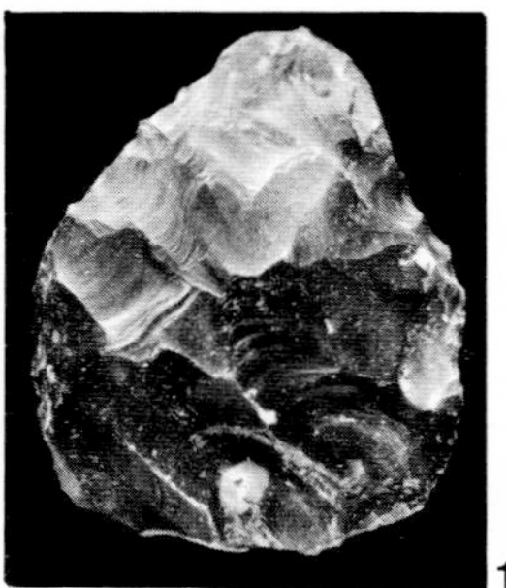
1

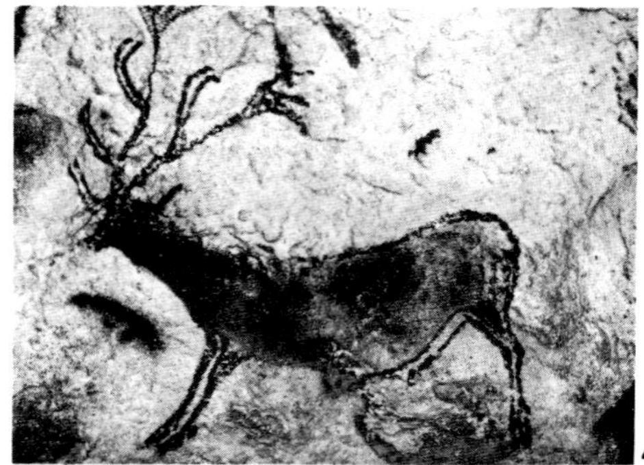
4

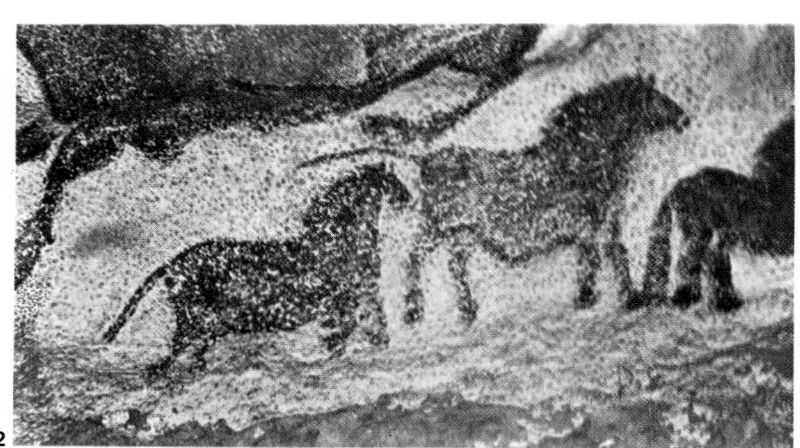
2

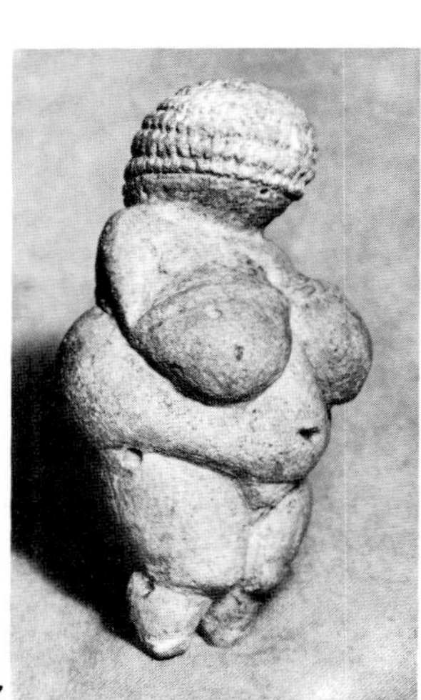
7

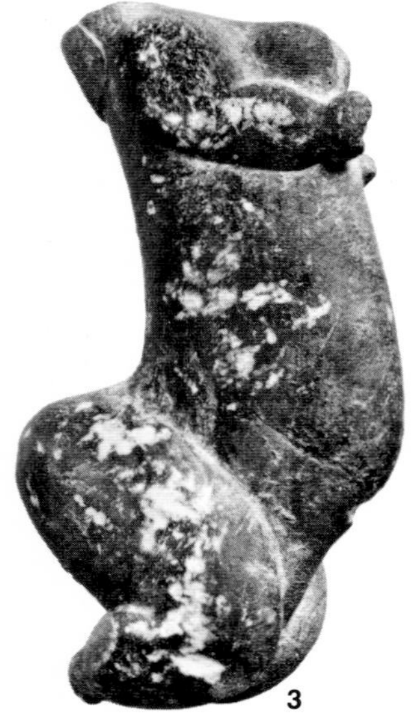
3

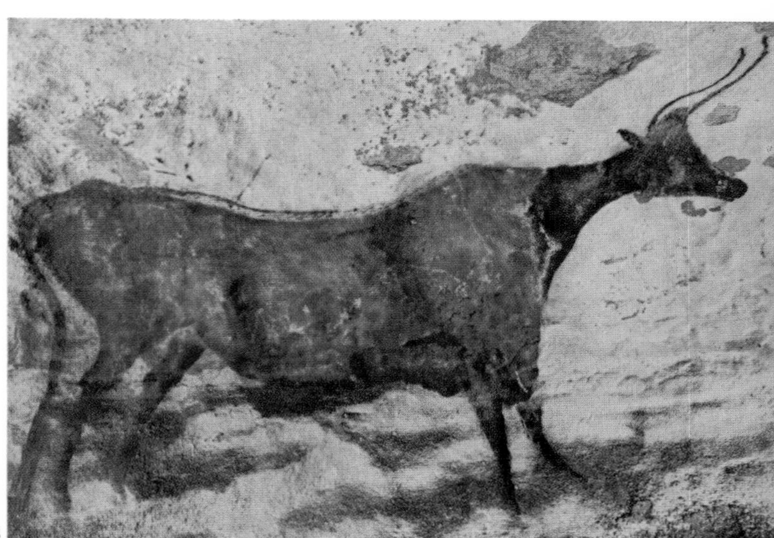
8

1. Wounded bison, traced in clay on the ground. Niaux cave, Ariège, France. Palaeolithic (Magdalenian)
2. Bison, painted and engraved. Niaux cave, Ariège, France. Palaeolithic (Magdalenian)
3. Horse. Mammoth ivory. Les Espeluges, Hautes-Pyrénées, France. Palaeolithic (Magdalenian). Musée des Antiquités Nationales, St-Germain-en-Laye
4. Two bison. Niaux cave, Dordogne, France. Palaeolithic (Magdalenian)
5. Pierced staff with bison head, carved from reindeer antler. Isturitz, Basses-Pyrénées, France. Palaeolithic (Magdalenian). Collection St-Perier
6. Bison. Ceiling of cave at Altamira, Spain. Palaeolithic (Magdalenian)
7. Hyena. Mammoth ivory. La Madeleine cave, Dordogne, France. Palaeolithic (Magdalenian). Musée des Antiquités Nationales, St-Germain-en-Laye
8. Silex scraper. Palaeolithic (Magdalenian)
9. Harpoon, carved from bone. Palaeolithic (Magdalenian)

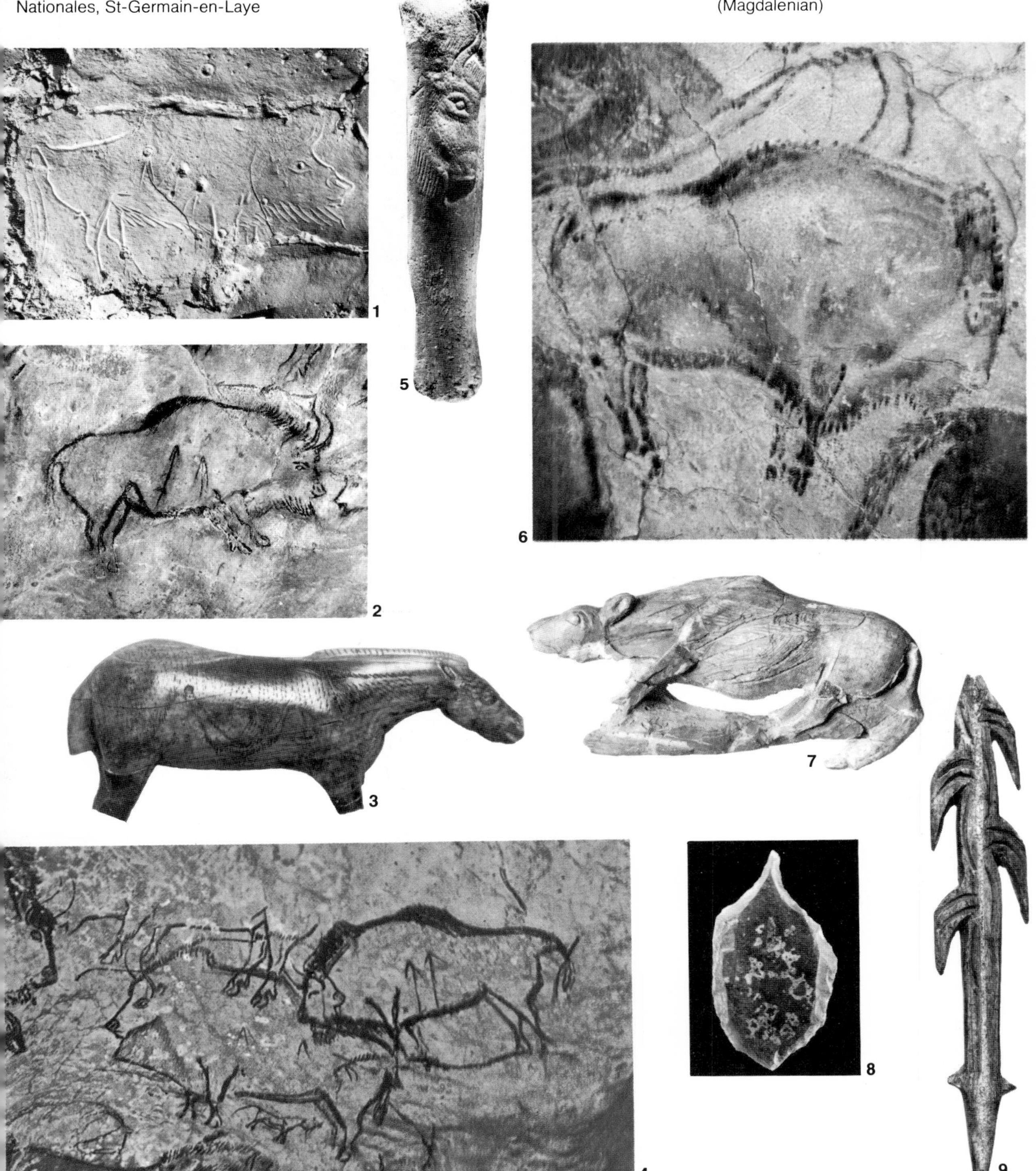

1. Sorcerer, painted black. Les Trois Frères cave, Ariège, France. Palaeolithic
2. Bull and hunters. Wall painting. Catal Hüyük, Turkey. Neolithic, about 5850 BC
3. Mound (model) at Los Millares, Spain. About 2000 BC. Museo Arqueológico, Barcelona
4. Painted pebble from Mas-d'Azil. Ariège. Mesolithic (Azilian). Musée des Antiquités Nationales, St-Germain-en-Laye
5. Human head, cut in amber. Västergötland, Sweden. Neolithic. Stadsmuseum, Stockholm
6. Human mask. Clay. Siberia. Neolithic. Academy of Sciences, Novosibirsk
7. Interior of tumulus at Gavrinis, Britanny. Neolithic, end of 3rd millennium BC
8. Fertility goddess. Clay. Hacilar, Turkey. Neolithic, 6th millennium. Archaeological Museum, Ankara

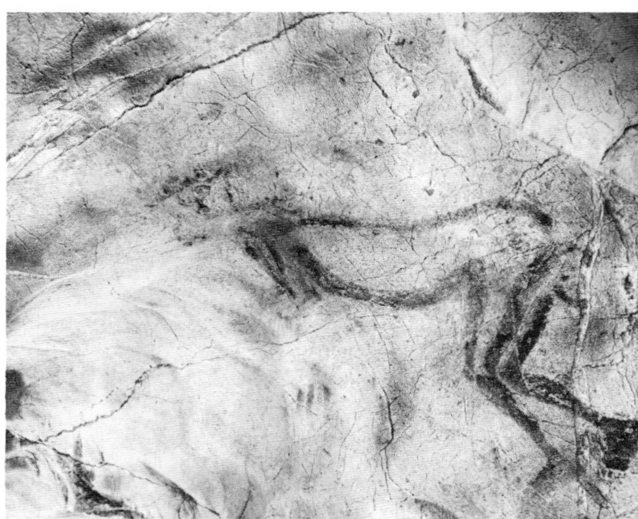
1

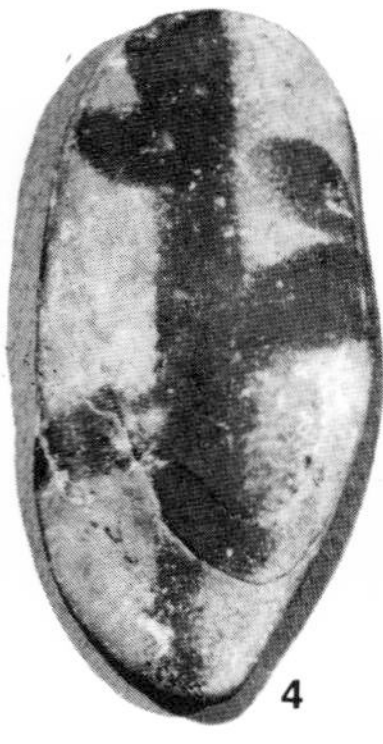
4

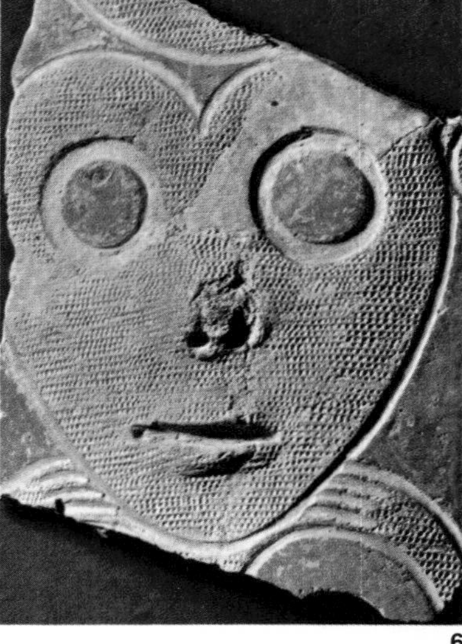
6

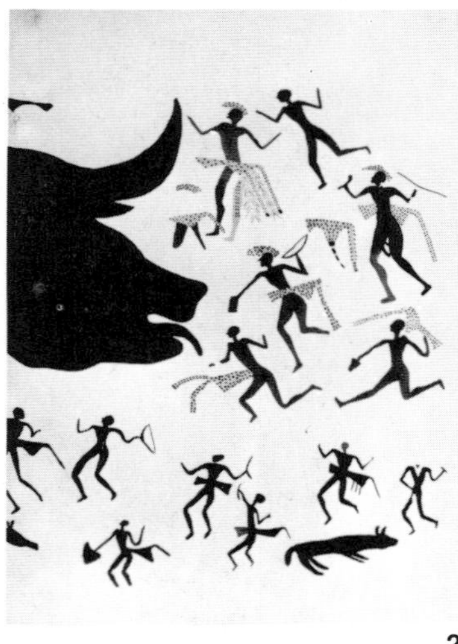
2

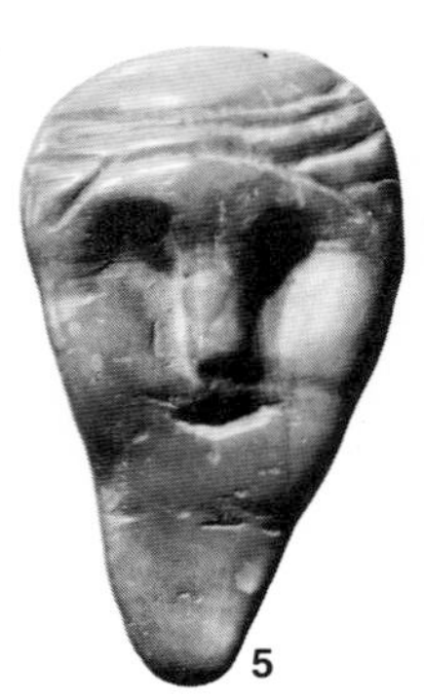
5

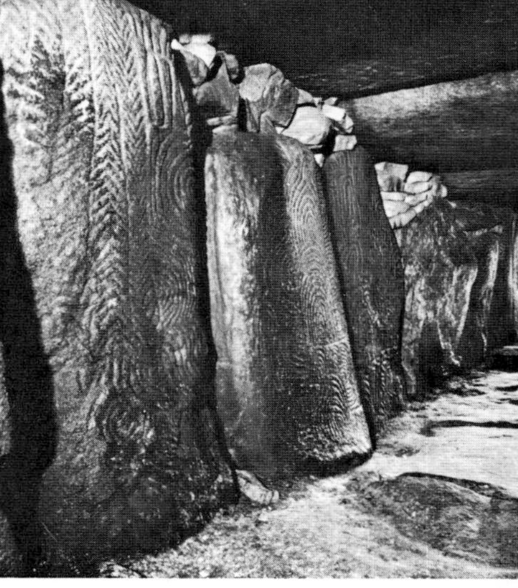
7

3

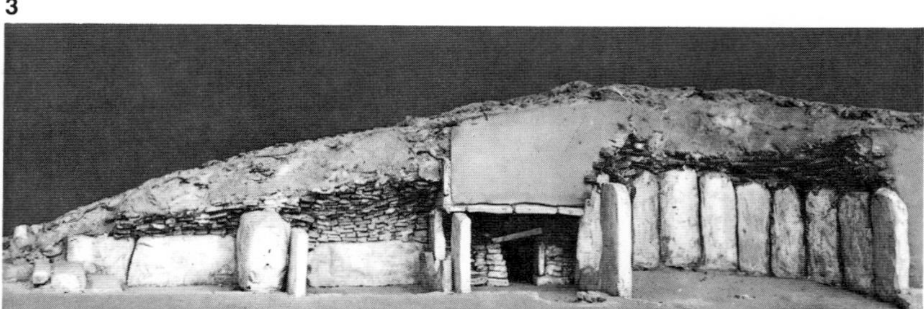

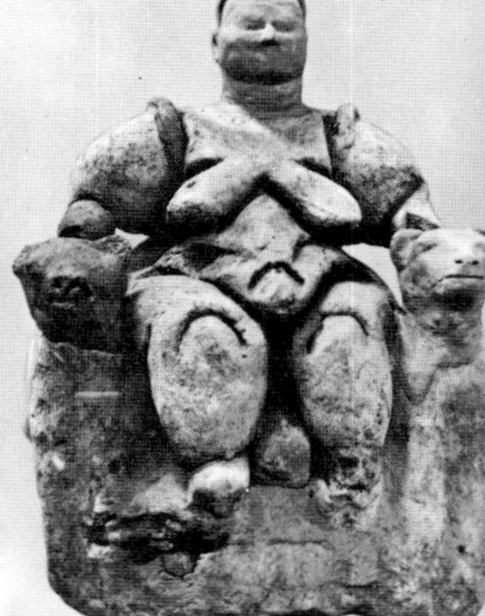
8

1. Menhir statue. Filitosa, Corsica. Neolithic, about 2000 BC
2. Cromlech at Stonehenge, Wiltshire, England. Neolithic, about 2000 BC
3. Female figure, painted on stone. Sefar, Tassili N'Ajjer, Sahara. Neolithic, about 3000 BC
4. Giraffes, engraved on stone. Oued Ajjal, Fessan, Libya. Neolithic
5. Cattle and herdsmen, painted on stone. Sefar, Tassili N'Ajjer, Sahara. Neolithic, about 3000 BC
6. Menhir statue of a woman. Sandstone. St-Sernin, France. Neolithic, about 2000 BC. Musée des Antiquités Nationales, St-Germain-en-Laye
7. Silex dagger. Hindsgavl, Denmark. Neolithic. Nationalmuseet, Copenhagen

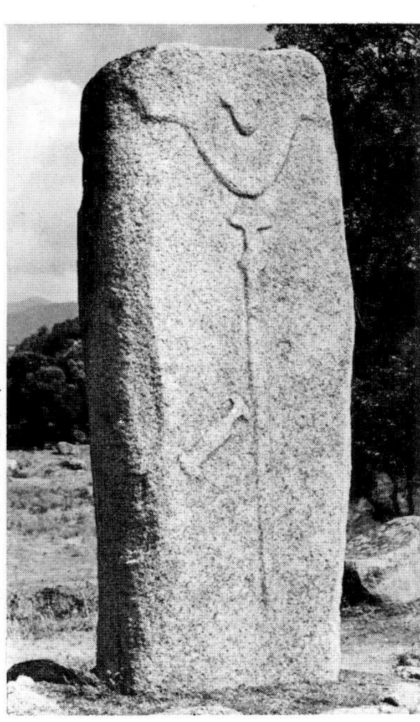
1

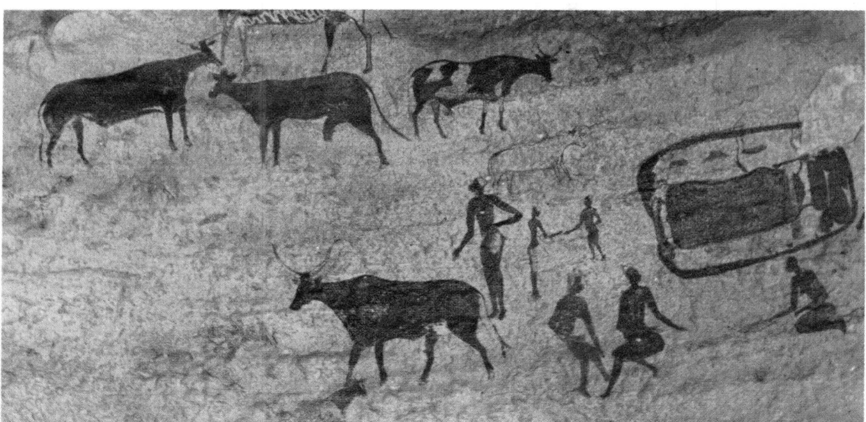
5

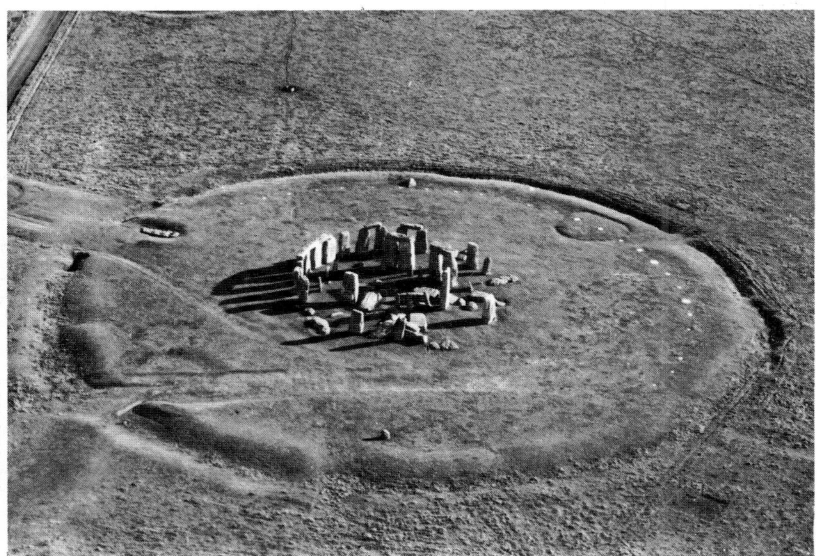
2

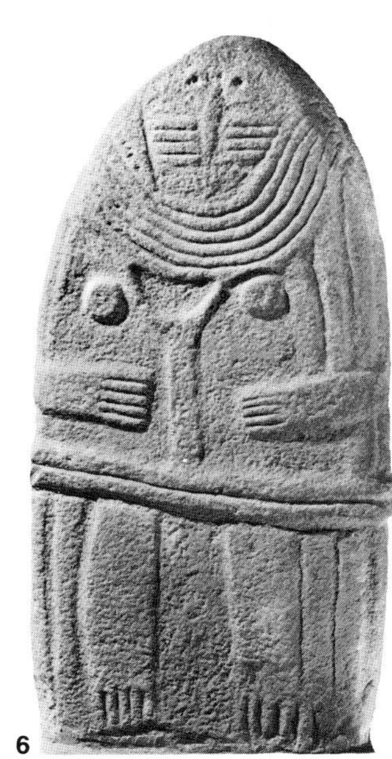
6

3
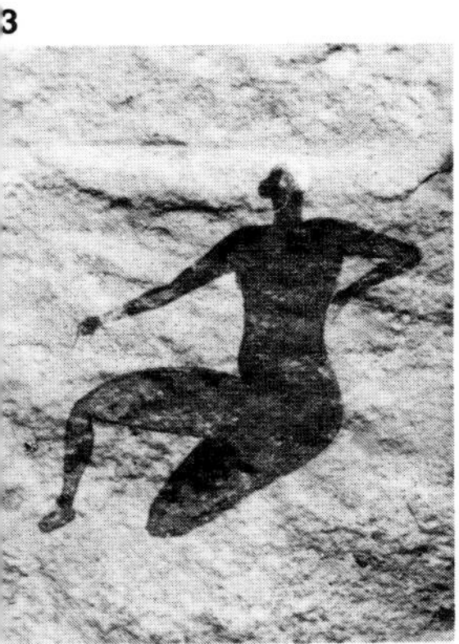

4
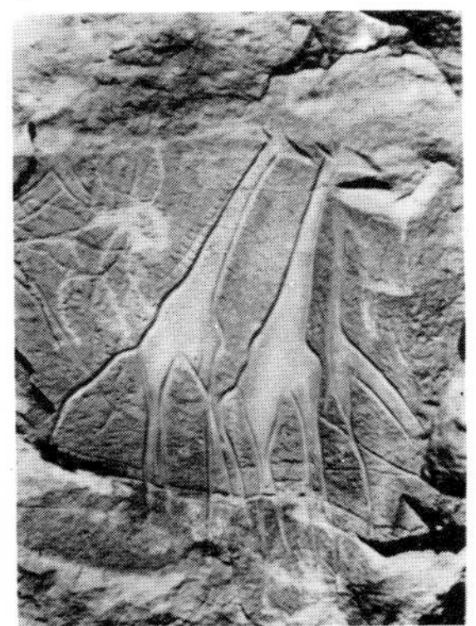

7
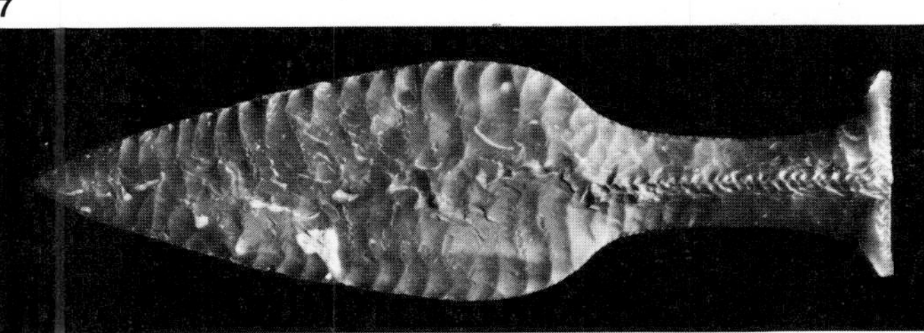

1. La Roche-aux-Fées. Dolmens in Ille-et-Vilaine. Bronze Age, about 1500 BC
2. Man building a chariot. Rock engraving. Val Camonica, Italy. 5th century BC
3. Pottery. Gomel', Belorussiya. Bronze Age, about 1500 BC. Gomel' Museum
4. Bark with stag's head on prow. Nuragic bronze. Bronze Age. Sardinia
5. Solar chariot. Bronze and laminated gold. Trundholm, Zealand, Denmark. About 14th century BC. Nationalmuseet, Copenhagen
6. Gold object. Schifferstadt, Germany. Bronze Age, end of 2nd millennium BC. Historisches Museum der Pfalz. Speyer
7. Bronze warrior. Sardinia. Bronze Age, 10th–5th century BC

6

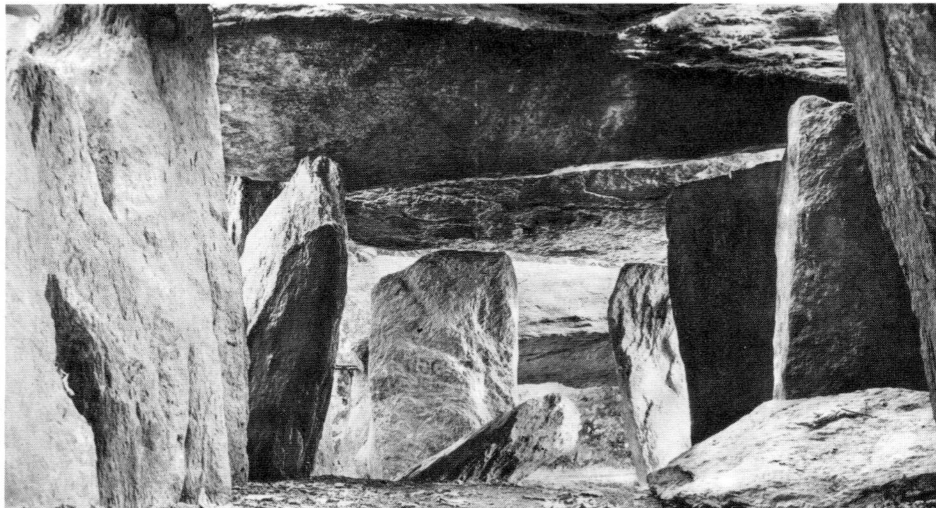

1

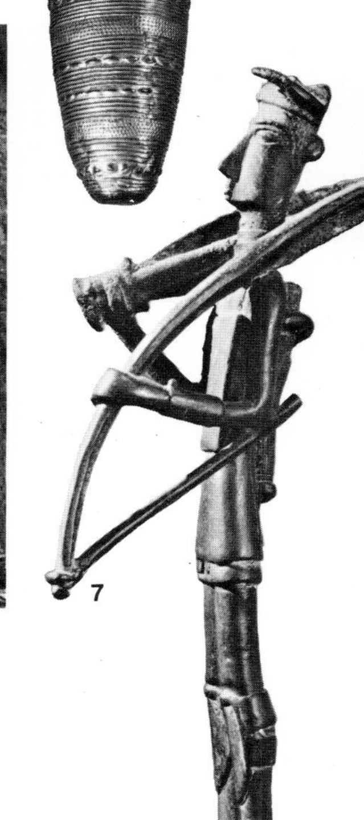

7

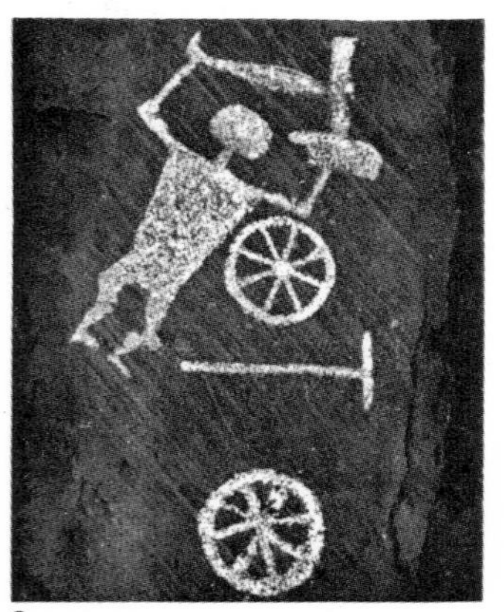

2

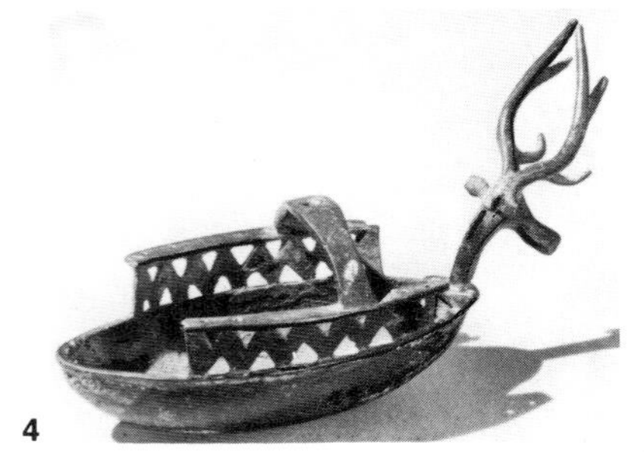

4

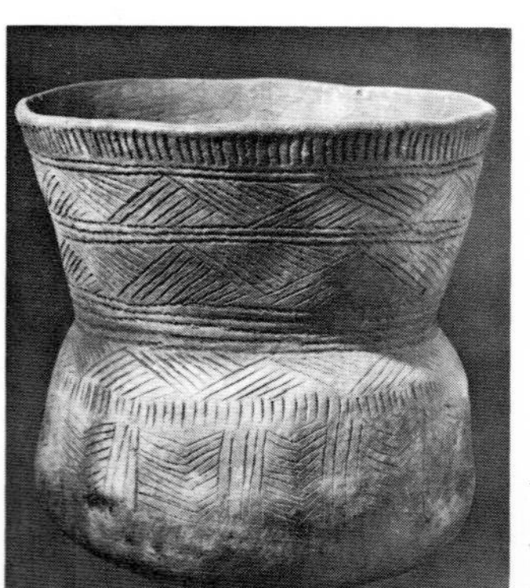

3

5

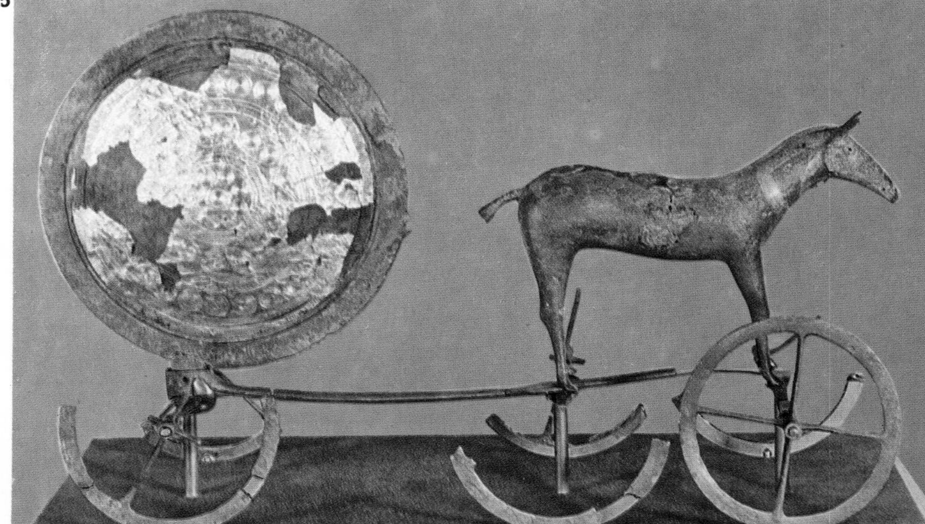

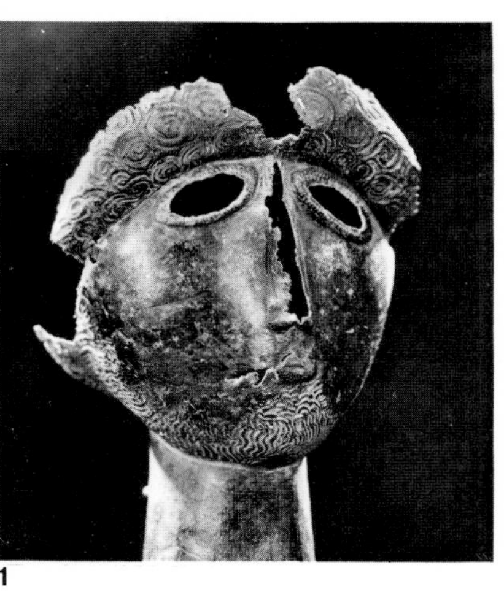
1

1. Divinity mask. Montousse, France. Iron Age, 3rd century BC. Musée Massey, Tarbes
2. War god. Nuragic bronze. Bronze Age. Sardinia
3. Bronze hydria. Detail. Graechwyl, Switzerland. Hallstatt period. Historisches Museum, Berne
4. Ritual chariot. Mérida, Spain. La Tène period, 1st century BC. Musée des Antiquités Nationales, St-Germain-en-Laye
5. Engraved bronze mirror. Desborough, England. La Tène period. British Museum
6. Clay idol. Klicevac, Yugoslavia. National Museum, Belgrade
7. Bronze disc. Ireland. La Tène period, 2nd century AD. British Museum, London
8. Hut. Rock engraving. Val Camonica, Italy. Iron Age
9. Limestone boar-god. Euffigneix, France. La Tène period, 3rd century BC. Musée d'Art et d'Histoire, Chaumont, France

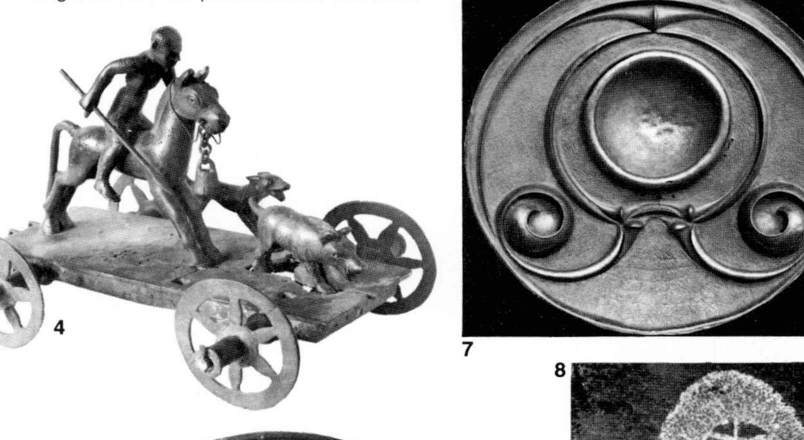
4

7

8

2

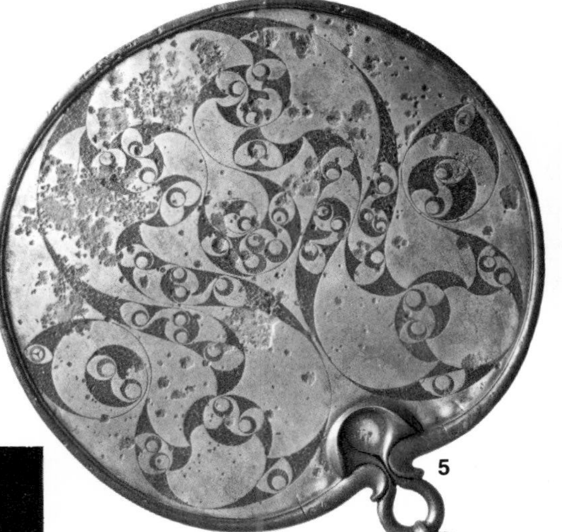
5

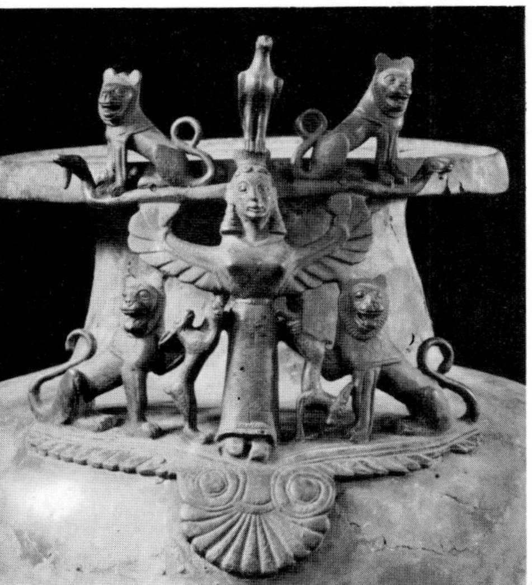
3

6

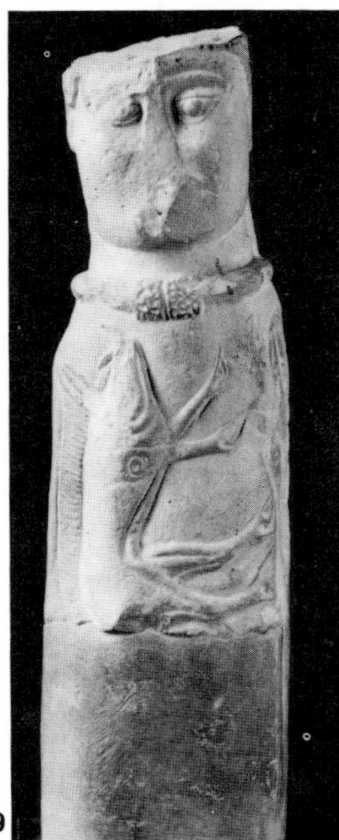
9

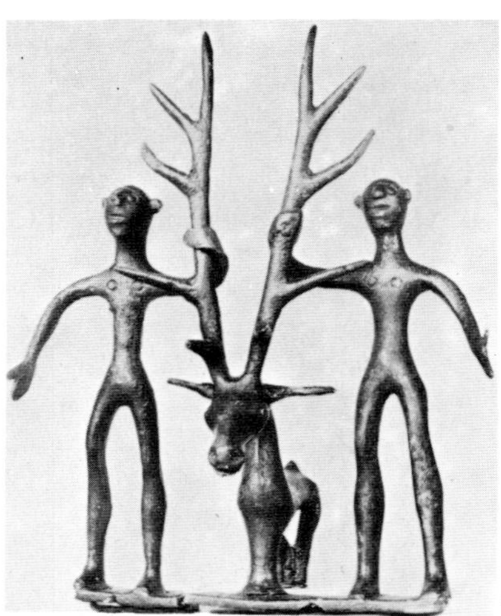

1

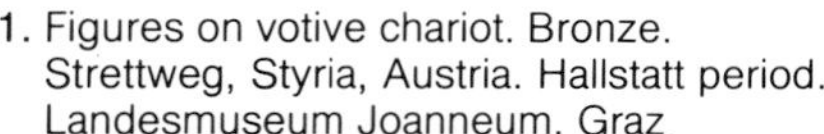

1. Figures on votive chariot. Bronze. Strettweg, Styria, Austria. Hallstatt period. Landesmuseum Joanneum, Graz
2. Gold diadem (detail) from the Vix treasure. Hallstatt period, 6th century BC. Musée Archéologique, Châtillon-sur-Seine, France
3. Bronze shield. River Thames, London. 1st century BC. British Museum, London
4. Situla from Vače, Yugoslavia. Hallstatt period. National Museum, Ljubljana
5. Bronze belt. Benacci tomb, Bologna. Villanovan culture. Iron Age. Museo Civico Bologna
6. Fragment of bronze cup from Törvegraving, Denmark. La Tène period. Nationalmuseet, Copenhagen
7. Bust of a god from Bouray. Beaten sheet bronze. 3rd–1st century BC. Musée des Antiquités Nationales, St-Germain-en-Laye

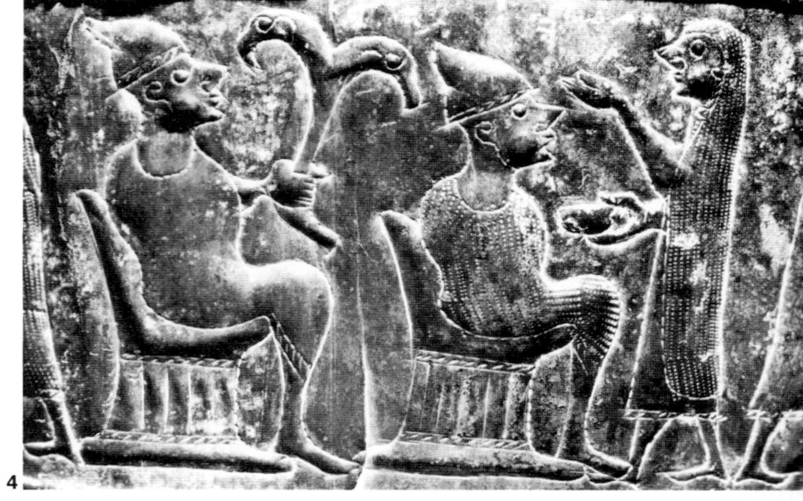

4

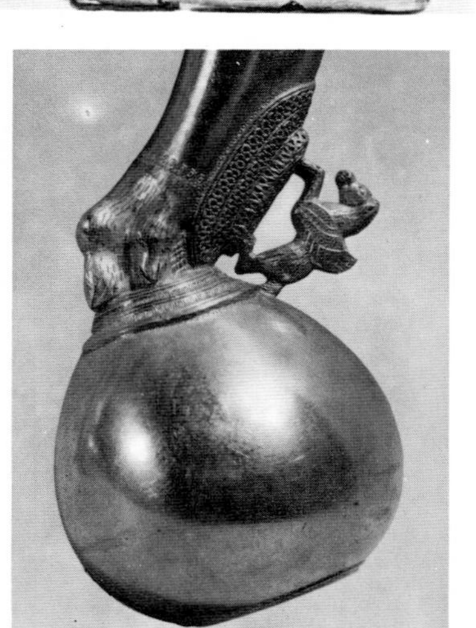

2

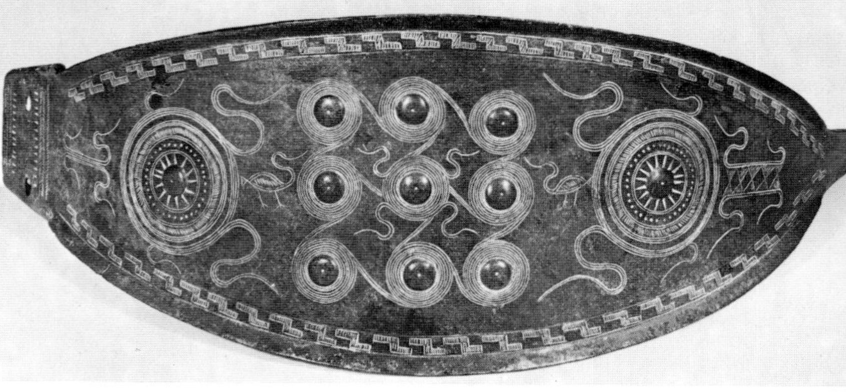

5

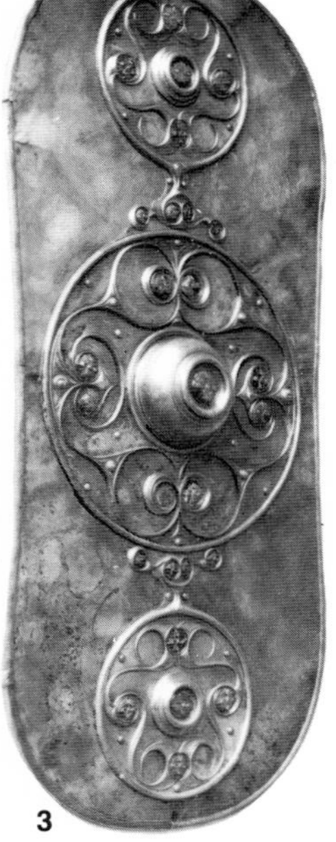

3

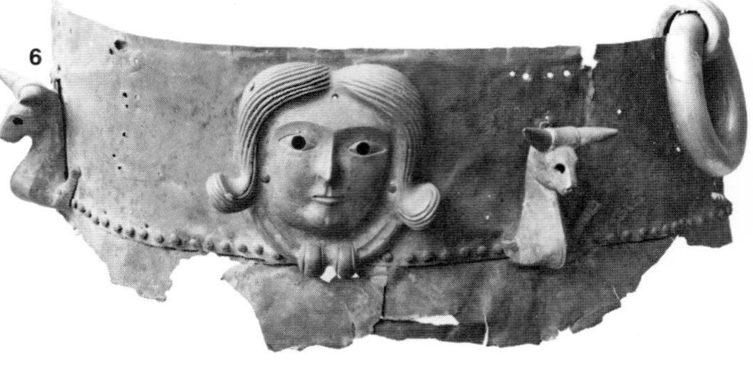

6

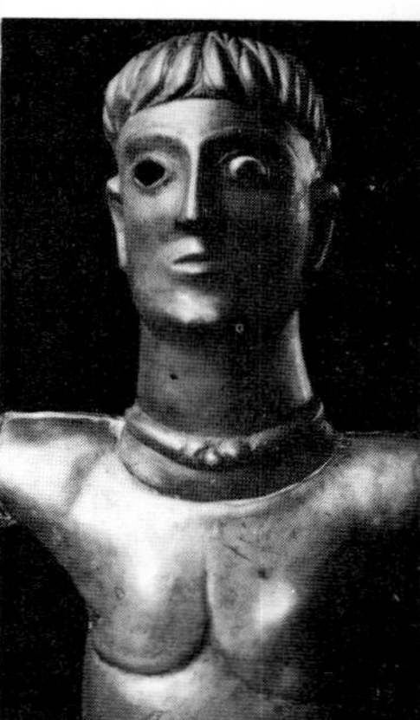

7

Part 2

The Ancient World

gyptian art is a comparatively self-contained henomenon. Ancient Egypt may be roughly efined as the cultivated valley of the Nile retching northwards from modern Aswan to airo, where the river fans out towards the elta – the whole distance amounting to some 50 miles. The Nile valley provided a wide rip of fertile land, forming a stark contrast 'th the dry desert on either side. Ancient gypt was therefore self-sufficient and hysically isolated. Trade was stimulated not much by necessity but, rather, by the esire felt by an increasingly sophisticated ociety for luxury goods. Geographical factors ave also influenced our knowledge of the t of Egypt: archaeologically the dry desert ands have preserved graves and temples xceptionally well, whereas the moisture has estroyed the human settlements in the alley. The isolation of Egypt persisted until e final dynasties, when the country was ccupied by the Persians and was then rongly influenced by the Greeks and omans. Egypt further lost some of its self-entification when Christianity was established the form of the Coptic Church, whose main ontribution to religion was the growth of onasticism.

The evolution of Egyptian art, including the ehistoric age, took place over some five ousand years. Prehistoric, or pre-dynastic, gyptian art was the work of settled ommunities dependent solely upon griculture, fishing and hunting. Products clude basket work and coarse pottery with decoration. The use of metals, an increasing ense of urbanization, and the evelopment of technical skills mark the end f the prehistoric period. Egyptian history is onventionally divided into Old Kingdom, iddle Kingdom, New Kingdom and the Late Period. The first pyramids were the creation of the Old Kingdom. The Middle Kingdom saw the stabilization of the language and literature of Egypt. The New Kingdom witnessed perhaps the greatest period of building in Egypt with the famous temples at Karnak and Luxor, and the royal tombs in the Valley of the Kings at Thebes.

One of the most important factors in the development of Egyptian art was the attitude to religion, and particularly to death. A multiplicity of deities was worshipped, each represented visually by a symbol, often in animal form. Human beings could also be deified. The Egyptian attitude to death was chiefly characterized by the refusal to accept its finality. Thus, there was the need to preserve the body and to provide it with essentials for survival in the after-life. Such aids included food, drink, and models representing servants. It was only during the New Kingdom, however, that the process of mummification was properly understood. Such religious customs gave Egyptian art a ritualistic quality.

The range and scale of objects surviving from Ancient Egypt is extensive: architecture in the forms of temples and tombs, sculpture of various categories, extending from the monumental to wooden models, painting in fresco and also on panel (usually portraits attached to mummies), pottery, glass, metalwork, weaving, leatherwork and, of great importance, the papyri. Our knowledge of Ancient Egypt is to a large extent derived from the inscriptions and reliefs found upon many of these works of art. The style of the figures, whether in two or three-dimensional forms, is hieratic as a result of the application of a standard geometrical grid pattern used for carving or drawing the human figure.

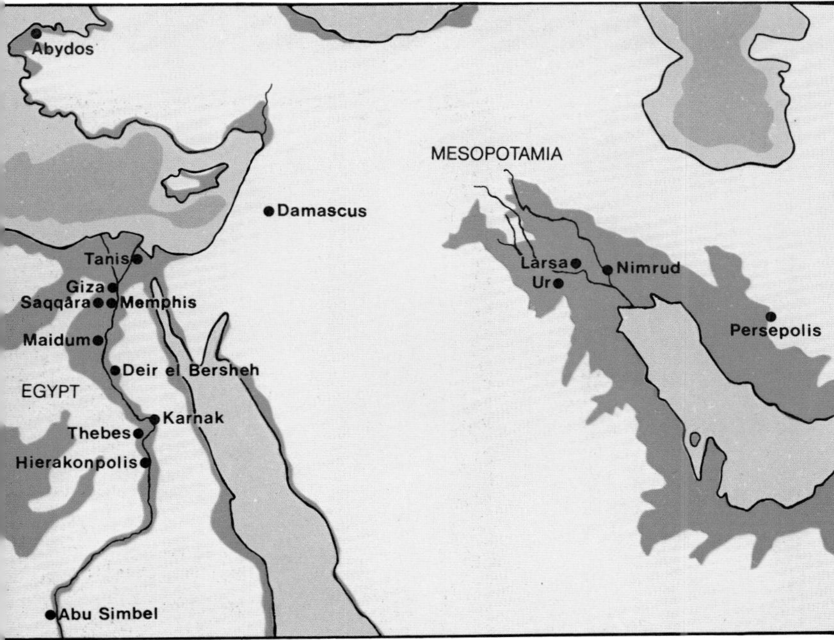

1. The Standard of Ur with scene of victory celebration. Royal tombs at Ur. Mosaic of shells, lapis lazuli and red limestone. Sumerian, 3000–2500 BC. British Museum
2. Terracotta lion head. Aqar Quf (Iraq). Kassite, 14th century BC. Iraq Museum, Baghdad
3. Bronze lion with limestone tablet. Hurrite, late 3rd millennium BC. Louvre, Paris
4. Relief from staircase at Persepolis. Achaemenian, 6th–5th century BC
5. Kneeling man. Bronze and gold. Larsa (Iraq). Babylonian, 18th century BC. Louvre, Paris
6. Cylinder-seal of Sharkalisharri. Jasper. Akkadian, 2500–2000 BC. Collection De Clercq, Paris
7. Hazael, king of Damascus. Ivory. Palace at Hadatu, Damascus. Aramaean, 9th century BC. Louvre, Paris
8. 'Mona Lisa' mask. Ivory. Nimrud. Assyrian, 8th century BC. Iraq Museum, Baghdad

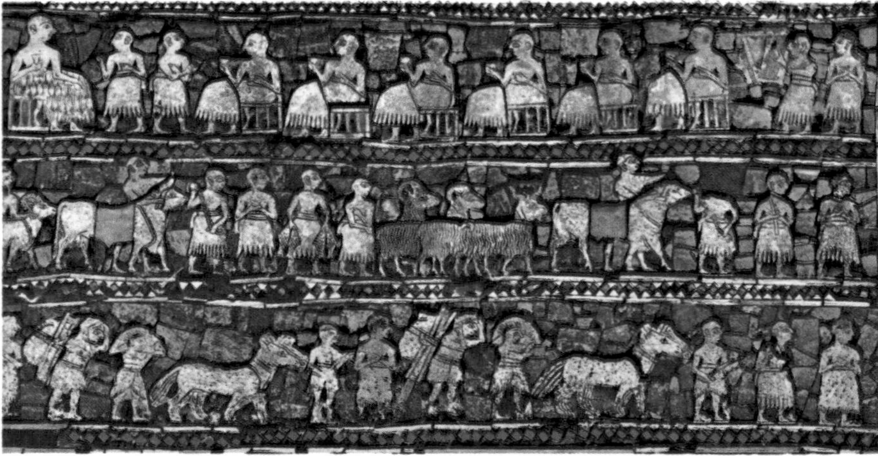
1

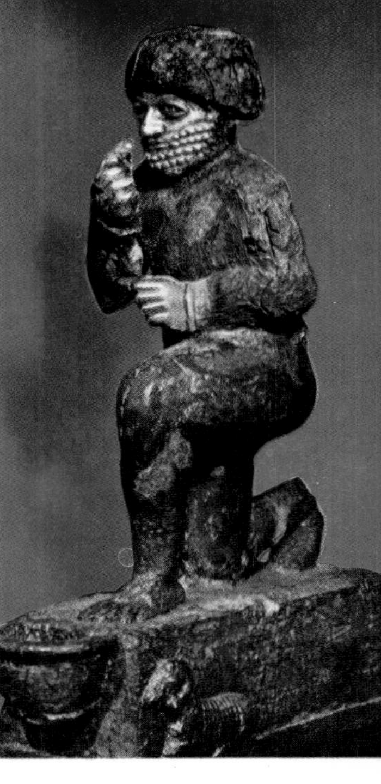

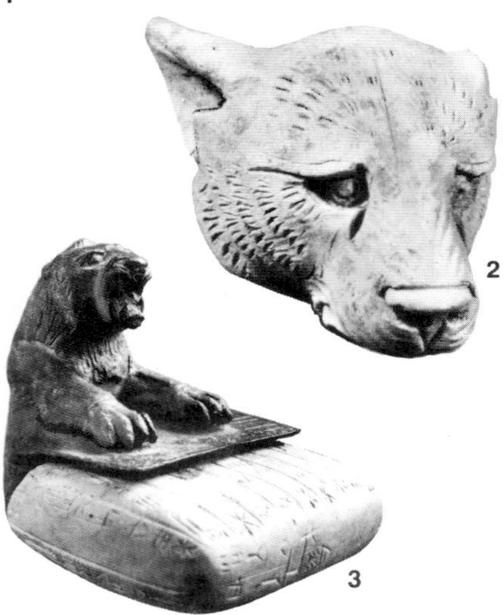
2

3

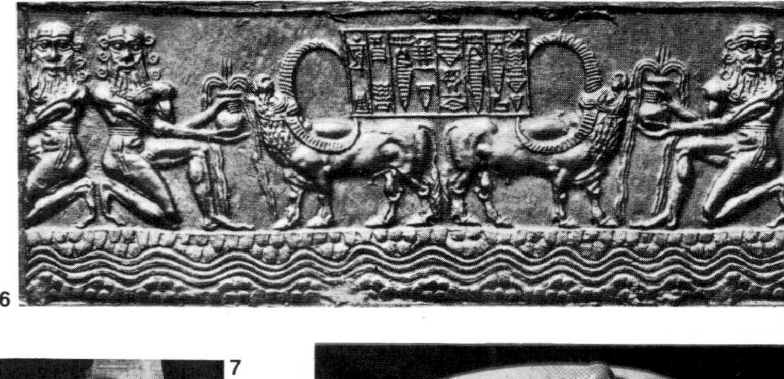
6

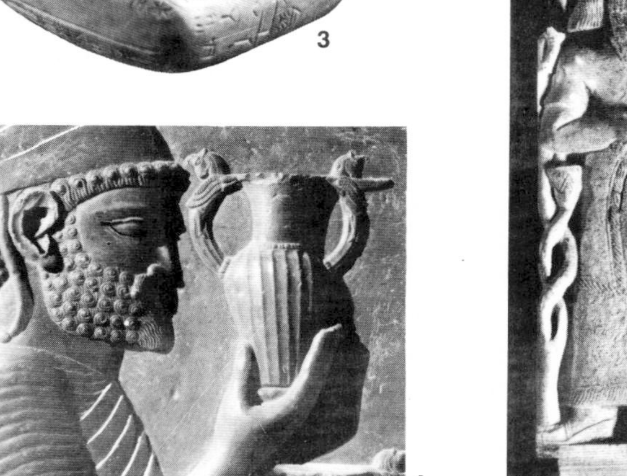
4

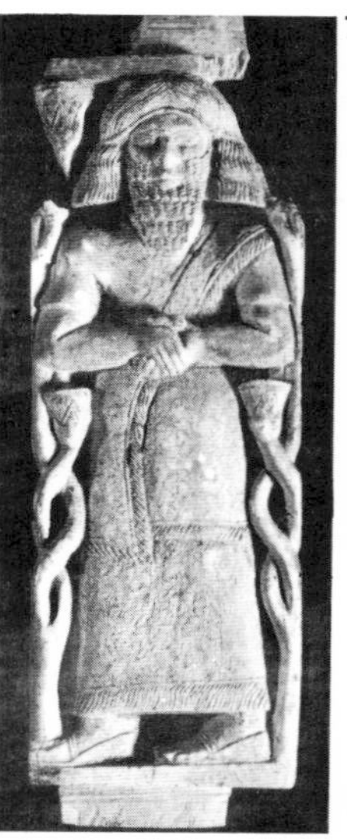
7

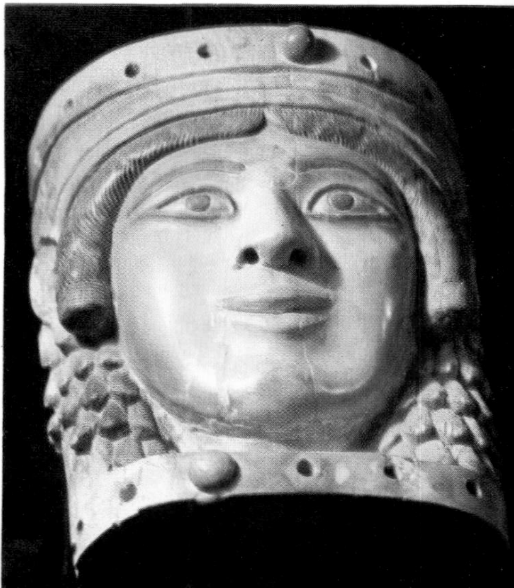
8

1. Magic figurine. Terracotta. Prehistoric. Brooklyn Museum, New York
2. Painted palette with animals of the steppes and fantastic beasts. Schist. Prehistoric. Ashmolean Museum, Oxford
3. Chest. Painted clay. On short side: ship; on long side: gazelles or giraffes. Gerzean ceramic. Prehistoric. British Museum
4. Cynocephalus. Clay. Hierakonpolis. Thinite period. Kestner-Museum, Hanover
5. Hippopotamus. Alabaster. Thinite period. Ny Carlsberg Glyptotek, Copenhagen
6. Stele of the Serpent King. Limestone. Abydos. Thinite period. Louvre, Paris

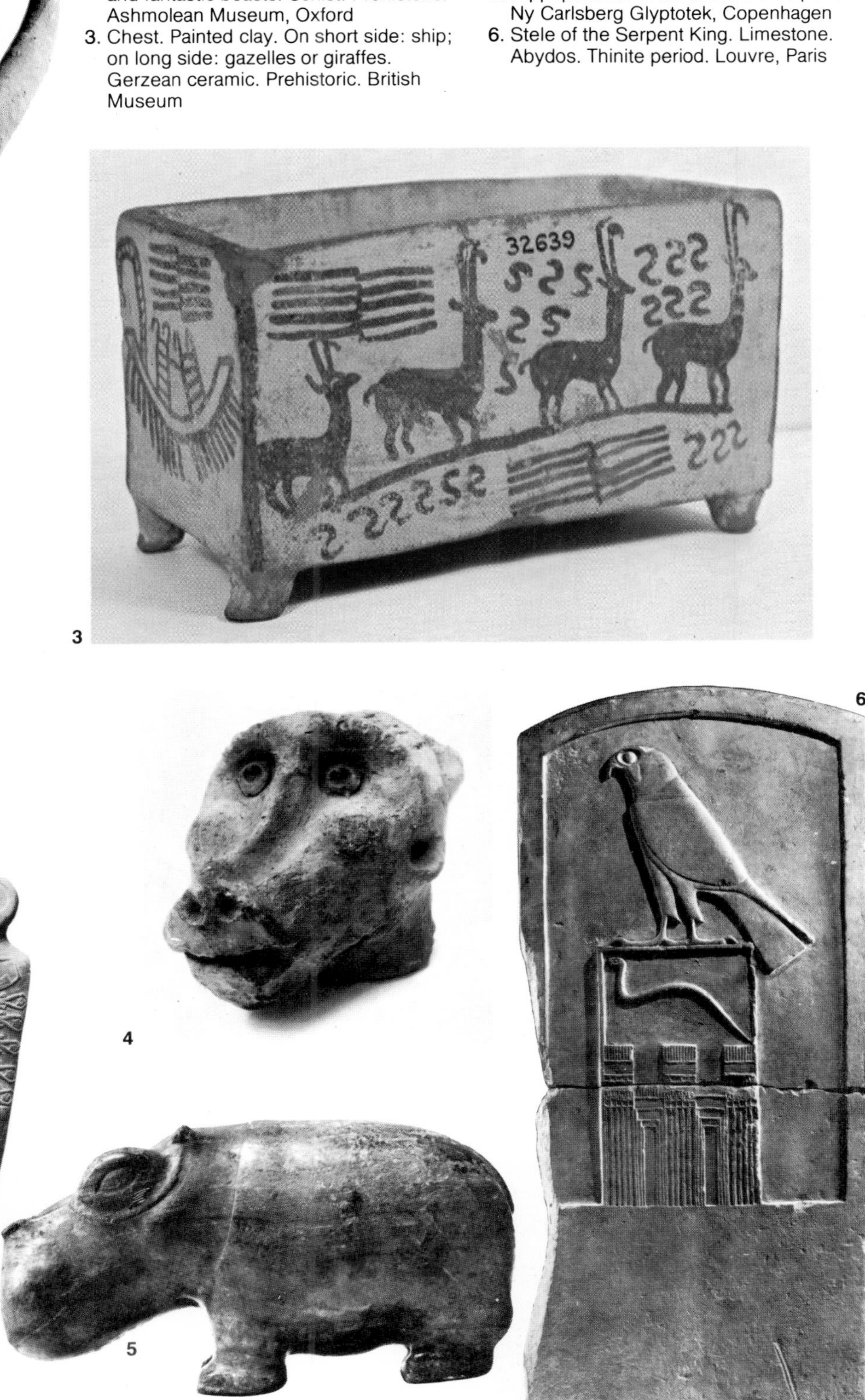

1. Geese. Painting on plaster. Detail. Mastaba of Nefermaat and Atet, Maidum. 4th Dynasty. Cairo Museum
2. Bas-relief of Akhoutaa. Limestone. 4th Dynasty. Louvre, Paris
3. Seated scribe. Painted limestone. Saqqâra. Early 5th Dynasty. Cairo Museum
4. Reserve head from Tomb of high official. Limestone. Giza. 4th Dynasty. Cairo Museum
5. Drovers and cattle crossing ford in Nile marshes. Carved and painted limestone relief. Tomb of Ti, Saqqâra. 5th Dynasty
6. Step pyramid of King Snofru at Maidum. Early 4th Dynasty
7. Hesire, a leading official under King Zoser, at the offering table. Detail of wooden relief from the mastaba of Hesire, Saqqâra. Cairo Museum

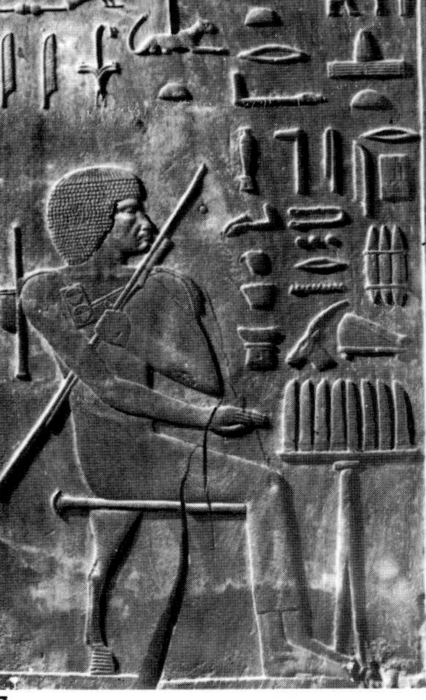

7

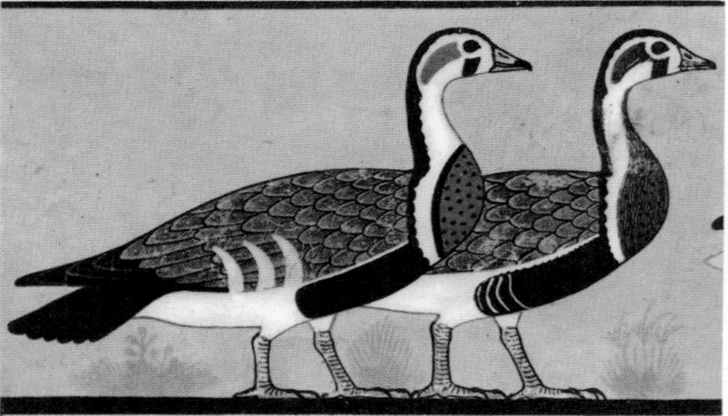

1

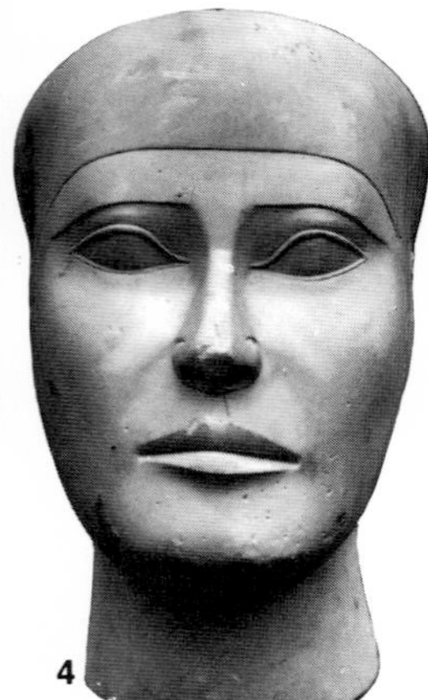

4

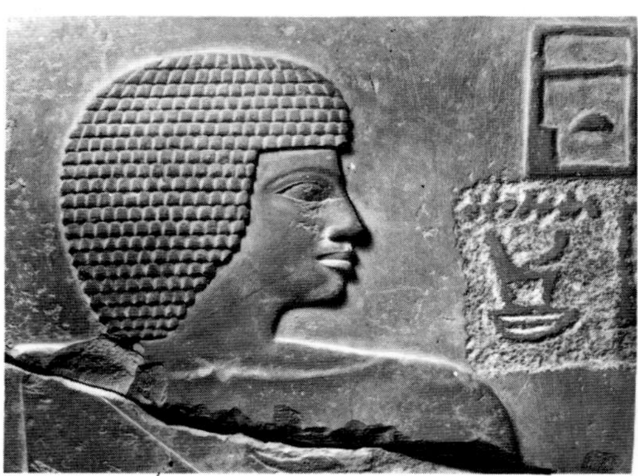

2

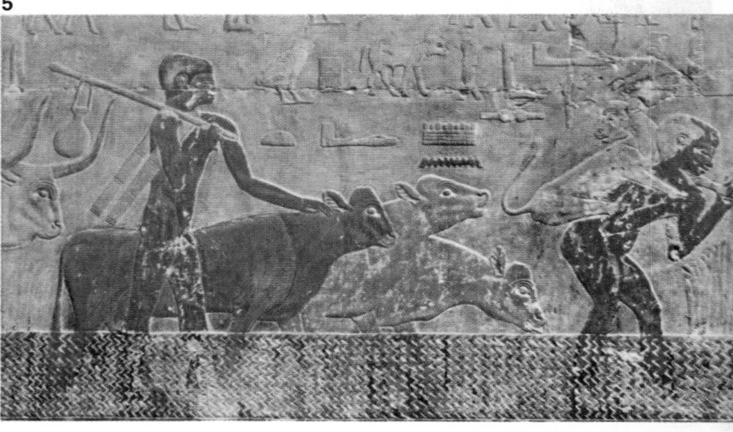

5

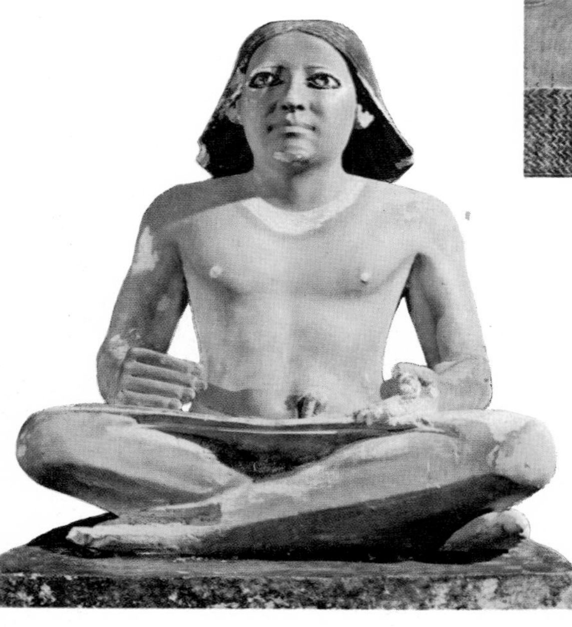

3

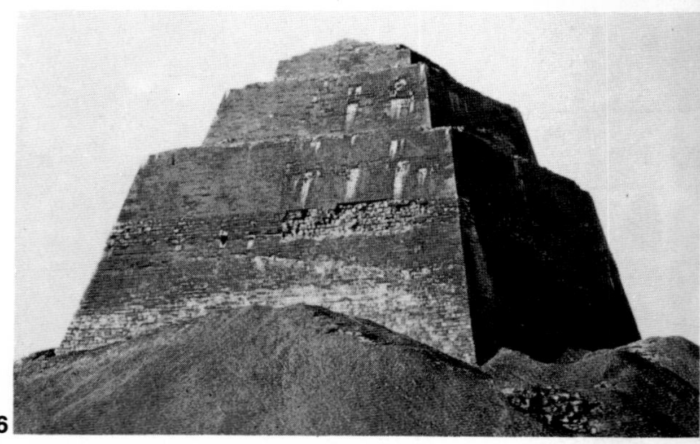

6

1. Khertihotep, an official. Crystalline sandstone. Late 12th Dynasty. Staatliche Museen, Berlin-Dahlem
2. Painting from the sarcophagus of Djehutinakht. Detail. Deir el Bersheh. 12th Dynasty. Museum of Fine Arts, Boston
3. Head of a queen. Middle of 12th Dynasty. Brooklyn Museum, New York
4. Head of unknown woman. Wood; hair covered with black paste and gold plates. Lisht. 12th Dynasty. Cairo Museum
5. Dancing scene. Painting from the tomb of a vizier of King Sesostris I. Thebes. 12th Dynasty
6. King Ammenemes III as maned sphinx. Granite. Tanis. 12th Dynasty

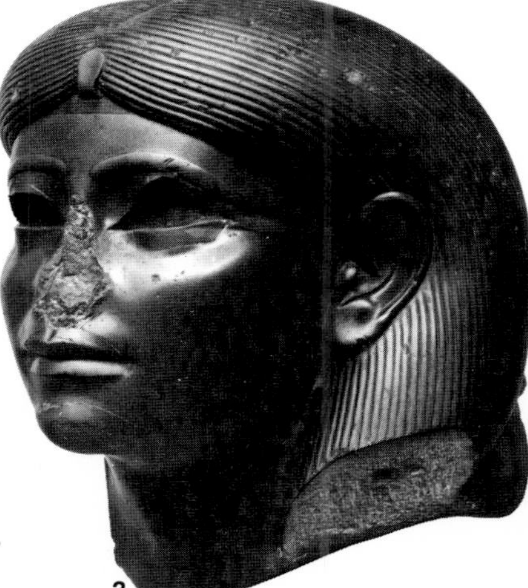

3

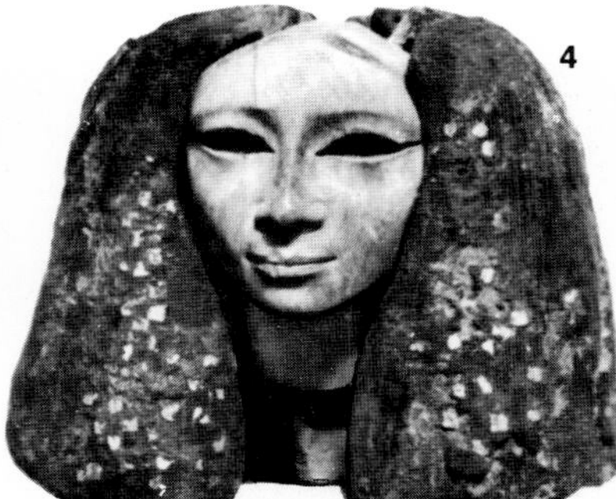

4

1

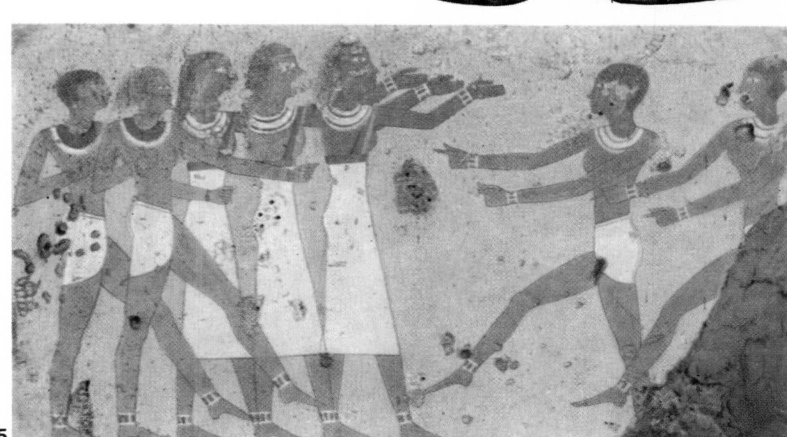

5

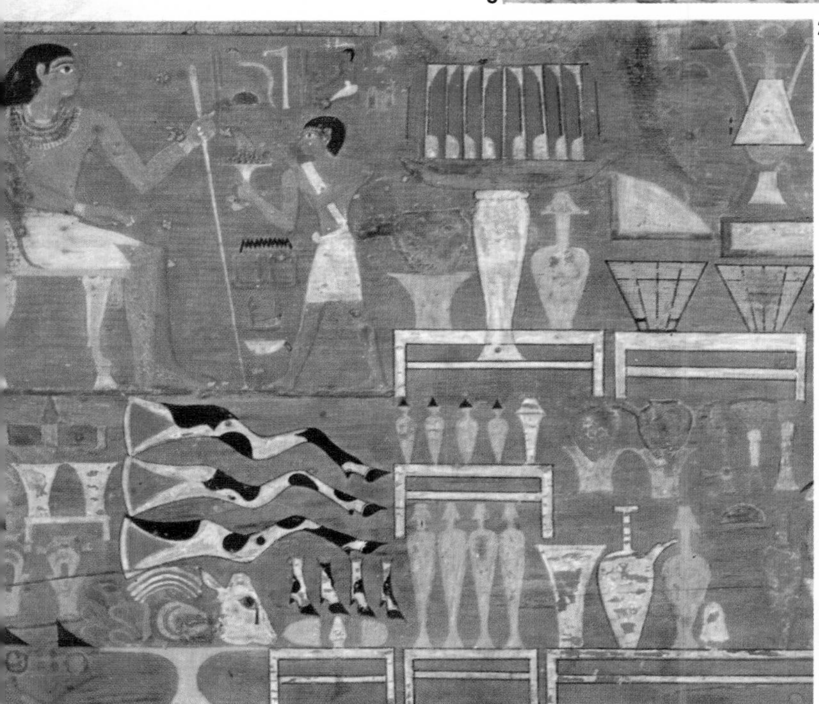

2

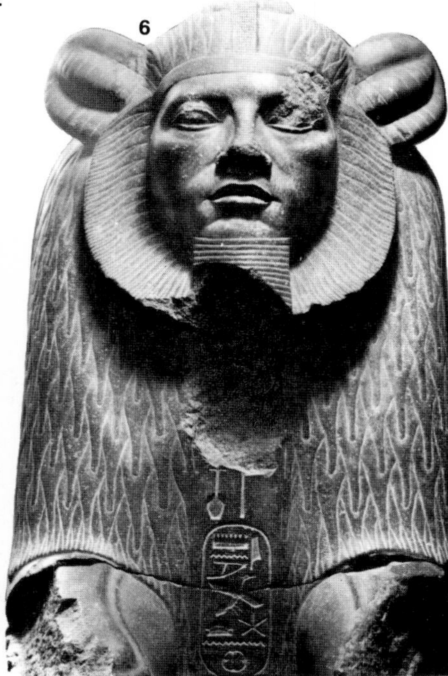

6

1. Second sarcophagus of Tutankhamun. Wood covered with gold leaf, inlaid with glass. Late 18th Dynasty. Cairo Museum.
2. Wine harvesting: gathering and pressing grapes. Tomb of Ipuy, Thebes. 19th Dynasty.
3. Amenhotep, Ramose's brother. Relief from the tomb of the vizier Ramose, Thebes. Early 18th Dynasty.
4. King Amenophis II in chariot, drawing his bow. Hollow relief. Karnak. 18th Dynasty.
5. Woman. Detail from painting in tomb of sculptors Nebamun and Ipuki, Thebes. 19th Dynasty.
6. Part of façade of small temple at Abu Simbel built by Ramesses II 19th Dynasty.
7. Royal head from time of Aton. Memphis. 18th Dynasty. Cairo Museum.

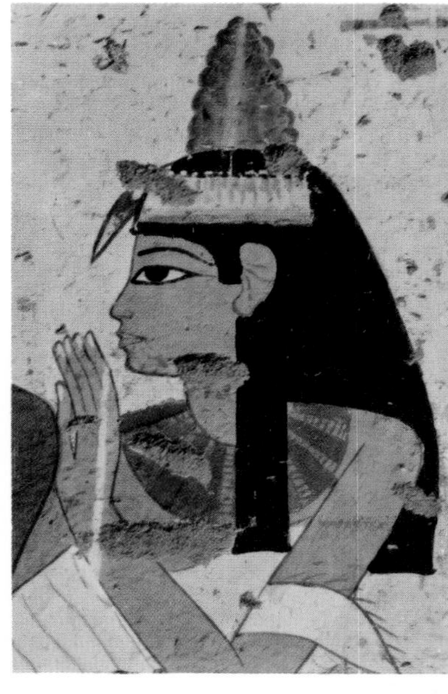

5

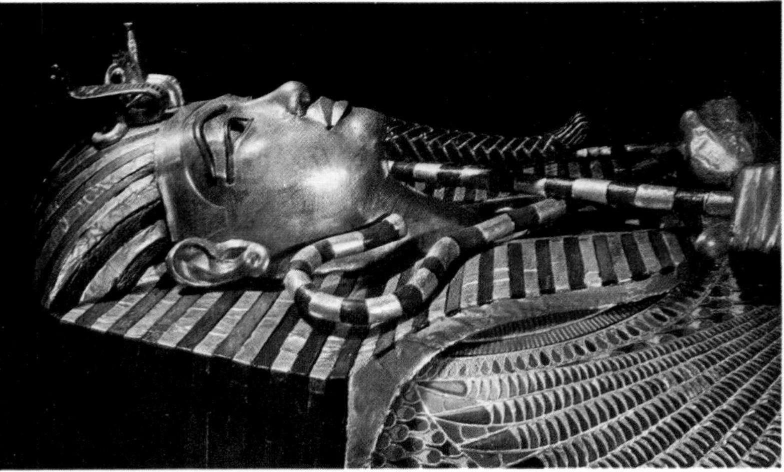

1

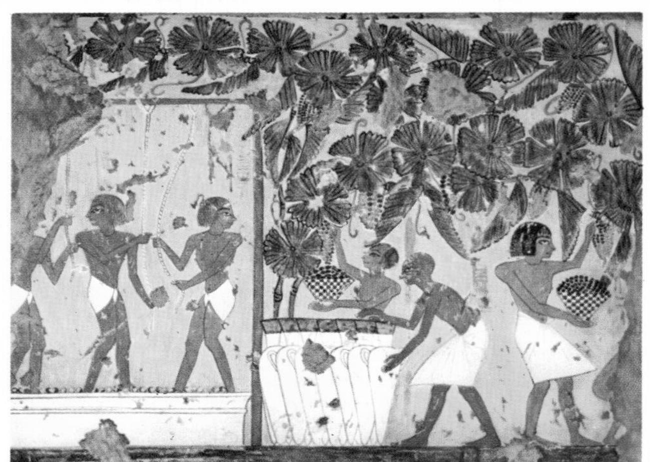

2

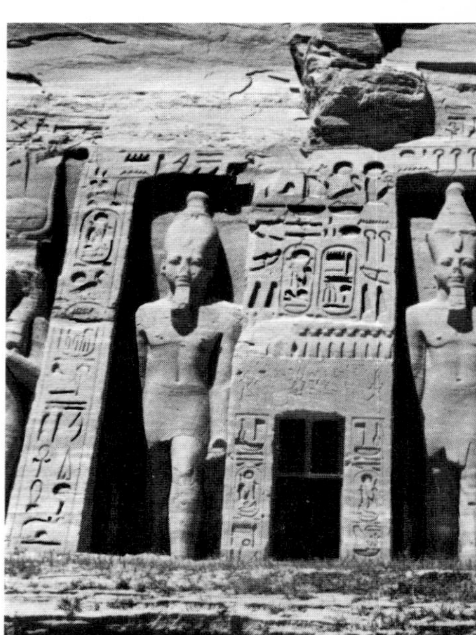

6

3

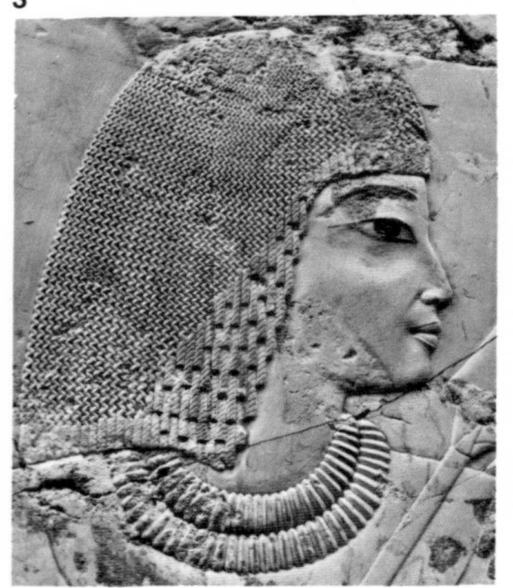

4

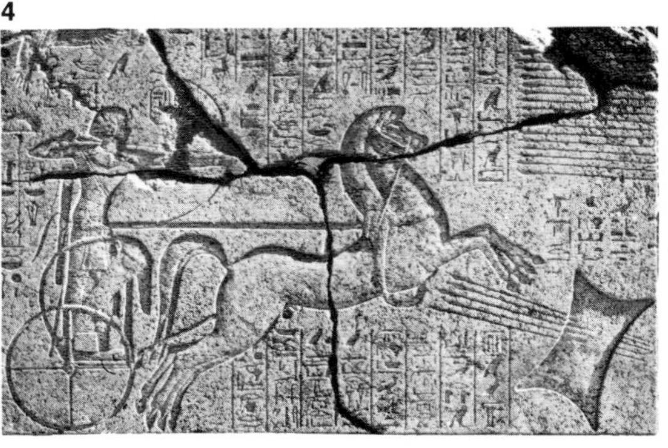

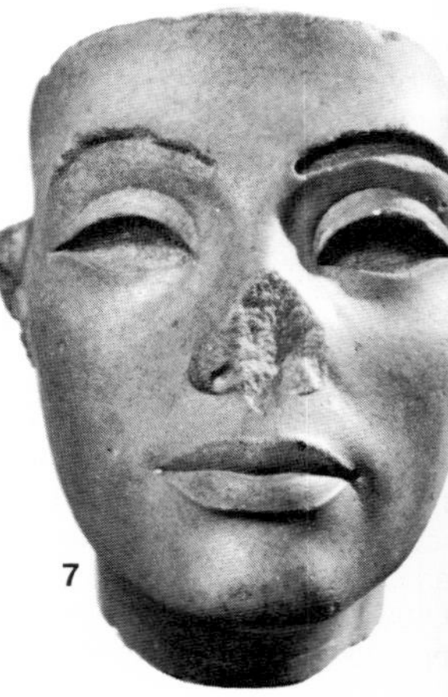

7

Part 3

The Greek World

Greek art was heir to the Minoan (Crete) and Mycenaean (Greek mainland) civilizations. Excavations have revealed that Minoan art in its maturity had developed an advanced system of architecture, particularly as regards palaces and tombs. Many of the palaces were decorated with wall paintings, in addition to which small sculptures in ivory, bronze and faience have been found, all exhibiting a lively interest in human and animal forms. The pottery, too, is plentiful and decorated with strong, simple designs.

At first Mycenaean art was subject to Minoan influences, but often the spontaneity was transformed into rigid, formal patterns. However, Mycenaean art was technically well executed and boldly conceived with a strong narrative element. The gradual fusion of these two artistic traditions led eventually to the mainstream of Greek art.

The Archaic period emerged from the century or so known as the Dark Ages, which was concluded by a phase of Oriental influence. The creation of the city state and an enlightened system of patronage led to a rapid advance in all the arts: sculpture in stone and bronze, modelling in terracotta, gems, coins, paintings and jewellery. All these artforms reveal an increasing concern with the natural representation of the human figure. The most significant development was in vase painting (black figure and red figure). The black-figure technique involved painting the design straight on to the clay with black paint. The red-figure technique called for the application of a black glaze over the surface of the vase leaving the design in the colour of the red clay. These vases were perfected in Attica, where they were virtually a monopoly. They were widely distributed, and a considerable amount of information has been discovered about the potters and painters, and their respective workshops. The Archaic period dispensed with the geometric designs that had decorated the vases of earlier Greece, and artists concerned themselves primarily with narrative scenes of everyday life and mythology. In fact, these vases are a vital source for our knowledge of daily life in Greece.

The classical age is placed in the fifth and fourth centuries BC. The self-identity of Greece during the fifth century was established by the threat of foreign invasion from Persia. During the fourth century, however, there was a certain amount of internal discord as this threat was lessened somewhat by the increasing desire of one particular Greek state to gain control over the rest of the mainland. The second half of the fifth century witnessed the creation of some of the masterpieces of Greek art, particularly the buildings on the Acropolis at Athens. We know the names of the most renowned sculptors – Phidias, Polycletus and Myron. In monumental sculpture there is a convincing rendering of human forms in various poses. Drapery is handled with greater subtlety as techniques of carving were improved, and nearly all sculpture was tinted with paint. This same century, however, saw the decline of vase painting, although a new type, known as white-ground vases, had been recently introduced in order to create greater variety in colour. On all types of vases during this final stage of the art the figures are remarkably expressive and often deployed in landscape settings.

The fourth century is perhaps best described as the Pre-Hellenistic Age. In all forms of art there is a continuing increase in skill and, in the work of sculptors such as Praxiteles, a more marked individuality. It is in this century more than in any other that the ideals of Greek artists are most apparent: the attempt to render human forms with the greatest accuracy, thereby establishing a canon of human proportions, the search for individuality in facial expressions and gestures with detailed modelling, and the location of figures in a realistic setting, often with a simple system of perspective. It is these features that became the standard measure for all European art during later periods right up to the nineteenth century, and it is in these respects that Greek art is the progenitor of the visual arts as we conceive them today.

The immediate influence of Greece in Egypt, Asia Minor and Syria led to the Hellenistic period. This was a time when artists were content to perfect what had been evolved by their immediate predecessors. Artists travelled much more widely and there was a tendency to honour established tradition.

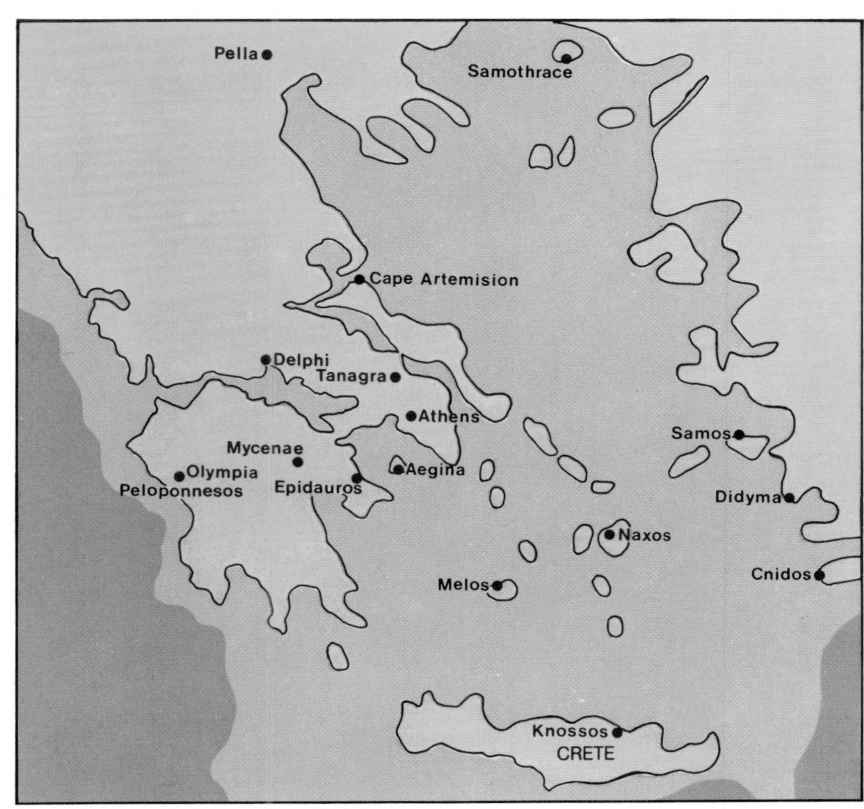

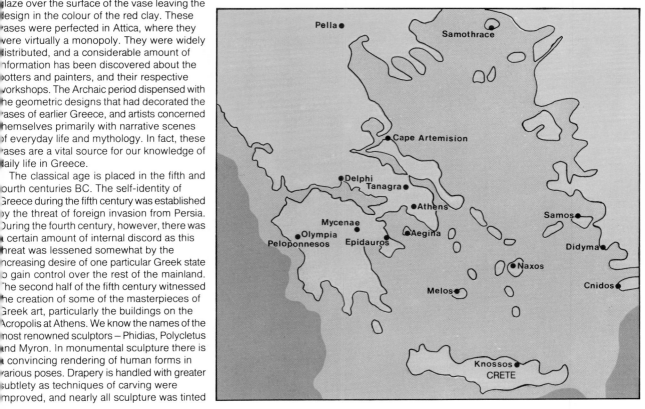

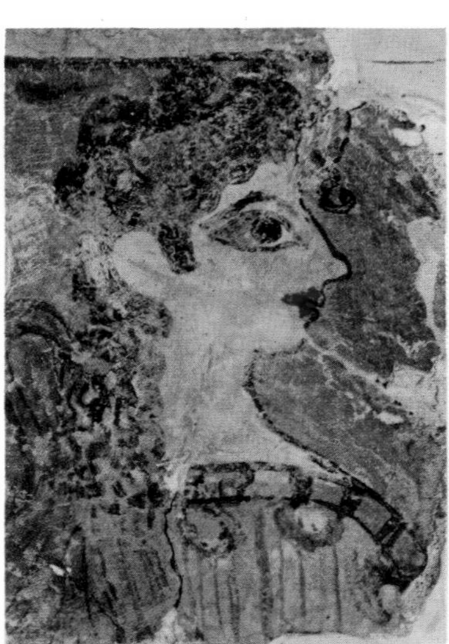

1. *'La Parisienne'.* Fresco fragment from Palace of Minos, Knossos, Crete. Late Minoan. Heraklion Museum
2. Plan of the small palace at Knossos
3. Libation procession. Detail of sarcophagus. Painted limestone. Hagia Triada. Late Minoan. Heraklion Museum
4. Vase with polychrome decoration. Terracotta. Palace at Phaistos. Kamares style, Middle Minoan. Heraklion Museum
5. Bull's head rhyton. Steatite. Knossos. Late Minoan. Heraklion Museum
6. Snake goddess. Faience. Treasure of palace sanctuary, Knossos. Middle Minoan, Heraklion Museum
7. Rhyton decorated with shell motifs. Terracotta. Zakro. Late Minoan. Heraklion Museum

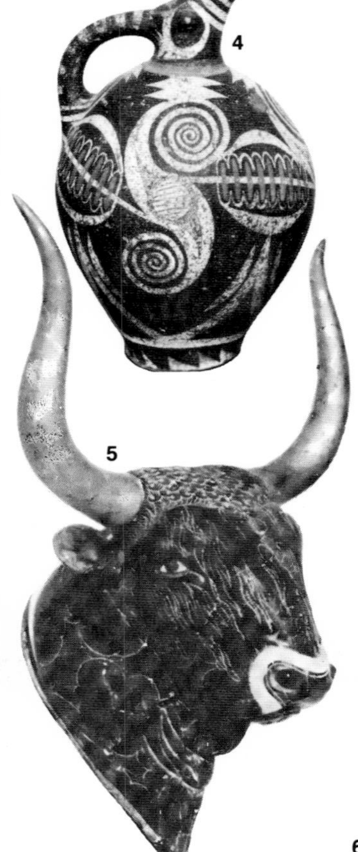

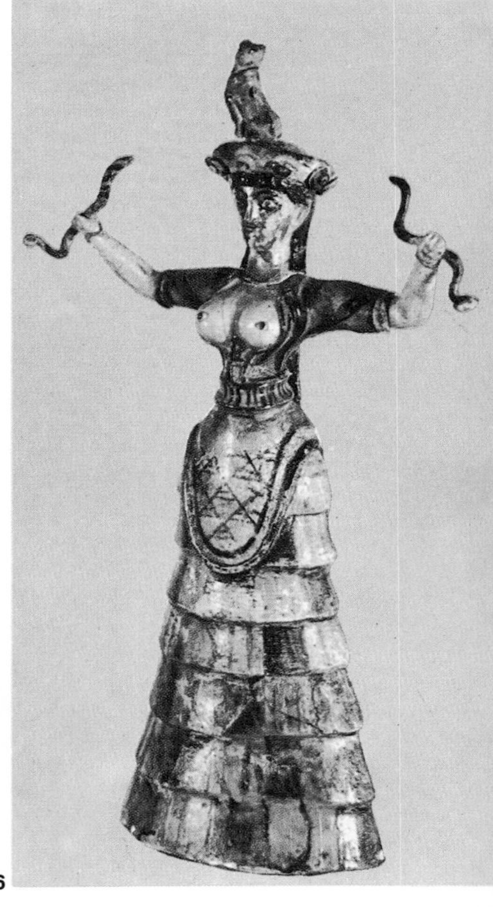

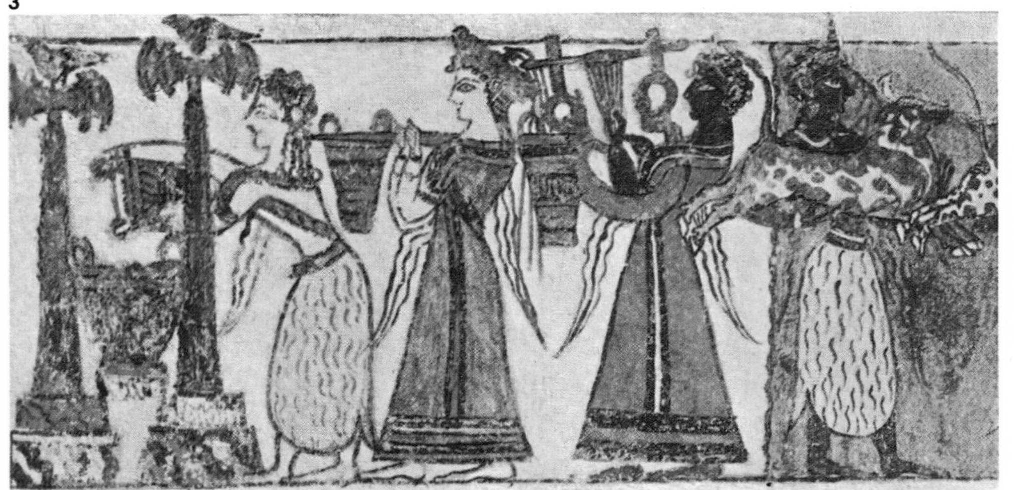

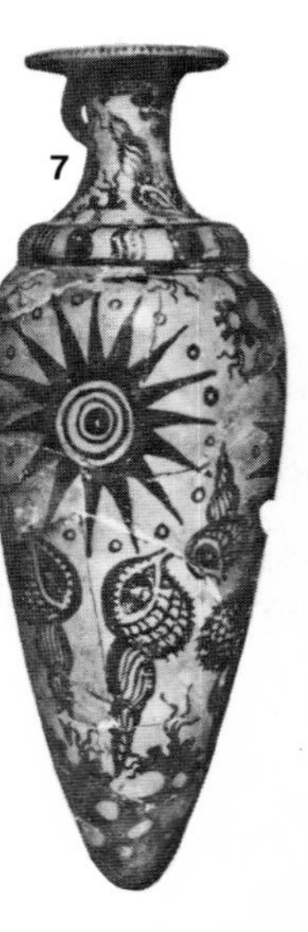

1. Lion Gate, Mycenae. 14th century BC
2. Poniard. Bronze encrusted with gold and silver. Royal tombs, Mycenae. 14th century BC. National Museum, Athens
3. Funerary stele. Circle of tombs, Mycenae. 16th century BC. National Museum, Athens
4. Funerary mask of a king or prince. Mycenae. 16th century BC. National Museum, Athens
5. Figures wearing donkey masks. Fresco. Acropolis, Mycenae. 14th century BC. National Museum, Athens
6. Circle of tombs, Acropolis, Mycenae. 14th century BC

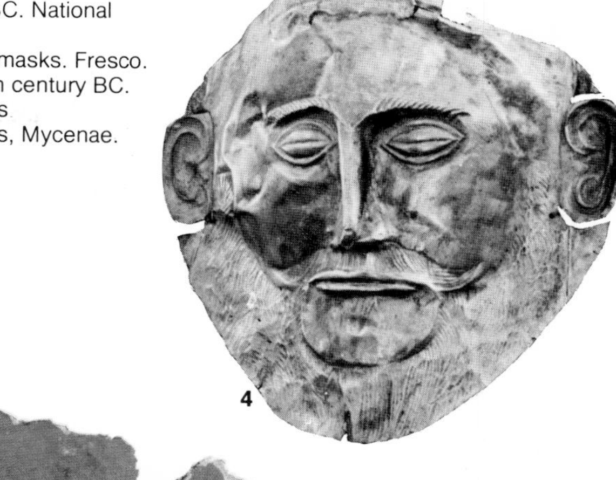

4

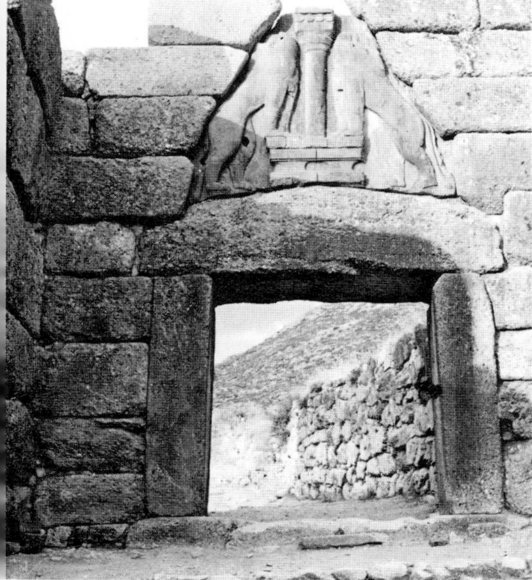

1

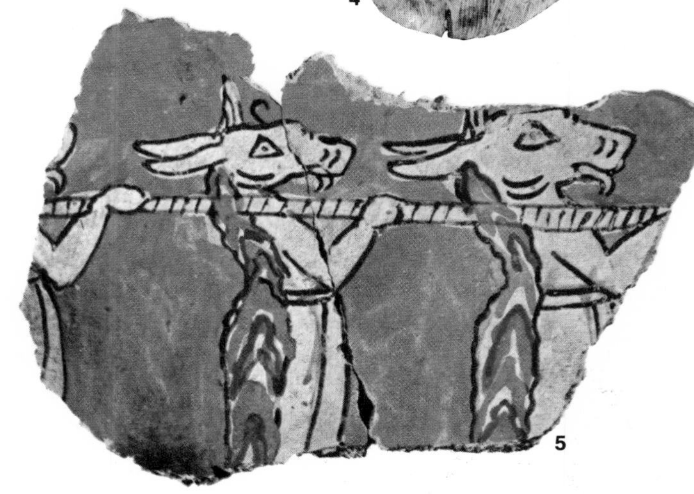

5

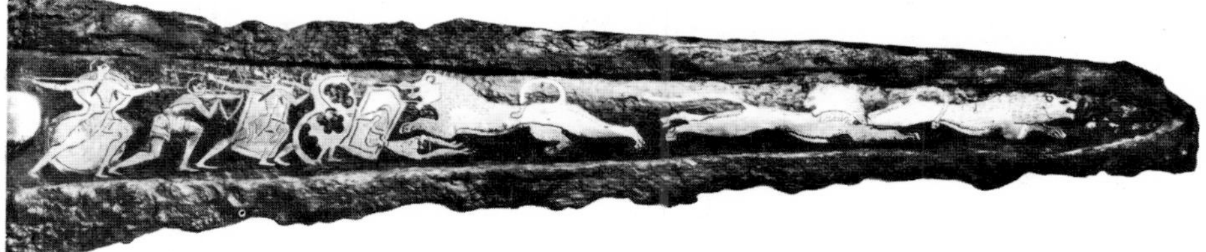

2

3

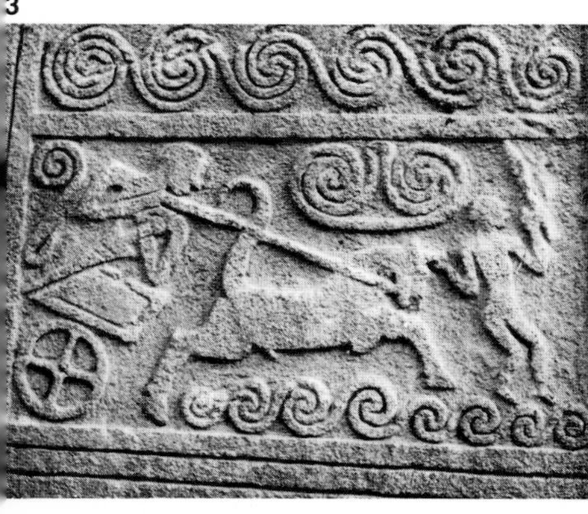

6

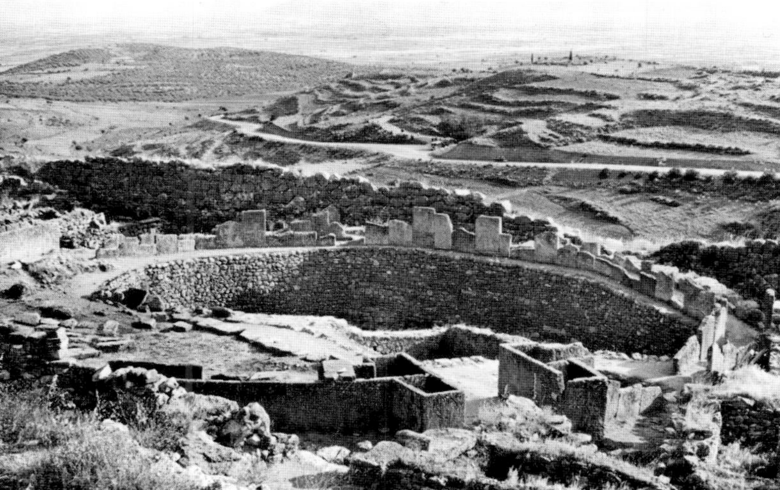

1. Horse. Bronze. Peloponnesos. 8th century BC. Staatliche Museen, Berlin-Dahlem
2. Funeral scene. Detail from a vase found in Athenian tomb. Geometric style. 8th century BC. Metropolitan Museum of Art. New York
3. Row of lions, Delos. Late 7th century BC
4. Boeotian idol. Terracotta. About 700 BC. Louvre, Paris
5. Cycladic pitcher. Aegina. Orientalizing style. 1st half of 7th century BC. British Museum, London
6. Kouros from Melos. Marble. About 550 BC. National Museum, Athens

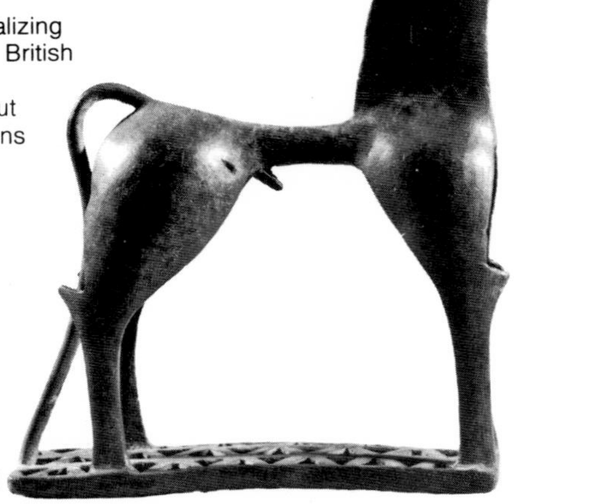
1

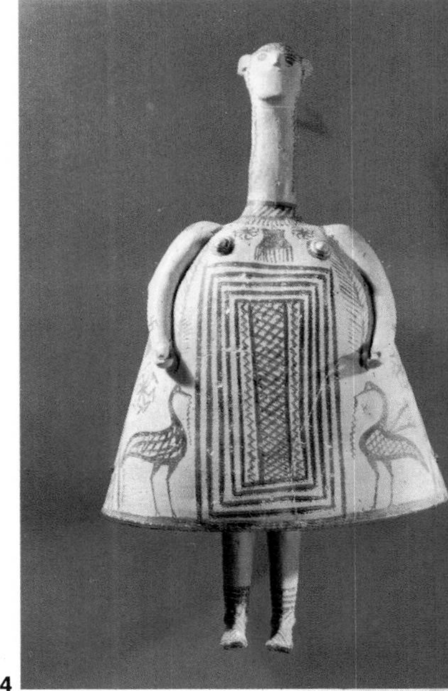
4

2
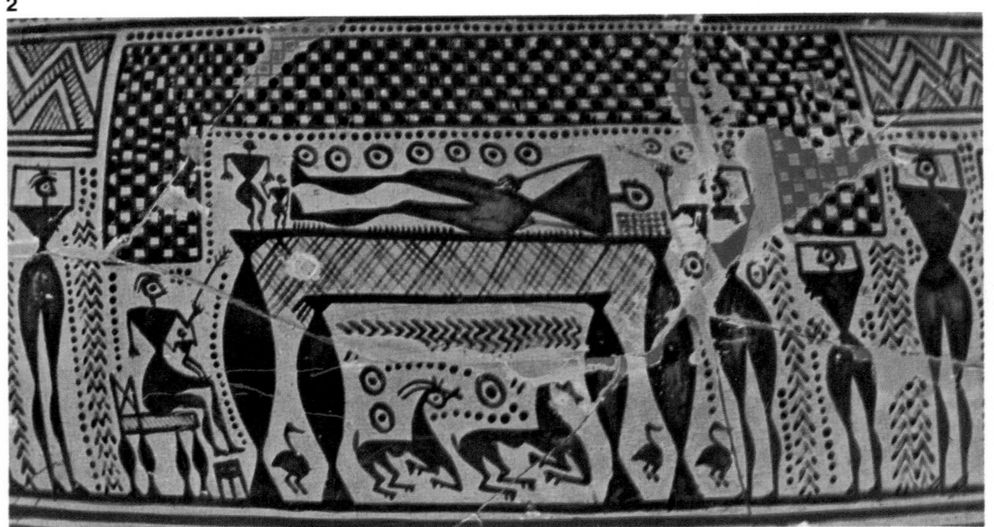

6
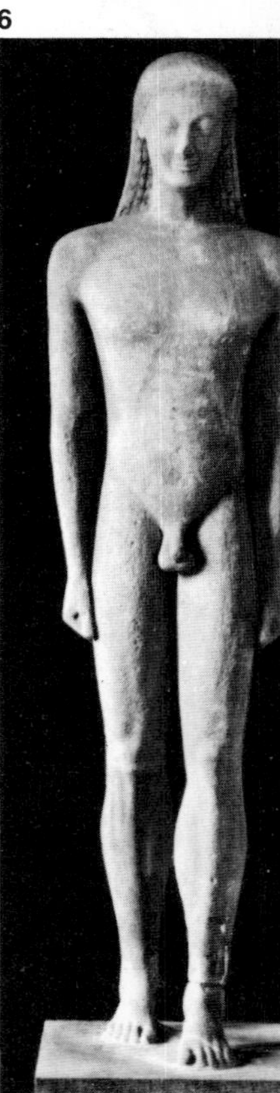

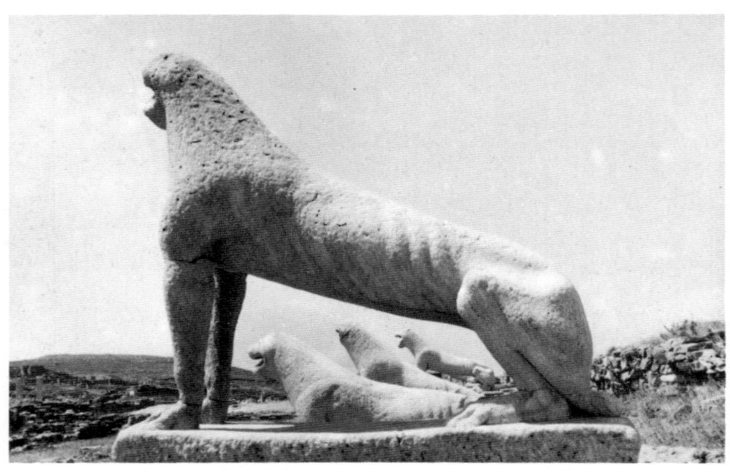
3

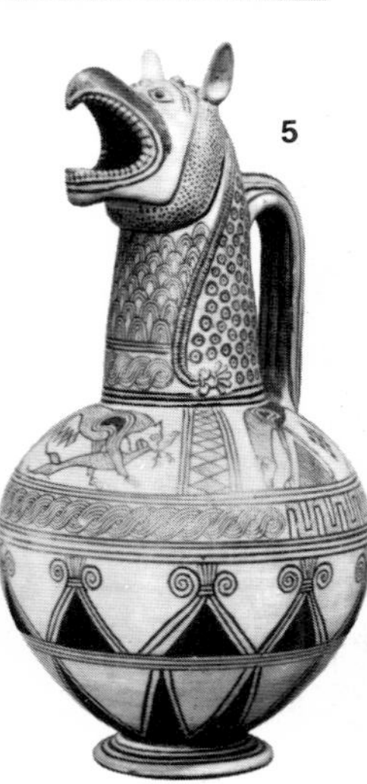
5

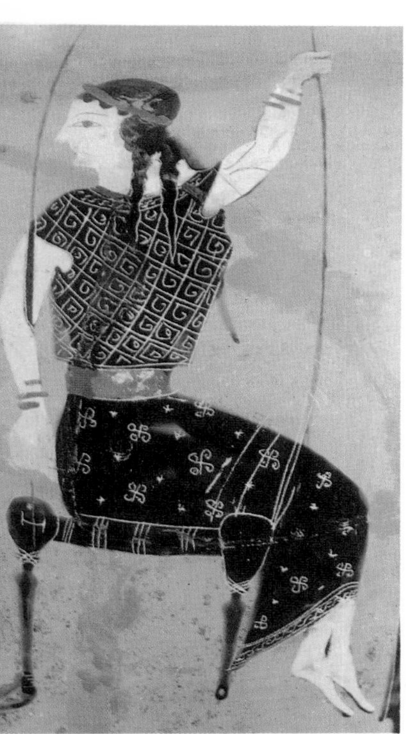

1. Woman on a swing. Detail from Attic amphora. About 540 BC. Louvre, Paris.
2. Female figure from Auxerre. Limestone. Daedalic style. About 625 BC. Louvre, Paris.
3. Exekias (*fl.* late 6th century BC): Achilles and Penthesilea. Detail from amphora. About 525 BC. British Museum, London.
4. Young musician. Interior of Attic cup. About 525 BC. Louvre, Paris.
5. Oltos (*fl.* late 6th century BC): Girl tying sandals. Detail from amphora. Etruria. About 520 BC. Louvre, Paris.
6. Hera of Samos. Marble. About 550 BC. Louvre, Paris.

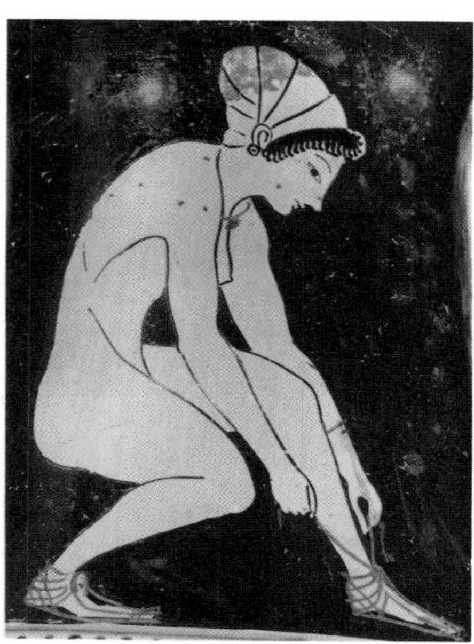

5

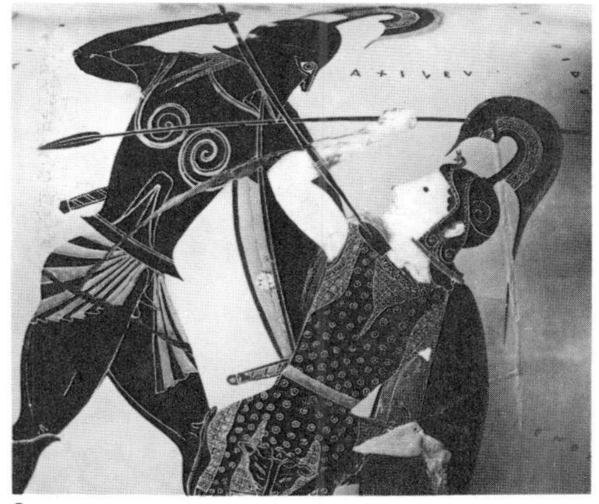

3

2

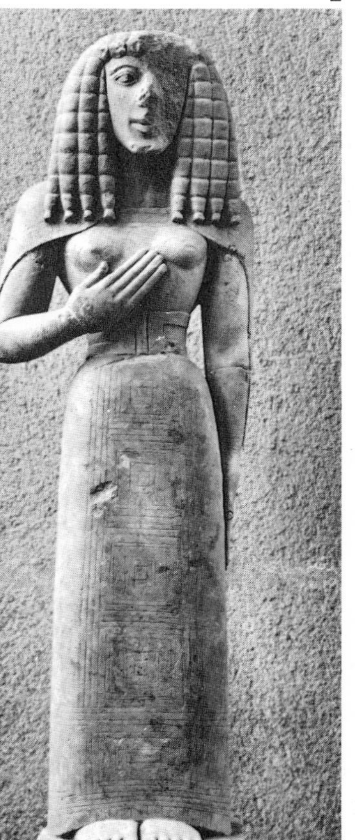

6

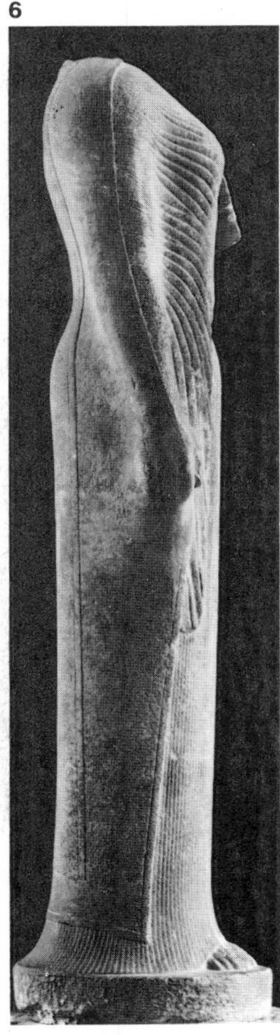

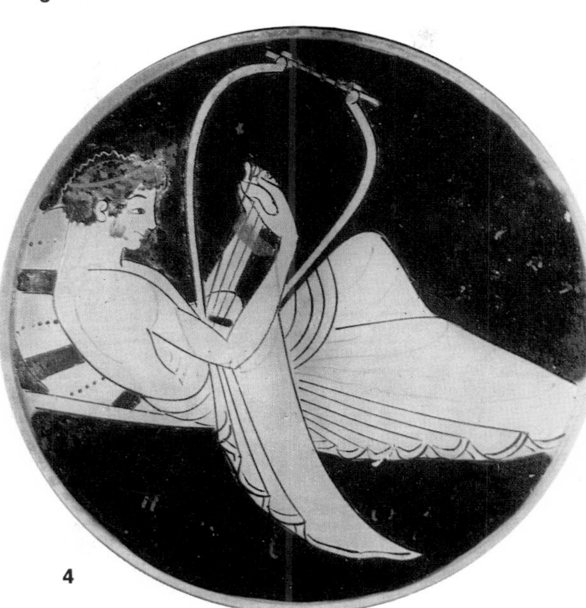

4

1. Onesimos (*fl.* early 5th century BC): Girl bathing. Interior of goblet. Chiusi. About 480 BC. Musées d'Art et d'Histoire, Brussels.
2. Horse from east pediment of the Parthenon, Athens. About 437–431 BC. British Museum, London
3. Cithern player. About 420 BC. Louvre.
4. Charioteer. Bronze. Delphi. About 470 BC. Delphi Museum.
5. Ball game. Marble relief on Attic statue base. About 510 BC. National Museum, Athens.
6. Head of a kore. Marble. About 525 BC. Acropolis Museum, Athens.
7. Zeus (or Poseidon?). Detail. Bronze. Found in sea off Cape Artemision. Abou 450 BC. National Museum, Athens.

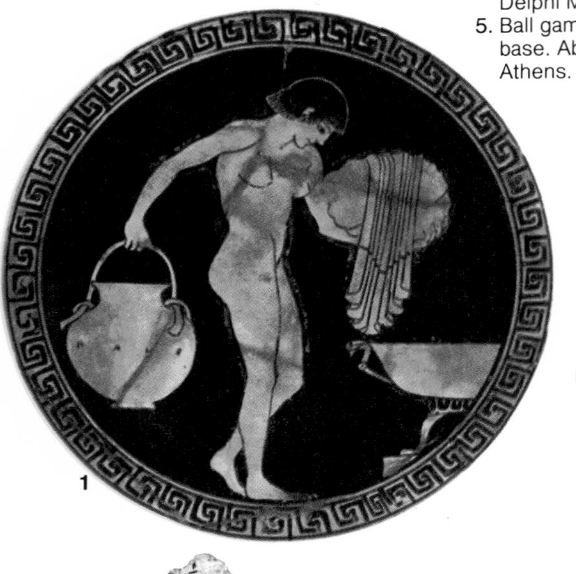
1

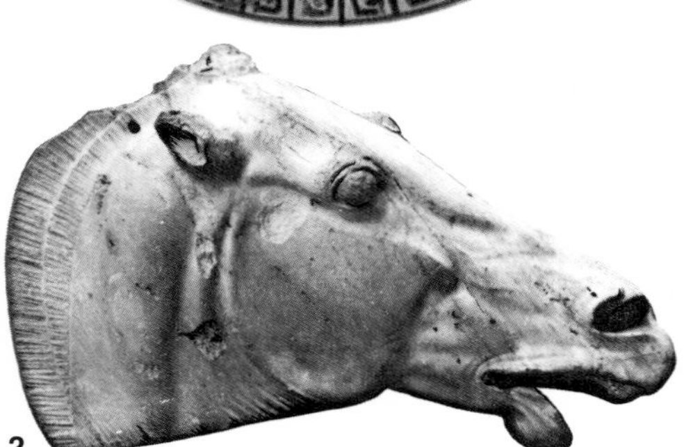
2

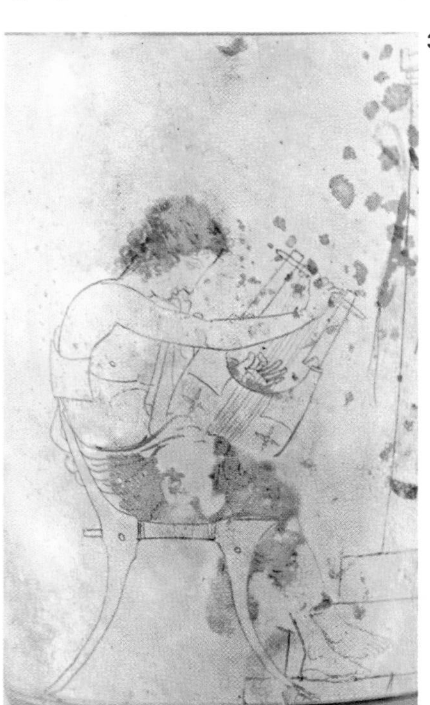
3

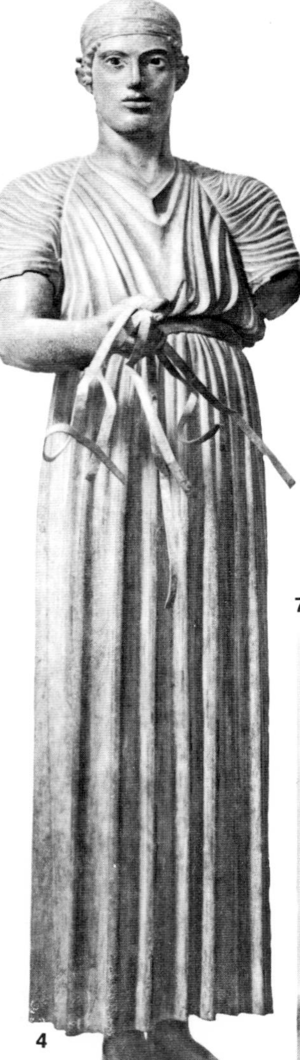
4

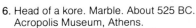

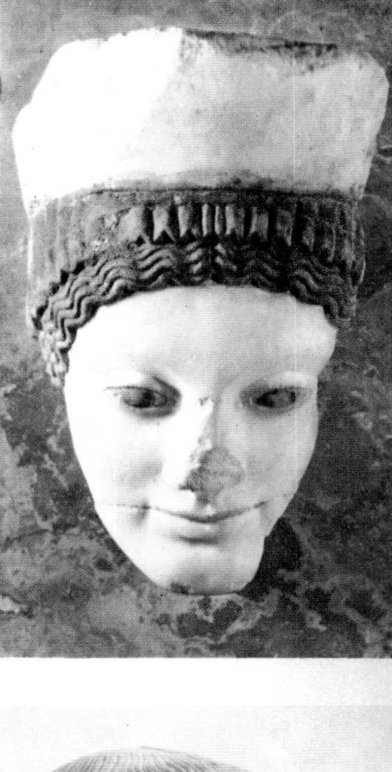
6

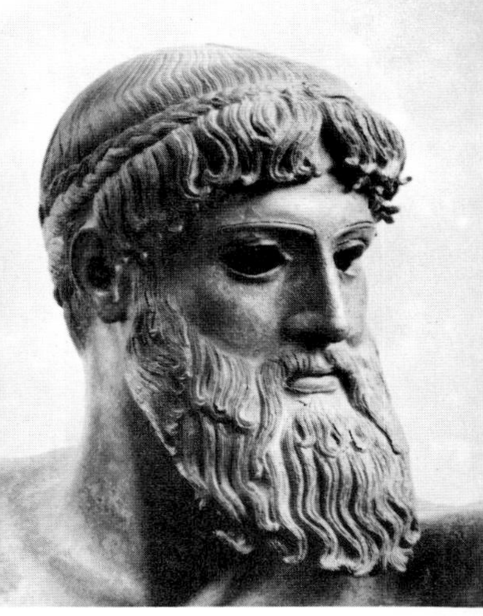
7

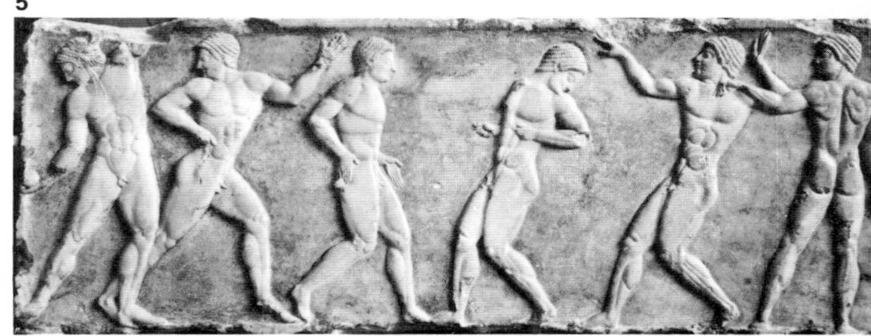
5

. Funeral stele of Hegeso. Detail. Marble. About 410 BC. National Museum, Athens.
. Discobolus (discus thrower). Roman marble copy after bronze original of about 450 BC by Myron. Museo delle Terme, Rome.
3. River Kladeos. Marble. East pediment of Temple of Zeus, Olympia. About 460 BC. Olympia Museum.
4. Doryphorus (spear bearer). Roman marble copy after original of about 450–440 BC by Polycletus. Museo Nazionale, Naples
5. Torso of Aphrodite. Roman marble copy after bronze original of about 450 BC. Louvre, Paris.
6. Temple of Poseidon, Paestum. About 460 BC.
7. Dying Niobid. Marble. Found in Rome. About 440 BC. Museo delle Terme, Rome.
8. Temple of Hera, Agrigento. About 440 BC. Doric

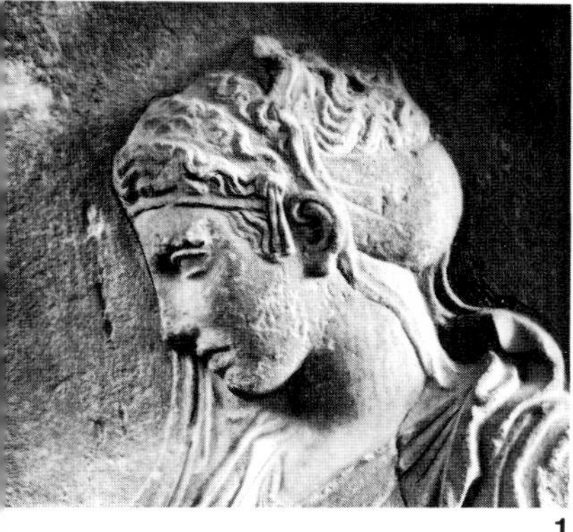
1

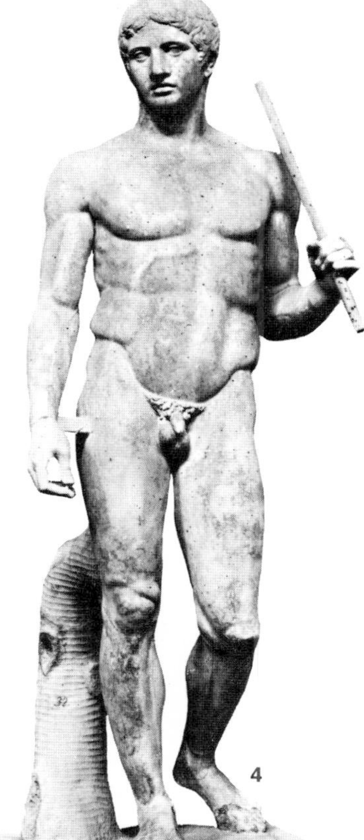
4

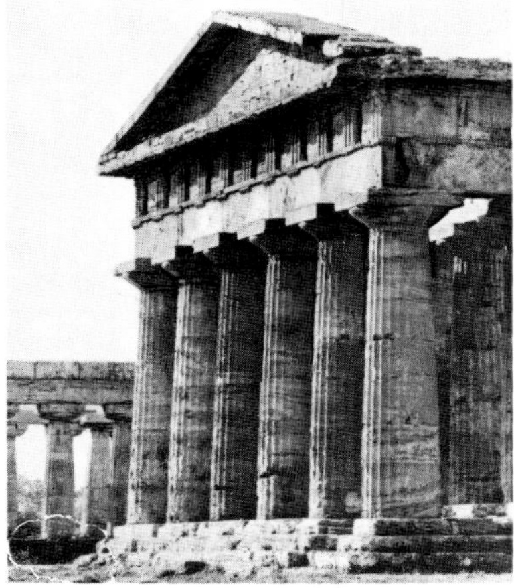
6

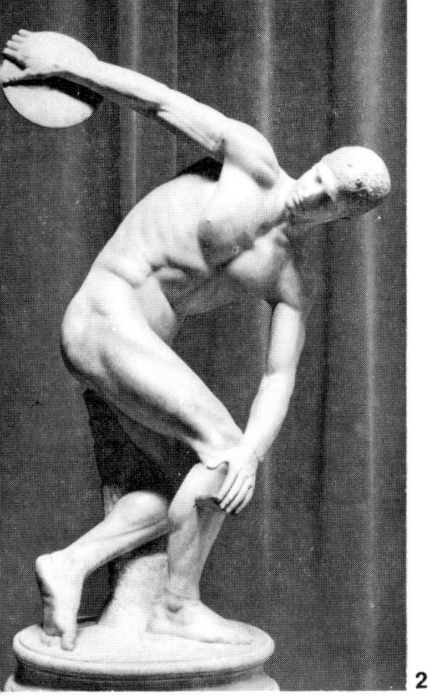
2

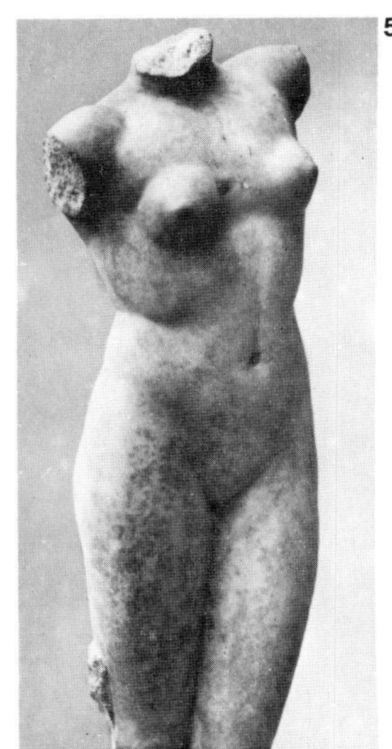
5

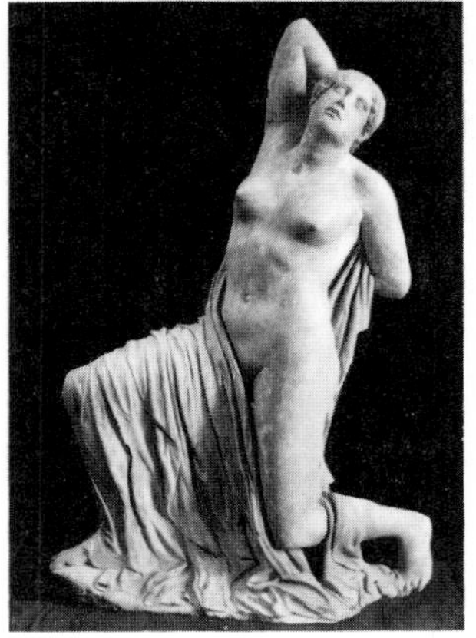
7

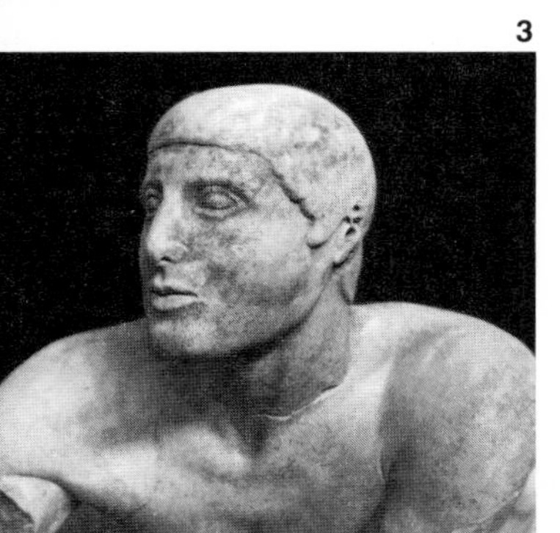
3

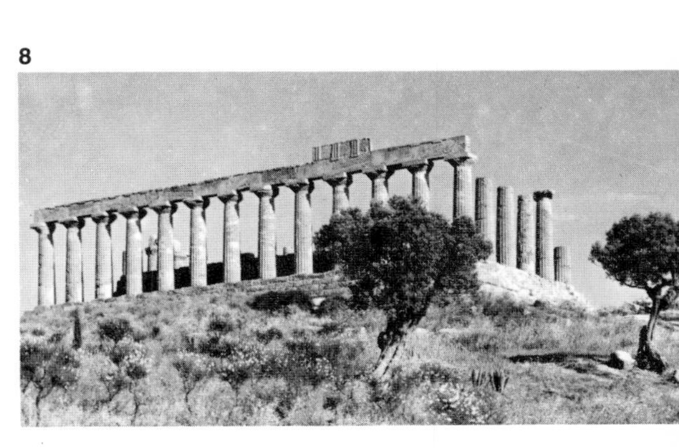
8

Phidias (c.500–430 BC) supervised the sculpture

1. Dione and Aphrodite. Marble. East pediment of the Parthenon, Athens. About 437–431 BC. British Museum, London.
2. Centaur and Lapith. Marble. South metope of the Parthenon, Athens. About 445 BC. British Museum, London.
3. Ephebi and horsemen. Marble. West frieze of the Parthenon, Athens. About 440–437 BC. British Museum, London.
4. Panathenaic procession. Marble. Fragment of east frieze of the Parthenon, Athens. About 442–438 BC. Louvre, Paris.
5. Dionysus (or Theseus?). Marble. East pediment of the Parthenon, Athens. About 437–431 BC. British Museum, London.

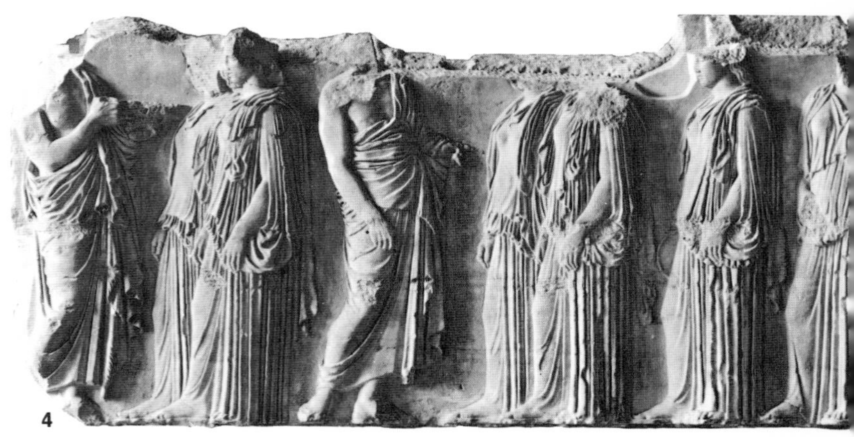

4

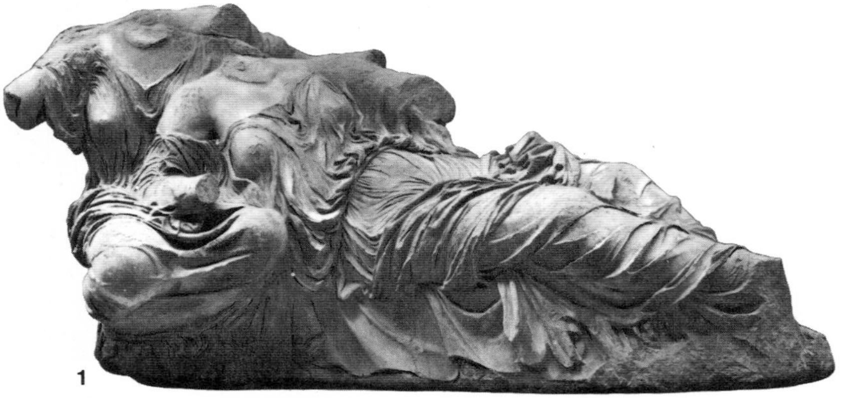

1

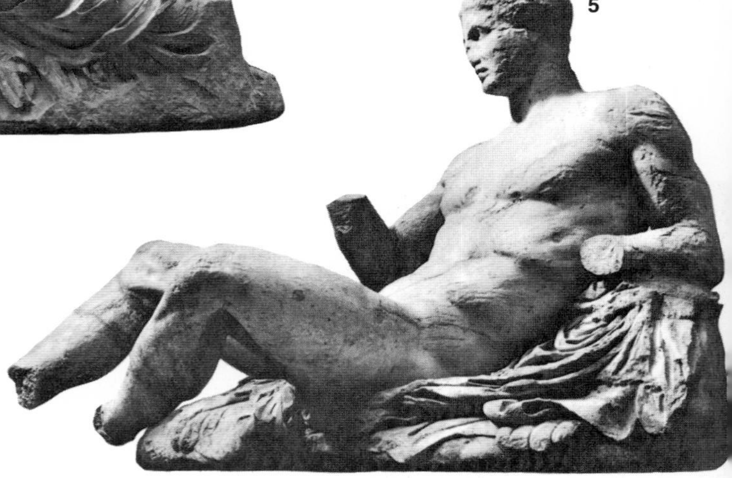

5

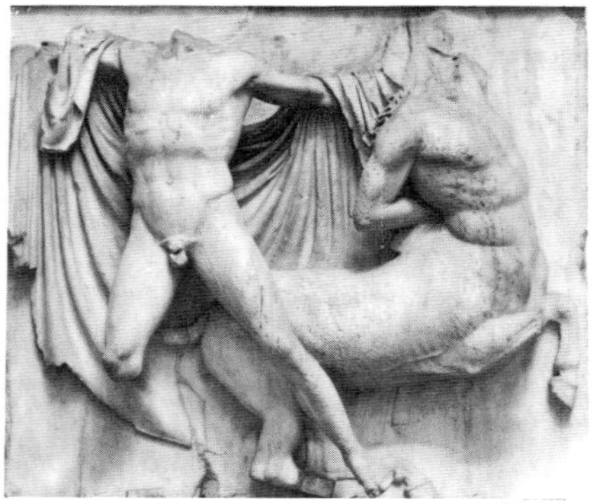

2

3

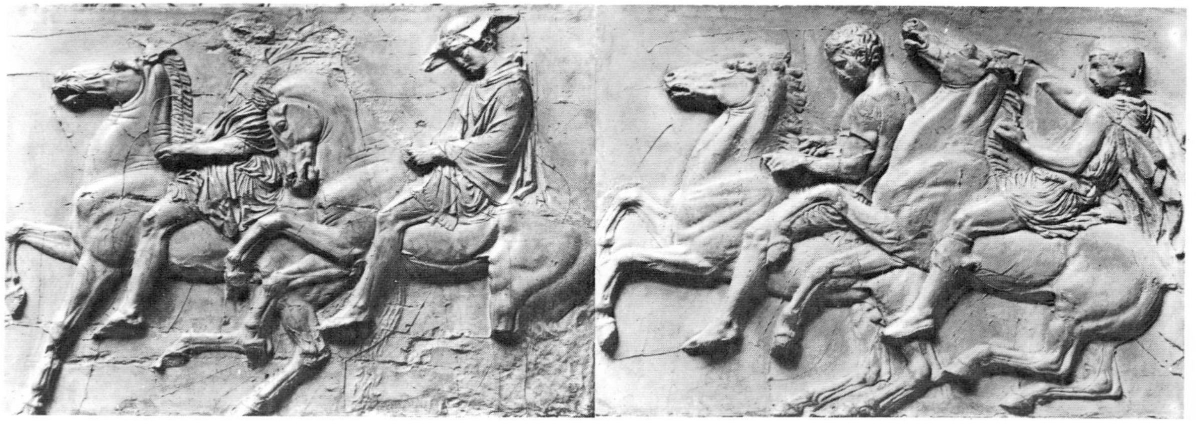

. Porch of the Caryatids. Erechtheion, Athens. About 421–406 BC.
. Plan of the Parthenon, Athens.

3. Temple of the Parthenon, Athens. View from the northwest. About 447–438 BC. Doric.

4. Temple of Athena Nike, Athens. Ionic columns. Probably designed by Callicrates (*fl.* mid-5th century BC).

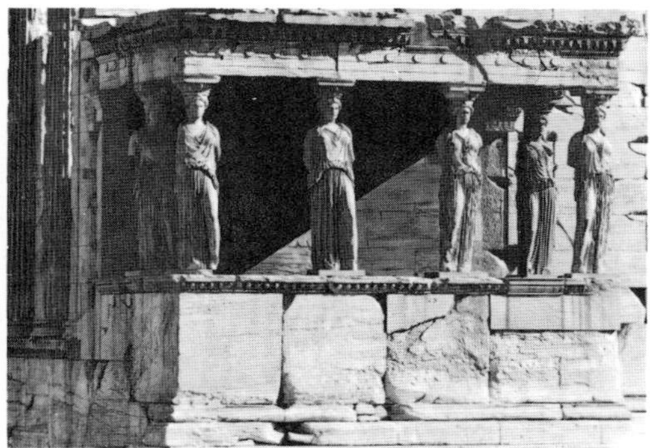

1

2

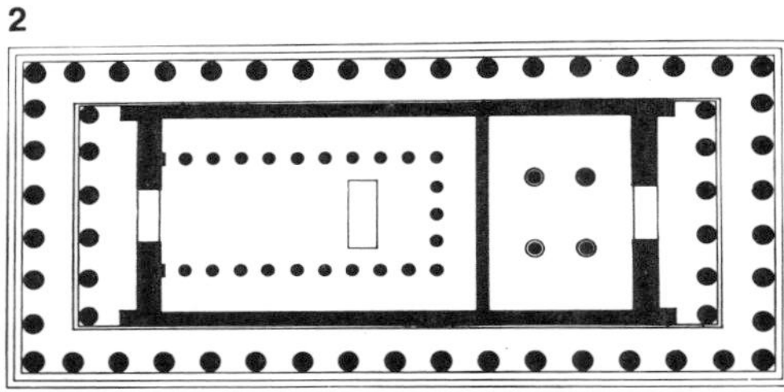

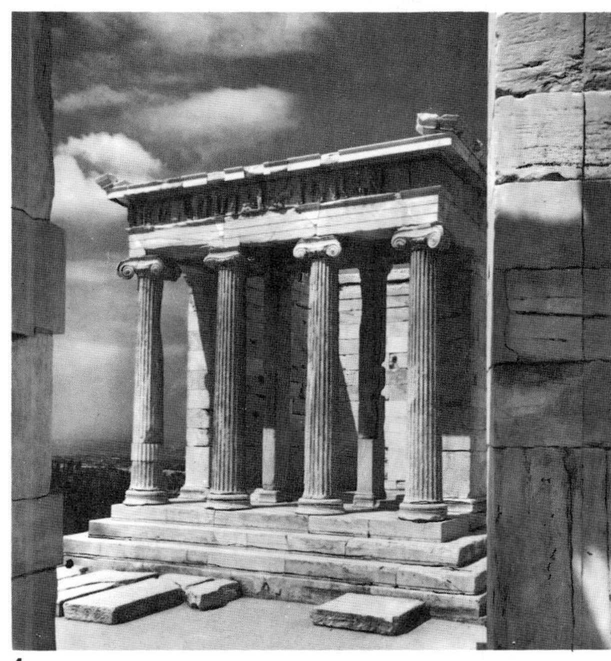

4

3

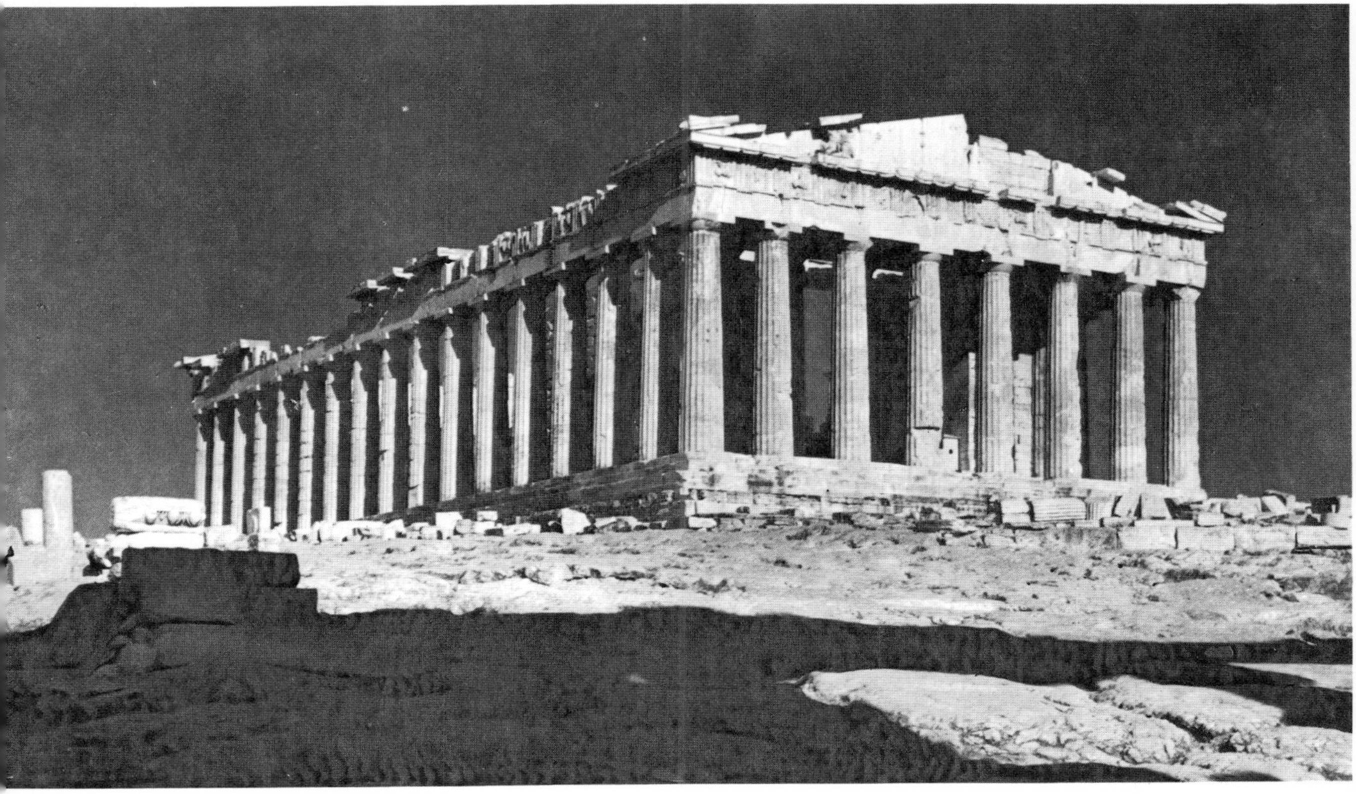

1. Praxiteles (1st half of 4th century BC): Hermes (or copy?). Paros marble. About 350–330 BC. Olympia Museum.
2. Demeter of Cnidos. Marble. About 340–330 BC. British Museum, London.
3. Goddess. Acroterion from a Peloponnesian temple. Marble. Early 4th century. Ny Carlsberg Glyptotek, Copenhagen.
4. Lion hunt. Mosaic of pebbles from Pella, Macedonia. Late 4th century BC.
5. Apollo Sauroktonos. Roman marble copy after original of about 350 BC by Praxiteles. Louvre, Paris.
6. Head of Aphrodite of Cnidos. Roman marble copy after original of about 350 BC by Praxiteles. Louvre, Paris.

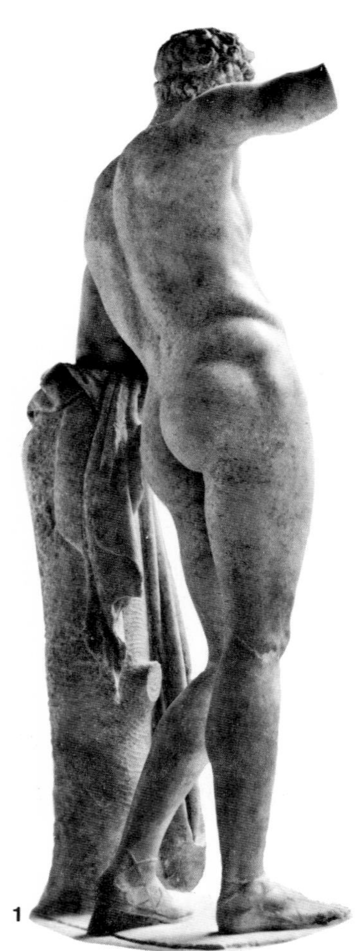
1

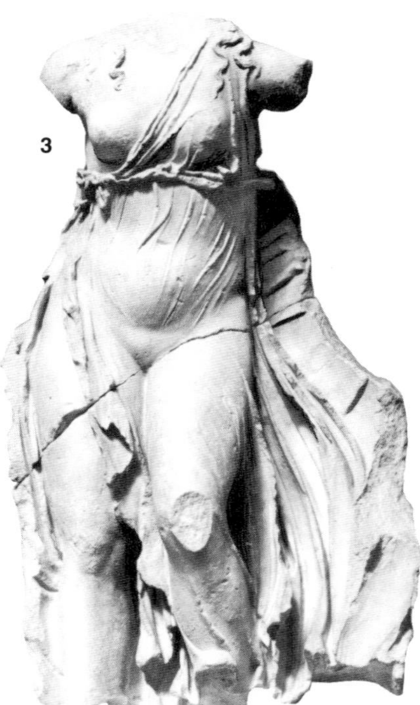
3

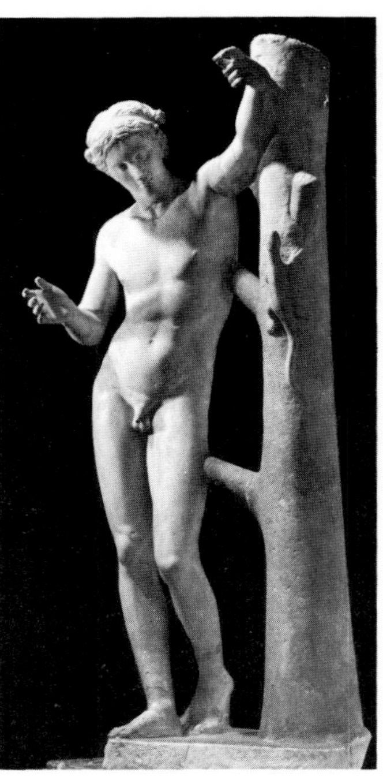
5

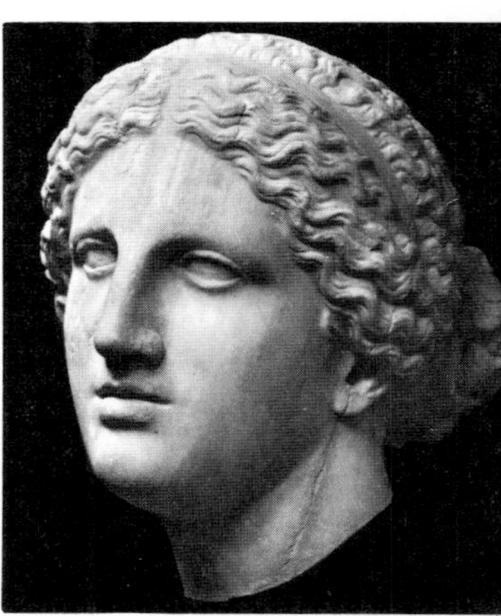
6

2
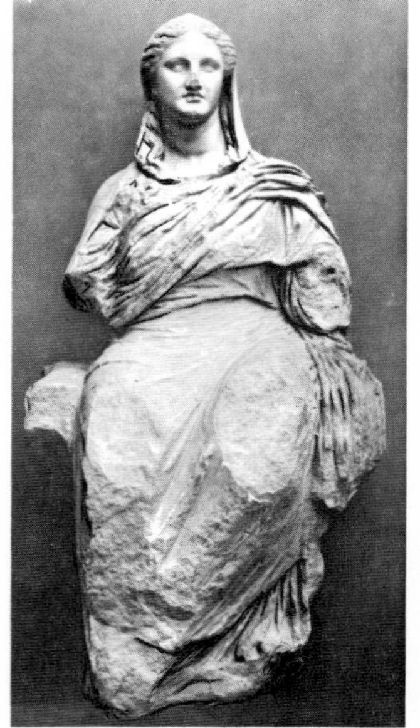

4
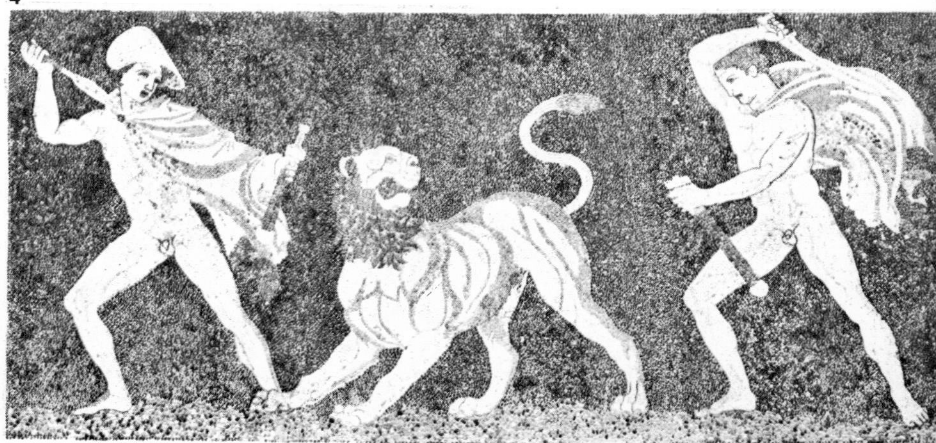

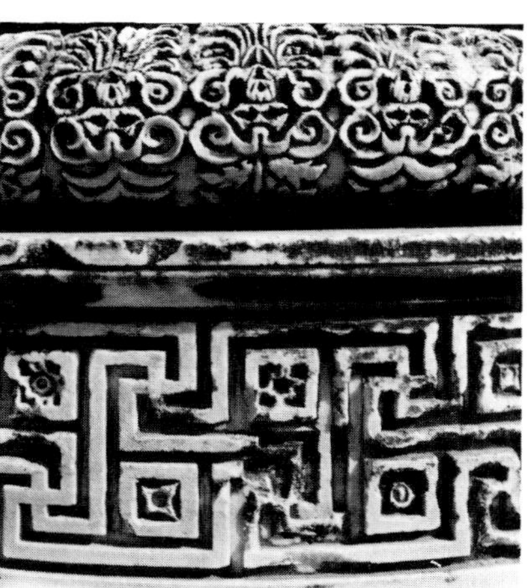

1. Base of Ionic column. Portico of the Temple of Apollo, Didyma
2. Polycletus the Younger (?): Theatre, Epidauros. About 350 BC
3. Central court of the Temple of Apollo, Didyma. About 330 BC–AD 40
4. Aphrodite from Syracuse. Roman marble copy after original of about 150 BC. Museo Archeologico Nazionale, Syracuse, Italy
5. Plan of tholos at Epidauros, probably designed by Polycletus the Younger about 350 BC
6. Apollo Belvedere. Roman marble copy after Greek original of about 350 BC. Vatican Museums

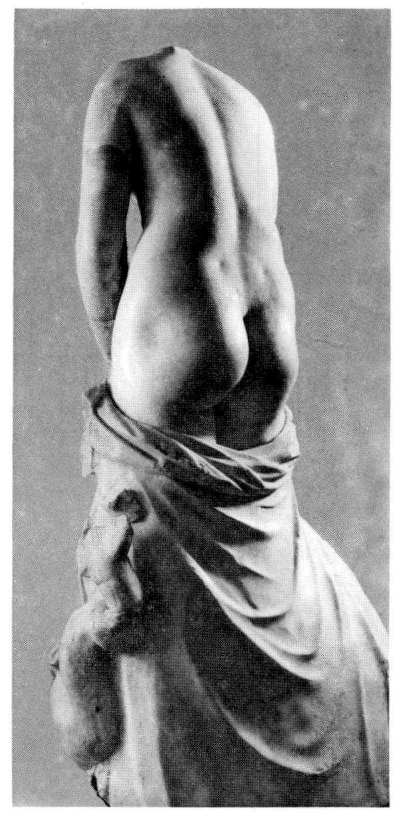

4

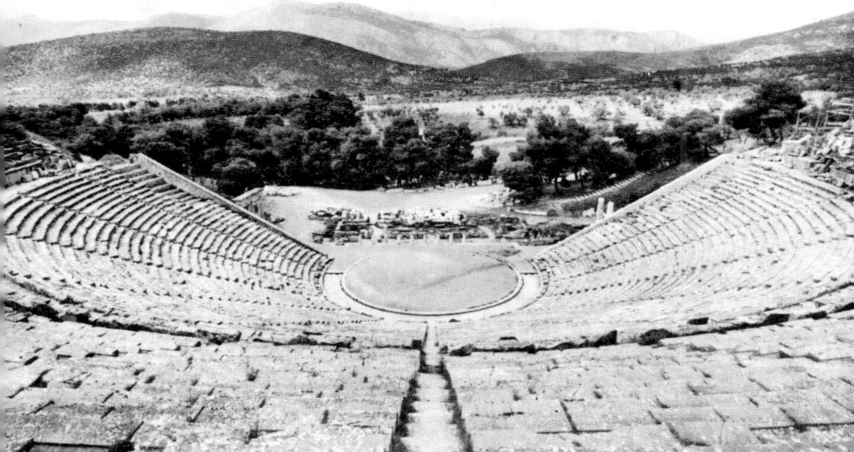

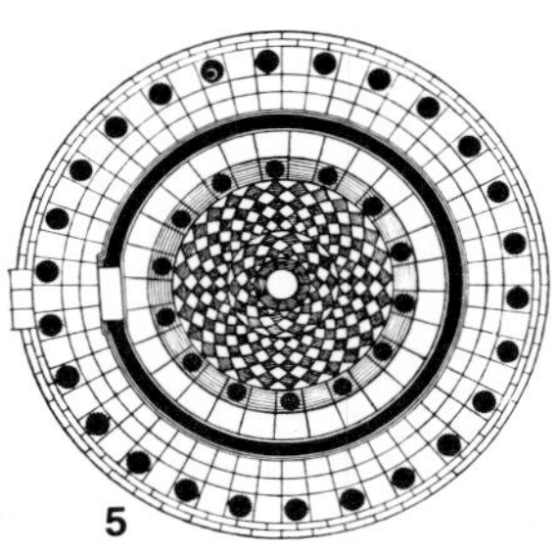

5

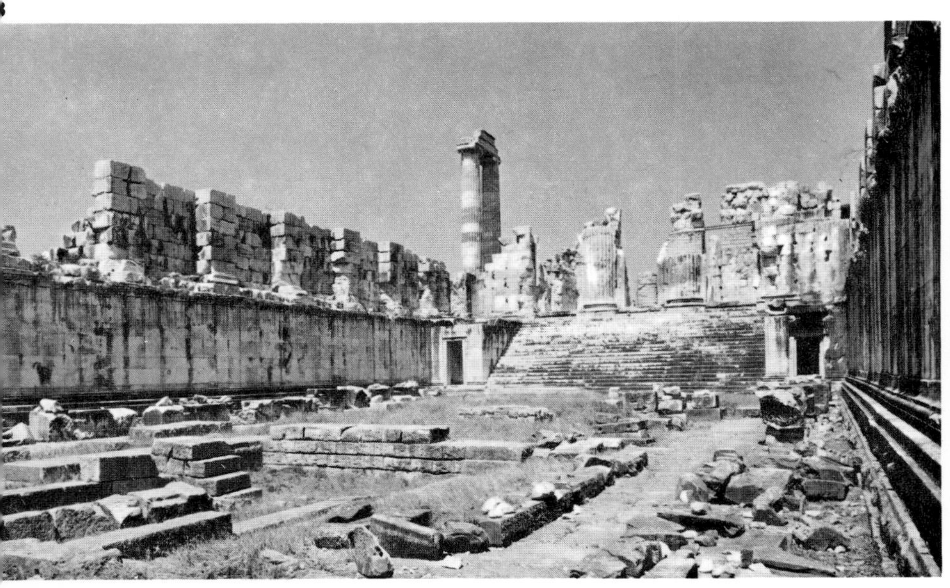

6

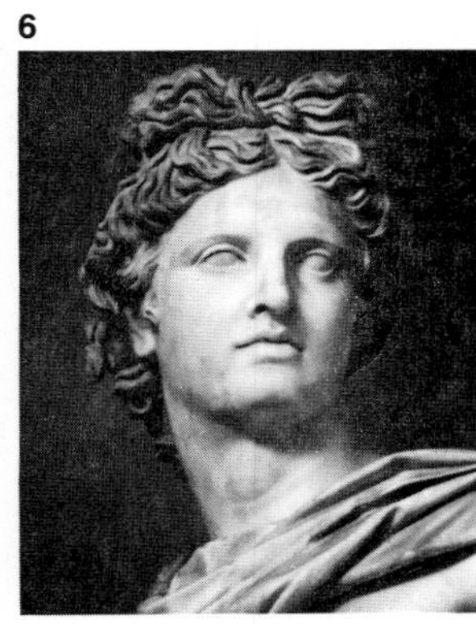

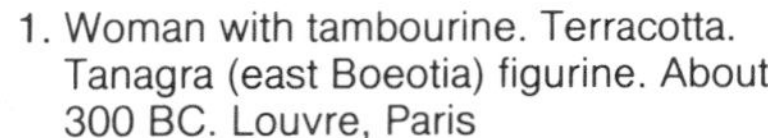

1. Woman with tambourine. Terracotta. Tanagra (east Boeotia) figurine. About 300 BC. Louvre, Paris
2. Woman. Terracotta. Tanagra (east Boeotia) figurine. About 300 BC. Louvre, Paris
3. Athenodoros, Hagesandros and Polydoros of Rhodes: Laocoön and his sons. Marble. About 50 BC or late 2nd century BC. Vatican Museums
4. Victory, or Nike, of Samothrace. Marble About 200 BC. Louvre, Paris
5. Venus of Melos. Detail. Late 2nd centu BC. Louvre, Paris
6. Demosthenes. About 280 BC. Ny Carlsberg Glyptotek, Copenhagen

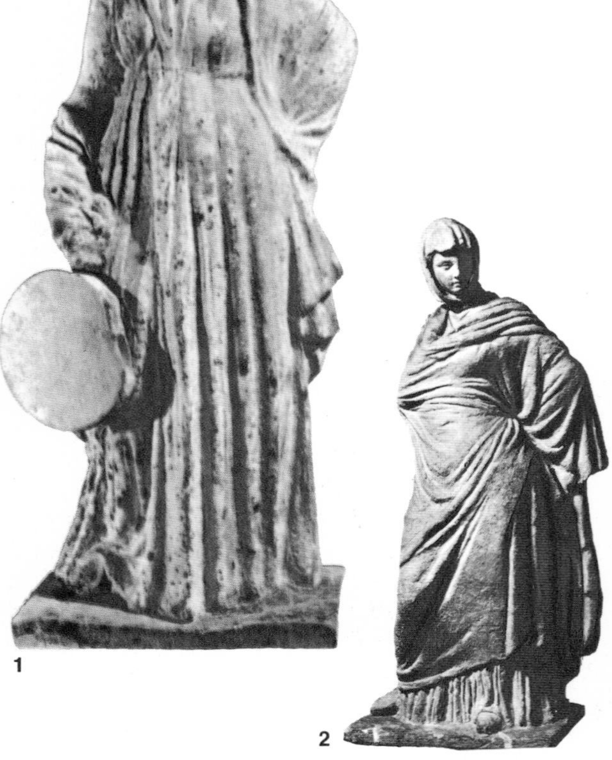

1

2

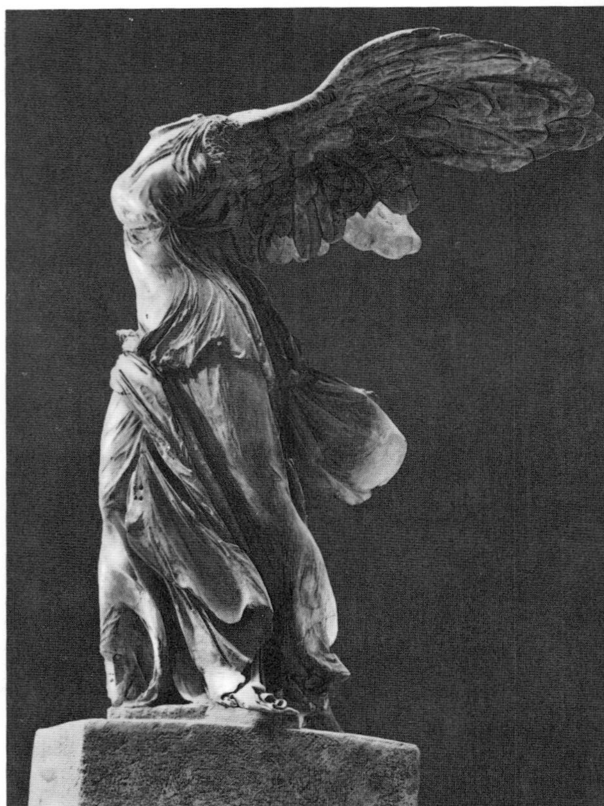

4

3

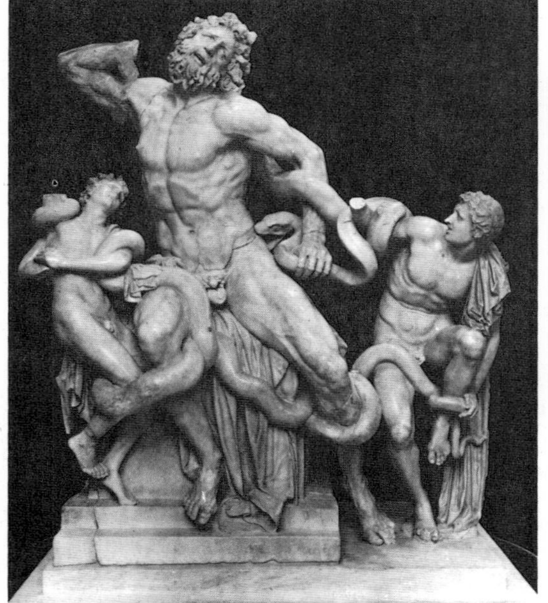

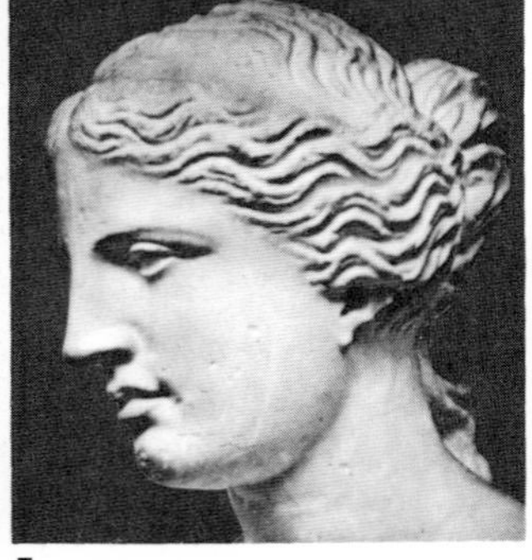

5

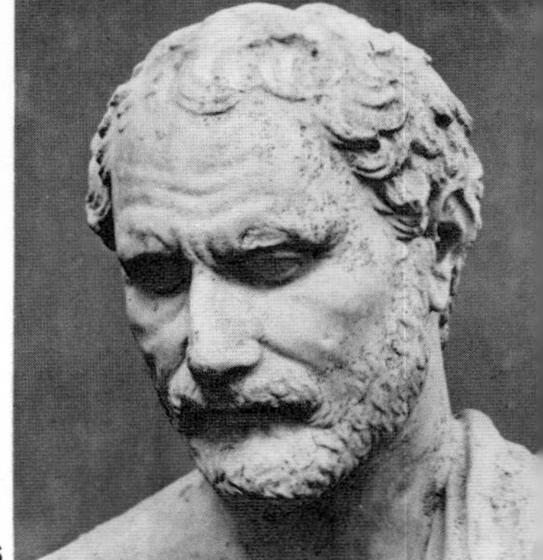

6

Part 4

The Roman World and the Early Middle Ages

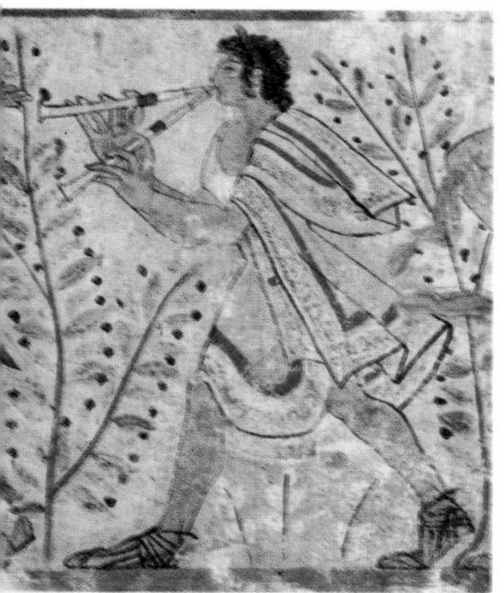

Flute Player. Etruscan art, *c.*470 BC. Tomb of the Leopards, Tarquinia

Supremacy in the Mediterranean eventually passed from Greece to Rome, whose empire included Britain, Gaul, Spain, North Africa, Syria and Asia Minor. It is hardly surprising that in their art the Romans would to some extent be influenced by the art of the Greek colonies in Italy. There was, however, also an art indigenous to the peninsula in the Etruscan settlements north of Rome. Etruscan art evolved in a similar way to that of Greece. It is chiefly characterized by a forceful execution and a primitive charm that tends to grasp the form of Greek art, but not always its dignity. While their vases were made in imitation of Greek work the Etruscans also developed their own pottery (known as black ware). Their traditional burial customs have led to the survival of frescoes, a great deal of bronze work and a number of terracottas. The jewellery perhaps exhibits the most lively and original expression of their skills.

In the art of republican and imperial Rome there is a greater concern for natural and realistic representation than the search for ideal form that Greek art had demonstrated. This is most apparent in the portraiture and historical reliefs decorating triumphal arches, columns and sarcophagi. The subjects of these reliefs were usually taken from religious and civic ritual. The scale of Roman art is, on the whole, more expansive, particularly in architecture, wall paintings, and mosaics. The wall paintings and mosaics again illustrate a wider range of subject matter, including pure landscape. If it is true to say that the Romans built to last, then it is hardly surprising that their architecture and other works of art have been so influential. Besides developing their own type of pottery, known as Arretine ware, on which the images are in raised relief, they also displayed a special interest in luxury goods such as gems, medallions, coinage and glass.

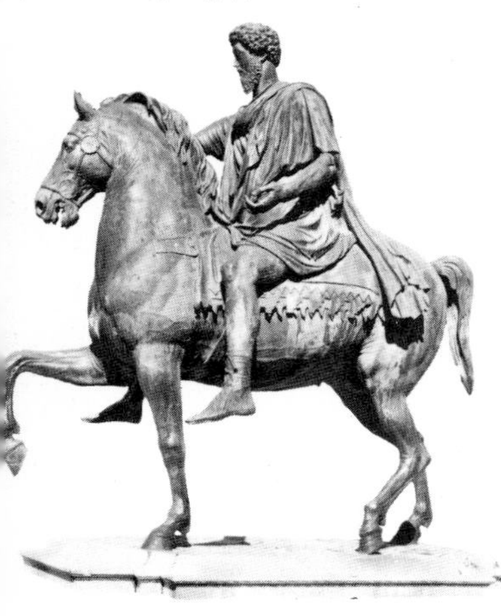

Equestrian statue of Marcus Aurelius. Roman art, *c.*170. Campidoglio, Rome

The conversion of Constantine the Great to Christianity and the official recognition of the religion in AD 312–13, followed in 330 by the foundation of a new capital, Constantinople, in the Eastern Empire, were momentous events both politically and artistically. Early Christian art grows directly out of Roman imperial art. The subject matter takes on a new meaning, but the iconography was often only adapted. The Carolingians and the Ottonians preserved Charlemagne's ideal of the Holy Roman Empire and their finest art is found in the form of architecture, ivories, manuscripts and precious metals, mostly used in an ecclesiastical context. More distant countries in northern Europe, where a similar transition from pagan to Christian themes can be observed, reacted no less ardently to the task of providing ecclesiastical furnishings and objects for liturgical use. It was, however, in Constantinople itself and throughout the Byzantine Empire, which for a time included Ravenna, that Christian art was nurtured in its purest vein. The development of a Byzantine style over a number of centuries can be traced in wall paintings, mosaics, manuscripts, architecture, and also in sculpture (mainly ivories). During this period Byzantine art was looked upon as the guardian of Greek ideals and learning and this belief was a potent factor in the evolution of European art right up to the Renaissance.

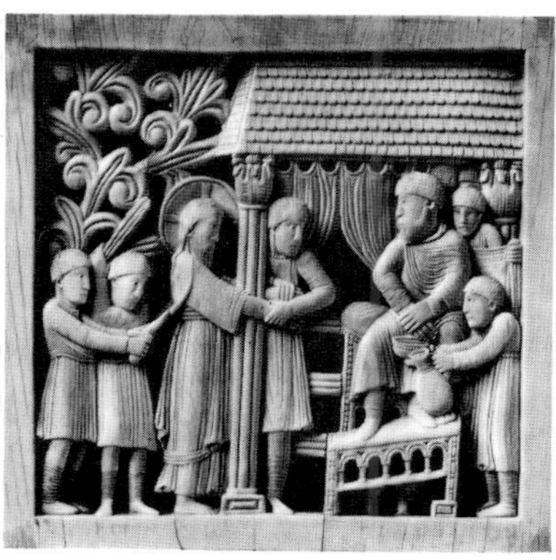

Christ before Pontius Pilate, and Flagellation. Ivory. Ottonian art. *c.*970. Bayerisches Nationalmuseum, Munich

Madonna and Child. Icon. Byzantine art, Byzantine Museum, Athens

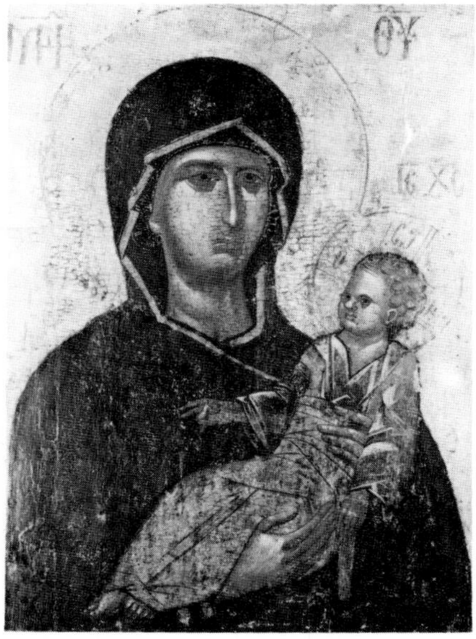

1. Cinerary urn. Terracotta. Sarteano. Late 7th century BC. Museo Archeologico, Florence
2. Sarcophagus. Stone. 3rd century BC. Museo Nazionale Tarquiniense, Tarquinia
3. Head of Hermes. Painted terracotta. Veii. About 500 BC. Museo Nazionale di Villa Giulia, Rome
4. Flute player. Tomb of the Leopards, Tarquinia. About 470 BC
5. Human mask. Bronze. Chiusi. 700–650 BC. Staatliche Antikensammlungen, Munich
6. Model of an Etruscan temple of the 6th century BC, decorated with revetmen and terracotta statues
7. Dancer. Tomb of the Triciinium. Museo Nazionale Tarquiniense, Tarquinia
8. Chimera from Arezzo. Bronze. 5th centu BC. Museo Archeologico, Florence

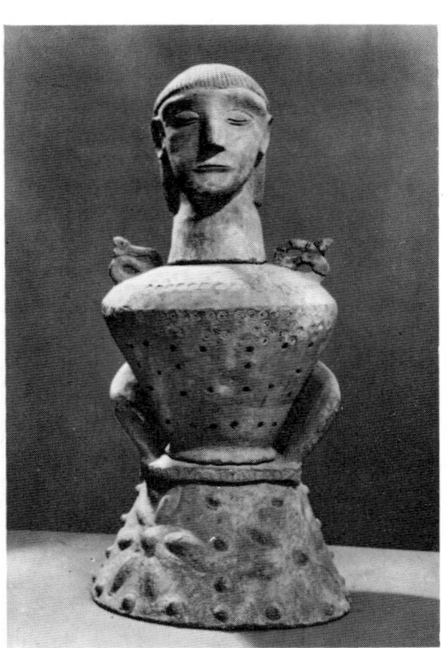

1

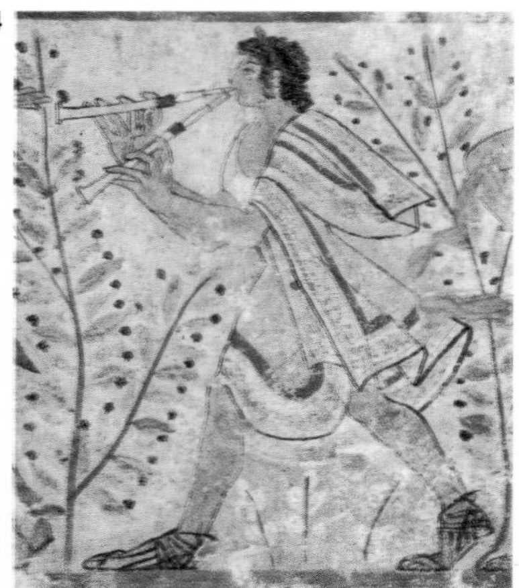

4

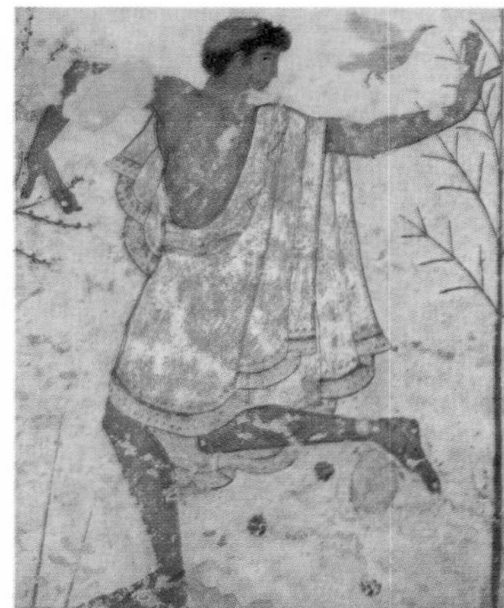

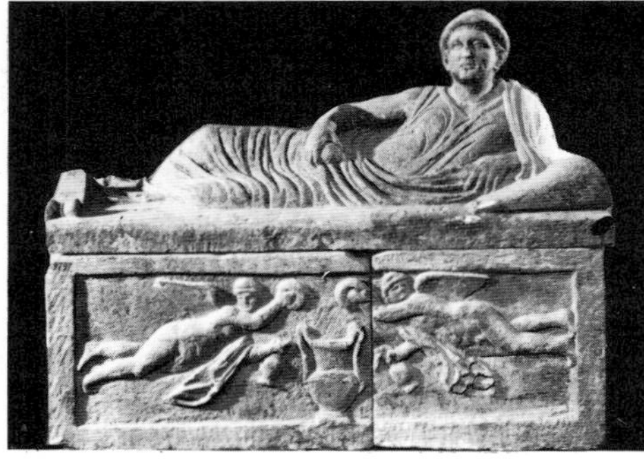

2

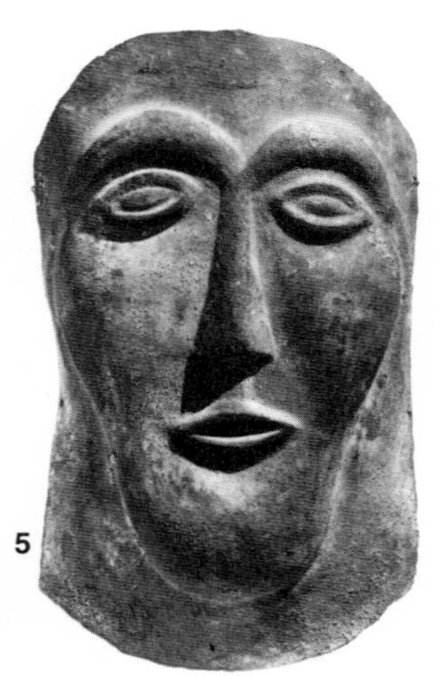

5

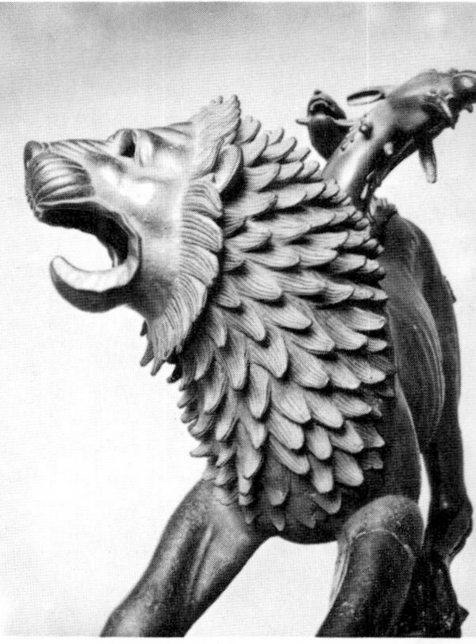

8

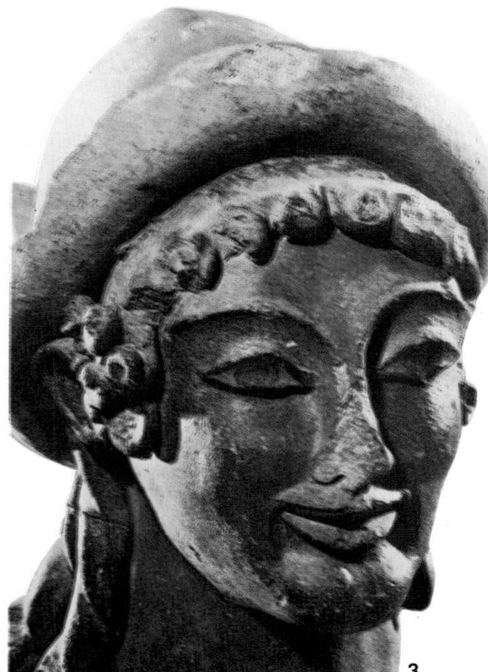

3

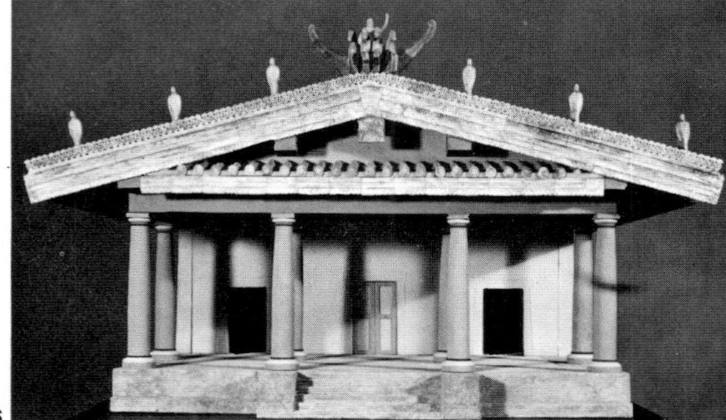

6

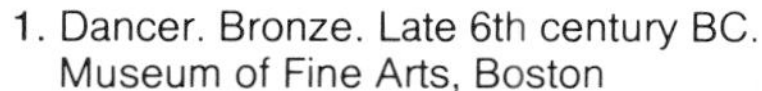

1. Dancer. Bronze. Late 6th century BC. Museum of Fine Arts, Boston
2. Female votive figure. Bronze. 4th–3rd century BC. Louvre, Paris
3. Head of warrior. Orvieto. 530–520 BC. Museo Archeologico, Florence
4. Spectator (or referee?) at funerary games. Tomb of the Augurs, Tarquinia. About 530 BC
5. Offering of the cup. Tomb of the Baron, Tarquinia. Late 6th century BC
6. Sarcophagus. Terracotta. Cerveteri. 6th century BC. Louvre, Paris
7. Mars of Todi. Bronze. 380–370 BC. Vatican Museums
8. Woman borne by winged being. Painted terracotta. Cerveteri. 6th century BC. Louvre, Paris

1

3

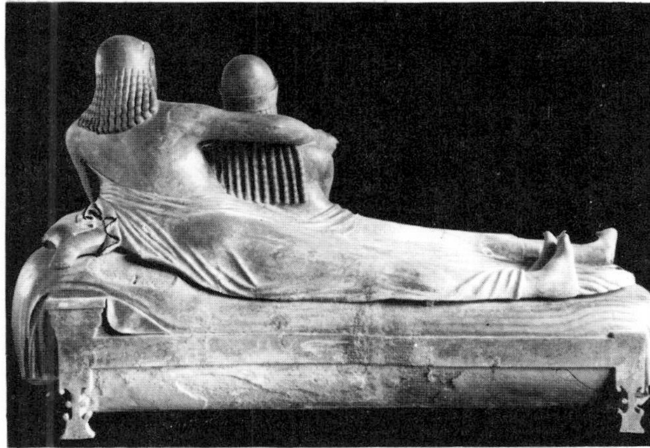

6

4

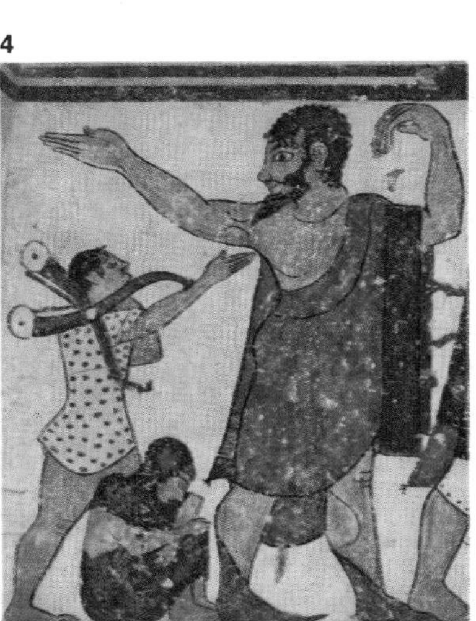

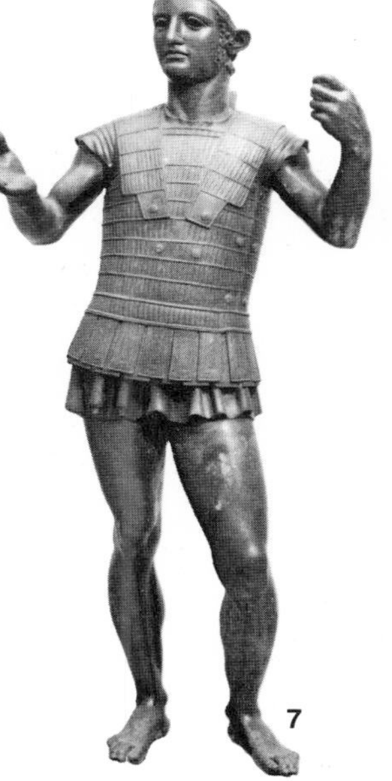

7

8

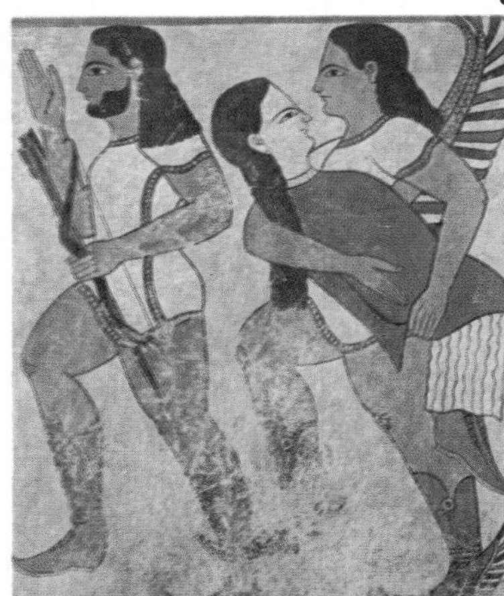

5

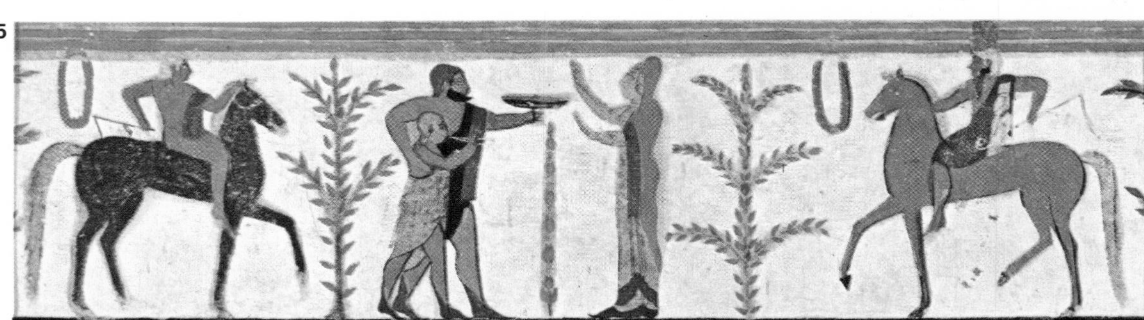

2

1. Funeral procession of women from a tomb at Ruvo di Puglia. Fresco. Late 5th century BC. Museo Nazionale, Naples
2. Unknown man. Marble. About 31 BC. Metropolitan Museum of Art, New York.
3. She-wolf with Romulus and Remus. Bronze. Wolf, by Etruscan artists, about 500 BC; twins added during the Renaissance. Museo Capitolino, Rome
4. Model of Temple of Fortune, Praeneste (Palestrina). About 80 BC. Museo Archeologico e Tempio della Fortuna Primigenia, Palestrina
5. Lucius Junius Brutus (?). Bronze. Etruscan, 3rd century BC. Museo Capitolino, Rome
6. Elevation of the Maison Carée, Nîmes. Pseudo-peripteral temple with podium

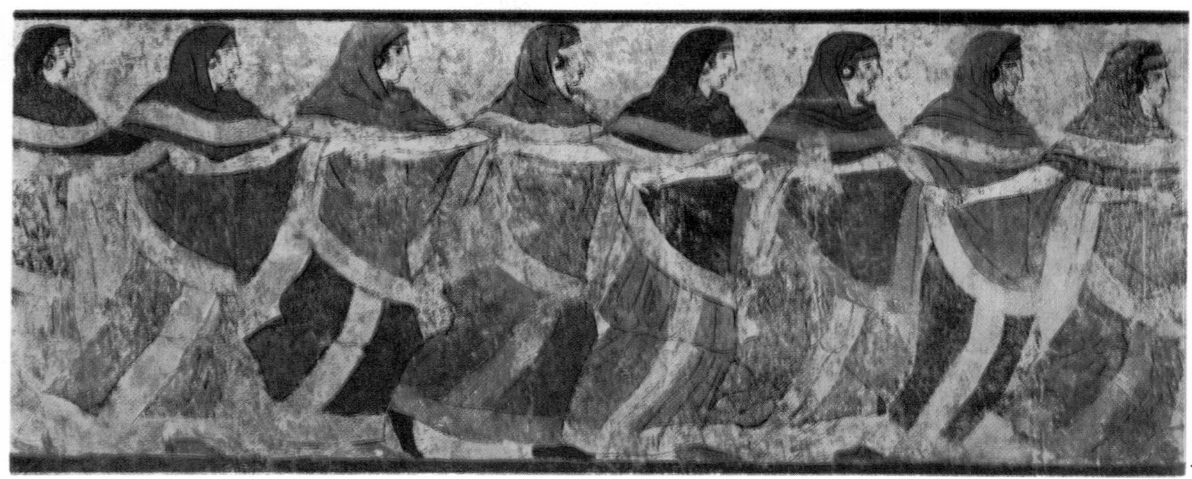

1

2

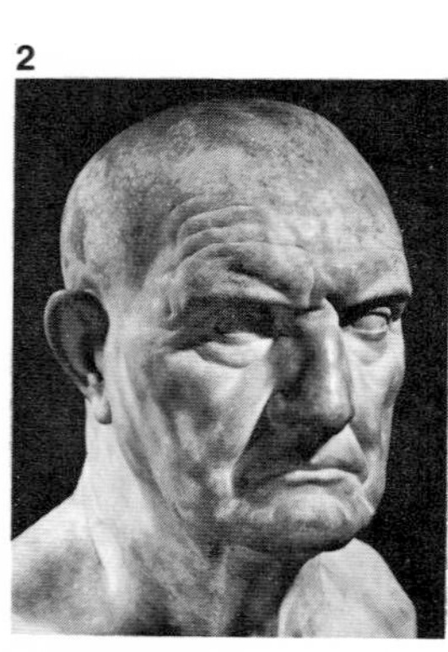

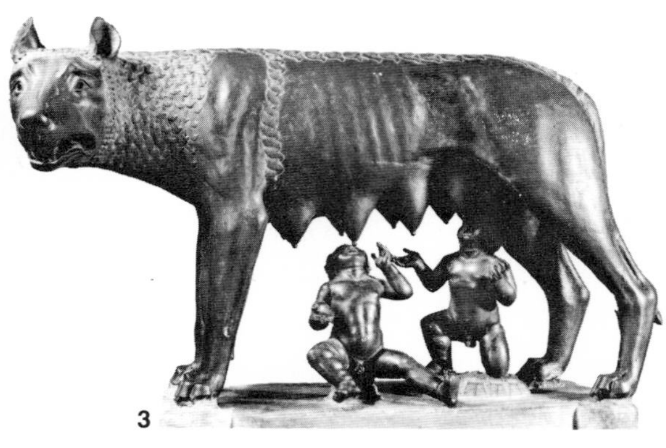

3

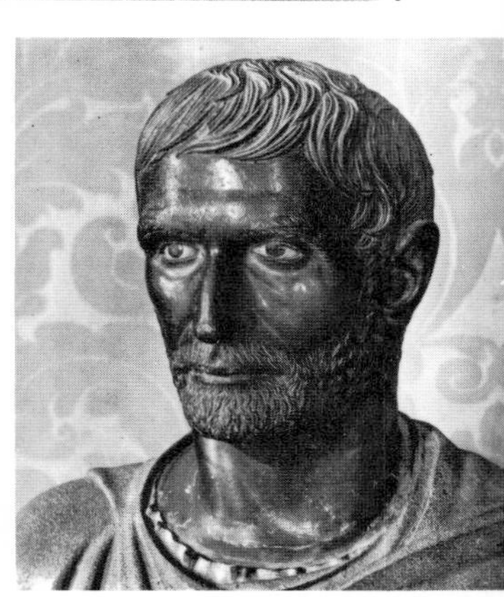

5

4

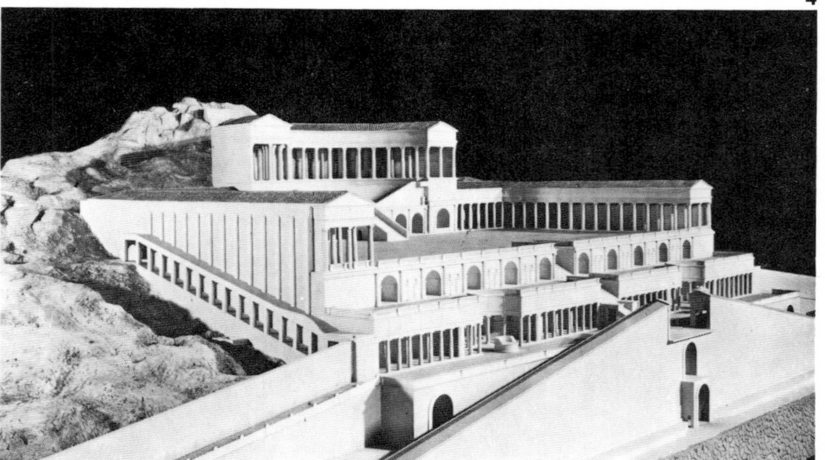

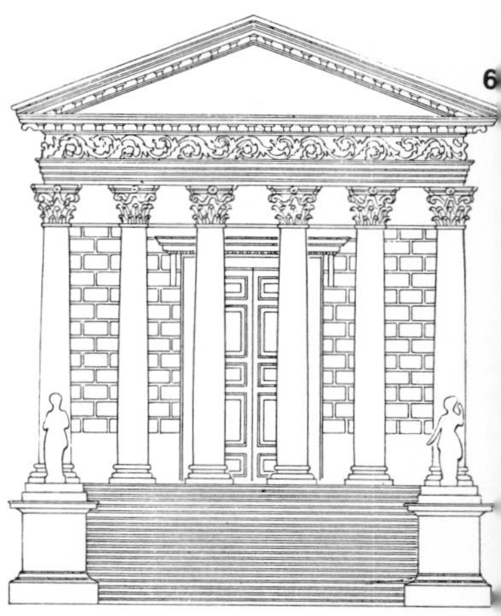

6

1. Temple of Fortuna Virilis, Rome. 1st century BC
2. Wandering musicians. Mosaic by Dioscurides of Samos from Cicero's villa, Pompeii. Late 1st century BC. Museo Nazionale, Naples
3. Venus. Wall painting from House of the Marine Venus, Pompeii. About AD 70
4. Portrait of the Domina (mistress of the household). Wall painting from the Villa of the Mysteries, Pompeii. Late 1st century BC
5. View of a port. Wall painting from Stabiae. About AD 50. Museo Nazionale, Naples

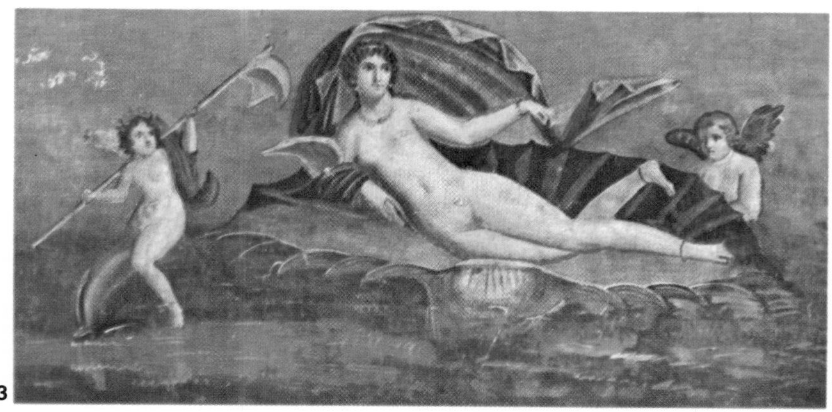

3

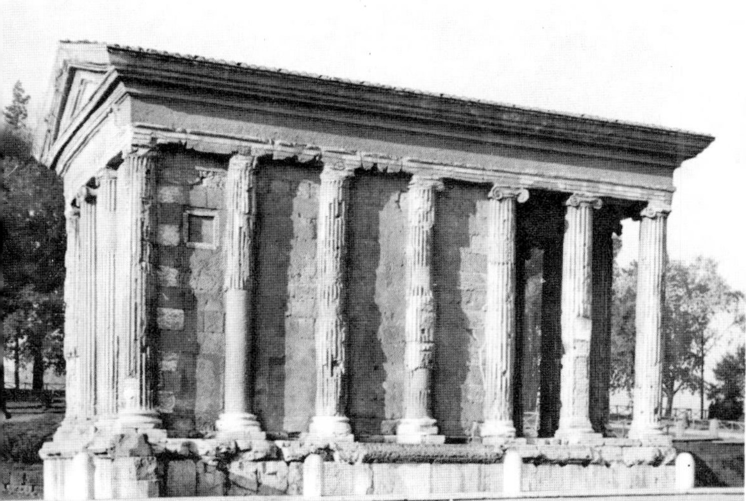

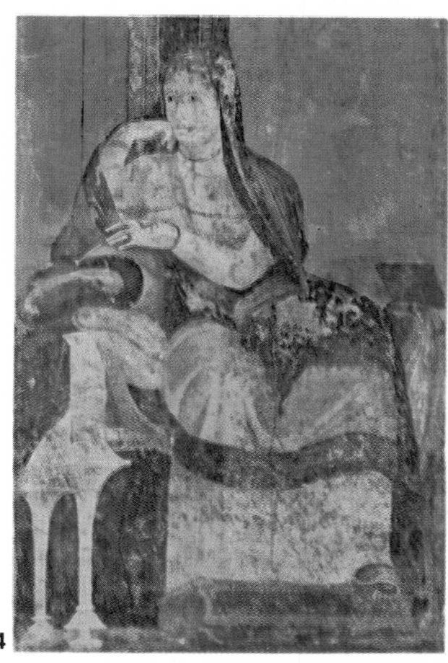

4

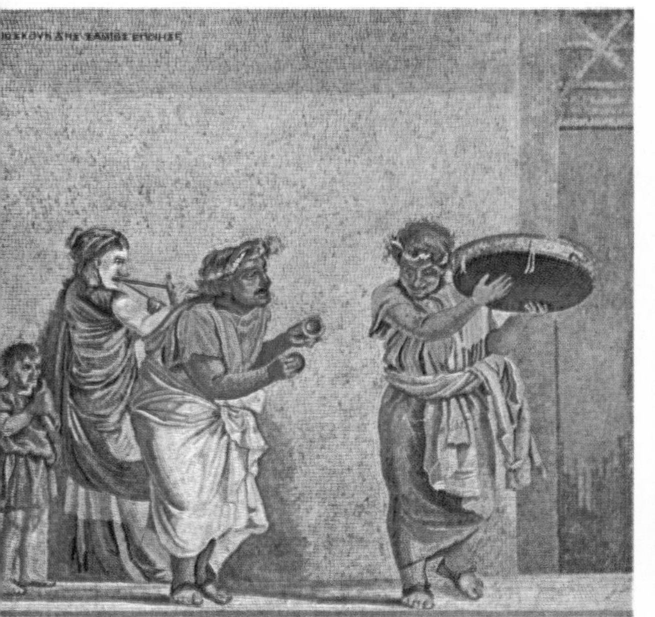

5

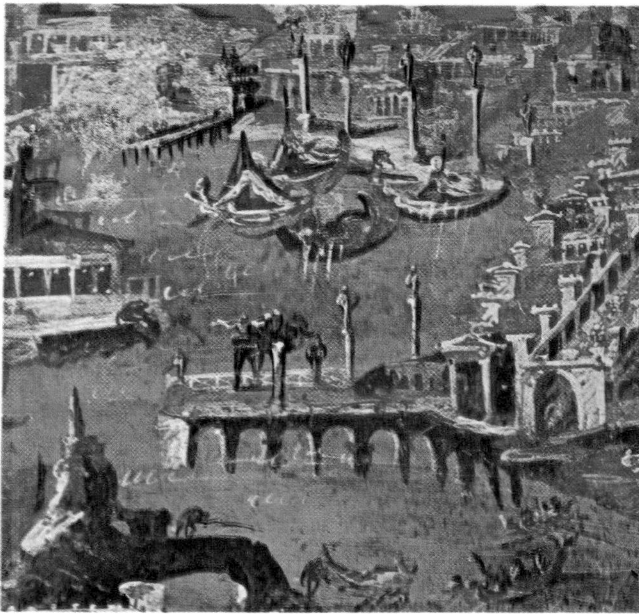

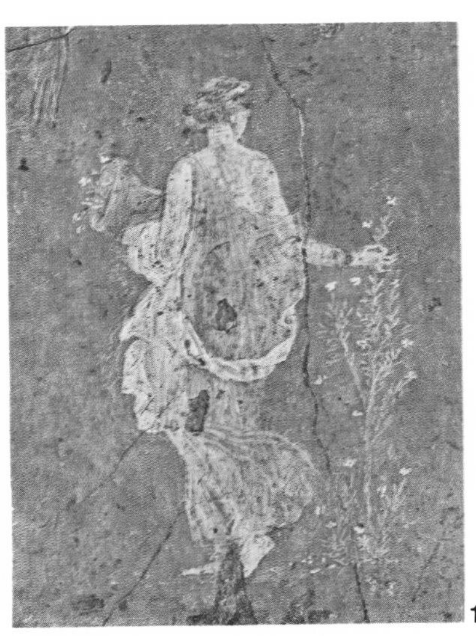

1

1. Young girl gathering flowers. Wall painting from Stabiae, a Roman resort on the Bay of Naples (on the site of present-day Castellammare di Stabia) destroyed in AD 79, with Pompeii and Herculaneum, by the eruption of Vesuvius. 1st century AD
2. House of the Faun, Pompeii. 2nd century BC. The statuette of the faun in the foreground
3. Dancing Bacchante. Wall painting from the Villa of the Mysteries, Pompeii. Late 1st century BC
4. Amazon. Wall painting from Herculaneum. 1st century AD. Museo Nazionale, Naples
5. Still life with game. Wall painting from the House of Julia Felix at Pompeii. 1st century BC. Museo Nazionale, Naples
6. View of Herculaneum, showing villas with atrium (central hall with an opening to the sky) and gardens

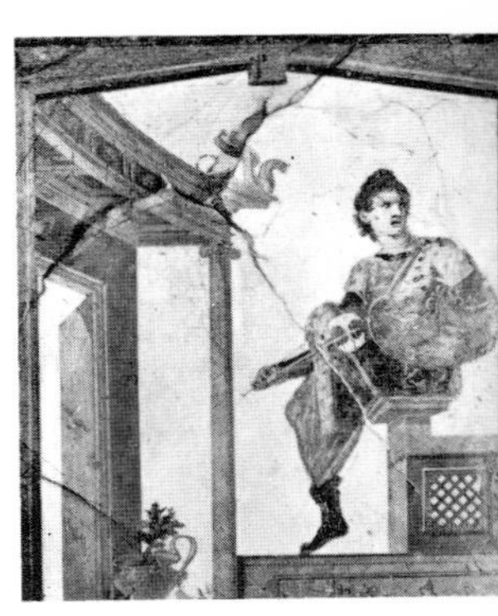

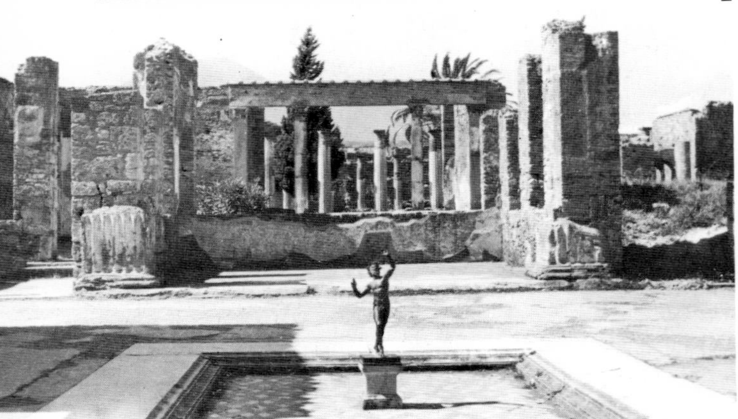

2

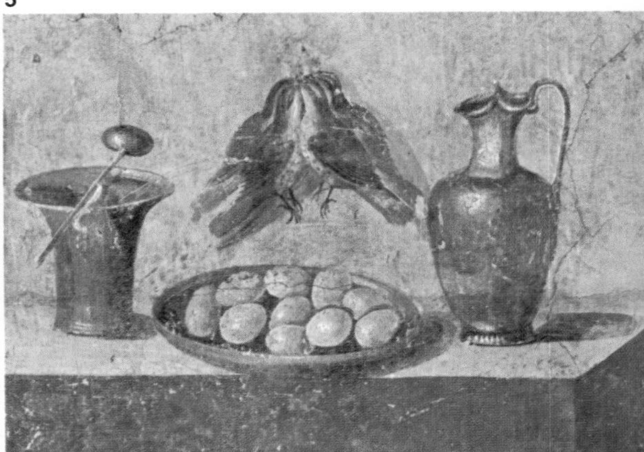

5

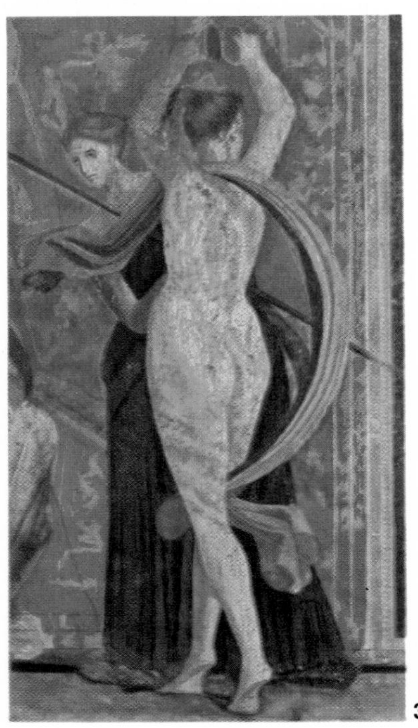

3

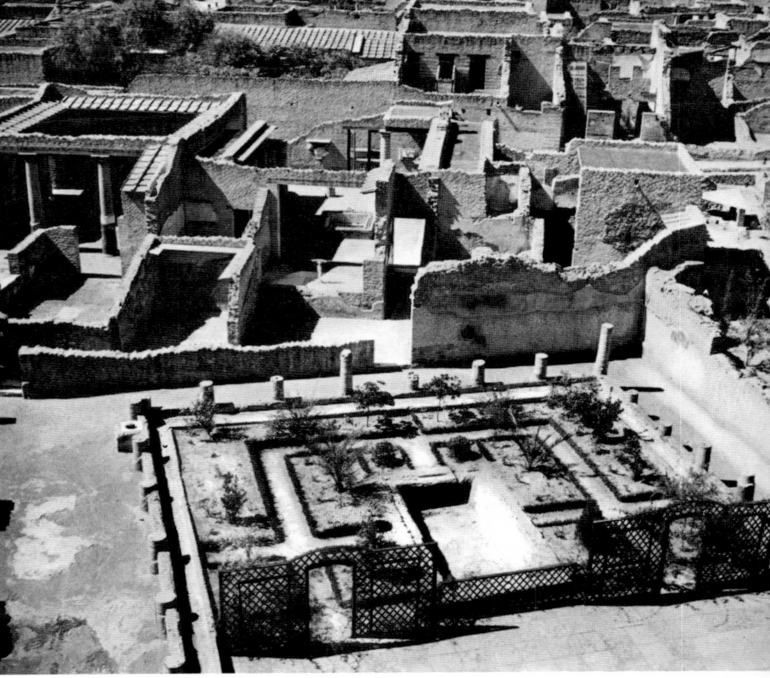

6

1. Roman patrician carrying busts of his ancestors. Marble. About 30 BC. Museo Capitolino, Rome
2. The Colosseum, or Flavian amphitheatre, Rome. AD 72–80
3. Aldobrandini wedding. Fresco. 1st century AD. Vatican Library
4. Statue of Augustus from Prima Porta, Rome. Detail. About 20 BC. Vatican Museums
5. Lower portion of Trajan's Column, Rome. Marble. Built, perhaps by Apollodorus of Damascus, to celebrate Trajan's victories over the Dacians, which are recounted in the spiral band of reliefs. AD 106–13

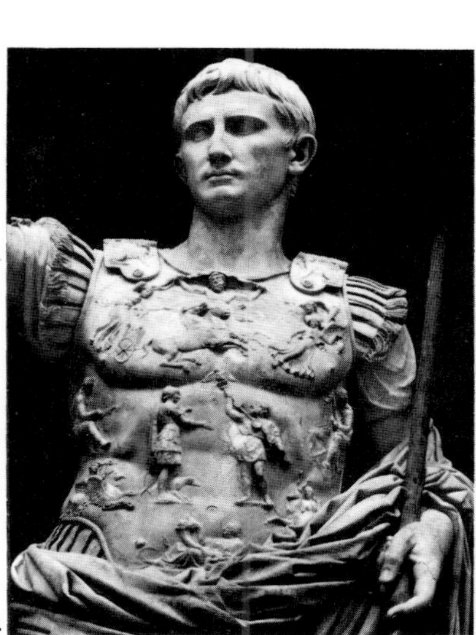
4

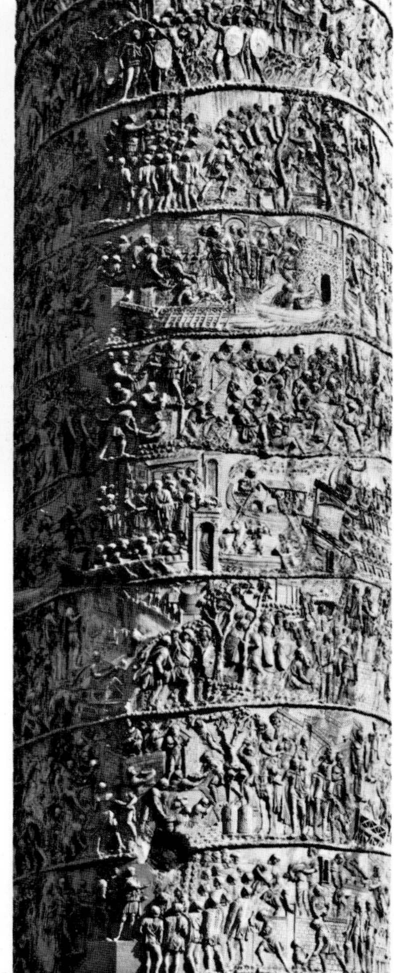
5

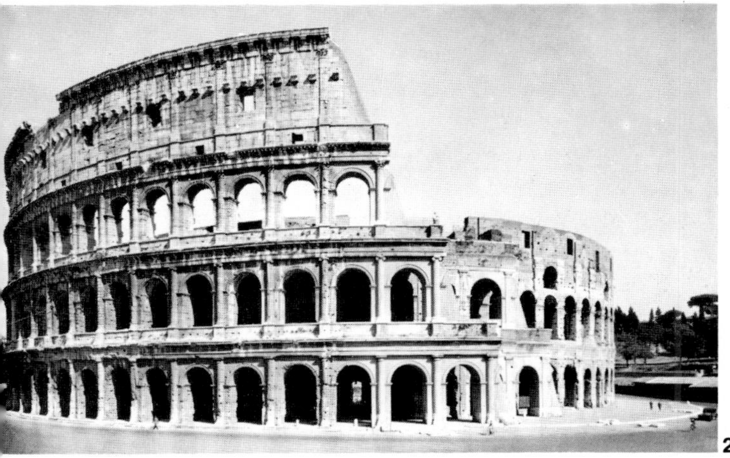
2

3
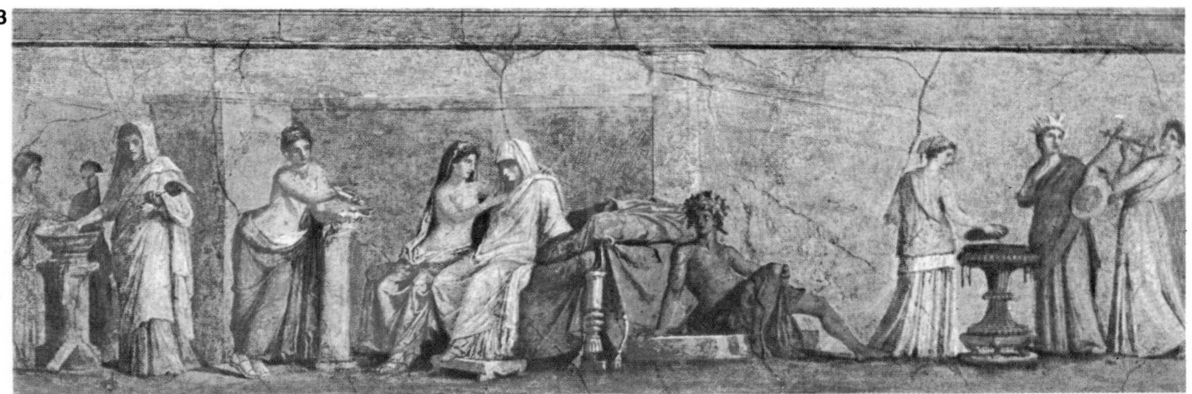

1. Amphitheatre, Nîmes. Early 1st century AD
2. Marcus Aurelius. Detail from equestrian statue on the Campidoglio, Rome. About AD 170
3. Lucius Caecilius Jucundus, Pompeian banker. Bronze. AD 41–54. Museo Nazionale, Naples
4. Thermopolium, Ostia, near Rome. 3rd century AD
5. Sea or river god. Bronze. Found at Bavaï, near Cambrai, France. 2nd century AD. Musée Archéologique du Centre Galloromain, Bavaï
6. The Arch of Constantine, Rome. AD 312–15
7. Young girl dressed as an acrobat. Mosaic. About AD 300. Piazza Armerina, Sicily
8. Empress Sabina, wife of Hadrian. Early 2nd century AD. Ostia Museum

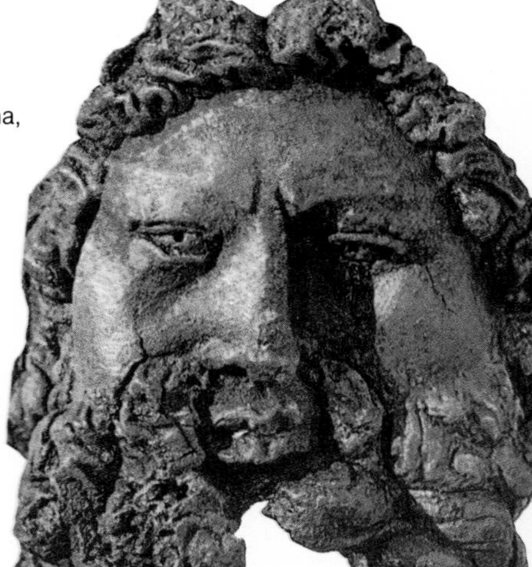

5

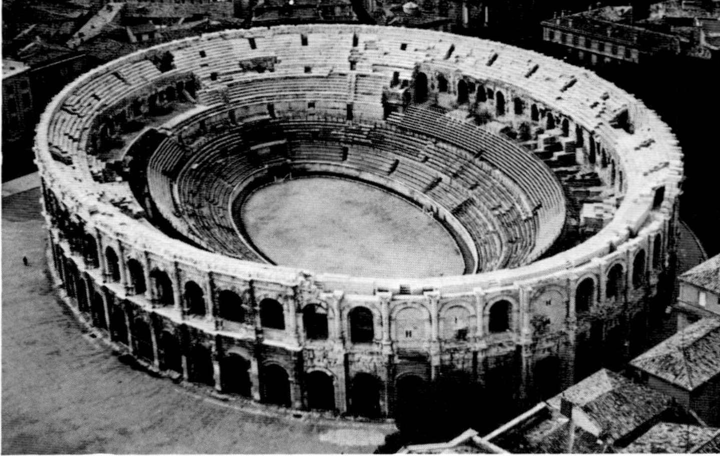

1

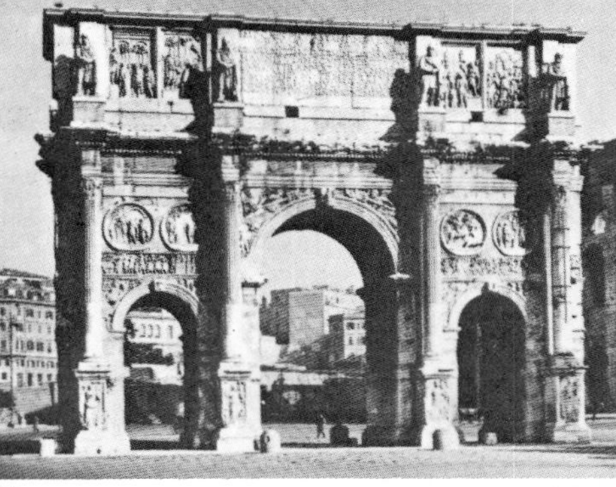

6

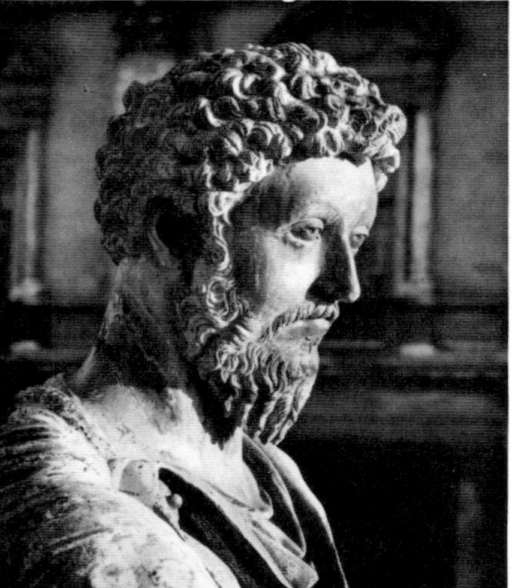

2

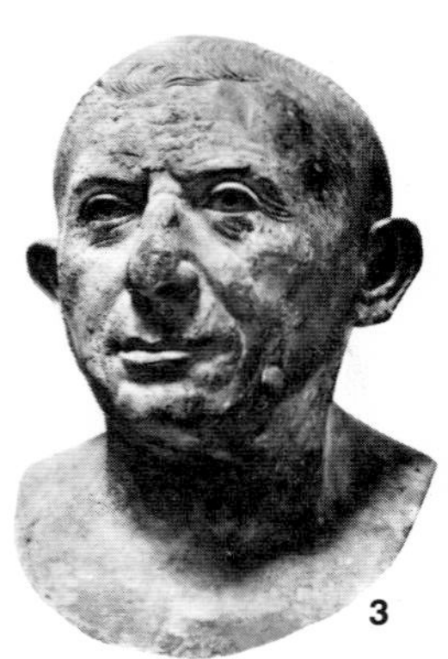

3

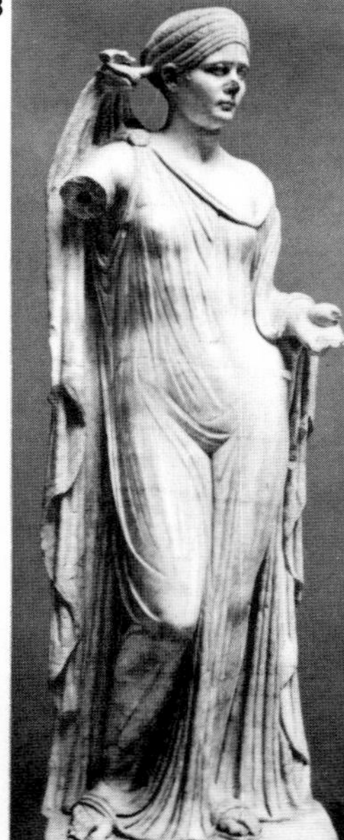

8

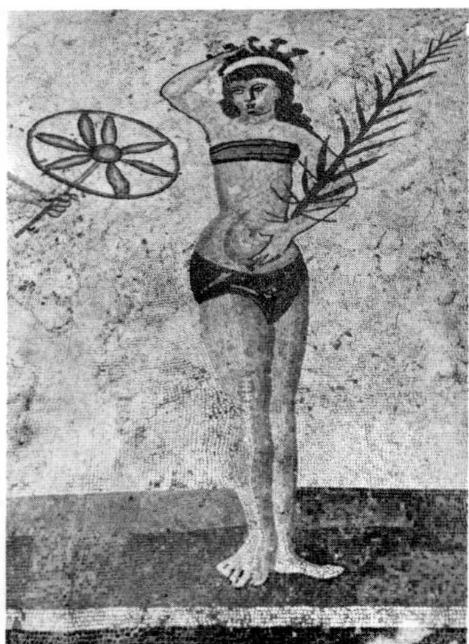

7

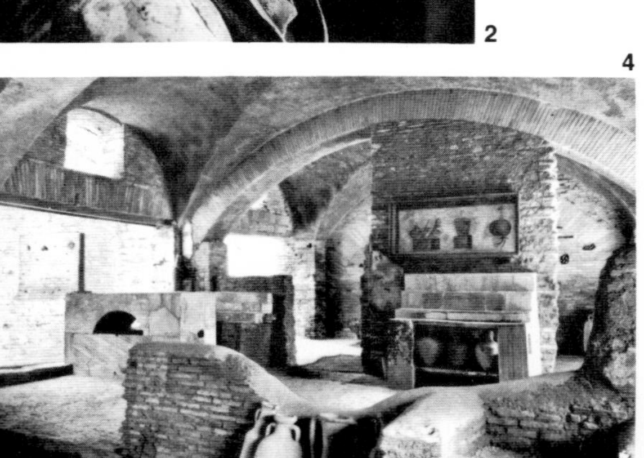

4

1. Christ as teacher. One of the earliest sculptural representations of Christ. 350–60. Museo delle Terme, Rome
2. The Good Shepherd. 3rd–4th century. Musée National du Bardo, Tunis
3. Mosaic pavement (detail) in the church of Shavei Zion, Israel. 5th century
4. Hospitality of Abraham. Mosaic (detail) in the nave of S. Maria Maggiore, Rome. 432–40
5. Scenes from the Passion. Detail of relief on a sarcophagus. About 350. Vatican Museums
6. S. Stefano Rotondo, Rome. About 475

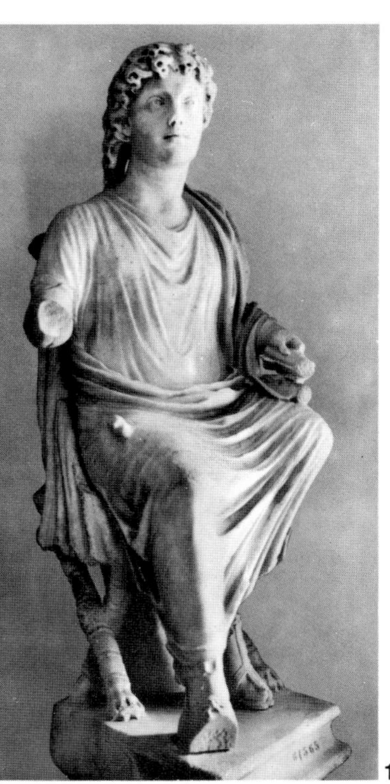

1

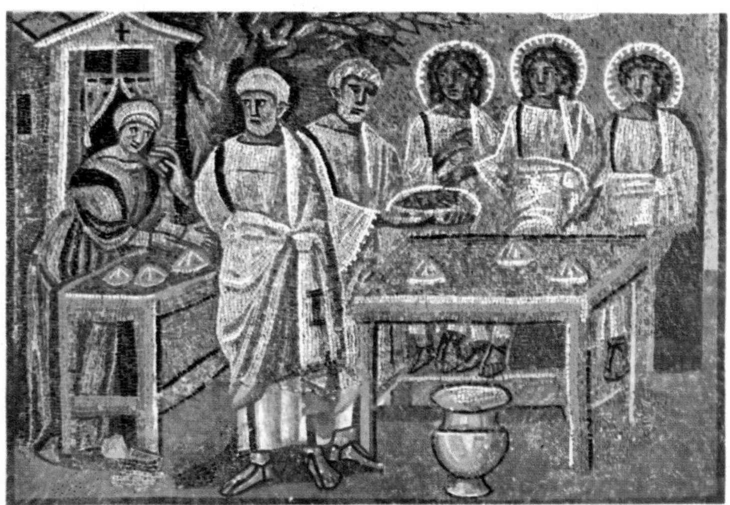

4

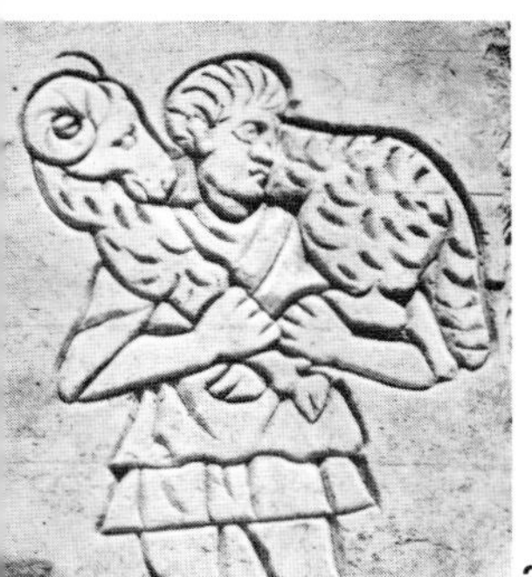

2

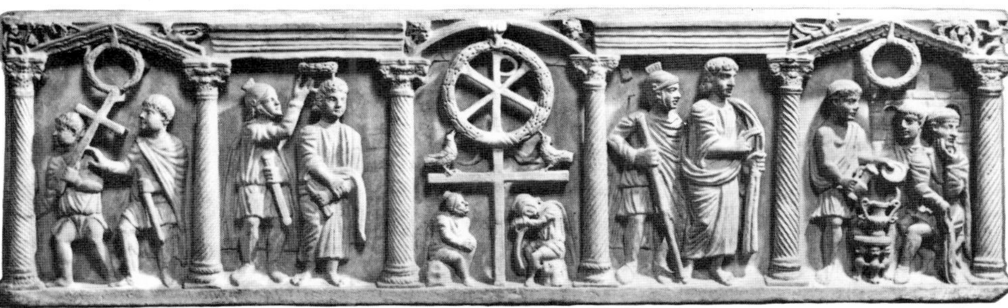

5

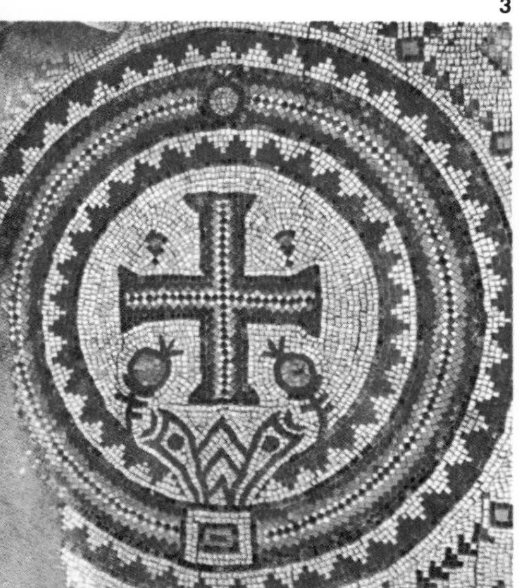

3

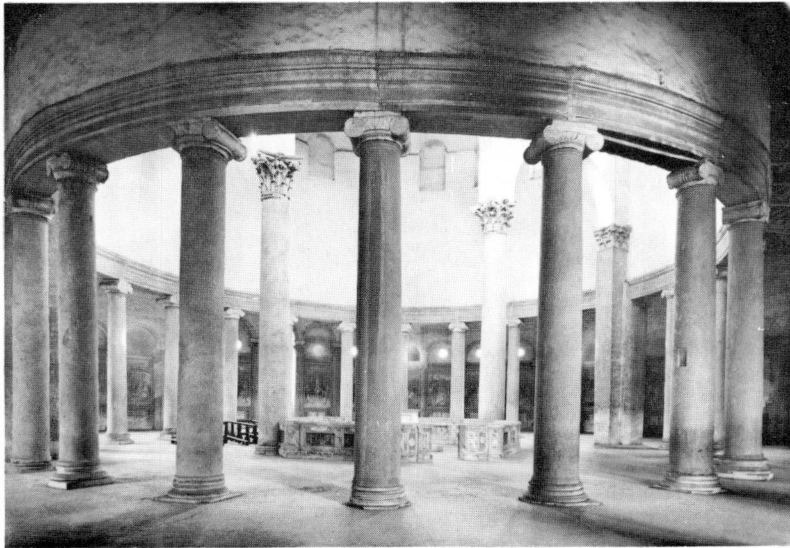

6

1. Ariadne. Ivory relief. 6th century. Musée de Cluny, Paris
2. Procession of the Holy Virgins. Mosaic in the nave of S. Apollinare Nuovo, Ravenna, Italy. After 526
3. Empress Theodora. Detail of mosaic in the choir of S. Vitale, Ravenna. About 546
4. Mosaic of the apse of S. Apollinare in Classe, Ravenna. In the centre: S. Apollinare. About 549
5. Capital in S. Vitale, Ravenna. 6th century
6. Head of an empress (Theodora?). 6th century. Castello Sforzesco, Milan
7. Triumph of an emperor (Justinian?). Det of the Barberini ivory. Early 6th century. Louvre, Paris

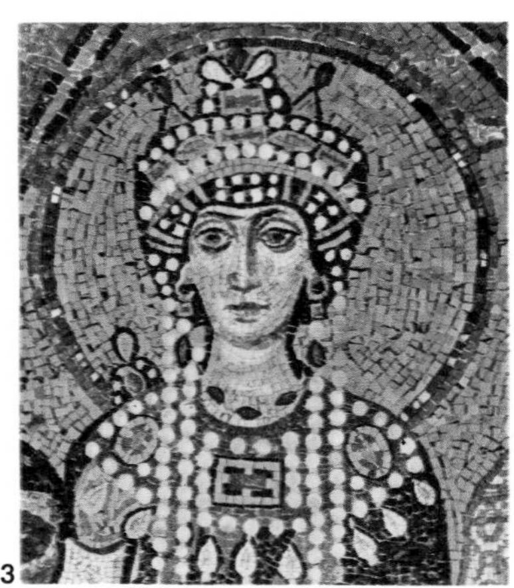

3

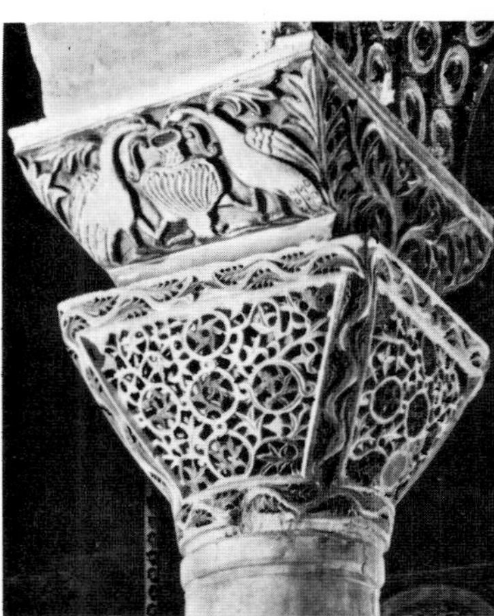

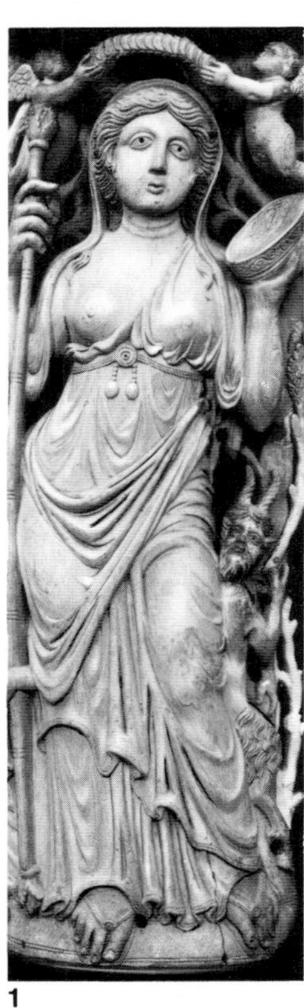

1

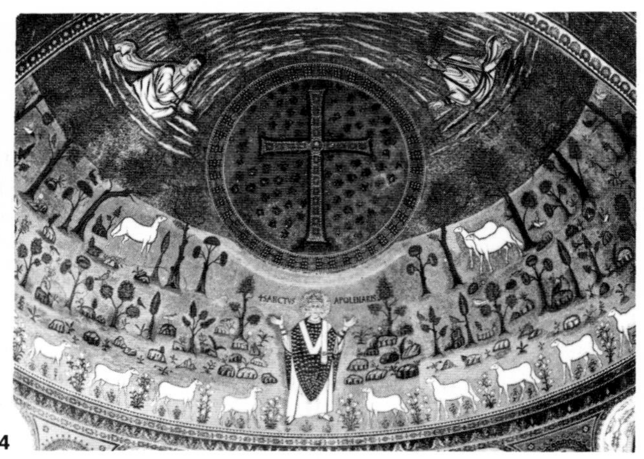

4

6

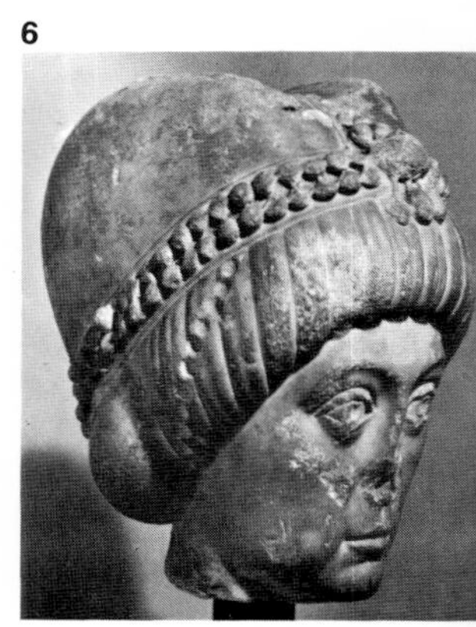

2

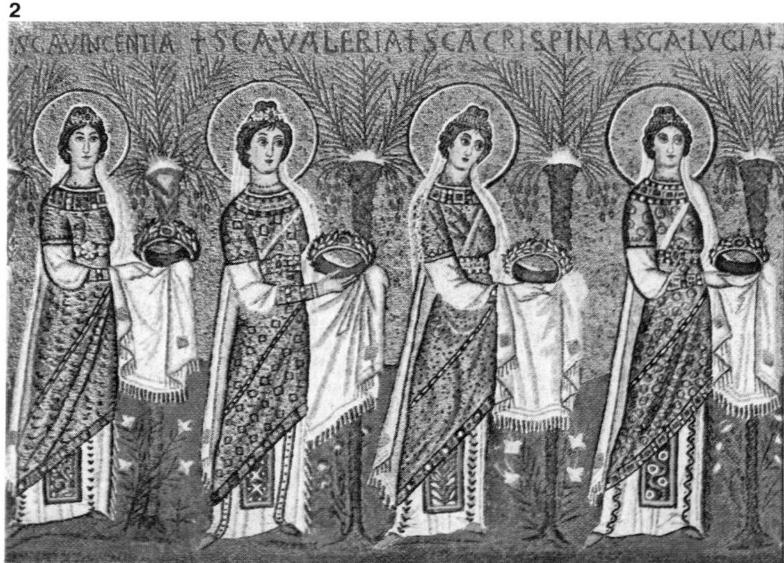

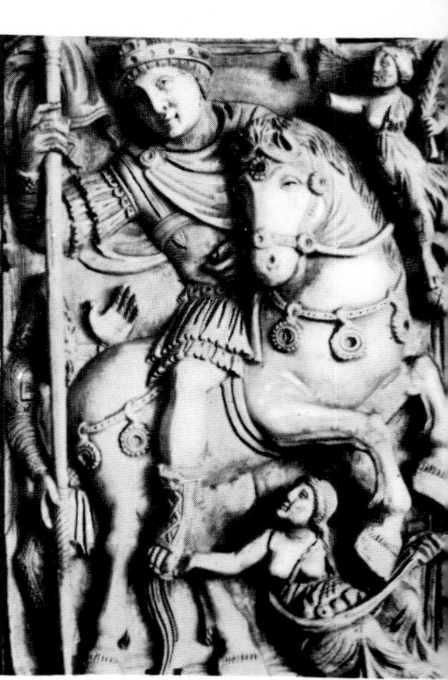

7

1. St Demetrius. Mosaic. 7th century. Church of St Demetrius, Salonika
2. Cross section of Hagia Sophia (*right*)
3. Christ symbolized by Orpheus. Marble. Late 4th century. Byzantine Museum, Athens
4. S. Vitale, Ravenna, Italy 526–47
5. Hagia Sophia, Istanbul. Built for Justinian between 532 and 537 by the Greek architects Anthemius of Tralles and Isidorus of Miletus. The minarets date from 1453

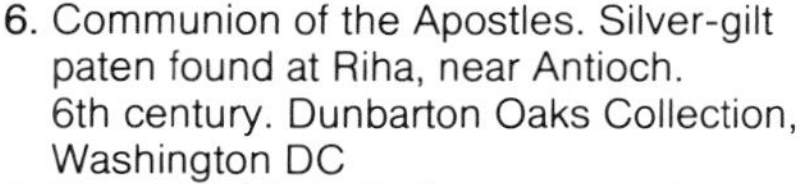

6. Communion of the Apostles. Silver-gilt paten found at Riha, near Antioch. 6th century. Dunbarton Oaks Collection, Washington DC
7. Plan of S. Vitale (*left*). 1 apse, 2 choir, 3 semicircular niches, 4 ambulatory, 5 narthex

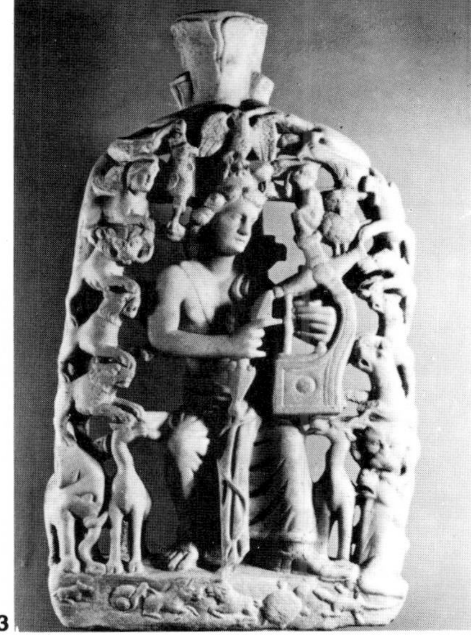

3

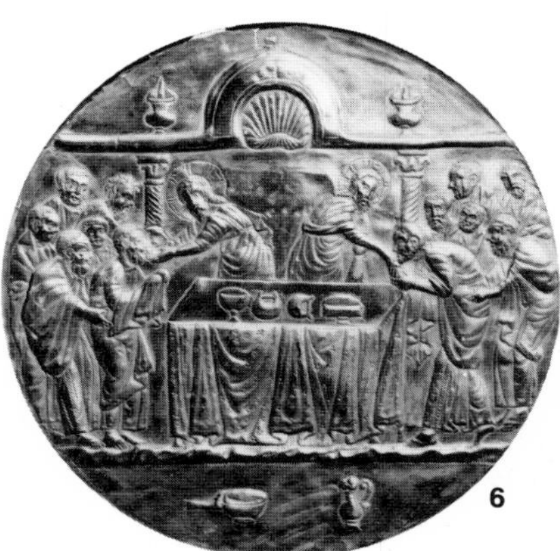

6

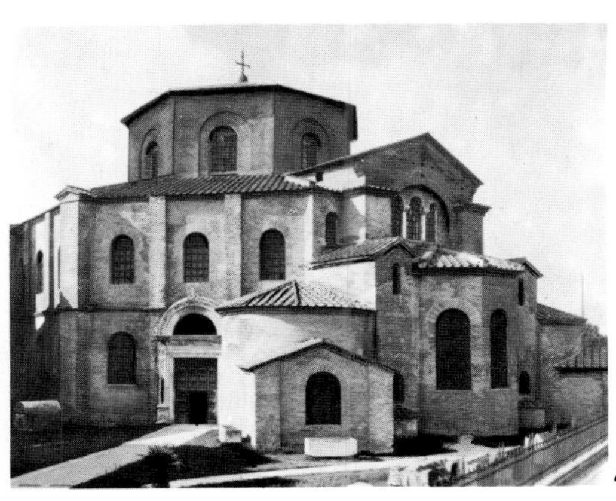

4

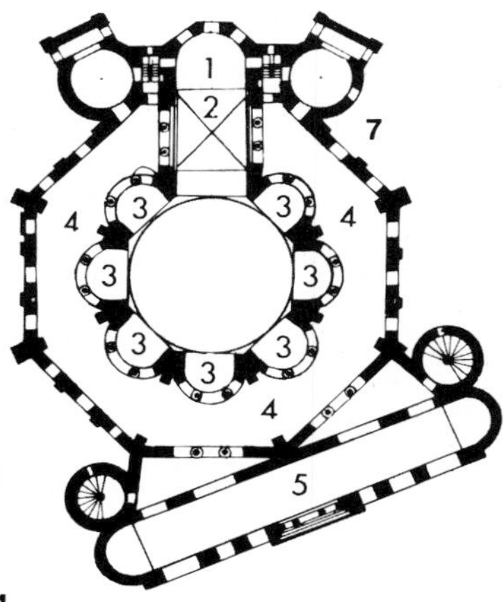

7

1

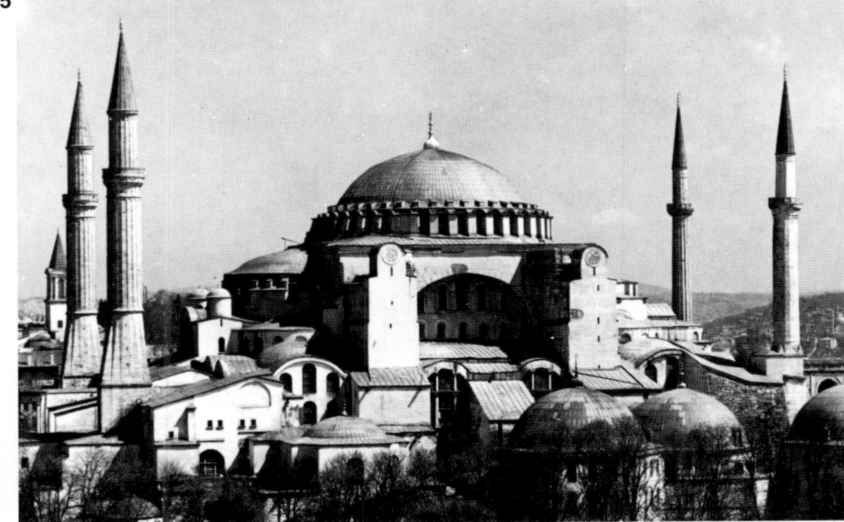

5

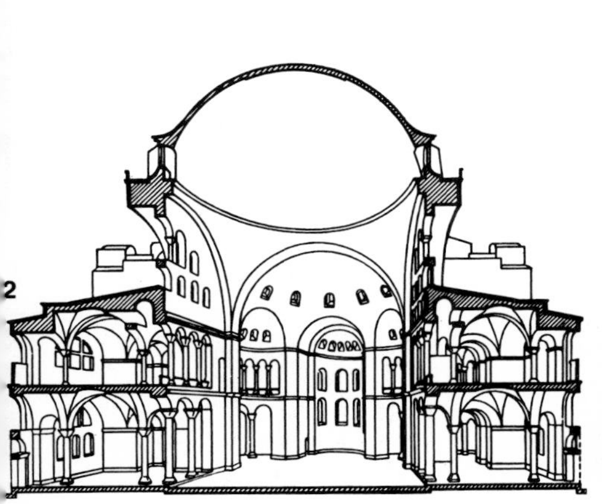

2

1. St John the Evangelist. Miniature on parchment. 10th century. National Library, Athens
2. Shroud of St Victor: Daniel in the Lions' Den (?). Silk. 8th century. Treasury of Sens Cathedral, France
3. Book cover with plaque of enamel, pearls and precious stones. 10th–11th century. Biblioteca Marciana, Venice
4. Relief with mythological subject. 10th–11th century. Byzantine Museum, Athens
5. Church of Hosios Lukas, near Delphi. 11th century
6. Archangel Gabriel. Detail from wing of a ivory triptych. 11th century. Benaki Museum, Athens

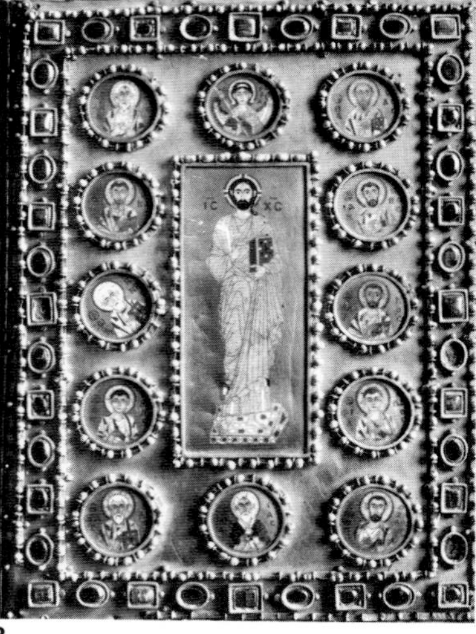

3

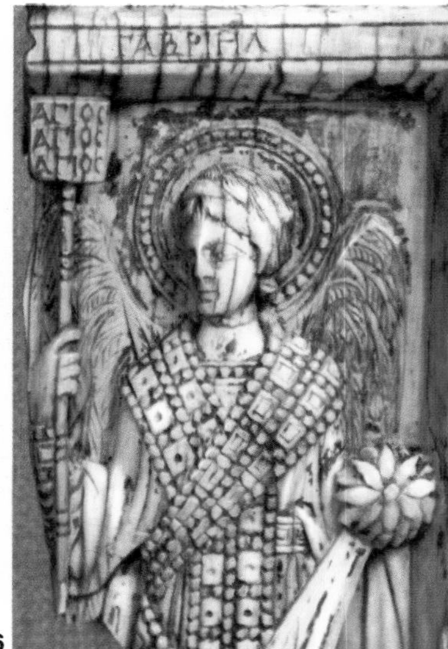

6

1

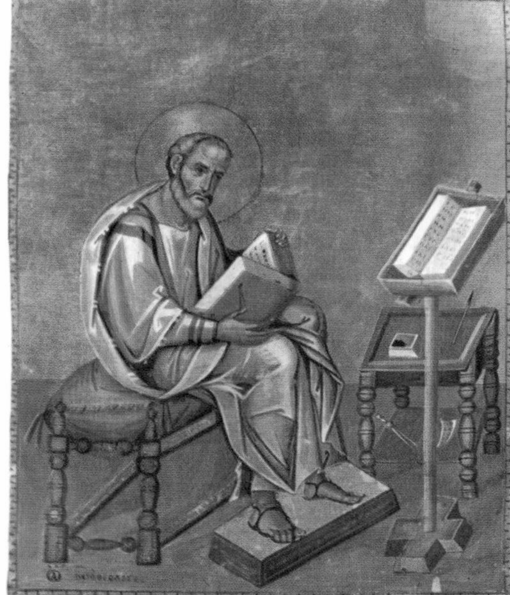

4

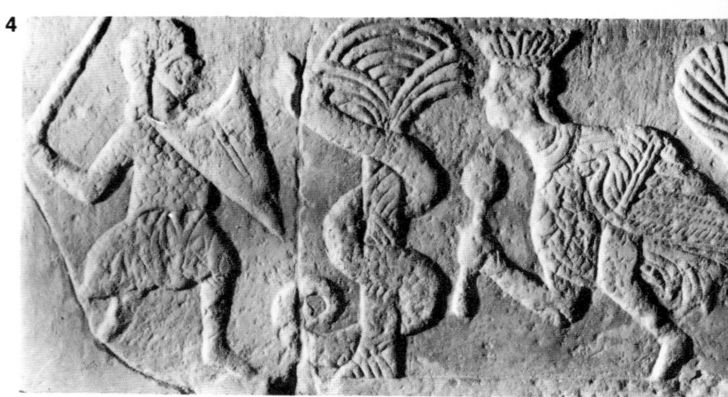

2

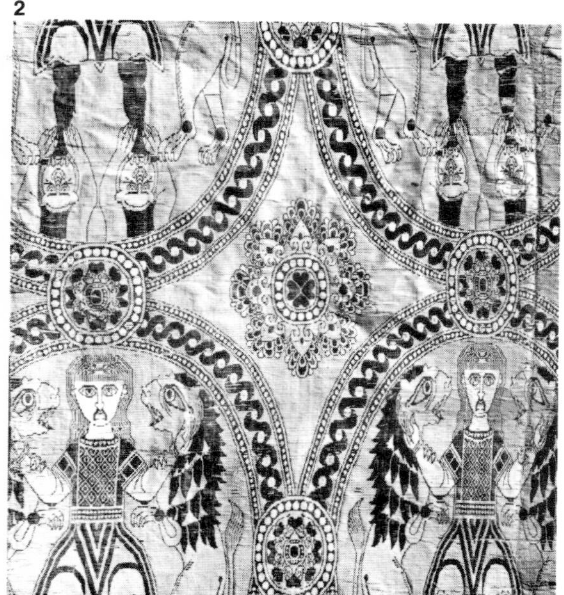

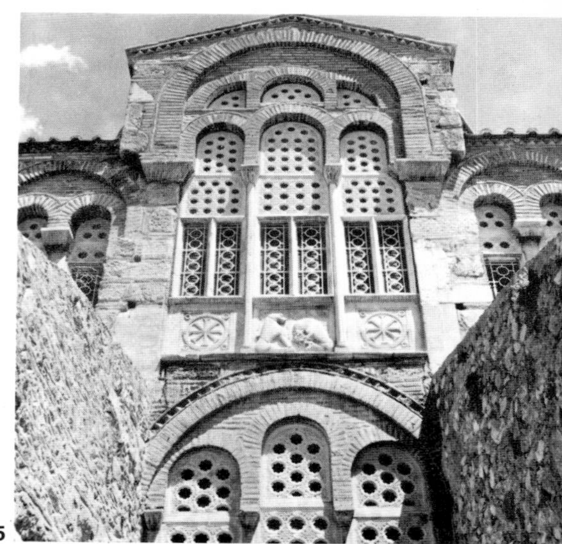

5

. Church of the Holy Apostles, Salonika. 1312–15. View of trilobed apse
. Virgin of Vladimir. Detail of an icon. 13th century. Tretyakov Gallery, Moscow
Noah releasing the Dove. Mosaic. 13th century. St Mark's Church, Venice
4. Christ Pantocrator. Enamel on bronze. 13th century. Museo di Palazzo Venezia, Rome
5. Flight into Egypt. Mosaic. 12th century. Palatine Chapel, Palermo, Sicily

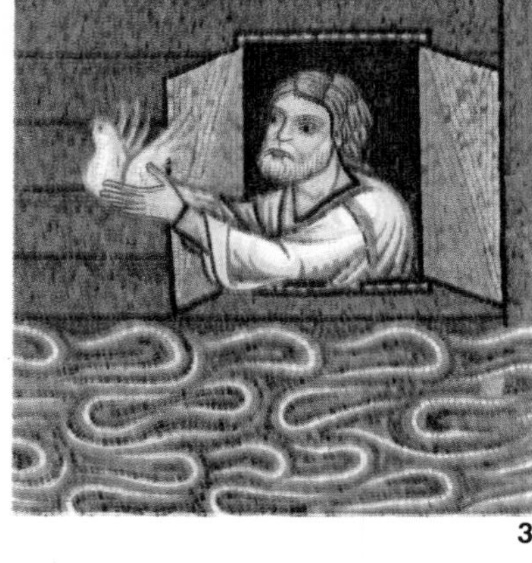

3

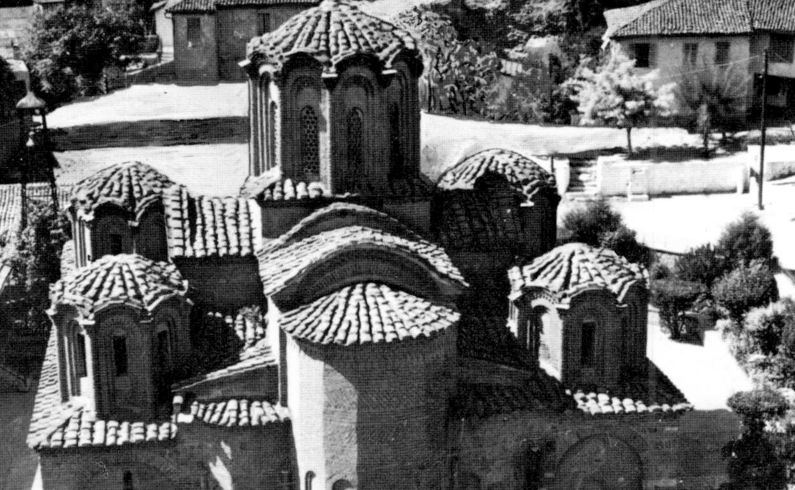

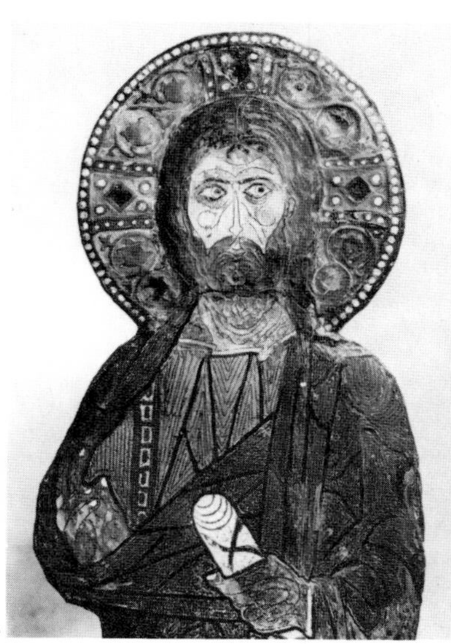

4

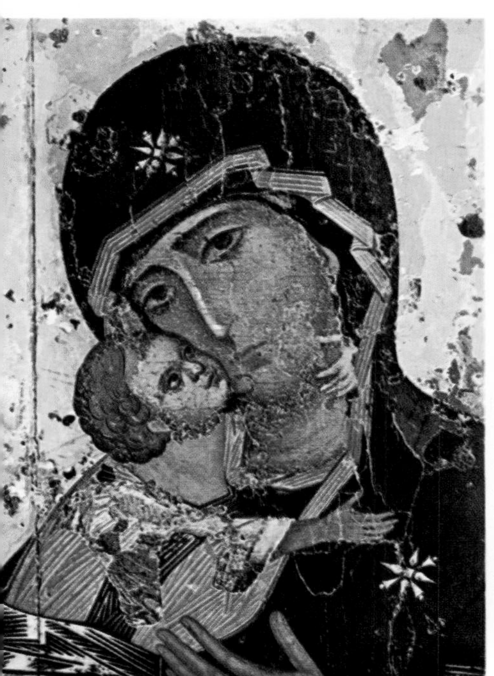

5

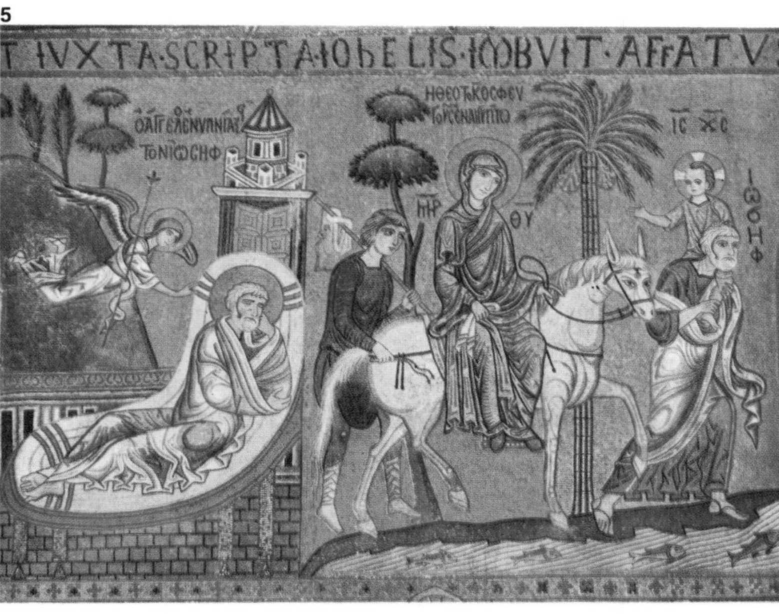

1. Monastery church of Gracanica, Yugoslavia. Built in 1321 during the reign of King Milutin
2. Head of colossal bronze statue of an emperor. 4th century. Barletta, Italy
3. Head of an angel. Fresco. 17th century. Byzantine Museum, Athens
4. Church of St Theodore, Mistra, Greece. Late 13th century
5. Trinity. Icon. 14th century (?). Benaki Museum, Athens

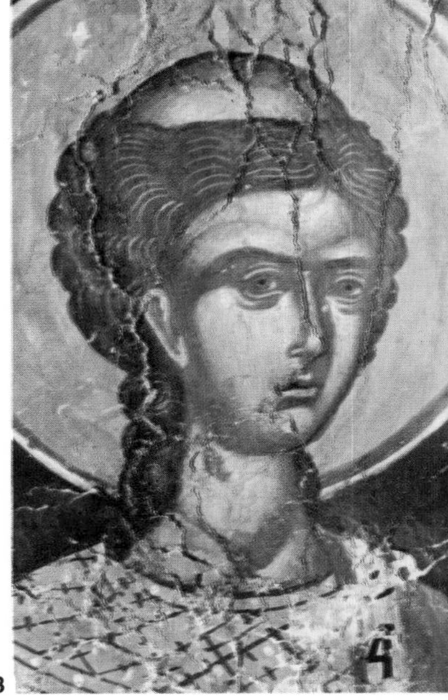

3

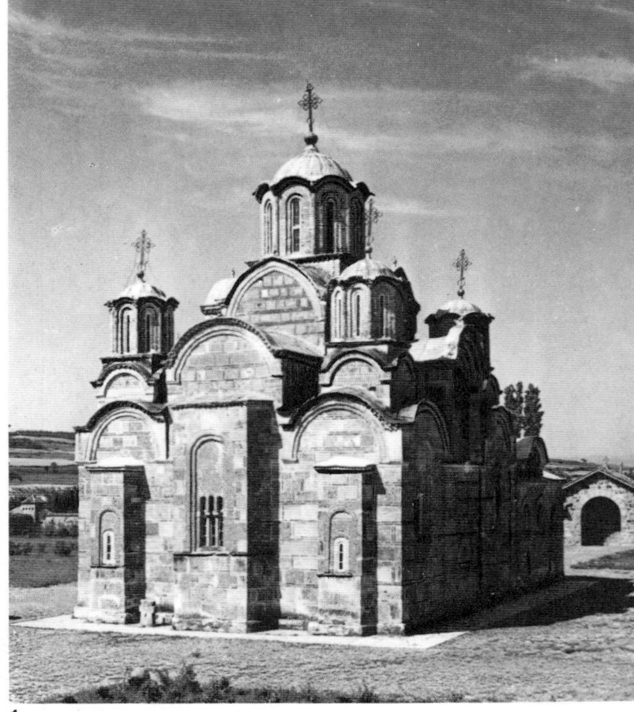

1

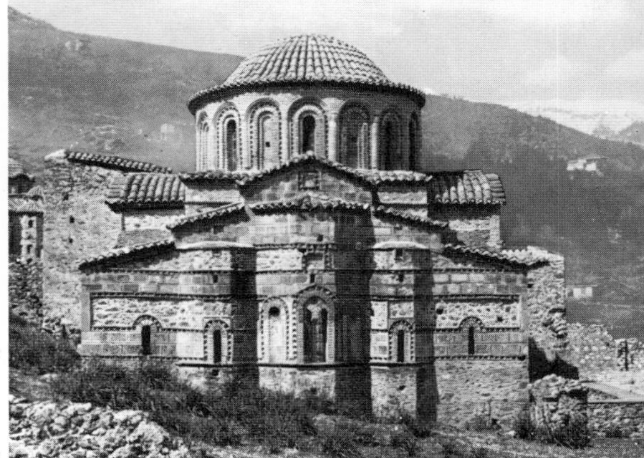

4

2

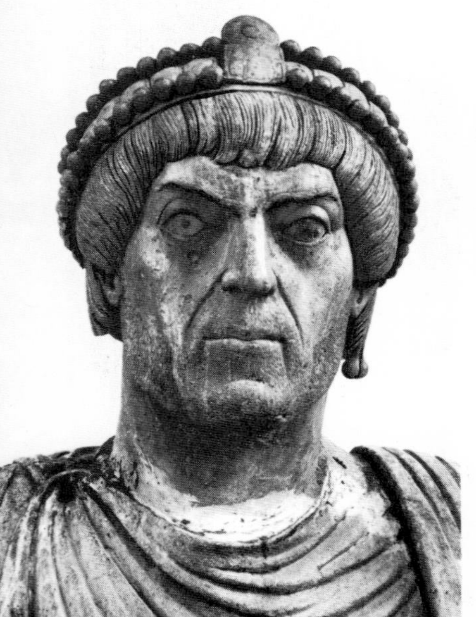

5

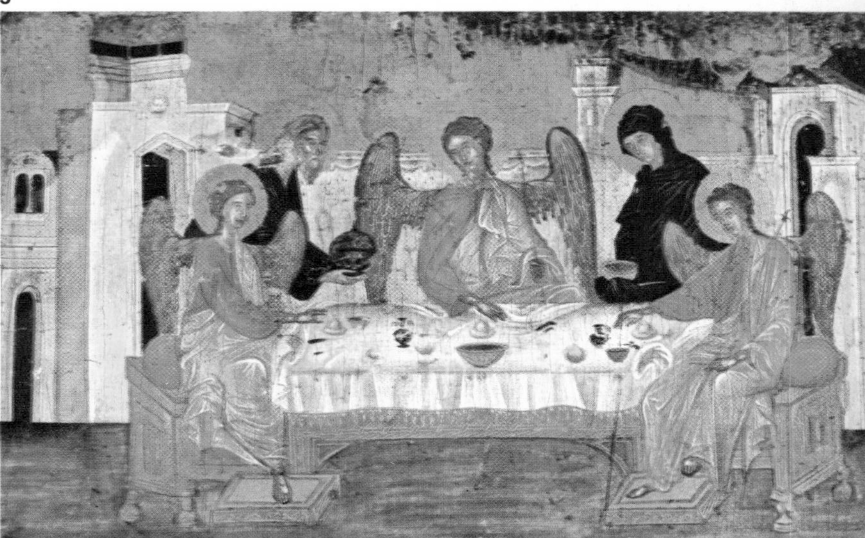

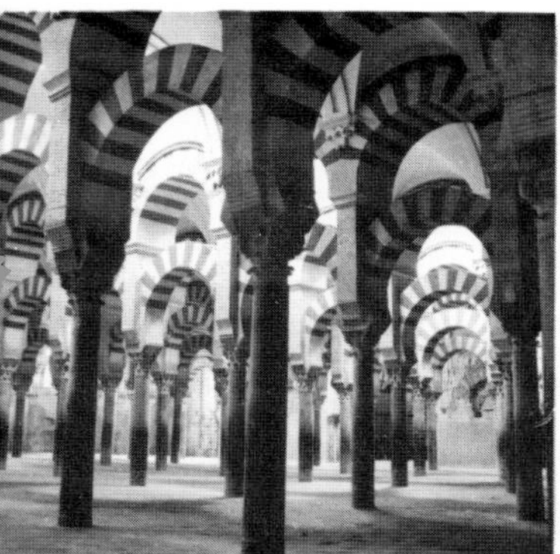

1. Mosque, Cordoba, Spain (now the cathedral). Hispano-Moresque, 8th–10th century
2. Plan of the Palatine Chapel (*below*)
3. Palatine Chapel, Aachen (Aix-la-Chapelle). Built for Charlemagne by Eudes of Metz. Carolingian period, 792–805
4. St Matthew. Carolingian miniature. 845–82. Pierpont Morgan Library, New York
5. Church of S. Maria de Naranco, near Oviedo, Spain. Consecrated 848
6. Oratory, Germigny-des-Prés, Loiret. Built for Bishop Theodulph of Orléans. Carolingian period, 806
7. Gateway at Lorsch monastery, Germany. Carolingian period, 800

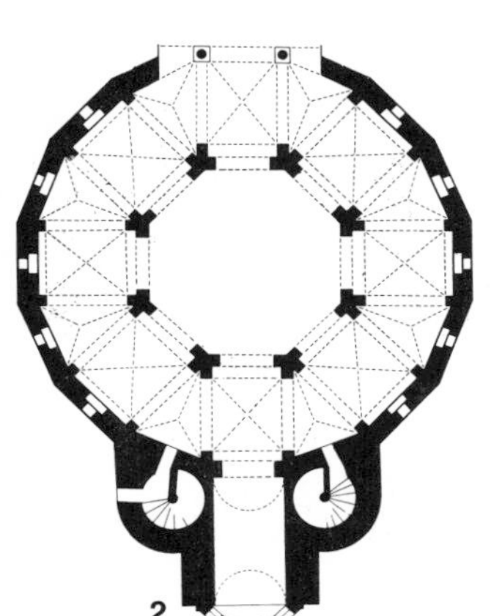

2

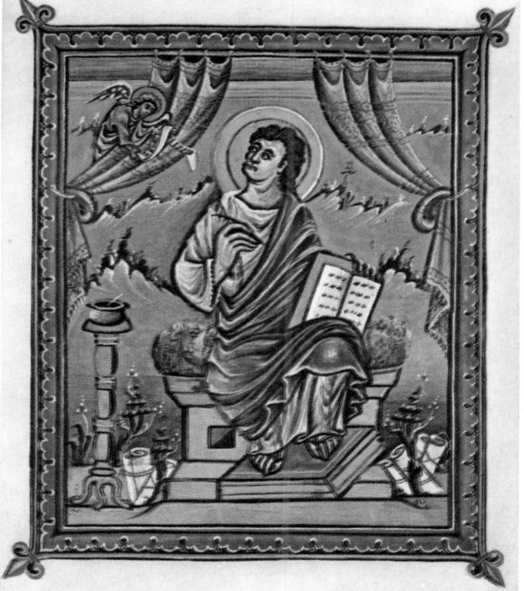

4

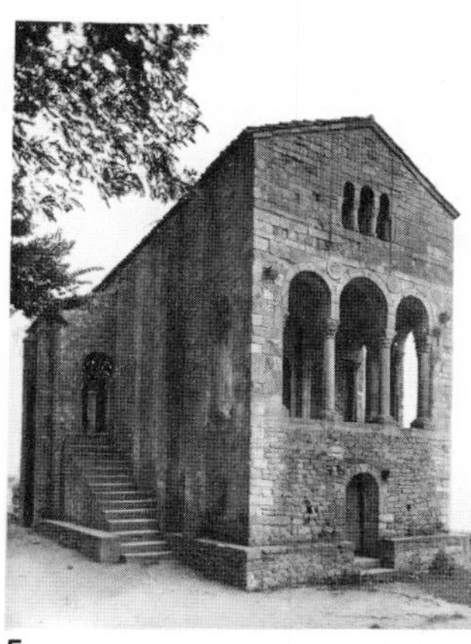

5

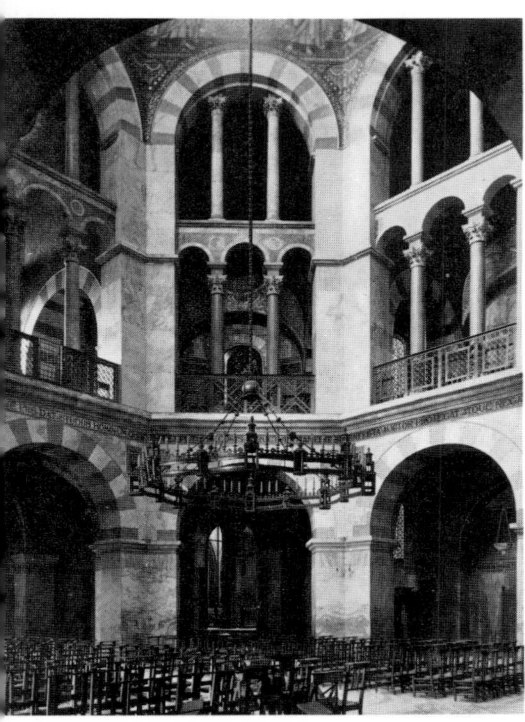

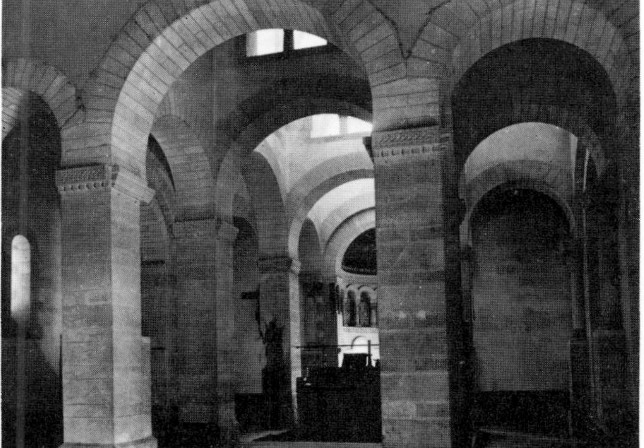

6

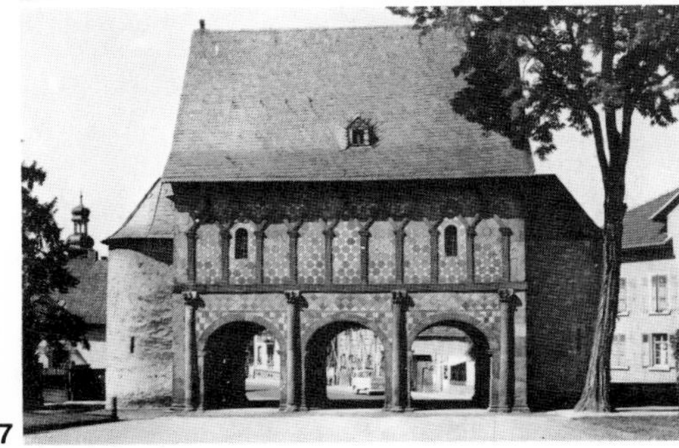

7

1. Church of St Michael, Hildesheim. Transept. 1010–34
2. St Matthew in ecstasy. Gospel Book of Otto III. Manuscript produced by the school of Reichenau. Late 10th century. Bayerische Staatsbibliothek, Munich
3. Christ before Pontius Pilate, and Flagellation. Ivory. About 970. Bayerisches Nationalmuseum, Munich
4. Christ addressing his Disciples. Book of Pericopes of Henry II. Reichenau. About 1007–14. Bayerische Staatsbibliothek, Munich
5. Adam and Eve picking the forbidden fruit. High relief (detail) from one of the bronze doors of Hildesheim Cathedral, commissioned by Bishop Bernward of Hildesheim and completed in 1015 (*see also below*)
6. Expulsion of Adam and Eve from Paradis High relief (detail) from one of the bronze doors of Hildesheim Cathedral. 1015 (*see above*)
7. Master of the Registrum Gregorii: Emper Otto II receiving homage from the four provinces. Miniature. About 985. Musée Condé, Chantilly

1

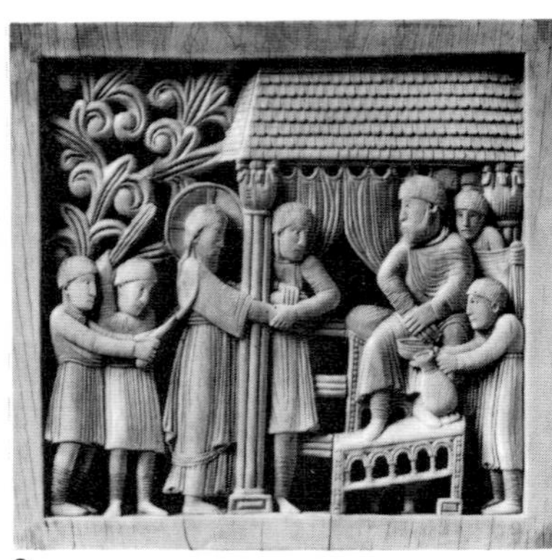

3

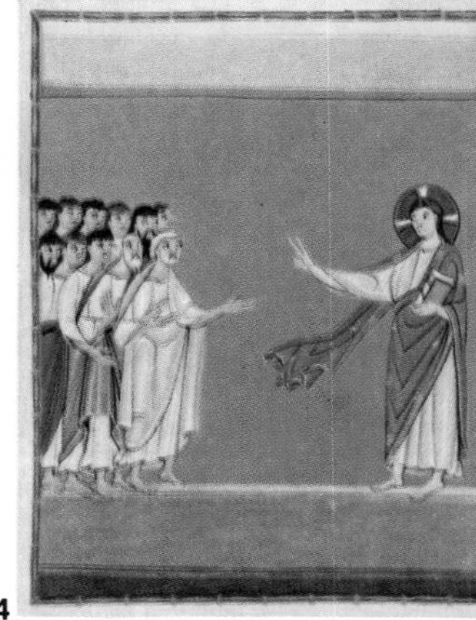

4

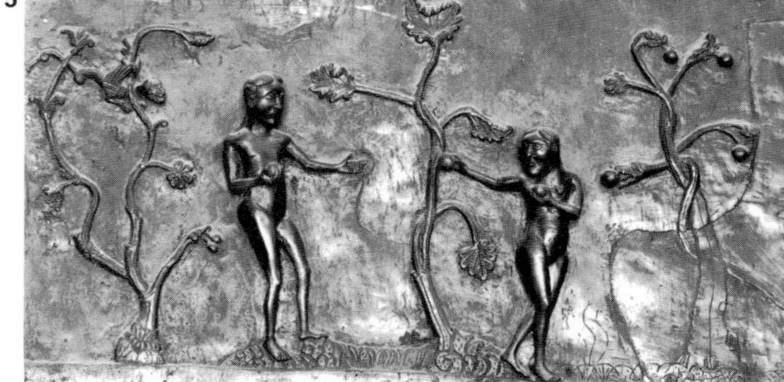

5

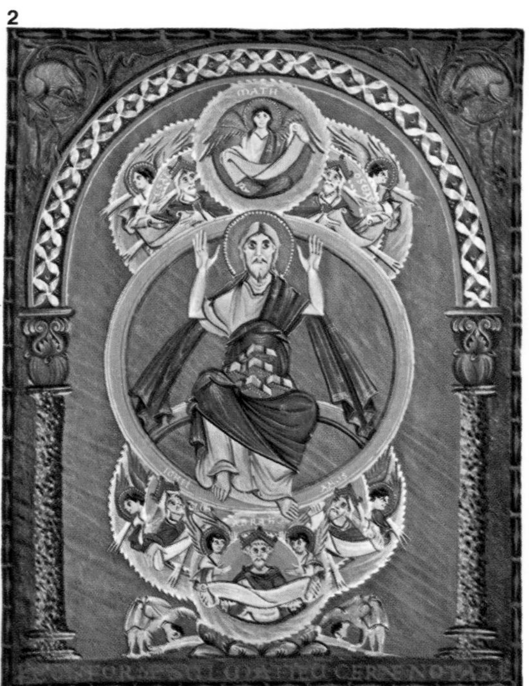

2

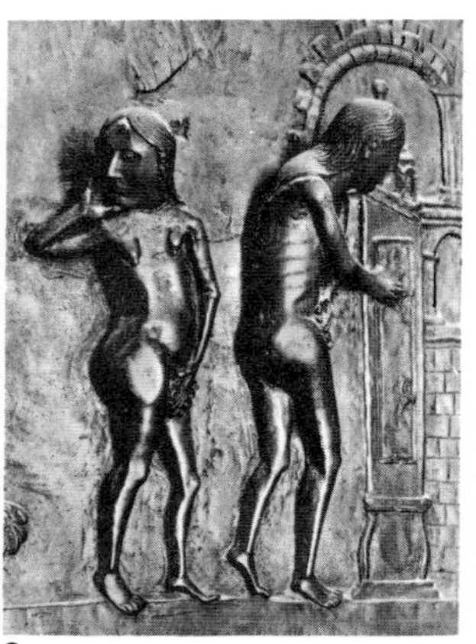

6

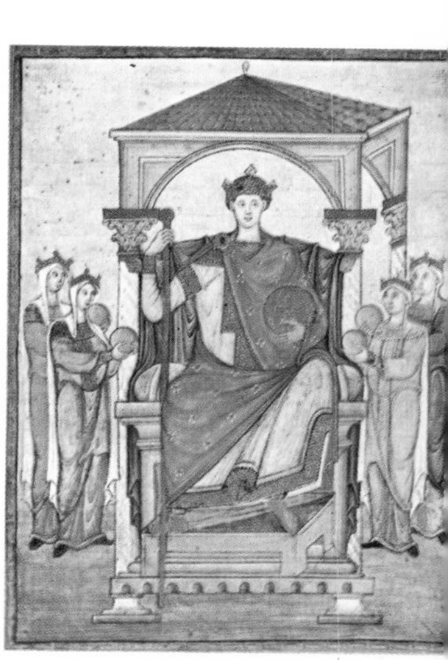

7

1. Detail of a horse collar found at Søllested, Denmark. Bronze. Nationalmuseet, Copenhagen
2. Detail of prow of ship unearthed at Oseberg, Norway. About 850. University Museum of Northern Antiquities, Oslo
3. Die stamper used for decorating helmets. Bronze. 7th century. Nationalmuseum, Stockholm
4. Gold bracteate. 7th–8th century. Nationalmuseum, Stockholm
5. The saga of Sigurd Fafnesbane, the dragon killer, engraved on a runic stone. Rasmus Rock, Sweden. About 1050
6. Tombstone from Tangelgarda, Gotland, Sweden. 8th century. Nationalmuseum, Stockholm
7. Dragon's head. Carved and encrusted wood. Oseberg, Norway. 9th century. University Museum of Northern Antiquities, Oslo
8. The Jelling stone, erected about 958 by Harold Bluetooth in memory of his parents and found at Jelling, Denmark. Nationalmuseet, Copenhagen

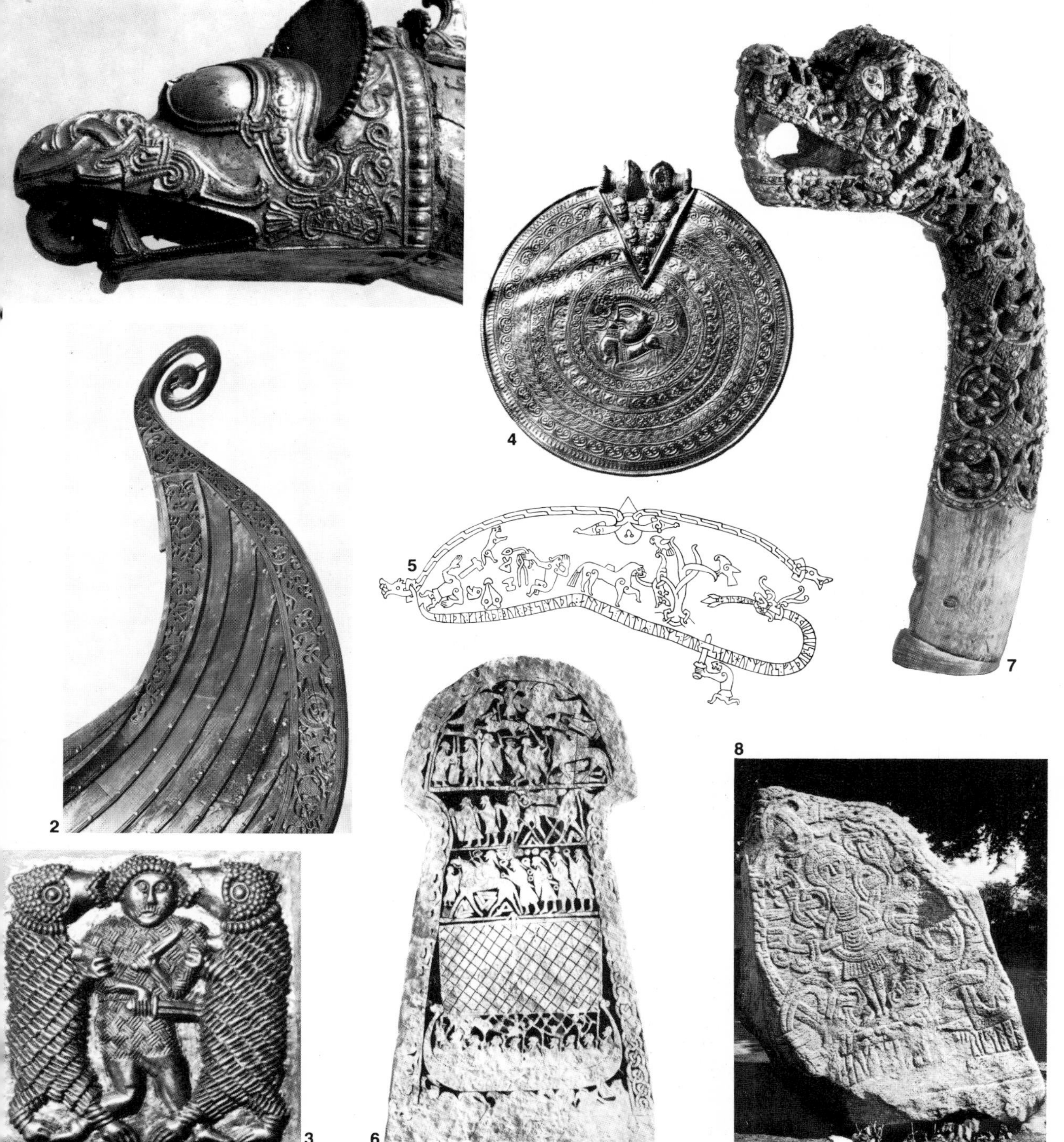

1. Portal of the abbey church of Clonfert, County Galway. Late 12th century
2. St John the Evangelist. Miniature from an Irish Gospel of the 8th century. Stifts-Bibliothek, St Gall, Switzerland
3. Chalice. Bronze and gold with enamel. Ardagh, County Limerick. Early 8th century. National Museum of Ireland, Dublin
4. The Crucifixion. Gilt bronze. Church of St John, Rinnagen, County Roscommon. 8th century. National Museum of Ireland, Dublin

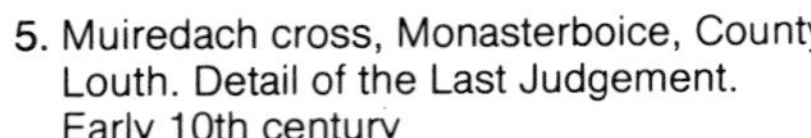

5. Muiredach cross, Monasterboice, County Louth. Detail of the Last Judgement. Early 10th century
6. Page from the Lindisfarne Gospels. Made by Irish missionaries in Northumbria in about 700. Hiberno-Saxon style. British Library, London

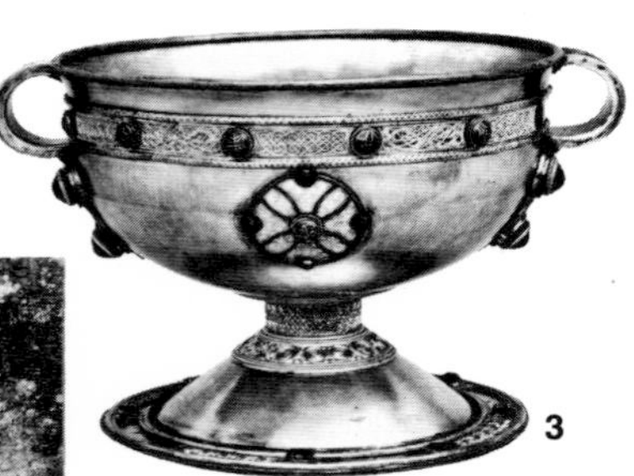

3

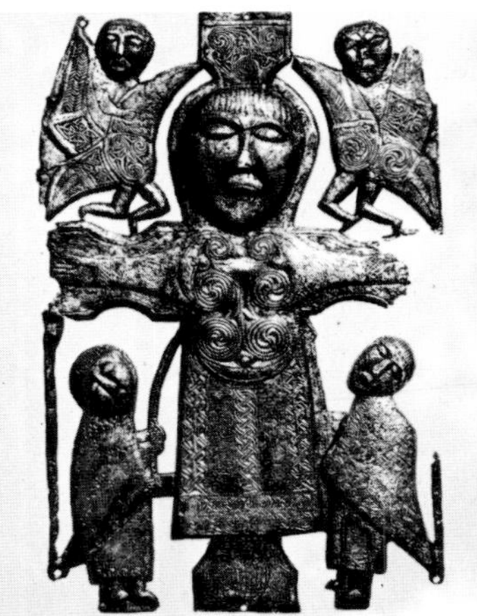

4

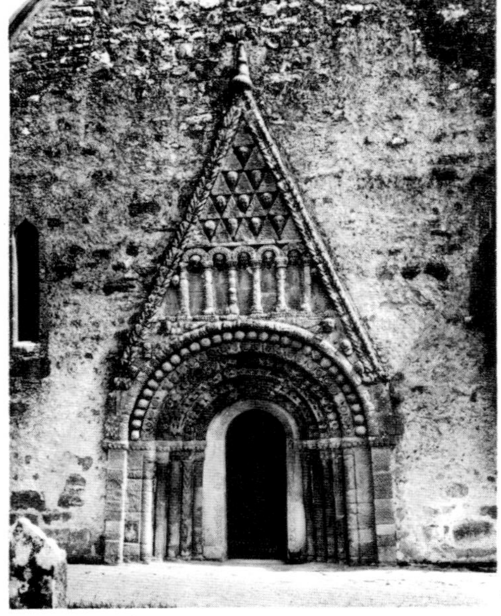

1

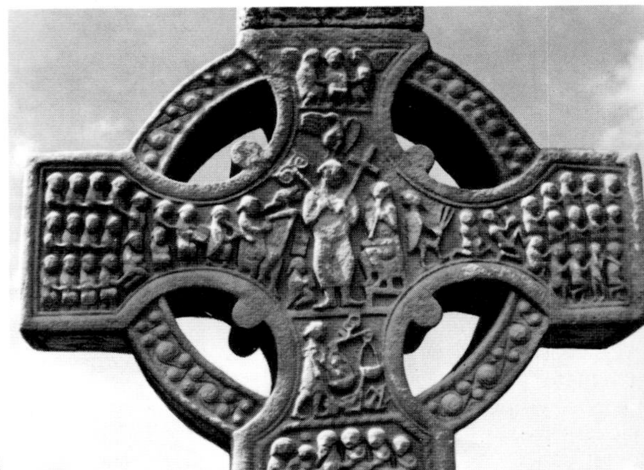

5

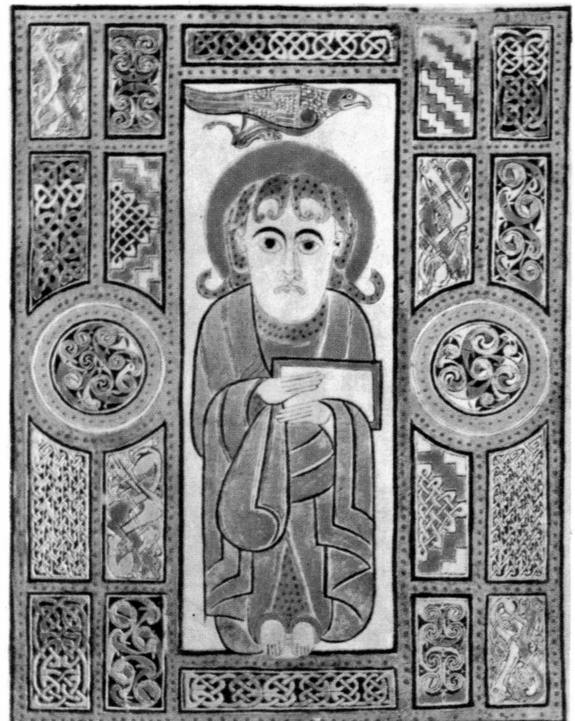

2

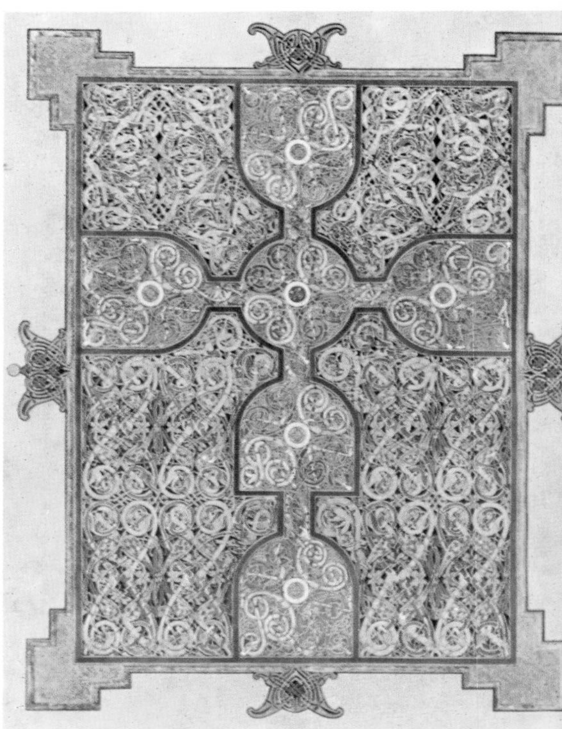

6

Part 5

The Late Middle Ages

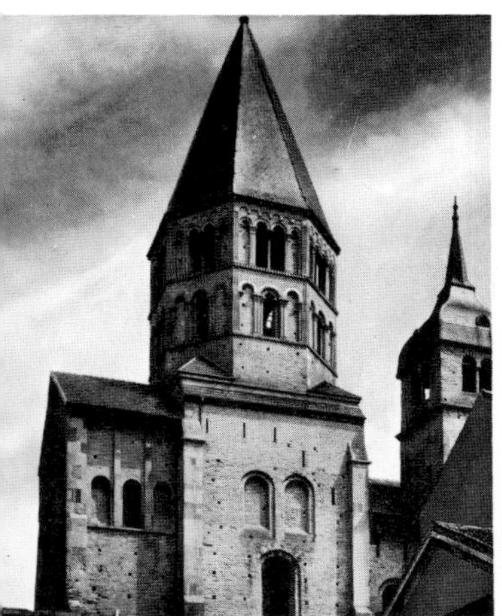

›wer 'of the Blessed Water'. Romanesque art,)88–1118. Abbey church of Cluny, France

ıe styles of the Romanesque and the Gothic eriods have a remarkable consistency. They e both primarily religious styles, but where ey were used in a secular context the same overning principles pertain. In short, both yles pervaded every artistic activity – chitecture, sculpture, metalwork, painting ıd manuscript illumination. A wide range of aterials was used and where objects were oduced for a rich patron the results were ten of a very high quality, particularly in the ıse of manuscripts and metalwork. The omanesque style dominated Europe during e eleventh century and lasted until the irteenth century: the Gothic from the twelfth ıtil the fourteenth century. In fact, so firmly ıtrenched did the Gothic style become that continued to exist in the fifteenth century ıring the Renaissance. Both the omanesque and Gothic builders were sponsible for constructing some of the ıest cathedrals in Europe. These show ɔt only a mastery of design, but also an credibly sophisticated application of ıilding techniques.

ıe principal difference between Romanesque ıd Gothic is that Romanesque designs are lditive – an accumulation of spatial units ɔ that the final building is a sum of its parts – hereas Gothic buildings always display a unity of design. Romanesque art in all its forms is primarily concerned with mass and shape. The architecture is notable for its rounded arches, powerful columns, radiating chapels, groin vaulting or simple rib vaulting, and restricted, often abstract, decoration. It is a style that is closely associated with Norman France and England, but it is found elsewhere in Europe: in Germany, northern Italy, Sicily and Spain. Above all it is important for its manipulation of space, which is firmly defined and carefully controlled. Romanesque art is always remarkably articulate.

ɜpital decorated with birds. Romanesque art, ıd of 12th century. St-Martin de Brive, France

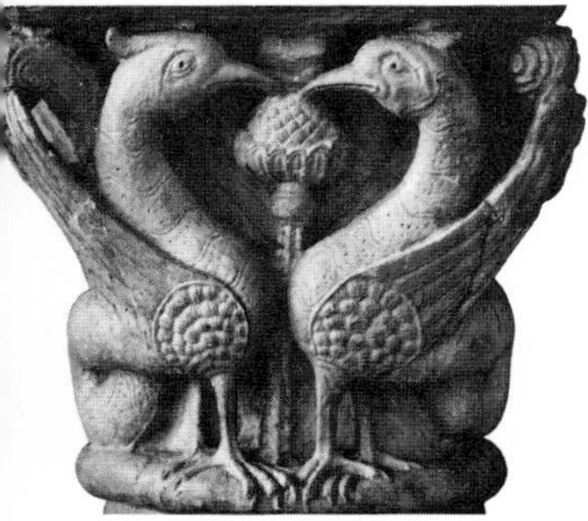

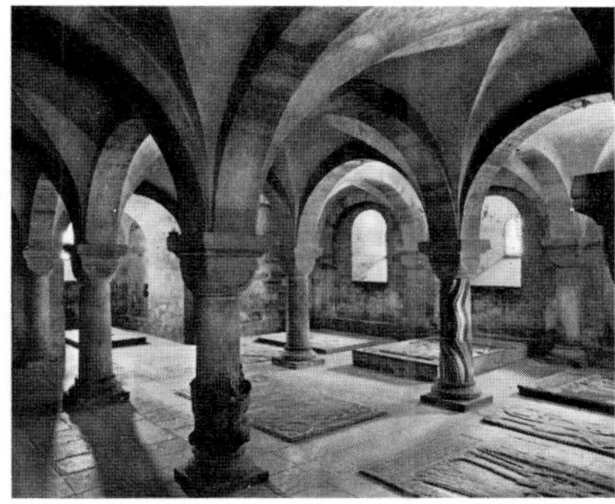

Crypt of Lund Cathedral, Sweden. Romanesque art, begun 1080

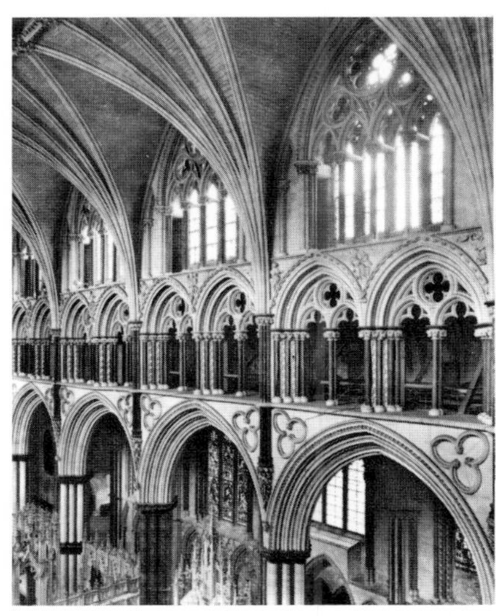

Triforium of Angel Choir. Gothic art, 1256–1320. Lincoln Cathedral

If the Romanesque style is earthbound, the Gothic style is the opposite. The soaring spires, high naves, flying buttresses, ribbed vaults and stained glass of Gothic cathedrals exude an intensely spiritual feeling. These buildings are totally dedicated to the worship of God, and their transcendental quality is comparable with the theological writings of St Thomas Aquinas or St Vincent of Beauvais. Since Gothic art persisted through so many centuries, it naturally developed fresh characteristics although it never lost its sense of line. Late Gothic art, for example, resorted to intricate surface patterns, thereby losing much of the clarity and precision of the earlier Gothic styles.

The portals and interiors of many Gothic cathedrals were adorned with sculpture. During the Romanesque period sculptural decoration was more limited and the figures were often stiff and hieratic, with the drapery represented in formal patterns. In Gothic sculpture one sees the evolution of a more natural style. The figures at Chartres, Reims or Naumburg foreshadow the treatment of the human figure as developed in the Renaissance: they are palpable human beings with convincing gestures and expressions, and with drapery that helps to define the forms beneath the surface.

Léon Cathedral. Gothic art, 1255–1303

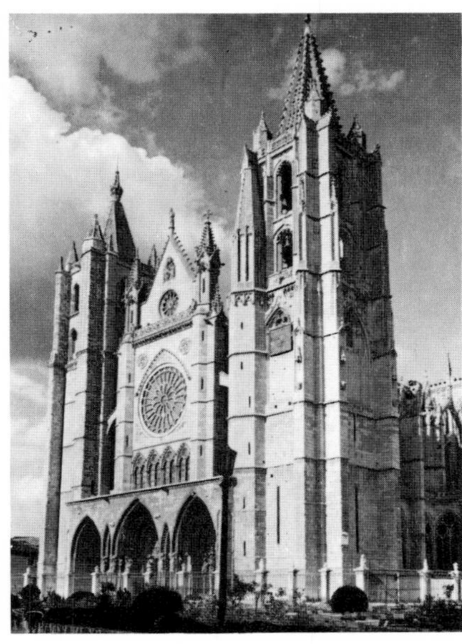

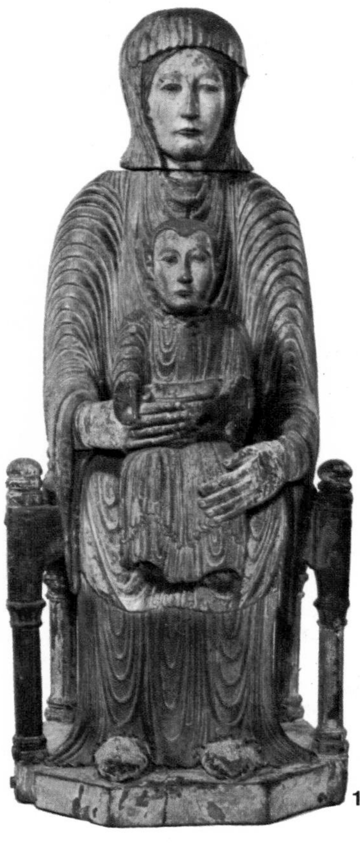
1

1. *The Virgin and Child.* Wood. Auvergne. Late 12th century. Metropolitan Museum of Art, New York
2. **Bernard Gilduin:** *Christ in Majesty.* Detail of marble relief on mensa of altar, church of St-Sernin, Toulouse. 1096
3. *The Annunciation to the Shepherds.* Detail from choir capital, church of St-Pierre, Chauvigny. About 1120
4. *Adam and Eve.* Capital, church of Ste-Radegonde, Poitiers. About 1090
5. *Bust of St Baudime.* Detail. Brass. Chu of St-Nectaire. End of 12th century
6. **Gislebertus:** *The Last Judgement.* Por tympanum, St-Lazare Cathedral, Autun. About 1135–40
7. *The Adoration of the Magi.* Tympanum c the old portal, church of La Charité-sur-Loire. Early 12th century

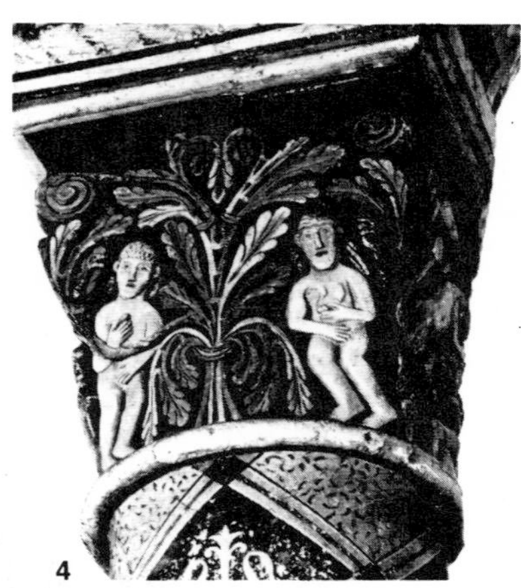
4

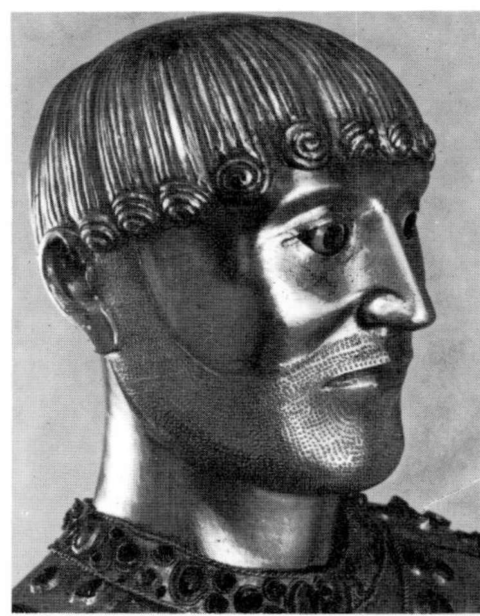
5

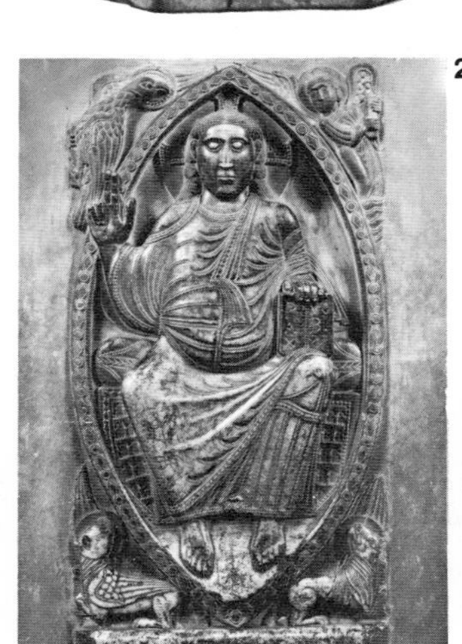
2

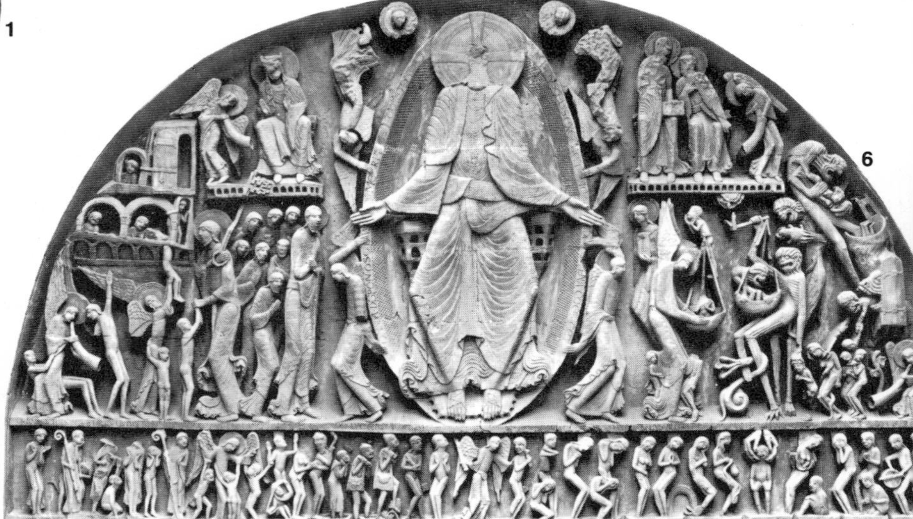
6

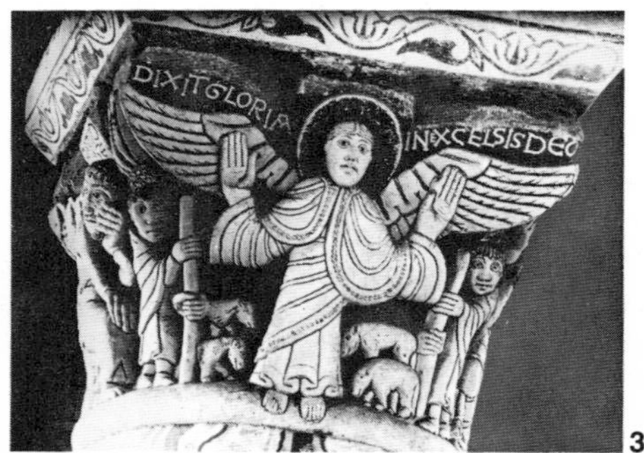

3

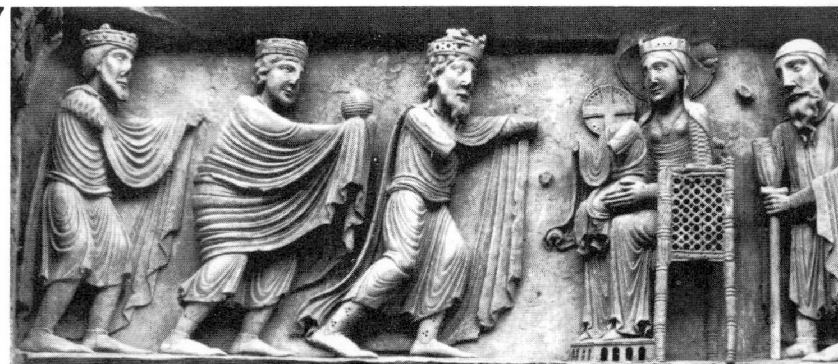
7

Choir of the abbey church of St-Benoit-sur-Loire. Begun about 1060; completed 12th century

Nave of the abbey church of Fontevrault. Founded about 1100

3. Apse exterior of the church at Rioux, Charente-Maritime. 12th century
4. Church of Ste-Trinité, Caen. 1062–6
5. Church of Ste-Fois, Conques. About 1050–1130
6. Cloister of the abbey church of St-Pierre, Moissac. About 1100

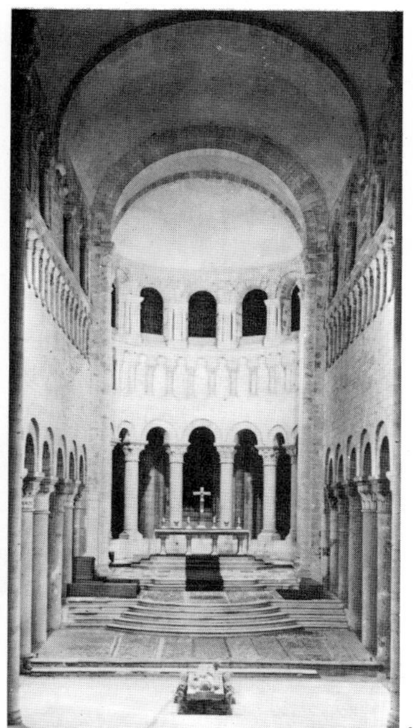

1

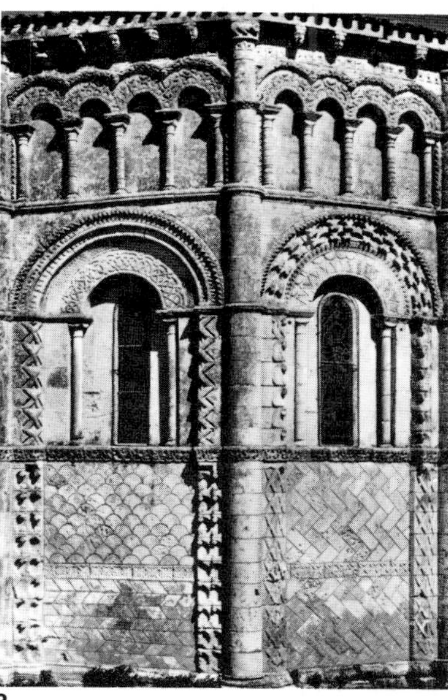

3

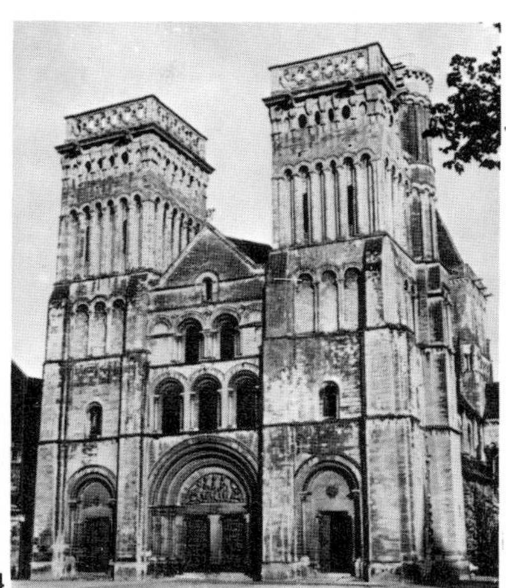

4

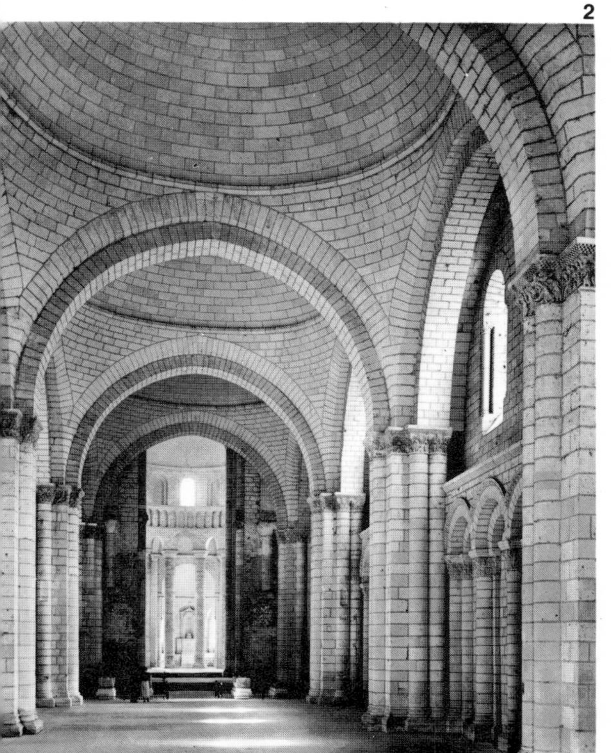

2

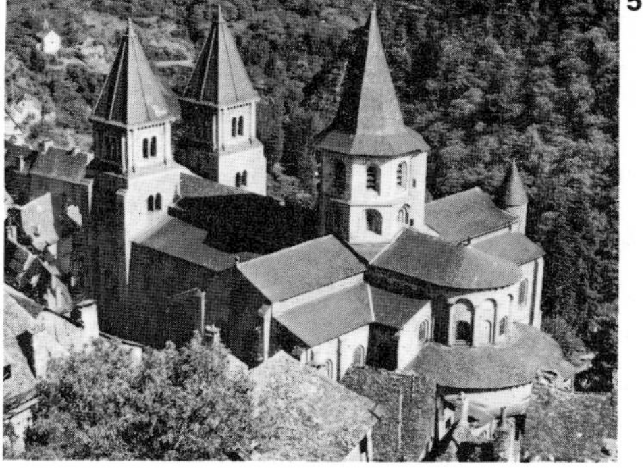

5

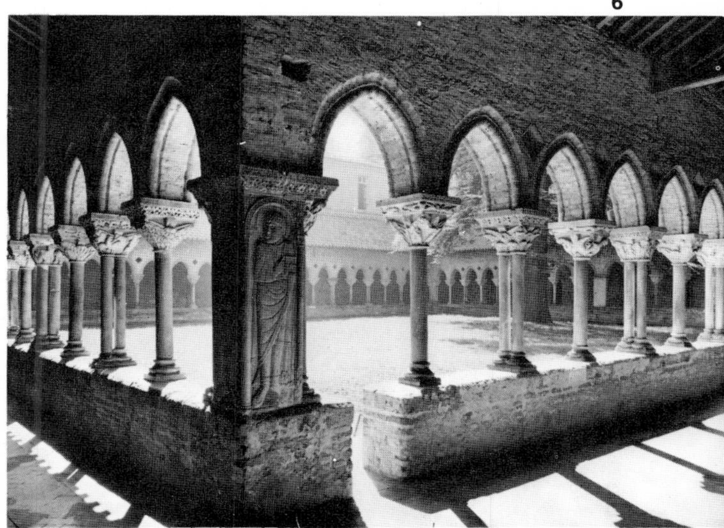

6

1. *The Fall of the Stars.* Apocalypse of St Sever. About 1050. Bibliothèque Nationale, Paris
2. *Dance of David.* Fresco in the crypt of the church of St-Nicolas, Tavant. 12th century
3. Book-cover plaque. Limoges champlevé enamel on copper. Late 12th century. Musée de Cluny, Paris
4. *Marriage at Cana.* Fresco on wall of the choir of the church of St-Aignan, Brinay. About 1150
5. *The Landing of the Normans in England.* Detail from the Bayeux Tapestry. Embroidery of wool on silk. About 1080. Bibliothèque Municipale, Bayeux

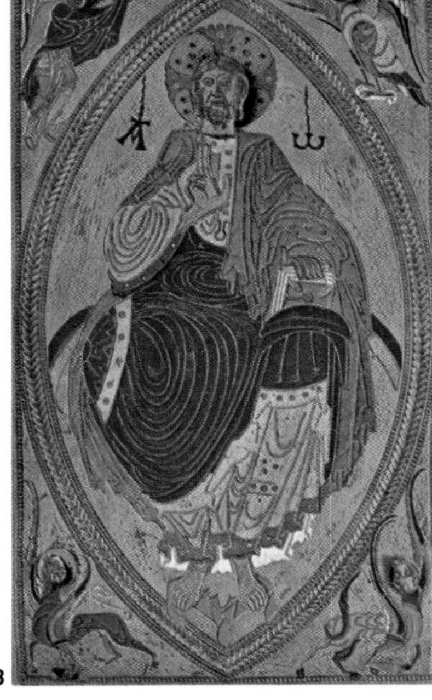

3

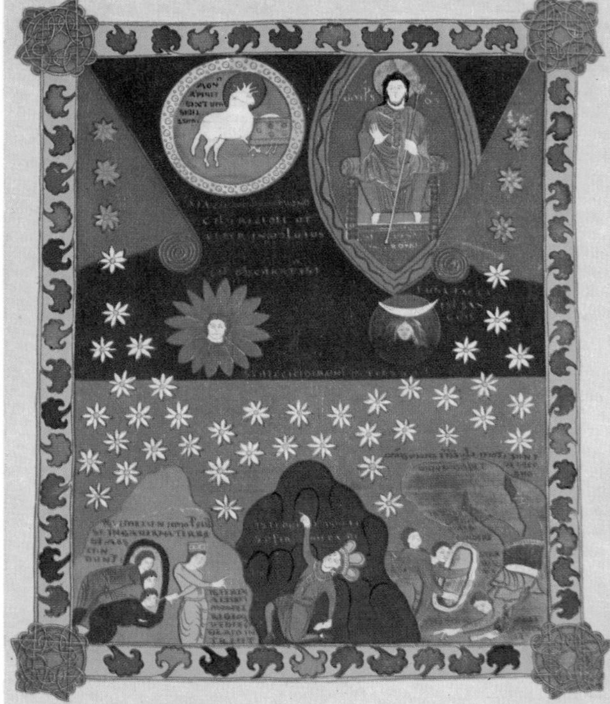

1

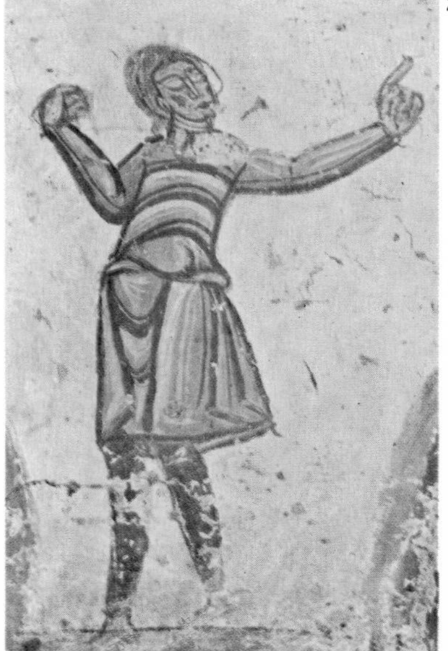

2

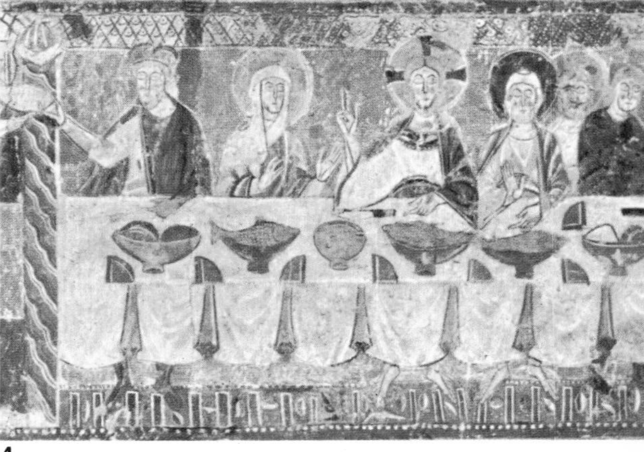

4

5

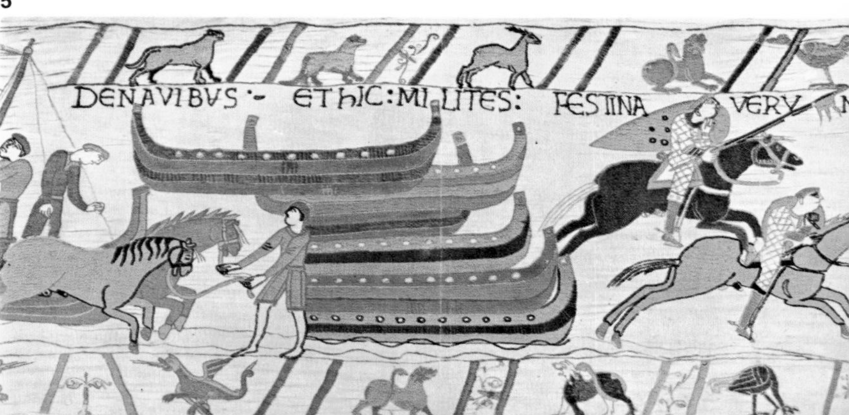

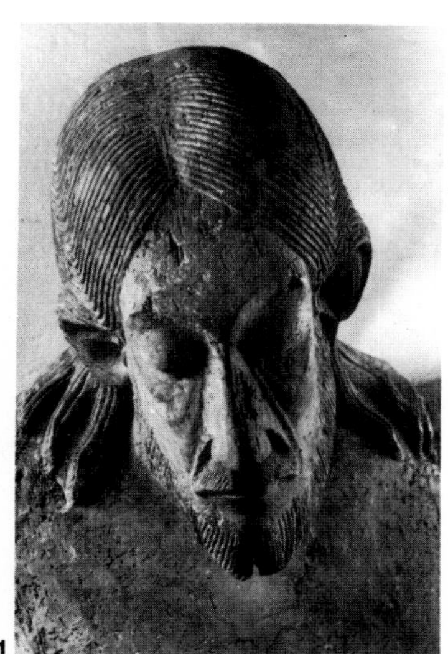

1

1. *The Crucifix.* Detail. Wood. About 1070. Church of St George, Cologne, Germany
2. Wooden church, Borgund, Norway. About 1150
3. Abbey church of Maria Laach, Germany. 1093–1156
4. *Virgin of Randers Fjord,* Denmark. Metal. Nationalmuseet, Copenhagen
5. Speyer Cathedral, Germany. Begun about 1030; completed 1853
6. Choir of Worms Cathedral, Germany. Early 13th century
7. Notre-Dame Cathedral, Tournai, Belgium. About 1110–1165

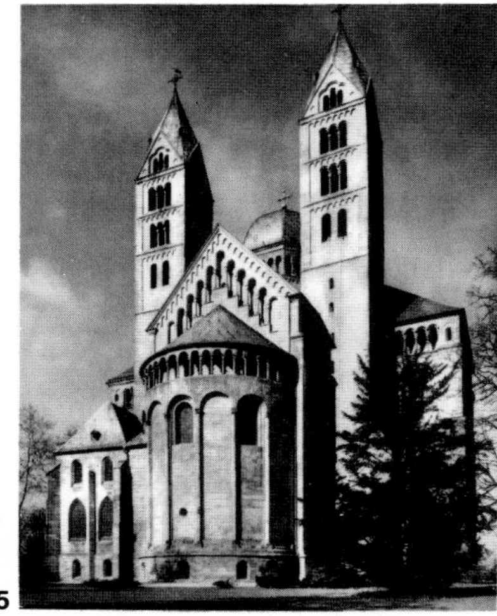

5

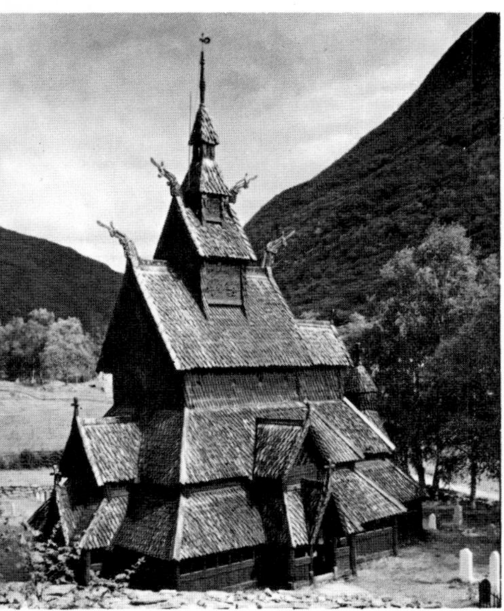

2

4

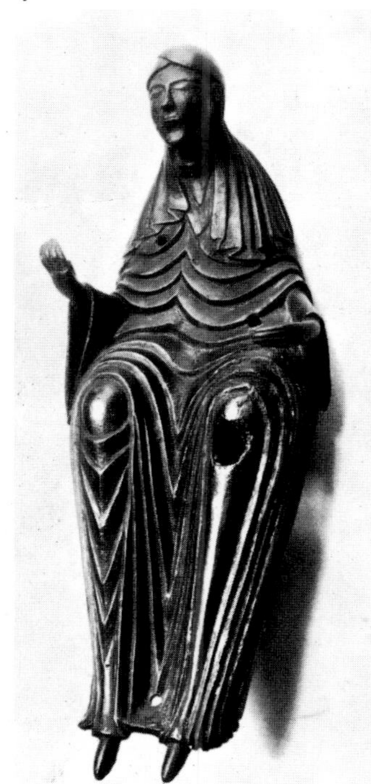

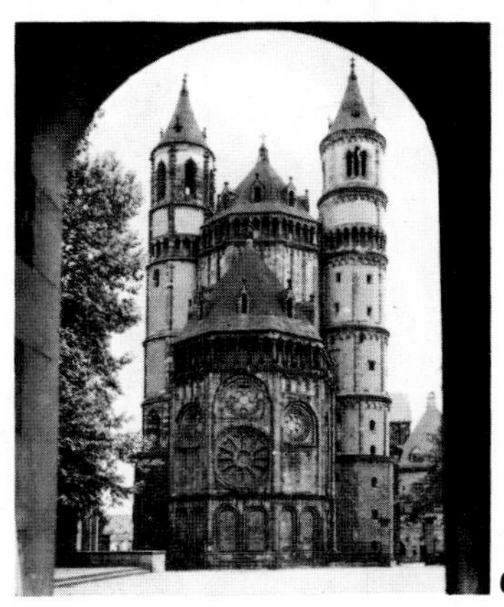

6

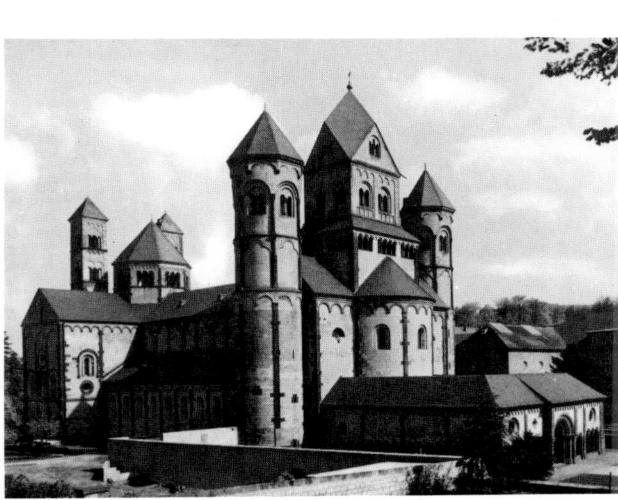

3

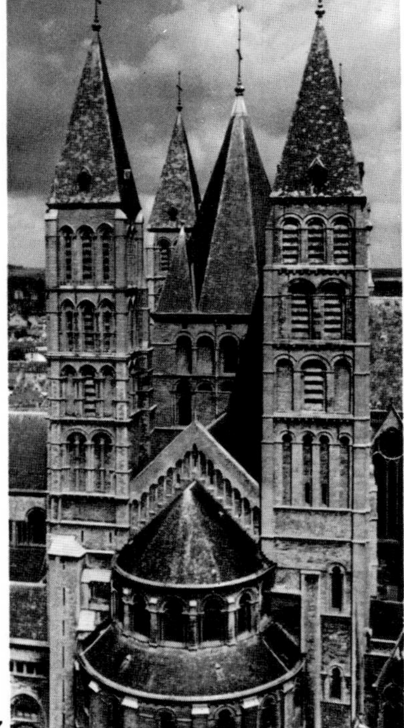

7

1. Lucca Cathedral, Italy. Façade and bell tower. About 1204
2. Ivory reliquary. Detail. 11th century. Church of S. Millán de la Cogolla, Spain
3. *Apostle.* Fresco from the apse of the church of Ginestarre de Cardos, Spain. About 1100. Museo de Arte de Cataluña, Barcelona
4. *The Last Supper.* Aisle fresco in S. Angel in Formis, Italy. Late 11th century
5. Pisa Cathedral. About 1261–72
6. **Bonanno of Pisa** (*fl.* 1174–86): *Massacr of the Innocents.* Detail of bronze relief o the S. Ranieri portal, Pisa Cathedral. 118
7. *The Annunciation to the Shepherds.* Fresco in the narthex of S. Isidoro de León, known as the 'Panteón de los Reyes', Spain. Between 1157 and 1188

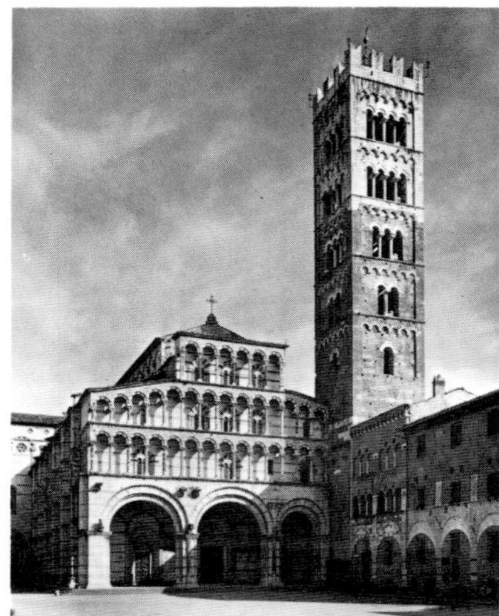
1

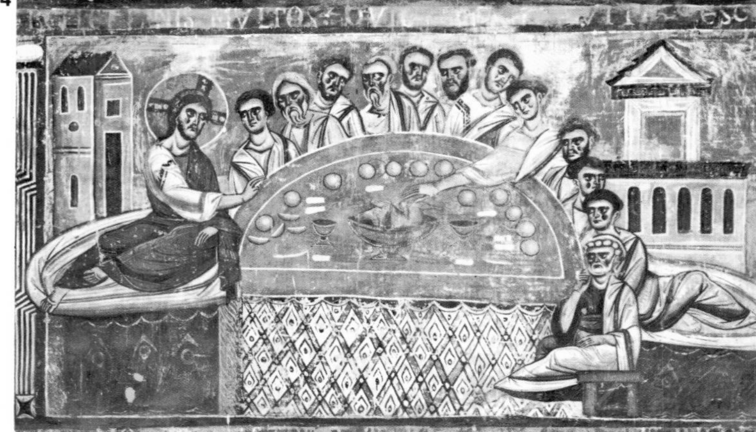
4

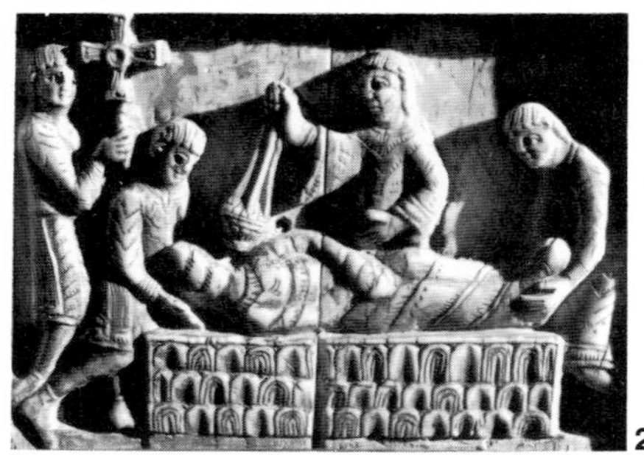
2

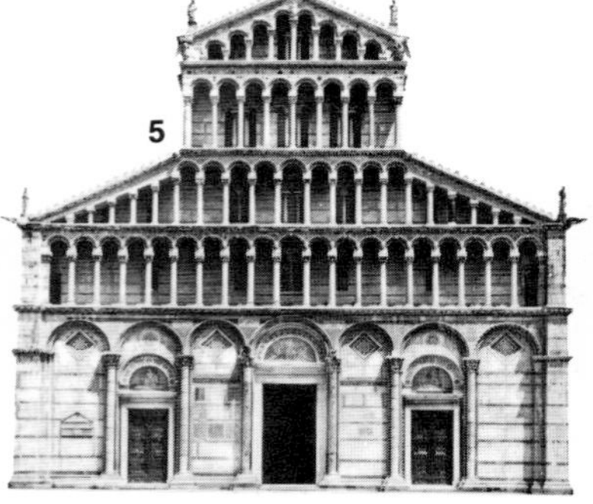
5

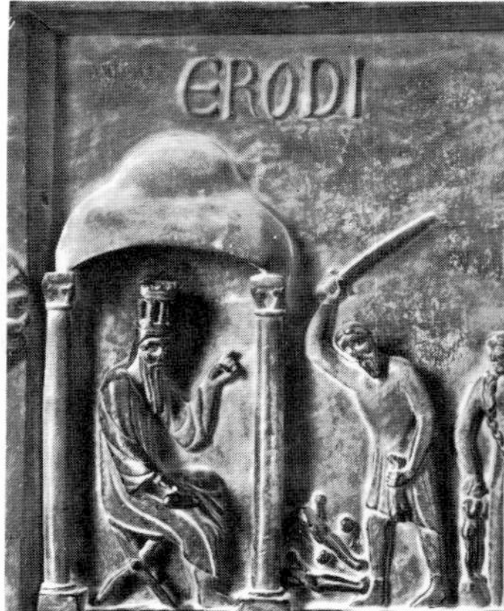

6

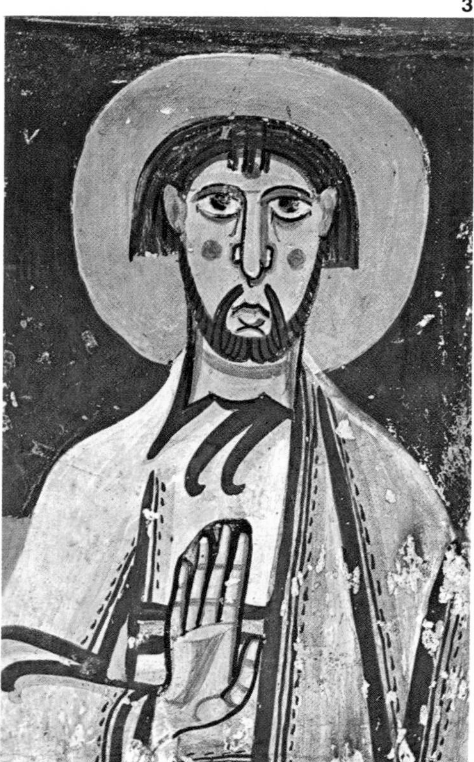
3

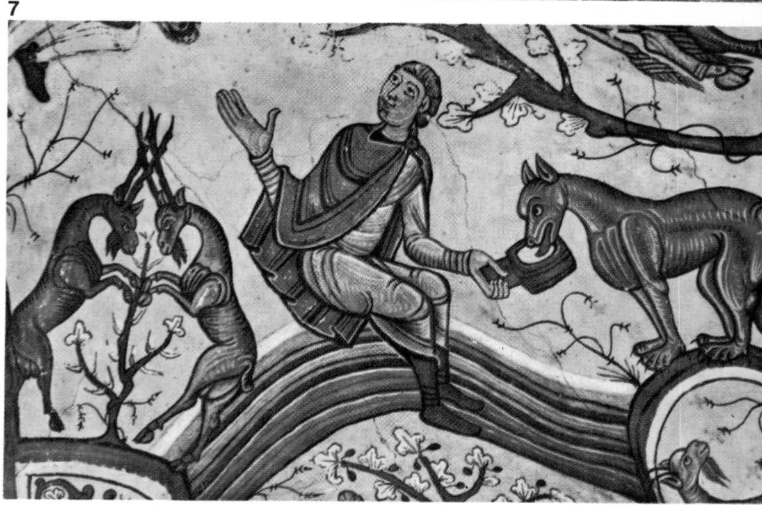
7

Virgin of the Cloister. Stone. Solsona Cathedral, Spain. About 1180

Church of SS. Maria e Donato, Murano, Italy. Completed 1140

The Nativity. Wing of an altarpiece from Sagas, Spain. About 1150. Museo Arqueologico Diocesano, Solsona

Gallery of Evora Cathedral, Portugal. Begun 1186

The Adoration of the Magi. Portal of S. Pedro, Huesca, Spain. 1134–7

Master of Pedret: *Vision of Ezekiel.* Detail from a fresco in the apse of S. Maria, Esterri de Aneu, Spain. About 1100. Museo de Arte de Cataluña, Barcelona

Master of the Last Judgement of Tahull: *Combat between David and Goliath.* Fresco from the church of S. Maria, Tahull, Lerida, Spain. About 1123. Museo de Arte de Cataluña, Barcelona

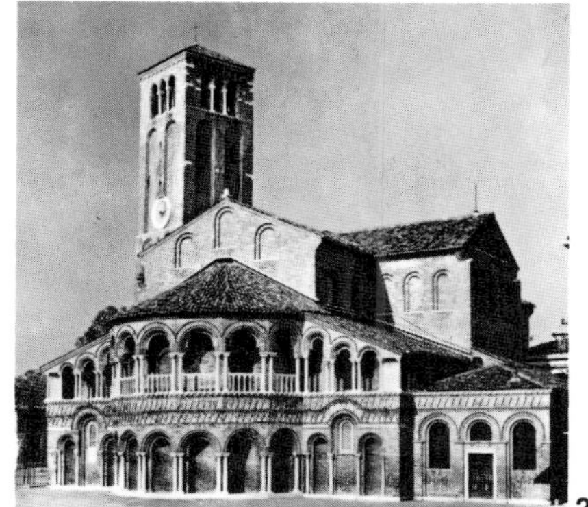

2

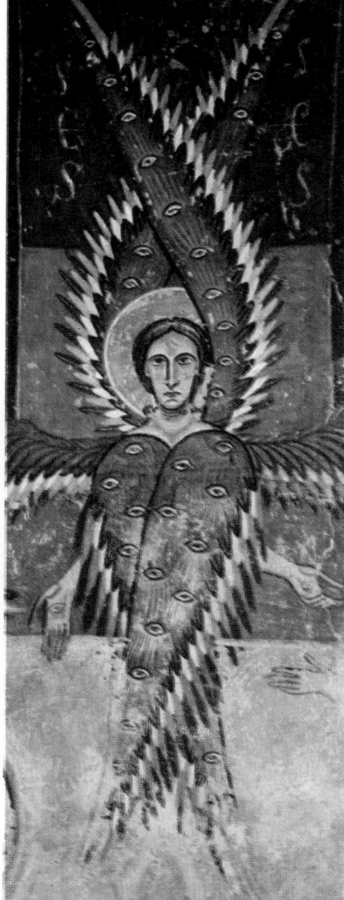

6

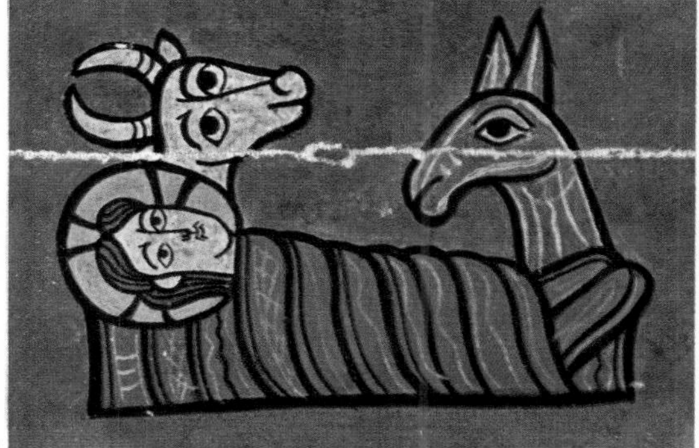

3

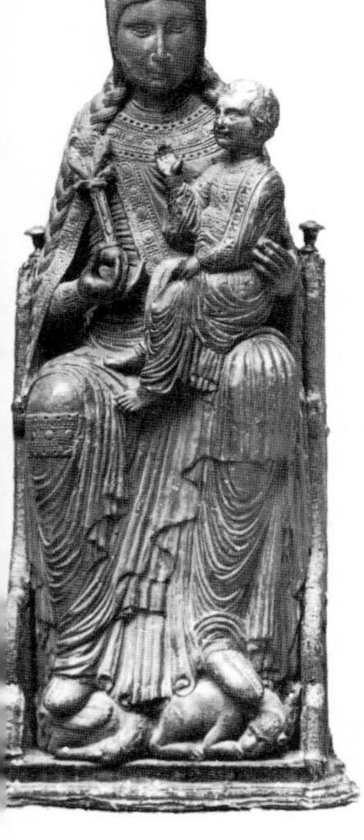

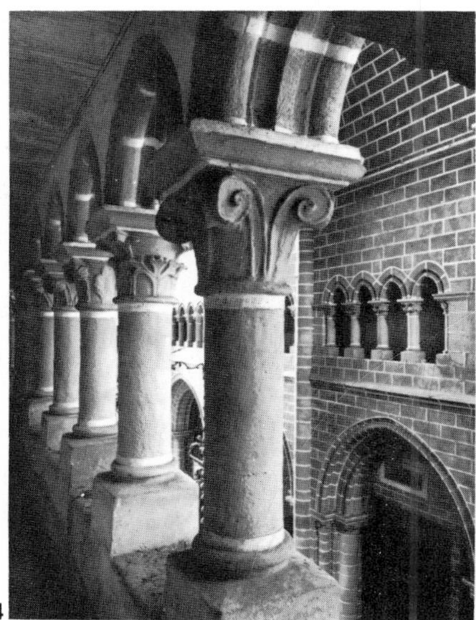

4

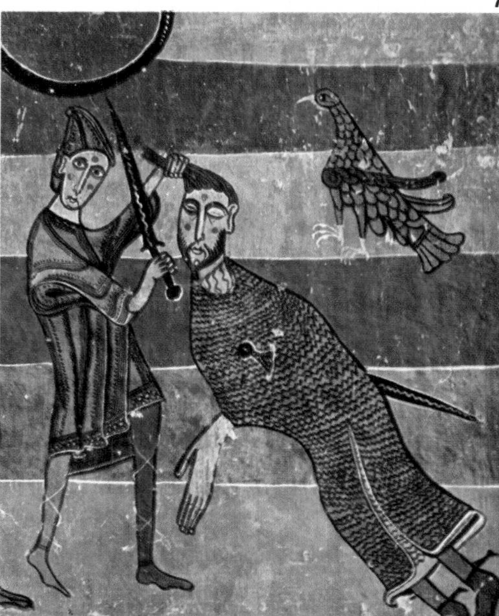

7

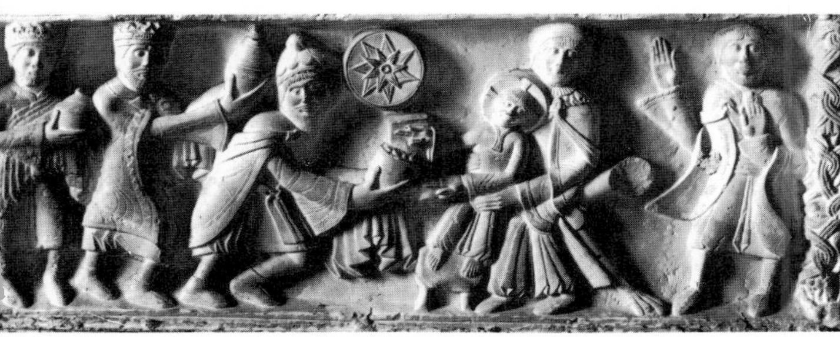

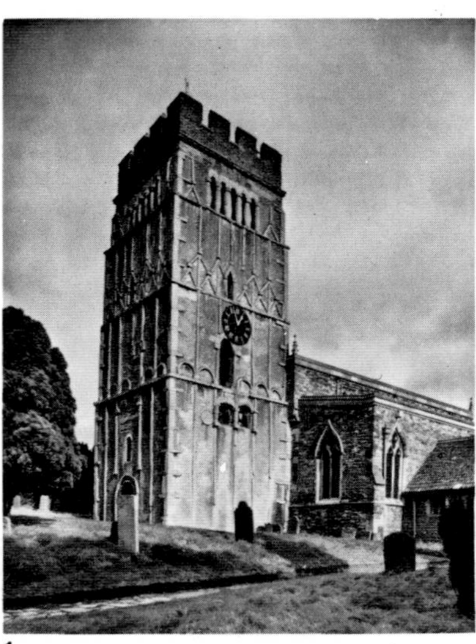
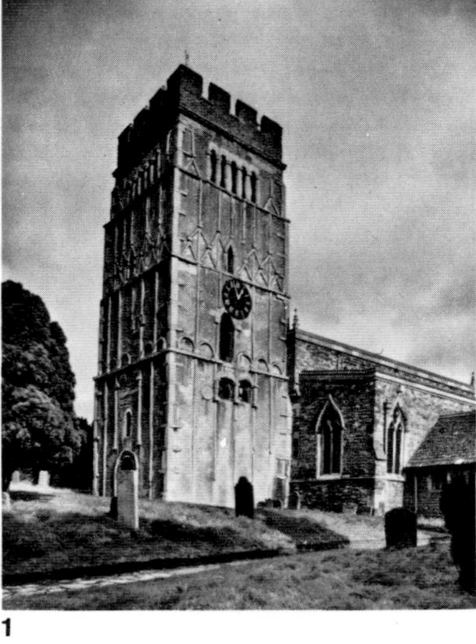

1

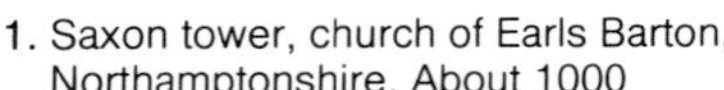

1. Saxon tower, church of Earls Barton, Northamptonshire. About 1000
2. White Tower, Tower of London. Begun late 11th century
3. Nave of Tewkesbury Abbey. Begun 1087
4. Ely Cathedral. About 1090–1180
5. Chapter House of Bristol Cathedral. 1155–70
6. Durham Cathedral. Begun 1093
7. Carved portal decoration on west façade of Lincoln Cathedral. About 1148

2

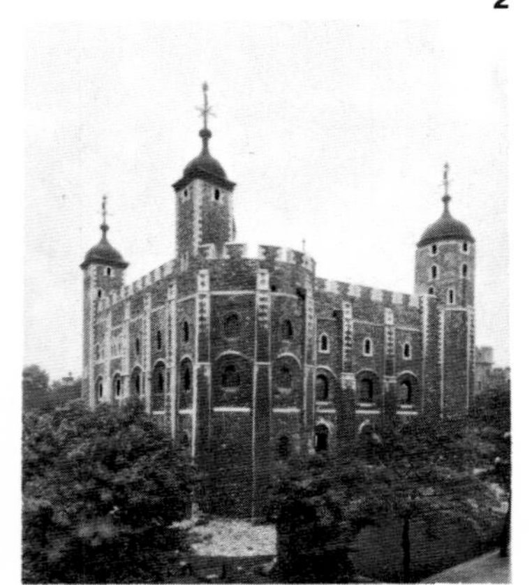

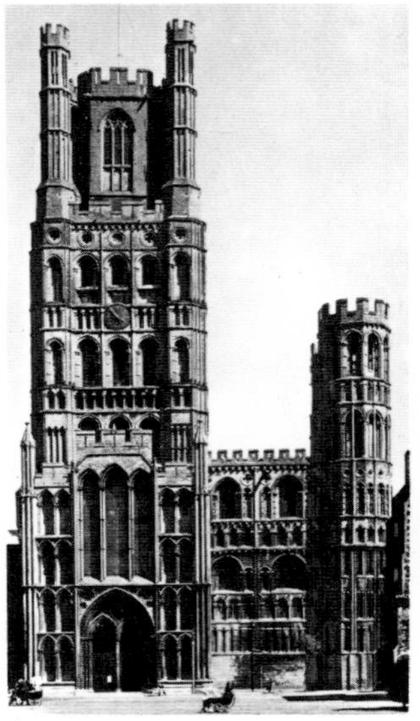

4

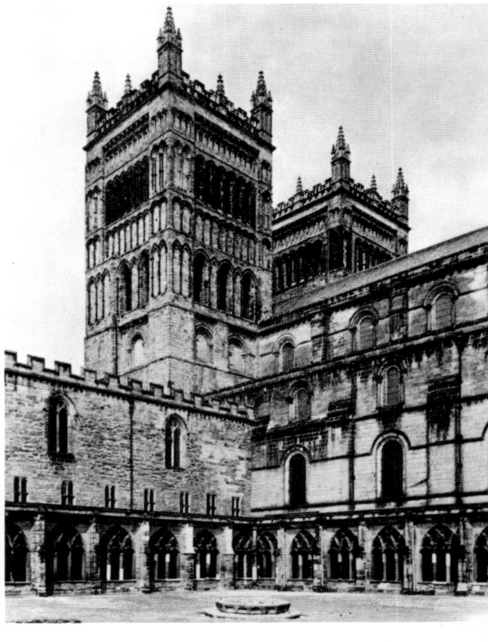

3

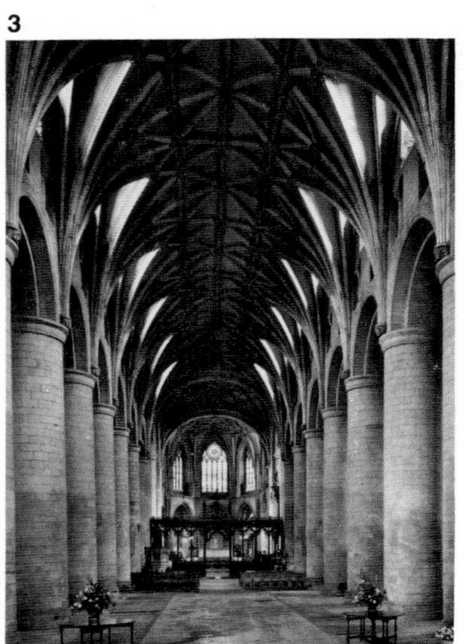

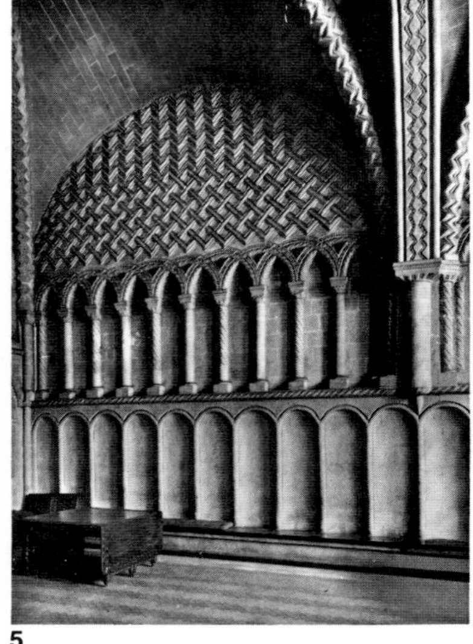

5

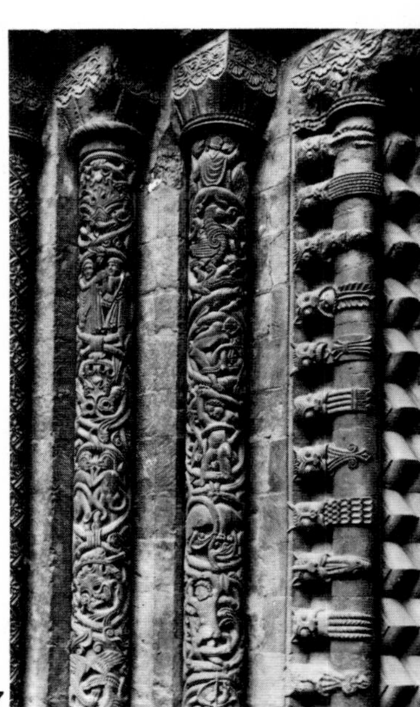

7

1. Notre-Dame Cathedral, Paris. West façade. About 1200–50
2. North transept crossing of Soissons Cathedral. About 1200
3. *The Virgin.* Trumeau, north portal, Notre-Dame Cathedral, Paris. About 1250
4. **Master to King René:** Scene showing Heart reading an inscription while Desire sleeps, from *Coeur d'Amour Épris.* About 1470–80. Bibliothèque Nationale, Paris
5. Chartres Cathedral. West façade. About 1134–1216
6. *Christ in Majesty.* Detail from central tympanum depicting the Second Coming of Christ, royal portal, Chartres Cathedral. 1145–55

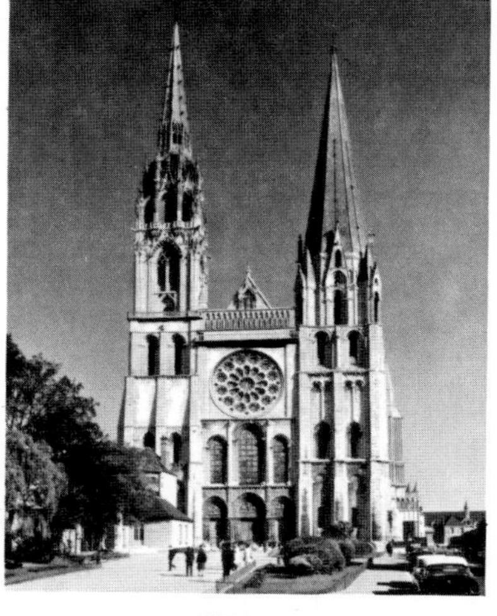

5

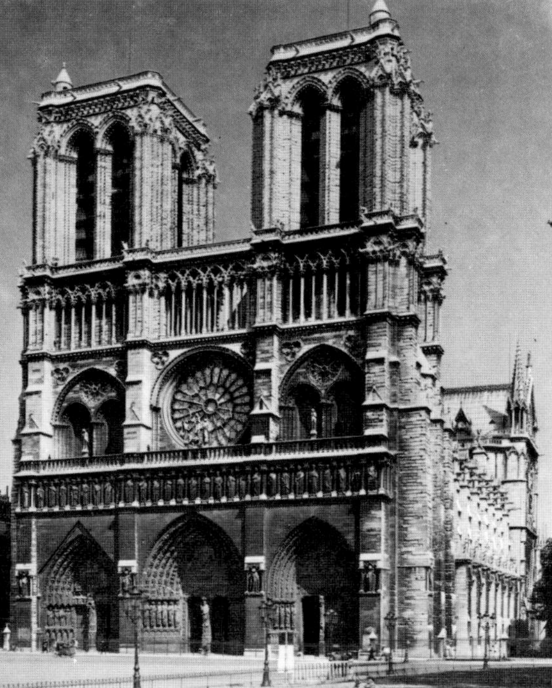

1

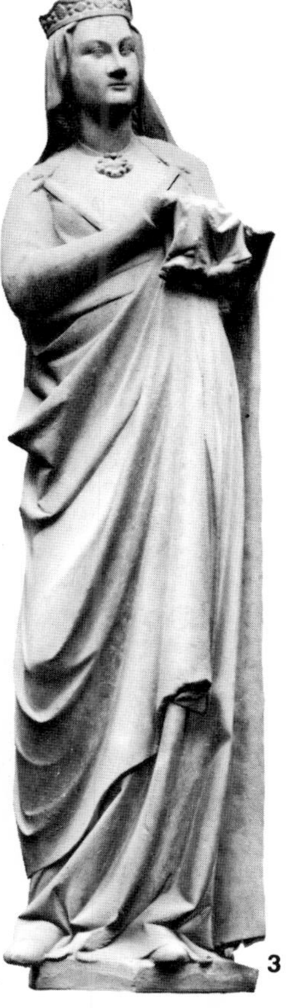

3

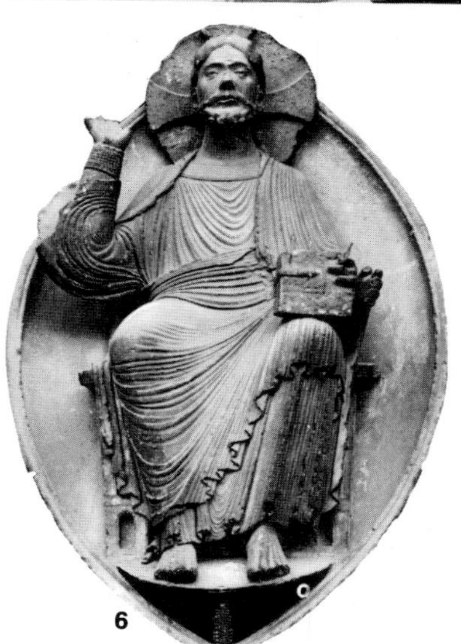

6

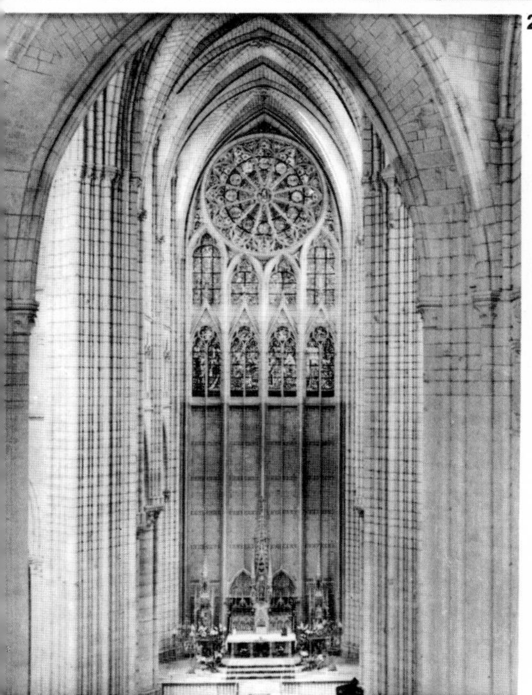

2

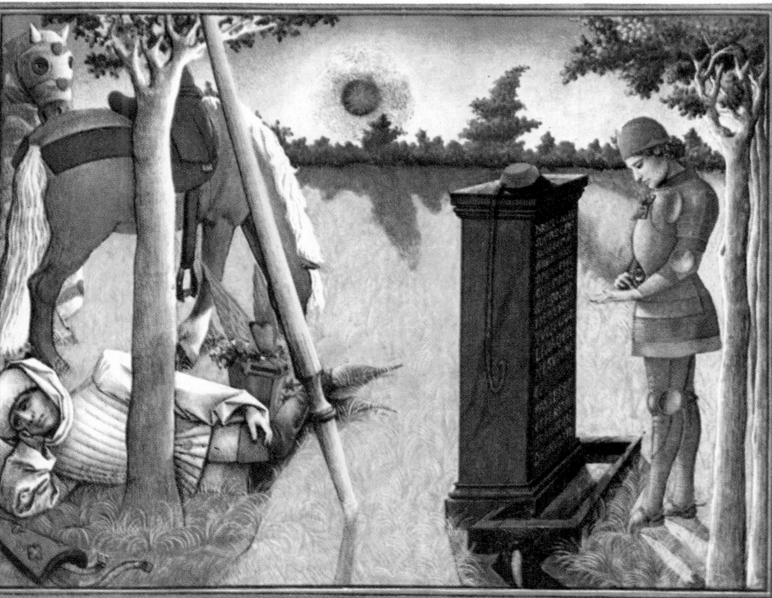

4

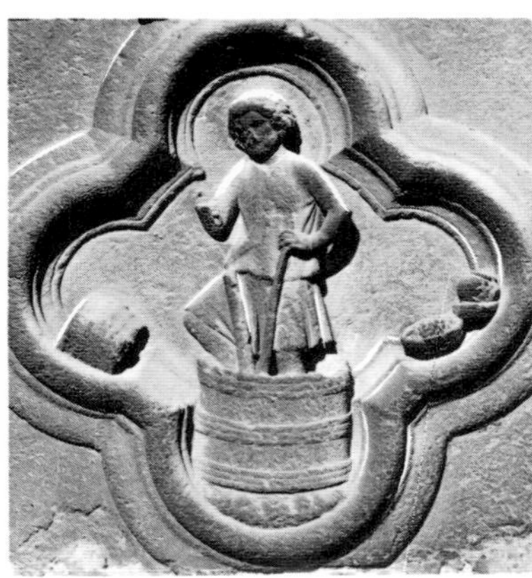

1

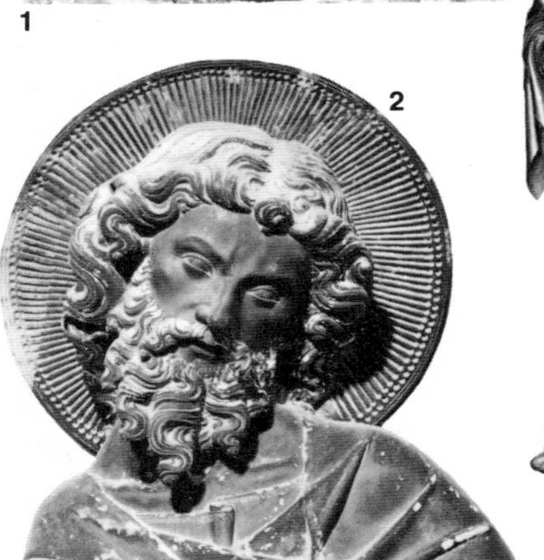

2

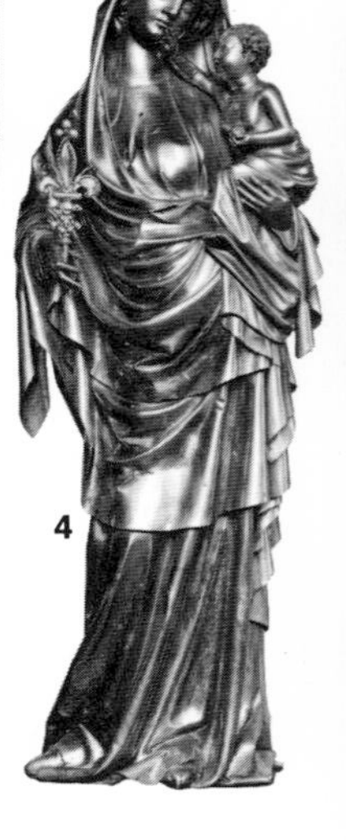

4

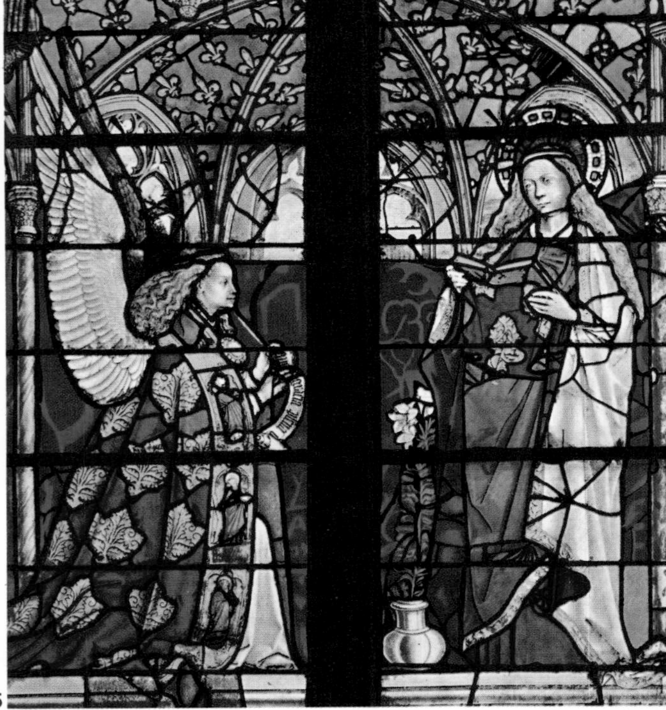

5

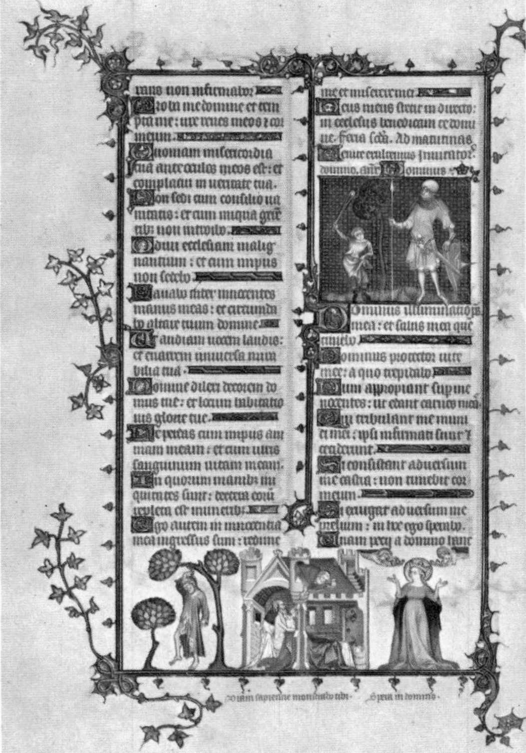

3

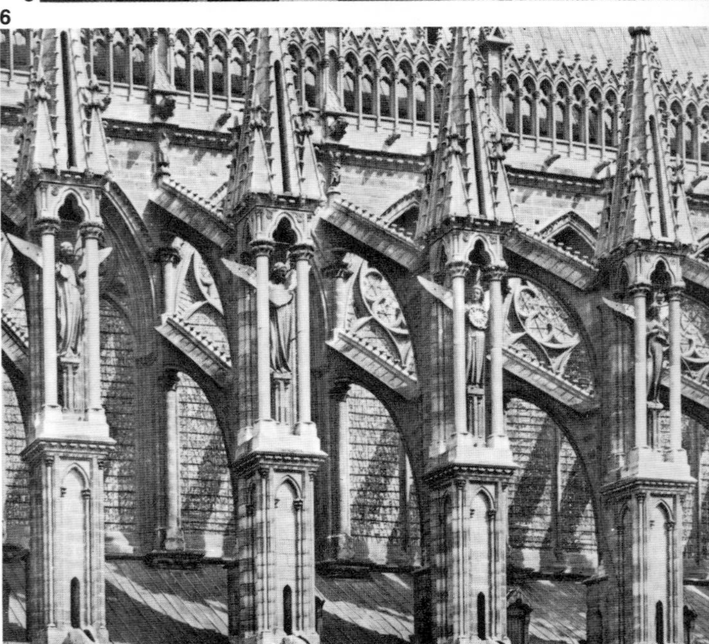

6

1. *Pressing Grapes.* One of the Labours of the Months on the west porch of Amiens Cathedral. About 1225–46
2. *St John the Apostle.* Chapel of Rieux. About 1340. Musée des Augustins, Toulouse
3. **Jean Pucelle** (*fl.* 1320s): Page from the Belleville Breviary. About 1323–6. Bibliothèque Nationale, Paris
4. *The Virgin and Child.* Silver gilt. Given by Jeanne d'Evreux to the abbey of St-Denis. 1339. Louvre, Paris
5. *The Annunciation.* Detail from stained-glass window in the chapel of Jacques Coeur, Bourges Cathedral. About 1447–50
6. Flying buttresses of double span, and pinnacles with statues of angels. Nave, Reims Cathedral. 1255–1311

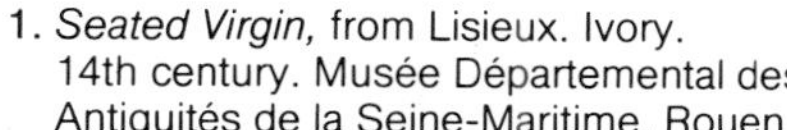

1. *Seated Virgin,* from Lisieux. Ivory. 14th century. Musée Départemental des Antiquités de la Seine-Maritime, Rouen
2. **Villard de Honnecourt** (*fl.* 1225–35): *Couple talking.* Drawing. Musée Condé, Chantilly
3. *Jacob's Ladder.* Psalter of St Louis. About 1260. Bibliothèque Nationale, Paris
4. **Jean de Bondol** (painter; *fl.* 1368–81) and **Nicolas Bataille** (weaver; *fl.* 1363–1400): *Apocalypse.* Detail from tapestry. 1375–81. Musée des Tapisseries, Angers
5. Ambulatory and radiating chapels of the abbey church of St-Denis. About 1140–3

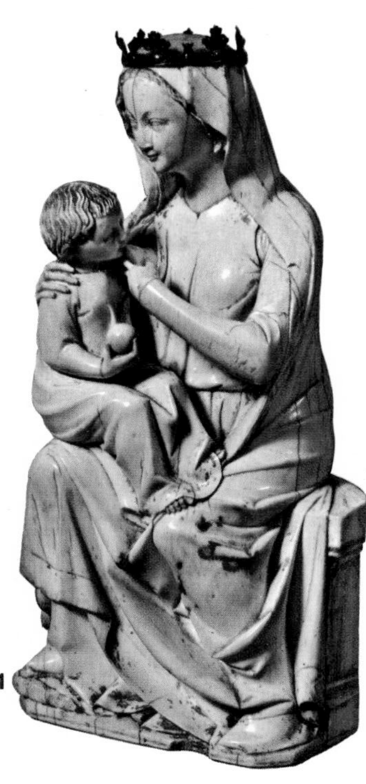

1

2

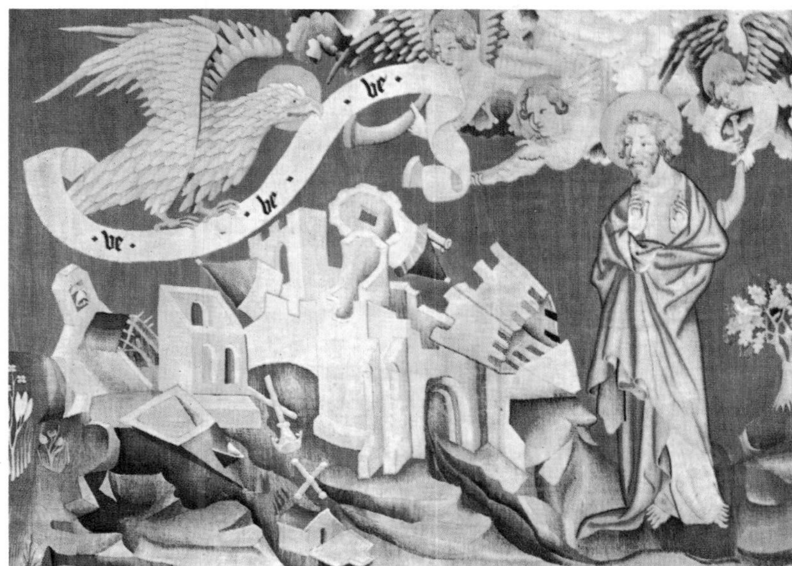

4

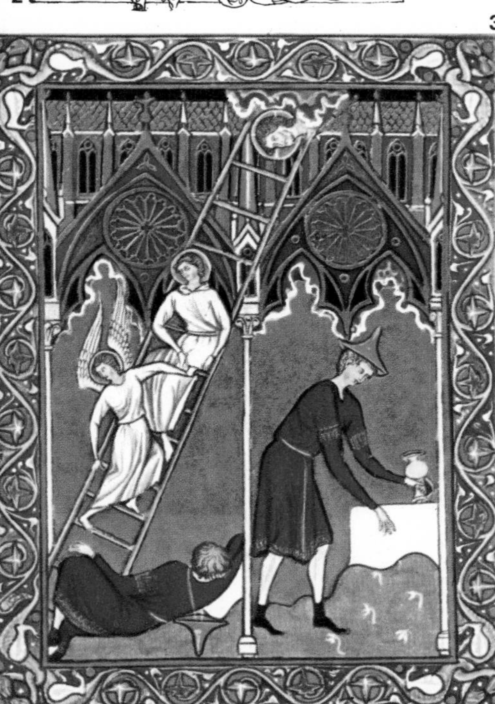

3

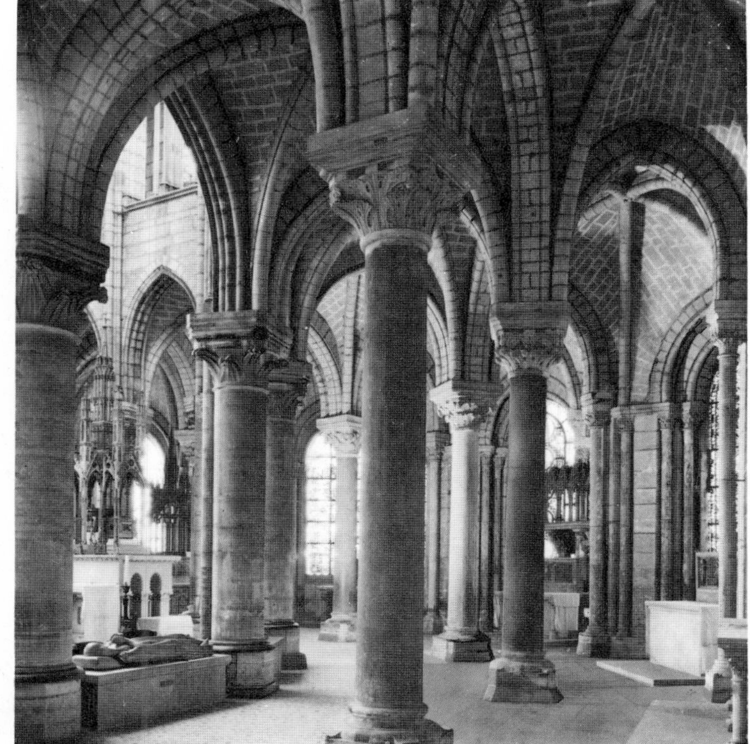

5

1. Rose window on south transept façade, Amiens Cathedral. About 1236–69. Tracery remade in the 15th century
2. Nave seen from ambulatory of the choir, Reims Cathedral. Begun 1210
3. *The Virgin and Child,* from Autun. Stone. 15th century. Musée Rolin, Autun
4. East end and south-porch, Ste-Cécile Cathedral, Albi. 1282–1390
5. Pierre d'Évreux-Navarre, Comte de Mortain. Detail from stained-glass windo depicting scene of Pierre d'Évreux-Navarr presented to the Virgin by St Peter and St Denis, Évreux Cathedral. About 1395

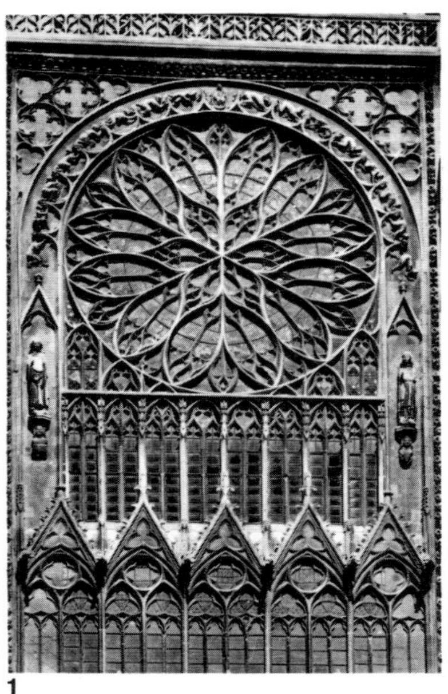

1

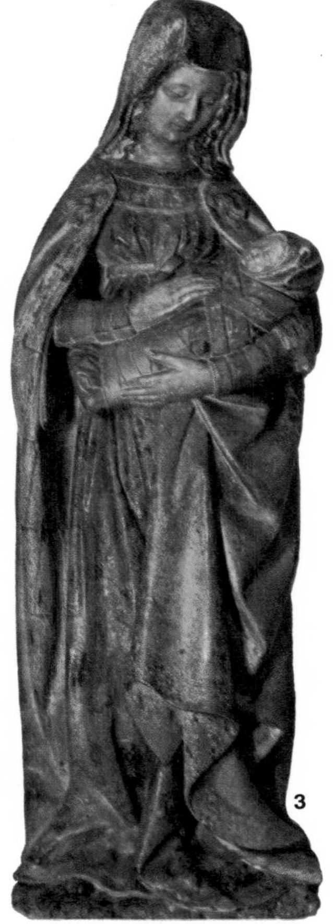

3

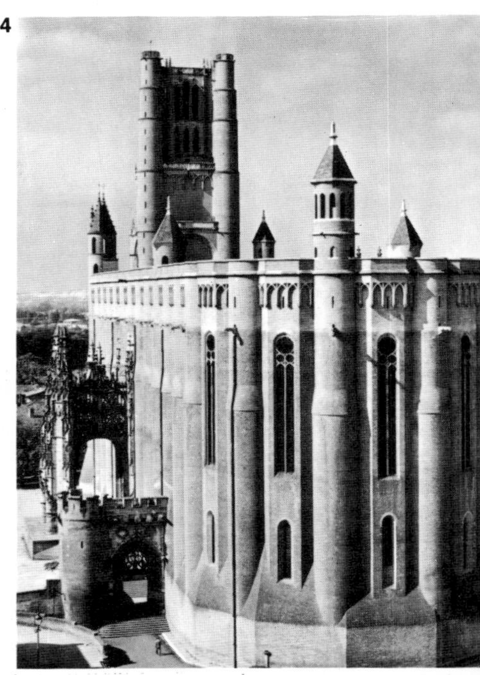

4

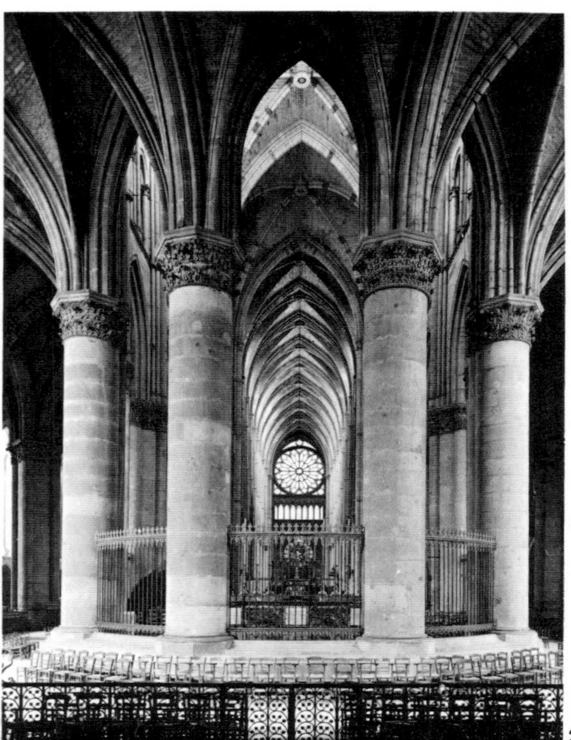

2

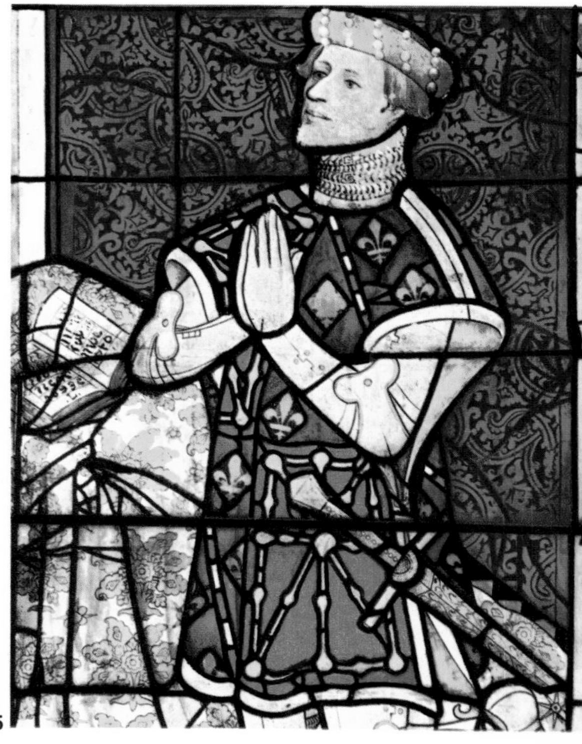

5

. Choir of Salisbury Cathedral. 1220–70
. Transept crossing with strainer arches, Wells Cathedral. 1338
. Plan of Salisbury Cathedral (*left*)
. Octagon at transept crossing, Ely Cathedral. 1323–30

5. Wells Cathedral. West façade. 1220–55
6. Beaumaris Castle, Wales. Aerial view. 1295–1330

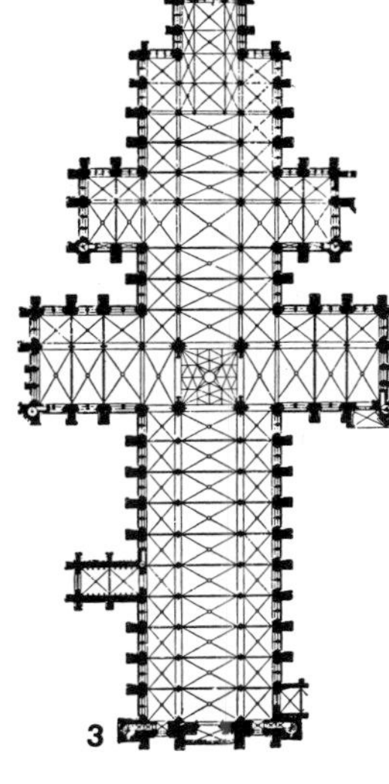

3

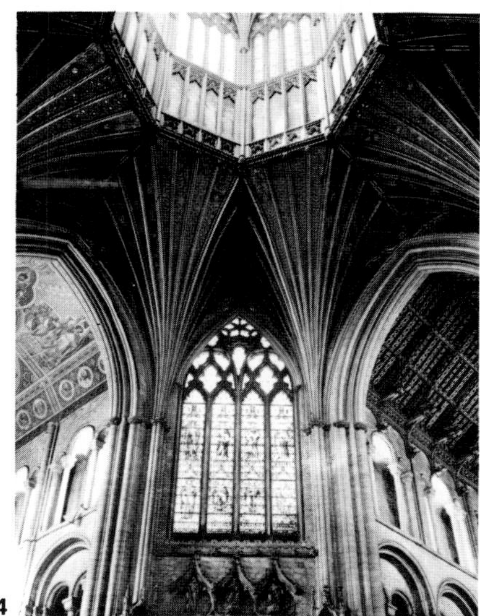

4

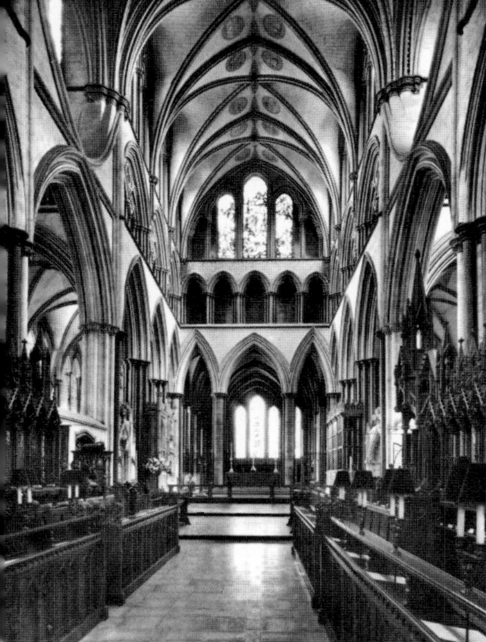

5

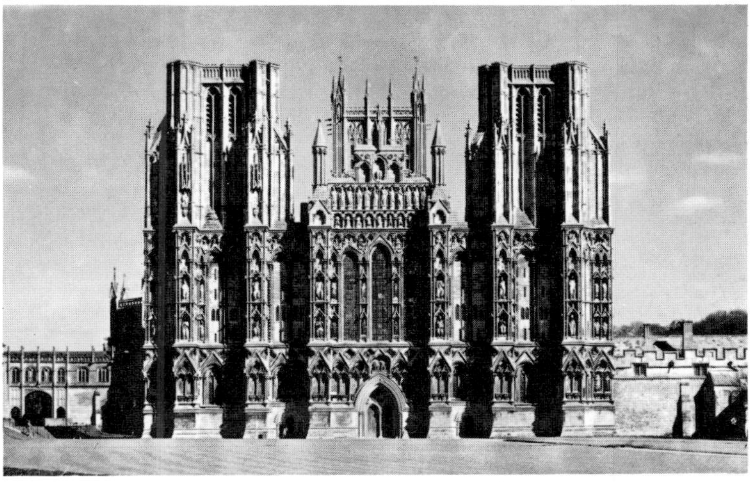

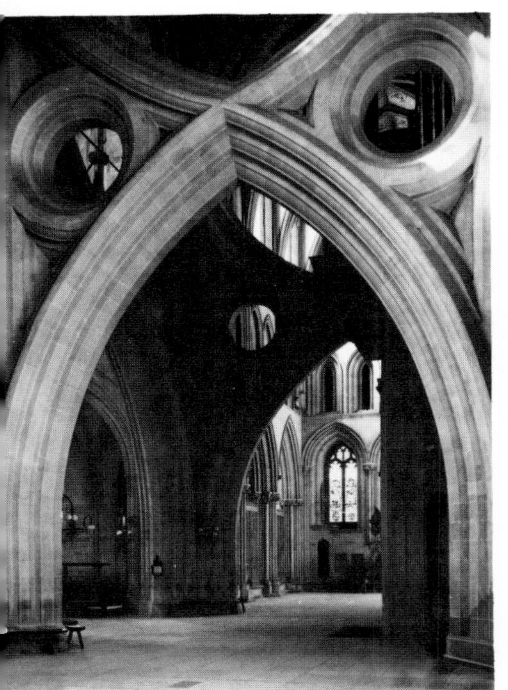

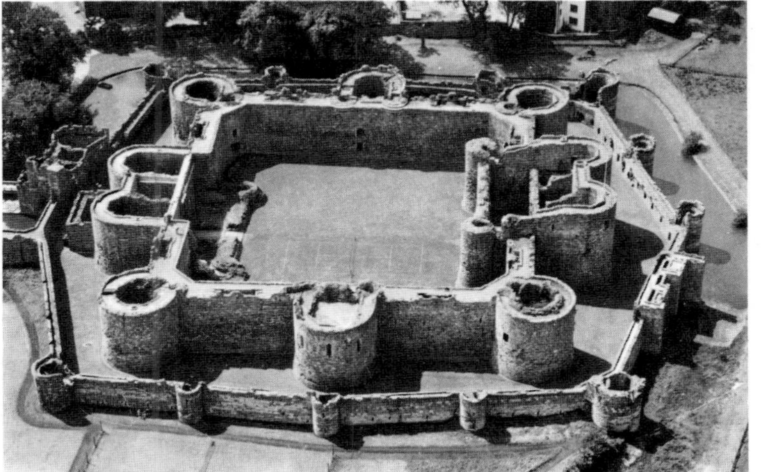

6

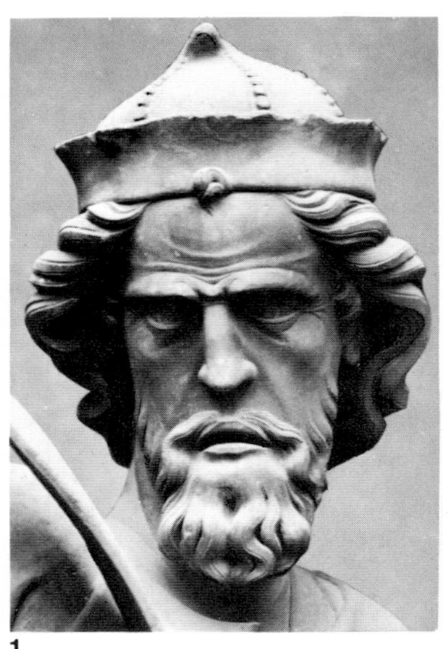

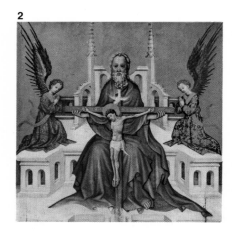

1

1. *Prophet.* Jamb in central portal of west façade, Strasbourg Cathedral. About 1290–1330
2. Austrian School: *Trinity with Christ Crucified.* 15th century. National Gallery, London
3. Choir of Cologne Cathedral, Germany. Begun 1248
4. **Hans von Burghausen** (d.1432): Hall church of St Martin, Landshut, Germany. Begun 1387
5. *Princess Uta.* Detail from painted limestone statue commemorating a founder. Choir of Naumburg Cathedral, Germany. About 1250
6. Ulm Cathedral, Germany. West façade. Begun 1377. Tower designed 1482, completed in the 19th century

2

4

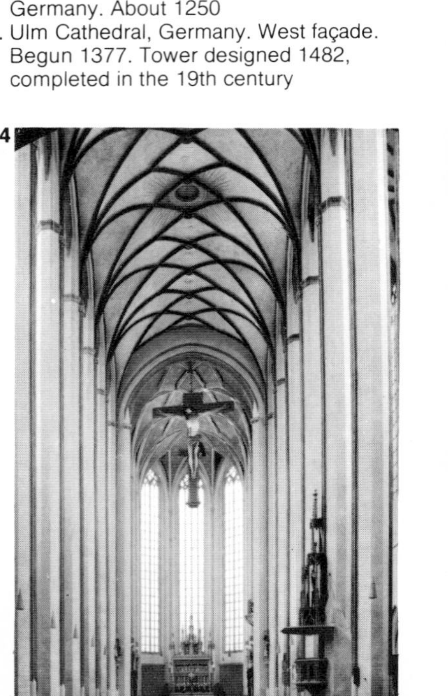

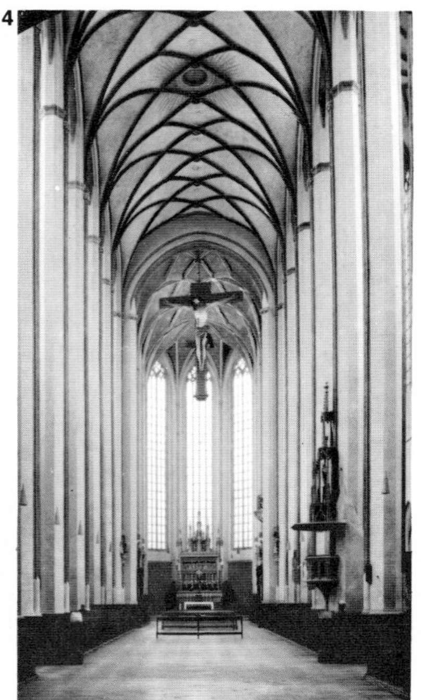

3

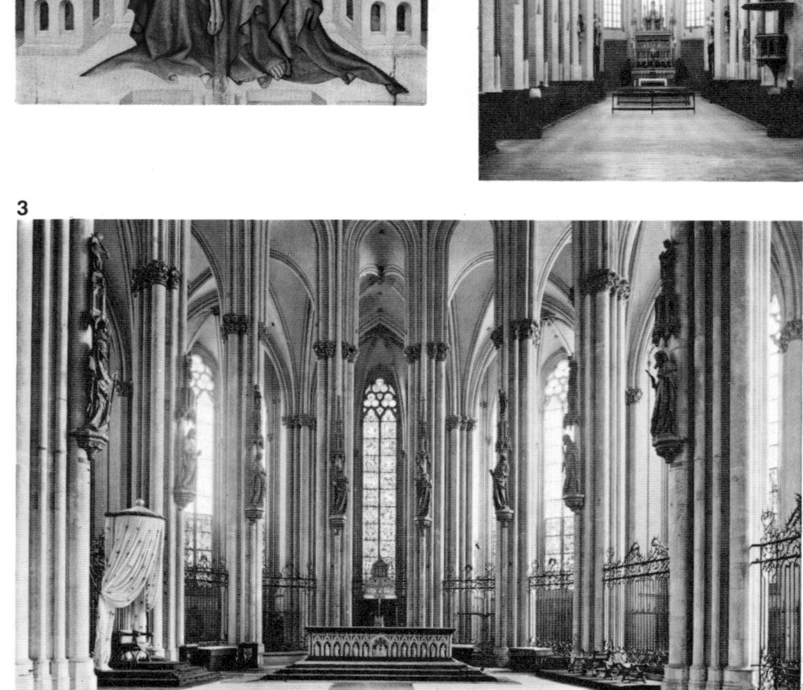

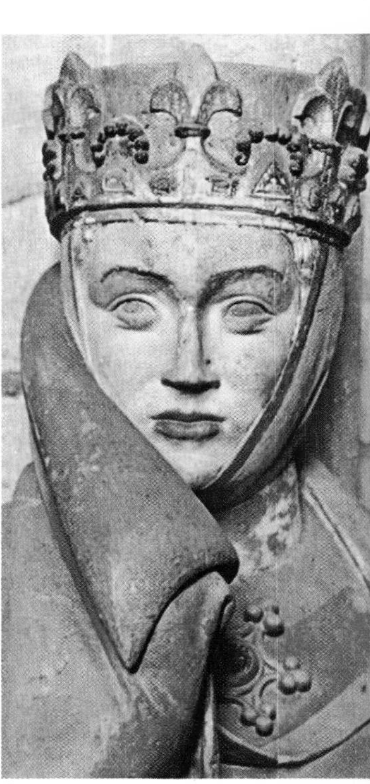

5

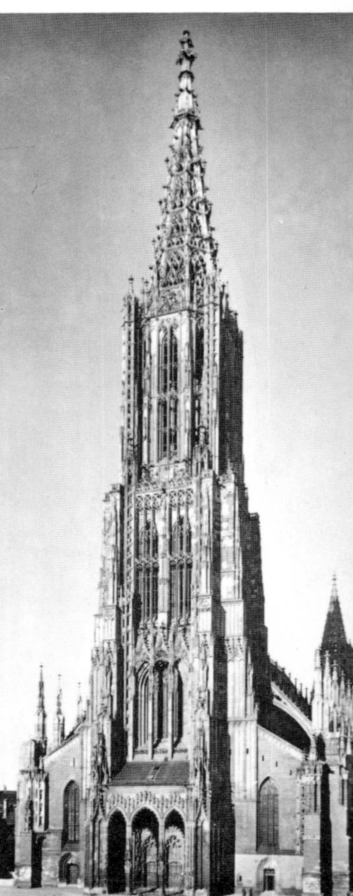

1. Pillar with Evangelists and Angels, south transept interior, Strasbourg Cathedral. About 1230–50
2. Royal figures on choir screen, York Minster. Late 15th century
3. English (or French?) School: Richard II with his patron saints: Edward the Confessor, St Edmund and St John the Baptist. Detail from *The Wilton Diptych.* About 1395. National Gallery, London
4. *Horse and Rider.* Magdeburg Cathedral, Germany. About 1240–50
5. Cologne Master: *The Annunciation.* About 1330. Wallraf-Richartz-Museum, Cologne

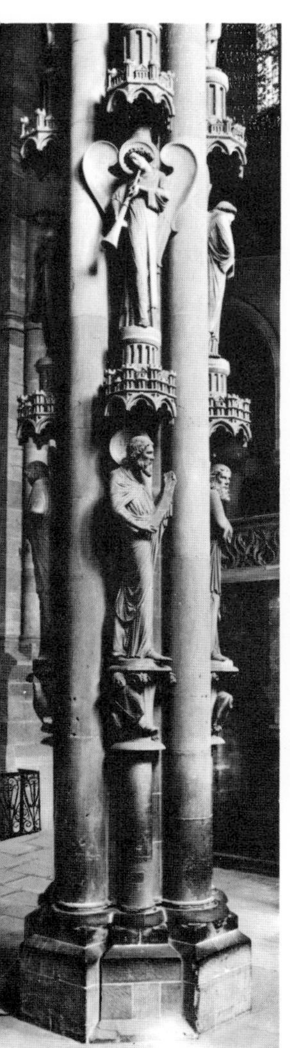

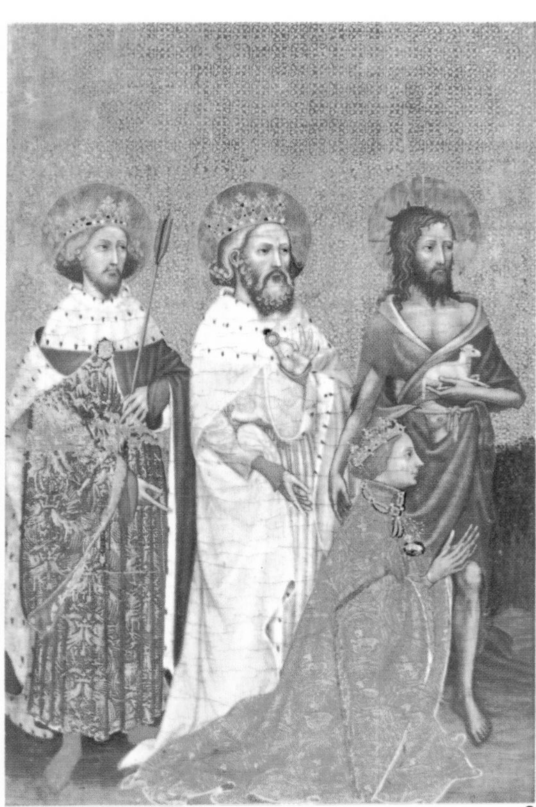

3

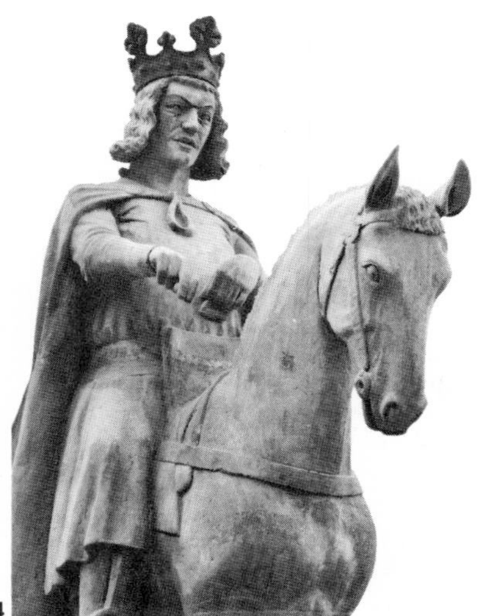

4

5

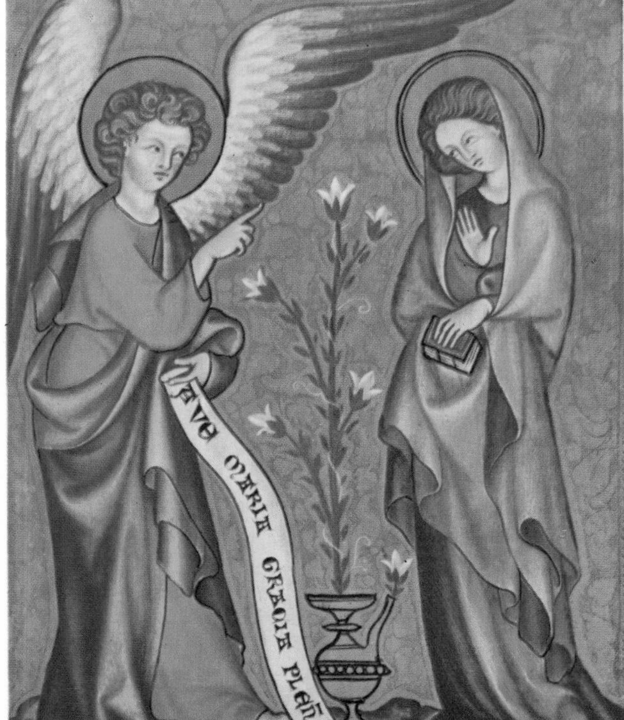

2

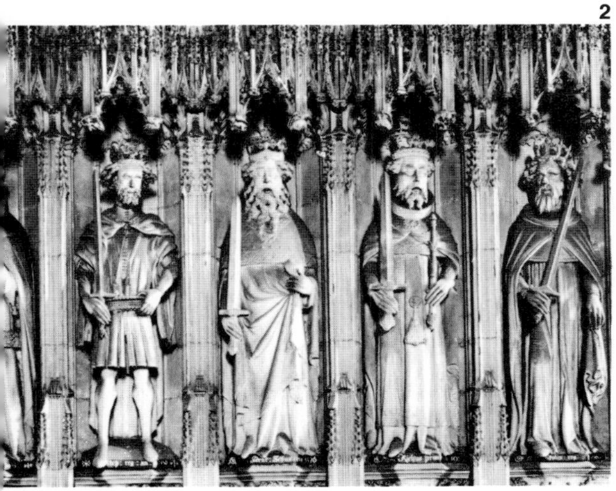

1. Palazzo dei Priori, Perugia, Italy. 1288–1309
2. Town Hall, Bruges, Belgium. Begun 1377
3. Church of S. Maria de Collemaggio, L'Aquila, Italy. Façade in red and white mosaic. 14th century
4. Refectory, abbey of Alcobaça, Portugal. 13th century
5. Vaulted interior, Toledo Cathedral, Spain. About 1227–1493
6. Doges' Palace, Venice. Second half of 14th century; balcony begun 1402
7. Siena Cathedral. Façade by Giovanni Pisano. Begun 1284

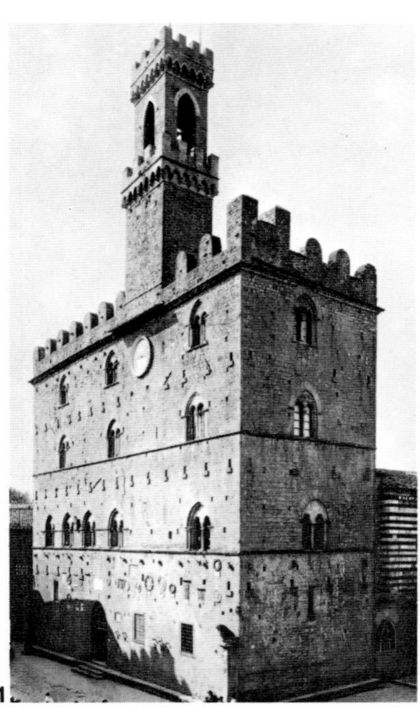

1

4

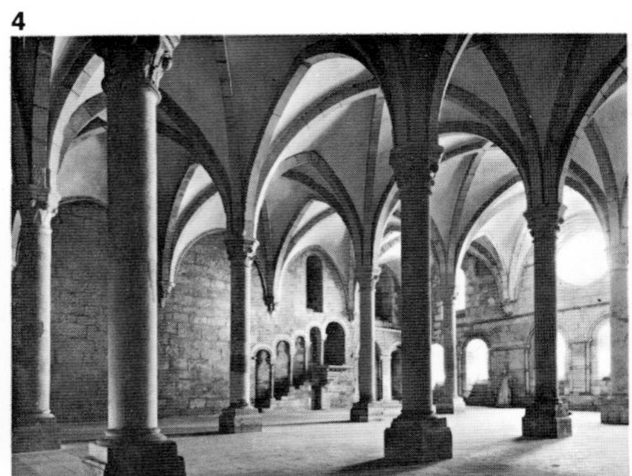

5

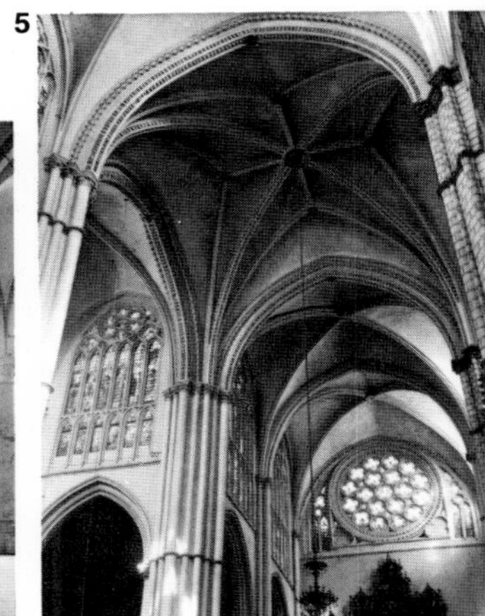

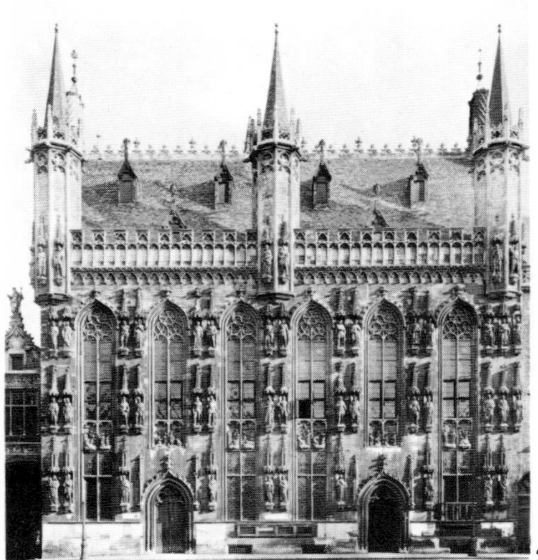

2

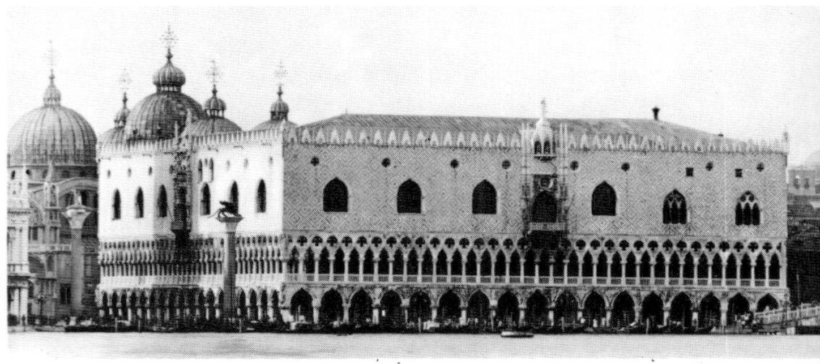

6

3

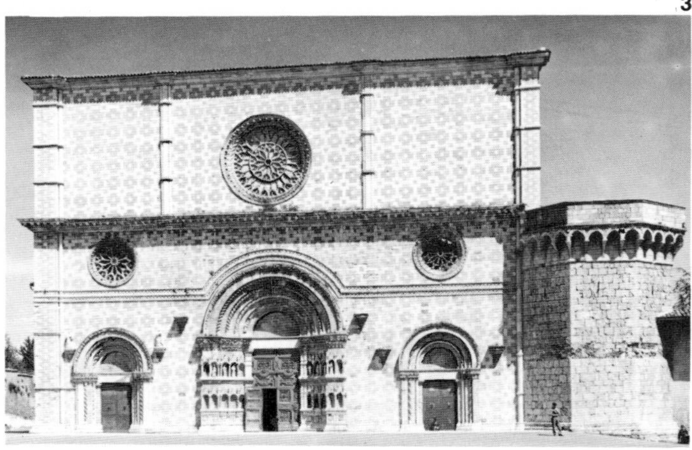

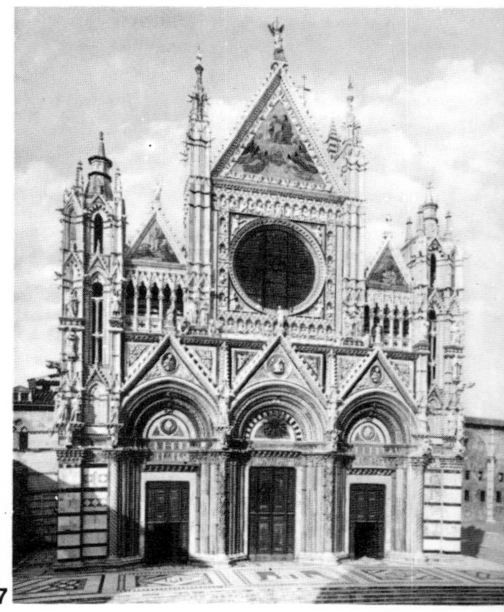

7

Part 6

The Italian Renaissance 1400–1600

Ɛuropean art of the fourteenth, fifteenth and sixteenth centuries firmly established man at he centre of the universe. Painters and sculptors both in Italy and north of the Alps leveloped a remarkable proficiency in the lepiction of individuals seen within their natural surroundings. The means of doing this was sought primarily with the aid of mathematical science. Linear perspective allowed an artist such as Uccello to depict scenes with a reater fidelity to nature, just as mathematically ased modules invested the architectural esigns of Brunelleschi and Palladio with a ense of unity. The rediscovery of antiquity nrough excavations and manuscripts was an dded impetus for painters, sculptors and rchitects alike in their search for verisimilitude. Vhile fifteenth-century artists, even allowing or local differences in various regions, ttempted to portray man with a gravity and sychological penetration that approximated to eal life, their world was still contained. ccuracy and meticulousness of style could e spellbinding, but also confining. Similarly, ne search for monumentality in the figures ainted by Masaccio and Piero della Francesca ould be constraining. Where, however, a ealistic rendering of the human form is ombined with a convincing handling of space, utstanding passages of narrative art can be ound, as in the work of Giotto, Duccio, hiberti or Donatello.

The sixteenth century, in contrast with the vo previous centuries, was essentially xpansionist. It was the age of discovery and ne period when landscape painting came to the fore. Artists were more determined to interpret the world about them than just to record it. The personalities of artists such as Leonardo da Vinci, Raphael, Michelangelo, Giorgione and Titian are closely related to their works. Now the unity of a composition was derived from the interlocking of its constituent elements as opposed to the sum of its various parts. Where, however, the classical sense of balance and order was swept aside, the elegant gestures and refined poses favoured by Mannerist artists such as Pontormo, Rosso and Parmigianino were preferred.

What is so remarkable about this period is the widespread wealth of artistic talent. This was partly due to an enlightened system of patronage and partly to the organization of workshops. At the beginning of the fourteenth century these aspects were primarily corporate, but by the sixteenth century they had become more individual. As a direct result of this cultural ascendancy, the social status of the artist improved so that those of the calibre of Michelangelo or of Titian kept the company of monarchs, princes and popes. It was also a period when a number of important theoretical and biographical writings relating to the arts were published. Nearly all of these were written by artists themselves – Alberti, Piero della Francesca, Leonardo da Vinci, Dürer and Vasari. There is, in short, a direct connection, it seems, between the fact that as art became more secular so artists became more self-conscious.

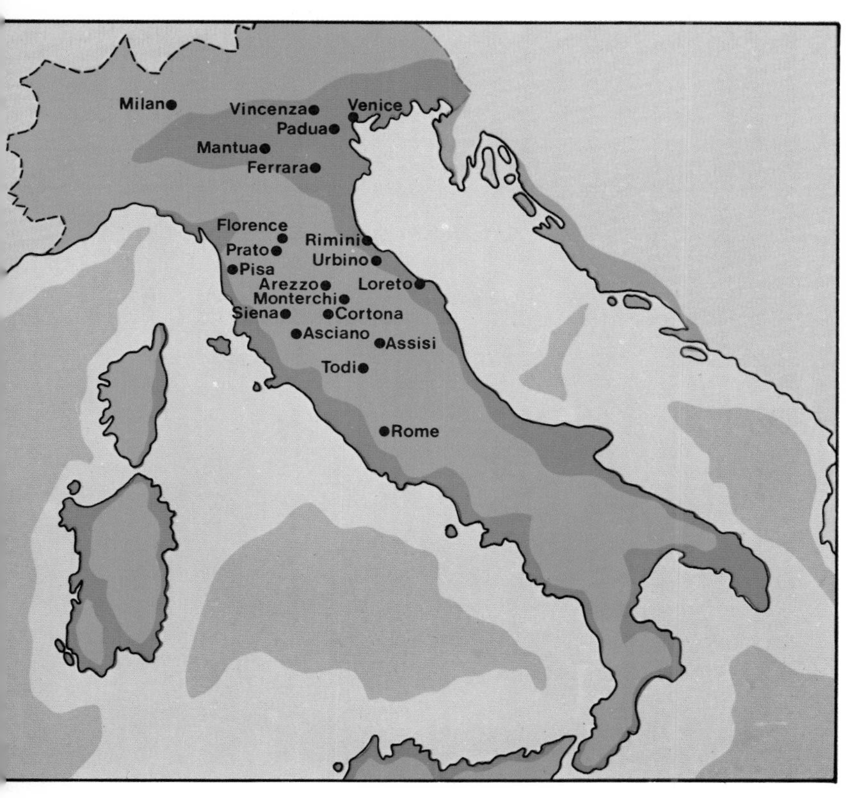

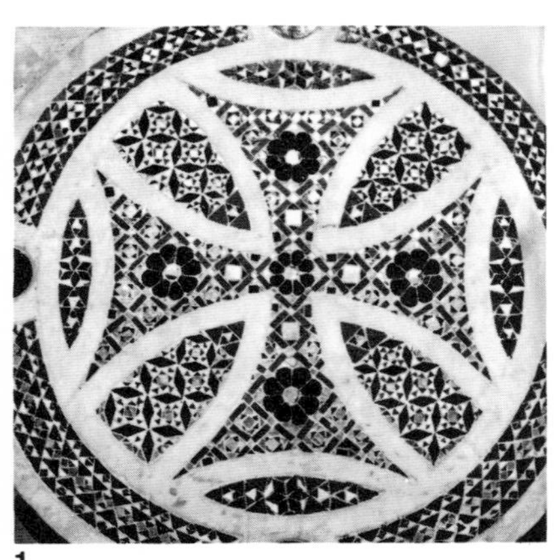

1

1. **Cosmati** artists: mosaic in the church of S. Saba, Rome. About 1200
2. **Bonanno of Pisa** (*fl.*1174–86): *Prophets.* Detail of bronze relief on the S. Ranieri portal, Pisa Cathedral. 1180
3. **The Vassalletti:** cloister of the Basilica di S. Paolo fuori le Mura, Rome. 1193–1241
4. **Bonanno of Pisa** (*fl.*1174–86): *The Adoration of the Magi.* Detail of bronze relief on the S. Ranieri portal, Pisa Cathedral. 1180
5. **Giovanni Pisano** (*c.*1245–after 1314): *The Nativity, and Angels appearing to the Shepherds.* Detail from pulpit of Pisa Cathedral. 1302–10
6. **Giovanni Pisano** (*c.*1245–after 1314): *Dancer.* Museo Nazionale di S. Matteo, Pisa

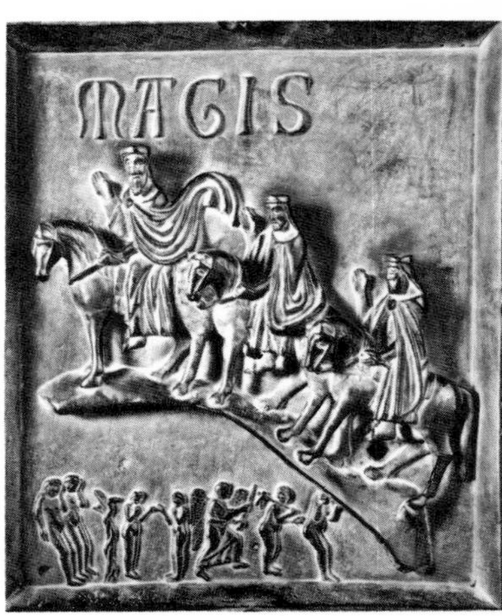

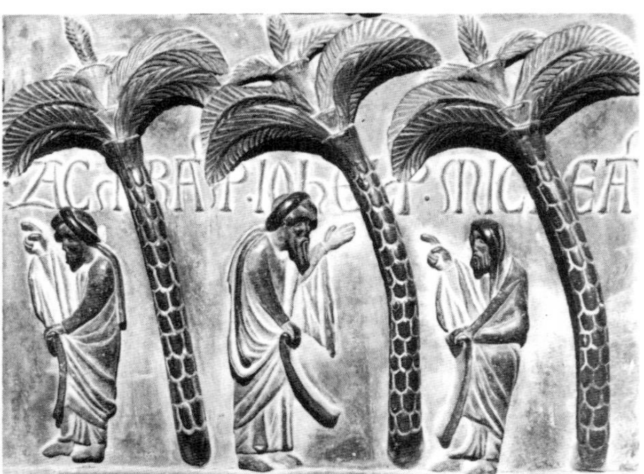

2

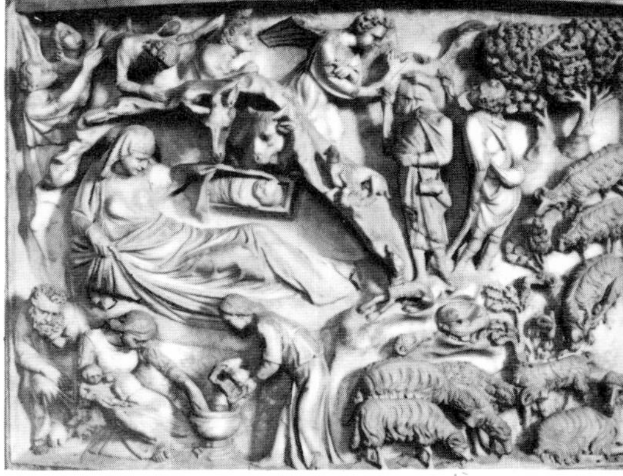

5

3

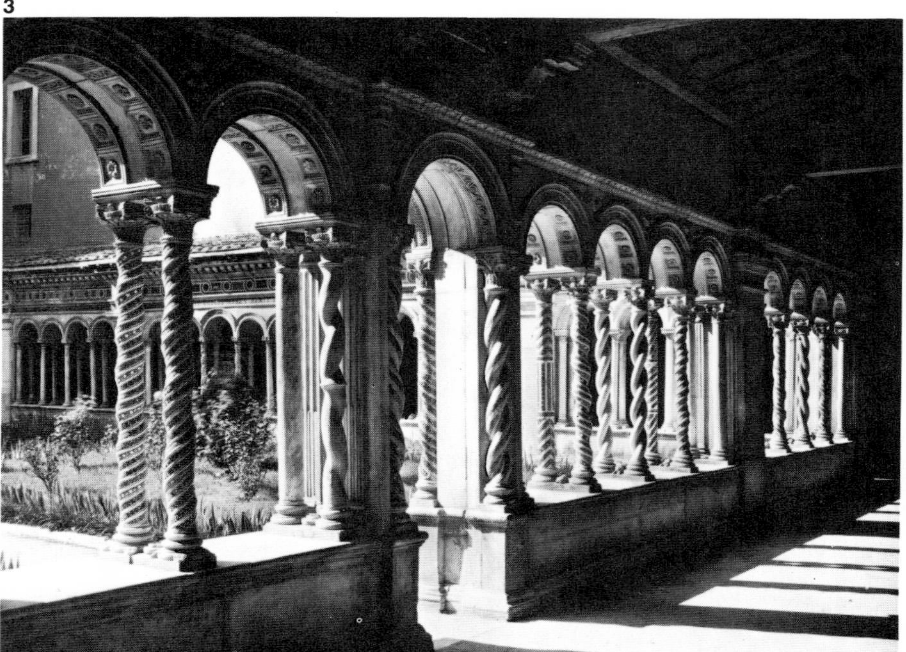

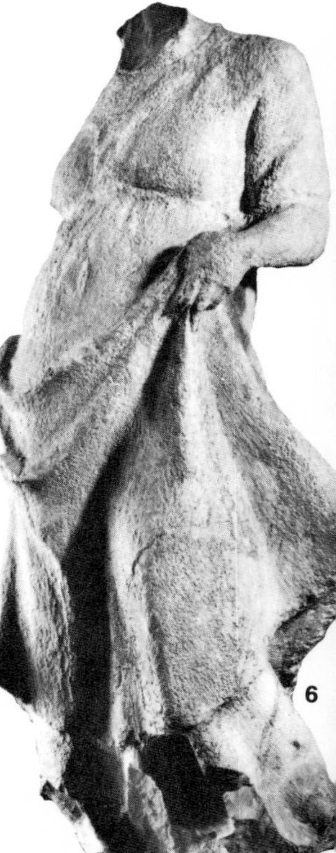

6

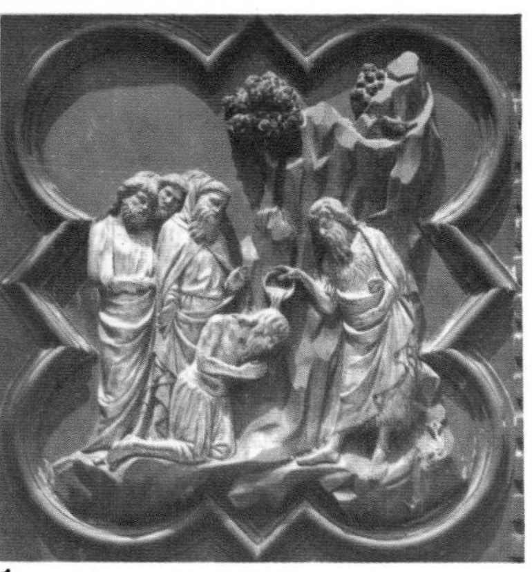

1

1. **Andrea Pisano** (*c.*1290–1348): *The Baptism of Christ.* Panel of bronze door, Florence Baptistery. 1330–6
2. **Giovanni di Balduccio** (*c.*1300–after 1360): Shrine of St Peter Martyr. Detail. Marble. 1335–9. Church of S. Eustorgio, Milan
3. **Pietro Cavallini** (*fl.*1273–1308); *Angels.* Detail from Last Judgement fresco in the church of S. Cecilia in Trastevere, Rome. About 1293
4. **Cimabue** (1240/50–1302?): *Maestà.* About 1285. Uffizi, Florence
5. **Nicola Pisano** (*fl.*1258–78): *The Adoration of the Magi.* Detail from marble pulpit of Pisa Baptistery. 1260
6. **Nicola Pisano** (*fl.*1258–78): *The Crucifixion.* Detail from marble pulpit of Siena Cathedral. 1265–8

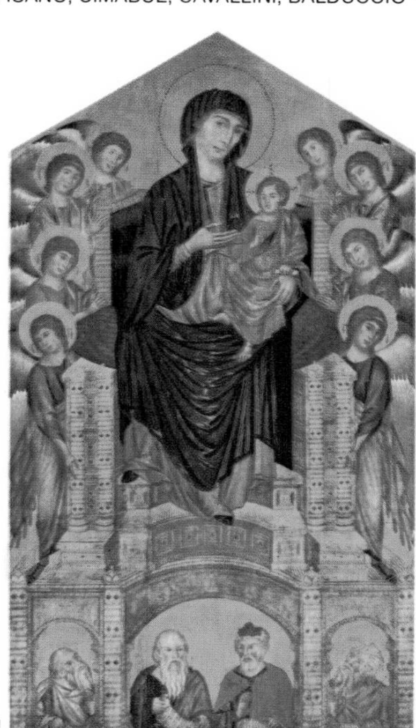

4

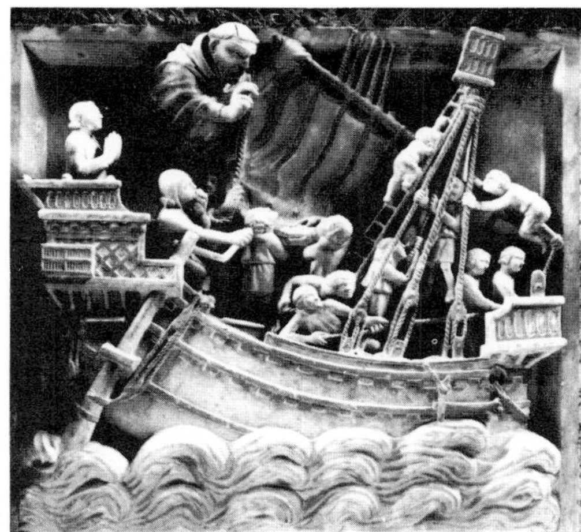

2

5

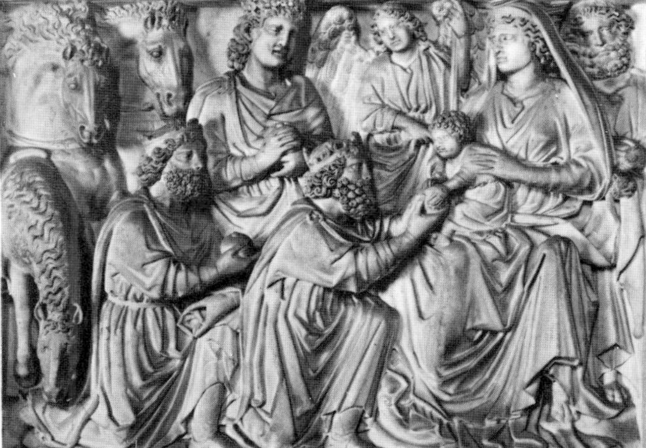

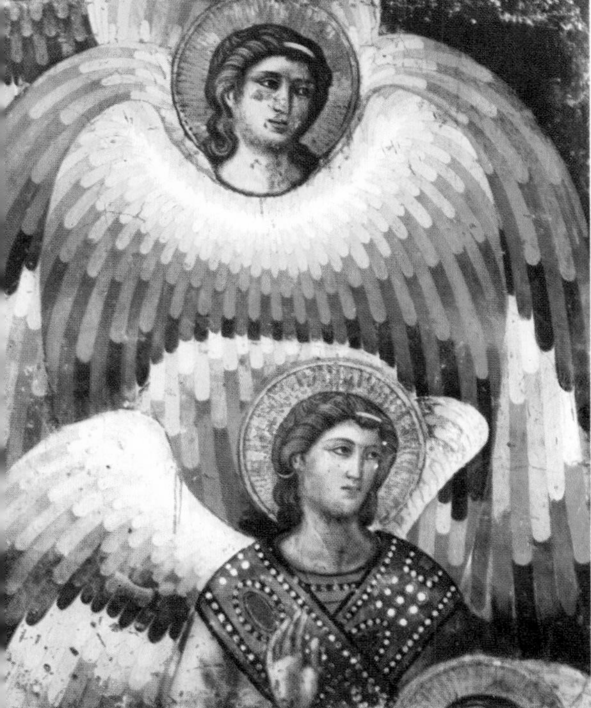

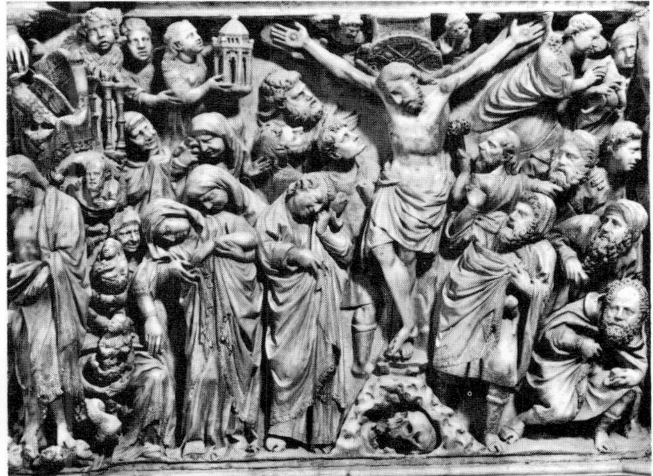

6

Giotto (1266?–1337)

1. *The Last Supper.* Alte Pinakothek, Munich
2. *St Francis preaching to the Birds.* Fresco. About 1297–1300. Upper Church, S. Francesco, Assisi
3. *Angel.* Detail from *The Last Judgement.* Fresco. 1304–12/13. Arena Chapel, Padua
4. *The Lamentation of Christ.* Fresco. 1305–6. Scrovegni Chapel, S. Maria Annunziata dell'Arena, Padua
5. *The Dream of Joachim.* Fresco. 1305–6. Scrovegni Chapel, S. Maria Annunziata dell'Arena, Padua

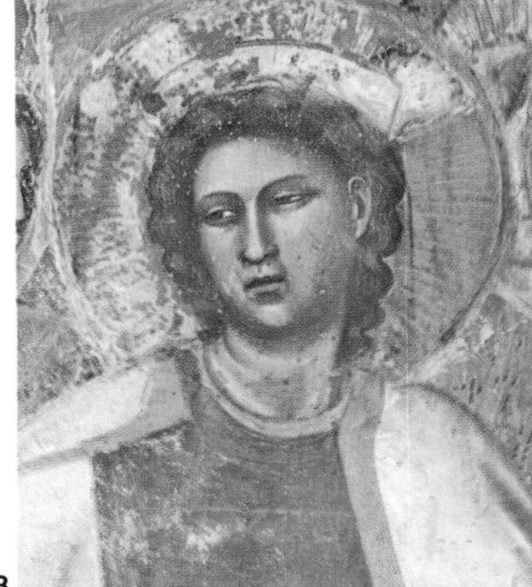

3

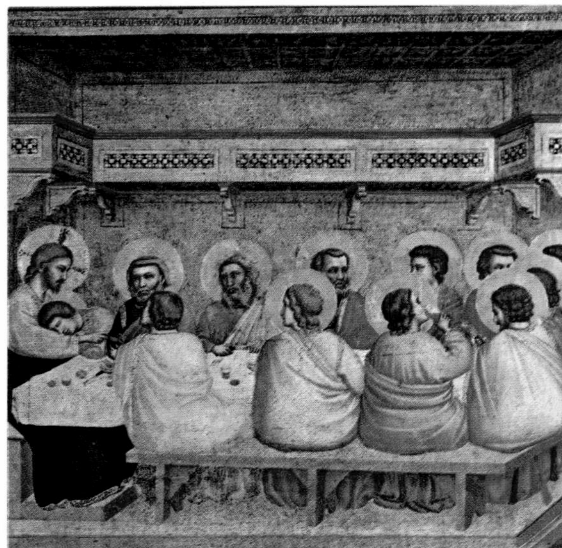

1

2

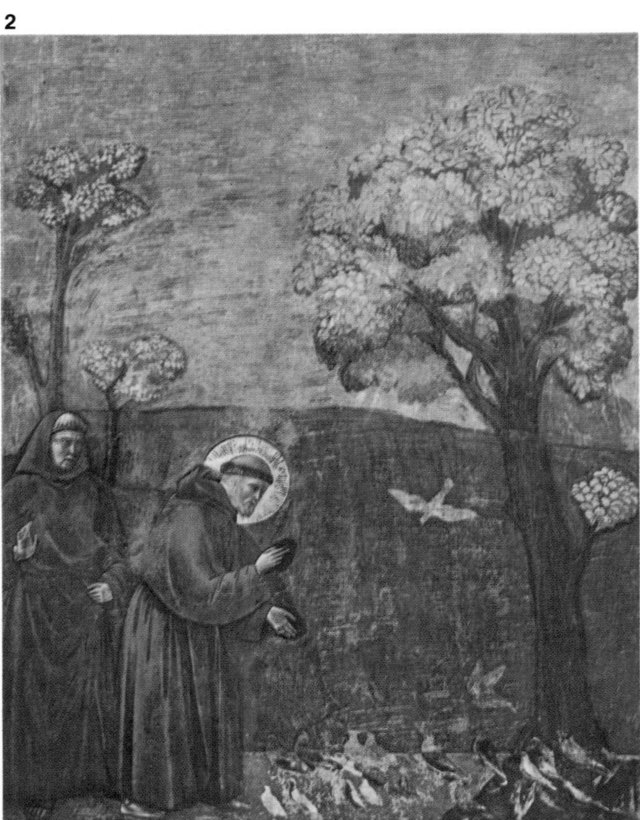

4

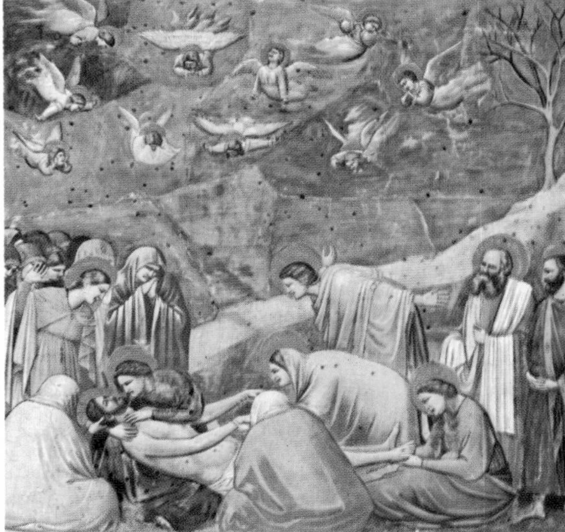

5

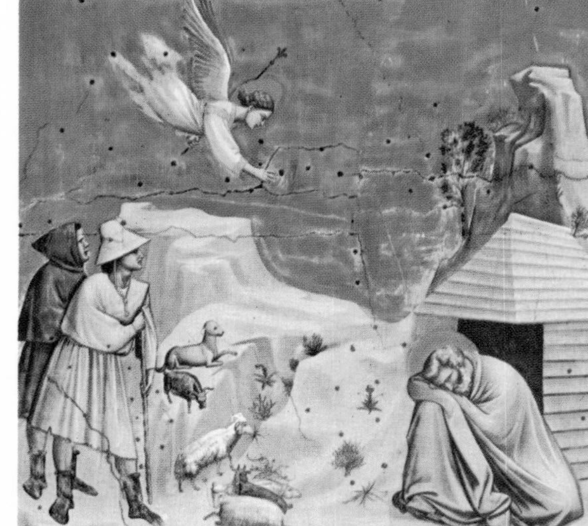

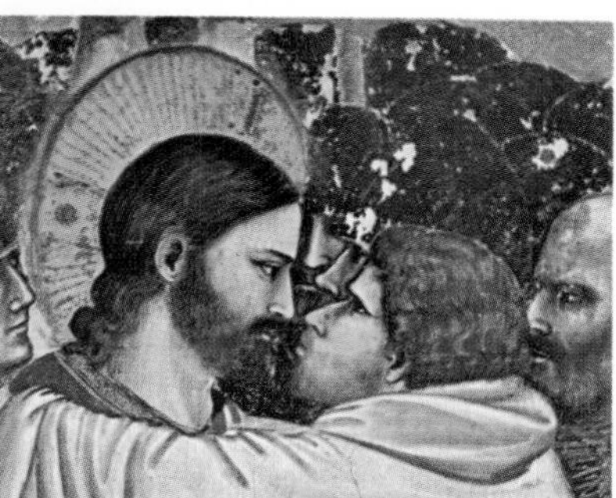

Giotto (1266?–1337)

1. *The Kiss of Judas.* Detail of fresco. 1305–6. Scrovegni Chapel, S. Maria Annunziata dell'Arena, Padua
2. *The Death of St Francis.* Fresco. About 1318. Bardi Chapel, S. Croce, Florence. Before restoration in 1958
3. *The Death of the Virgin.* About 1310? Staatliche Museen, Berlin-Dahlem
4. Detail of fig. 2. After restoration in 1958
5. *The Crucifixion of St Peter.* Left panel of triptych. Pinacoteca, Vatican
6. *The Meeting of Joachim and Anna at the Golden Gate.* Fresco. 1305–6. Scrovegni Chapel, S. Maria Annunziata dell'Arena, Padua

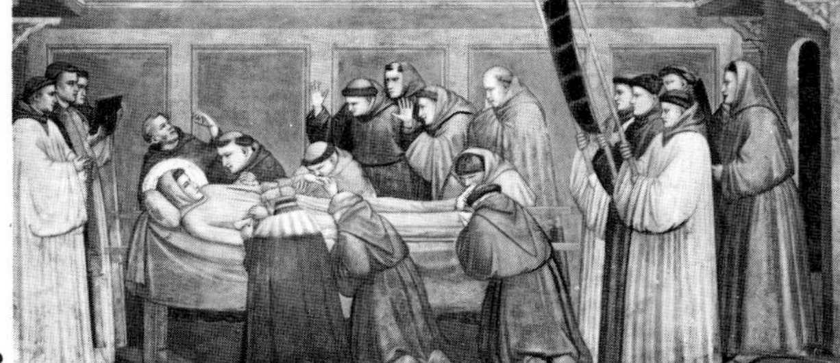

2

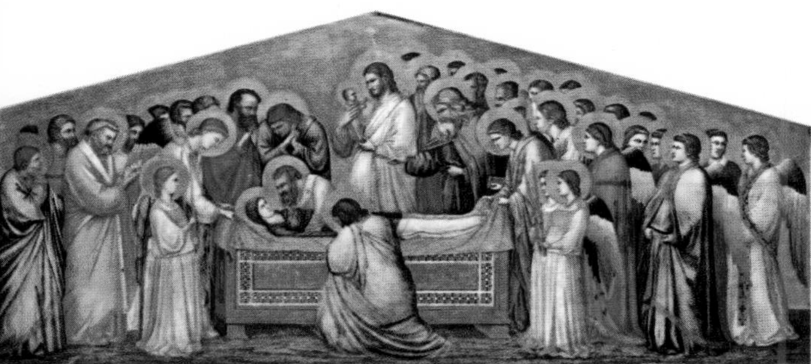

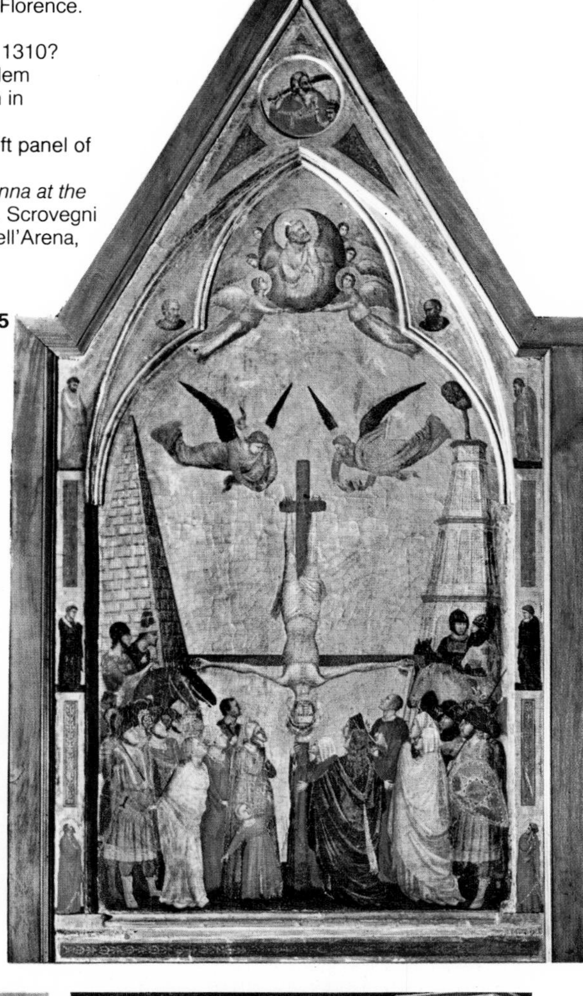

5

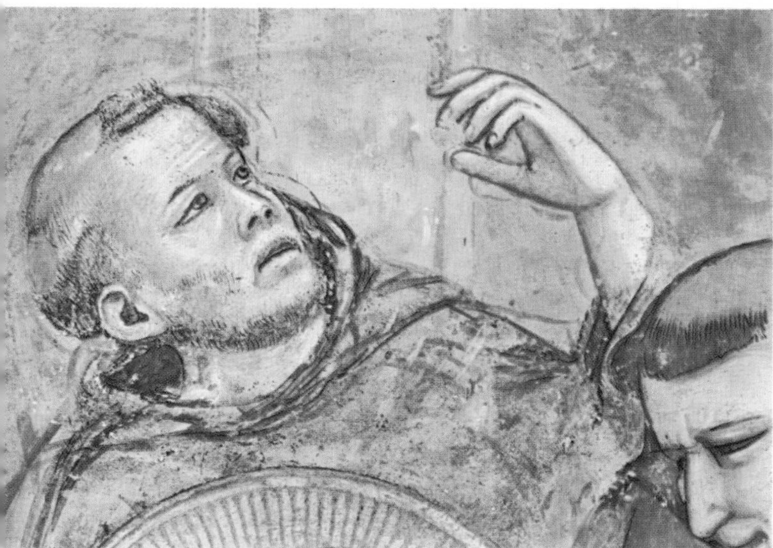

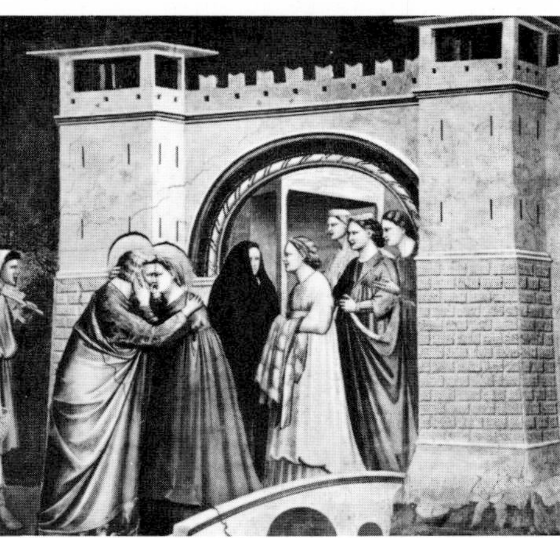

6

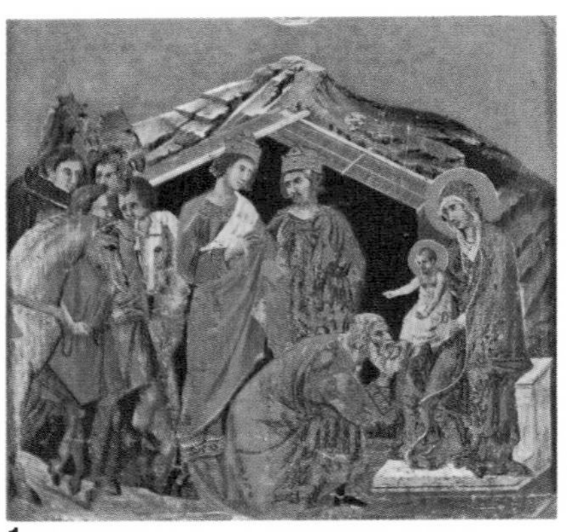

1

Duccio (*c.*1255–*c.*1319)

1. *The Adoration of the Magi.* The Maestà Altarpiece. 1308–11. Museo dell'Opera del Duomo, Siena
2. *The Temptation of Christ.* The Maestà. 1308–11. Frick Collection, New York
3. *The Calling of St Peter and St Andrew.* The Maestà. 1308–11. National Gallery of Art (Samuel H. Kress Collection), Washington DC
4. *Christ washing the Disciples' Feet.* The Maestà. 1308–11. Museo dell'Opera del Duomo, Siena
5. *The Annunciation.* The Maestà. 1308–11. Museo dell'Opera del Duomo, Siena
6. *The Holy Women at the Sepulchre.* The Maestà. 1308–11. Museo dell'Opera del Duomo, Siena
7. *Madonna surrounded by Saints.* The 1308–11. Museo dell'Opera del Duomo, Siena

4

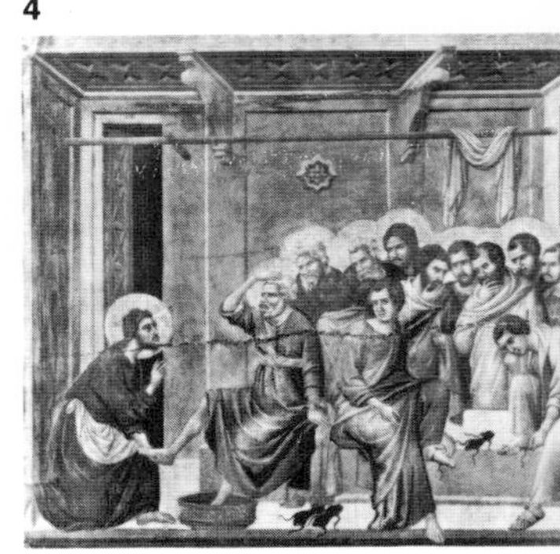

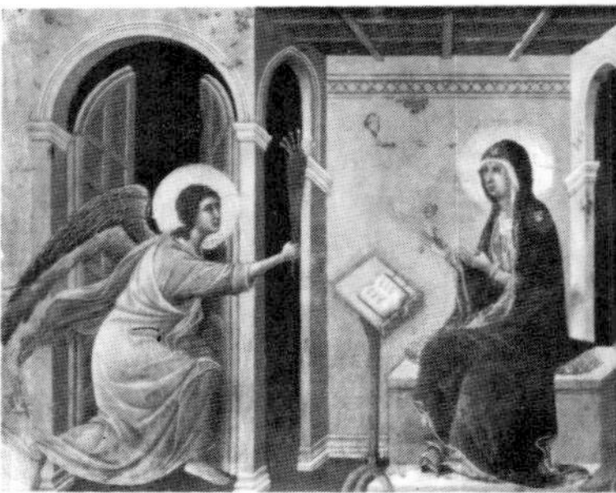

5

2

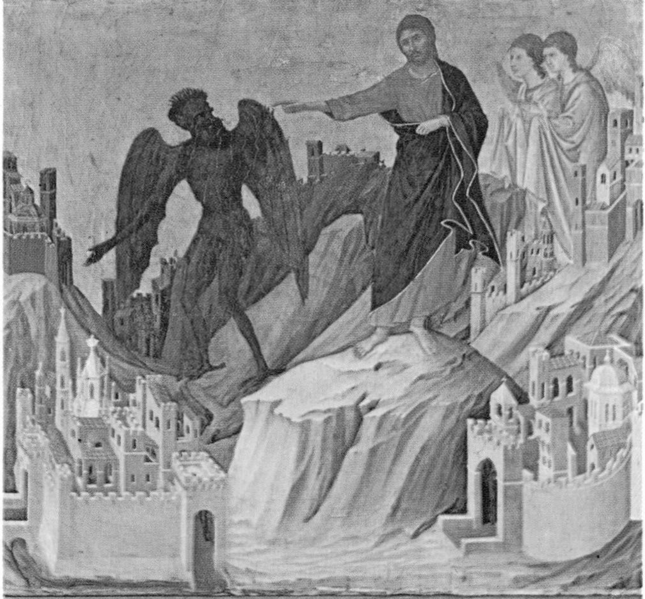

6

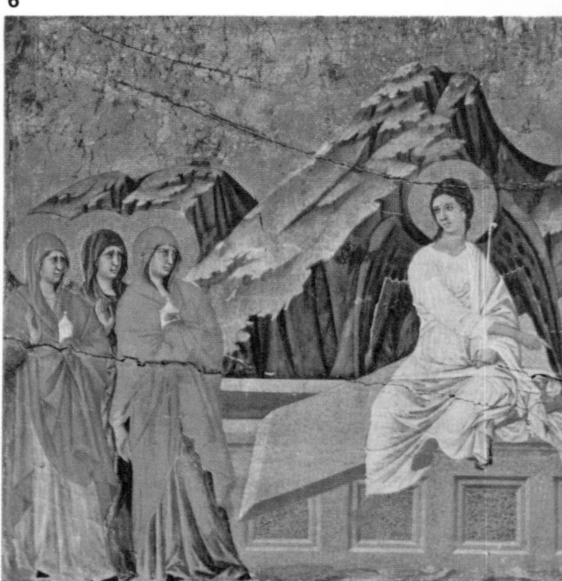

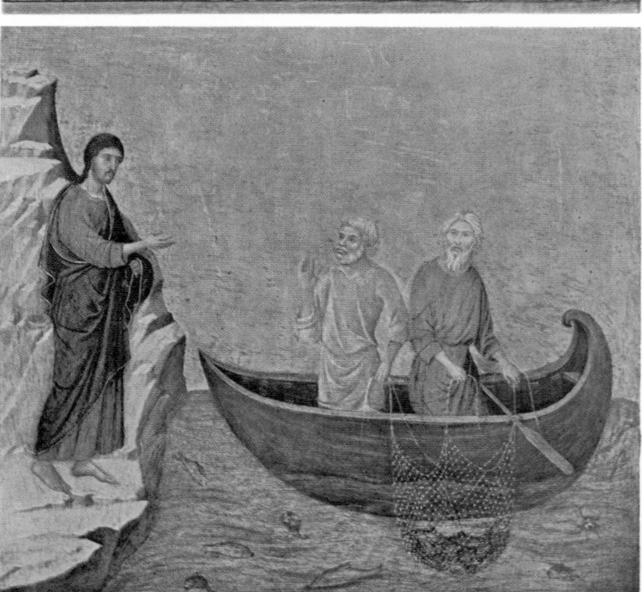

3

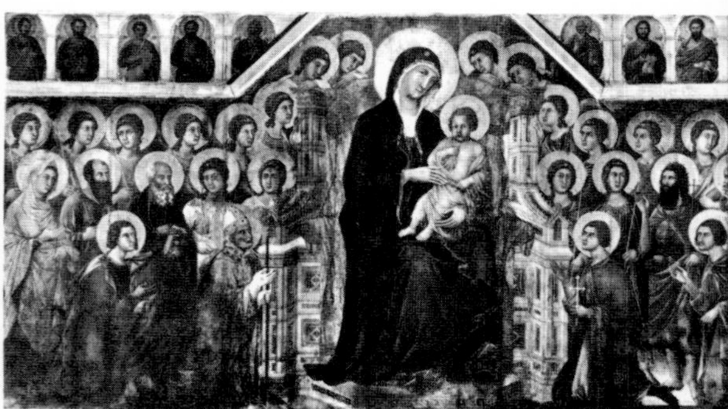

7

1. **Andrea Orcagna** (*fl.* 1344–68): *The Triumph of Death.* Fresco fragment. 1360s. Museo dell'Opera di S. Croce, Florence
2. **Andrea Orcagna** (*fl.* 1344–68): *St Lawrence saving the Soul of Emperor Henry II.* Detail from Strozzi Altarpiece. 1354–7. S. Maria Novella, Florence
3. **Maso di Banco** (*fl.* 1340s): *Scenes from the Life of St Sylvester.* Fresco. About 1341. Bardi di Vernio Chapel, S. Croce, Florence
4. **Bernardo Daddi** (*c.* 1290–1348?): *The Madonna and Child Enthroned.* Late 1330s? National Gallery of Art (Samuel H. Kress Collection), Washington DC
5. **Andrea Orcagna,** style of: *The Birth of the Virgin.* Ashmolean Museum, Oxford

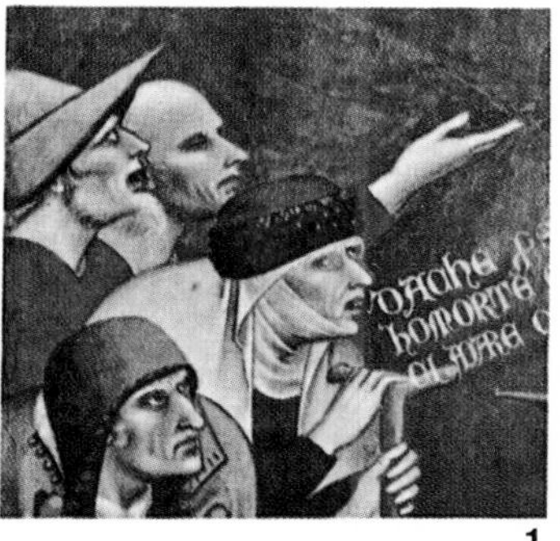

1

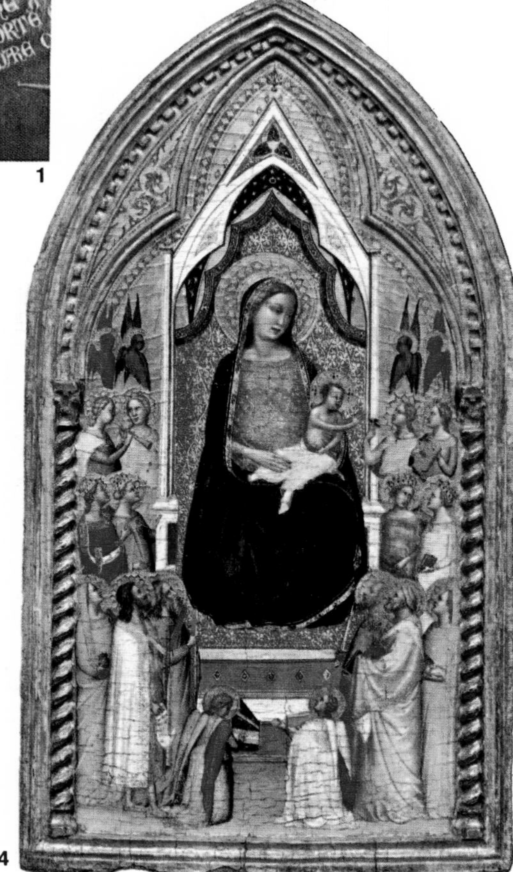

4

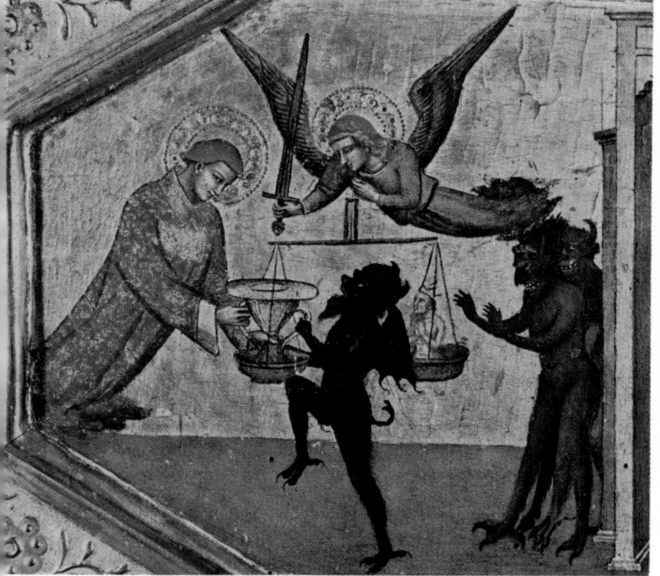

2

3

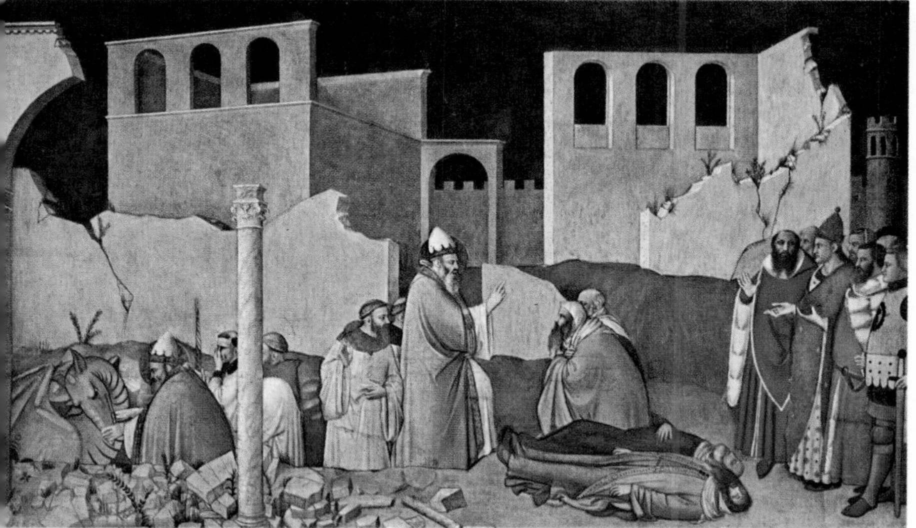

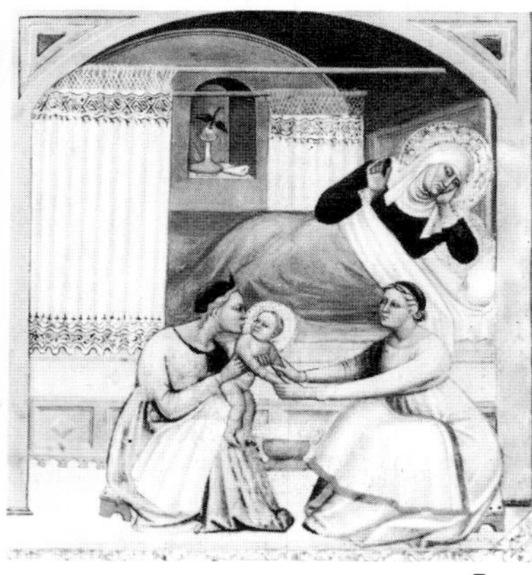

5

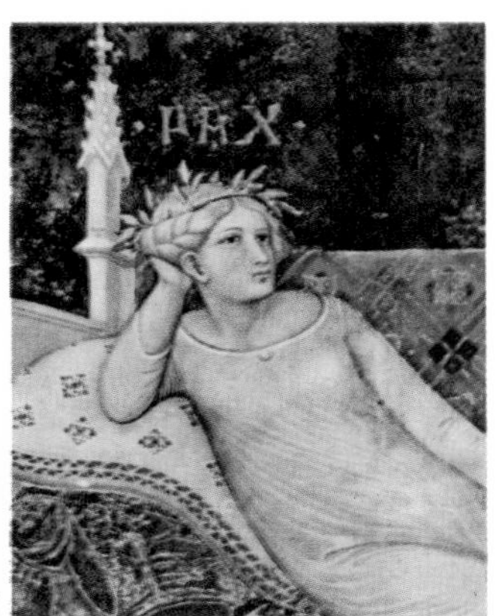

1

1. **Ambrogio Lorenzetti** (*fl.*1319–47): *Peace.* Detail from *Good Government.* Fresco. About 1338–40. Palazzo Pubblico, Siena
2. **Pietro Lorenzetti** (*fl.*1306?–1348): *The Descent from the Cross.* About 1330. Lower Church, S. Francesco, Assisi
3. **Pietro Lorenzetti** (*fl.*1306?–1348): Panel from *The Life of the Blessed Umilita.* Polyptych. 1341. Uffizi, Florence
4. **Pietro Lorenzetti** (*fl.*1306?–1348): *The Birth of the Virgin.* Detail. 1342. Museo dell'Opera del Duomo, Siena
5. **Ambrogio Lorenzetti** (*fl.*1319–47): *Work in the Fields.* Detail from *Good Government.* Fresco. About 1338–40. Palazzo Pubblico, Siena

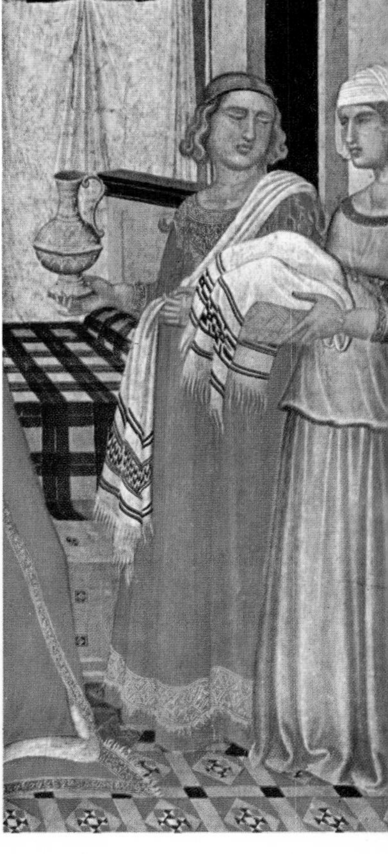

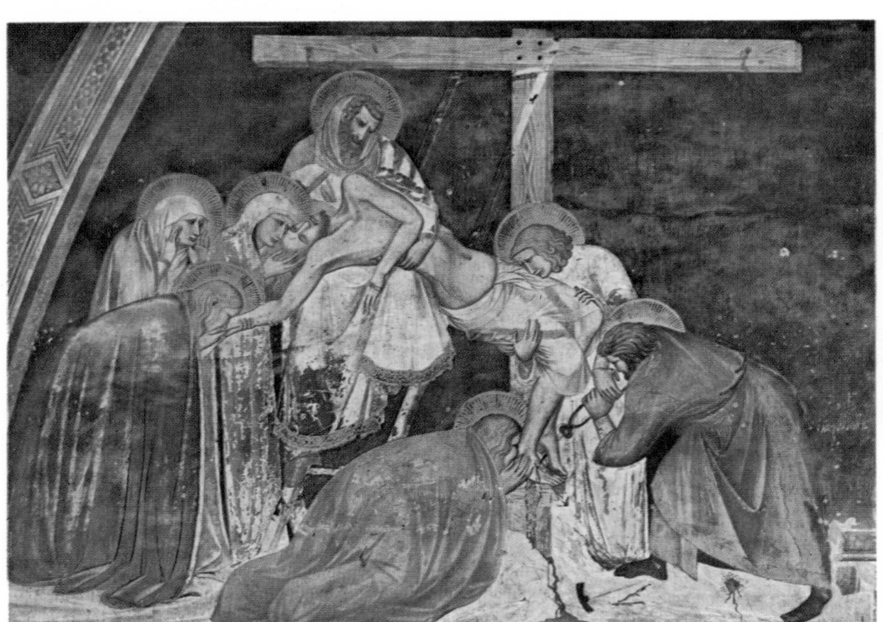
2

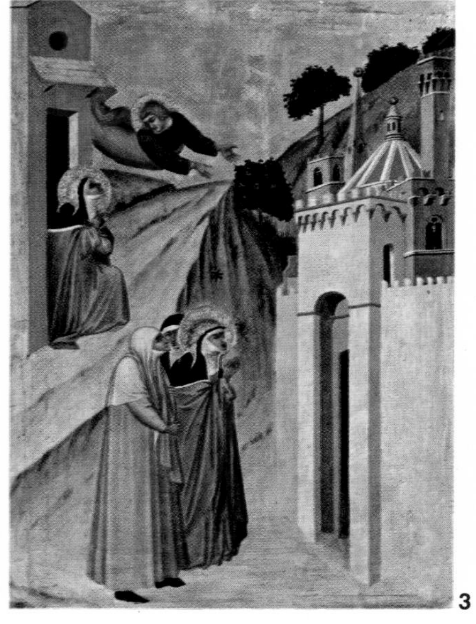
3

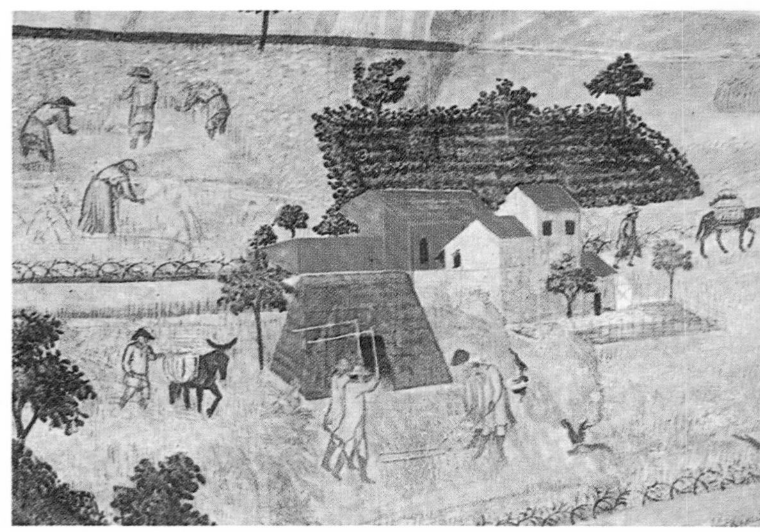

1. **Simone Martini** (*c.*1284–1344) or **Lippo Memmi** (*fl.*1317–47): *Virgin of the Annunciation.* Early 1340s? Koninklijk Museum voor Schone Kunsten, Antwerp
2. **Lorenzo Veneziano** (*fl.*1356–72): *The Conversion of St Paul.* Predella panel from the polyptych of St Peter. Staatliche Museen, Berlin-Dahlem
3. **Simone Martini** (*c.*1284–1344): *Guidoriccio da Fogliano.* Fresco. 1328. Palazzo Pubblico, Siena
4. **Simone Martini** (*c.*1284–1344): *The Blessed Agostino Novello rescuing a Child bitten by a Wolf.* Panel from the altarpiece of the Miracles of the Blessed Agostino. About 1333–6. Church S. Agostino, Siena
5. **Simone Martini** (*c.*1284–1344): *The Entombment.* Panel from triptych of the Passion. About 1340? Staatliche Museen, Berlin-Dahlem

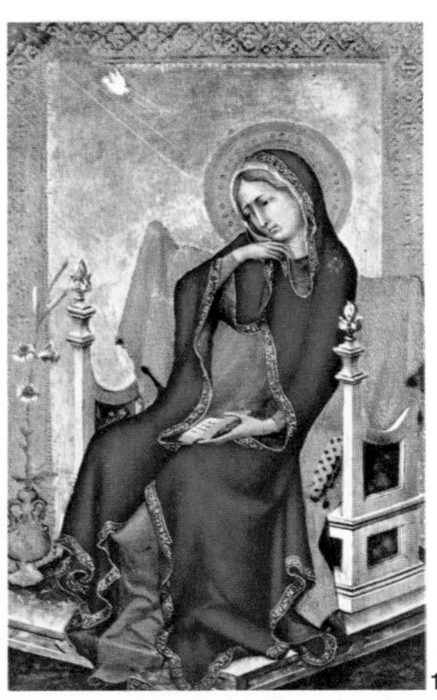
1

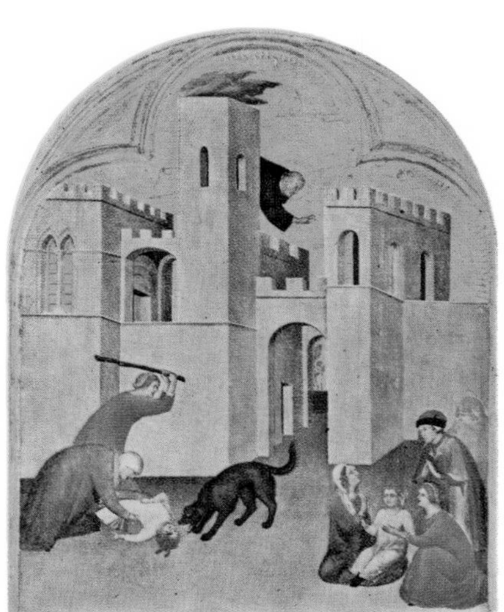
4

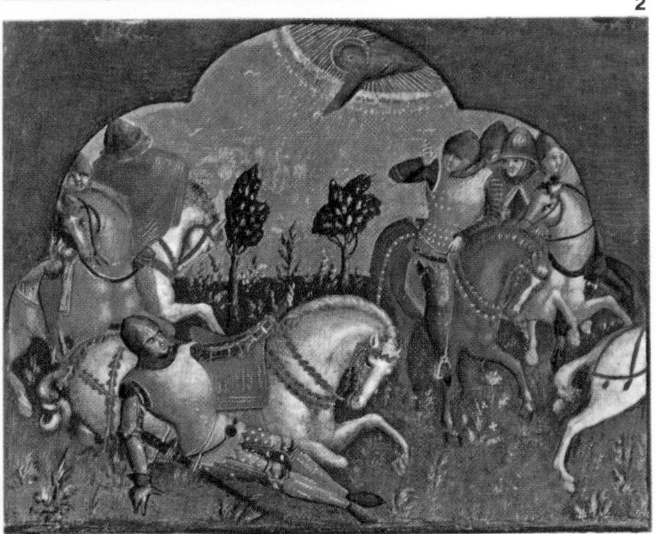
2

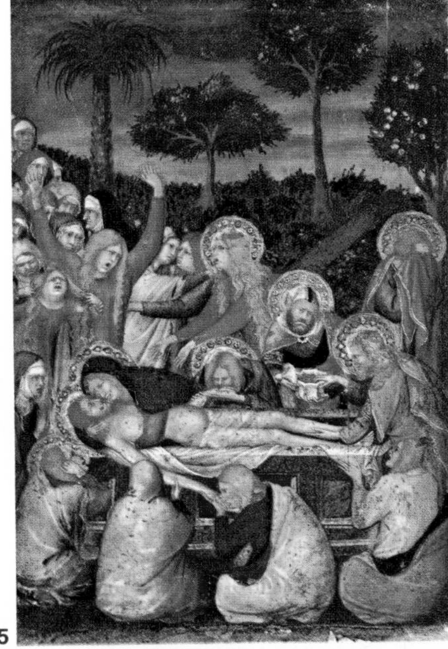
5

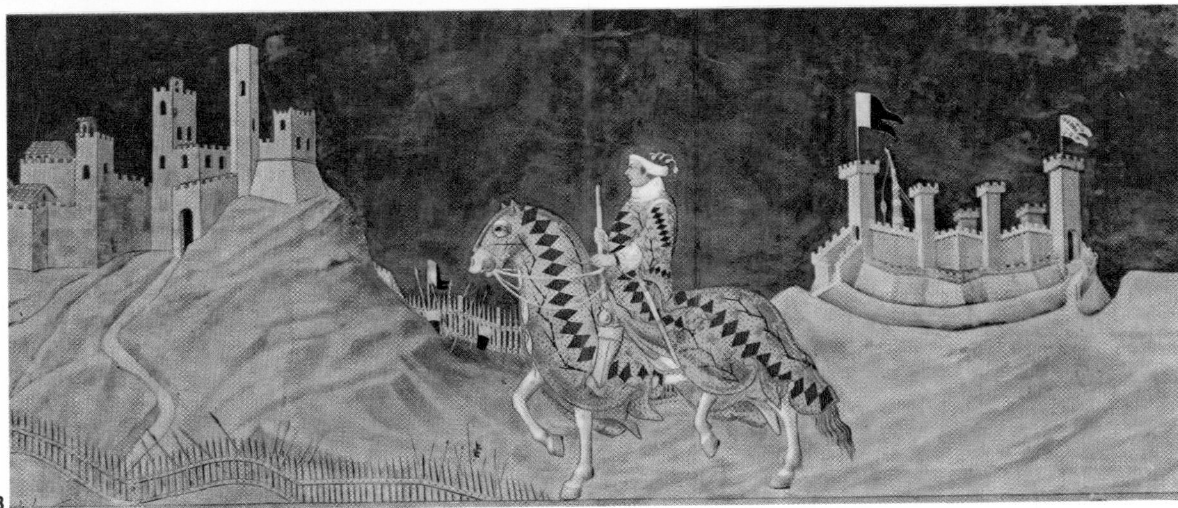
3

1. **Taddeo Gaddi** (*c.*1300–66): *The Nativity.* Detail from fresco. 1332–8. S. Croce, Florence
2. **Giovanni da Milano** (*fl. c.*1346–69): *The Martyrdom of St Catherine.* Predella panel from polyptych of Prato. Museo Comunale, Prato
3. **Nanni di Banco:** Detail of fig. 4
4. **Nanni di Banco** (*c.*1384–1421): *Quattro Coronati.* About 1410–15. Or S. Michele, Florence
5. **Lorenzo Monaco** (*c.*1370–*c.*1422): *The Crucifixion.* Pinacoteca, Vatican
6. **Masolino** (*c.*1383–after 1432): *Story of St Peter: Resurrection of Tabitha, and Healing of the Cripple.* Fresco. About 1425. Brancacci Chapel, S. Maria del Carmine, Florence

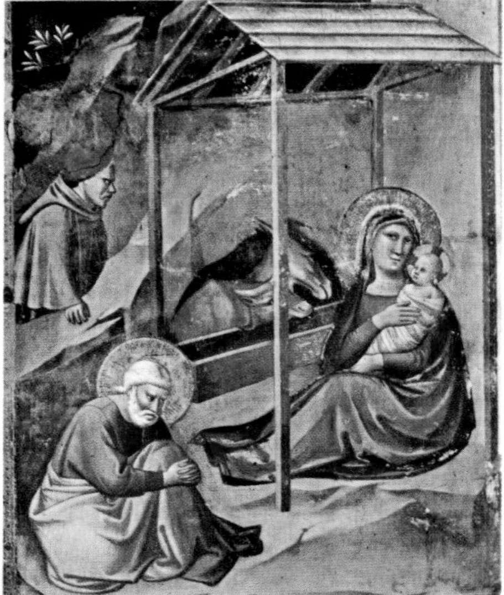

1

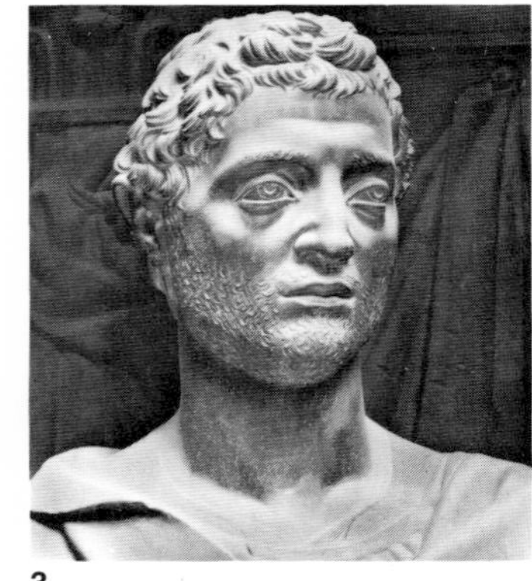

3

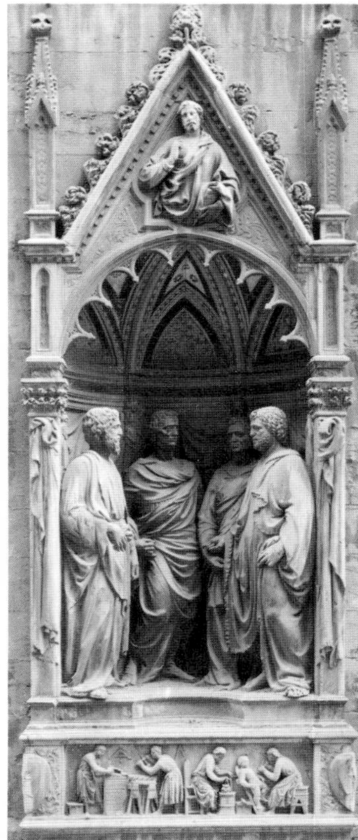

4

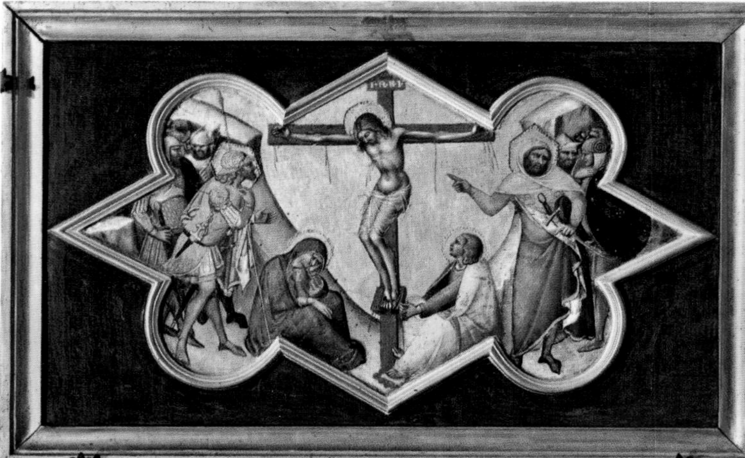

5

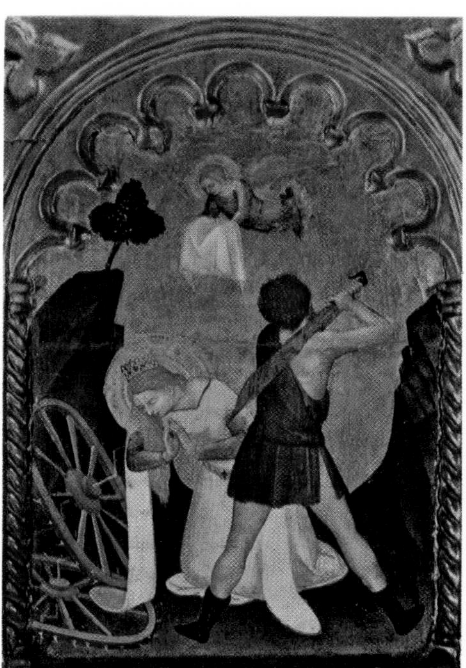

2

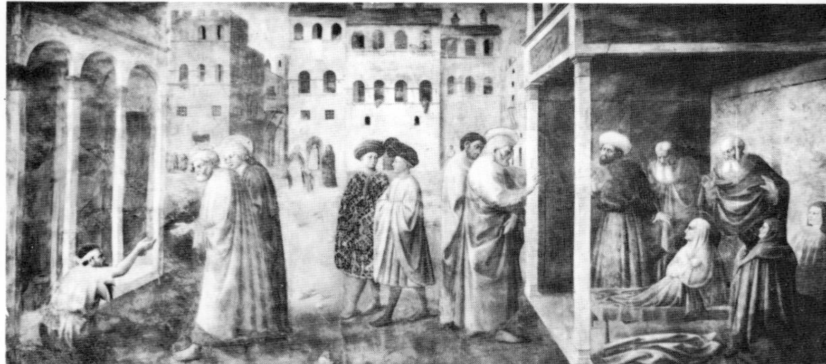

6

Gentile da Fabriano (*c.*1370–1427): *Presentation in the Temple.* Detail from predella panel. 1423. Louvre, Paris
Jacopo della Quercia (1374/5–1438): *The Creation of Adam.* Bas-relief on central portal, S. Petronio, Bologna. 1425–38
Jacopo della Quercia (1374/5–1438): *Tomb of Ilaria del Carretto.* Marble. About 1406. Lucca Cathedral

4. **Gentile da Fabriano** (*c.*1370–1427): *The Madonna and Child Enthroned, with two Saints.* About 1395–1400. Staatliche Museen, Berlin-Dahlem
5. **Pisanello** (*c.*1395–*c.*1455): *Allegory of Luxury.* Drawing. Albertina, Vienna
6. **Pisanello** (*c.*1395–*c.*1455): *Portrait of a Princess of the House of Este (Ginevra d'Este?).* About 1443. Louvre, Paris

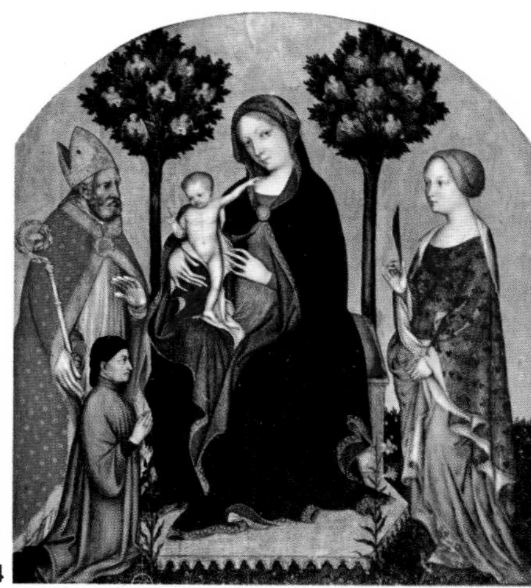
4

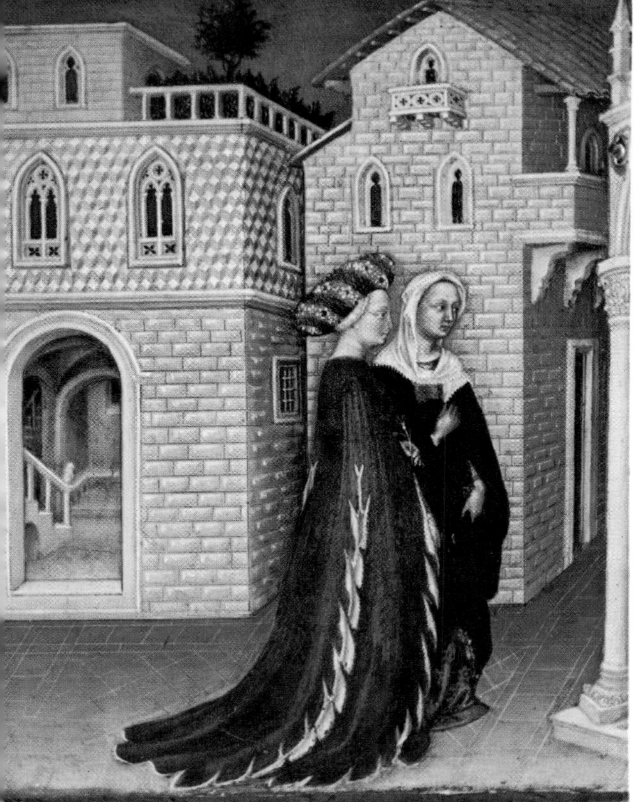

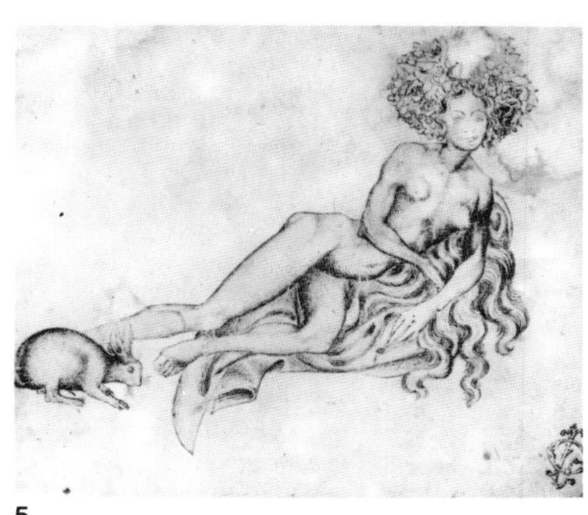
5

6
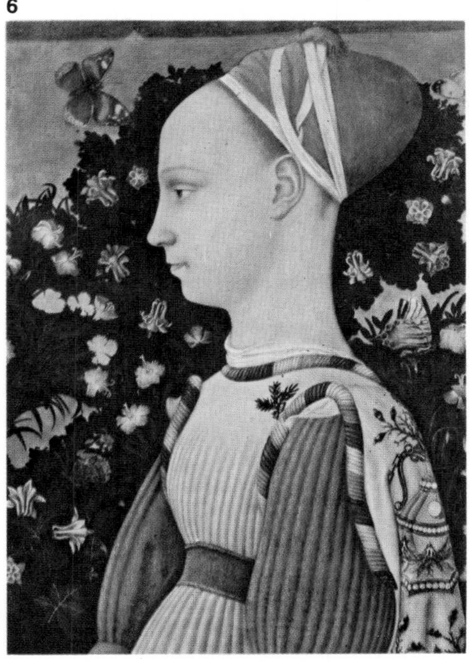

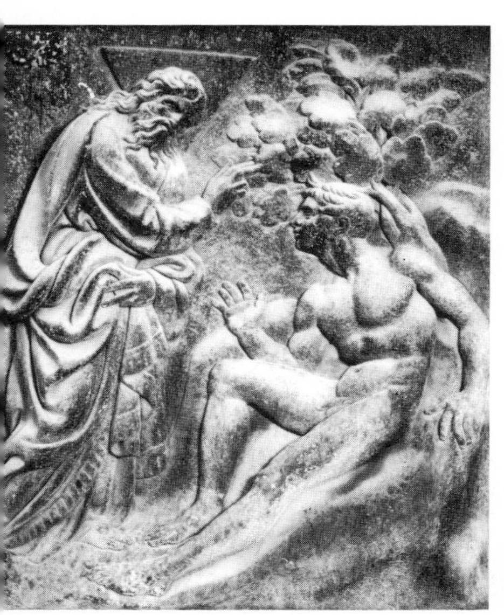

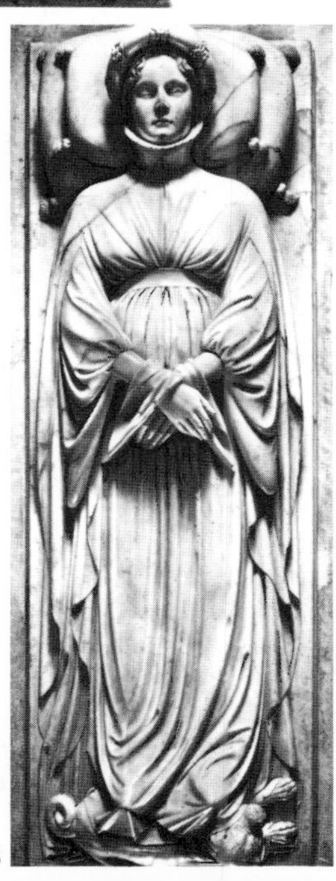
3

Fra Angelico (*c.*1400–55)

1. *The Deposition.* About 1440. Museo di S. Marco, Florence
2. *The Birth and the Calling of St Nicholas of Bari.* Detail from predella of the Perugia altarpiece. 1437. Pinacoteca, Vatican
3. *The Lamentation over the dead Christ.* About 1436. Museo di S. Marco, Florence
4. *The Annunciation.* Fresco. About 1440–7. Convent of S. Marco, Florence
5. *The Mocking of Christ.* Fresco. After 1437. Convent of S. Marco, Florence
6. *The Martyrdom of St Mark.* Detail from predella of the Linaiuoli Triptych. 1433. Museo di S. Marco, Florence
7. *St Peter preaching.* Detail from predella of the Linaiuoli Triptych. 1433. Museo di S. Marco, Florence

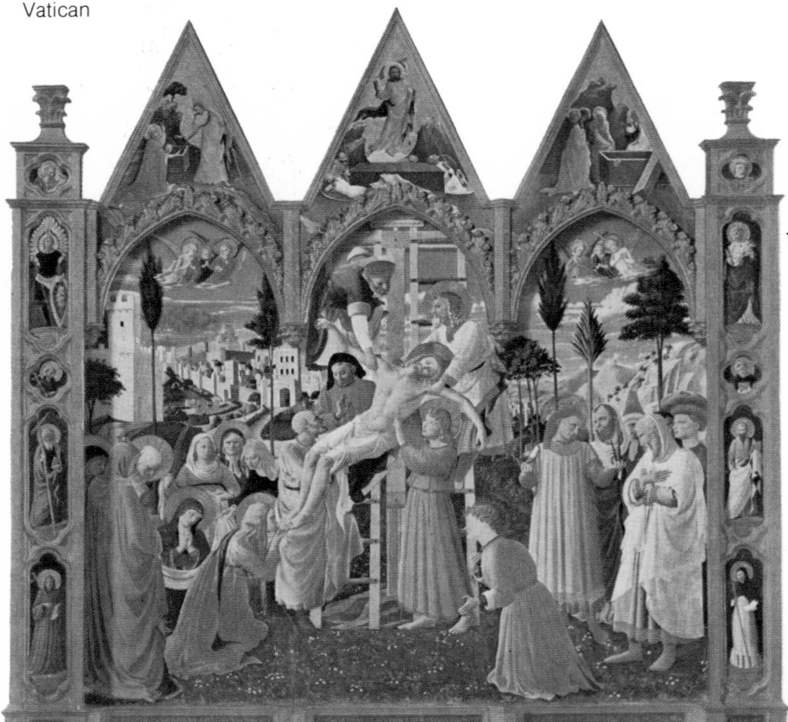
1

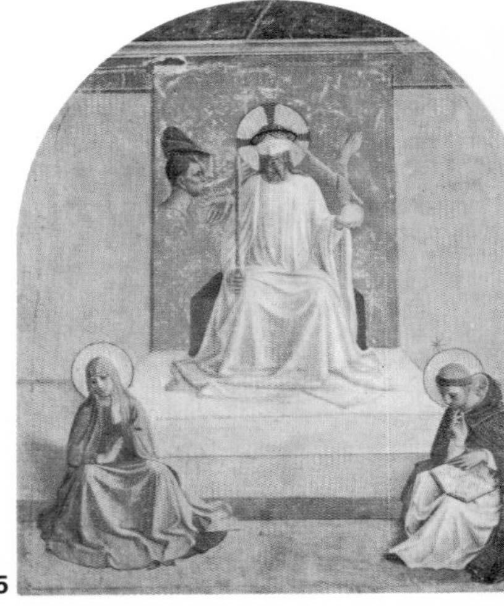
5

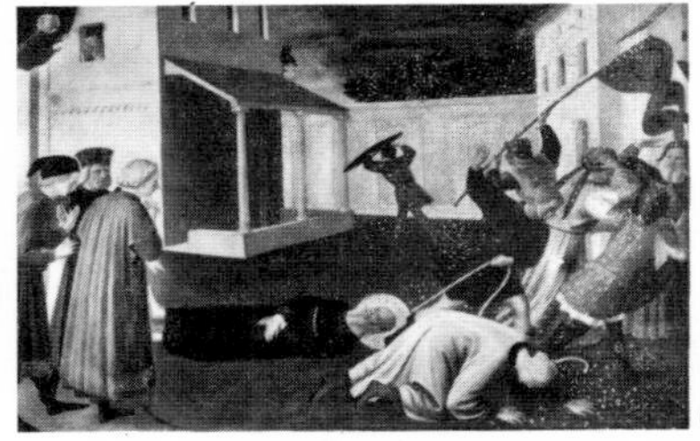
6

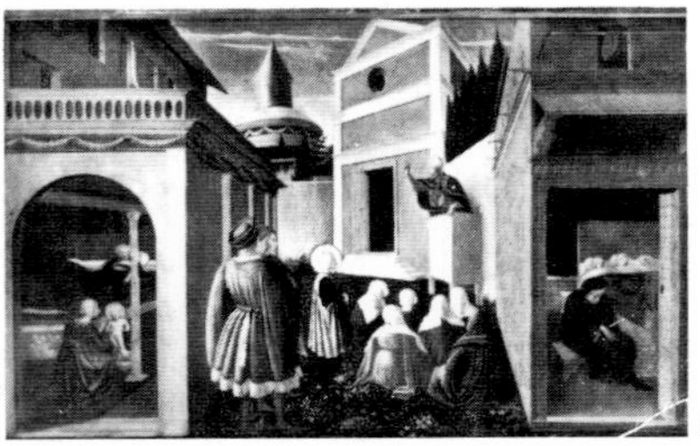
2

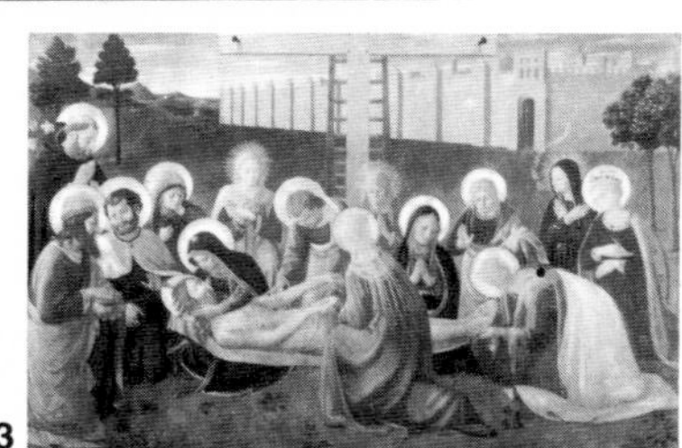
3

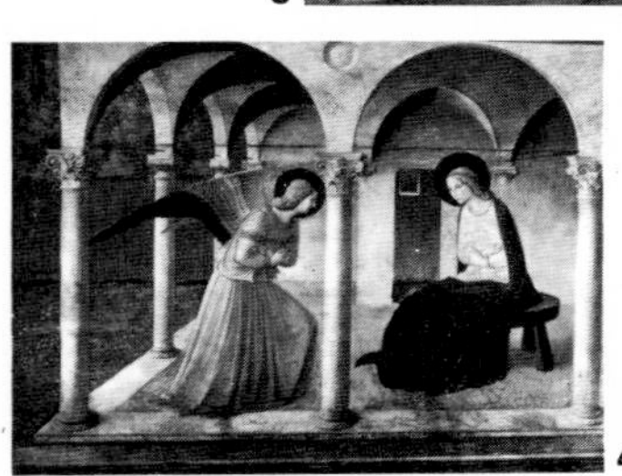
4

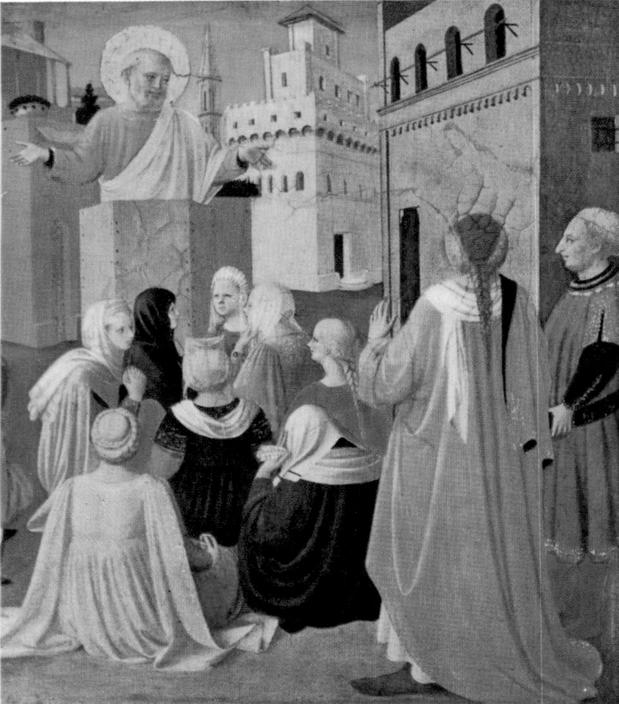
7

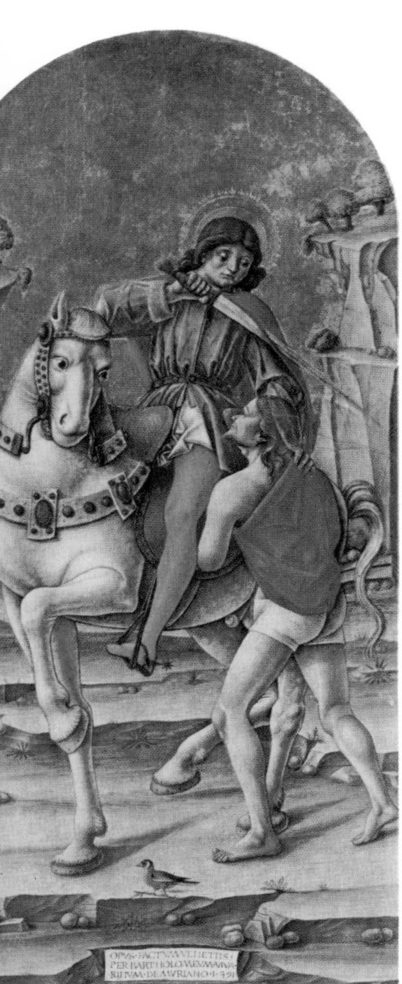

1. **Bartolomeo Vivarini** (*c.*1432–*c.*1499): *St Martin and the Beggar.* 1491. Accademia Carrara, Bergamo
2. **Paolo Uccello** (*c.*1397–1475): Perspective study. Uffizi, Florence
3. **Marco Zoppo** (*c.*1432–*c.*1478): *Pietà.* Musei Civici, Pesaro
4. **Paolo Uccello** (*c.*1397–1475): *St George and the Dragon.* About 1460. National Gallery, London
5. **Paolo Uccello** (*c.*1397–1475): *Niccolò Mauruzi da Tolentino at the Battle of San Romano.* About 1455–60. National Gallery, London

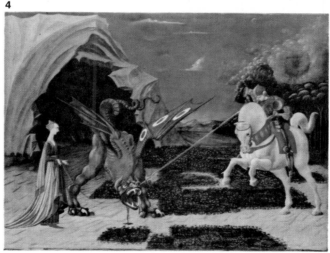

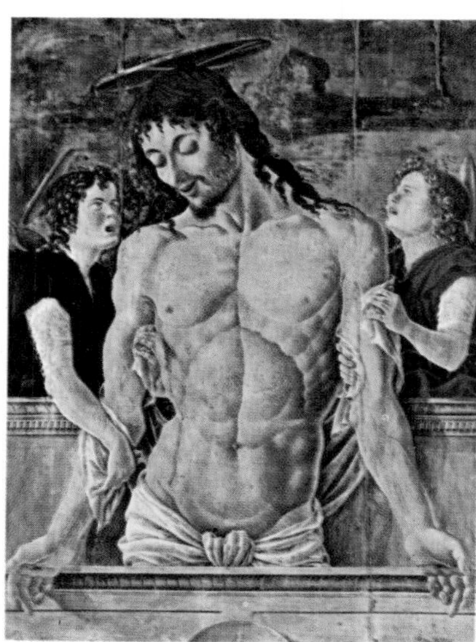

3

4

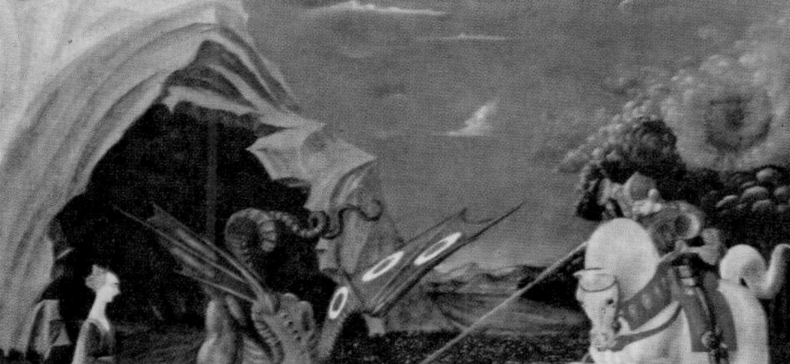

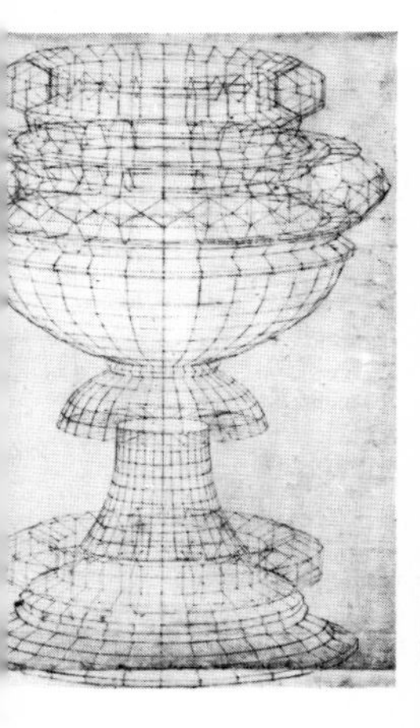

5

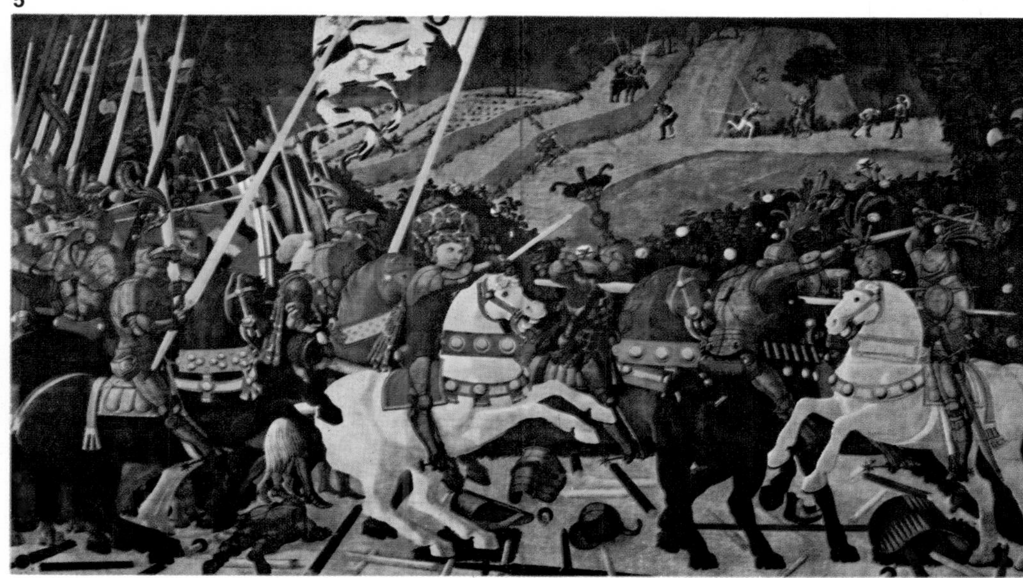

Masaccio (1401–*c.*1428)

1. *St Peter giving Alms.* Detail of fig. 6
2. *St Peter.* Detail of fig. 3
3. *The Tribute Money.* Fresco. 1425–7. Brancacci Chapel, S. Maria del Carmine, Florence
4. *Adam and Eve being expelled from Paradise.* Fresco. 1425–7. Brancacci Chapel, S. Maria del Carmine, Florence
5. *St John.* Detail of fig. 3
6. *St Peter giving Alms.* Fresco. 1425–7. Brancacci Chapel, S. Maria del Carmine, Florence

1

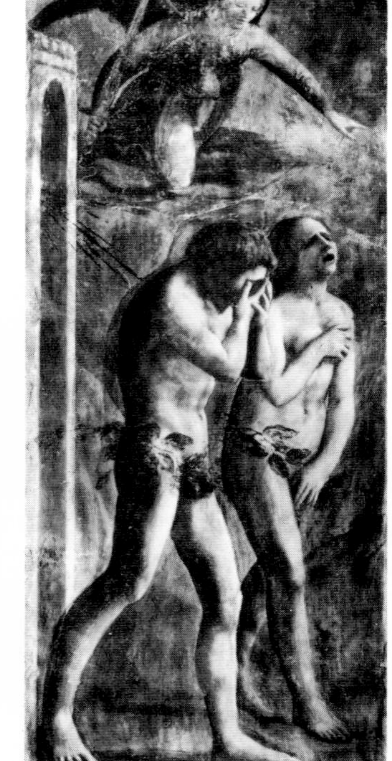

4

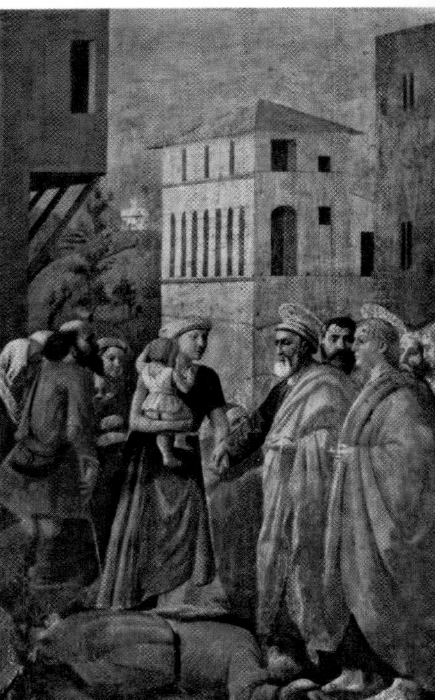

2

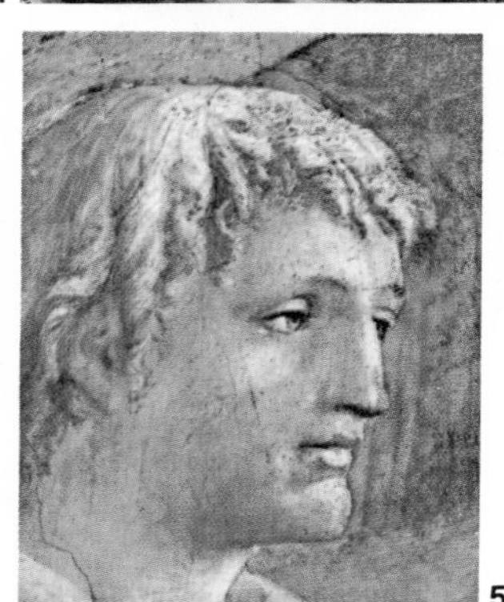

5

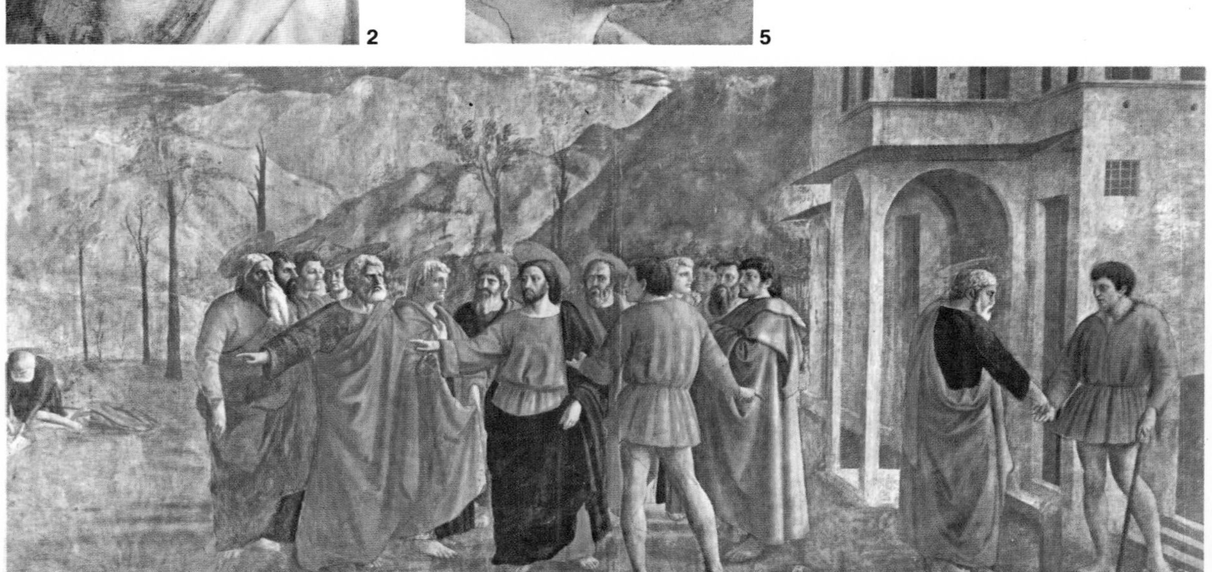

3

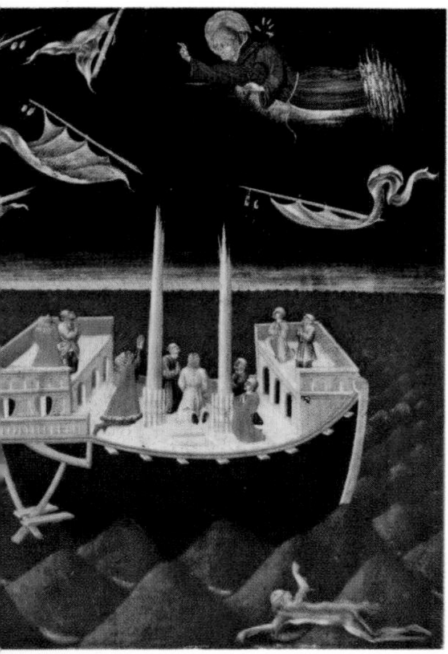
1

1. **Giovanni di Paolo** (*c.*1400–82): *A Miracle of St Nicholas of Tolentino.* About 1455. John G. Johnson Collection, Philadelphia
2. **Giovanni di Paolo** (*c.*1400–82): *The Adoration of the Magi.* National Gallery of Art (Mellon Collection), Washington DC
3. **Domenico Veneziano** (*c.* 1410–61): The *Madonna and Child with St Francis, St John the Baptist, the Bishop St Zenobius, and St Lucy.* The altarpiece of S. Lucia de' Magnoli. About 1445. Uffizi, Florence
4. **Fra Filippo Lippi** (*c.*1406–69): The Bartolini Tondo: *Madonna and Child with scenes from the life of the Madonna.* 1452. Palazzo Pitti, Florence
5. **Luca della Robbia** (1399/1400–82): *The Madonna of the Lilies.* Glazed terracotta. About 1480. Boston Museum of Fine Arts

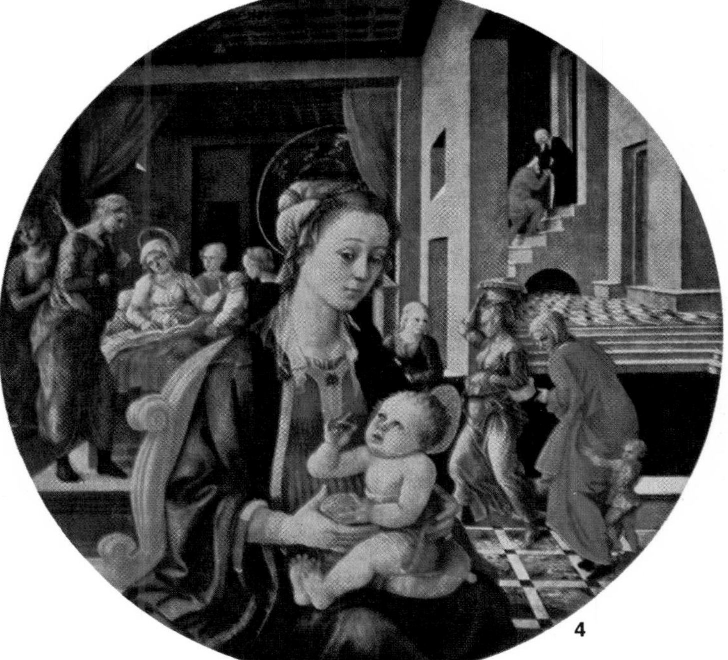
4

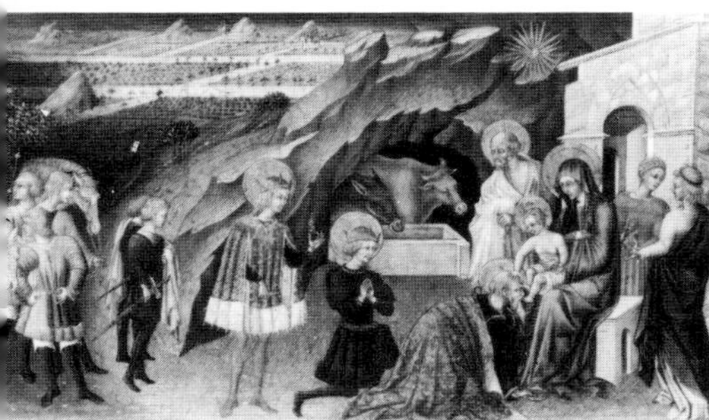

5

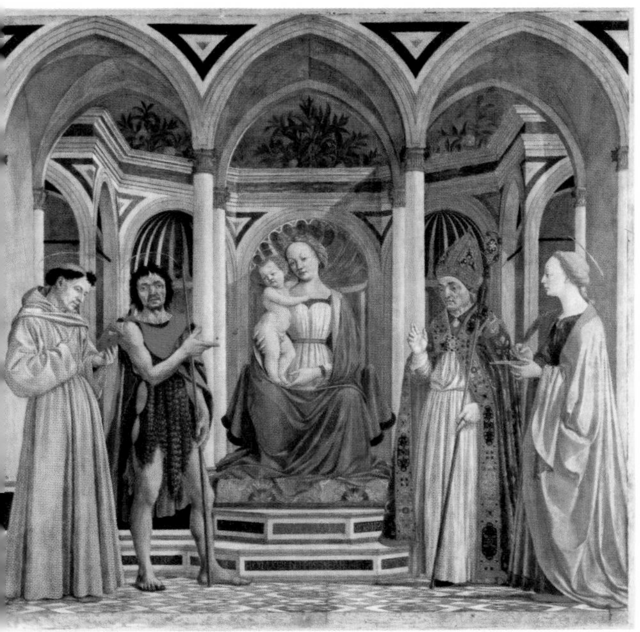

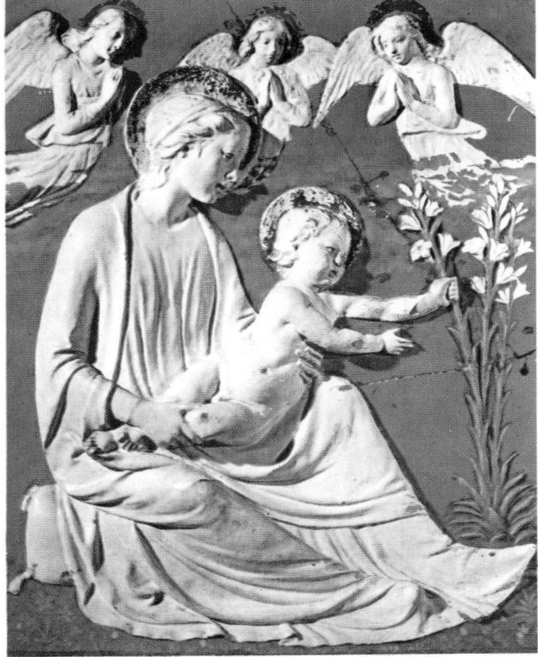

Filippo Brunelleschi (1377–1446)

1. Pazzi Chapel, S. Croce, Florence. Begun about 1430 for Andrea de' Pazzi
2. Basilica of S. Lorenzo, Florence. Central nave, remodelled after Brunelleschi's plans. Begun 1421; Brunelleschi's collaboration dates from about 1425; unfinished at Brunelleschi's death
3. Old Sacristy, S. Lorenzo, Florence. Built for the Medici, 1419–28
4. Elevation of Florence Cathedral (*see also dome, opposite*)
5. Plan of S. Spirito, Florence. Begun 1436; unfinished at Brunelleschi's death and extensively remodelled

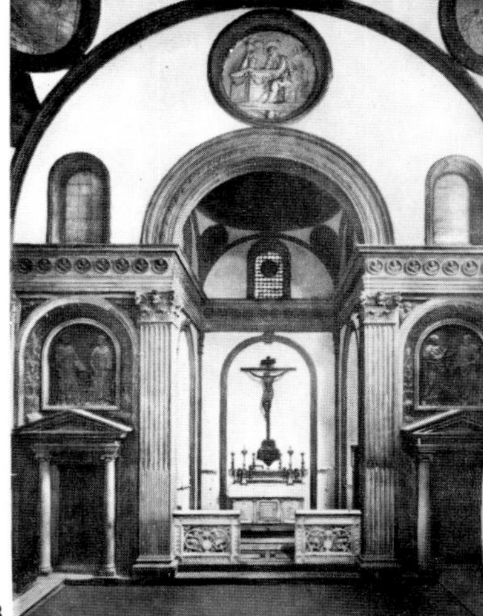

3

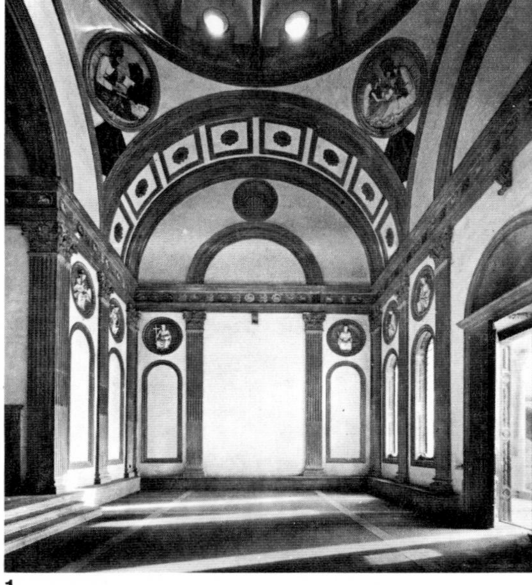

1

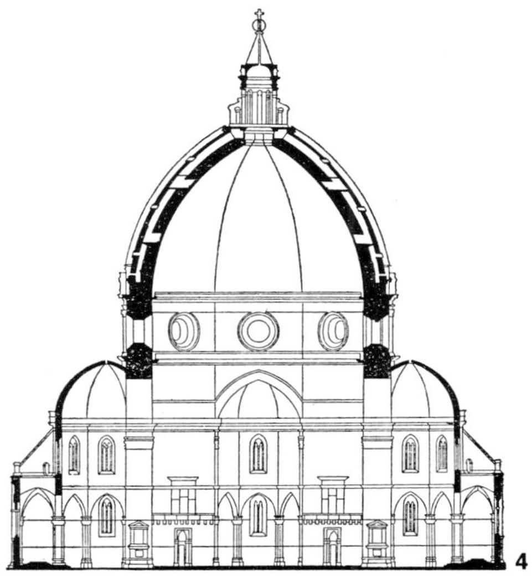

4

2

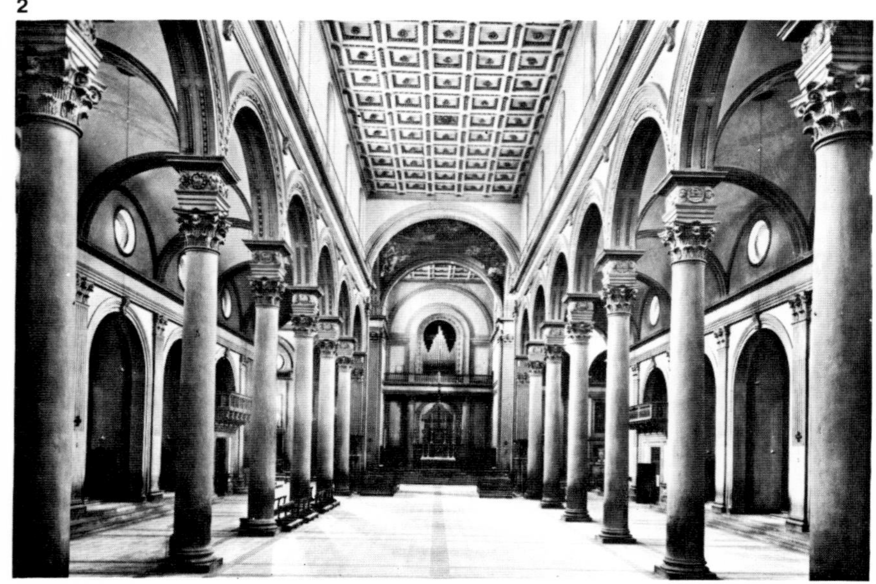

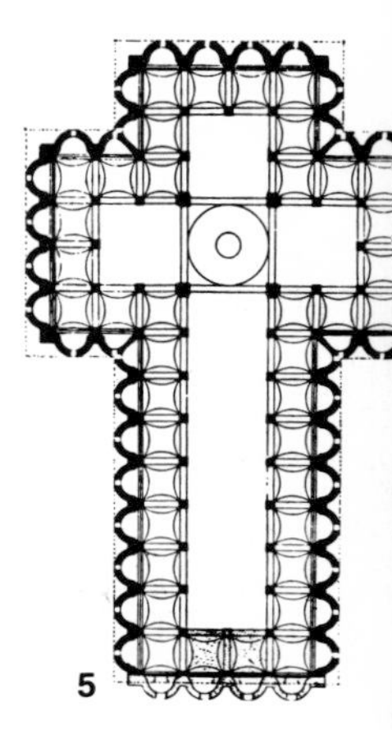

5

ıdrea della Robbia (1435–1525)
Figure of a Child. Glazed terracotta. One of the roundels, depicting foundlings, in the spandrels of the loggia of the Ospedale degli Innocenti (*below*); they were added by Andrea della Robbia long after the death of Brunelleschi, in about 1463

ippo Brunelleschi (1377–1446)
Loggia of the Ospedale degli Innocenti (foundling hospital), Florence. Commissioned by the silk-weavers guild in 1419; inaugurated in 1445
The dome of Florence Cathedral. 1420–36; the lantern completed in 1461 after Brunelleschi's design
Pazzi Chapel, S. Croce, Florence (*interior view on opposite page*)

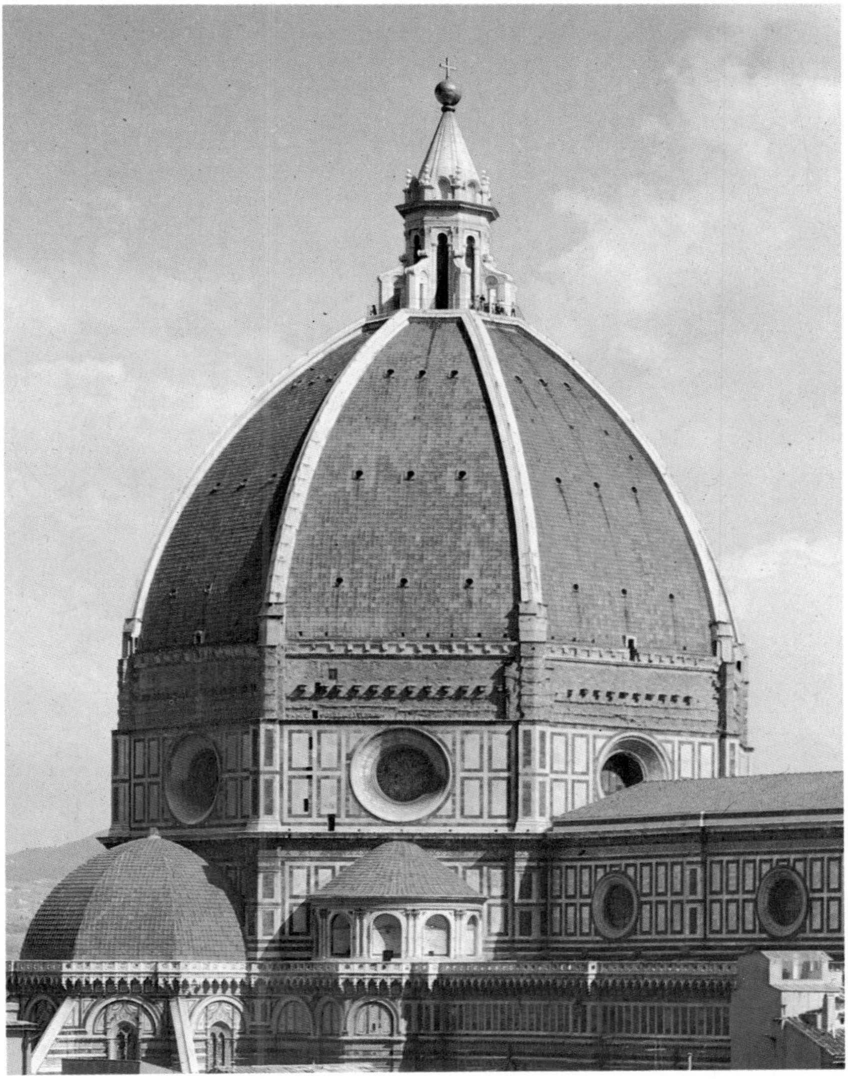

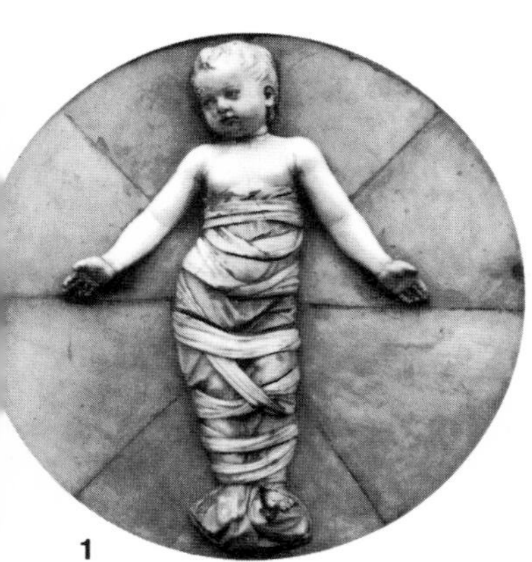

1

3

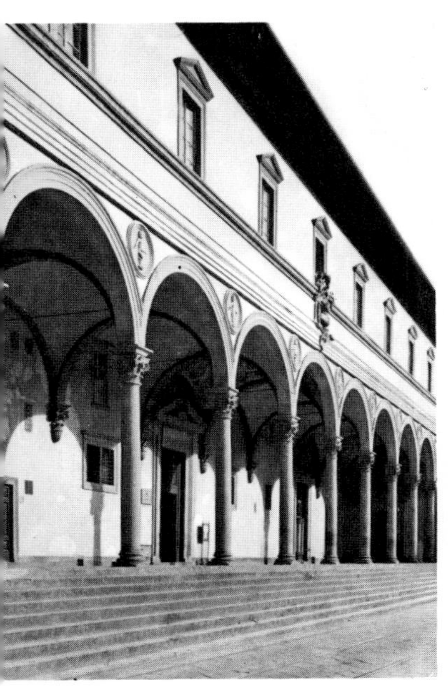

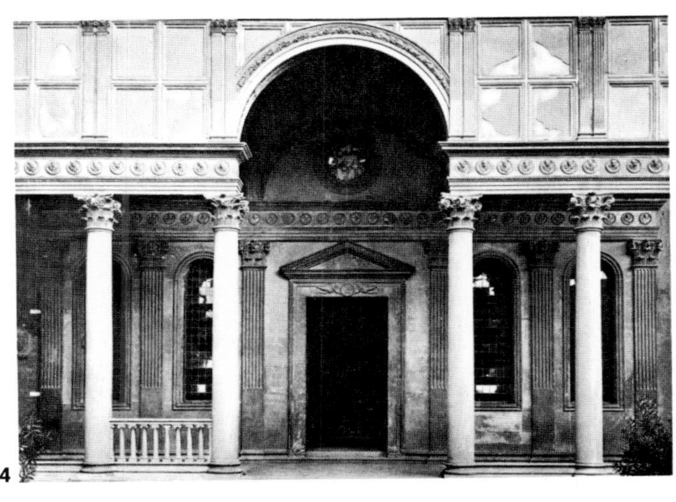

4

1. **Lorenzo Ghiberti** (1378–1455): *The Annunciation.* Bronze panel from north portal of Florence Baptistery. 1403–24
2. **Lorenzo Ghiberti** (1378–1455): *The Story of Abraham.* Bronze panel from the Doors of Paradise, Florence Baptistery. 1425–52
3. **Michelozzo** (1396–1472): Palazzo Medici-Riccardi, Florence. Built for Cosimo de' Medici, 1444–59 (*see interior court, right*)
4. **Lorenzo Ghiberti** (1378–1455): *The Story of Jacob and Esau.* Bronze panel from the Doors of Paradise, Florence Baptistery. 1425–52
5. **Michelozzo** (1396–1472): Interior court the Palazzo Medici-Riccardi. 1444–59 (*see façade, left*)

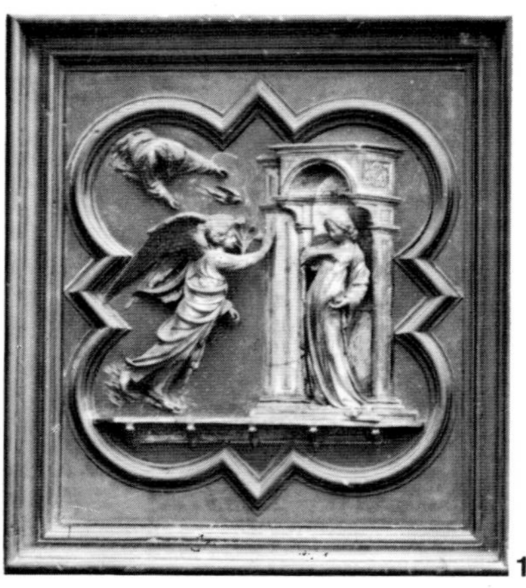
1

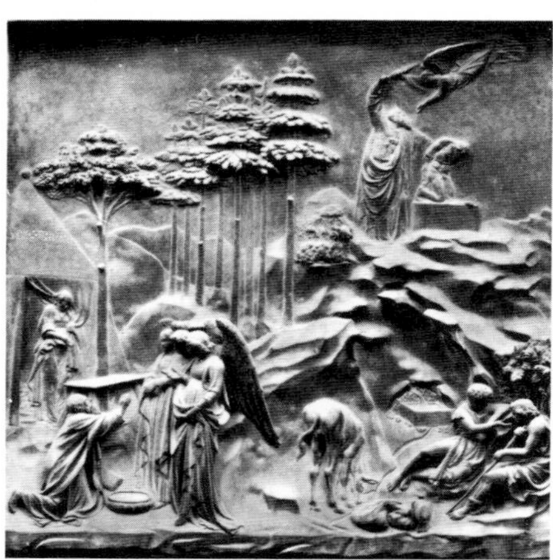
2

4

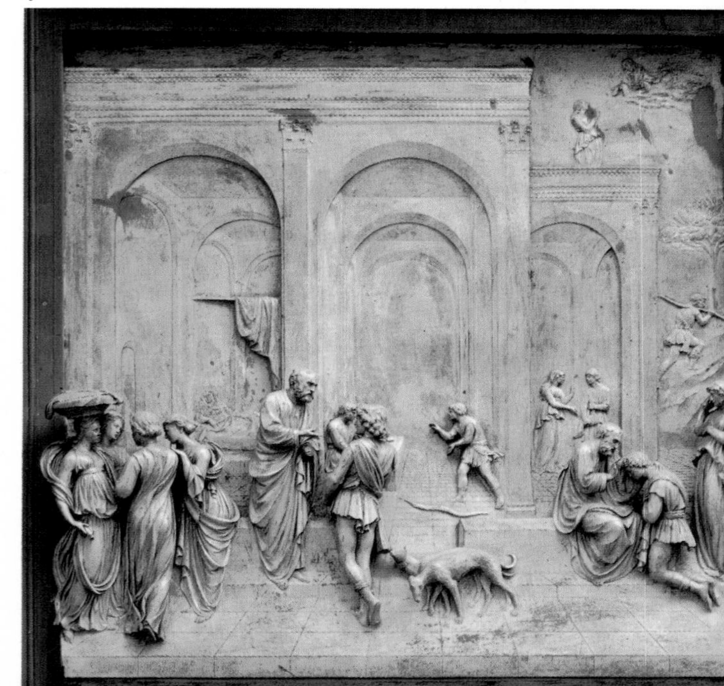

3

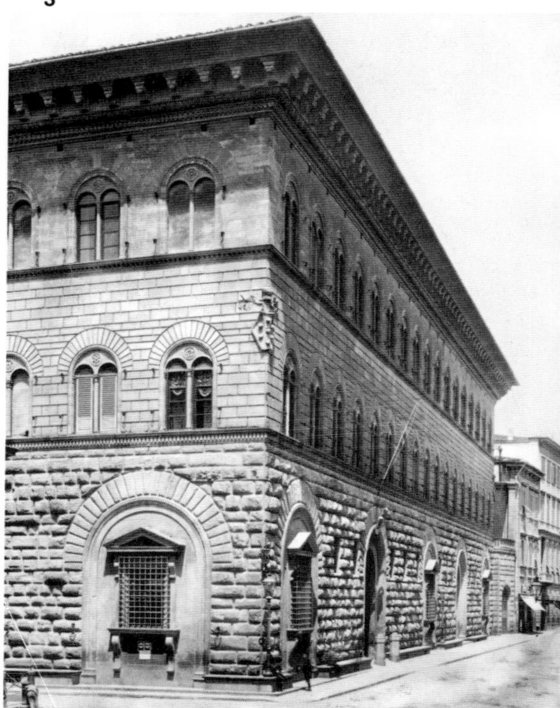

5

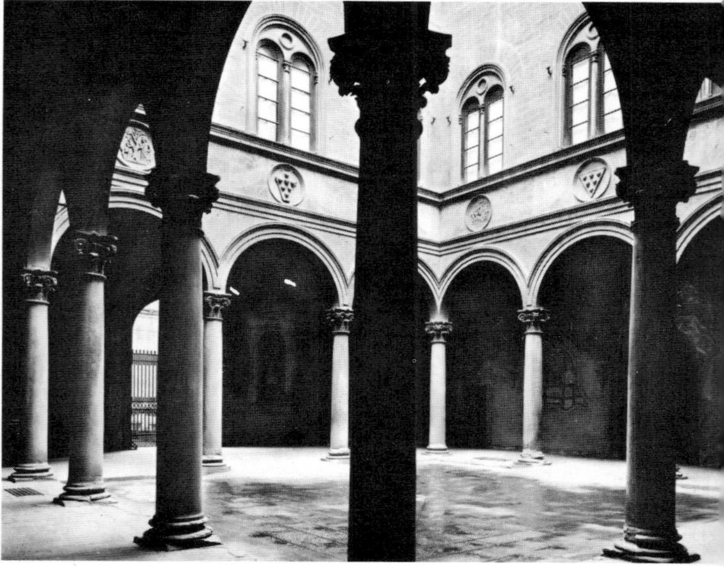

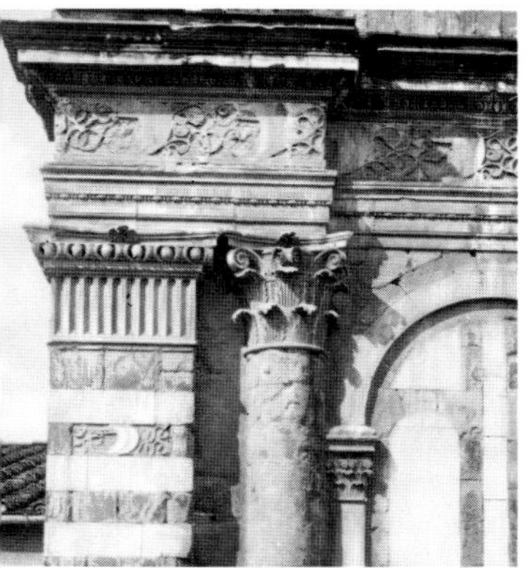

Leon Battista Alberti (1404–72)

1. Detail of façade of S. Maria Novella (*below*)
2. Façade of S. Maria Novella, Florence. About 1456–70
3. Façade of the church of S. Francesco, or Tempio Malatestiano, Rimini. The marble shell encases a Gothic church. Commissioned by Sigismondo Malatesta, prince of Rimini, 1450; executed by Matteo de' Pasti after Alberti's designs, 1450–5
4. *Self-portrait.* Cabinet des Médailles, Louvre, Paris
5. Façade of S. Andrea, Mantua. Designed 1470; execution begun 1472 by Luca Fancelli
6. Detail of façade of Tempio Malatestiano (fig. 3)
7. Façade of the Palazzo Rucellai, Florence. Detail. Executed by Bernardo Rossellino after Alberti's designs, 1446–51

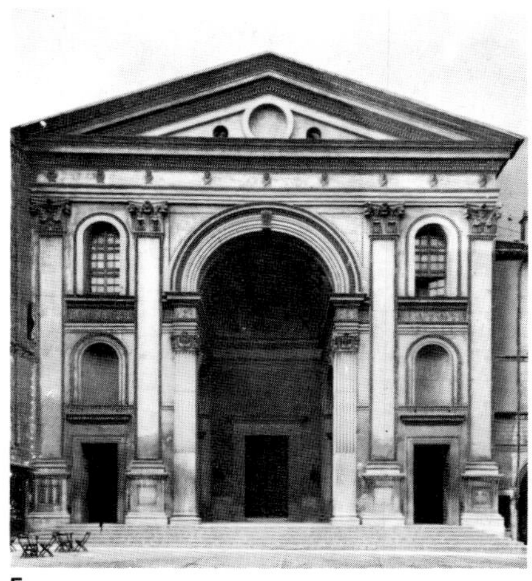

5

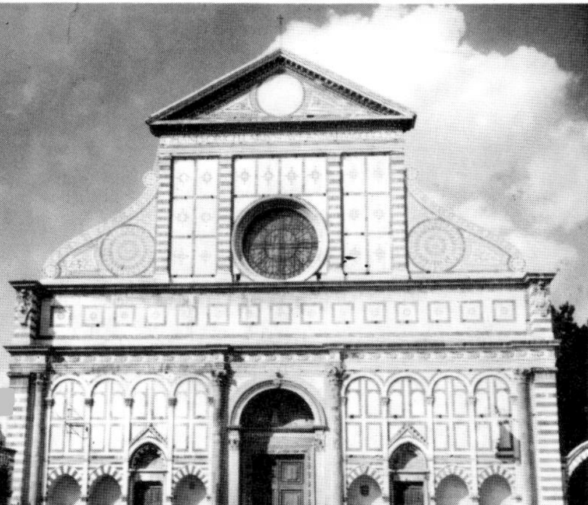

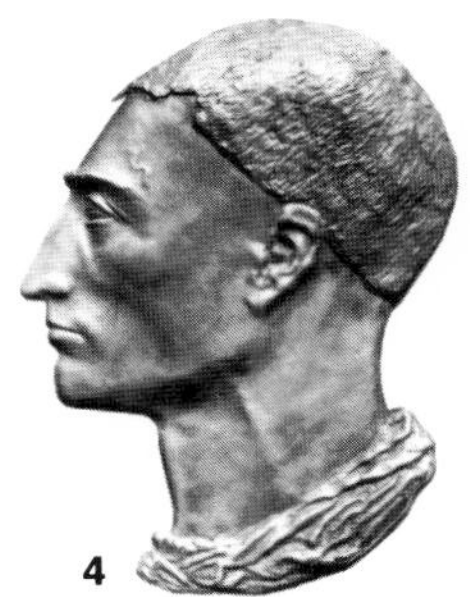

4

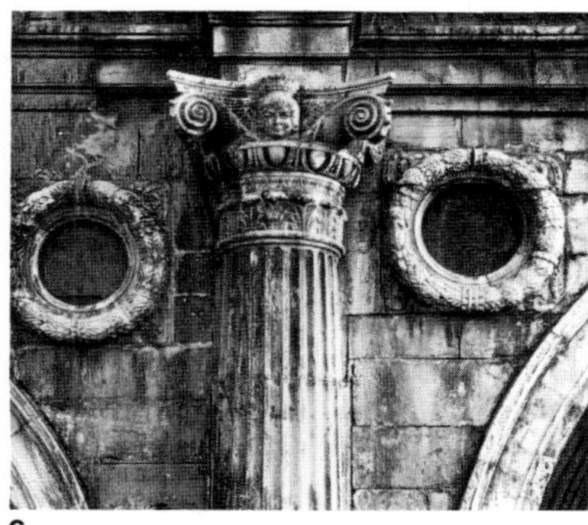

6

7

3

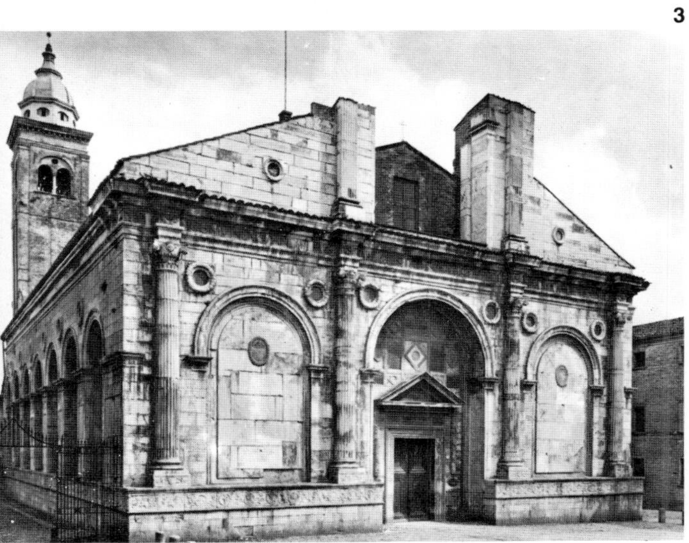

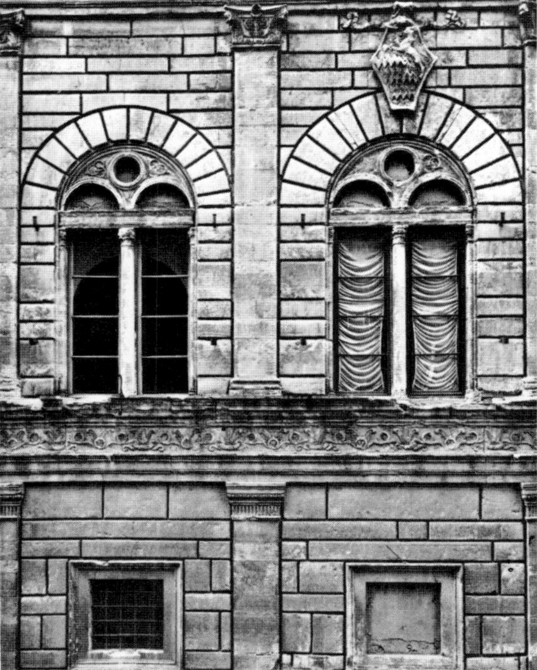

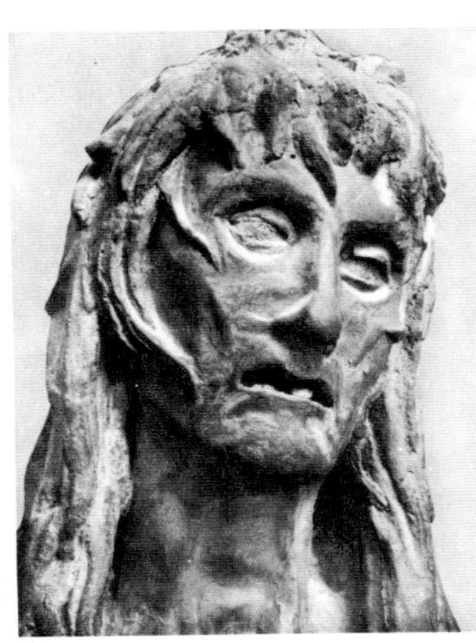
1

Donatello (*c.*1386–1466)

1. *St Mary Magdalene.* Detail. Painted wood. About 1456. Florence Baptistery
2. *Miracle of the Mule.* Bronze relief on high altar of St Anthony, Padua. 1445–8
3 & 4. *The condottiere Gattamelata.* Details from bronze equestrian statue (fig. 3 on opposite page)
5. *Judith.* Detail from bronze statue of Judith and Holofernes, Piazza della Signoria, Florence. About 1453–5

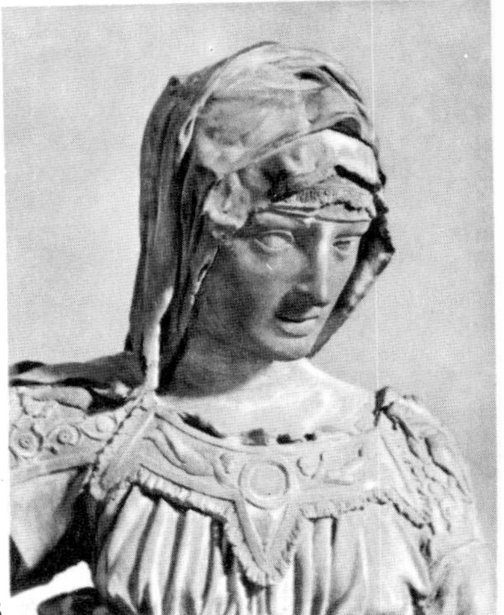
5

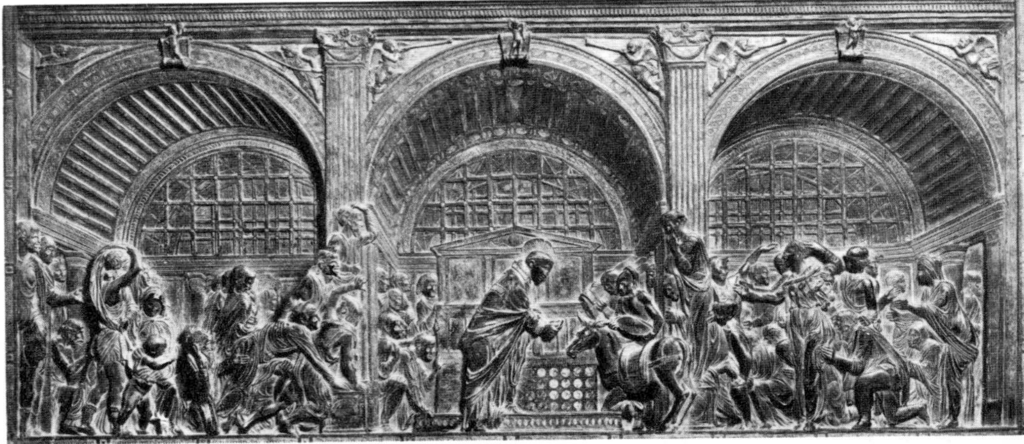
2

3

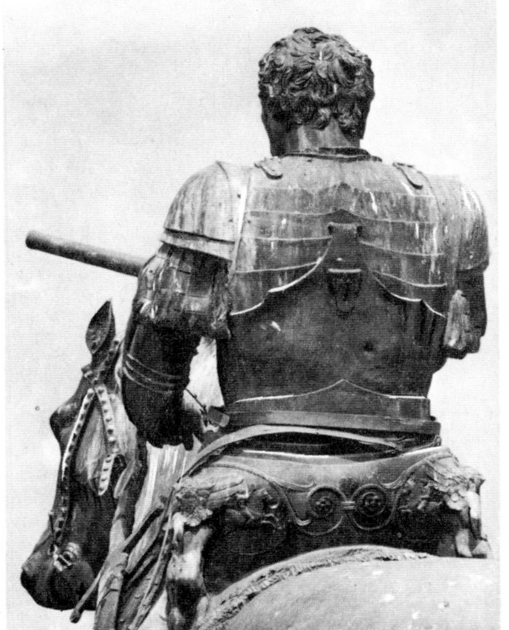

4

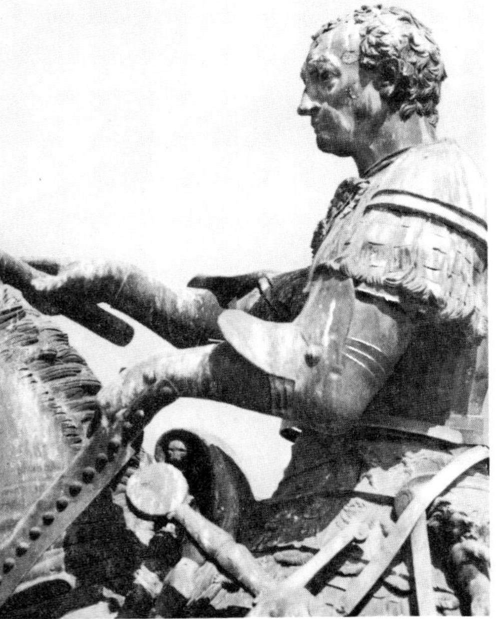

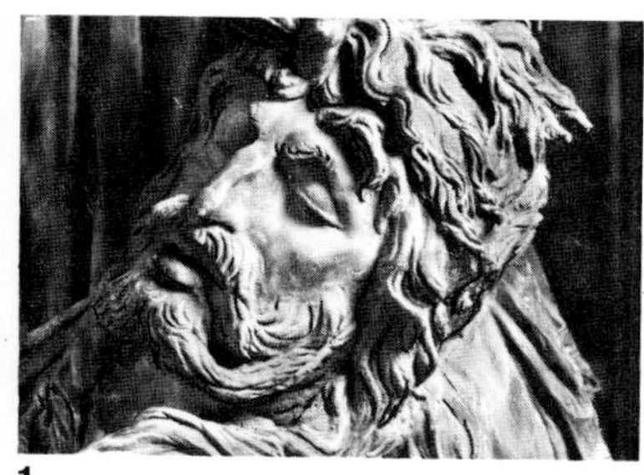
1

Donatello (*c.*1386–1466)

1. *Head of Holofernes.* Detail from bronze statue of Judith and Holofernes, Piazza della Signoria, Florence. About 1453–5
2. *Habakkuk.* A prophet formerly in a niche on the west side of the Campanile of Florence Cathedral. Marble. About 1427–36. Museo dell'Opera del Duomo, Florence
3. *Equestrian statue of the condottiere Gattamelata.* Bronze. 1447–53. Piazza del Santo, Padua
4. *St George.* Detail of a marble statue carved for a niche in Or S. Michele, Florence. About 1415–16. Museo Nazionale, Florence
5. *Prophet.* Detail of marble statue formerly in a niche on the east side of the Campanile of Florence Cathedral. About 1420. Museo dell'Opera del Duomo, Florence
6. *The Presentation of St John the Baptist's Head to Herod,* Gilt bronze relief from a baptismal font, Siena Baptistery. 1423–7

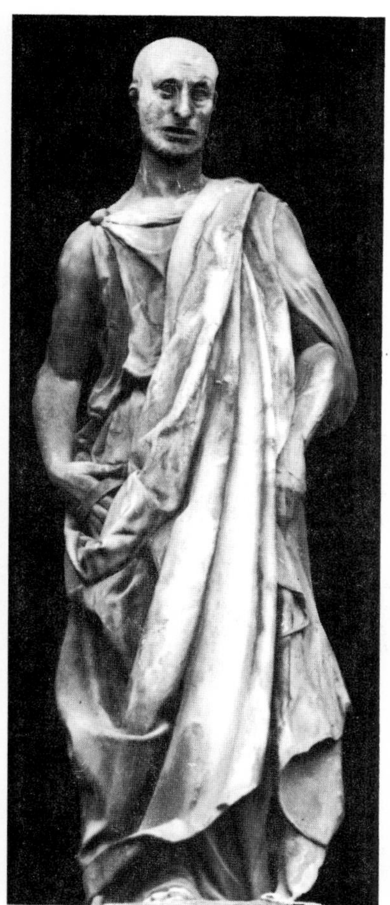
2

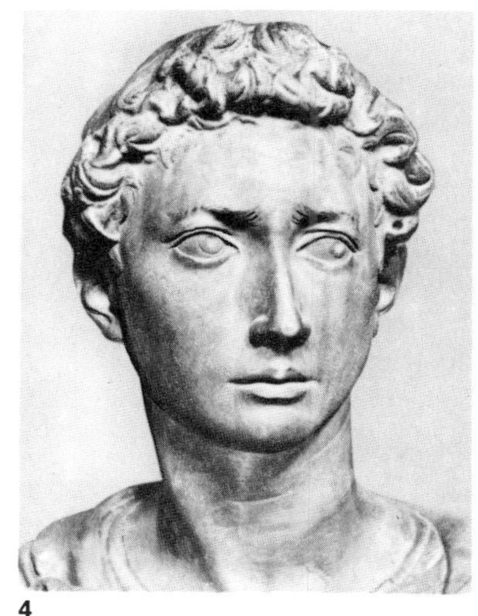
4

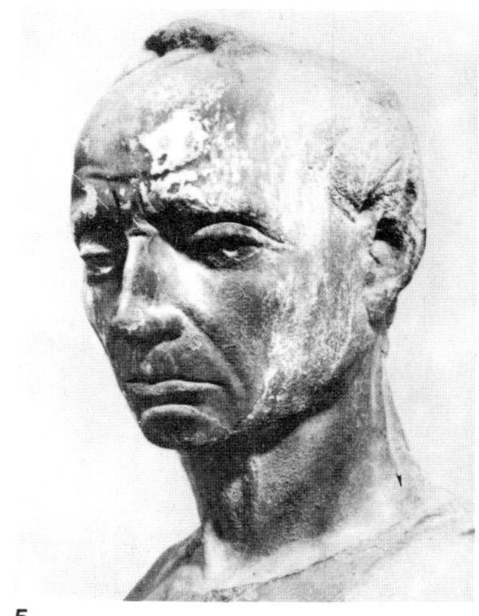
5

6
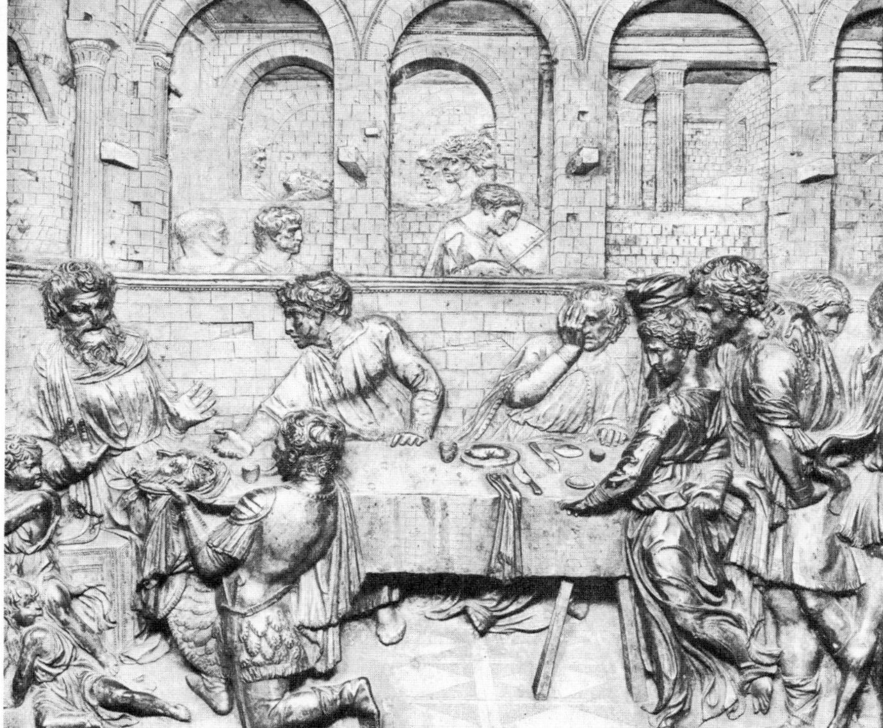

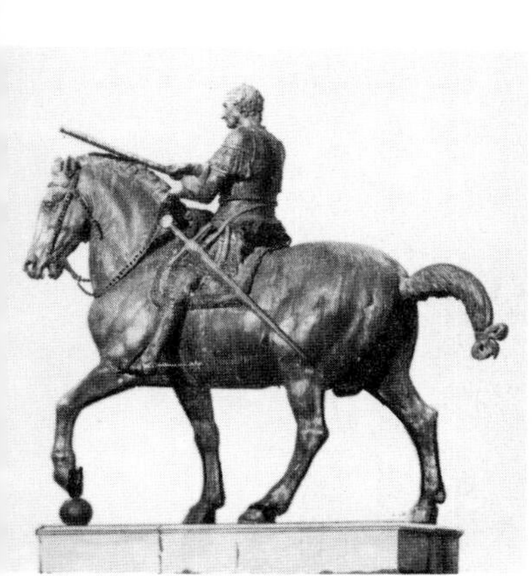
3

1. **Antonio Rossellino** (1427–*c.*1479): *The Stoning of St Stephen*. Bas-relief. 1473. Prato Cathedral
2. **Antonio Rossellino** (1427–*c.*1479): Tomb of the Cardinal of Portugal. 1461–6. S. Miniato, Florence
3. **Antonio Rossellino** (1427–*c.*1479), attributed to: *Bust of a Lady*. Staatliche Museen, Berlin-Dahlem
4. **Andrea del Verrocchio** (1435–88): *David*. Bronze. About 1475. Museo Nazionale, Florence
5. **Niccolò dell'Arca** (*c.*1435–94): *Weeping Woman*. Terracotta. 1463. S. Maria della Vita, Bologna
6. **Andrea del Verrocchio:** Detail of fig. 8
7. **Desiderio de Settignano** (*c.*1430–64): Altar of the Sacrament. Completed 1461. S. Lorenzo, Florence
8. **Andrea del Verrocchio** (1435–88): *The Colleoni Monument*. Bronze. Campo di SS. Giovanni e Paolo, Venice

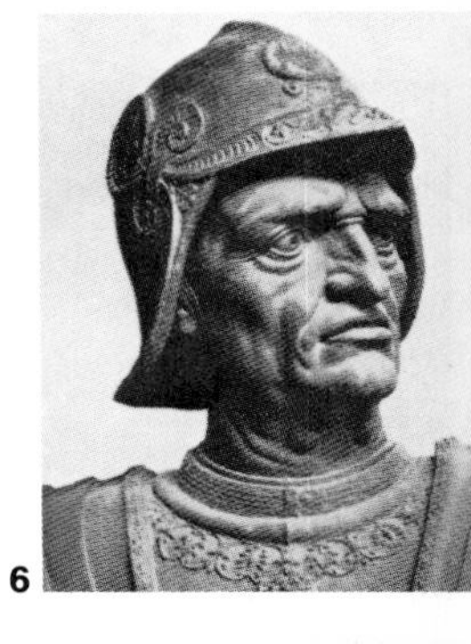

6

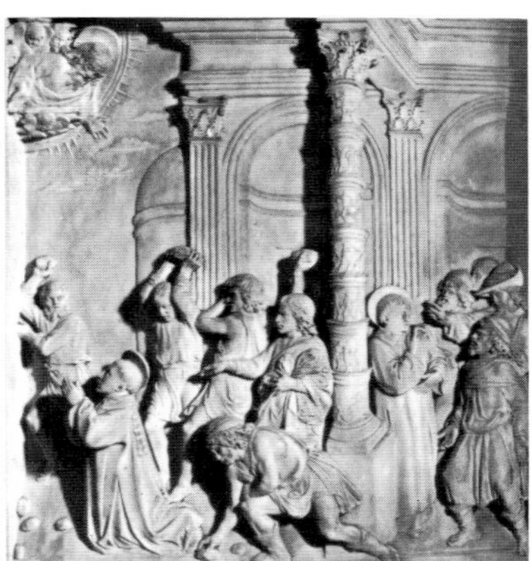

1

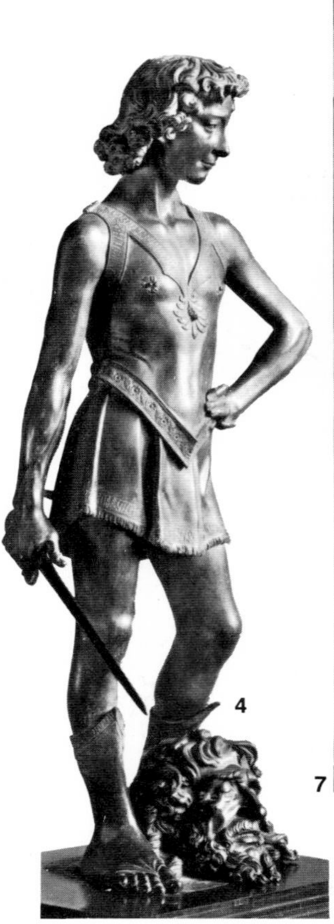

4

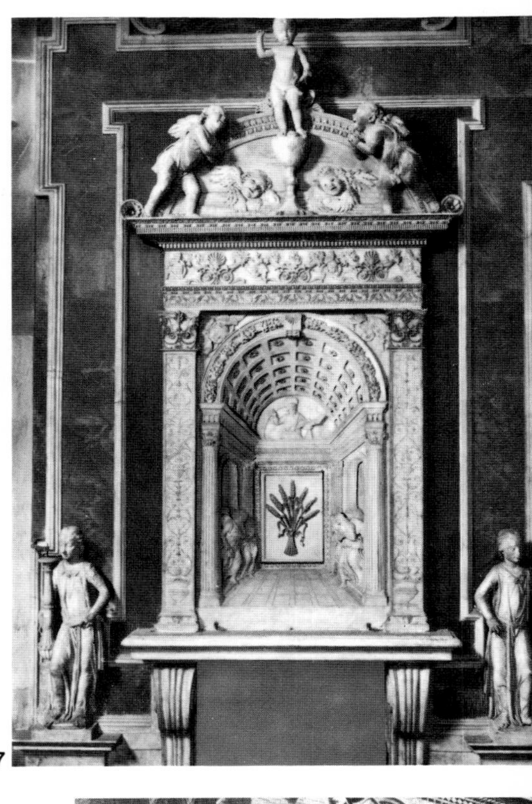

7

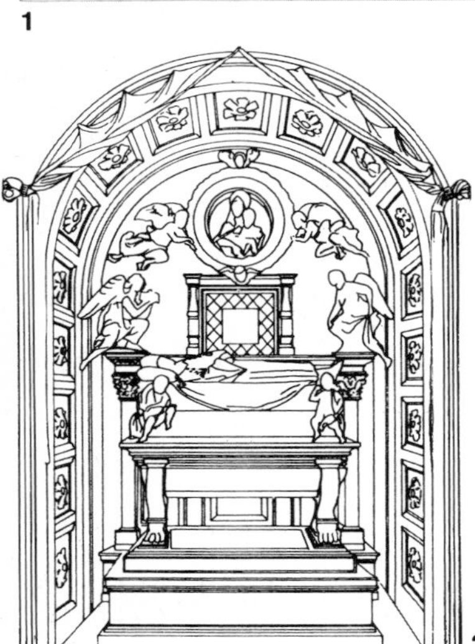

2

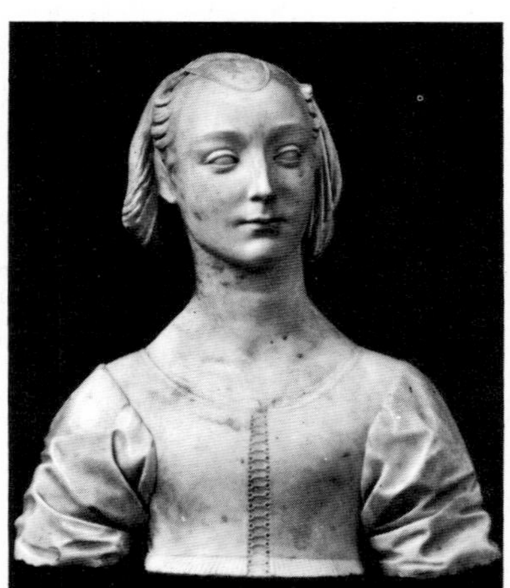

3

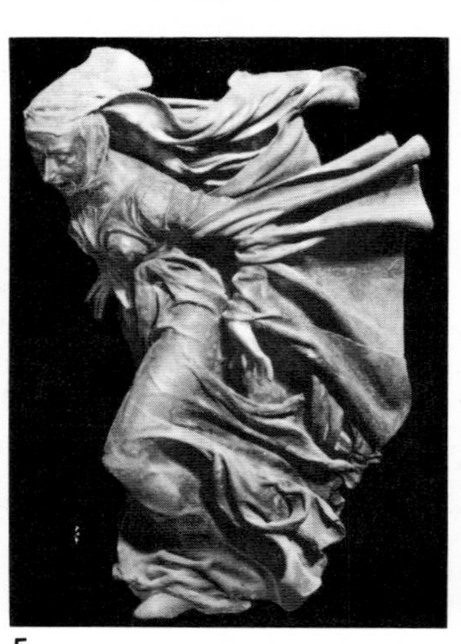

5

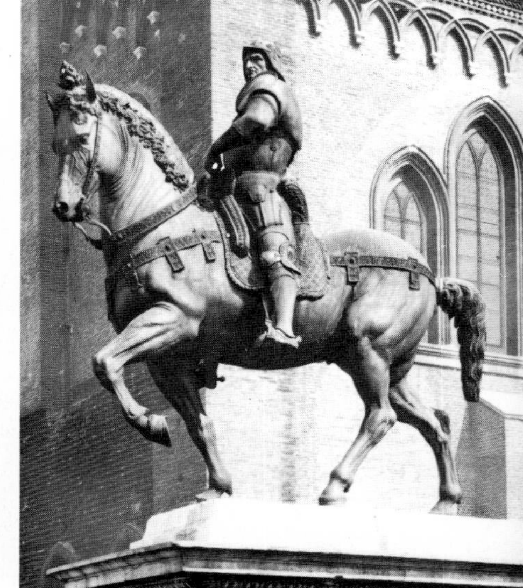

8

1 & 2. **Ercole de'Roberti** (*c.*1450–96): *Portraits of Giovanni II Bentivoglio and his Wife Ginevra.* About 1480. National Gallery of Art (Samuel H. Kress Collection), Washington DC
3. **Pesellino** (*c.*1422–57): *St Cosmas and St Damian visiting a sick Man.* Panel of a predella. About 1442–5. Louvre, Paris
4. **Vecchietta** (*c.*1412–80): *Martyrdom of St Biagio.* Detail of a predella. 1457–60. Museo della Cattedrale, Pienza
5. **Antonio Rizzo** (*c.*1430–1499/1500): *Eve.* Marble. About 1491. Doges' Palace, Venice
6. **Vincenzo Foppa** (1427/30–1515/16): *Madonna of the Book.* Castello Sforzesco, Milan
7. **Giovanni Ambrogio de Predis** (*c.*1455–*c.*1517): *Portrait of Beatrice d'Este* (?). Biblioteca Ambrosiana, Milan

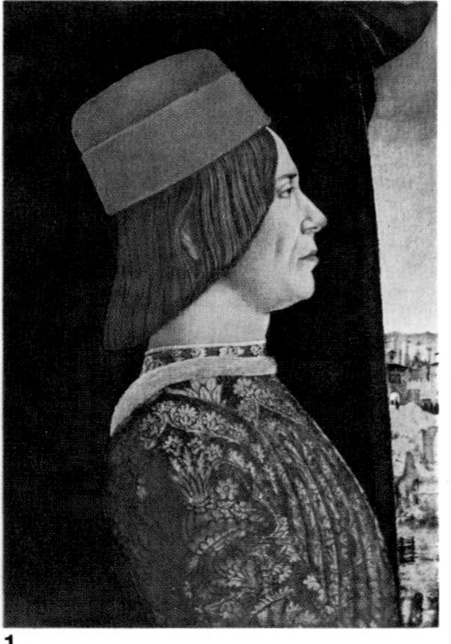

1

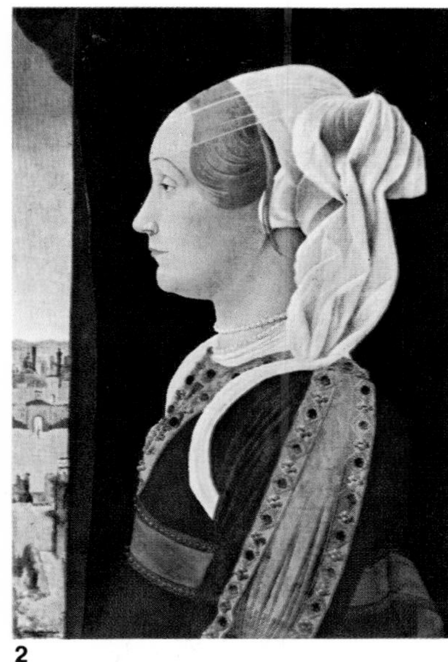

2

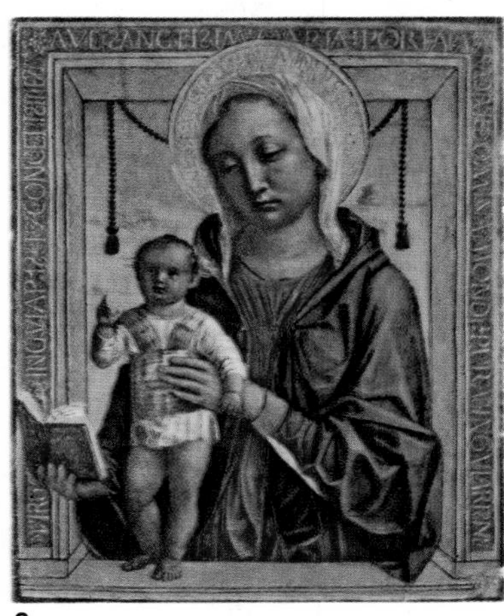

6

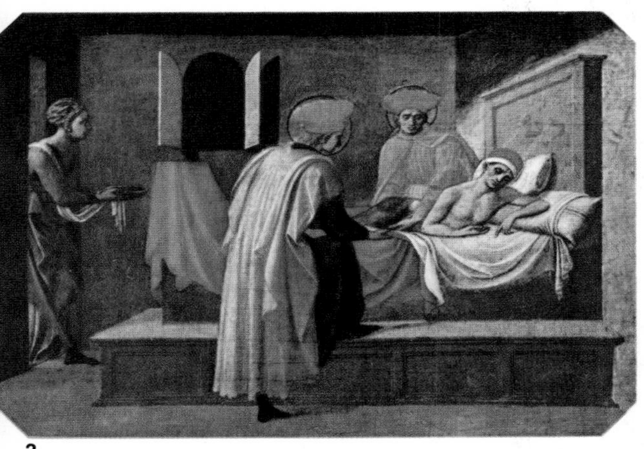

3

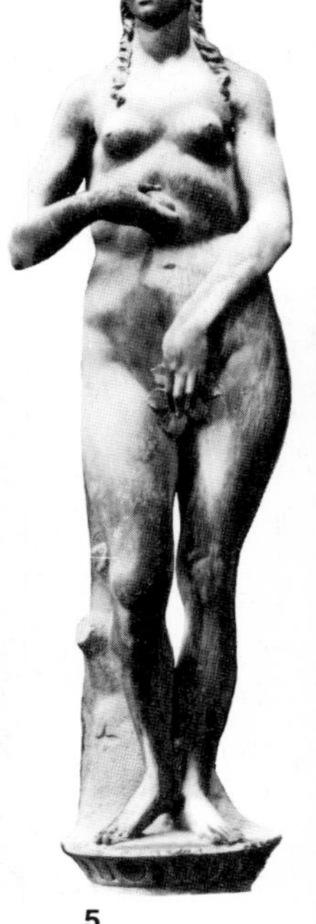

5

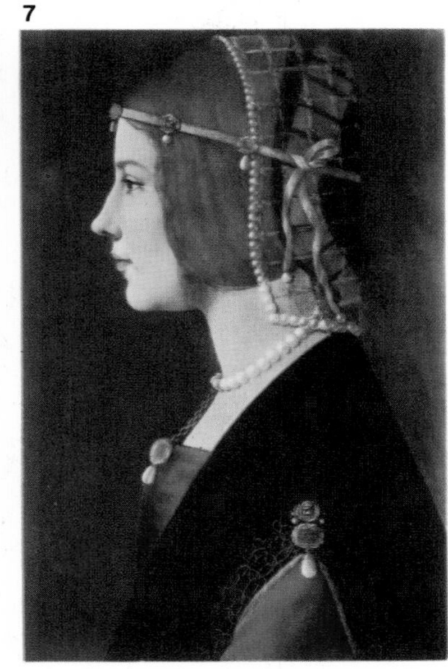

7

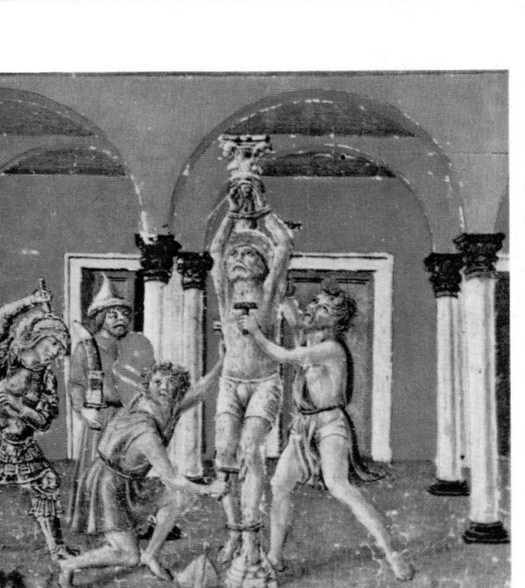

1. **Sassetta** (1392?–1450): *Mystic Marriage of St Francis.* 1437–44. Musée Conde, Chantilly
2. **Perugino** (*c.*1445–1523): *Delivery of the Keys to St Peter.* Fresco. 1481. Sistine Chapel, Vatican
3. **Sassetta** (1392?–1450): *St Martin and the Beggar.* 1433. Chigi-Saracini Collection, Siena
4. **Filippino Lippi** (*c.*1457–1504): *Portrait of a young Man.* National Gallery of Art, Washington DC
5. **Pintoricchio** (*c.*1454–1513): *Portrait of a young Boy.* Gemäldegalerie, Dresden
6. **Perugino** (*c.*1445–1523): *Apollo and Marsyas.* About 1496. Louvre, Paris

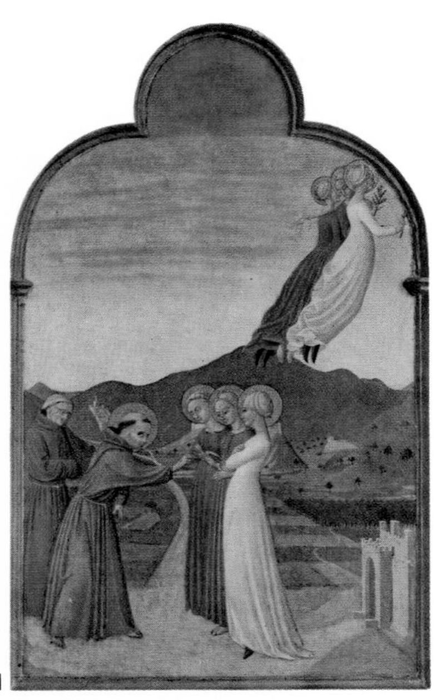

1

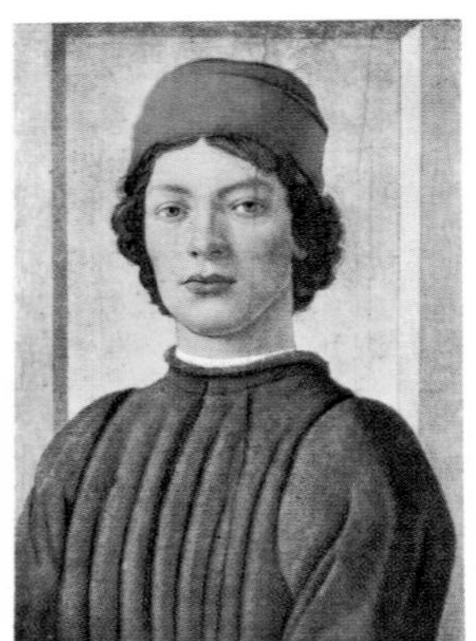

4

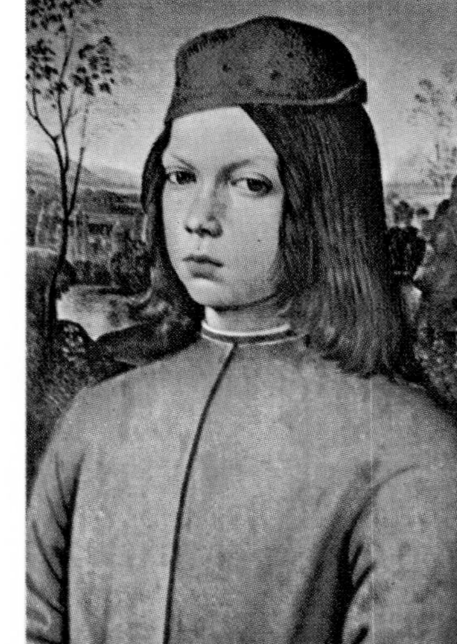

5

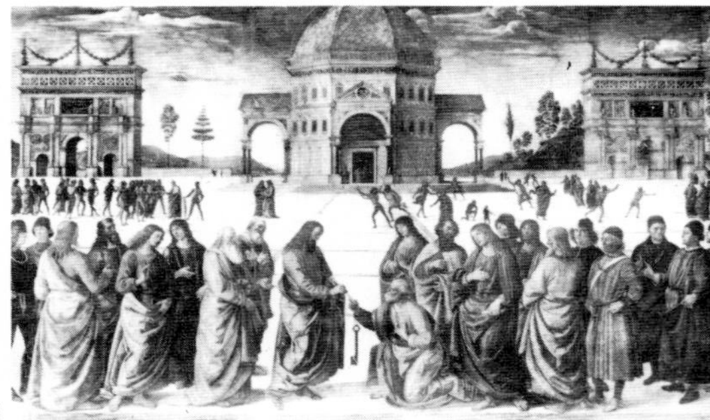

2

6

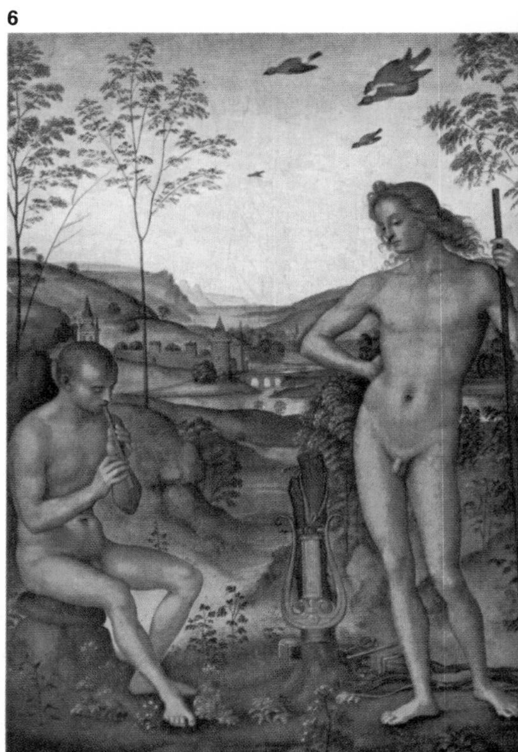

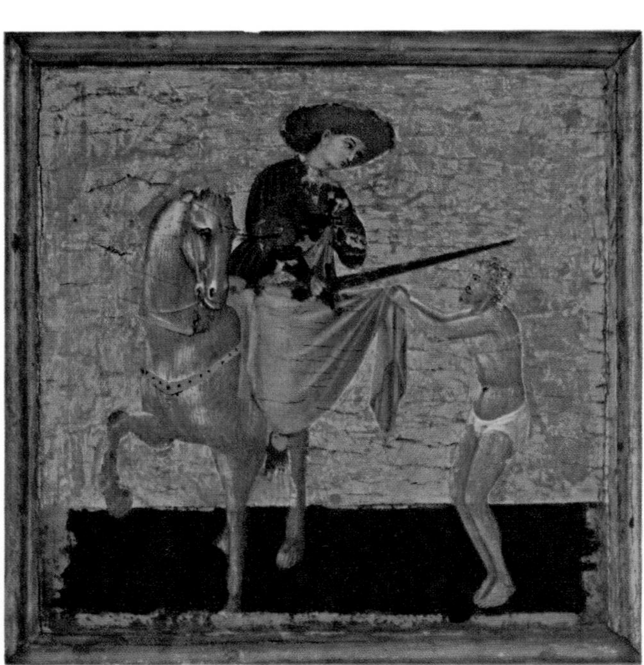

3

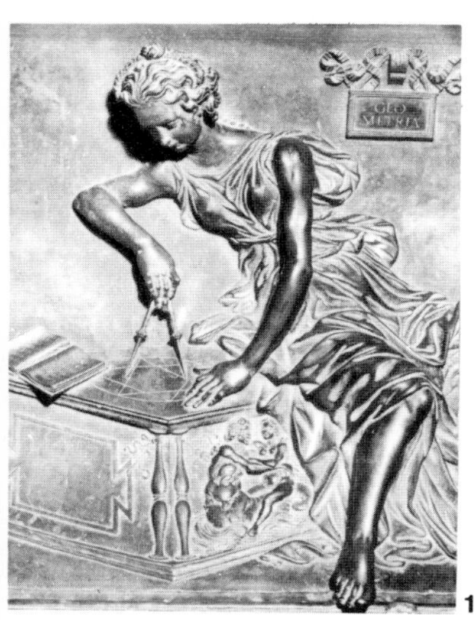

1

1. **Antonio Pollaiuolo** (*c.*1432–98): *Geometry.* Bronze relief on the tomb of Pope Sixtus IV, St Peter's, Rome. Completed 1493
2. **Antonio Pollaiuolo** (*c.*1432–98): *The Battle of the ten Nudes.* Engraving. About 1471–2. Uffizi, Florence
3. **Antonio Pollaiuolo** (*c.*1432–98): *David.* Staatliche Museen, Berlin-Dahlem
4. **Antonio** or **Piero** (*c.*1441–96) **Pollaiuolo,** attributed to: *Portrait of a Lady.* Museo Poldi-Pezzoli, Milan
5. **Benozzo Gozzoli** (1420–97): *The Dance of Salome.* 1461–2. National Gallery of Art (Samuel H. Kress Collection), Washington DC
6. **Benozzo Gozzoli** (1420–97): *The Journey of the Magi.* Detail of fresco. 1459–61. Palazzo Medici-Riccardi, Florence

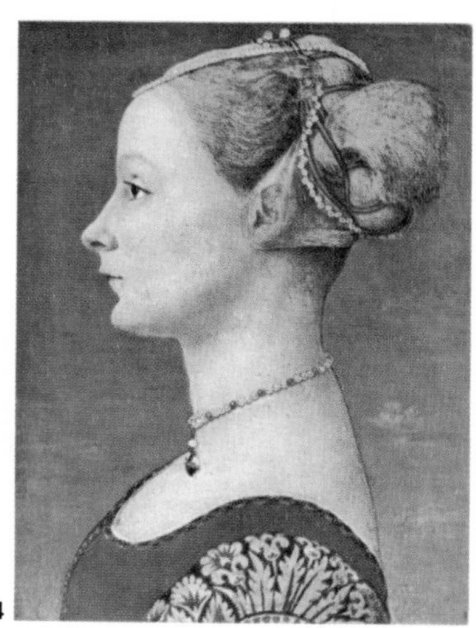

4

2

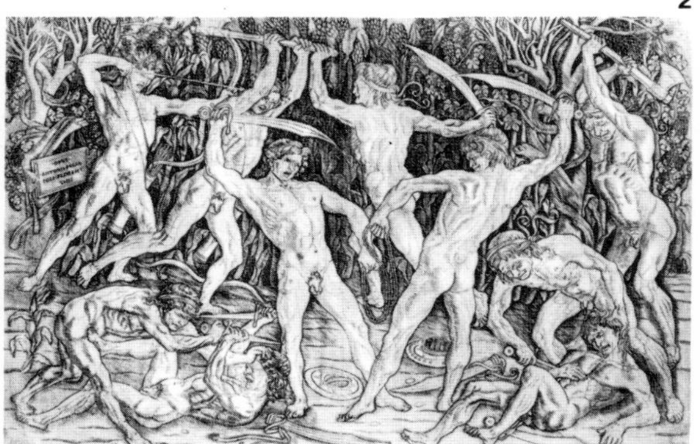

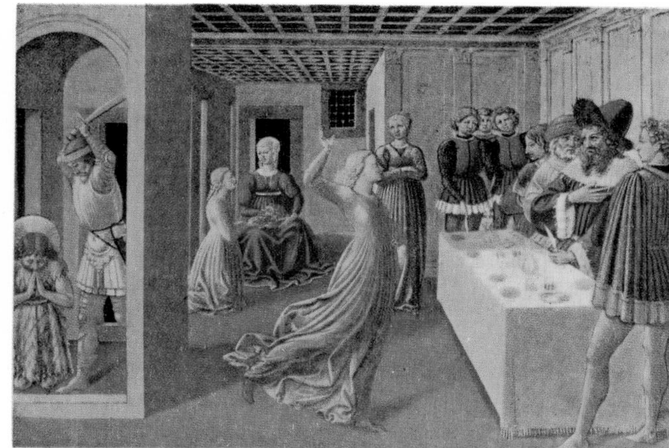

5

3

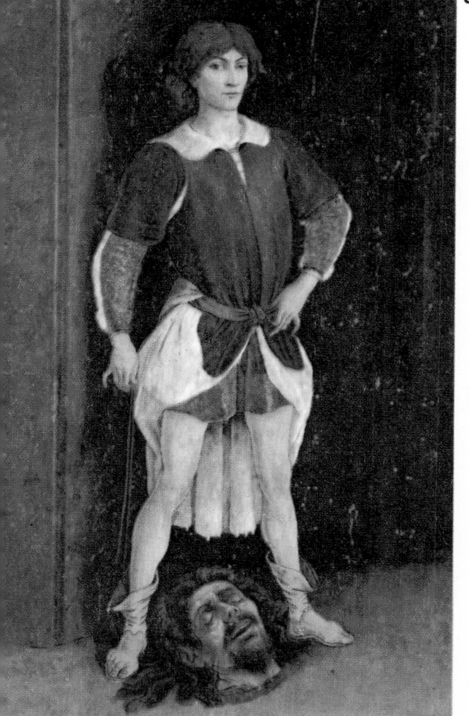

6

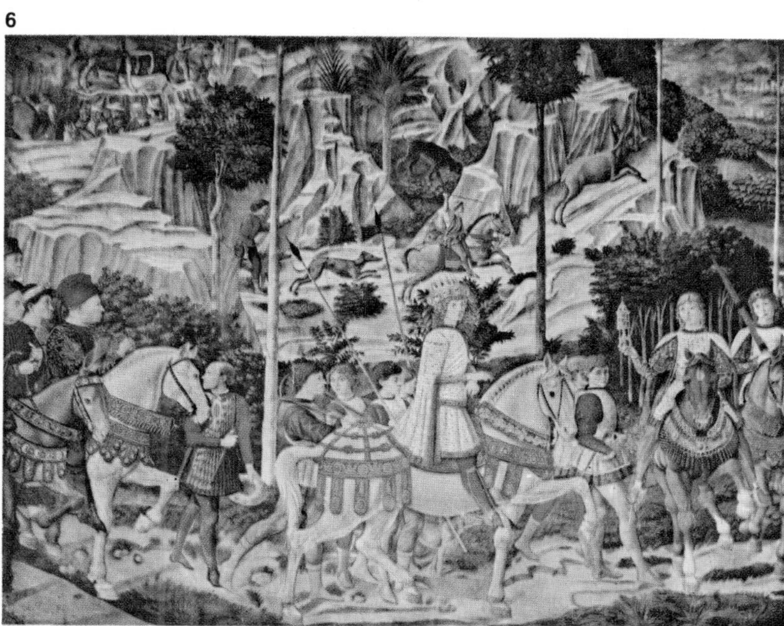

Piero della Francesca (1410/20–92)

1. *Sinigallia Madonna.* About 1474–8. Galleria Nazionale delle Marche, Urbino
2. *The Dream of Constantine.* 1452–9. S. Francesco, Arezzo
3. *The Flagellation of Christ.* About 1445 or 1456–7. Galleria Nazionale delle Marche, Urbino
4. *The Baptism of Christ.* National Gallery, London
5. *The Nativity.* National Gallery, London
6. *The Virgin.* Detail from *The Annunciation.* Fresco. 1452–9. S. Francesco, Arezzo

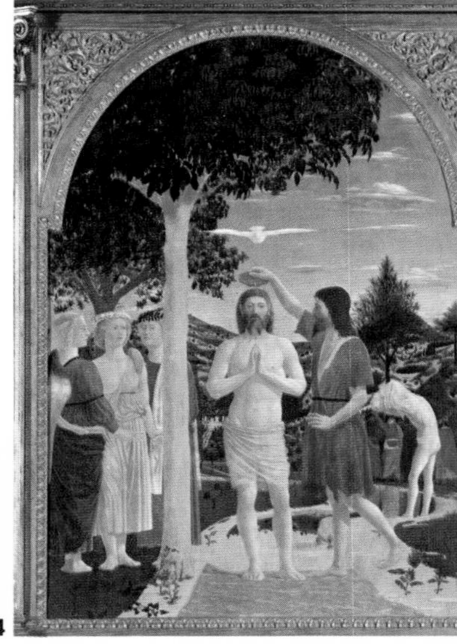

4

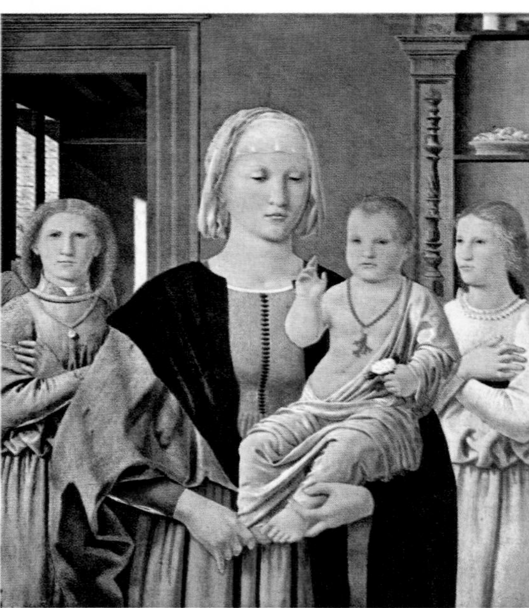

1

2

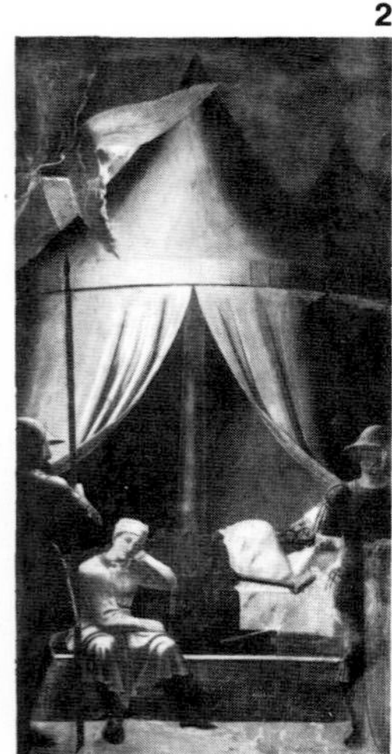

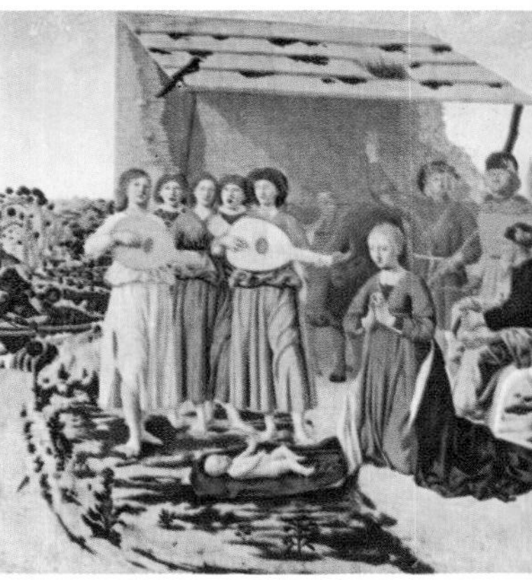

5

3

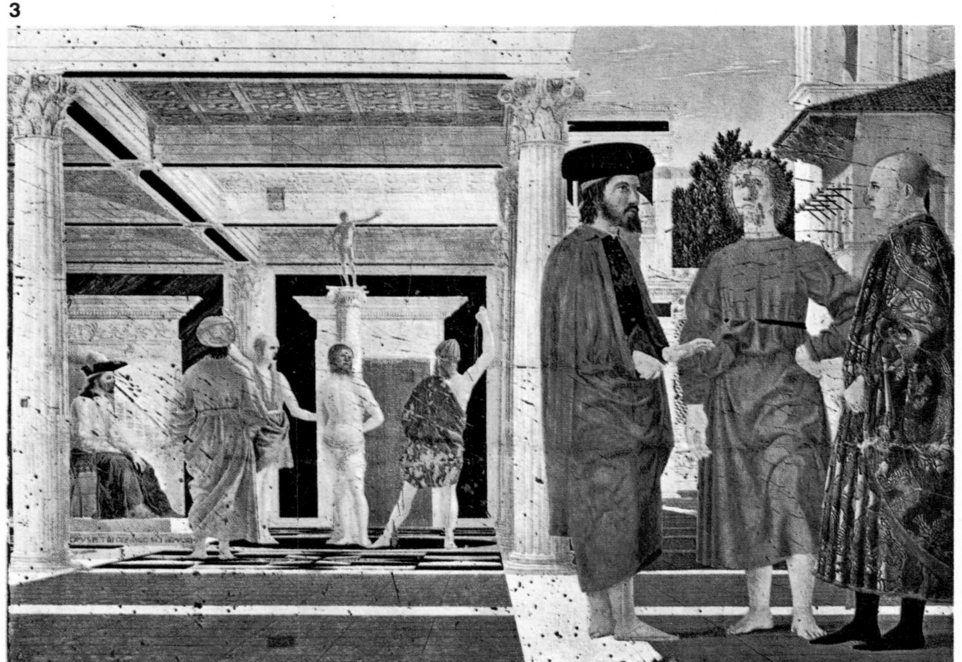

6

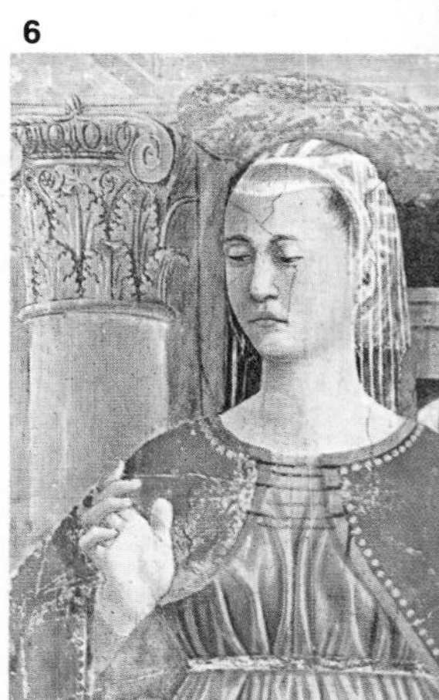

ero della Francesca (1410/20–92)
& 2. *Portraits of Federigo da Montefeltro, Duke of Urbino, and his Wife, Battista Sforza.* Diptych. About 1465. Uffizi, Florence
workshop of: *St Apollonia.* National Gallery of Art (Samuel H. Kress Collection), Washington DC
4. *The Legend of the True Cross: The Queen of Sheba and her Retinue.* Fresco. 1452–9. S. Francesco, Arezzo
5. *Madonna del Parto.* Detail. 1460–70. Chapel of the Campo Santo, Monterchi

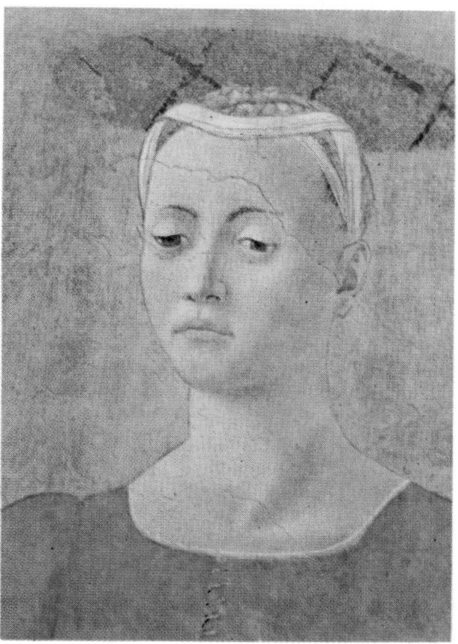

5

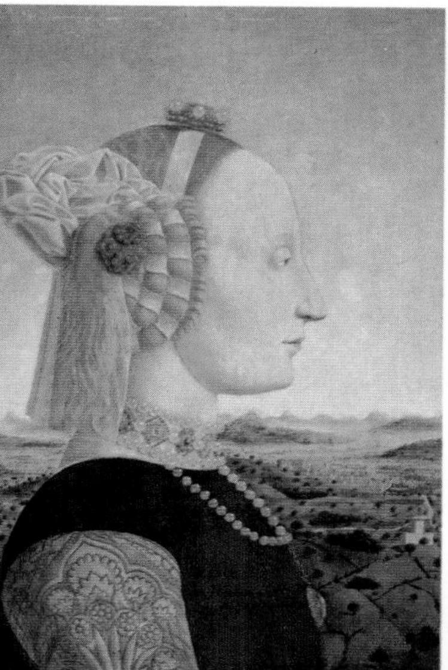

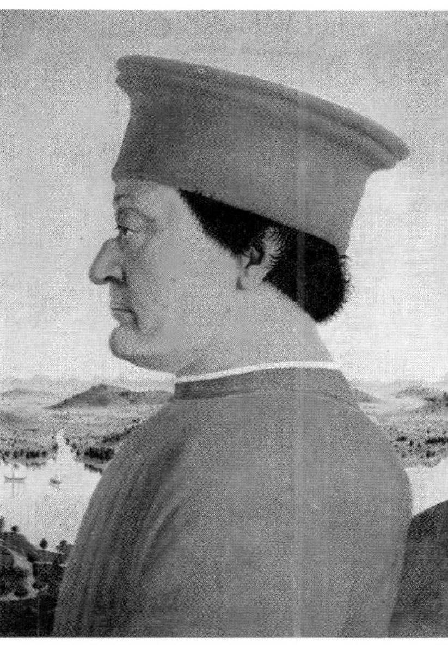

2

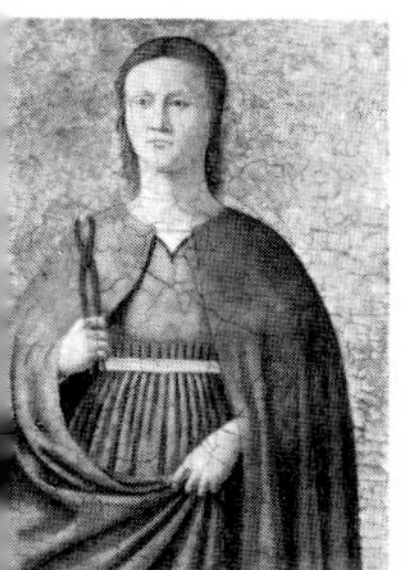

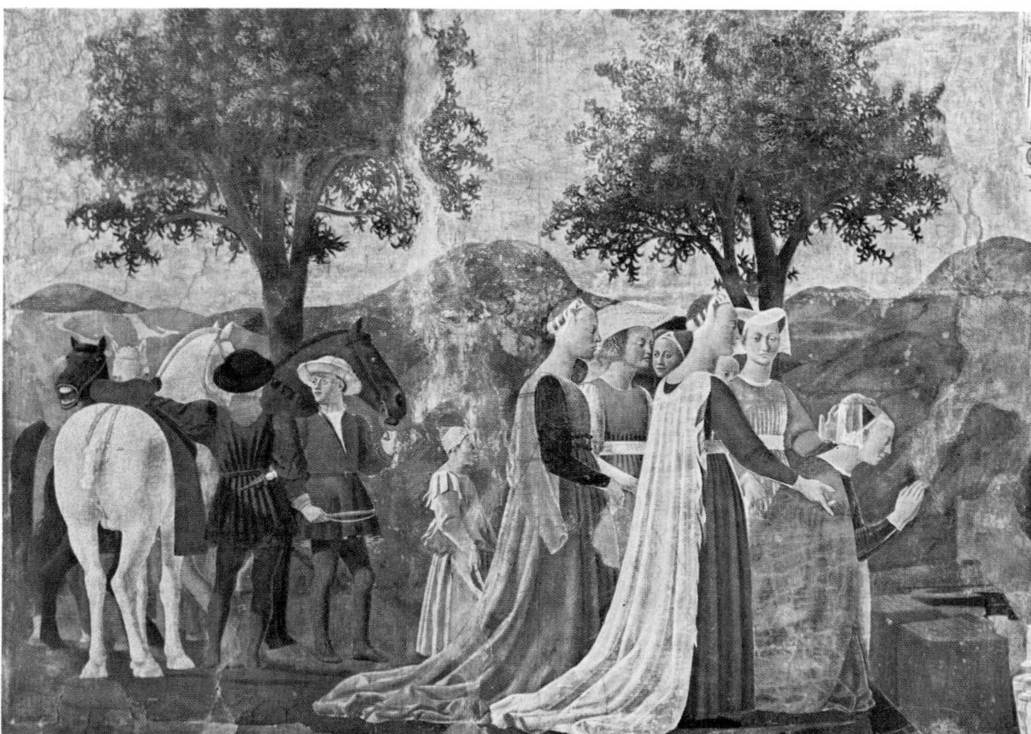

4

Sandro Botticelli (*c.*1445–1510)

1. *St Augustine in his Cell.* Uffizi, Florence
2. *The Virgin and Child with St John the Baptist.* Louvre, Paris
3. *The Adoration of the Kings.* About 1472–6. National Gallery, London
4. *The Virgin and Child with singing Angels.* About 1477. Staatliche Museen, Berlin-Dahlem
5. *Pietà.* Early 1490s. Alte Pinakothek, Munich

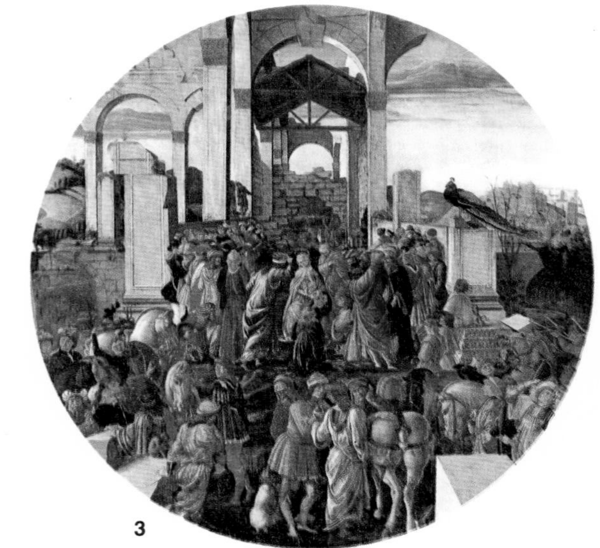

3

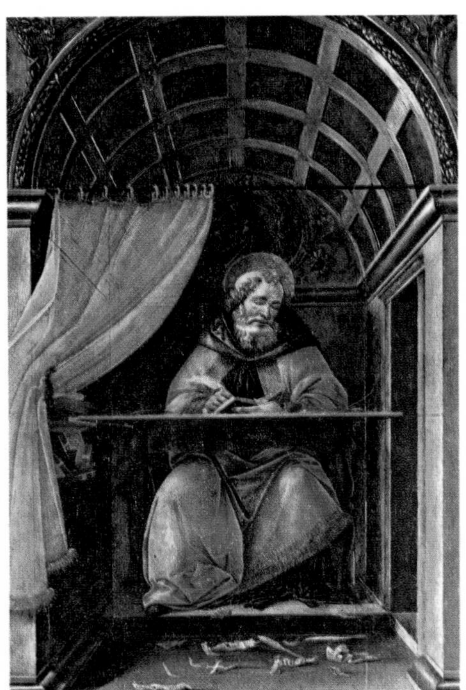

1

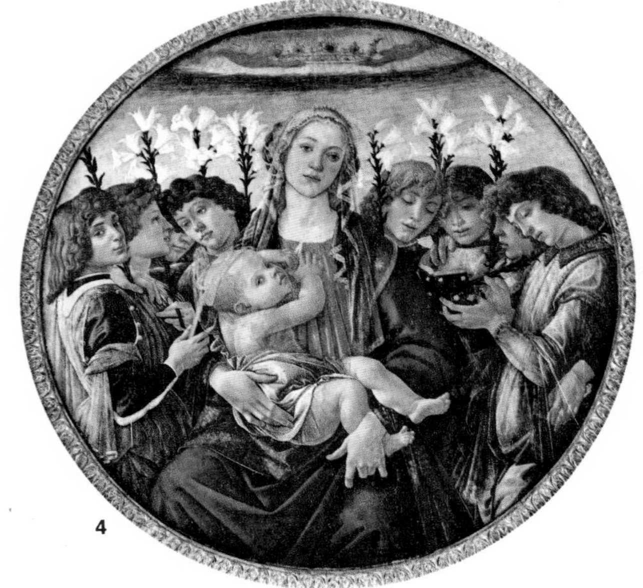

4

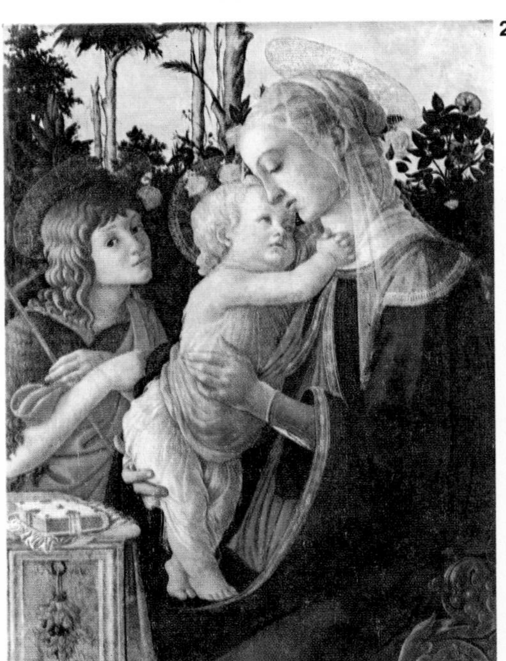

2

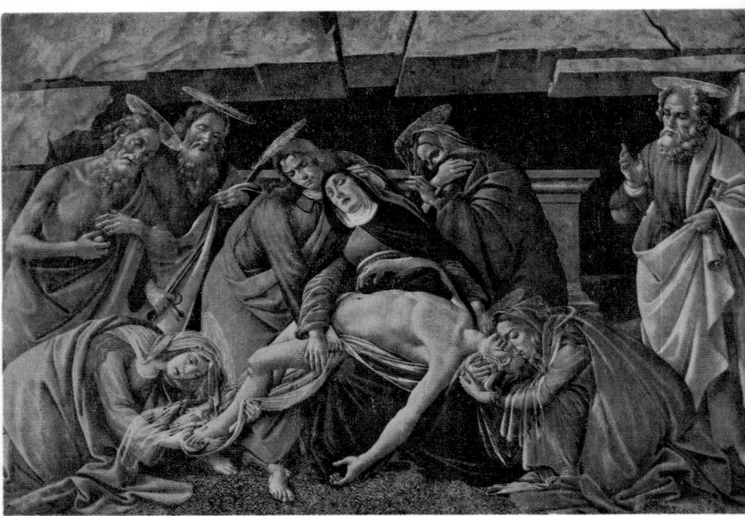

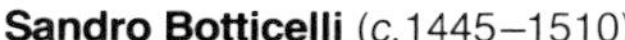

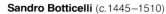

Sandro Botticelli (*c.*1445–1510)
1. *The Virgin and Child.* Galleria Borghese, Rome
2. *The Annunciation.* 1490. Uffizi, Florence
3. *Judith with the Head of Holofernes.* 1470s. Uffizi, Florence
4. *Pallas and the Centaur.* Uffizi, Florence
5. *La Primavera.* 1477–8. Uffizi, Florence

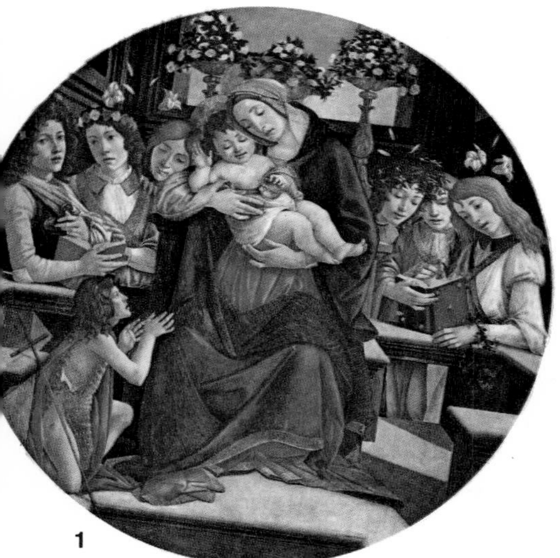

1

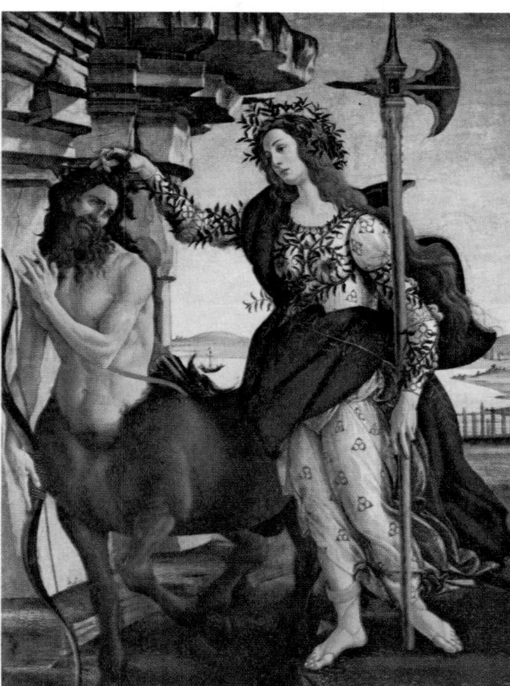

4

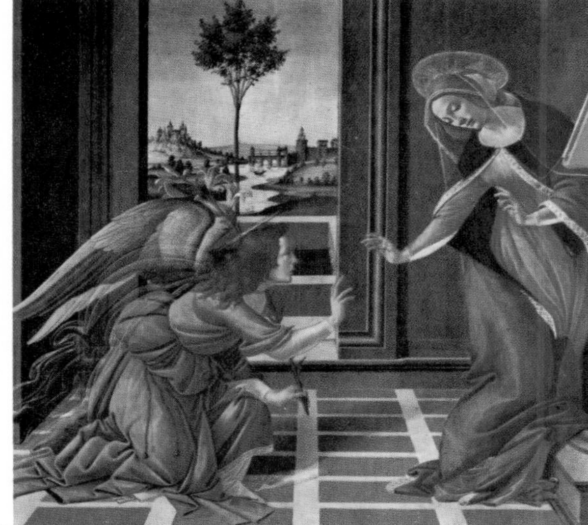

2

5

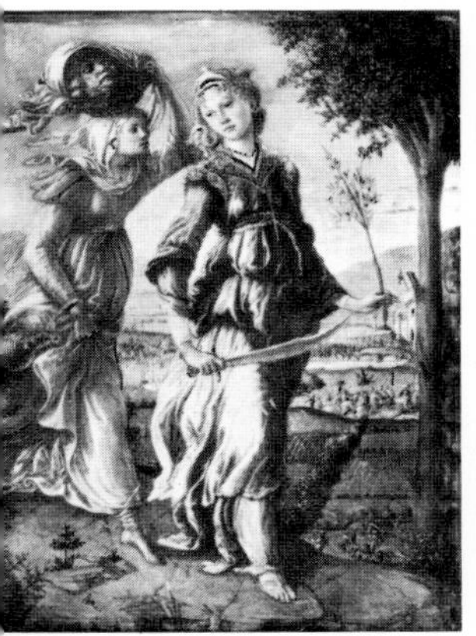

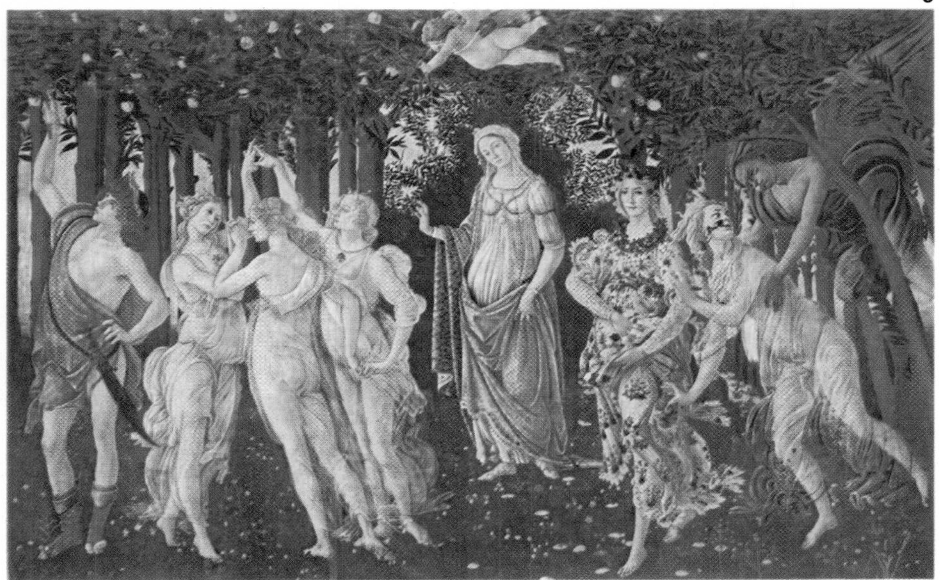

Andrea Mantegna (1430/1–1506)

1. *The Crucifixion.* Predella panel of the S. Zeno Altarpiece. 1456–9. Louvre, Paris
2. *Judith with the Head of Holofernes.* About 1480. National Gallery of Art, Washington DC
3. Detail from *The Martyrdom of St Christopher.* Fresco. About 1456. Ovetari Chapel, church of the Eremitani, Padua
4. *The dead Christ.* About 1465. Brera, Milan
5. *The Agony in the Garden.* About 1460. National Gallery, London
6. *Federigo I Gonzaga* (right). Detail from frescoes in the Camera degli Sposi, Palazzo Ducale, Mantua. 1473–4

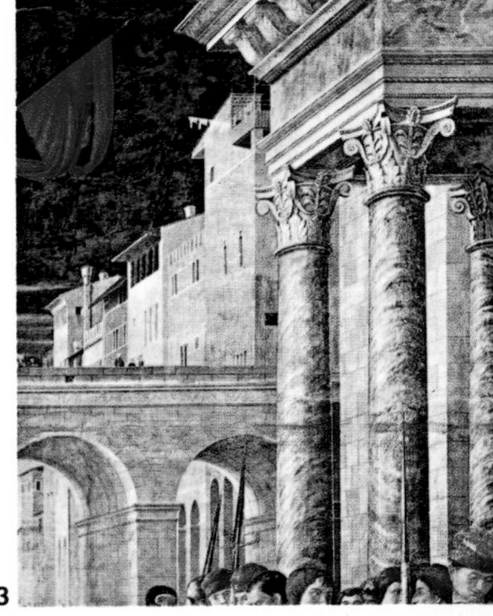

3

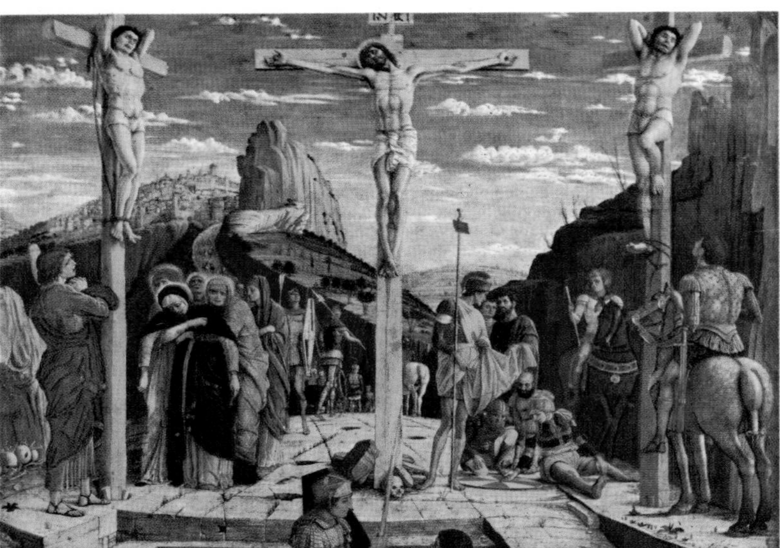

1

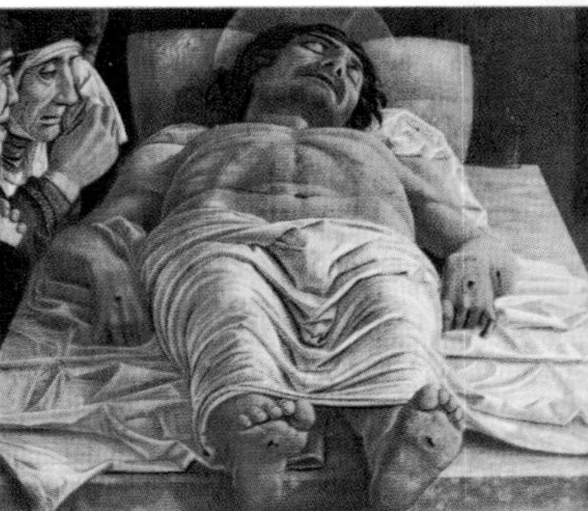

4

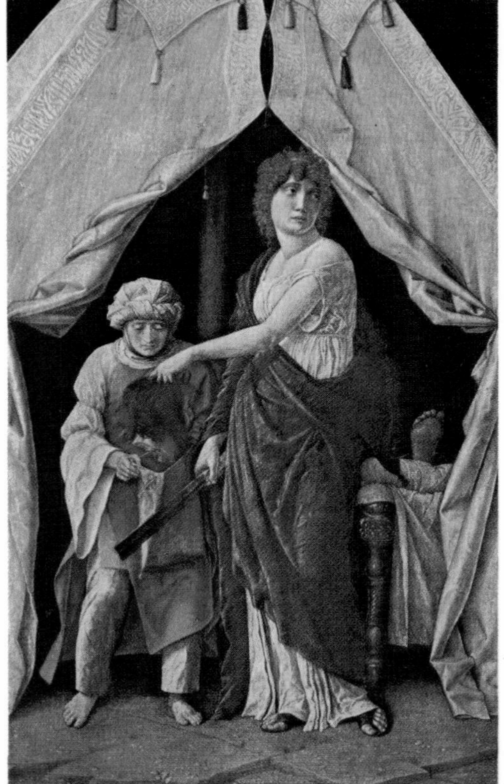

2

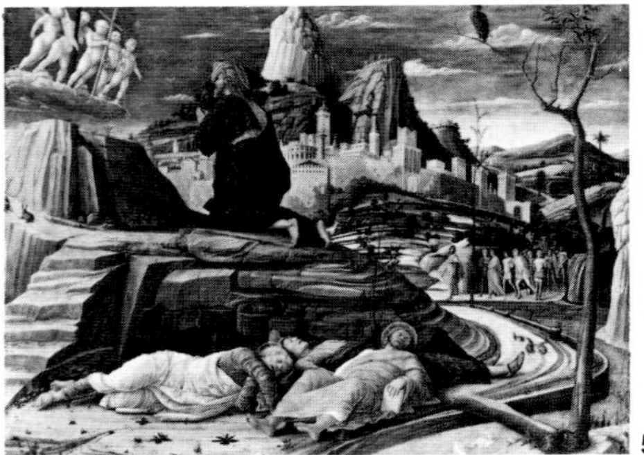

5

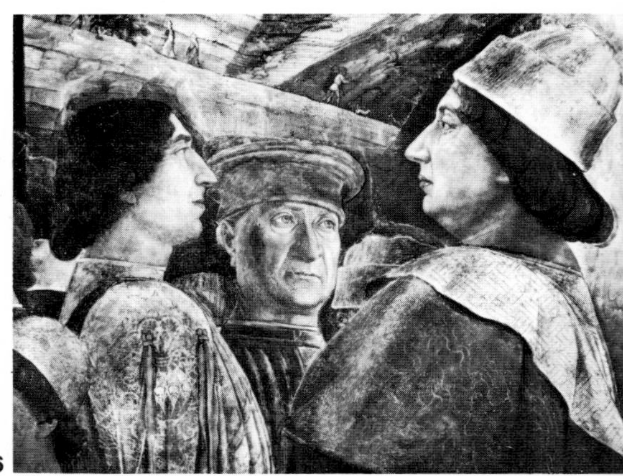

6

1 **Domenico Ghirlandaio** (1449–94): *Old Man and his Grandson.* About 1480. Louvre, Paris

2 **Domenico Ghirlandaio** (1449–94): *Ludovica Tornabuoni and her Attendants.* Detail from *The Birth of the Virgin.* Fresco. 1485–90. S. Maria Novella, Florence

3 **Andrea del Castagno** (*c.*1419–57): *The Last Supper.* Fresco. 1445–50. Cenacolo di S. Apollonia, Florence

4 **Domenico Ghirlandaio** (1449–94): *A Lady of the Sassetti Family.* Metropolitan Museum of Art, New York

5 **Andrea del Castagno** (*c.*1419–57): *David.* About 1450–7. National Gallery of Art (Widener Collection), Washington DC

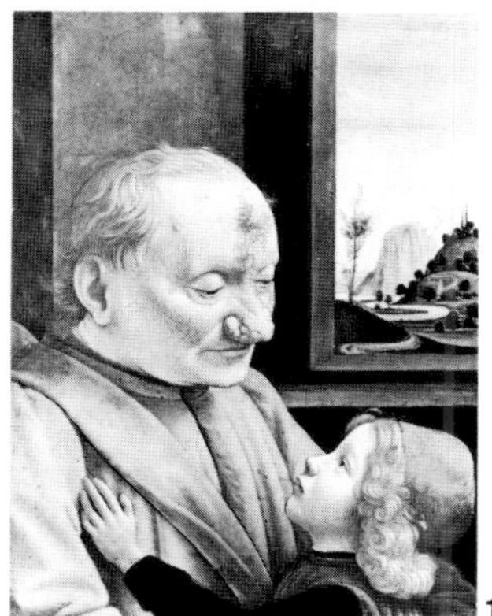

1

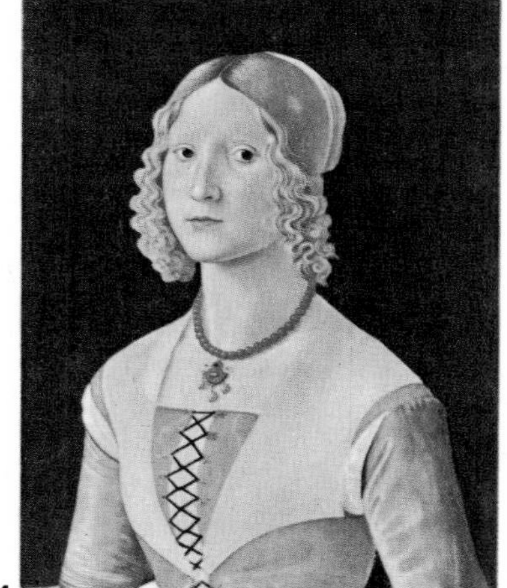

4

2

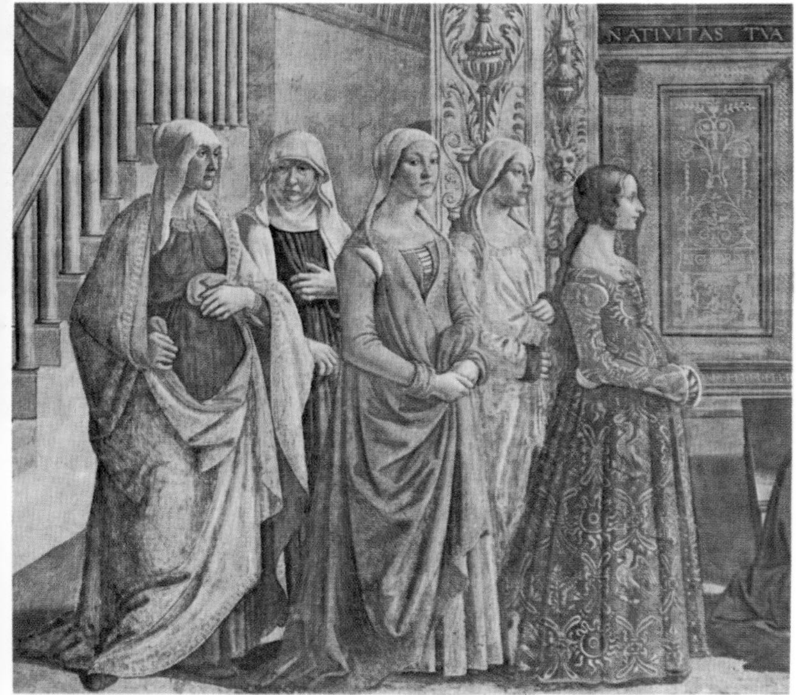

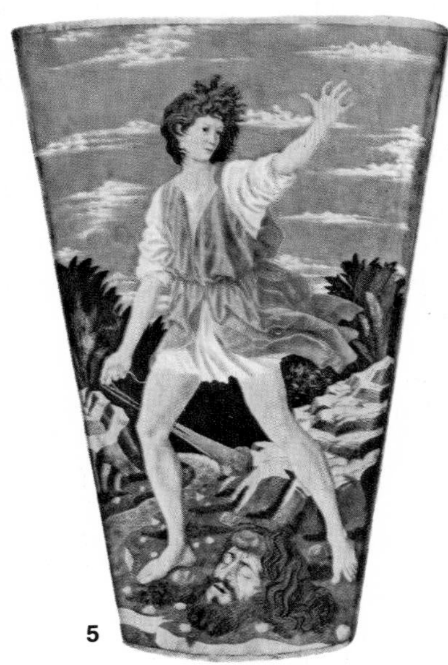

5

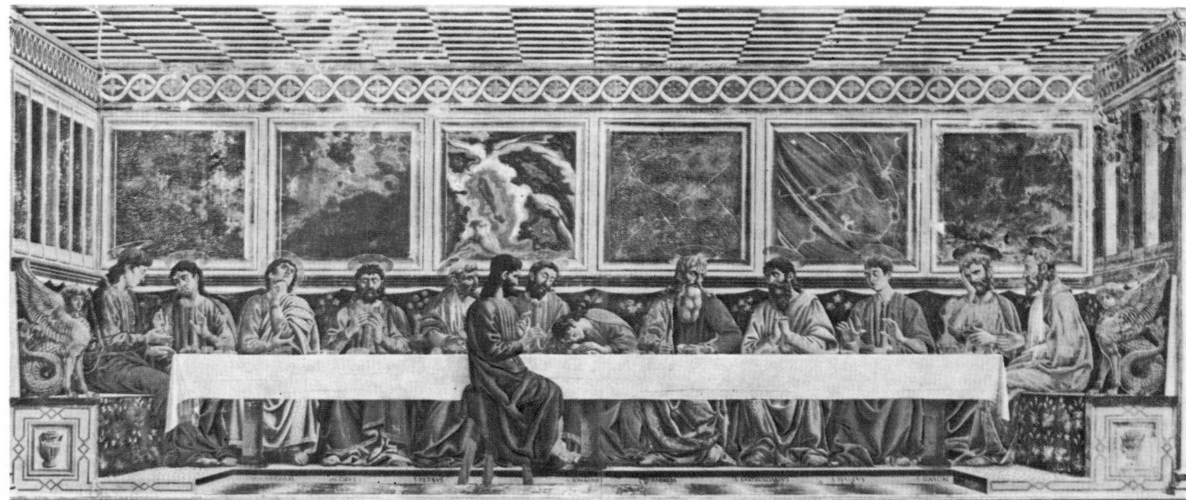

3

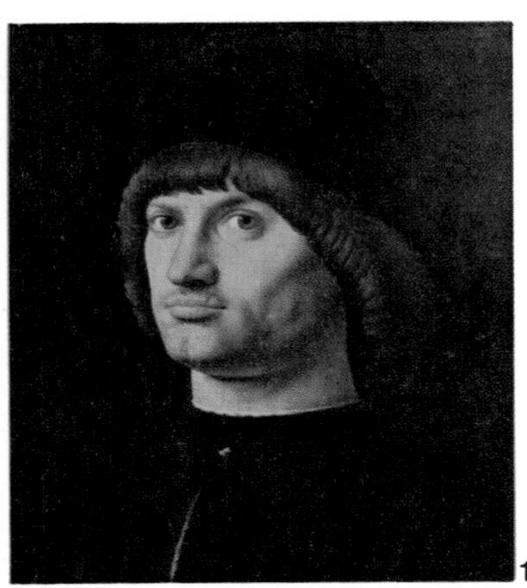
1

1. **Antonello da Messina** (*c.*1430–79): *Portrait of a Condottiere.* 1475. Louvre, Paris
2. **Antonello da Messina** (*c.*1430–79): Detail from *St Sebastian.* Gemäldegalerie, Dresden
3. **Antonello da Messina** (*c.*1430–79): *Virgin of the Annunciation.* Galleria Nazionale, Palermo
4. **Piero di Cosimo** (*c.*1462–*c.*1521): *The Death of Procris.* National Gallery, London
5. **Luca Signorelli** (1441?–1523): Detail f *The Life of St Benedict.* Fresco. 1497- Monastery of Monte Oliveto Maggiore, Asciano
6. **Cristoforo Solari** (*c.*1460–*c.*1527): Recumbent figure of Lodovico il Moro. Marble. 1497–9. Certosa di Pavia
7. **Piero di Cosimo** (*c.*1462–*c.*1521): *Simonetta Vespucci.* Musée Condé, Chantilly
8. **Luca Signorelli** (1441?–1523): *Nymp and Satyrs.* Drawing. Uffizi, Florence

2

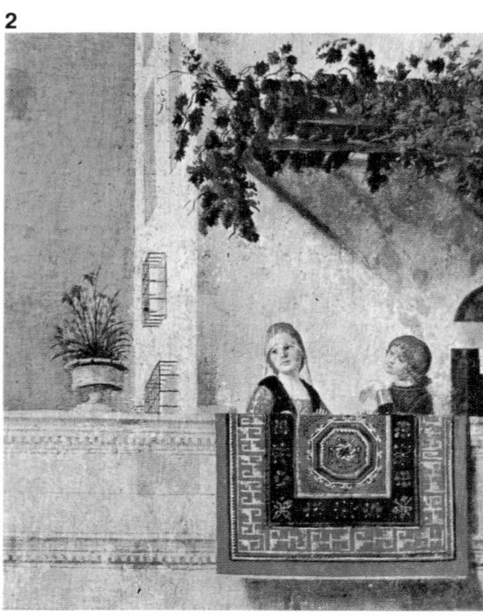

4

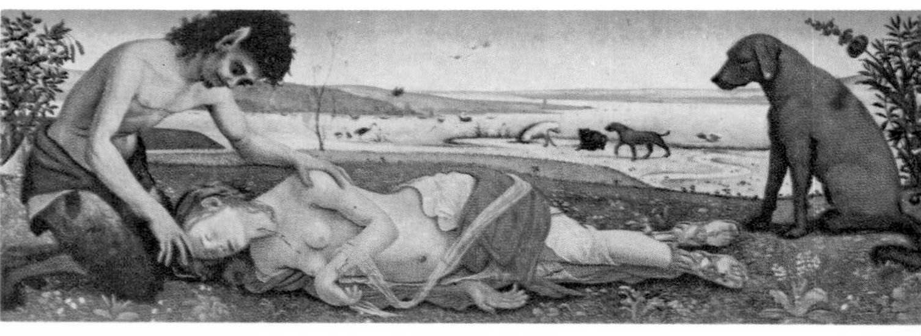

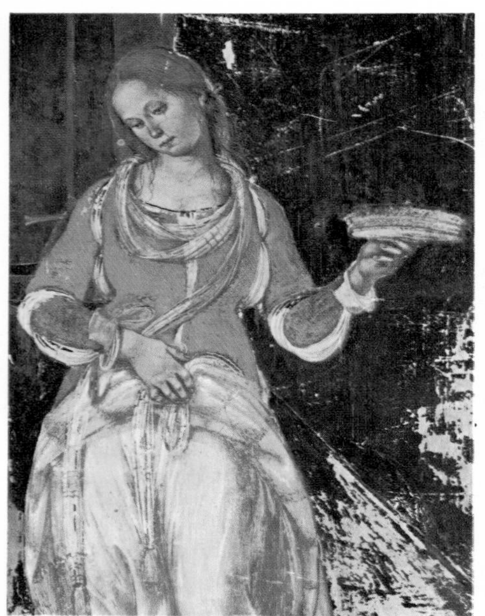
5

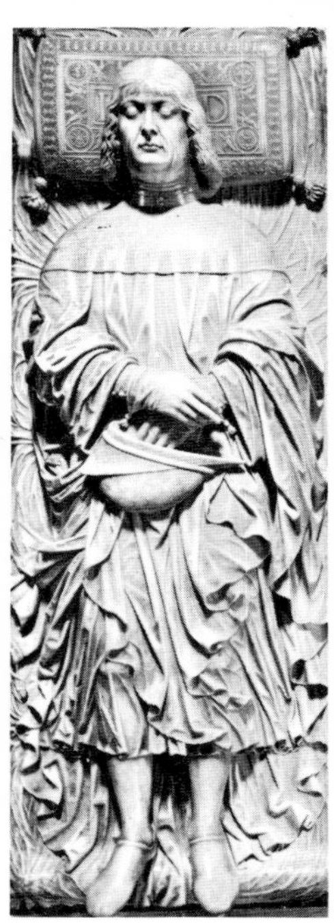
6

3

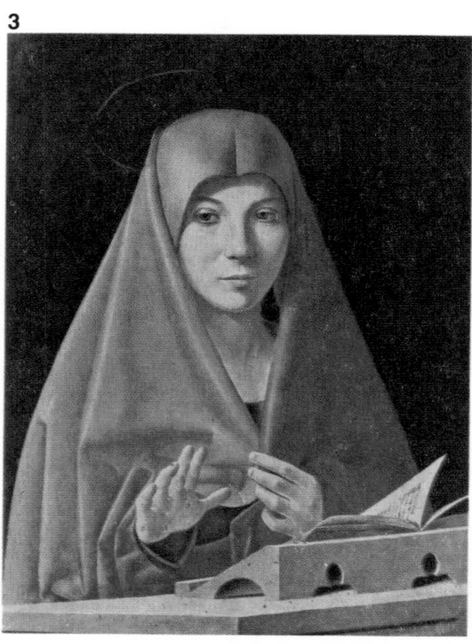

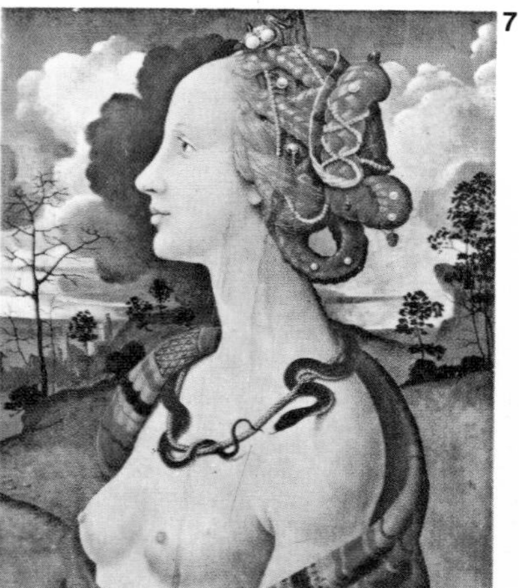
7

8

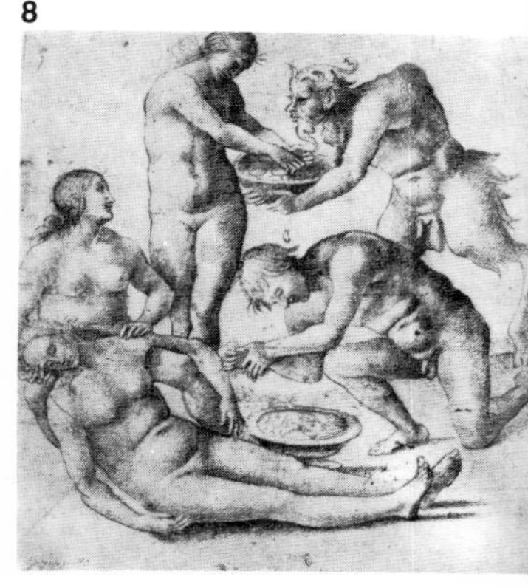

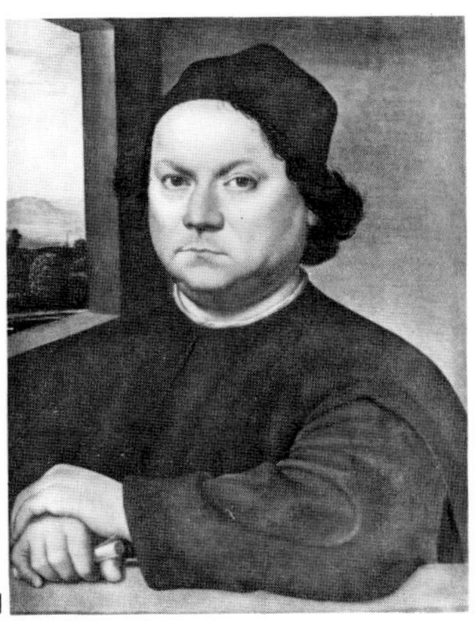
1

1. **Lorenzo di Credi** (*c.*1458–1537), attributed to: *Portrait of Verrocchio* (?). Uffizi, Florence
2. **Melozzo da Forli** (1438–94): *Angel Musician.* Fragment of fresco. About 1480. Pinacoteca, Vatican
3. **Mariotto Albertinelli** (1474–1515): *The Adoration.* Detail from predella of The Visitation. Uffizi, Florence
4. **Matteo Civitali** (1436–1501): *Madonna della Tosse.* Marble. 1480. S. Trinita, Lucca
5. **Andrea del Sarto** (1486–1530): *Portrait of Lucretia, the Painter's Wife.* Prado, Madrid
6. **Andrea Solari** (*c.*1470–1524): *Virgin with the green Cushion.* About 1500. Louvre, Paris
7. **Fra Bartolommeo** (*c.*1472–1517): *Pietà.* About 1516–17. Palazzo Pitti, Florence

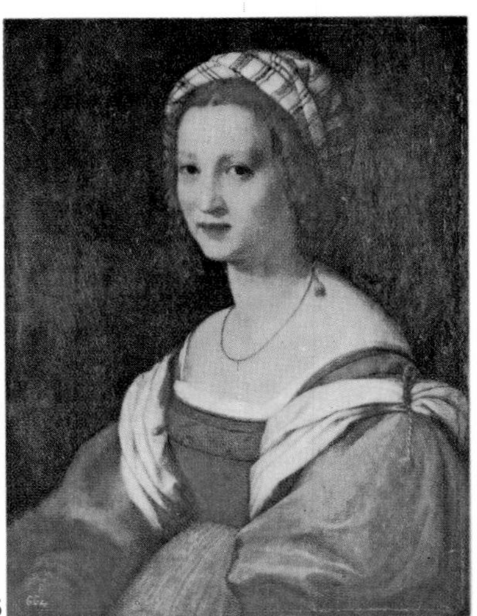
5

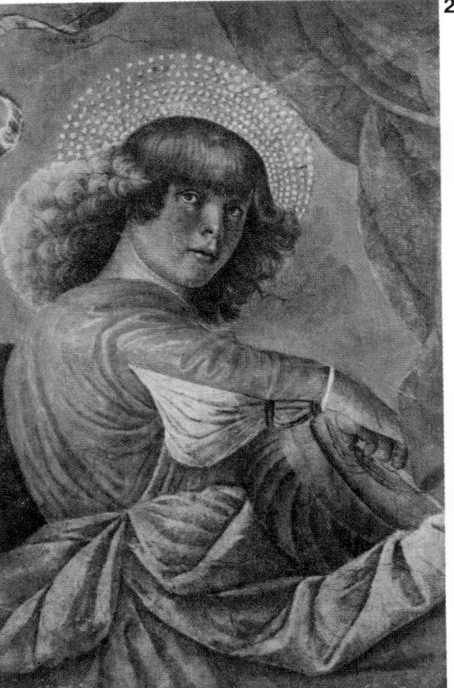
2

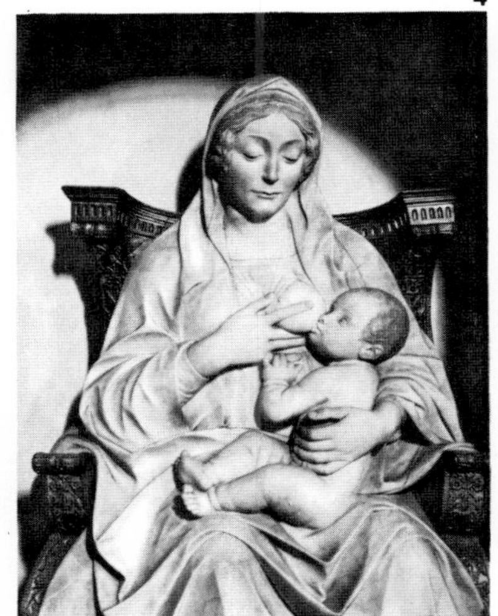
4

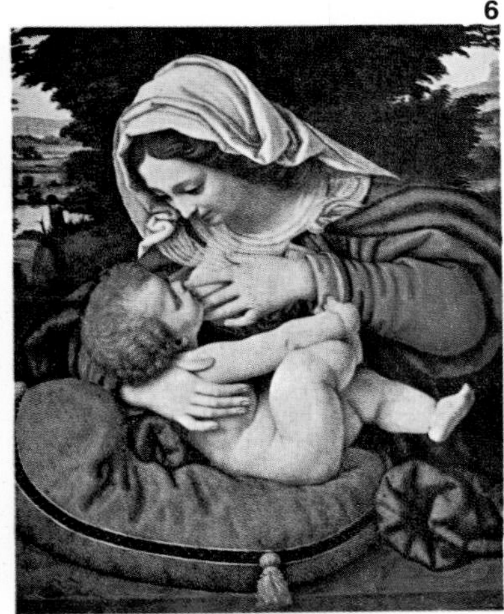
6

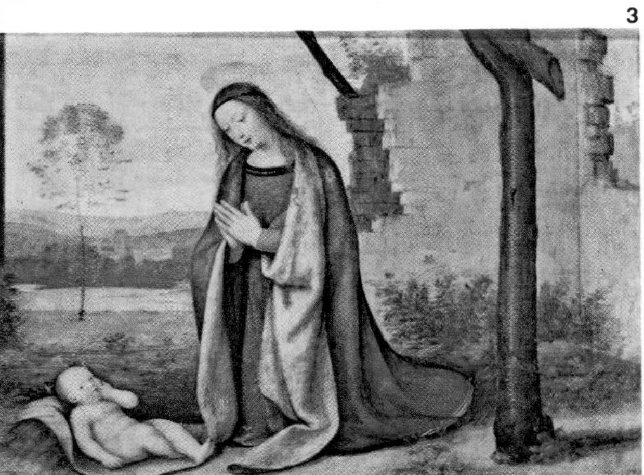
3

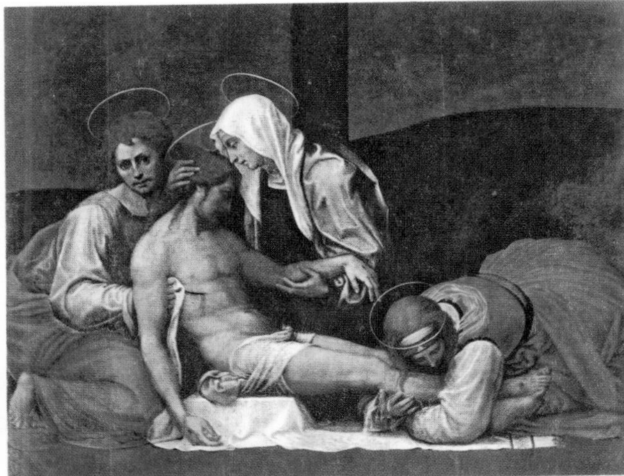
7

1. **Giovanni Bellini** (*c.*1430–1516): *Pietà.* About 1470. Brera, Milan
2. **Giovanni Bellini** (*c.*1430–1516): *Orpheus.* National Gallery of Art (Widener Collection), Washington DC
3. **Giovanni Bellini** (*c.*1430–1516): *The Entombment.* Pinacoteca, Vatican
4. **Gentile Bellini** (*c.*1429–1507), attributed to: *Portrait of Sultan Mehmet II.* 1480. National Gallery, London
5. **Gentile Bellini** (*c.*1429–1507): *The Mira of the True Cross.* 1500. Accademia, Ven
6. **Gentile and Giovanni Bellini:** *St Mark preaching in Alexandria.* Begun 1505. Brera, Milan

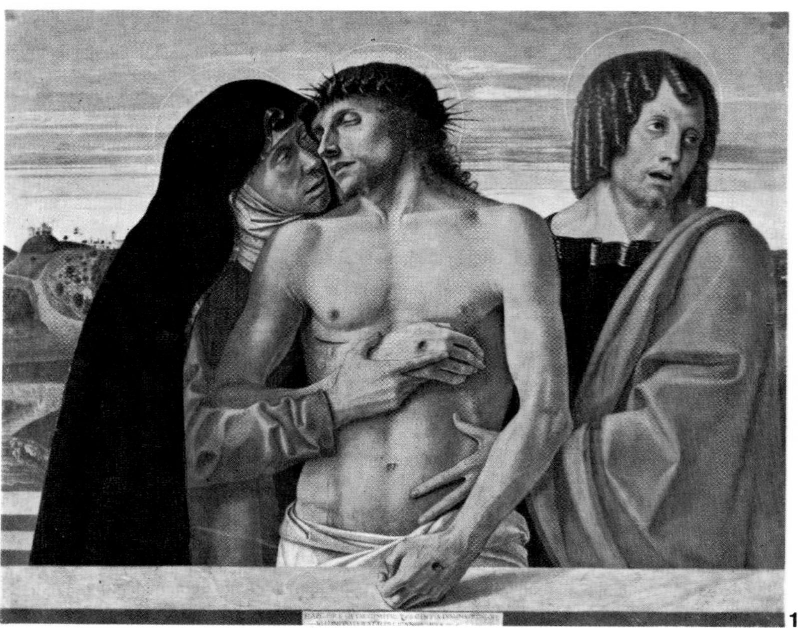
1

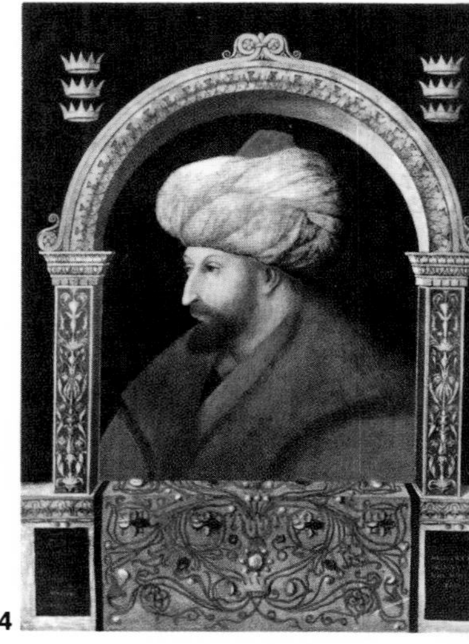
4

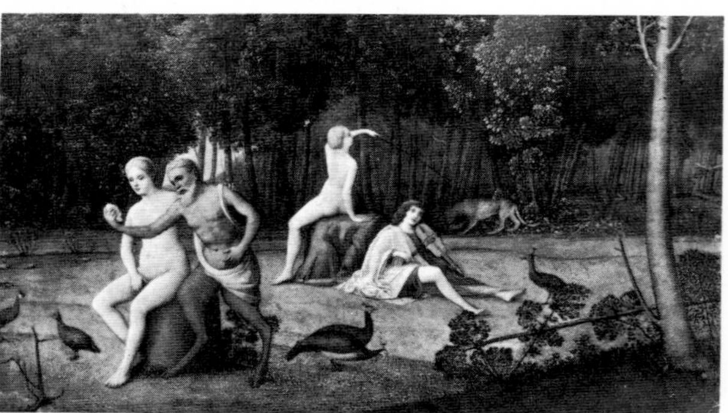
2

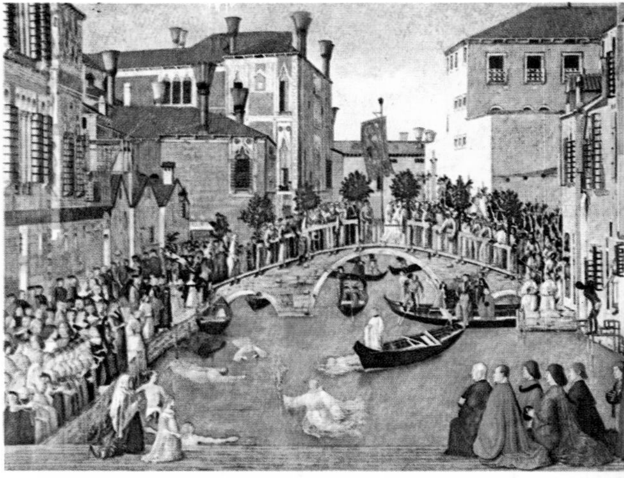
5

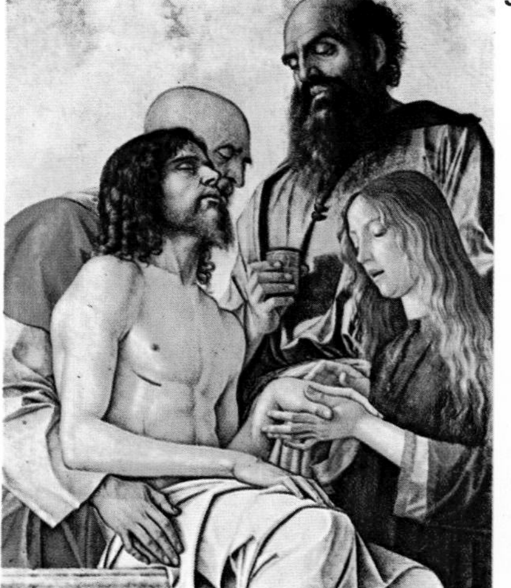
3

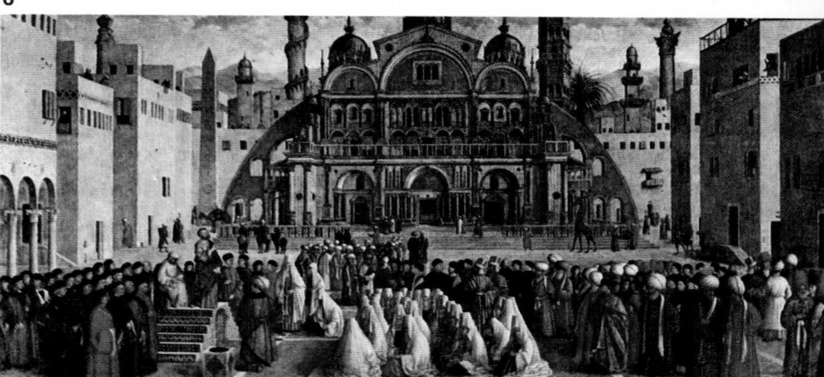
6

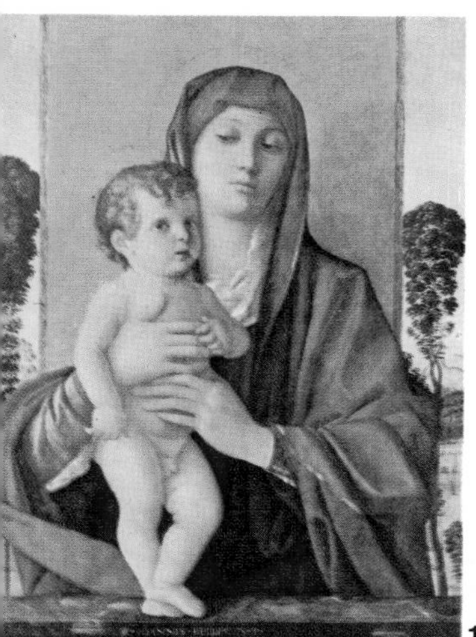

1

Giovanni Bellini (*c.*1430–1516)

1. *Madonna of the Trees.* 1487. Accademia, Venice
2. *An Allegory.* About 1485. Uffizi, Florence
3. *St Jerome reading.* 1505? National Gallery of Art (Samuel H. Kress Collection), Washington DC
4. *Allegory of Inconstancy* (?). About 1490–1500. Accademia, Venice
5. *Portrait of Doge Leonardo Loredan.* About 1503–4. National Gallery, London
6. *A young Woman at her Toilet.* 1515. Kunsthistorisches Museum, Vienna

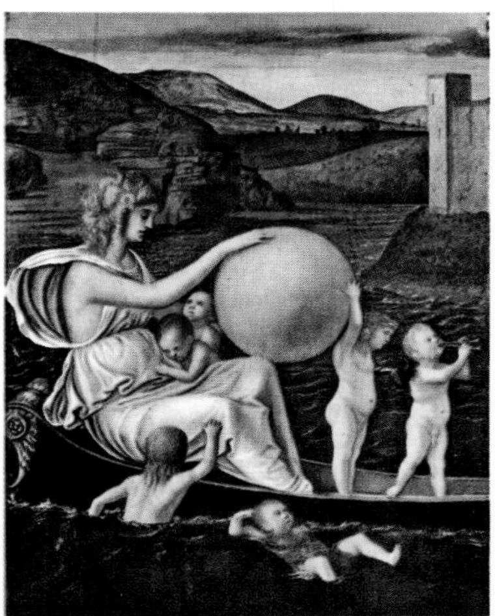

4

2

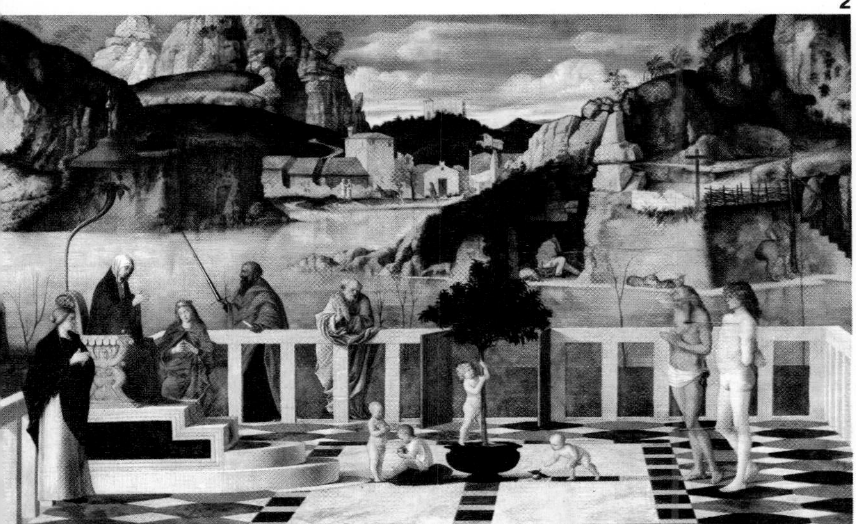

5

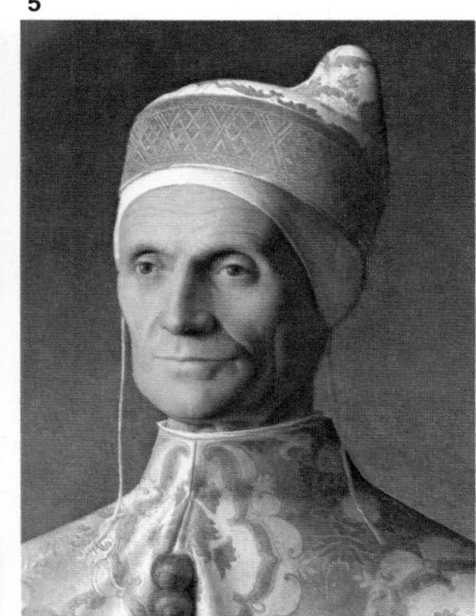

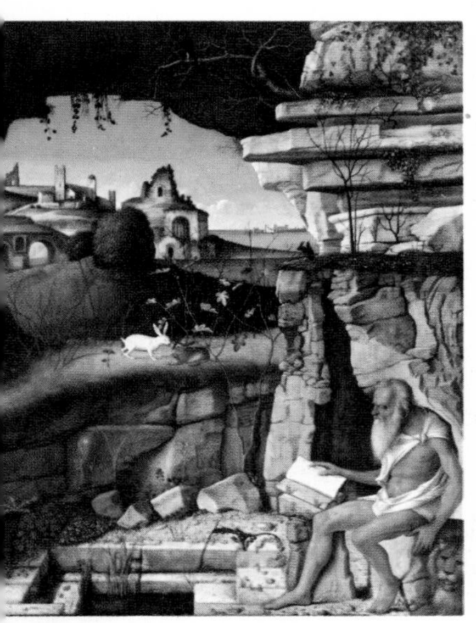

6

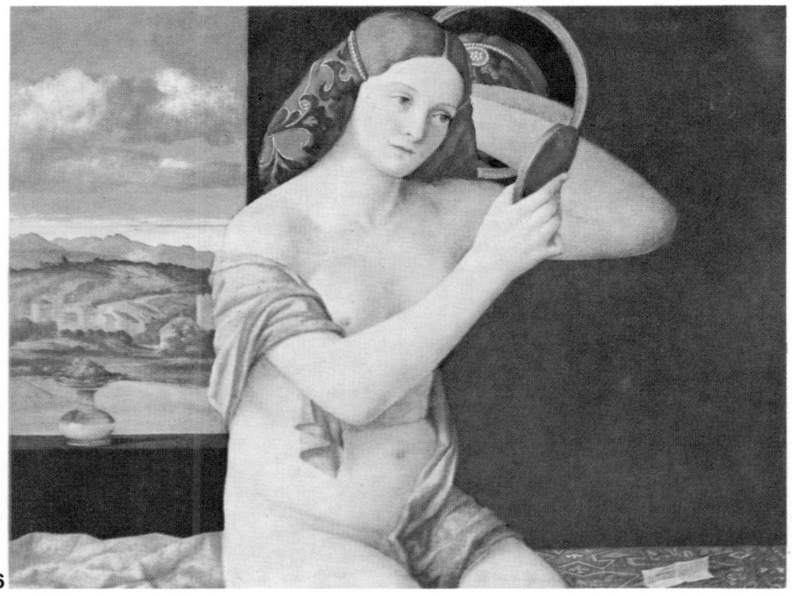

Vittore Carpaccio (*c.*1465/7–1525/6)

1. *The Legend of St Ursula: St Ursula and the Prince taking leave of their Parents.* Detail. 1495. Accademia, Venice
2. *The Vision of St Augustine.* 1502–7. Scuola di S. Giorgio degli Schiavoni, Venice
3. *The Legend of St Ursula: Martyrdom and Funeral of St Ursula.* 1493. Accademia, Venice
4. *Two Courtesans.* About 1510. Museo Correr, Venice
5. *The Legend of St Ursula: Dream of St Ursula.* 1495? Accademia, Venice
6. Detail of fig. 5

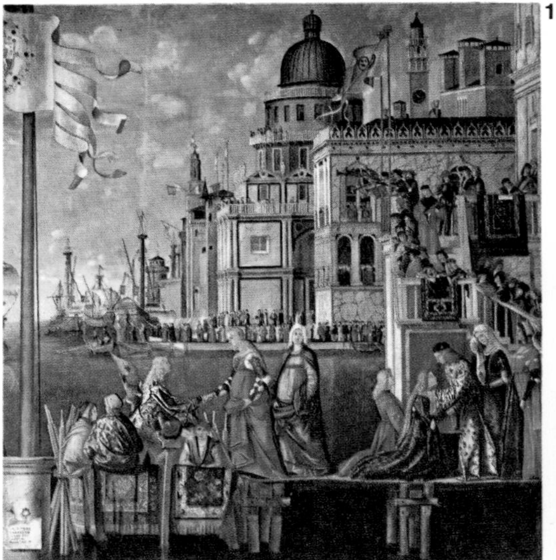
1

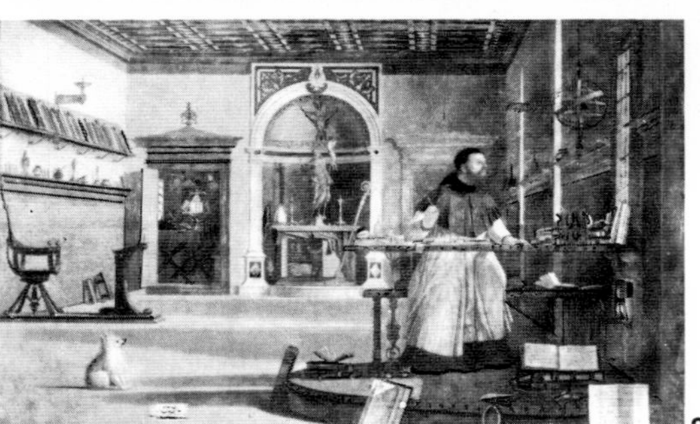
2

4

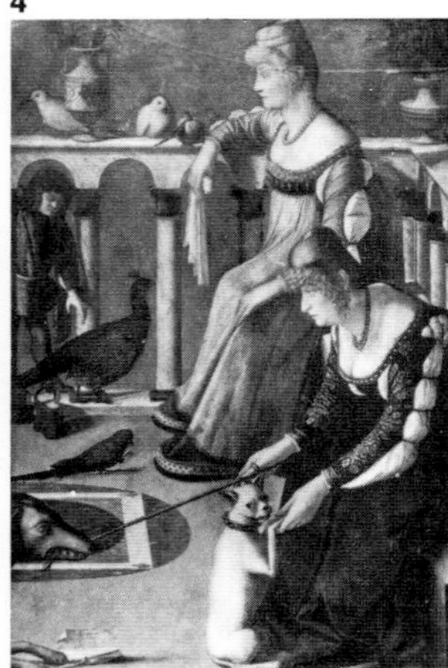

5

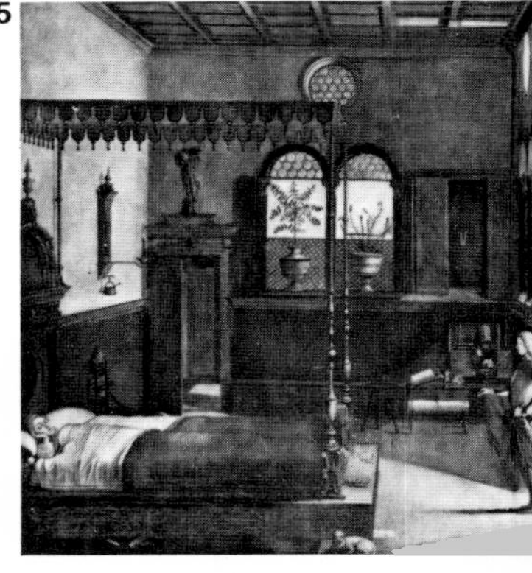

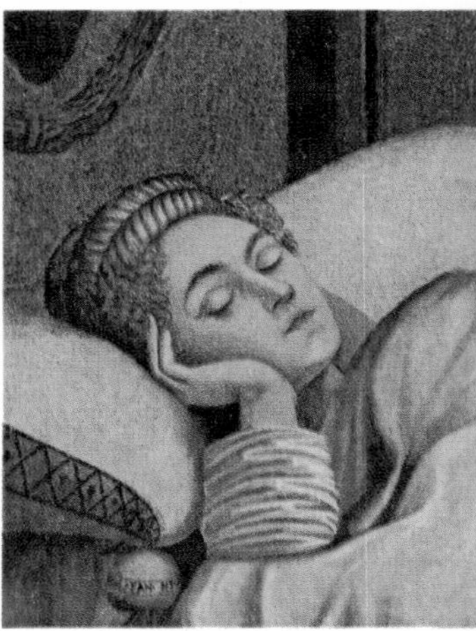
6

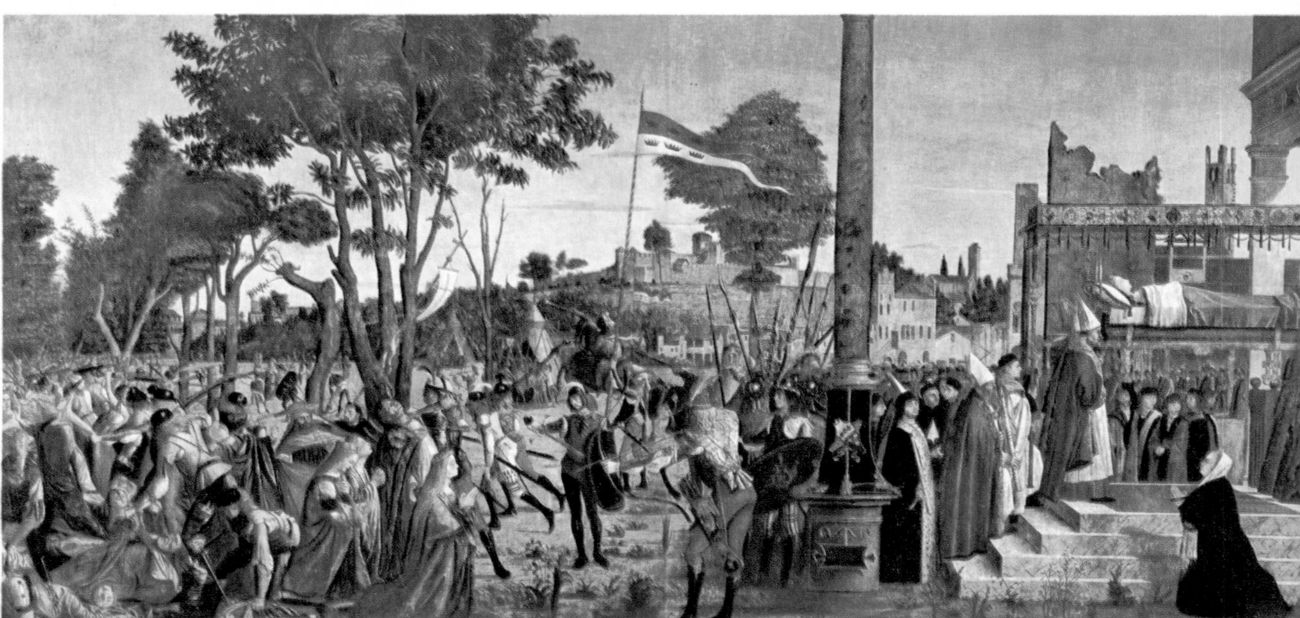

1. **Cosimo Tura** (*c.*1430–95): *St Anthony of Padua.* 1484. Galleria Estense, Modena
2. **Carlo Crivelli** (*c.*1435–*c.*1495): *The Virgin and Child.* Metropolitan Museum of Art, New York
3. **Francesco del Cossa** (*c.*1435–*c.*1477): *The Miracles of St Vincent Ferrer.* Predella panel. About 1473. Pinacoteca, Vatican
4. **Francesco del Cossa** (*c.*1435–*c.*1477): *Symbolic Figure.* Detail from *Month of March.* Fresco. About 1469–70. Palazzo Schifanoia, Ferrara
5. **Cosimo Tura** (*c.*1430–95): *Portrait of a Member of the Este Family.* About 1451. Metropolitan Museum of Art, New York
6. **Carlo Crivelli** (*c.*1435–*c.*1495): *St Mary Magdalene.* Rijksmuseum, Amsterdam

1

2

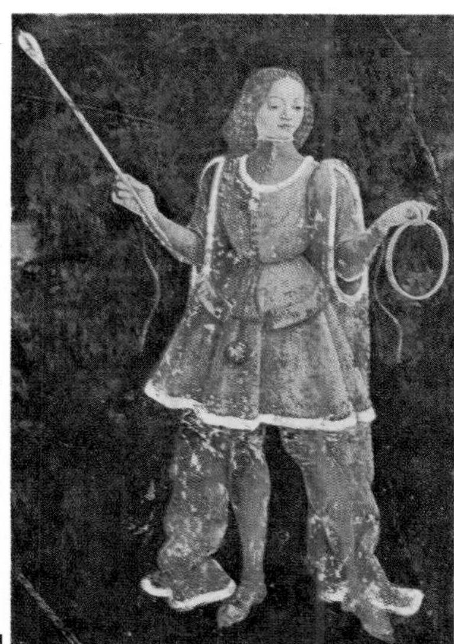

4

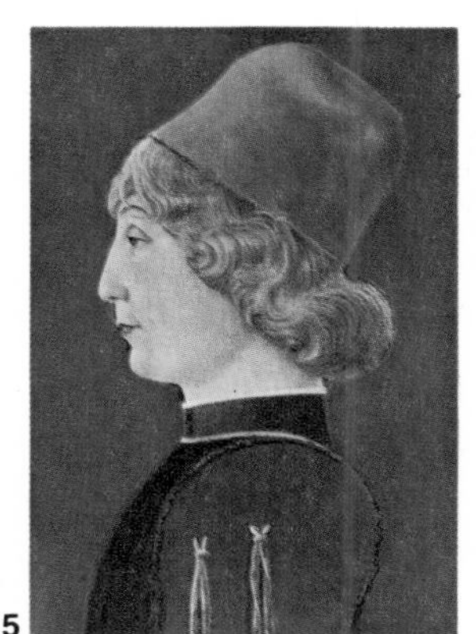

5

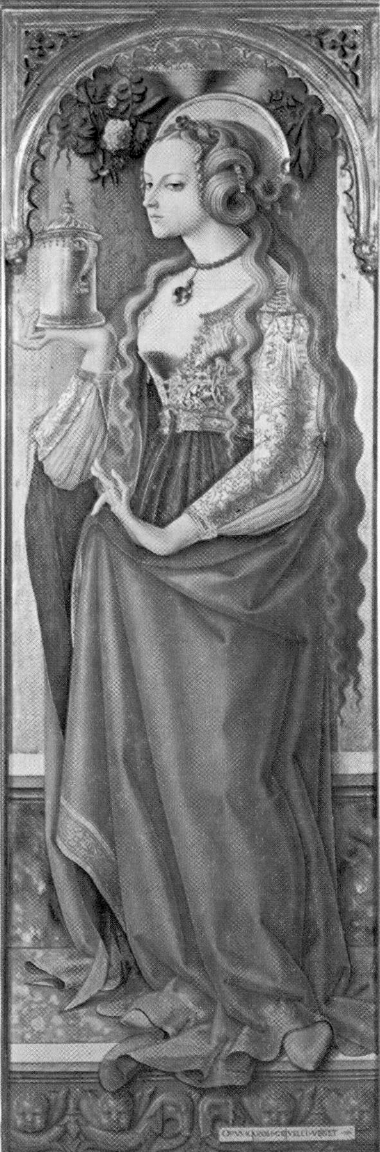

6

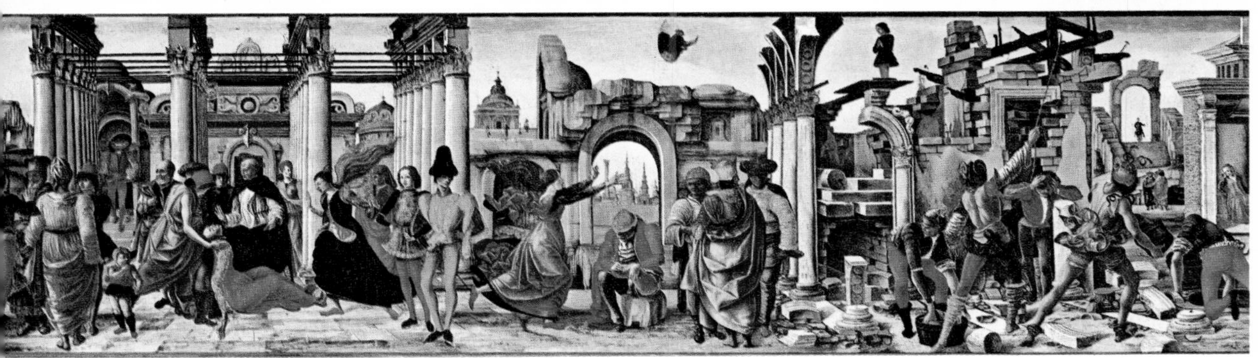

Leonardo da Vinci (1452–1519)

1. *St Anne.* Detail from *The Virgin and Child with St Anne.* About 1508–10. Louvre, Paris
2. After Leonardo: *Leda and the Swan.* Galleria Borghese, Rome
3. *The Proportions of the human Body,* after Vitruvius. Pen and ink. About 1492. Accademia, Venice
4. *The Last Supper.* Fresco. About 1495–8. S. Maria delle Grazie, Milan
5. *Christ.* Detail of fig. 4

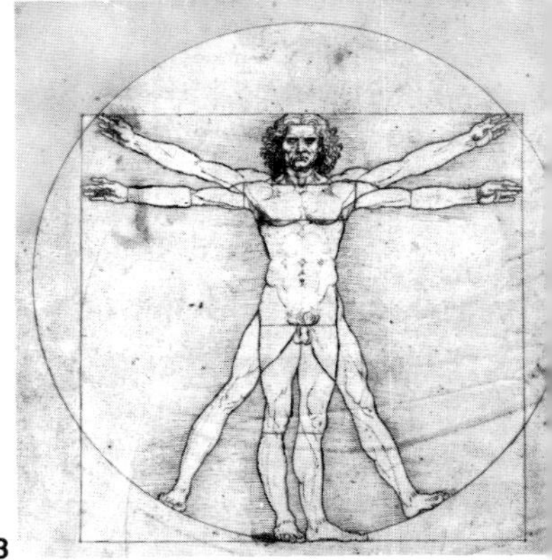

3

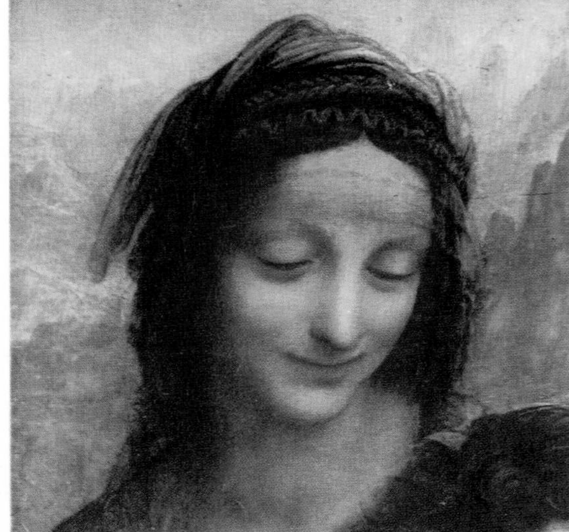

1

4

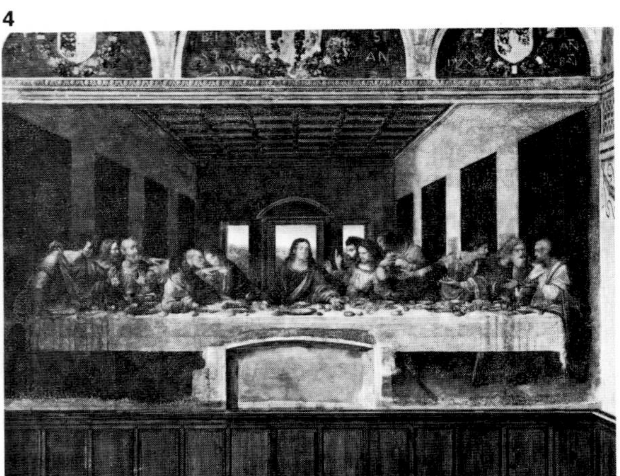

2

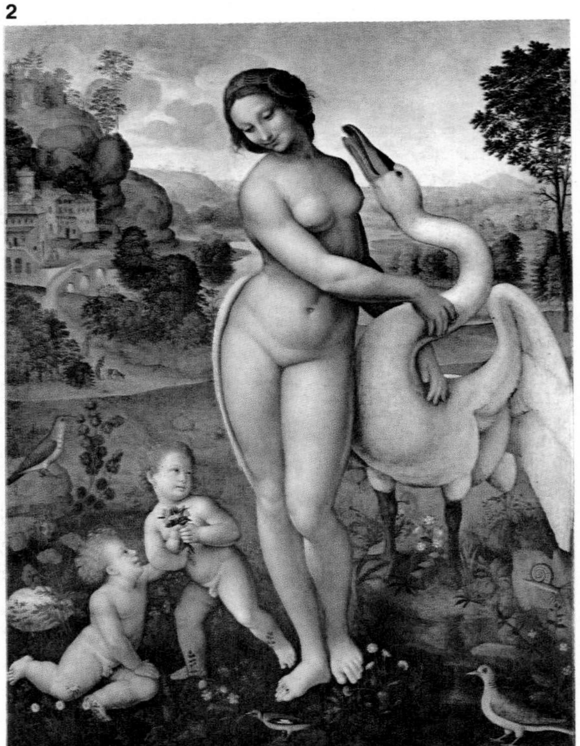

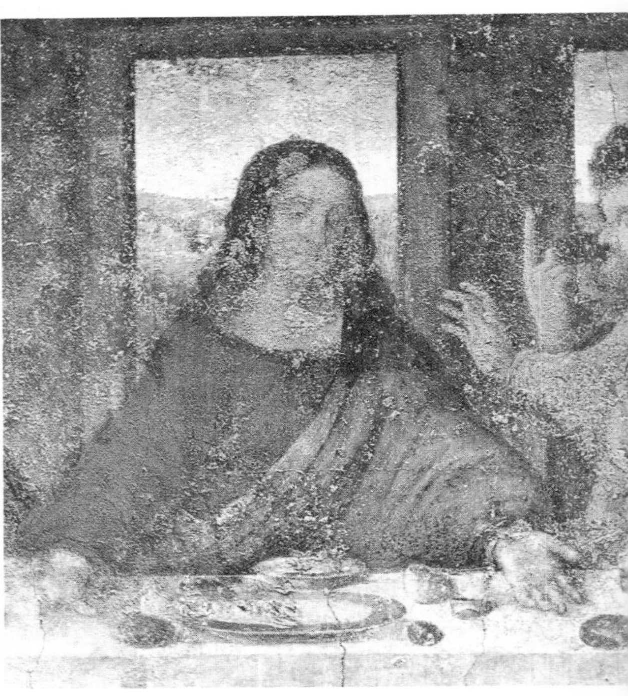

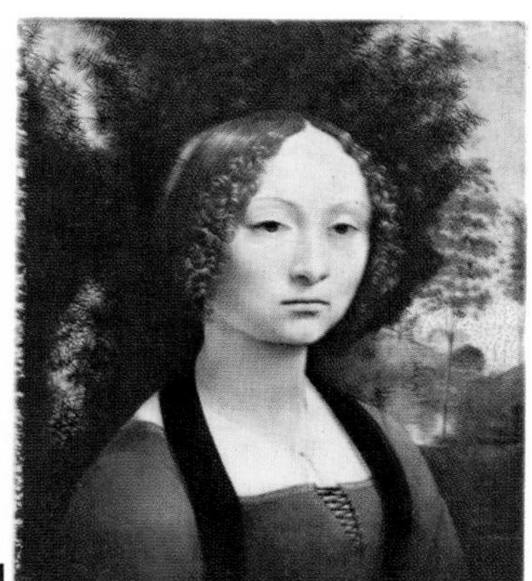

1

Leonardo da Vinci (1452–1519)

1. *Portrait of Ginevra de'Benci.* About 1478. National Gallery of Art, Washington DC
2. Project for a domed church. About 1488–9. Institut de France, Paris
3. *A Study of Flowers.* Pen and ink and red chalk. About 1506. Royal Library, Windsor Castle
4. *The Adoration of the Magi.* 1481. Uffizi, Florence
5. *Study for Leda and the Swan.* Pen and ink. About 1506. Royal Library, Windsor Castle
6. *Mona Lisa.* 1503. Louvre, Paris
7. *The Virgin of the Rocks.* National Gallery, London

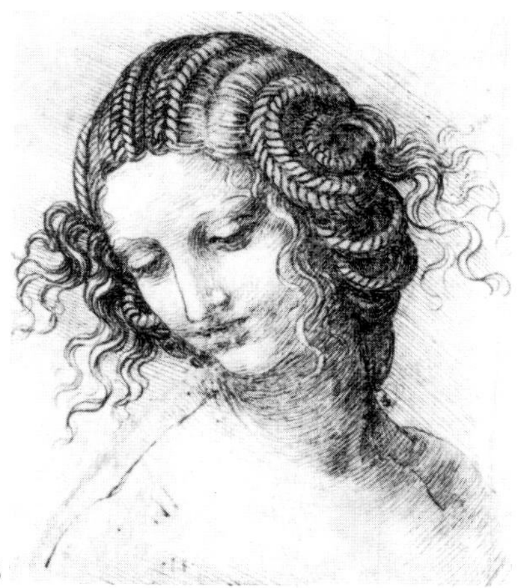

5

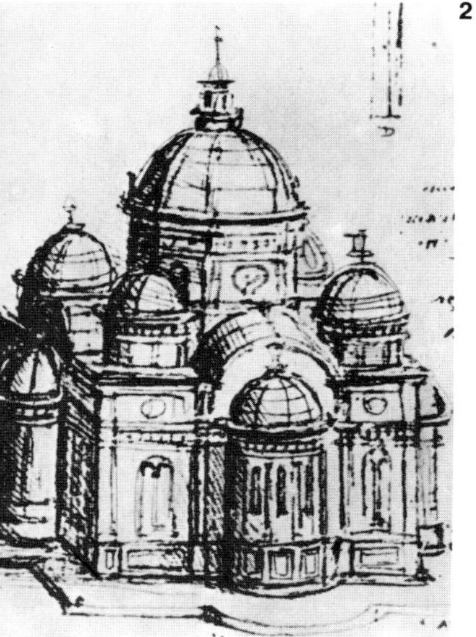

2

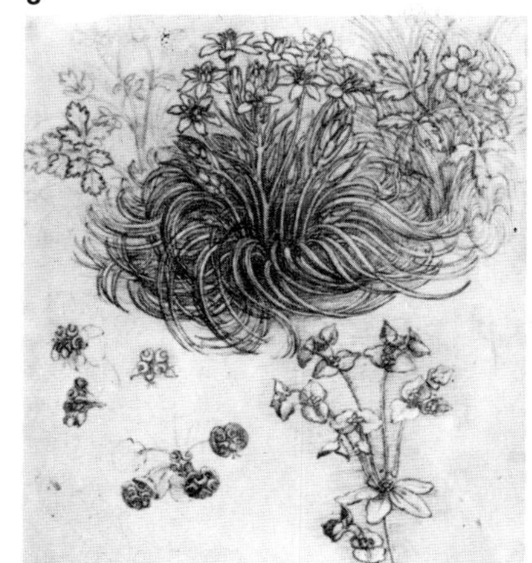

3

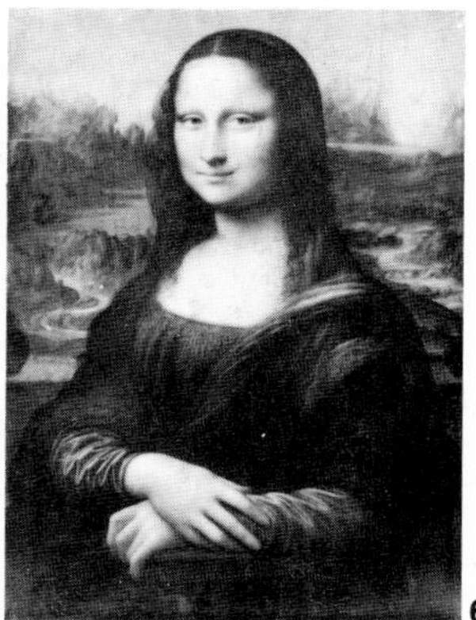

6

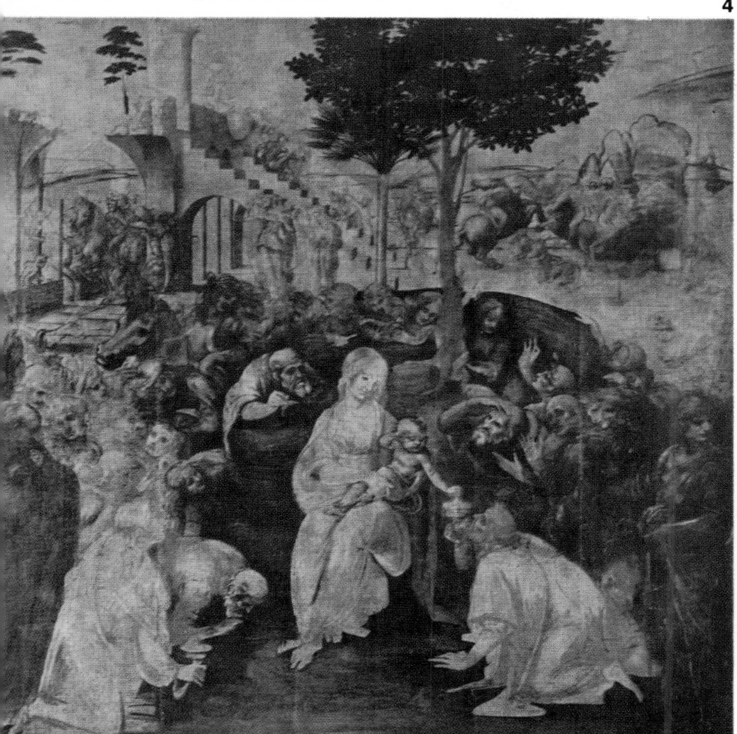

4

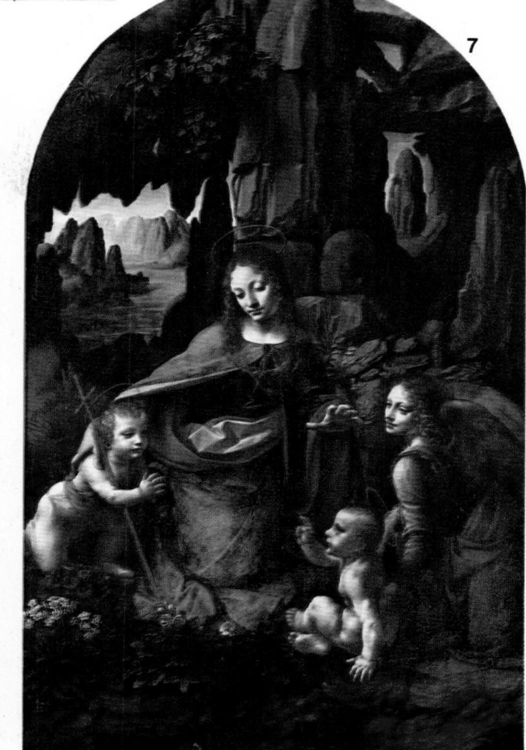

7

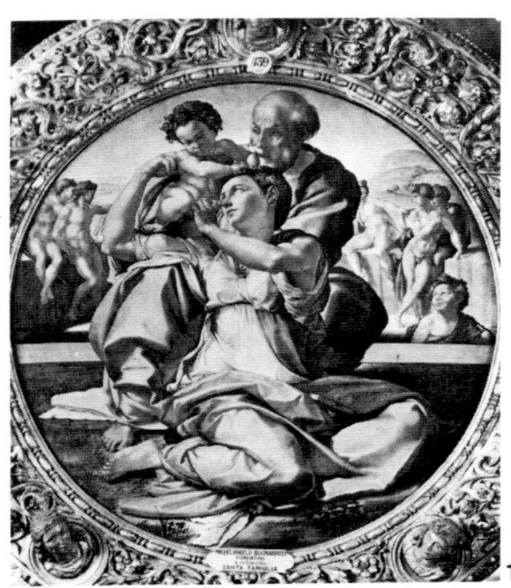
1

Michelangelo (1475–1564)

1. *The Holy Family* (Doni Tondo). 1504–5. Uffizi, Florence
2. *Dawn*. Detail from tomb of Lorenzo de'Medici. 1524–31. New Sacristy of S. Lorenzo, Florence
3. *Pietà*. Detail. About 1548–56. Florence Cathedral
4. *Ignudi*. Detail from ceiling fresco. About 1511. Sistine Chapel, Vatican
5. *David*. 1501–4. Accademia, Florence
6. *Bound Slave*. 1513–14. Louvre, Paris

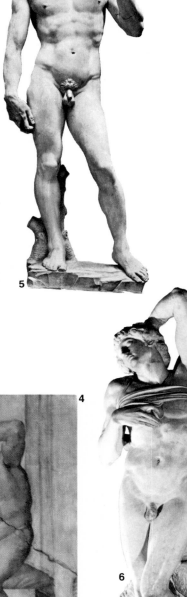

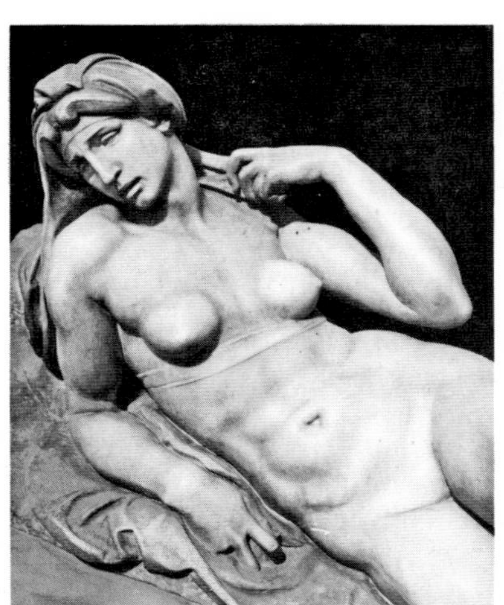
2

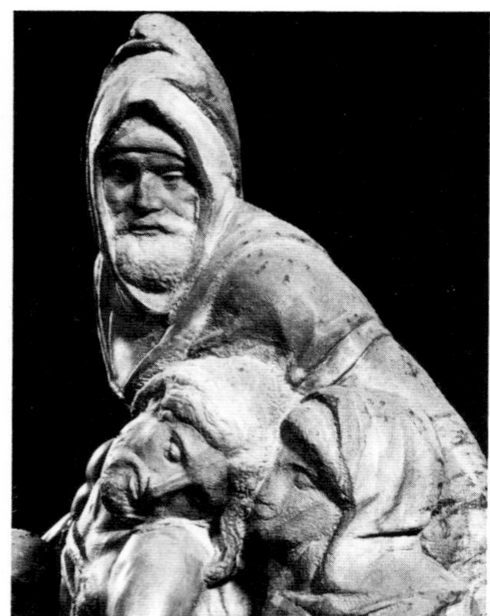
3

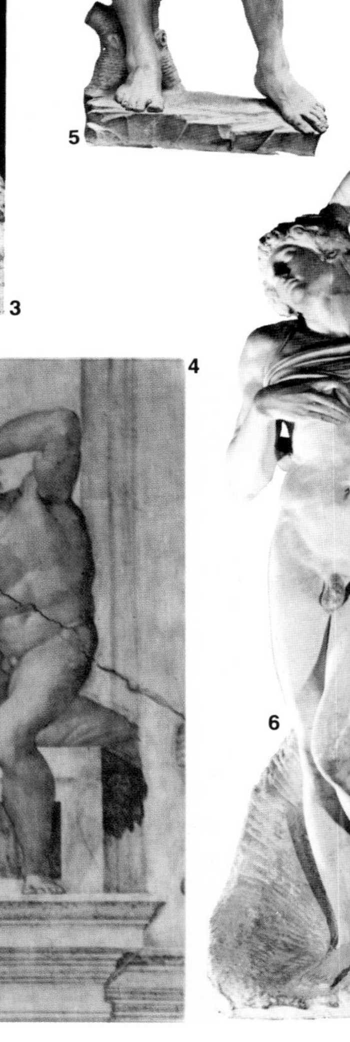
5

6

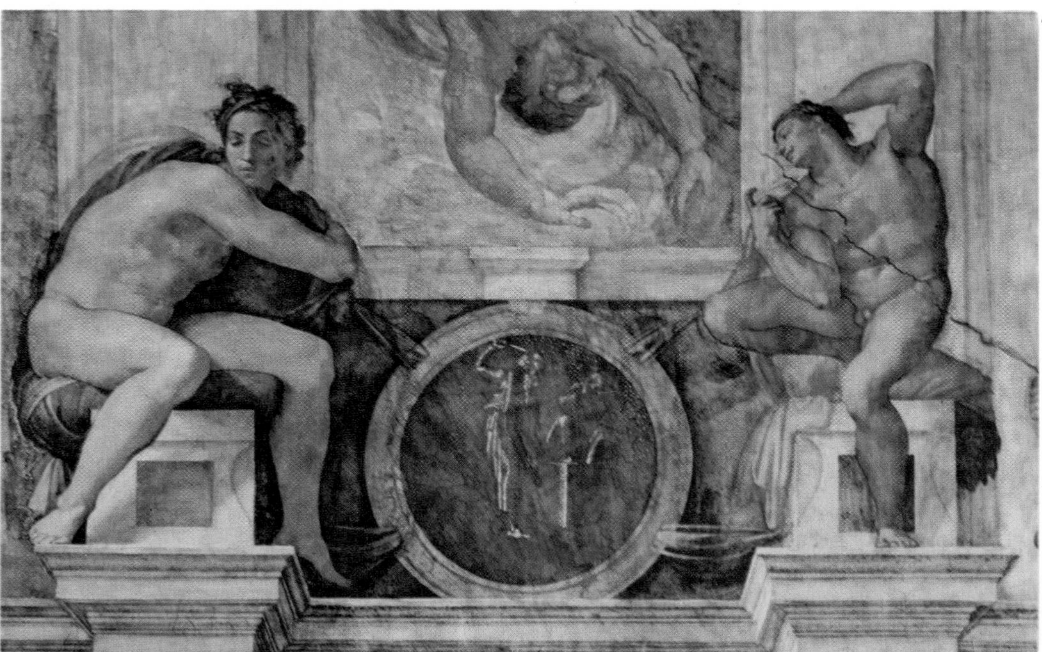
4

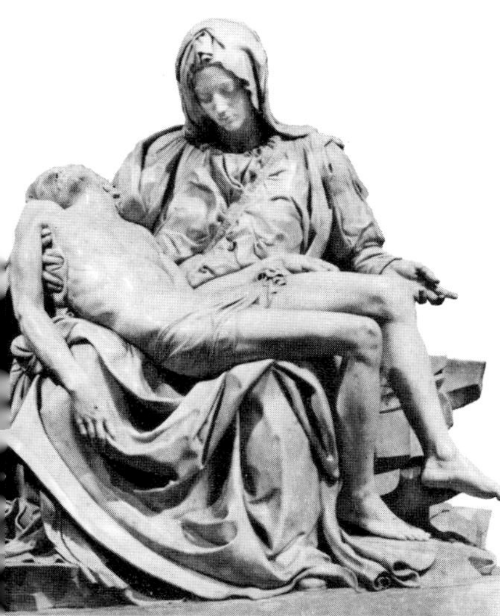
1

Michelangelo (1475–1564)

1. *Pietà.* 1497–9. St Peter's, Rome
2. *Archers shooting at a Herm.* Red chalk. Royal Collection. Reproduced by gracious permission of Her Majesty The Queen
3. *The Entombment.* About 1508. National Gallery, London
4. *The Prophet Joel.* Detail from ceiling fresco. About 1509. Sistine Chapel, Vatican
5. *The Creation of the Sun and Moon.* Detail from ceiling fresco. 1508–12. Sistine Chapel, Vatican
6. *The Damned.* Detail from *The Last Judgement* fresco. 1536–41. Sistine Chapel, Vatican

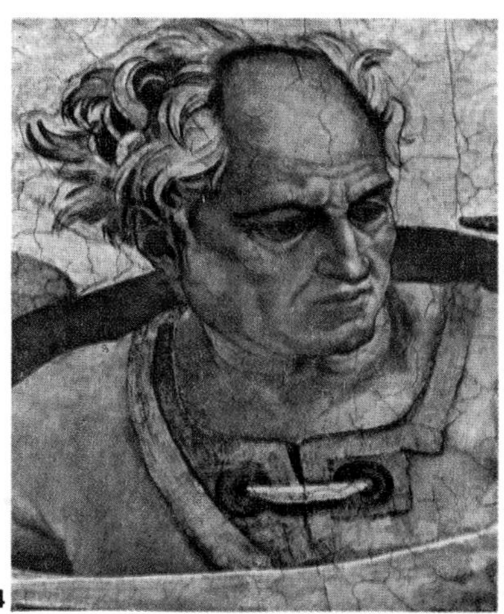
4

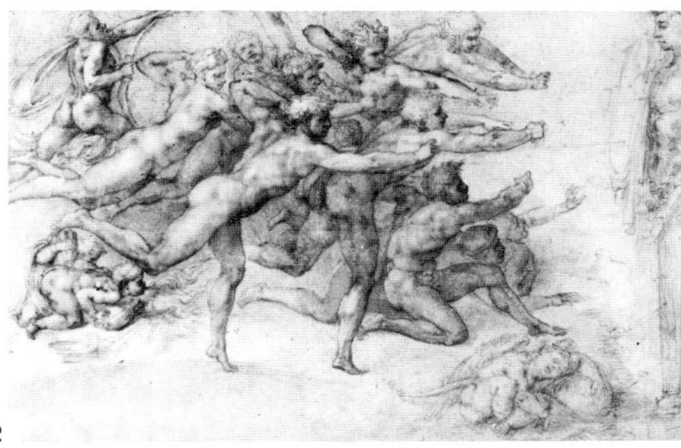
2

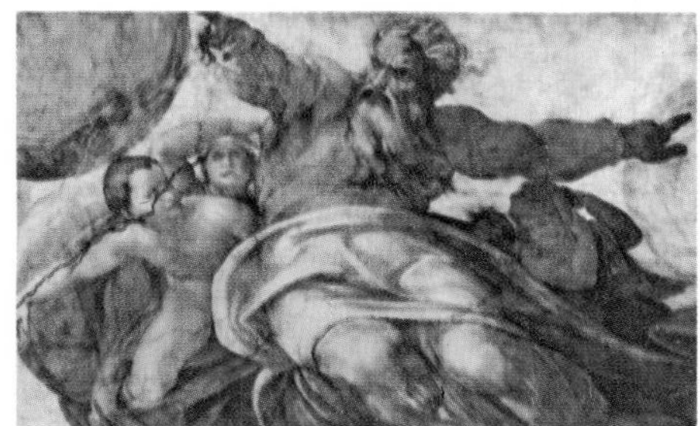
5

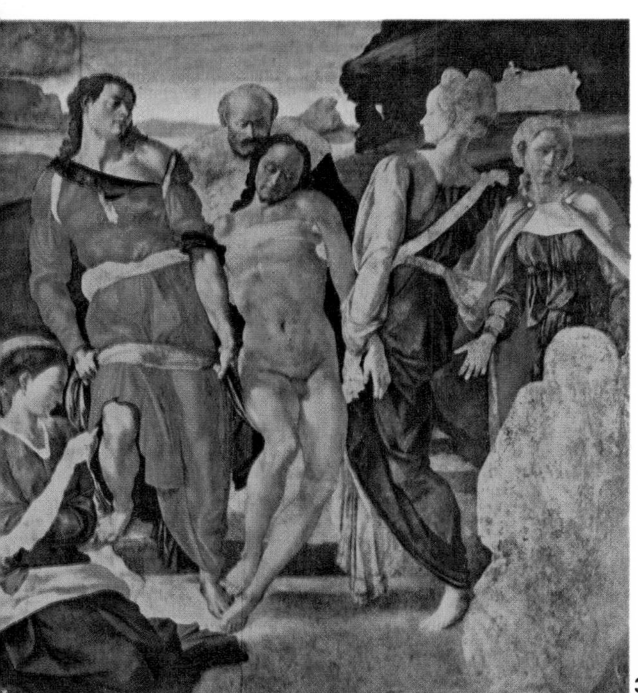
3

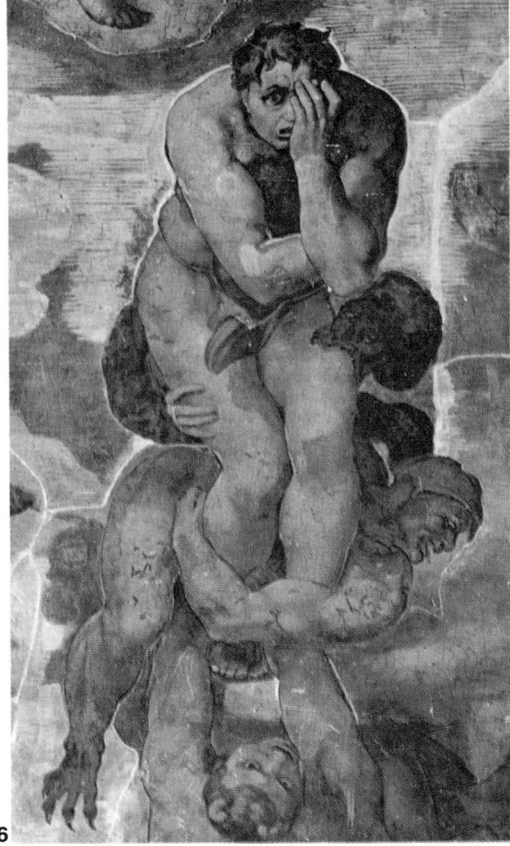
6

Michelangelo (1475–1564)

1. Biblioteca Laurenziana, Florence. Detail of vestibule. Begun 1524; completed 1560 by Bartolommeo Ammanati
2. St Peter's, Rome. Detail of west elevation
3. Dome of St Peter's, Rome. 1558–61. Remodelled by Giacomo della Portà in 1588–90
4. Piazza del Campidoglio, Rome. Begun 1544. Statue of Marcus Arelius in the centre

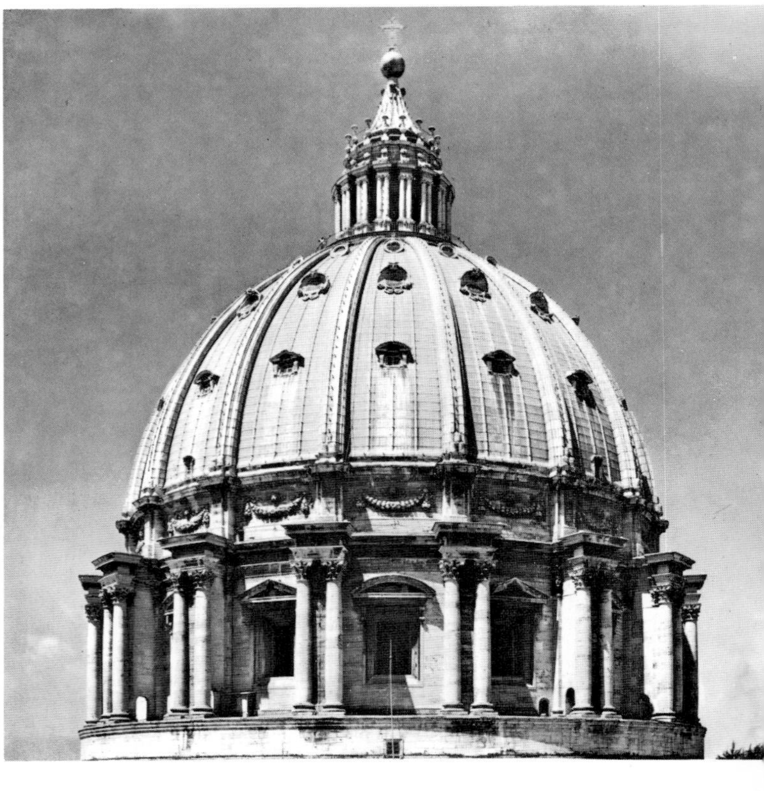

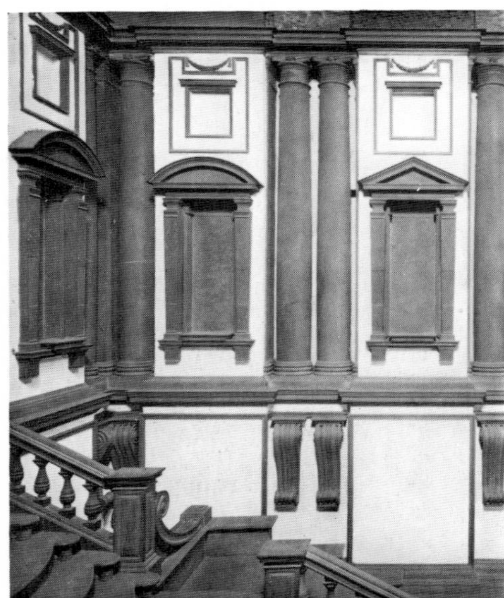

1

4

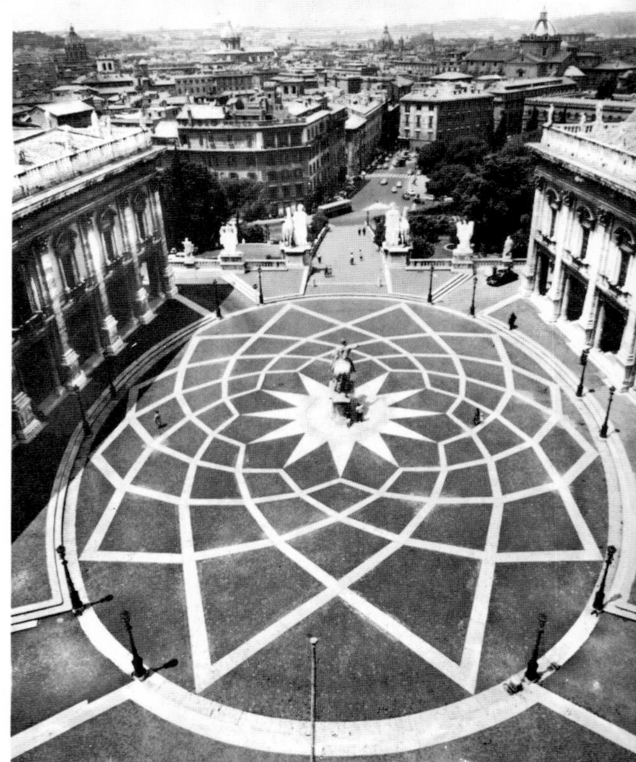

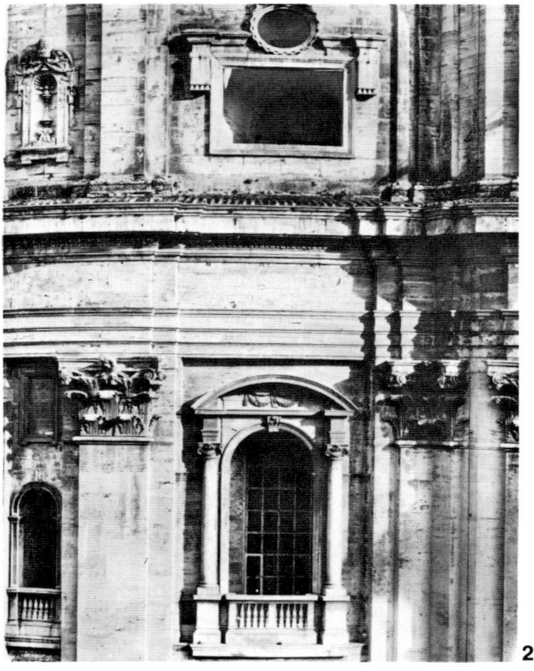

2

ramante (1444–1514)

, Exterior decoration of the apse, S. Maria delle Grazie, Milan. About 1492–5

Plan for St Peter's, Rome (not used). 1506

3. with Cola di Matteuccio: S. Maria della Consolazione, Todi. Completed early 17th century
4. *Christ at the Pillar.* Brera, Milan
5. Cloister, S. Maria della Pace, Rome. 1504
6. Tempietto, S. Pietro in Montorio, Rome. 1502

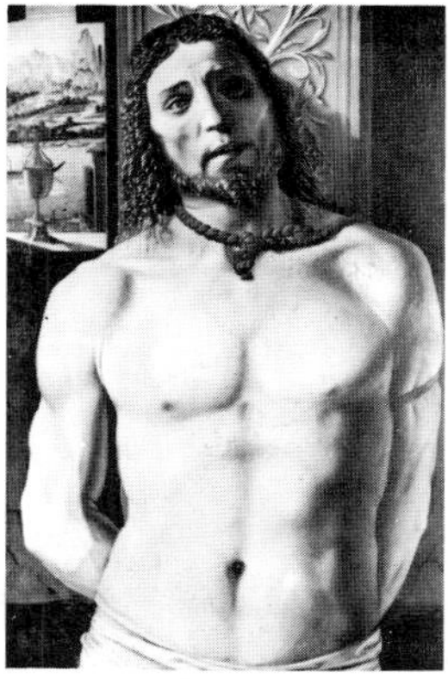

4

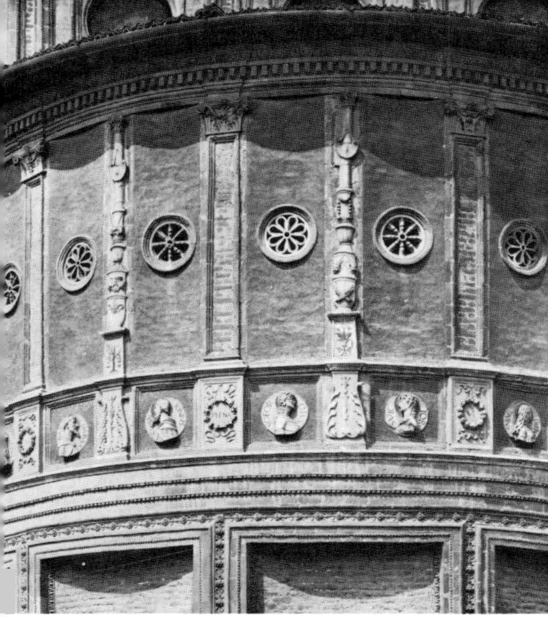

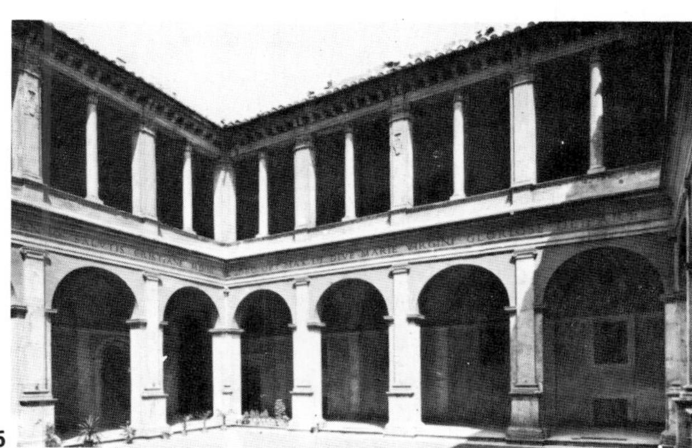

5

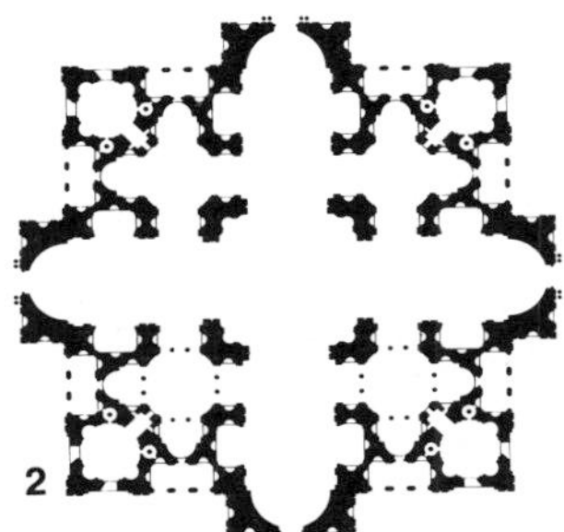

2

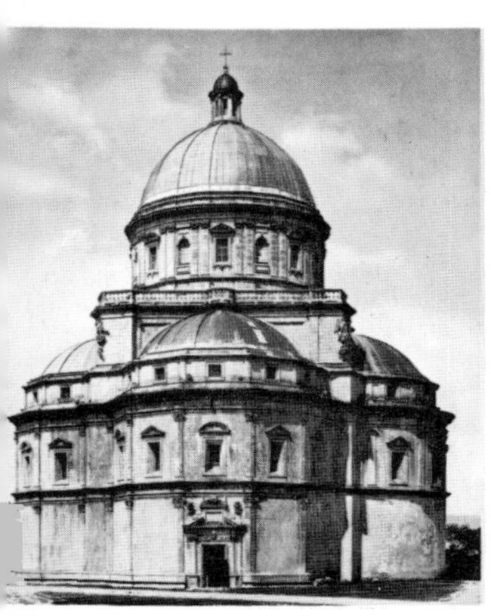

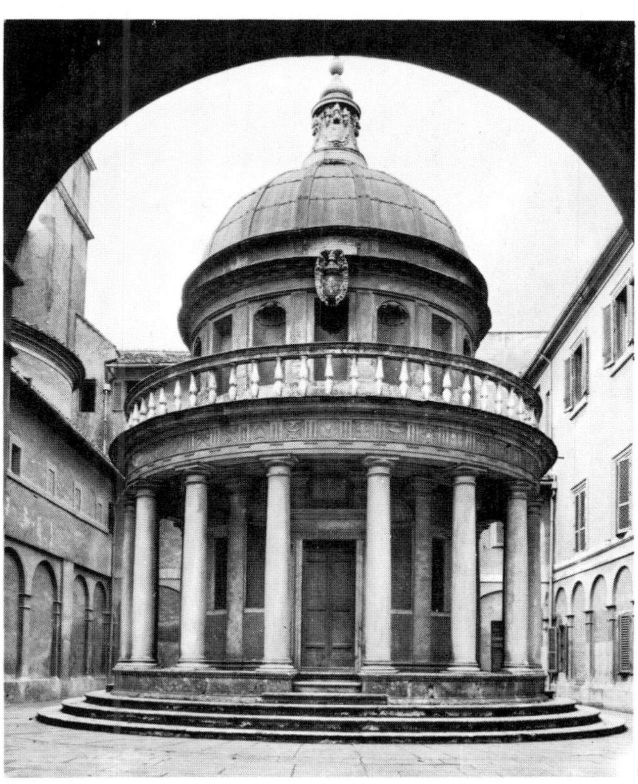

6

Raphael (1483–1520)
1. Perspective drawing. Uffizi, Florence
2. *The Marriage of the Virgin.* 1504. Brera, Milan
3. *The Tempi Madonna.* About 1505. Alte Pinakothek, Munich
4. *Madonna of the Goldfinch.* About 1506. Uffizi, Florence
5. *Swiss Guards.* Detail from the *Mass at Bolsena.* Fresco. 1512. Stanza d'Eliodo[r]o, Vatican

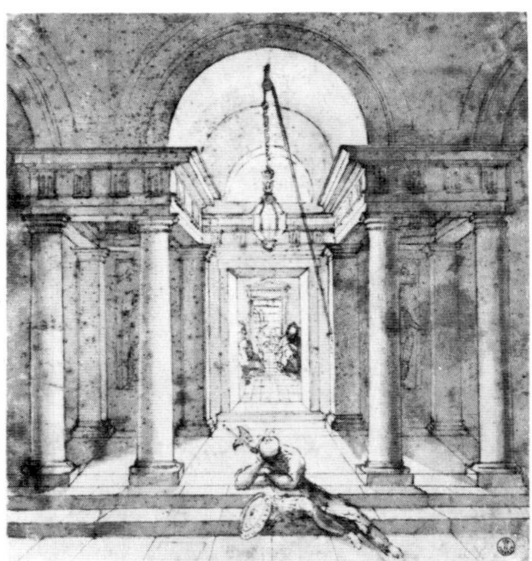

1

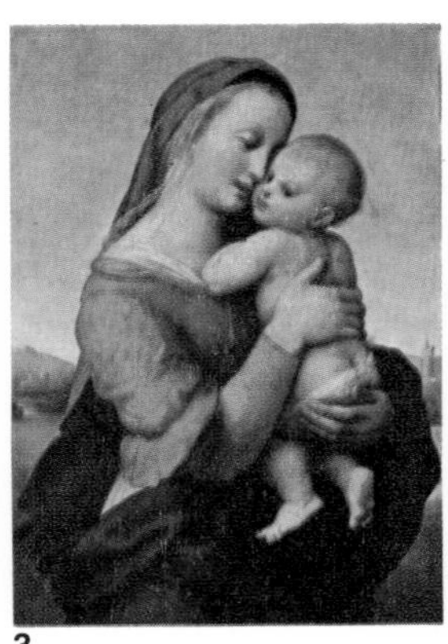

3

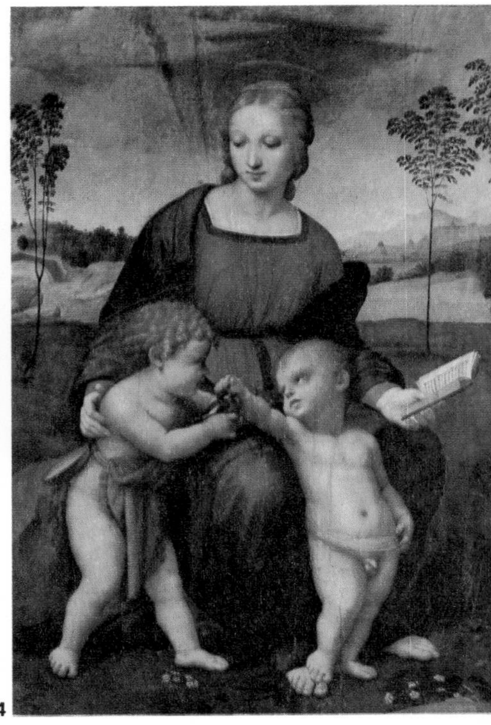

4

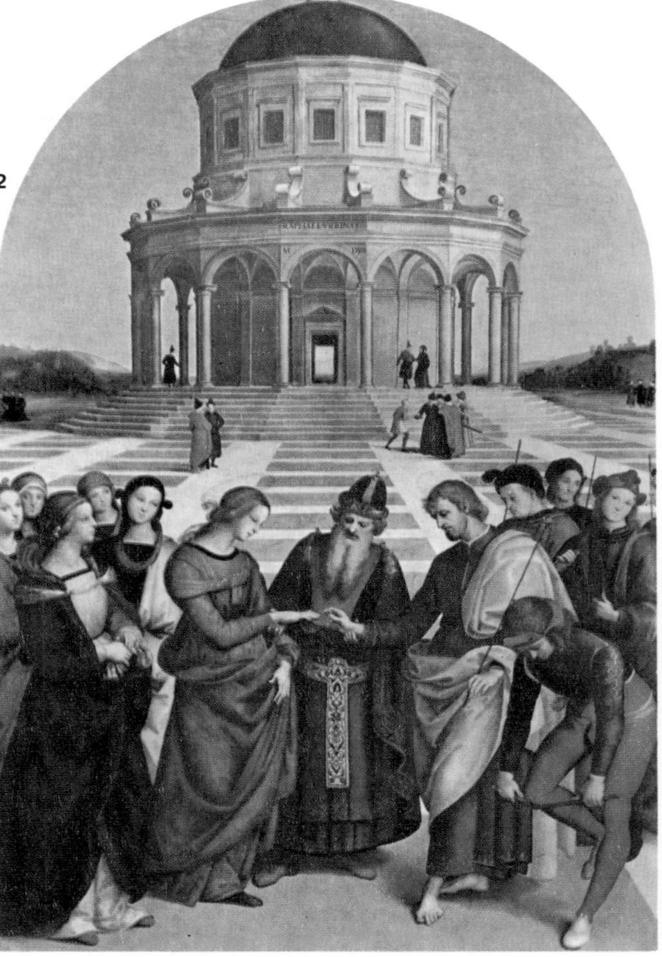

2

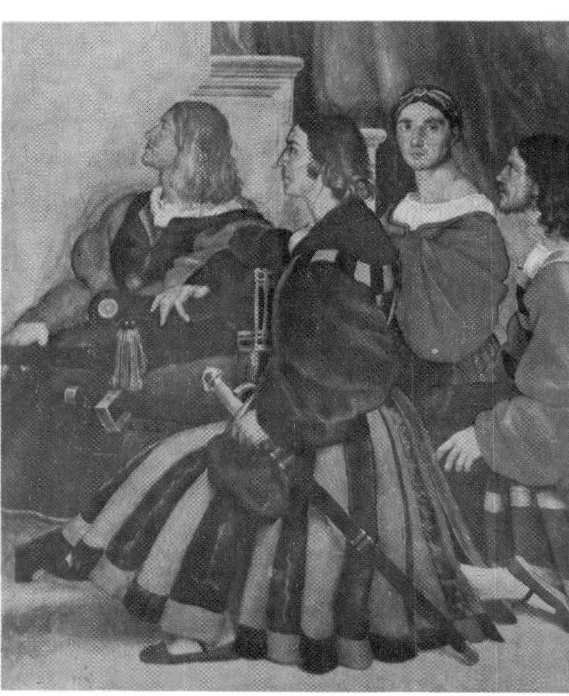

Raphael (1483–1520)

1. *Portrait of Agnolo Doni.* About 1506. Palazzo Pitti, Florence
2. *The School of Athens.* Detail. Fresco. 1509–11. Stanza della Segnatura, Vatican
3. Palazzo Vidoni, Rome. About 1515–20. Subsequently altered
4. *Galatea.* Fresco. 1511–12. Villa Farnesina, Rome
5. *The Madonna della Sedia.* 1514–15. Palazzo Pitti, Florence
6. *La Fornarina.* About 1515. Galleria Nazionale (Palazzo Barberini), Rome
7. *Pope Leo X (Medici) with two Cardinals.* About 1518. Palazzo Pitti, Florence

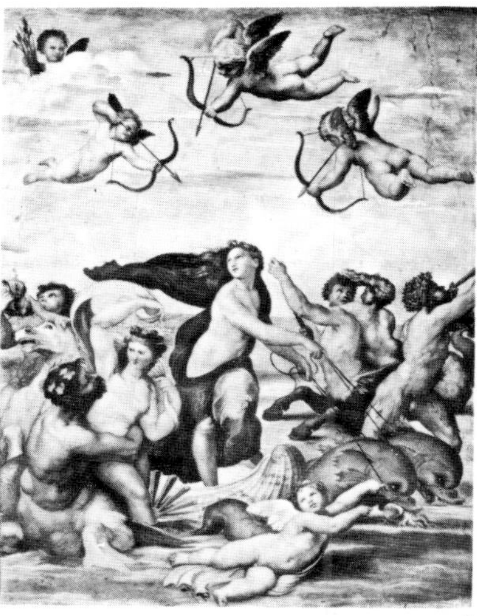

4

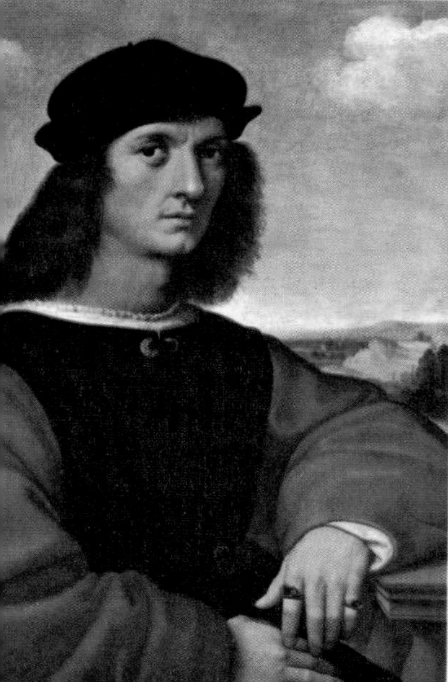

1

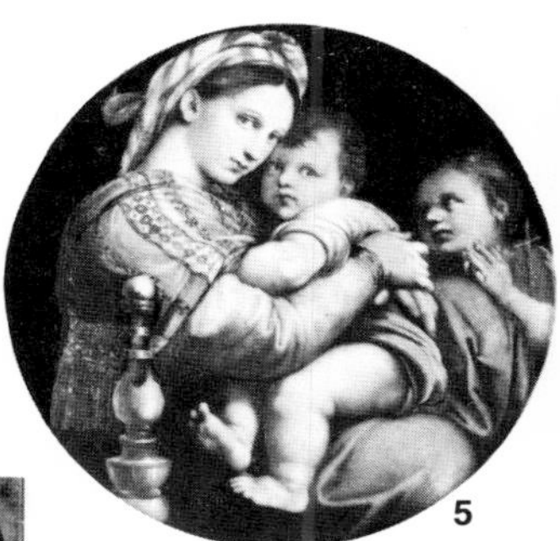

5

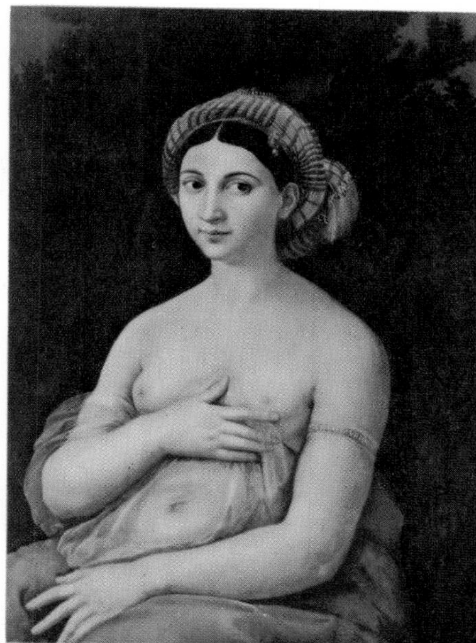

6

2

3

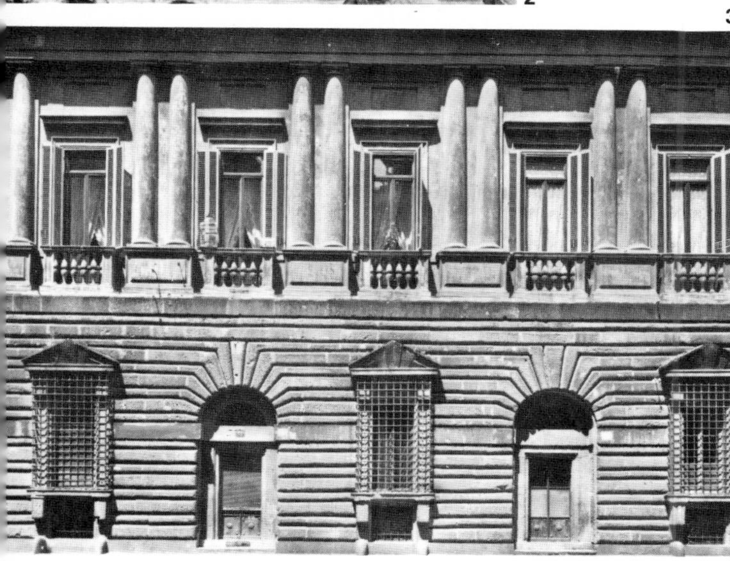

7

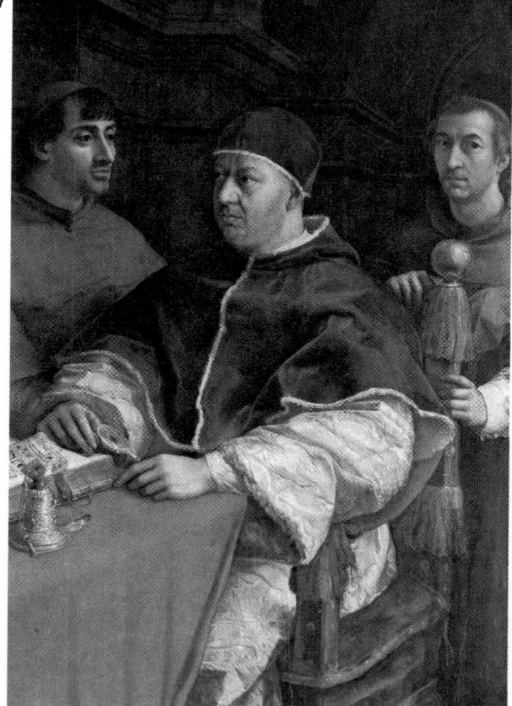

1. **Francesco di Giorgio Martini** (1439–1501/2): Church of S. Maria del Calcinaio, near Cortona. Commissioned 1484; completed 1516
2. **Antonio da Sangallo the Younger** (1485–1546): Palazzo Farnese, Rome. Begun 1534; completed after 1546 by Michelangelo
3. **Giuliano da Sangallo** (1445–1516): Courtyard of the Palazzo Gondi, Florence. 1490–4
4. **Giuliano da Sangallo** (1445–1516): Cupola of S. Maria delle Carceri, Prato. Begun 1485
5. **Jacopo Sansovino** (1486–1570): Libreria Vecchia, Venice. Begun 1536; completed 1588 by Scamozzi

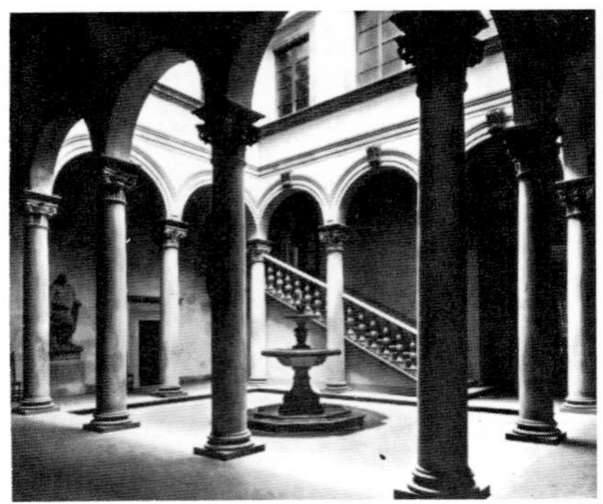

3

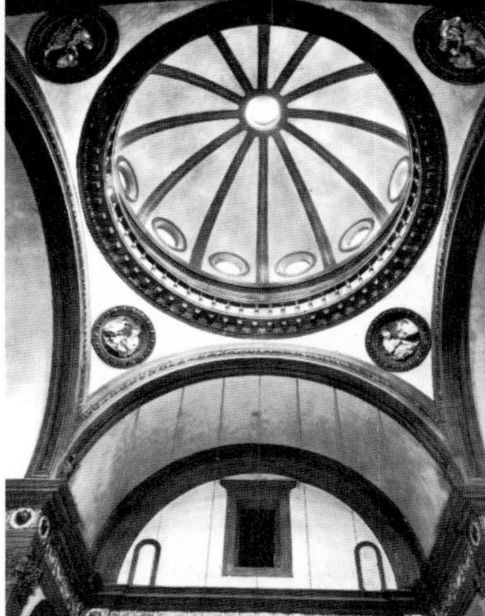

4

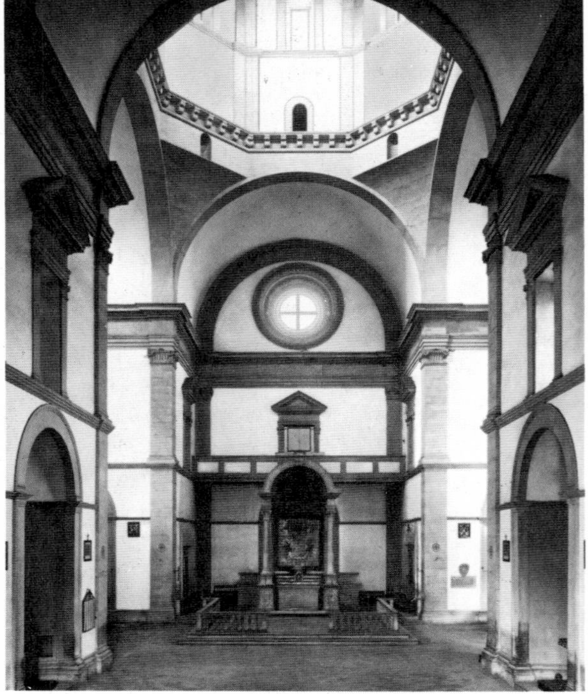

1

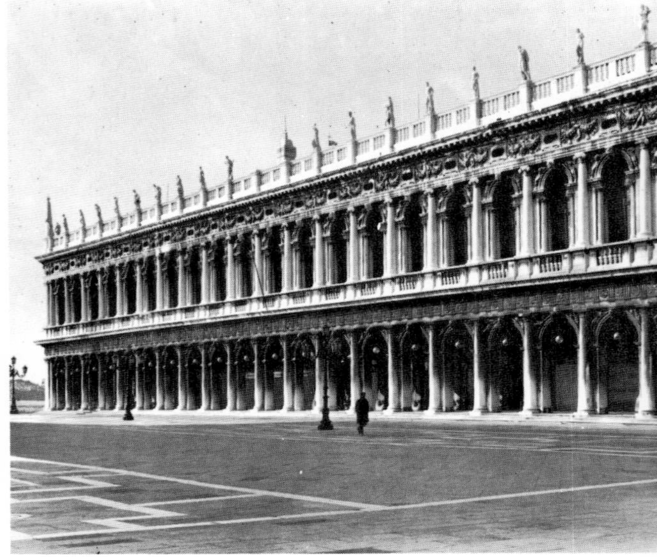

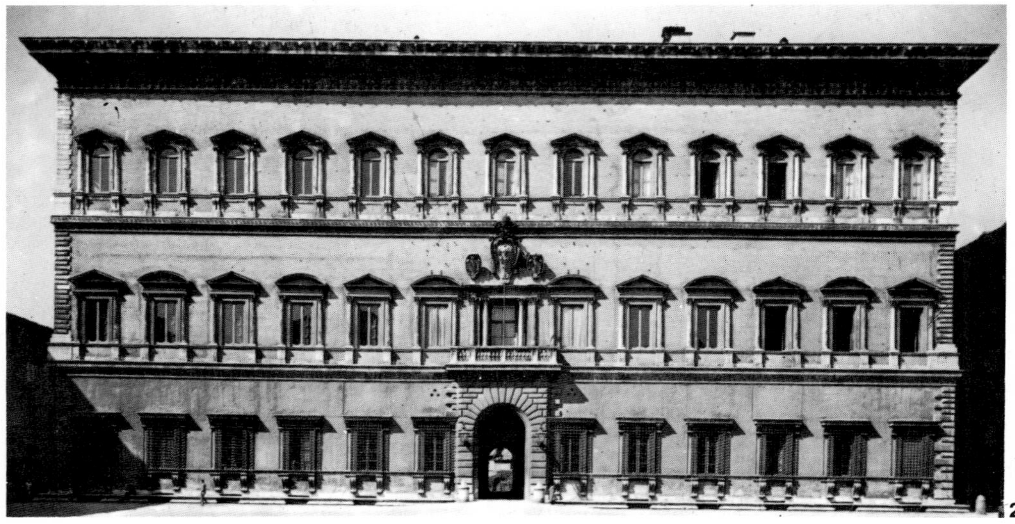

2

rreggio (1489/94–1534)
The Madonna and Child with St Catherine. Galleria Nazionale di Capodimonte, Naples
Danaë. 1530–2. Galleria Borghese, Rome
Madonna della Scodella. About 1530. Pinacoteca, Parma
4. *Leda and the Swan.* About 1530. Staatliche Museen, Berlin-Dahlem
5. *Jupiter and Io.* About 1530. Kunsthistorisches Museum, Vienna
6. Ceiling of the abbess's chamber, Convent of S. Paolo, Rome. Detail. About 1519

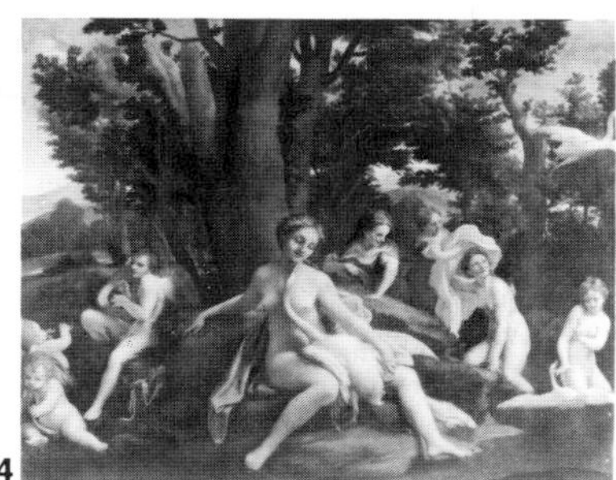
4

1
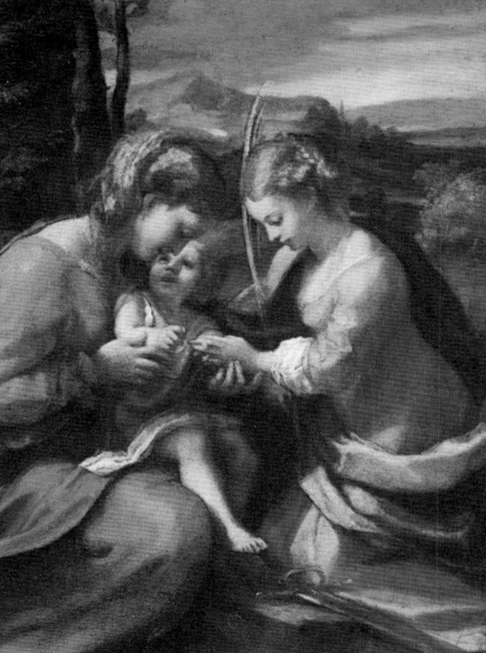

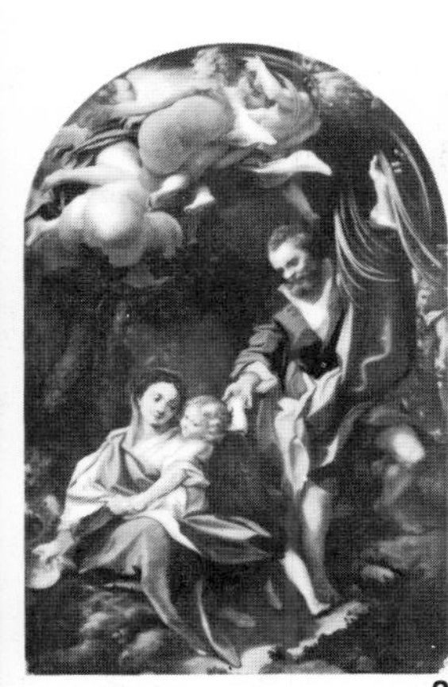
3

5
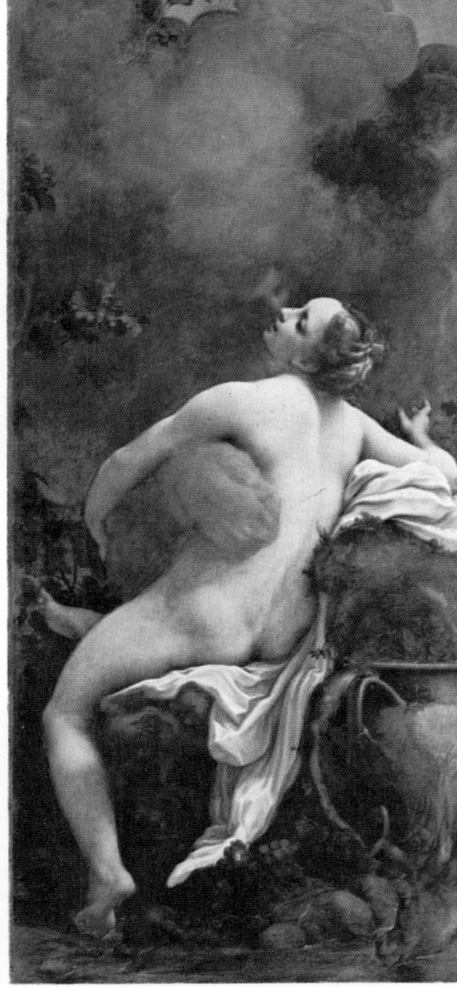

2
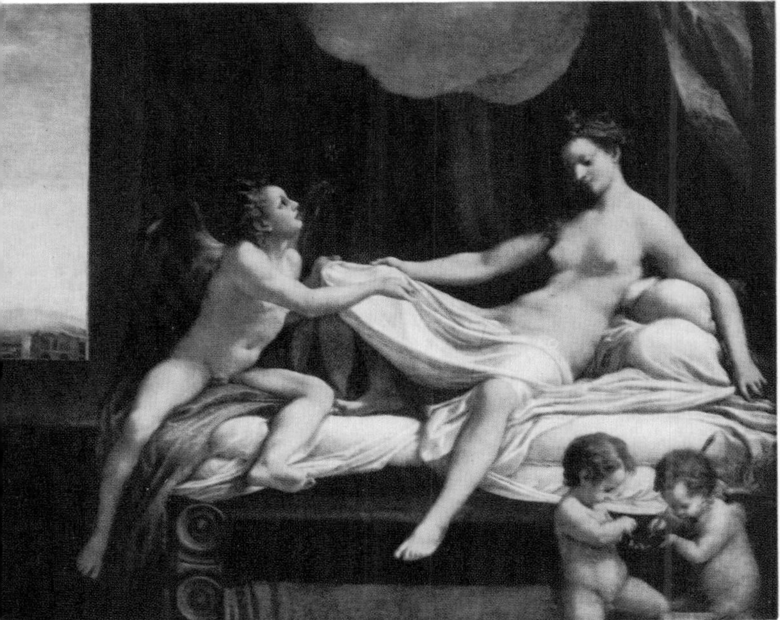

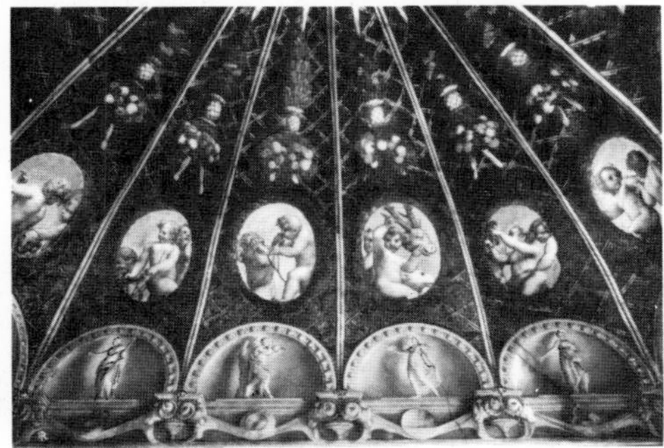
6

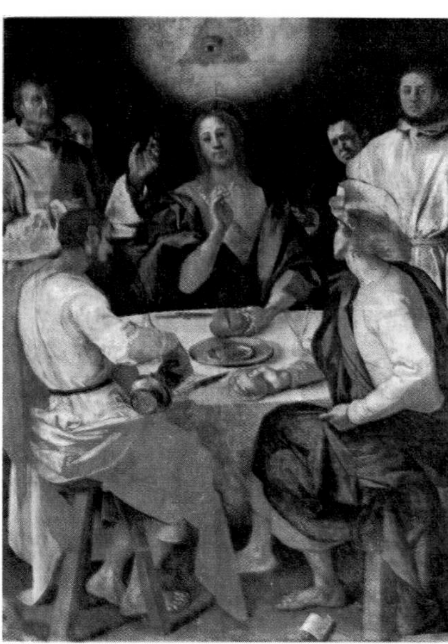

1

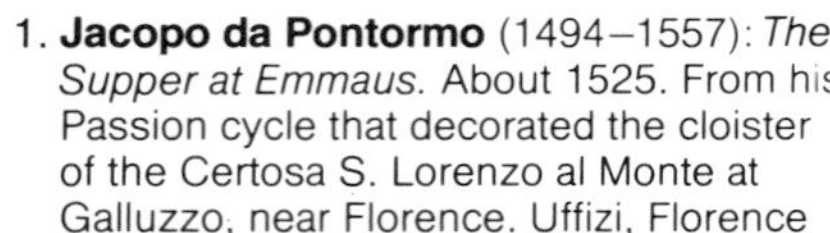

1. **Jacopo da Pontormo** (1494–1557): *The Supper at Emmaus.* About 1525. From his Passion cycle that decorated the cloister of the Certosa S. Lorenzo al Monte at Galluzzo, near Florence. Uffizi, Florence
2. **Giovanni Battista Rosso** (1494–1540): *Cherub playing a Lute.* Uffizi, Florence
3. **Jacopo da Pontormo** (1494–1557) or follower: *Portrait of Ugolino Martelli.* About 1445/50. National Gallery of Art (Samuel H. Kress Collection), Washington DC
4. **Giovanni Battista Rosso** (1494–1540 *The Deposition.* 1521. Pinacoteca, Volte
5. **Parmigianino** (1503–40): *The Madonr with the long Neck.* 1534–40 (unfinishe his death). Uffizi, Florence
6. **Giulio Romano** (1499?–1546): Palazz del Tè, Mantua. Courtyard façade. 1525–35

2

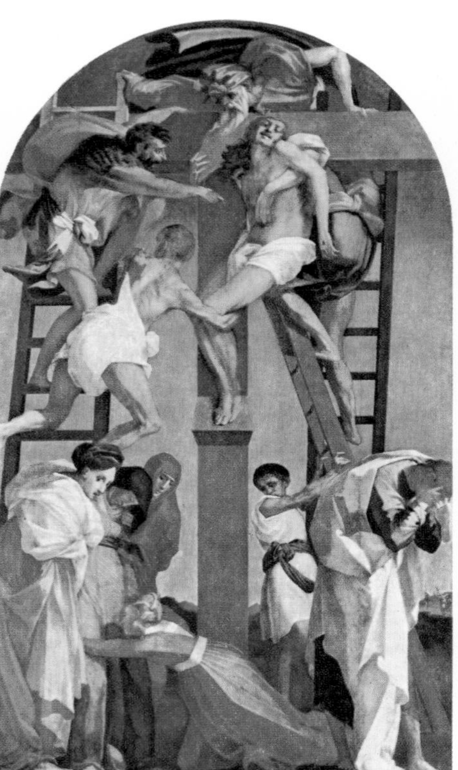

4

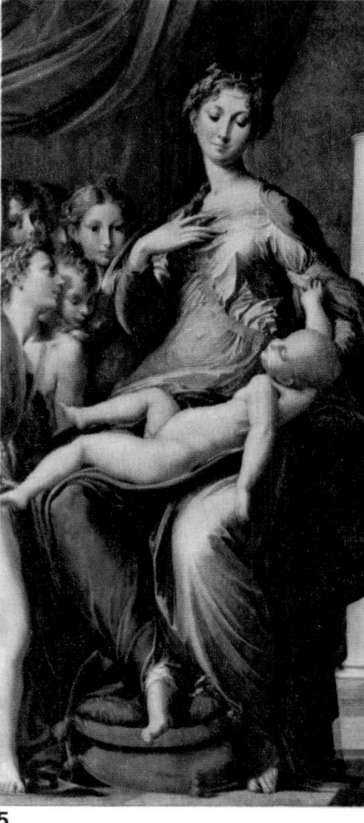

5

3

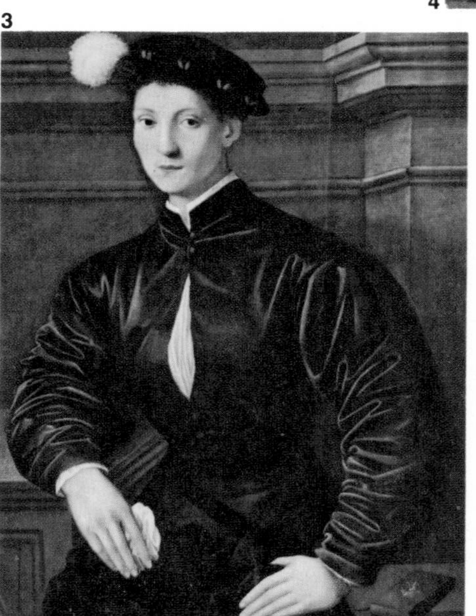

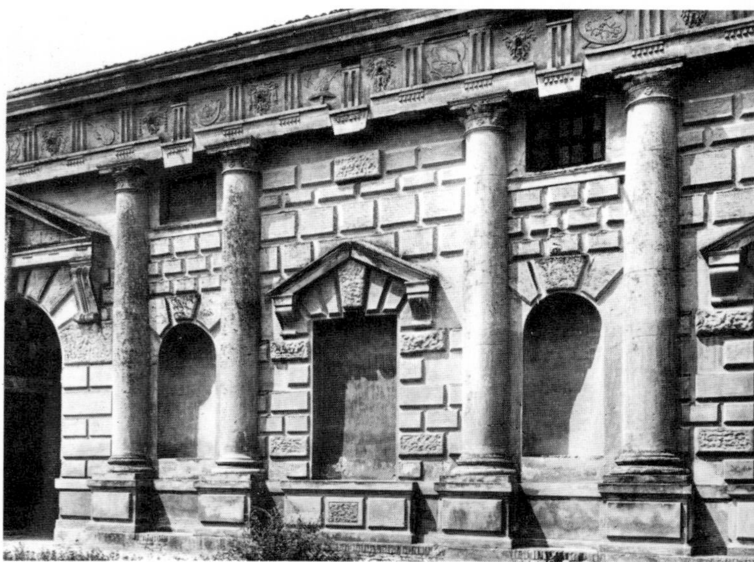

ɜiulio Romano (1499?–1546): *The Wedding of Psyche and Amor*. Fresco 1527–31. Palazzo del Tè, Mantua
Parmigianino (1503–40): *The Madonna of the Rose.* 1528–30. Gemäldegalerie, Dresden

3. **Agnolo Bronzino** (1503–72): *Portrait of Giovanni de' Medici.* 1475. Uffizi, Florence
4. **Giorgio Vasari** (1511–74): The Uffizi, Florence. Begun 1560
5. **Agnolo Bronzino** (1503–72): Detail from *Descent from the Cross.* 1545. Musée des Beaux-Arts, Besançon

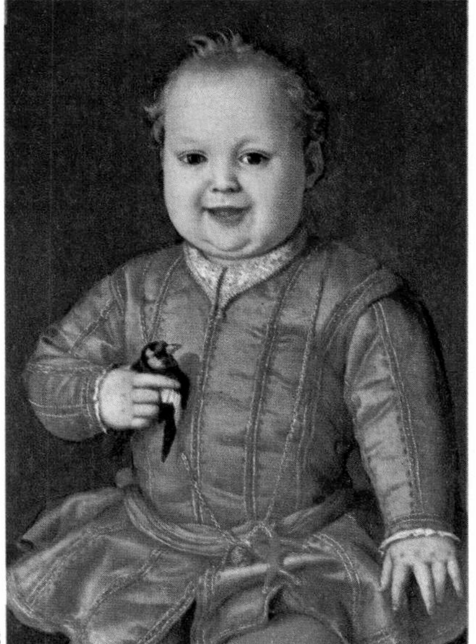
3

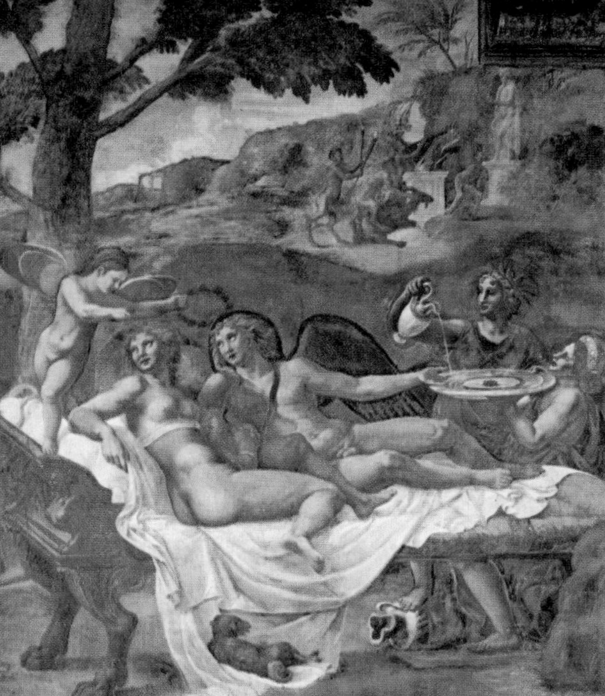
2

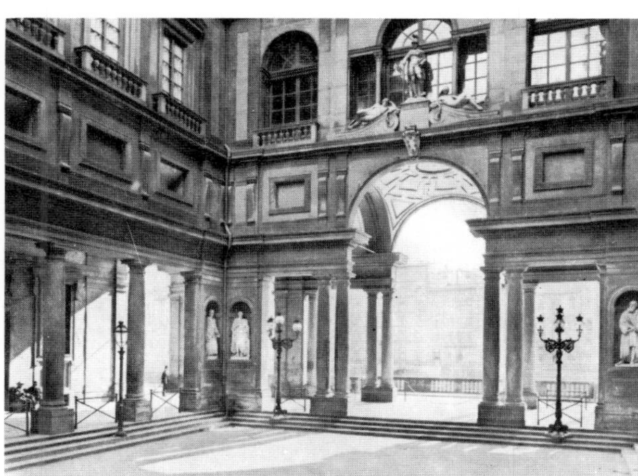
4

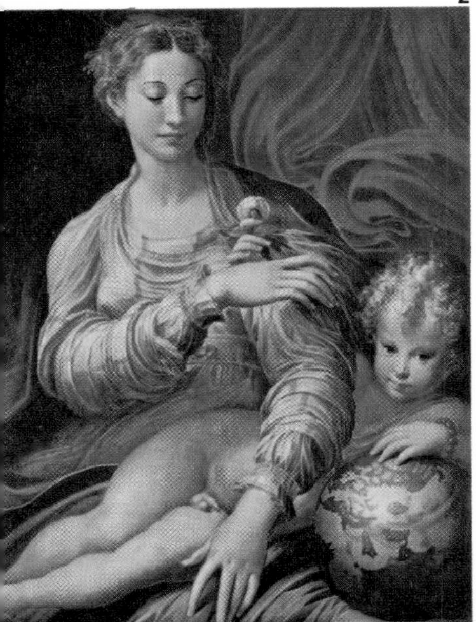

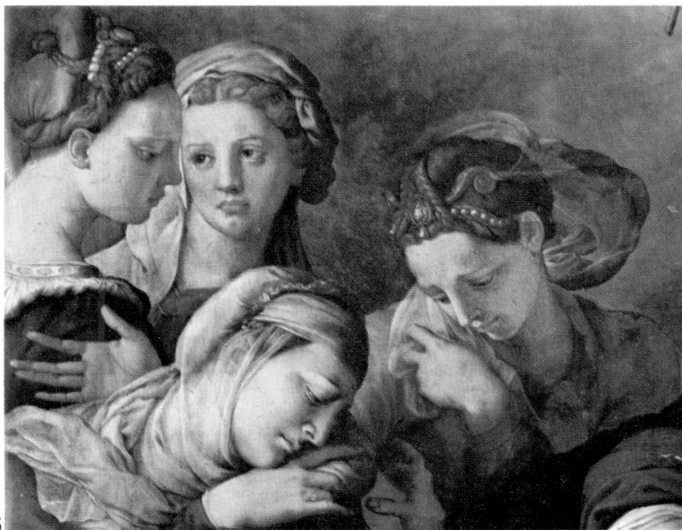
5

1. **Benvenuto Cellini** (1500–71): *Danaë with young Perseus.* Loggia dei Lanzi, Florence
2. **Benvenuto Cellini** (1500–71): *Head of Medusa.* Detail from *Perseus with the Head of Medusa.* 1545–54. Loggia dei Lanzi, Florence
3. **Giovanni Bologna** (1529–1608): *Mercury.* Bronze. Museo Nazionale, Florence
4. **Benvenuto Cellini** (1500–71): *Cosimo I de'Medici.* Bronze. 1546–7. Museo Nazionale, Florence
5. **Andrea Sansovino** (*c.*1467–1529): *Prudence.* Marble. 1505. S. Maria del Popolo, Rome
6. **Andrea Sansovino** (*c.*1467–1529): *The Annunciation.* Marble bas-relief from the S. Casa, Loreto. 1518–24
7. **Giovanni Bologna** (1529–1608): *La Fiorenza.* Bronze. About 1570–1. Villa Petraia, near Florence

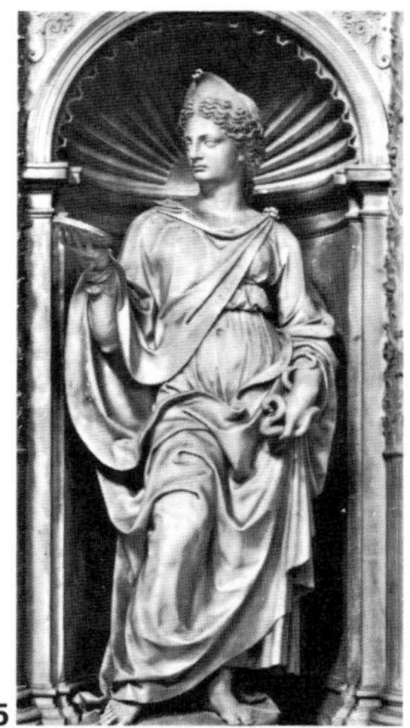
5

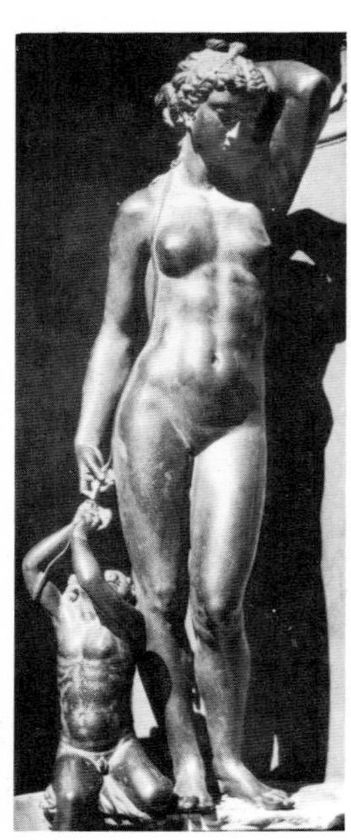
1

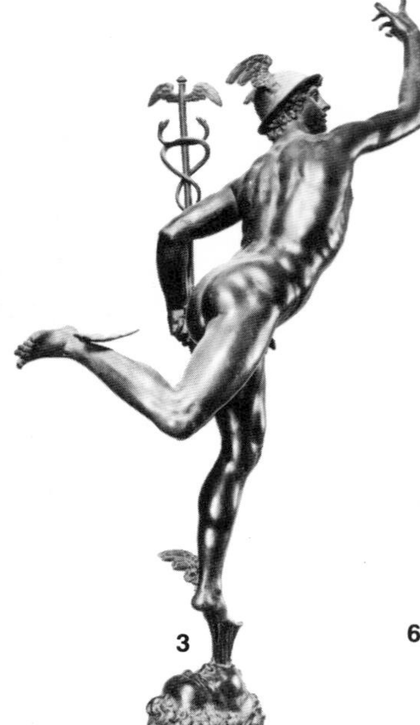
3

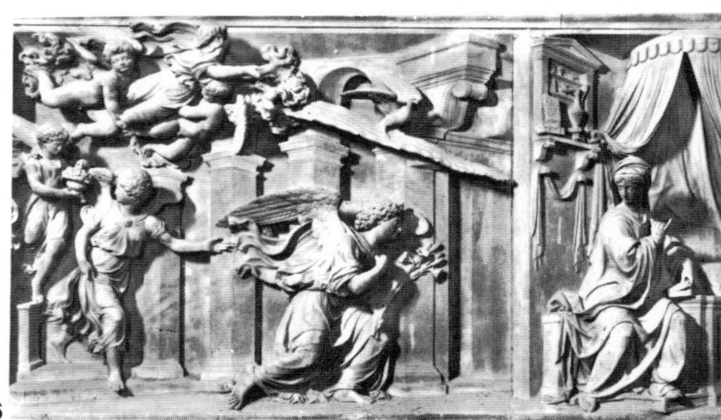
6

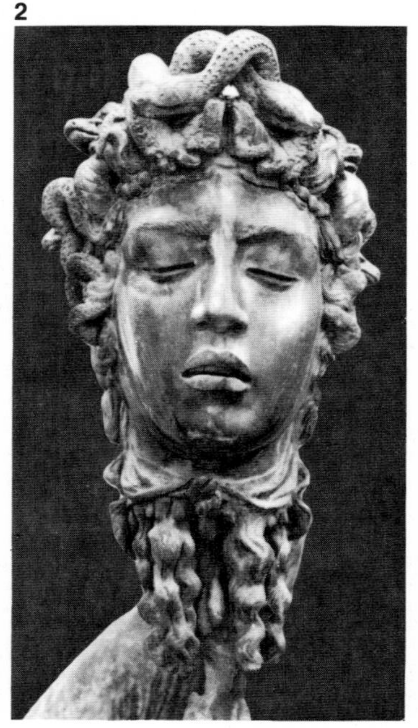
2

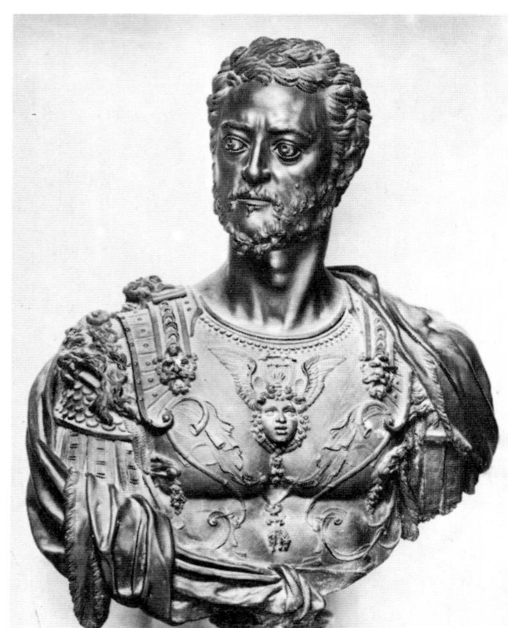
4

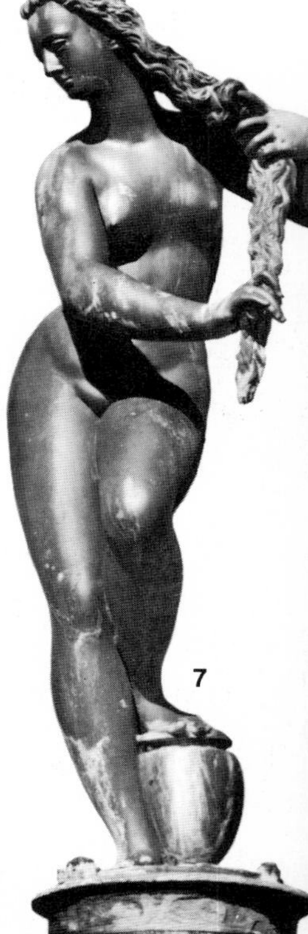
7

Giorgione (1477/8–1510)
1. *Le Concert champêtre.* Louvre, Paris
2. *The Tempest.* About 1505. Accademia, Venice
3. *Sleeping Venus.* Gemäldegalerie, Dresden
4. or **Titian:** *Portrait of a Venetian.* National Gallery of Art, Washington DC
5. *Judith.* About 1500. Hermitage, Leningrad

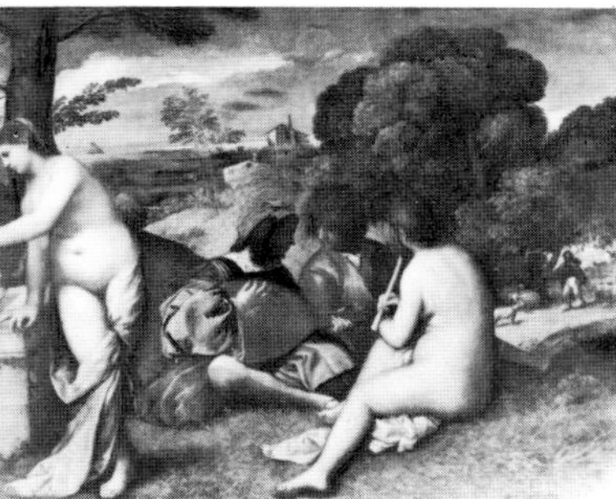

1

2

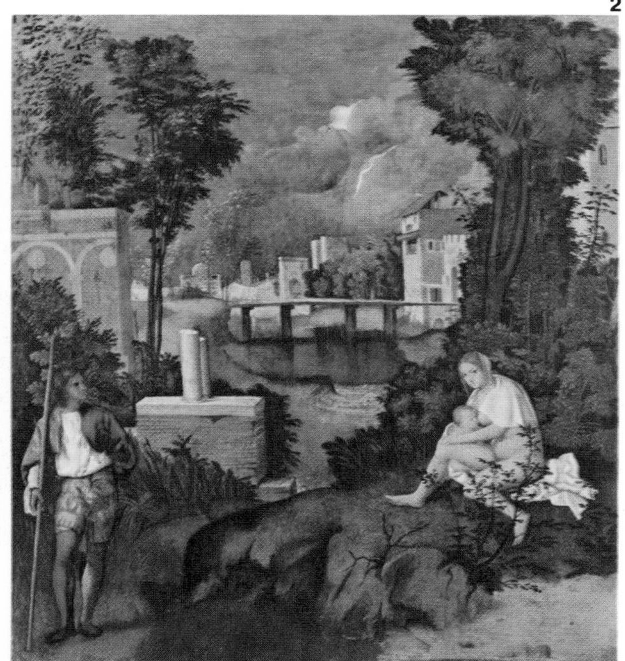

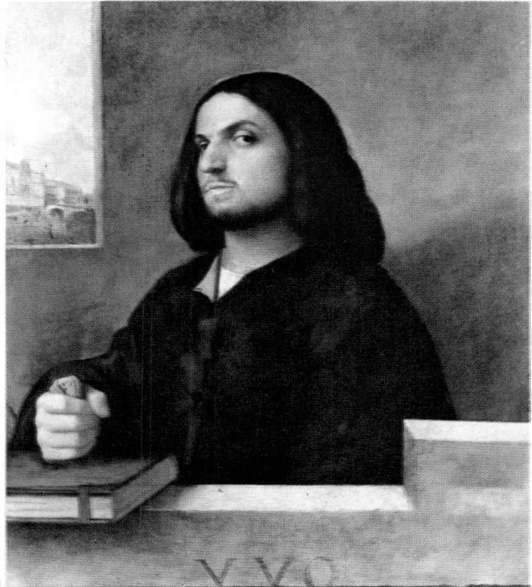

4

3

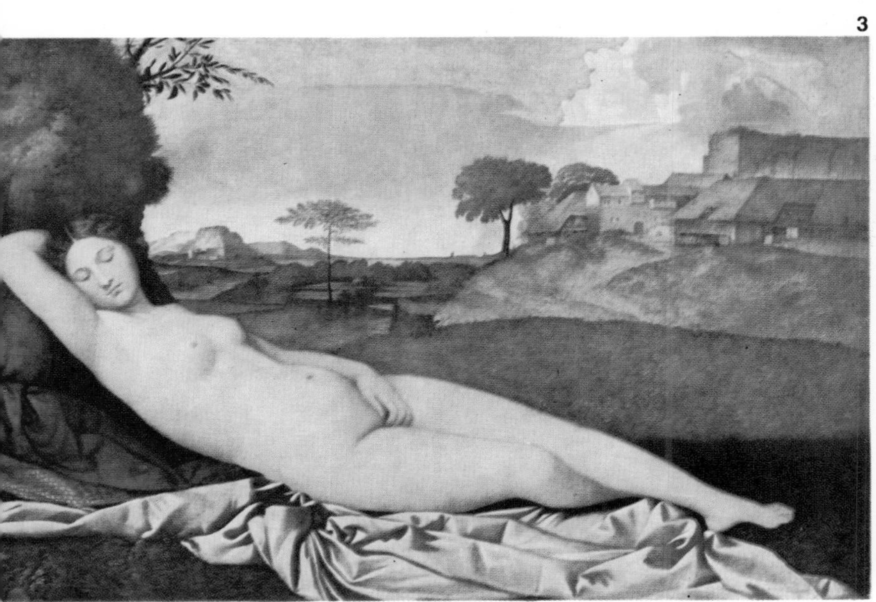

5

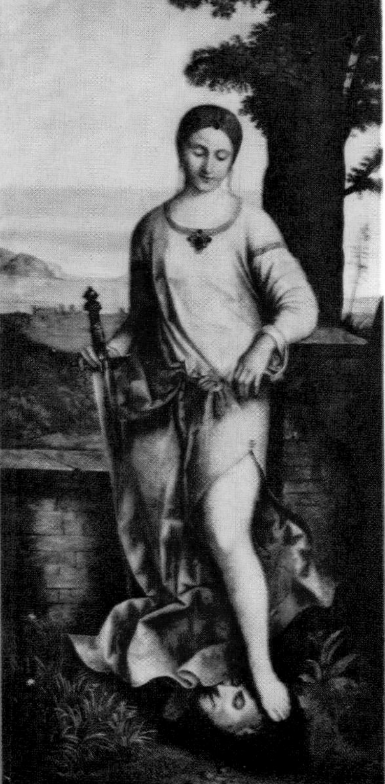

Titian (*c.*1489–1576)

1. *Landscape.* Pen and ink drawing. About 1516. Cabinet des Dessins, Louvre, Paris
2. *Venus and Adonis.* Detail. About 1554. Metropolitan Museum of Art, New York
3. *Venus of Urbino.* 1538. Uffizi, Florence
4. *Portrait of a Man.* Detail. 1540–5. Palazzo Pitti, Florence
5. *The Vendramin Family.* About 1550. National Gallery, London
6. *Emperor Charles V.* 1548. Alte Pinakothek, Munich

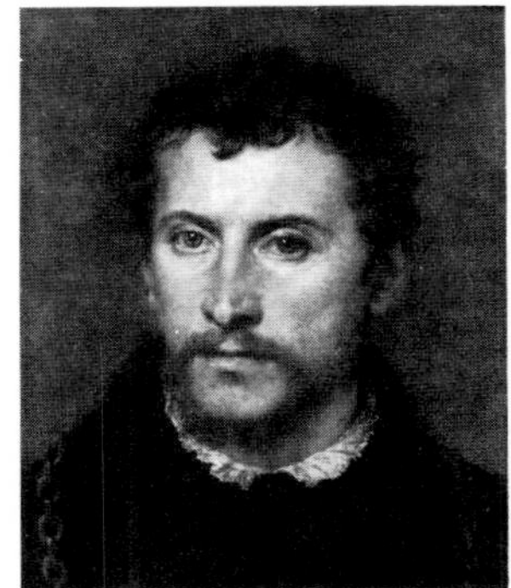
4

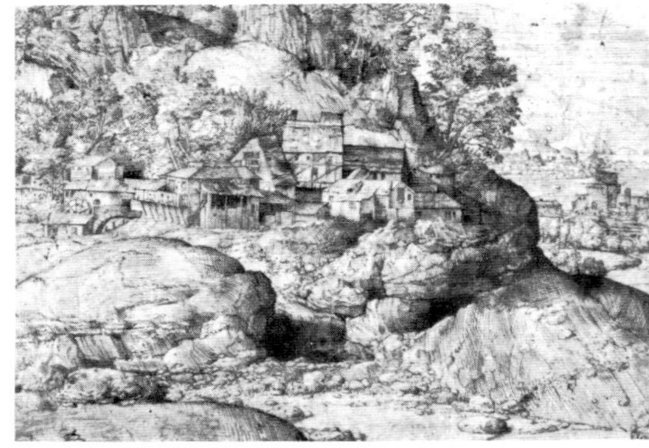
1

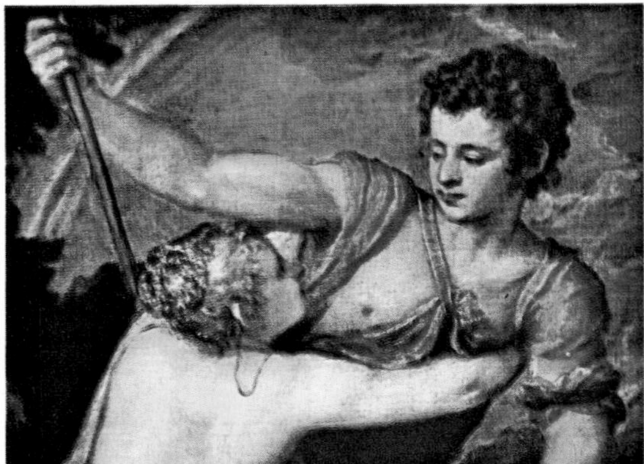
2

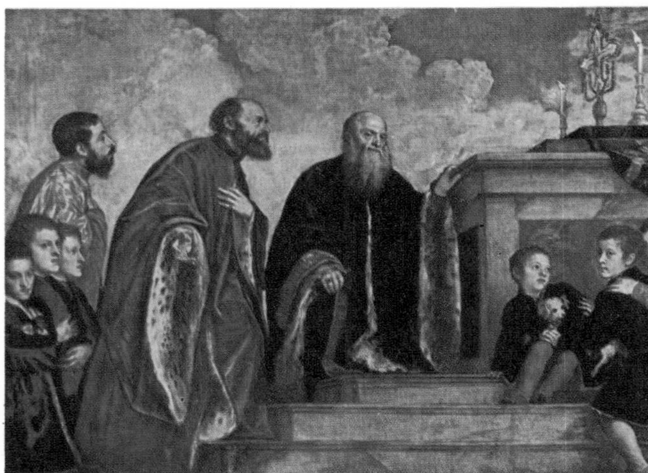

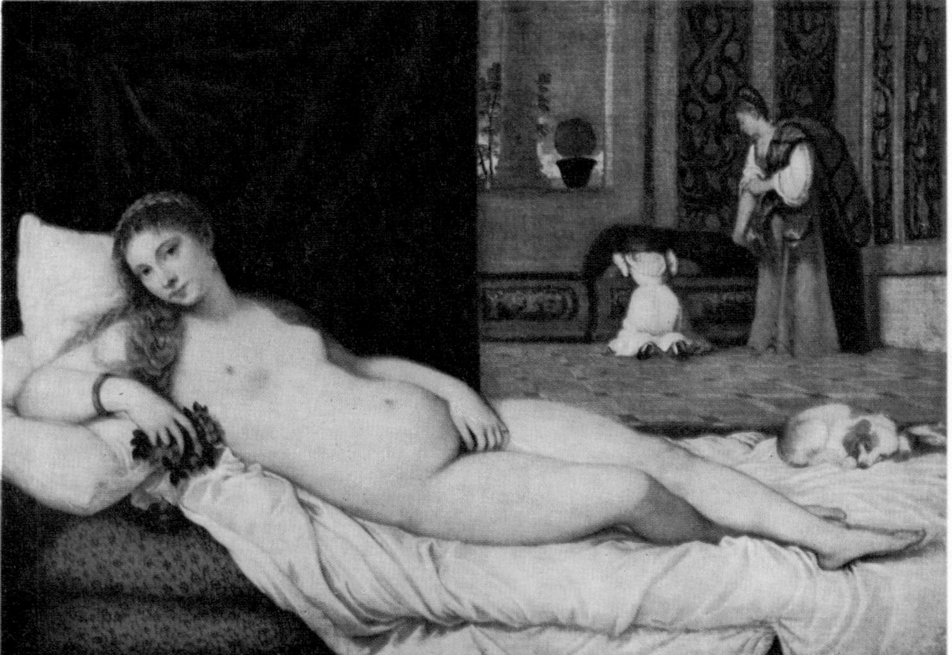
3

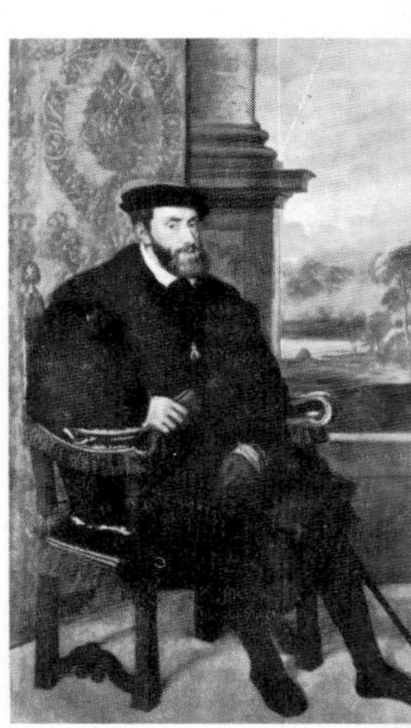

tian (*c.*1489–1576)
Empress Isabella. 1548. Prado, Madrid
Self-portrait. About 1565–70. Prado, Madrid
Sacred and Profane Love. About 1515. Galleria Borghese, Rome
4. *Pope Paul III and his Grandsons, Alessandro and Ottaviano Farnese.* 1545–6. Galleria Nazionale di Capodimonte, Naples
5. *Danaë.* 1554. Prado, Madrid

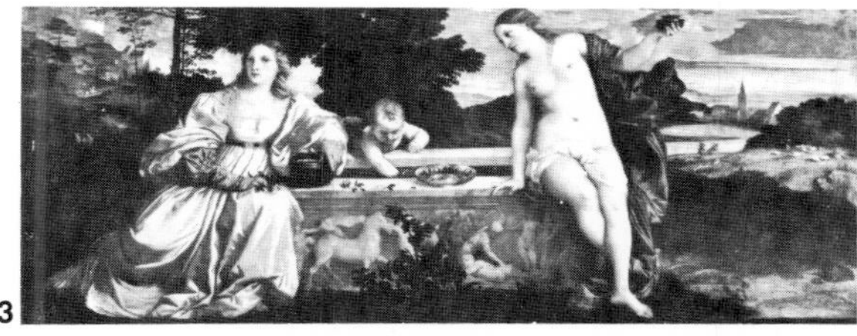

3

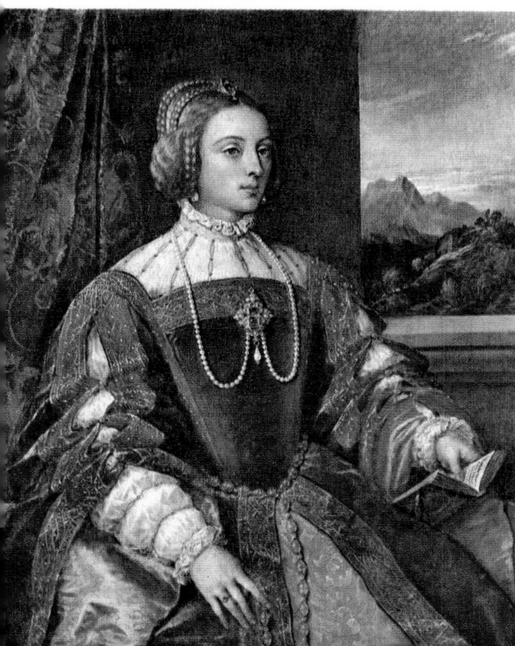

1

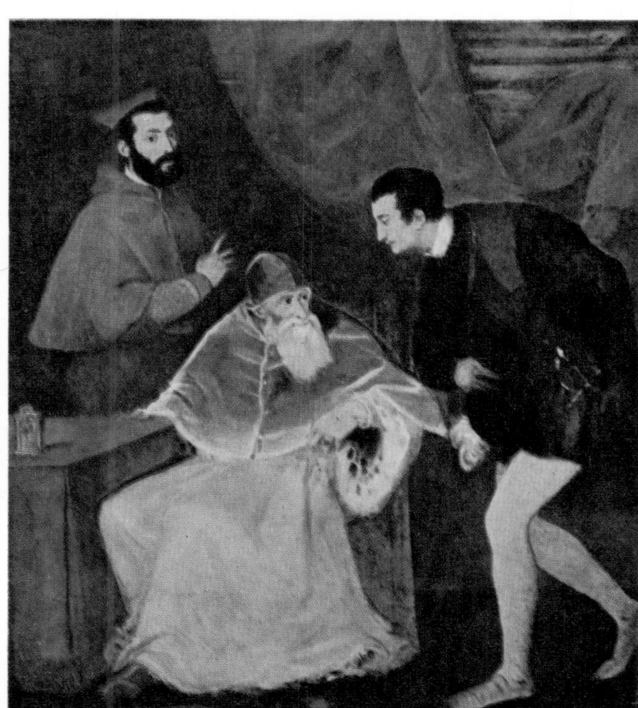

4

2

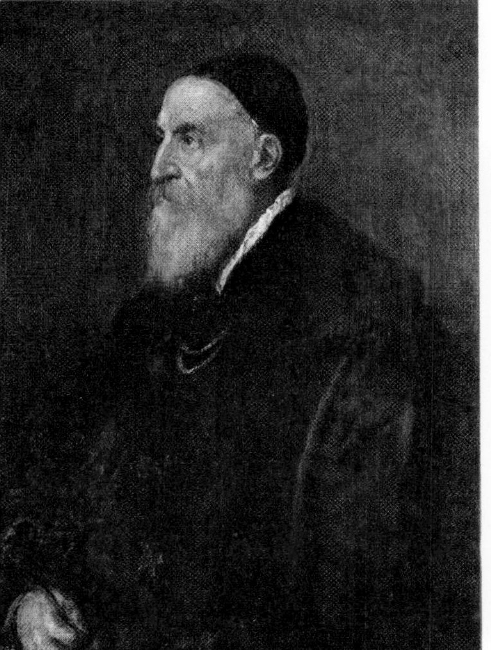

5

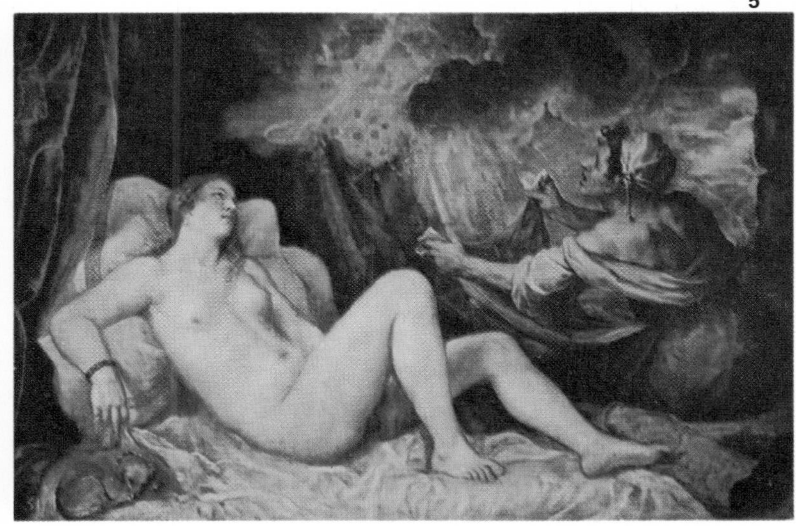

Tintoretto (1518–94)

1. *Christ washing the Disciples' Feet.* About 1550. Prado, Madrid
2. *Mars and Venus surprised by Vulcan.* Alte Pinakothek, Munich
3. *Christ at the Sea of Galilee.* National Gallery of Art (Samuel H. Kress Collection), Washington DC
4. *Susanna and the Elders.* About 1560–70. Kunsthistorisches Museum, Vienna
5. *Portrait of Jacopo Soranzo.* Accademia, Venice
6. *Christ in the House of Martha and Mary.* Alte Pinakothek, Munich
7. *Portrait of a Woman.* Prado, Madrid

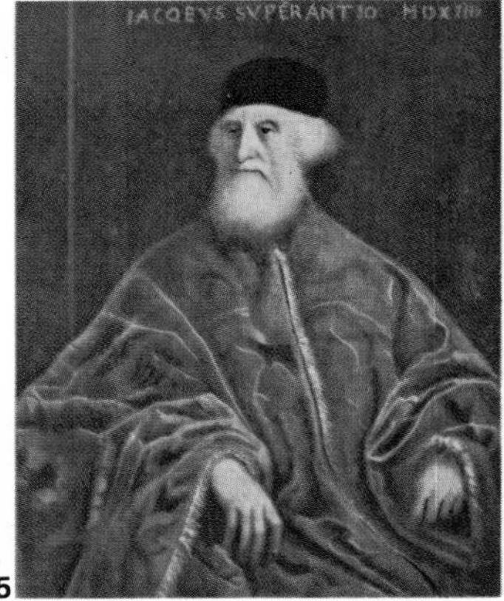

5

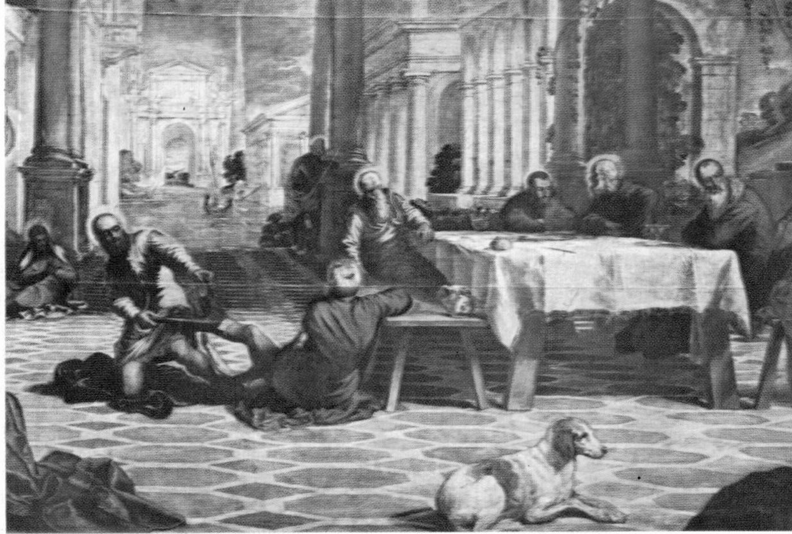

1

6

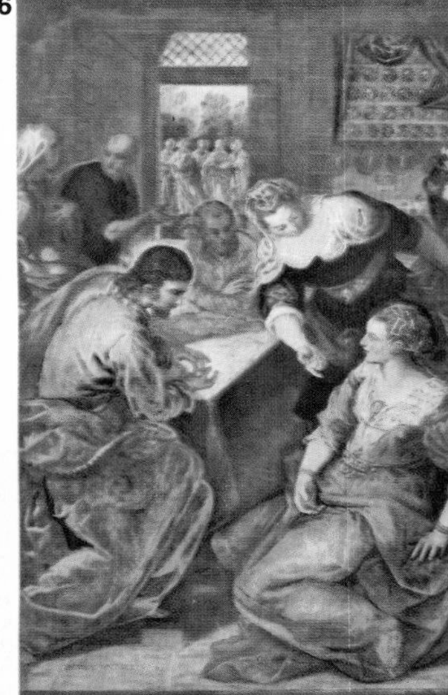

2

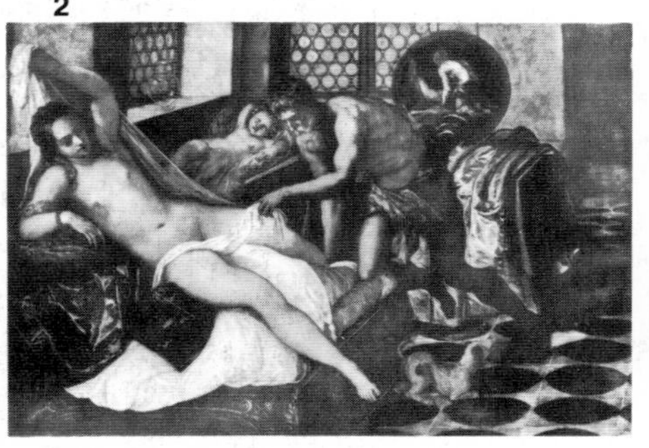

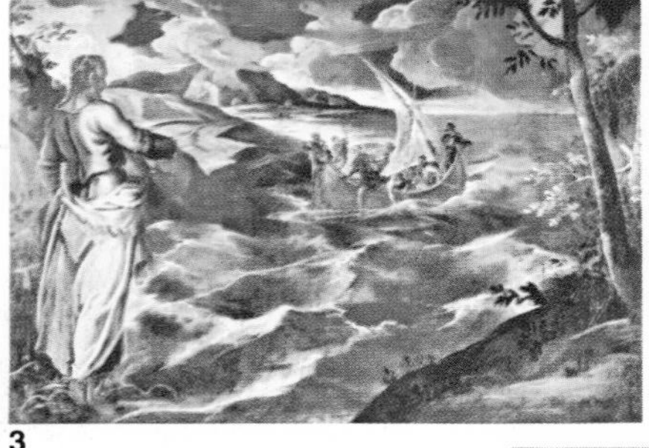

3

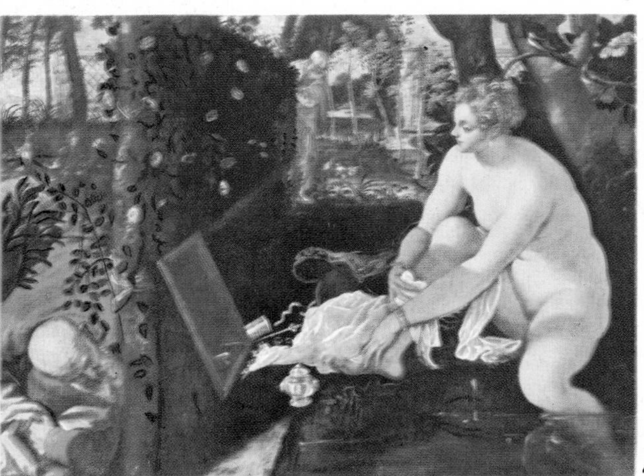

4

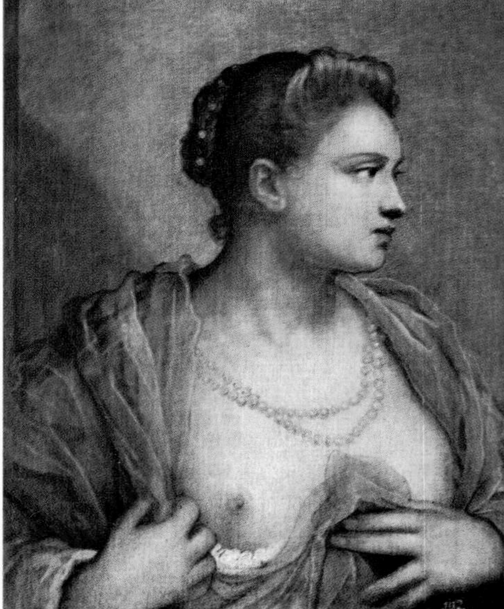

olo Veronese (1528?–1588)
Calvary. About 1570. Louvre, Paris
The Feast in the House of Levi. 1573. Accademia, Venice
The Baptism of Christ. Detail. Brera, Milan
The Finding of Moses. 1570–80. Prado, Madrid

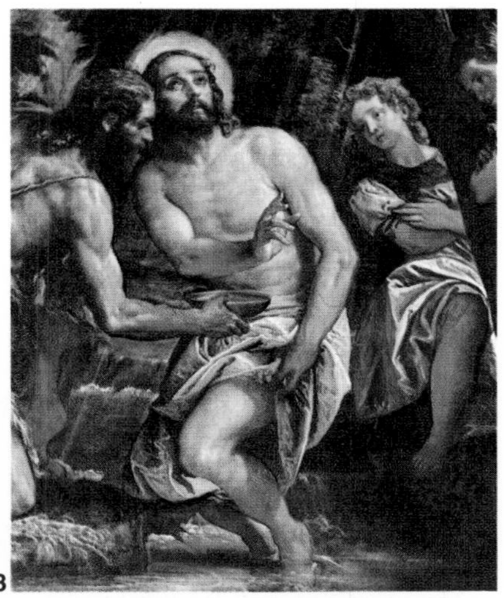

3

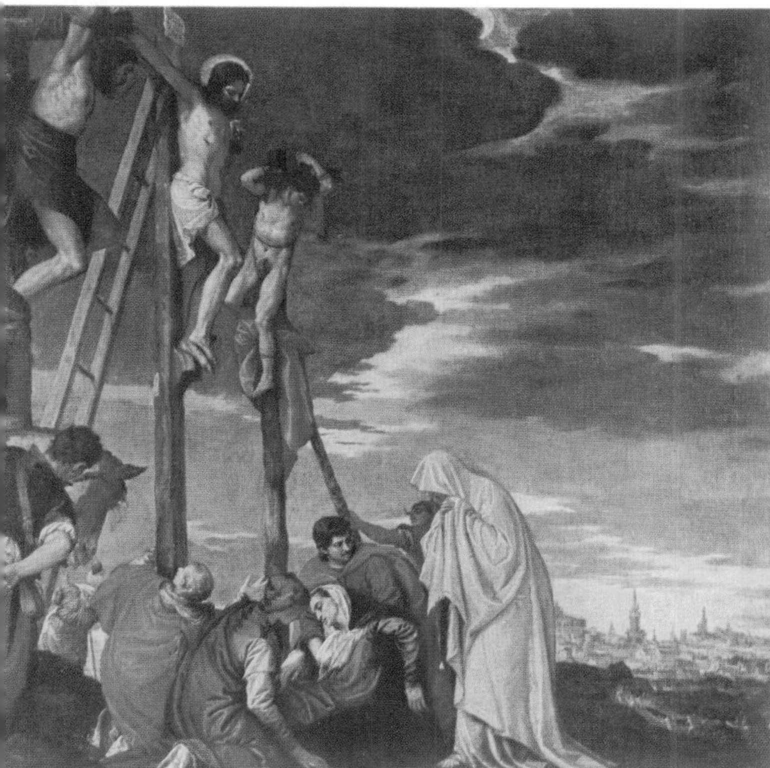

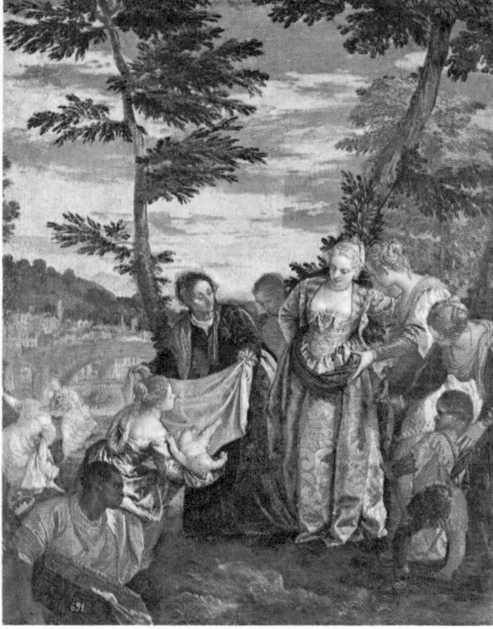

4

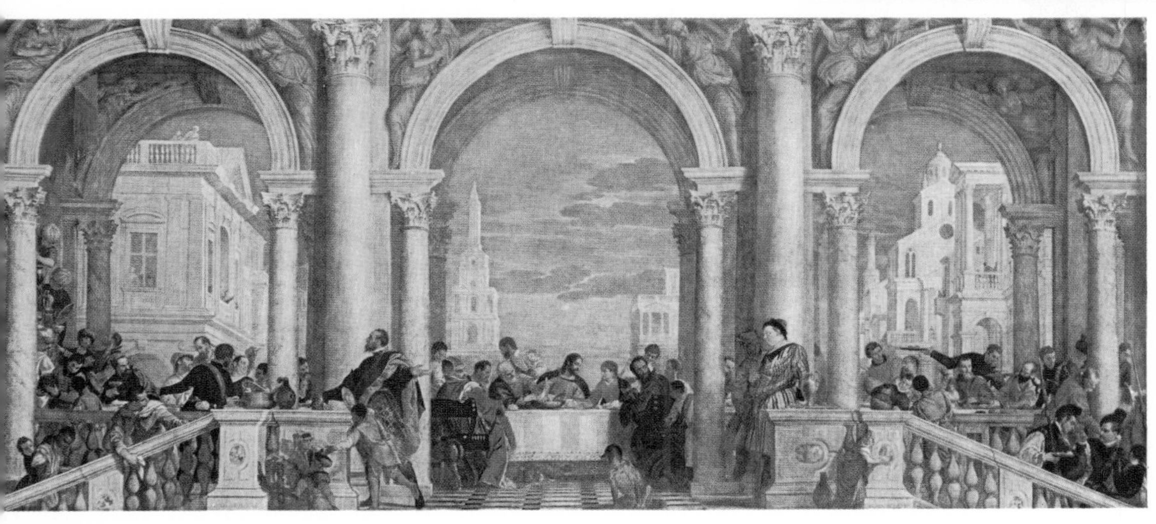

1. **Cima da Conegliano** (1459/60–1517/18): *Endymion.* Pinacoteca, Parma
2. **Giuseppe Arcimboldo** (1527–93): *The Cook.* Pen and ink drawing. Ecole des Beaux-Arts, Paris
3. **Giuseppe Arcimboldo** (1527–93): *Summer.* 1563. Kunsthistorisches Museum, Vienna
4. **Sodoma** (1477–1549): *St Sebastian.* 1526. Palazzo Pitti, Florence
5. **Dosso Dossi** (*fl.*1512–d.1542): *Circe.* National Gallery of Art (Samuel H. Kress Collection), Washington DC
6. **Sebastiano del Piombo** (*c.*1485–1547): *Pietà.* About 1515. Museo Civico, Viterbo
7. **Sebastiano del Piombo** (*c.*1485–1547): *Dorothea.* About 1512/13. Staatliche Museen, Berlin-Dahlem

2

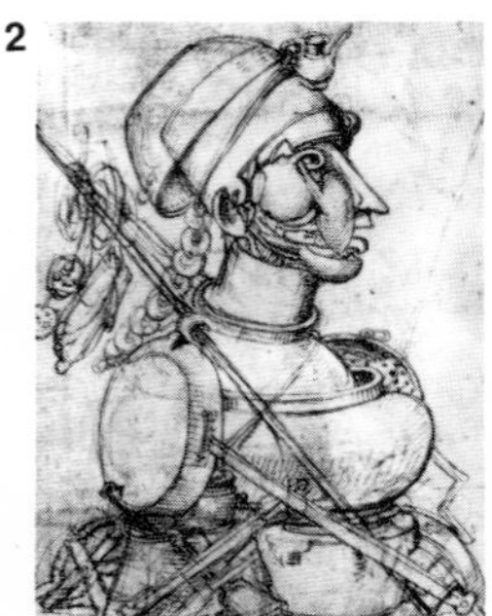

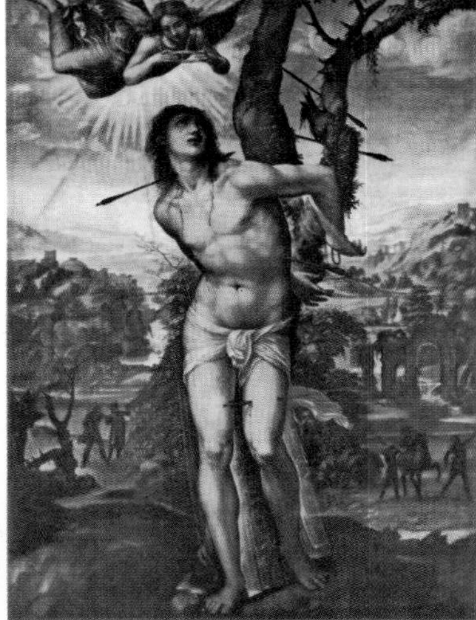

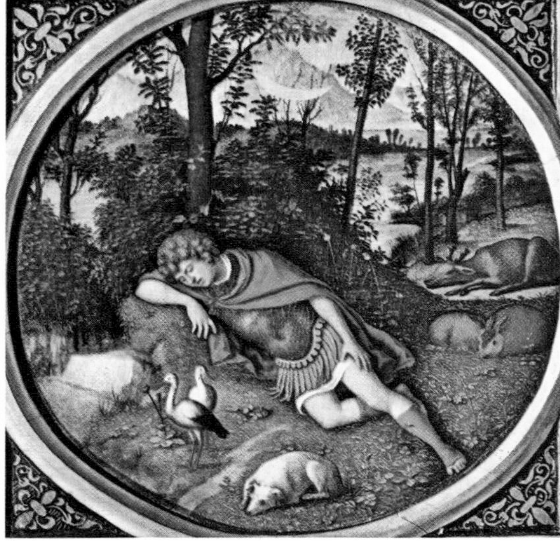

1

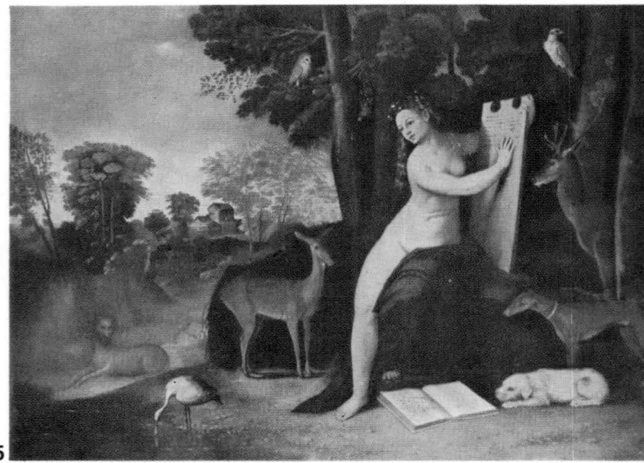

5

3

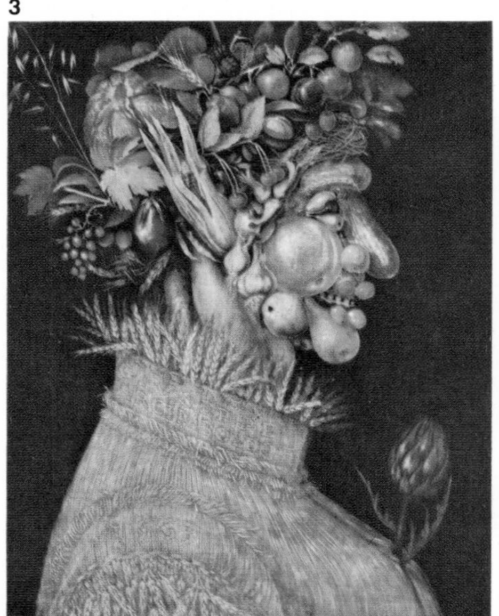

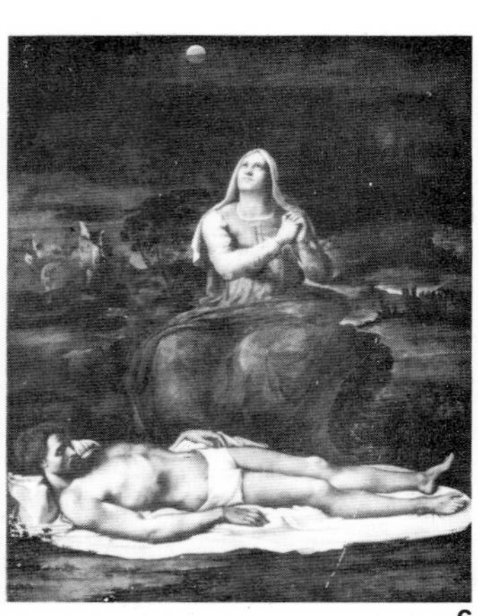

6

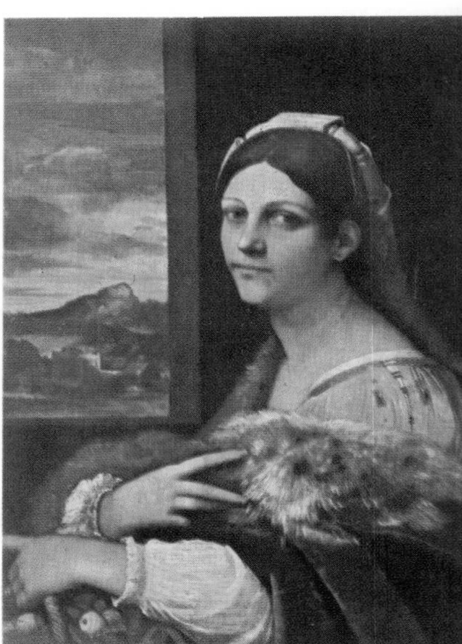

7

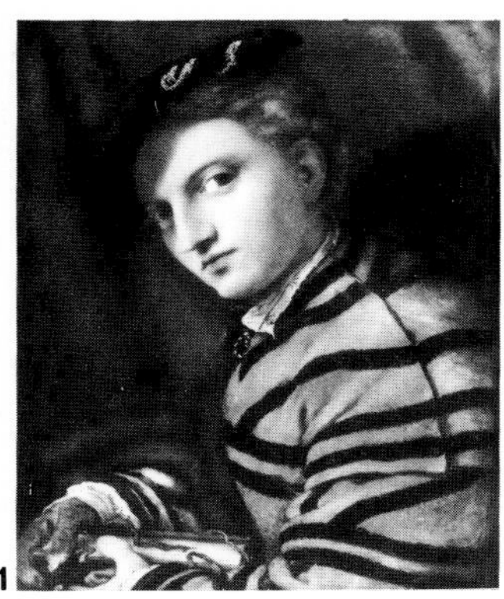
1

Lorenzo Lotto (*c.*1480–1556)

1. *Portrait of a young Man in a striped Coat.* 1526. Castello Sforzesco, Milan
2. *Portrait of a Man.* About 1525. Isaac Delgado Museum of Art (Samuel H. Kress Collection), New Orleans
3. *St Jerome in the Wilderness.* 1506. Louvre, Paris
4. *Susanna and the Elders.* 1517. Contini-Bonacossi Collection, Florence

Jacopo Bassano (*c.*1510–92)

5. *The Crucifixion.* 1562. Museo Civico, Treviso
6. *Penelope.* Musée des Beaux-Arts, Rennes
7. *The Adoration of the Shepherds.* Galleria Borghese, Rome

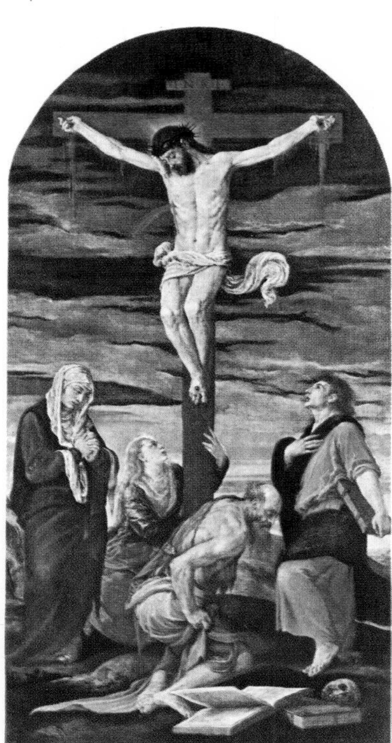
5

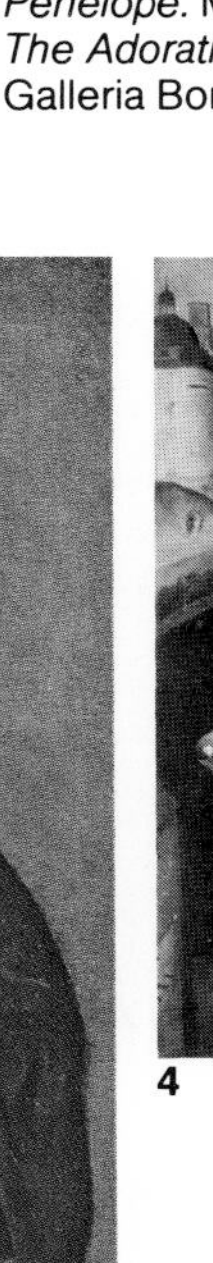

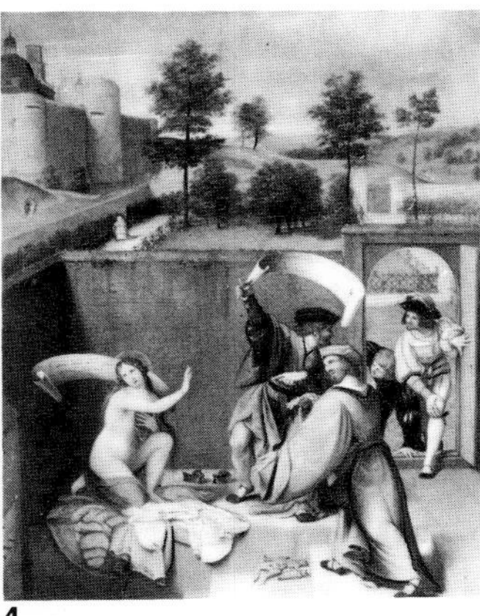
4

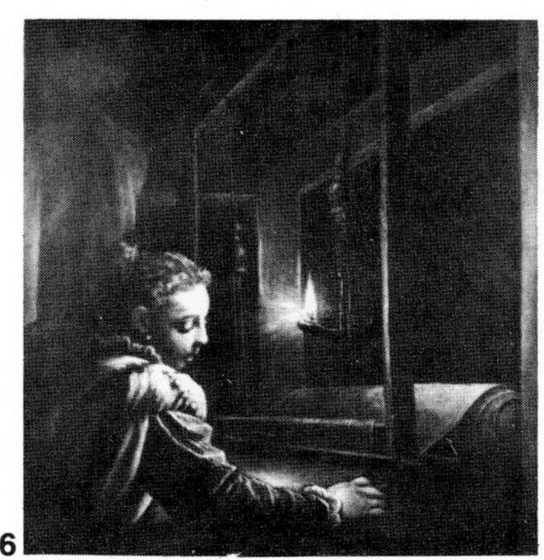
6

3

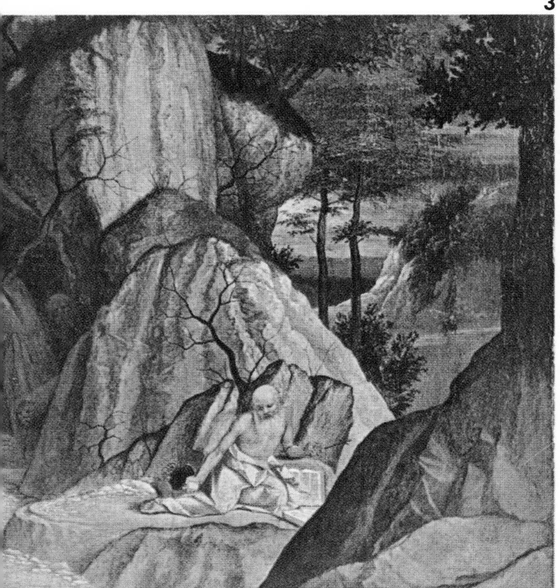

7

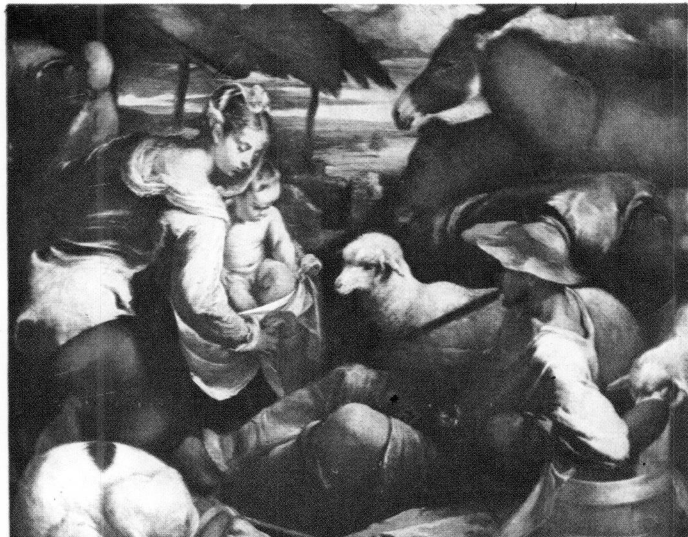

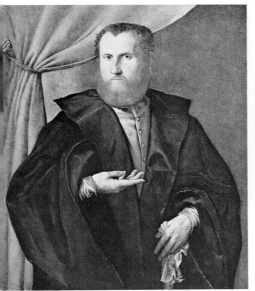

1. **Andrea Palladio** (1508–80): Church of Giorgio Maggiore, Venice. 1566–80
2. **Andrea Palladio** (1508–80): Palazzo Chiericati, Vicenza. Begun 1550
3. **Andrea Palladio** (1508–80): Villa Cap (Villa Rotonda), near Vicenza. 1550–1
4. **Andrea Palladio** (1508–80): Church c Redentore, Venice. Begun 1577
5. **Vincenzo Scamozzi** (1552–1616), a follower of Palladio: Procuratie Nuove, Venice. 1586–1611 (second order modif in 1640 by Longhena)

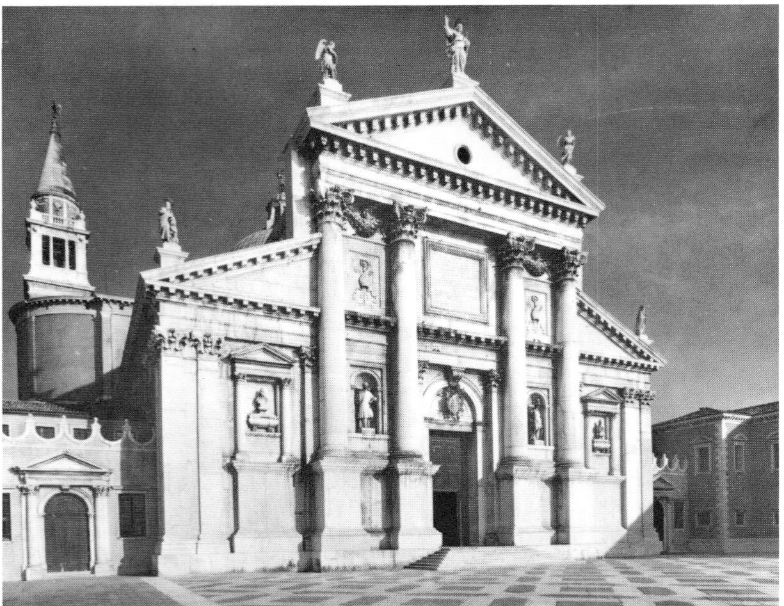

1

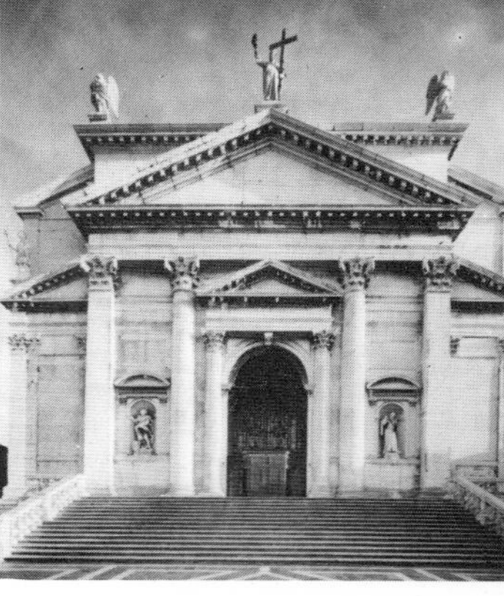

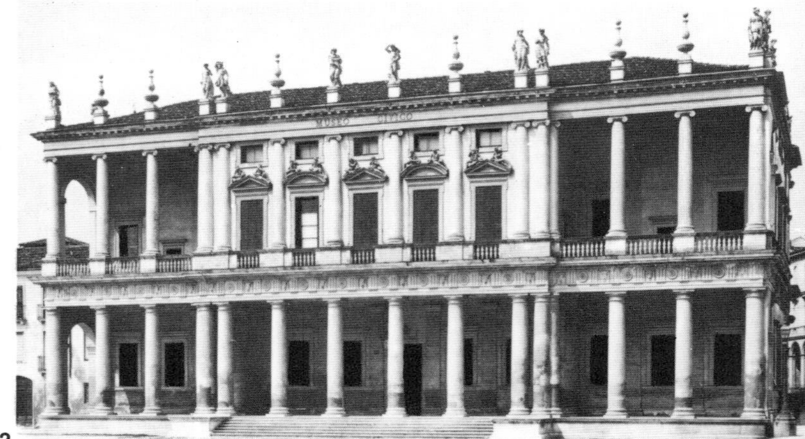

2

5

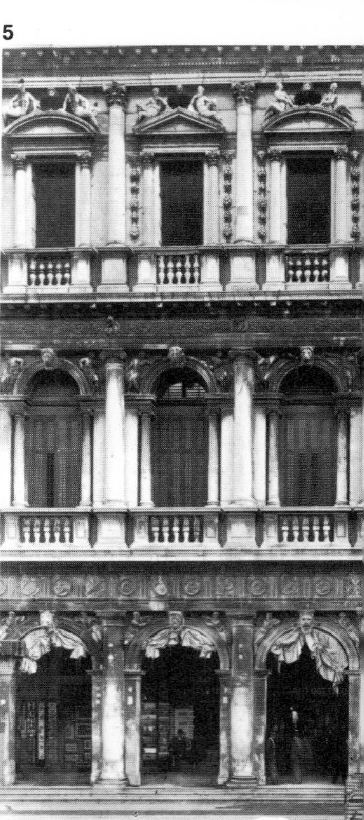

3

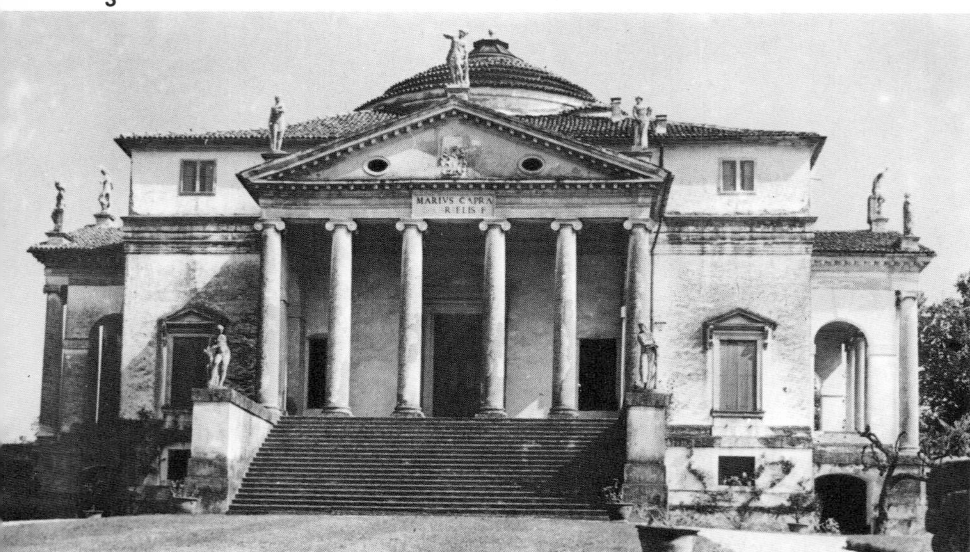

Part 7

The Renaissance outside Italy 1400–1600

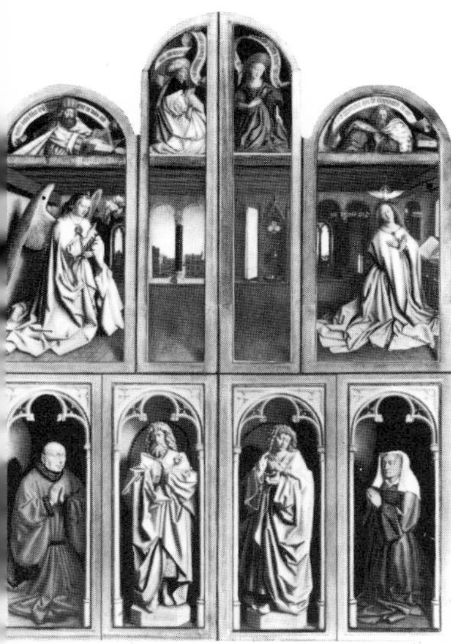

an and Hubert van Eyck: *Polyptych of the 'ystic Lamb* (closed). 1426–32. St-Bavon athedral, Ghent

ne Northern Renaissance effected a technical volution in the art of painting on panel. The our of the classical tradition was not so ominent as in Italy, with the result that ny transition from the Gothic period had be resolved on the panel itself. The Van yck brothers, Jan and Hubert, working the Netherlands, are often credited with e discovery of painting in oil. Although e introduction of oil in place of tempera was ot as sudden or as clear-cut as is often ought, there can be no doubt that the loption of the new medium was a significant evelopment in European art. The Ghent altarpiece painted by the Van Eycks initiated a fresh examination of the world and is notable for its accuracy of observation, as well as for its precise rendering. Painters like Rogier van der Weyden, Robert Campin, Petrus Christus and Memling set out to depict both people and objects, as well as landscape, with the utmost fidelity to nature. Their paintings are a literal interpretation of the world about them, moulded above all by a treatment of light that defined space as well as created atmosphere. This style of painting in the Netherlands persisted throughout the fifteenth century and was certainly influential in Italy. Indeed, contacts between these two parts of Europe were quite common as a result of trade, banking and diplomacy. Germany stood somewhat aloof from the Netherlands and Italy. There a more emotional response to religious subject matter is detectable, reaching a climax in an artist like Matthias Grünewald (Isenheim altarpiece). Compared with Netherlandish artists, German painters were far more hidebound by local traditions, but in general there is a greater freedom in their style of painting or carving and a wider range in their colouring. This is particularly apparent in the Danube school (Altdorfer) and in the south of Germany.

All these strands in northern European art are united in Albrecht Dürer, the outstanding master of the Northern Renaissance. In a considerable output (paintings, drawings, but above all prints) he displays great creative ability combined with considerable intellectual powers. He visited both the Netherlands and Italy (Venice) and his prints were widely circulated, becoming, as a result, immensely influential. Like the works of Leonardo da Vinci, Raphael and Michelangelo, those of Dürer were thoroughly absorbed into the European artistic consciousness.

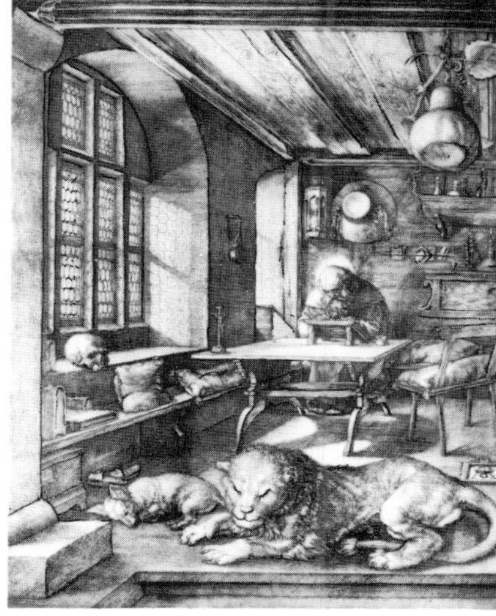

Durer: *St Jerome in His Study.* Copperplate engraving. 1514. Galleria Corsini, Rome

rünewald: Detail of landscape from the *emptation of St Anthony.* Isenheim Altarpiece. 1512–15. Underlinden Museum, Colmar

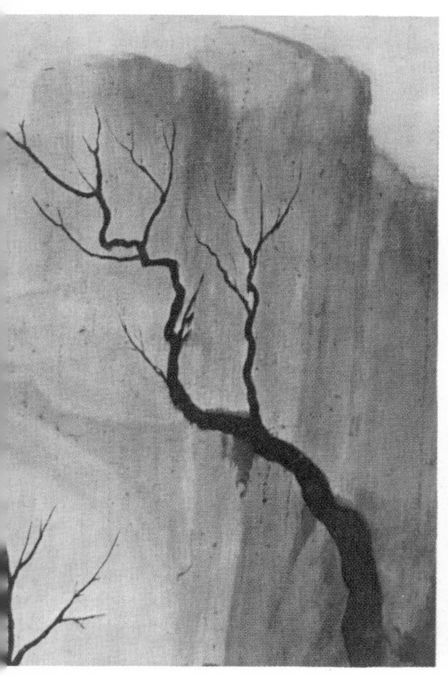

Altdorfer: *Battle of Arbela.* Detail. 1529. Alte Pinakothek, Munich

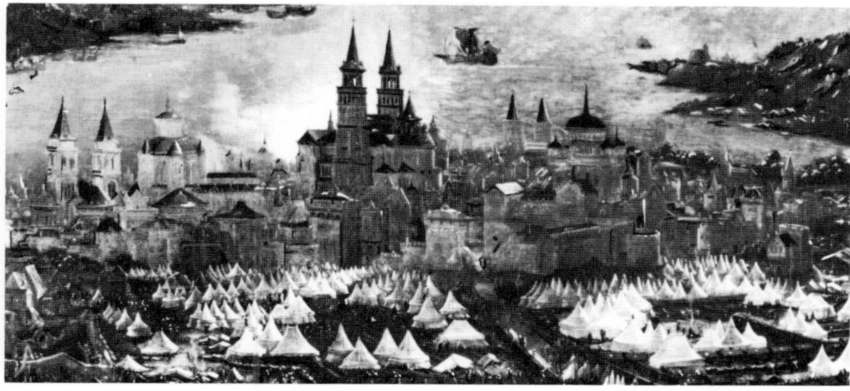

Jan van Eyck (*c.*1390–1441)

1. *St Barbara.* Brush drawing on chalk ground. 1437. Koninklijk Museum voor Schone Kunsten, Antwerp
2. *The Madonna and Chancellor Rolin.* About 1434–5. Louvre, Paris
3. with **Hubert van Eyck** (d.1426): The Gh Altarpiece (wings closed). Above: *The Annunciation;* below: *St John the Bapti and St John the Evangelist flanked by Donor, Burgomaster of Ghent, and his W* Completed 1432. St-Bavon, Ghent
4. *Angel playing the Organ.* Detail from Th Ghent Altarpiece (wings open) St-Bavo Ghent
5. *The Madonna in the Church.* About 14 Staatliche Museen, Berlin-Dahlem

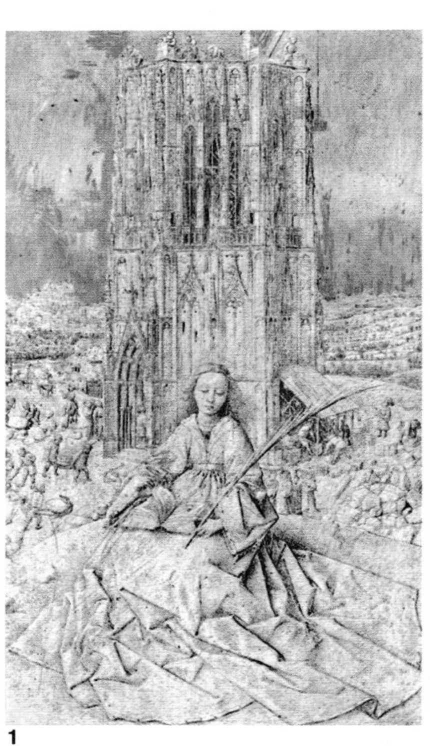

1

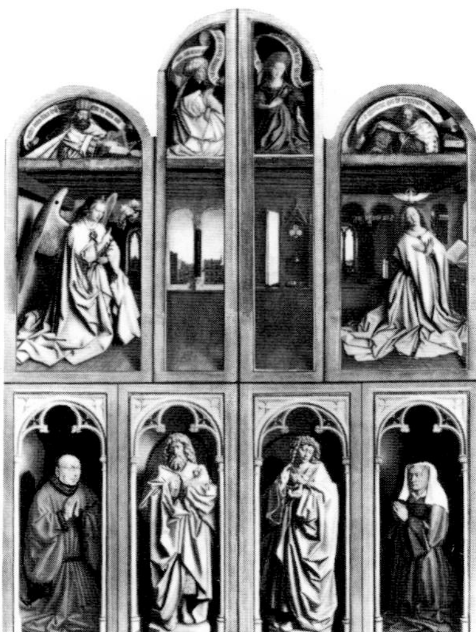

3

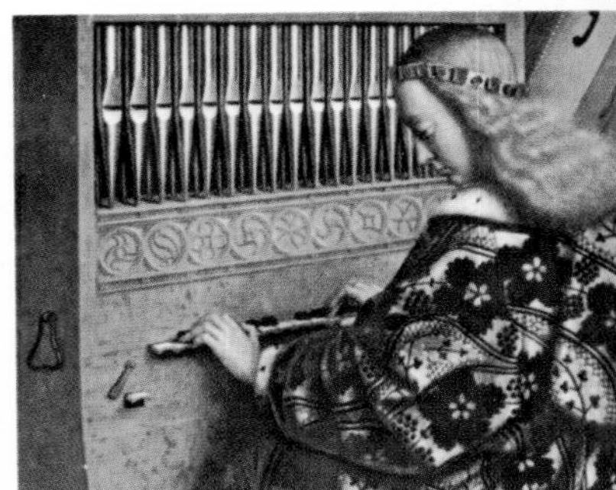

4

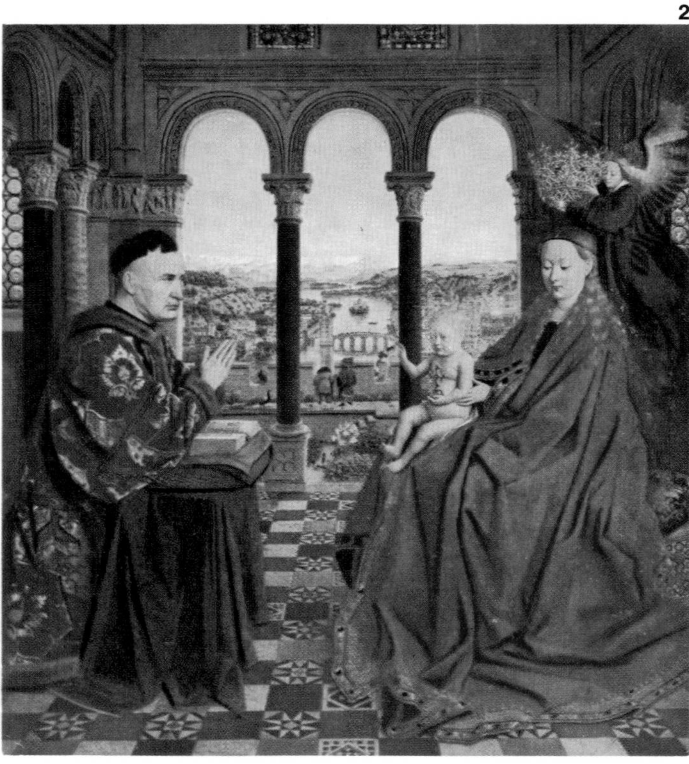

2

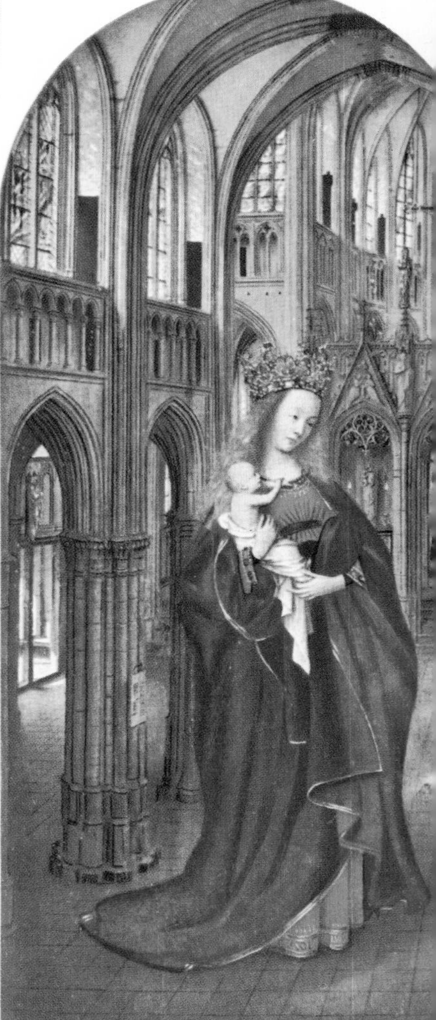

5

van Eyck (c.1390–1441)
he Marriage of Giovanni (?) Arnolfini nd Giovanni Cenami (?). 1434. National Gallery, London
vith **Hubert van Eyck** (d.1426): *The doration of the Lamb.* Central panel of he Ghent Altarpiece. Completed 1432. St-Bavon, Ghent

3. *The Madonna by the Fountain.* 1439. Koninklijk Museum voor Schone Kunsten, Antwerp
4. Detail of fig. 1

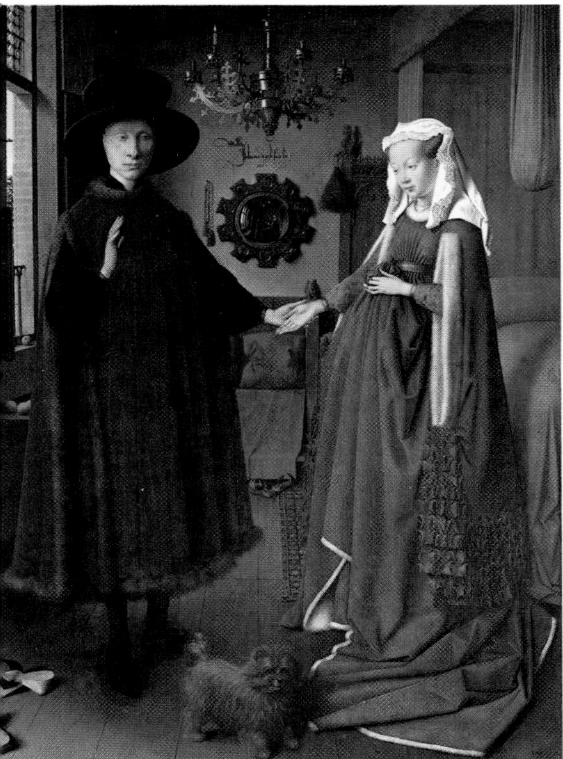

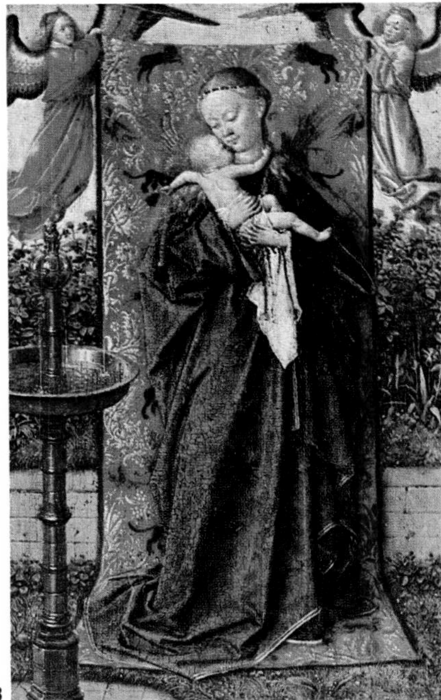

3

4

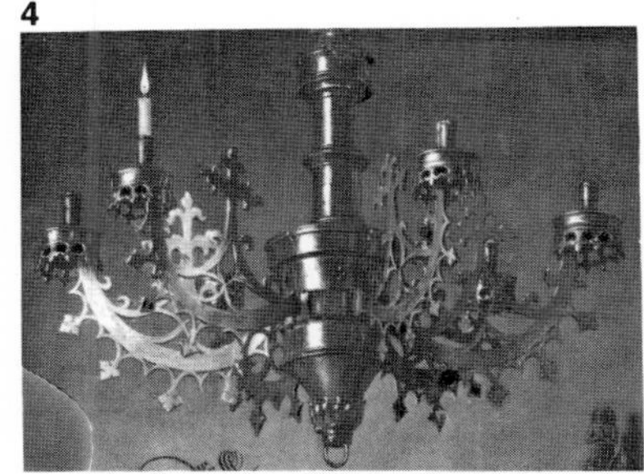

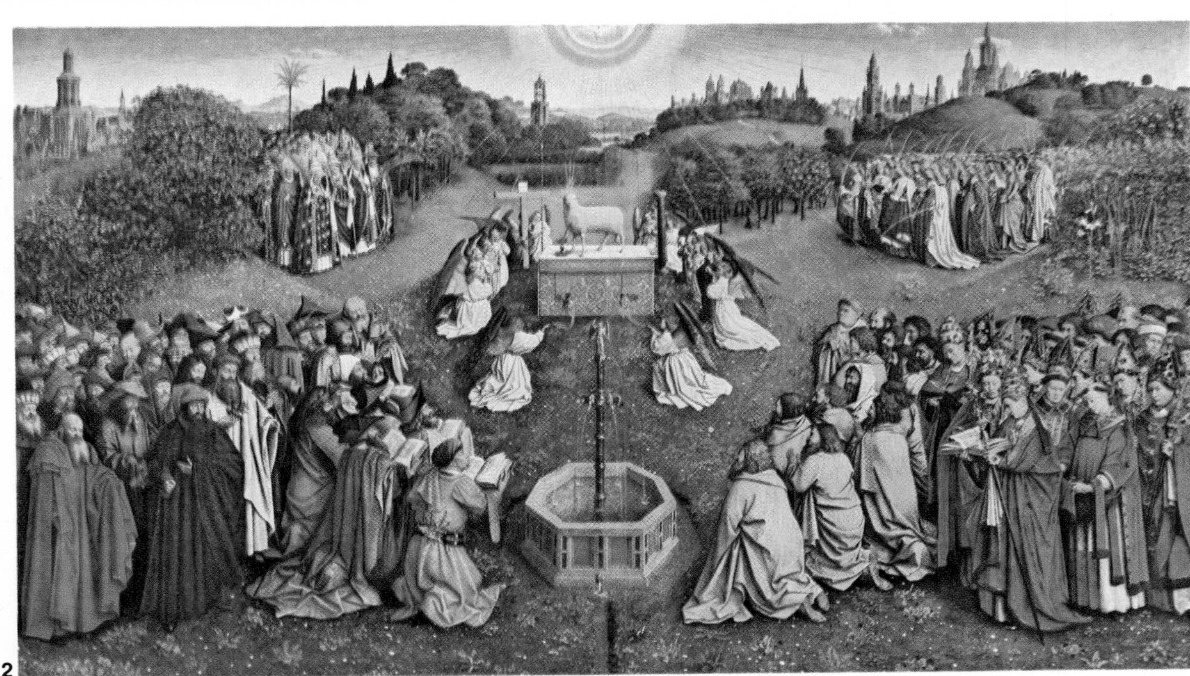

2

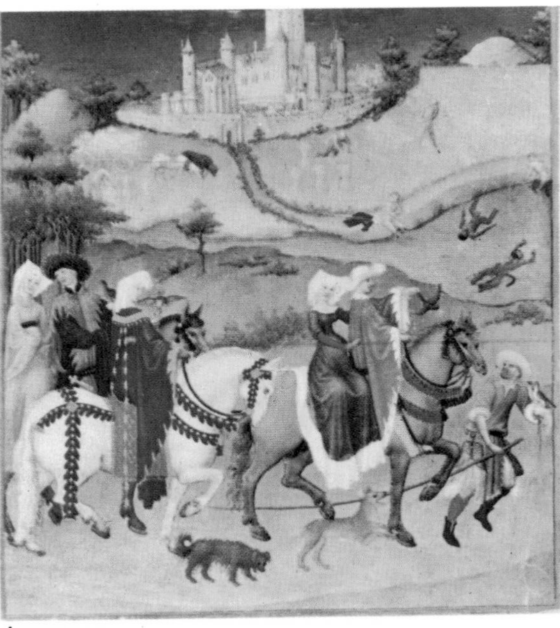

1

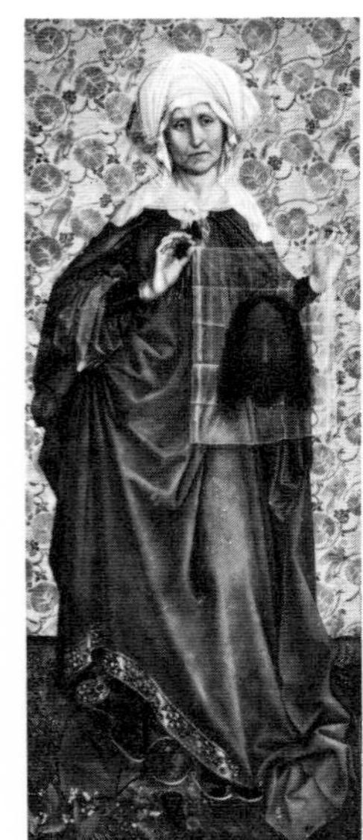

3

1. **Paul, Herman and Jean de Limbourg** (d.1416): *The Month of August.* Scene w the Chateau d'Etampes, residence of th Duc de Berry. Miniature from the *Très Riches Heures du Duc de Berry.* 1415-
2. **Robert Campin,** also called Master of Flémalle (*c.*1378–1444): *St Joseph.* Ri wing of the Mérode triptych. 1420–30. T Cloisters, Metropolitan Museum of Art, New York
3. **Robert Campin,** also called Master of Flémalle (*c.*1378–1444): *St Veronica.* 1430–5. Städelsches Kunstinstitut, Frankfurt
4. **Jean Le Tavernier** (*fl.*early 15th centur *Combat in the Lists between Charlemag and Doon de Mayence.* Miniature from *Chronicles and Conquests of Charlemag* 1458–61. Bibliothèque Royale, Brusse
5. **Henri Bellechose** (*c.*1380–1440/4): *L Communion and Martyrdom of St Denis* 1416. Louvre, Paris

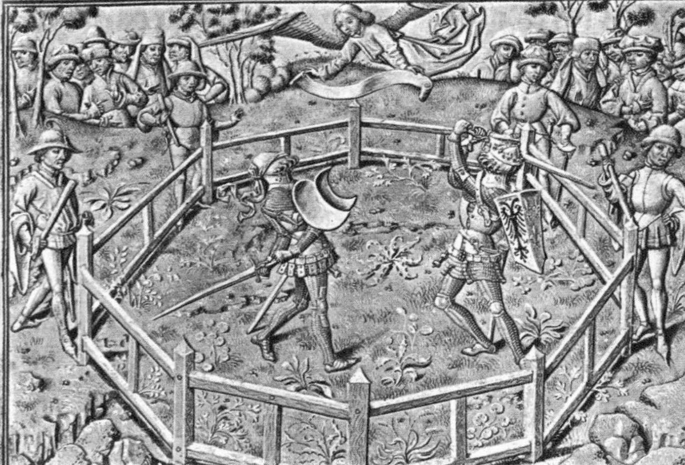

2

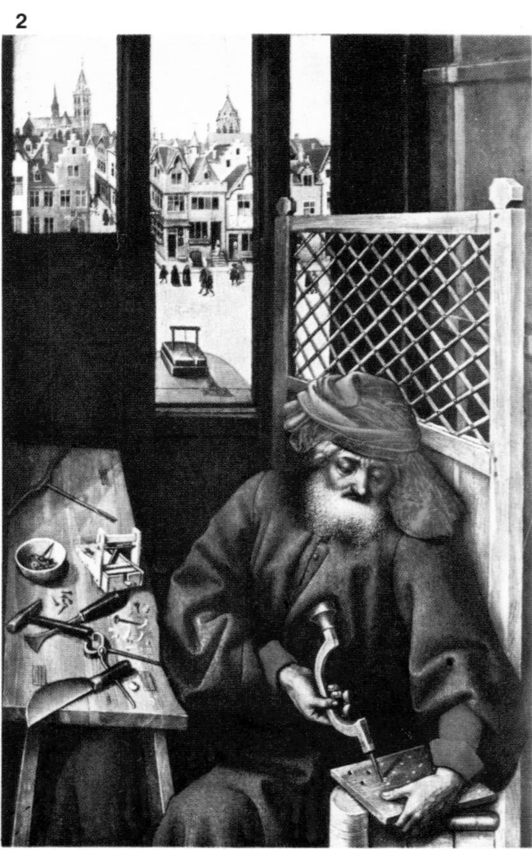

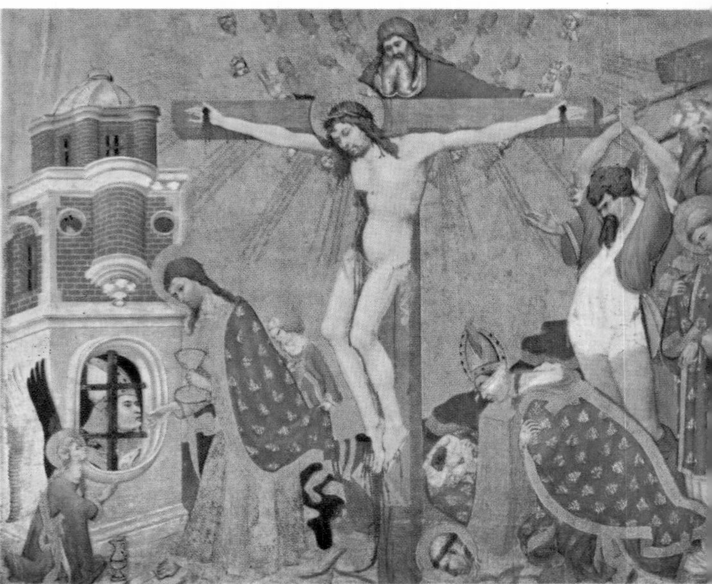

5

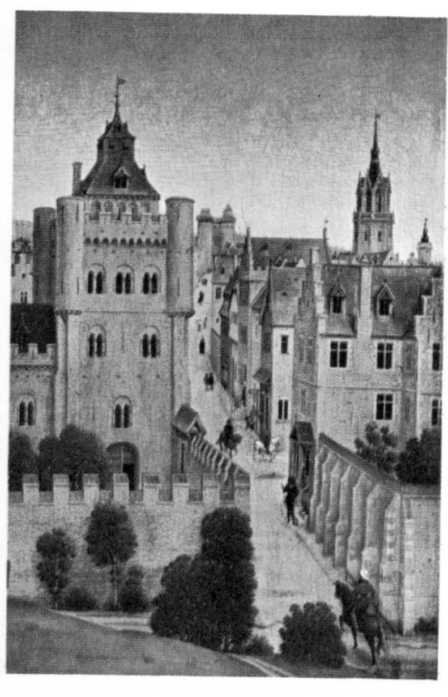

Rogier van der Weyden (1399/1400–64)

1. *Pierre Bladelin's Castle* (?). Detail from the central panel of the Bladelin triptych. After 1456. Staatliche Museen, Berlin-Dahlem
2. *The Virgin supported by St John* and *Christ on the Cross.* Two panels, possibly from a triptych. John G. Johnson Collection, Philadelphia
3. *The Descent from the Cross.* About 1435. Prado, Madrid
4. *Portrait of Francesco d'Este.* About 1460. Metropolitan Museum of Art, New York
5. *Ordination, Marriage and Extreme Unction.* Right wing of the altarpiece of the Sacraments. About 1460. Koninklijk Museum voor Schone Kunsten, Antwerp
6. *The Virgin.* Detail of fig. 7
7. *Christ on the Cross.* Central panel: *St John, the Virgin and two Donors;* left panel: *St Mary Magdalene;* right panel: *St Veronica.* About 1440–5. Kunsthistorisches Museum, Vienna

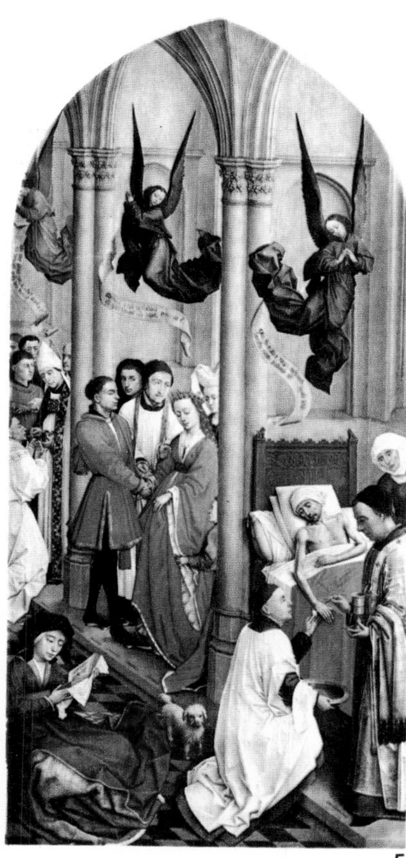

5

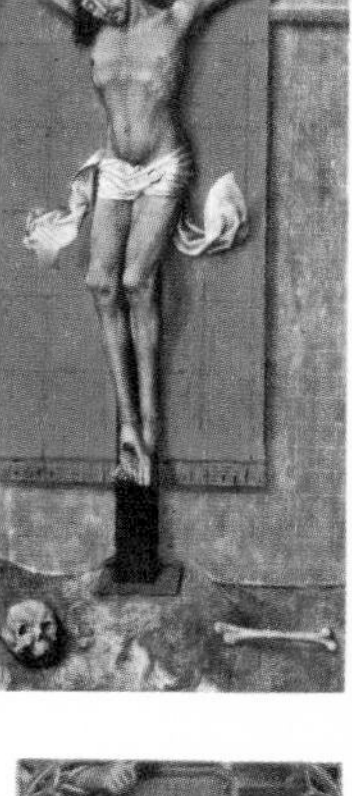

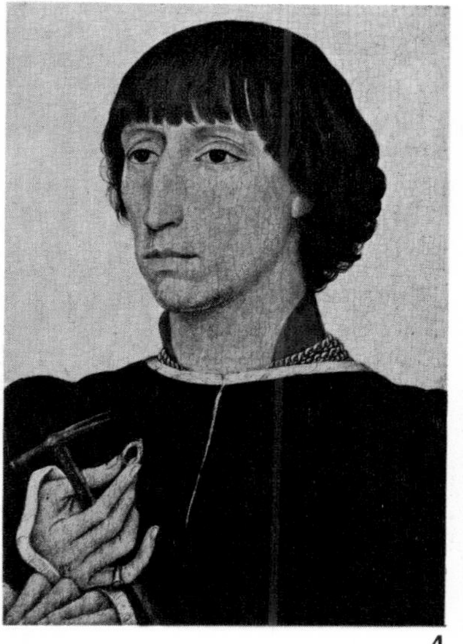

4

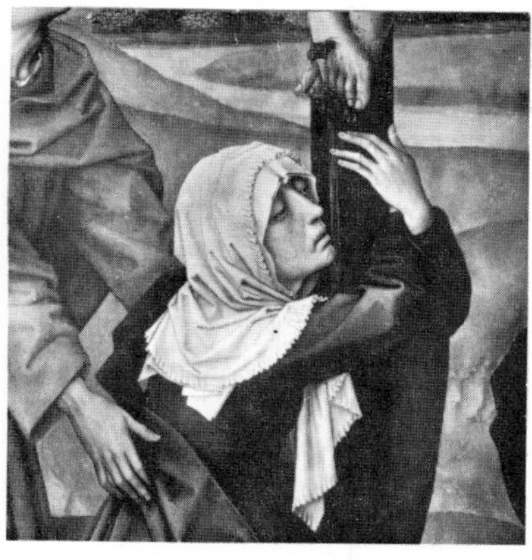

6

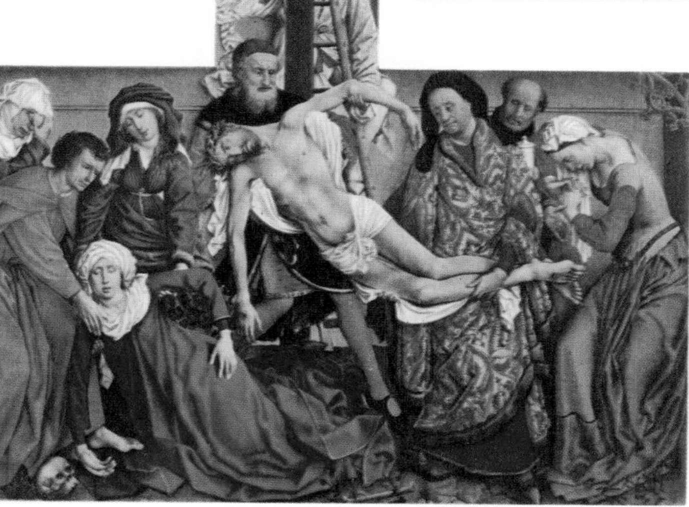

7

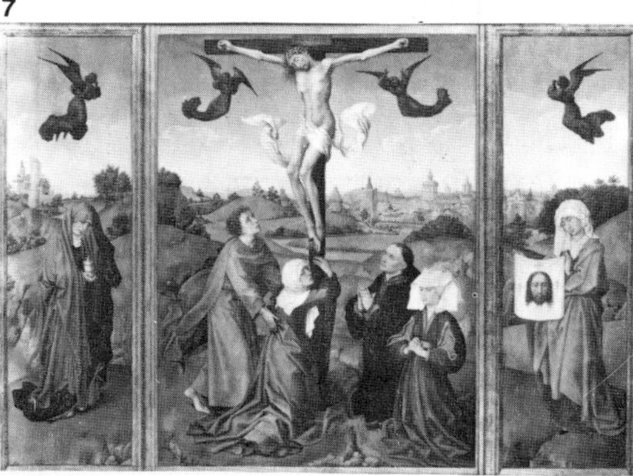

1. **Claes Sluter** (*c.*1350–1405/6): Mourning figure from the tomb of Philip the Bold. Late 14th century. Musée des Beaux-Arts, Dijon
2. **Petrus Christus** (*c.*1410–72/3): *St Eligius weighing the Wedding Rings of a Bridal Couple.* 1449. Metropolitan Museum of Art (Robert Lehman Collection), New York
3. **Claes Sluter (***c.*1350–1405/6): *Moses.* Stone statue from the Well of Moses, Chartreuse de Champmol, Dijon. 1395–1403
4. **Petrus Christus** (*c.*1410–72/3): *Portrait of a young Lady.* About 1446? Staatliche Museen, Berlin-Dahlem
5. **Dieric Bouts** (*c.*1415–75): *The Last Supper.* Central panel of altarpiece, church of St-Pierre, Louvain, Belgium. 1467
6. **Dieric Bouts** (*c.*1415–75): *Justice of Emperor Otto: Ordeal by Fire.* About 1473. Musées Royaux des Beaux-Arts, Brussels

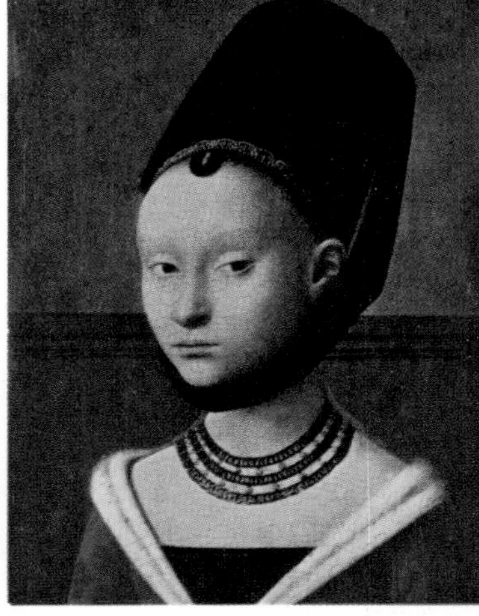

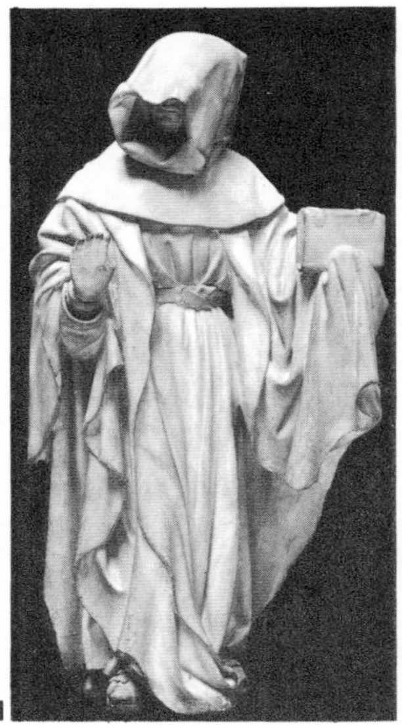
1

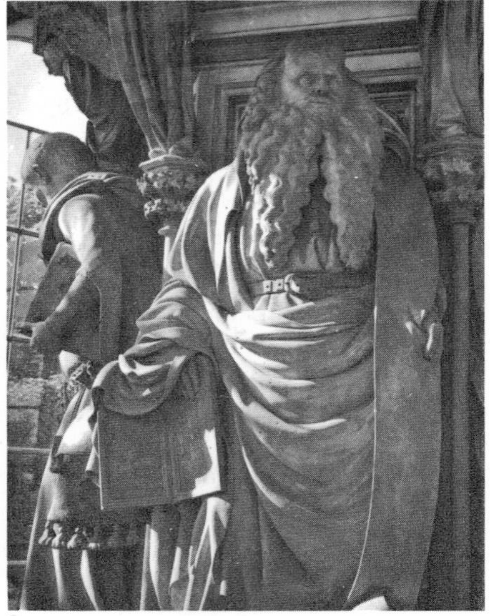
3

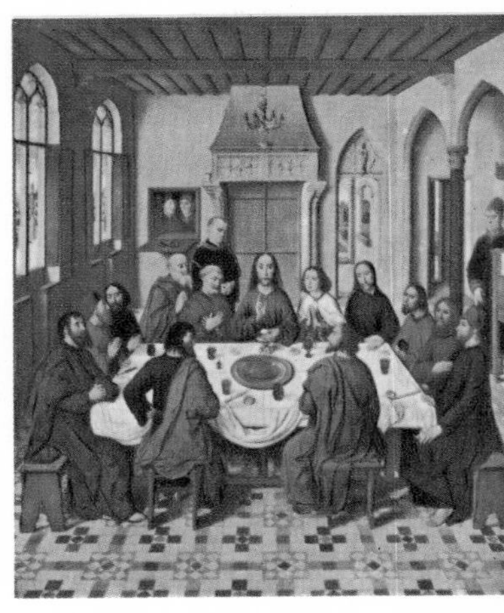

2
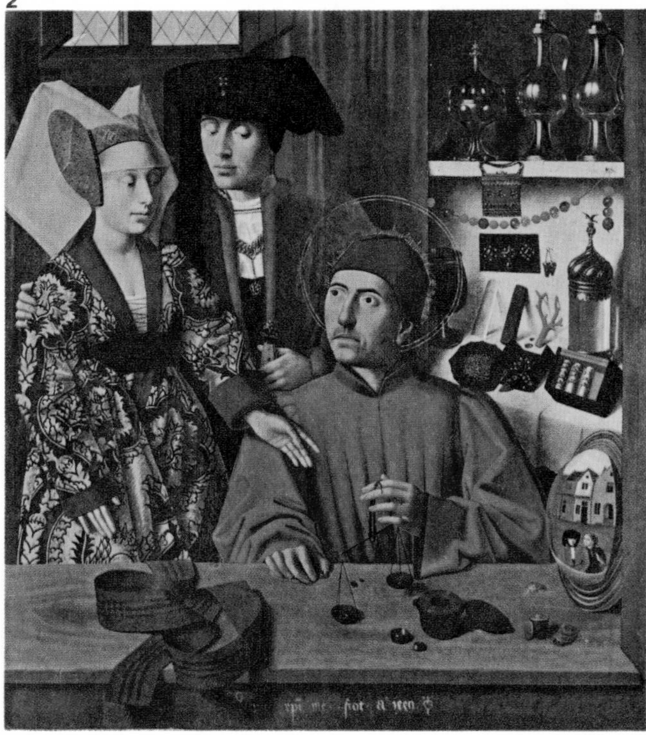

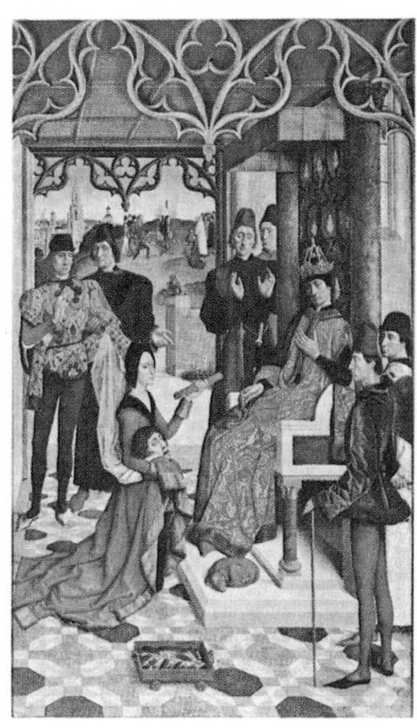
6

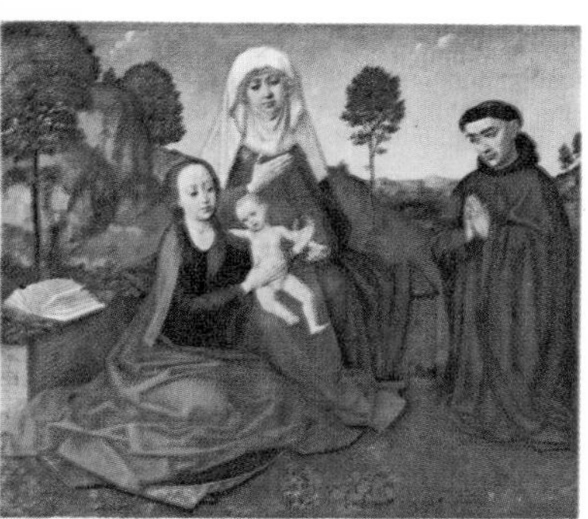

1. **Hugo van der Goes** (*c.*1440/5–82): *The Virgin and Child, St Anne and Donor.* Musées Royaux des Beaux-Arts, Brussels
2. **Hugo van der Goes** (*c.*1440/5–82): *The Adoration of the Shepherds.* Central panel of the Portinari Altarpiece. About 1476. Uffizi, Florence
3. **Hans Memling** (*c.*1435–94): *Portrait of Martin van Nieuwenhove.* 1487. Hôpital St-Jean, Bruges
4. **Hans Memling** (*c.*1435–94): *Barbara van Vlaenderberghe.* Right wing of the triptych of Guillaume Moreel. 1484. Hôpital St-Jean, Bruges
5. **Hugo van der Goes** (*c.*1440/5–82): *St Margaret and St Mary Magdalene with Maria Portinari and her Daughter.* Right wing of the Portinari Altarpiece. About 1476. Uffizi, Florence
6. **Hans Memling** (*c.*1435–94): *St Ursula.* Detail from the shrine of St Ursula. 1489. Hôpital St-Jean, Bruges

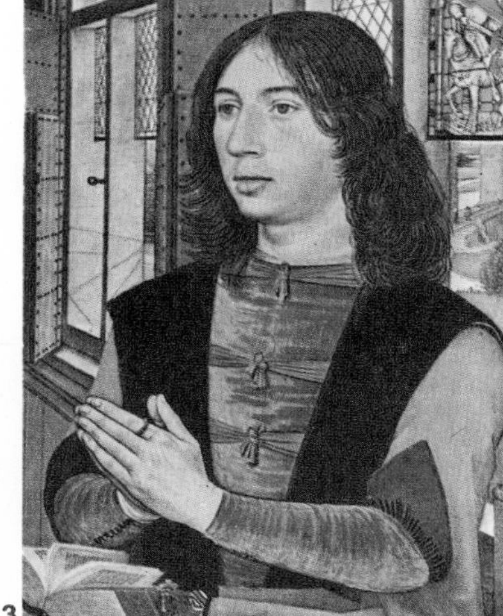

3

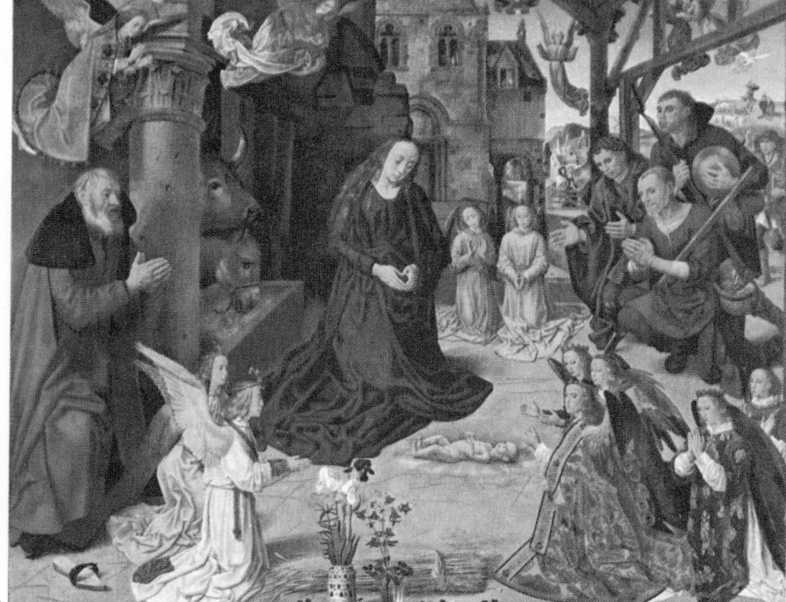

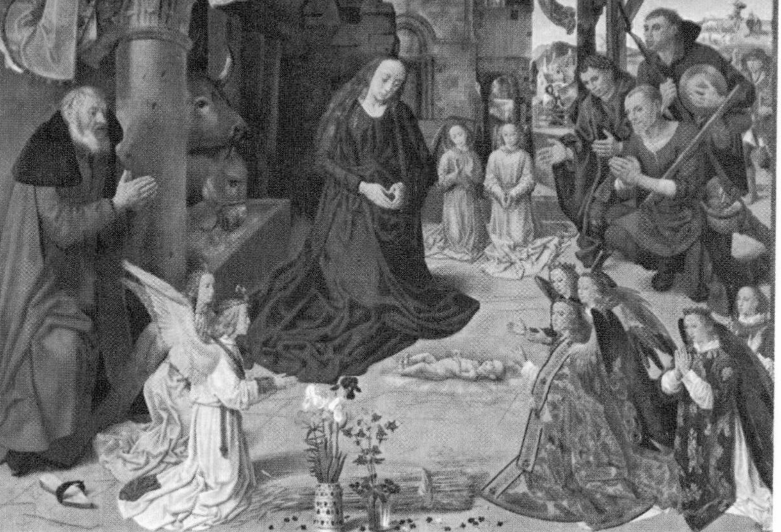

2

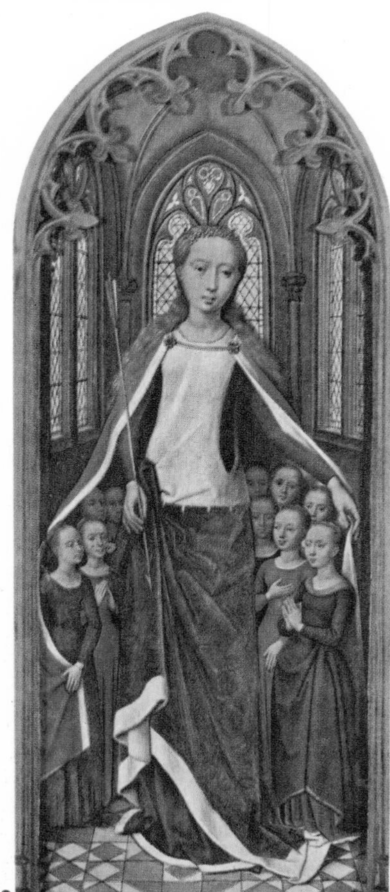

6

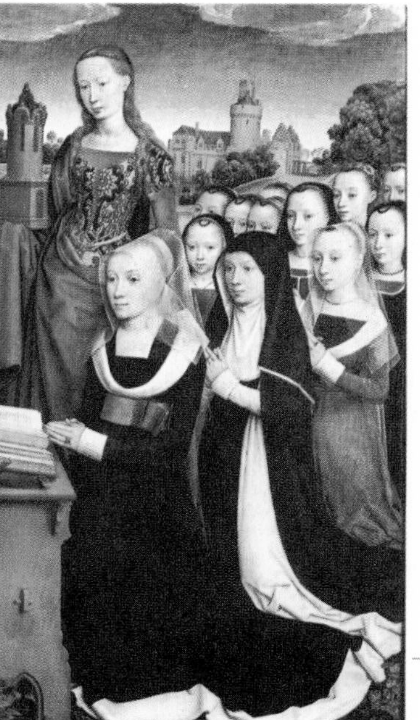

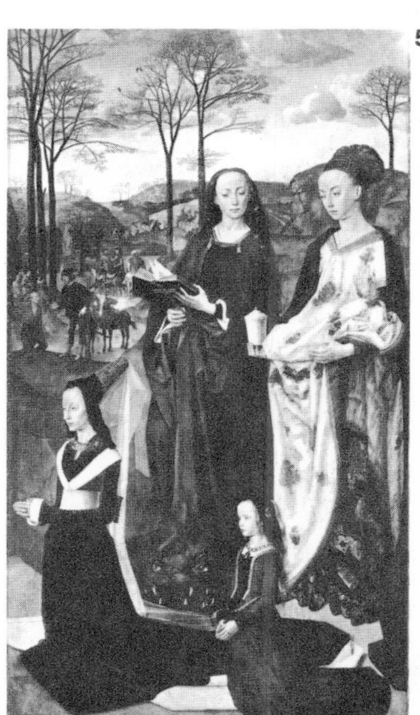

5

Hieronymus Bosch (*c.*1450–1516)

1. *The Conjurer.* About 1480. Musée Municipal, St-Germain-en-Laye
2. *Amorous Couples.* Detail from central panel of the *Haywain* triptych. About 1505. Prado, Madrid
3. *Garden of Earthly Delights.* Detail from central panel of the triptych. Between 1485 and 1505. Prado, Madrid
4. *The Errant Fool.* Detail from exterior of the *Haywain* triptych, wings closed. About 1505. Prado, Madrid
5. *The Prodigal Son.* After 1505. Museum Boymans-van Beuningen, Rotterdam
6. *St John on Patmos.* About 1490. Staatlic Museen, Berlin-Dahlem
7. *The Creation of Eve.* Detail from right wing of the *Garden of Earthly Delights* triptych. Between 1485 and 1505. Prad Madrid

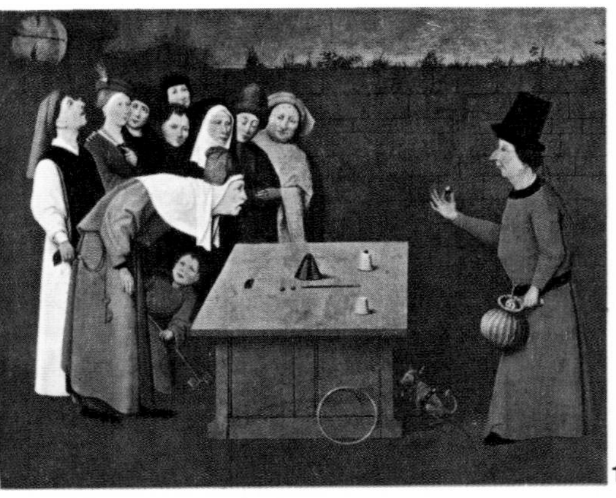
1

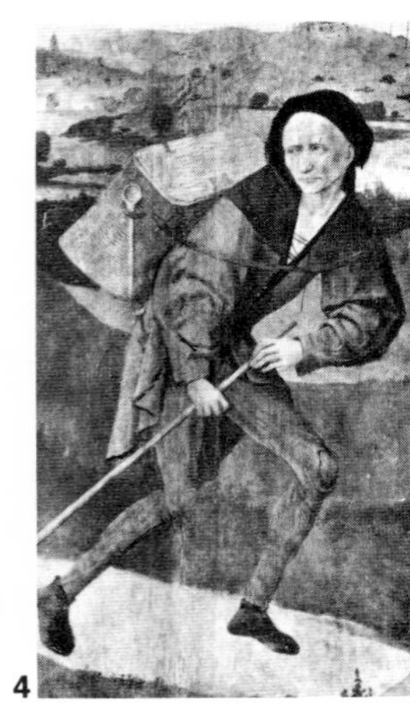
4

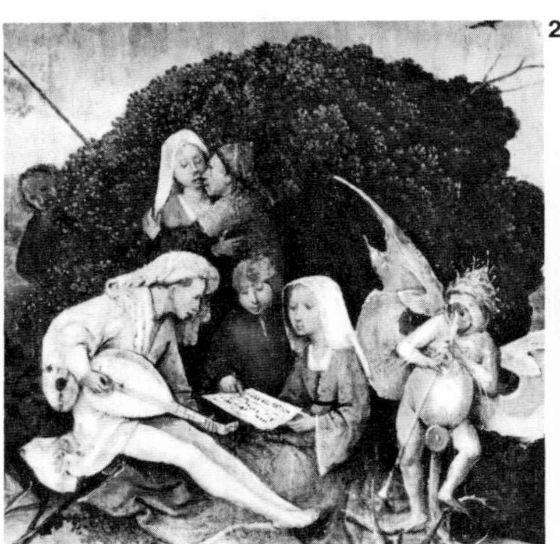
2

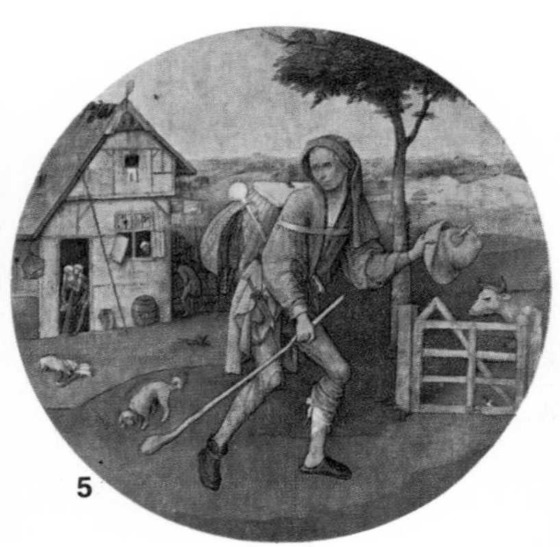
5

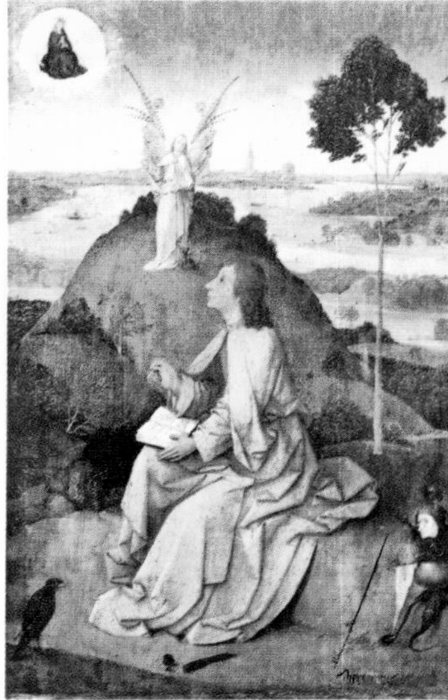
6

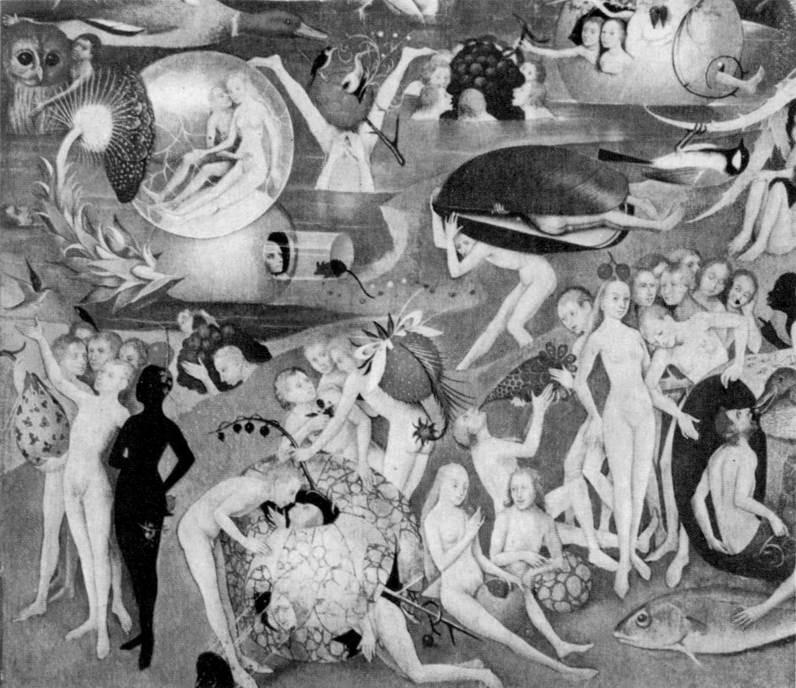
3

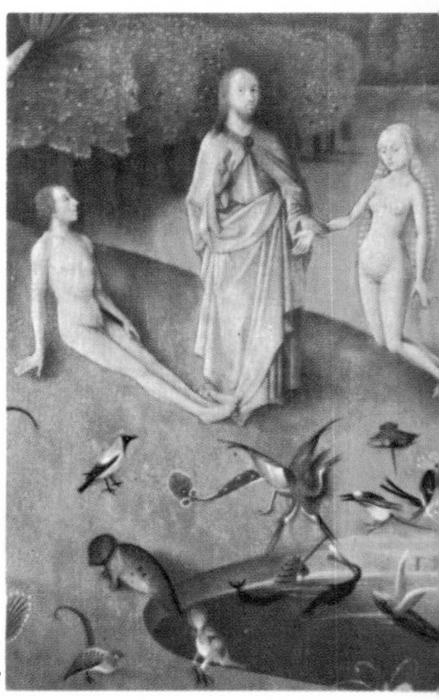
7

Jan Gossaert (1470/80–1532): *Danaë*. 1527. Alte Pinakothek, Munich
Master of the View of St Gudule (*fl.* 1470–1500): *The Virgin and Child with St Mary Magdalene and Donor*, Musée Diocesan, Liège
Lucas van Leyden (*c.* 1494?–1533): *Portrait of a Man*. Engraving. 1521. Stedelijk Museum, Leiden

4. **Lucas van Leyden** (*c.* 1494?–1533): *Lot and his Daughters*. Louvre, Paris
5. **Joos van Cleve** (*c.* 1480/5–1540): *Portrait of Queen Eleanor of France*. 1530–1. Kunsthistorisches Museum, Vienna
6. **Jan Gossaert** (1470/80–1532): *Neptune and Amphitrite*. 1516. Staatliche Museen, Berlin-Dahlem

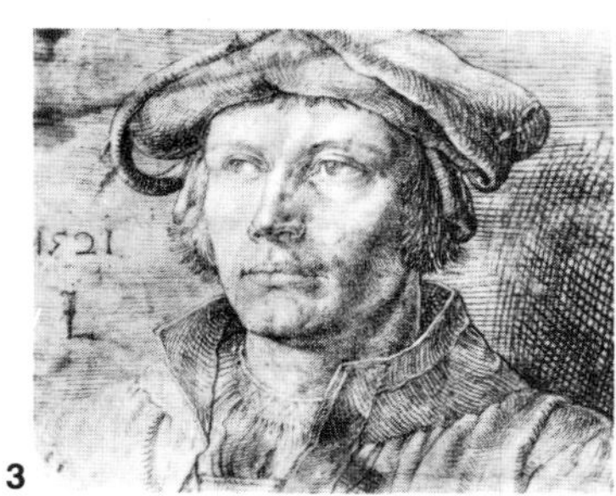

3

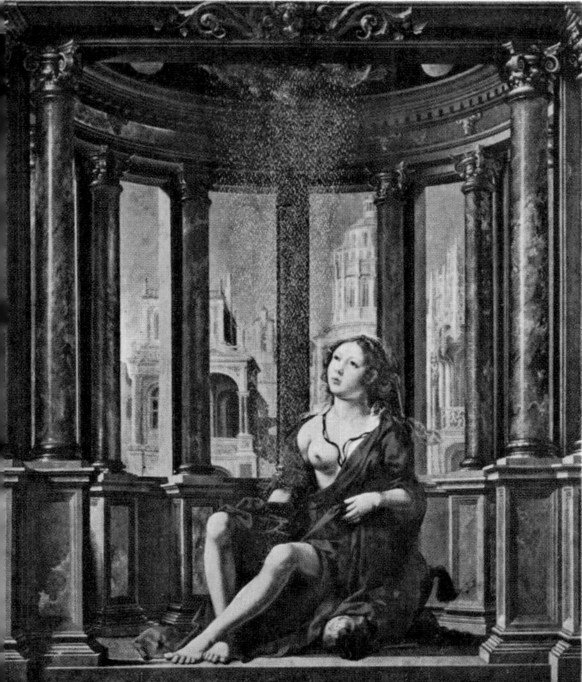

1

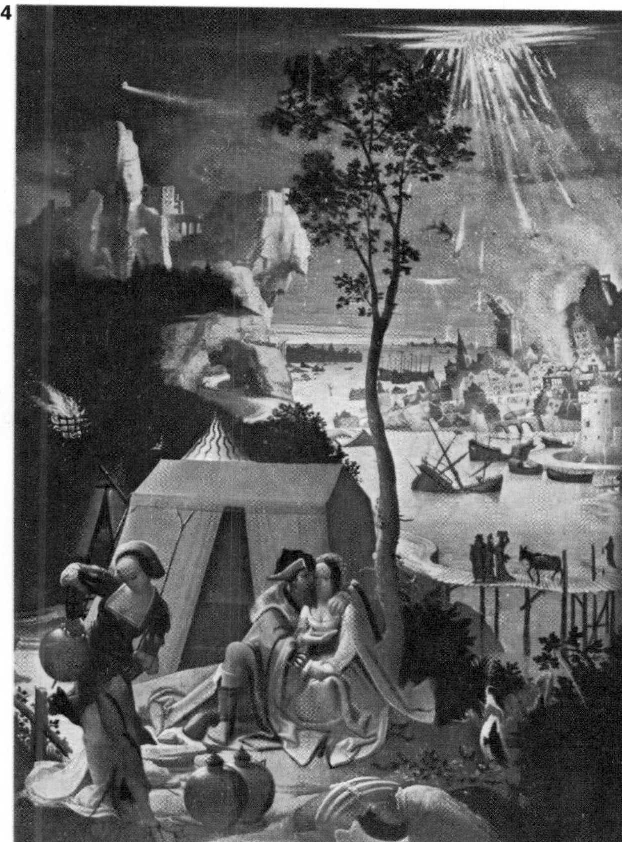

4

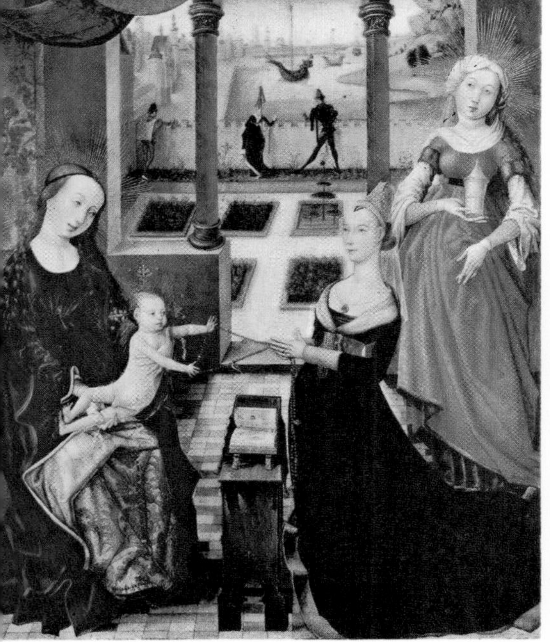

2

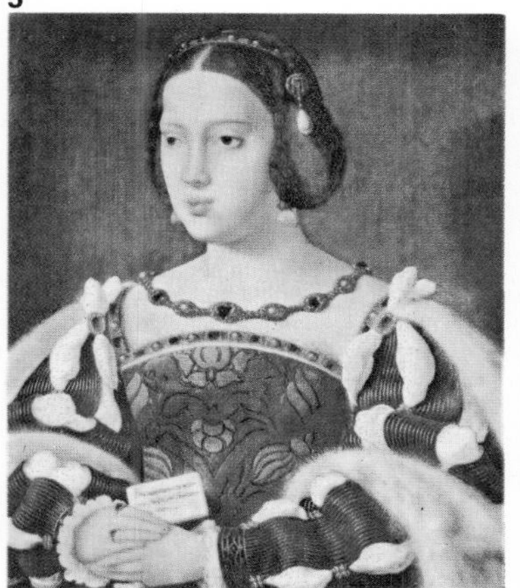

5

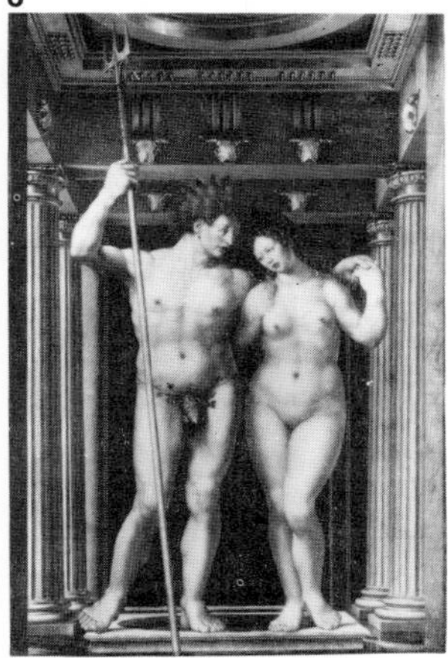

6

1. **Gerard David** (*c.*1460–1523): *The Annunciation.* About 1520. Städelsches Kunstinstitut, Frankfurt
2. **Joachim Patenier** (*c.*1480–*c.*1524): *Landscape with Flight into Egypt.* About 1520. Koninklijk Museum voor Schone Kunsten, Antwerp
3. **Jan van Scorel** (1495–1562): *Portrait of a young Student.* 1531. Museum Boymans-van Beuningen, Rotterdam
4. **Jan van Scorel** (1495–1562): *St Mary Magdalene.* About 1529. Rijksmuseum, Amsterdam
5. **Joachim Patenier** (*c.*1480–*c.*1524): *The Rest on the Flight into Egypt.* About 1520. Staatliche Museen, Berlin-Dahlem

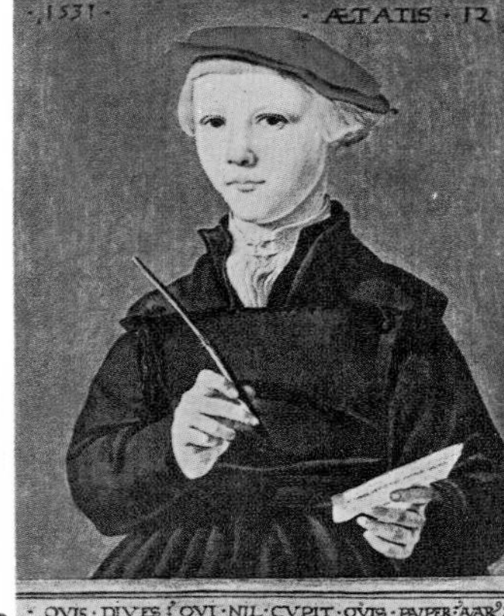

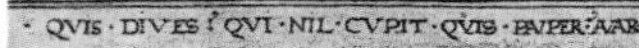

3

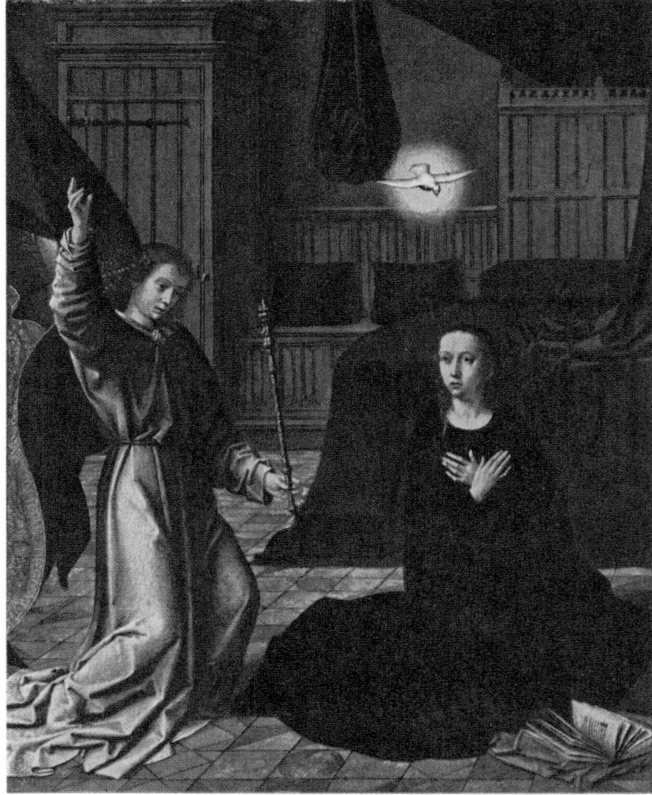

1

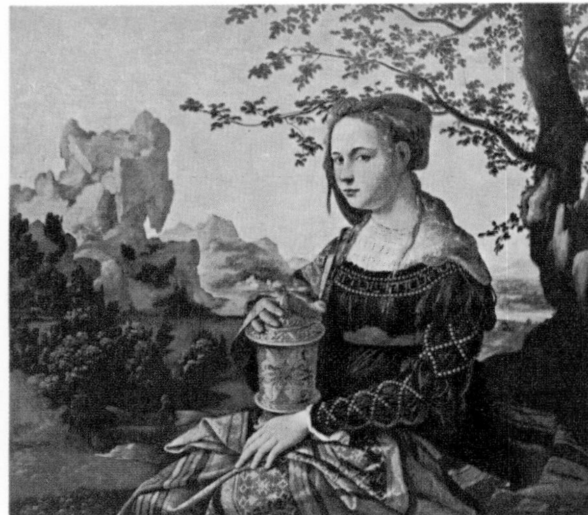

2

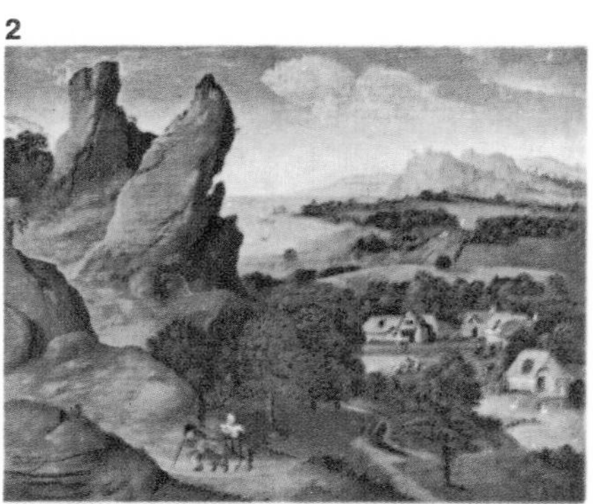

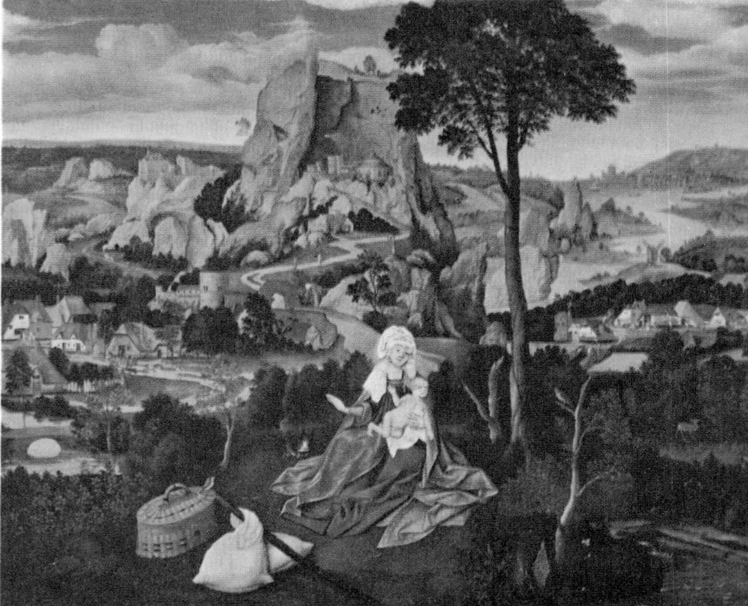

5

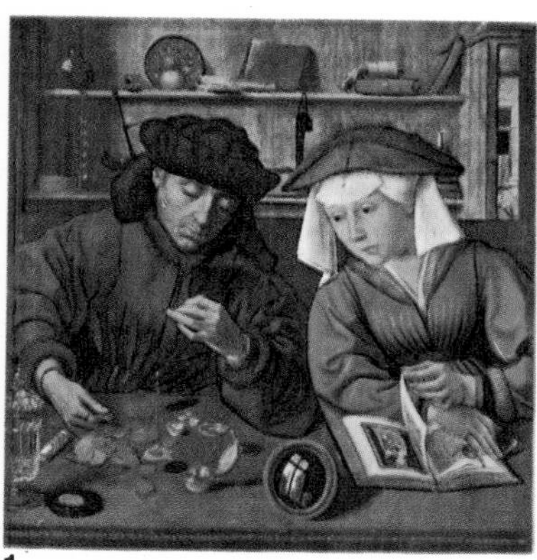
1

1. **Quinten Massys** (1465/6–1530): *The Banker and his Wife.* 1514. Louvre, Paris
2. **Quinten Massys** (1465/6–1530): *The Lamentation.* 1508–11. Koninklijk Museum voor Schone Kunsten, Antwerp
3. **Jan Massys** (*c.*1509–75): *Flora before the Bay of Naples.* 1561. Nationalmuseum, Stockholm
4. **Master of the Female Half-lengths** (*fl.* early 16th century): *Lady Musicians.* Graf Harrach'sche Gemäldegalerie, Vienna
5. **Quinten Massys** (1465/6–1530): *Portrait of Erasmus.* 1517. Galleria Nazionale, Rome
6. **Jan Mostaert** (*c.*1472/3–1555/6): *Portrait of a Man.* Musées Royaux des Beaux-Arts, Brussels

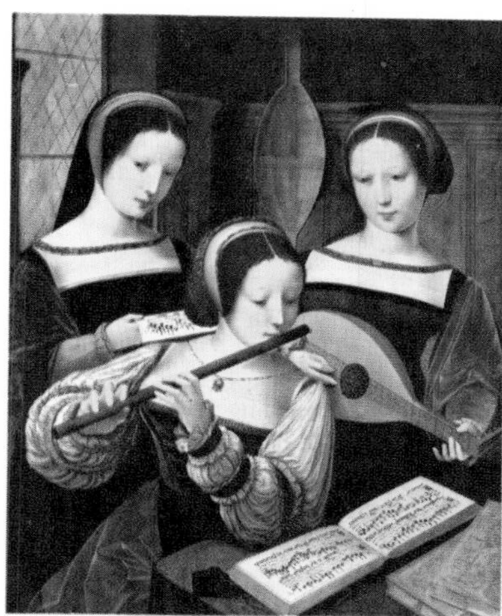
4

2

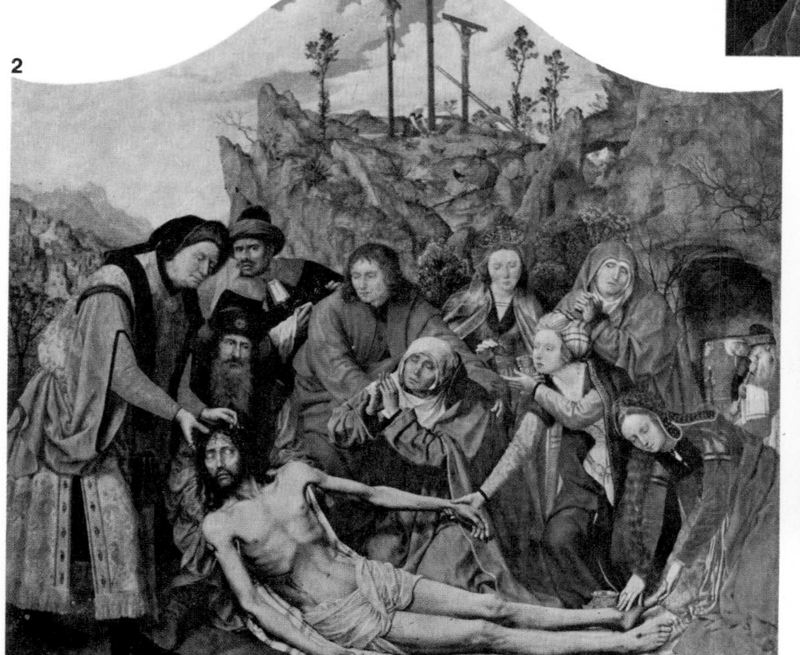

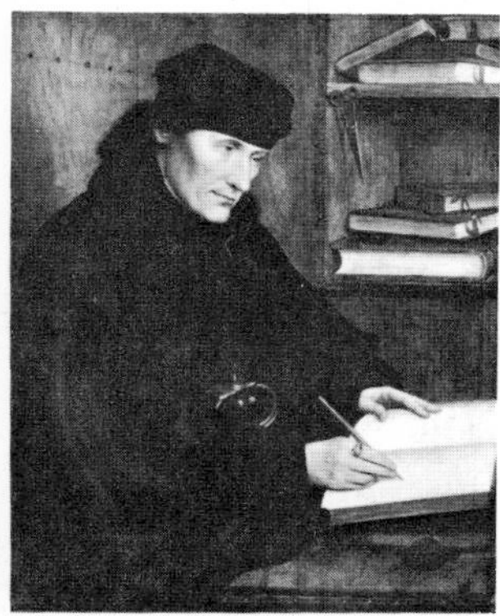
5

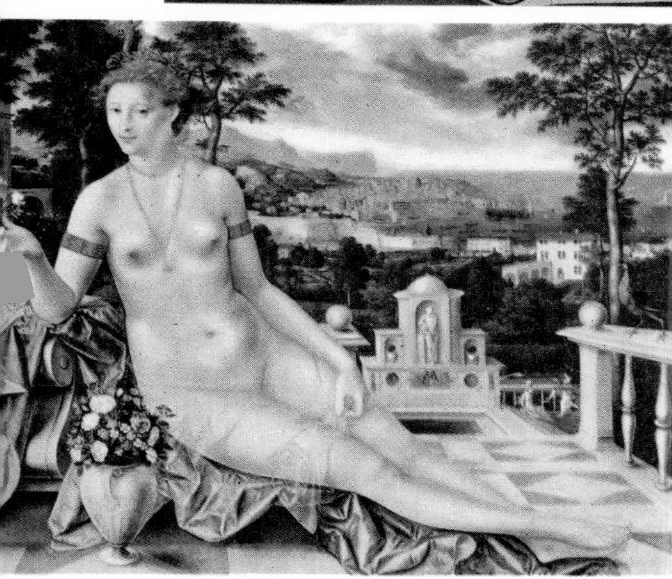

6

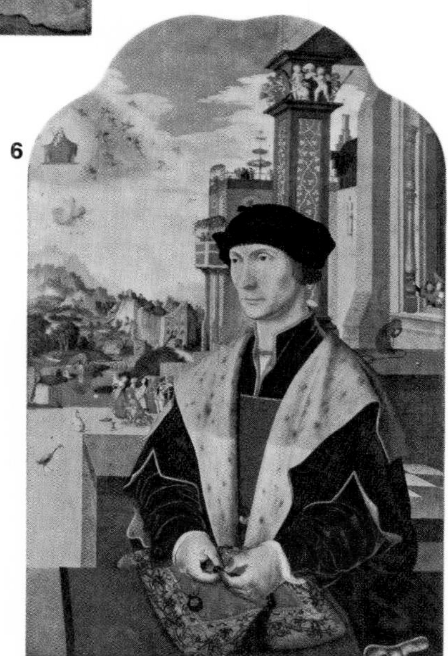

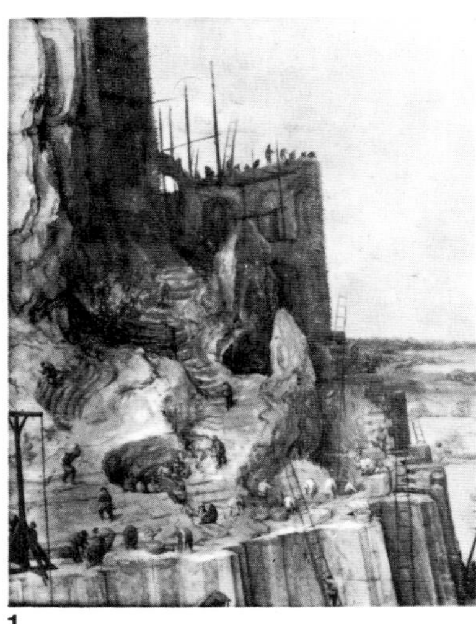
1

Pieter Bruegel (*c.*1525–69)
1. *The Tower of Babel.* Detail. 1563. Kunsthistorisches Museum, Vienna
2. *The Tower of Babel.* Detail. 1563. Kunsthistorisches Museum, Vienna
3. *The Return of the Herd.* 1565. Kunsthistorisches Museum, Vienna
4. *The Parable of the Blind.* 1568. Galleria Nazionale di Capodimonte, Naples
5. Detail from *The Return of the Herd* (fig. 3)
6. *The Fall of Icarus.* About 1565. Musées Royaux des Beaux-Arts, Brussels

4
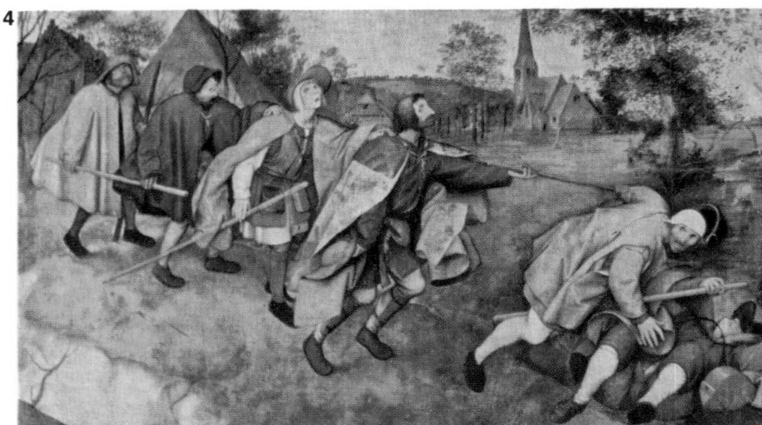

2
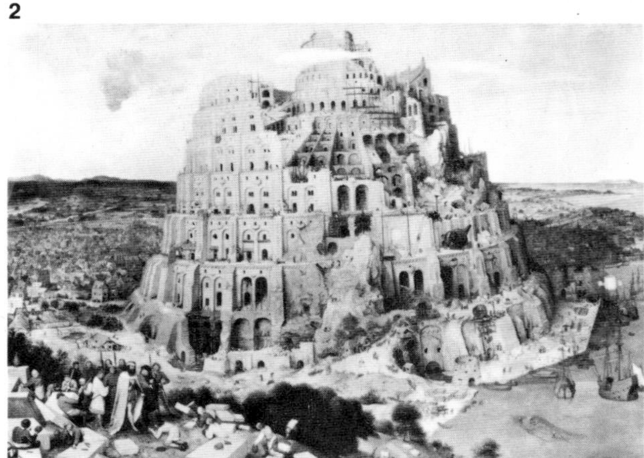

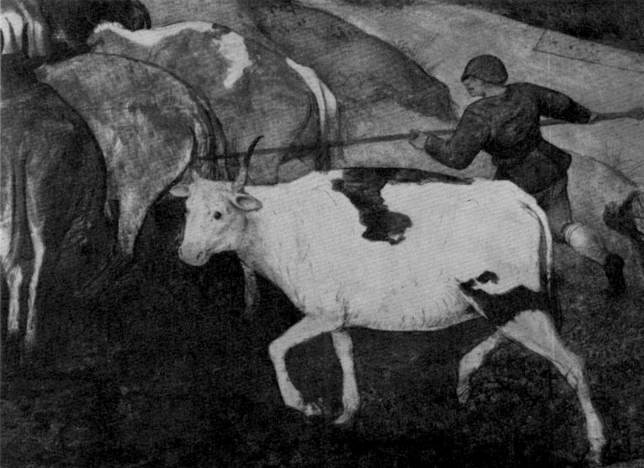

3
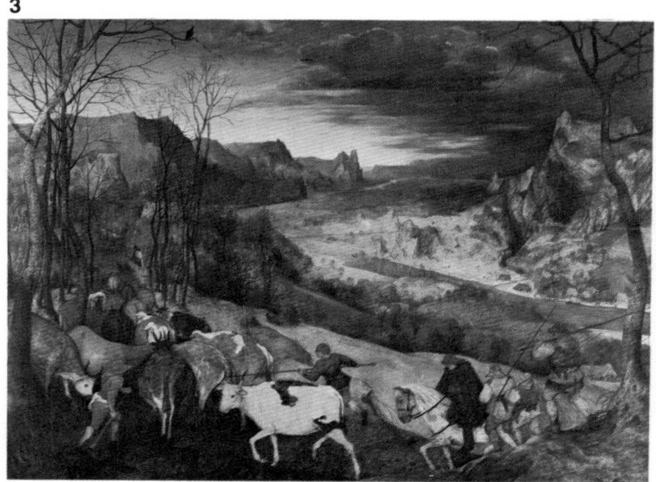

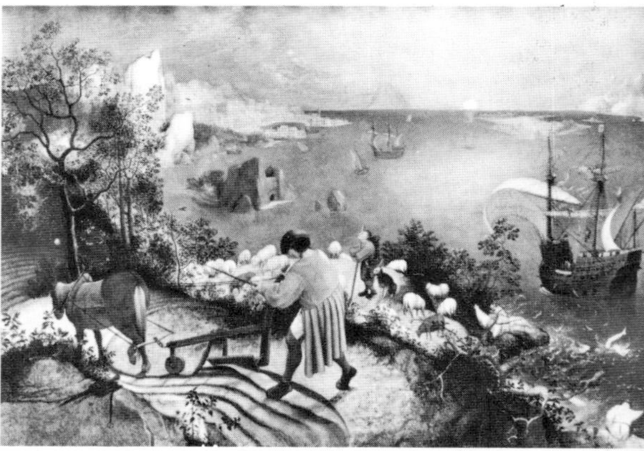

eter Bruegel (*c.*1525–69)
Peasant Wedding. About 1567. Kunsthistorisches Museum, Vienna
Detail from the *Peasant Wedding.* (fig. 1)
The Hunters in the Snow. 1565. Kunsthistorisches Museum, Vienna
Self-portrait. Detail from a drawing. About 1565. Albertina, Vienna
Detail from *The Hunters in the Snow* (fig. 3)

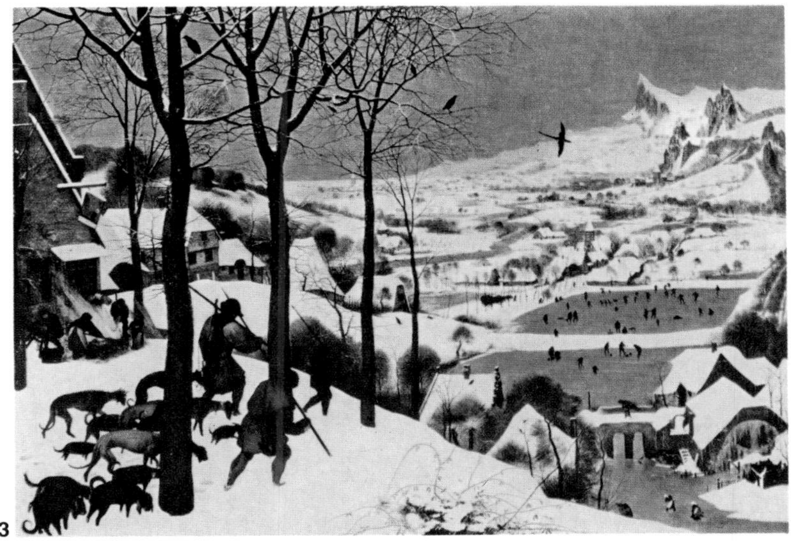

3

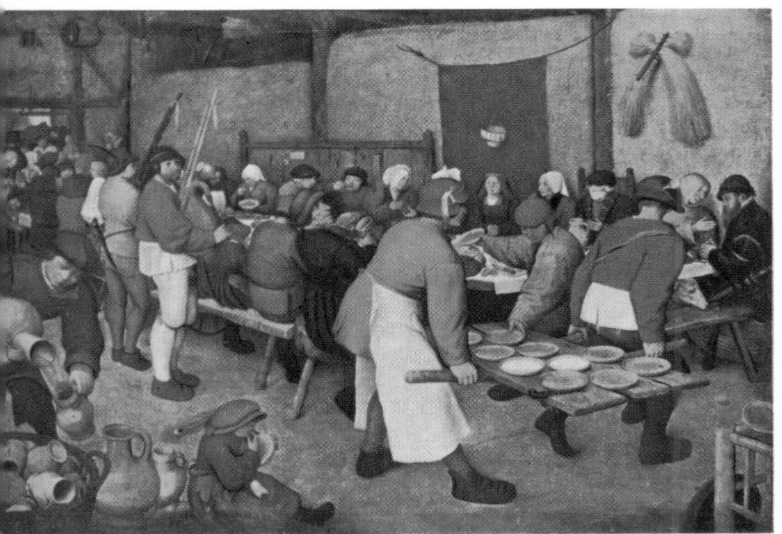

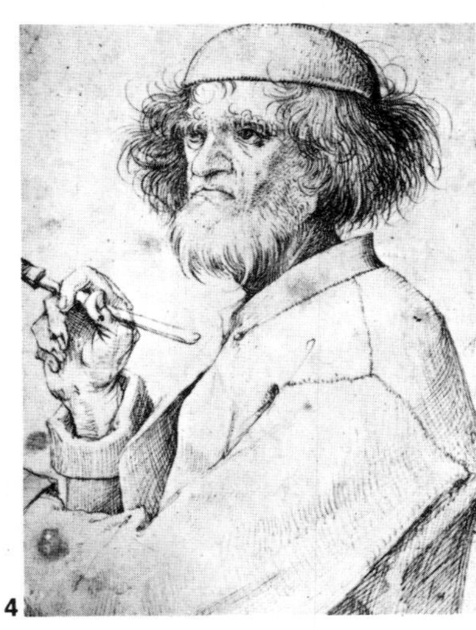

4

5

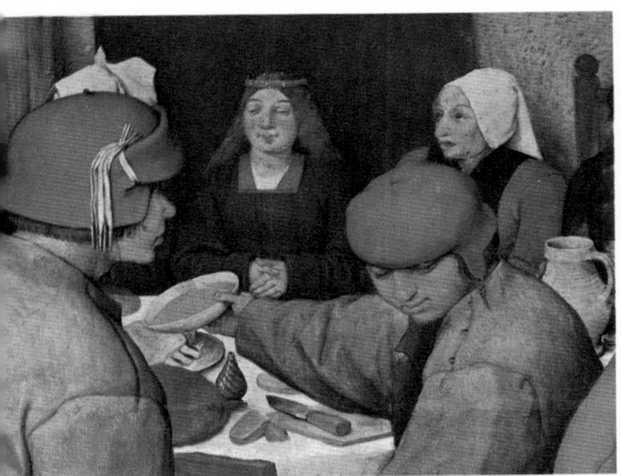

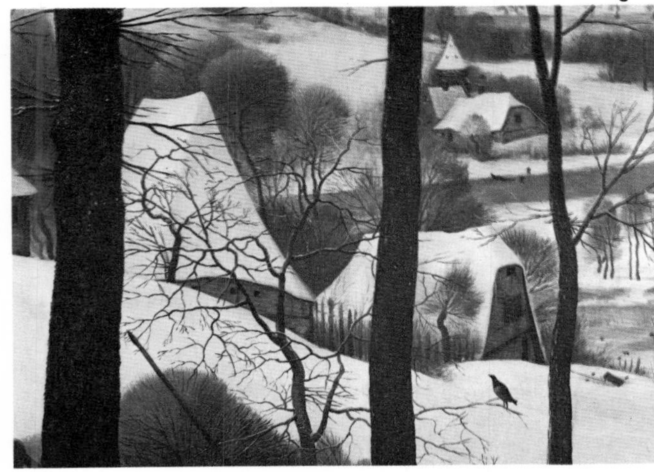

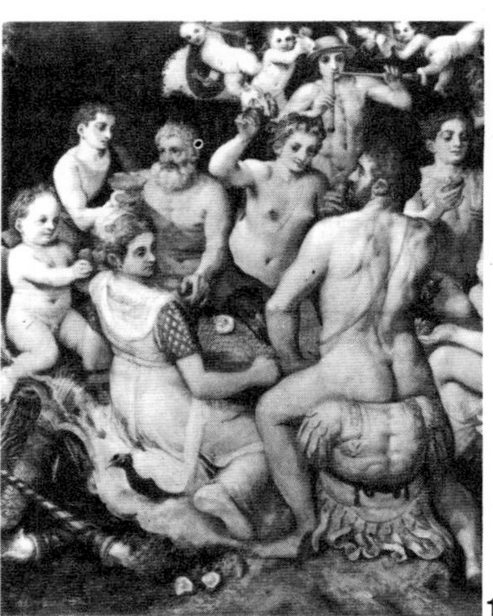

1

1. **Frans Floris** (1516–70): *Feast of the Gods.* Detail. 1550. Koninklijk Museum voor Schone Kunsten, Antwerp
2. **Bernaert van Orley** (*c.*1492–1541): *Hunts of Maximilian.* Detail from tapestry series. 1521–30
3. **Bernaert van Orley** (*c.*1492–1541): *Portrait of Doctor Georg de Zelle.* 1519. Musées Royaux des Beaux-Arts, Brussels
4. **Adriaen de Vries** (*c.*1560–1626): *Mercury carrying off Psyche.* Bronze. 1593. Louvre, Paris
5. **Pieter Aertsen** (*c.*1507/8–75): *The Co* 1559. Musées Royaux des Beaux-Arts, Brussels
6. **Master Francke** (*fl. c.*1405–after 1424 Panel from the Thomas à Becket Altarpie 1424. Kunsthalle, Hamburg

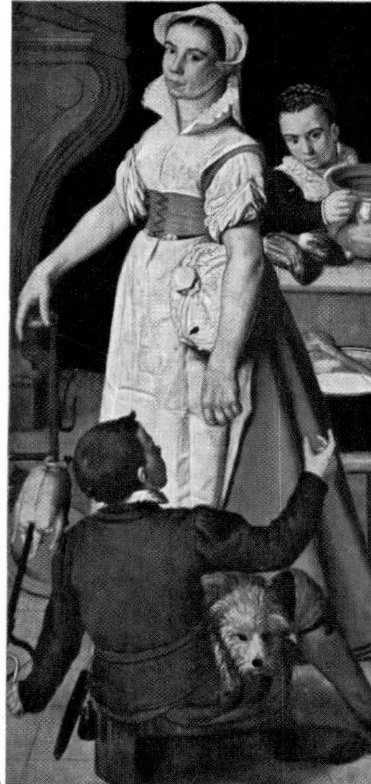

5

2

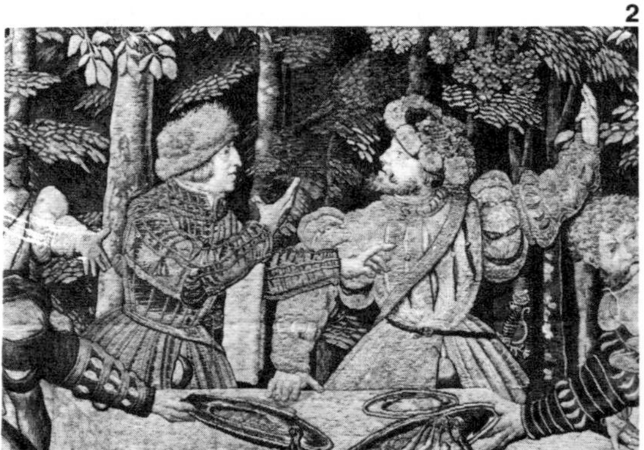

4

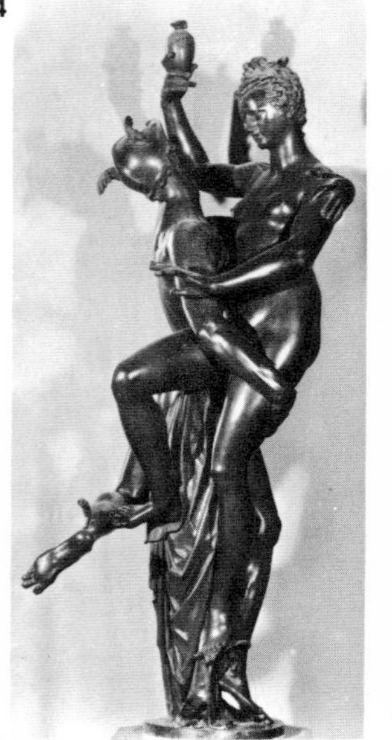

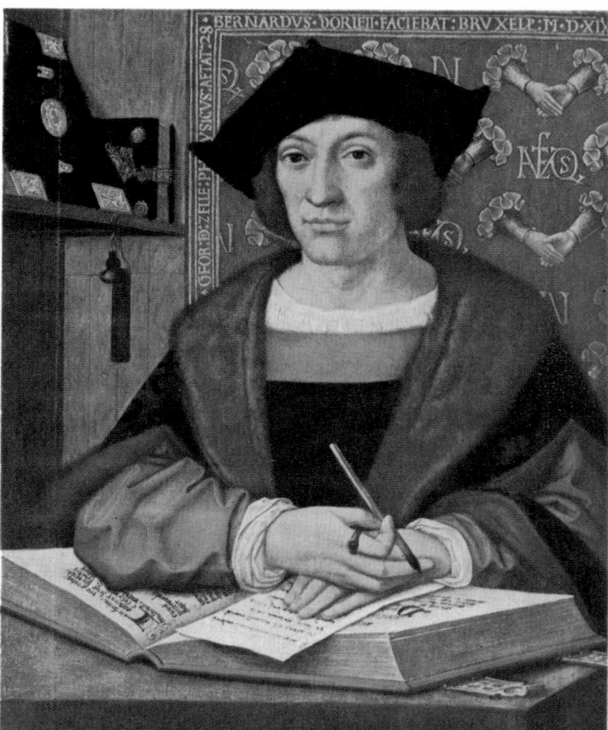

3

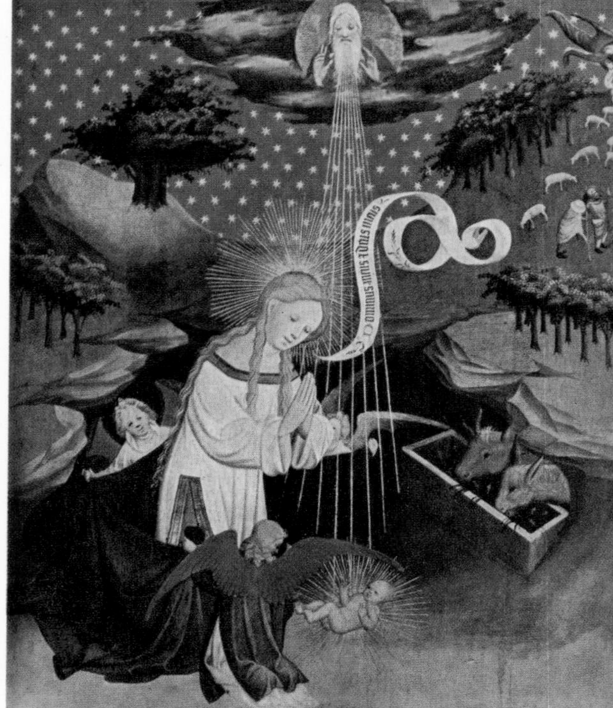

6

Stefan Lochner (d.1451): *Virgin of the Rosebush.* Wallraf-Richartz-Museum, Cologne

Konrad Witz (c.1400–c.1445): *The Miraculous Draught of Fishes.* Panel from the St Peter Altarpiece. 1444. Musée d'Art et d'Histoire, Geneva

Master of the St Bartholomew Altarpiece (*fl.* late 15th century): *St Mary Magdalene.* Detail from central panel of the St Thomas Altarpiece. About 1499. Wallraf-Richartz-Museum, Cologne

4. **Lukas Moser** (*fl.* first half of 15th century): *Wise Virgins.* Detail from predella of the Magdalene Altarpiece. 1431. Parish church, Tiefenbronn
5. **Konrad Witz** (c.1400–c.1445): *Esther before Ahasuerus.* Panel from the *Heilspiegelaltar* (altarpiece of the Redemption). About 1435–6. Kunstmuseum, Basle

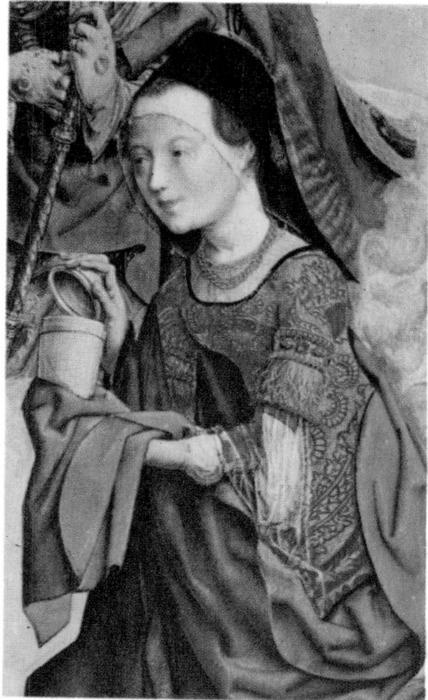

3

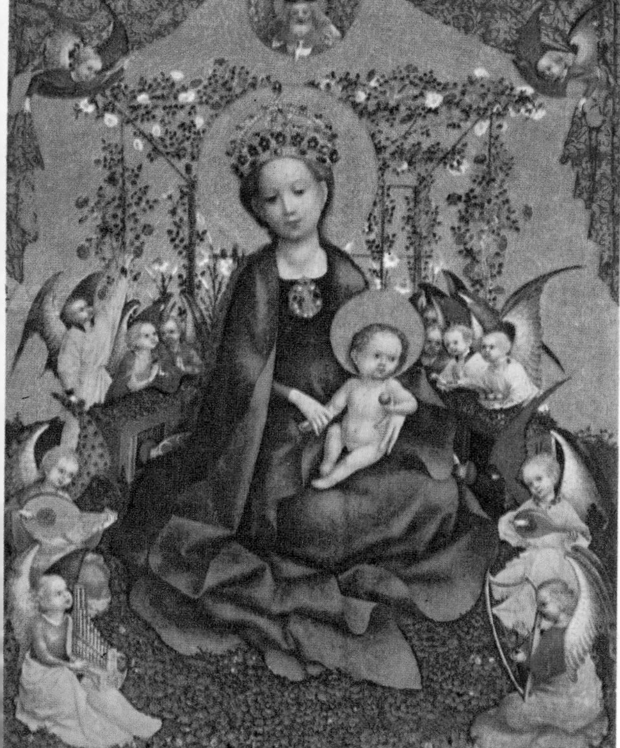

4

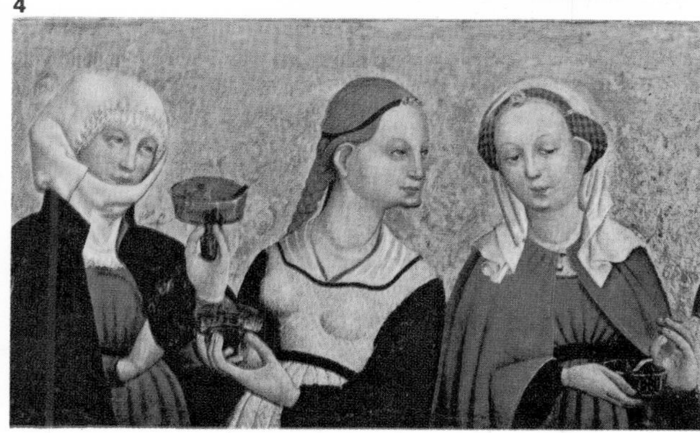

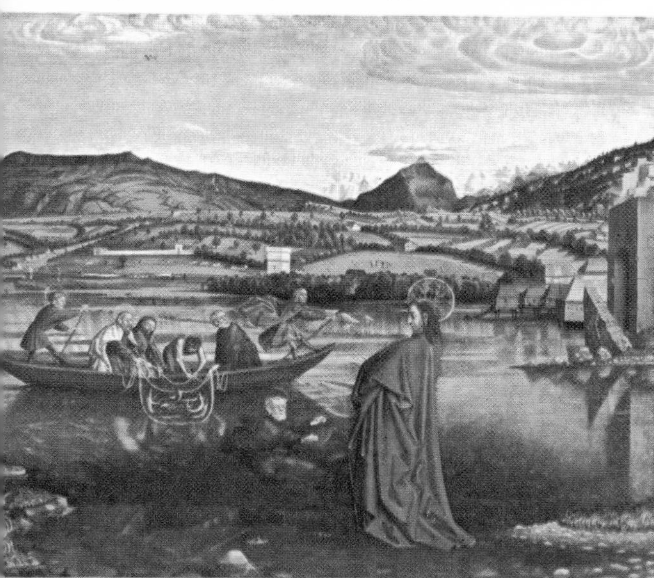

5

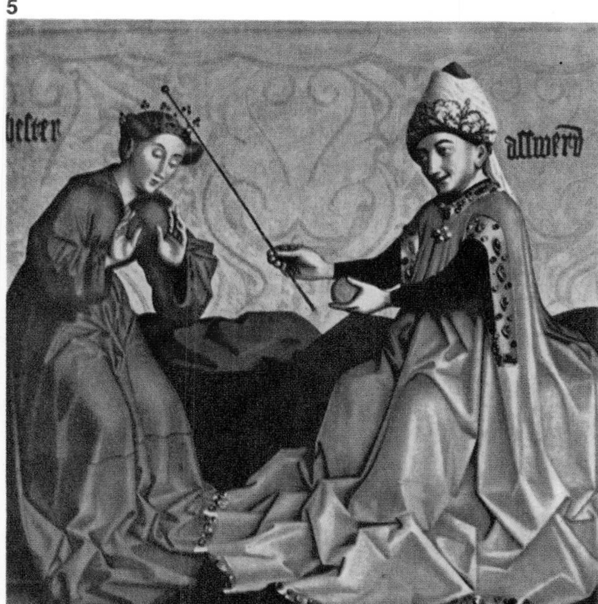

1. **Nicolaus Gerhaert van Leyden** (d.*c.*1473): *Bärbel von Ottenheim* (?). 1464. Städtische Skulpturensammlung, Frankfurt
2. **Nicolaus Gerhaert van Leyden** (d.*c.*1473): *Self-portrait* (?). About 1467. Musée de l'Oeuvre Notre Dame, Strasbourg
3. **Master of the Housebook** (*fl.*1475–90): *Christ falling under the Cross.* Engraving. Print Room, Rijksmuseum, Amsterdam
4. **Michael Pacher** (*fl.*1465?–1498): *St Jerome, St Augustine, St Gregory* and *St Ambrose.* About 1483. Alte Pinakothek, Munich
5. **Master of the Aix-la-Chapelle Altarpiece** (*fl. c.*1480–1520): *The Virgin and Child.* About 1515–20. Alte Pinakothek, Munich
6. **Martin Schongauer** (*c.*1450–91), workshop of: *Noli me tangere.* Panel from the altarpiece of the Dominicans. About 1475. Unterlinden Museum, Colmar

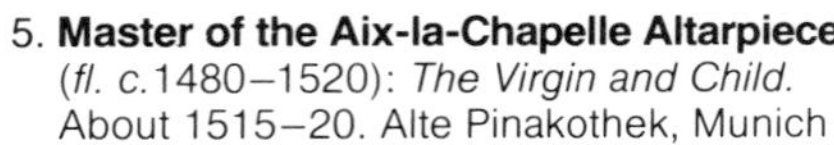

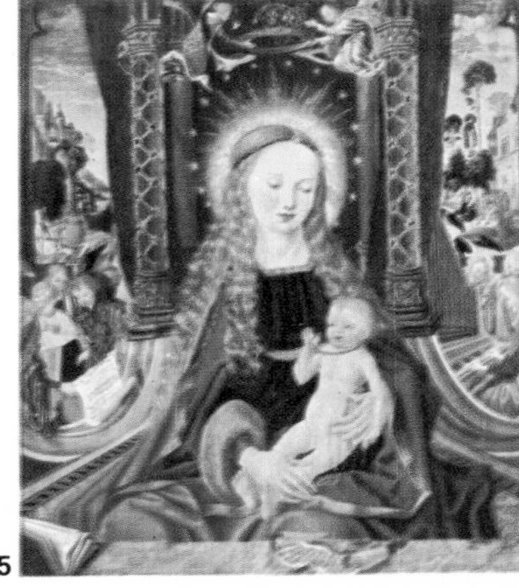

5

1

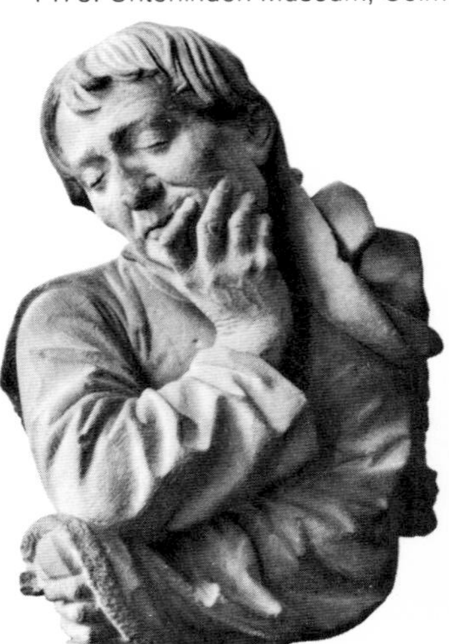

2

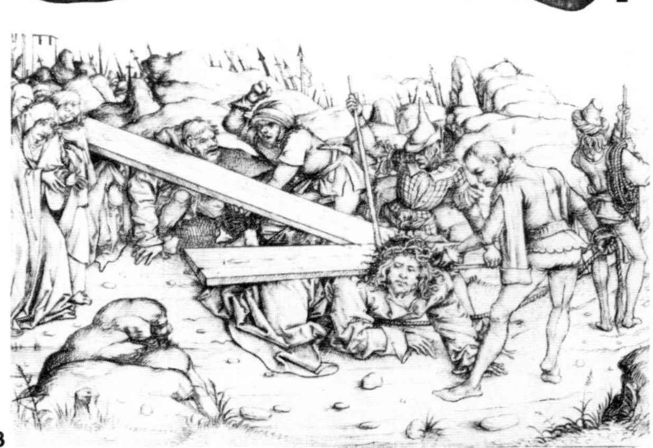

3

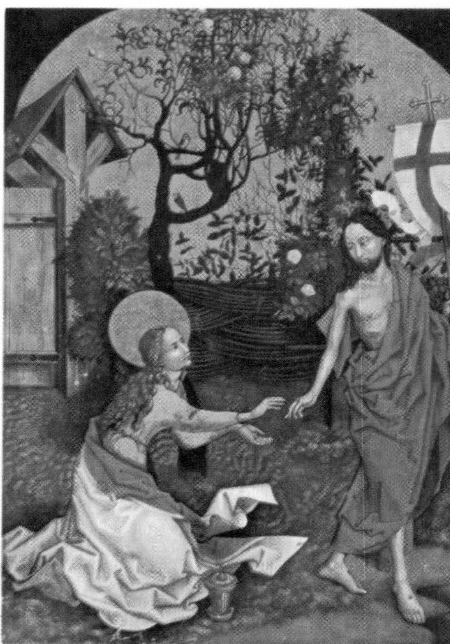

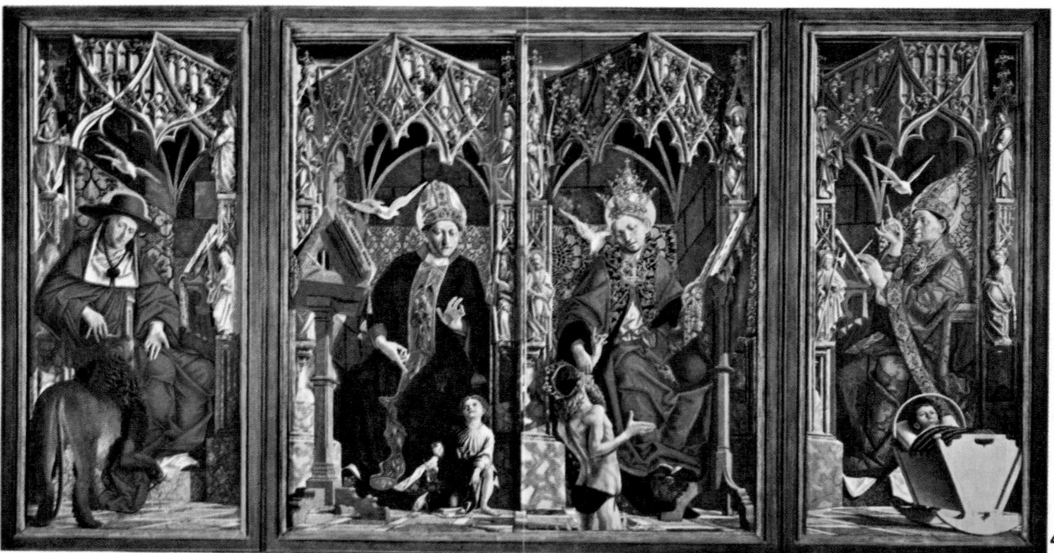

4

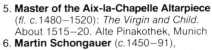

. **Tilman Riemenschneider** (*c.*1460–1531): *Adam.* Detail. 1491–3. Mainfränkisches Museum, Würzburg

. **Master of the Garden of Paradise** (*fl.* early 15th century): *Garden of Paradise.* About 1410. Städelsches Kunstinstitut, Frankfurt

3. **Tilman Riemenschneider** (*c.*1460–1531): *The Last Supper.* Detail from the altarpiece of the Holy Blood. Wood. 1501–5. Jacobskirche, Rothenburg

4. **Master of the Life of the Virgin** (*fl. c.*1460–80/90): *The Annunciation.* About 1470. Alte Pinakothek, Munich

5. **Tilman Riemenschneider** (*c.*1460–1531): Tomb of Bishop Rudolf von Scherenberg. Detail. Stone. 1496–9. Würzburg Cathedral

6. **Veit Stoss:** *St Peter.* Detail of fig. 7

7. **Veit Stoss** (1438/47–1533): *The Death of the Virgin.* Detail from the high altar of St Mary's Church, Cracow. Wood. 1477–89

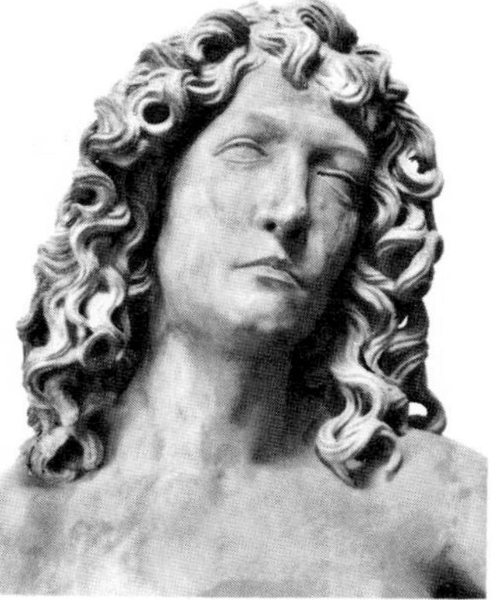
1

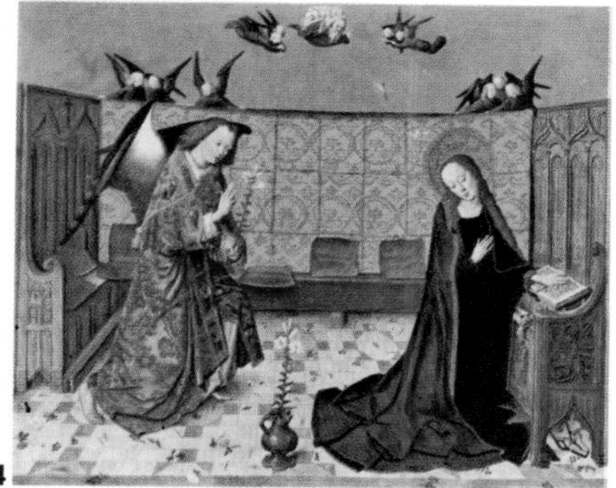
4

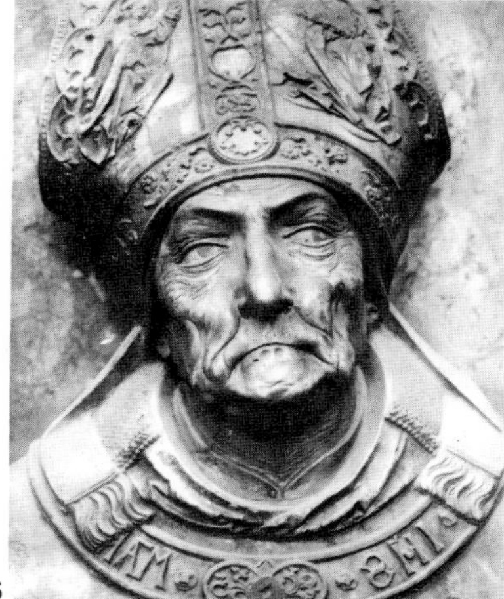
5

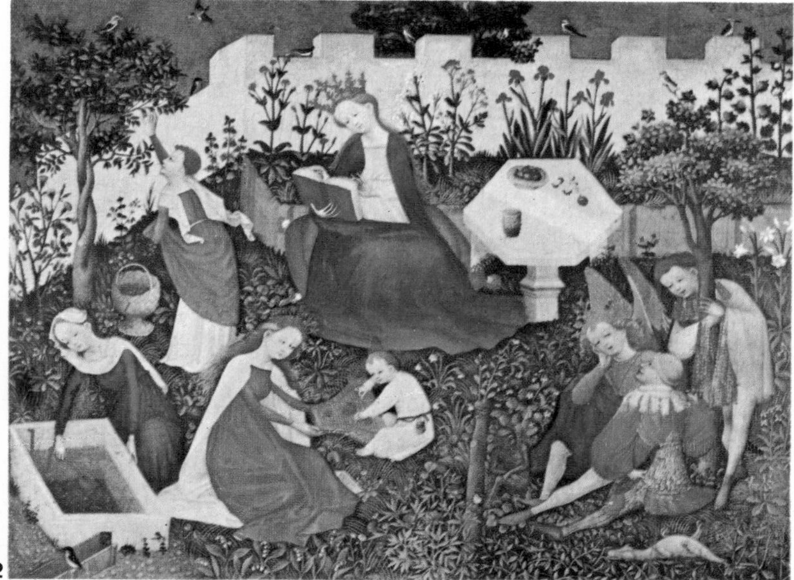
2

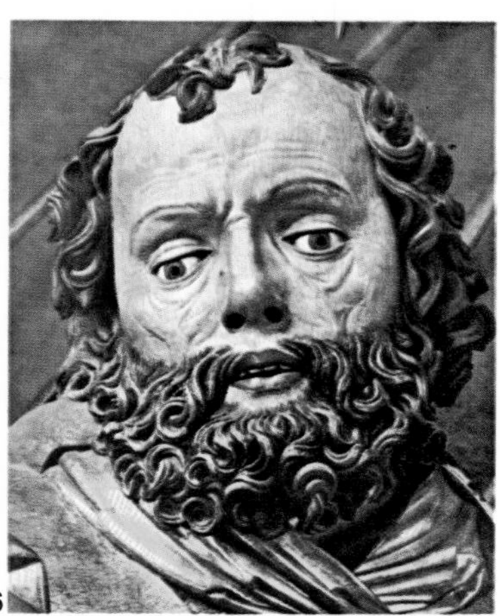
6

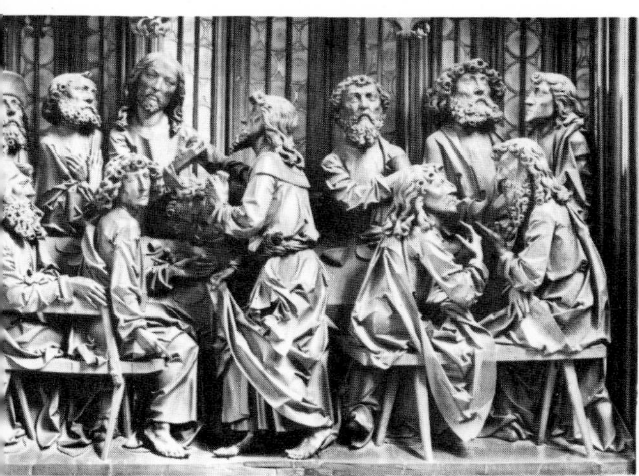

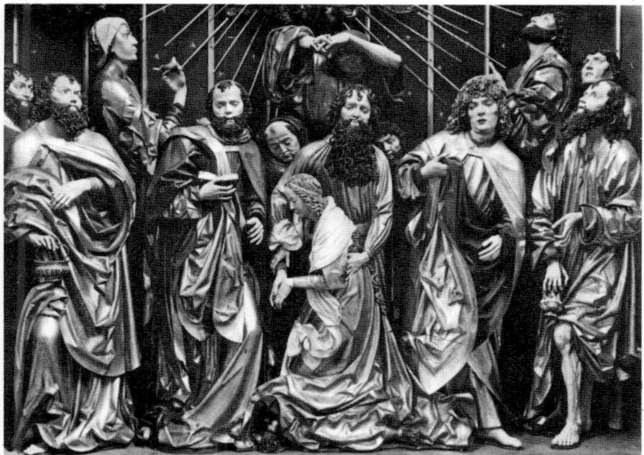
7

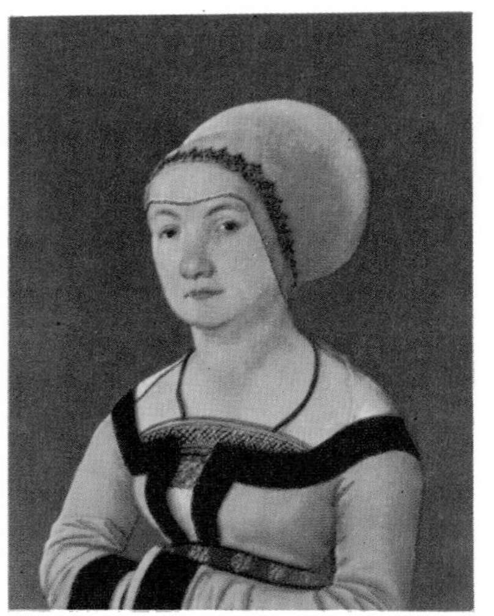

1

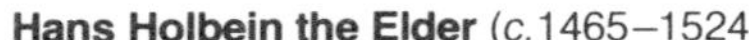

Hans Holbein the Elder (*c.*1465–1524)

1. *Portrait of a Woman.* 1516–17. Kunstmuseum, Basle

Hans Holbein the Younger (1497/8–1543)

2. *Portrait of Jane Seymour.* 1536–7. Kunsthistorisches Museum, Vienna
3. *Portrait of Anne of Cleves.* 1539. Louvre, Paris
4. *Portrait of Hermann Wedigh.* 1532. Metropolitan Museum of Art, New York
5. *Portrait of Dorothea Kannengiesser.* 1516. Kunstmuseum, Basle
6. *Portrait of Magdalen Offenburg as Lais of Corinth.* 1526. Kunstmuseum, Basle
7. *The Ambassadors: Jean de Dinteville and Georges de Selve.* 1533. National Gallery, London

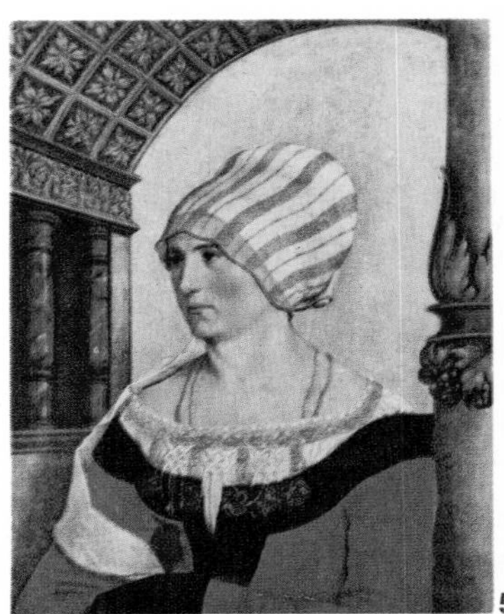

5

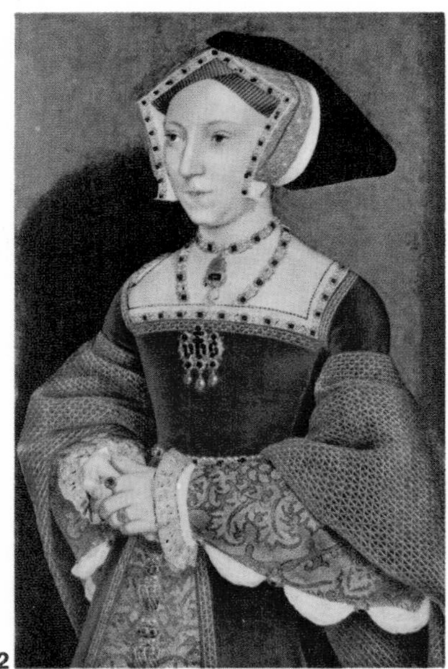

2

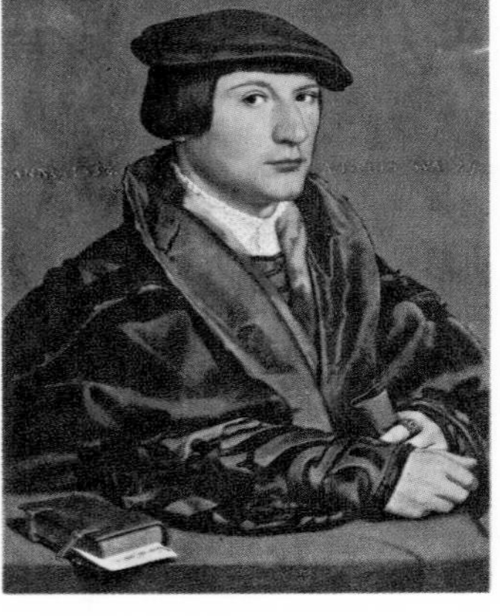

4

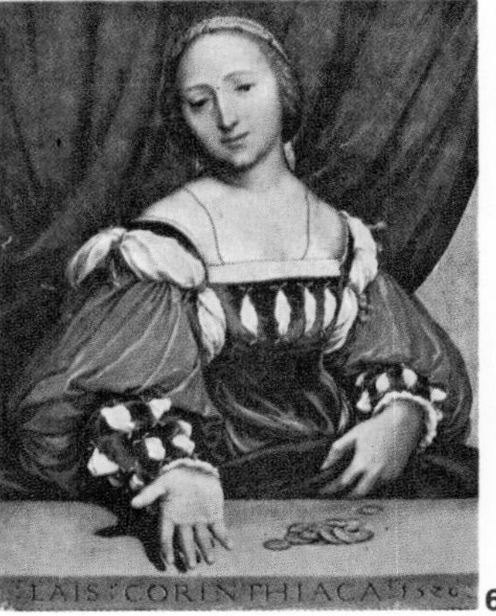

6

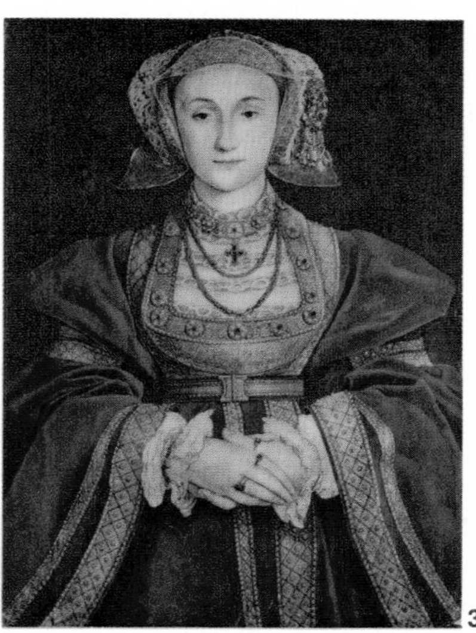

3

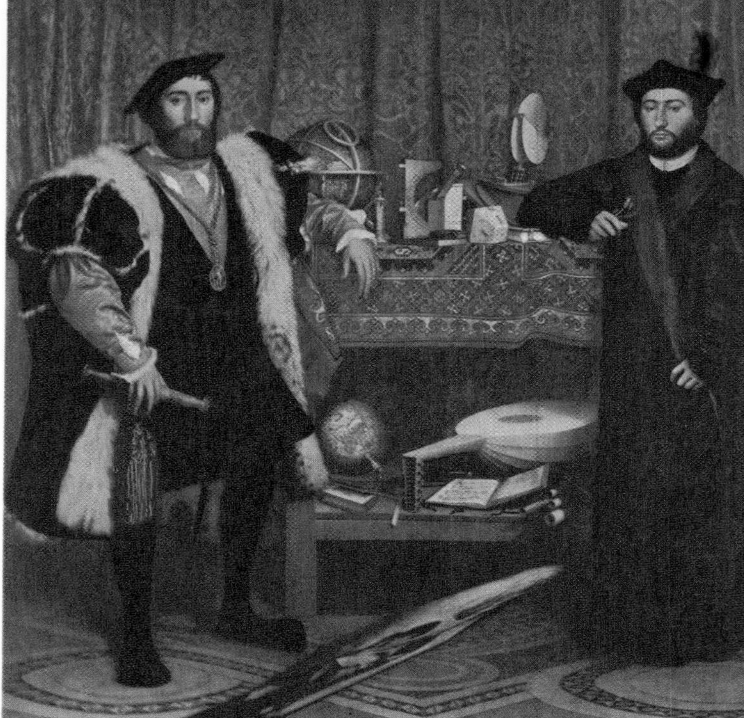

7

latthias Grünewald (*c.*1470–1528): *St ;rasmus and St Maurice.* Alte Pinakothek, lunich
latthias Grünewald (*c.*1470–1528): *The ;rucifixion.* Central panel (wings closed) f the Isenheim Altarpiece. About 1512–15. Interlinden Museum, Colmar
latthias Grünewald (*c.*1470–1528): *;oncert of Angels and Nativity.* Central anel (wings open) of the Isenheim ltarpiece. About 1512–15. Unterlinden luseum, Colmar
'eter Vischer the Younger (1487–1528): *)rpheus and Eurydice.* Bronze. About 515–20. Staatliche Museen, erlin-Dahlem

5. **Peter Vischer the Elder** (*c.*1460–1529): *Self-portrait.* Detail from bronze shrine of St Sebald. 1507–19. Church of St Sebald, Nuremberg

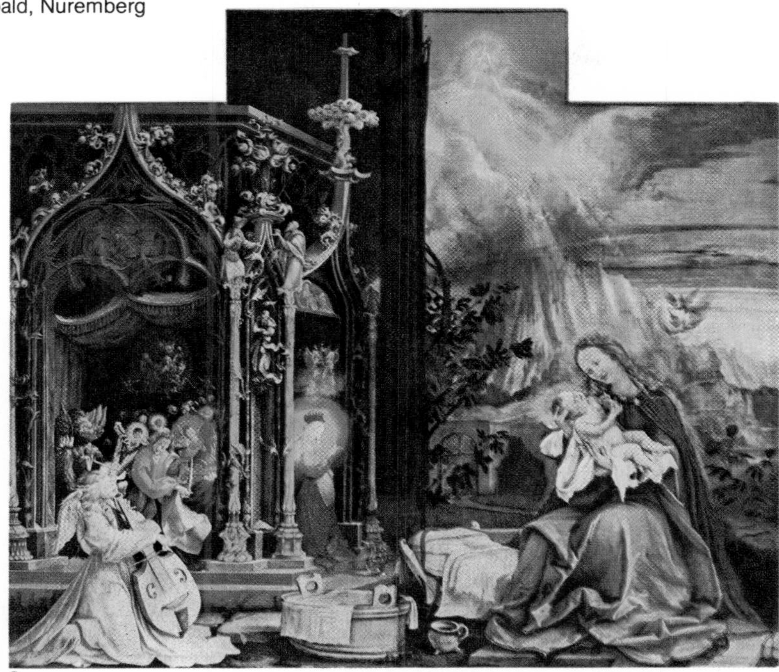
3

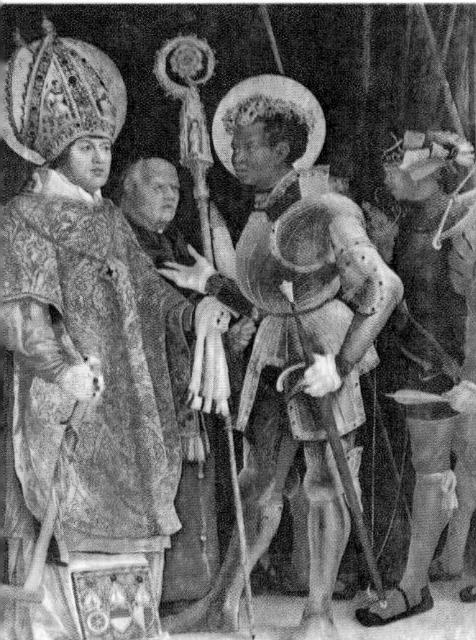
1

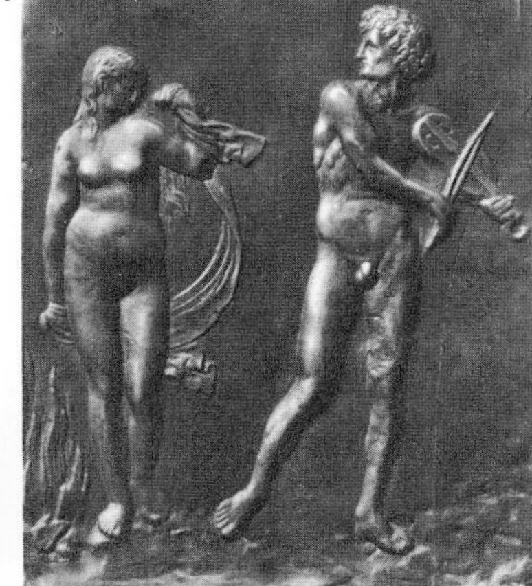
4

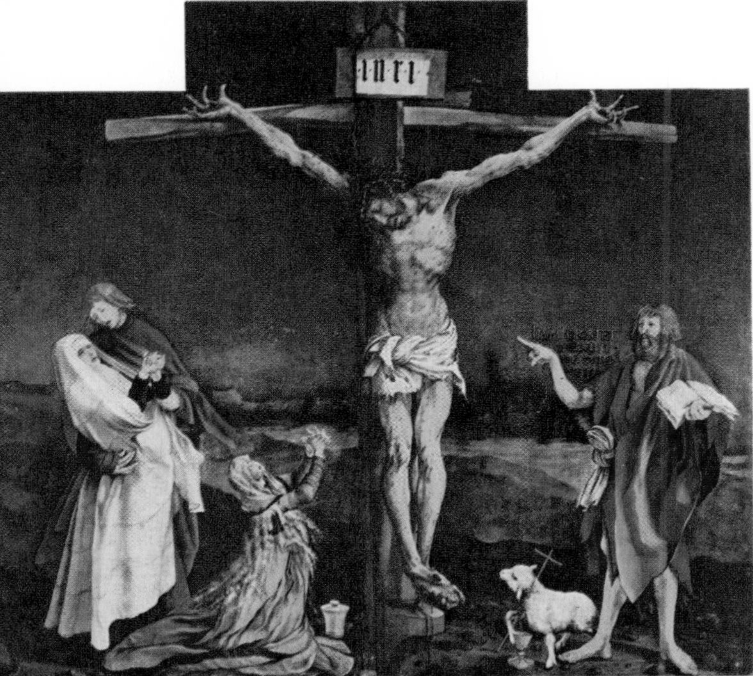

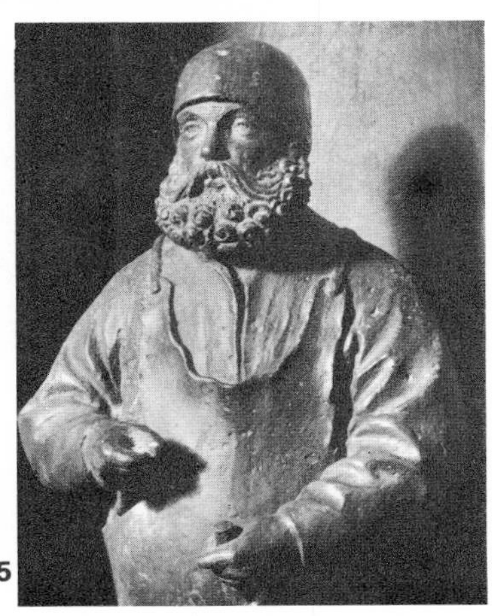
5

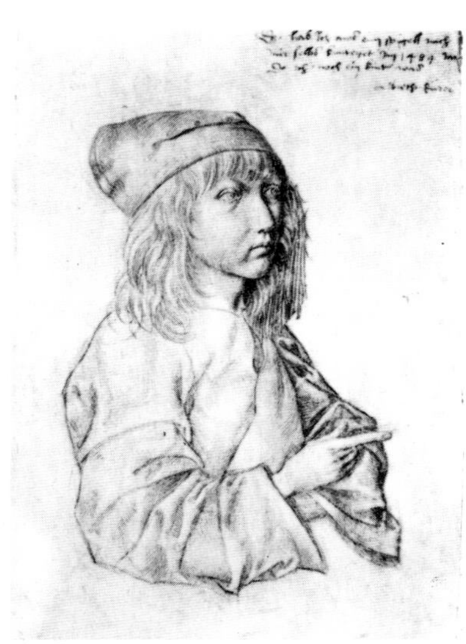

1

Albrecht Dürer (1471–1528)

1. *Self-portrait.* Silverpoint drawing. 1484. Albertina, Vienna
2. *Abduction of Amymone.* Copperplate engraving. 1498. Musée du Petit Palais, Paris
3. *Hare.* Watercolour and body-colour. 1502. Albertina, Vienna
4. *St Jerome in his Study.* Copperplate engraving. 1514. Galleria Corsini, Rome
5. *View of the Arco Valley.* 1495. Cabinet des Dessins, Louvre, Paris
6. *Portrait of Oswolt Krel.* 1499. Alte Pinakothek, Munich
7. *St Anthony.* Copperplate engraving. 1519. Musée du Petit Palais, Paris

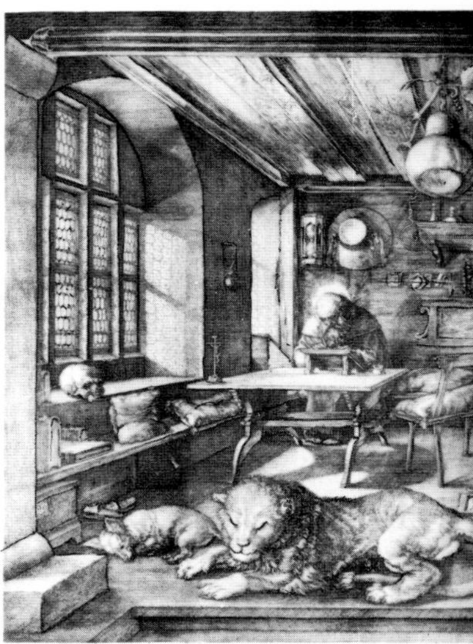

4

5

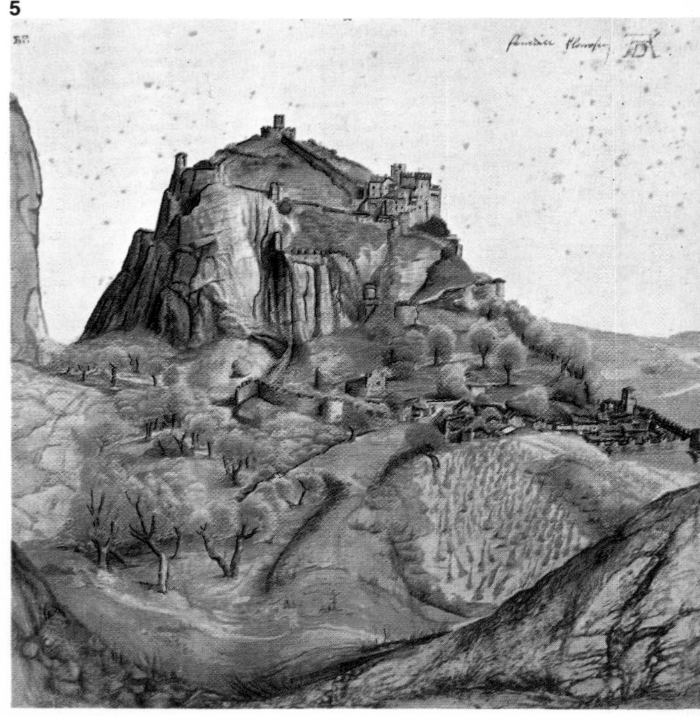

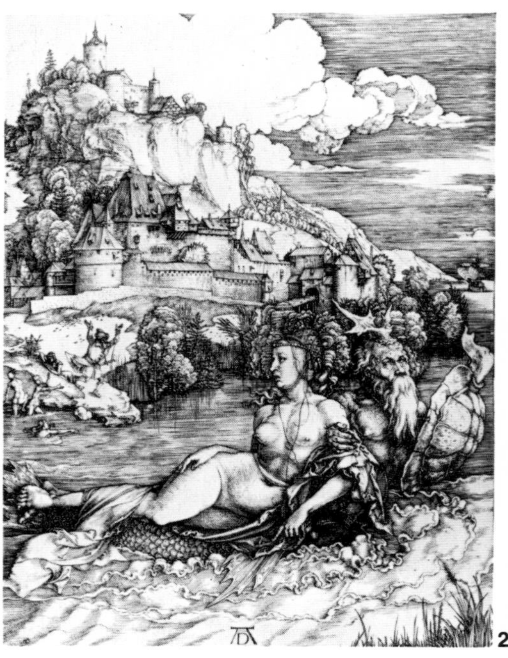

2

3

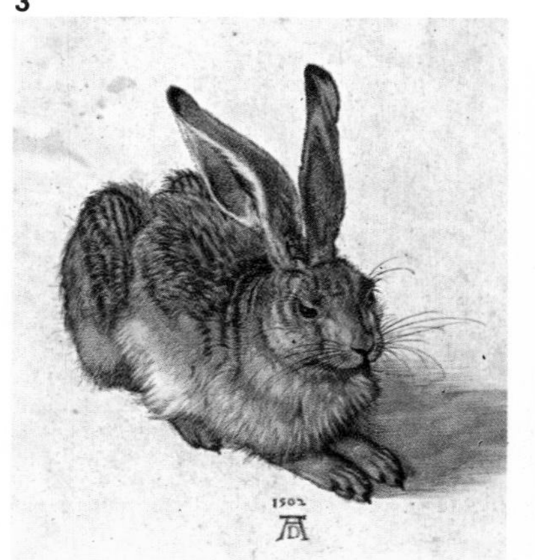

6

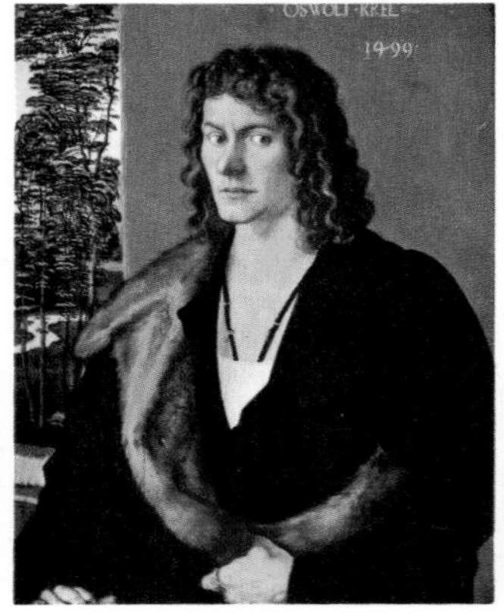

7

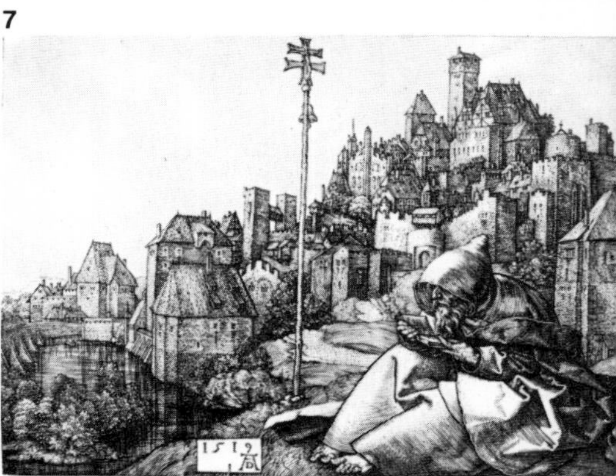

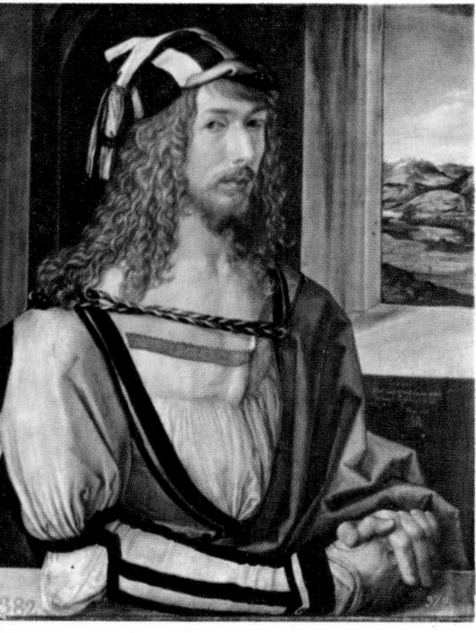

Albrecht Dürer (1471–1528)
1. *Self-portrait.* 1498. Prado, Madrid
2. *St John and St Peter.* Left panel of the *Four Apostles.* 1526
3. *The Virgin and Child.* 1512. Kunsthistorisches Museum, Vienna
4. attributed to: *Portrait of a Man.* National Gallery of Art, Washington DC
5. *Adam and Eve.* 1507. Prado, Madrid

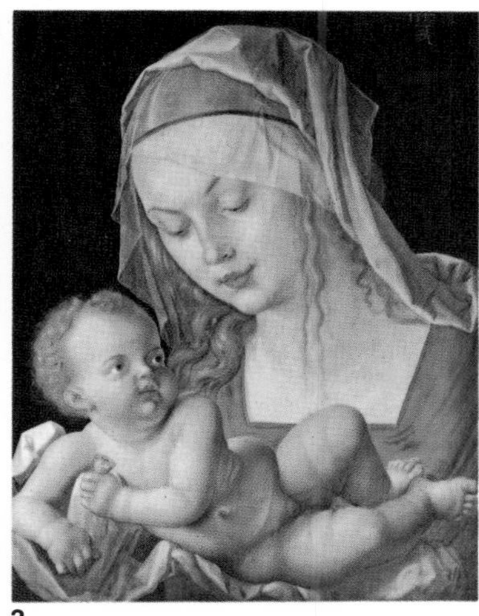

3

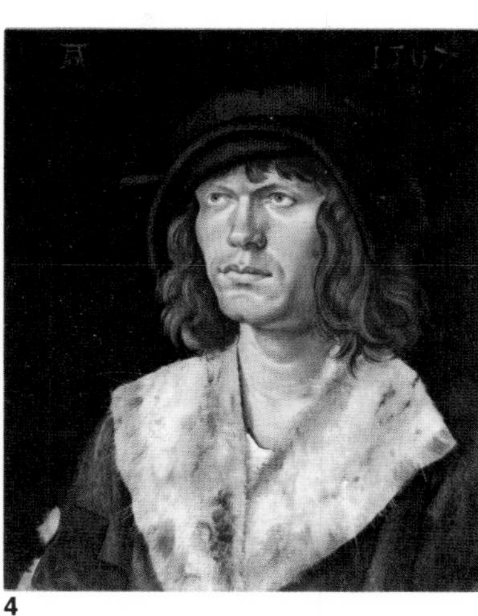

4

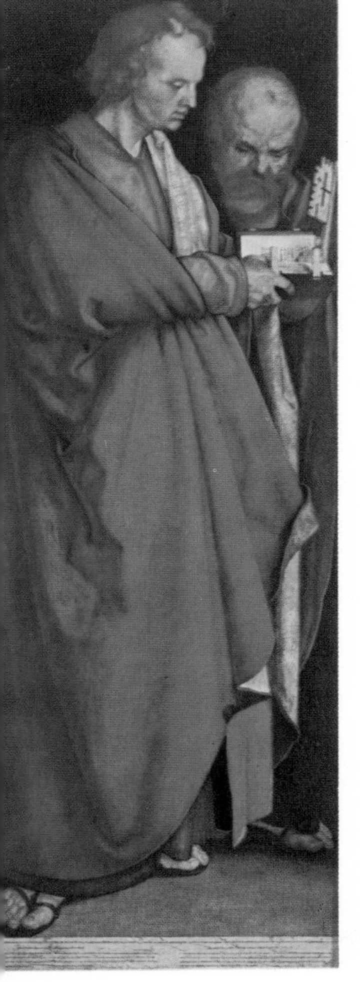

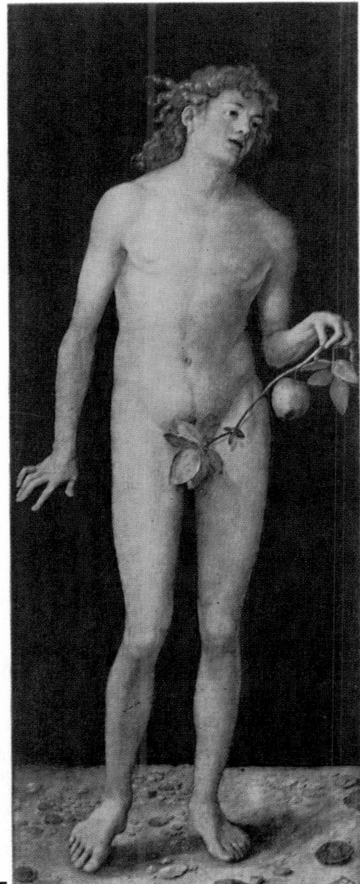

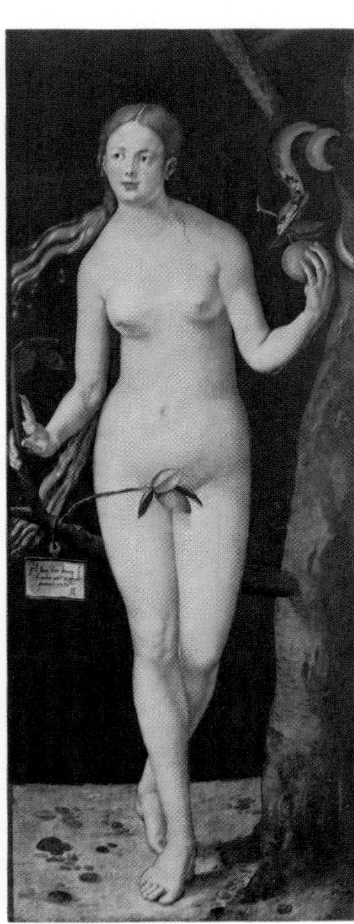

5

1. **Albrecht Altdorfer** (*c.*1480–1538): *Landscape with Church.* Watercolour. Albertina, Vienna
2. **Hans Baldung Grien** (1484/5–1545): *Bewitched Groom.* Woodcut. About 1544
3. **Hans Baldung Grien** (1484/5–1545): *The Three Graces.* About 1540. Prado, Madrid
4. **Albrecht Altdorfer** (*c.*1480–1538): *Wild Men of the Forest.* Drawing. 1510. Albertina, Vienna
5. **Albrecht Altdorfer** (*c.*1480–1538): Detail from *Susanna at the Bath.* 1526. Alte Pinakothek, Munich
6. **Hans Baldung Grien** (1484/5–1545): *Saturn.* Drawing. 1516. Albertina, Vienna
7. **Hans Baldung Grien** (1484/5–1545): *Two Witches.* 1523. Städelsches Kunstinstitut, Frankfurt

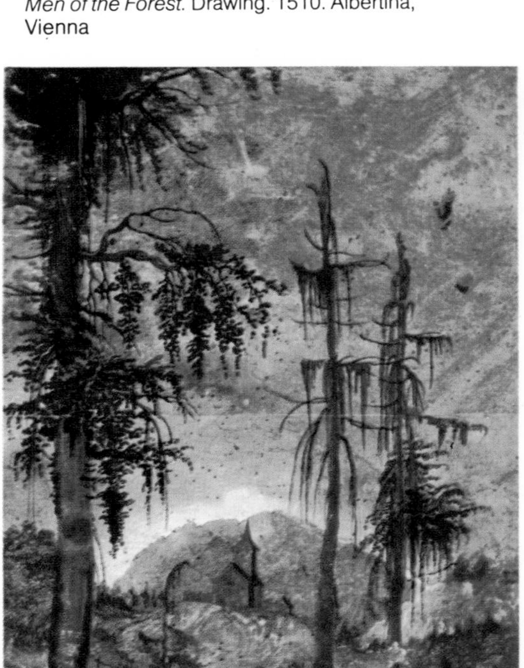

1

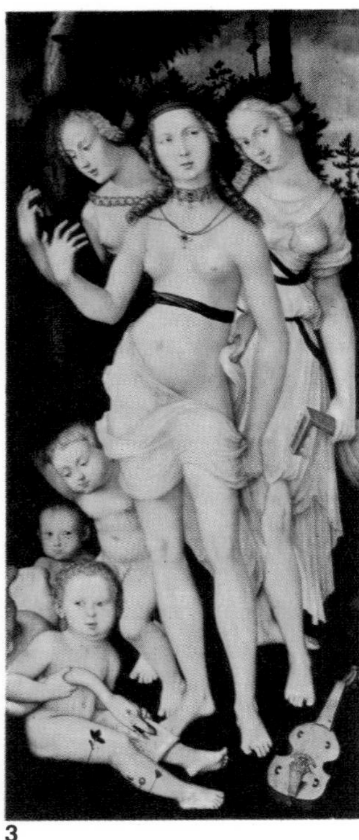

3

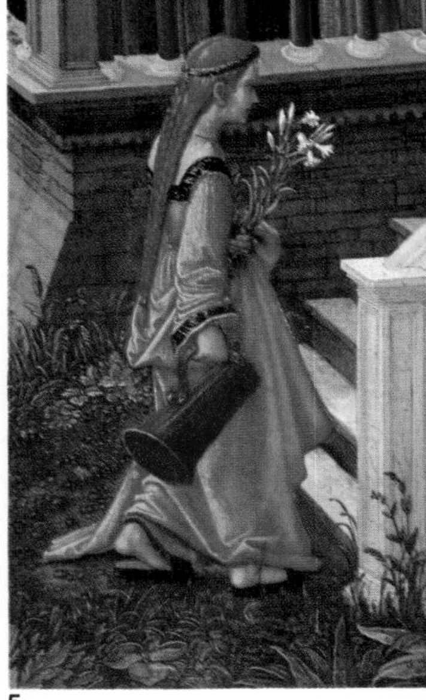

5

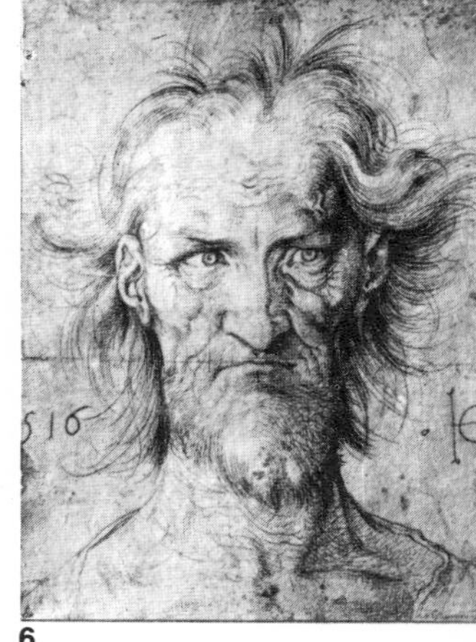

6

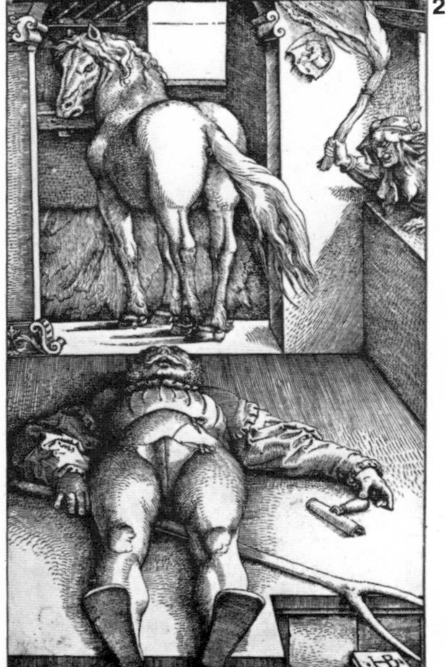

2

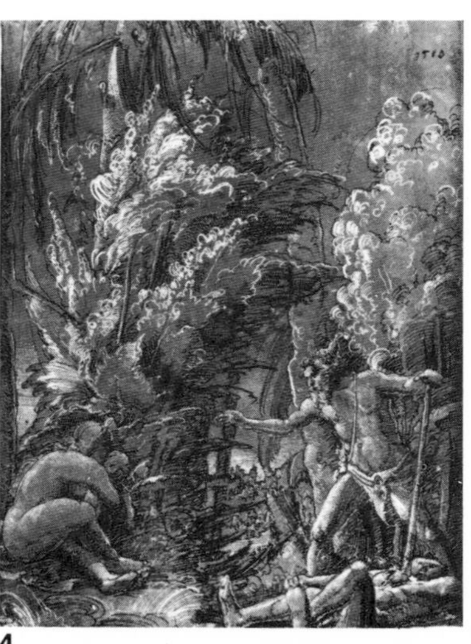

4

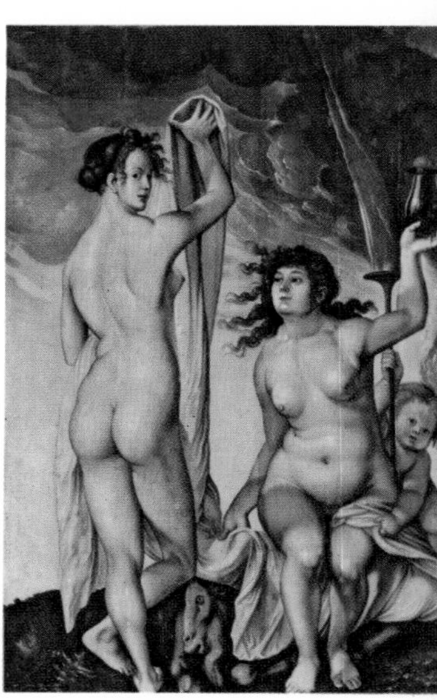

7

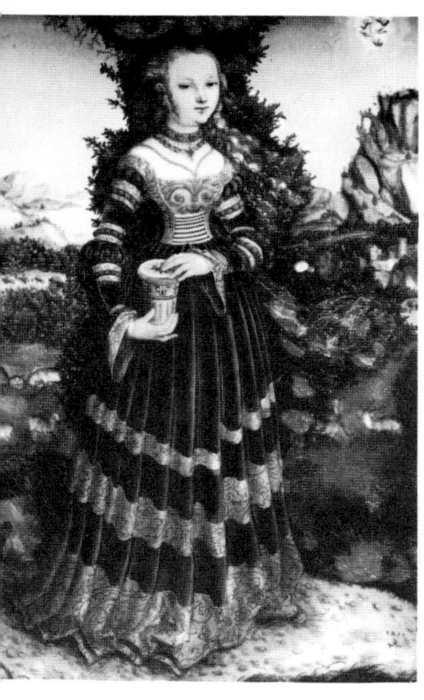

Lucas Cranach the Elder (1472–1553)

1. *St Mary Magdalene.* 1525. Wallraf-Richartz-Museum, Cologne
2. *The Judgement of Paris.* 1530. Staatliche Kunsthalle, Karlsruhe
3. *Portrait of Hans Luther.* Drawing. Albertina, Vienna
4. *Judith with the Head of Holofernes.* After 1526. Staatsgalerie, Stuttgart

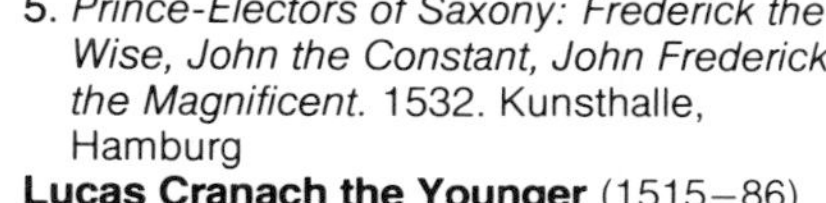

5. *Prince-Electors of Saxony: Frederick the Wise, John the Constant, John Frederick the Magnificent.* 1532. Kunsthalle, Hamburg

Lucas Cranach the Younger (1515–86)

6. *Venus and Cupid.* Alte Pinakothek, Munich
7. *Portrait of a Woman.* 1564. Boston Museum of Fine Arts

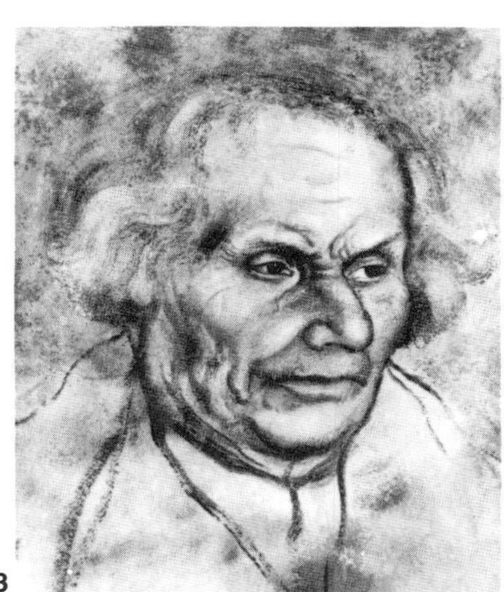

3

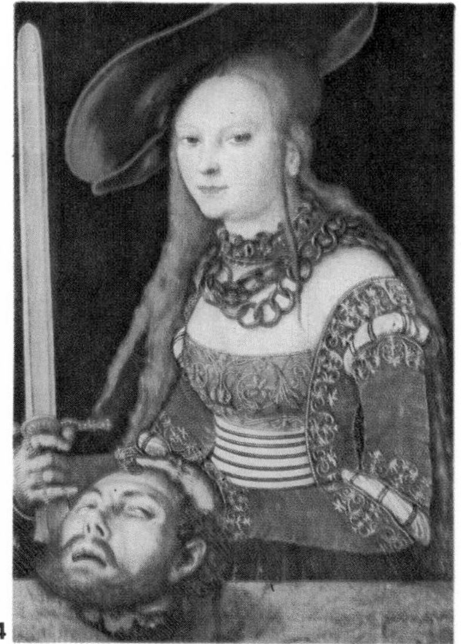

4

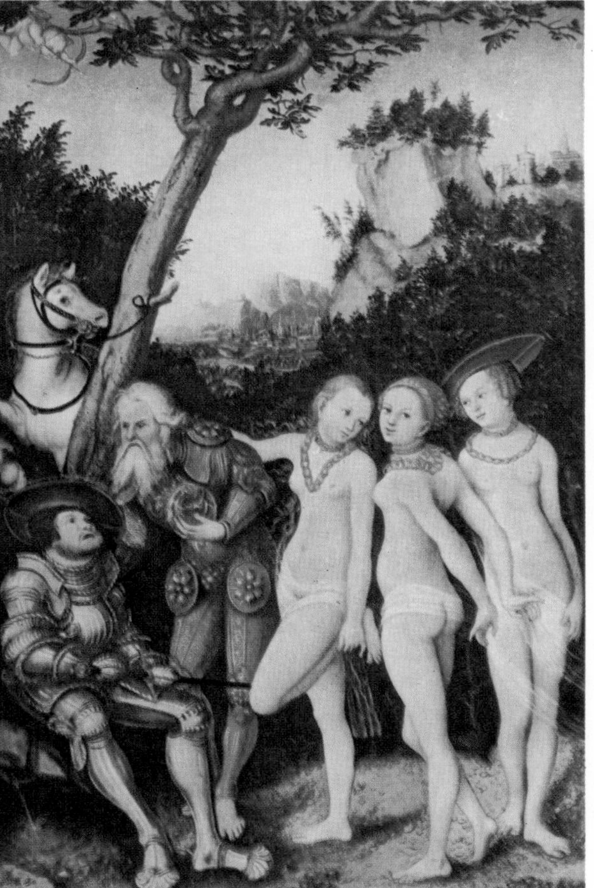

5

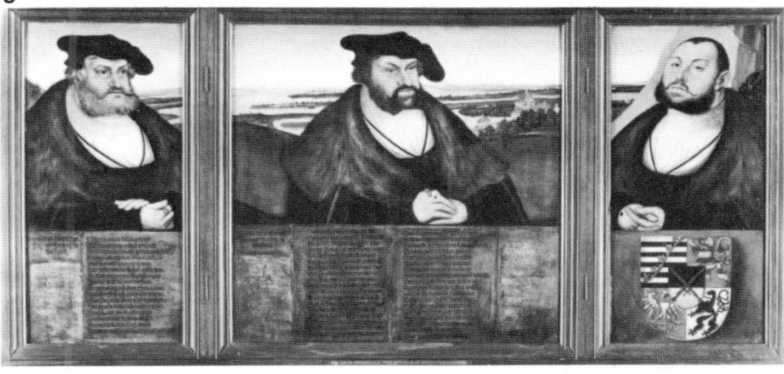

6

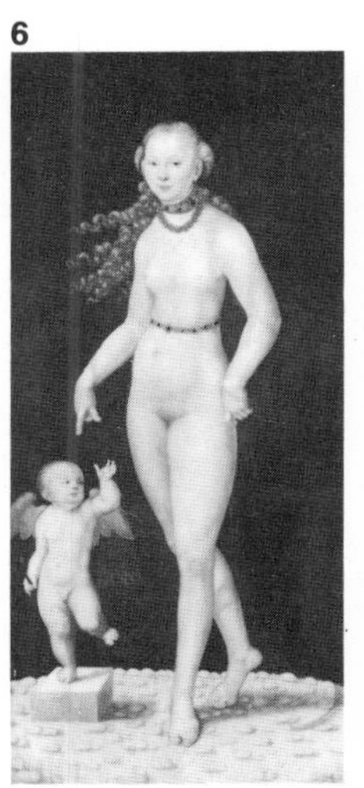

7

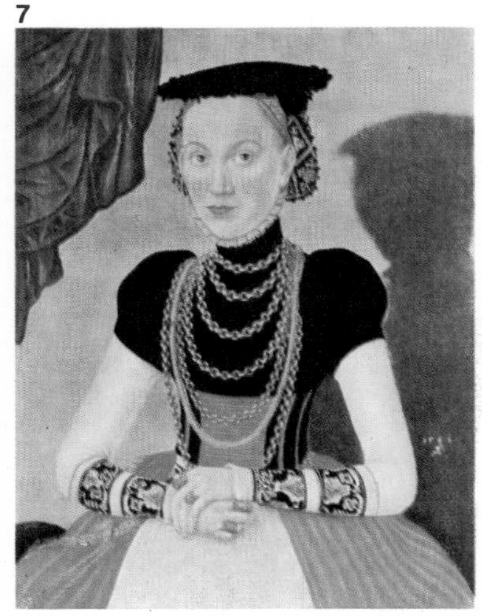

Jean Fouquet (*c.*1420–*c.*1480)

1. *Self-portrait.* Enamel. About 1450. Louvre
2. *Virgin and Child with Angels.* Right half of Melun Diptych. About 1450. Koninklijk Museum voor Schone Kunsten, Antwerp
3. *Etienne Chevalier presented by St Stephen.* Left half of Melun Diptych. About 1450. Staatliche Museen, Berlin-Dahlem
4. *Birth of St John the Baptist.* Miniature from the Book of Hours of Etienne Chevalier. About 1450. Musée Condé, Chantilly
5. *Pietà with Donor.* About 1470–80. Parish church, Nouans

Nicolas Froment (*c.*1425–83/6)

6. Central panel of altarpiece of the Burning Bush. 1475–6. Cathedral, Aix-en-Provence

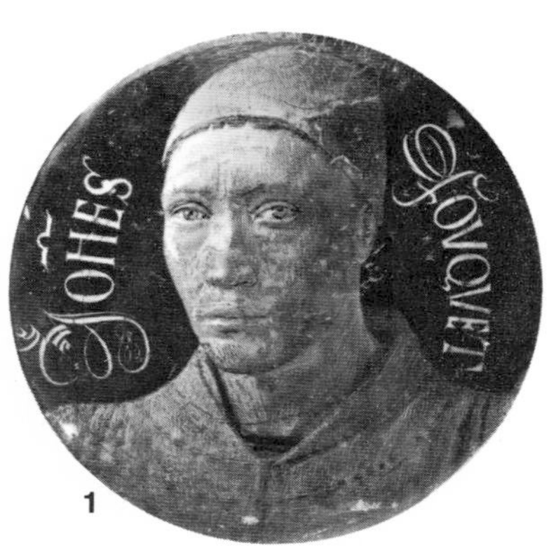

1

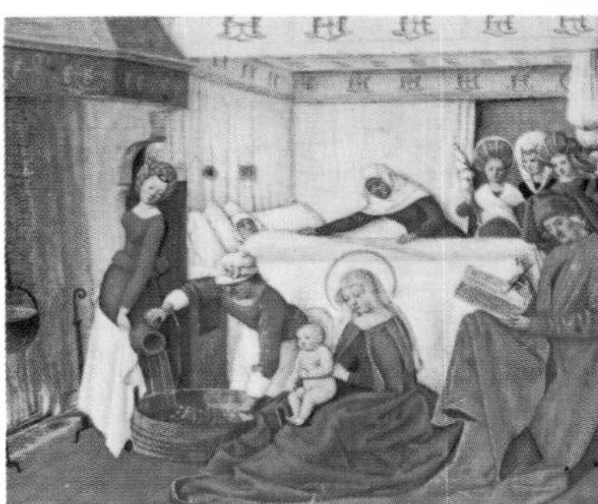

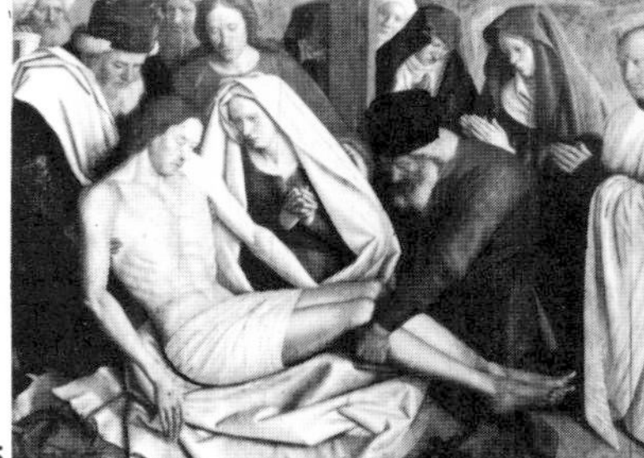
5

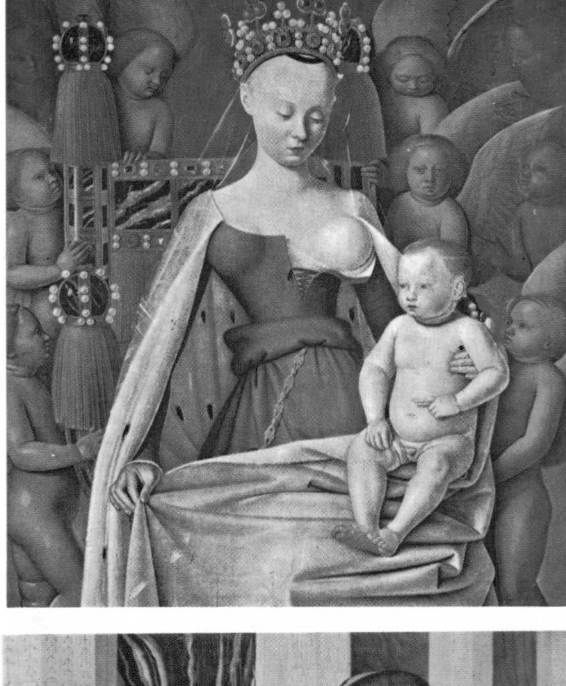
2

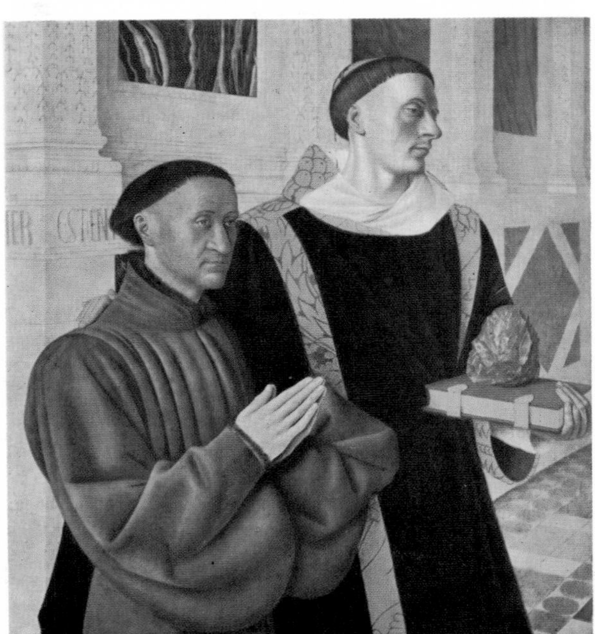
3

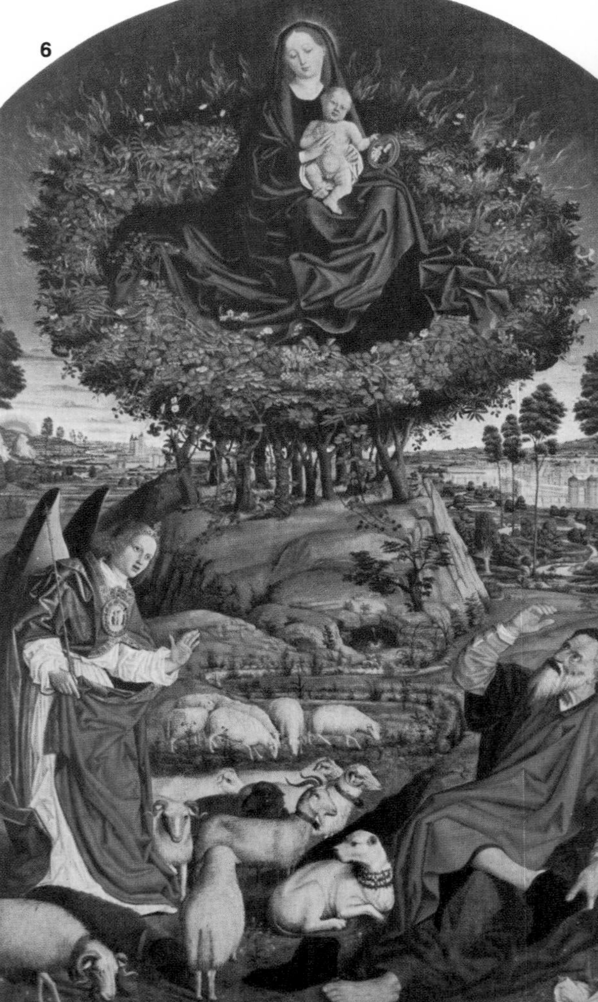
6

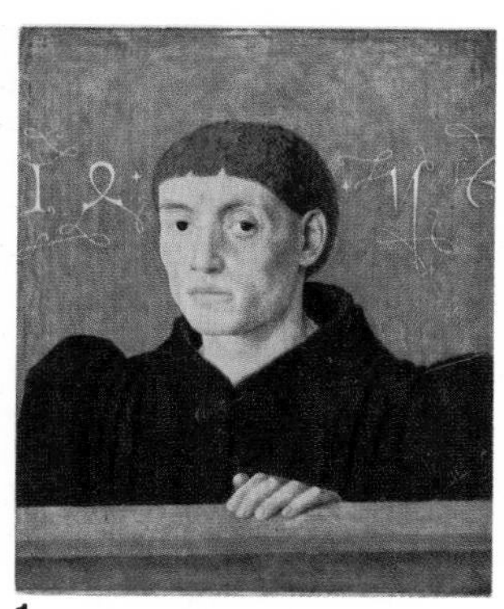
1

1. **Master of 1456** (*fl.* mid-15th century): *Portrait of a Man.* Fürst Liechtensteinische Gemäldegalerie, Vaduz
2. **Master of Moulins** (*fl. c.*1480–99): *The Nativity, with Cardinal Jean Rolin.* 1480–3. Musée des Beaux-Arts, Autun
3. **Enguerrand Charton** (*c.*1410–after 1462): *The Coronation of the Virgin.* 1454. Hospice, Villeneuve-les-Avignon
4. **Germain Pilon** (*c.*1531–90): *Chancellor René de Birague praying.* Bronze. 1584–5. Louvre, Paris
5. **Germain Pilon** (*c.*1531–90): Tomb of Valentine Balbiani. Detail. 1584–5. Louvre, Paris
6. **Master of St Giles** (*fl.*1490–1510): *St Remigius blessing the People.* 1490–1510. National Gallery of Art (Samuel H. Kress Collection), Washington DC

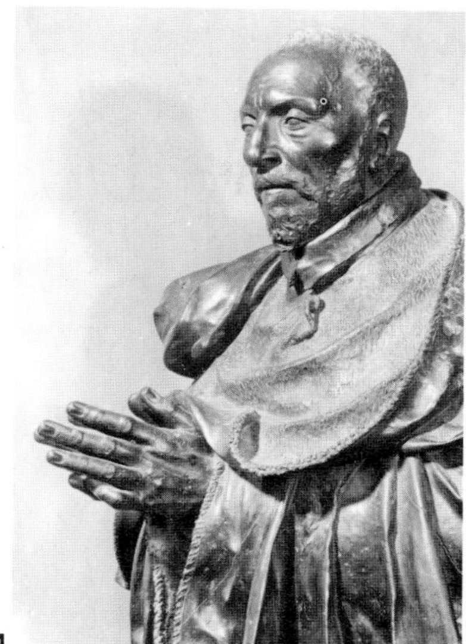
4

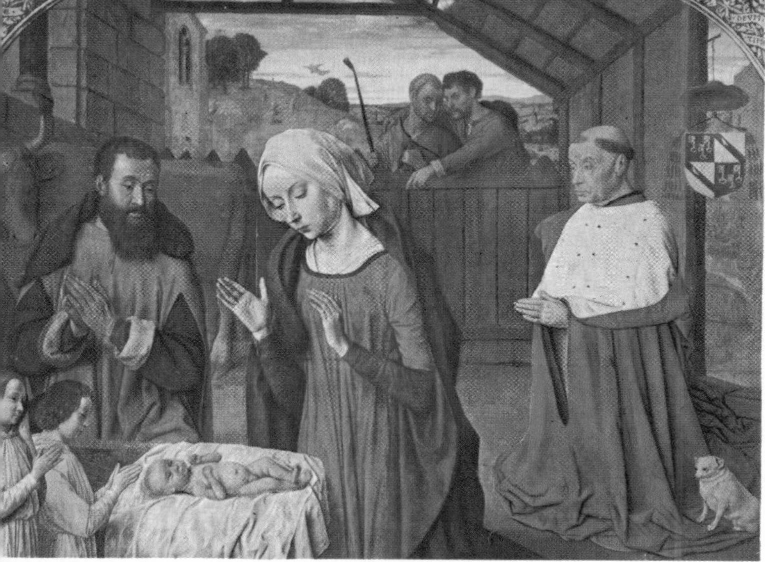

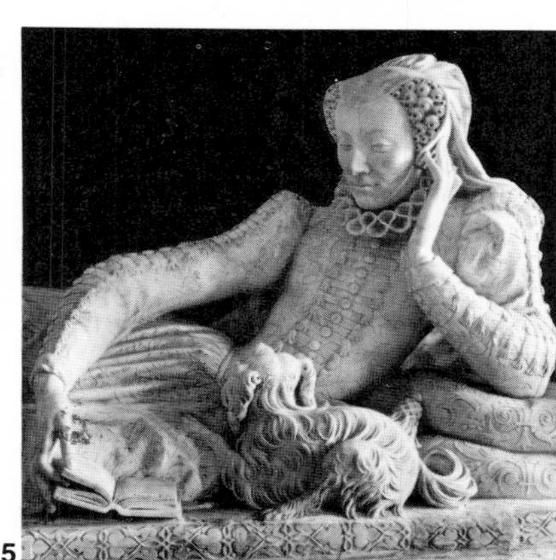
5

6

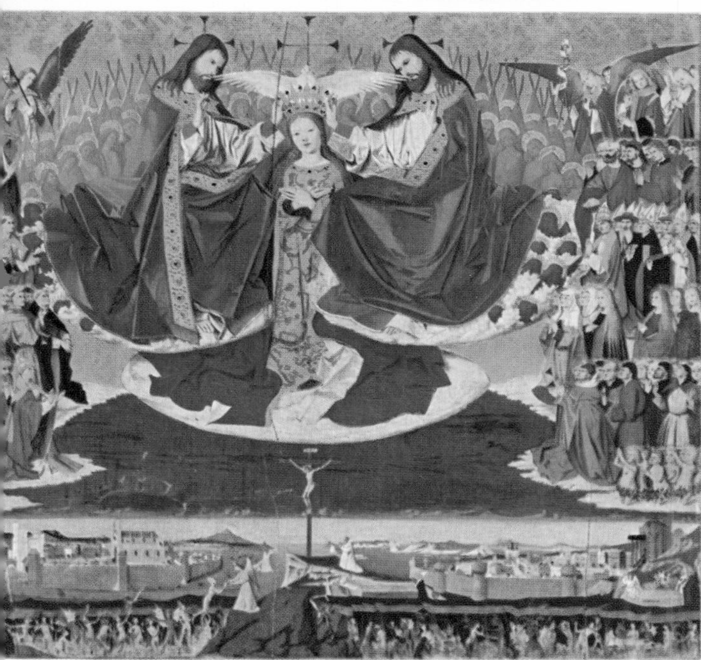
3

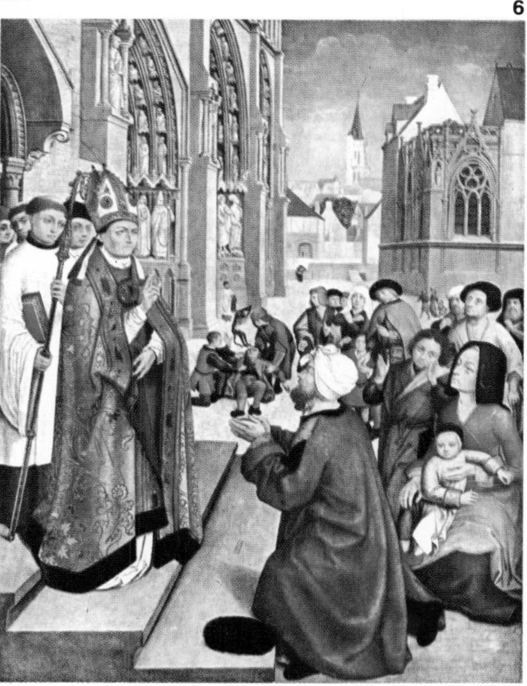

1. **Jean Clouet** (*c.*1485–*c.*1540): *Portrait of Maréchal Lautrec.* Black and red chalk drawing. About 1516. Musée Condé, Chantilly
2. **Niccolò dell'Abbate** (*c.*1509–71): *Rape of Persephone.* Detail. 1557? Louvre, Paris
3. Château of Fontainebleau. François I wing. 1528–40.
4. **François Clouet** (*c.*1522–72): *Portrait of Elizabeth of Austria.* 1571. Louvre, Paris
5. **François Clouet** (*c.*1522–72): *Lady in her Bath.* About 1570. National Gallery of Art (Samuel H. Kress Collection), Washington DC
6. **François Clouet** (*c.*1522–72): *Portrait of Charles IX as a Child.* 1561. Kunsthistorisches Museum, Vienna

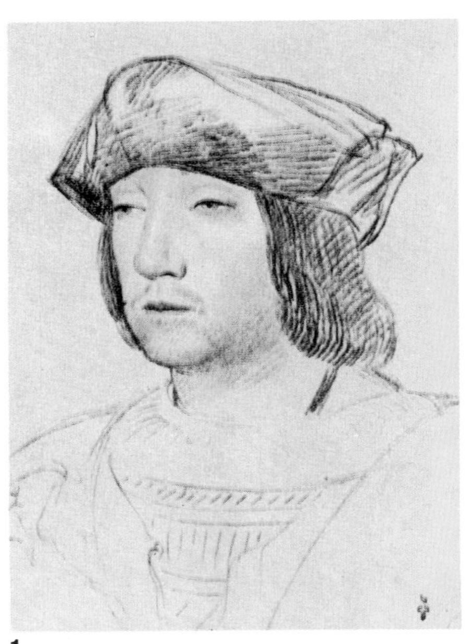
1

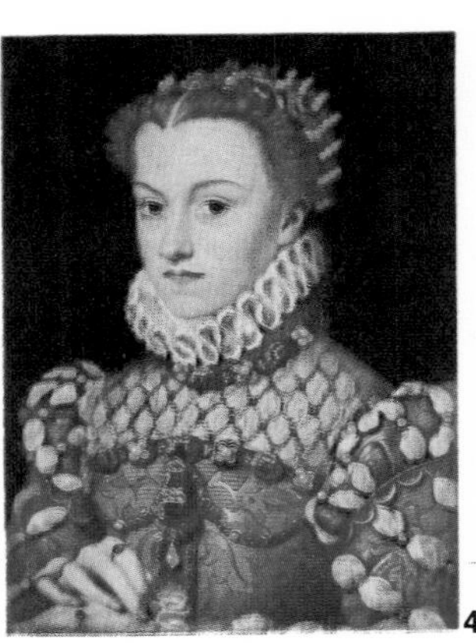
4

2

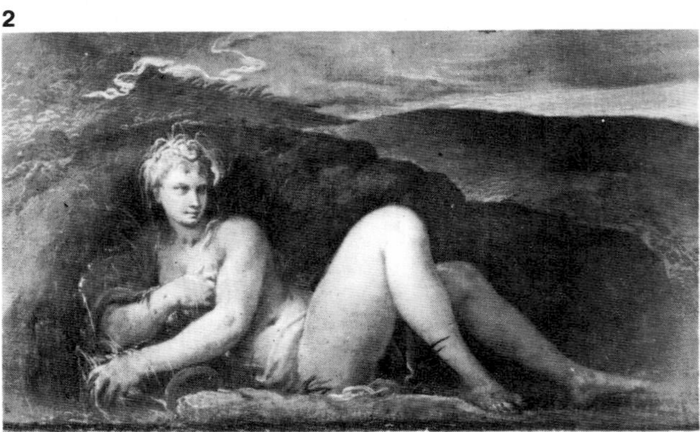

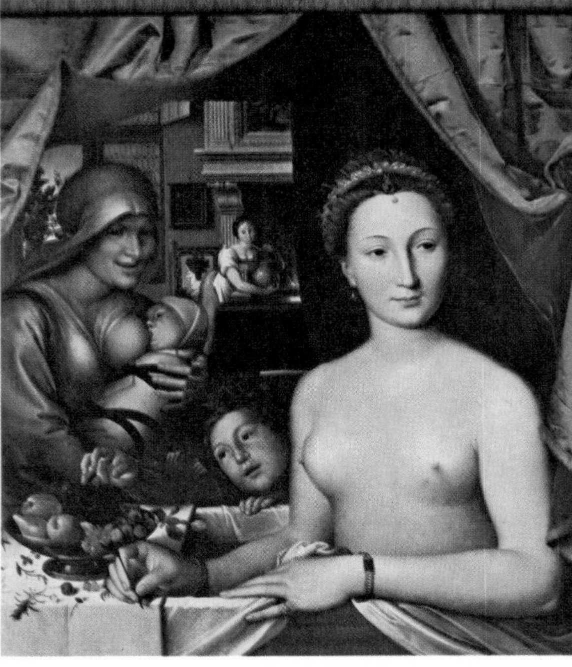
5

3

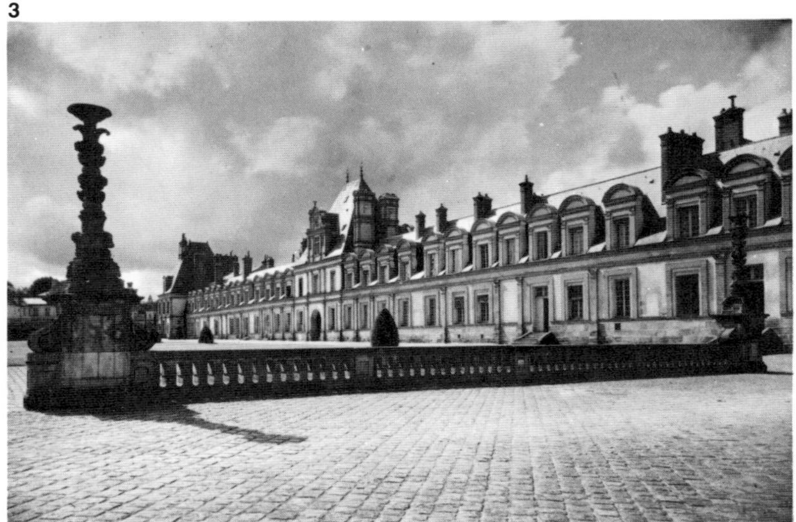

6

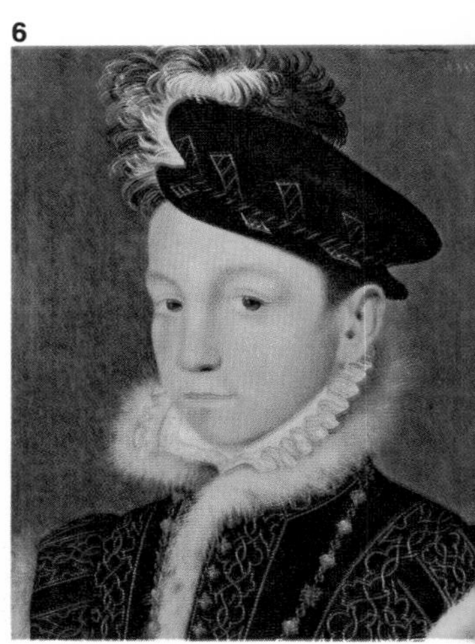

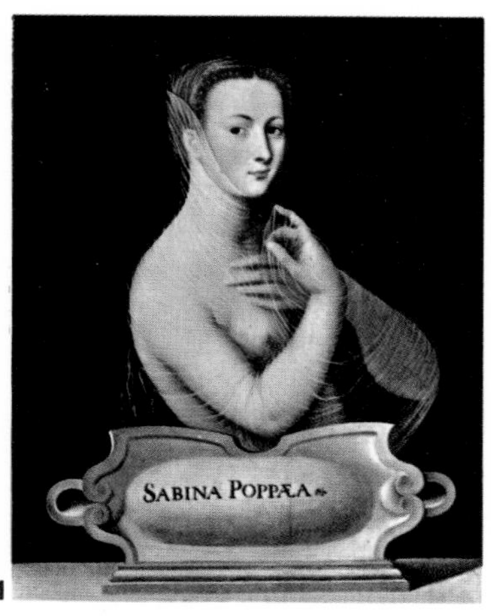

1

1. **School of Fontainebleau:** *Portrait of Sabina Poppaea.* About 1560. Musée d'Art et d'Histoire, Geneva
2. **School of Fontainebleau:** *The Duchesse de Villars and Gabrielle d'Estrées in the Bath.* About 1596. Louvre, Paris
3. **School of Fontainebleau:** *Diana of Anet.* Marble. Before 1554. Louvre, Paris
4. **Francesco Primaticcio** (1504–70): Stucco decoration in the bedroom of the Duchesse d'Etampes, Château of Fontainebleau. About 1541–5
5. **School of Fontainebleau:** *Diana the Huntress.* About 1550. Louvre, Paris
6. **Francesco Primaticcio** (1504–70): *Ulysses and Penelope.* About 1545. Collection Wildenstein Galleries, New York

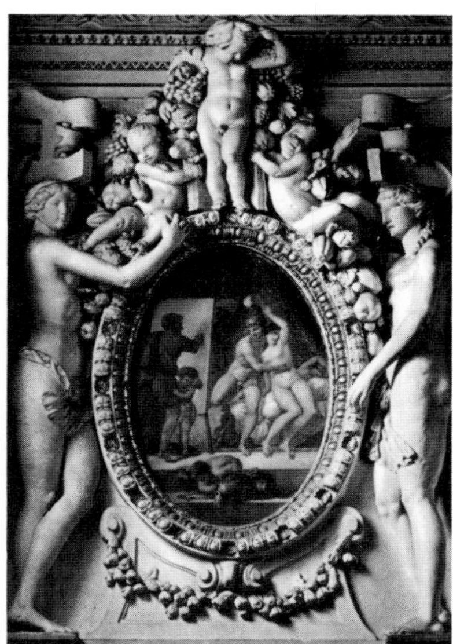

4

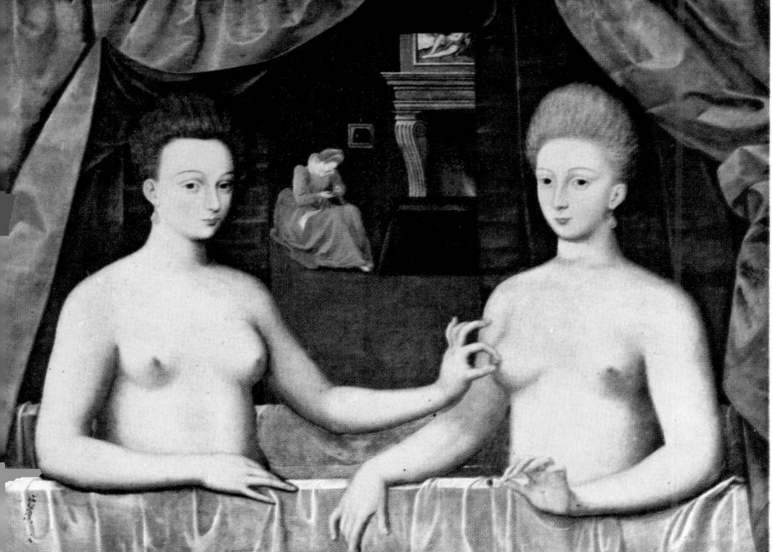

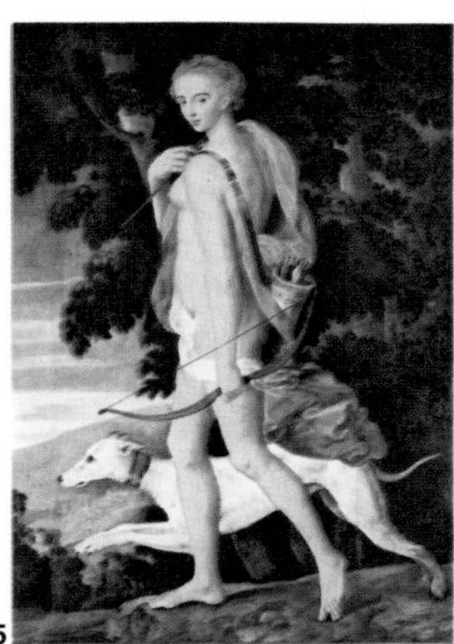

5

6

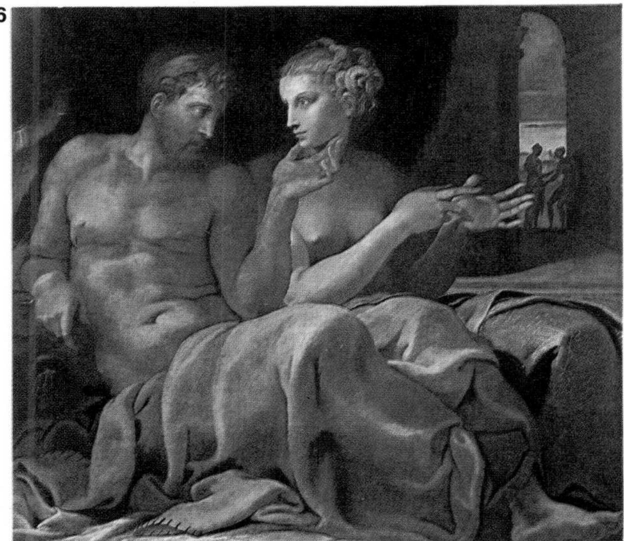

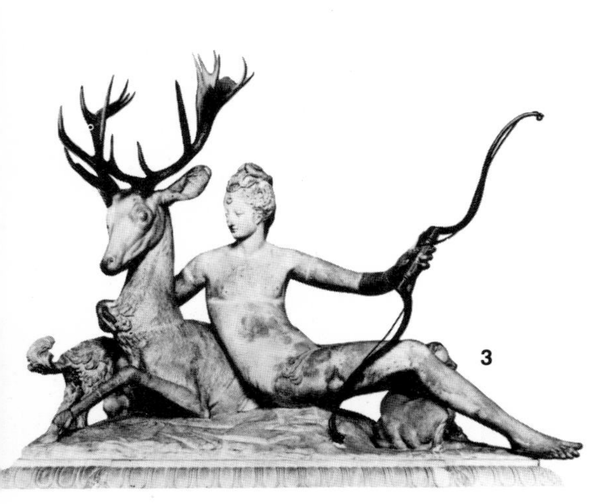

3

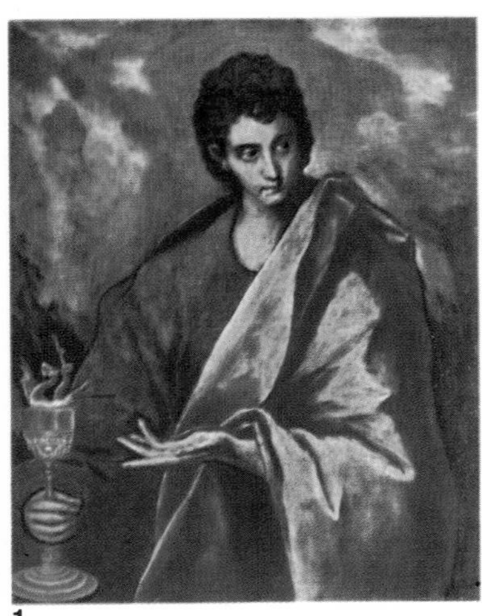

1

El Greco (1541–1614)

1. *St John the Evangelist.* About 1604. Prado, Madrid
2. *Christ driving the Traders from the Temple.* National Gallery, London
3. *The Vision of the Apocalypse: Breaking the Fifth Seal.* 1608–14. Museo Zuloaga, Zumaya
4. *St Andrew and St Francis.* About 1603. Prado, Madrid
5. *The Adoration of the Shepherds.* About 1612–14. Prado, Madrid

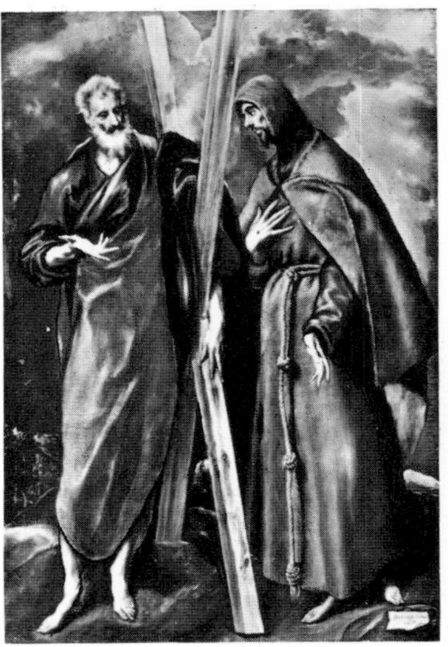

4

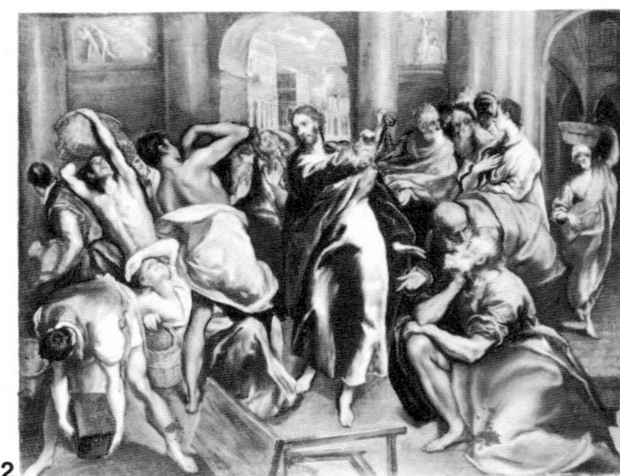

2

3

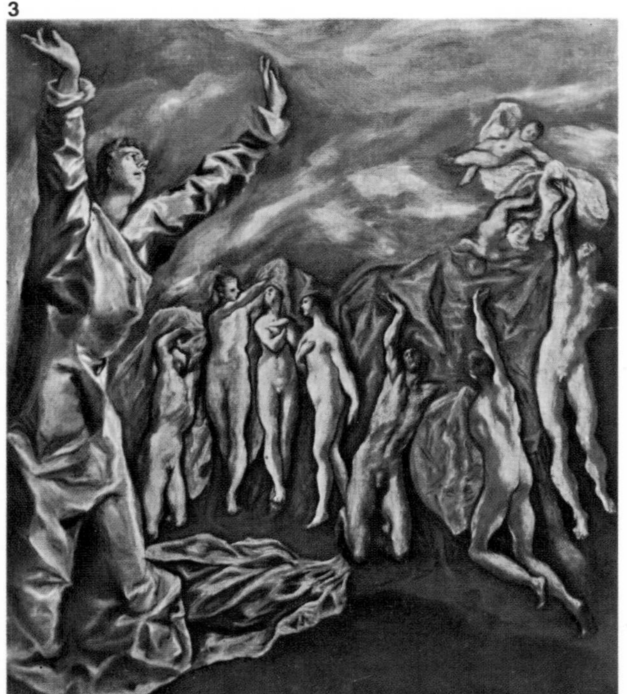

5

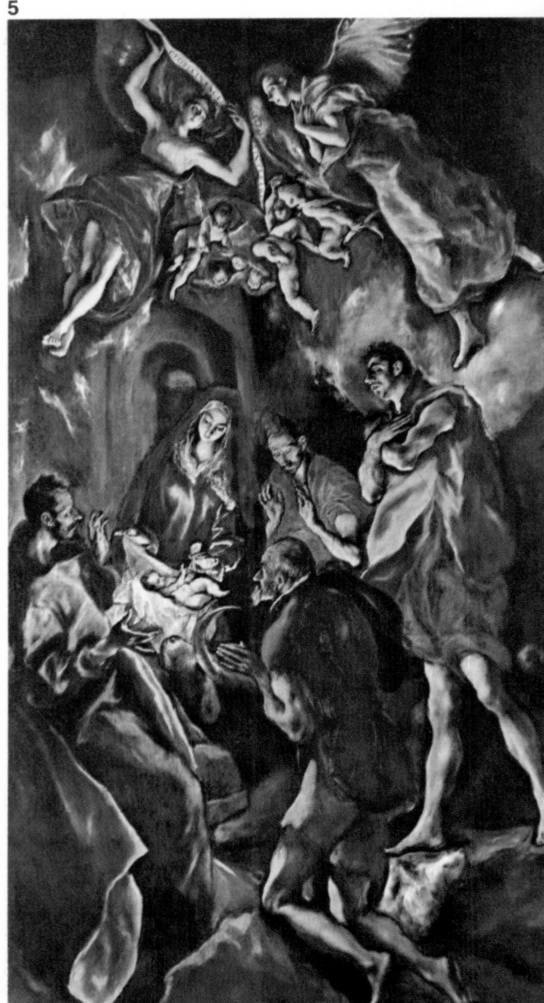

Greco (1541–1614)
View of Toledo. 1608. Metropolitan Museum of Art, New York
Portrait of a Man with Hand on Breast. About 1585. Prado, Madrid
Mater Dolorosa. About 1595–1600. Musée des Beaux-Arts, Strasbourg

4. *St Martin and the Beggar.* 1597–9. National Gallery of Art (Widener Collection), Washington DC
5. *The Burial of the Count of Orgaz.* 1586–8. S. Tomé, Toledo

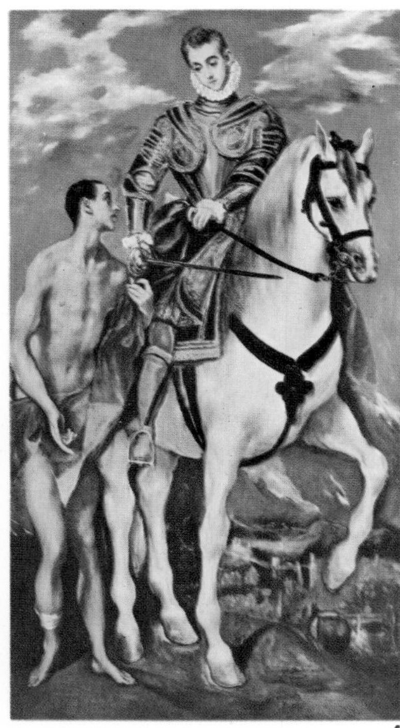

4

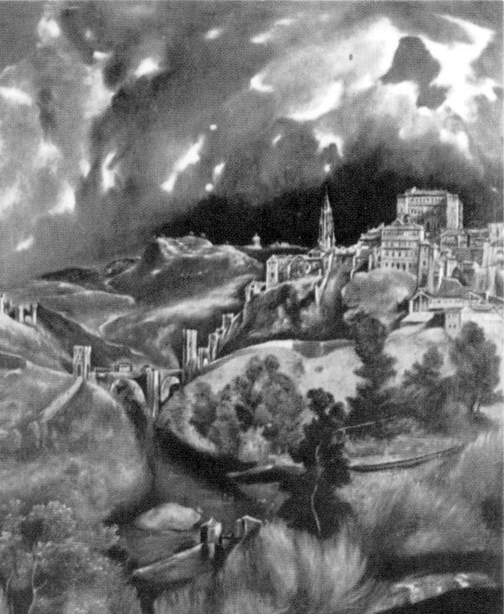

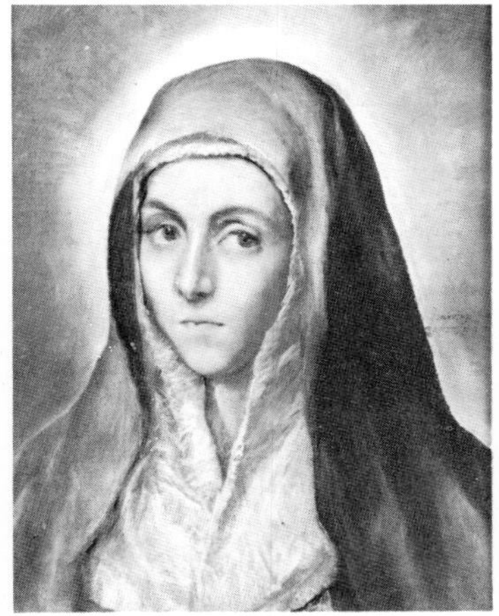

3

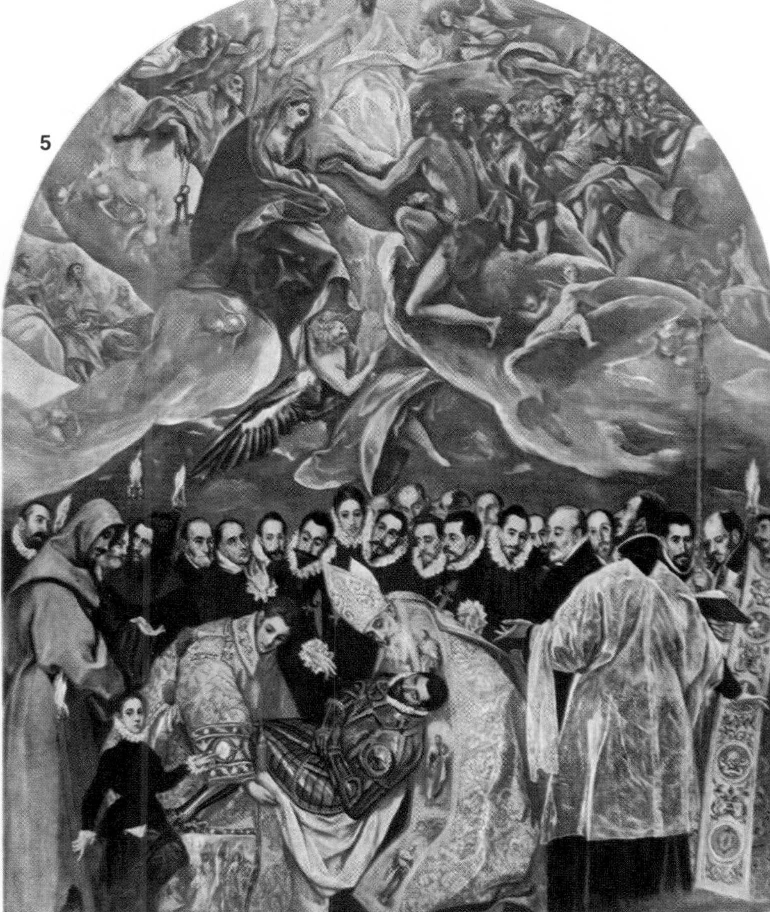

5

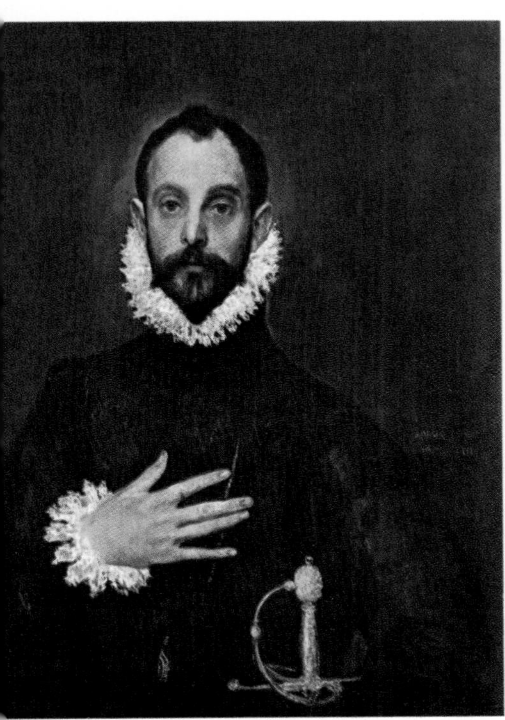

1. **Francisco Ribalta** (1565–1628): *St Bruno.* 1627. Museo S. Carlos, Valencia
2. **Bartolomé Bermejo** (*c.*1440–*c.*1500): *St Dominic of Silos.* 1467–74. Prado, Madrid
3. **Pedro de Berruguete** (*c.*1450–*c.*1503): *Duke Federigo da Montefeltro and his Son.* Palazzo Ducale, Urbino
4. **Alonso de Berruguete** (1489?–1561): *Eve.* Detail from stalls, Toledo Cathedral. 1543
5. **Alonso de Berruguete** (1489?–1561): *The Sacrifice of Isaac.* 1526–32. Museo Nacional de Escultura, Valladolid
6. **Bartolomé Bermejo** (*c.*1440–*c.*1500): *The Descent into Limbo.* Museo de Arte de Cataluña, Barcelona
7. **Nuno Gonçalves** (*fl.*1450–80): *Prince John of Portugal.* Detail. 1465–7. Museu de Arte Antiga, Lisbon

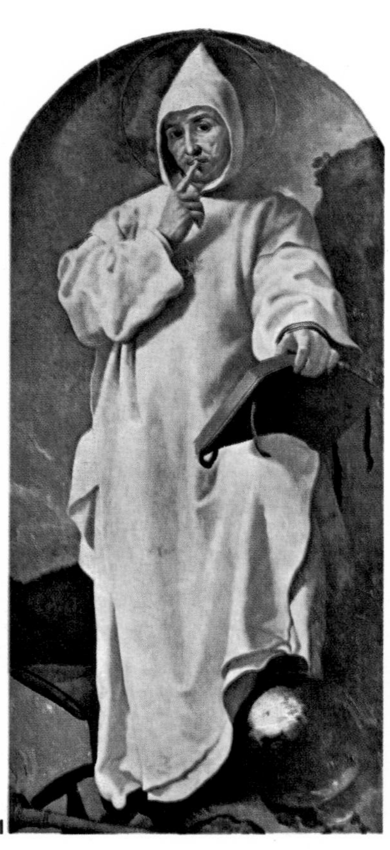
1

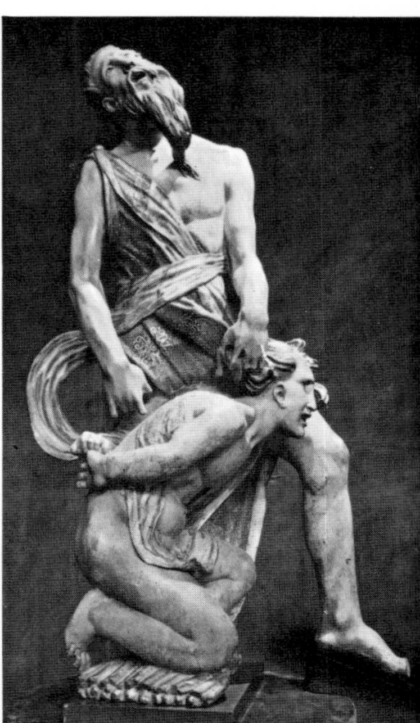
5

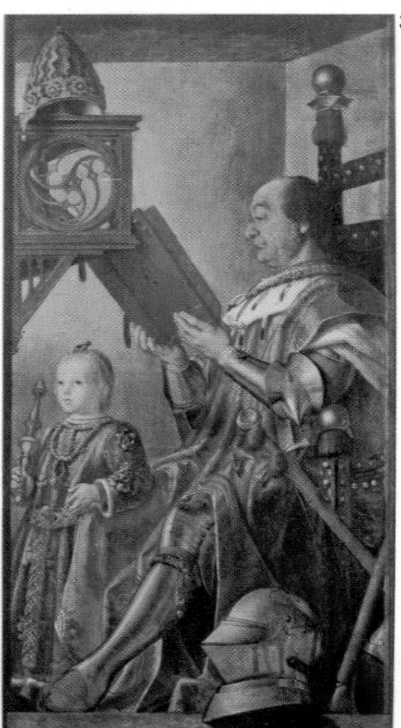
3

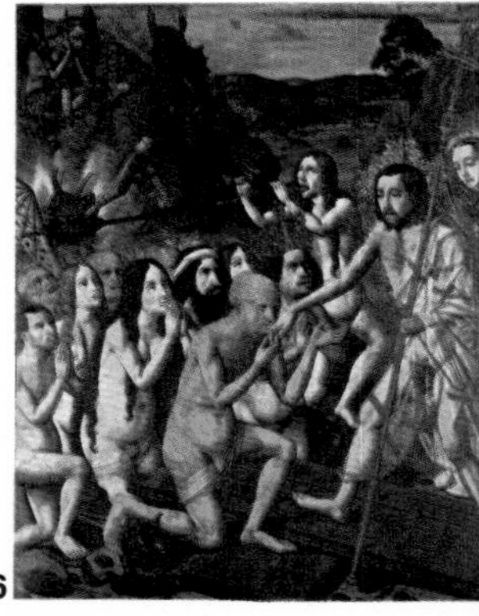
6

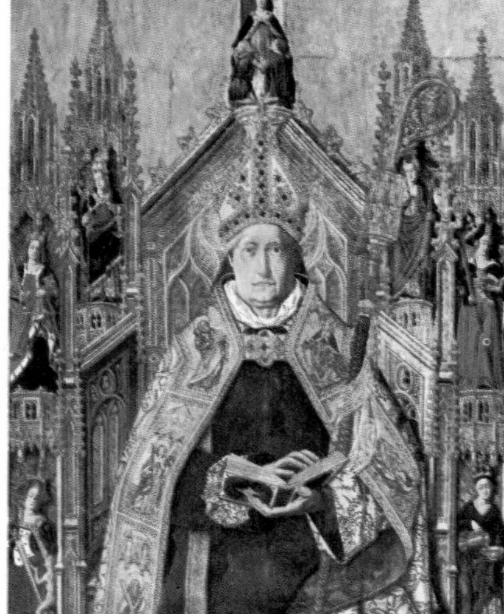
2

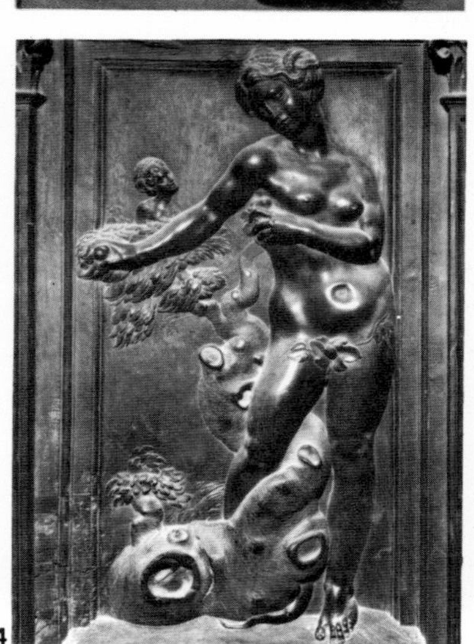
4

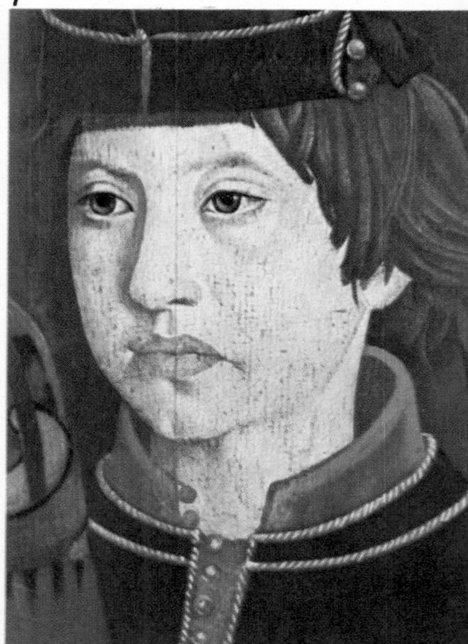
7

e art of seventeenth and eighteenth-ntury Europe hardly presents a united front. ere was a great deal more mobility, and er parts of the world, notably America and East, were being extensively explored. In y, Rome and the papacy played an influential e as patrons and arbiters of taste. This was time when painters demonstrated their ility by covering vast areas with fresco coration, often of an esoteric kind as regards subject matter. Annibale Carracci,

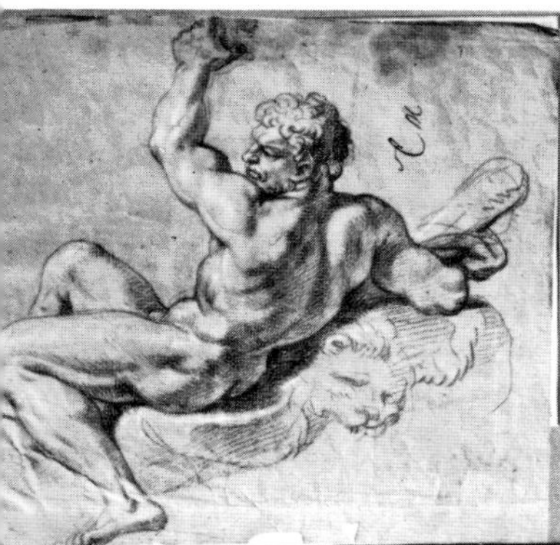

nibale Carracci: *Astronomer.* Cabinet des ssins, Louvre, Paris

ercino, Lanfranco, Domenichino and etro da Cortona were amongst those who rformed prodigious feats in the palaces and urches of Italy. It is, however, Bernini who itomizes Baroque Italy, his sculpture and chitecture moving freely and effortlessly ough space. The Baroque style was sentially characterized by swirling drapery, aying poses, wild gesticulating, eddying, stless movements, which echo the rvilinear contours of the buildings and create nasterly feeling of illusion. These vast corative schemes absorb the eye and, nost physically, suck the viewer into the iral rhythms that transport one upwards vards the heavens and impress upon one sense of unity. The most important feature seventeenth-century fresco decoration is at it is perfectly integrated with the chitectural setting, although when such hemes lacked a true source of inspiration e result tended to be no more than rhetoric. e architecture of both centuries lent itself ry easily to institutional projects sometimes coming formal and stereotyped.

In the full tide of Baroque art nothing is er still or silent, but while this was the icial style of the seventeenth century it was no means the only one. In Italy Caravaggio d his followers are an important exception, eferring to paint in a more realistic vein. e same dichotomy existed in northern rope where the prolific Rubens, the debonair n Dyck and the burly Hals have to be ntrasted with the firmer Protestant resolve Rembrandt. In the work of Rembrandt e various strands of Dutch art meet –

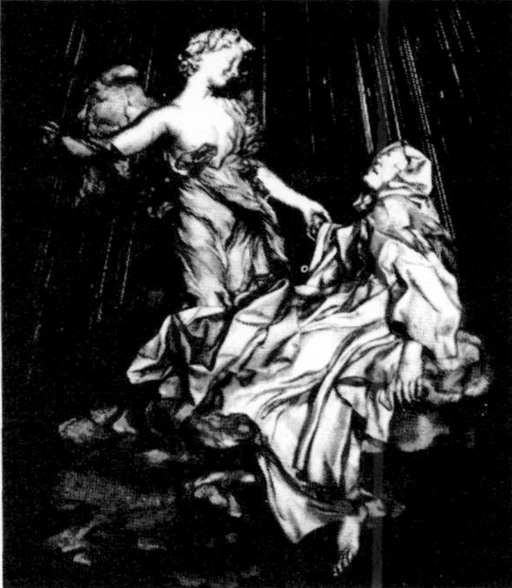

Gian Lorenzo Bernini: *The Ecstasy of St Theresa.* Marble. 1645–52. Cornaro Chapel, S. Maria della Vittoria, Rome

portraiture, religious painting, landscape and genre. The intimate mood of domestic genre painting in Holland finds its perfect expression in the work of Vermeer, de Hooch, Steen or ter Borch, whilst the landscape of the country was memorably depicted by Jacob van Ruisdael, Cuyp and Hobbema. Flower painting was another specialist interest of Dutch painters. In France and Spain also one has to balance the achievements of Poussin and Claude against the realism of the Le Nain brothers and Georges de La Tour, or those of Murillo with Velazquez. Only in southern Germany, and primarily in architecture, was the full force of the Baroque experienced, where, however, it had a late flowering.

The eighteenth century shows even less consistency. Several artists continued established trends: Giovanni Battista Tiepolo and Canaletto in Venice; Boucher, Fragonard and Chardin in France; Reynolds and Gainsborough in England. Yet, it was also a century in which artists such as Goya, Fuseli,

Rembrandt: *Self-portrait.* Detail. 1659. National Gallery of Art (Mellon Collection), Washington DC

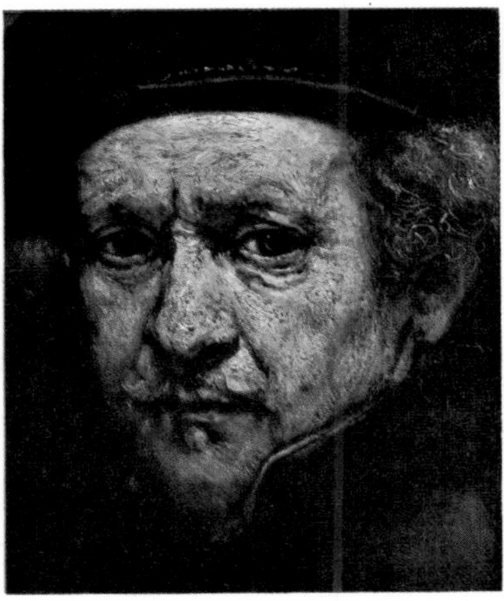

Part 8

Europe and America 1600–1800

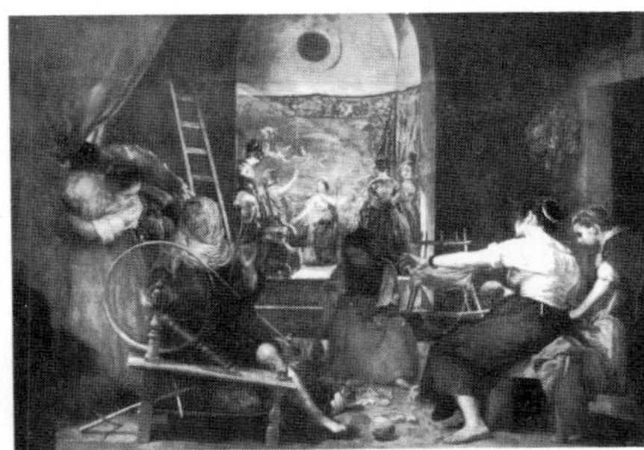

Velazquez: *The Spinners. c.*1657. Prado, Madrid

Hogarth and Watteau flourished, the mood and subject matter of whose work cannot be so easily categorized. Movements like Romanticism and Neoclassicism, which emerged during the last half of the eighteenth century, were partly reactions against the elegant and pretty Rococo style entrenched in the courts of Europe. It was, in fact, these movements that ushered in a new spirit of scepticism and radicalism, heralding developments that were to take place in the next century. The secularization of art was now complete.

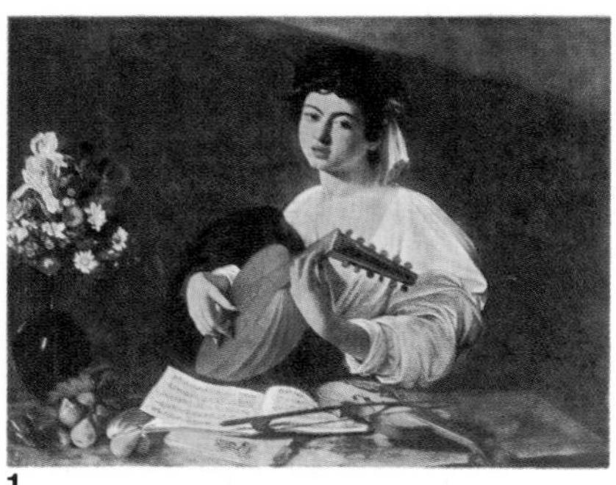
1

Caravaggio (1571–1610)
1. *The Lute Player.* About 1595. Hermitage, Leningrad
2. *Boy with a Basket of Fruit.* Galleria Borghese, Rome
3. *Bacchus.* Galleria Borghese, Rome
4. *St Mary Magdalene.* About 1590. Galleria Doria-Pamphili, Rome
5. *The Conversion of St Paul.* 1600–1. Cerasi Chapel, S. Maria del Popolo, Rome
6. *The Crucifixion of St Peter.* 1600–1. Cerasi Chapel, S. Maria del Popolo, Rome
7. *The Death of the Virgin.* Detail. About 1605–7. Louvre, Paris

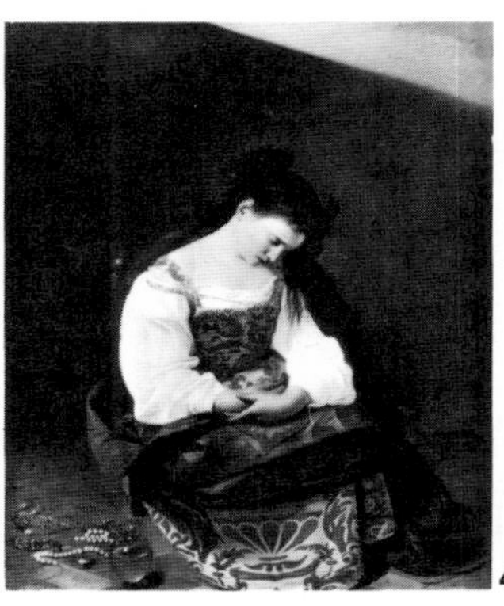
4

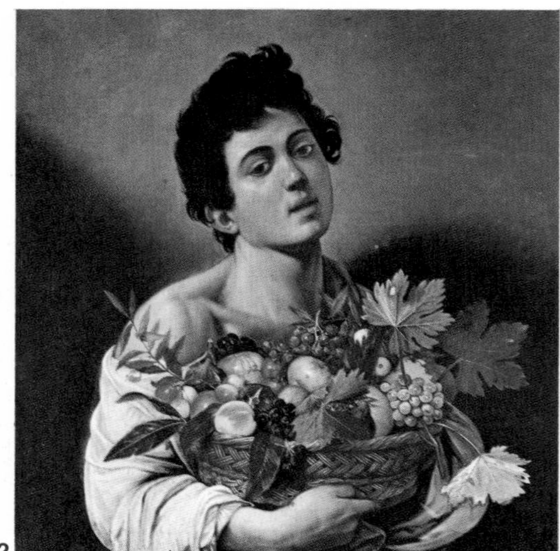
2

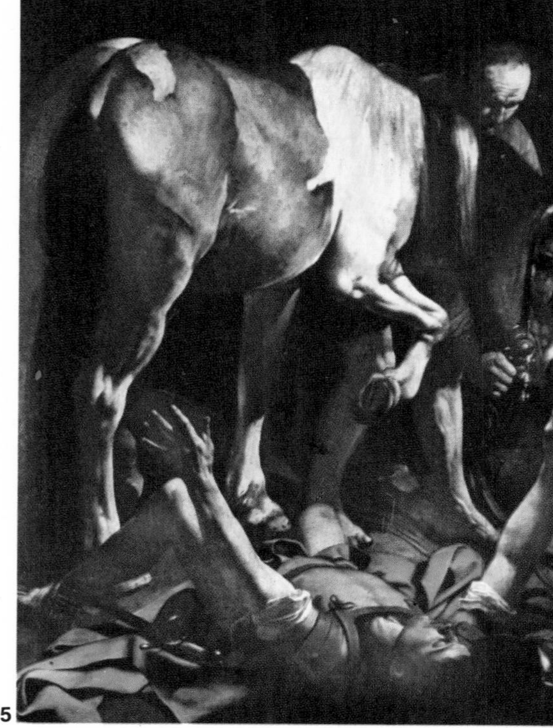
5

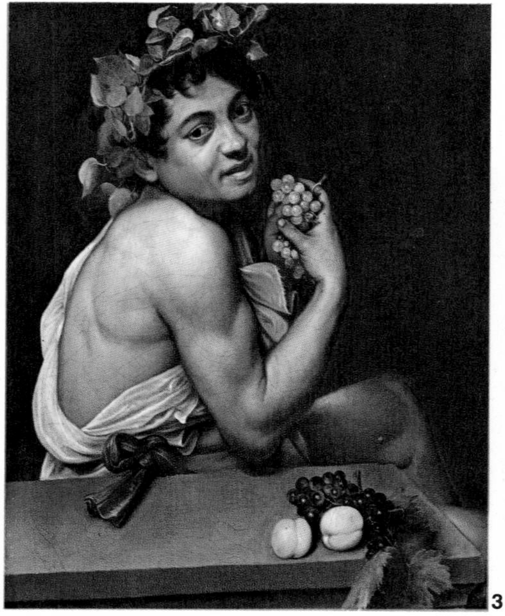
3

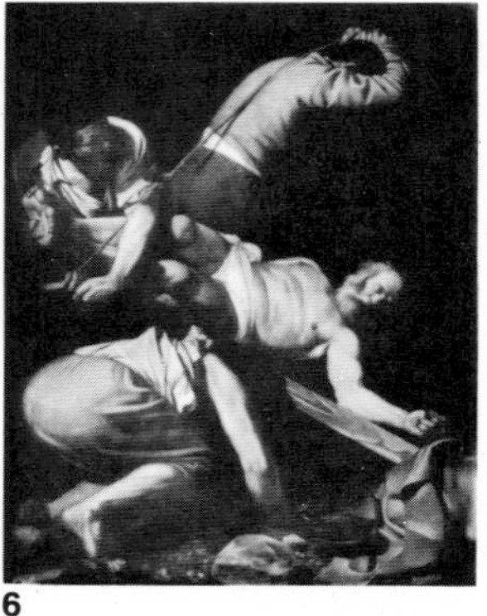
6

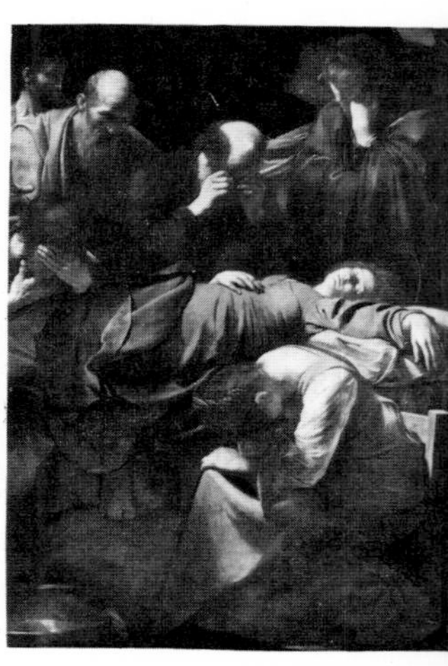
7

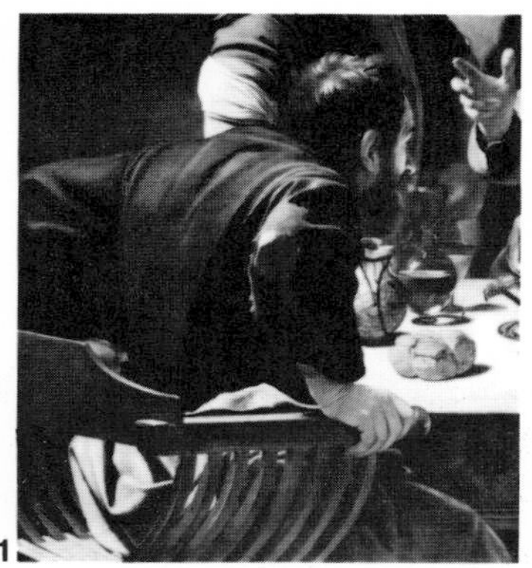
1

Caravaggio (1571–1610)

1. *The Supper at Emmaus.* Detail. About 1600. National Gallery, London
2. *The Supper at Emmaus.* Brera, Milan
3. Detail of fig. 6, opposite
4. *The Entombment.* 1604. Pinacoteca, Vatican
5. *The Calling of St Matthew.* About 1598. Contarelli Chapel, S. Luigi dei Francesi, Rome
6. *David with the Head of Goliath.* About 1604. Galleria Borghese, Rome

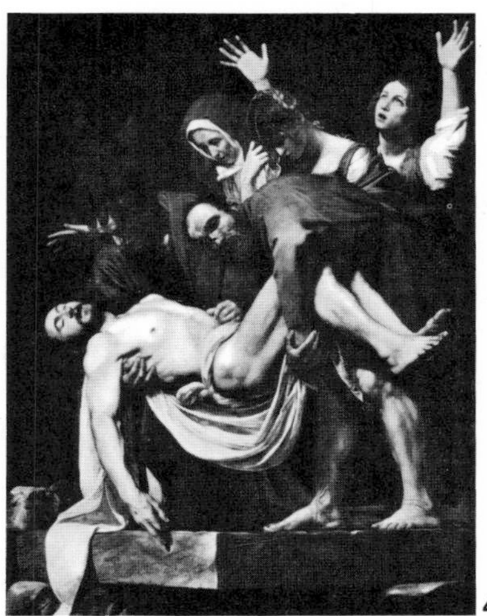
4

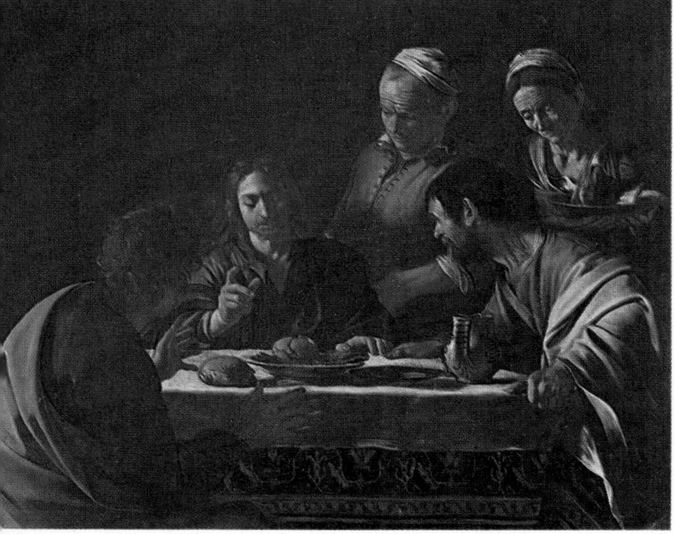

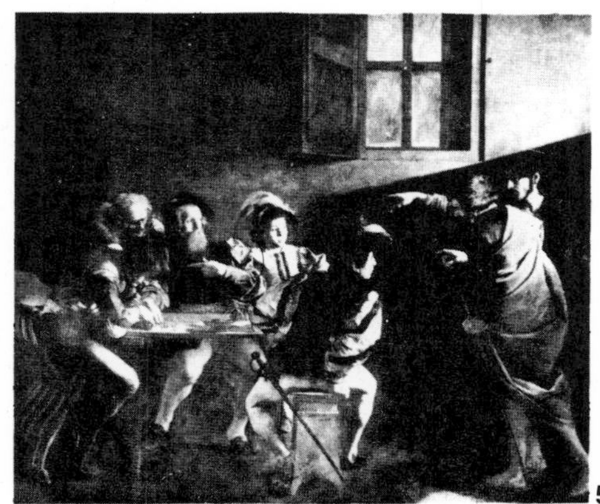
5

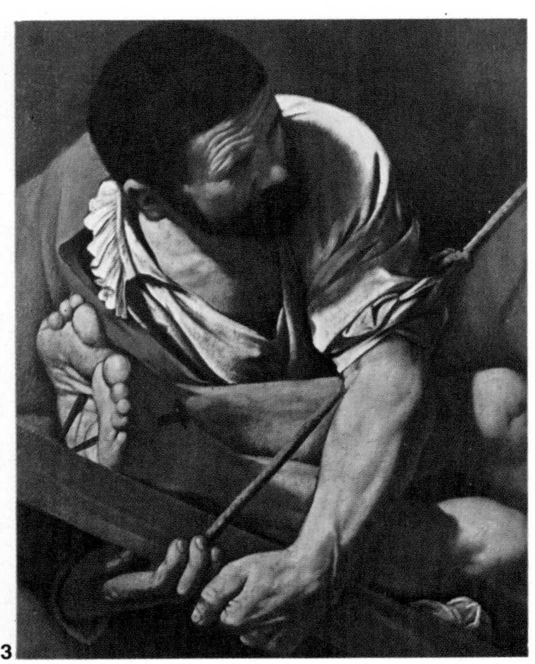
3

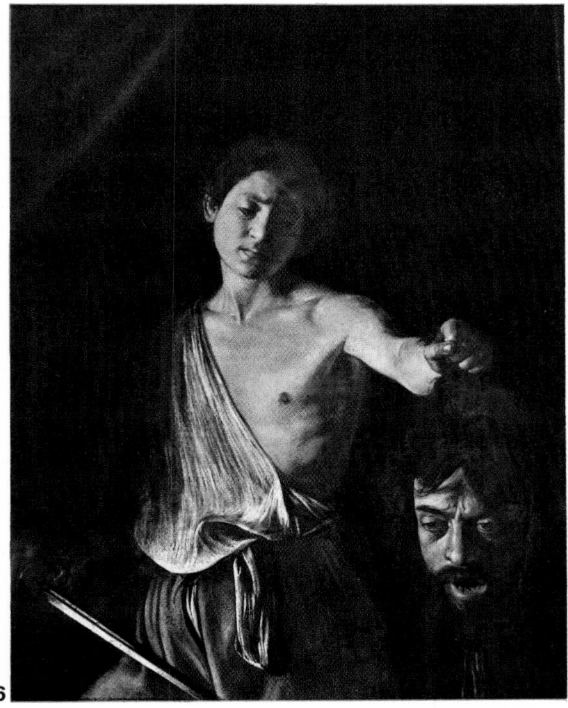
6

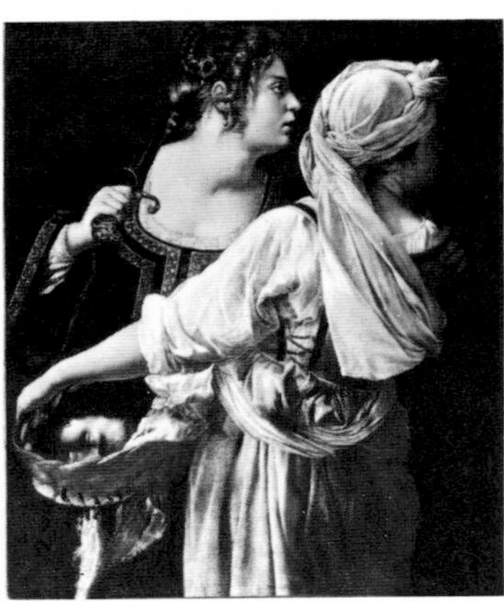
1

1. **Artemisia Gentileschi** (1593–*c.*1652): *Judith and a Servant with the Head of Holofernes.* Palazzo Pitti, Florence
2. **Orazio Gentileschi** (1563–1639): *The Rest on the Flight into Egypt.* Before 1626. Louvre, Paris
3. **Orazio Gentileschi** (1563–1639): *The Lute Player.* About 1626. Liechtenstein Collection, Vaduz
4. **Bartolomeo Schedoni** (1578–1615) *Sebastian and Irene.* About 1614. Galleria Nazionale di Capodimonte
5. **Bartolomeo Manfredi** (*c.*1587–1620 *The Fortune-teller.* Palazzo Pitti, Florence
6. **Simon Vouet** (1590–1649): *Amor an Psyche.* About 1625. Musée des Bea Arts, Lyons

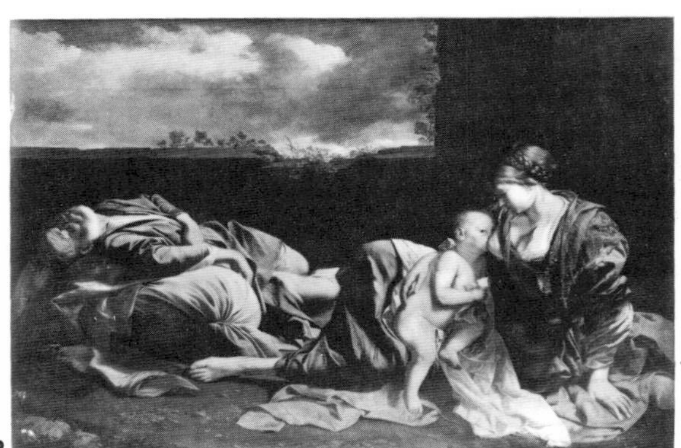
2

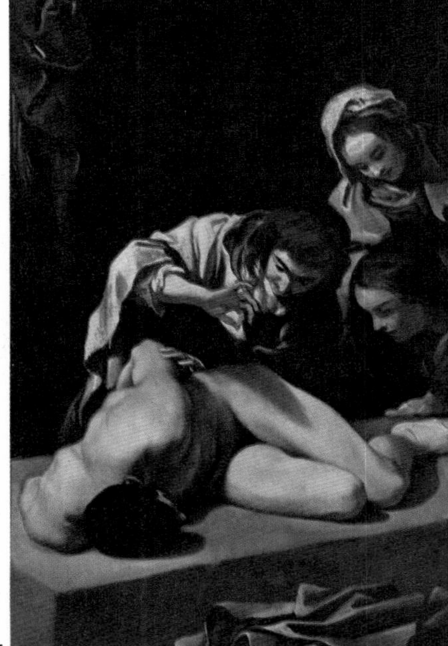
4

3

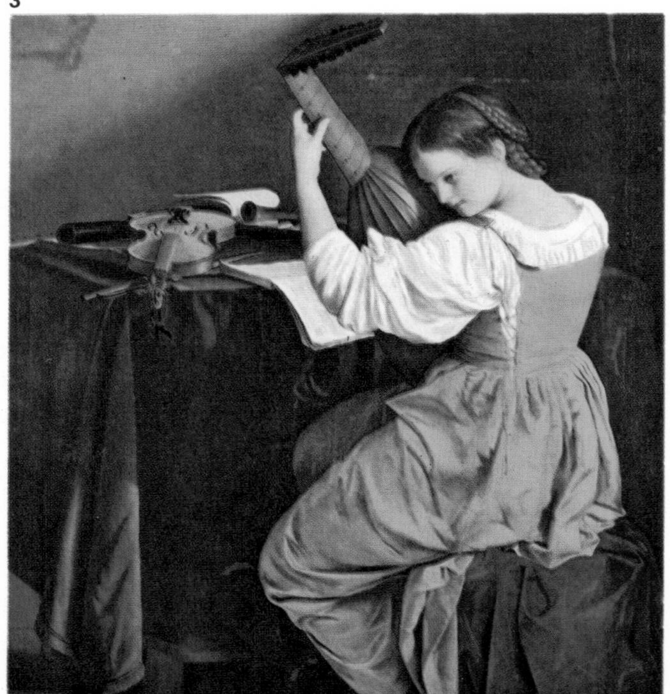

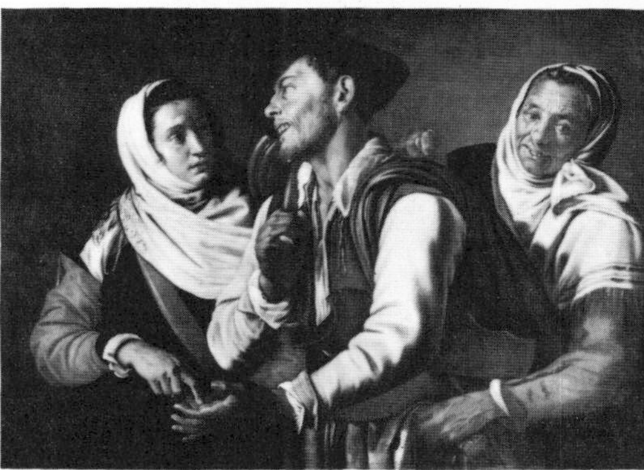

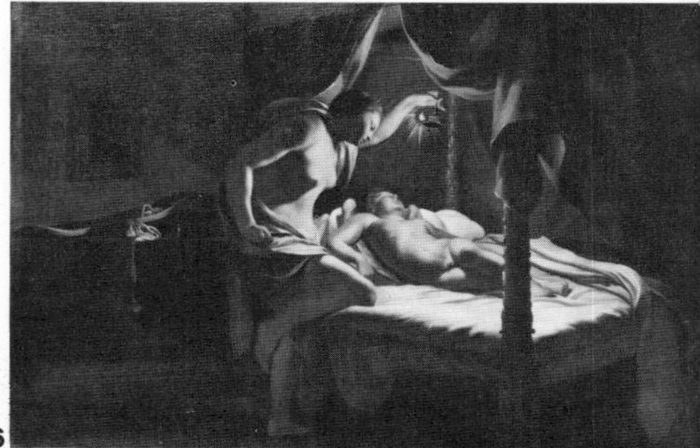
6

Annibale Carracci (1560–1609): *Landscape with Fishing Scene.* About 1587–8. Louvre, Paris
Annibale Carracci (1560–1609): *The Triumph of Bacchus and Ariadne.* Fresco. 1597–1604. Palazzo Farnese, Rome
Annibale Carracci (1560–1609): *The Bean-eater.* Galleria Colonna, Rome

4. **Agostino Carracci** (1557–1602): *The Communion of St Jerome.* About 1590. Pinacoteca, Bologna
5. **Annibale Carracci** (1560–1609): *Adonis discovering Venus.* About 1594–5. Kunsthistorisches Museum, Vienna
6. **Annibale Carracci** (1560–1609): *Polyphemus and Acis.* Fresco. 1597–1604. Palazzo Farnese, Rome

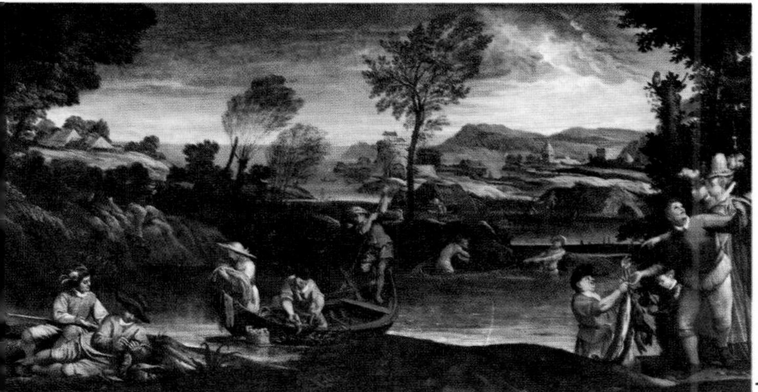

1

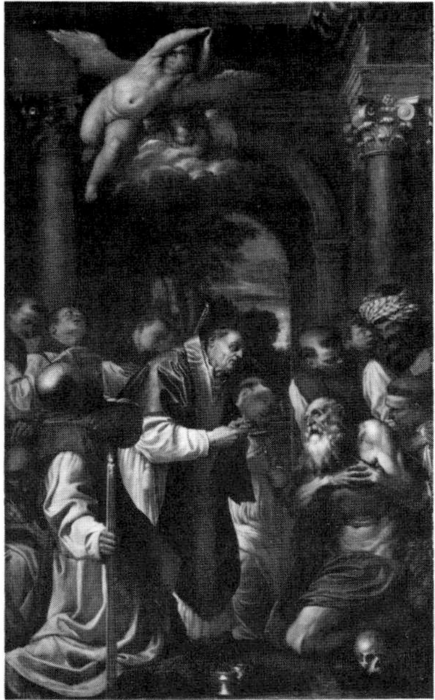

4

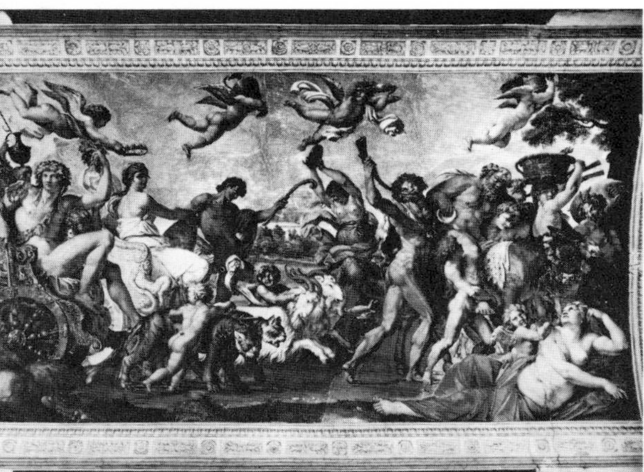

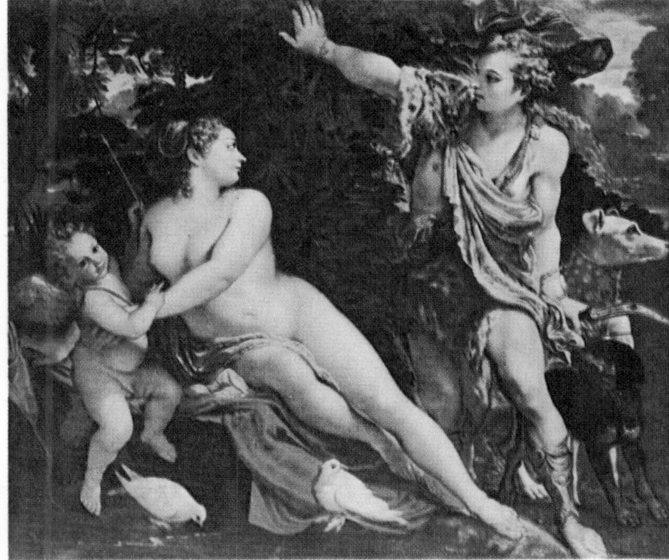

5

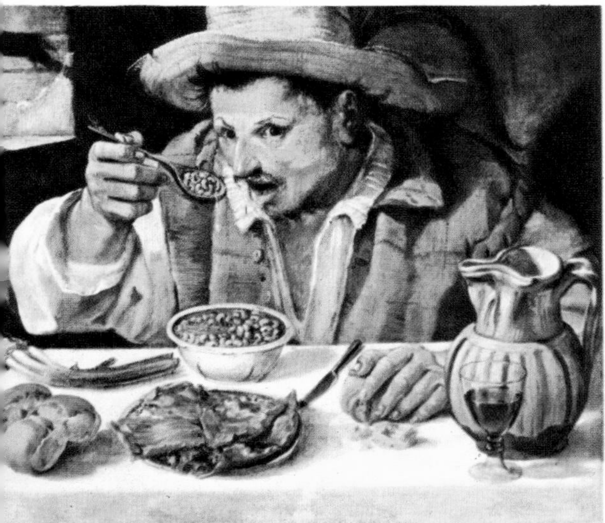

3

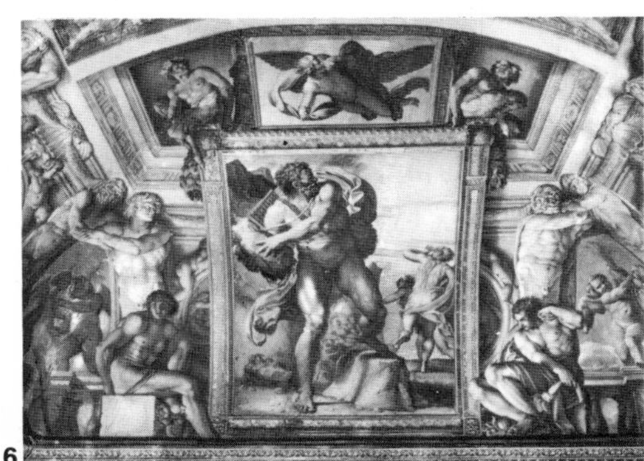

6

1. **Guido Reni** (1575–1642): *Atalanta and Hippomenes.* About 1625. Galleria Nazionale di Capodimonte, Naples
2. **Pietro da Cortona** (1596–1669): *The Apotheosis of Aeneas.* Fresco. 1651–4. Galleria Doria-Pamphili, Rome
3. **Giovanni Lanfranco** (1582–1647): *The Funeral of an Emperor.* Prado, Madrid
4. **Guido Reni** (1575–1642): *St Jerome.* About 1635. Kunsthistorisches Museum, Vienna
5. **Pietro da Cortona** (1596–1669): *The Silver Age.* Detail from *The Four Ages of Man.* Fresco. 1637–40. Sala della Stufa, Palazzo Pitti, Florence

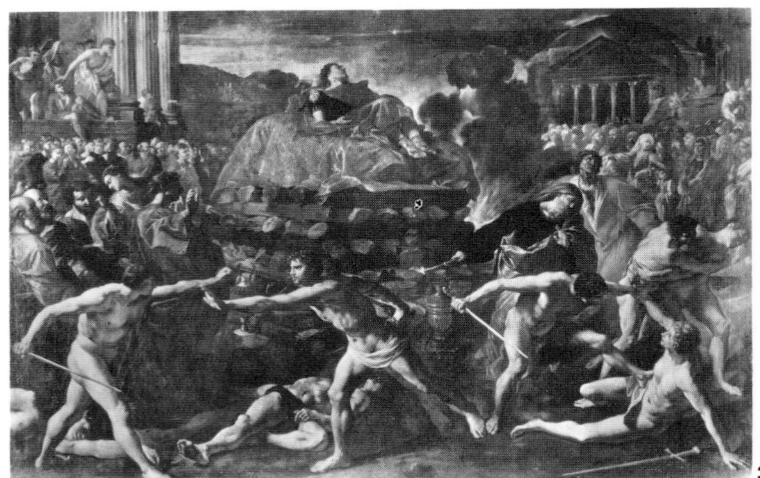
3

1
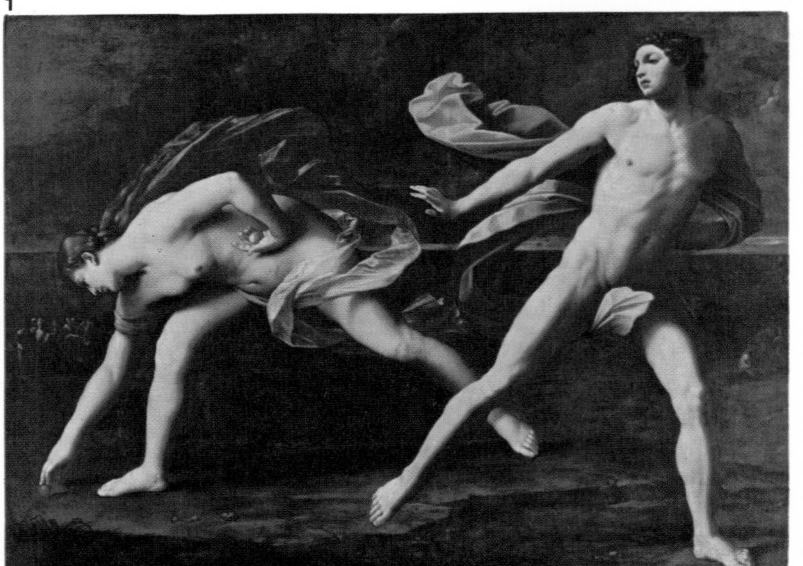

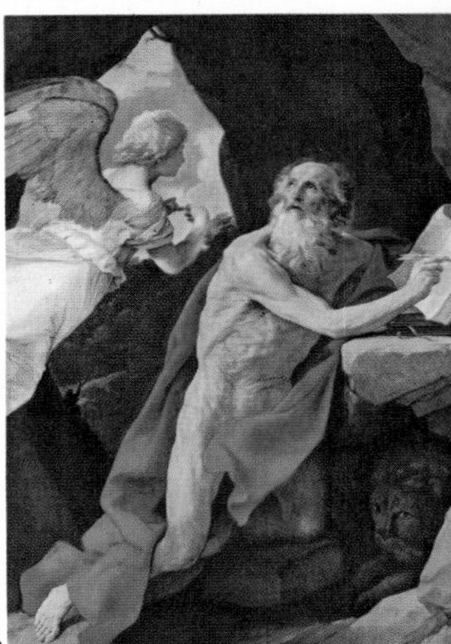
4

2
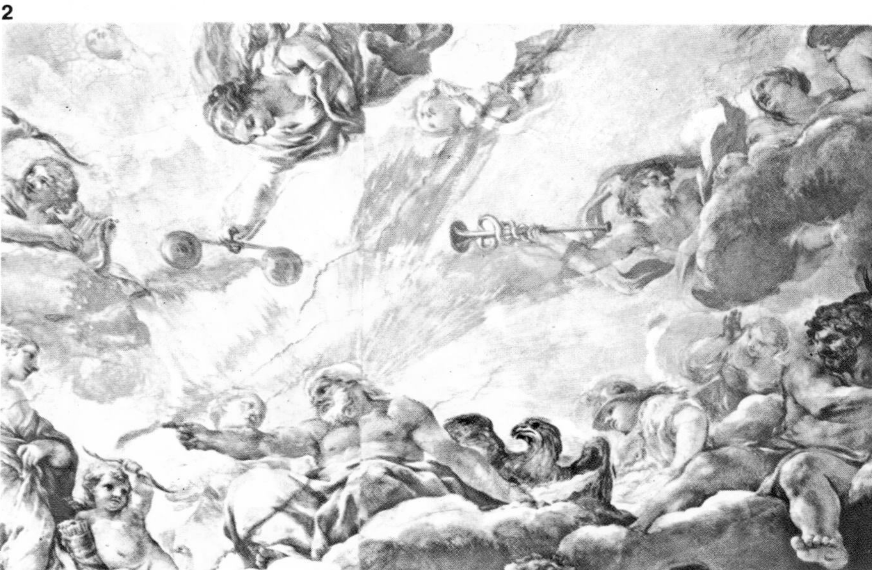

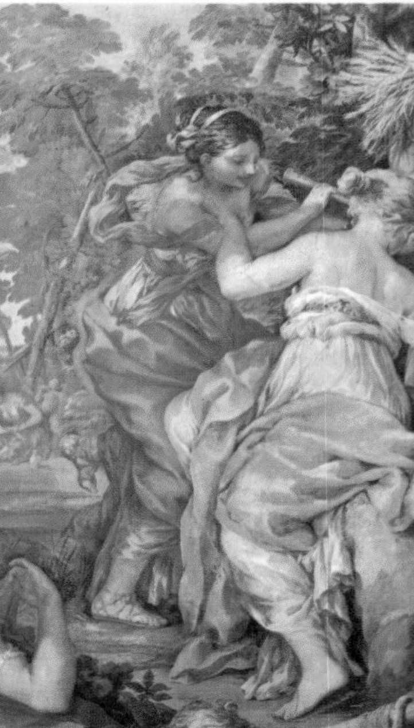
5

1. **Pietro da Cortona** (1596–1669): S. Maria della Pace, Rome. 1656–7
2. **Guercino** (1591–1666): *Venus and Adonis*. Wash drawing. Musée des Beaux-Arts, Bayonne
3. **Domenico Feti** (*c.*1589–1624): *The lost Piece of Silver*. Palazzo Pitti, Florence
4. **Domenichino** (1581–1641): *Lady with a Unicorn*. About 1602. Palazzo Farnese, Rome
5. **Andrea Sacchi** (1599/1600–61): *Portrait of Monsignore Clemente Merlini*. 1631–2. Galleria Borghese, Rome

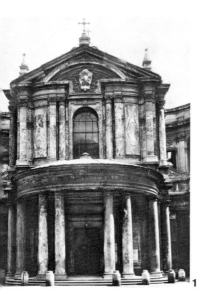

1

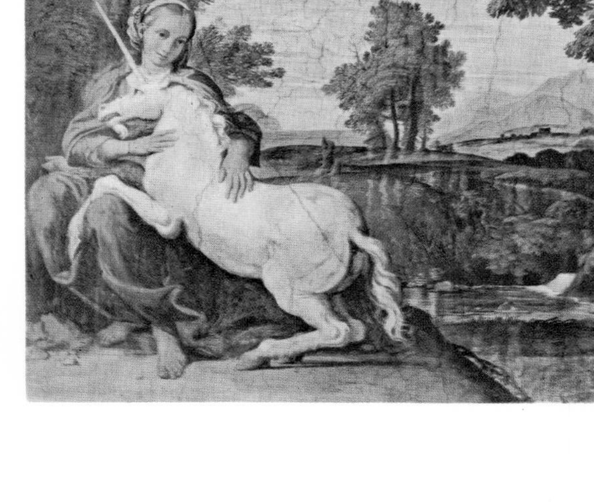

4

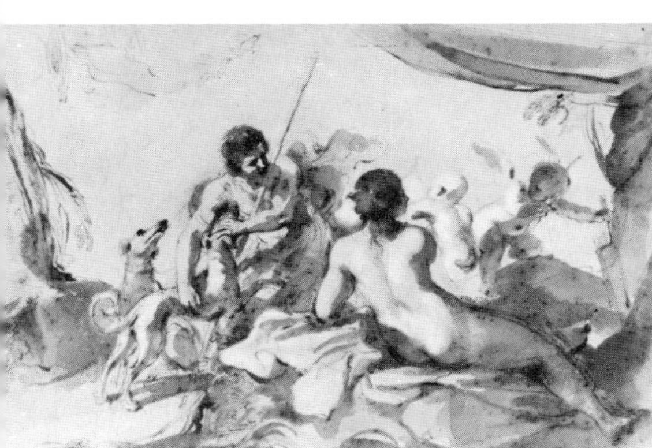

5

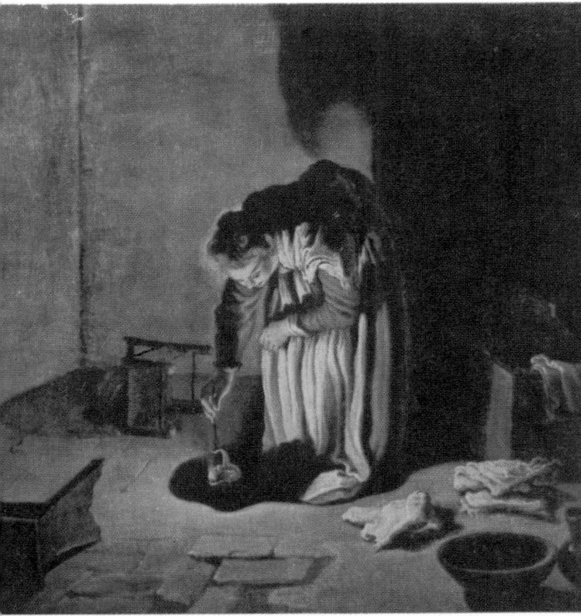

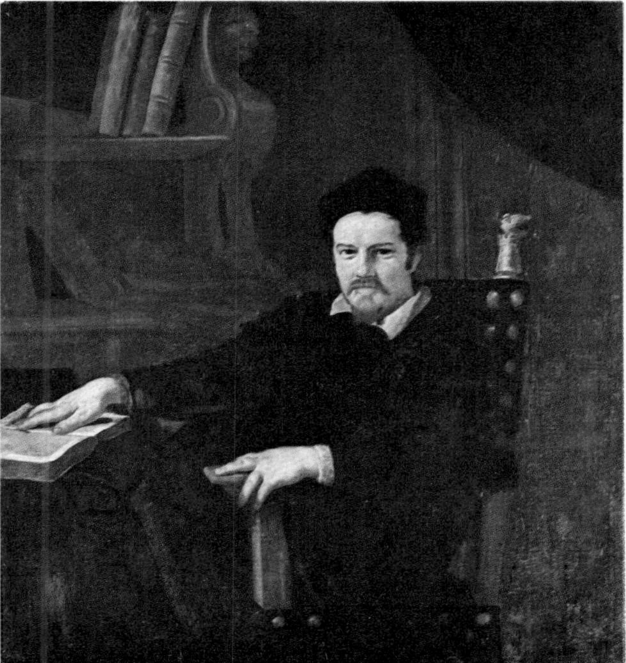

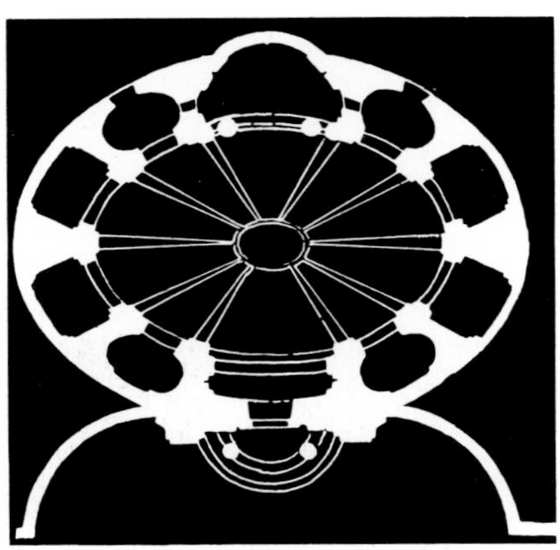

Gian Lorenzo Bernini (1598–1680)

1. Plan of S. Andrea al Quirinale, Rome (*see figs 2 and 5*)
2. Cupola of church of S. Andrea al Quirinale, Rome. 1658–70
3. The Colonnade of St Peter's, Rome. 1656–67
4. *Apollo and Daphne.* Marble. 1622–5. Galleria Borghese, Rome
5. Church of S. Andrea al Quirinale, Rome. 1658–70
6. *The Blessed Ludovica Albertoni.* Marble. 1671–4. Altieri Chapel, S. Francesco a Ripa, Rome

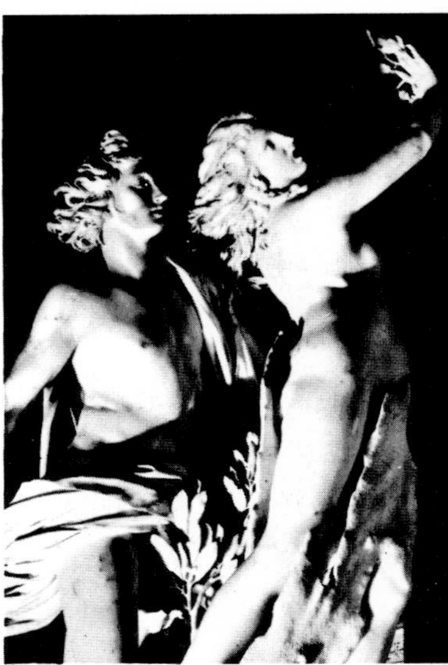

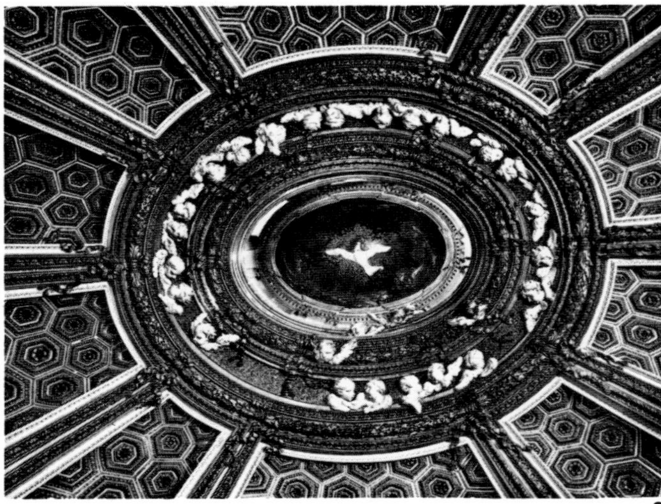

2

3

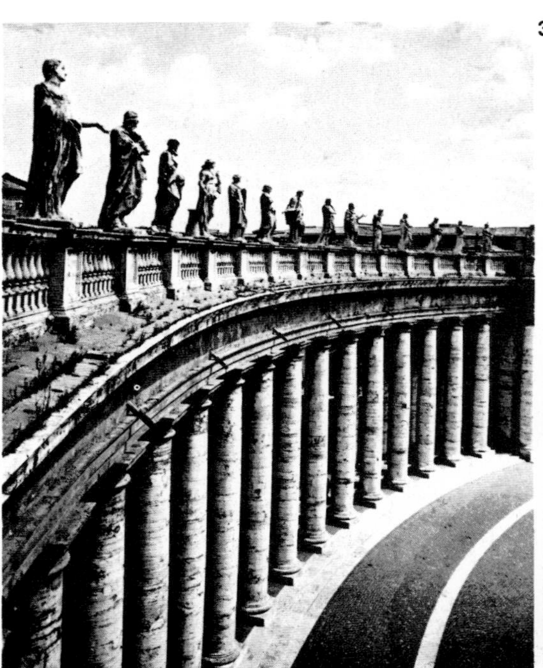

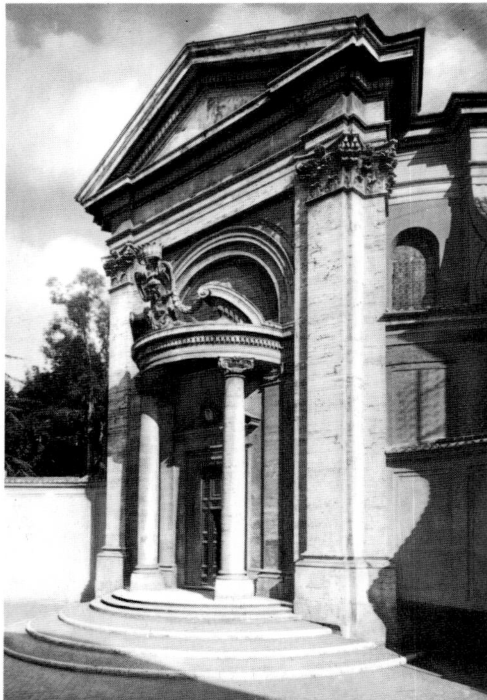

5

6

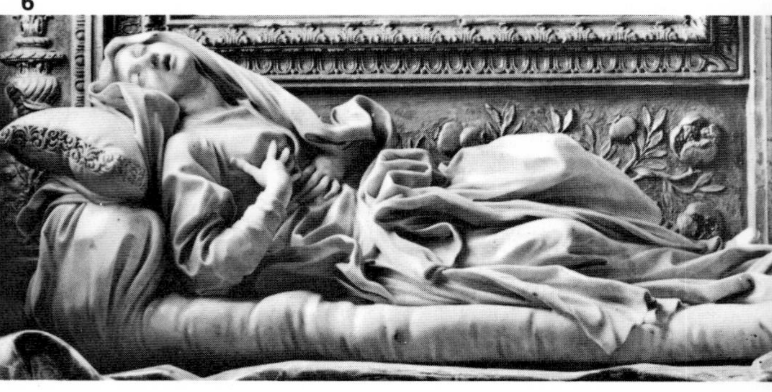

Gian Lorenzo Bernini (1598–1680)

1. *The Ecstasy of St Teresa.* Marble. 1645–52. Cornaro Chapel, S. Maria della Vittoria, Rome
2. *Fountain of the four Rivers: the Ganges.* Marble. 1651. Piazza Navona, Rome. The fountain was designed by Bernini; the *Ganges River* was sculpted by Claude Poussin
3. *The Blessed Ludovica Albertoni.* Detail of fig. 6, opposite
4. with pupils: *Members of the Cornaro Family.* Marble. 1645–52. Cornaro Chapel, S. Maria della Vittoria, Rome
5. *David.* Detail of marble statue. 1623–4. Galleria Borghese, Rome
6. Baldacchino in St Peter's, Rome. 1624–33
7. Façade of the Palazzo Barberini, Rome. 1628–33

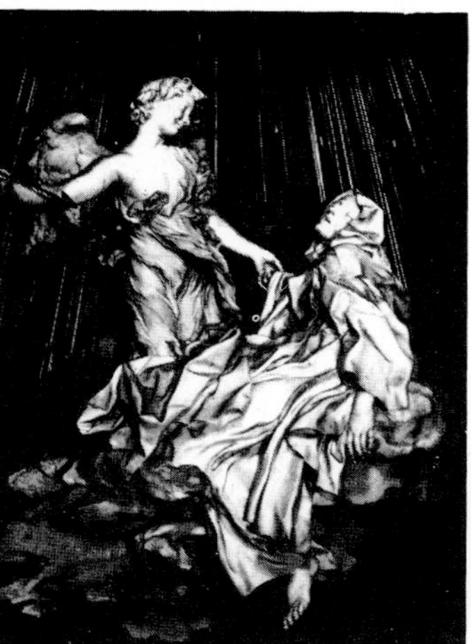

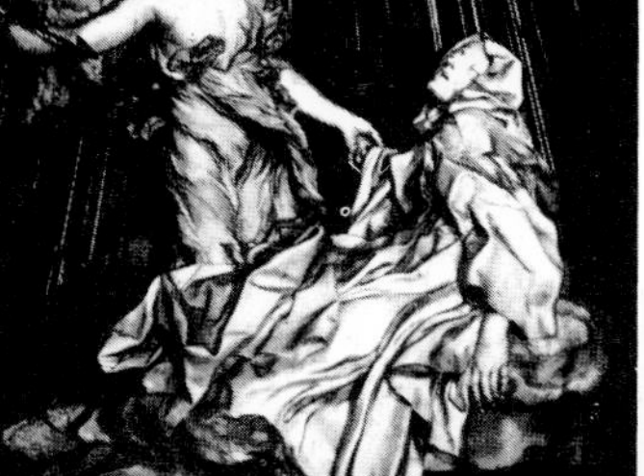

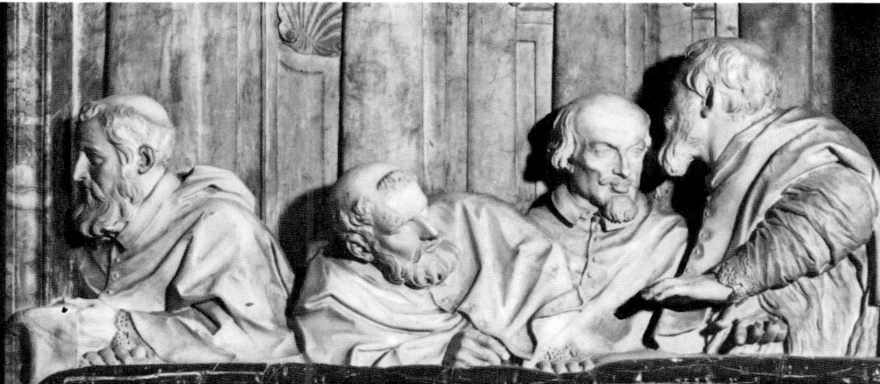

4

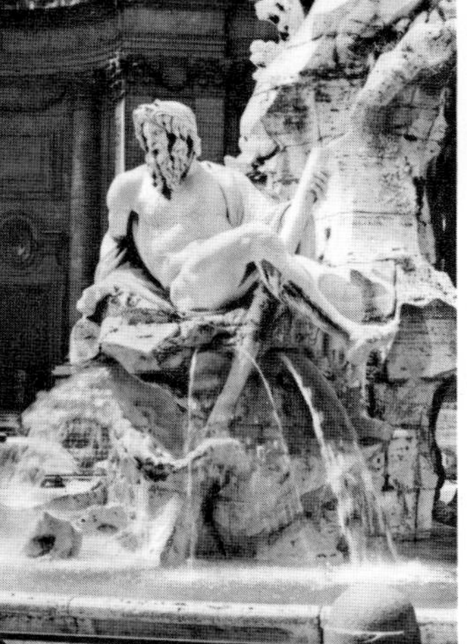

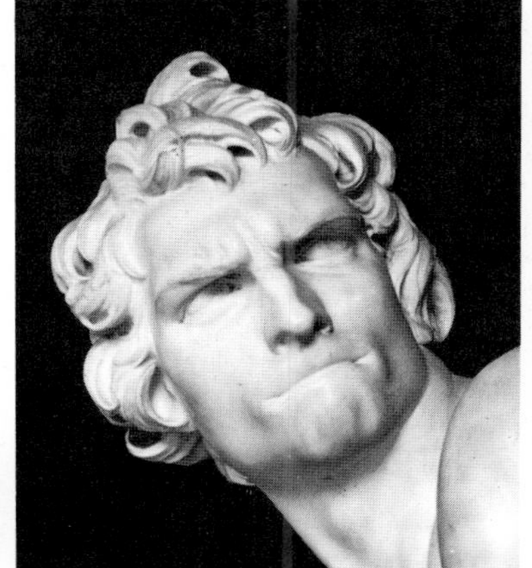

5

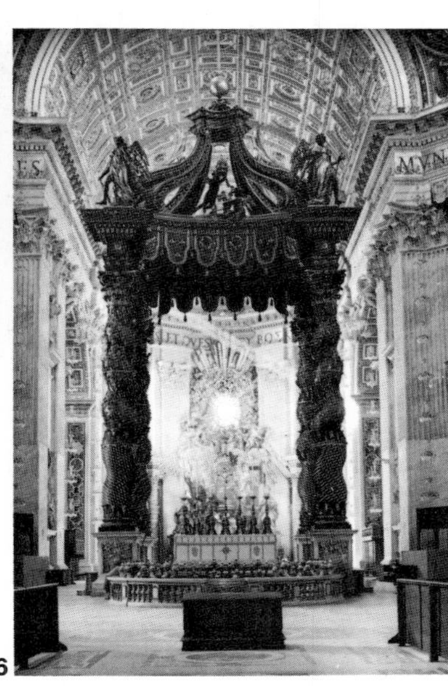

6

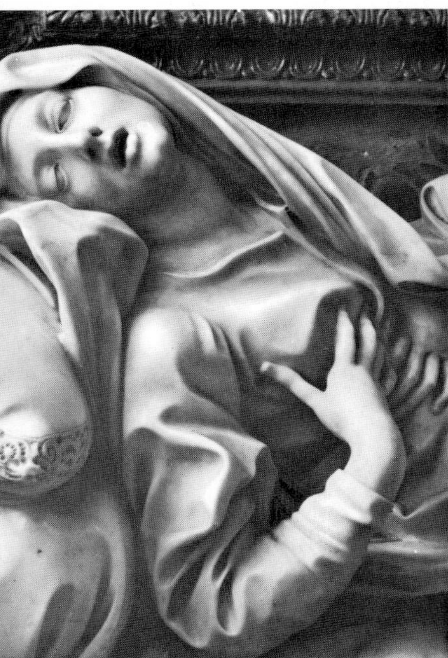

3

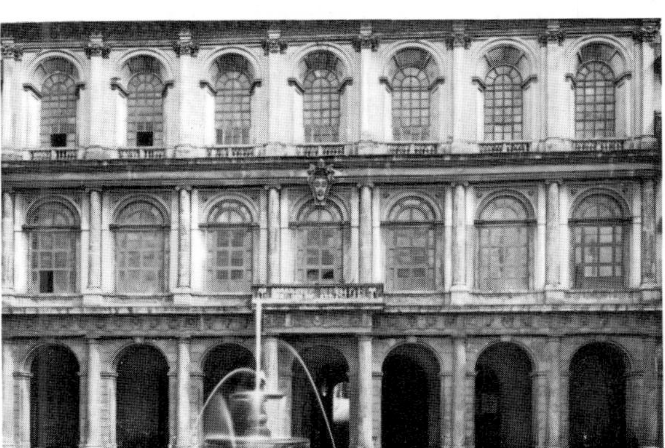

7

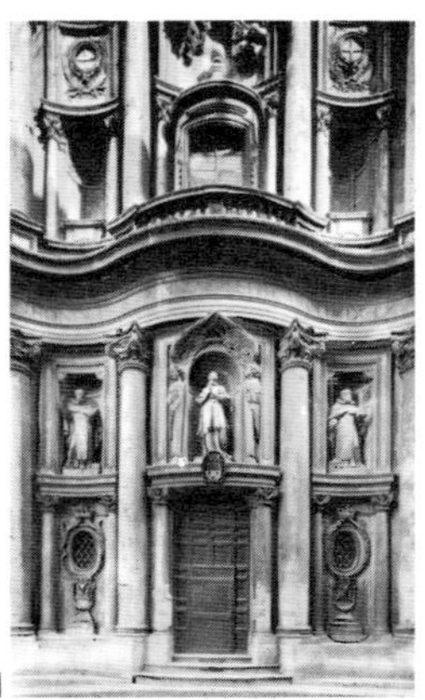
1

Francesco Borromini (1599–1667)

1. Façade of S. Carlo alle Quattro Fontane, Rome. Detail. 1667
2. Cupola of S. Ivo della Sapienza, Rome. 1642–50
3. Courtyard and church of S. Ivo della Sapienza, Rome. 1642–50
4. Gallery of the Palazzo Spada, Rome. 1634–6
5. Cupola of S. Carlo alle Quattro Fontane, Rome. 1638–41
6. Interior of S. Ivo della Sapienza, Rome. 1642–50

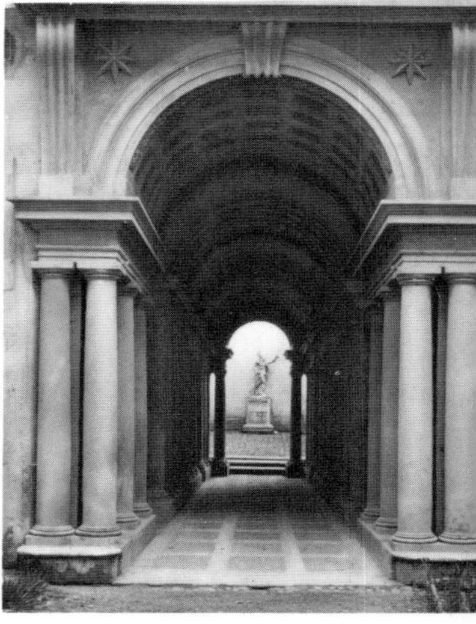

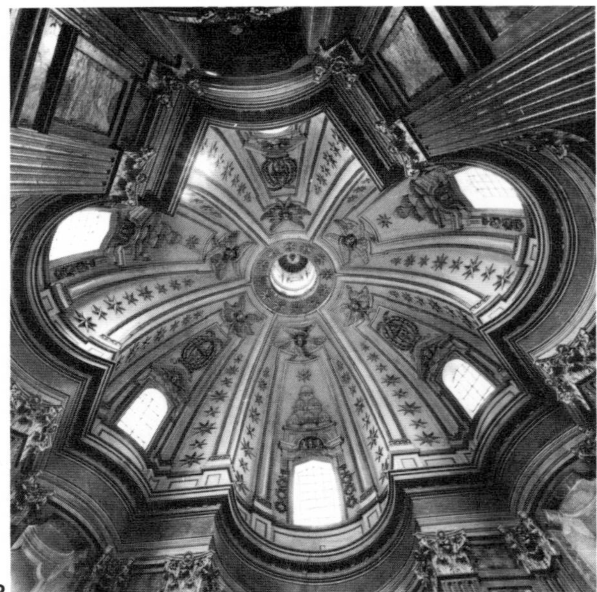
2

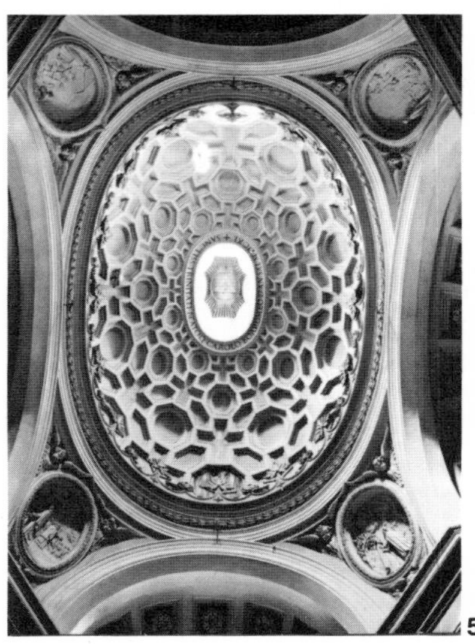
5

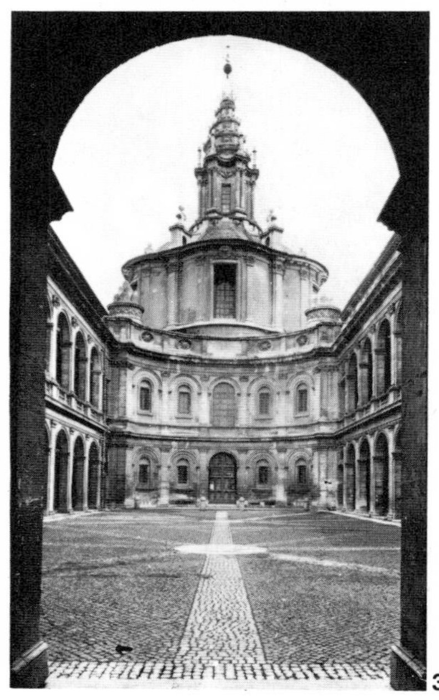
3

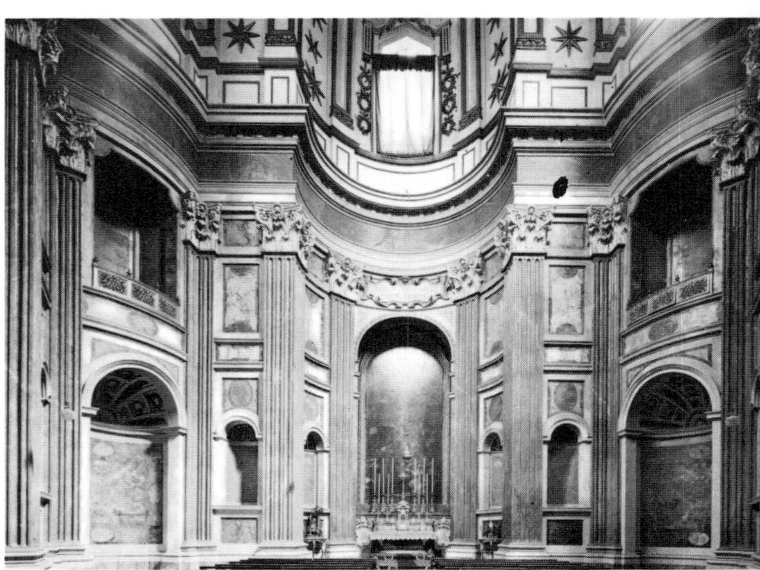

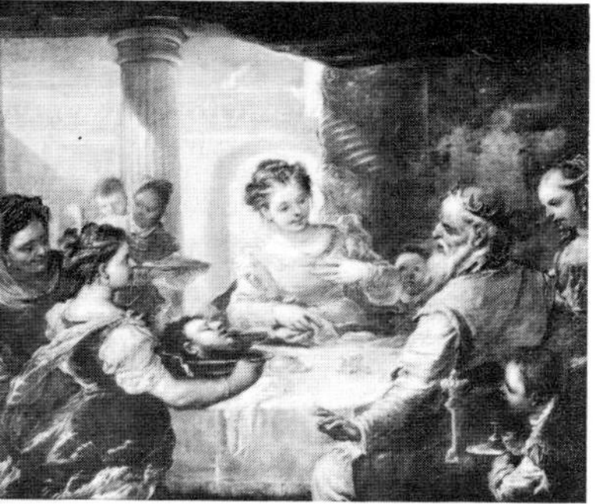

1. **Luca Giordano** (1634–1705): *The Feast of Herod.* Galleria Nazionale di Capodimonte, Naples
2. **Guarino Guarini** (1624–83): Palazzo Carignano, Turin. Begun 1679
3. **Baldassare Longhena** (1598–1682): Staircase of the monastery of S. Giorgio Maggiore, Venice. 1643–5
4. **Andrea Pozzo** (1642–1709): *The Triumph of St Ignatius of Loyola.* Fresco on nave ceiling, church of S. Ignazio, Rome. 1691–4
5. **Baldassare Longhena** (1598–1682): S. Maria della Salute, Venice. 1631–48
6. **Baldassare Longhena** (1598–1682): Palazzo Rezzonico on the Grand Canal, Venice. 1660–7

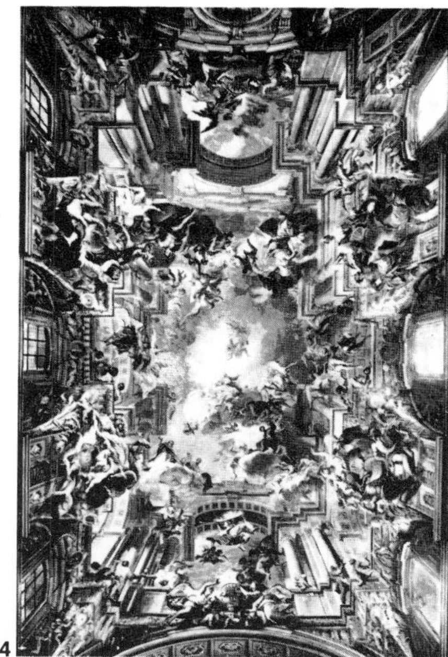

4

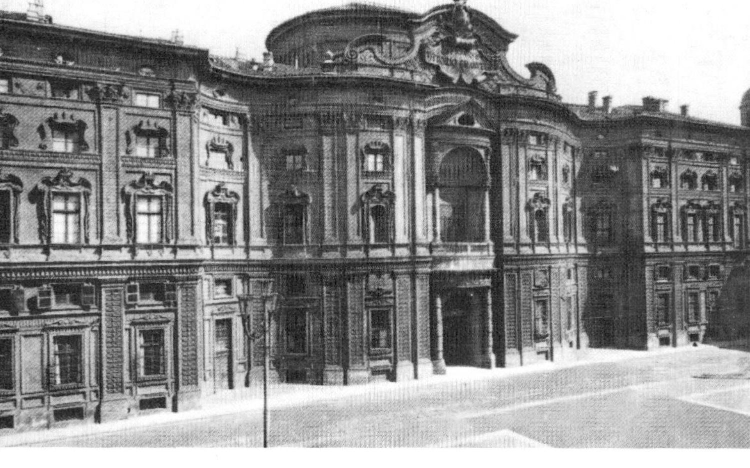

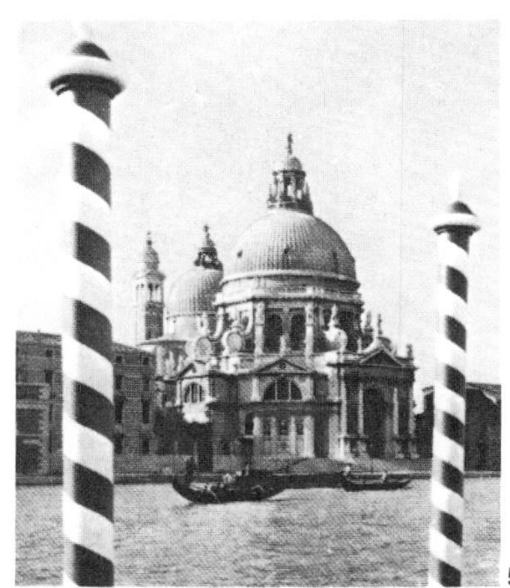

5

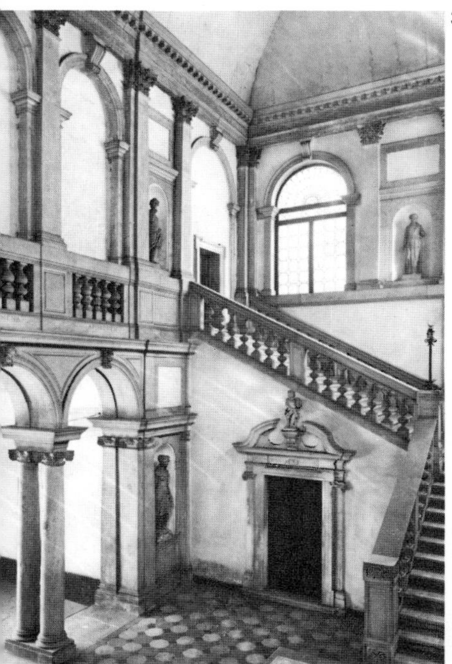

3

6

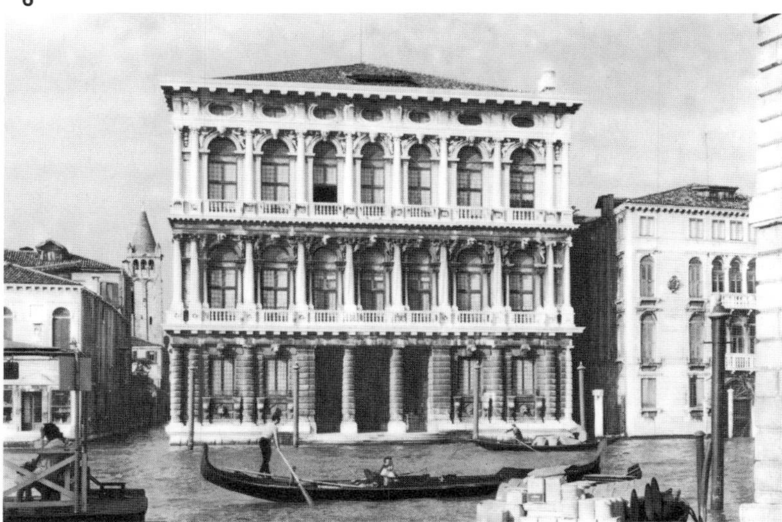

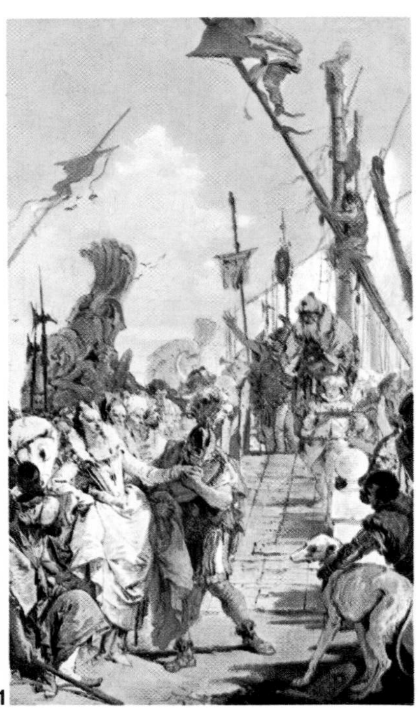

1

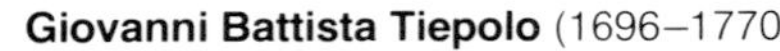

Giovanni Battista Tiepolo (1696–1770)

1. *Antony and Cleopatra.* About 1745–50. National Gallery of Scotland, Edinburgh
2. *Timocleia and the Thracian Commander.* About 1750. National Gallery of Art (Samuel H. Kress Collection), Washington DC
3. *Danaë.* 1736. University Museum, Stockholm
4. *Portrait of the Procurator Giovanni Querini.* About 1749? Galleria Querini-Stampalia, Venice
5. *The Embarkation of Cleopatra.* About 1745–50. Palazzo Labia, Venice
6. *Aurora dispersing the Clouds of Night.* About 1755–60. Boston Museum of Fine Arts

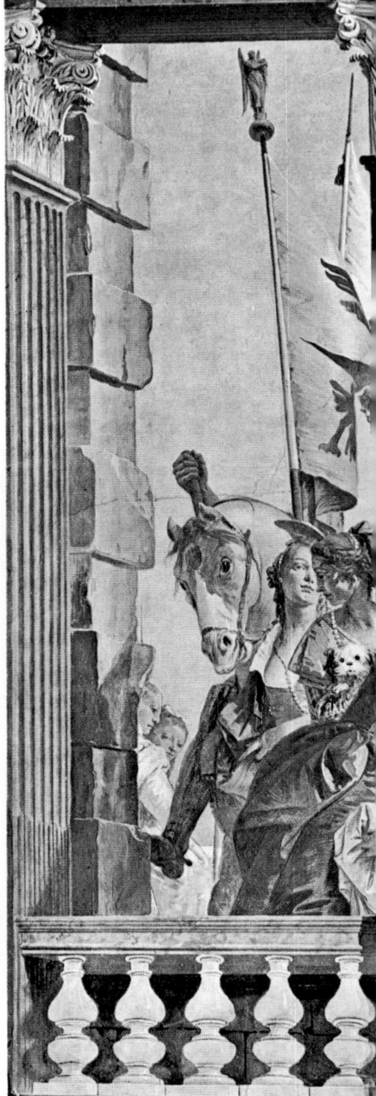

5

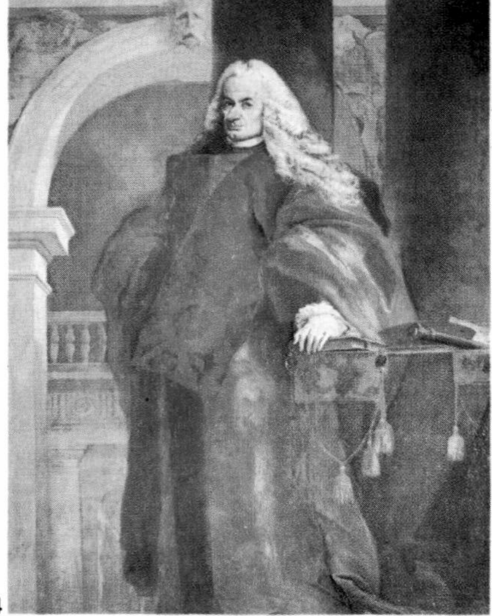

4

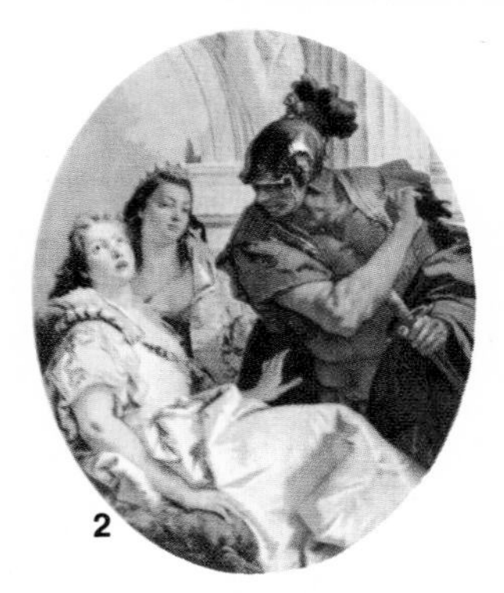

2

3

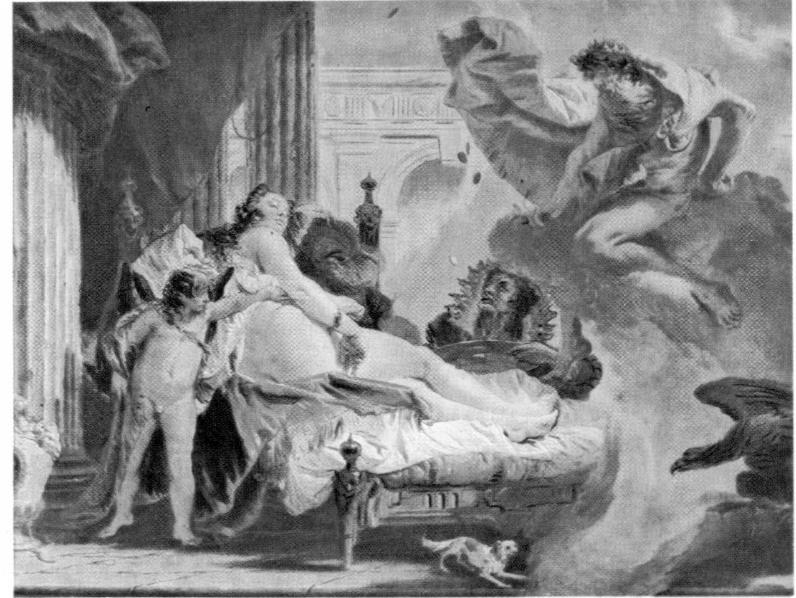

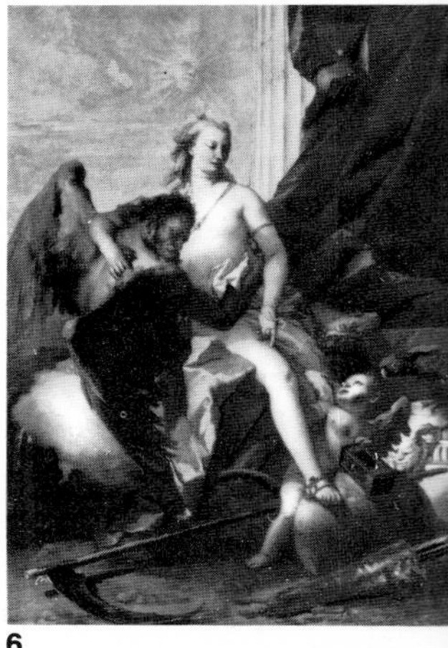

6

Giovanni Paolo Panini (1691/2–1765): *The Interior of the Pantheon.* About 1730–5. National Gallery of Art (Samuel H. Kress Collection), Washington DC

2. **Sebastiano Ricci** (1659–1734) and **Marco Ricci** (1676–1730): Detail from *Memorial to Admiral Sir Clowdisley Shovell.* About 1725. National Gallery of Art (Samuel H. Kress Collection), Washington DC
3. **Marco Ricci** (1676–1730): *Park of a Villa.* Accademia, Venice
4. **Giovanni Battista Piranesi** (1720–78): Imaginary reconstruction of an antique temple, based on the Temple of Vesta, Rome, Engraving
5. **Giovanni Paolo Panini** (1691/2–1765): *Procession of Carriages across the water-filled Piazza Navona.* 1756. Landesgalerie, Hanover
6. **Giovanni Battista Piazzetta** (1683–1754): *Rebecca at the Well.* About 1740. Brera, Milan

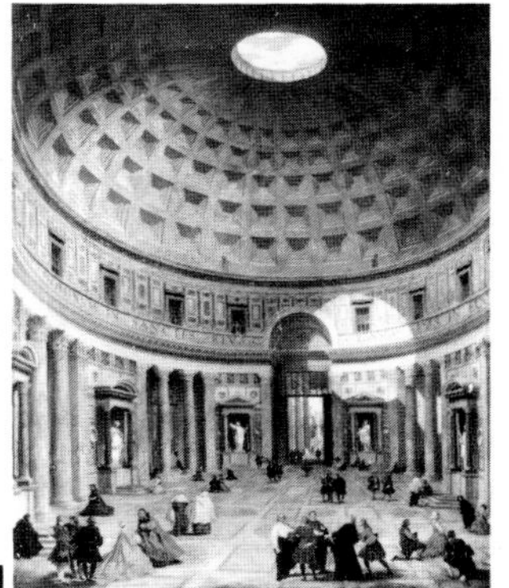

1

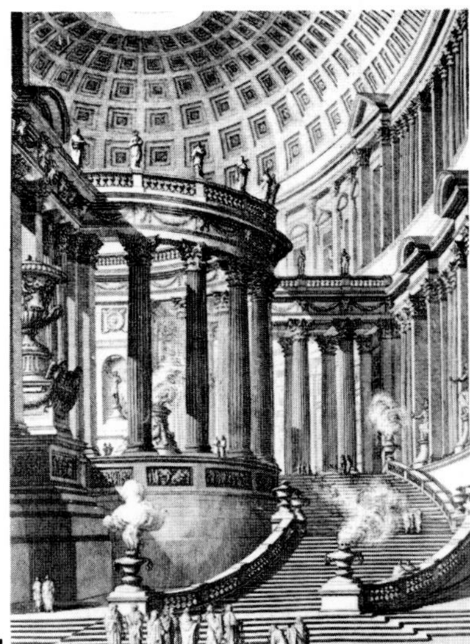

4

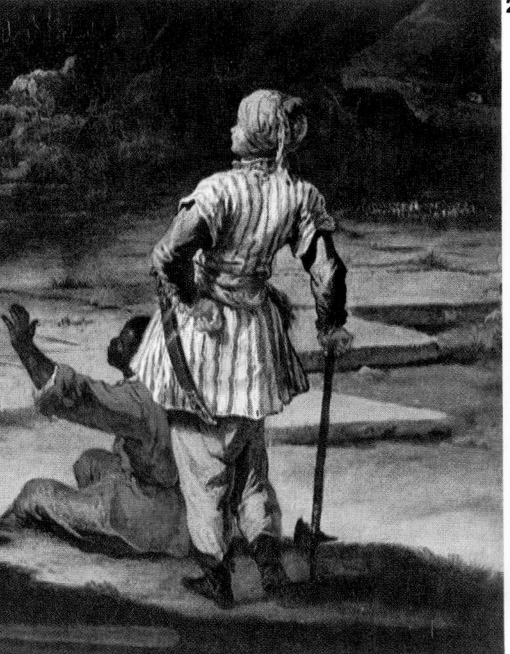

2

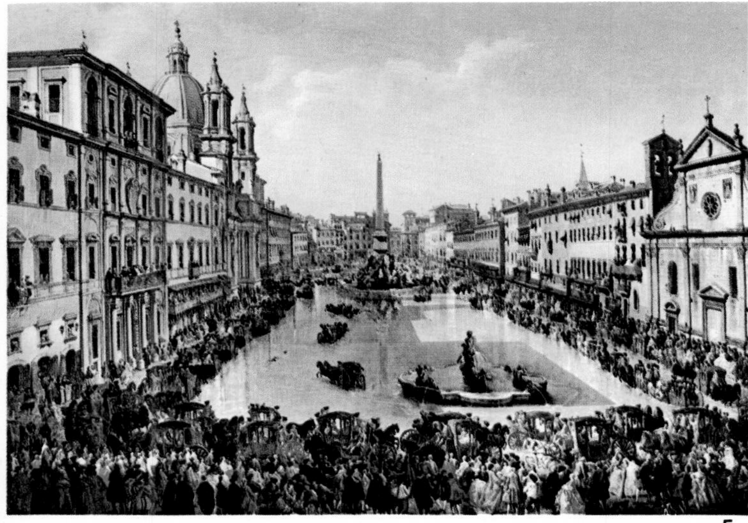

5

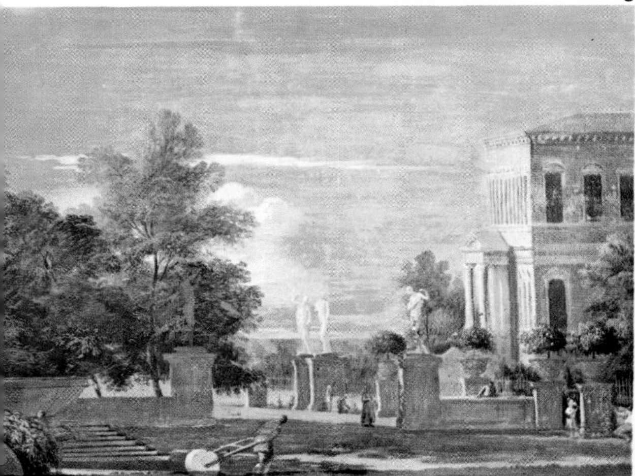

3

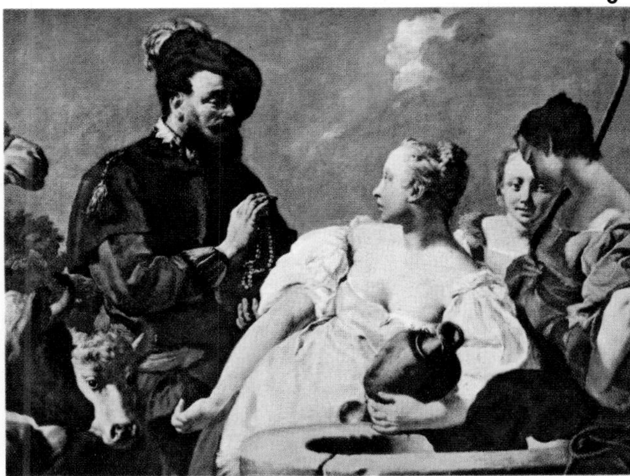

6

1. **Canaletto** (1697–1768): *The Grand Canal, Venice.* National Gallery, Prague
2. **Canaletto** (1697–1768): *The Bucintoro returning to the Molo on Ascension Day.* About 1730. Crespi Collection, Milan
3. **Francesco Guardi** (1712–93): *Strollers in Venice.* Drawing
4. **Francesco Guardi** (1712–93): *Feast of the Ascension in Venice.* About 1763. Louvre, Paris

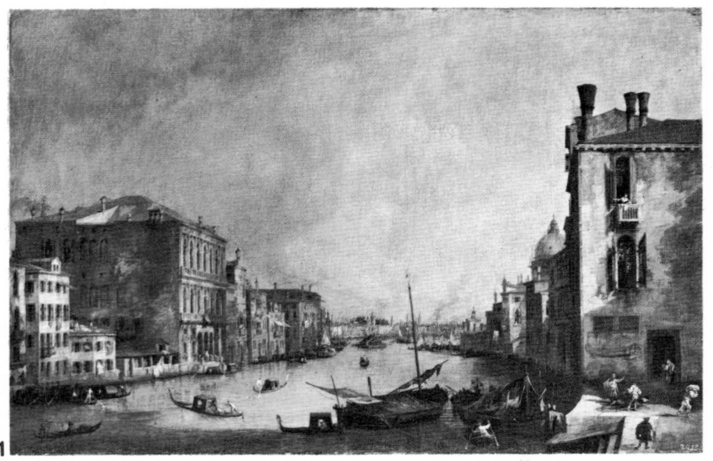

1

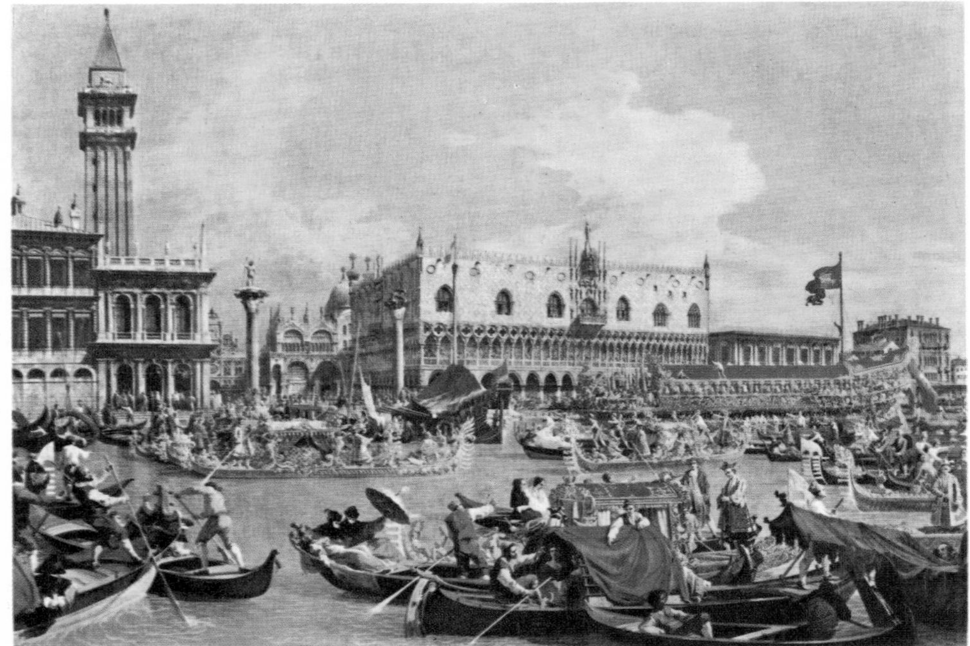

2

3

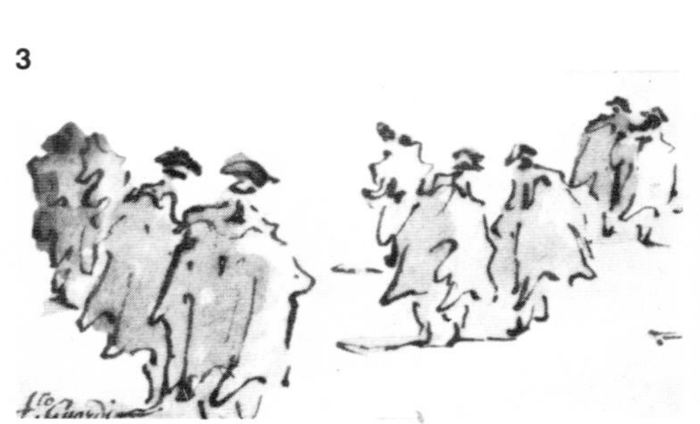

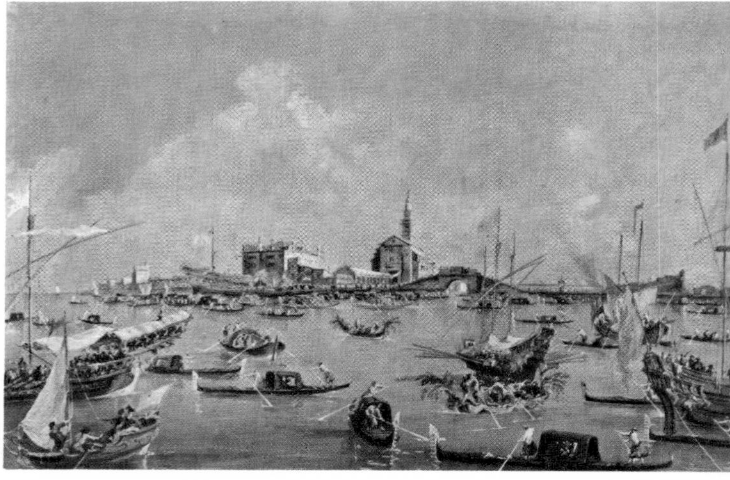

Pietro Longhi (1702–85): *Rhinoceros.* 1751. Ca'Rezzonico, Venice

Canaletto (1697–1768): *Perspective.* Accademia, Venice

3. **Francesco Guardi** (1712–93): *Feast of the Ascension in St Mark's Square, Venice.* About 1770. Gulbenkian Foundation, Lisbon
4. **Francesco Guardi** (1712–93): *The Entrance to the Arsenale, Venice.* Kunsthistorisches Museum, Venice
5. **Bernardo Bellotto** (1720–80): *Vienna from the Belvedere.* 1758–61. Kunsthistorisches Museum, Vienna
6. **Pietro Longhi** (1702–85): *Duck Hunting.* Galleria Querini-Stampalia, Venice

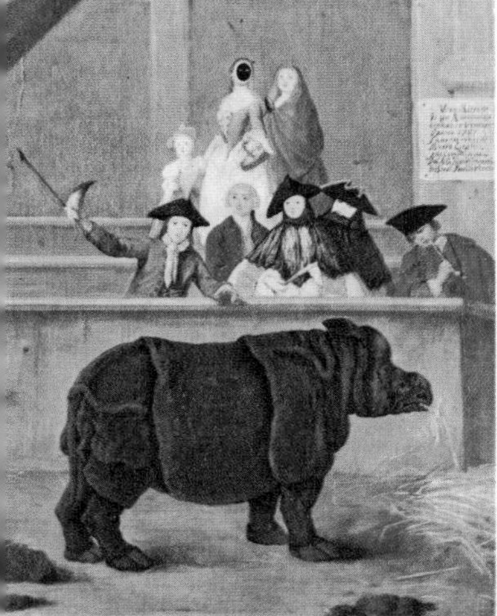

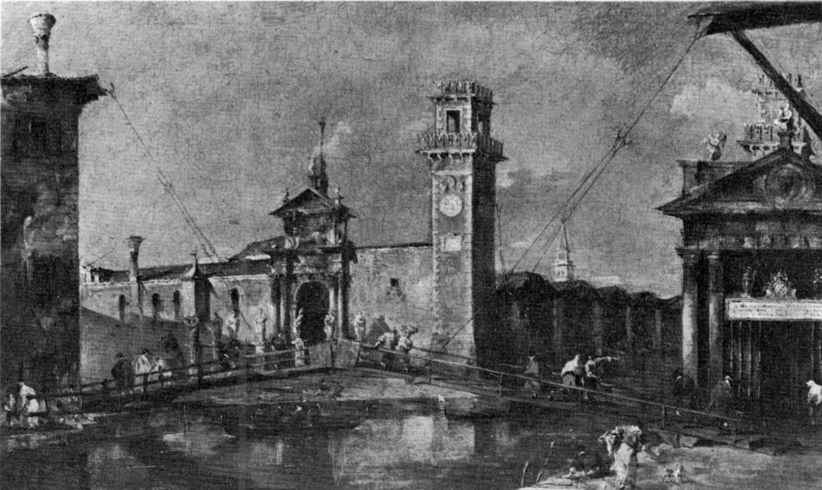

4

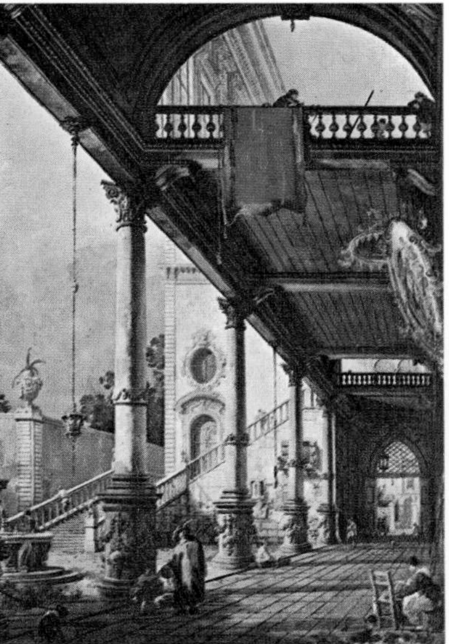

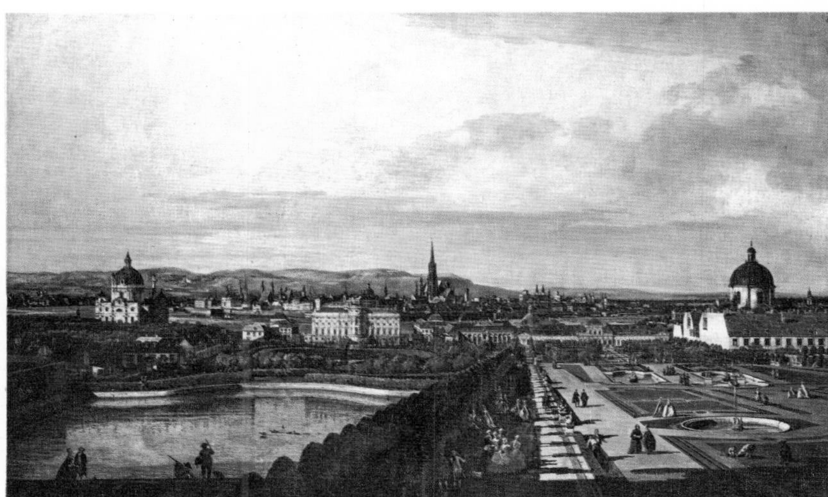

5

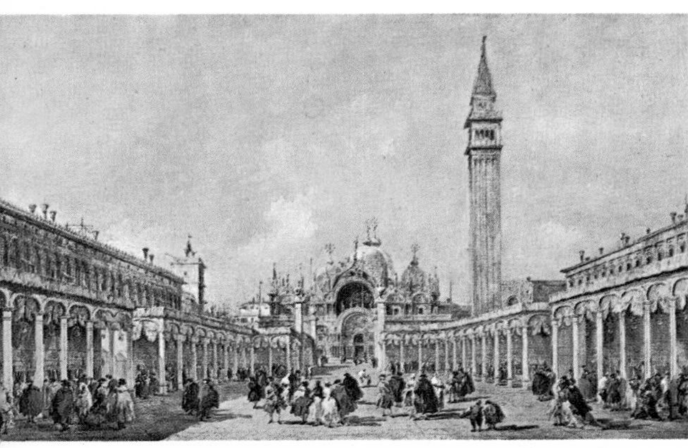

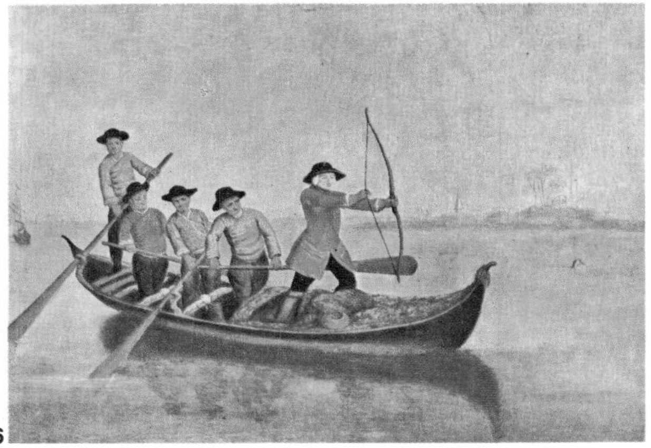

6

Sir Peter Paul Rubens (1577–1640)

1. *Hélène Fourment, the Artist's second Wife, in her Wedding Dress.* About 1631. Alte Pinakothek, Munich
2. *Portrait of the Artist and Isabella Brant, his first Wife.* About 1609. Alte Pinakothek, Munich
3. *The Rape of the Daughters of Leucippus* About 1618. Alte Pinakothek, Munich
4. *The Descent from the Cross.* About 161 Antwerp Cathedral

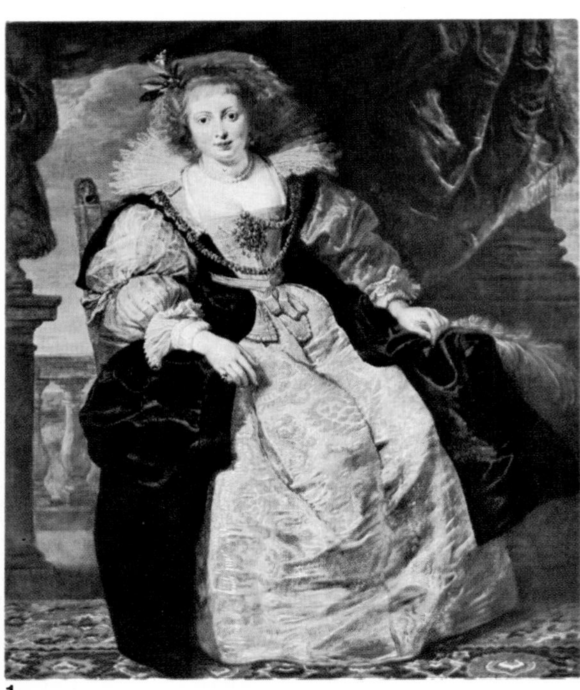

1

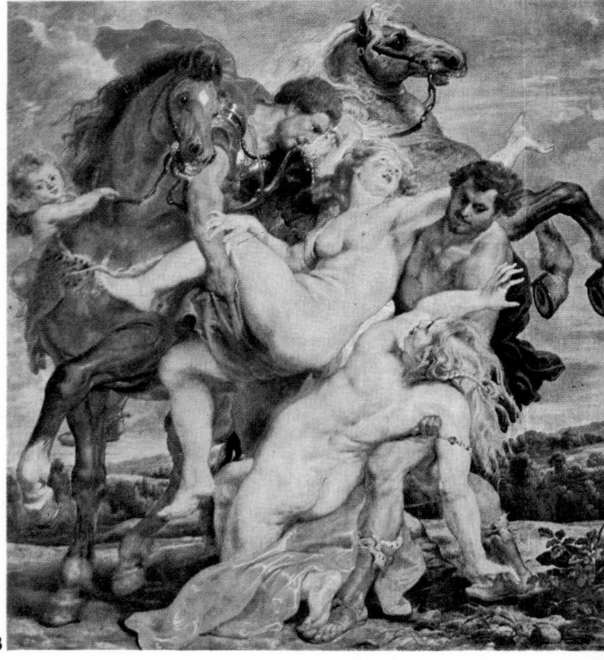

3

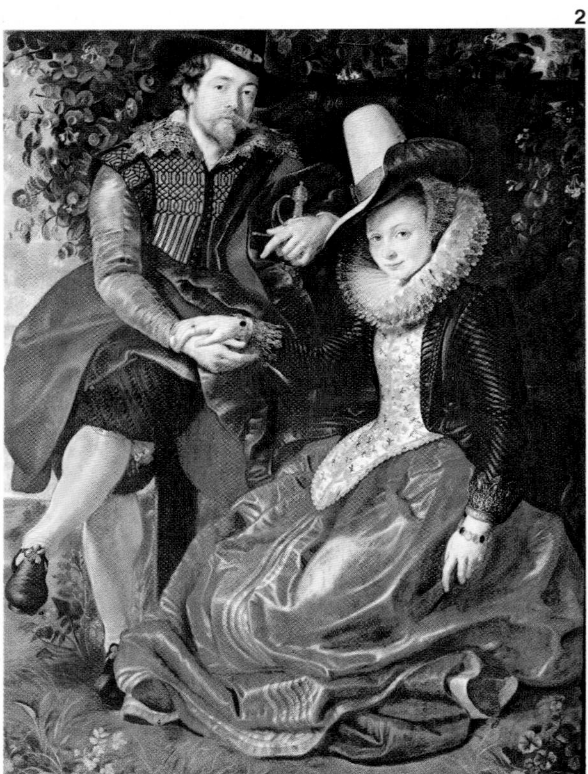

2

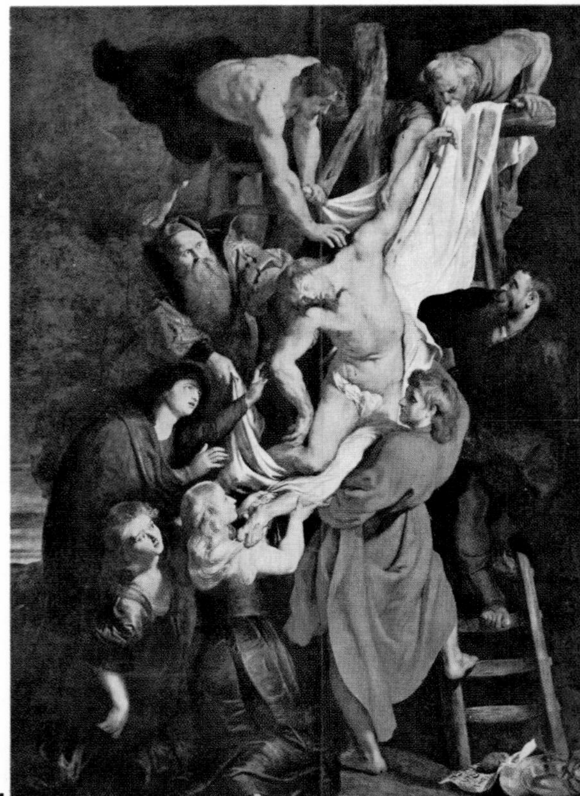

4

ir Peter Paul Rubens (1577–1640)

Self-portrait. Detail of fig. 2, opposite

Archduke Albert presented by his Patron Saint. Left wing of the Ildefonso Altarpiece. 1630–2

Studies of a Negro Head. Musées Royaux des Beaux-Arts, Brussels

The Judgement of Paris. About 1638–9. Prado, Madrid

La Kermesse. About 1636–8. Louvre, Paris

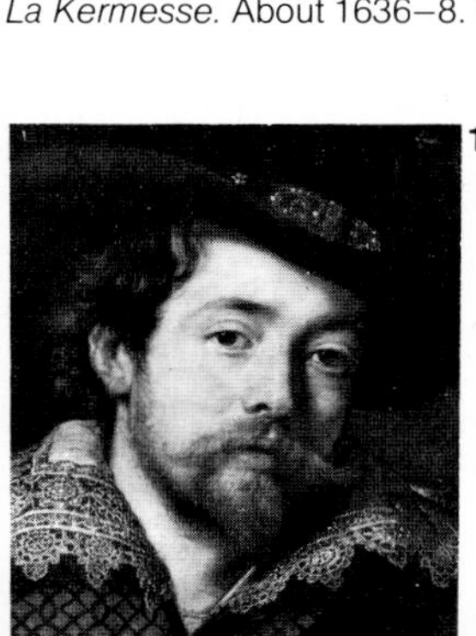
1

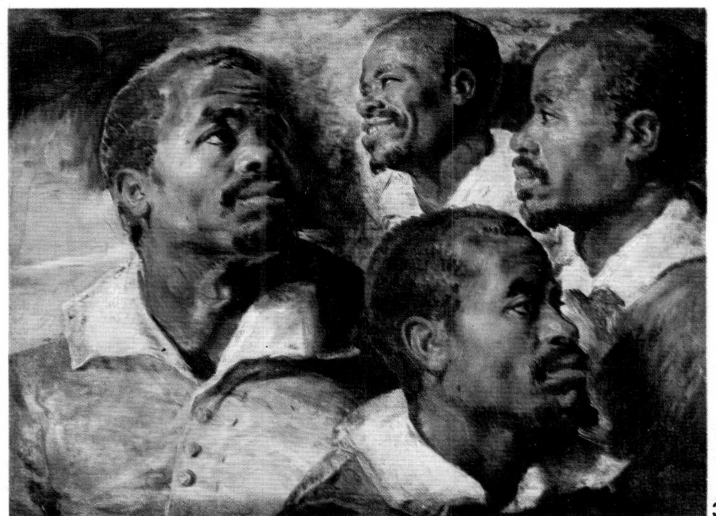
3

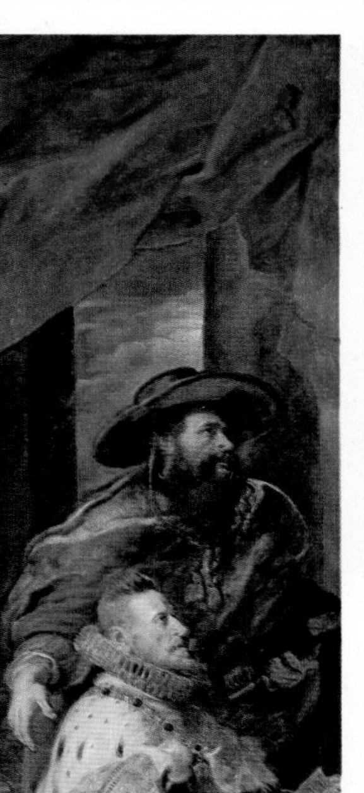

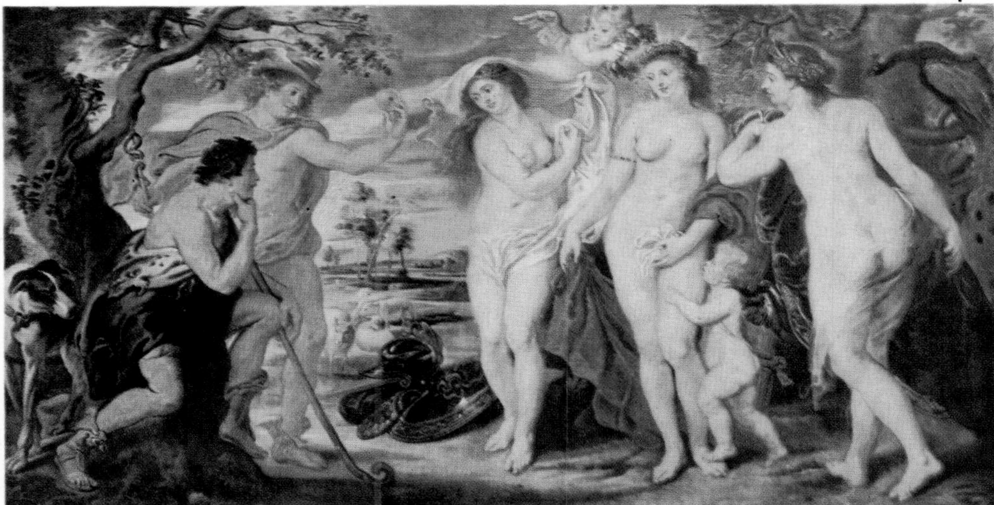
4

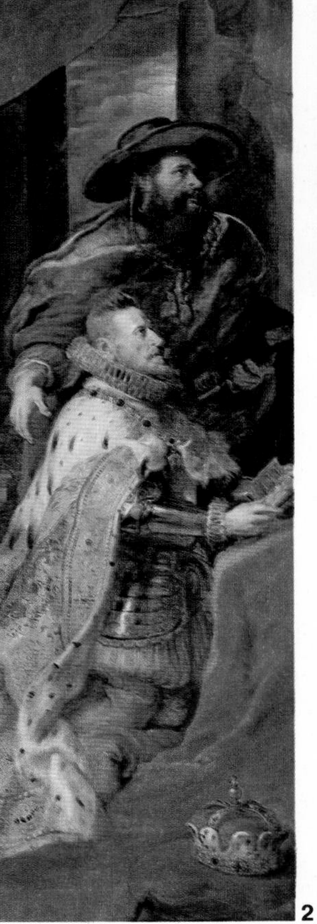
2

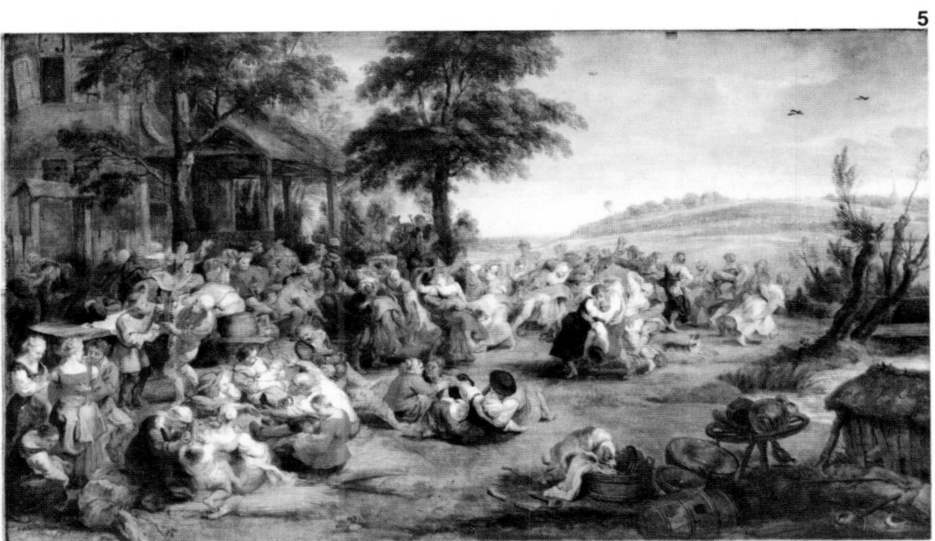
5

Sir Anthony van Dyck (1599–1641)

1. *Portrait of Lady d'Aubigny.* About 1638. National Gallery of Art (Widener Collection), Washington DC
2. *Portrait of Charles I.* 1635. Louvre, Paris
3. *Portrait of Endymion Porter and the Artist.* Prado, Madrid
4. *Self-portrait.* Detail. About 1621–2. Alte Pinakothek, Munich
5. *Portrait of William II of Nassau and Orange.* About 1640. National Gallery of Art (Mellon Collection), Washington DC
6. *Portrait of Philip, Lord Wharton.* 1632. National Gallery of Art (Mellon Collection), Washington DC

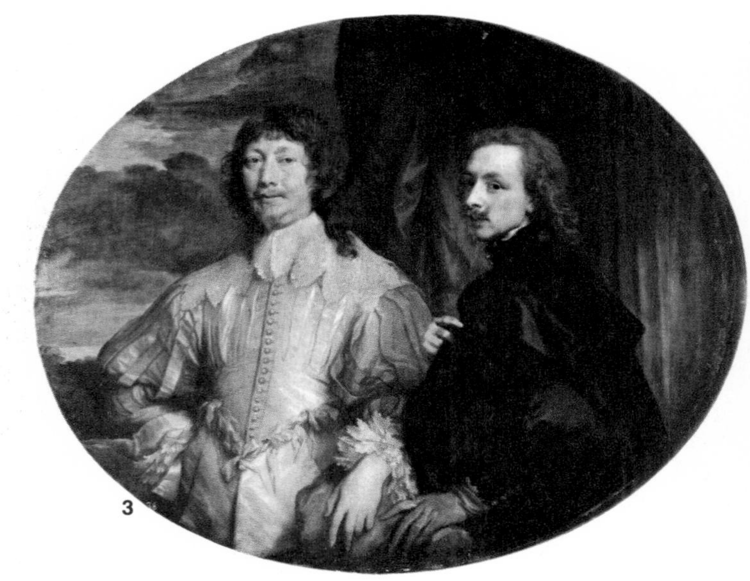

3

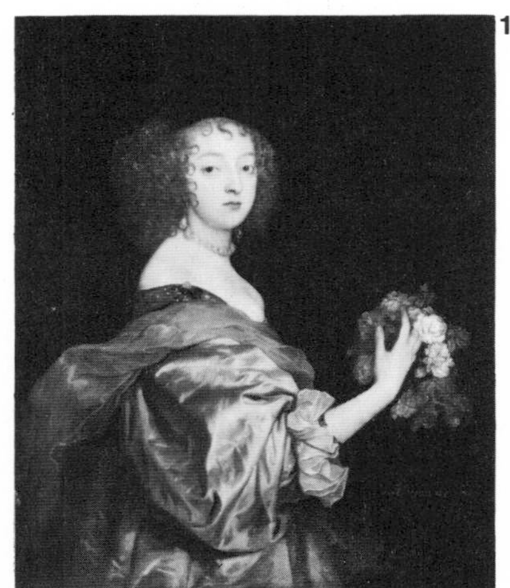

1

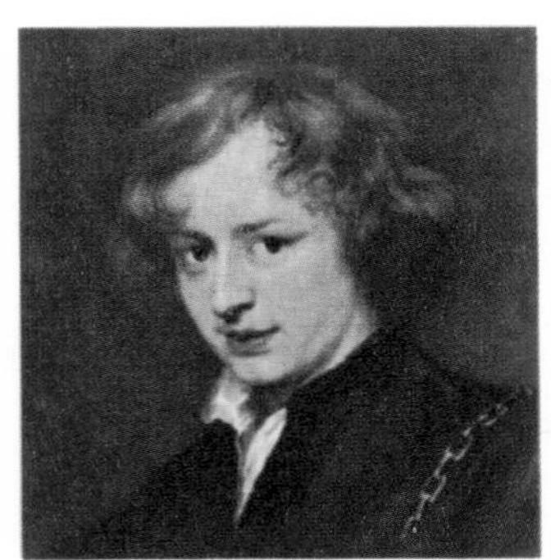

4

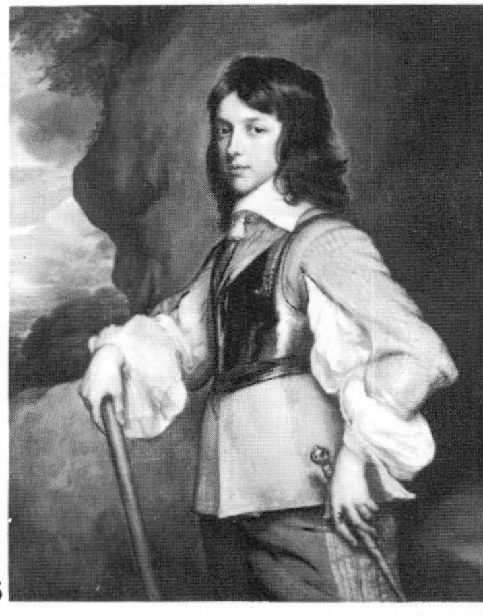

5

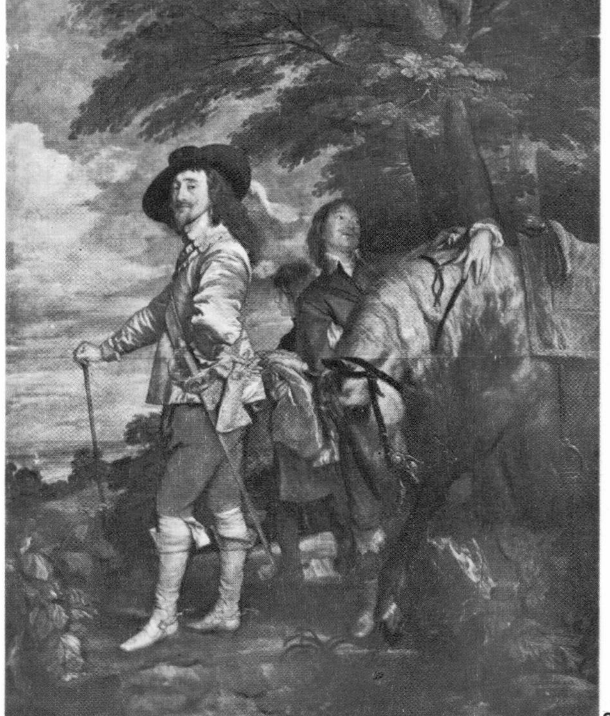

2

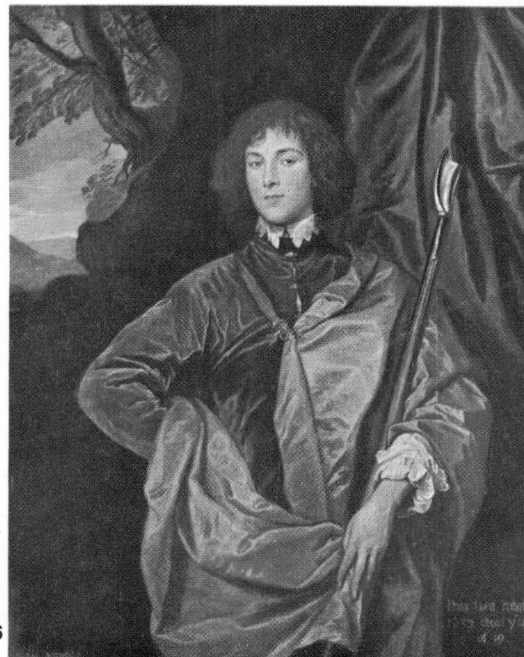

6

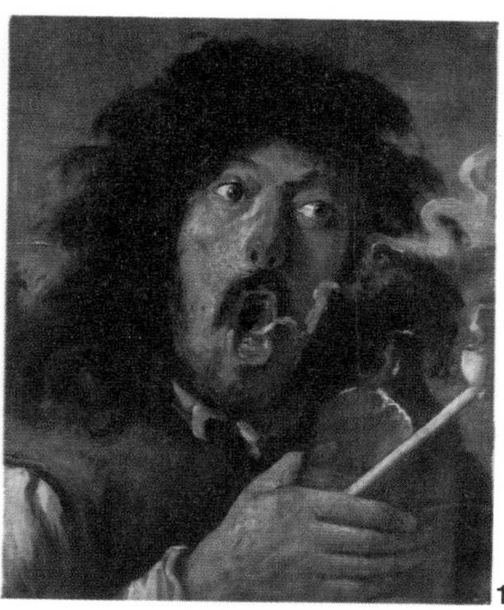

1

1. **Adriaen Brouwer** (1605/6–38): *The Smoker.* About 1626. Louvre, Paris
2. **Jan Bruegel** (1568–1625): *Still Life with Bowl and Jewels.* 1618. Musées Royaux des Beaux-Arts, Brussels
3. **Paul Bril** (1554–1626): *The Baptism of Christ.* Galleria Borghese, Rome
4. **Hendrick ter Brugghen** (1588–1629): *The Flute Player.* 1621. Gemäldegalerie, Kassel
5. **Hendrick Avercamp** (1585–1634): *Winter Landscape with Skaters.* Detail. Rijksmuseum, Amsterdam
6. **Adriaen Brouwer** (1605/6–38): *Cardplayers in a Tavern.* Alte Pinakothek, Munich

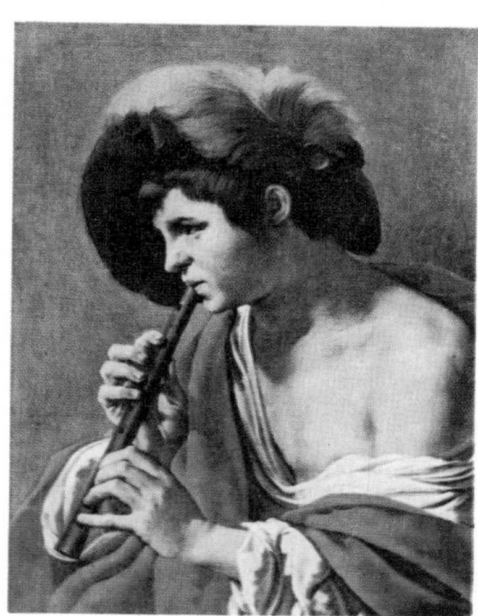

4

2

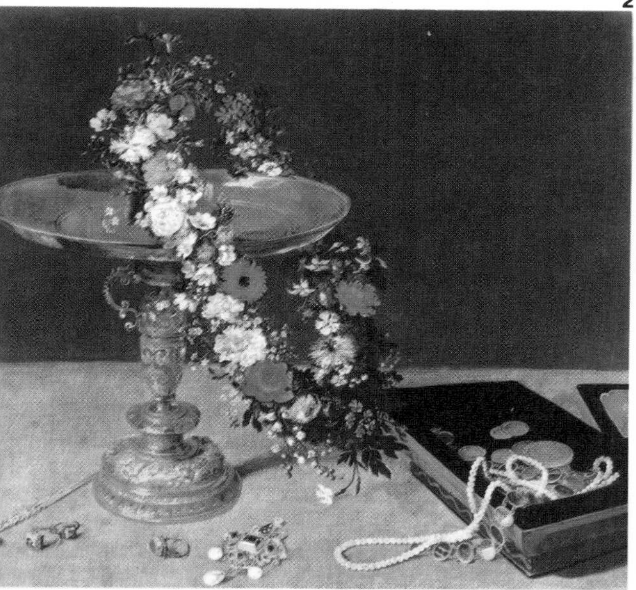

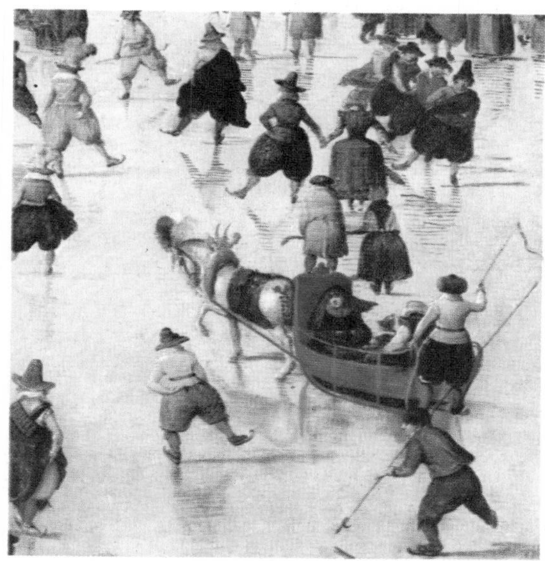

5

3

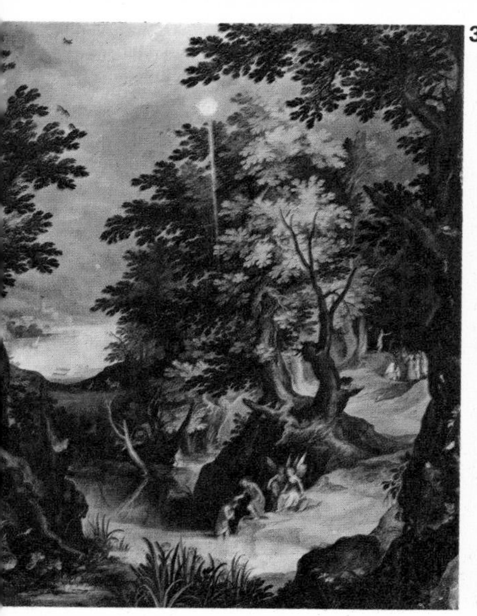

6

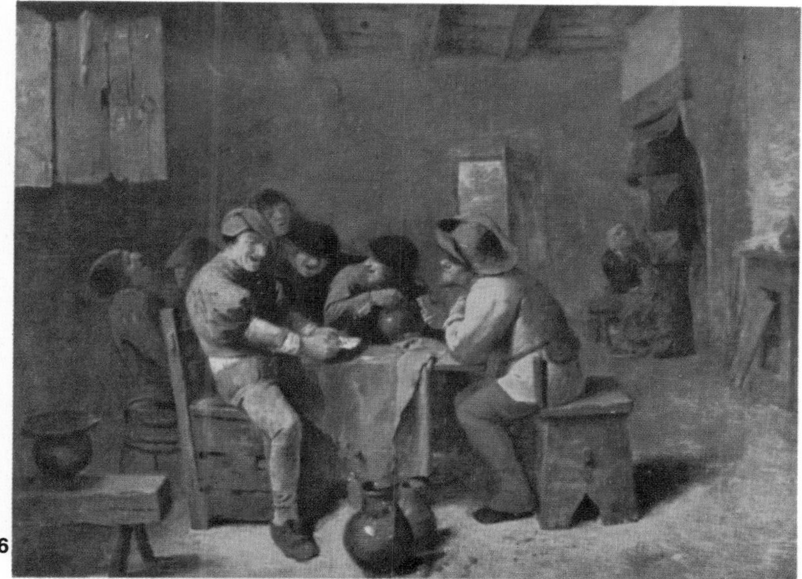

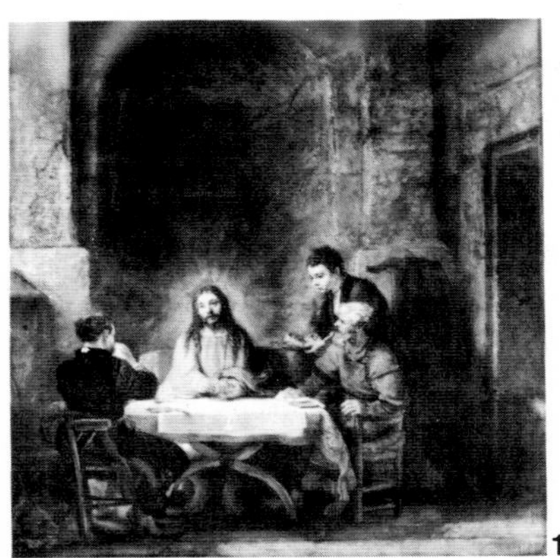

1

Rembrandt (1606–69)

1. *Christ at Emmaus.* 1648. Louvre, Paris
2. *The Jewish Bride (Isaac and Rebecca?).* About 1666. Rijksmuseum, Amsterdam
3. *The Militia Company of Captain Frans Banning Cocq* (*The Night Watch*). 1642. Rijksmuseum, Amsterdam
4. *Portrait of Jan Six.* 1654. Six Collection, Amsterdam
5. *Portrait of Titus.* 1655. Museum Boymans-van Beuningen, Rotterdam
6. *Self-portrait.* Detail. 1640. National Gallery, London
7. *Jeremiah mourning over the Destruction of Jerusalem.* 1630. Rijksmuseum, Amsterdam

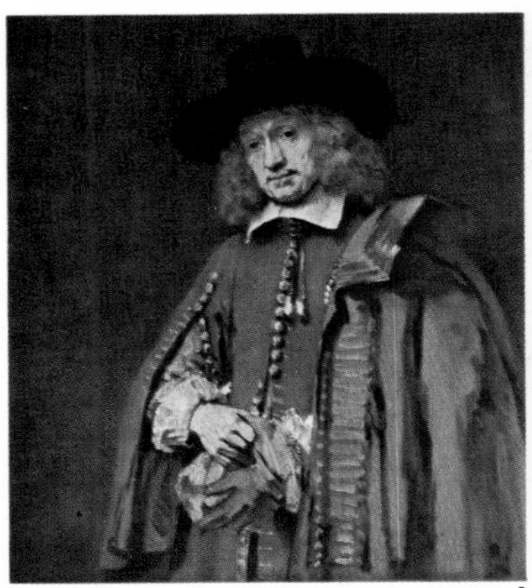

4

2

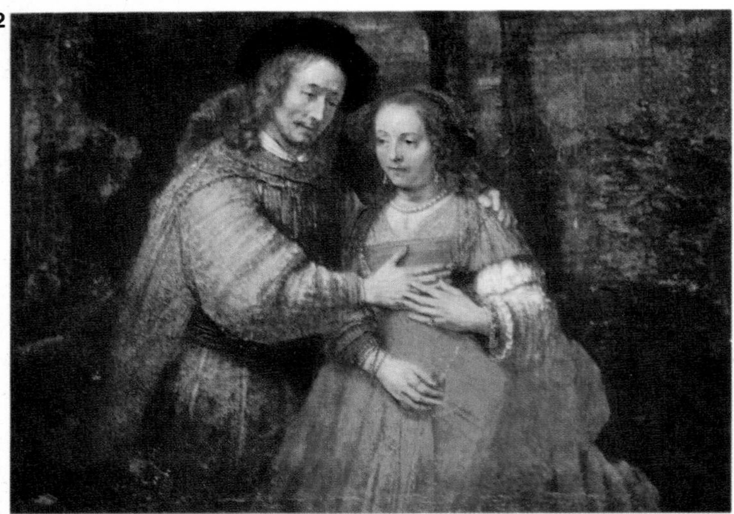

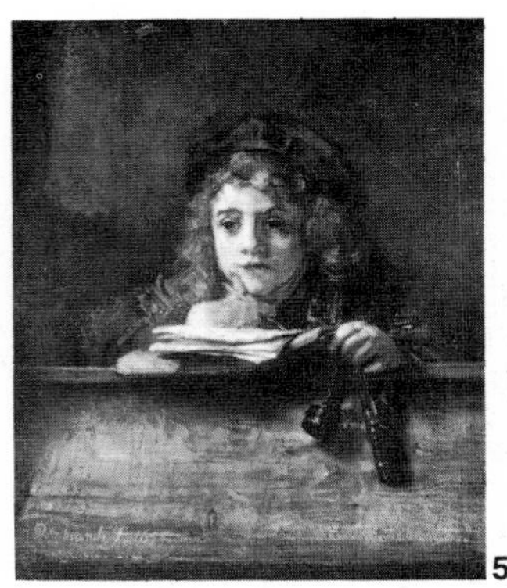

5

3

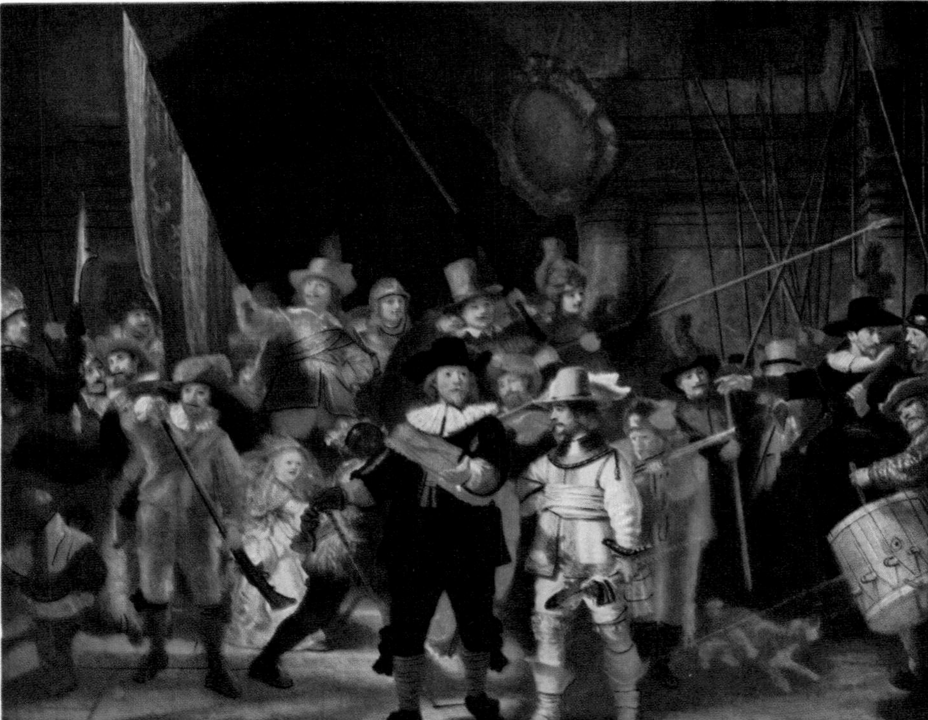

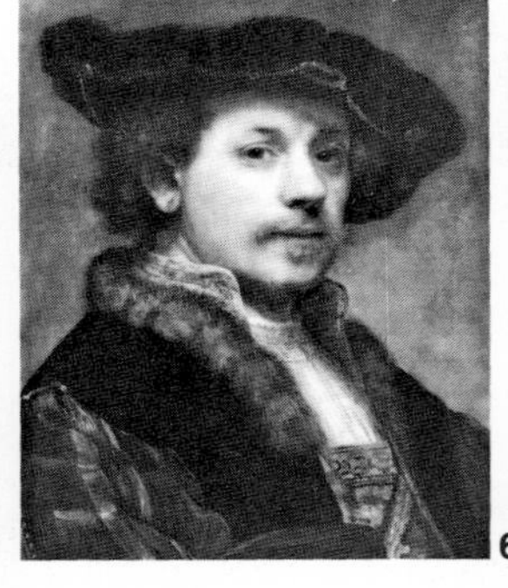

6

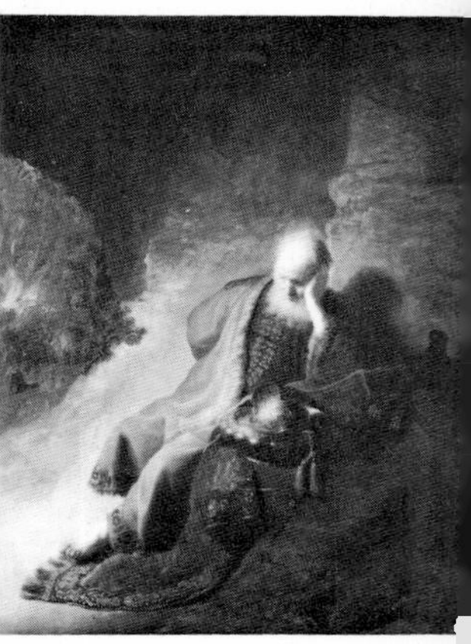

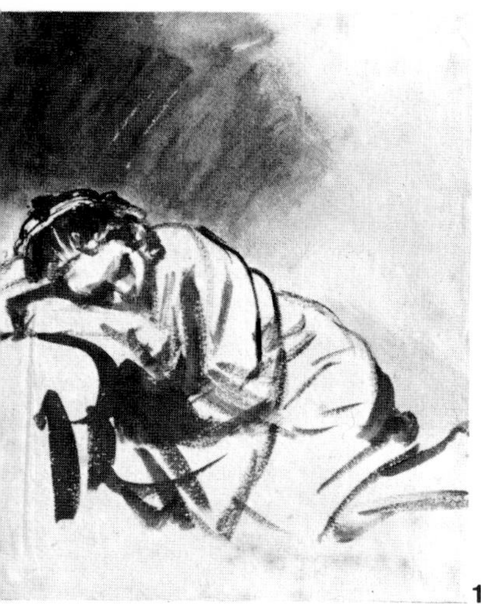

1

Rembrandt (1606–69)

1. *Sleeping Woman.* Wash. British Museum, London
2. *Doctor Nicolaes Tulp demonstrating the Anatomy of the Arm.* 1632. Mauritshuis, The Hague
3. *Self-portrait.* Detail. 1659. National Gallery of Art (Mellon Collection), Washington DC
4. *The three Crosses.* Detail. Etching. 1653. Rijksmuseum, Amsterdam
5. *Danaë.* 1636. Hermitage, Leningrad
6. *The Sampling Officials of the Clothmakers' Guild in Amsterdam* (*De Staalmeesters*). 1662. Rijksmuseum, Amsterdam

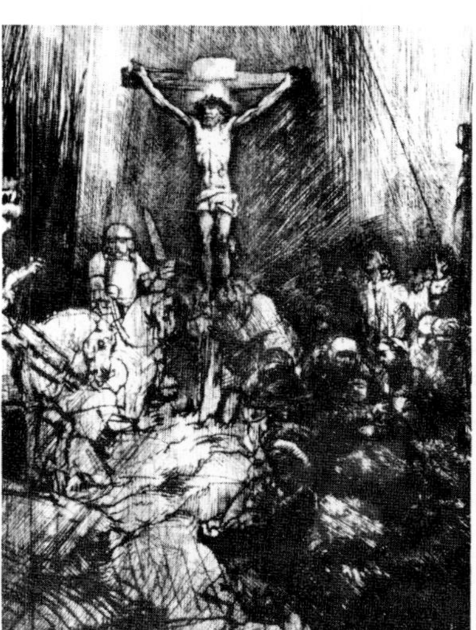

4

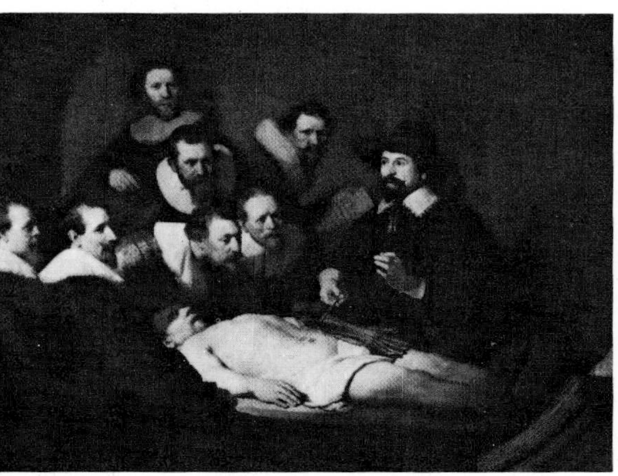

2

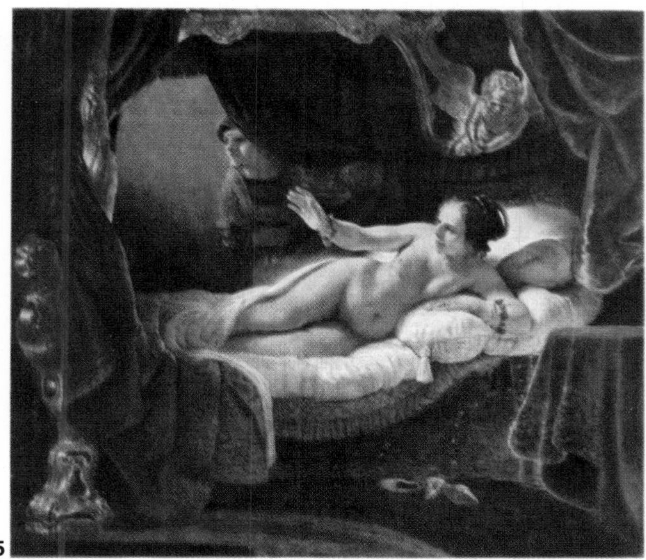

5

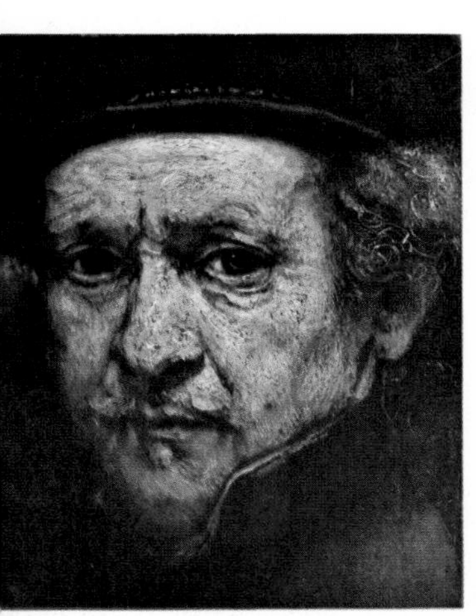

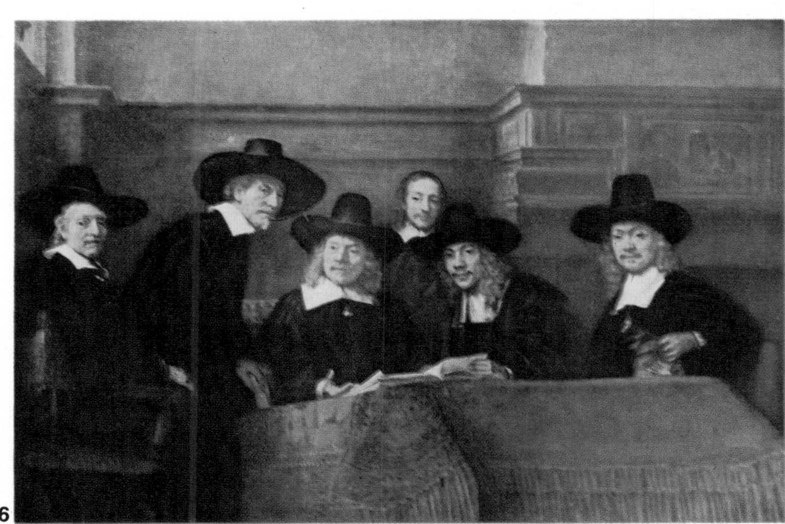

6

1. **Gerrit Dou** (1613–75): *The Doctor.* 1653. Kunsthistorisches Museum, Vienna
2. **Pieter Jansz Saenredam** (1597–1665): *Old Town Hall, Amsterdam.* 1657. Rijksmuseum, Amsterdam
3. **Gabriel Metsu** (1629–67): *The Vegetable Market, Amsterdam.* About 1660–5. Louvre, Paris
4. **Hercules Pietersz Seghers** (1589/90–1633/8): *Rocky Landscape with a Plateau.* Engraving. Metropolitan Museum of Art (gift of Henry Walters), New York
5. **Gerrit van Honthorst** (1590–1656): *A Concert.* About 1619–21. Galleria Borghese, Rome
6. **Frans Snyders** (1579–1657): *Still Life with Game and Fruit.* About 1613. Gemäldegalerie, Kassel

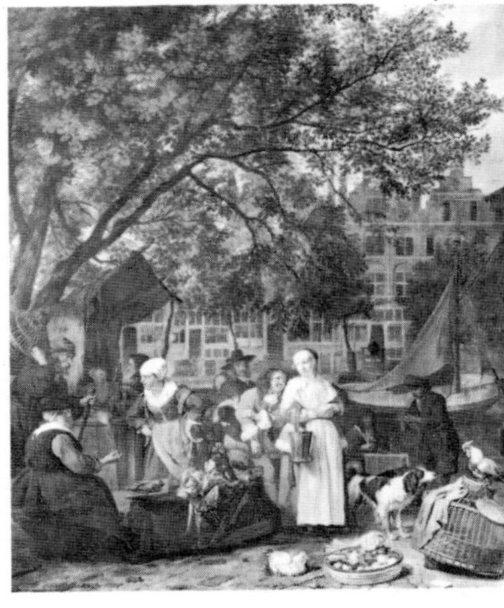

3

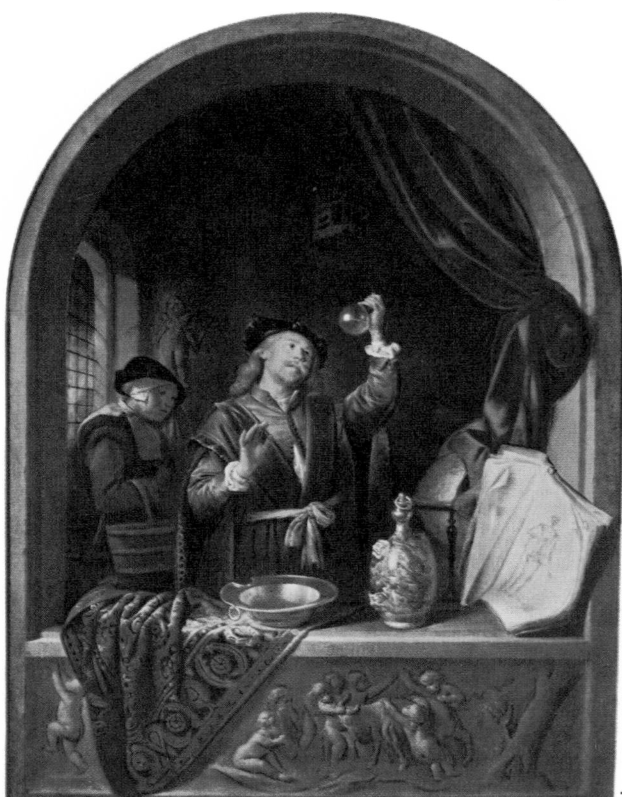

1

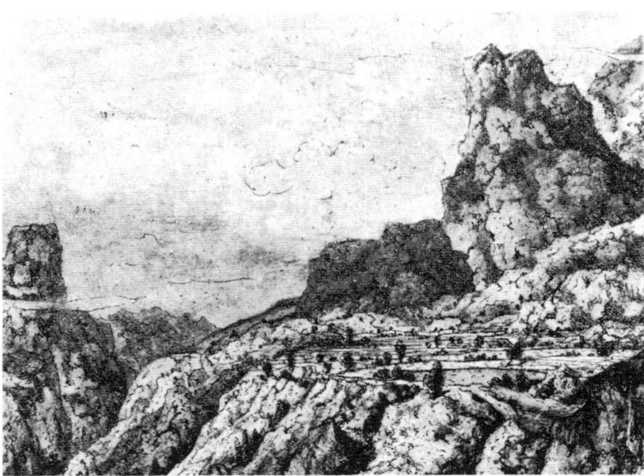

4

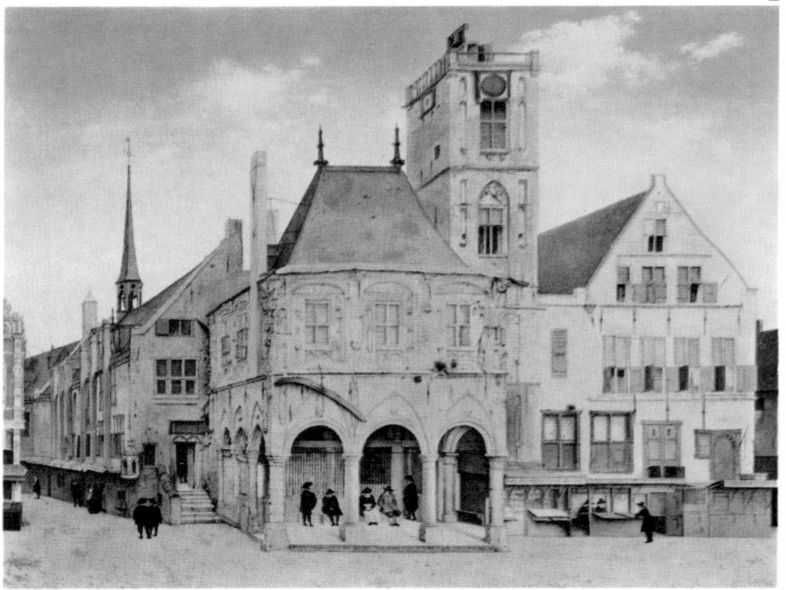

2

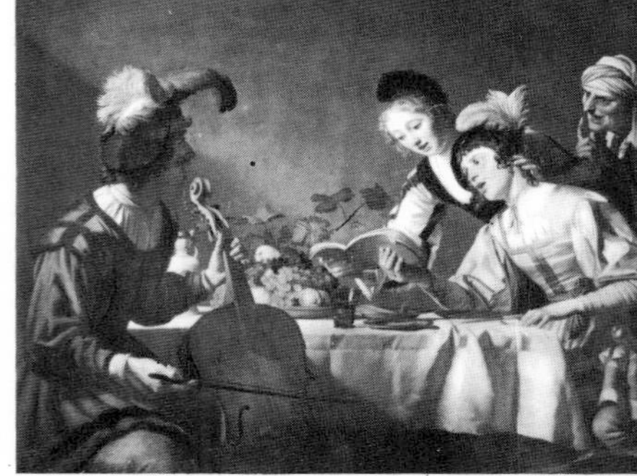

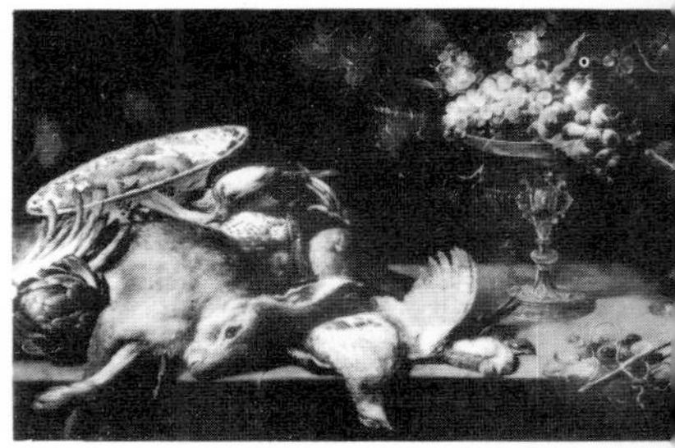

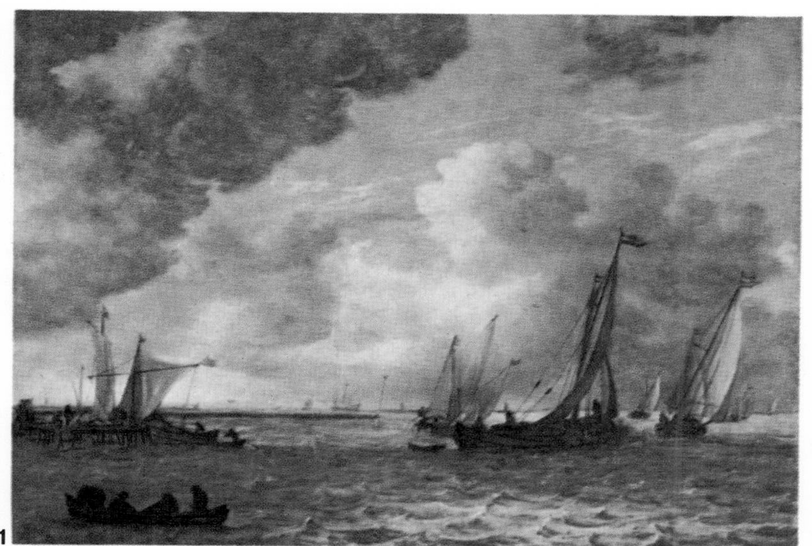

1

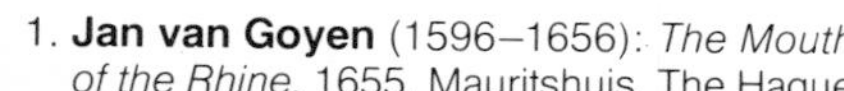

1. **Jan van Goyen** (1596–1656): *The Mouth of the Rhine.* 1655. Mauritshuis, The Hague
2. **Carel Fabritius** (1622–54): *Goldfinch.* 1654. Mauritshuis, The Hague
3. **Gerard ter Borch** (1617–81): *A Woman writing.* About 1665. Mauritshuis, The Hague
4. **Gerard ter Borch** (1617–81): *The Duet.* About 1675. Staatliche Museen, Berlin-Dahlem
5. **Jan van Goyen** (1596–1656): *Landscape with two Oaks.* 1641. Rijksmuseum, Amsterdam
6. **Jacob Jordaens** (1593–1678): *The Painter's Family.* 1622–3. Prado, Madrid
7. **Jacob Jordaens** (1593–1678): *Allegory of Fertility.* About 1625. Musées Royaux des Beaux-Arts, Brussels

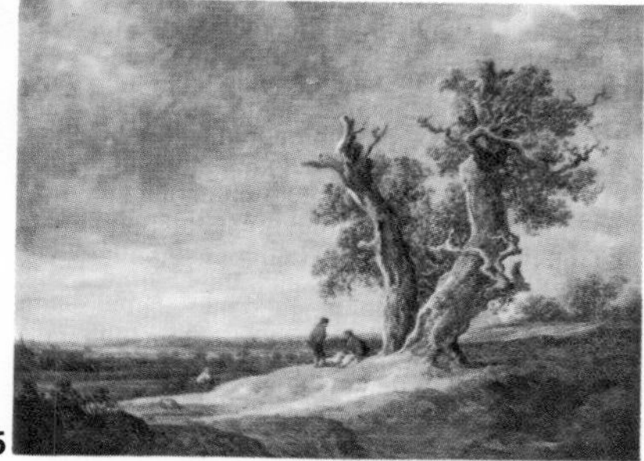

5

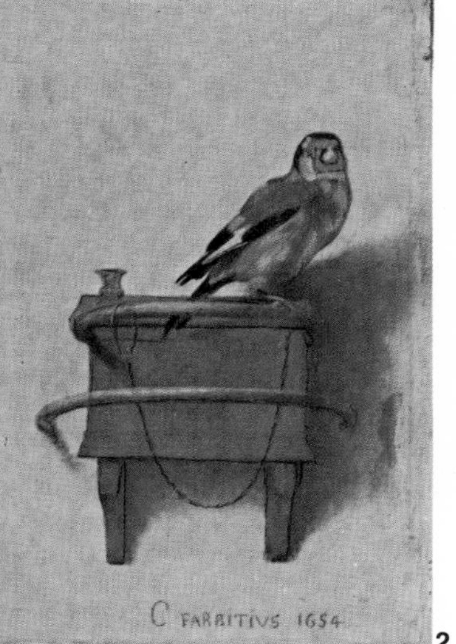

2

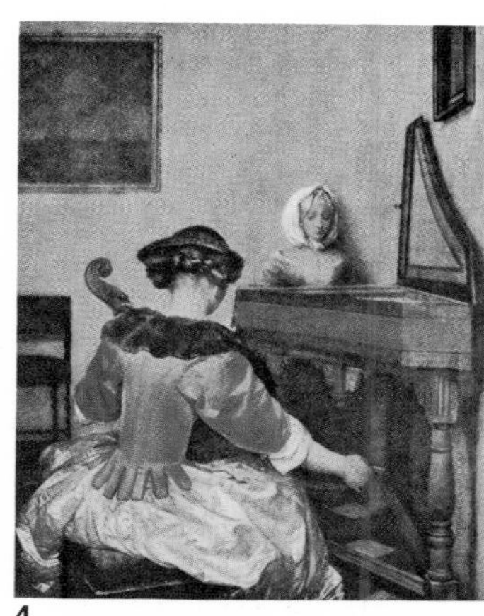

4

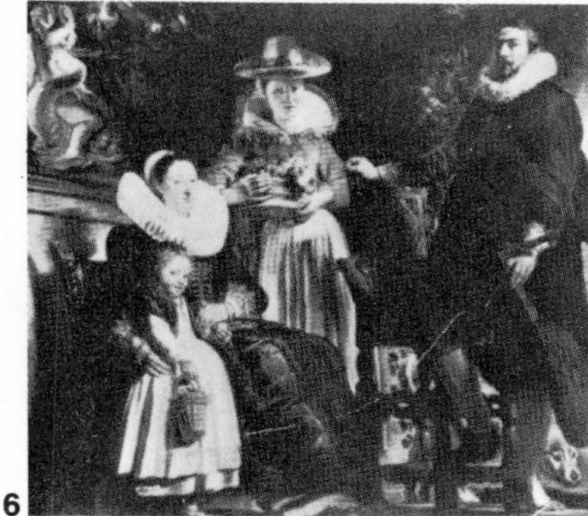

6

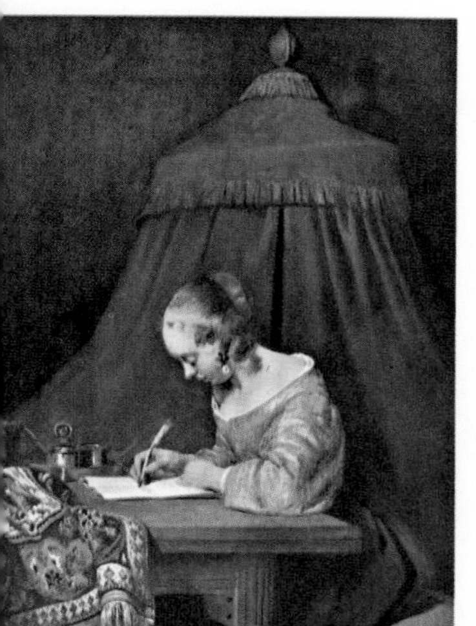

3

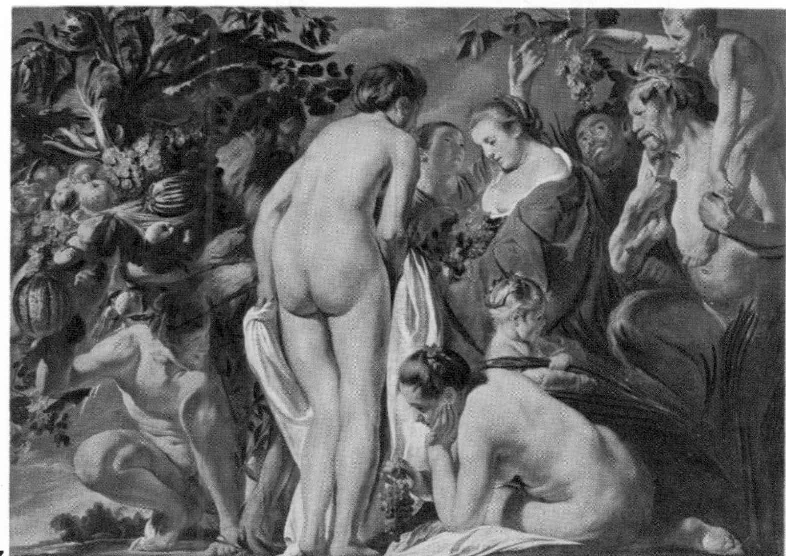

7

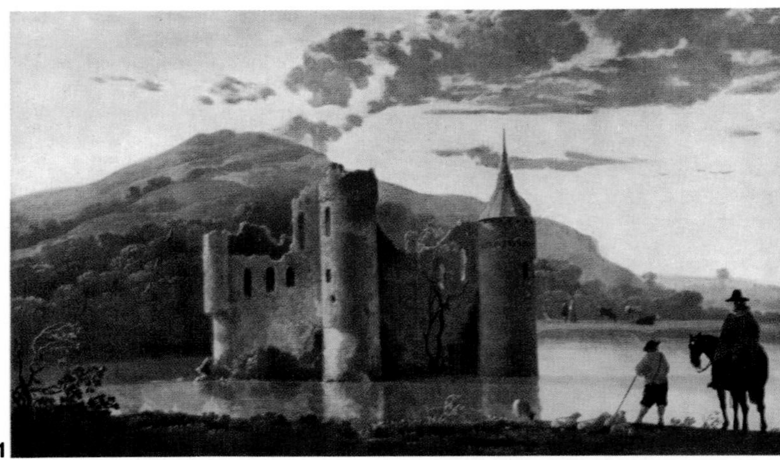

1. **Aelbert Cuyp** (1620–91): *Ubbergen Castle.* National Gallery, London
2. **Jacon van Ruisdael** (1628/9–82): *Landscape with Ruins.* About 1670. National Gallery, London
3. **Willem Kalf** (1619–93): *Still Life.* 165 Metropolitan Museum of Art (Maria De Jesup Fund), New York
4. **Jacob van Ruisdael** (1628/9–82): *Th Wheat Field.* About 1670. Metropolitan Museum of Art, New York
5. **Jacob van Ruisdael** (1628/9–82): *Th Windmill at Wijk bij Duurstede.* About 1665. Rijksmuseum, Amsterdam
6. **Meindert Hobbema** (1638–1709): *Th Avenue, Middelharnis.* 1689. National Gallery, London

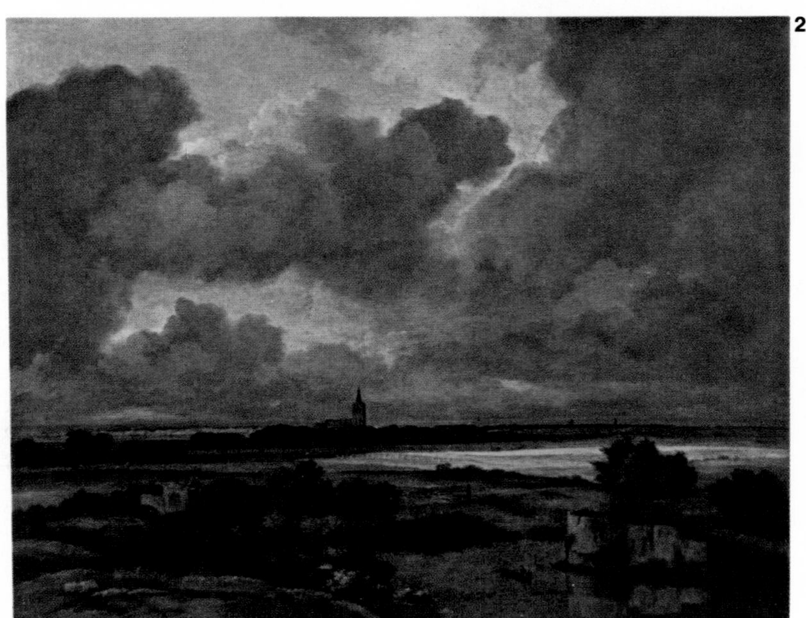

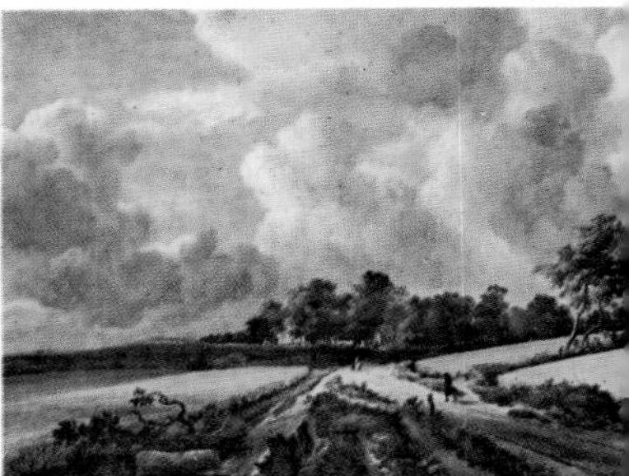

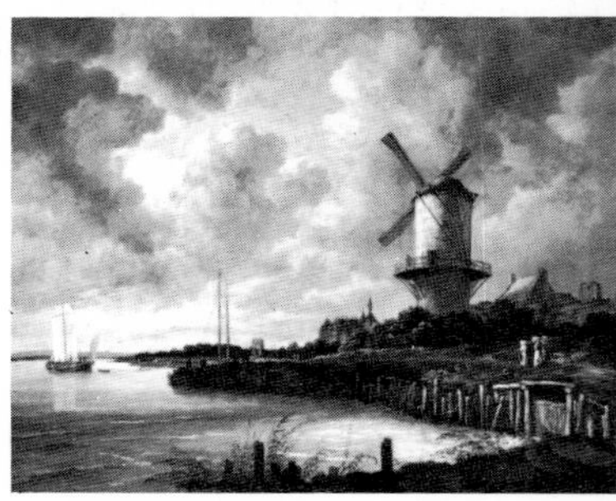

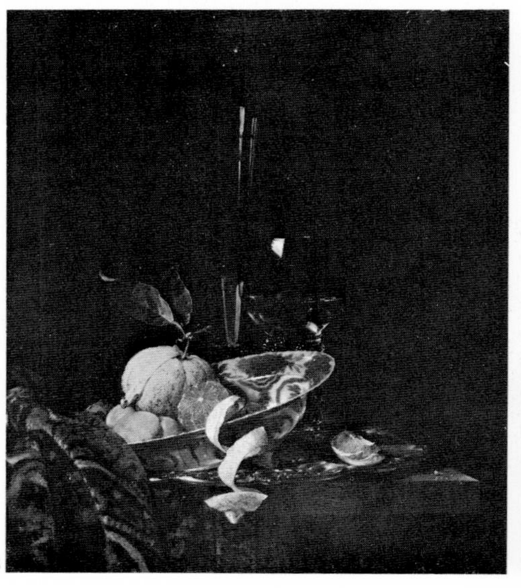

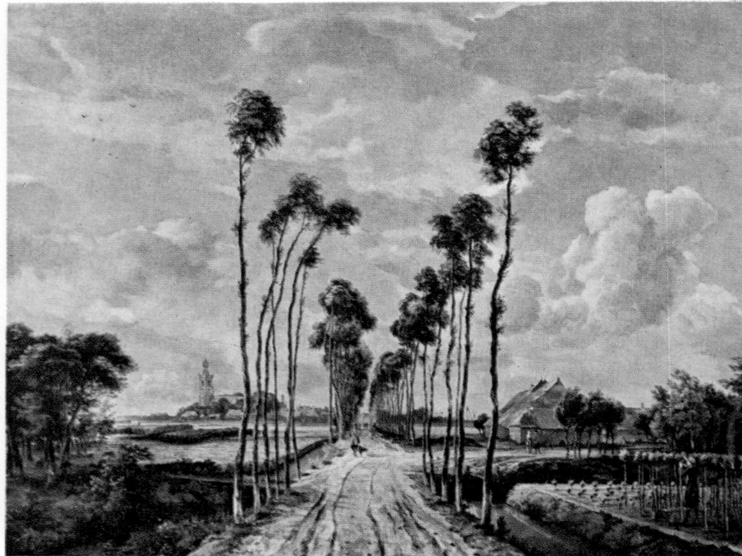

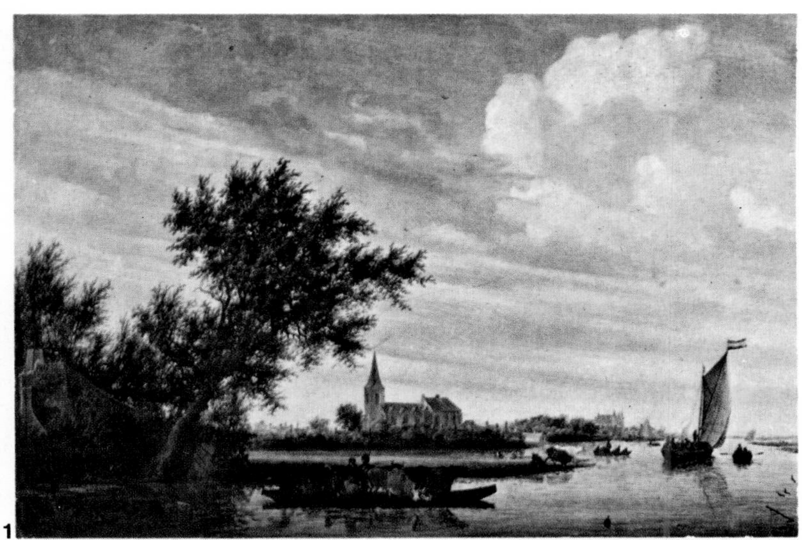

1

1. **Salomon van Ruysdael** (1600/3–70): *View of a River in the Province of Gelderland.* 1644 or 1647. Mauritshuis, The Hague
2. **Willem Claesz Heda** (1594–1680): *Dessert.* 1637. Louvre, Paris
3. **Emanuel de Witte** (1616/18–92): *Woman at the Clavichord.* Museum Boymans-van Beuningen, Rotterdam
4. **Jan Steen** (1625/6–79): *The World Topsy-turvy.* 1663. Kunsthistorisches Museum, Vienna
5. **Jan van der Heyden** (1637–1712): *View of Veere.* John G. Johnson Collection, Philadelphia

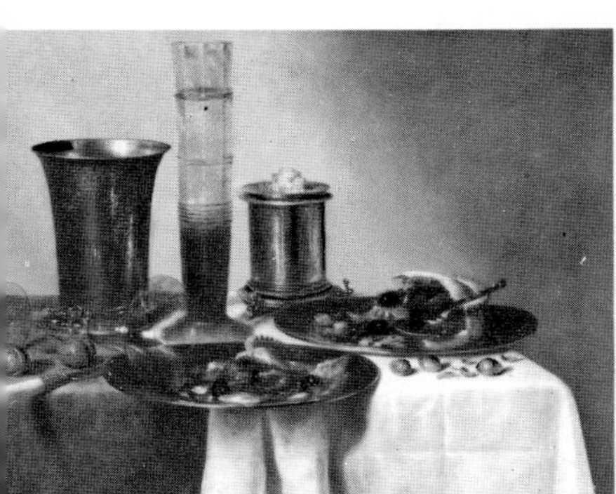

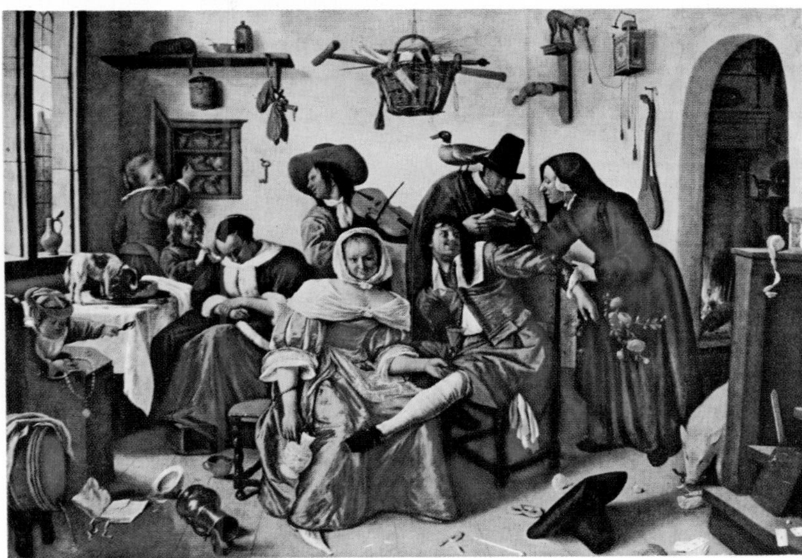

4

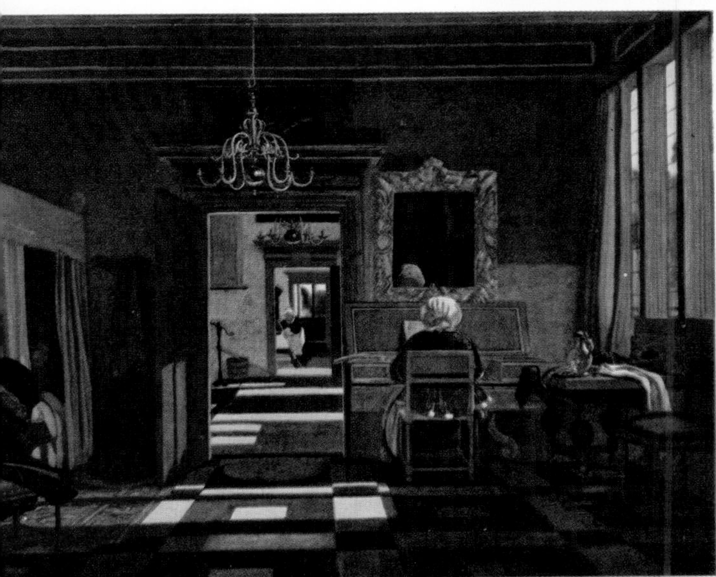

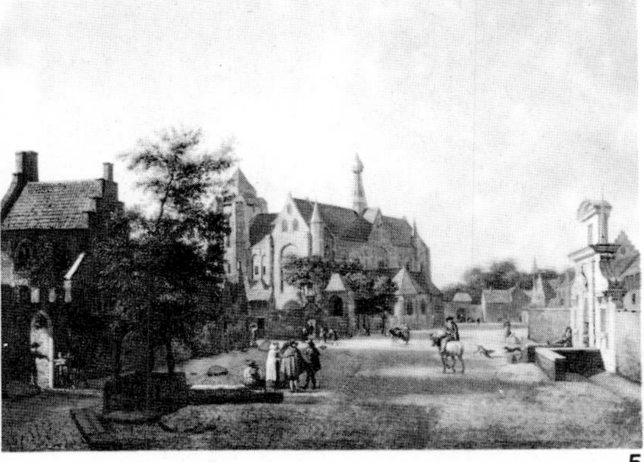

5

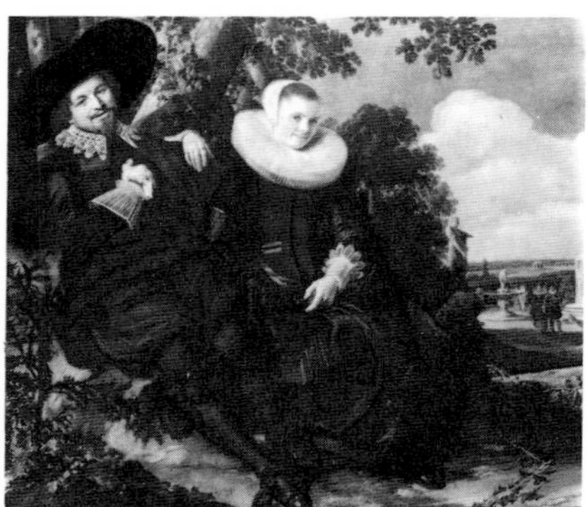
1

Frans Hals (1581/5–1666)

1. *A married Couple in a Garden* (*Isaac Massa and Beatrix van der Laen?*). About 1622. Rijksmuseum, Amsterdam
2. *Willem van Heythuyzen*. About 1637–9. Musées Royaux des Beaux-Arts, Brussels
3. *Banquet of the Officers of the St George Civic Guard Company*. About 1627. Frans Hals Museum, Haarlem
4. *The Merry Drinker*. About 1628–30. Rijksmuseum, Amsterdam
5. *The Gipsy Girl*. About 1628–30. Louvre, Paris
6. *Malle Babbe*. About 1630–3. Staatliche Museen, Berlin-Dahlem
7. *Three Children with a Goat Cart*. About 1620. Musées Royaux des Beaux-Arts, Brussels

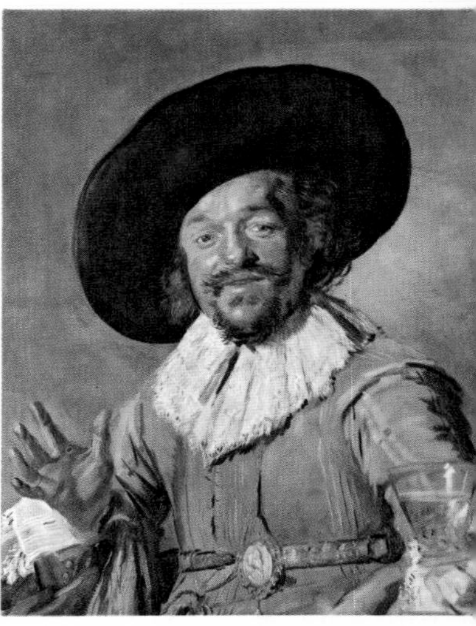
4

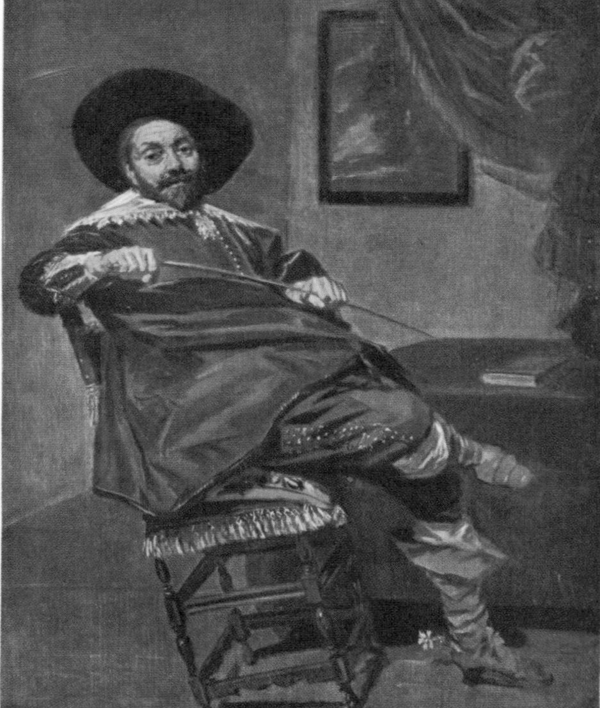
2

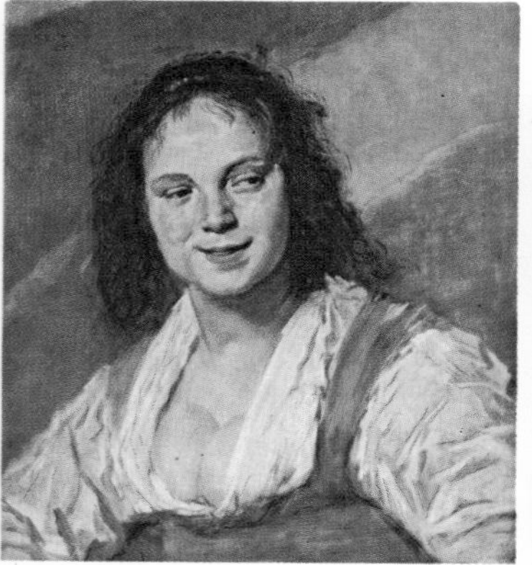
5

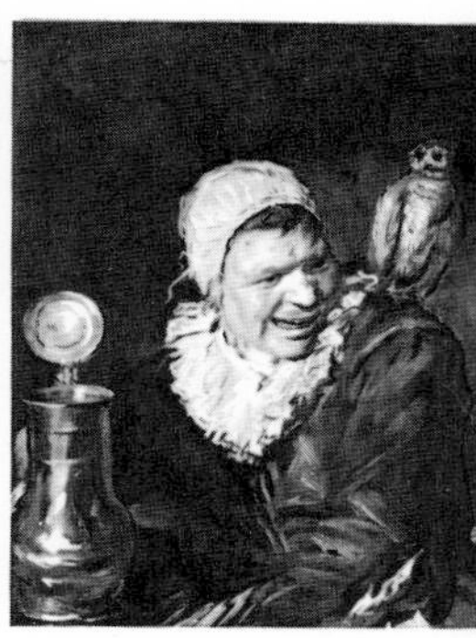

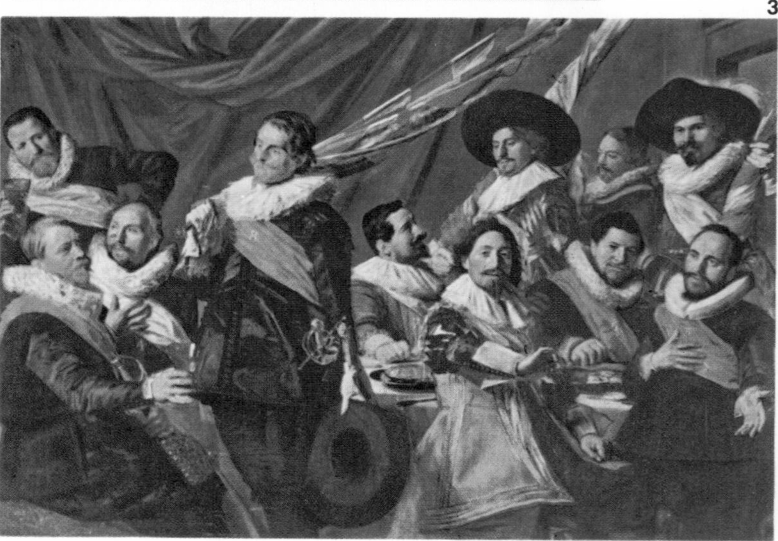
3

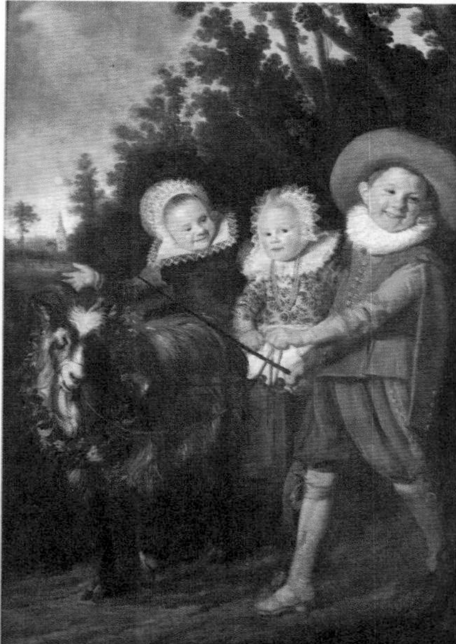

hannes Vermeer (1632–75)
The Milkmaid. About 1660. Rijksmuseum, Amsterdam
A Painter in his Studio. About 1666. Kunsthistorisches Museum, Vienna
Girl with a pearl Ear-ring. About 1665. Mauritshuis, The Hague
4. *Woman with a Water Jug.* About 1662. Metropolitan Museum of Art, New York
5. *The Procuress.* 1656. Gemäldegalerie, Dresden
6. *The Lacemaker.* 1670–1. Louvre, Paris
7. *A Street in Delft.* About 1661. Rijksmuseum, Amsterdam

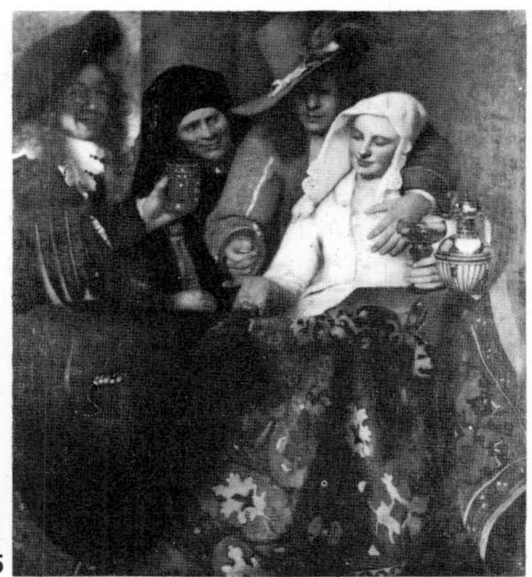

5

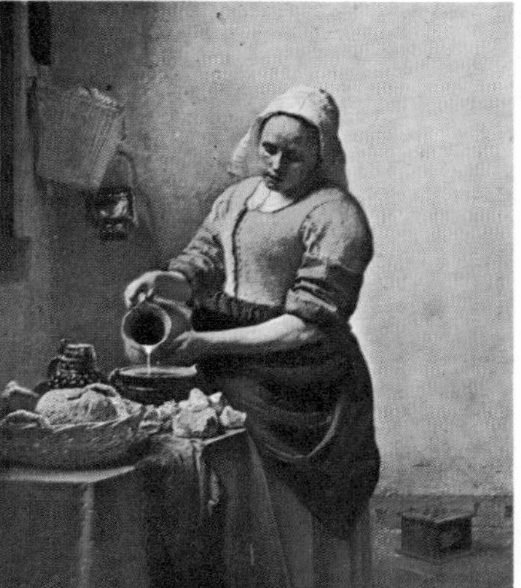

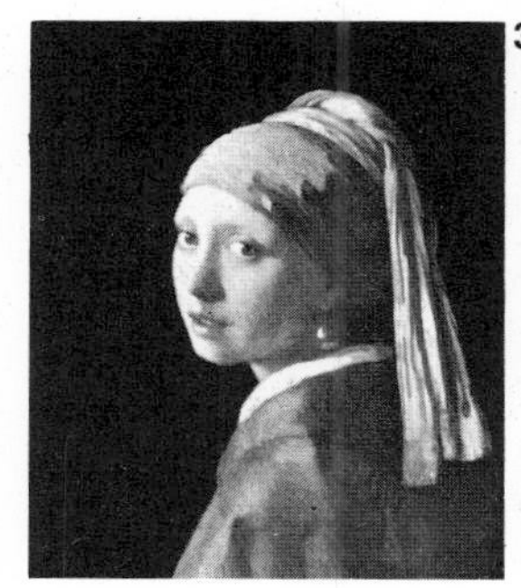

3

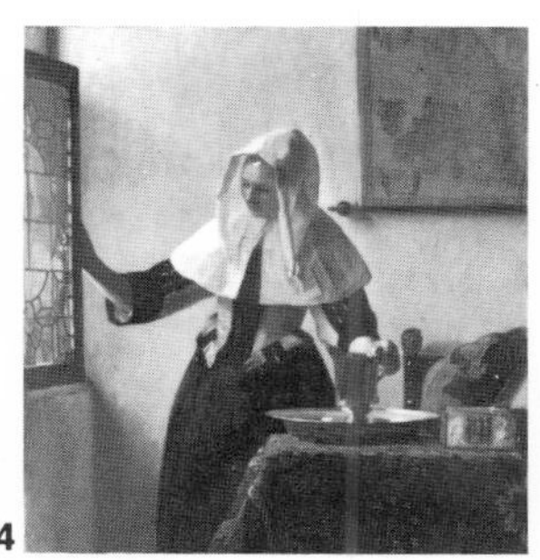

4

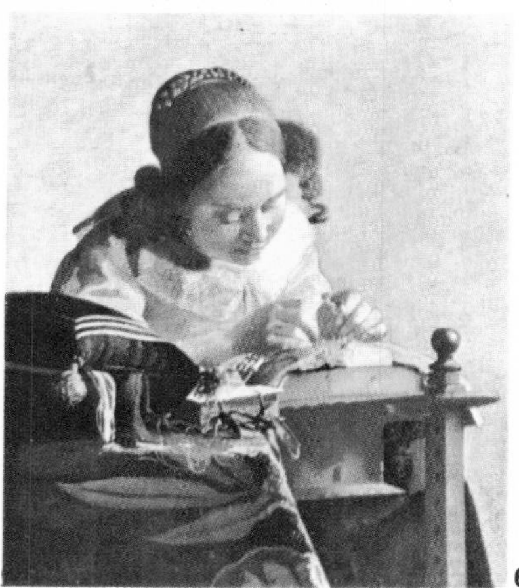

6

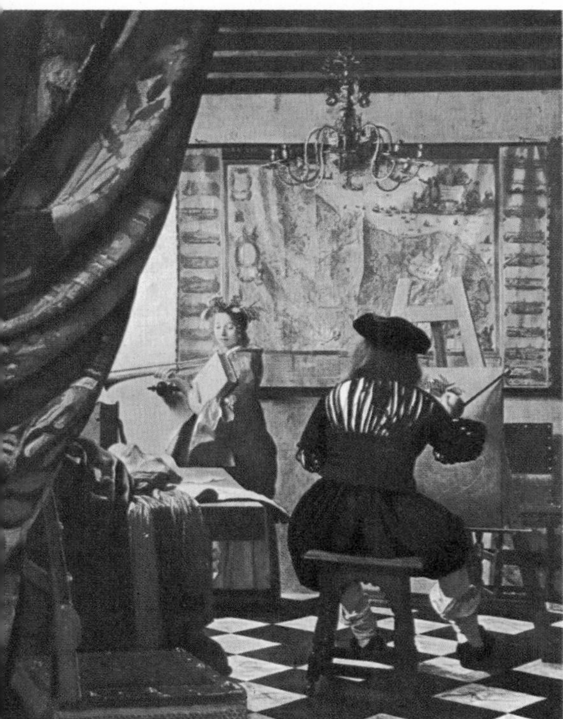

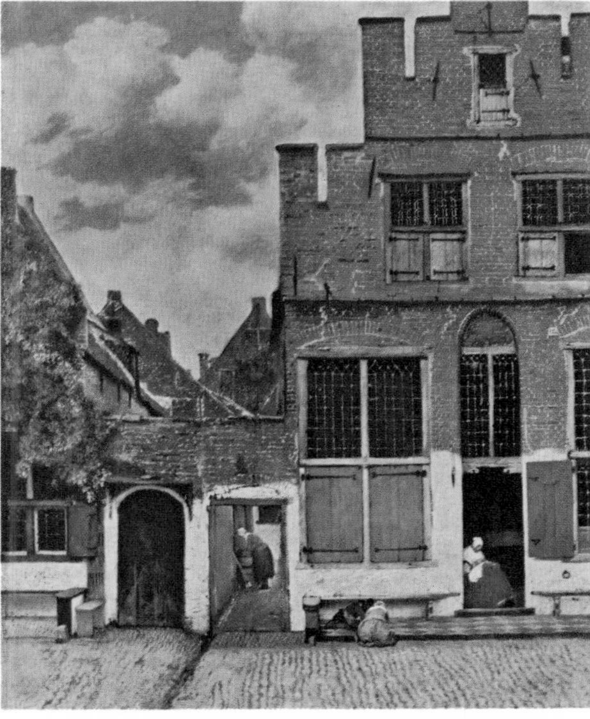

7

1. **David Teniers the Younger** (1610–90): *The Cardplayers.* Musées Royaux des Beaux-Arts, Brussels
2. **Gerrit Berckheyde** (1638–98): *The Flo Market, Amsterdam.* Rijksmuseum, Amsterdam
3. **Willem van de Velde the Younger** (163 1707): *The Cannon Shot.* About 1660. Rijksmuseum, Amsterdam
4. **Adriaen van Ostade** (1610–85): *Landscape with an old Oak.* Rijksmuseu Amsterdam
5. **Pieter de Hooch** (1629–84): *Interior Scene.* About 1658. National Gallery, London

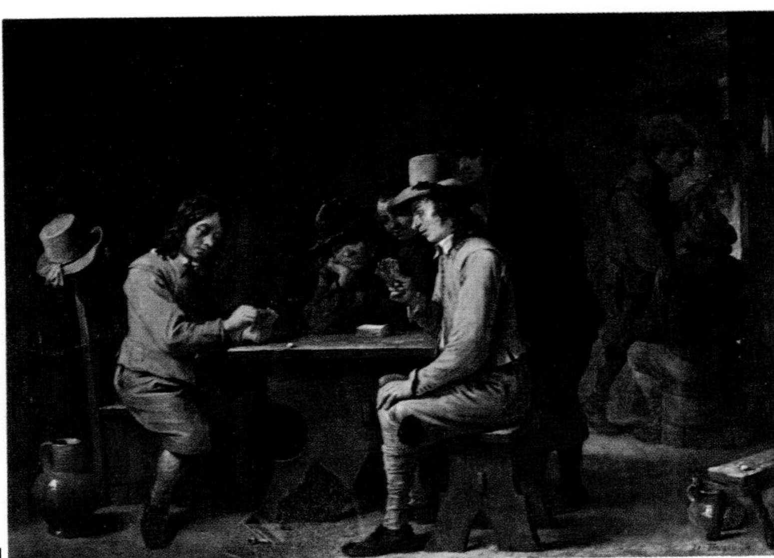

1

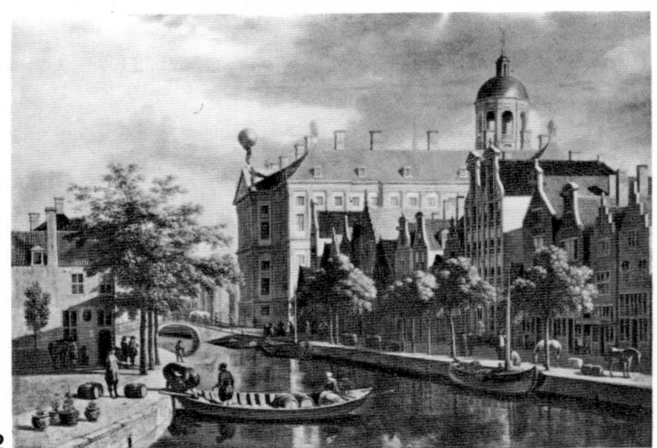

2

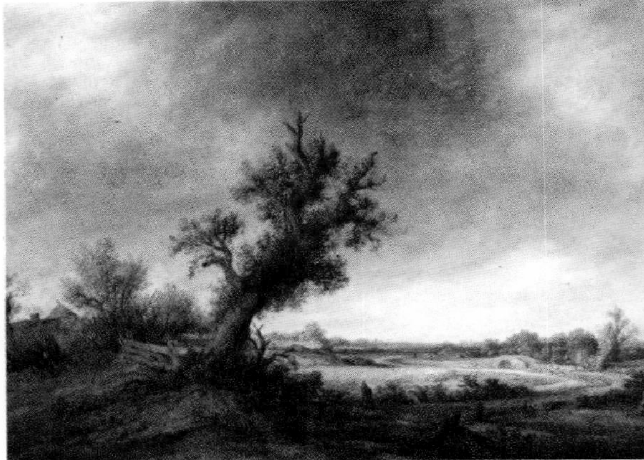

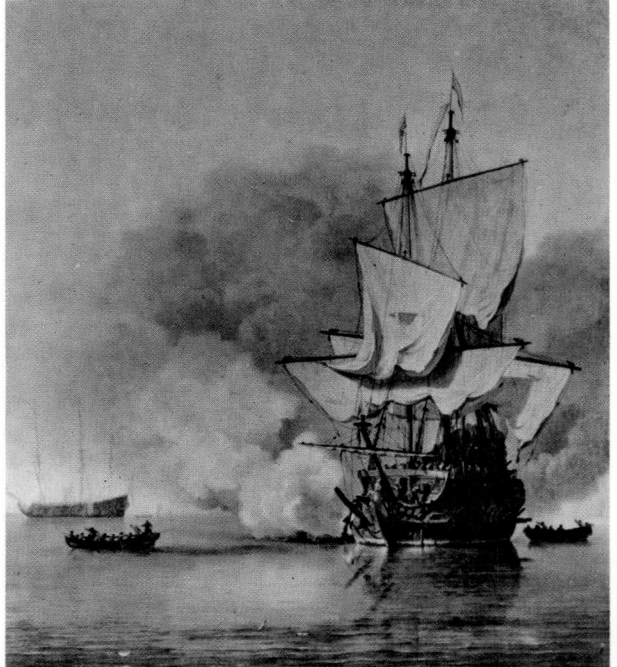

3

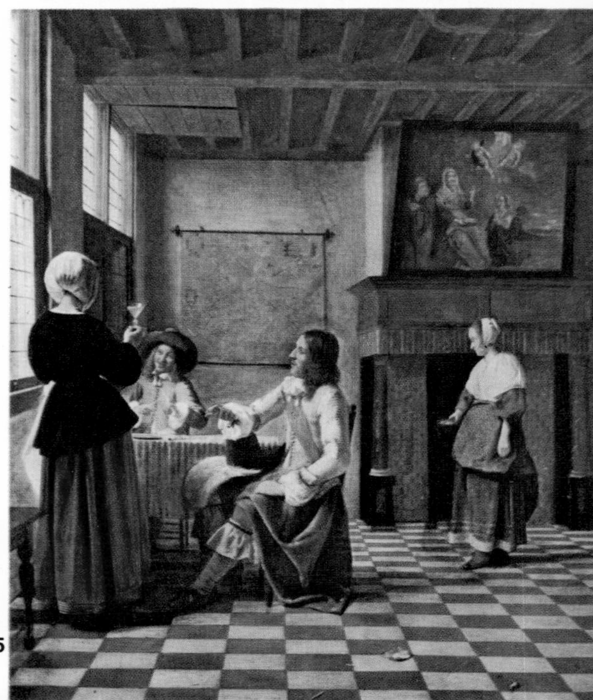

5

Andreas Schlüter (1662/9–1760): *Head of a dying Warrior.* About 1696. Arsenal, Berlin

2. **Joseph Anton Feuchtmayer** (1696–1770): *Angel with a Lute.* Painted wood. About 1730. Landesmuseum, Karlsruhe
3. **Ignaz Günther** (1725–75): *The Virgin of the Annunciation.* Detail. 1764. Abbey church, Weyarn
4. **Joseph Anton Feuchtmayer** (1696–1770): *The Virgin of the Annunciation.* Detail. About 1760. Staatliche Museen, Berlin-Dahlem
5. **Ignaz Günther** (1725–75): *St Cunegonde.* Painted wood. 1762. Abbey church, Rott am Inn
6. **Balthasar Permoser** (1651–1732): *The Apotheosis of Prince Eugene of Savoy.* Marble. 1718–21. Österreichisches Barockmuseum, Vienna
7. **Ignaz Günther** (1725–75): *Pietà.* Painted wood. 1774. Cemetery chapel, Nenningen

1

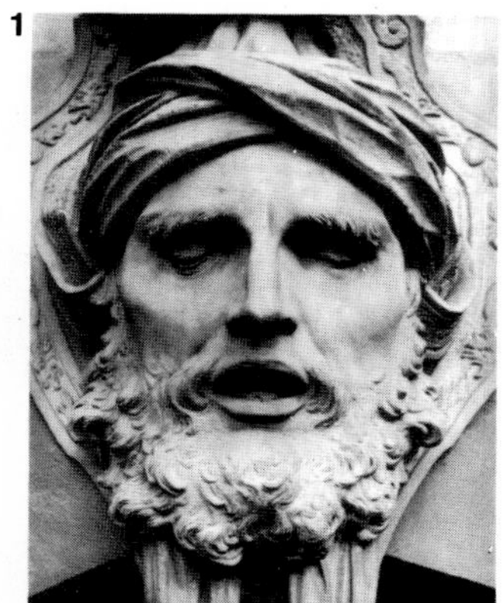

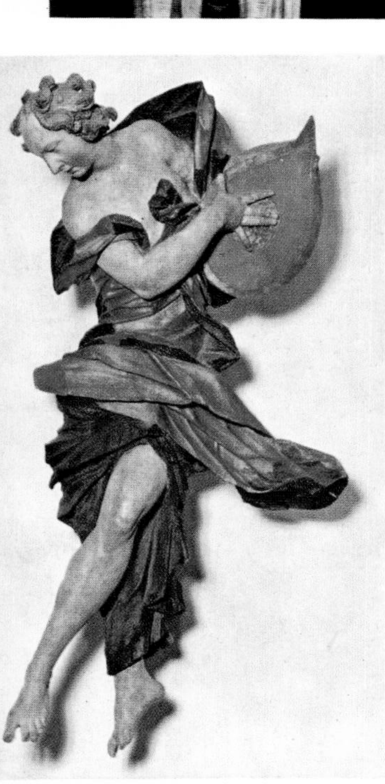

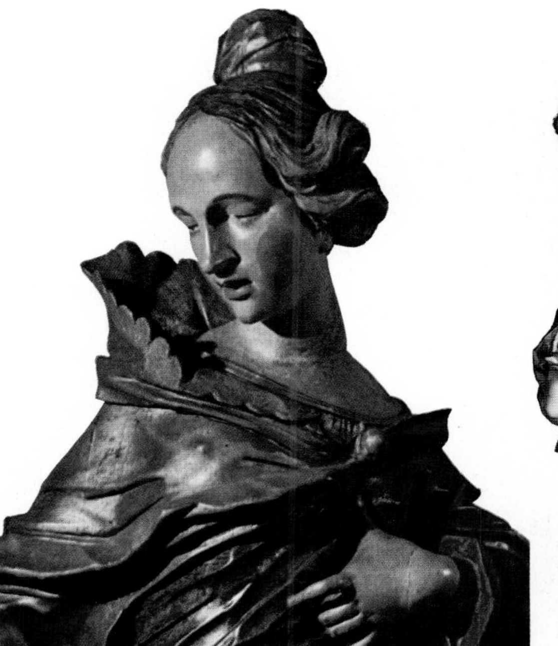

4

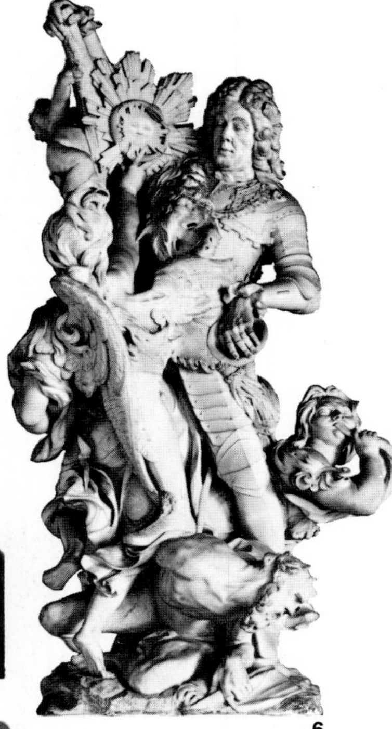

6

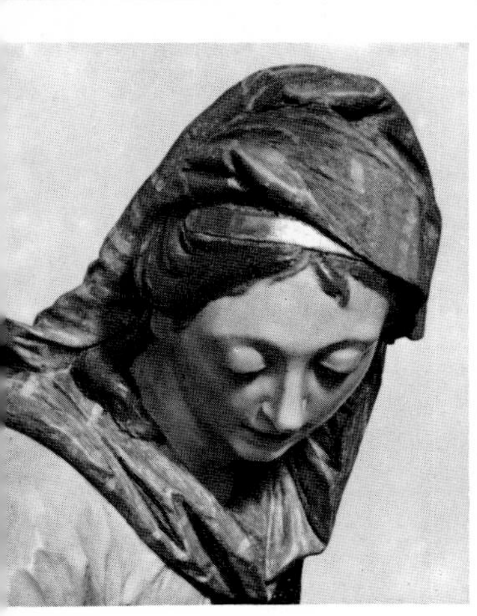

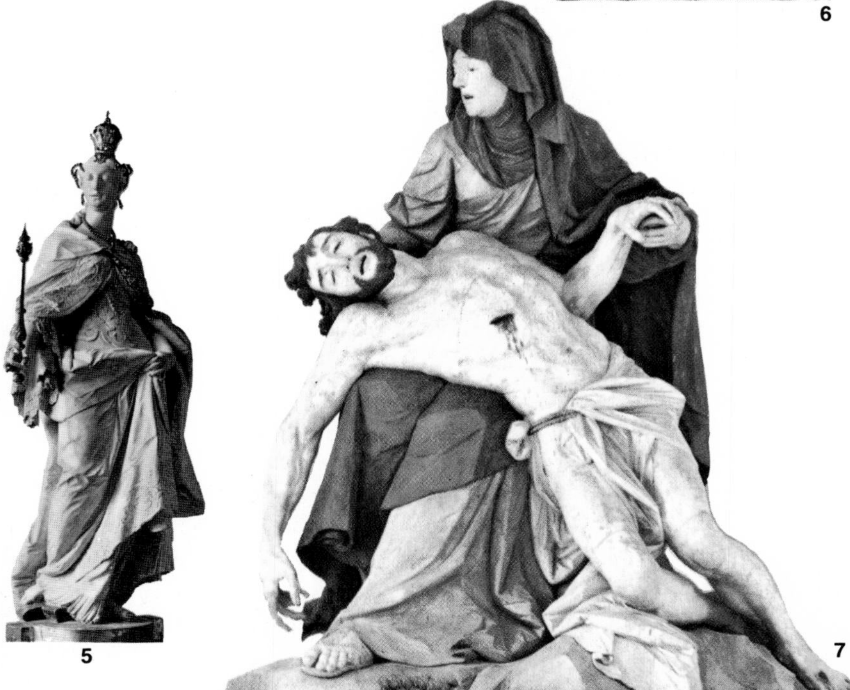

5

7

1. **Johann Balthasar Neumann** (1687–1753): Pilgrimage church, Vierzehnheiligen, Franconia. Begun 1743
2. **Johann Lukas von Hildebrandt** (1668–1745): The Upper Belvedere, Vienna. Garden façade. 1721–4
3. **Jakob Prandtauer** (1660–1726): Melk Abbey. 1701–26
4. **Johann Balthasar Neumann** (1687–1753): Residenz, Würzburg. About 1719–44
5. **Georg Wenzeslaus von Knobelsdorff** (1699–1753): Colonnade, Palace of Sanssouci, Potsdam. 1747–7

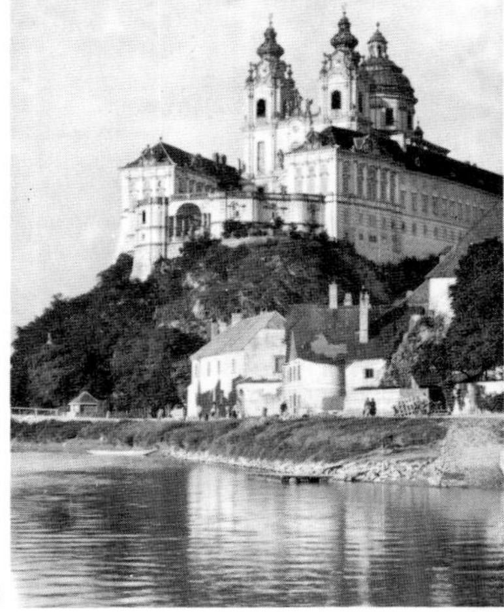

3

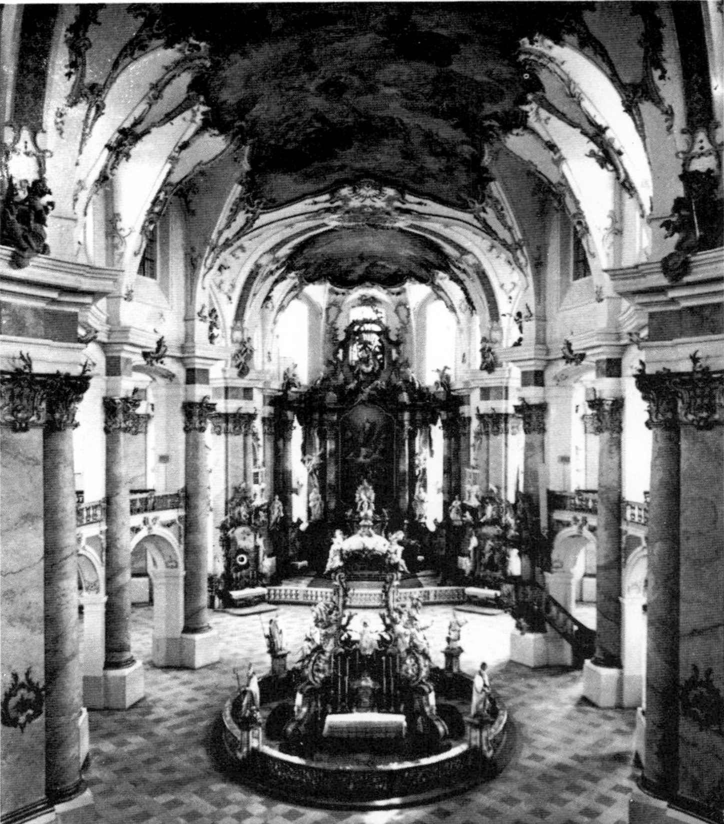

1

4

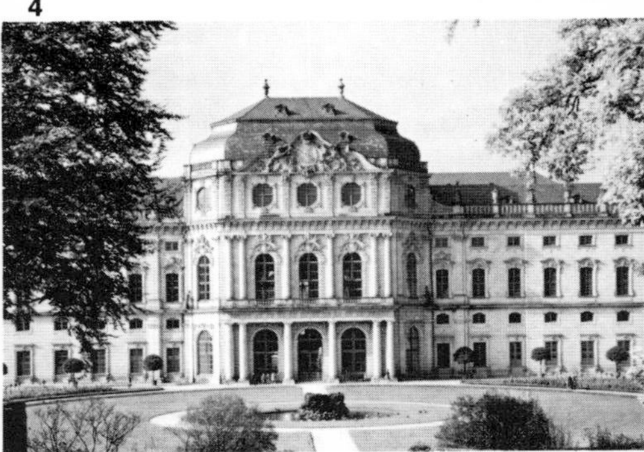

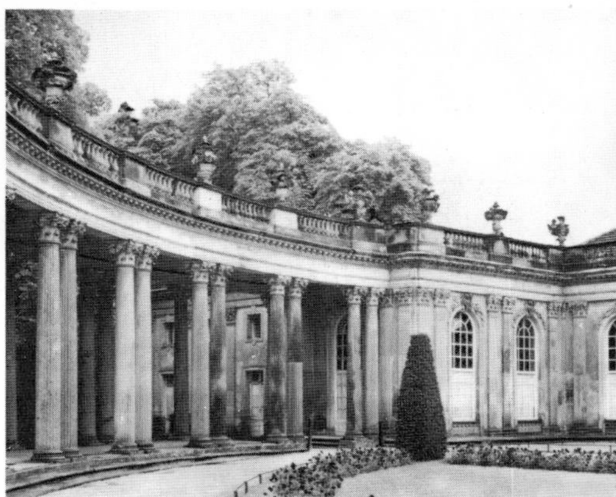

2

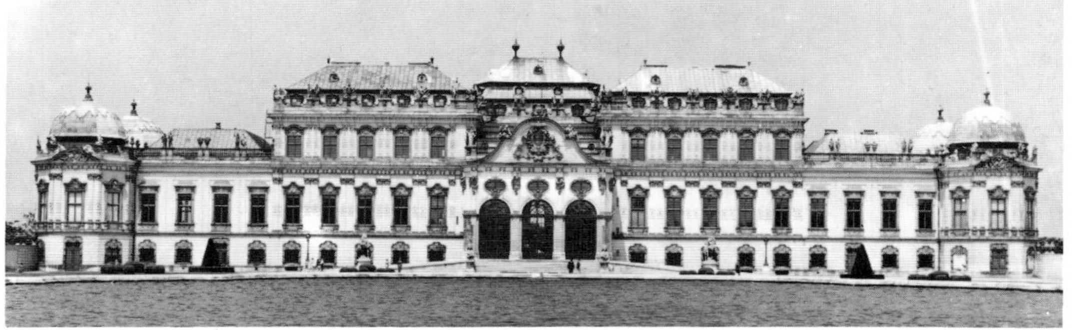

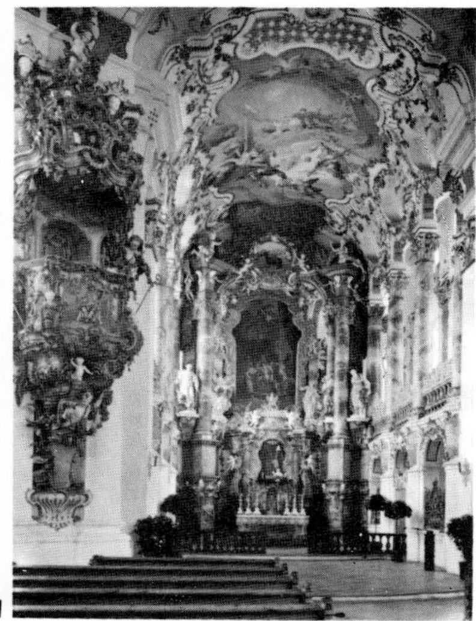

1

1. **Dominikus Zimmermann** (1685–1766): Pilgrimage church, Die Wies, near Steingaden, Upper Bavaria. 1745–54
2. **Johann Bernhard Fischer von Erlach** (1656–1723): Church of the Holy Trinity, Salzburg. 1694–1702
3. **Matthäus Daniel Pöppelmann** (1662–1736): The Zwinger, Dresden. Aerial view. 1711–22
4. **Carl Gotthard Langhans** (1732–1808): The Brandenburg Gate, Berlin. 1788–9
5. **Johann Michael Fischer** (1692–1766): Abbey church at Ottobeuren. 1737–66

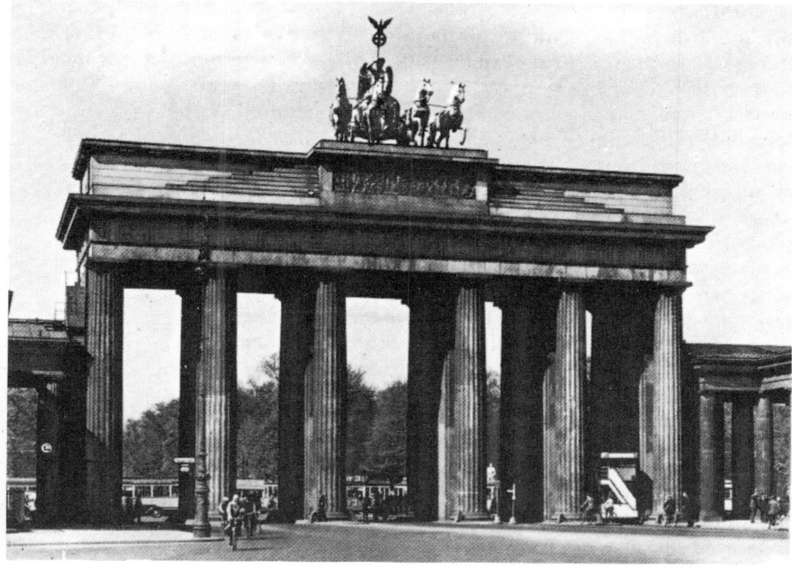

4

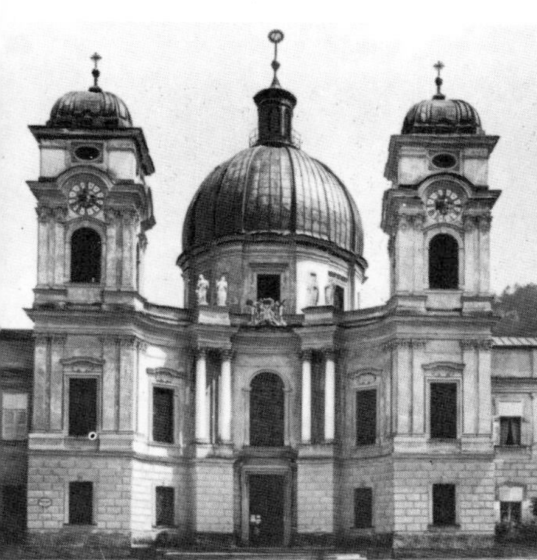

2

5

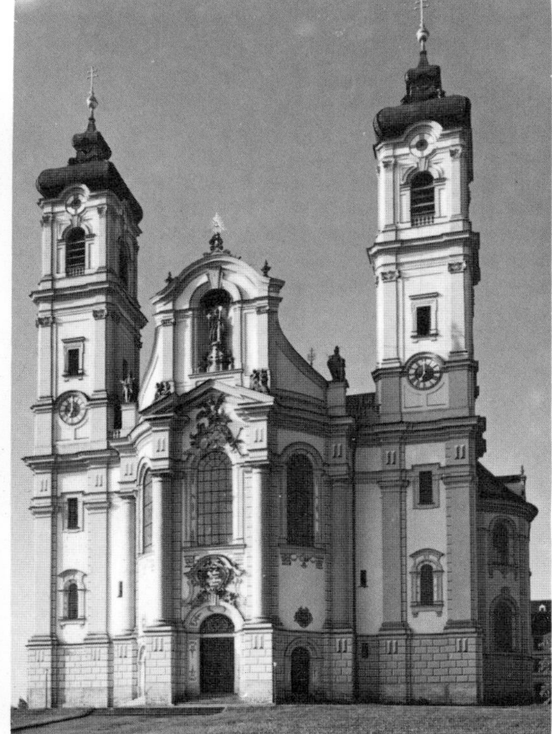

3

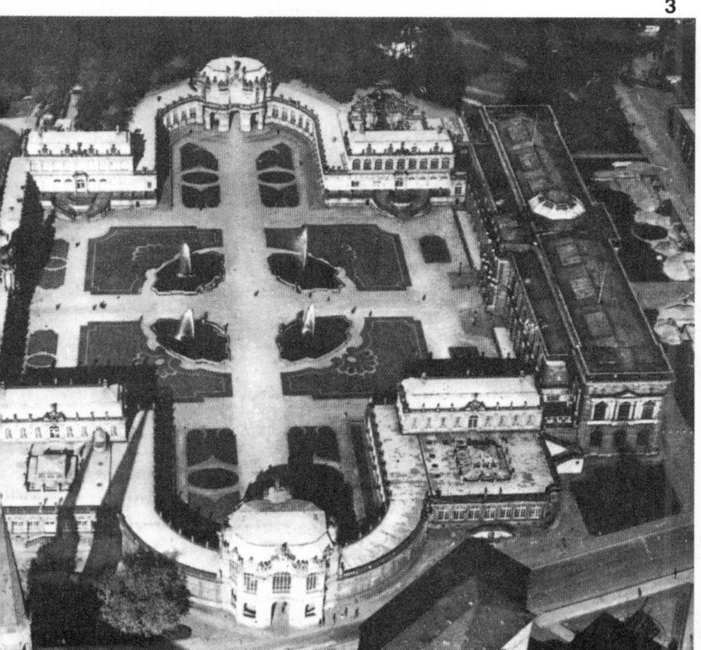

1. **Francisco de Zurbarán** (1598–1664): *St Hugo of Grenoble visiting the Refectory of the Carthusians.* About 1633. Museo Provincial de Bellas Artes, Seville
2. **Jusepe de Ribera** (1591?–1652): Jacob's Dream. 1639. Prado, Madrid
3. **Jusepe de Ribera** (1591?–1652): *Club-footed Boy.* 1652. Louvre, Paris
4. **Jusepe de Ribera** (1591?–1652): *A Hermit Saint.* Prado, Madrid
5. **Jusepe de Ribera** (1591?–1652): *St Peter.* Hermitage, Leningrad
6. **Francisco de Zurbarán** (1598–1664): *Still Life with Oranges.* 1633. Contini-Bonacossi Collection, Florence

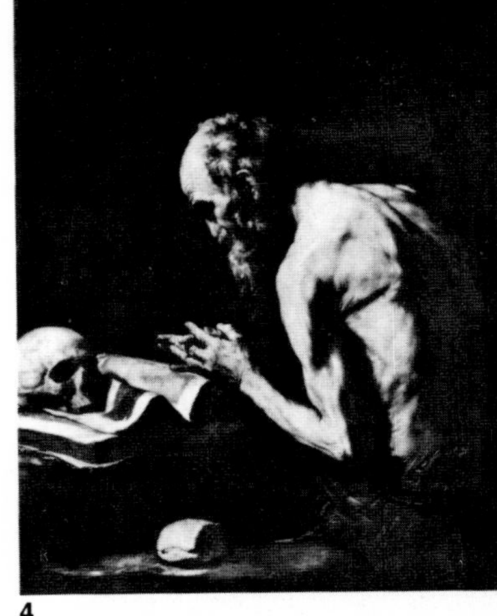

4

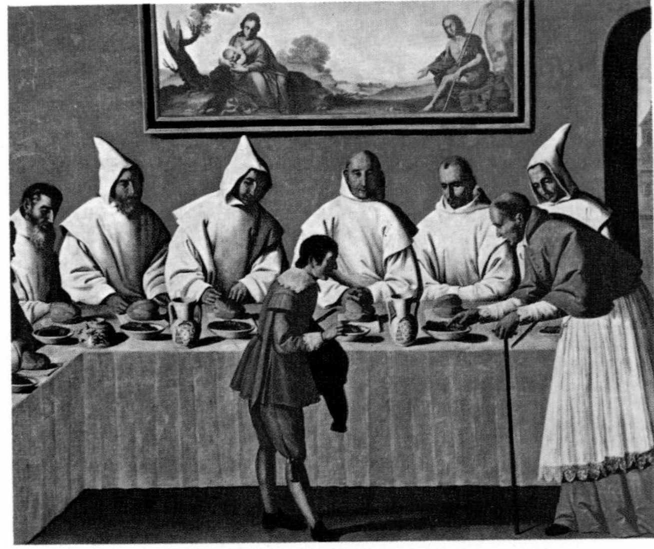

1

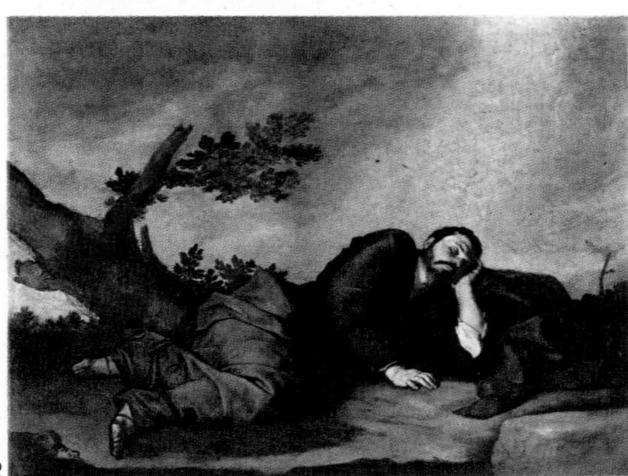

2

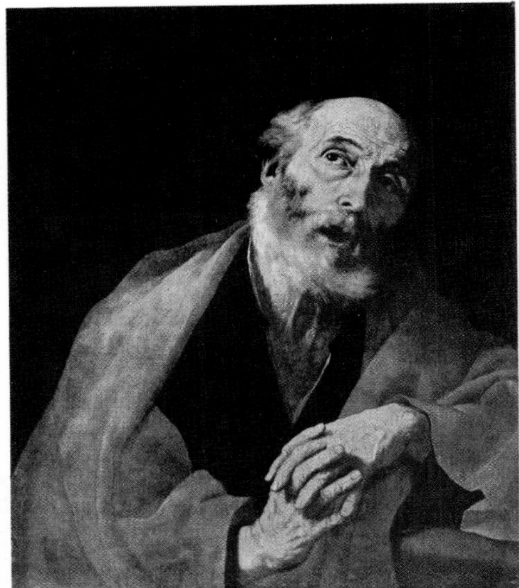

5

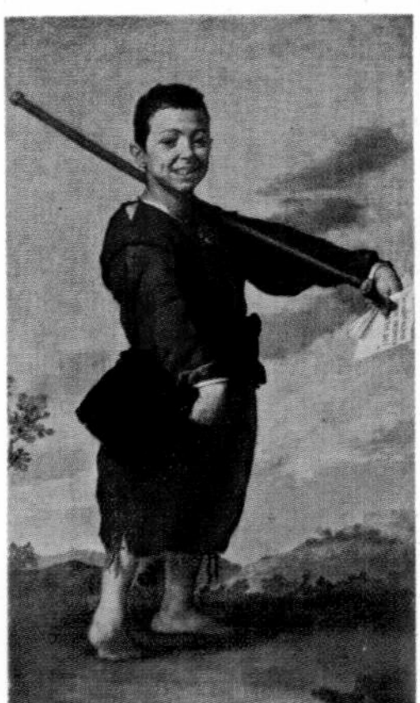

3

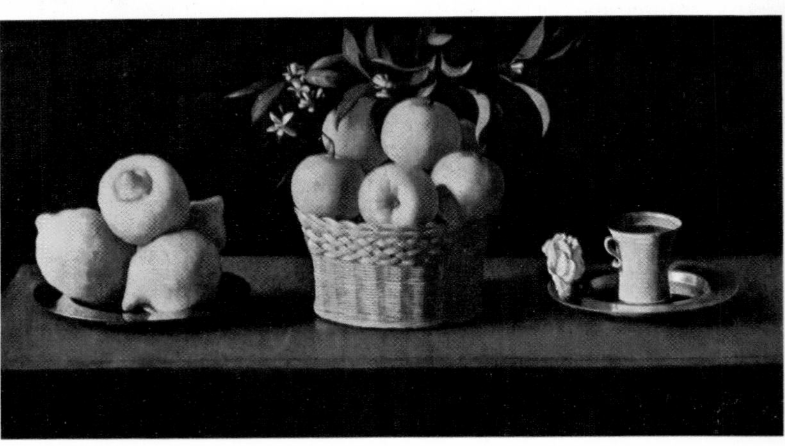

6

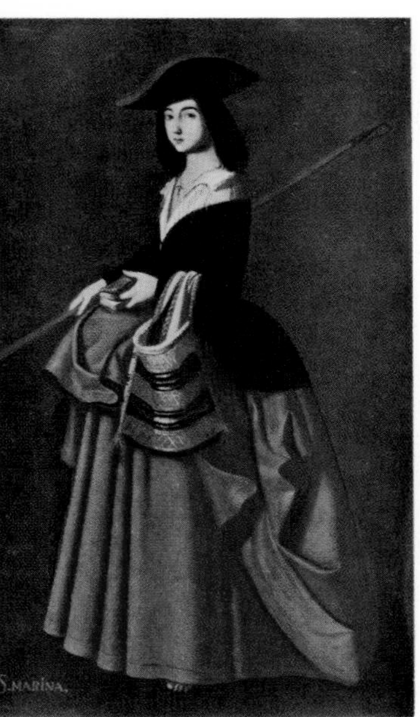

1. **Francisco de Zurbarán** (1598–1664): *St Marina.* Museo Provincial de Bellas Artes, Seville
2. **Bartolomé Estéban Murillo** (1617–82): *The Adoration of the Shepherds.* Prado, Madrid
3. **Bartolomé Estéban Murillo** (1617–82): *The Holy Family.* Prado, Madrid
4. **Bartolomé Estéban Murillo** (1617–82): *St Joseph and the Infant Jesus.* Wash drawing and gouache. Cabinet des Dessins, Louvre, Paris
5. **Francisco de Zurbarán** (1598–1664): *St Luke before the Crucified Christ.* Prado, Madrid
6. **Bartolomé Estéban Murillo** (1617–82): *The Beggar Boy.* Louvre, Paris

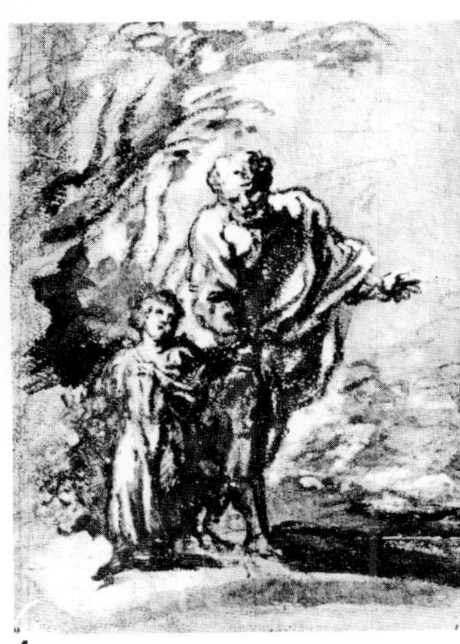

4

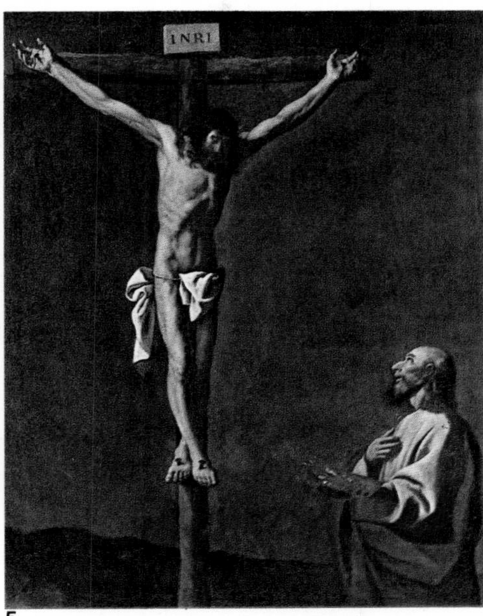

5

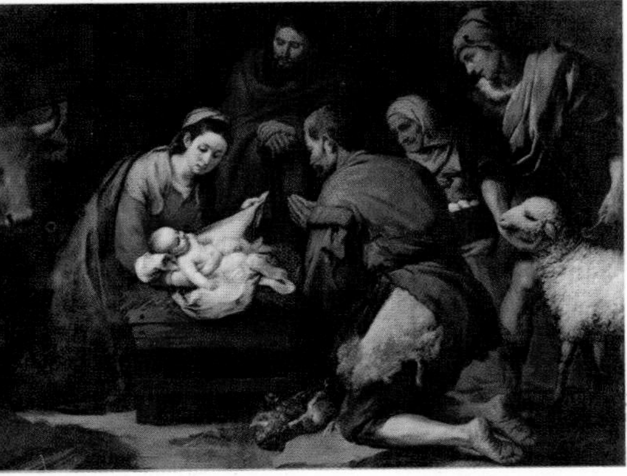

2

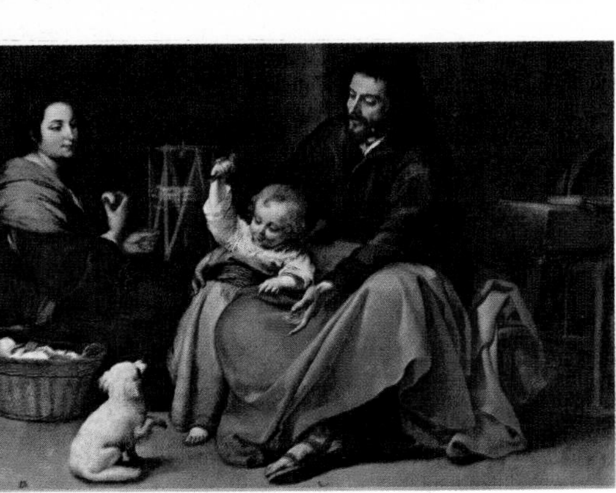

3

6

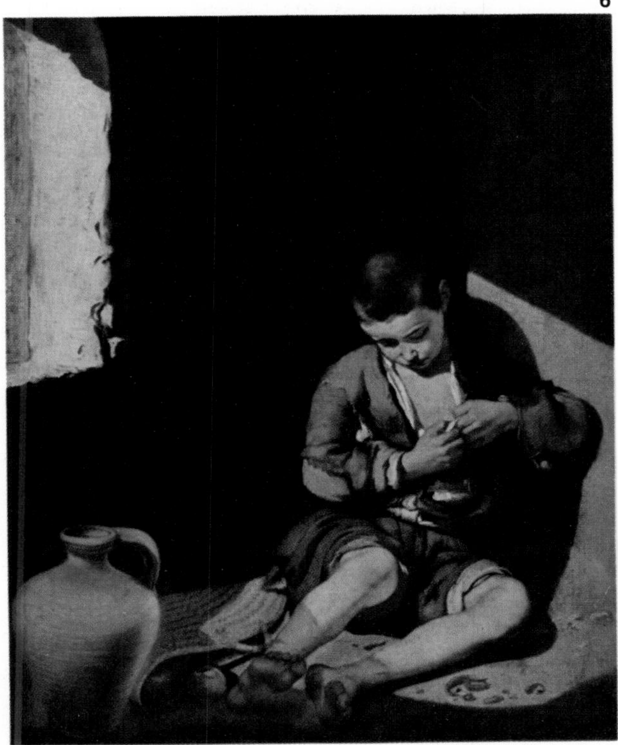

Diego de Silva y Velázquez (1599–1660)

1. *Court Jester Juan Calabazas* (*Calabacillas*). About 1647. Prado, Madrid
2. *The Infante Carlos.* Prado, Madrid
3. *Christ on the Cross.* About 1631–2. Prado, Madrid
4. *St Paul.* Museo de Arte de Cataluña, Barcelona
5. *The Water Seller of Seville.* About 1619. Wellington Museum, London
6. *Lady with a Fan.* About 1648. Wallace Collection, London
7. *The Rokeby Venus.* About 1650. National Gallery, London

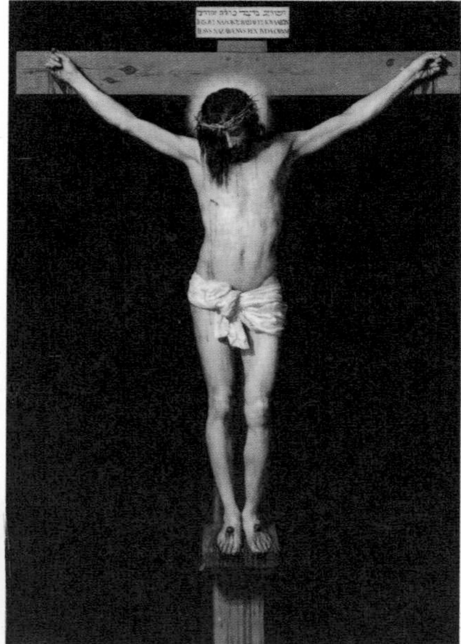

3

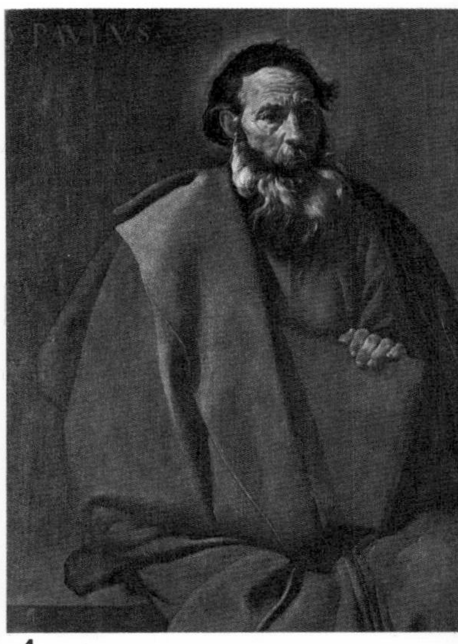

4

1

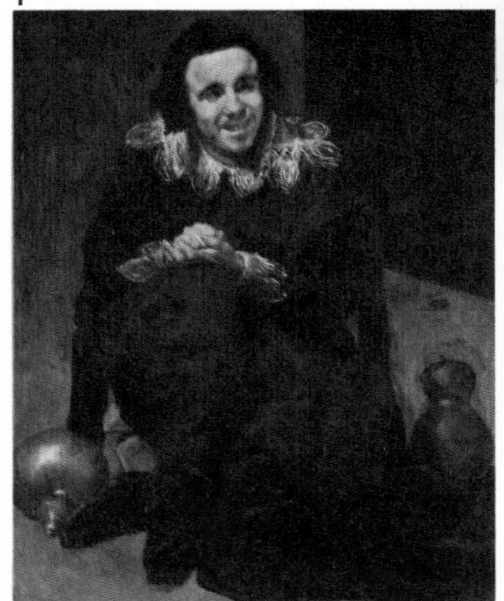

2

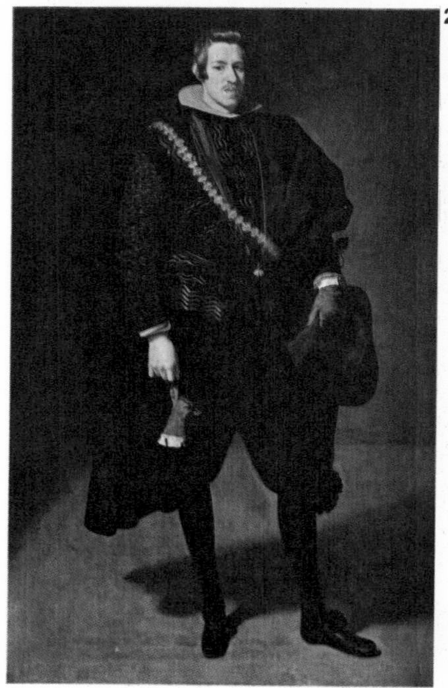

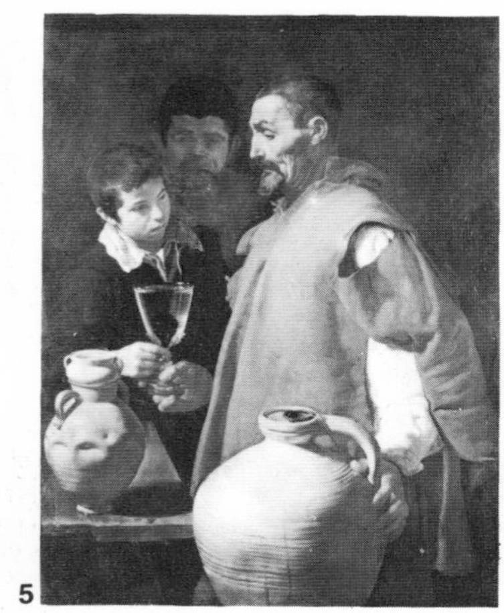

5

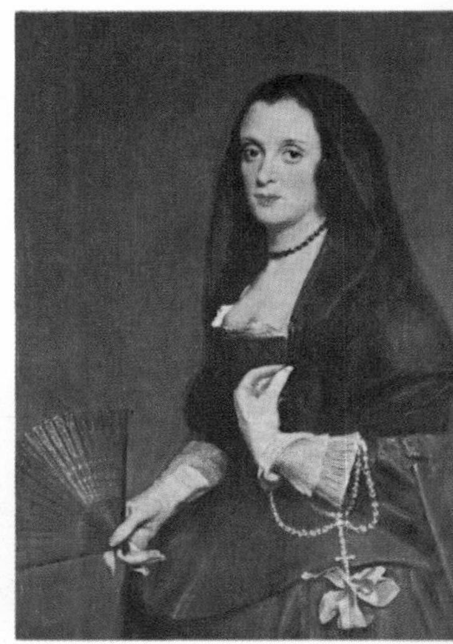

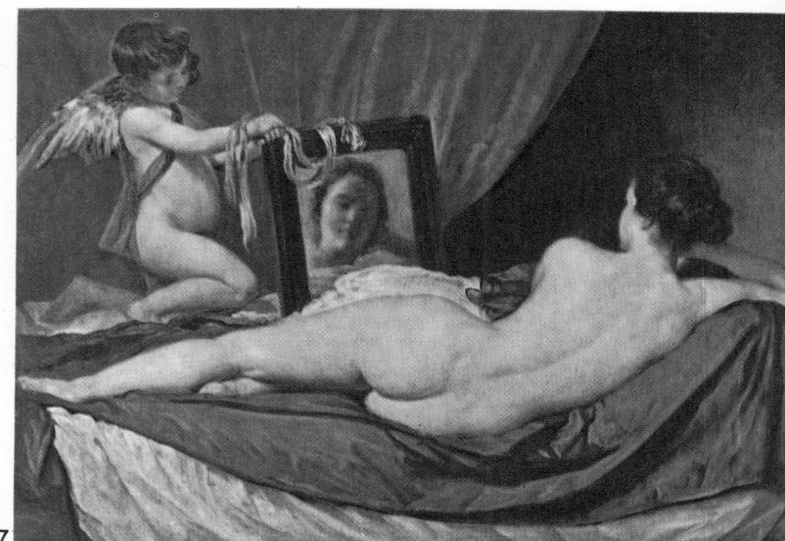

7

Diego de Silva y Velázquez (1599–1660)

1. *The Infanta Margarita.* About 1660. Prado, Madrid
2. *The Infanta Margarita.* About 1656. Kunsthistorisches Museum, Vienna
3. *Portrait of Luis de Gongora.* 1622. Boston Museum of Fine Arts
4. *The three Musicians.* About 1616–20. Staatliche Museen, Berlin-Dahlem
5. *Las Meninas* (*Maids of Honour*). 1656. Prado, Madrid
6. *The Infante Philip Prosper.* 1659. Kunsthistorisches Museum, Vienna
7. *Portrait of Gaspar de Guzman, Count-Duke of Olivares.* About 1634. Prado, Madrid

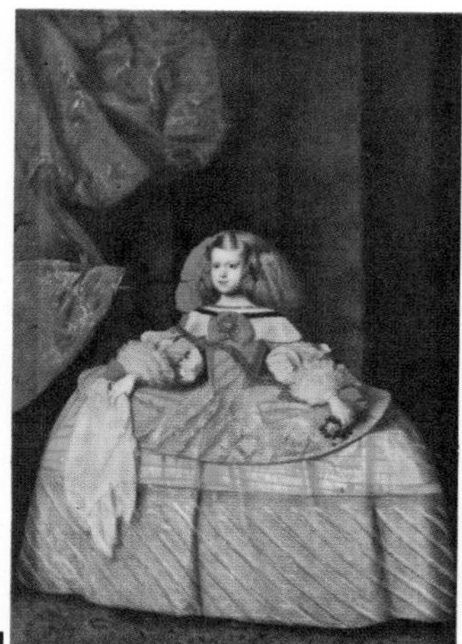
1

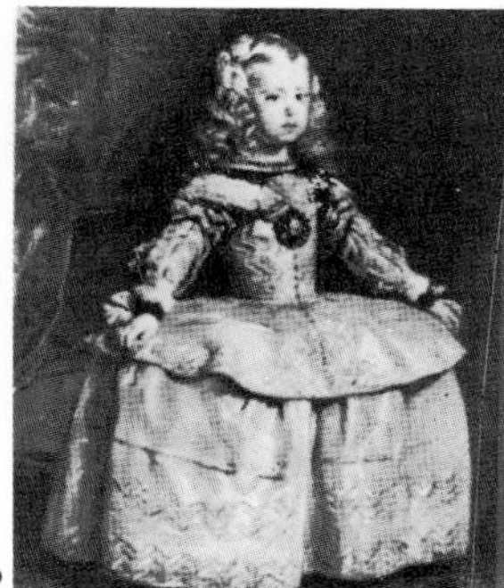
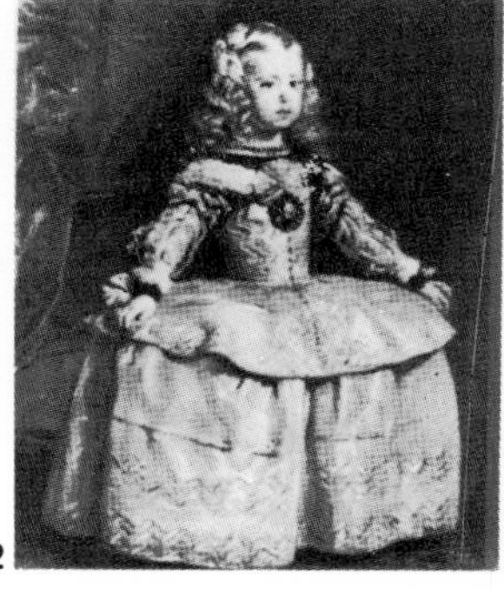
2

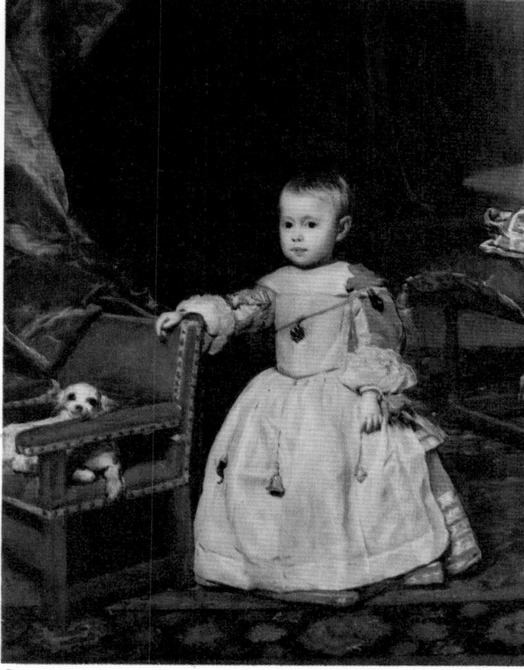

3

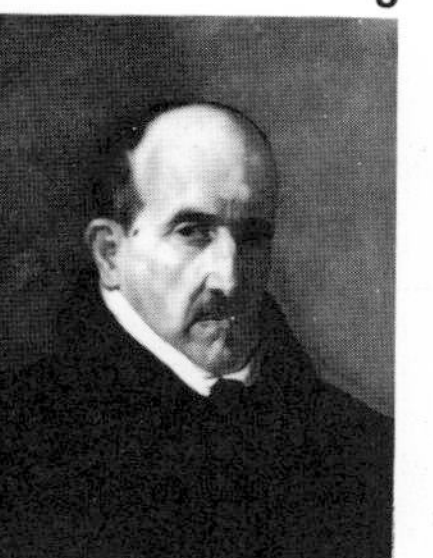

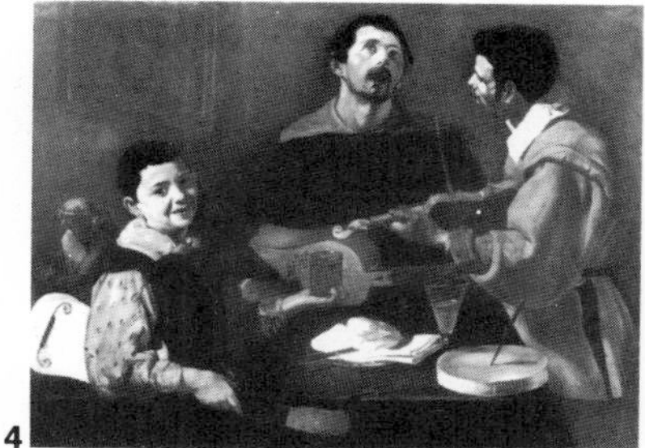
4

5

6

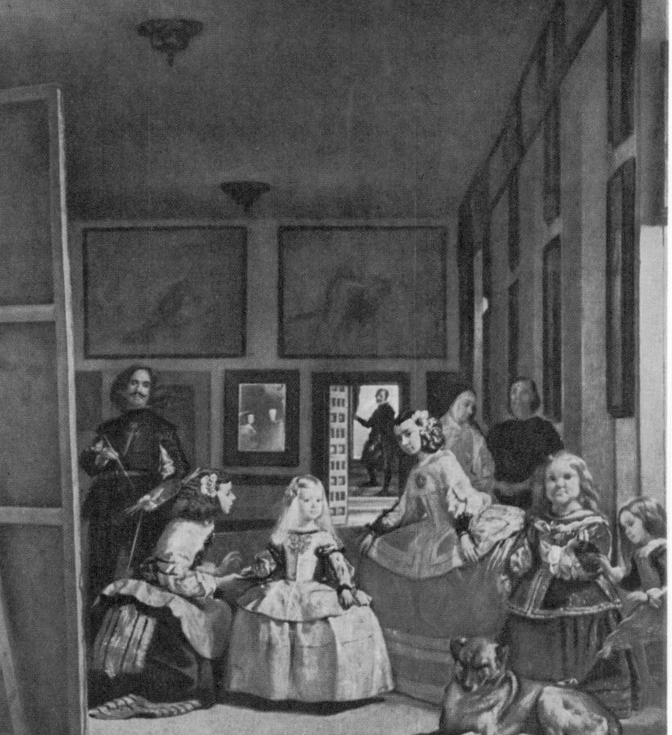

7

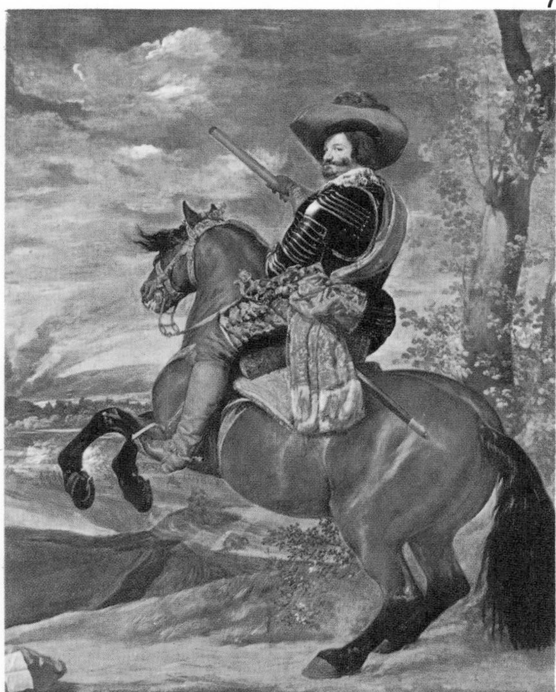

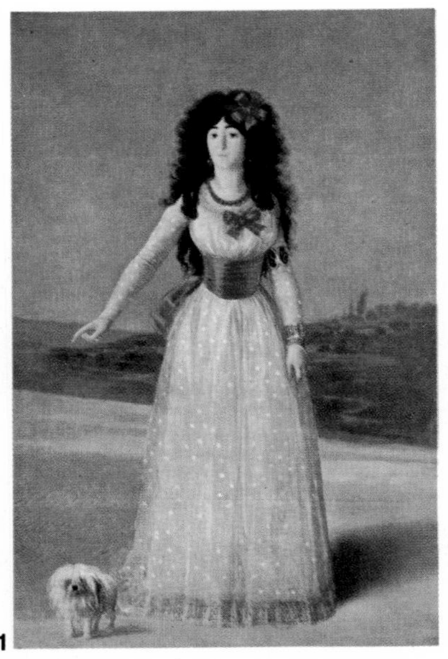
1

Francisco de Goya y Lucientes (1746–1828)

1. *The Duchess of Alba.* 1795. Duke of Alba Collection, Madrid
2. *'Volaverunt'.* 1793–8. Aquatint from *Los Caprichos*
3. *The Shooting of 3 May 1808.* 1814. Prado, Madrid
4. *Lovely Advice.* Etching from *Los Caprichos.* 1793–8
5. *The Clothed Maja.* About 1800–3. Prado, Madrid
6. *The Naked Maja.* About 1800–3. Prado, Madrid
7. *The Family of Charles IV.* Detail. 1800. Prado, Madrid

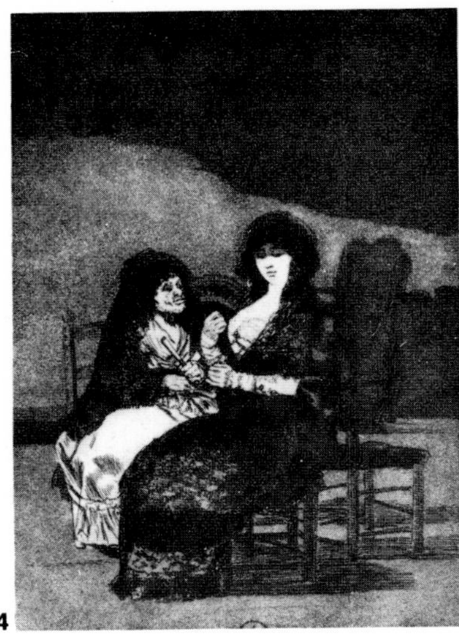
4

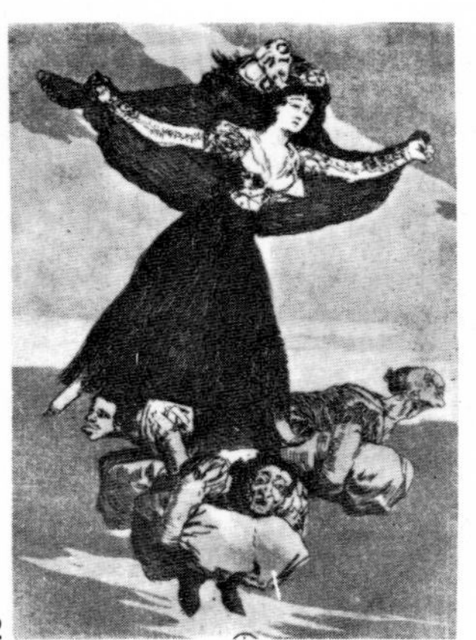
2

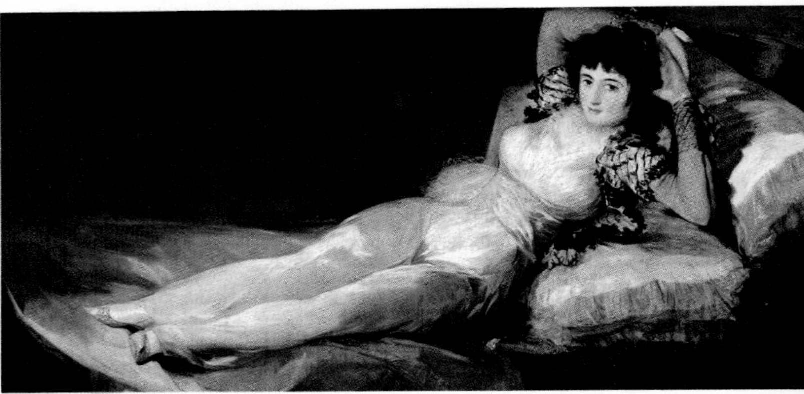
5

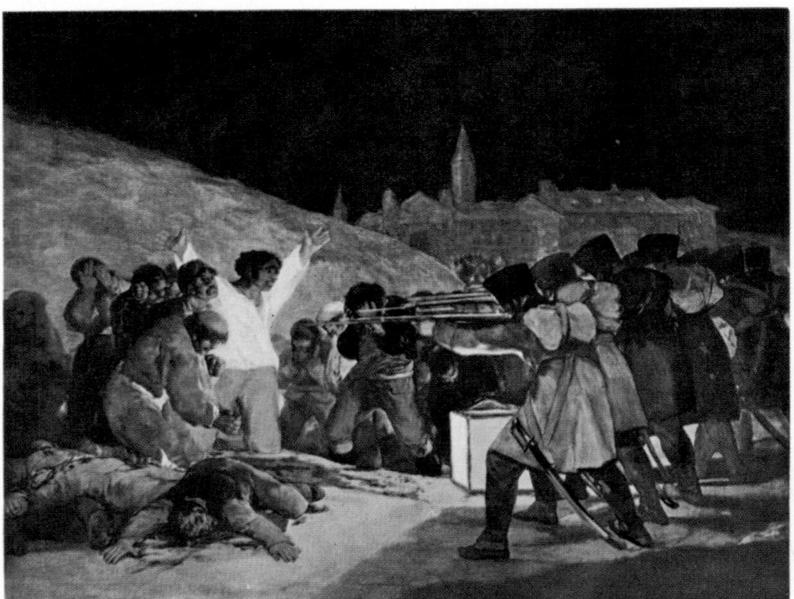
3

6
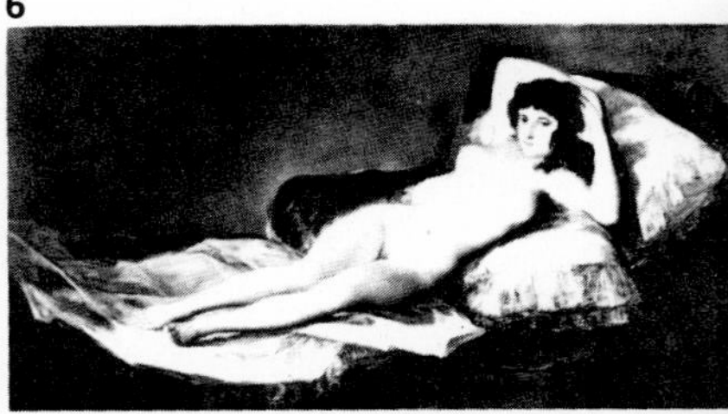

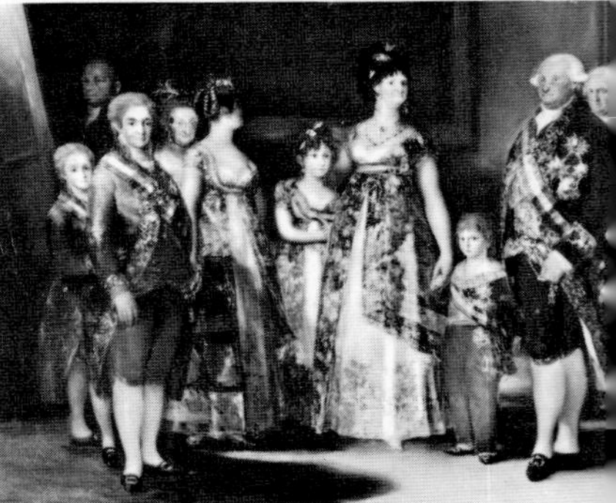
7

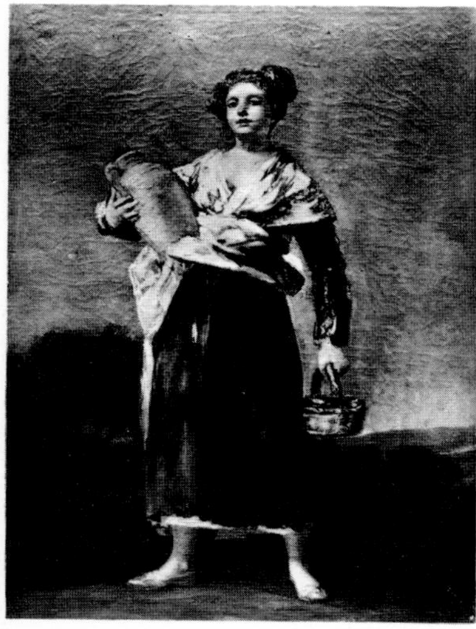

1

Francisco de Goya y Lucientes (1746–1828)

1. *The Water Carrier.* About 1815. Museum of Fine Arts, Budapest
2. *Blindman's Buff.* 1789. Prado, Madrid
3. *Fantastic Vision.* About 1819. Prado, Madrid
4. *The Parasol.* Tapestry cartoon. 1778. Prado, Madrid
5. *The Bandit Maragato attacking Fray de Zaldivia, a Monk.* About 1806–7. Art Institute of Chicago

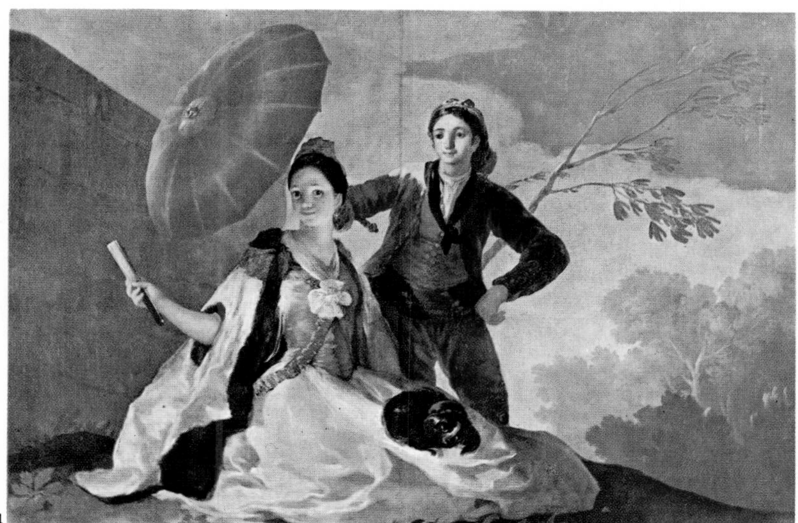

4

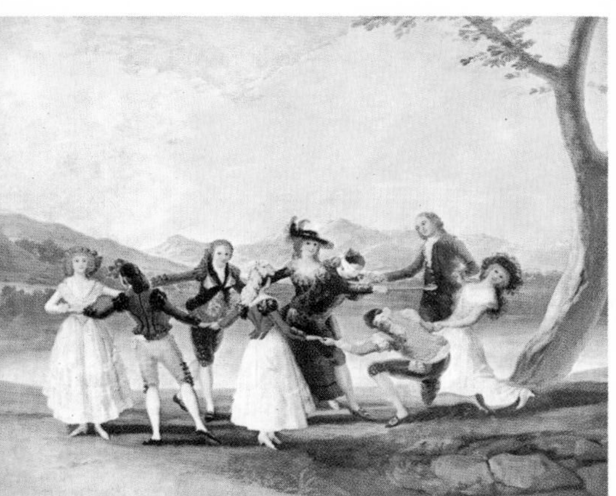

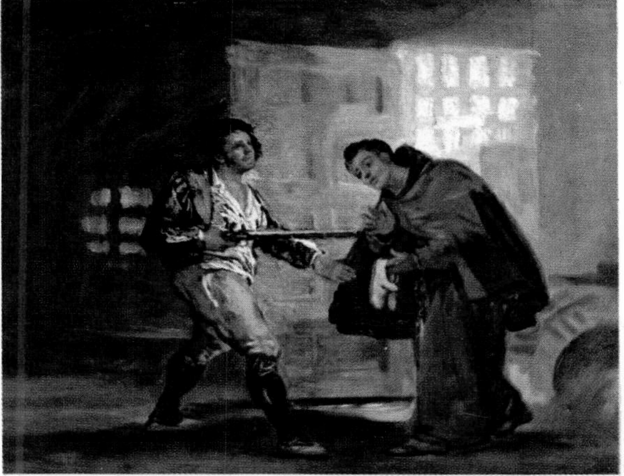

5

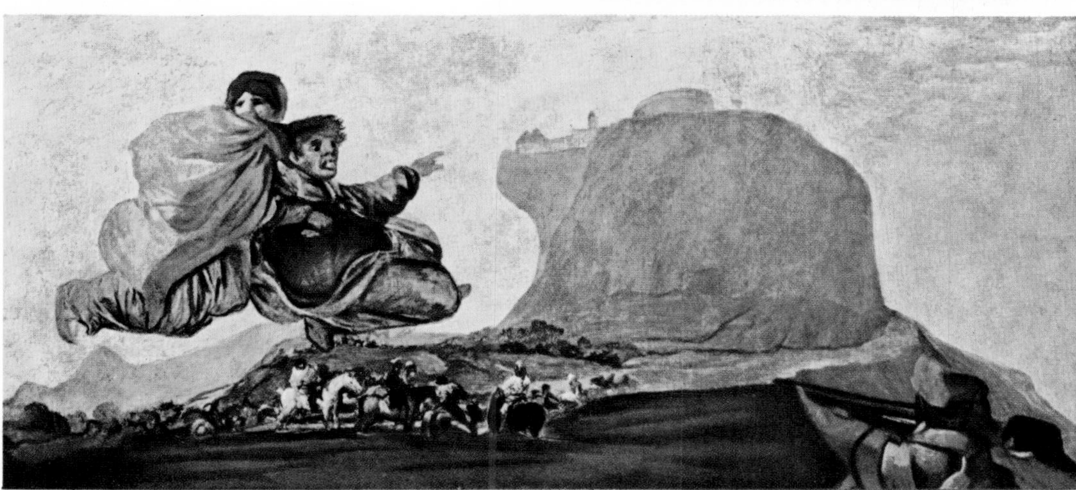

3

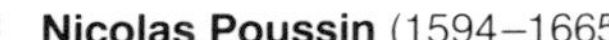

Nicolas Poussin (1594–1665)

1. *Autumn* (*The Spies with the Grapes of t Promised Land*). From *The Four Seaso* series. 1660–4. Louvre, Paris
2. *The Rape of the Sabine Women.* About 1637. Metropolitan Museum of Art, New Y
3. *Self-portrait.* 1649–50. Louvre, Paris
4. *The Finding of Moses.* 1638. Louvre, Pa
5. *Study for a Bacchanal.* Drawing. École des Beaux-Arts, Paris
6. *A Bacchanalian Revel before a Term of P* About 1635–8. National Gallery, London

1

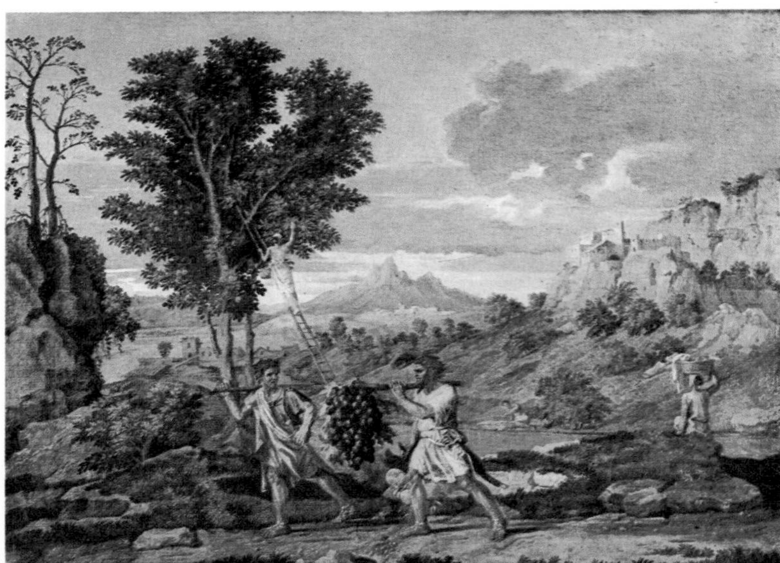

2

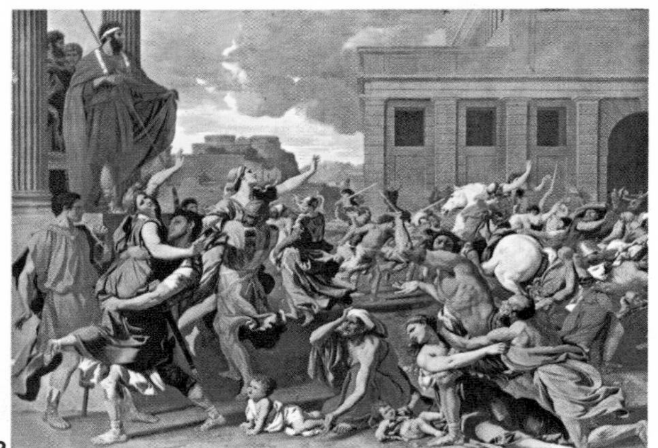

4

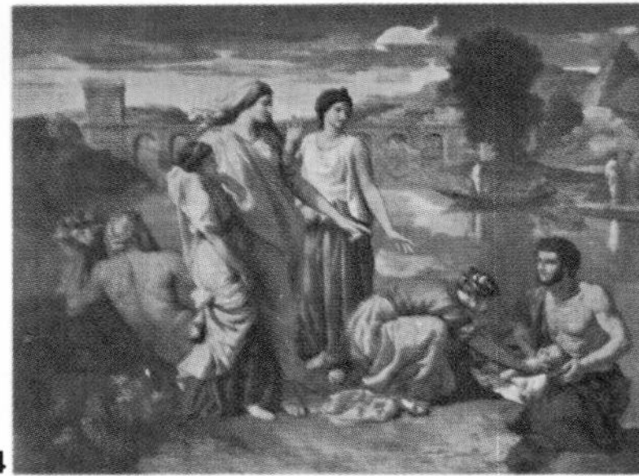

5

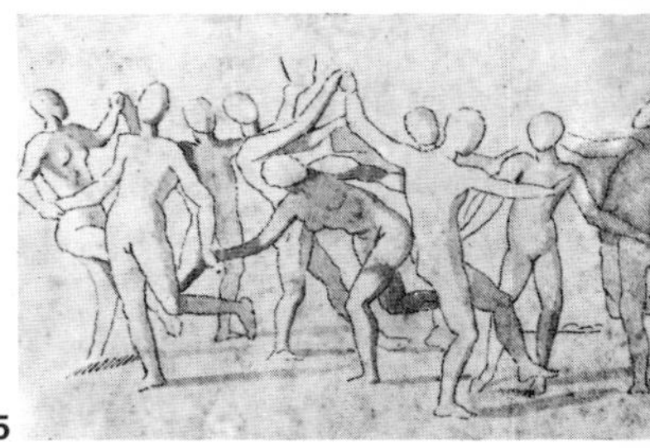

3

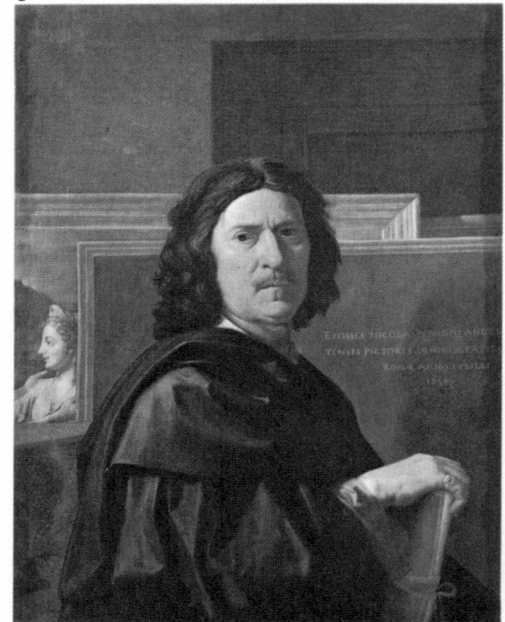

6

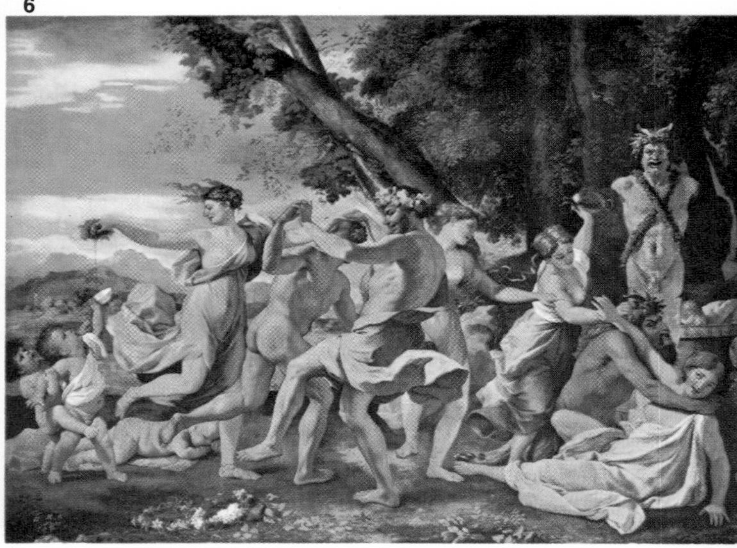

laude Lorrain (1600–82)
. *Landscape with Hagar and the Angel.* 1646. National Gallery, London
. *Seaport.* Bayerische Staatsgemäldesammlungen, Munich
. *Landscape with David at the Cave of Adullam.* 1658. National Gallery, London
4. *Trees and Foliage.* Wash drawing. Musée des Beaux-Arts, Besançon
5. *The Tiber Valley, near Rome.* Sepia drawing. About 1645. Formerly Georges Wildenstein Collection
6. *The Finding of Moses.* Prado, Madrid

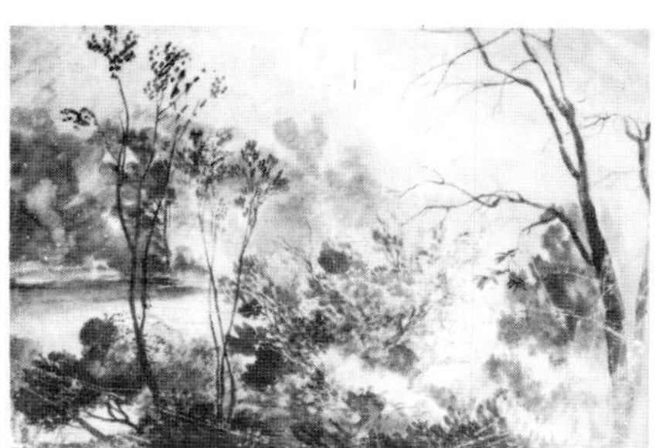
4

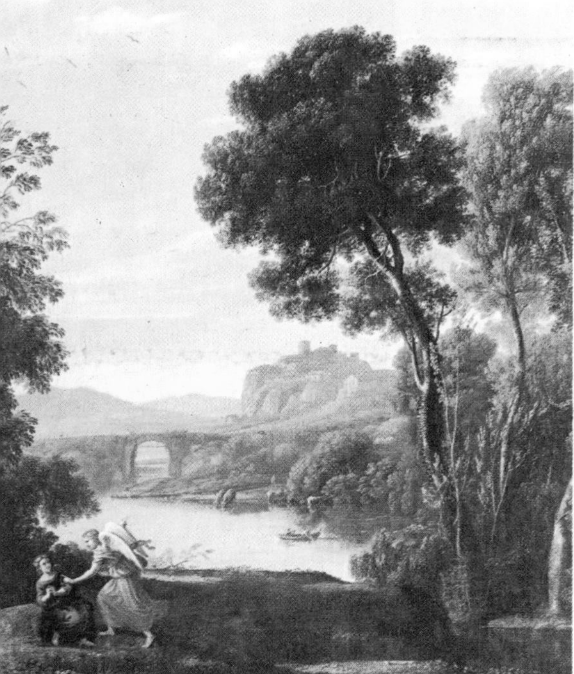

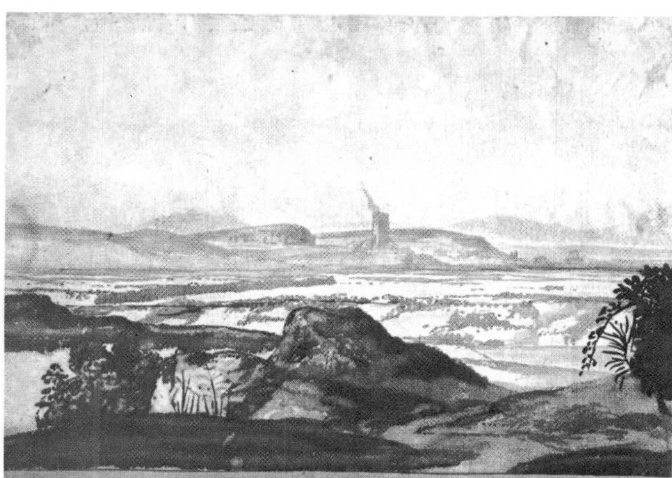
5

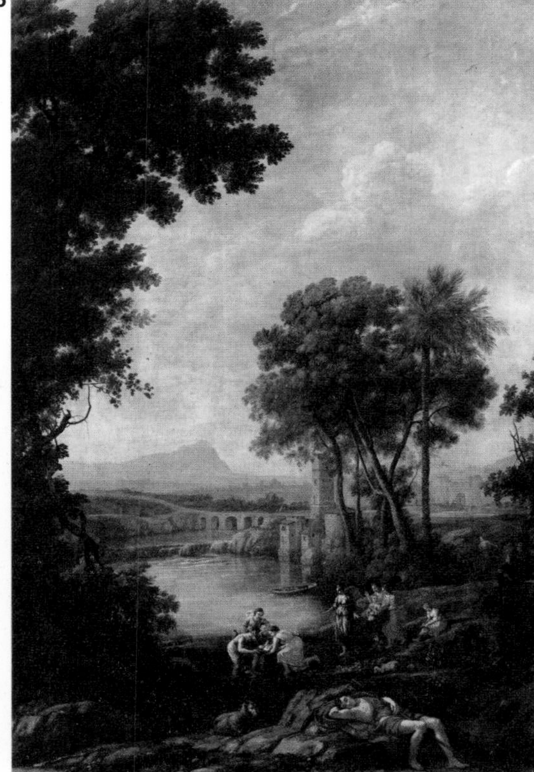
6

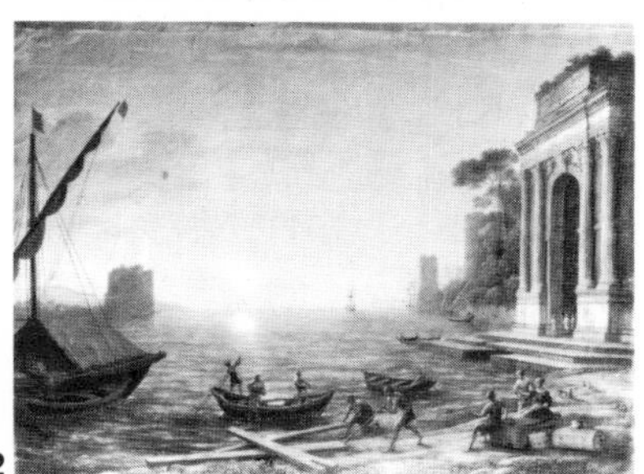
2

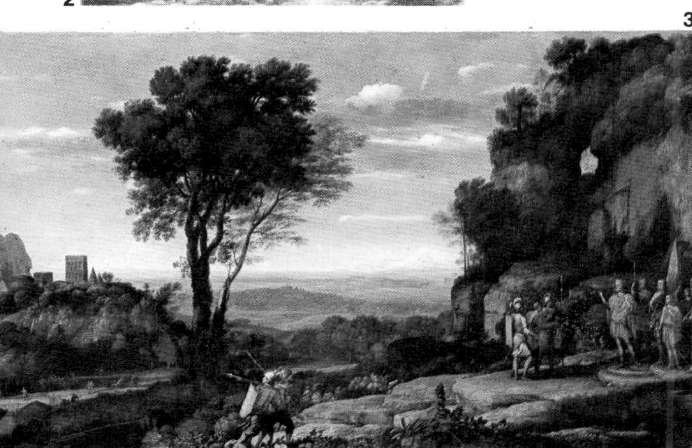
3

Georges de La Tour (1593–1652)

1. *The Fortune-teller.* About 1620–1. Metropolitan Museum of Art, New York
2. *St Sebastian being tended by Irene.* About 1650. Staatliche Museen, Berlin-Dahlem
3. *The penitent Magdalene.* About 1635–40. Louvre, Paris

Louis Le Nain (1593–1648)

4. *A Peasant.* Detail from *Peasants at Supper.* About 1645–8. Louvre, Paris
5. *Peasants in a Landscape.* About 1641. Wadsworth Atheneum, Hartford, Connecticut

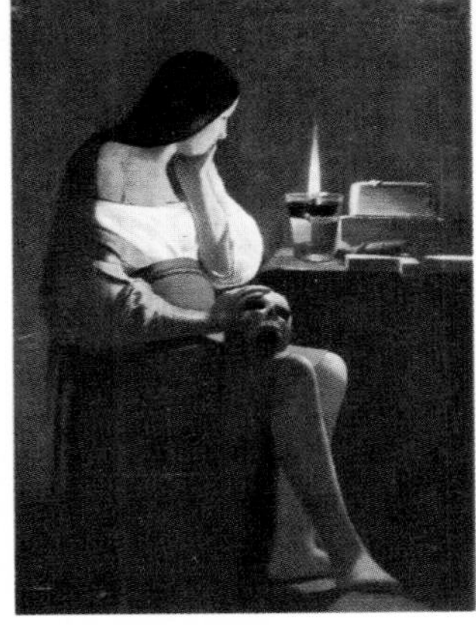

3

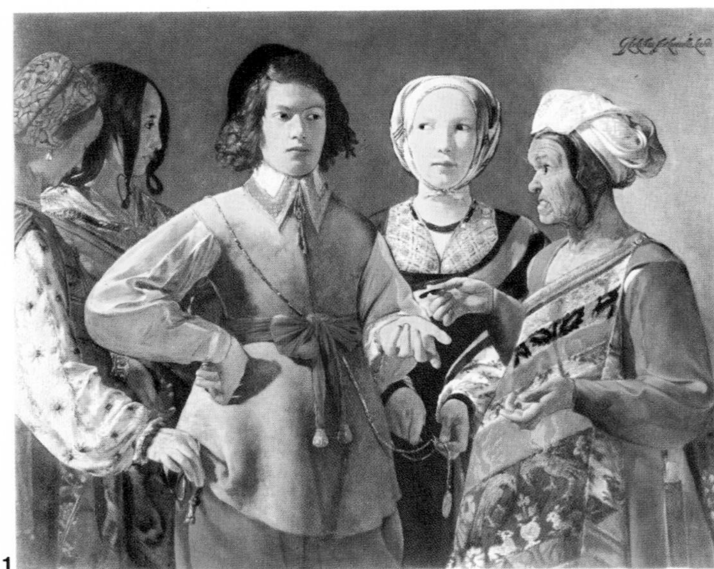

1

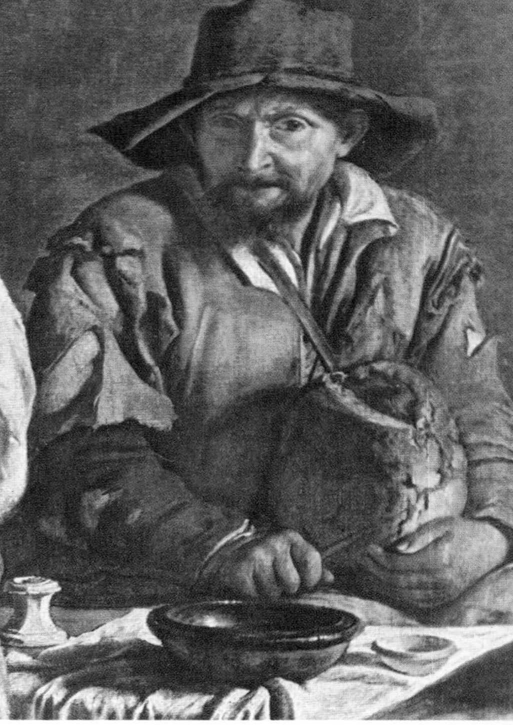

4

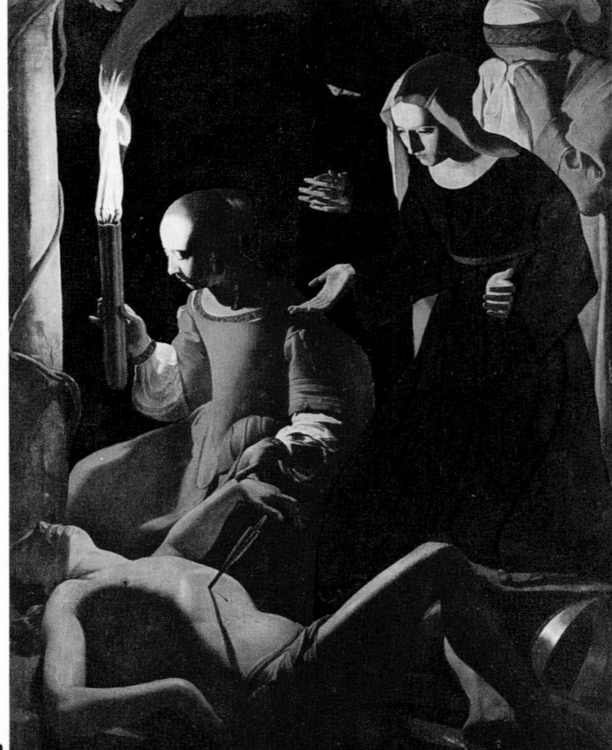

2

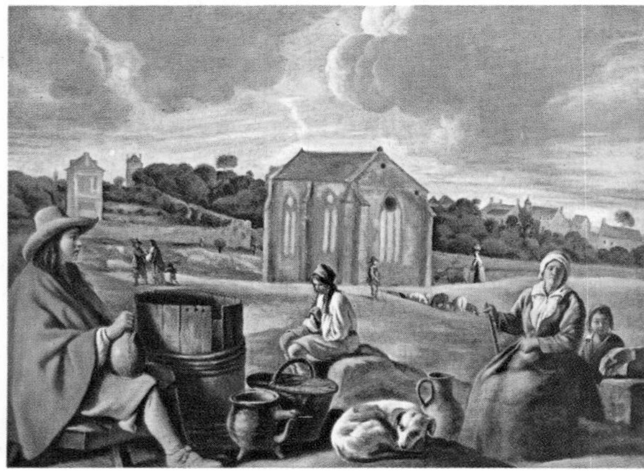

5

Charles Le Brun (1619–90): *Head of Astonishment.* Drawing. Louvre, Paris
Eustache Le Sueur (1616–55): *The Death of Raymond Diocrès.* Panel from the series on the Life of St Bruno. 1645–8. Louvre, Paris
Charles Le Brun (1619–90): *Chancellor Séguier in the Retinue of Maria Teresa on her Entry into Paris, 26 August 1660.* Louvre, Paris
Jacques Callot (1592/3–1635): *Tree of the Hanged.* Engraving from *Troubles of War.* 1633. Cabinet des Estampes, Bibliothèque Nationale, Paris
Simon Vouet (1590–1649): *The Muses Urania and Calliope.* National Gallery of Art (Samuel H. Kress Collection), Washington DC

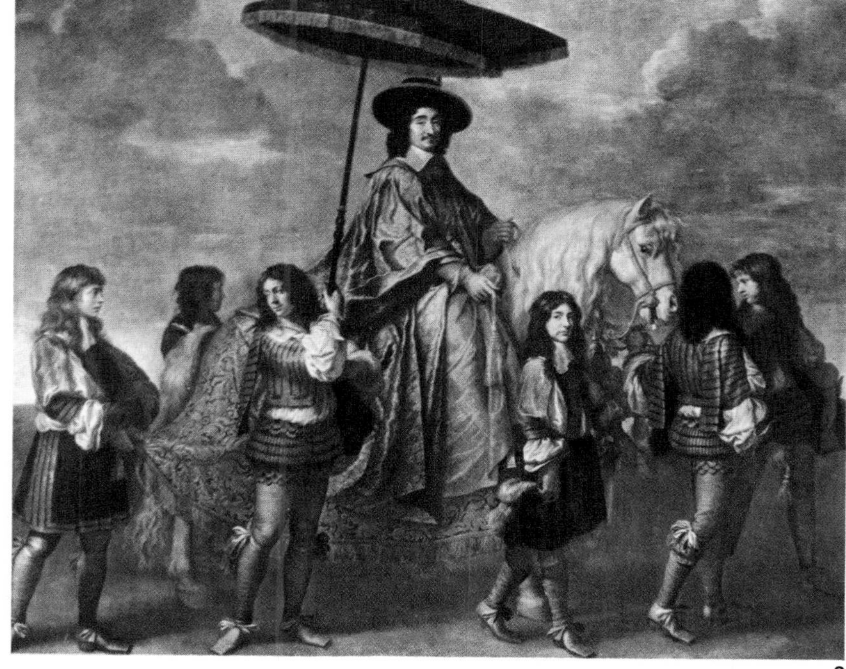

3

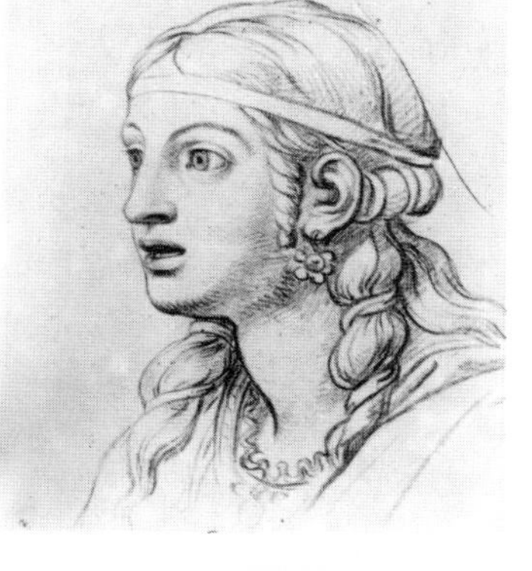

1

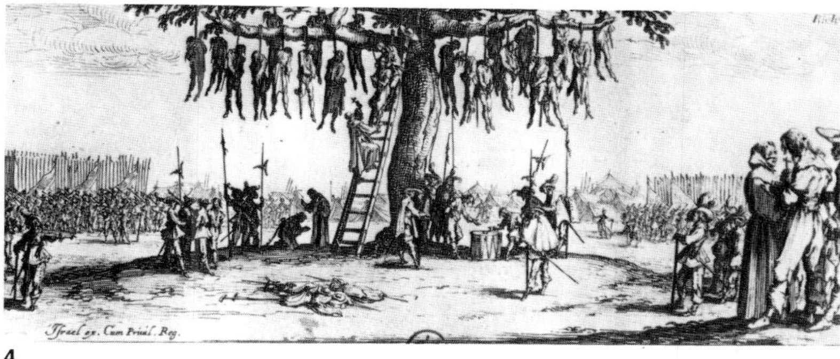

4

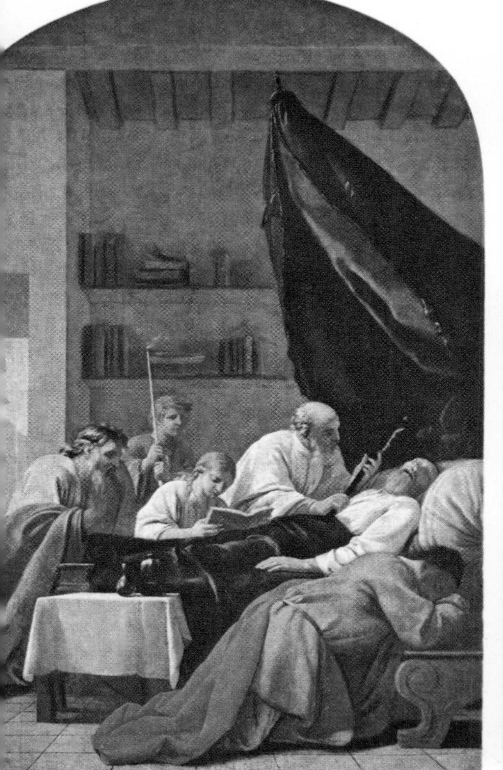

2

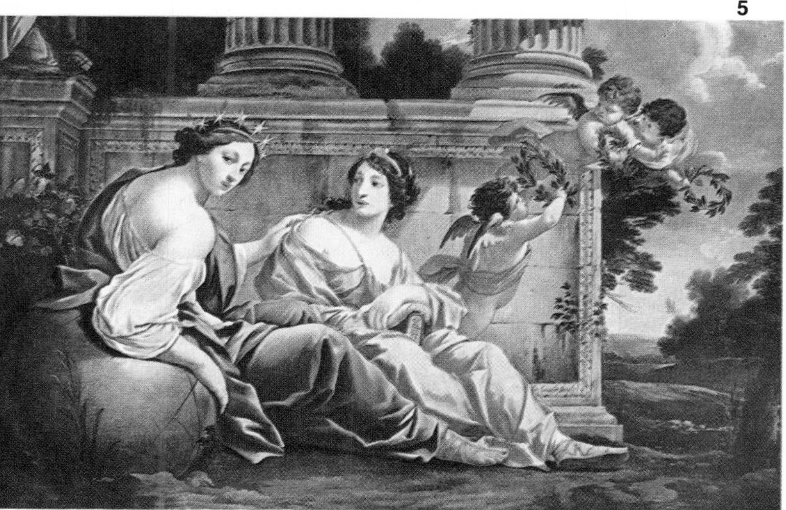

5

1. **François Mansart** (1598–1666): Orléans wing of the Château at Blois. 1635–8
2. **François Mansart** (1598–1666): Hall of the Château at Maisons-Laffitte. 1642–8
3. **Louis Le Vau** (1612–70): Château of Versailles. Begun 1668; completed 1678 by Jules Hardouin-Mansart
4. **Liberal Bruant** (*c.*1635–97): Main entrance gate. Hôtel des Invalides, Paris. 1670–7
5. **Louis Le Vau** (1612–70): Dome of the Institut de France (formerly the Collège des Quatre-Nations), Paris. 1663–74

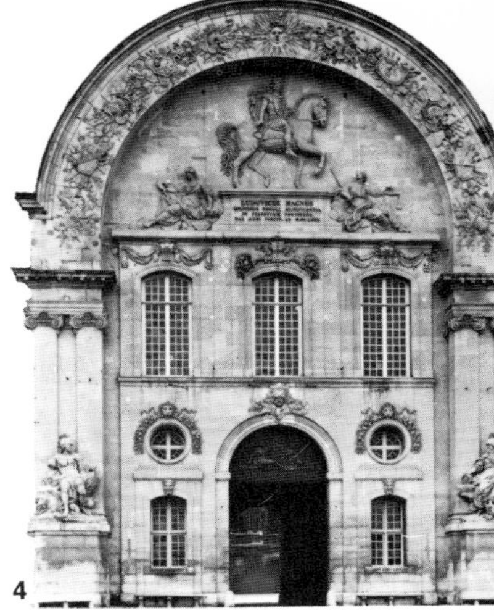

4

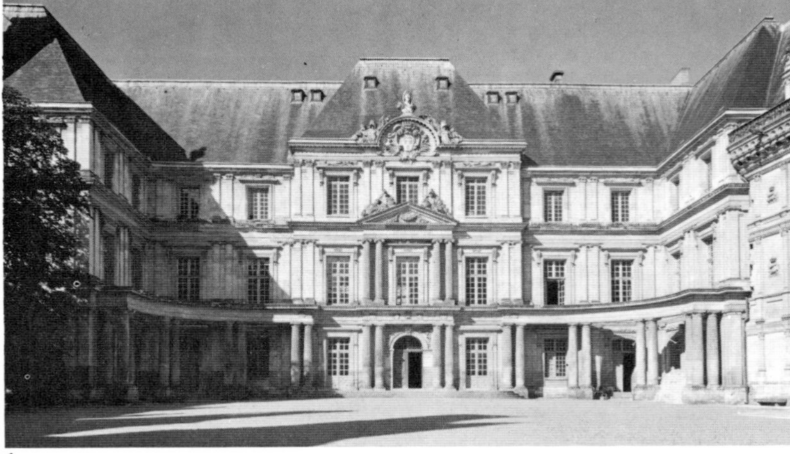

1

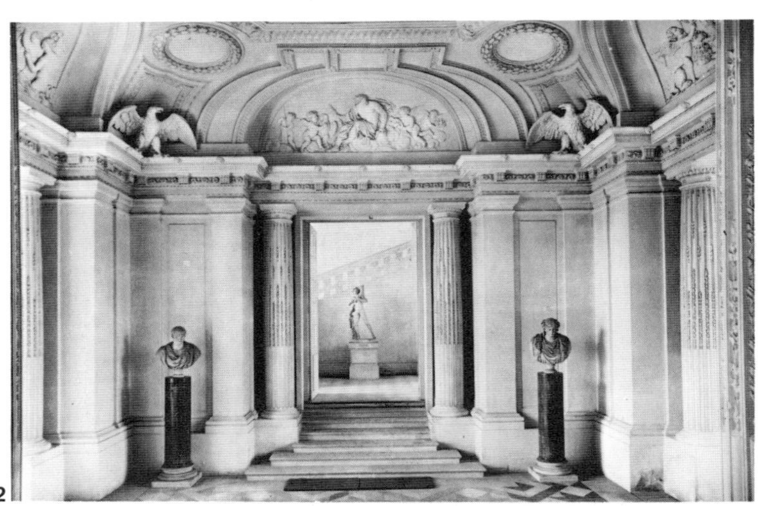

2

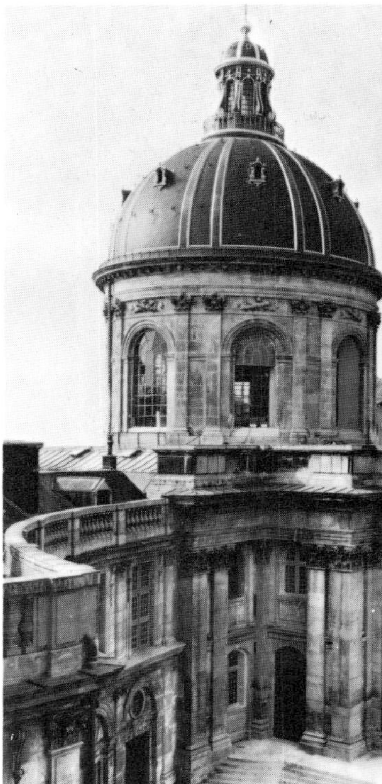

3

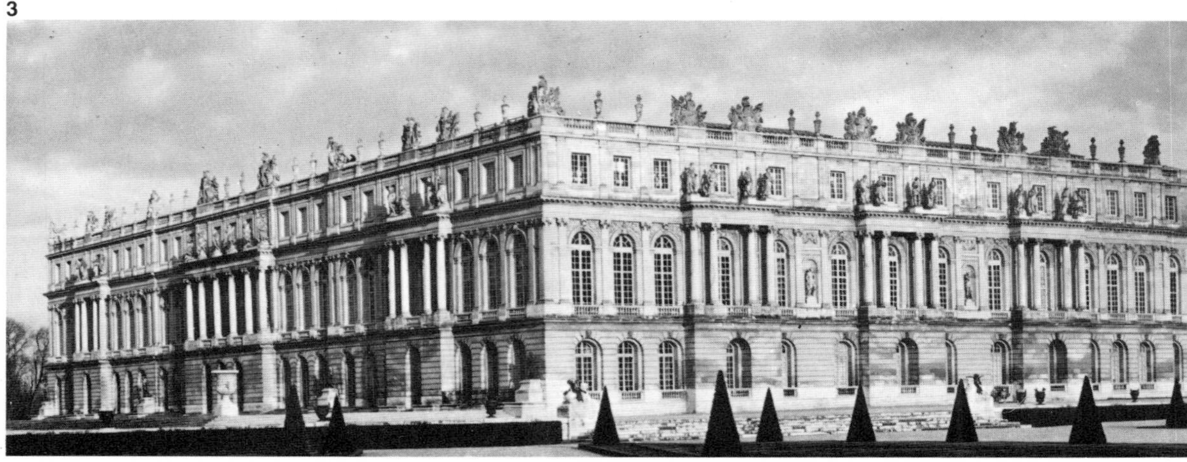

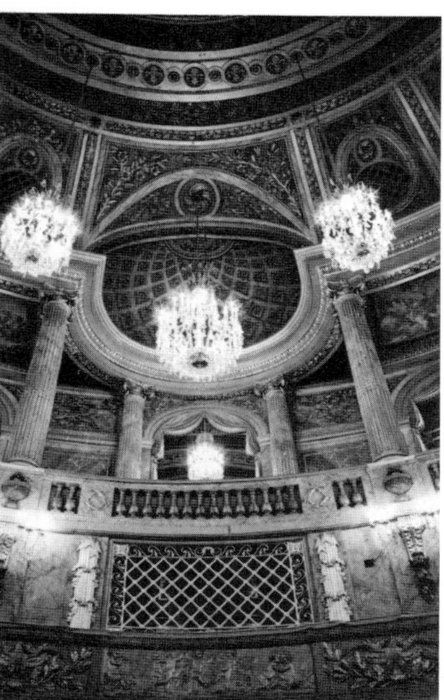

1. **Jacques-Ange Gabriel** (1698–1782): Opera house, Château of Versailles. Royal box. Completed in 1753
2. **Jules Hardouin-Mansart** (1646–1708): Hall of Mirrors, Château of Versailles. Ceiling by Charles Le Brun. 1678–86
3. **Claude Perrault** (1613–88) with **Louis Le Vau** and **Charles Le Brun**: Colonnade of the Louvre (east façade), Paris. 1667–73
4. **Jacques Gabriel** (1667–1742): Elevation of the Place Royale, Rennes: town hall with clock tower. 1726–44
5. **Jacques-Ange Gabriel** (1698–1782): Petit Trianon, Versailles. Courtyard façade. 1762–8

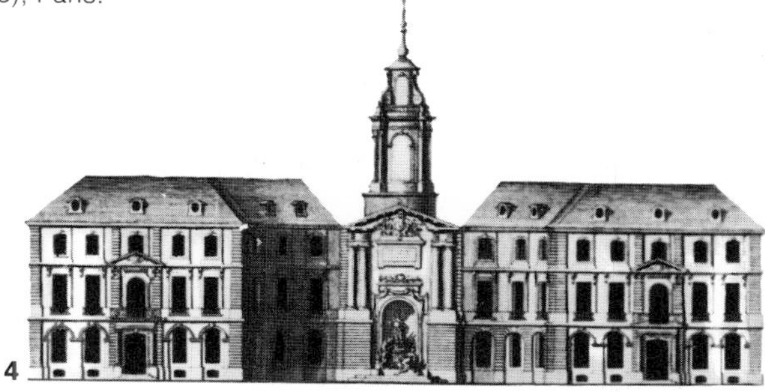

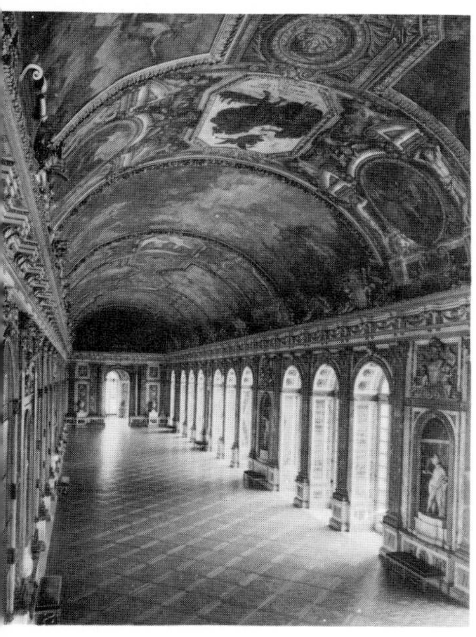

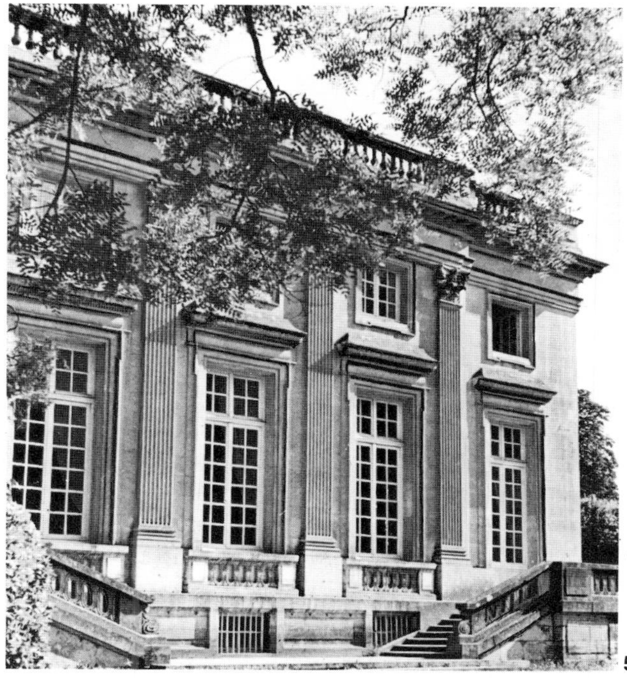

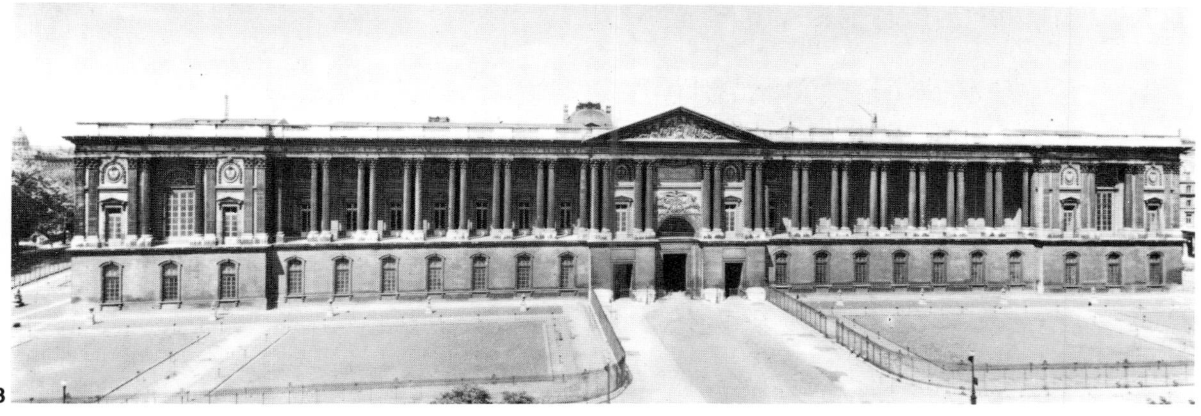

1. **Pierre Puget** (1620–94): *Alexander and Diogenes.* Detail of marble bas-relief. 1687–92. Louvre, Paris
2. **Pierre Puget** (1620–94): *Head of Medusa.* Louvre, Paris
3. **François Girardon** (1628–1715): *Bath of the Nymphs.* Detail from bas-relief. 1675. Park of Versailles
4. **François Girardon** (1628–1715): *Equestrian statue of Louis XIV.* Château of Versailles
5. **Jean-Baptiste Lemoyne** (1704–78): *Bust of the playwright Prosper Crébillon.* Musée des Beaux-Arts, Algiers
6. **Pierre Puget** (1620–94): *Milo of Crotona.* Marble. 1682. Louvre, Paris
7. **Jean-Baptiste Lemoyne** (1704–78): *Bust of the physicist Réaumur.* 1751. Louvre, Paris
8. **François Girardon** with **Thomas Regnaudin**: *Apollo served by the Nymphs.* 1666–75. Grove of the Bains d'Apollon, Versailles

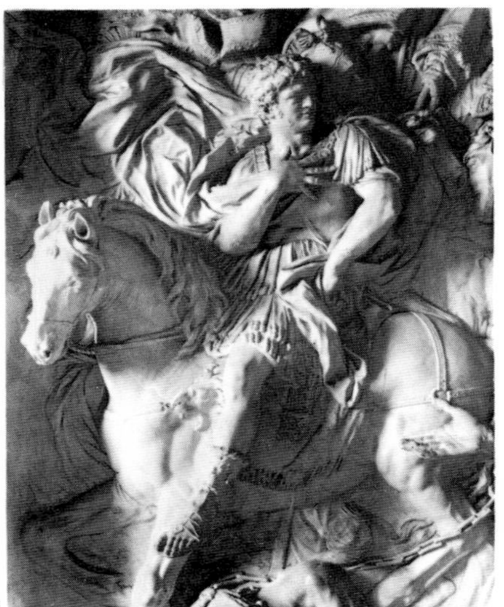
1

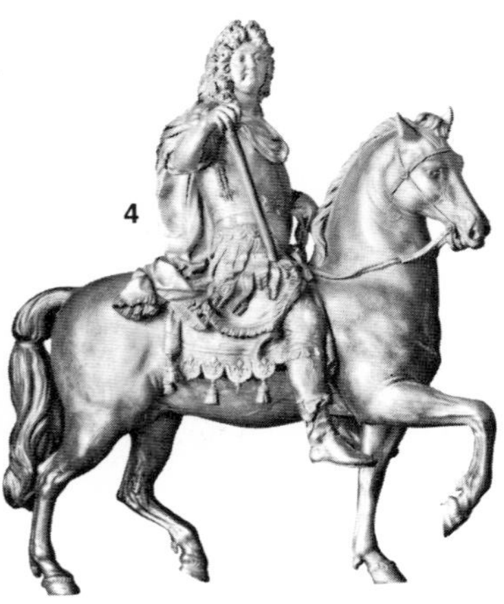
4

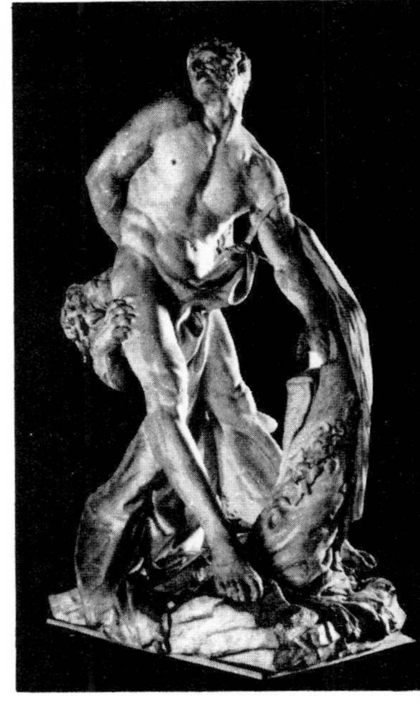

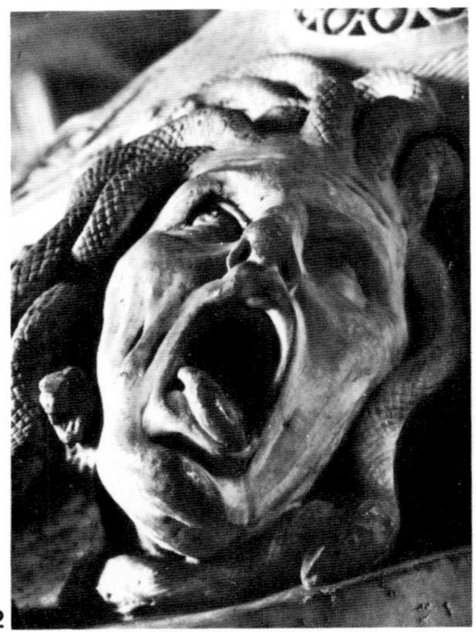
2

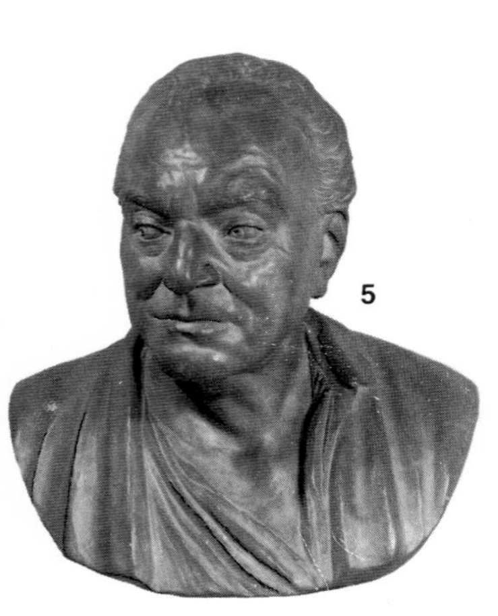
5

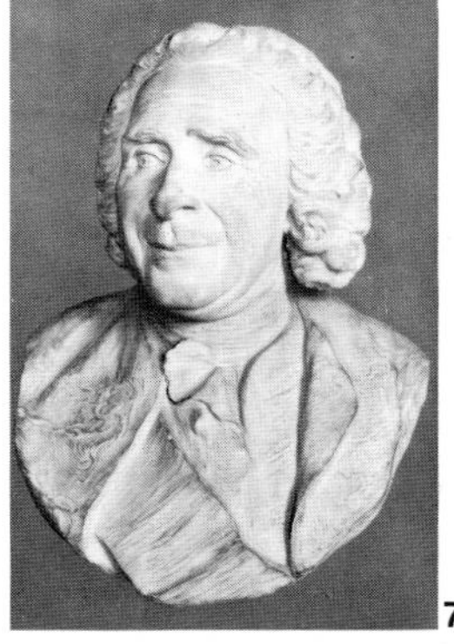
7

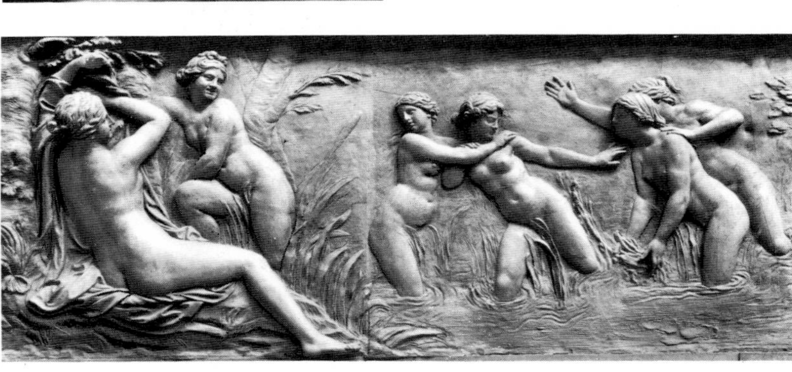
3

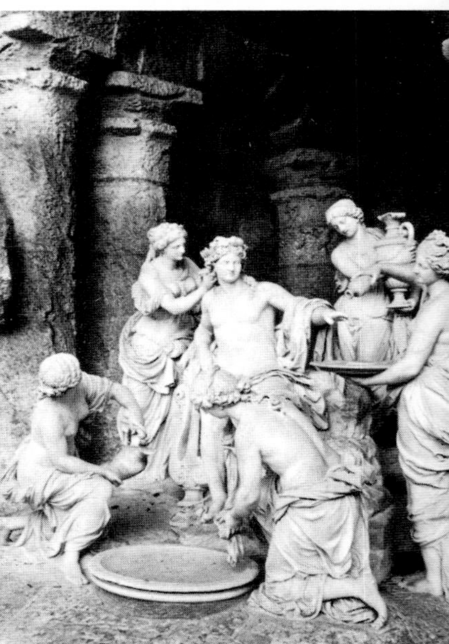
8

1. **Jean-Antoine Houdon** (1741–1828): *Shivering Girl.* Marble. 1783. Musée Fabre, Montpellier
2. **Jean-Antoine Houdon** (1741–1828): *Louise Brongniart.* Terracotta. 1777. Louvre, Paris
3. **Edmé Bouchardon** (1698–1762): *Summer.* Detail from bas-relief on the Fountain of the Four Seasons, Paris. 1739–45
4. **Jean-Antoine Houdon** (1741–1828): *Diana.* Bronze. 1776. Musée des Beaux-Arts, Tours
5. **Edmé Bouchardon** (1698–1762): *The River Marne.* Terracotta. Louvre, Paris
6. **Étienne-Maurice Falconet** (1716–91): *Equestrian statue of Peter the Great,* Leningrad. 1766–78
7. **Jean-Baptiste Pigalle** (1714–85): *Denis Diderot.* Bronze. 1777. Louvre, Paris
8. **Jean-Antoine Houdon** (1741–1828): *Voltaire in antique Drapery.* Marble. 1781. Comédie-Française, Paris

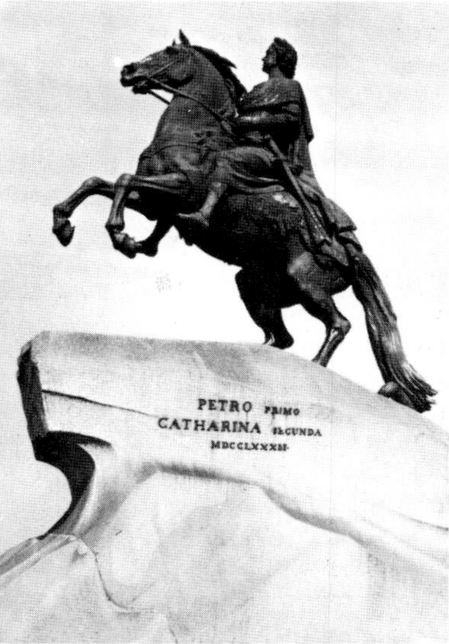

6

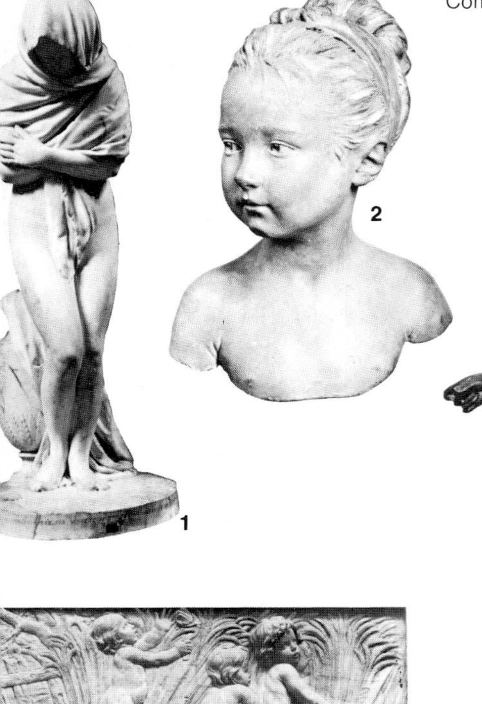

2

1

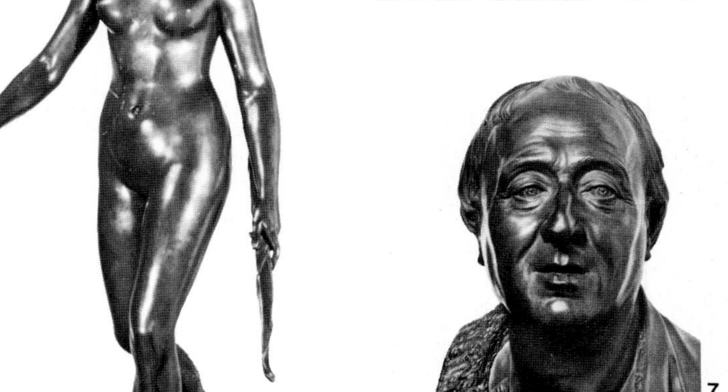

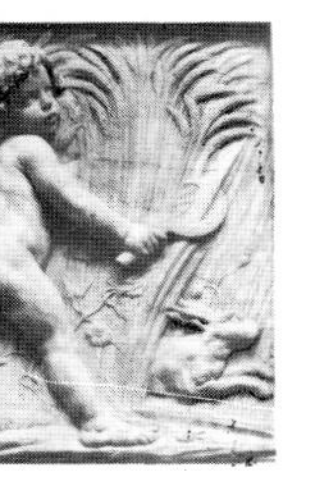

4

7

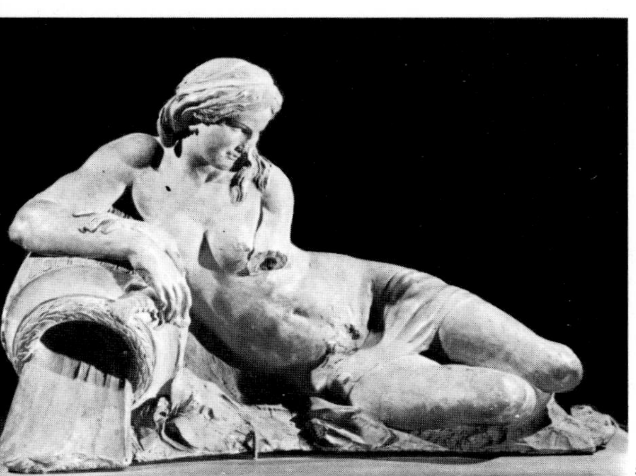

5

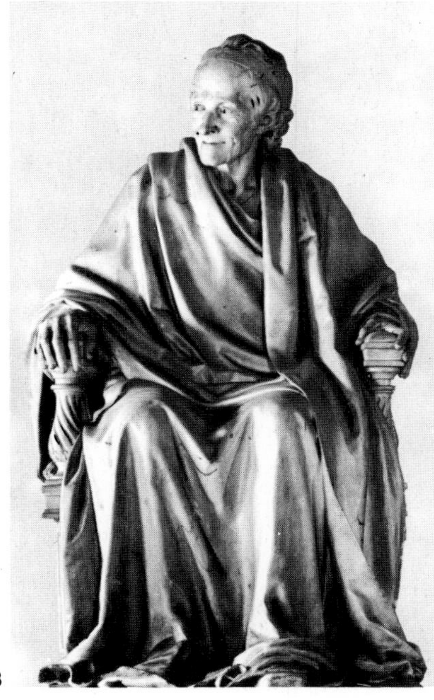

8

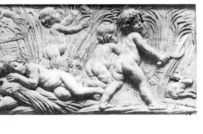

1. **Jean-Baptiste Chardin** (1699–1779): *The Cellar Boy.* 1738. Hunterian Museum, University of Glasgow
2. **Hyacinthe Rigaud** (1659–1743): *Portrait of Louis XIV.* 1701. Louvre, Paris
3. **Jean-Baptiste Chardin** (1699–1779): *Pipes and Drinking Vessels.* Louvre, Paris
4. **Hyacinthe Rigaud** (1659–1743): *Portrait of the Artist's Mother.* 1695. Louvre, Paris
5. **François Desportes** (1661–1743): *Landscape.* Musée National du Palais de Compiègne, Oise
6. **Jean-Baptiste Chardin** (1699–1779): *The young Draughtsman.* 1737. Staatliche Museen, Berlin-Dahlem
7. **Jean-Baptiste Chardin** (1699–1779): *Girl with a Shuttlecock.* 1741. Philippe de Rothschild Collection, Paris
8. **Jean-Baptiste Chardin** (1699–1779): *The House of Cards.* National Gallery of Art (Mellon Collection), Washington DC

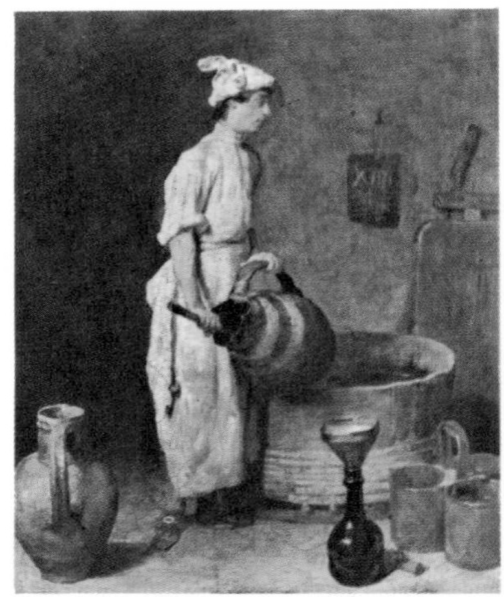

1

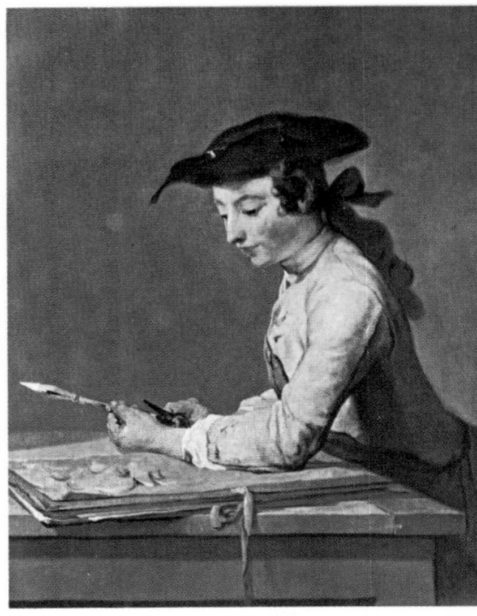

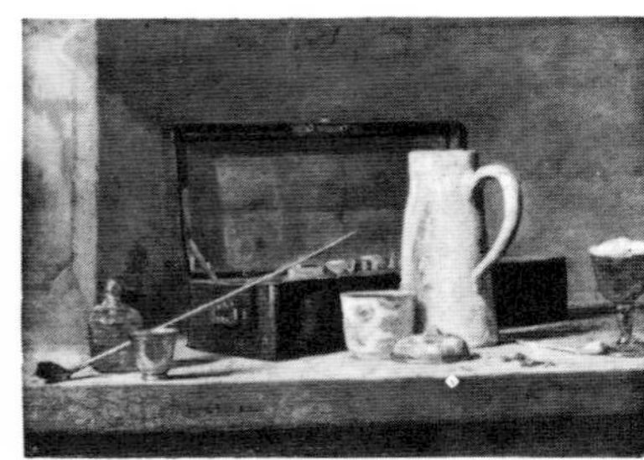

3

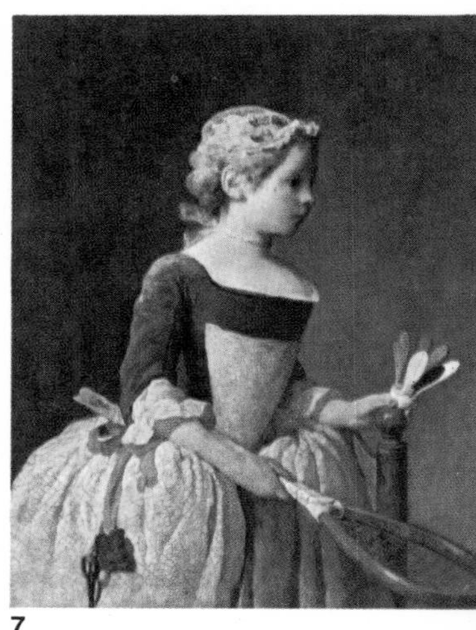

7

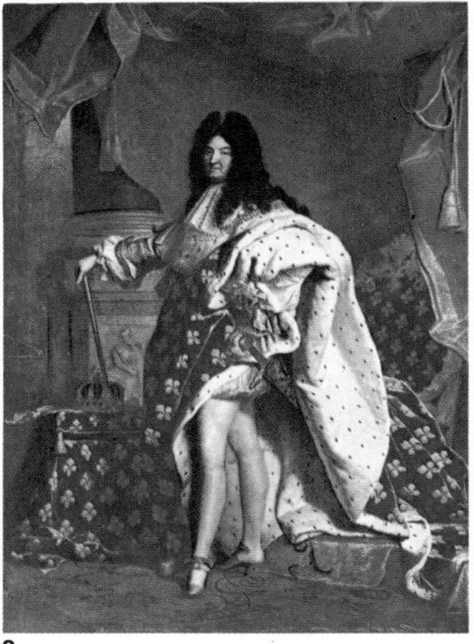

2

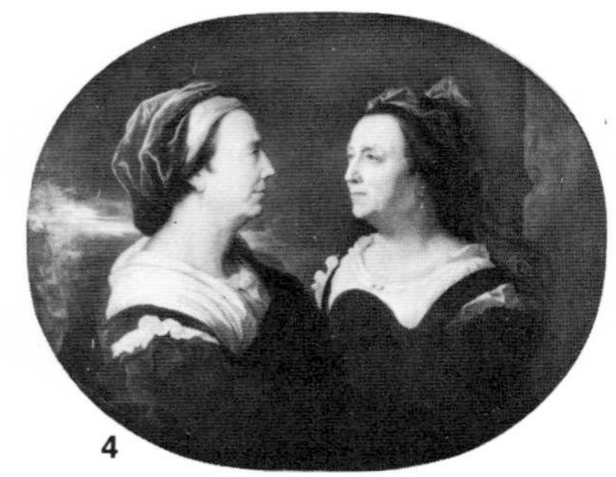

4

5

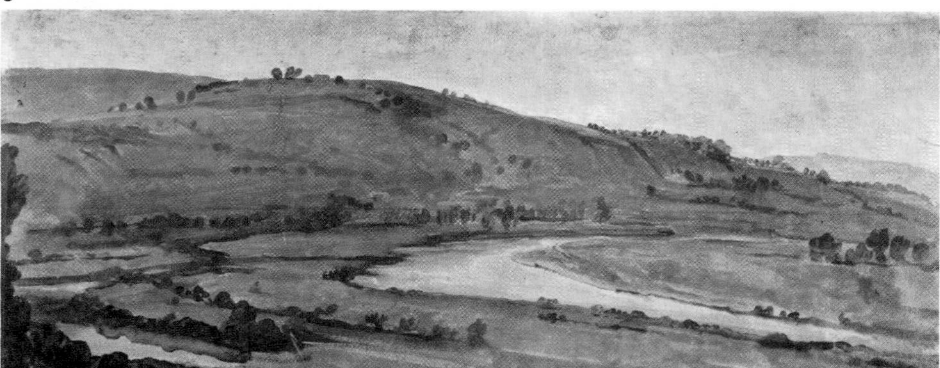

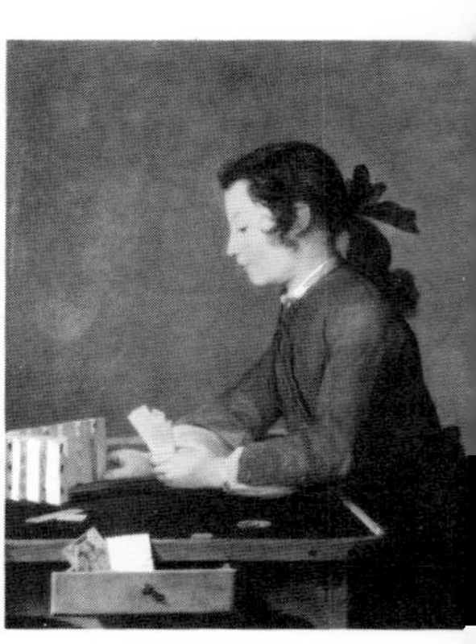

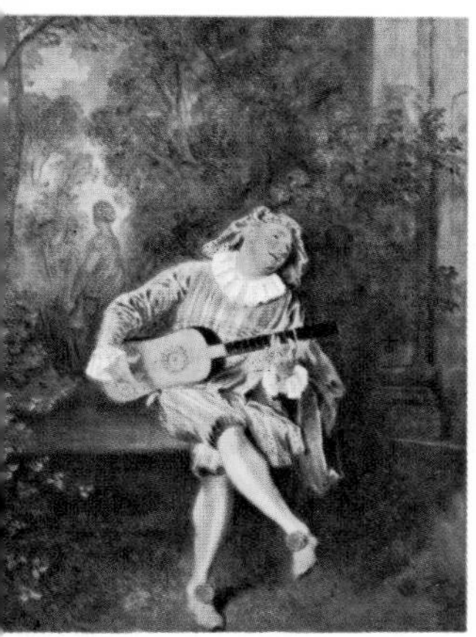

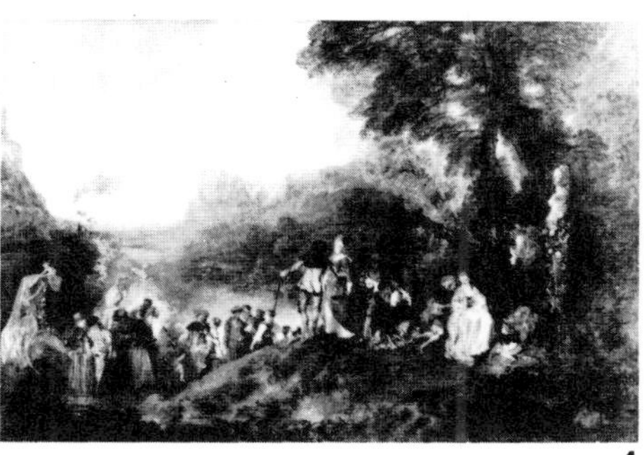

4

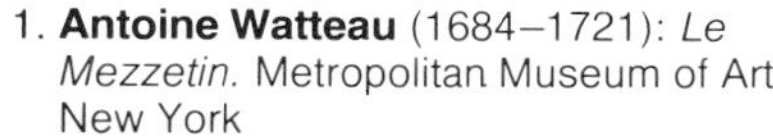

1. **Antoine Watteau** (1684–1721): *Le Mezzetin.* Metropolitan Museum of Art, New York
2. **Antoine Watteau** (1684–1721): *La Gamme d'Amour.* National Gallery, London
3. **Antoine Watteau** (1684–1721): *Le Gilles.* About 1718? Louvre, Paris
4. **Antoine Watteau** (1684–1721): *The Embarkation for Cythera.* 1717. Louvre, Paris
5. **Nicolas de Largillière** (1656–1746): *La belle Strasbourgeoise.* 1703. Musée des Beaux-Arts, Strasbourg
6. **Antoine Watteau** (1684–1721): *Les Champs-Élysées.* Between 1717 and 1719. Wallace Collection, London

5

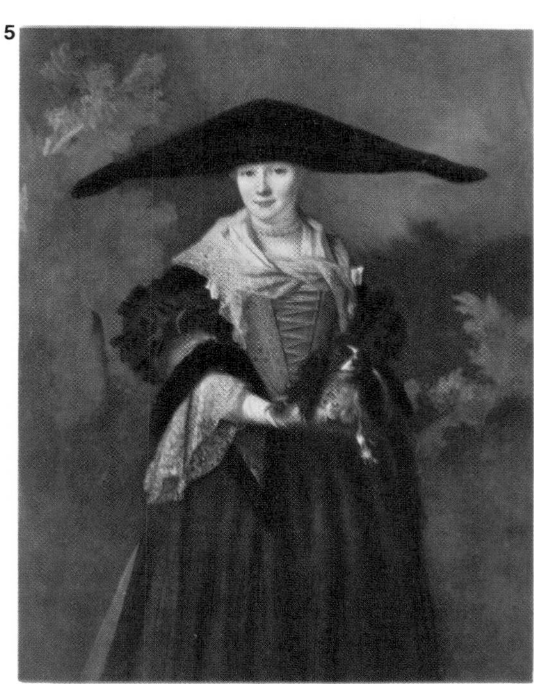

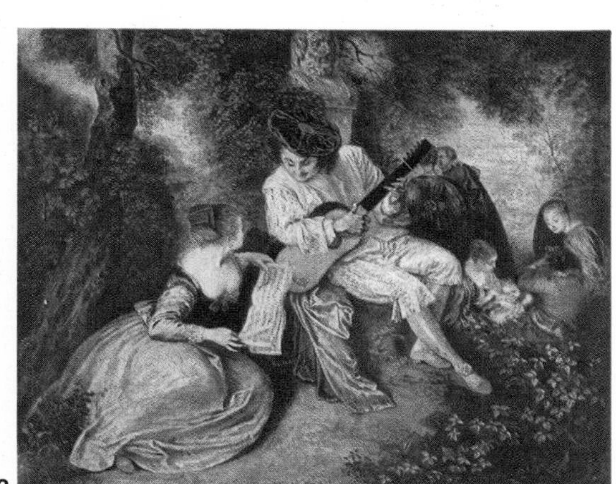

2

3

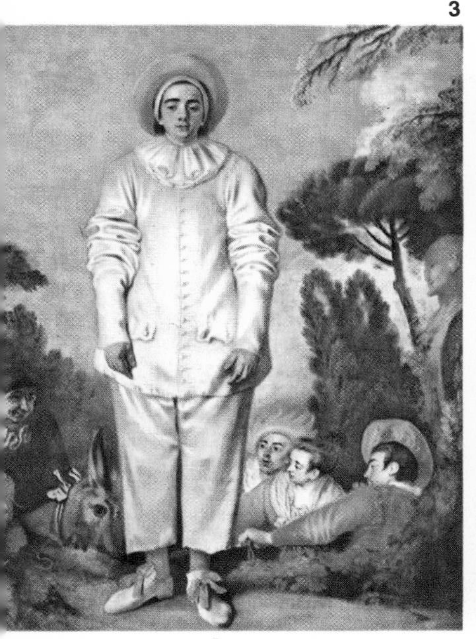

6

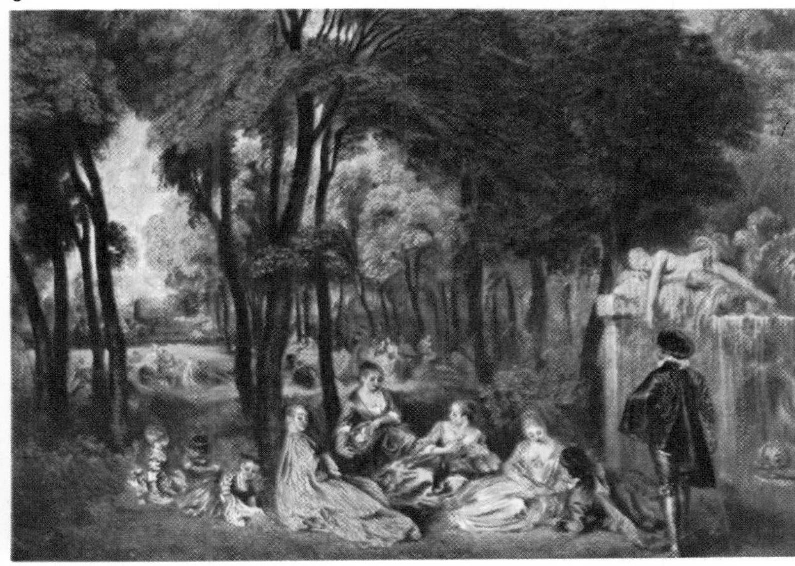

1. **Nicolas Lancret** (1690–1743): *The Music Lesson.* Louvre, Paris
2. **Philippe Mercier** (1689 or 1691–1760): *The Conjurer.* Louvre, Paris
3. **Jean-Baptiste Pater** (1695–1736): *Women bathing.* About 1735. Musée de Peinture et de Sculpture, Grenoble
4. **Jean-Baptiste Oudry** (1686–1755): *Swans and a Dog.* 1731. Musée d'Art et d'Histoire, Geneva
5. **Jean-Baptiste Oudry** (1686–1755): *Before the Fireplace: the lacquered Footstool.* Paul Cailleux Collection, Paris
6. **Jean-Marc Nattier** (1685–1766): *La Marquise d'Antin.* 1738. Musée Jacquemart-André, Paris

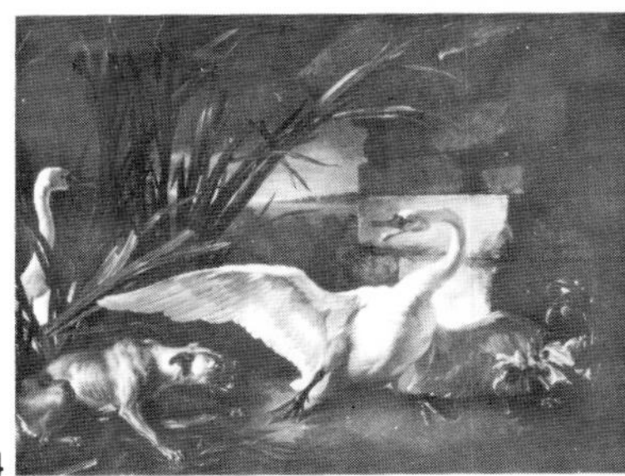
4

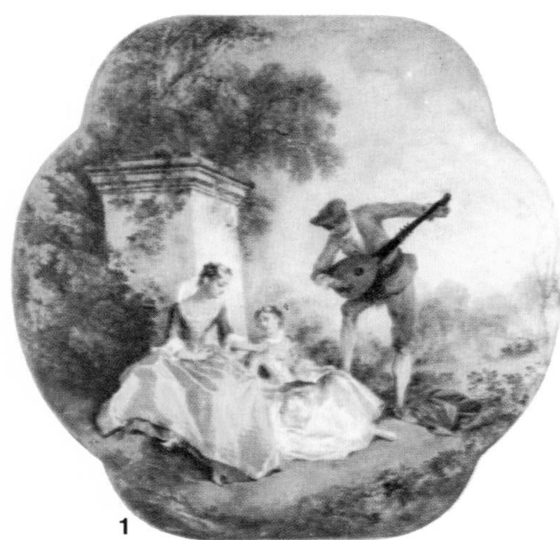
1

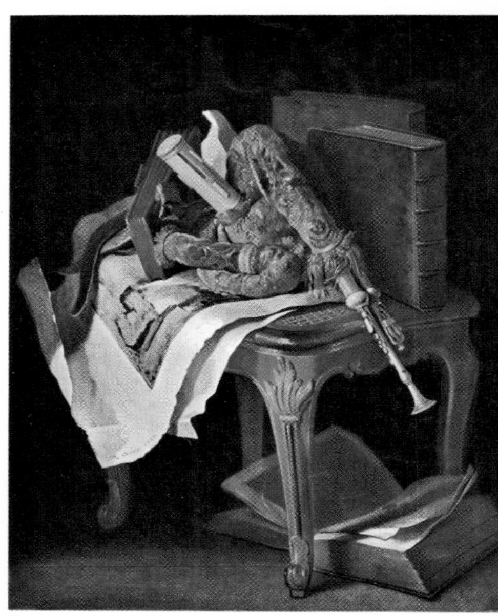
5

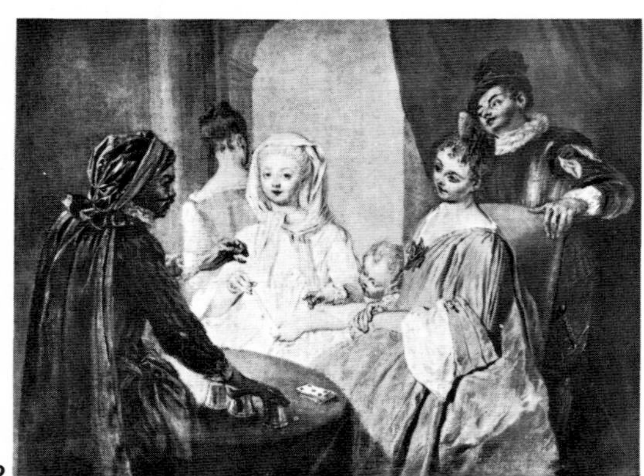
2

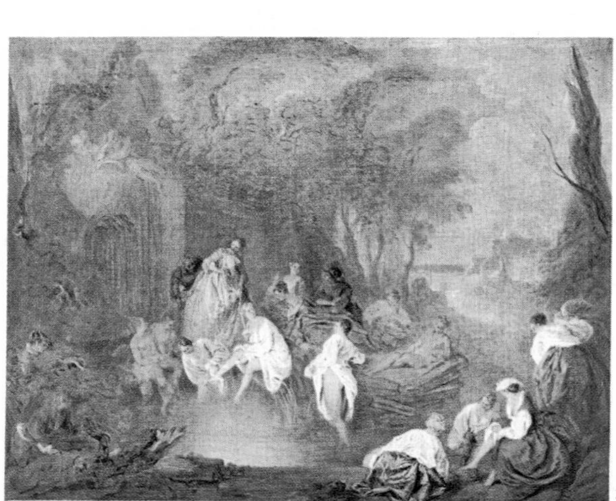
3

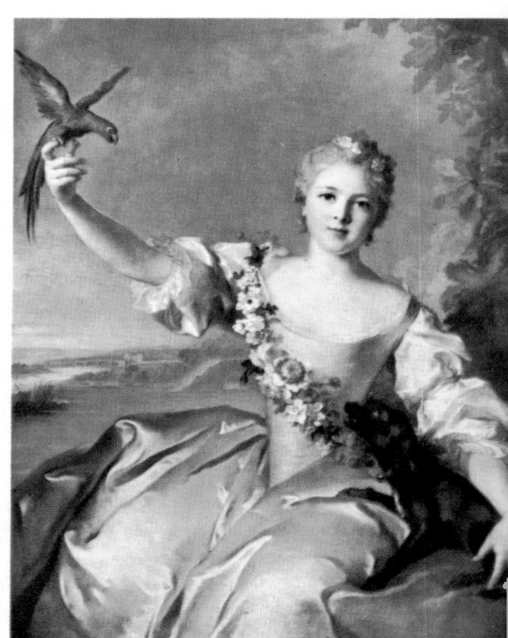

1. **Jean-Baptiste Greuze** (1725–1805): Detail from *The broken Pitcher.* About 1773. Louvre, Paris
2. **François Boucher** (1703–70): *La Marchande de Modes.* 1746. Nationalmuseum, Stockholm
3. **François Boucher** (1703–70): *Madame Bergeret.* 1746. National Gallery of Art (Samuel H. Kress Collection), Washington DC
4. **François Boucher** (1703–70): *Rustic Luncheon.* Detail from Beauvais tapestry
5. **Carle van Loo** (1705–65): *Sultana taking Coffee.* 1755. Musée des Arts Décoratifs, Paris
6. **François Boucher** (1703–70): *Louise O'Murphy.* 1752. Alte Pinakothek, Munich

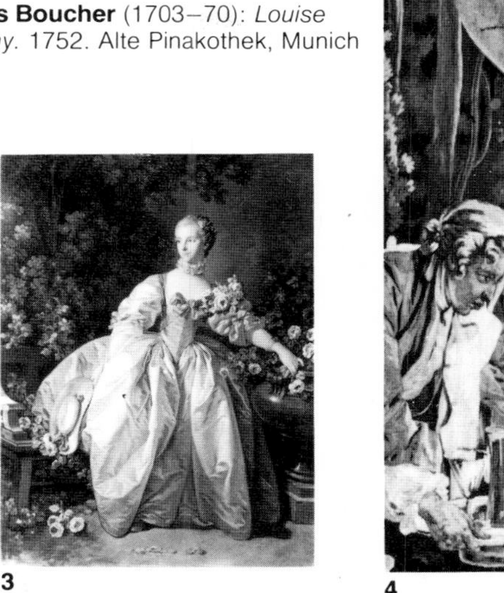

3

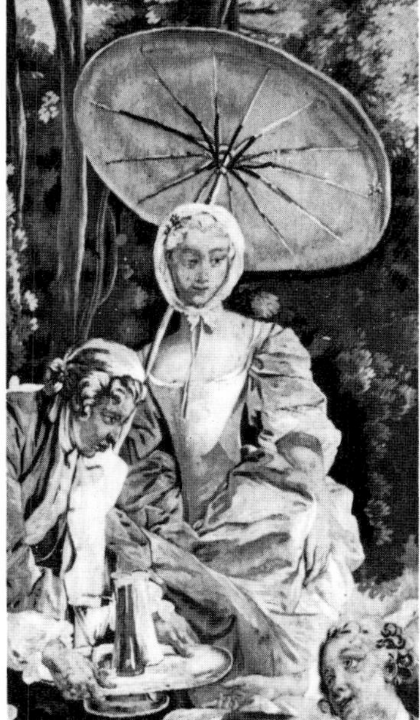

4

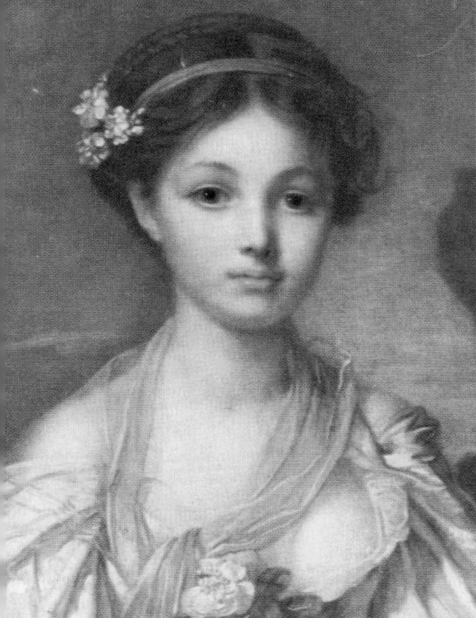

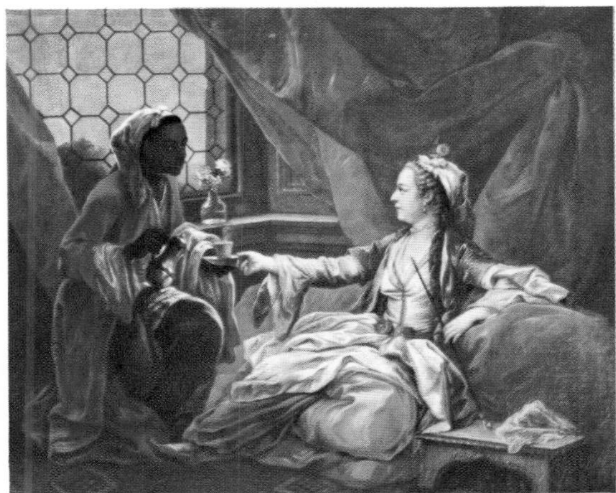

5

2

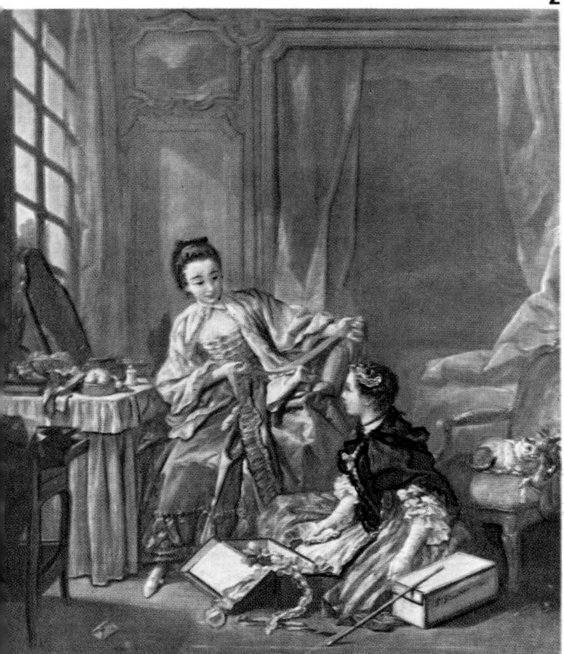

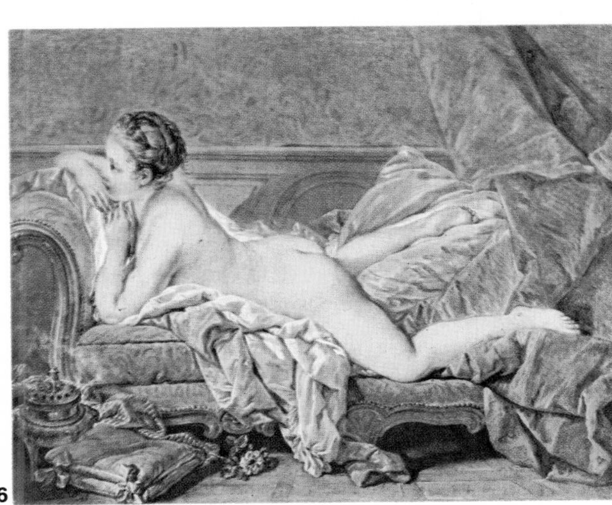

6

1. **Maurice-Quentin de La Tour** (1704–88): *Portrait of Madame de Pompadour.* 1755. Louvre, Paris
2. **Jean-Baptiste Perronneau** (1715?–1783): *Portrait of Abraham van Robais.* 1767. Louvre, Paris
3. **Claude-Joseph Vernet** (1714–89): *The Ponte Rotto.* 1745. Louvre, Paris
4. **Elisabeth-Louise Vigée-Lebrun** (1755–1842): *Self-portrait.* About 1791. Uffizi, Florence
5. **Hubert Robert** (1733–1808): *Project for the rearrangement of the Grande Galerie of the Louvre.* About 1796. Louvre, Paris
6. **Alexandre Roslin** (1718–93): *Lady with a Fan.* 1768. Nationalmuseum, Stockholm

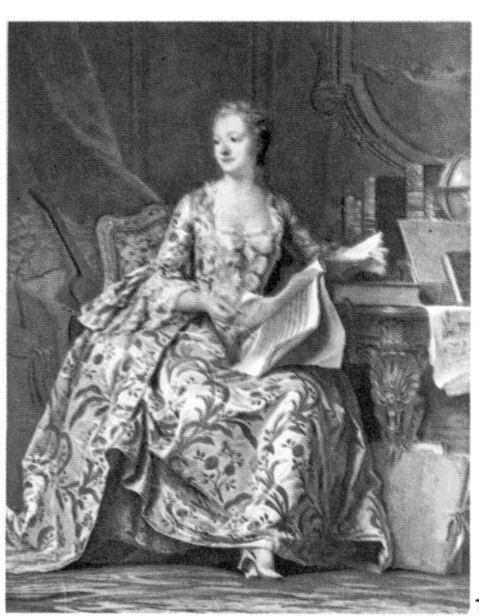
1

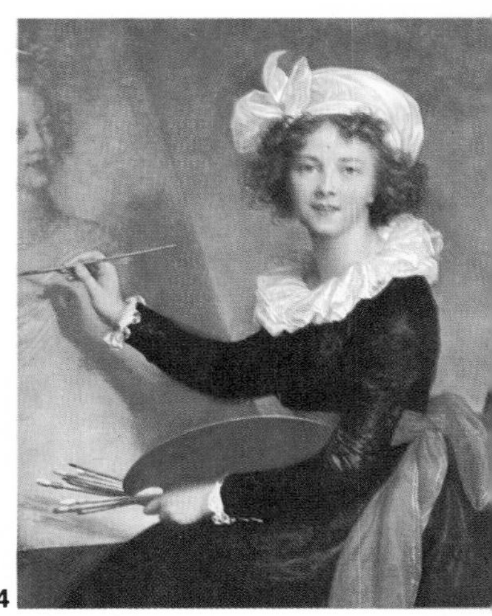
4

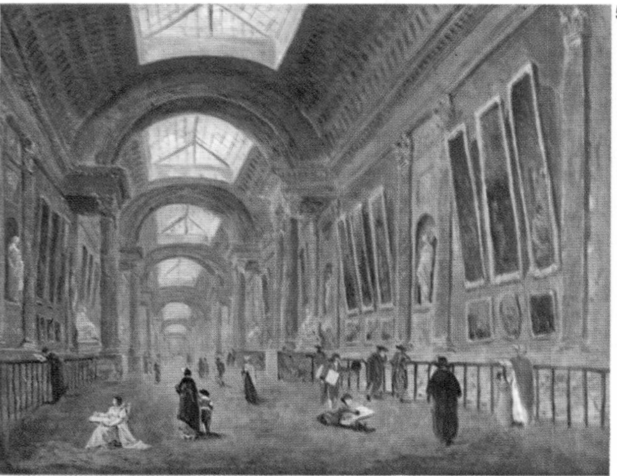
5

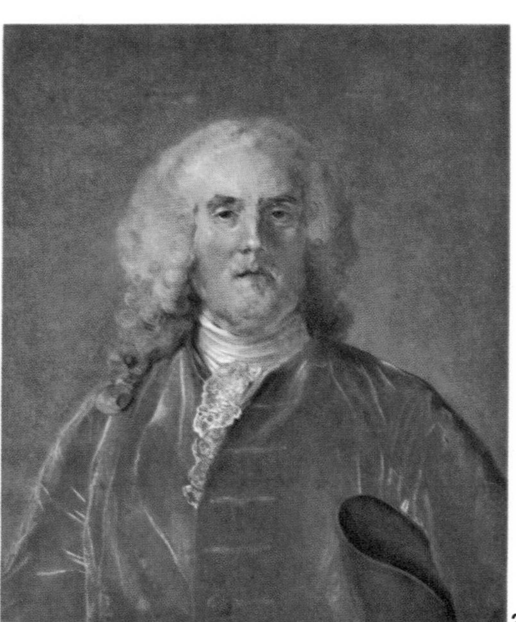
2

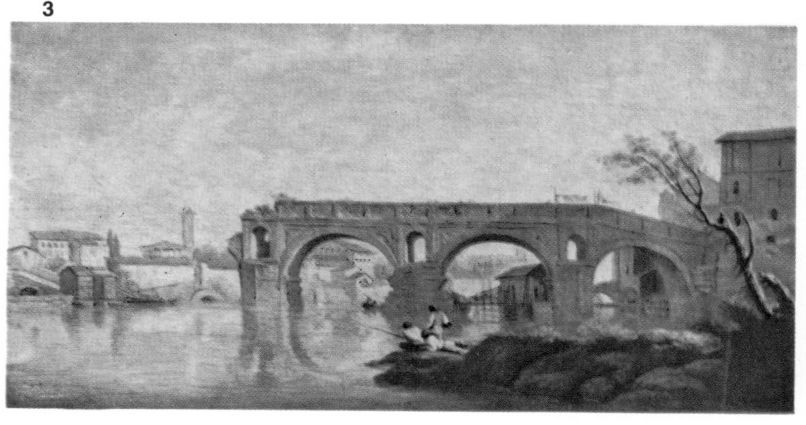
3

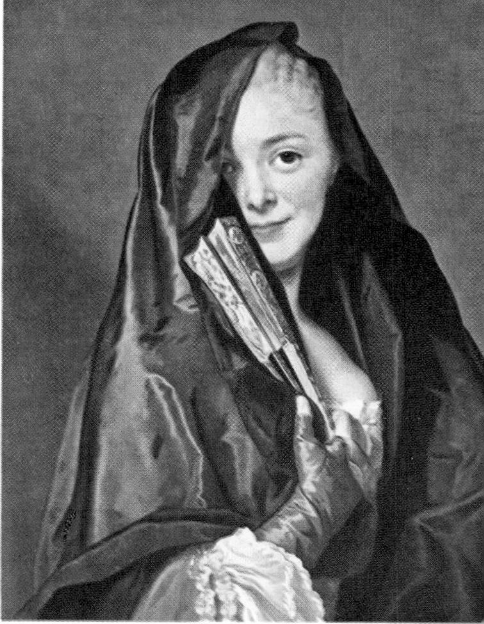

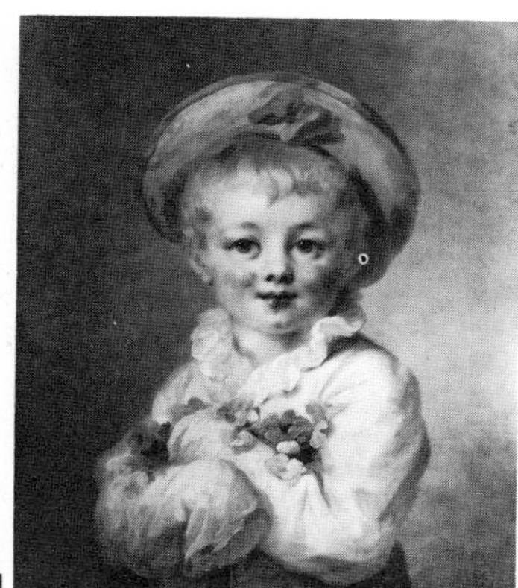

1

Jean-Honoré Fragonard (1732–1806)

1. *A Boy as Pierrot.* 1789–91. Wallace Collection, London
2. *The Useless Resistance* or *The Surprise.* Nationalmuseum, Stockholm
3. *Women bathing.* 1775. Louvre, Paris
4. *The Swing.* About 1768. Wallace Collection, London
5. *Blindman's Buff.* About 1775. National Gallery of Art (Samuel H. Kress Collection), Washington DC
6. *The Reader.* Private Collection, New York

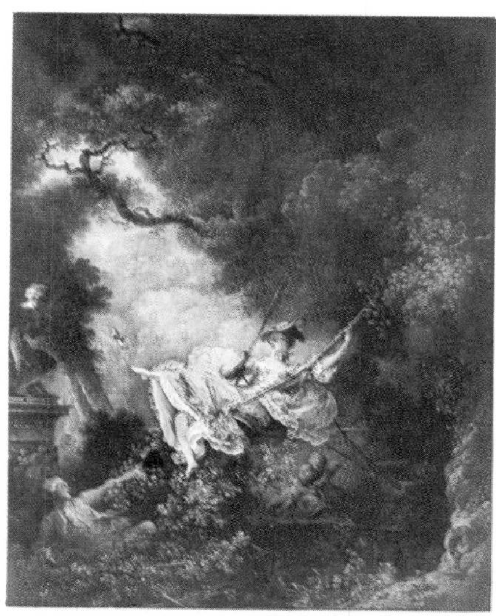

4

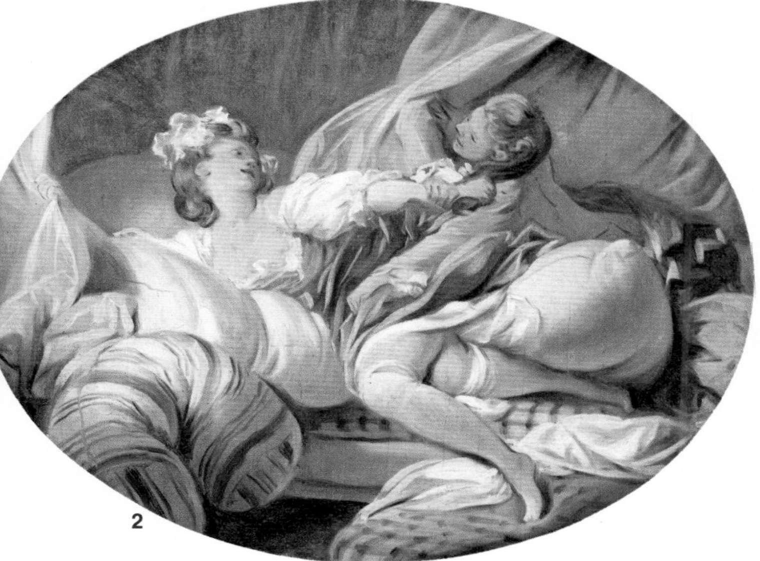

2

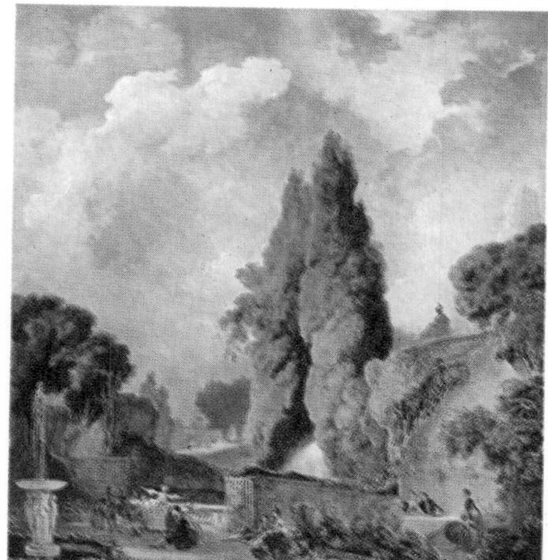

5

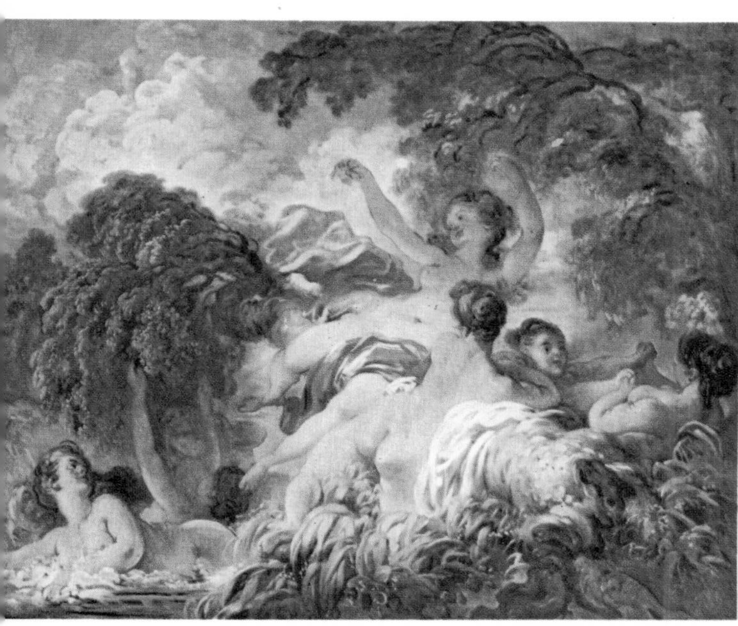

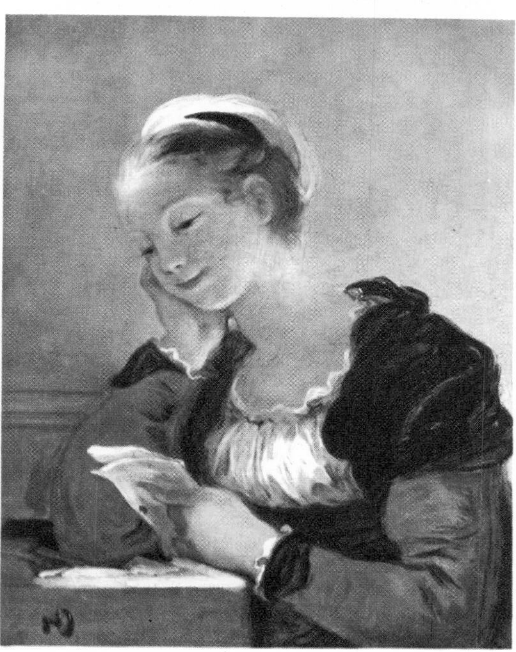

6

Jacques-Louis David (1748–1825)
1. *The Sabines.* 1799. Louvre, Paris
2. *The Death of Marat.* 1793. Musées Royaux des Beaux-Arts, Brussels
3. *Portrait of Madame Sériziat.* 1795. Louvre, Paris
4. *Napoleon crossing the Alps.* 1801. Museum, Versailles
5. *The Oath of the Horatii.* 1784. Louvre, Paris

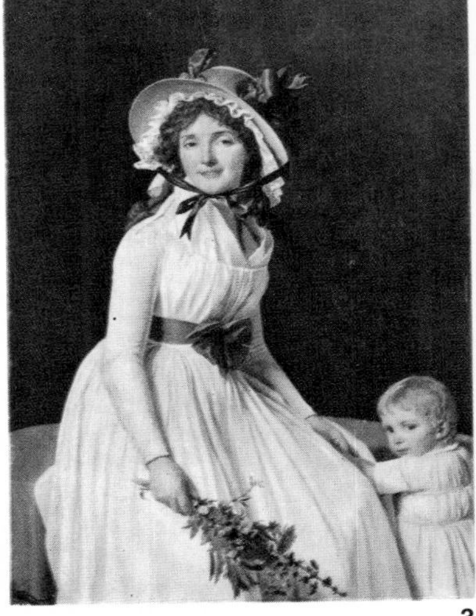

3

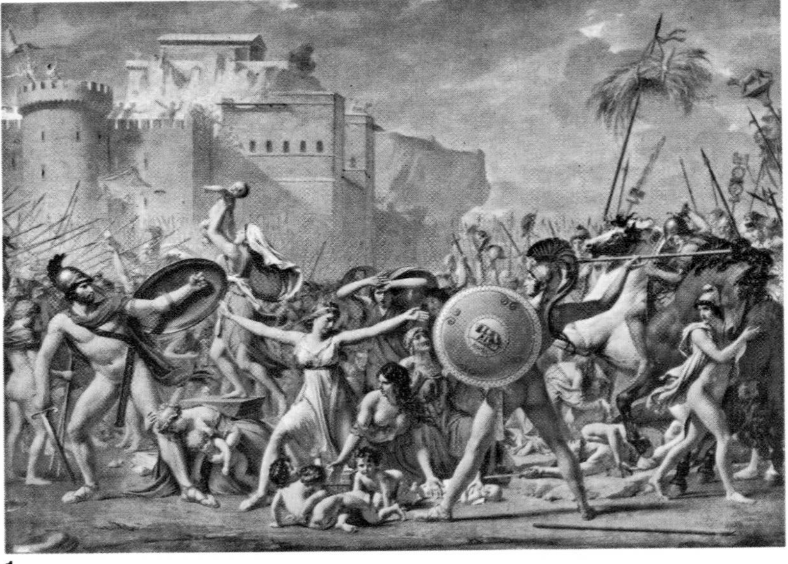

1

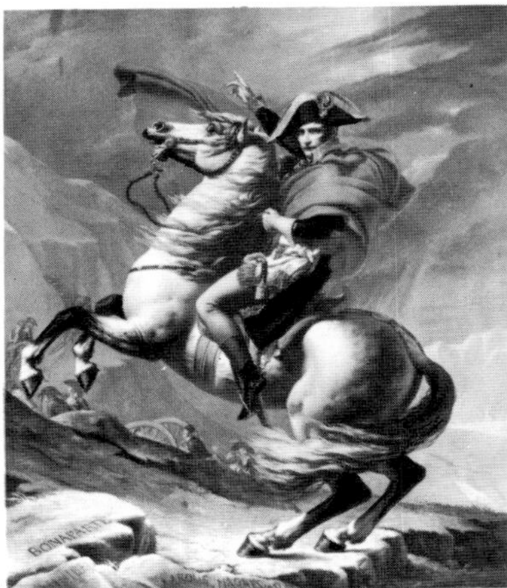

4

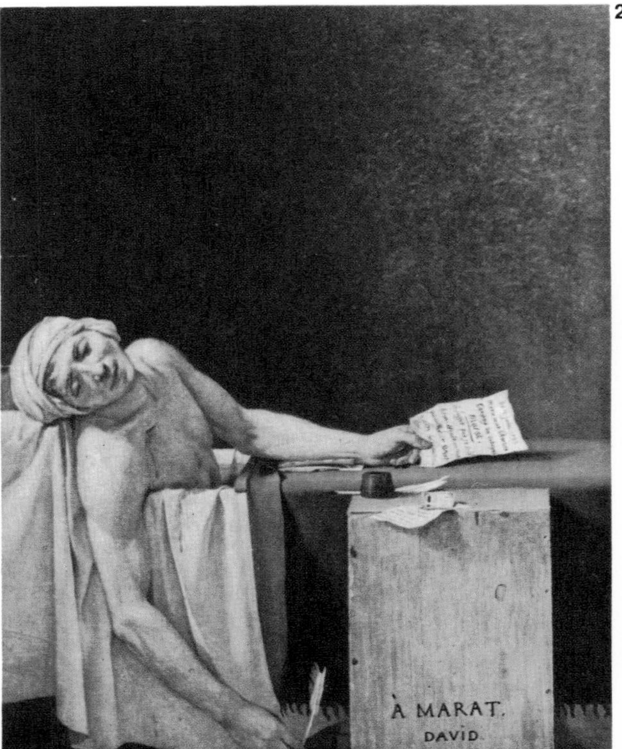

2

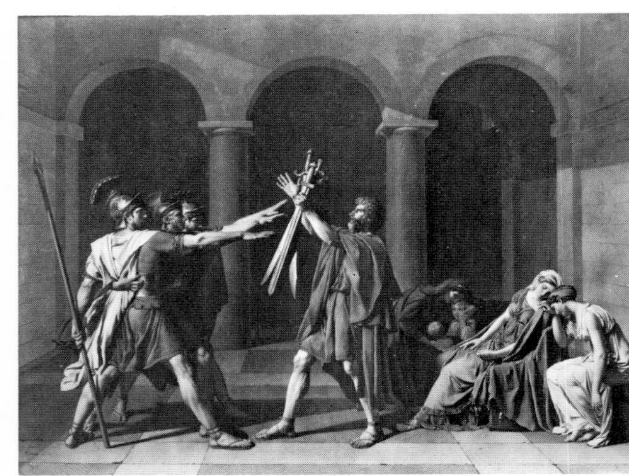

5

1

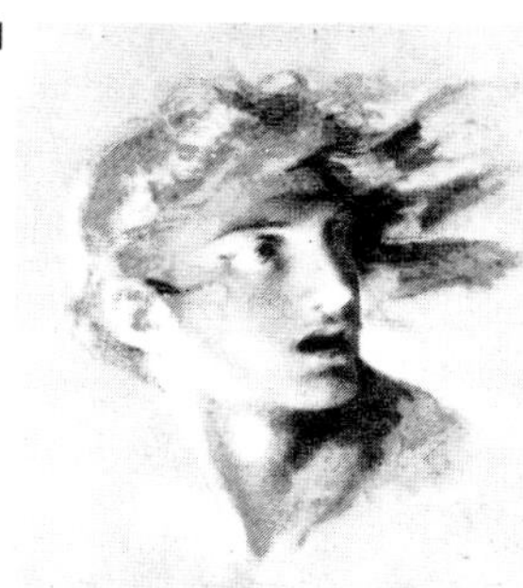

1. **Pierre-Paul Prud'hon** (1758–1823): Study for *Justice and Divine Vengeance pursuing Crime*. Pencil. About 1808. Art Institute of Chicago
2. **Pierre-Paul Prud'hon** (1758–1823): *Portrait of Empress Josephine*. 1805. Louvre, Paris
3. **Pierre-Alexandre Vignon** (1763–1828): Church of La Madeleine, Paris. Begun 1806
4. **Anne-Louis Girodet-Trioson** (1767–1824): *The Entombment of Atala*. 1808. Louvre, Paris
5. **Charles Percier** (1764–1838) and **Pierre Fontaine** (1762–1853): Arc de Triomphe du Carrousel, Paris. 1806–7
6. **Baron Antoine-Jean Gros** (1771–1835): *Napoleon on the Battlefield at Eylau*. Detail. 1808. Louvre, Paris

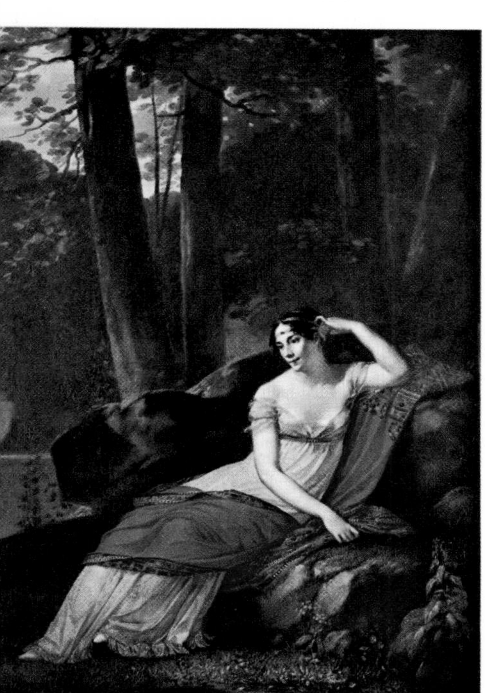

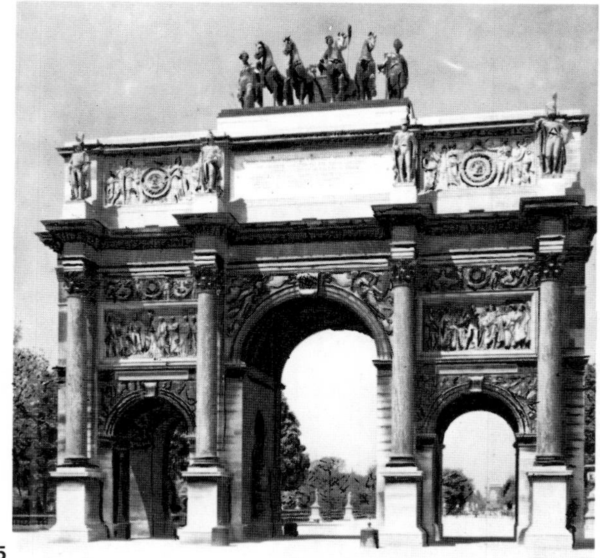

5

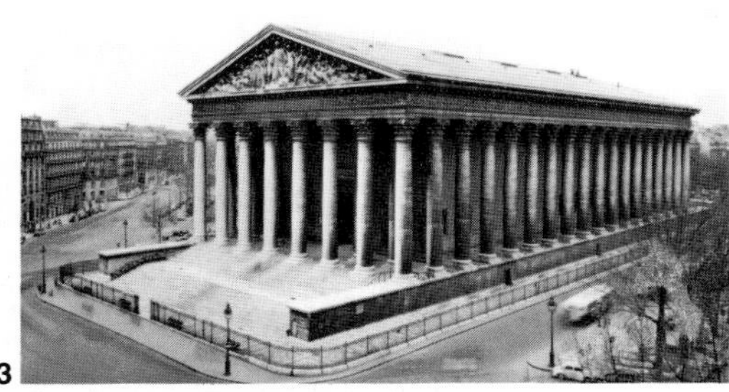

3

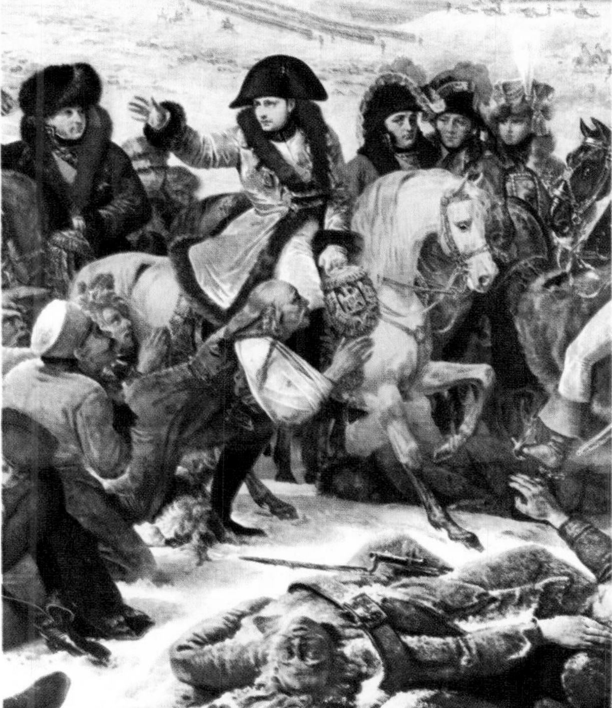

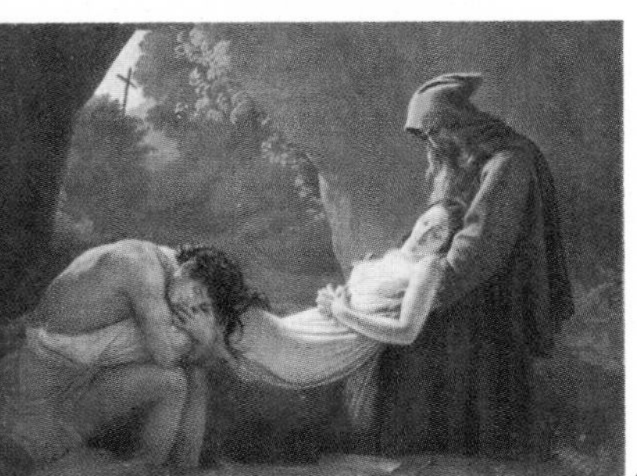

4

6

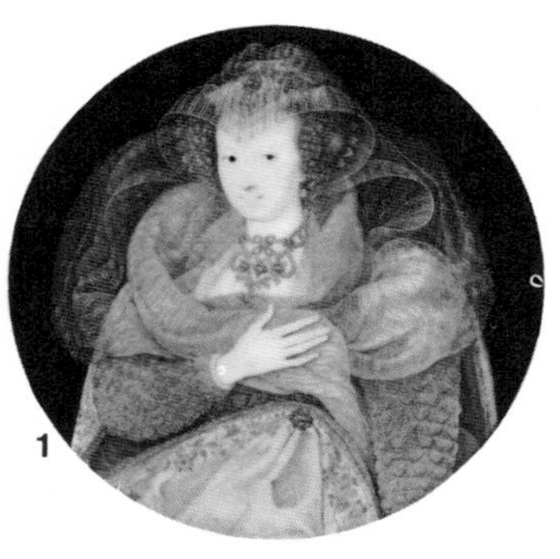

1. **Isaac Oliver** (d.1617): *Portrait of Frances Howard, Countess of Essex and Somerset.* About 1595. Earl of Derby Collection, Knowsley Hall
2. **Nicholas Hilliard** (*c.*1547–1619): *An unknown Man against a Background of Flames.* Victoria and Albert Museum, London
3. **Isaac Oliver** (d.1617): *Portrait of a young Man (Sir Philip Sidney?).* Royal Collection. Reproduced by gracious permission of Her Majesty The Queen
4. **Sir Peter Lely** (1618–80): *Two Ladie the Lake Family.* About 1660. Tate Gall London
5. **Samuel Cooper** (1609–72): *Portrait c Thomas Alcock.* Drawing. Ashmolean Museum, Oxford
6. **Nicholas Hilliard** (*c.*1547–1619): *A yo Man leaning against a Tree.* About 158 Victoria and Albert Museum, London

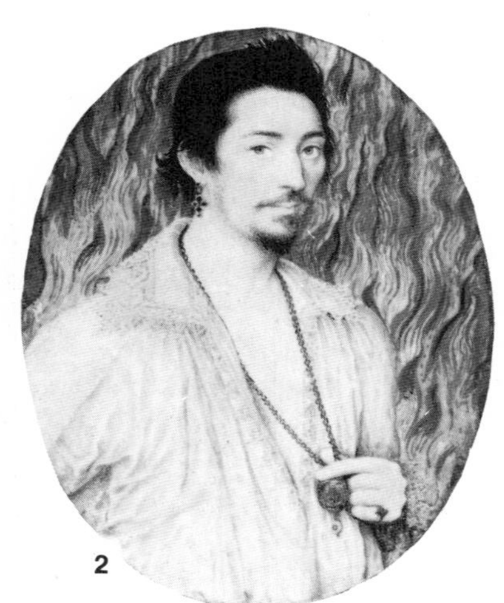

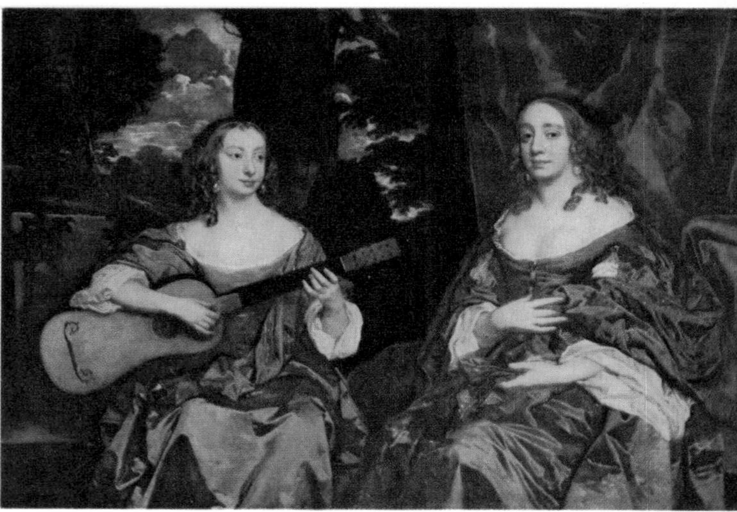

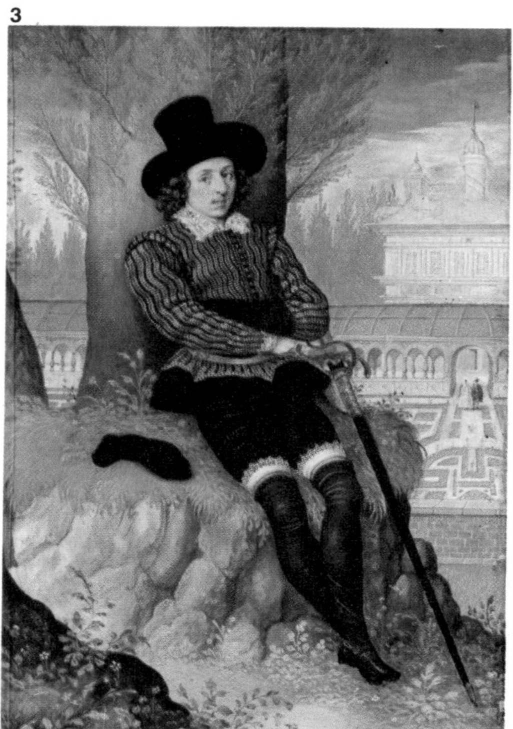

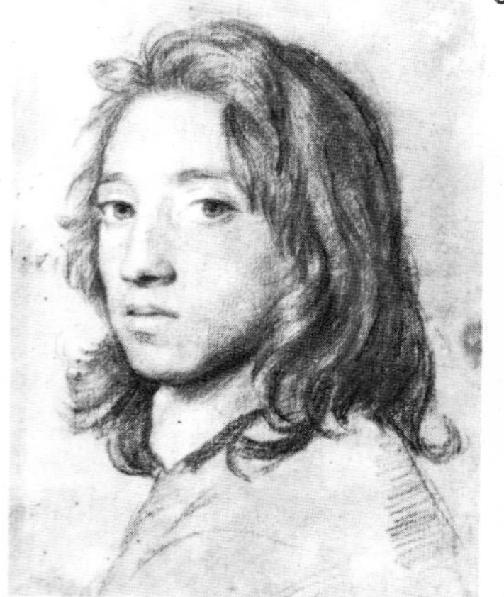

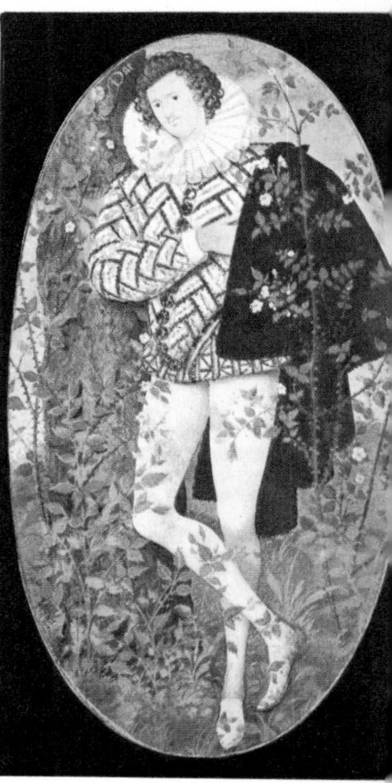

Inigo Jones (1573–1652): The Banqueting House, Whitehall, London. Interior view (with ceiling paintings by Rubens). 1619–22

Inigo Jones (1573–1652): The Banqueting House, Whitehall, London. Exterior view. 1619–22

3. **Sir Christopher Wren** (1632–1723): Church of St Stephen Walbrook, London. 1672–9
4. **Inigo Jones** (1573–1652): The Queen's House (now the National Maritime Musuem), Greenwich. 1616–35
5. **Sir Christopher Wren** (1632–1723): St Paul's Cathedral, London. 1675–1709

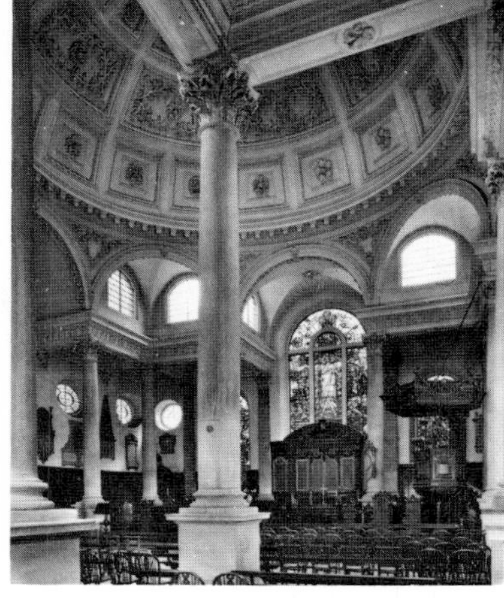

3

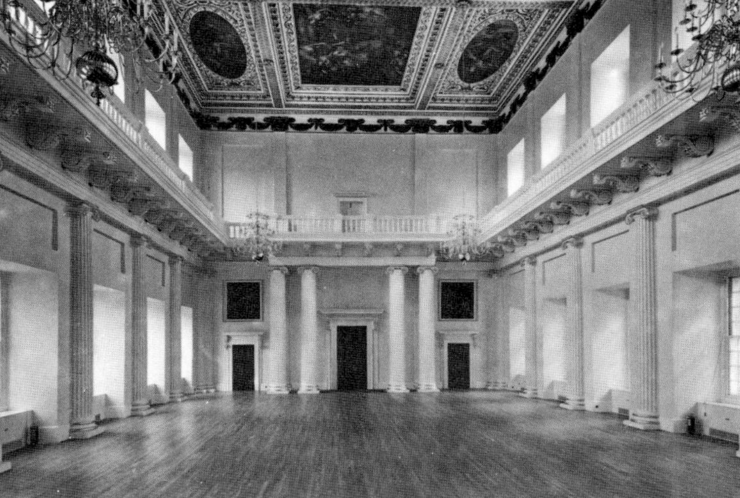

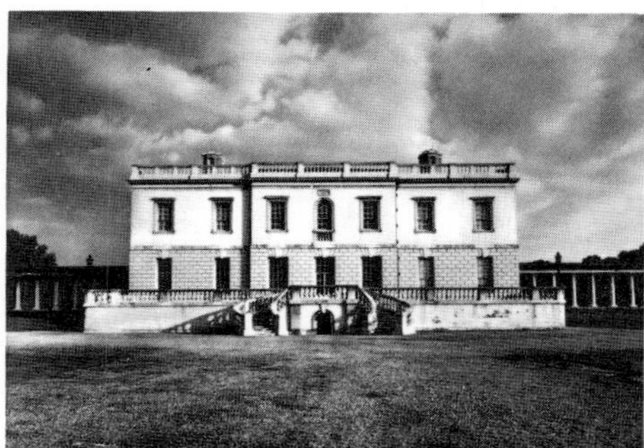

4

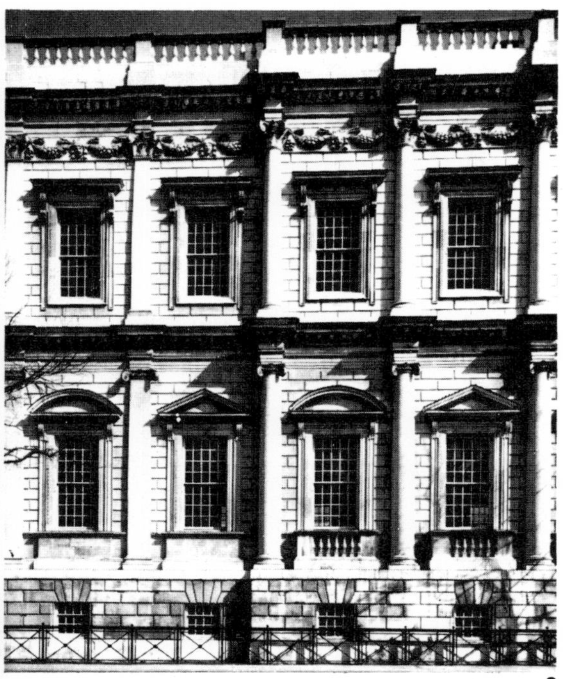

2

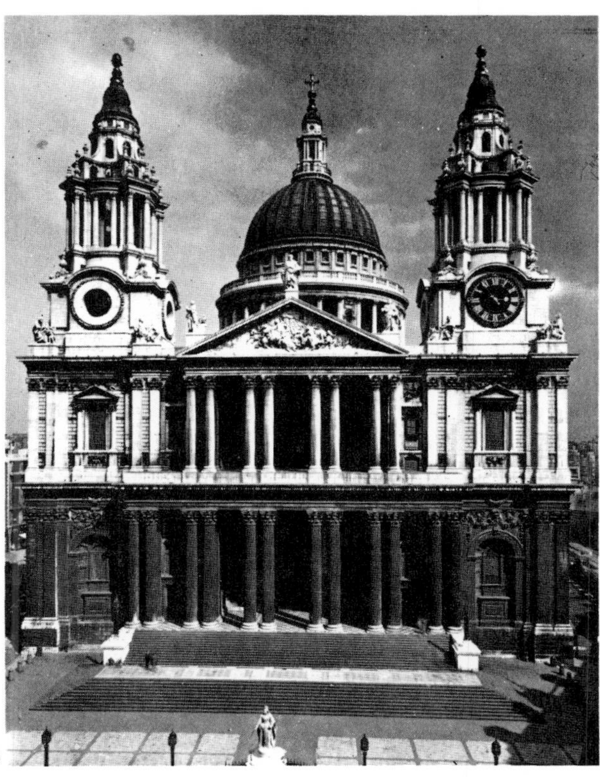

5

1. **Sir John Vanbrugh** (1664–1726): Cas Howard, Yorkshire. 1699–1726
2. **William Kent** (1685–1748): Holkham H Norfolk. Begun 1734
3. **Nicholas Hawksmoor** (1661–1736): Mausoleum at Castle Howard, Yorkshir 1729–36
4. **James Gibbs** (1682–1754): Senate House, Cambridge. 1722–30
5. **Sir William Chambers** (1723–96): Pag in Kew Gardens, Surrey. 1763

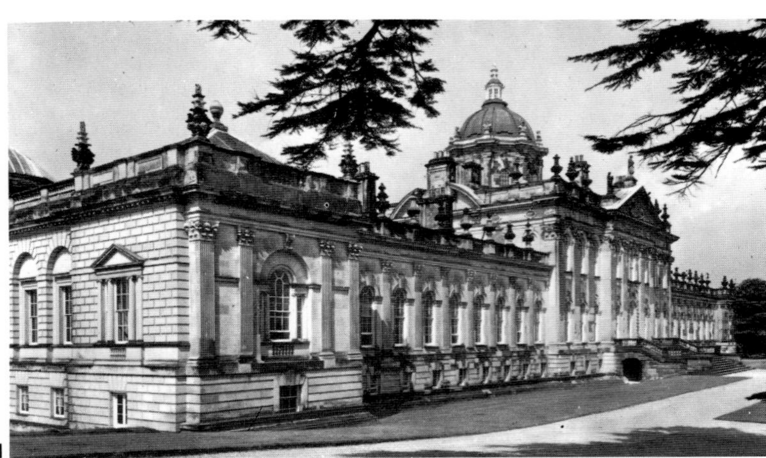

1

2

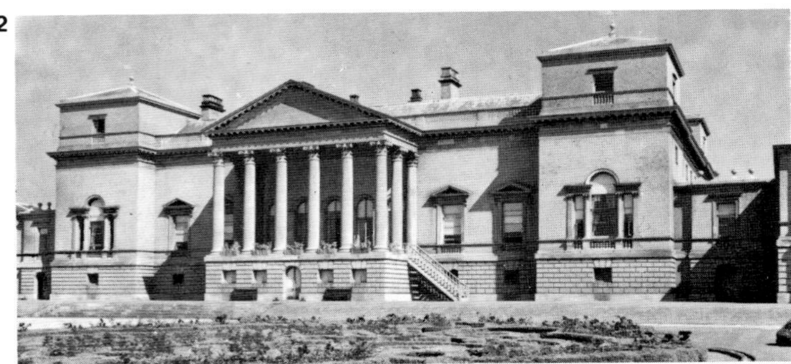

3

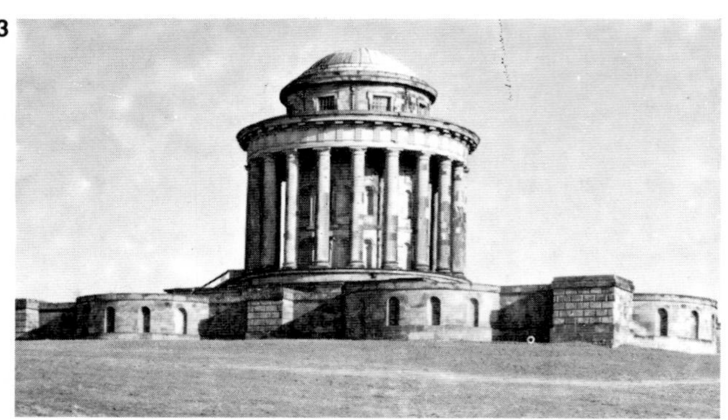

4

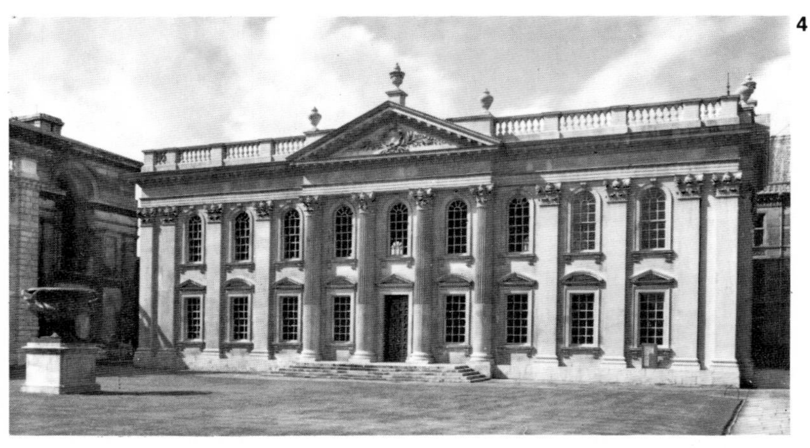

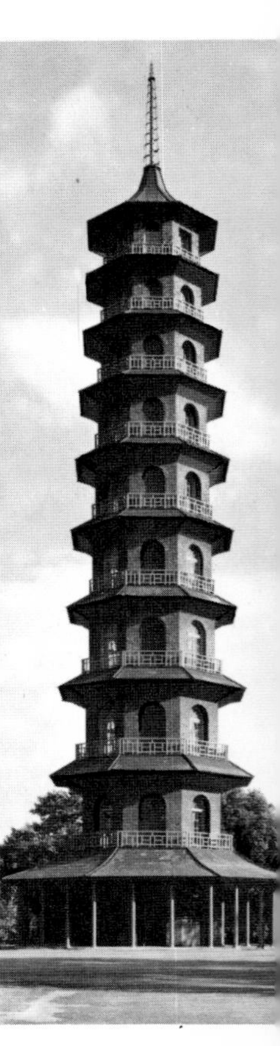

5

ames Wyatt (1746–1813)
Bowden Park, Wiltshire. South façade
obert Adam (1728–92)
Staircase, Osterley Park, Middlesex. After 1761
Entrance hall, Osterley Park, Middlesex. Remodelled 1761–80
4. with his brothers: No. 7 Adam Street, The Adelphi, London. 1768–72
5. Portico, Osterley Park. Remodelled 1761–80
6. Staircase, Home House (now the Courtauld Institute of Art), London. 1775–7

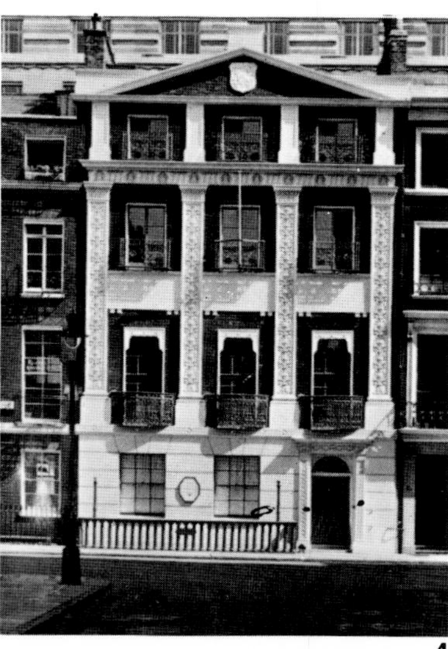

4

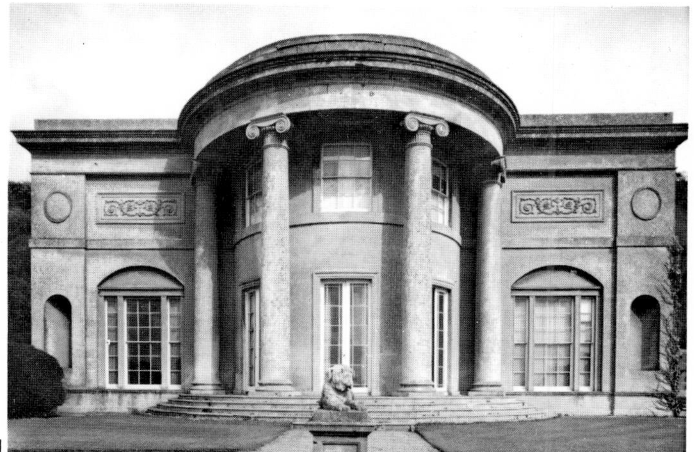

1

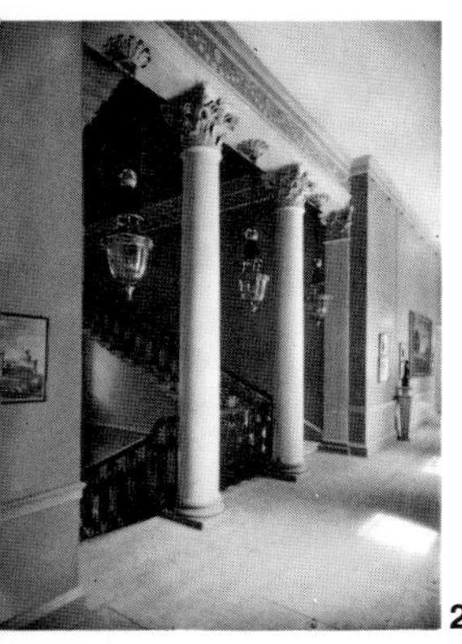

2

5

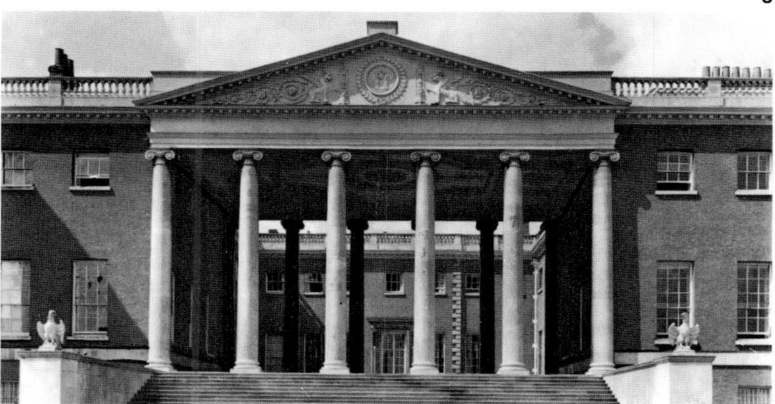

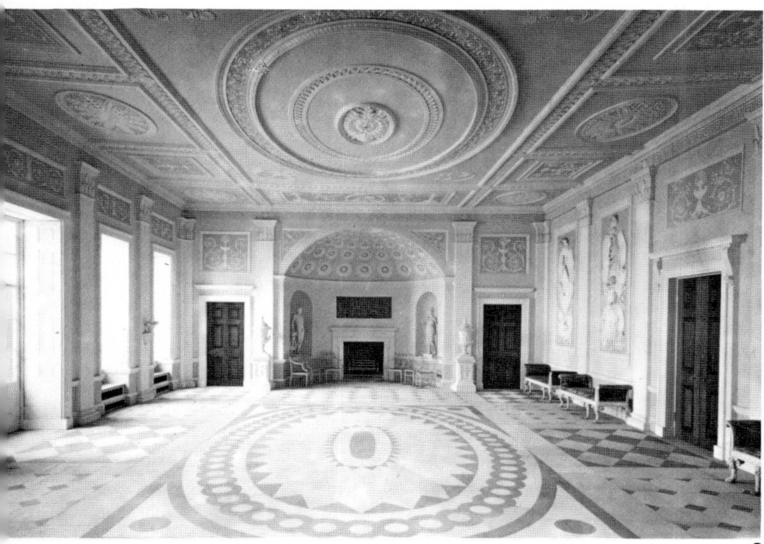

3

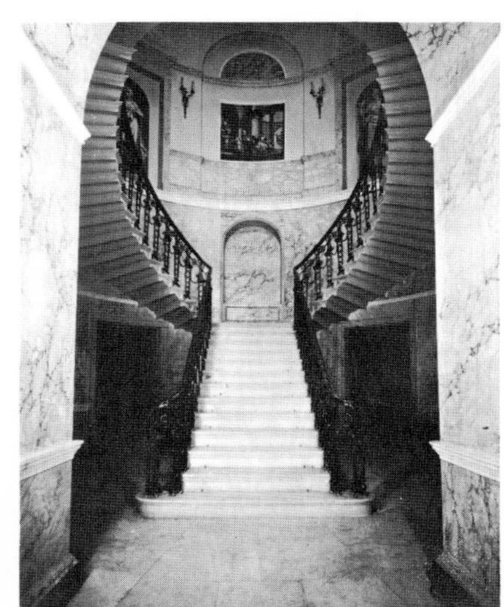

6

1. **Thomas Girtin** (1775–1802): *The White House, Chelsea.* Watercolour. 1800. Tate Gallery, London
2. **Thomas Rowlandson** (1756–1827): *Drawing Class from the living Model, at the Royal Academy, London.* Engraving. About 1808
3. **Samuel Scott** (*c.*1702–72): The Thames at Deptford. Tate Gallery, London
4. **Sir Godfrey Kneller** (1646–1723): *Portrait of Sir Christopher Wren.* 1711. National Portrait Gallery, London
5. **James Gillray** (1756–1815): *Dido in Despair.* Etching. 1801
6. **Allan Ramsay** (1713–84): *Portrait of Jean-Jacques Rousseau in Armenian Costume.* 1766. National Gallery of Scotland, Edinburgh

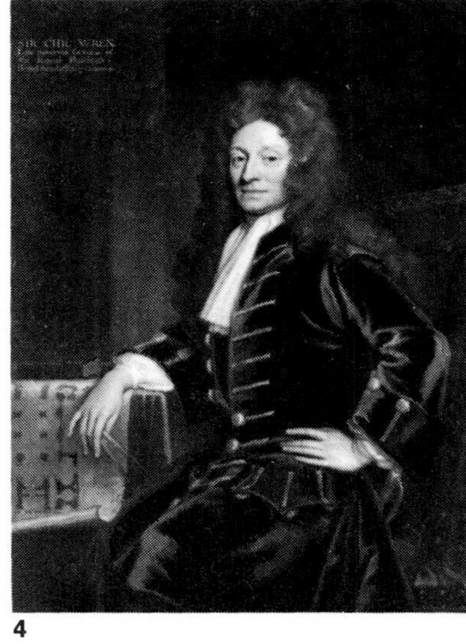

4

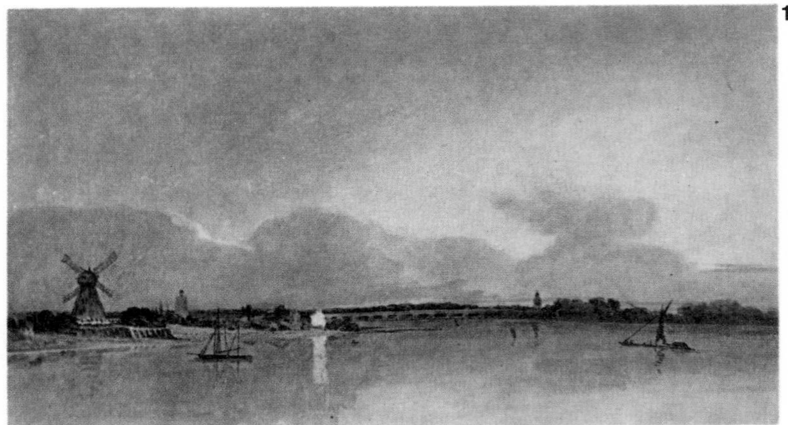

1

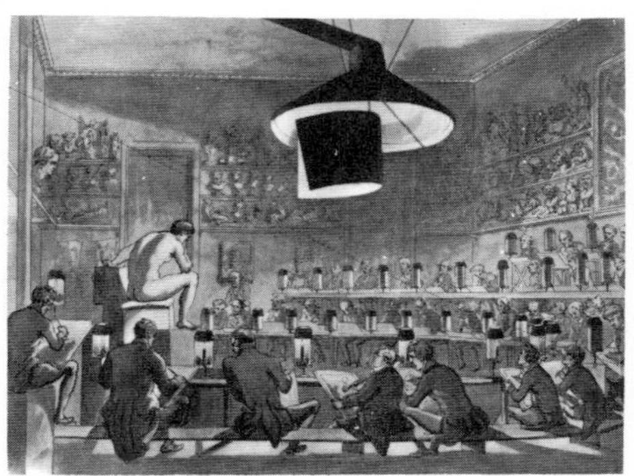

2

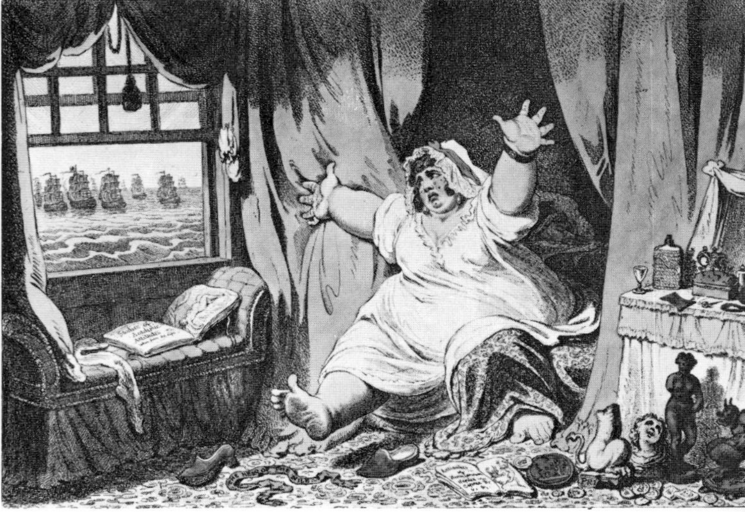

3

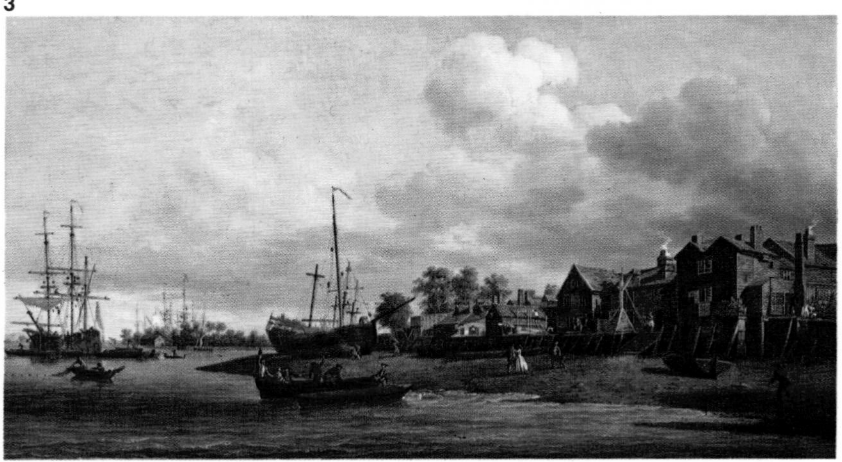

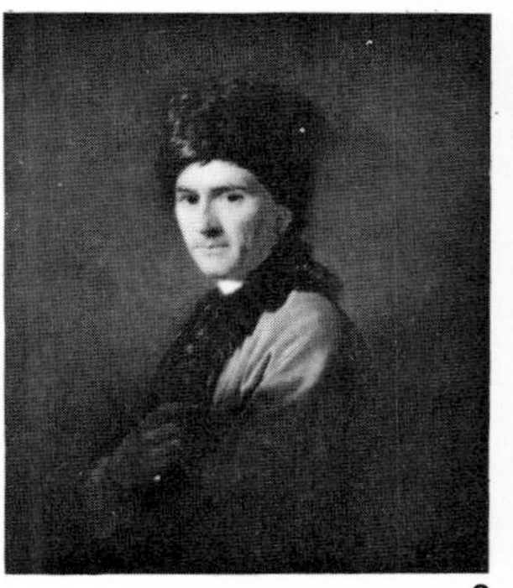

6

1. **Richard Wilson** (1714–82): *Llyn-y-Cau, Cader Idris.* 1774? Tate Gallery, London
2. **William Marlow** (1740–1813): *Capriccio: St Paul's Cathedral and a Venetian Canal.* About 1795? Tate Gallery, London
3. **John Crome** (1768–1821): *Slate Quarries.* About 1802–5. Tate Gallery, London
4. **Joseph Wright of Derby** (1734–97): *Experiment with the Air Pump.* About 1768. Tate Gallery, London
5. **Arthur Devis** (1711–87): *The James Family.* 1751. Tate Gallery, London

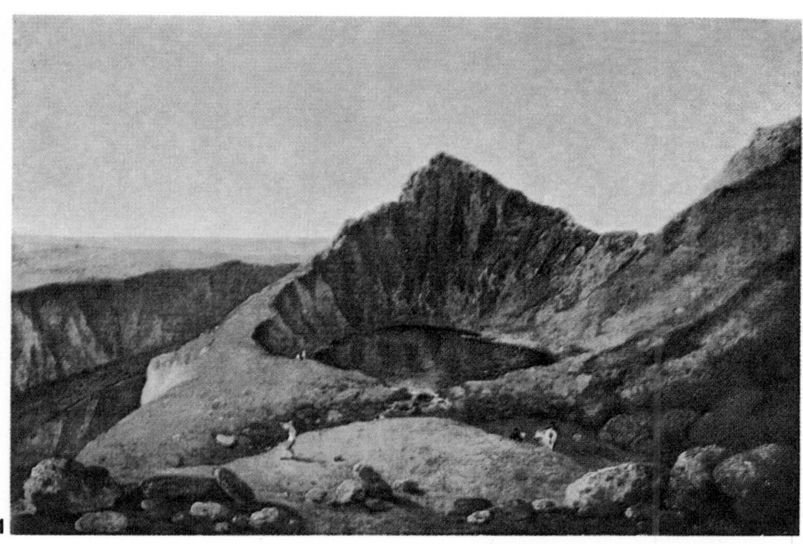

1

2

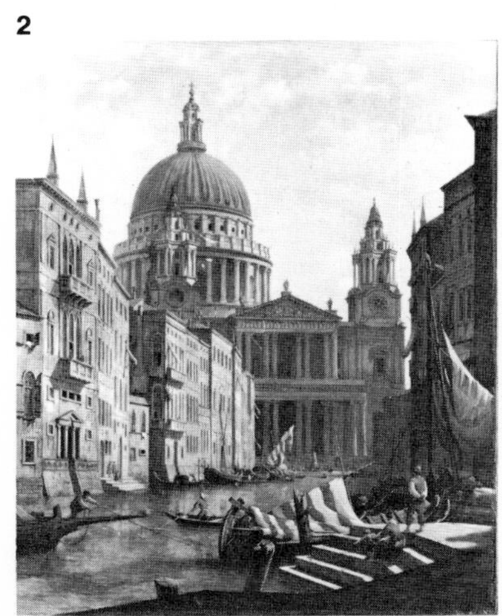

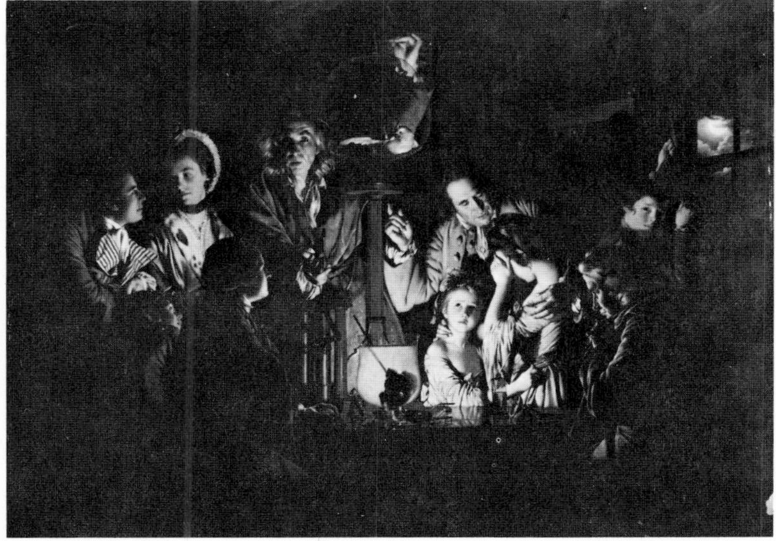

4

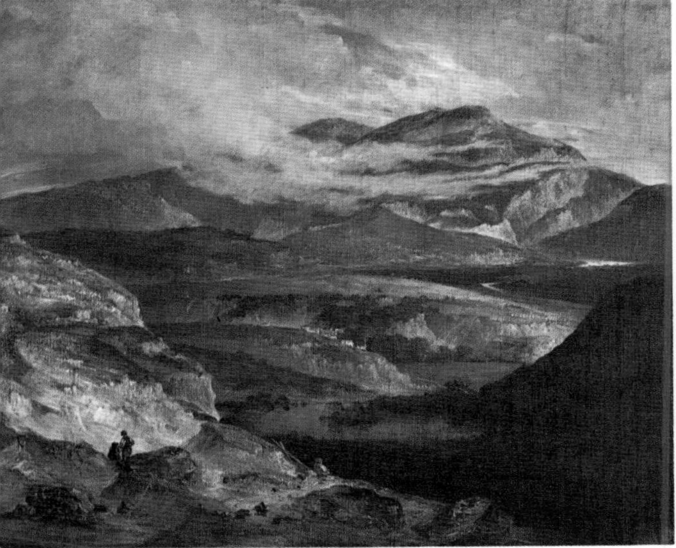

3

5

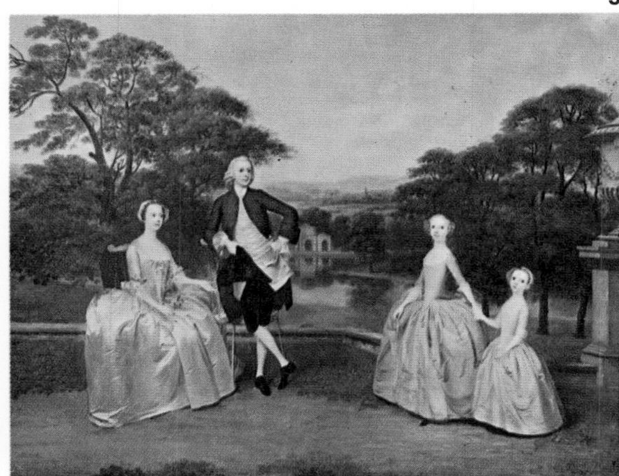

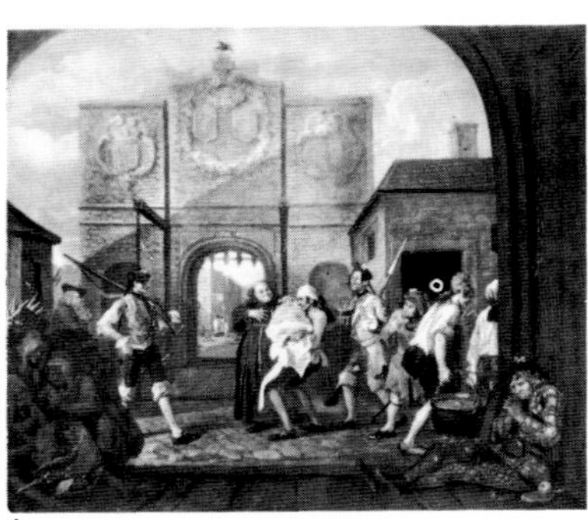
1

1. **William Hogarth** (1697–1764): *The Roast Beef of Old England* (*Calais Gate*). 1748–9. Tate Gallery, London
2. **George Stubbs** (1724–1806): *Mares and Foals in a Landscape.* 1763–8. Tate Gallery, London
3. **William Hogarth** (1697–1764): *The Shrimp Girl.* National Gallery, London
4. **William Hogarth** (1697–1764): *Heads of Six of the Artist's Servants.* About 1750–5. Tate Gallery, London
5. **George Stubbs** (1724–1806): *A Lady and a Gentleman in a Carriage.* 1787. National Gallery, London

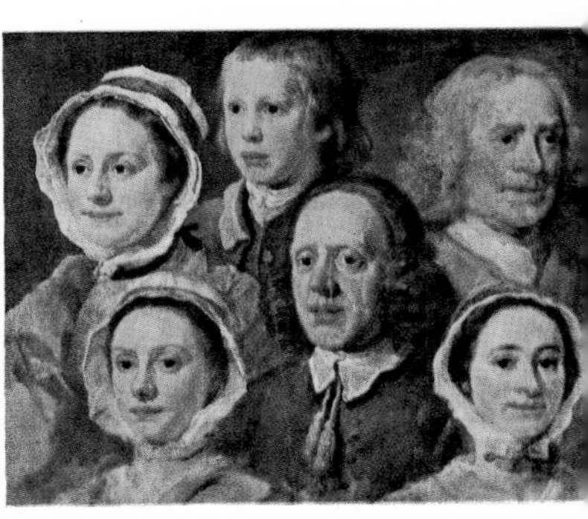

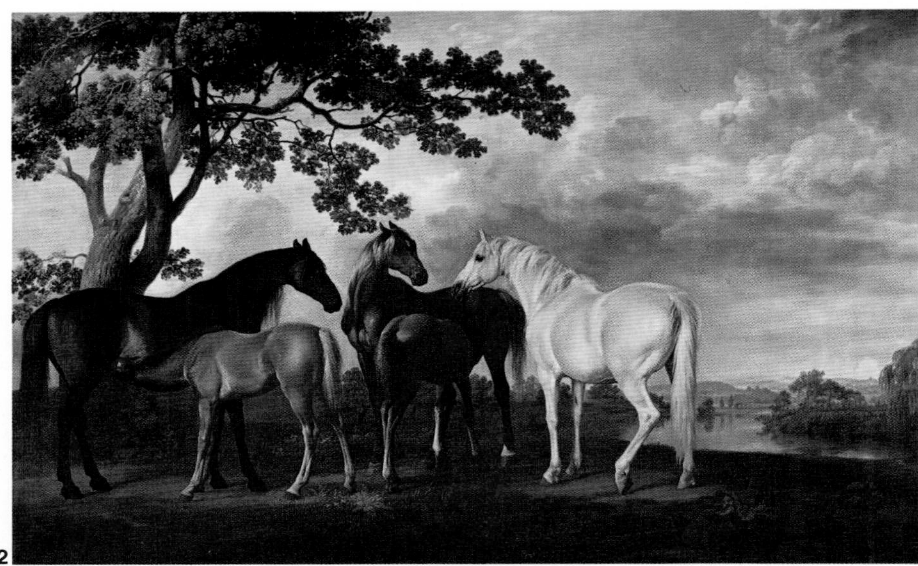
2

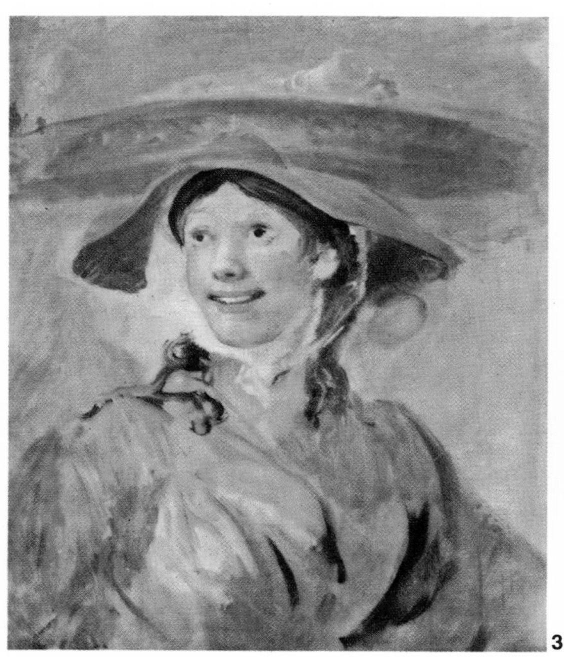
3

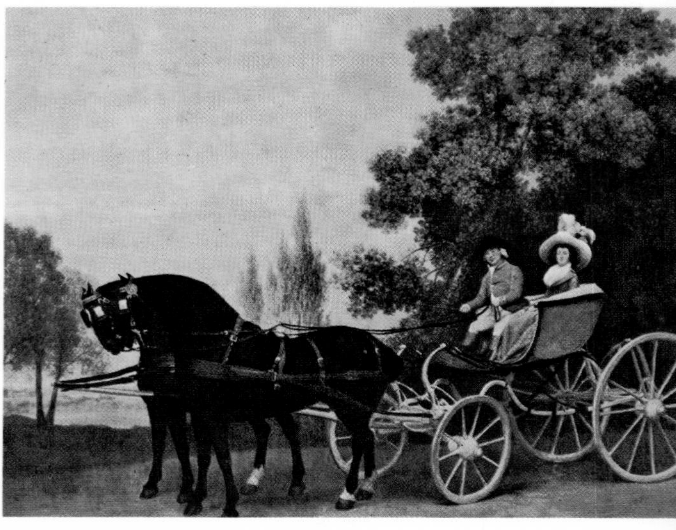

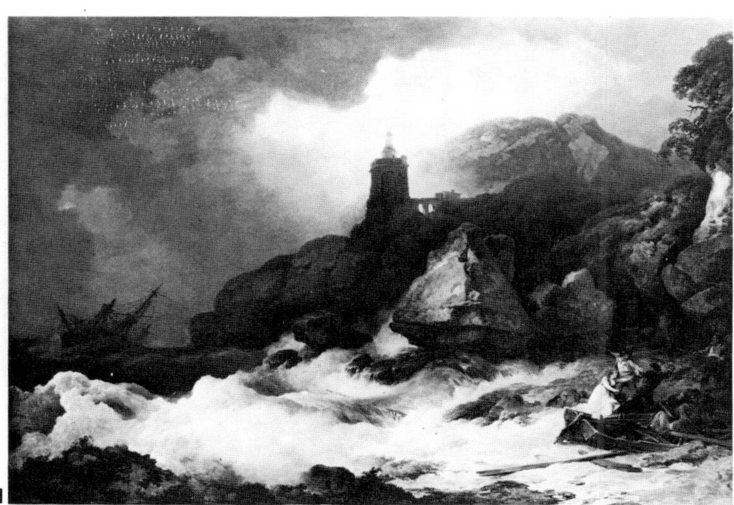

1. **Philip James de Loutherbourg** (1740–1812): *The Shipwreck.* 1793. Southampton Art Gallery
2. **Francis Wheatley** (1747–1801): *Lord Spencer Hamilton.* About 1778. Royal Collection. Reproduced by gracious permission of Her Majesty The Queen
3. **Johann Zoffany** (1733–1810): *Queen Charlotte with her two eldest Sons.* About 1794. Royal Collection. Reproduced by gracious permission of Her Majesty The Queen
4. **George Lambert** (1700–65): *Hilly Landscape with a Cornfield.* 1733. Tate Gallery, London

1

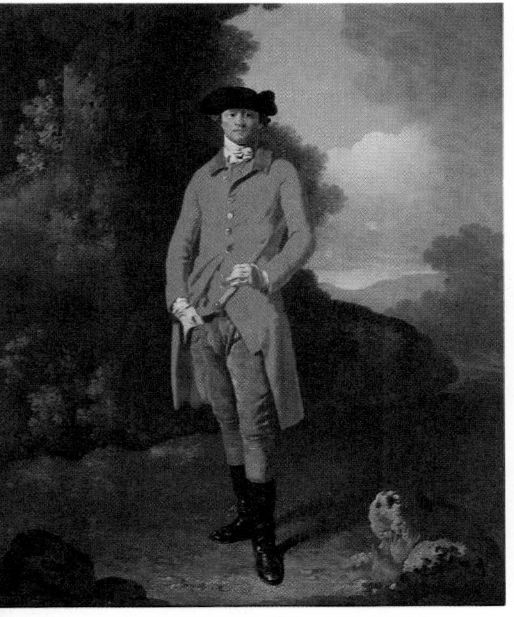

3

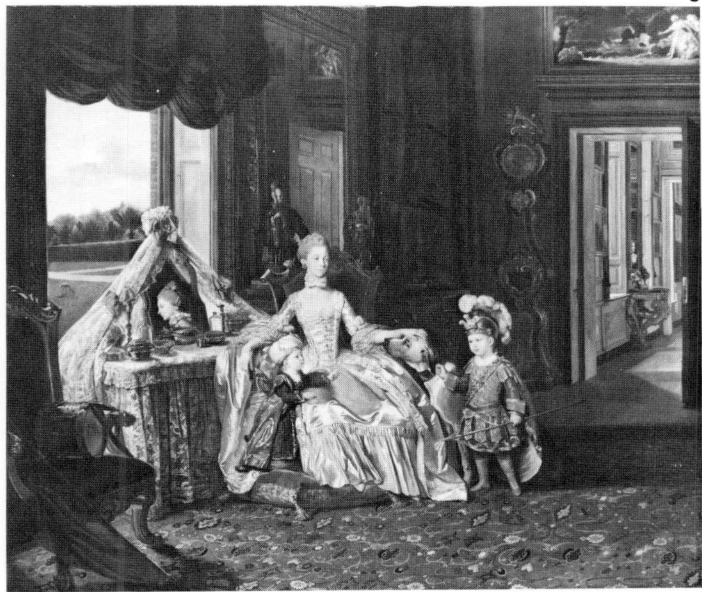

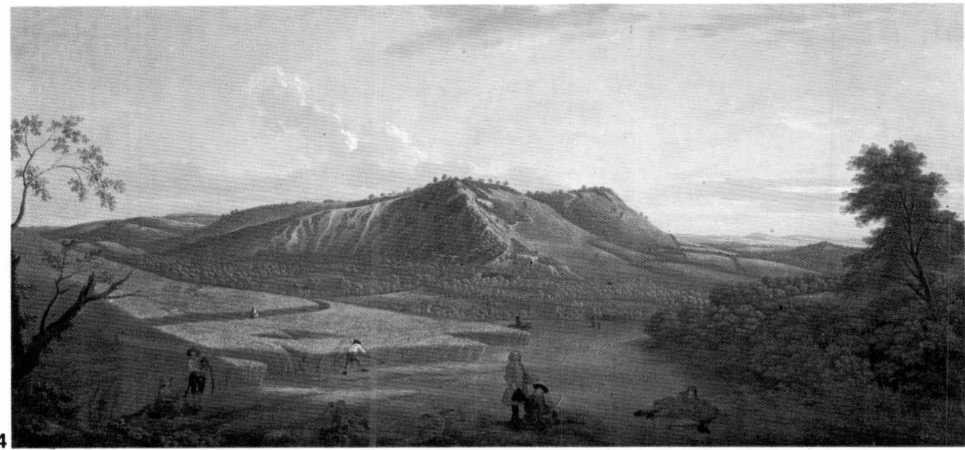

4

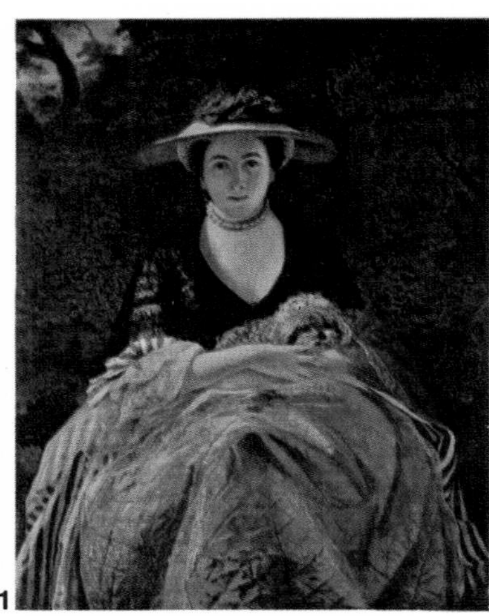
1

Sir Joshua Reynolds (1723–92)
1. *Portrait of Nelly O'Brien.* 1763. Wallace Collection, London
2. *Portrait of Mrs Thomas Meyrick.* 1782. Ashmolean Museum, Oxford
3. *Portrait of Lady Betty Hamilton.* National Gallery of Art (Widener Collection), Washington DC
4. *Portrait of Lord Heathfield, Governor of Gibraltar.* 1787. National Gallery, London
5. *Portrait of Georgiana, Countess Spencer, with her Daughter Georgiana, later Duchess of Devonshire.* Earl Spencer Collection, Althorp
6. *Portrait of Master Francis George Hare.* 1788. Louvre, Paris

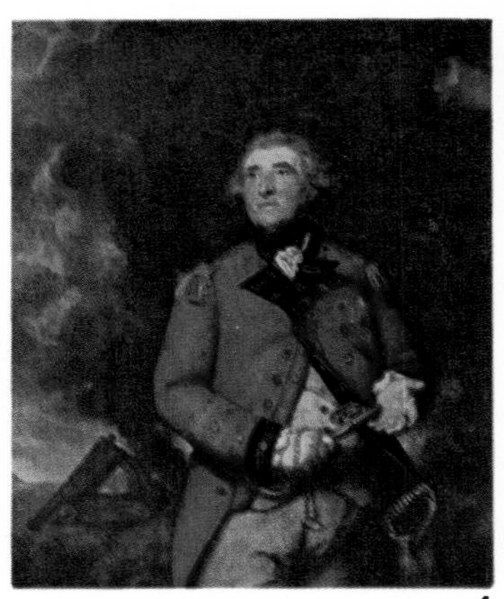
4

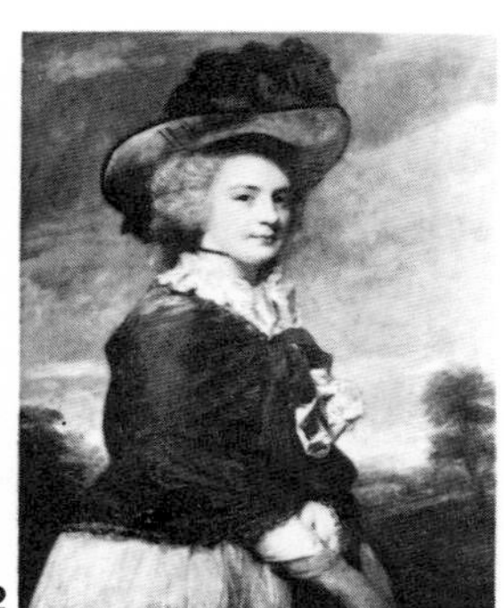
2

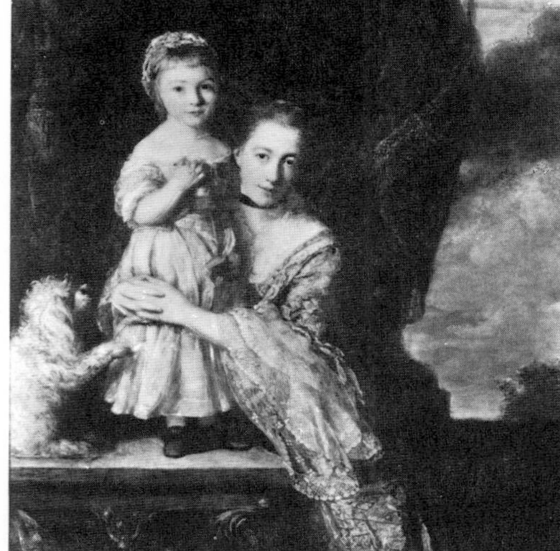
5

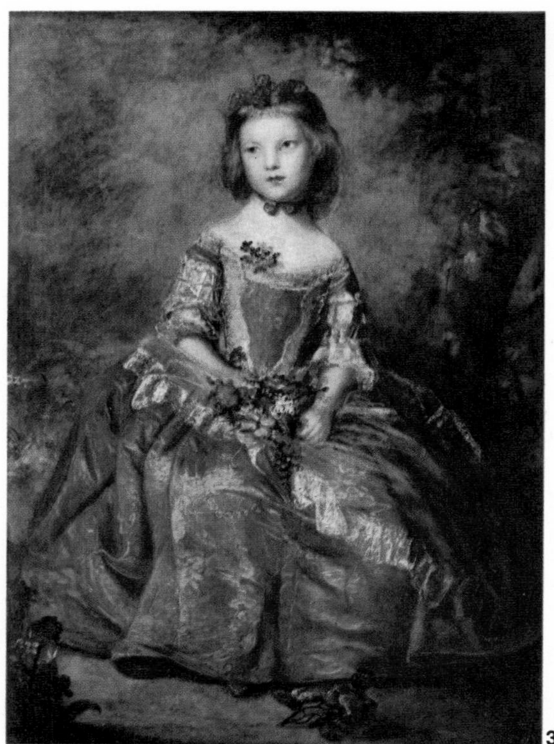
3

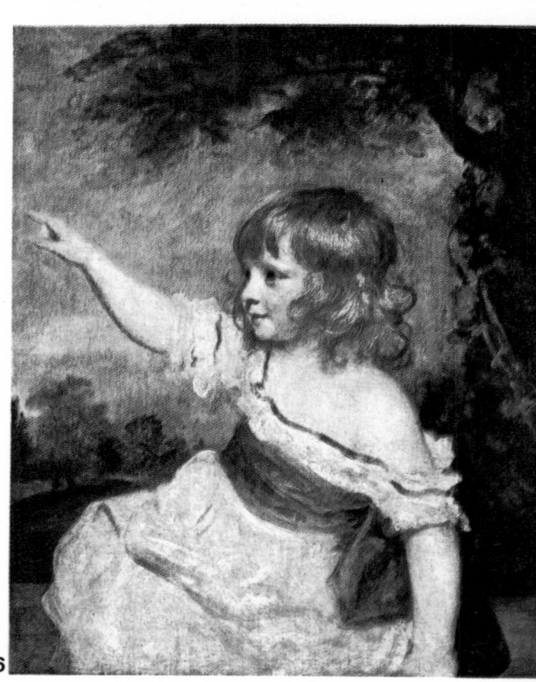
6

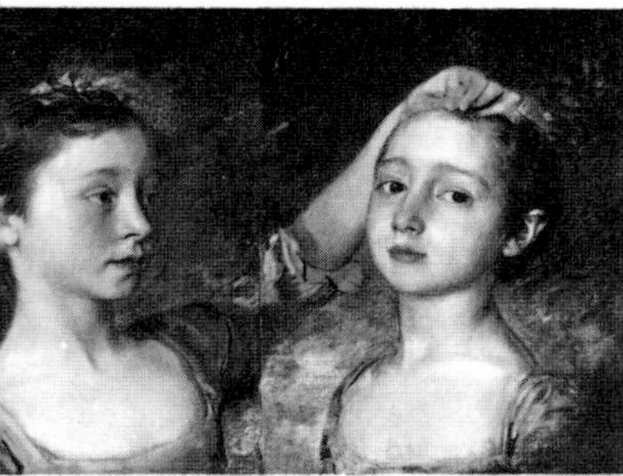

Thomas Gainsborough (1727–88)

1. *The Artist's Daughters, Mary and Margaret.* About 1758. Victoria and Albert Museum, London
2. *Portrait of Mrs Richard Brinsley Sheridan.* 1785–6. National Gallery of Art, Washington DC
3. *Portrait of Mr and Mrs Robert Andrews.* About 1748–9. National Gallery, London
4. *The Market Cart.* 1786–7. Tate Gallery, London
5. *Portrait of Mary, Countess Howe.* Detail. About 1763–4. Kenwood (Iveagh Bequest), London

1

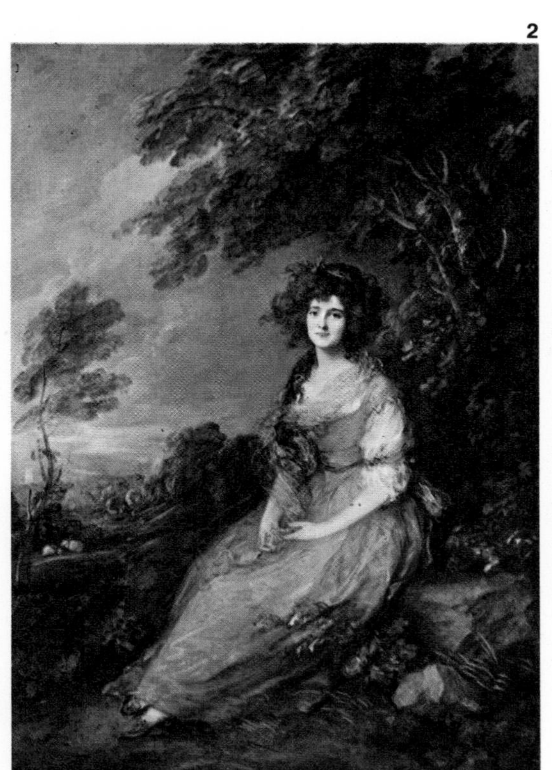

2

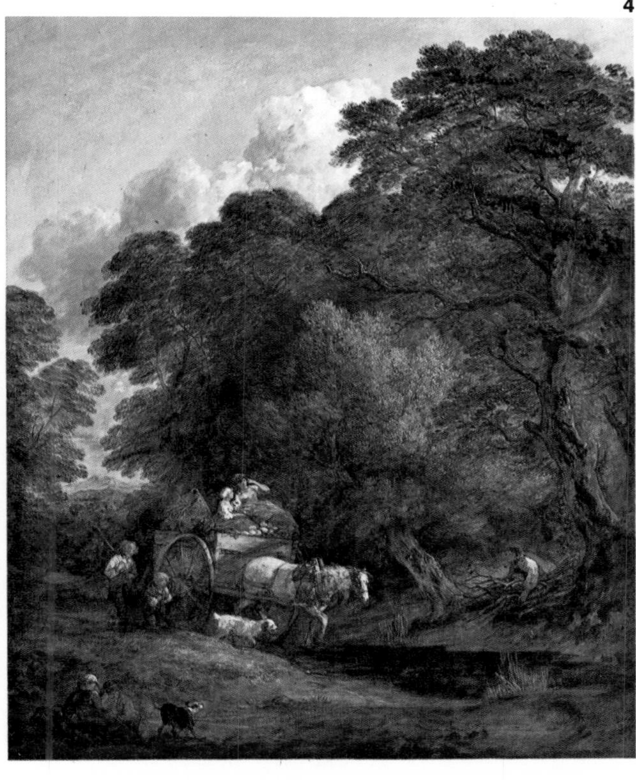

4

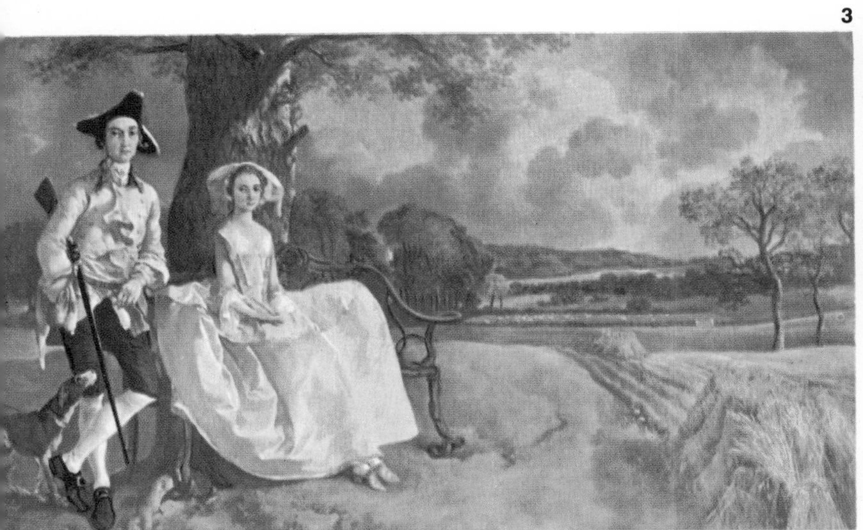

3

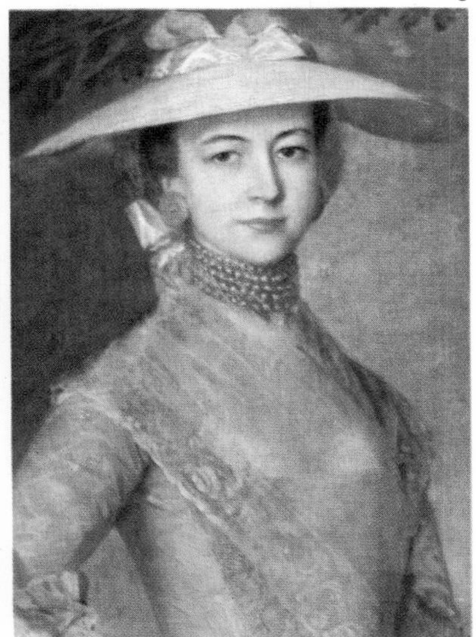

5

1. **George Romney** (1734–1802): *Portrait of Mrs Davenport.* 1782–4. National Gallery of Art (Mellon Collection), Washington DC
2. **George Romney** (1734–1802): *The Leveson-Gower Children.* 1776–7. Duke of Sutherland Collection
3. **Sir Thomas Lawrence** (1769–1830): *Portrait of Princess Lieven.* About 1820. Tate Gallery, London
4. **Sir Thomas Lawrence** (1769–1830): *The Fluyder Children.* Before 1805. Mus de Arte de São Paulo
5. **Sir Henry Raeburn** (1756–1823): *Port of Mrs Eleanor Urquhart.* About 1795. National Gallery of Art (Mellon Collectio Washington DC

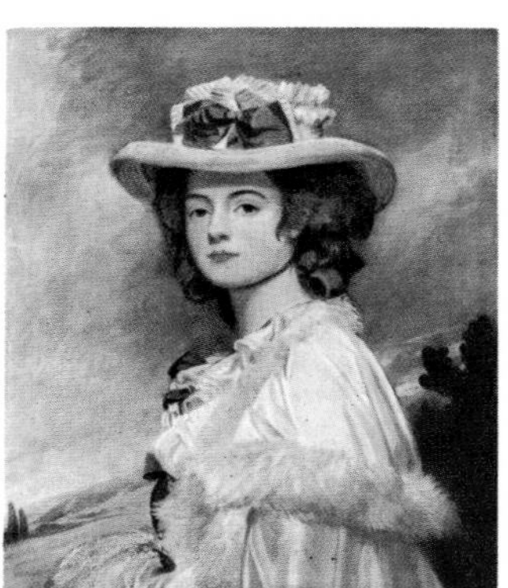

1

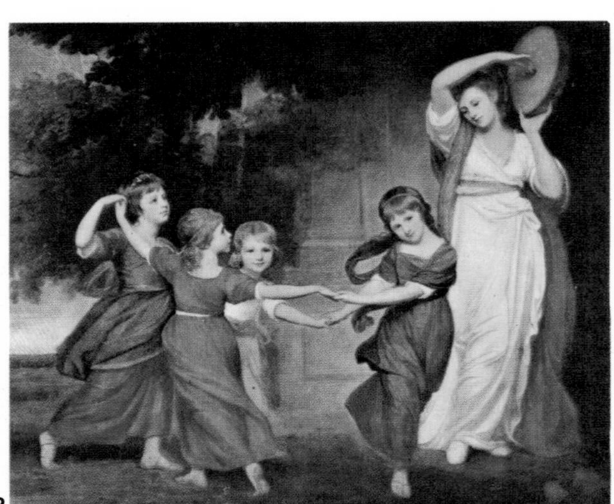

2

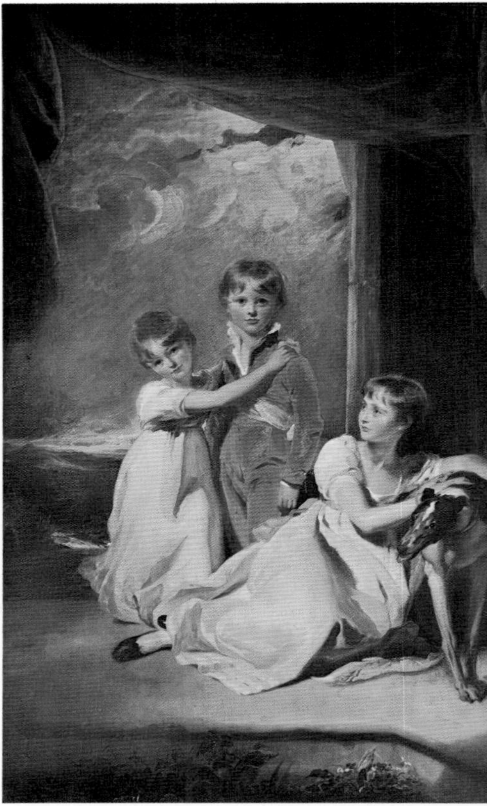

4

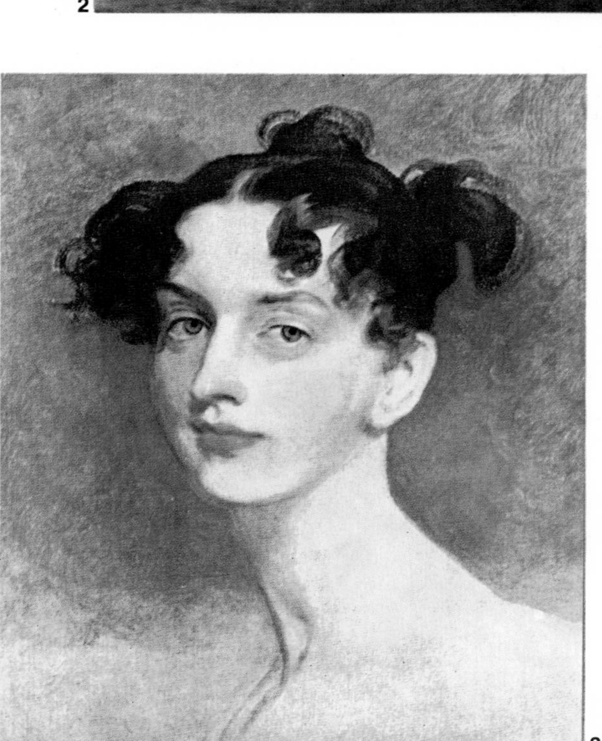

3

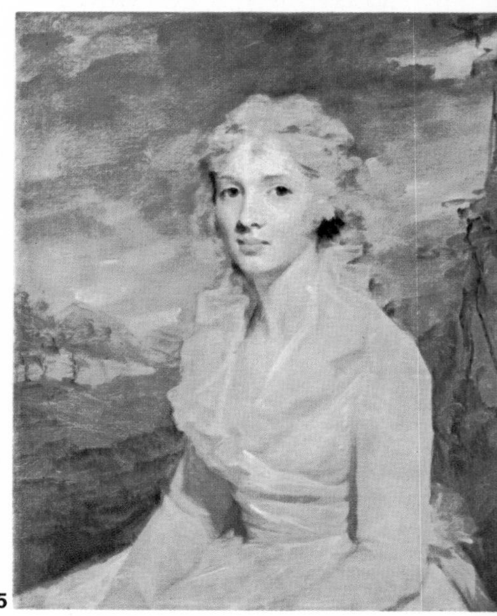

5

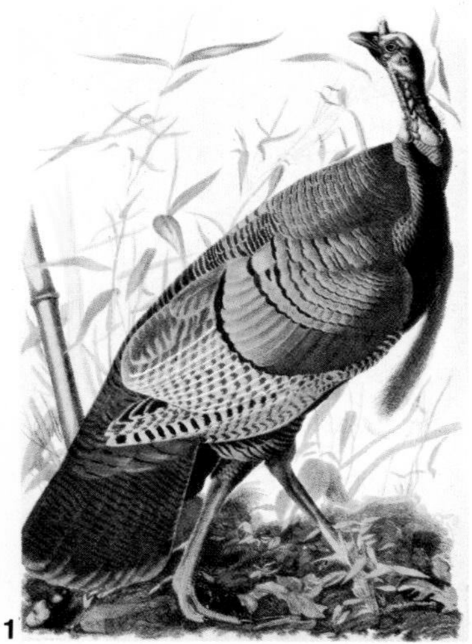
1

1. **John James Audubon** (1785–1851): *Wild Turkey.* Coloured engraving from *The Birds of America* (published 1827–38)
2. **Benjamin West** (1738–1820): *The Golden Age.* 1776. Tate Gallery, London
3. **Thomas Jefferson** (1743–1826): The Rotunda (formerly library) of the University of Virginia, Charlottesville. 1822–6. Reconstructed after the fire of 1895
4. **Gilbert Stuart** (1755–1828): *Portrait of Mrs Richard Yates.* 1793. National Gallery of Art, Washington DC
5. **John Trumbull** (1756–1843): *Portrait of George Washington.* 1780. Metropolitan Museum of Art (Charles Allen Munn Bequest), New York
6. **John Singleton Copley** (1738–1815): *Portrait of Mrs Seymour Fort.* Wadsworth Atheneum, Hartford, Connecticut

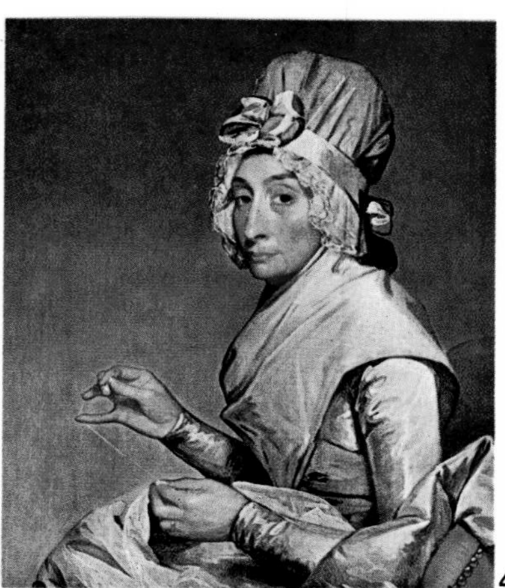
4

5

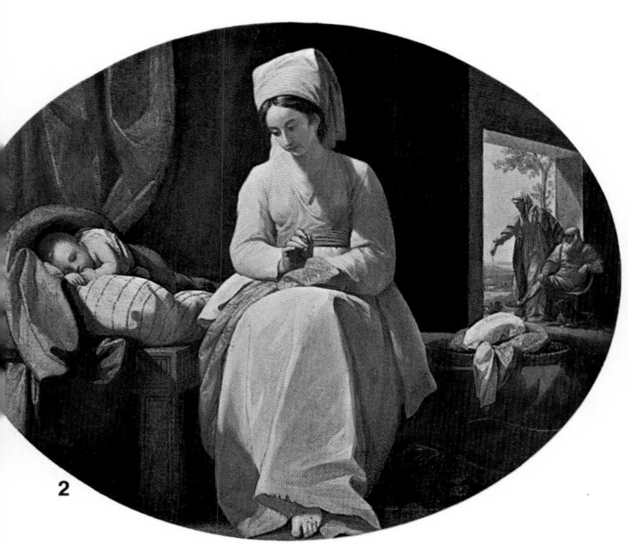
2

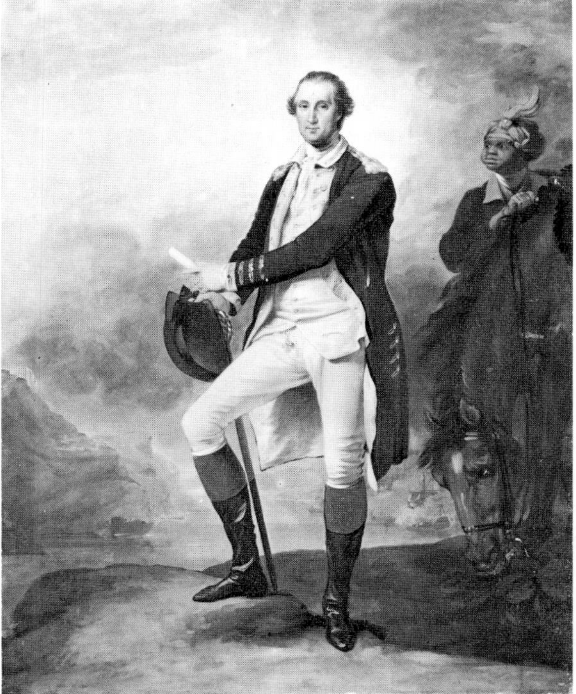

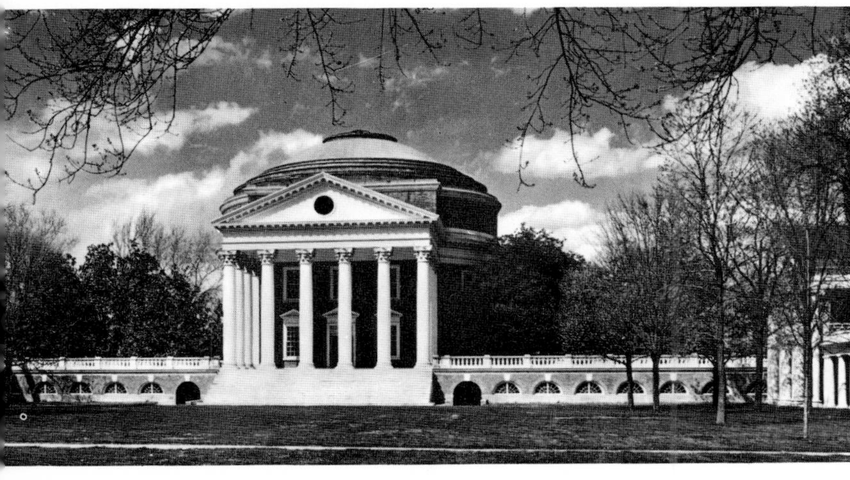

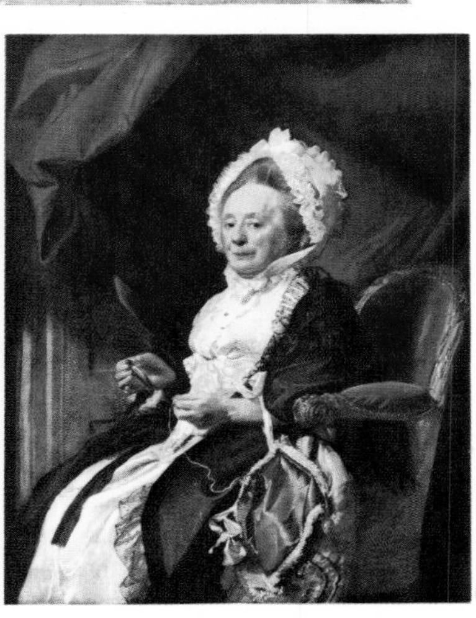
6

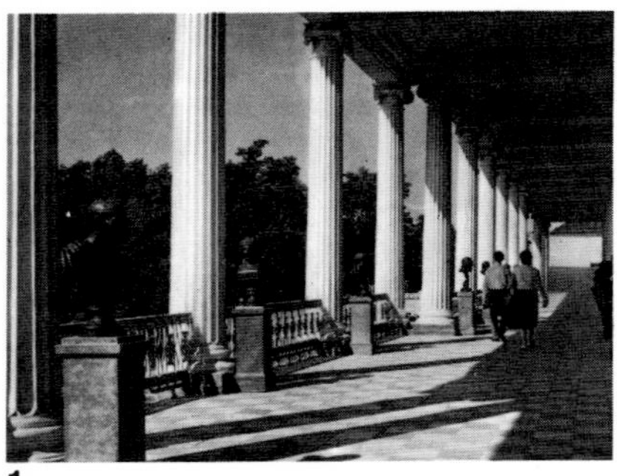
1

1. **Charles Cameron** (*c.*1740–1812): Gallery, Little Apartments of the empress at Tsarskoe Selo. 1782–5
2. Cathedral of the Blessed Basil, Red Square, Moscow. 1555–60. Built by Barma and Posnik
3. Palace at Peterhof. Designed by Jean-Baptiste Le Blond, 1717; remodelled by Bartolomeo Rastrelli, 1747–52
4. **Bartolomeo Francesco Rastrelli** (1700–71): Church of St Andrew, Kiev. 1749–56
5. The Gate of the Redeemer and the walls of the Kremlin, Moscow. 15th-17th century
6. **Bartolomeo Francesco Rastrelli** (1700–71): The Winter Palace, Leningrad (formerly St Petersburg). 1754–62. The Alexander Column, centre, is by Richard de Montferrand, 1829

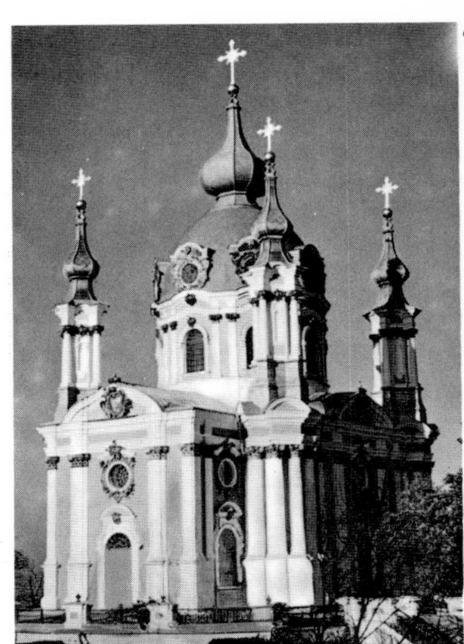
4

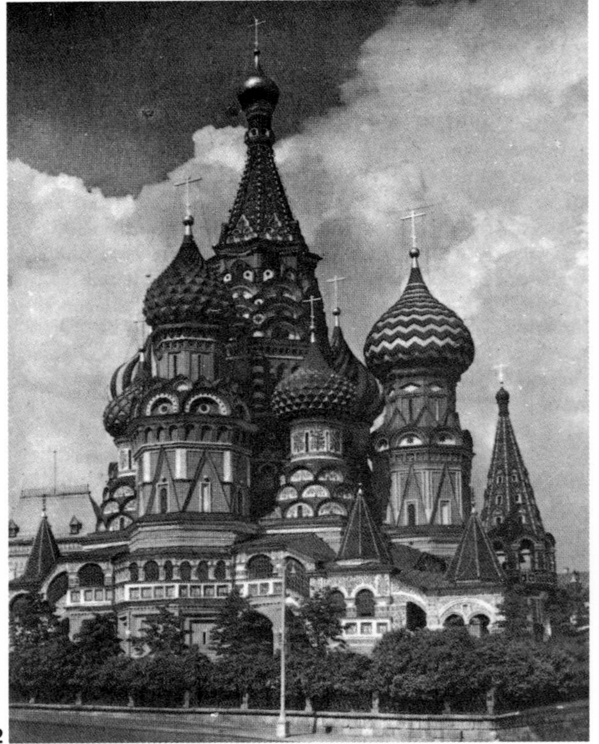
2

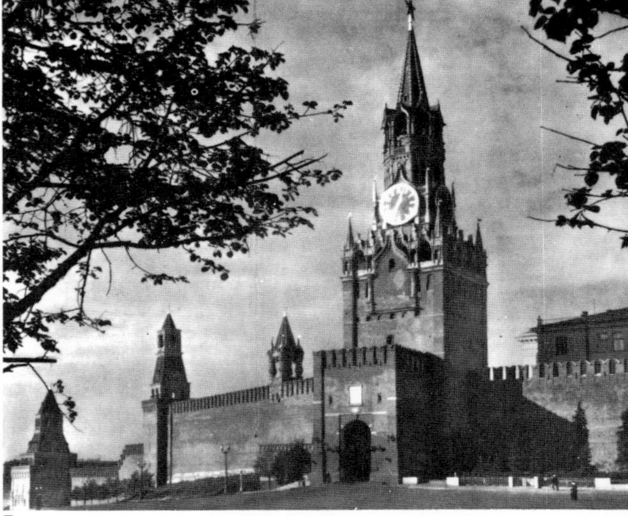
5

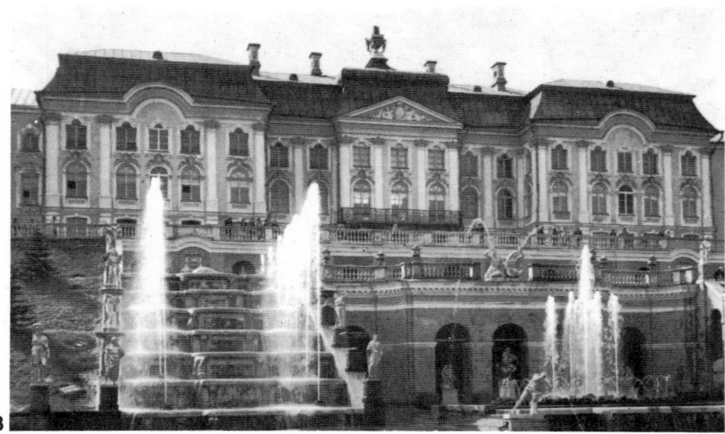
3

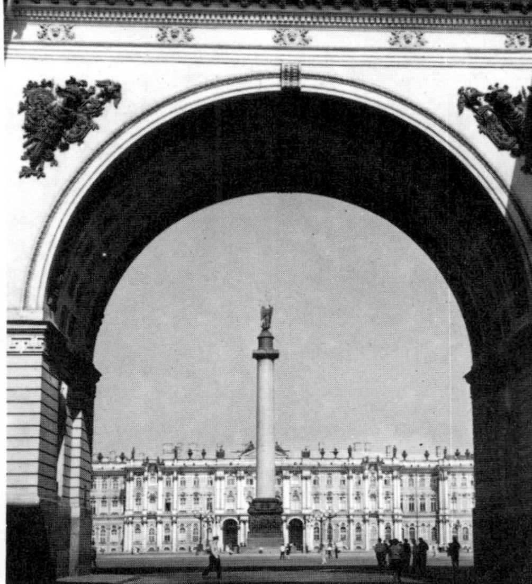
6

Part 9

Europe and America 1800–1900

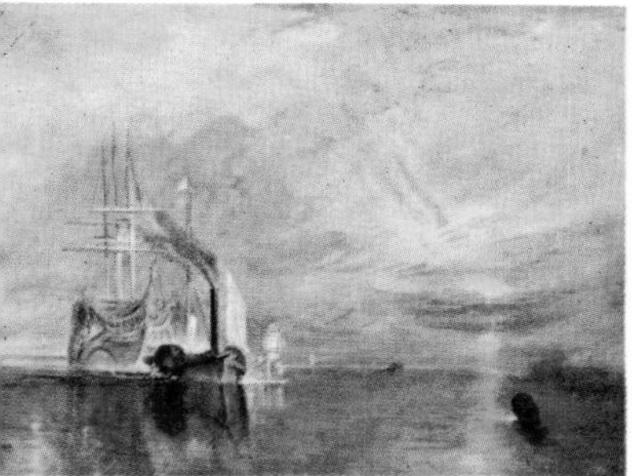

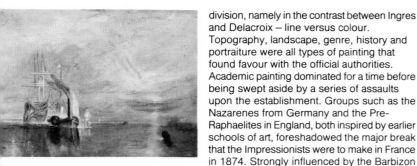

M.W. Turner: *The Fighting Téméraire.* 1838. ıtional Gallery, London

ıe nineteenth century was a period of bitter ntrasts. The political rifts in the structure of ciety are reflected in the art of the period and :en formed the subject matter of art itself, in the growth of Realism associated with ɔurbet. While at the beginning of the century ıglish artists, specifically J. M. W. Turner, ɔnstable and Bonington, were influential on

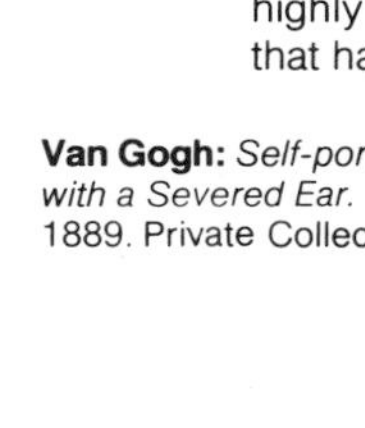

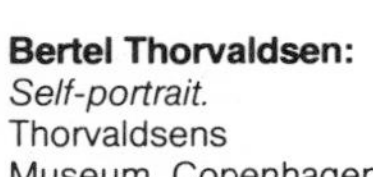

Bertel Thorvaldsen: *Self-portrait.* Thorvaldsens Museum, Copenhagen

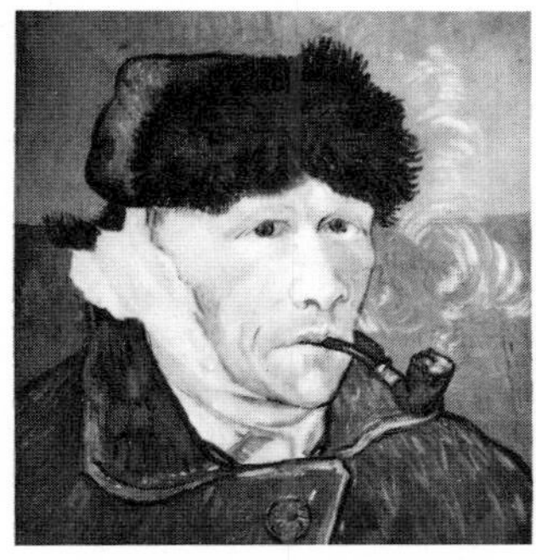

Van Gogh: *Self-portrait with a Severed Ear.* 1889. Private Collection

e Continent, France soon regained the tiative. The identity of national schools ırdened; American painters emerged, erman and Swiss artists again played gnificant roles in European art. Indeed, the :ernational flavour is perhaps at its most ɔminent in the field of sculpture, where the ɔrk of the Italian Canova, the Dane ıorwaldsen and the Frenchman Rodin was ıch vaunted. The century began with a division, namely in the contrast between Ingres and Delacroix – line versus colour. Topography, landscape, genre, history and portraiture were all types of painting that found favour with the official authorities. Academic painting dominated for a time before being swept aside by a series of assaults upon the establishment. Groups such as the Nazarenes from Germany and the Pre-Raphaelites in England, both inspired by earlier schools of art, foreshadowed the major break that the Impressionists were to make in France in 1874. Strongly influenced by the Barbizon school, the Impressionist painters revitalized art by placing greater emphasis on spontaneity and on the necessity of recording their sensations as experienced before nature. Their desire to depict freely what they saw about them and to paint contemporary subject matter, primarily in the urban context, represents a release from a tyranny and led to a number of subsequent developments in modern art. The freedom with which the Impressionists handled paint, their use of colour, their interest in Japanese painting and the character of their compositions were highly influential for virtually every movement that has followed, and Impressionism is therefore the true precursor of art in the twentieth century, as is indicated by the numerous strands for which the term Post-Impressionism is used. Cézanne, whose careful analysis of shape and structure was to be so essential for the emergence of abstract painting, belonged to the Impressionist movement for a time, as did Seurat and Gauguin. Neo-Impressionism, of which Seurat is the chief representative, reduced the creative brushstroke to a series of dots, but in doing this sought for purity of form and colour. Gauguin adopted Symbolism as his chief means of expression, finally rejecting contemporary values and seeking inspiration in the South Seas. Perhaps no artist anticipates the twentieth century more than Van Gogh, who worked and died in France. The intensity of his emotions was matched by the fevered activity of his brushwork and by the strength of his colour. Art was, for Van Gogh, an expression of an inner state of mind. Directly related to all these developments that took place in Paris during the last quarter of the nineteenth century is the advent of Picasso, Braque and Matisse.

ıuguin: *Where Do We Come From? What Are We? Where Are We Going?* 1897. ston Museum of Fine Arts

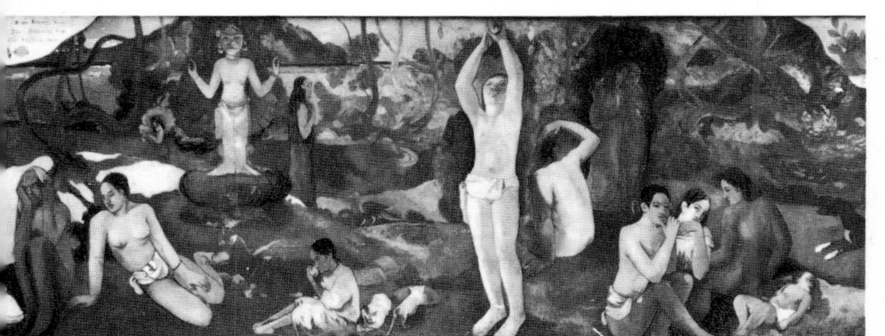

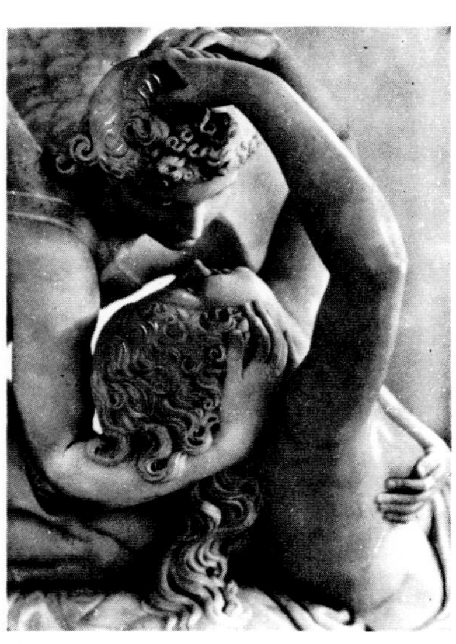

1

1. **Antonio Canova** (1757–1822): *Cupid and Psyche.* Detail. Marble. Villa Carlotta, Lake Como
2. **Giovanni Segantini** (1858–99): *The Homecoming.* Before 1898. Kunstmuseum, Berne
3. **Antonio Canova** (1757–1822): *Pauline Bonaparte Borghese as Venus.* Marble. 1808. Galleria Borghese, Rome
4. **Giovanni Fattori** (1825–1908): *La Rotonda di Palmieri.* 1866. Galleria d'Arte Moderna, Florence
5. **Giovanni Boldini** (1845–1931): *Portrait of the poet Hanvin.* Museu de Arte de São Paulo
6. **Francesco Hayez** (1791–1882): *Melancholy.* Brera, Milan

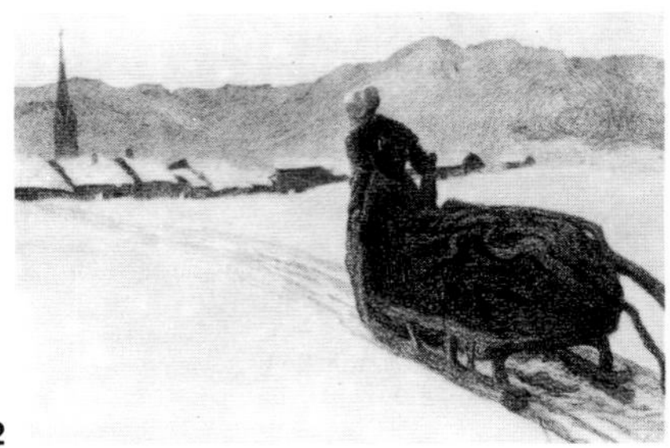

2

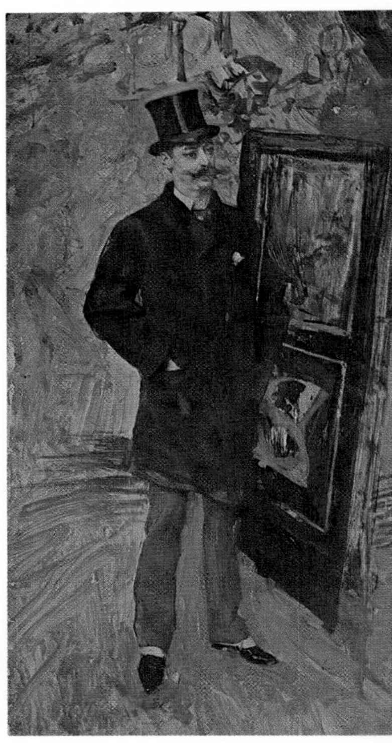

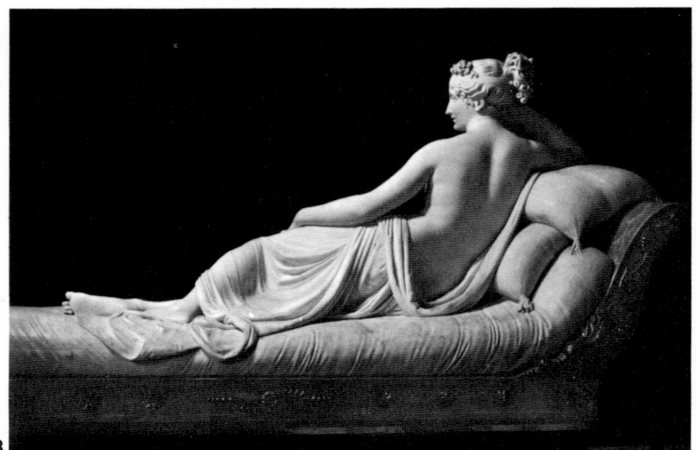

3

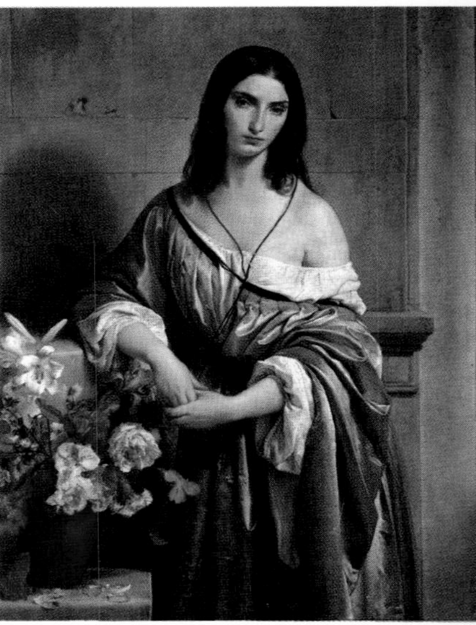

6

4

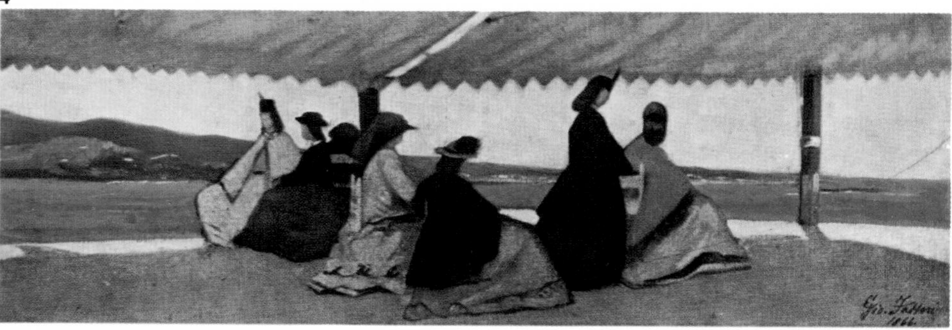

John Nash (1752–1835): Cronkhill, Shropshire. East façade. About 1802
Joseph Paxton (1803–65): The main exhibition hall of the Crystal Palace, London. 1851. Taken down and re-erected in Sydenham, 1852–4; destroyed by fire in 1936
John Nash (1752–1835): The Royal Pavilion, Brighton. 1816–21
Sir Charles Barry (1795–1860), assisted by Augustus Welby Pugin (1812–52): The Palace of Westminster (the Houses of Parliament), London. River front. 1836–65
Sir John Soane (1753–1837): The Bank of England, London. The Rotunda. 1796–1833

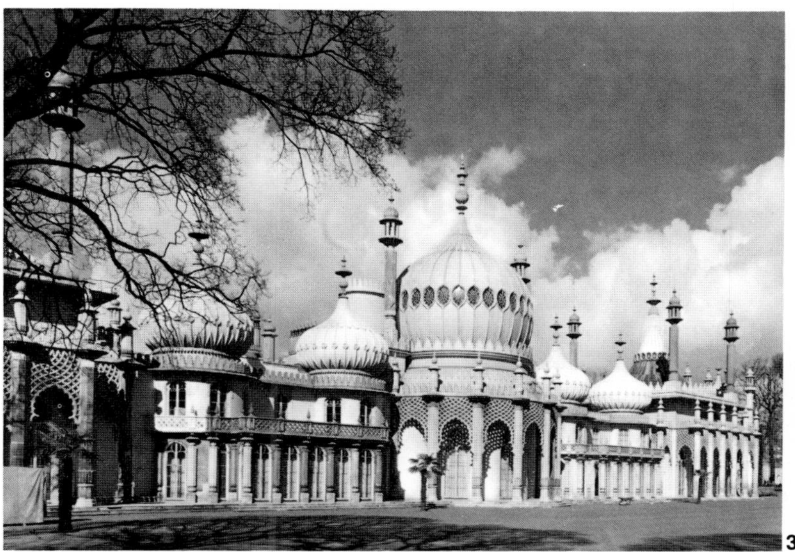
3

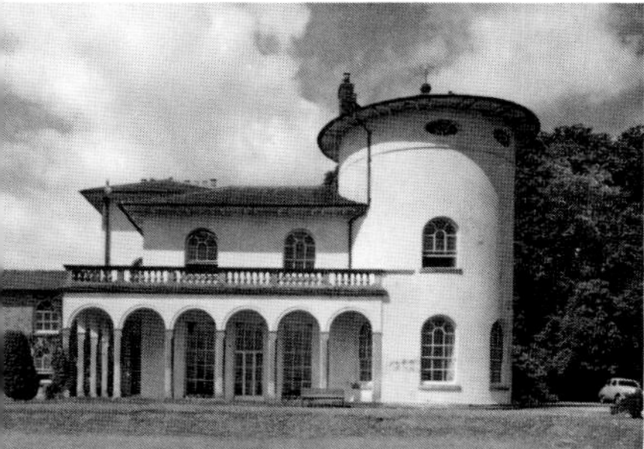
1

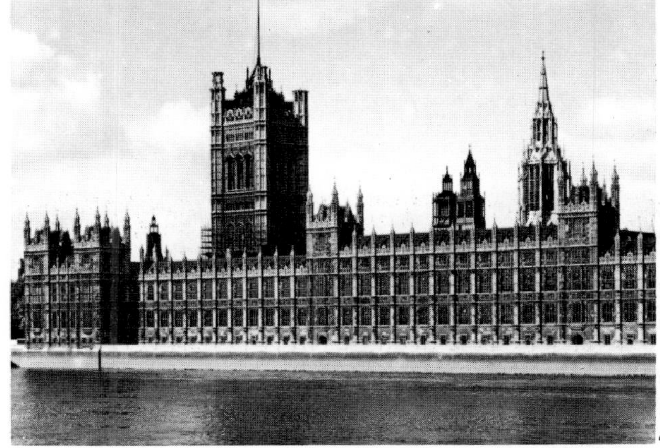
4

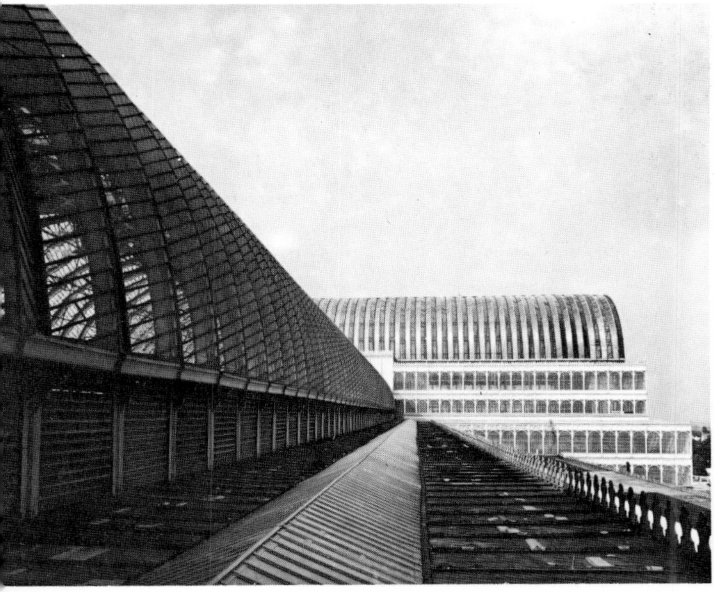

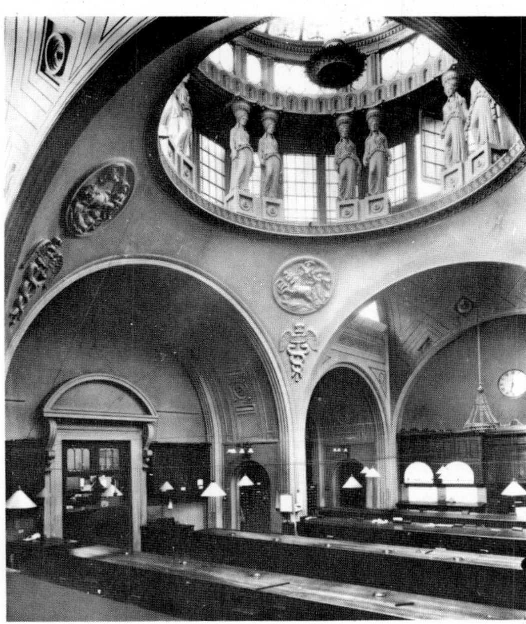
5

1. **Henry Fuseli** (1741–1825): *Succubus.* Watercolour. 1810. Kunsthaus, Zurich
2. **Henry Fuseli** (1741–1825): *Lady Macbeth seizing the Daggers.* 1812? Tate Gallery, London
3. **John Martin** (1789–1854): *Project for a Babylonian Triumphal Arch in Regent's Park, London.* Watercolour. 1820. British Museum, London
4. **William Blake** (1757–1827): *Dante and Virgil at the Entrance to Hell.* Pen and watercolour. Illustration for the *Divine Comedy.* 1824–7. Tate Gallery, London
5. **William Blake** (1757–1827): *The Simoniac Pope.* Illustration for the *Divine Comedy.* About 1824–7. Tate Gallery, London
6. **John Martin** (1789–1854): *The Fall of Babylon.* Engraving. 1820. British Museum, London

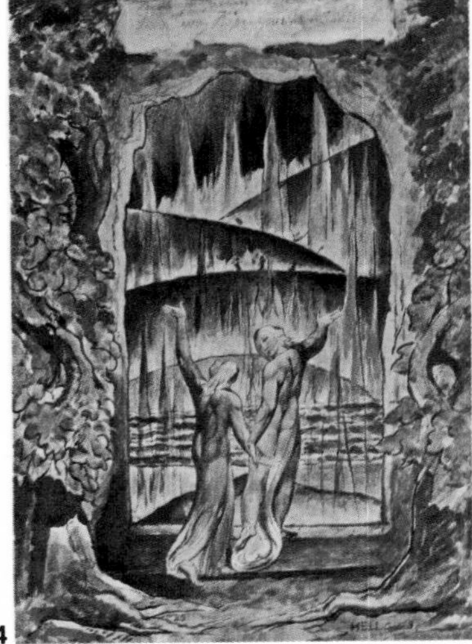
4

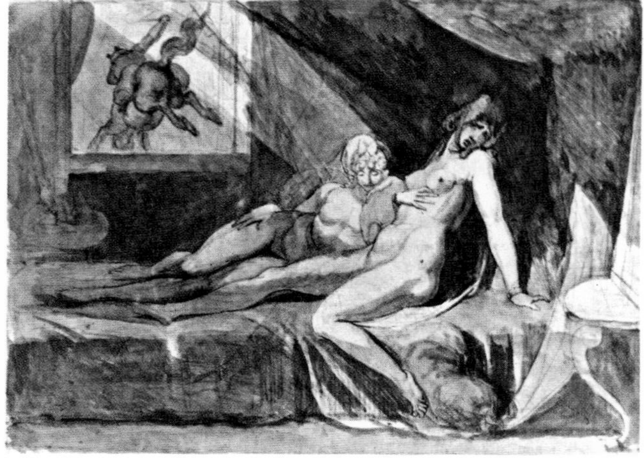
1

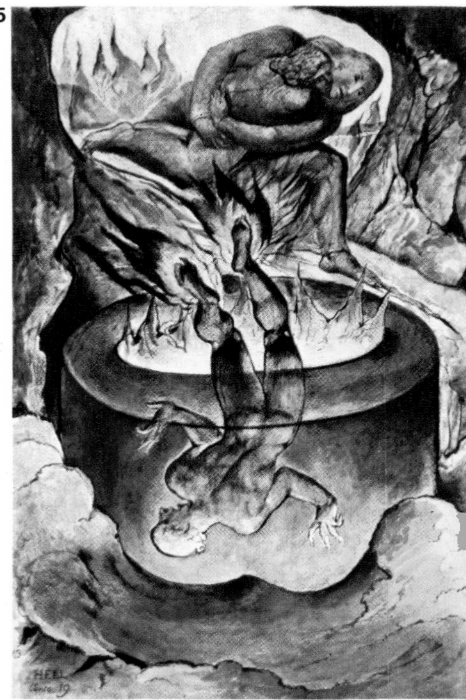
5

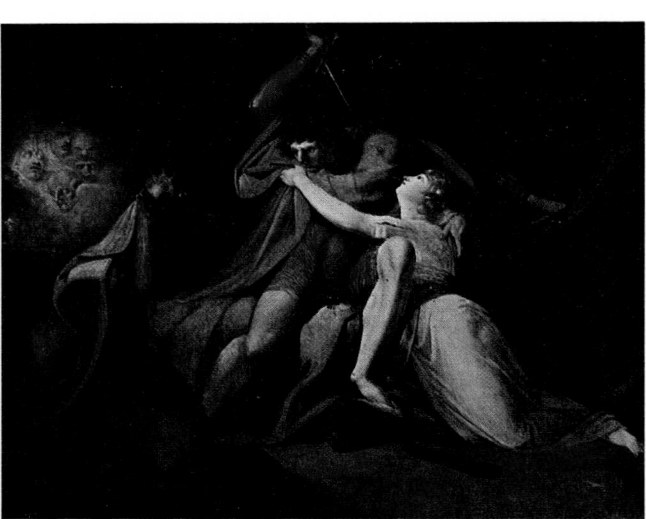
2

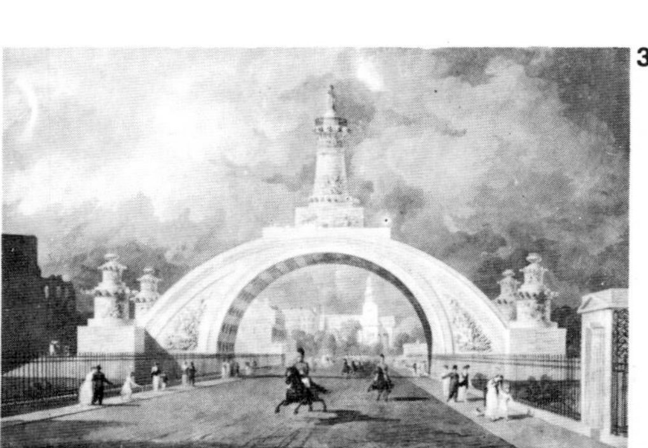
3

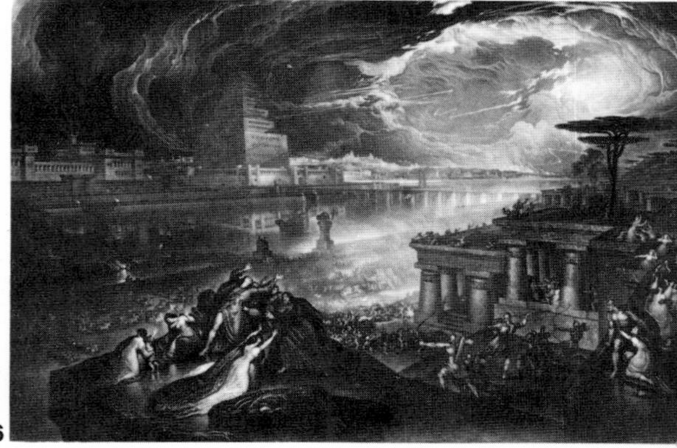
6

1. **Samuel Palmer** (1805–81): *In a Shoreham Garden.* About 1829. Victoria and Albert Museum, London
2. **William Powell Frith** (1819–1909): *Derby Day.* Detail. 1856–8. Tate Gallery, London
3. **John Sell Cotman** (1782–1842): *Greta Bridge.* Watercolour. 1805. British Museum, London
4. **Alfred Stevens** (1817–75): *Portrait of Mary Ann, wife of Leonard Collman.* About 1854. Tate Gallery, London
5. **Richard Parkes Bonington** (1802–28): *View of the Parterre d'Eau at Versailles.* 1825. Louvre, Paris

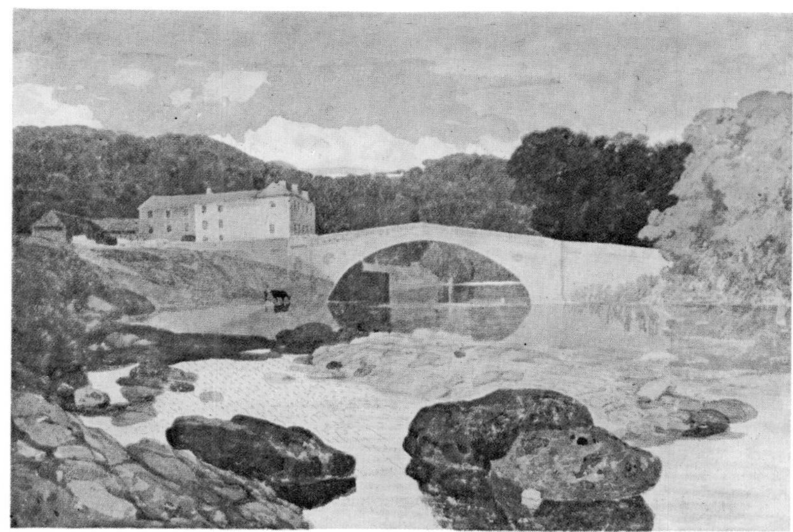
3

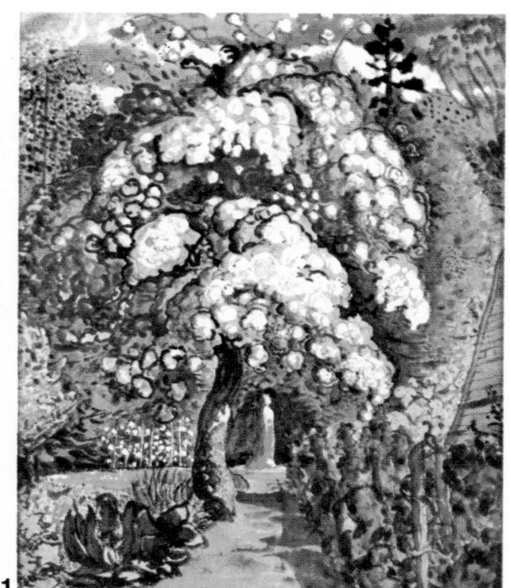
1

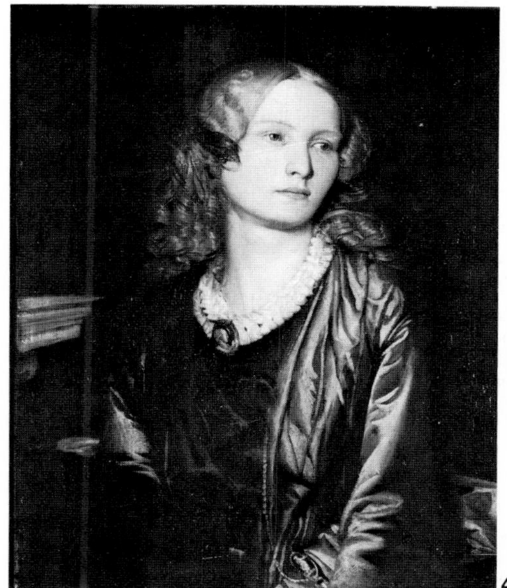
4

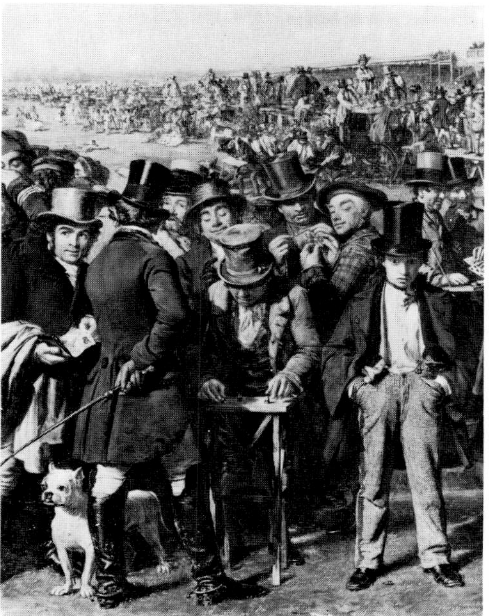
2

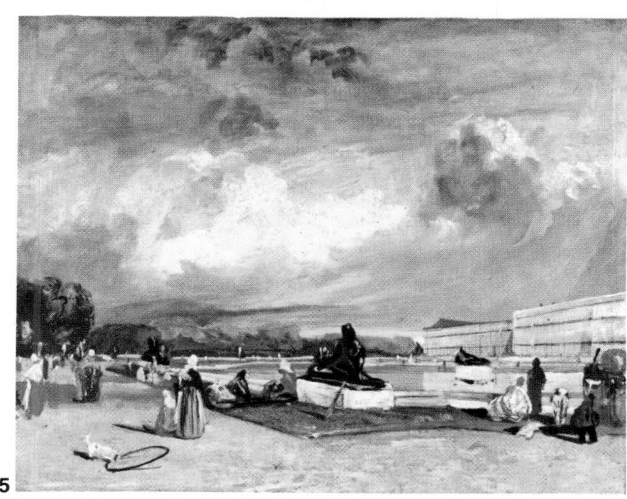
5

John Constable (1776–1837)

1. *Salisbury Cathedral.* 1820. National Gallery, London
2. *Wivenhoe Park, Essex.* 1816. National Gallery of Art (Widener Collection), Washington DC
3. *Willy Lott's House.* About 1810–15. Victoria and Albert Museum, London
4. *Salisbury Cathedral.* Museu de Arte de São Paulo
5. *Stonehenge.* Watercolour. 1836. Victoria and Albert Museum, London
6. *Weymouth Bay.* About 1817. National Gallery, London

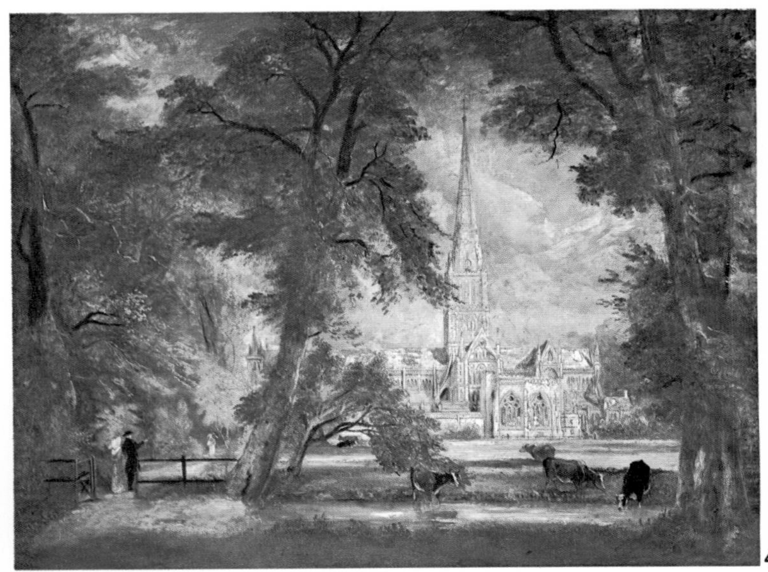

4

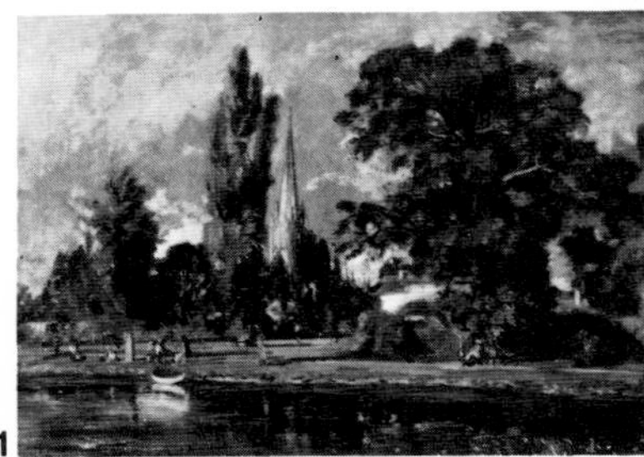

1

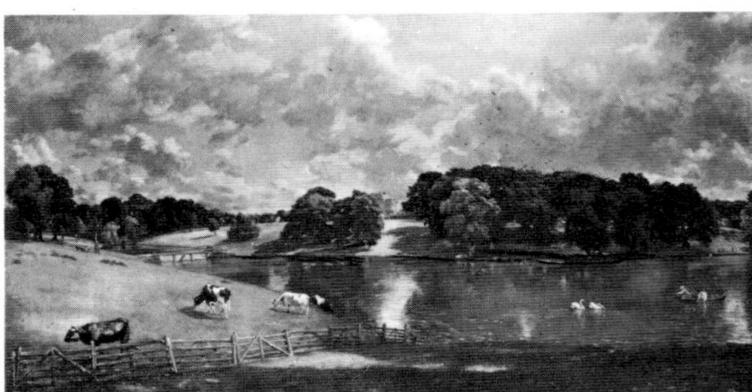

2

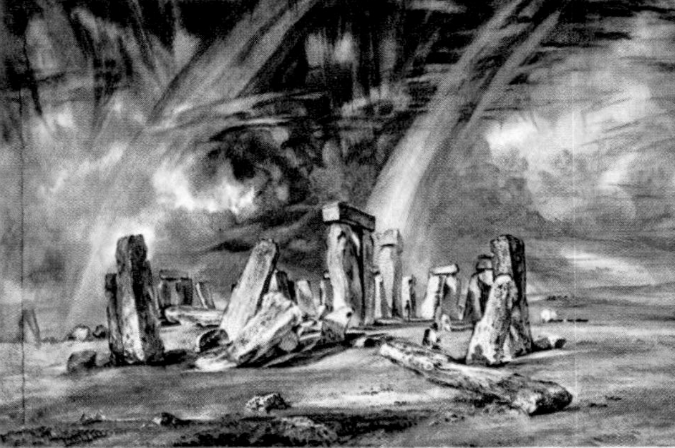

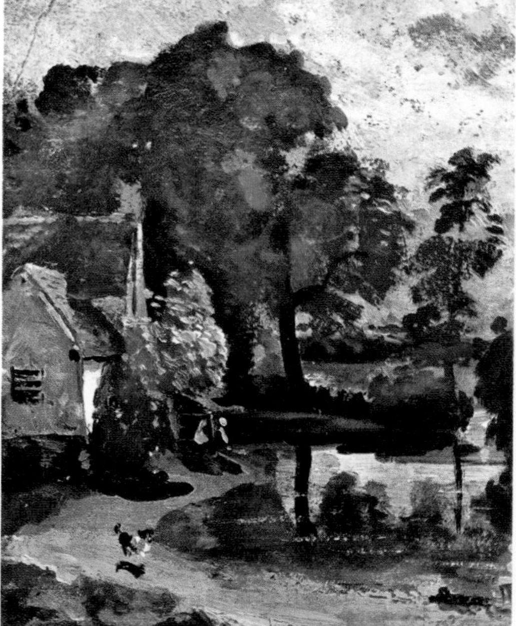

3

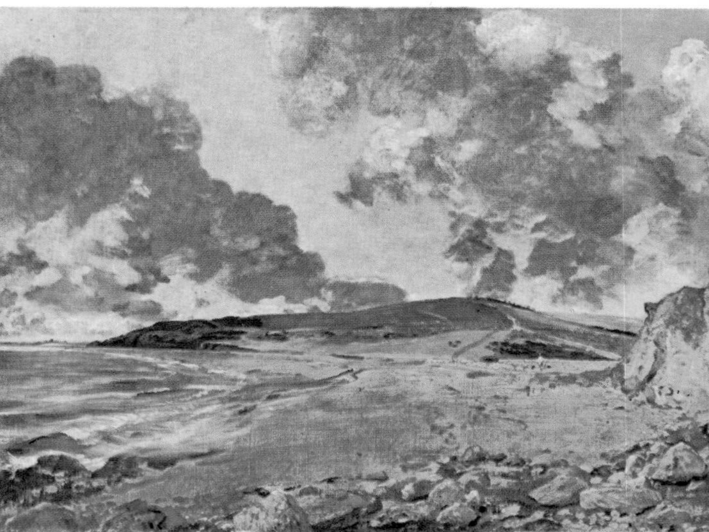

seph Mallord William Turner (1775–
51)

Interior of Petworth House. Gouache. 1830–1. British Museum, London

The Fighting Téméraire tugged to her last Berth to be broken up. 1838. National Gallery, London

The Shipwreck. 1805. Tate Gallery, London

Yacht approaching the Coast. About 1842. Tate Gallery, London

Interior at Petworth House. Gouache. 1830–1. British Museum, London

Interior at Petworth House (unfinished). About 1837. Tate Gallery, London

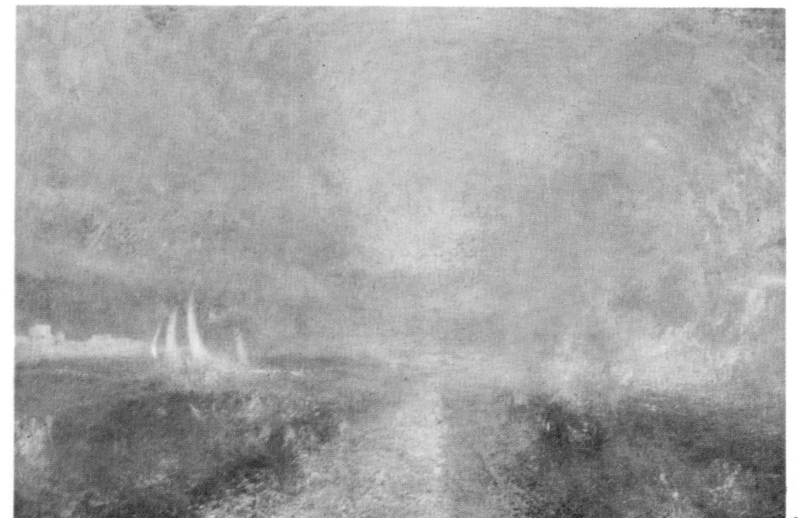

4

5

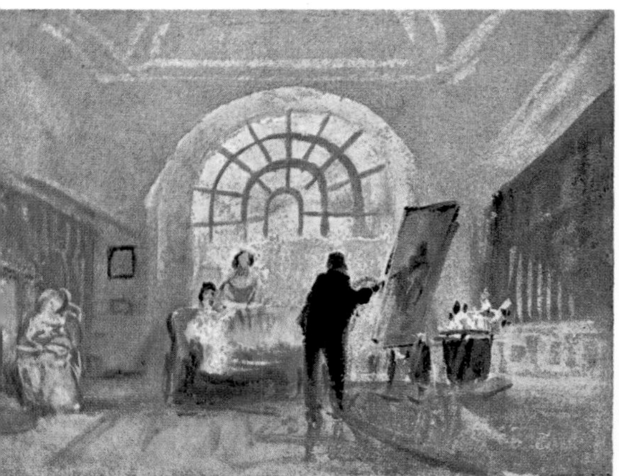

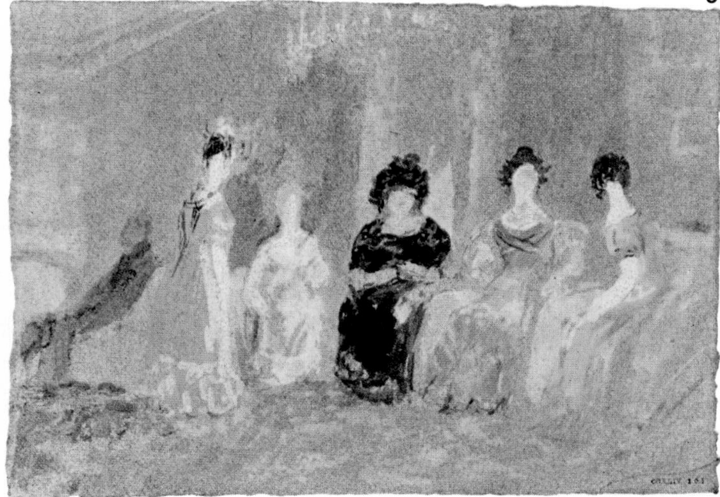

2

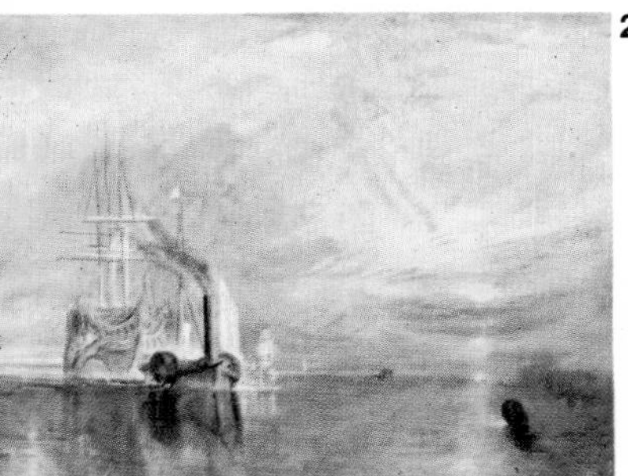

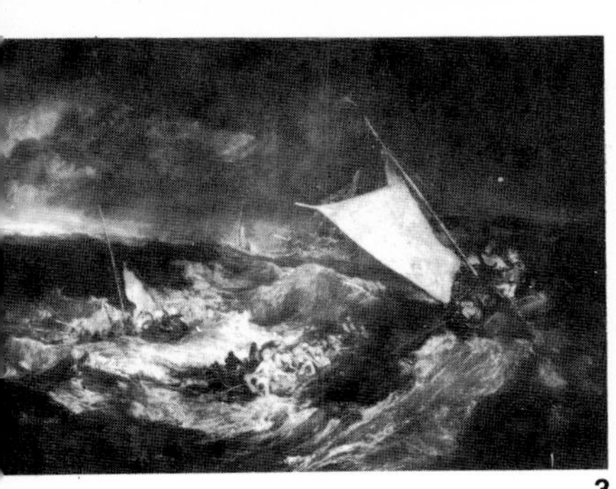

3

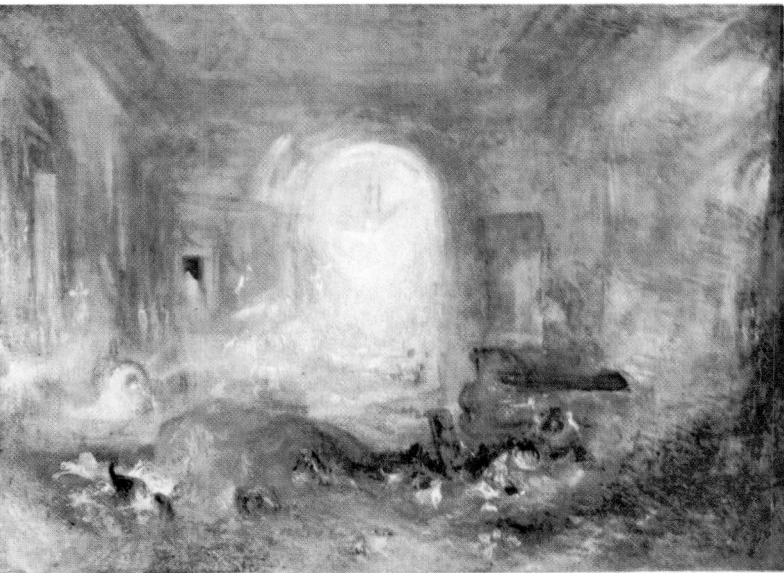

6

1. **Dante Gabriel Rossetti** (1828–82): *Reverie.* Victoria and Albert Museum, London
2. **Dante Gabriel Rossetti** (1828–82): *The Wedding of St George and Princess Sabra.* 1857. Tate Gallery, London
3. **Sir Edward Burne-Jones** (1833–98): *The Love Song.* Metropolitan Museum of Art, New York
4. **William Holman Hunt** (1827–1910): *Our English Coasts, 1852 ('Strayed Sheep').* 1852. Tate Gallery, London
5. **Sir Edward Burne-Jones** (1833–98): *The Golden Stairs.* 1880. Tate Gallery, London
6. **Sir John Everett Millais** (1829–96): *Ophelia.* 1851–2. Tate Gallery, London

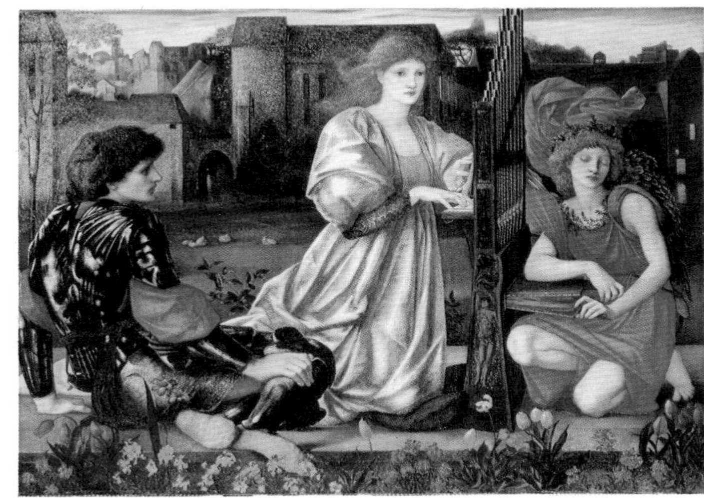
3

1
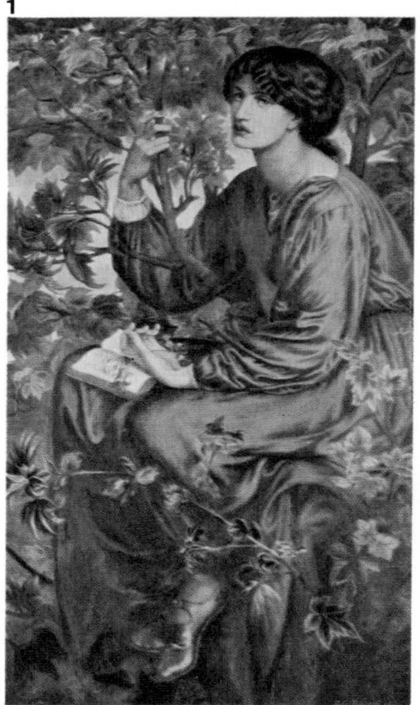

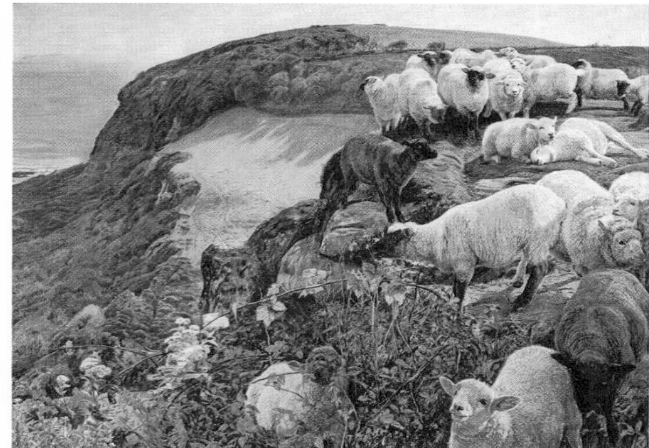
4

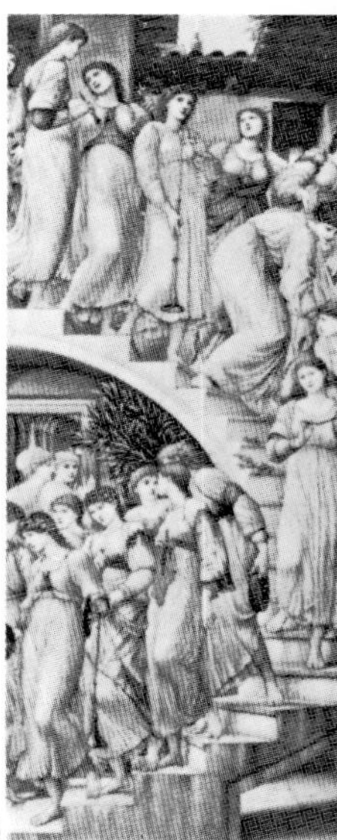
5

2
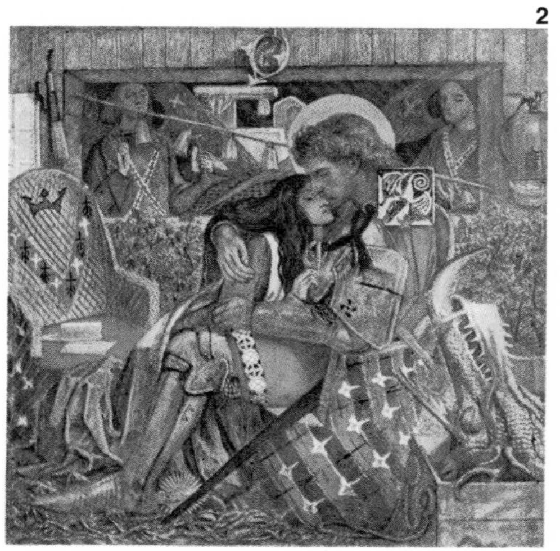

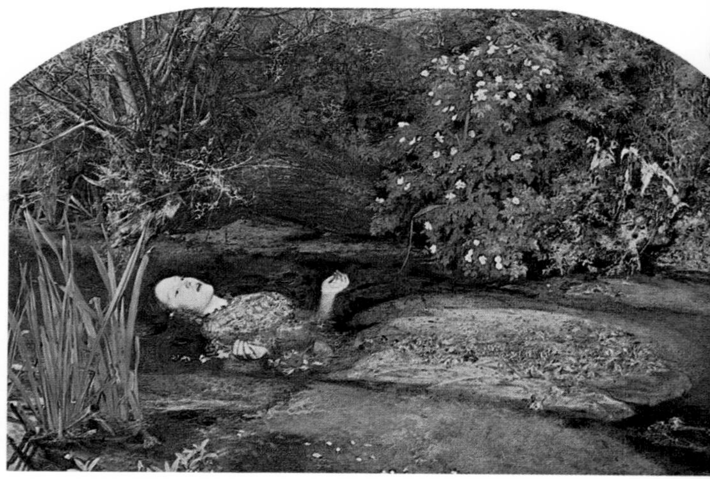
6

1. **George Frederic Watts** (1817–1904): *Cardinal Manning.* 1882. National Portrait Gallery, London
2. **William Morris** (1834–96): Wallpaper design
3. **Sir Edwin Henry Landseer** (1802–73): *The old Shepherd's Chief Mourner.* 1837. Victoria and Albert Museum, London
4. **Frederic, Lord Leighton** (1830–96): *Captive Andromache.* About 1887. City Art Gallery, Manchester
5. **Ford Madox Brown** (1821–93): *Work.* 1852–65. City Art Gallery, Manchester
6. **Arthur Hughes** (1830–1915): *April Love.* 1855–6. Tate Gallery, London

1

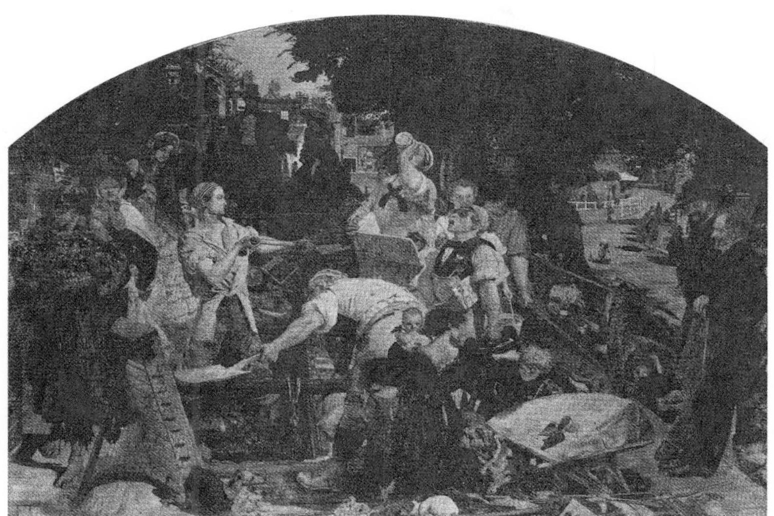

5

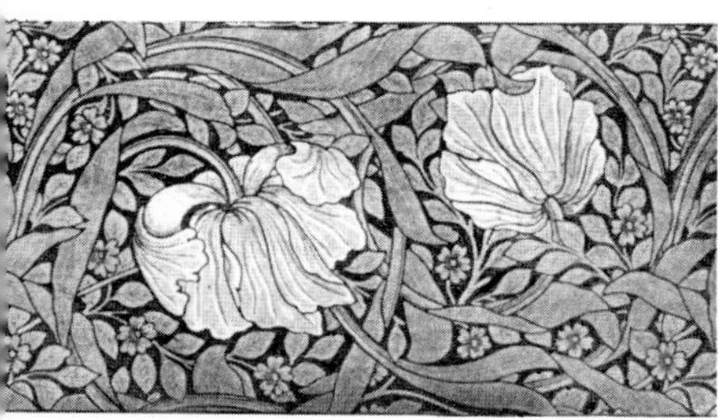

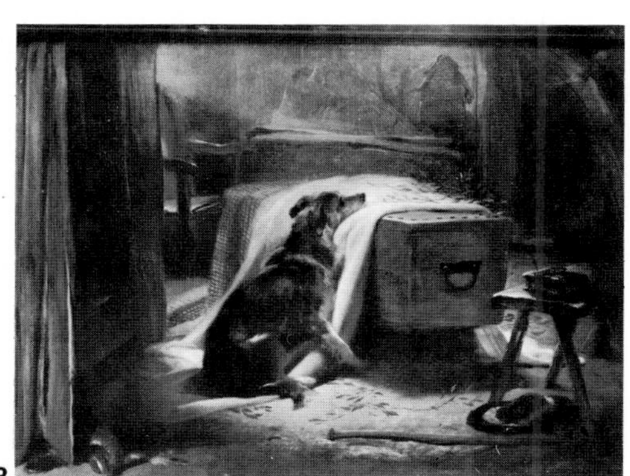

3

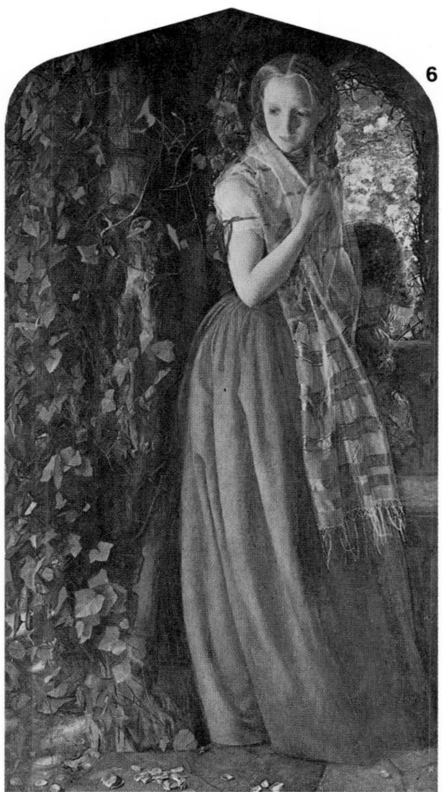

6

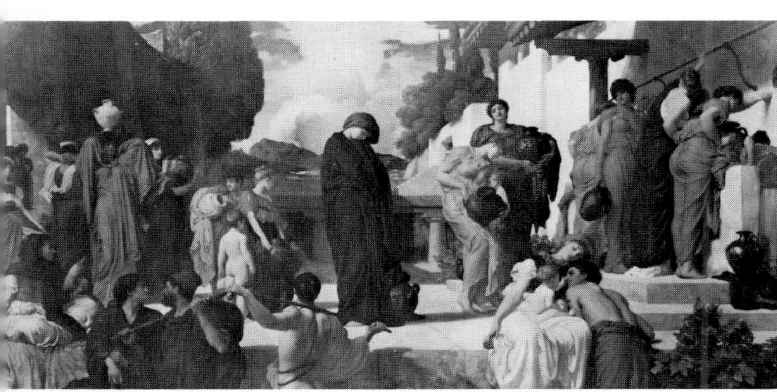

1. **Aubrey Beardsley** (1872–98): *Isolde.* Gouache. About 1890. Fogg Art Museum, Harvard University, Cambridge, Massachusetts
2. **Aubrey Beardsley** (1872–98): *Camille.* Drawing for *The Yellow Book.* 1894. Tate Gallery, London
3. **Philip Wilson Steer** (1860–1942): *The Bridge.* 1887. Tate Gallery, London
4. **Philip Wilson Steer** (1860–1942): *Girl running: Walberswick Pier.* 1888–94. Tate Gallery, London
5. **Walter Richard Sickert** (1860–1942): *T Interior of St Mark's, Venice.* 1896. Tate Gallery, London
6. **Walter Richard Sickert** (1860–1942): *rue Pecquet (St-Jacques).* 1900. City A Gallery, Birmingham

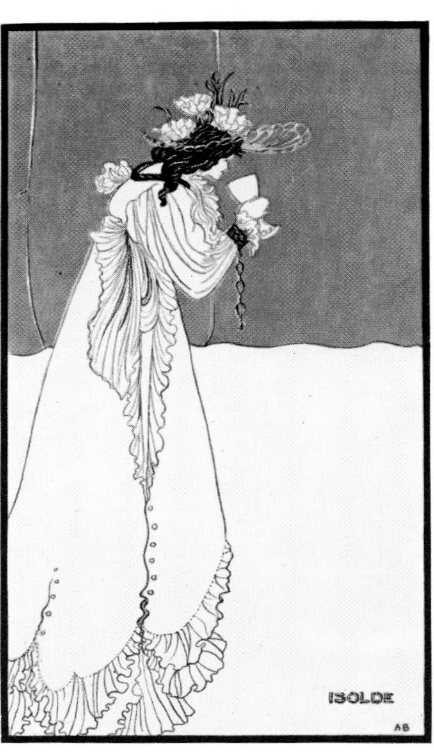

1

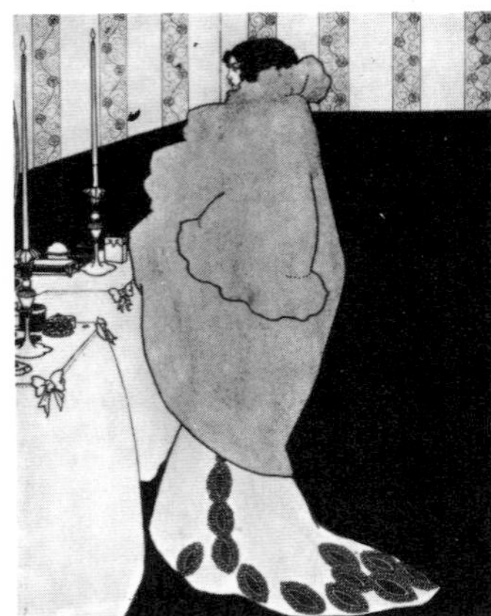
2

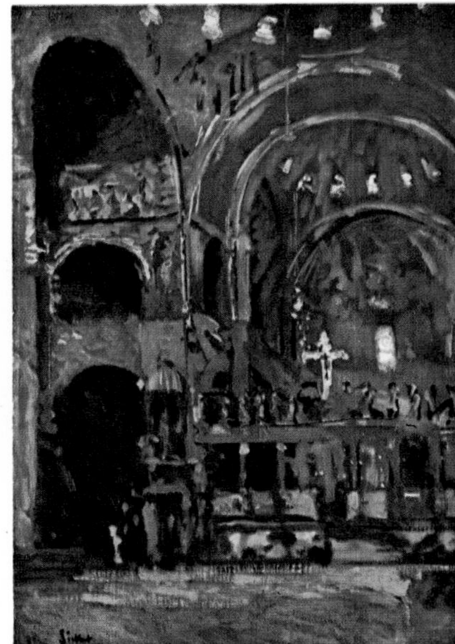
5

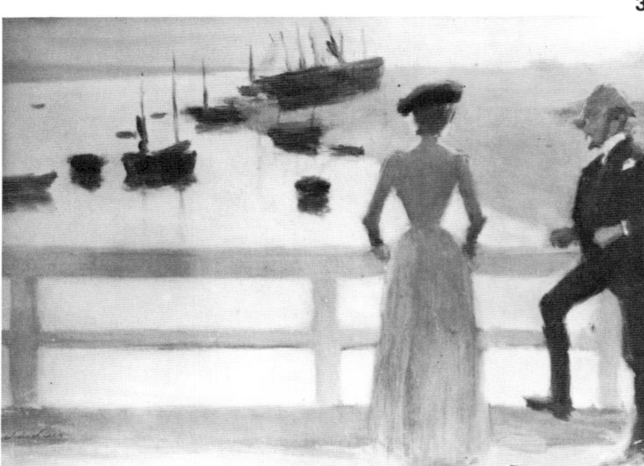
3

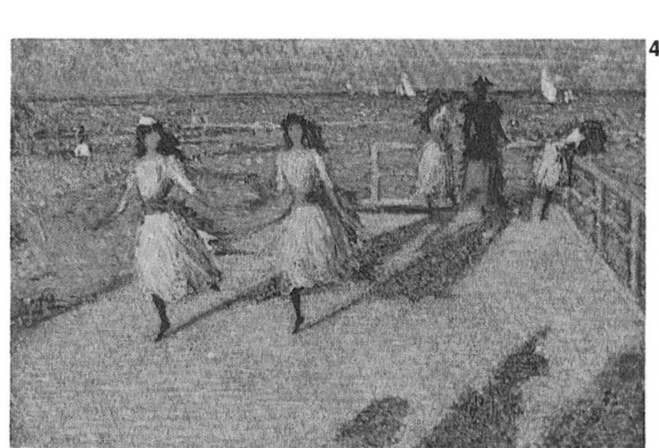
4

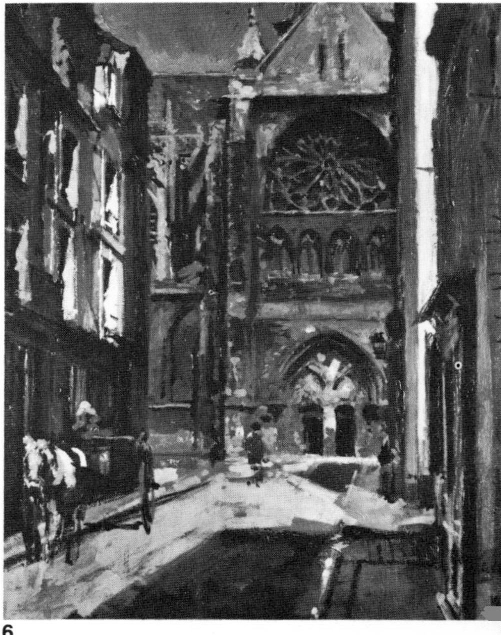
6

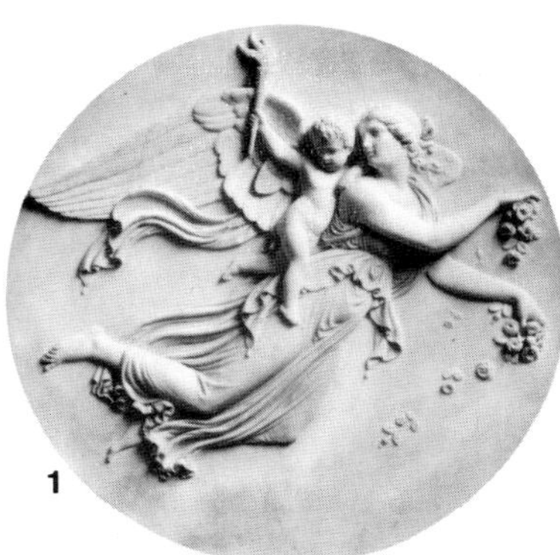
1

1. **Bertel Thorvaldsen** (1768–1844): *Dawn carrying Day.* Marble medallion. 1815. Thorvaldsens Museum, Copenhagen
2. **Leo von Klenze** (1784–1864): The Glyptothek, Munich. 1816–30
3. **Karl Friedrich Schinkel** (1781–1841): Altes Museum, Berlin. 1823–30
4. **Karl Friedrich Schinkel** (1781–1841): Design for the reception hall of King Otto's palace on the Acropolis, Athens (not used). 1834. Staatliche Museen, Berlin-Dahlem
5. **Bertel Thorvaldsen** (1768–1844): *The three Graces and Cupid.* 1819. Thorvaldsens Museum, Copenhagen
6. **Gottfried Semper** (1803–79): The Dresden Opera. 1837–41

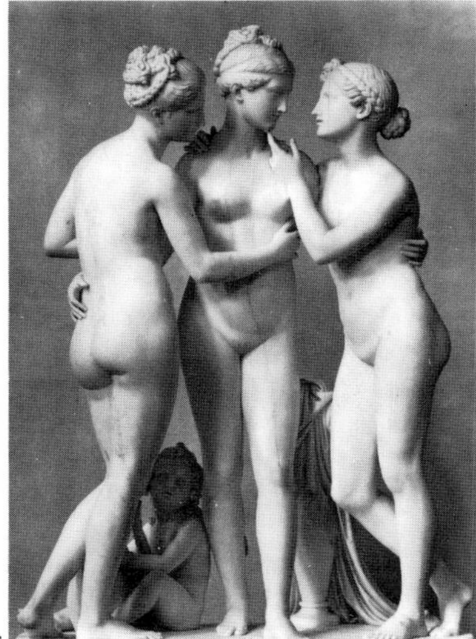
5

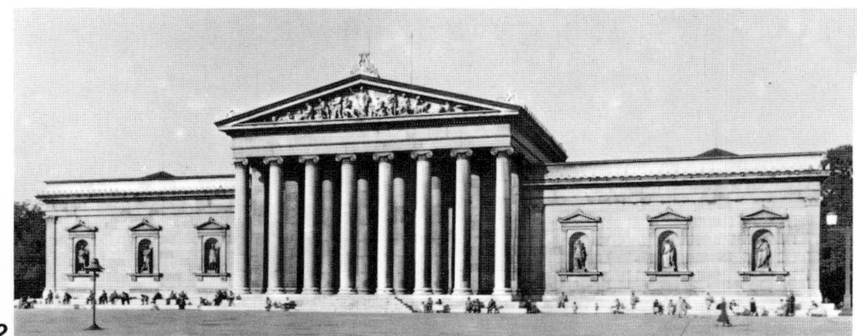
2

3

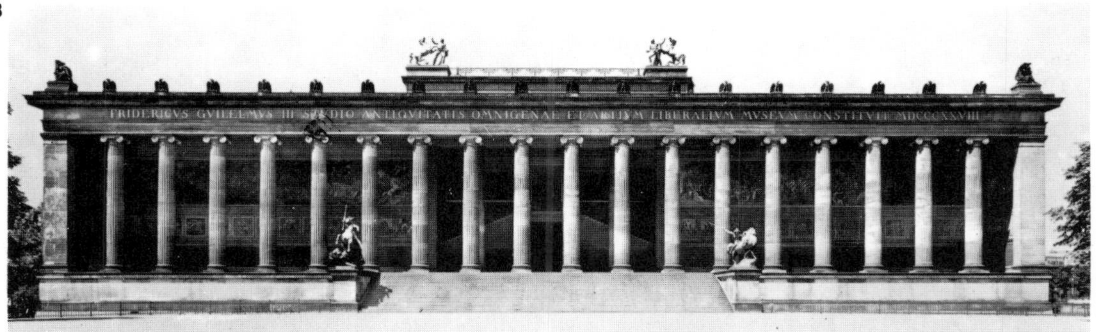

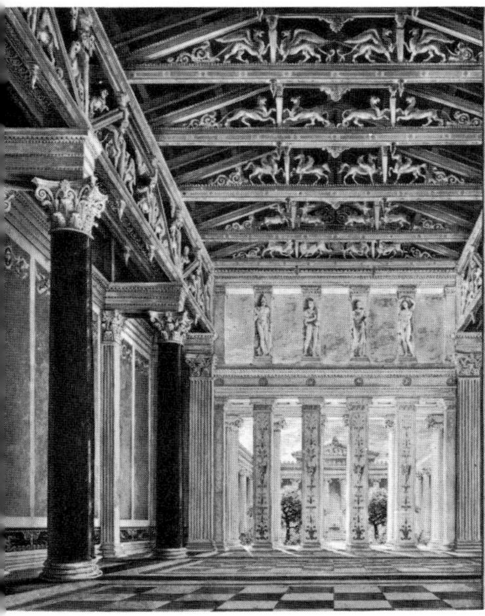

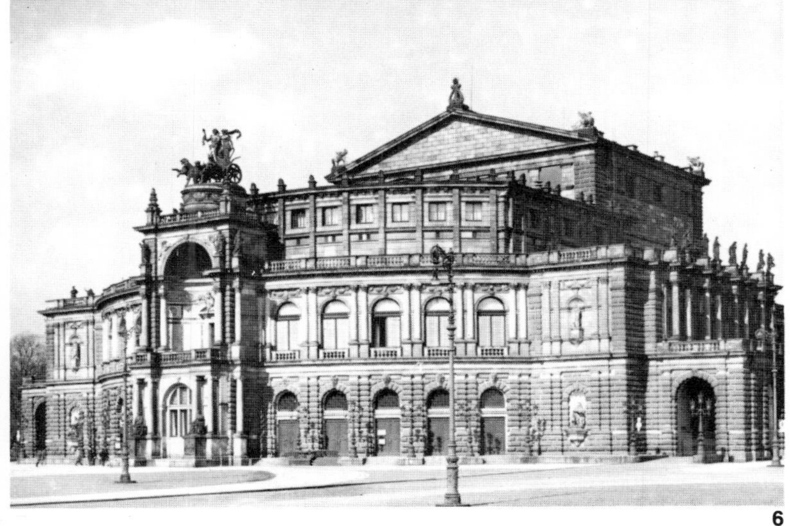
6

1. **Edward Hicks** (1780–1849): *The Peaceable Kingdom.* About 1833. Philadelphia Museum of Art
2. **Thomas Cole** (1801–48): *In the Catskill Mountains.* 1857. Metropolitan Museum o Art, New York
3. **Winslow Homer** (1836–1910): *In the Bermudas.* Watercolour. 1899. Metropolita Museum of Art, New York
4. **Mary Cassatt** (1845–1926): *The Toilet.* Print. 1891
5. **Winslow Homer** (1836–1910): *Breezin Up.* 1876. National Gallery of Art (Mellon Collection), Washington DC

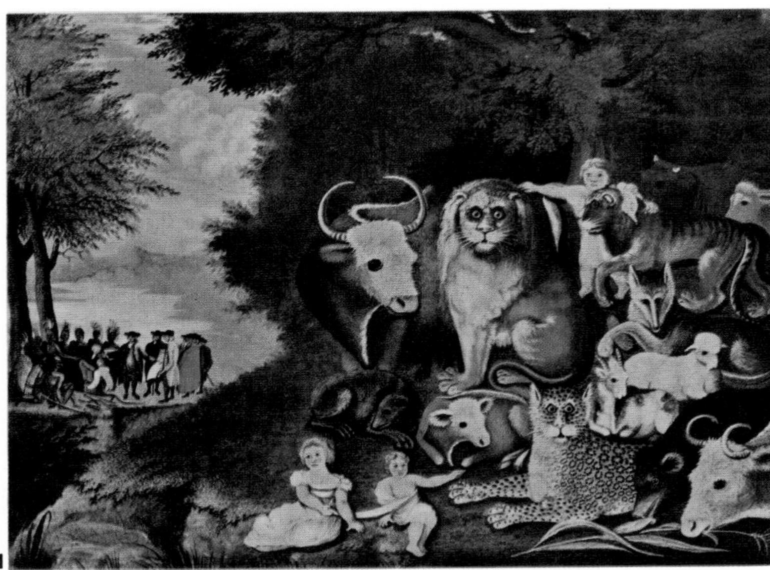

1

2

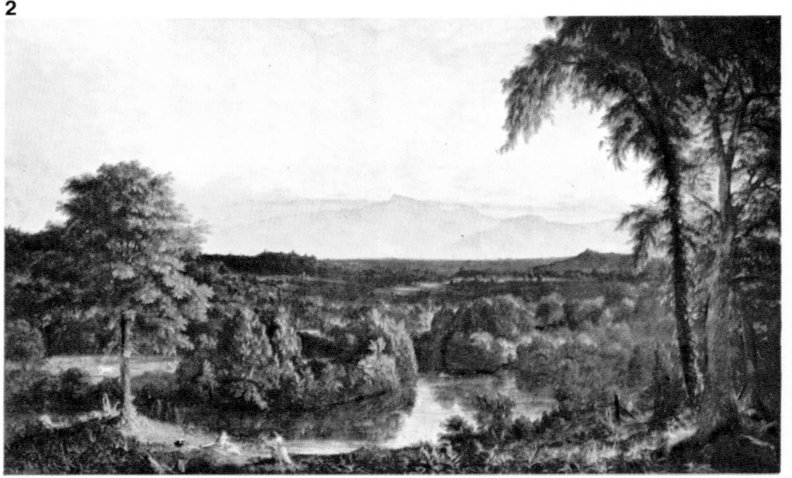

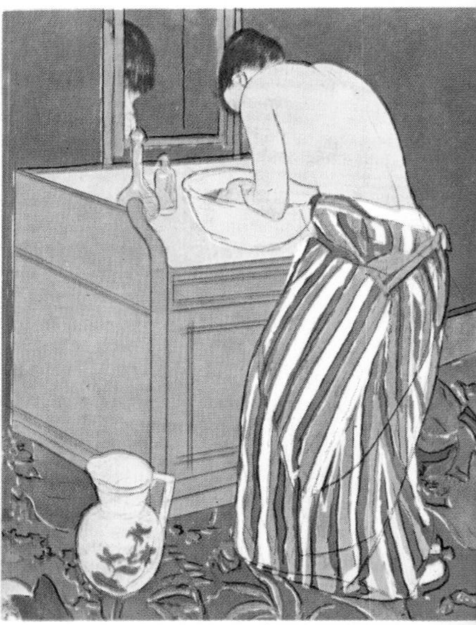

3

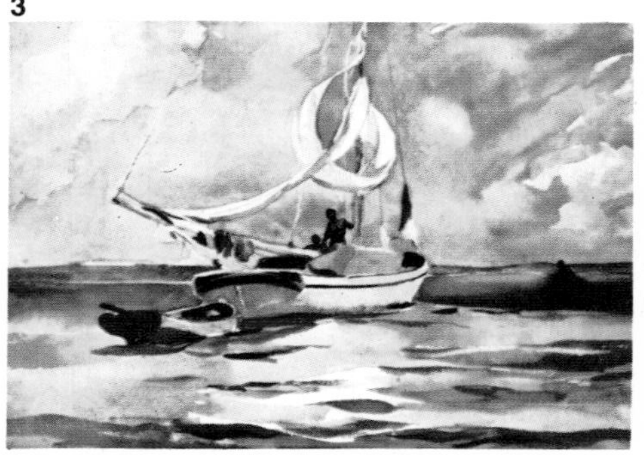

5

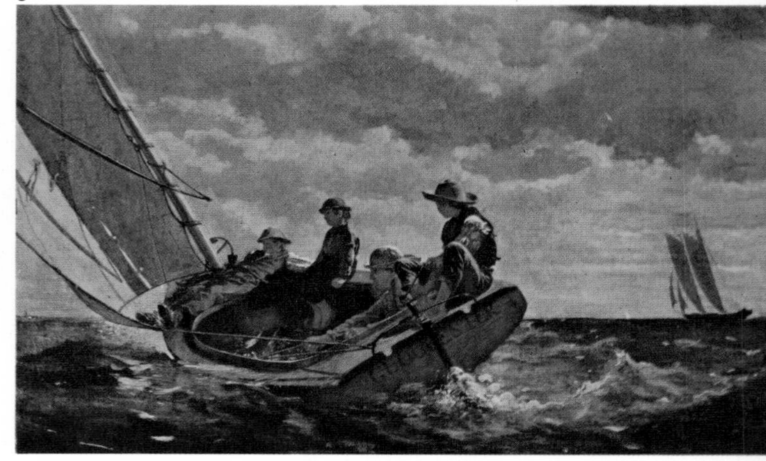

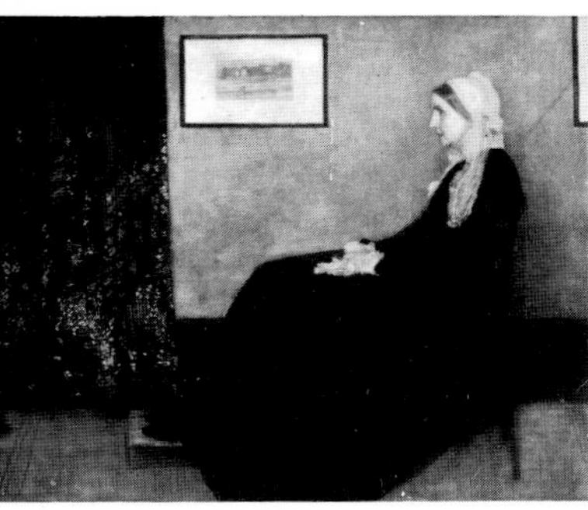

1. **James Abbott McNeill Whistler** (1834–1903): *Arrangement in Black and Grey, No. 1: the Artist's Mother.* 1871–2. Louvre, Paris
2. **J.A.M. Whistler** (1834–1903): *On the Beach.* About 1875. Art Institute of Chicago
3. **John Singer Sargent** (1856–1925): *Portrait of Mrs Charles Gifford Dyer.* Art Institute of Chicago
4. **J.A.M. Whistler** (1834–1903): *Portrait of Mrs Leyland.* 1872–3. Frick Collection, New York
5. **Thomas Eakins** (1844–1916): *Fishing: Repairing of the Nets.* 1881. Philadelphia Museum of Art
6. **John Singer Sargent** (1856–1925): *Paul Helleu sketching with his Wife.* 1889. Brooklyn Museum, New York

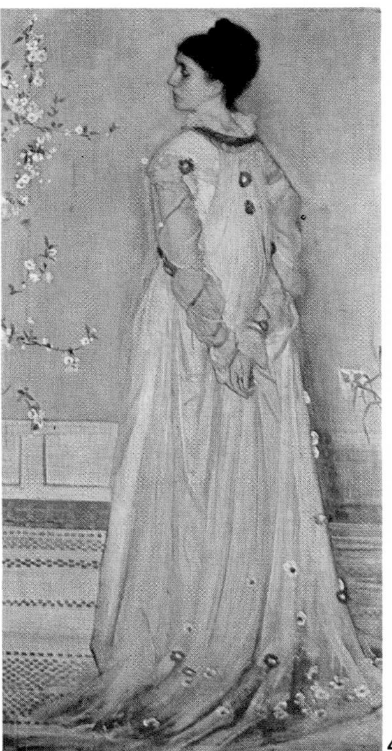

4

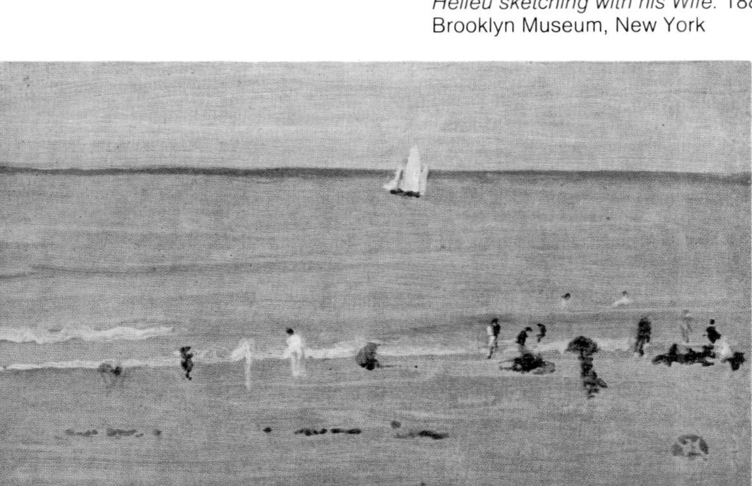

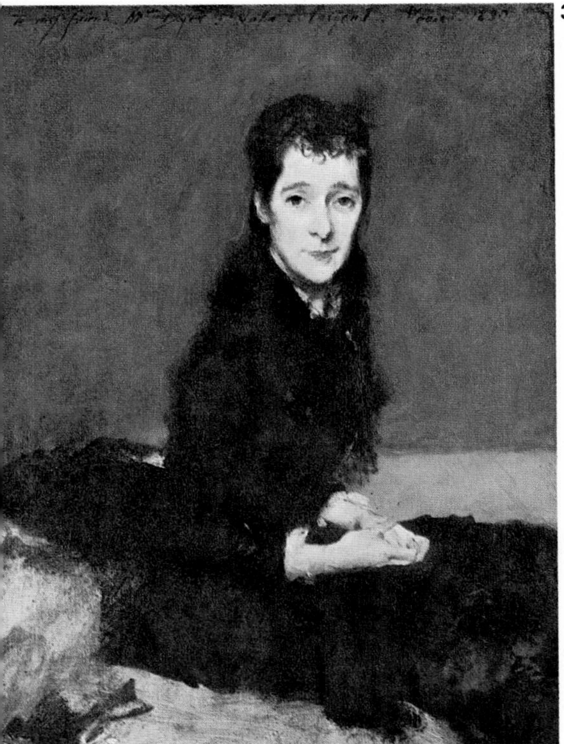

3

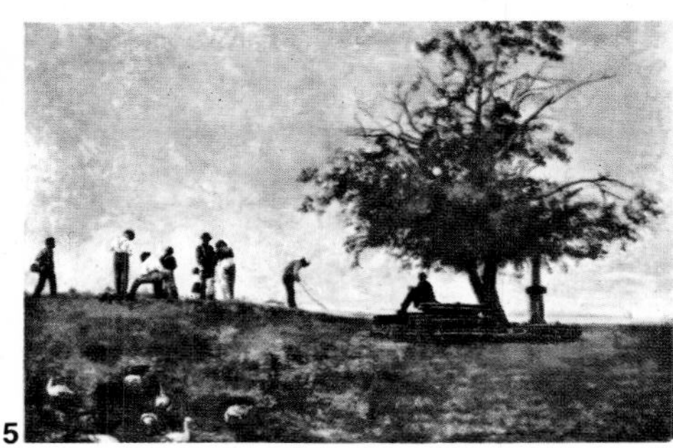

5

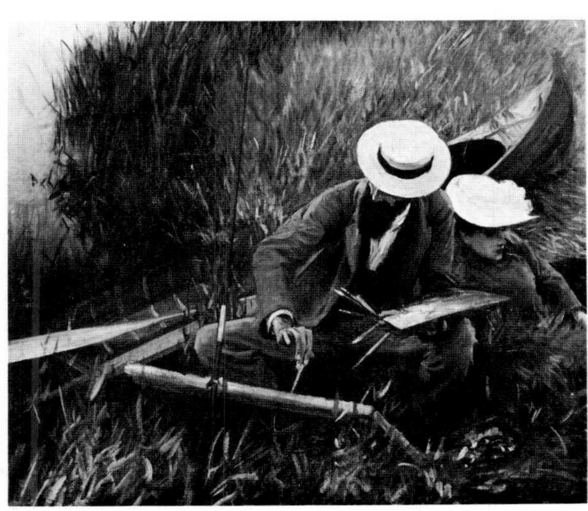

6

1. **Joseph Anton Koch** (1768–1839): *The Schmadribachfall.* 1811. Museum der bildenden Künste, Leipzig
2. **Caspar David Friedrich** (1774–1840): *Two Men contemplating the Moon.* 1819. Gemäldegalerie, Dresden
3. **Ferdinand Hodler** (1853–1918): *The Watercourse.* 1904. Kunsthaus, Zurich
4. **Ferdinand Hodler** (1853–1918): *Day.* 1900. Kunstmuseum, Berne
5. **Philipp Otto Runge** (1777–1810): *The Rest on the Flight into Egypt.* 1805–6. Kunsthalle, Hamburg
6. **Caspar David Friedrich** (1774–1840): *Morning Light.* 1808. Folkwang Museu Essen
7. **Arnold Böcklin** (1827–1901): *The Isle of the Dead* (first version). Tempera. 18 Kunstmuseum (Gottfried Keller Collectio Basle

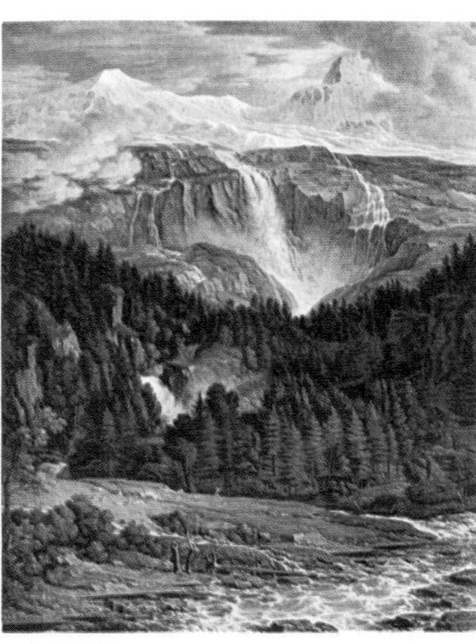
1

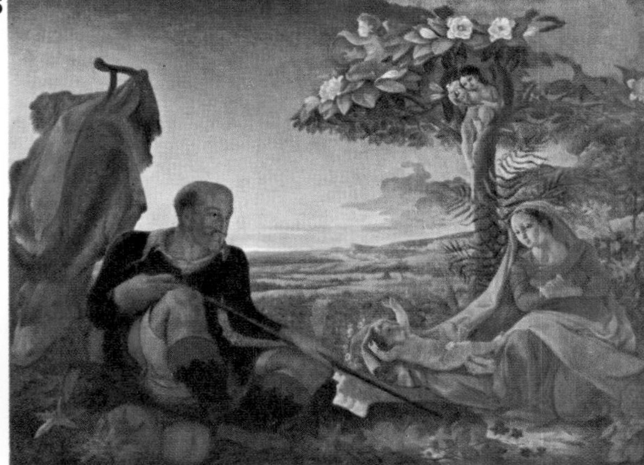
5

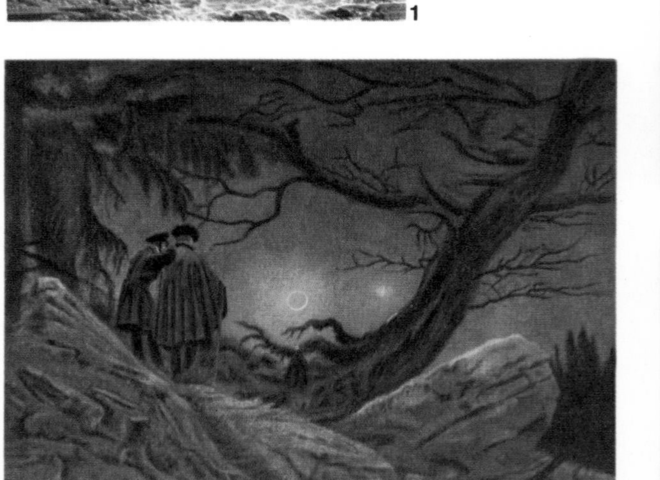
2

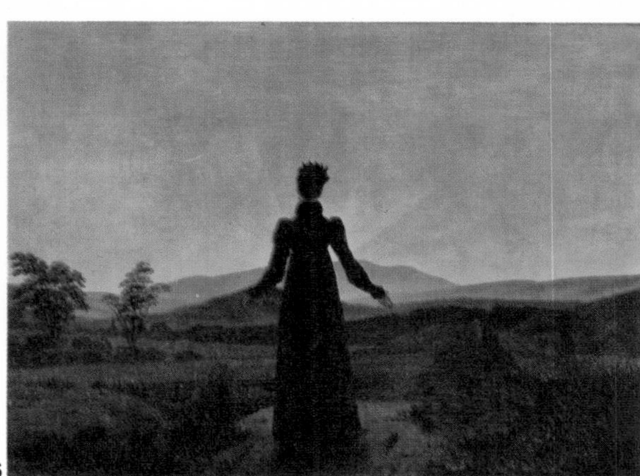
6

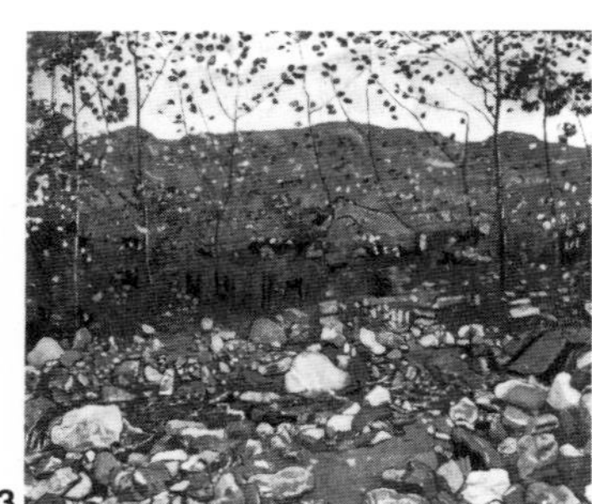
3

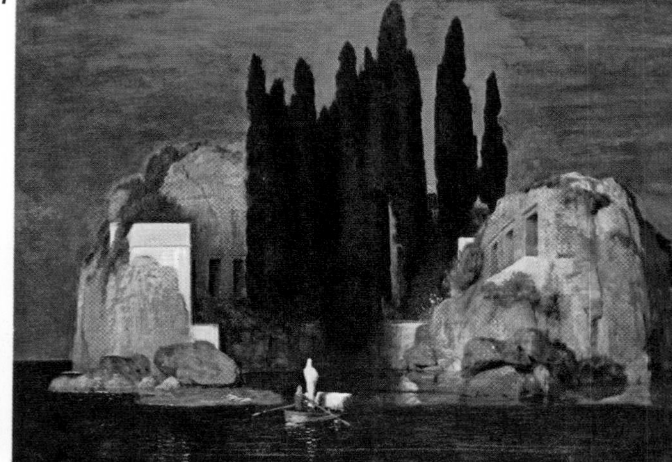
7

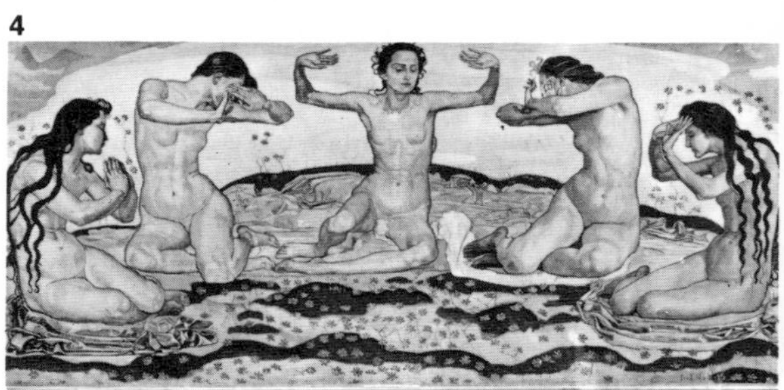
4

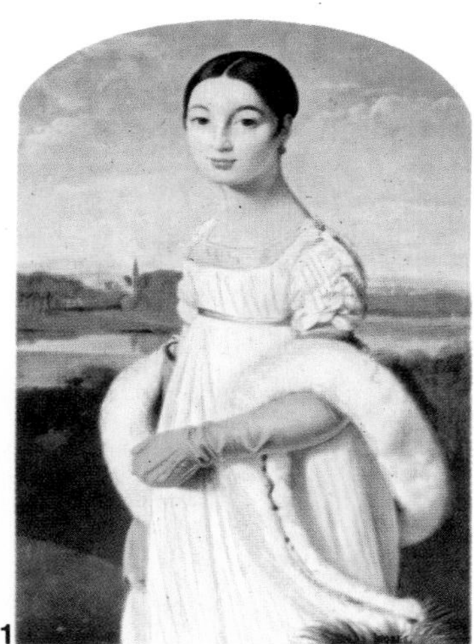
1

Jean-Auguste-Dominique Ingres
(1780–1867)

1. *Portrait of Mademoiselle Rivière.* 1805. Louvre, Paris
2. *Portrait of the painter François-Marius Granet.* 1807. Musée Granet, Aix-en-Provence
3. *The Guillon-Lethière Family.* Drawing. 1819. Boston Museum of Fine Arts
4. *The Bather of Valpinçon.* 1808. Louvre, Paris
5. *Thetis entreating Jupiter.* 1811. Musée Granet, Aix-en-Provence
6. *The Turkish Bath.* 1859–63. Louvre, Paris
7. *Odalisque with Slave.* 1842. Walters Art Gallery, Baltimore

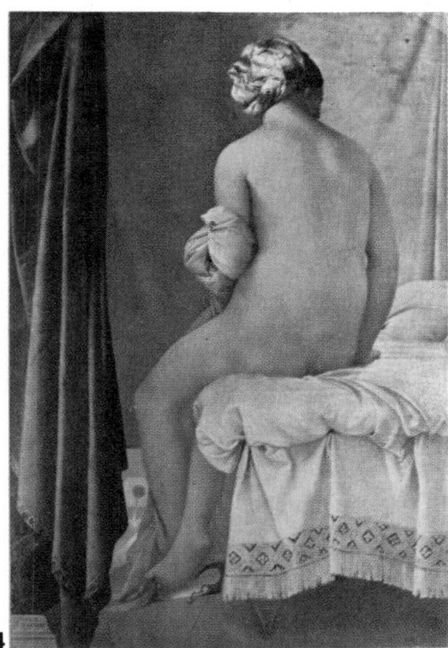
4

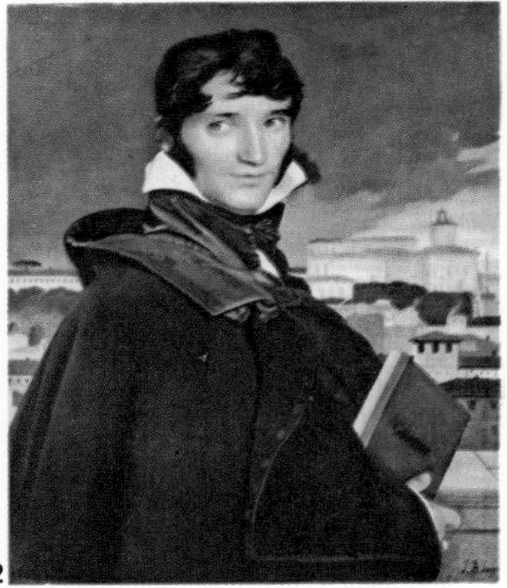
2

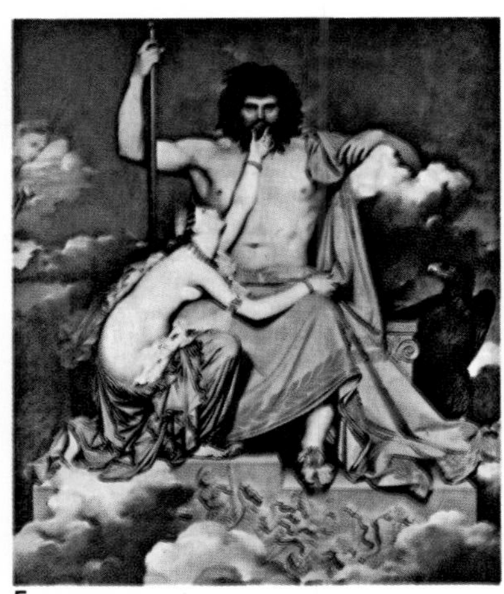
5

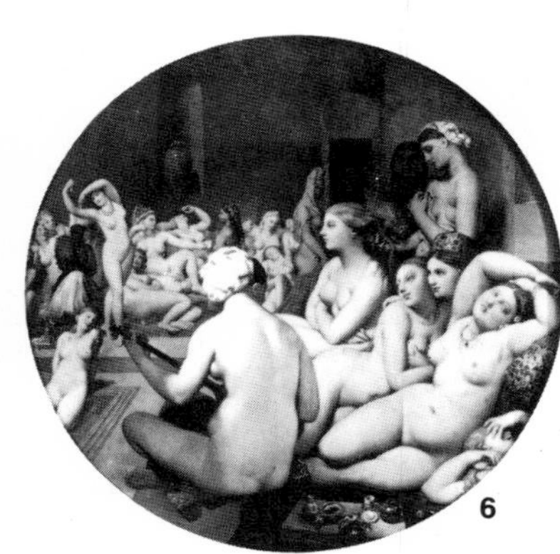
6

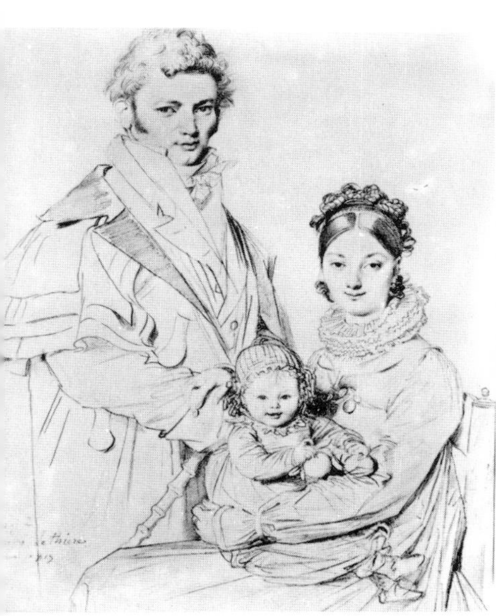

7

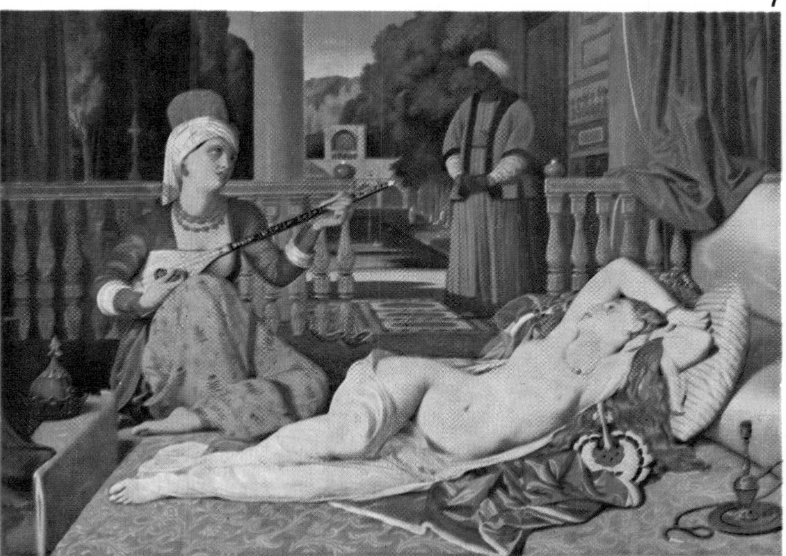

Jean-Baptiste-Camille Corot (1796–1875)

1. *The Belfry of Douai.* 1871. Louvre, Paris
2. *The Port of La Rochelle.* 1851. Private Collection, New York
3. *Gipsy with a Mandolin.* 1874. Museu de Arte de São Paulo
4. *Chartres Cathedral.* 1830. Louvre, Paris
5. *Rocks in the Forest of Fontainebleau.* 1860–5. National Gallery of Art (Chester Dale Collection), Washington DC
6. *The Environs of Barbizon.* Drawing. Bibliothèque Nationale, Paris
7. *Marietta, the Roman Odalisque.* 1843. Musée des Beaux-Arts de la Ville de Paris
8. *Trees at the Bank of a Lake.* Pencil and ink. Louvre, Paris

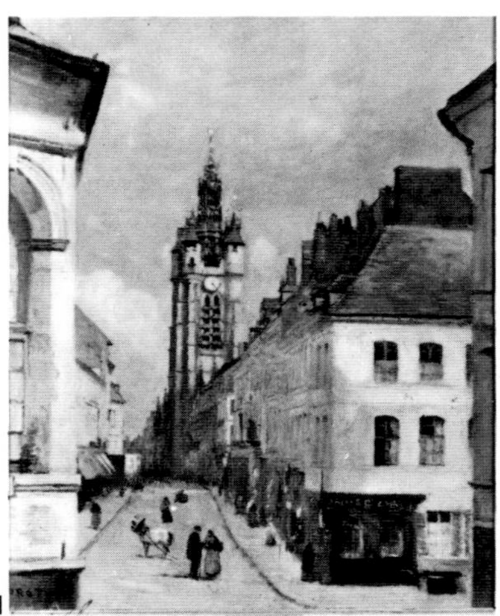
1

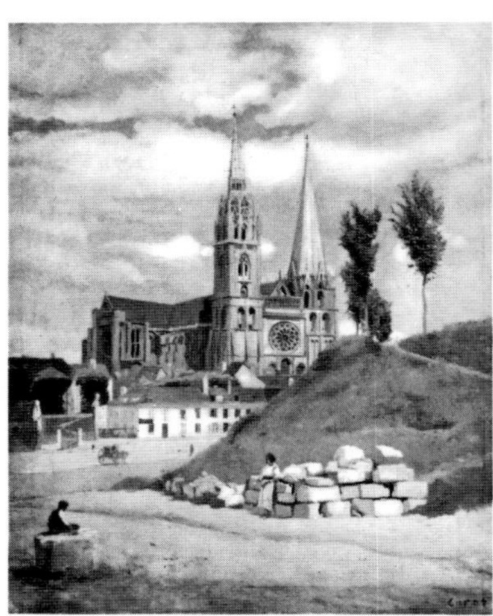
4

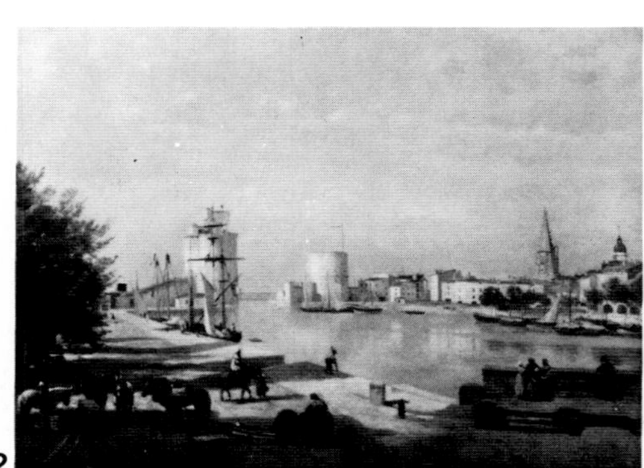
2

5
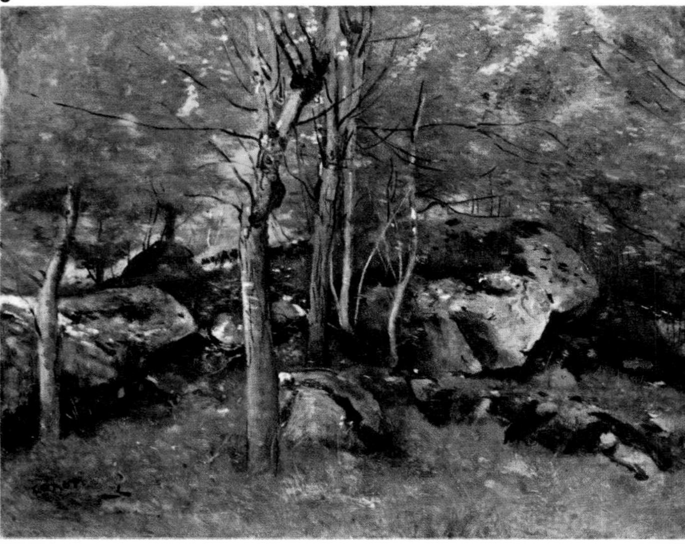

3
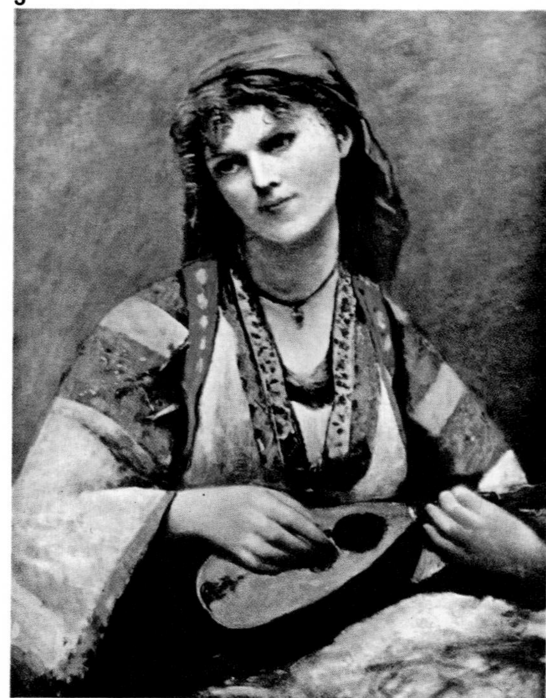

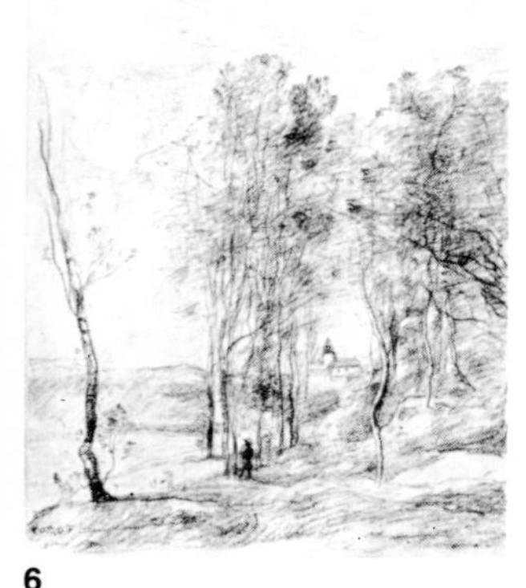
6

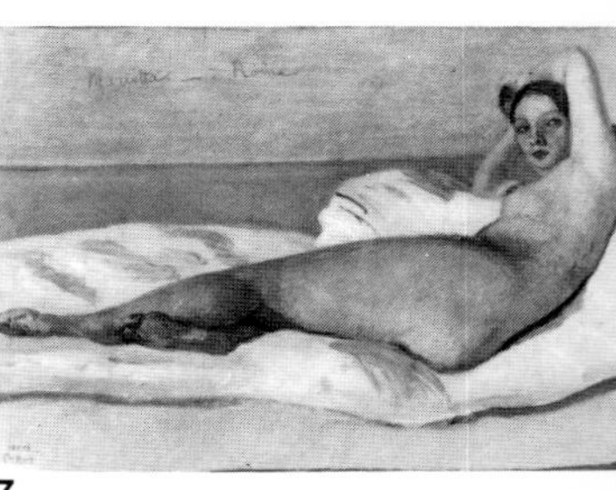
7

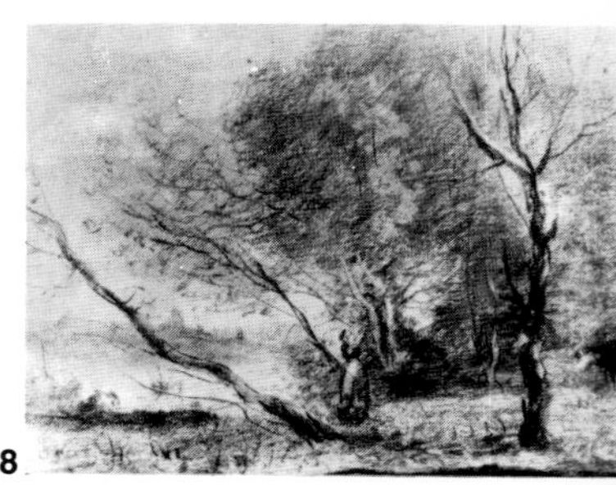
8

Gustave Courbet (1819–77)
1. *The Painter's Studio.* Detail. 1855. Louvre, Paris
2. *A Covert of Roedeer by the Stream of Plaisir-Fontaine, Doubs.* 1866. Louvre, Paris
3. *The Cliff at Étretat after the Storm.* 1869. Louvre, Paris
4. *The Corn Sifters.* 1855. Musée des Beaux-Arts, Nantes
5. *The Stonebreaker.* 1849. Private Collection
6. *The Meeting* or *Bonjour, Monsieur Courbet!* 1854. Musée Fabre, Montpellier

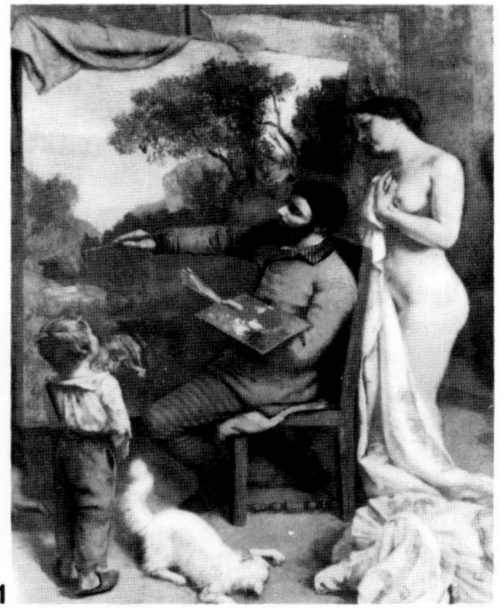
1

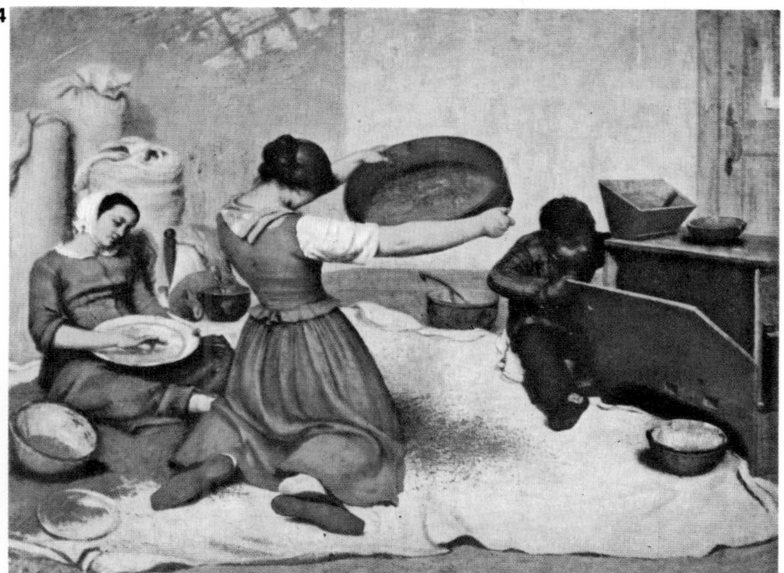
4

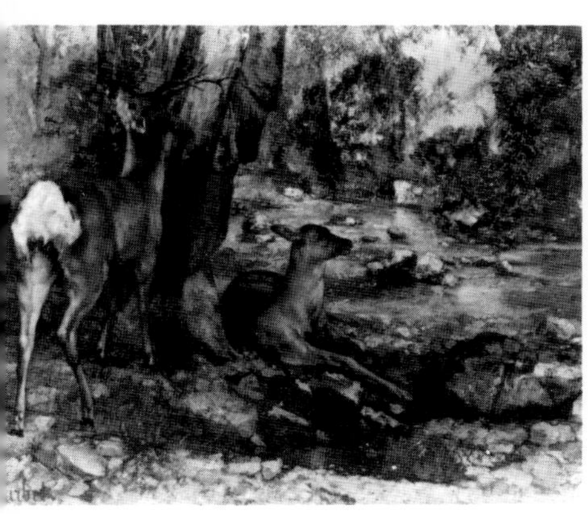

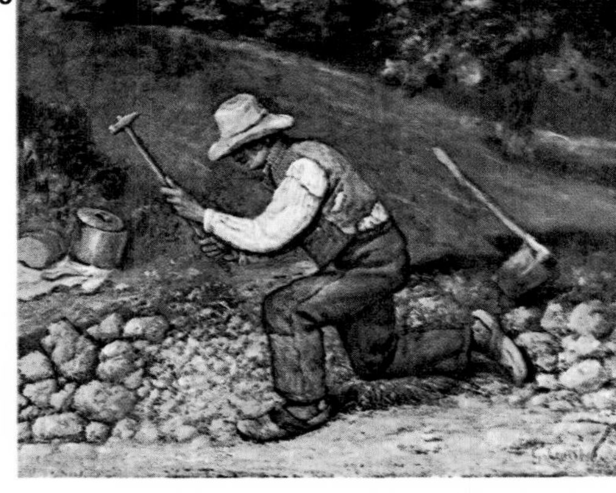
5

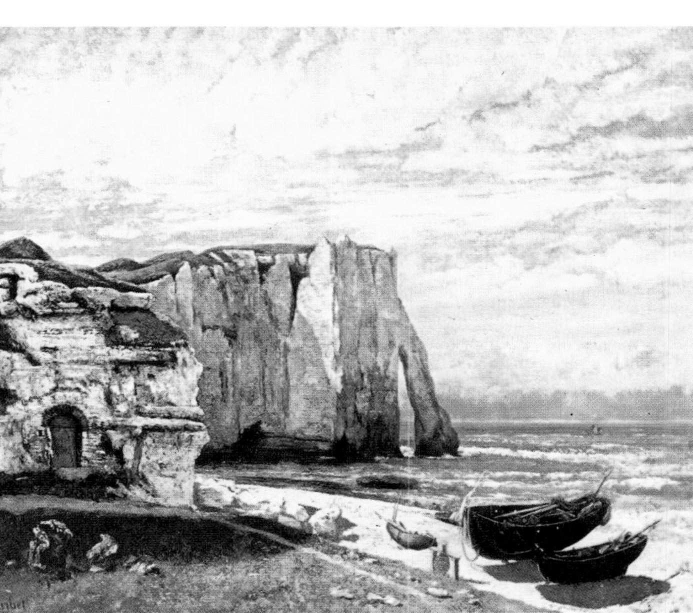

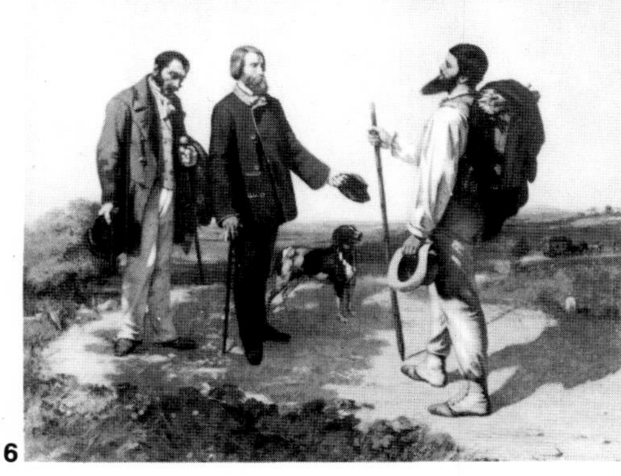
6

Théodore Géricault (1791–1824)

1. *Light Cavalry Officer charging.* 1812. Louvre, Paris
2. *The Capture of a wild Horse.* About 1817. Musée des Beaux-Arts, Rouen
3. *The Epsom Derby.* 1821. Louvre, Paris
4. *Hussar Trumpeter.* 1813. Kunsthistorisches Museum, Vienna
5. *An insane Woman from the Paris asylur of La Salpêtrière: Envy* (*The Hyena of Salpêtrière*). 1822–3. Musée des Beau Arts, Lyons
6. *The Raft of the Medusa.* Unfinished sketc 1818. Louvre, Paris

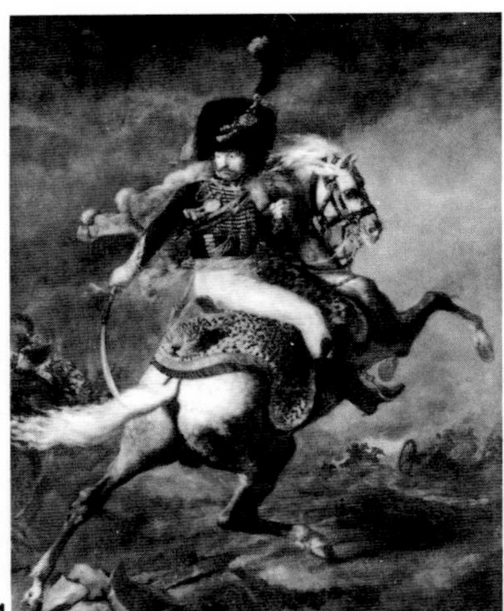
1

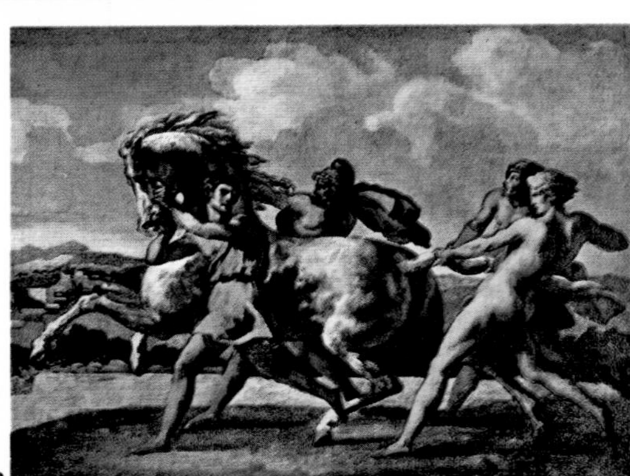
2

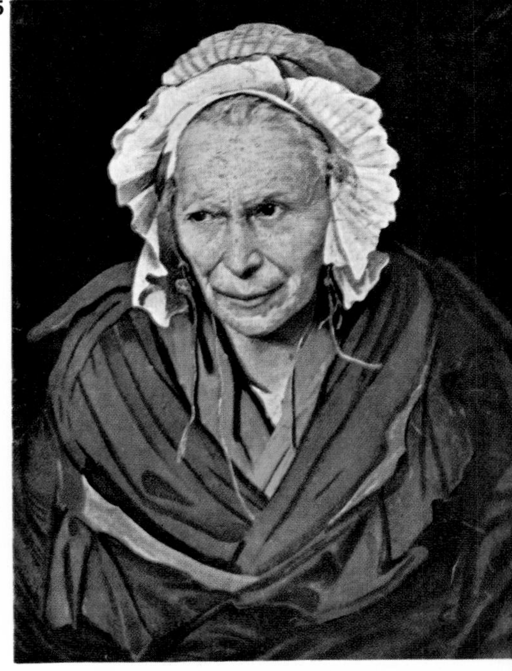
5

3
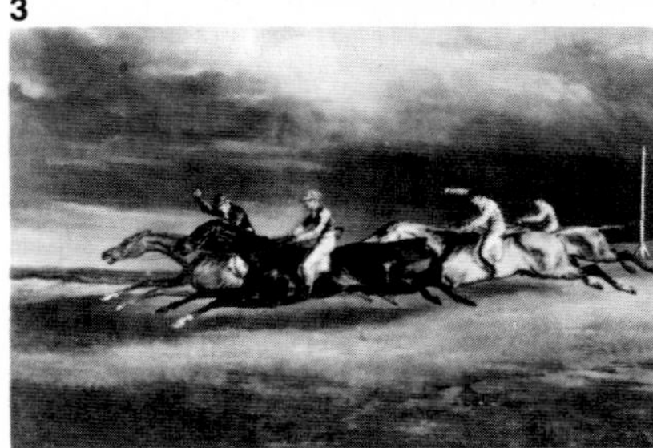

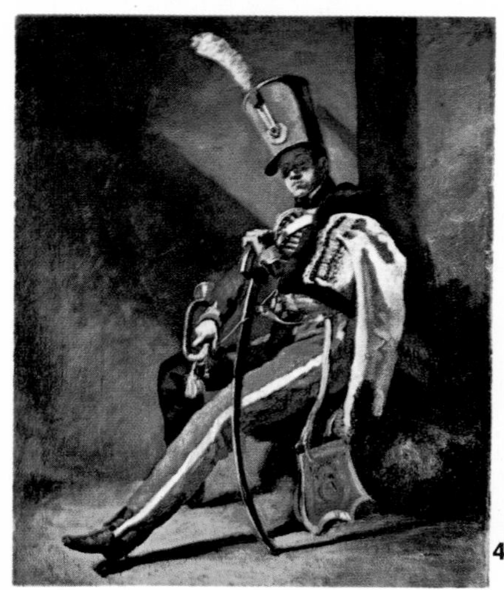
4

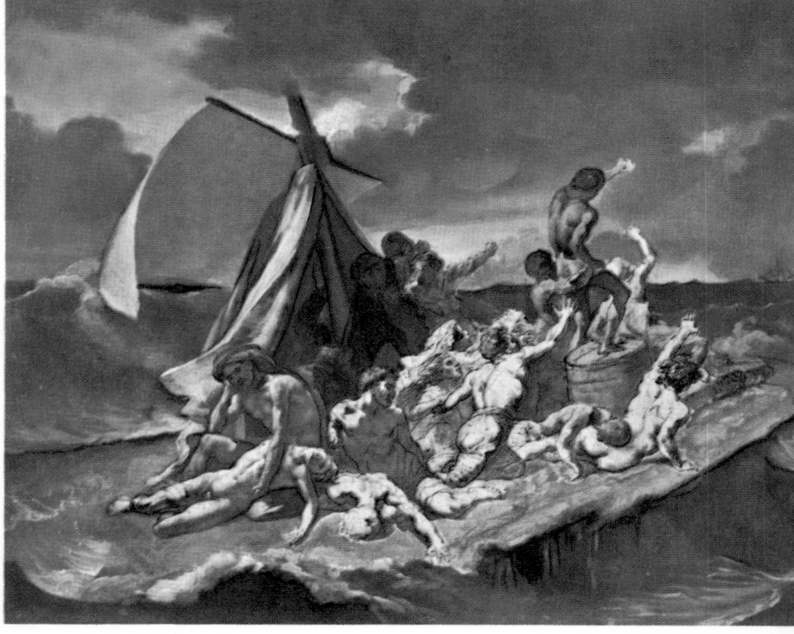

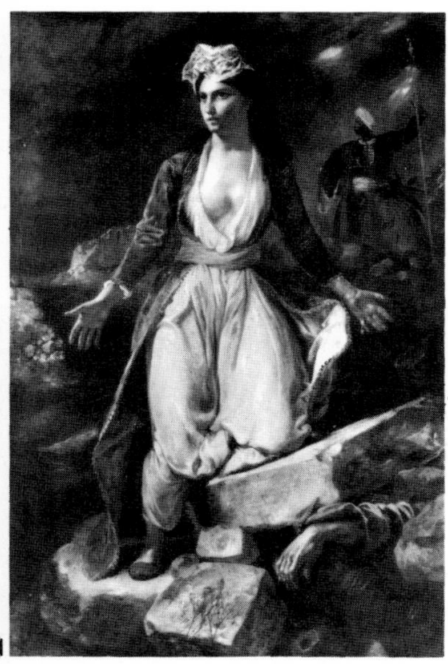

Eugène Delacroix (1798–1863)

1. *Greece expiring on the Ruins of Missolonghi.* About 1827. Musée des Beaux-Arts, Bordeaux
2. *Lion's Head.* Watercolour and gouache. Louvre, Paris
3. *Liberty leading the People.* 1830. Louvre, Paris
4. *Combat of the Giaour and the Pasha.* 1827. Art Institute of Chicago
5. *Horse attacked by a Tiger.* Watercolour. Louvre, Paris
6. *Orphan Girl in the Graveyard.* About 1823. Louvre, Paris

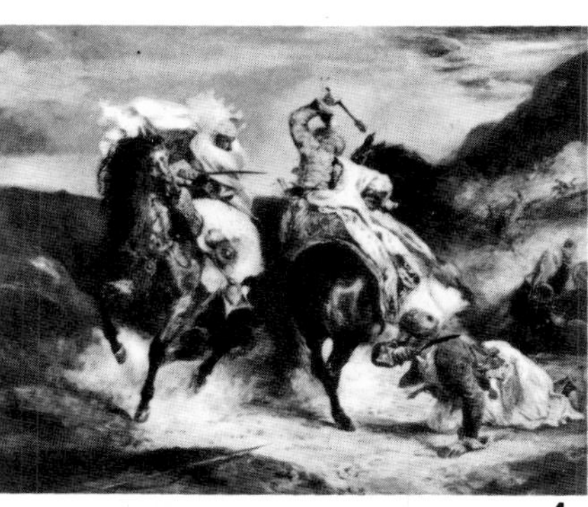

4

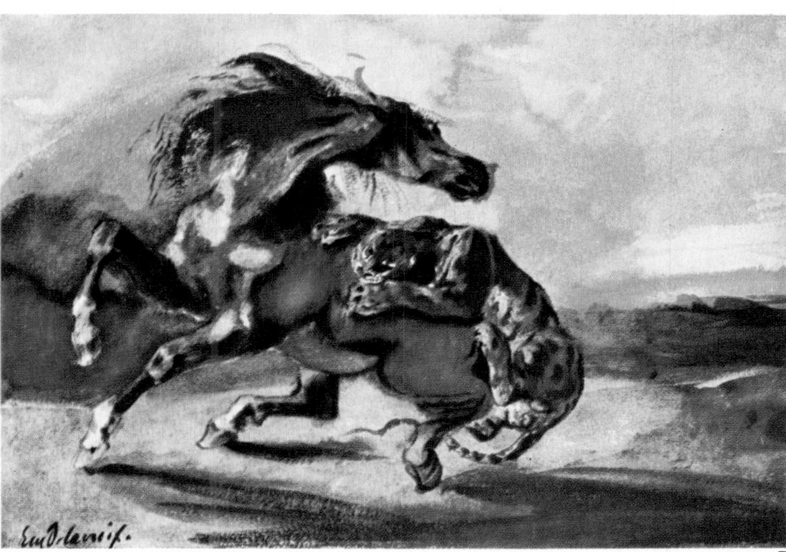

5

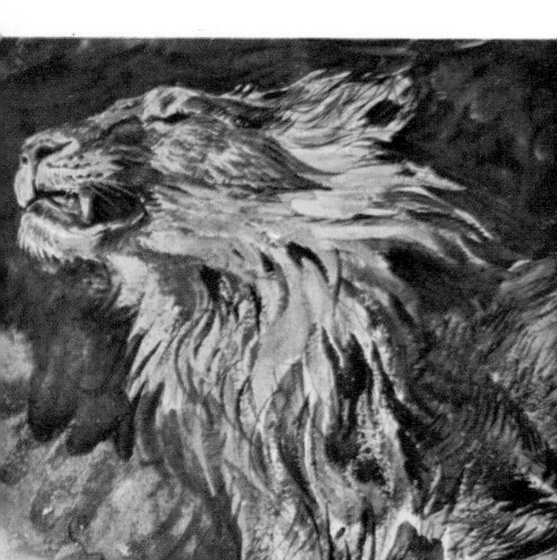

2

3

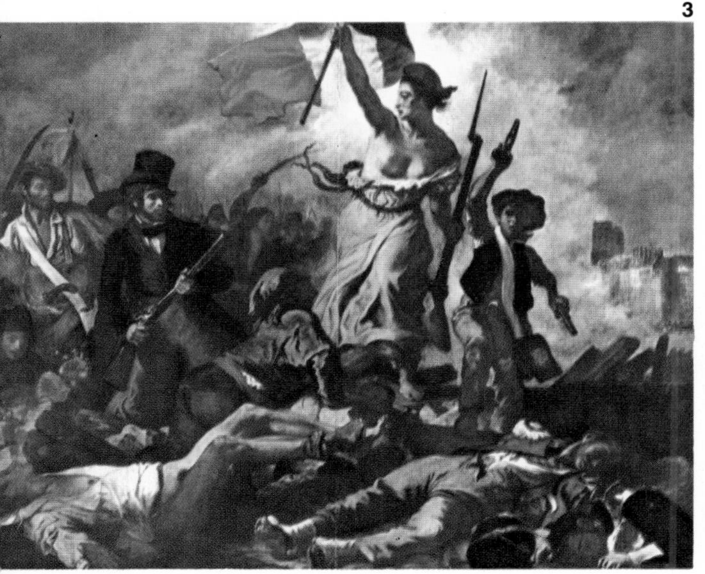

6

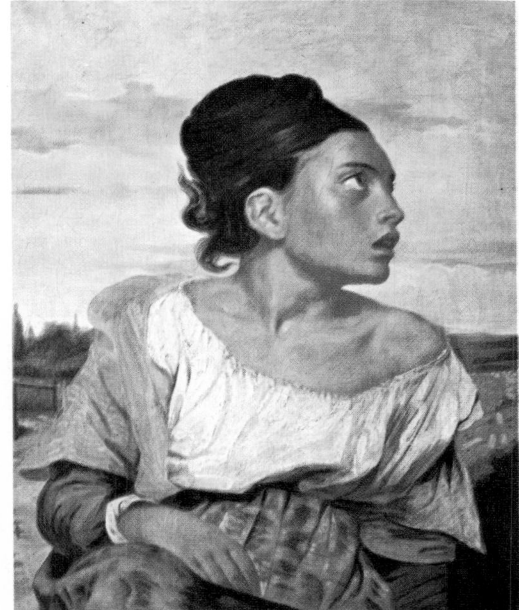

1. **Théodore Rousseau** (1812–67): *The little Fisherman.* 1848–9. Louvre, Paris
2. **Jean-François Millet** (1814–75): *The Gleaners.* 1857. Louvre, Paris
3. **Charles-François Daubigny** (1817–78): *Sunset on the Oise.* 1865. Louvre, Paris
4. **Théodore Rousseau** (1812–67): *Under the Birches* (*The Parish Priest*). Toledo Museum of Art, Ohio
5. **Jean-François Millet** (1814–75): *The Laundress.* About 1861. Louvre, Paris
6. **Jean-François Millet** (1814–75): *Woman with a Rake.* Metropolitan Museum of Art, New York

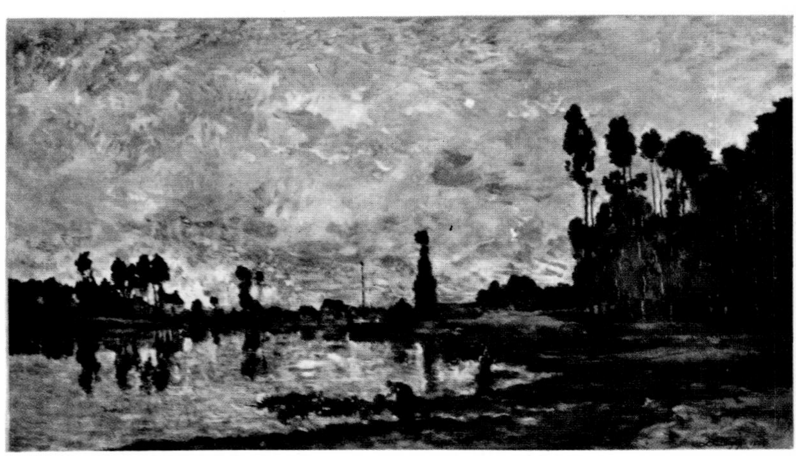

3

1

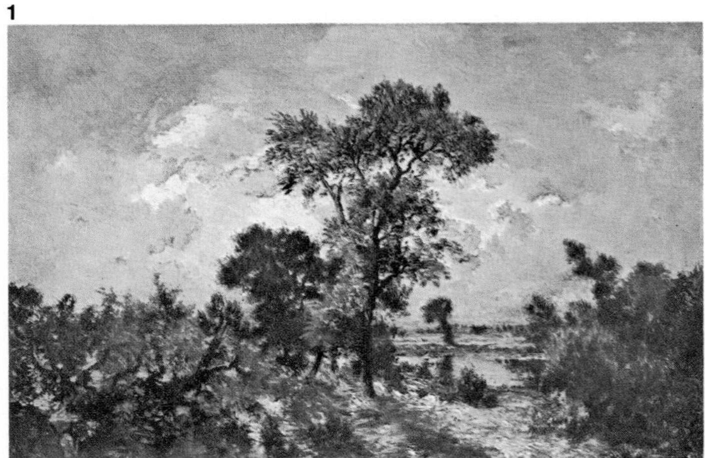

4

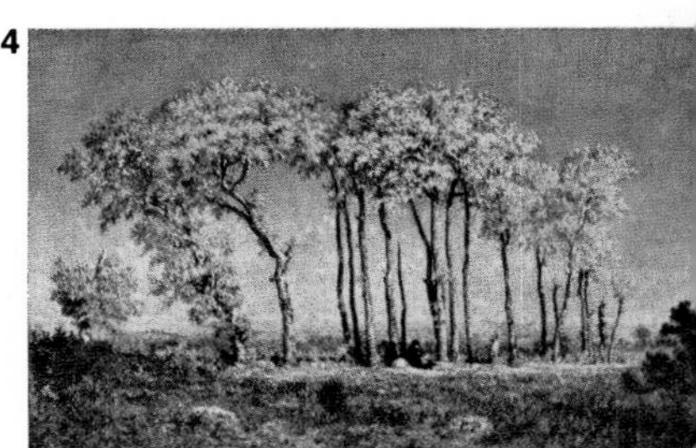

5

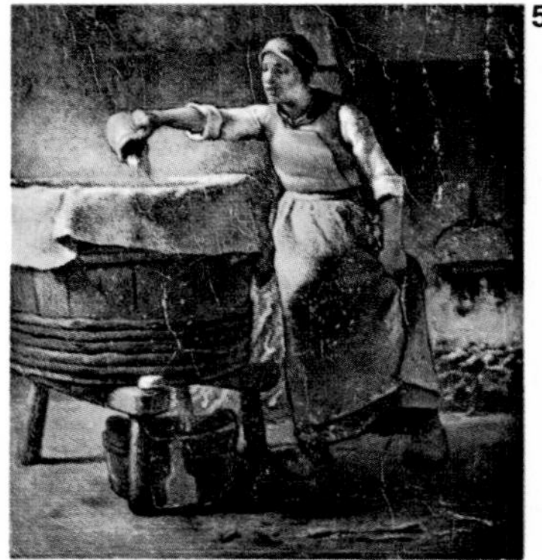

2

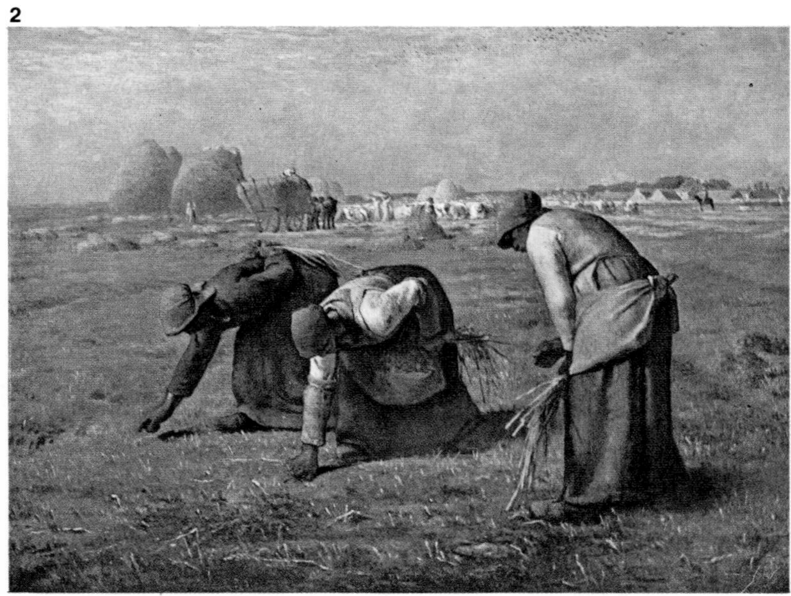

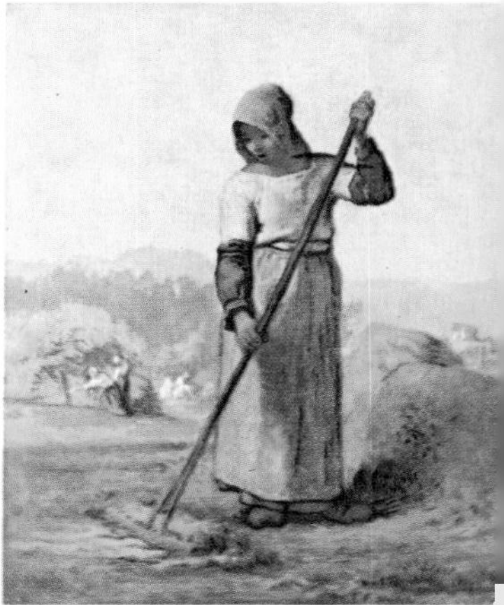

Honoré Daumier (1808–79): *A Third-class Carriage.* About 1862. Metropolitan Museum of Art, New York
Henri Rousseau (1844–1910): *Cart of Père Juniet.* 1908. Louvre, Paris
Pierre Puvis de Chavannes (1824–98): *The poor Fisherman.* 1881. Louvre, Paris
Honoré Daumier (1808–79): *The fine Bottle.* Aquarelle. Nationalmuseum, Stockholm
Henri Rousseau (1844–1910): *The sleeping Gipsy.* 1897. Museum of Modern Art, New York
Henri Rousseau (1844–1910): *The Snake Charmer.* 1907. Musée de l'Impressionnisme, Paris

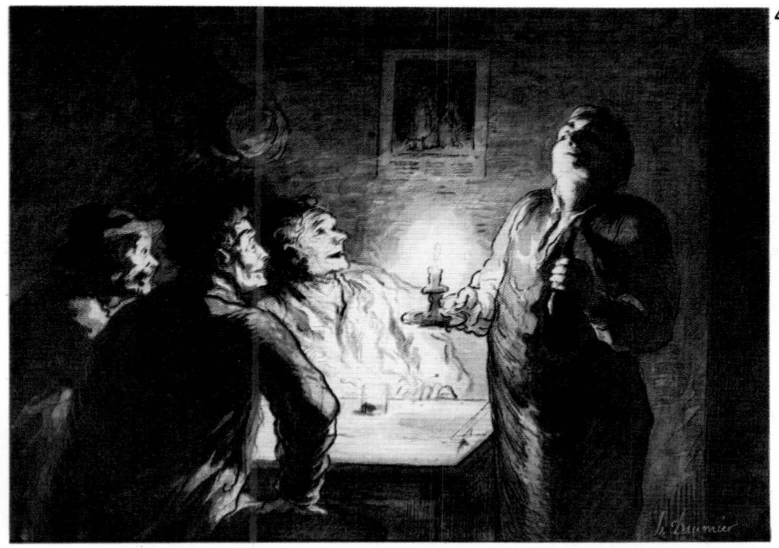

4

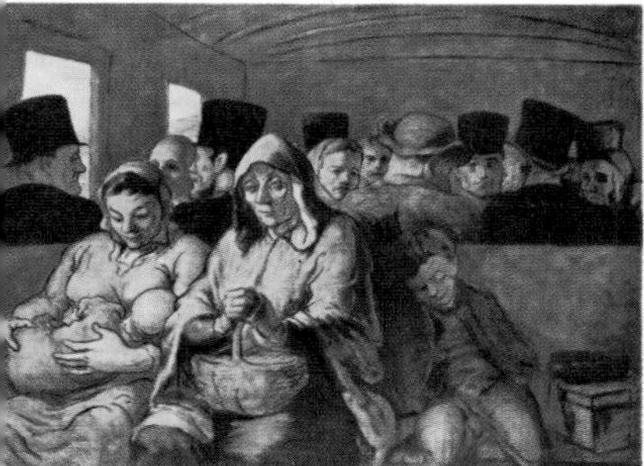

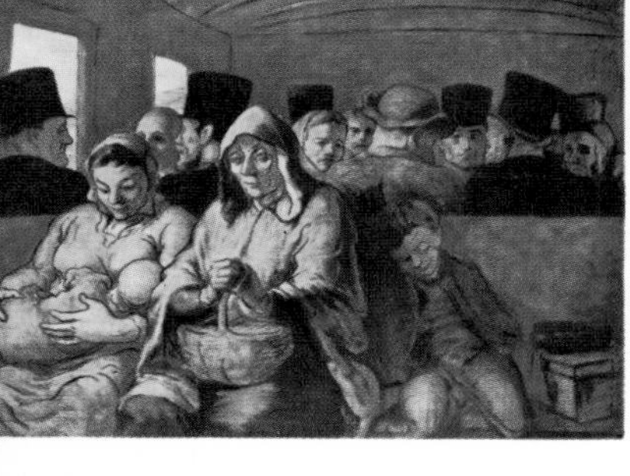

1

2

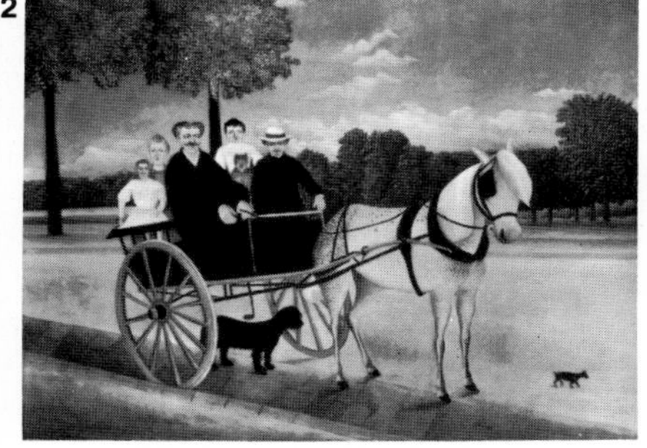

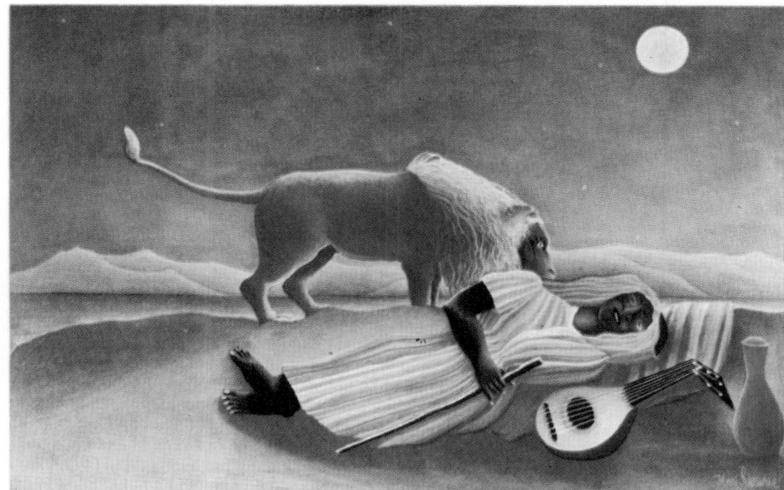

5

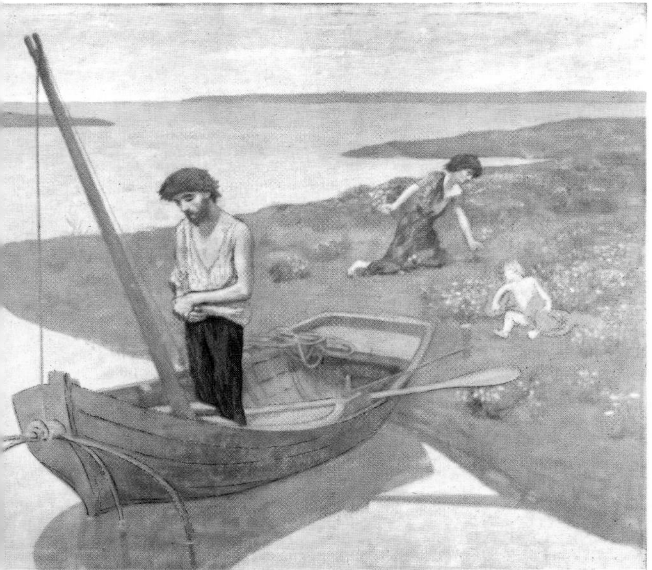

6

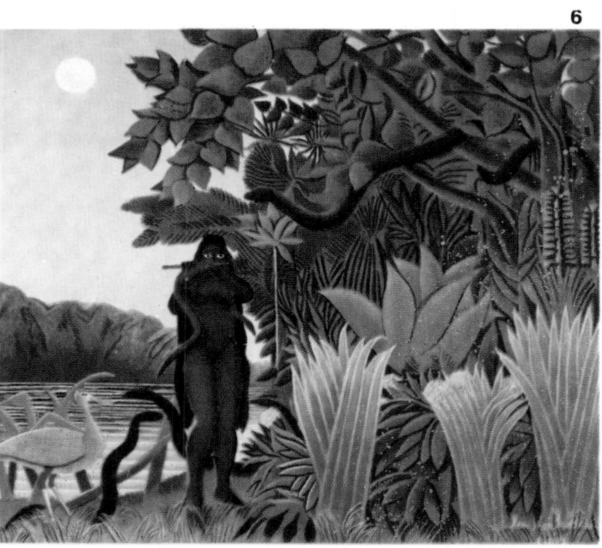

Édouard Manet (1832–83)
1. *Portrait of Stéphane Mallarmé.* 1876. Musée de l'Impressionnisme, Paris
2. *Portrait of Émile Zola.* 1868. Musée de l'Impressionnisme, Paris
3. *Le Déjeuner sur l'Herbe.* 1863. Musée de l'Impressionnisme, Paris
4. *Spring: Jeanne de Marsy.* Sketch. 1881. Fogg Art Museum, Harvard University, Cambridge, Massachusetts
5. *Olympia.* 1863. Musée de l'Impressionnisme, Paris
6. *Torero saluting.* 1866. Metropolitan Museum of Art, New York
7. *The Fifer.* 1866. Musée de l'Impressionnisme, Paris
8. *Woman with a black Hat: Irma Brunner.* Pastel. 1882. Musée de l'Impressionnisme, Paris

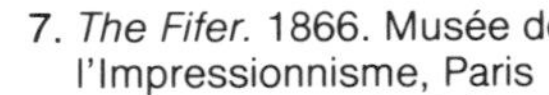

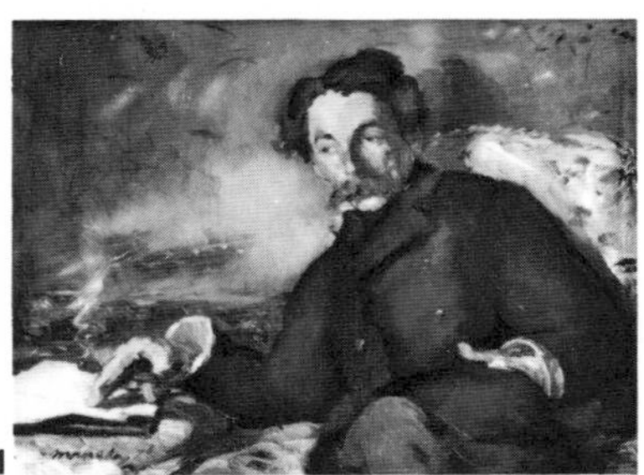

1

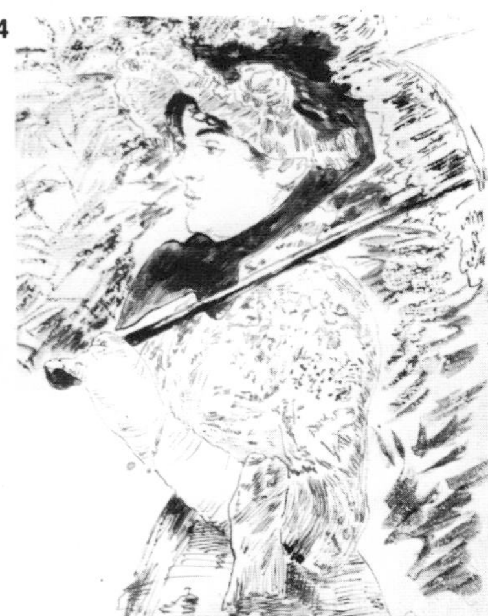

4

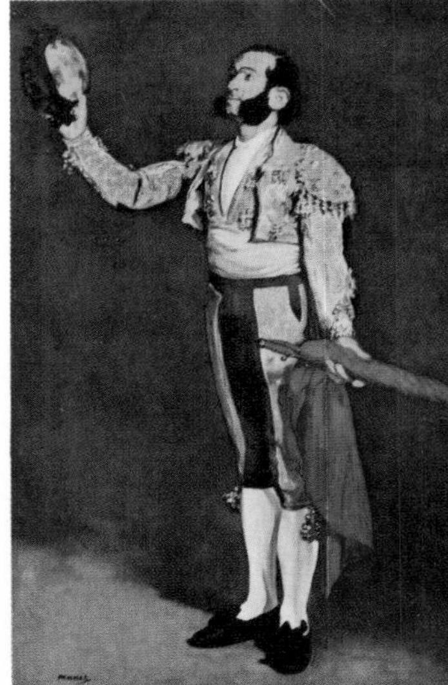

6

2

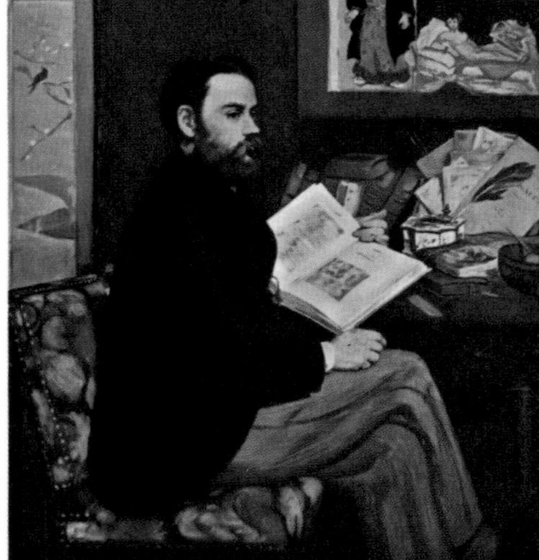

7

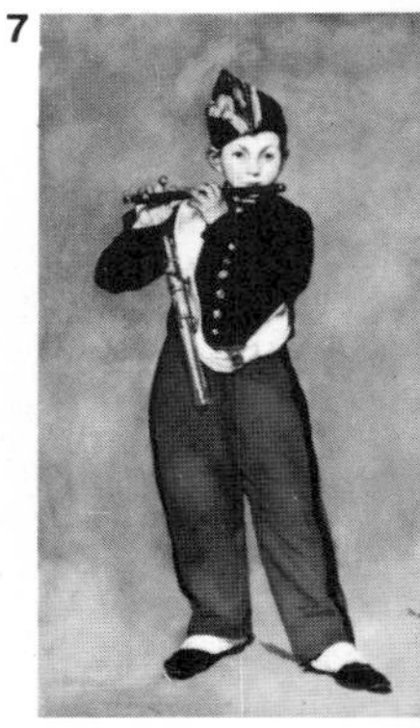

5

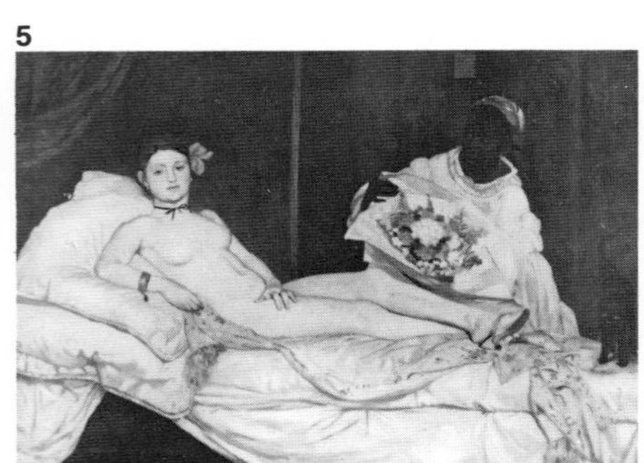

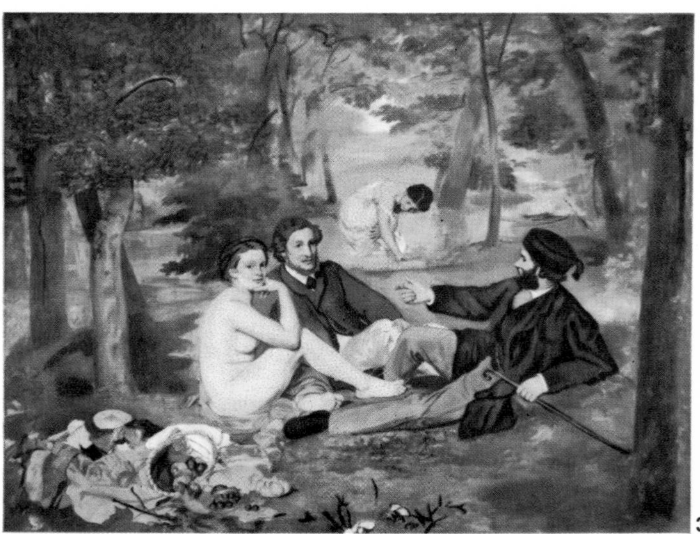

3

8

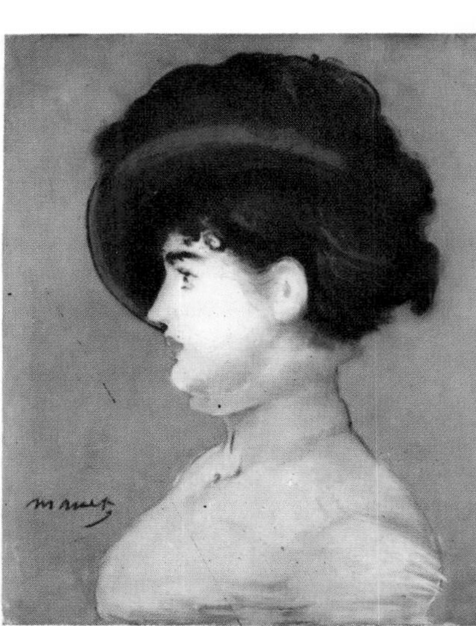

Berthe Morisot (1841–95): *The Cherry Picker.* 1891. Private Collection
Camille Pissarro (1830–1903): *Ile Lacroix, Rouen, in the Fog.* 1888. Philadelphia Museum of Art
Eugène Boudin (1824–98): *The Beach at Trouville.* 1863. Private Collection, Paris
Camille Pissarro (1830–1903): *The Road from Versailles to Louveciennes.* 1870. Emil G. Bührle Foundation, Zurich
Alfred Sisley (1839–99): *Snow at Louveciennes.* 1878. Musée de l'Impressionnisme, Paris
Frédéric Bazille (1841–70): *The Family Reunion.* 1867. Louvre, Paris

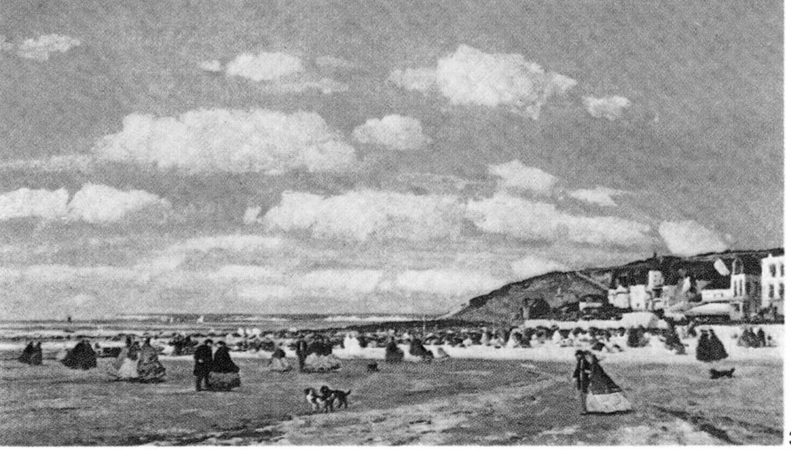

3

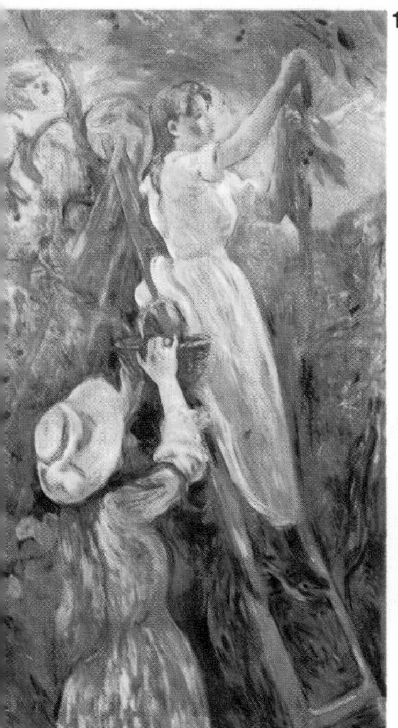

1

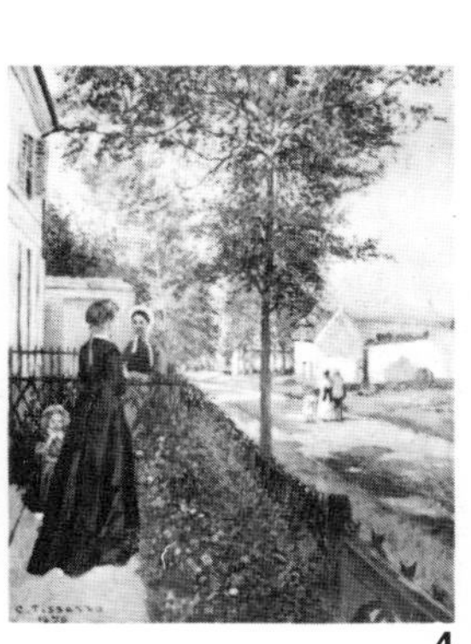

4

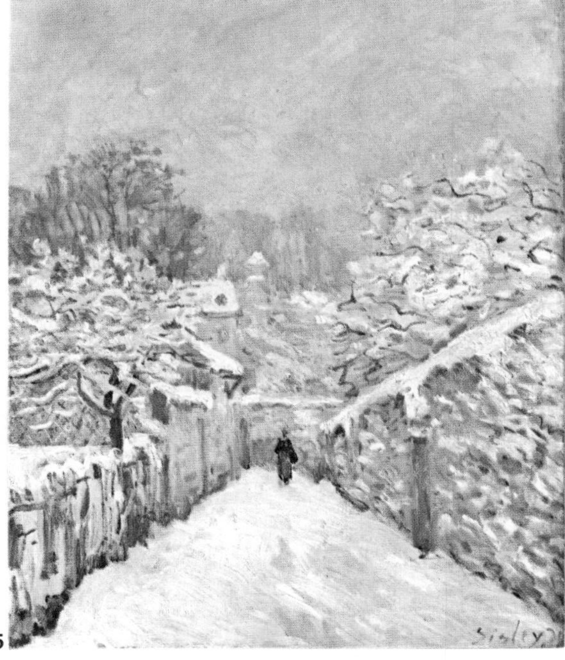

5

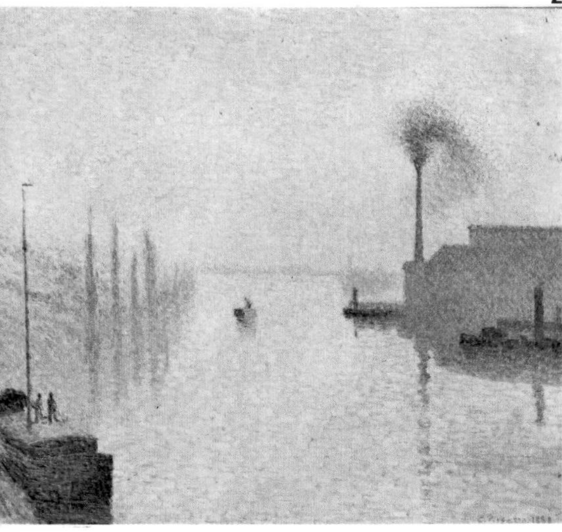

2

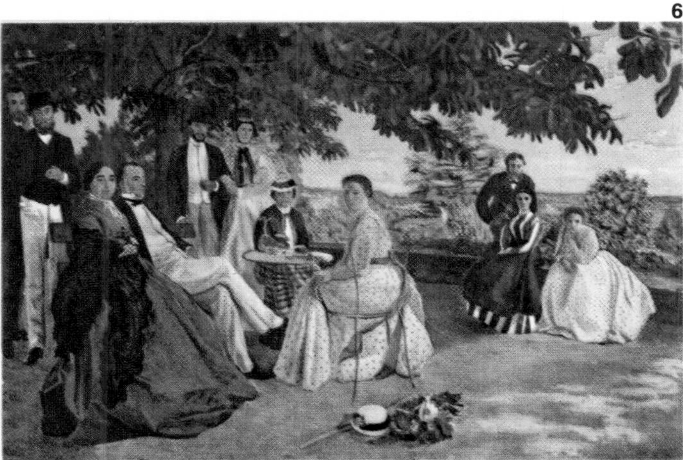

6

Pierre-Auguste Renoir (1841–1919):
1. *Young Girls at the Piano.* 1892. Metropolitan Museum of Art (Robert Lehman Collection), New York
2. *The Swing.* 1876. Musée de l'Impressionnisme, Paris
3. *Lise as Diana.* 1867. National Gallery of Art (Chester Dale Collection), Washington DC
4. *Portrait of Claude Monet.* 1875. Musée de l'Impressionnisme, Paris
5. *Grandes Baigneuses.* 1884–7. Philadelphia Museum of Art
6. *Young Girl combing her Hair.* 1894. Metropolitan Museum of Art (Robert Lehman Collection), New York
7. *Landscape of the Midi.* 1901–5. Private Collection

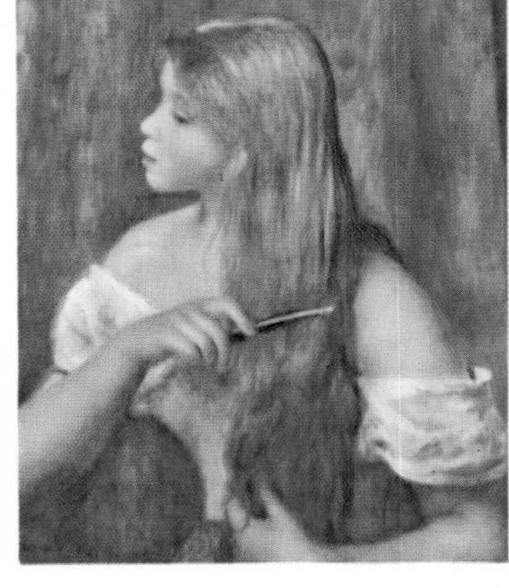
6

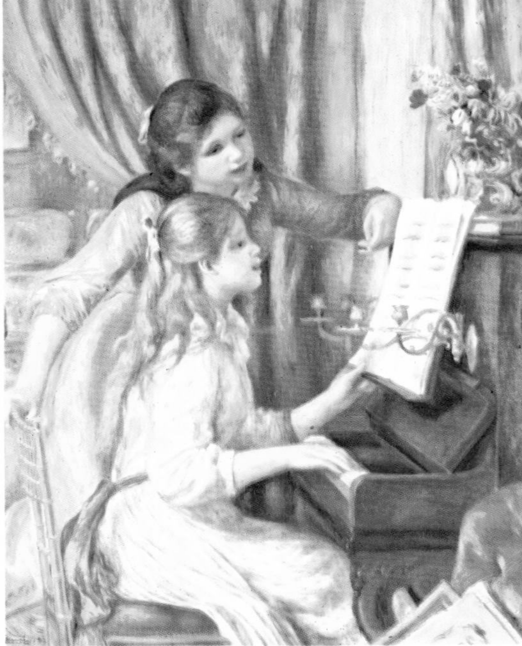
1

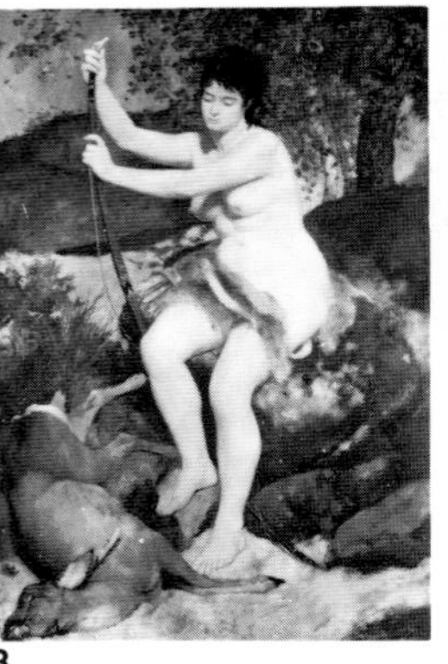
3

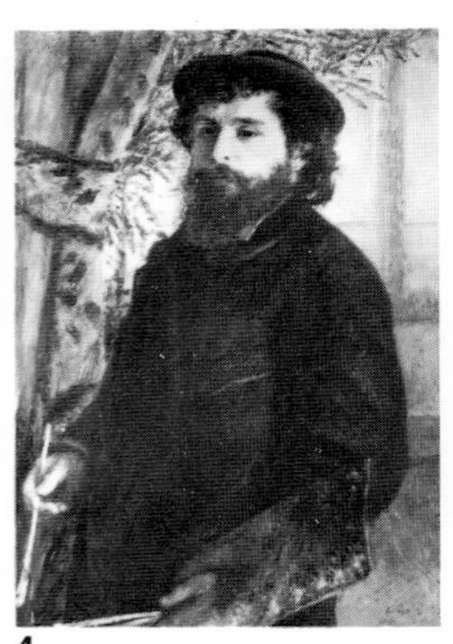
4

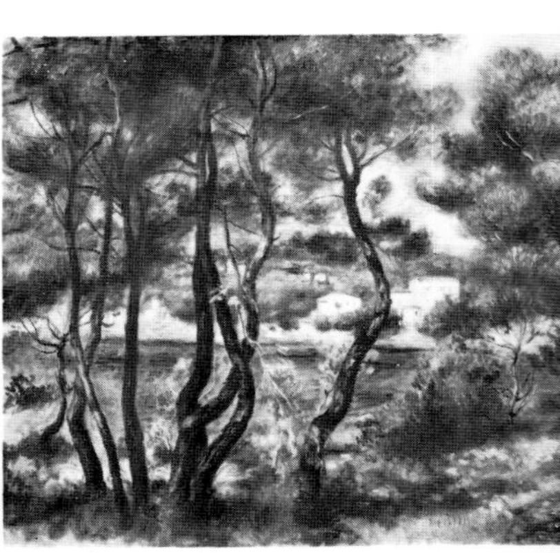

2

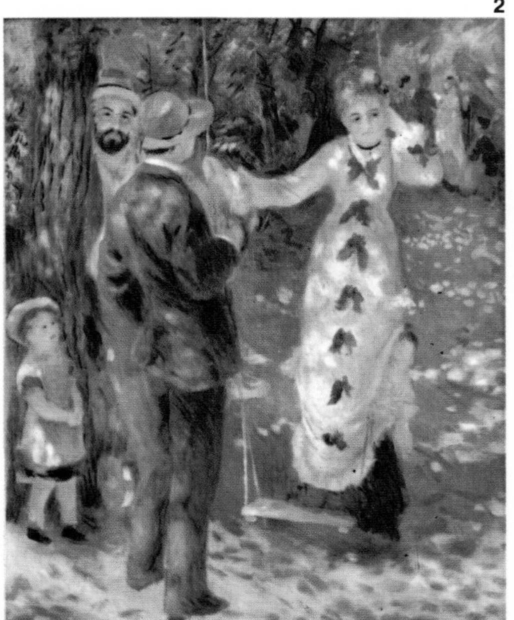

5

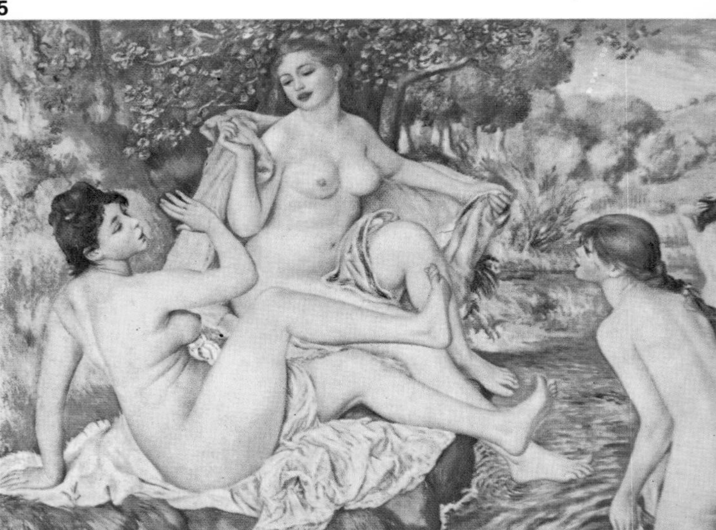

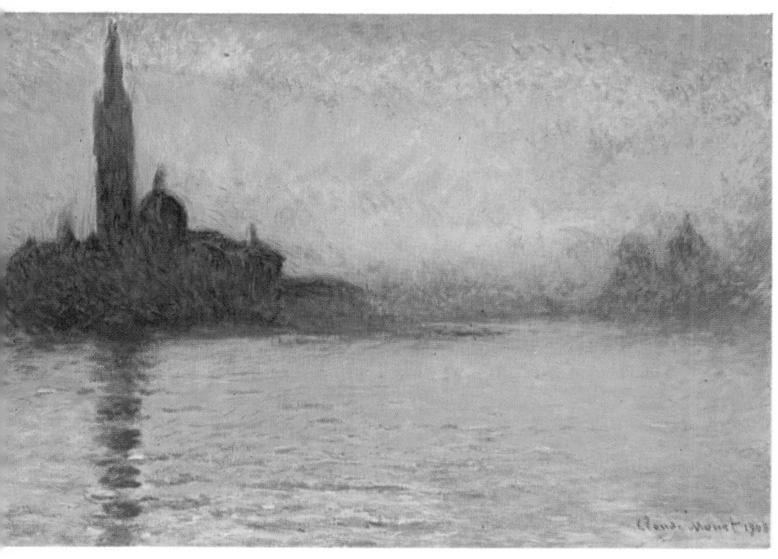

Claude Monet (1840–1926)
1. *Twilight, S. Giorgio Maggiore, Venice.* 1908. National Museum of Wales, Cardiff
2. *The Houses of Parliament, London.* 1904. Musée de l'Impressionnisme, Paris
3. *Water Lilies, Giverny.* 1919. Private Collection, Paris
4. *La Grenouillère.* 1869. Metropolitan Museum of Art, New York
5. *The Regatta at Argenteuil.* About 1872. Musée de l'Impressionnisme, Paris
6. *Rouen Cathedral in full Sunlight.* 1894. Musée de l'Impressionnisme, Paris

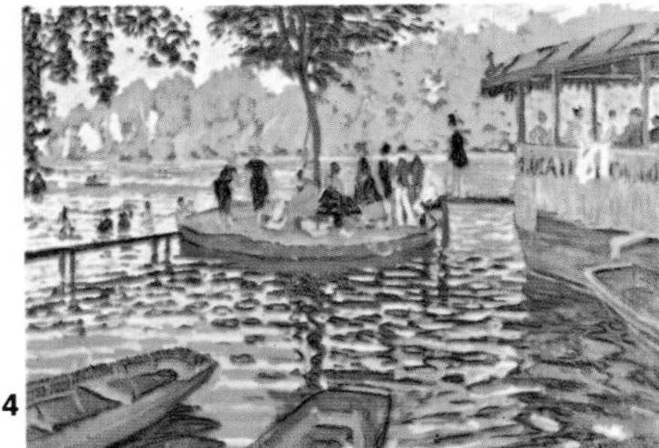

4

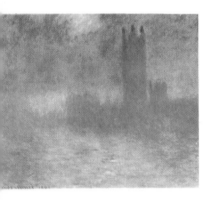

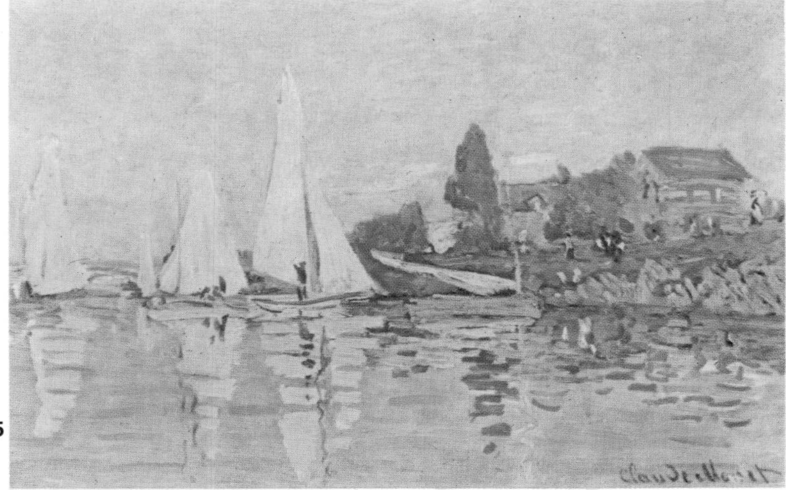

5

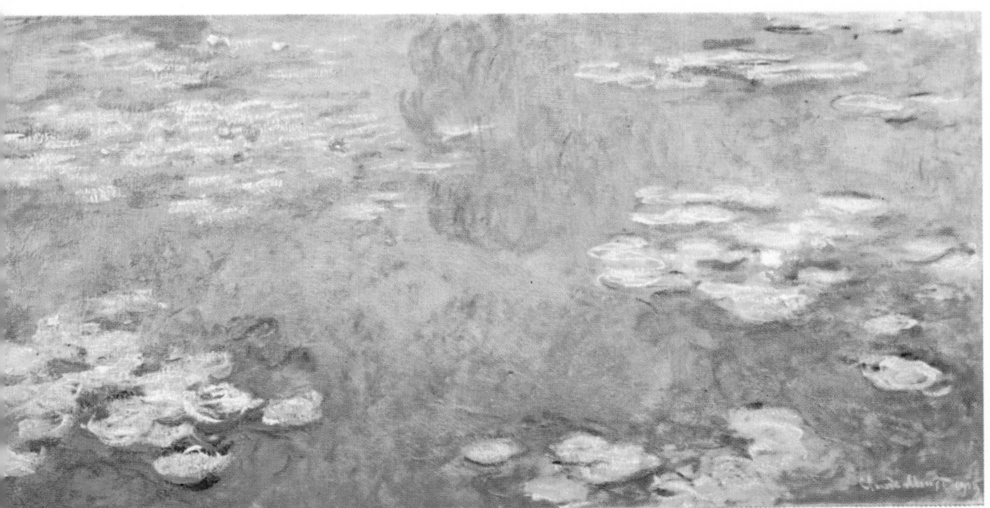

6

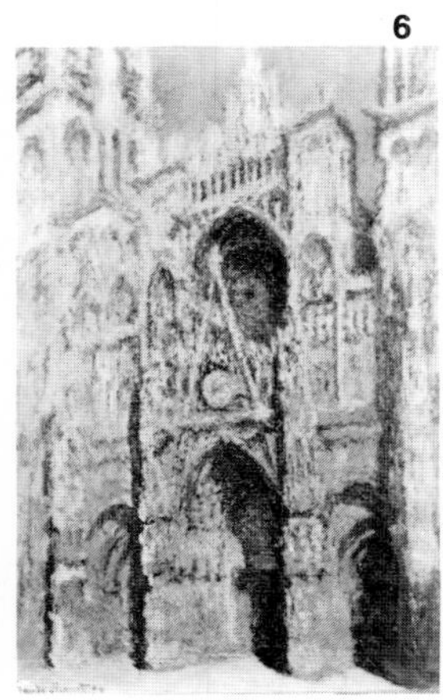

Edgar Degas (1834–1917)

1. *Racecourse Scene, with Jockeys in front of the Stands.* 1869–72. Musée de l'Impressionnisme, Paris
2. *The Bellelli Family.* About 1858–60. Musée de l'Impressionnisme, Paris
3. *Dancers adjusting their Slippers.* About 1883. Cleveland Museum of Art
4. *Young Dancer.* Bronze and fabric. About 1880. Musée de l'Impressionnisme, Paris
5. *Portrait of a young Woman.* 1867. Musée de l'Impressionnisme, Paris
6. *Woman in a Tub.* Bronze. About 1890.
7. *The Cotton Market in New Orleans.* 1873. Musée des Beaux-Arts, Pau

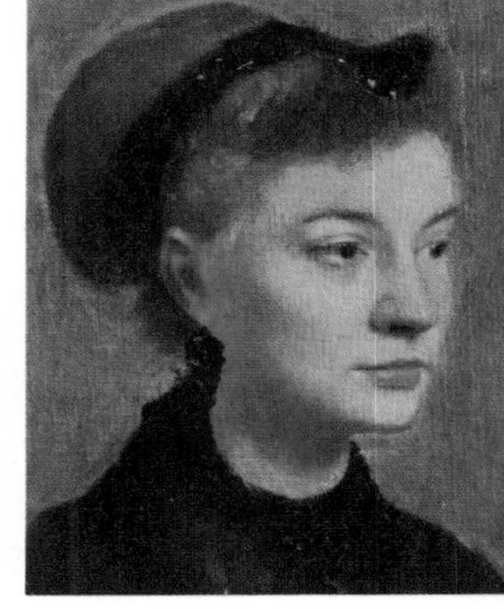

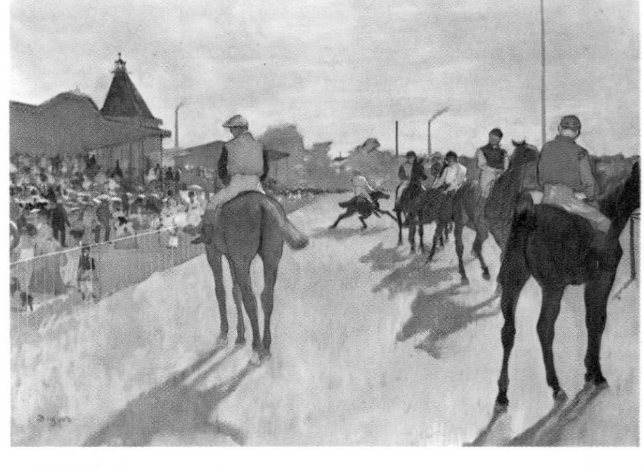

1

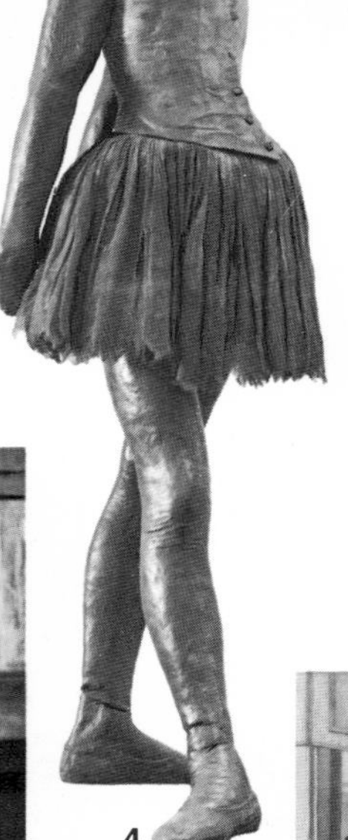

4

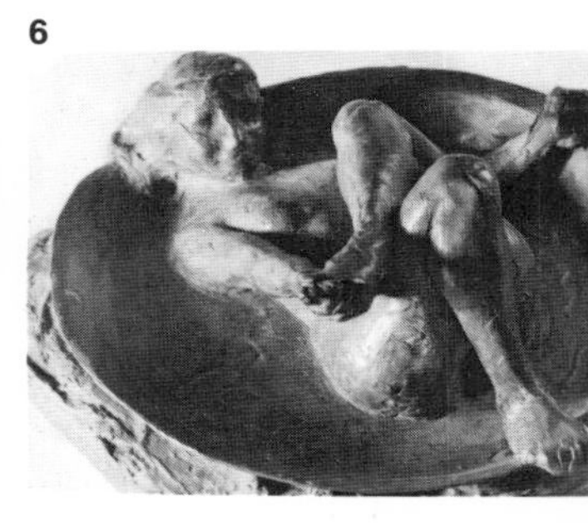

6

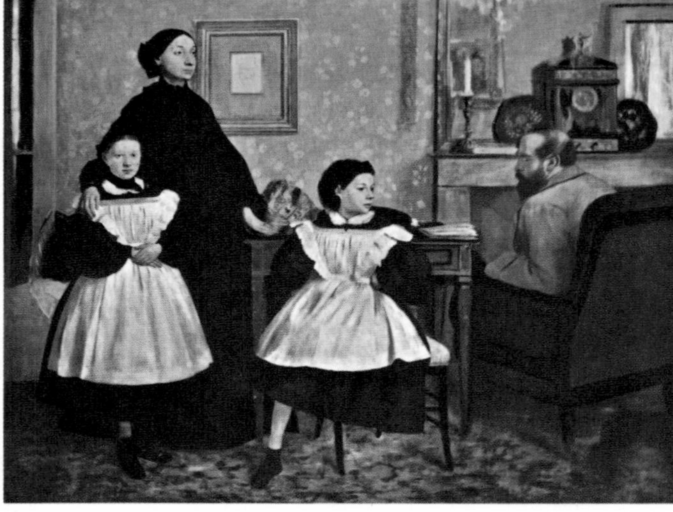

2

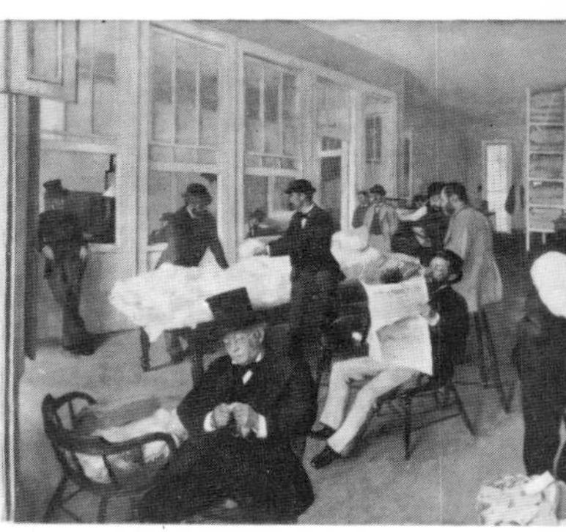

7

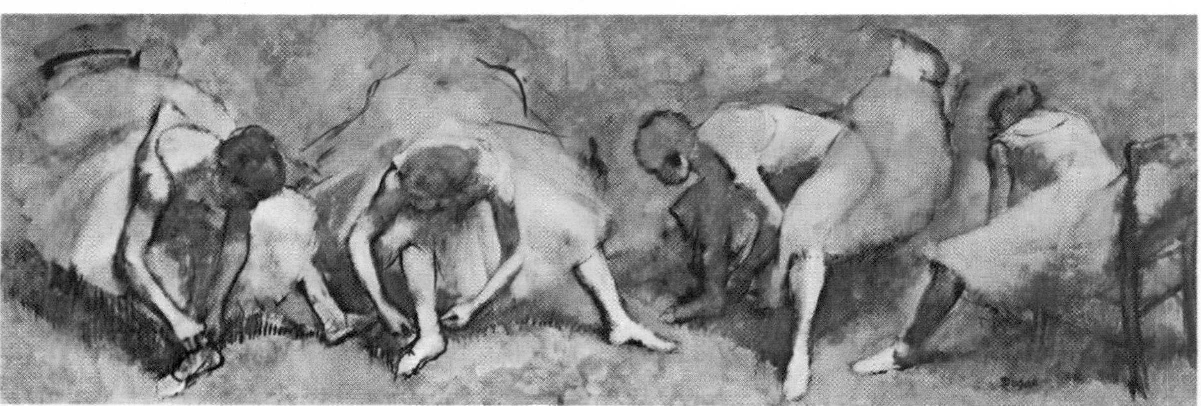

3

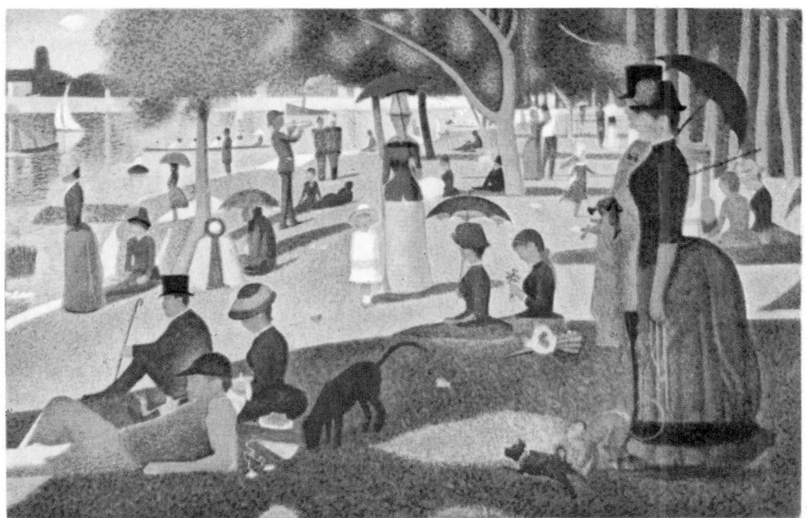

Georges Seurat (1859–91)
1. *Sunday Afternoon on the Island of La Grande Jatte.* 1886. Art Institute of Chicago
2. *Café-concert.* Pencil and gouache. 1887. Rhode Island School of Design, Providence
3. *Bathers at Asnières.* 1883–4. National Gallery, London

Paul Signac (1863–1935)
4. *The Port of St-Tropez.* 1894. Musée de l'Annonciade, St-Tropez
5. *Portrait of Félix Fénéon.* 1890. Private Collection

1

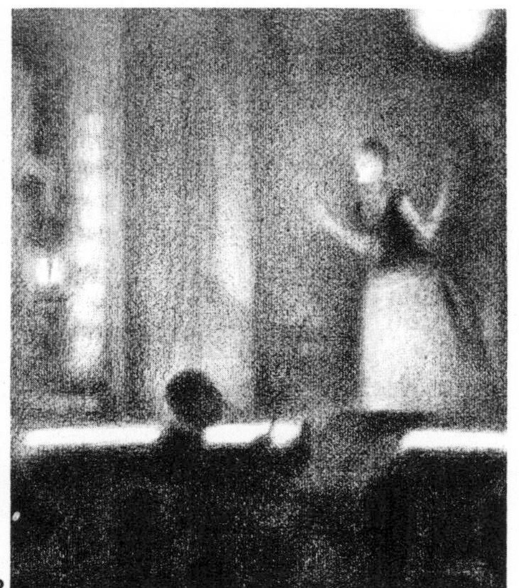

2

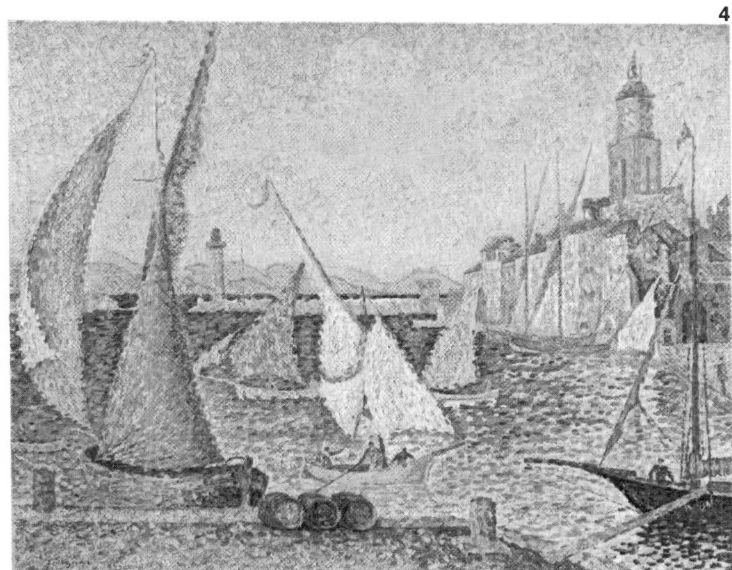

4

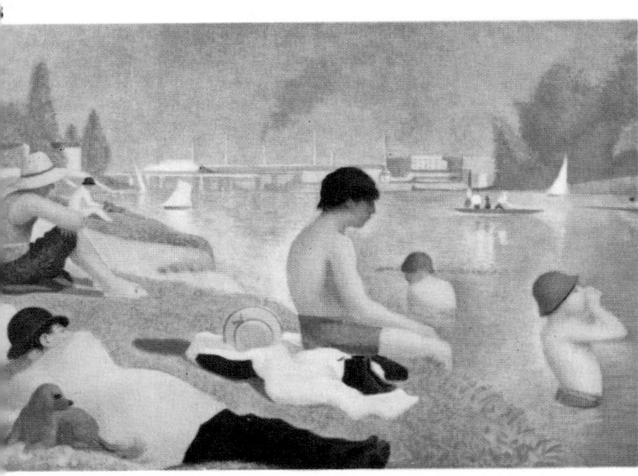

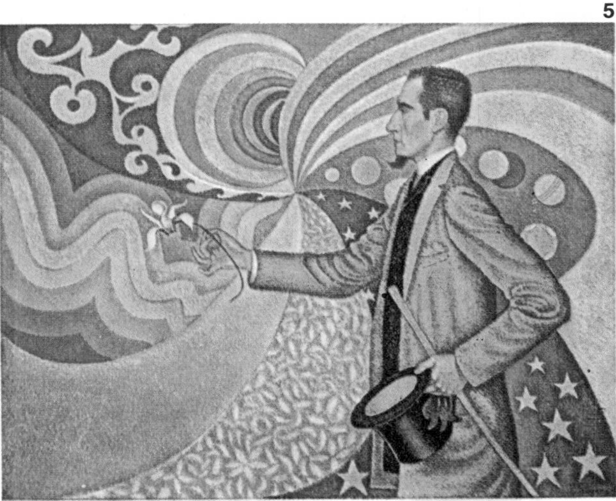

5

Paul Gauguin (1848–1903)
1. *The Yellow Christ.* 1889. Albright-Knox Art Gallery, Buffalo, New York
2. *Two Women on the Beach.* 1891. Musée d l'Impressionnisme, Paris
3. *Riders on the Beach.* 1902. Folkwang Museum, Essen
4. *Portrait of Madeleine Bernard.* 1888. Musée des Beaux-Arts, Grenoble
5. *The Vision after the Sermon.* 1888. National Gallery of Scotland, Edinburgh
6. *Annah the Javanese.* 1893. Private Collection

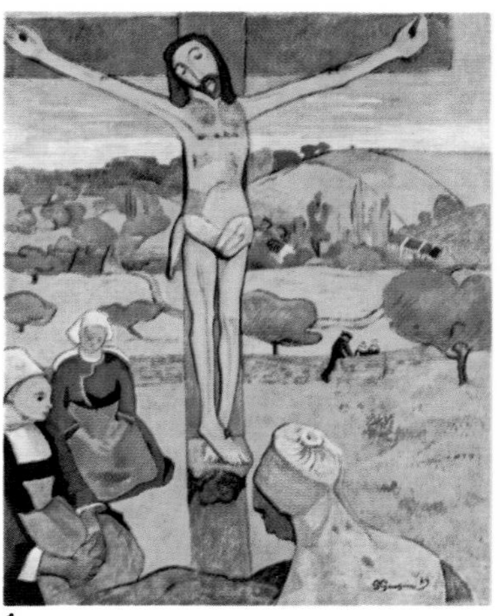

1

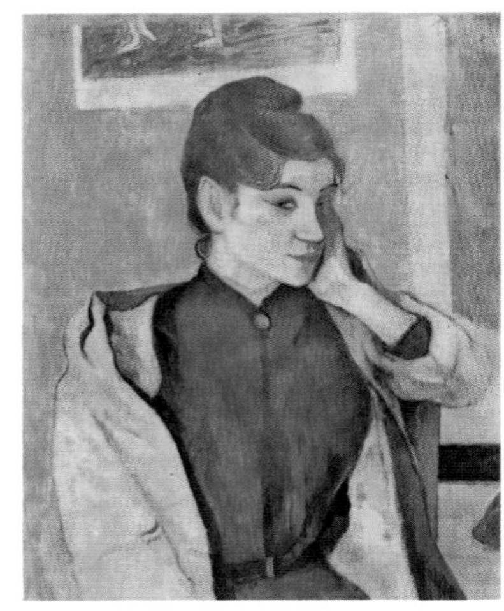

4

2

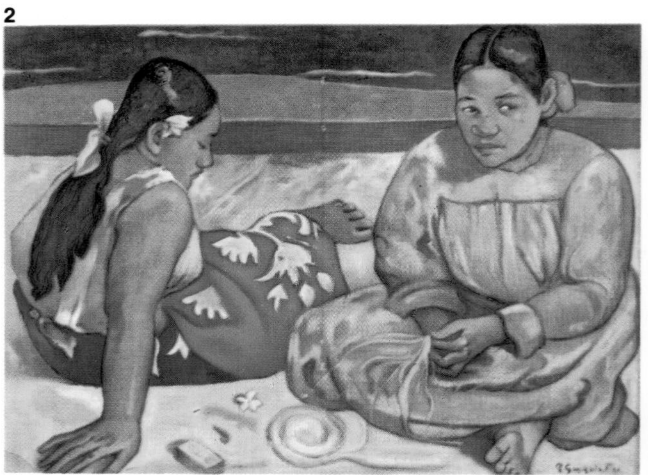

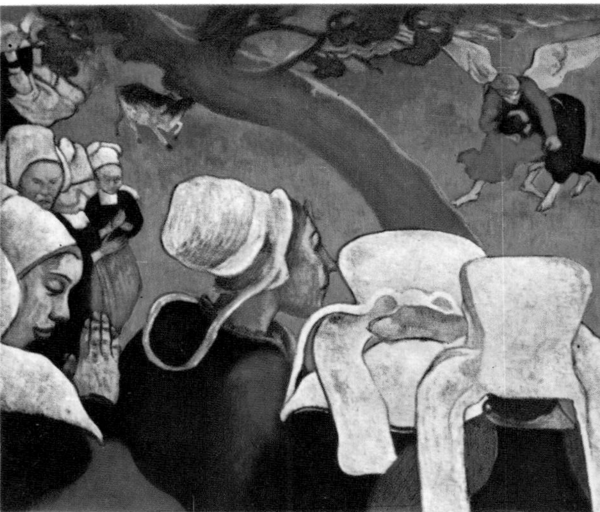

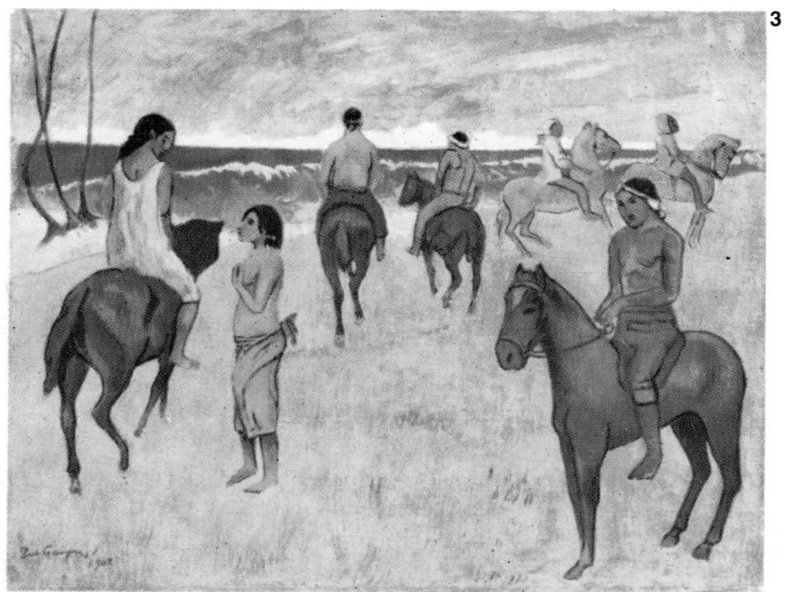

3

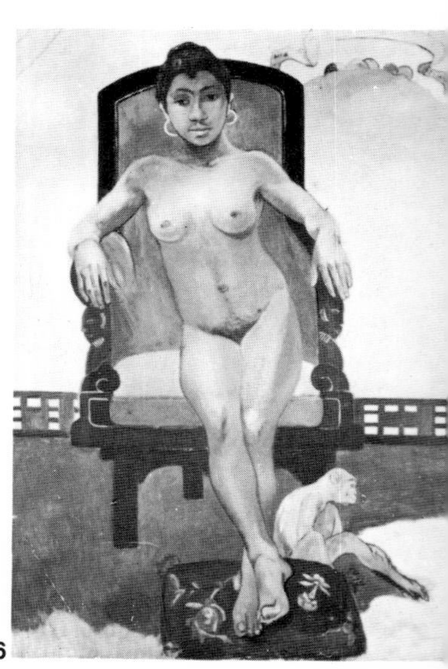

6

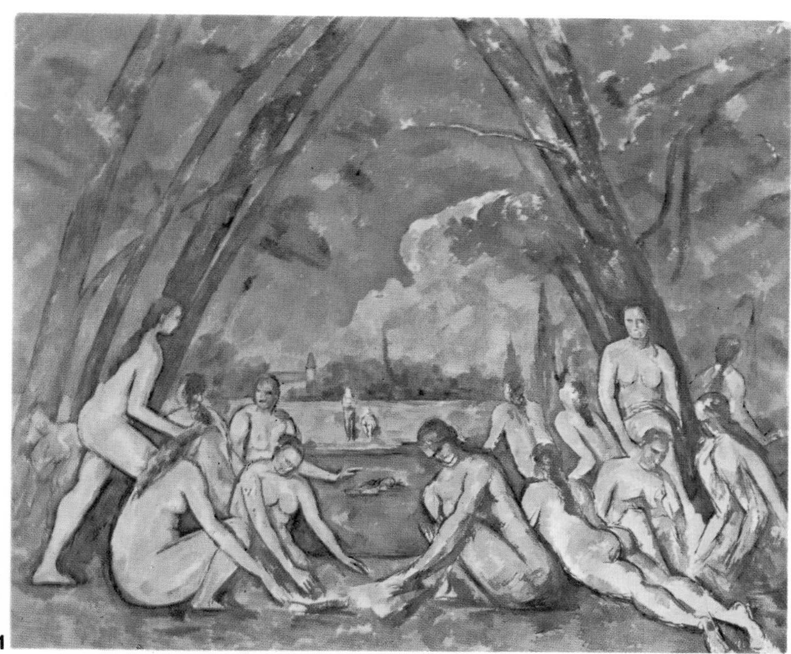
1

Paul Cézanne (1839–1906)
1. *Les grandes Baigneuses.* 1898–1905. Philadelphia Museum of Art (Wilstach Collection)
2. *The Blue Vase.* 1885–7. Musée de l'Impressionnisme, Paris
3. *Still Life with plaster Cupid.* About 1895. Courtauld Institute of Art, London
4. *The Cardplayers.* About 1890–2. Private Collection, Paris
5. *View of L'Éstaque.* About 1885. Private Collection
6. *Still Life with Apples.* 1890–1900. Museum of Modern Art (Lillie P. Bliss Collection), New York

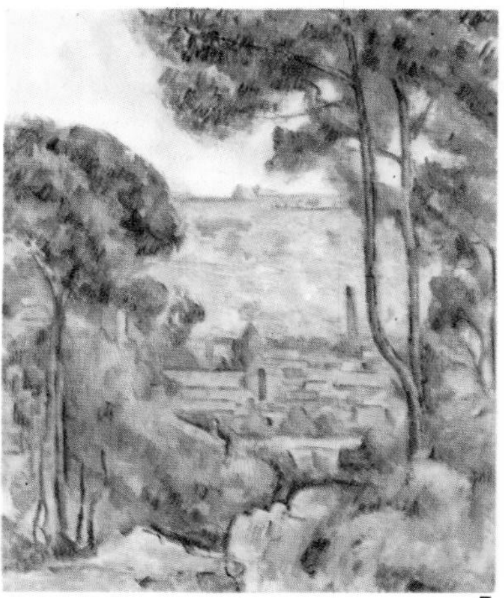
5

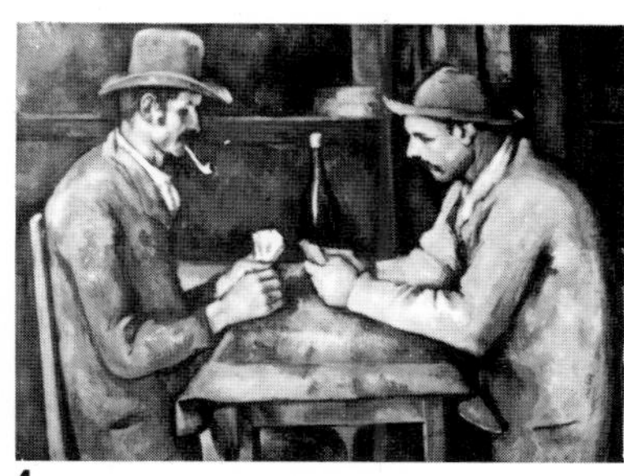
4

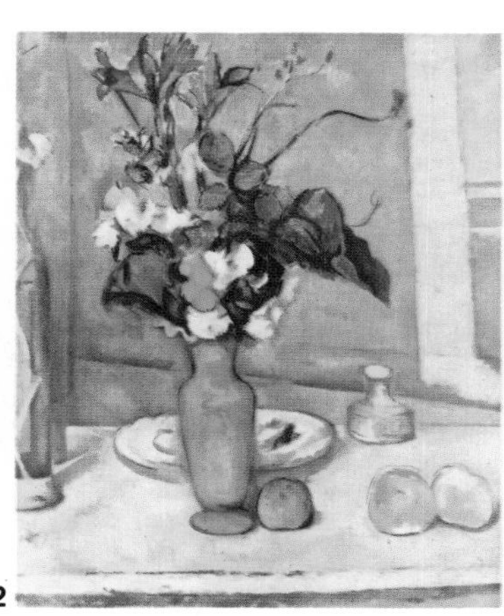
2

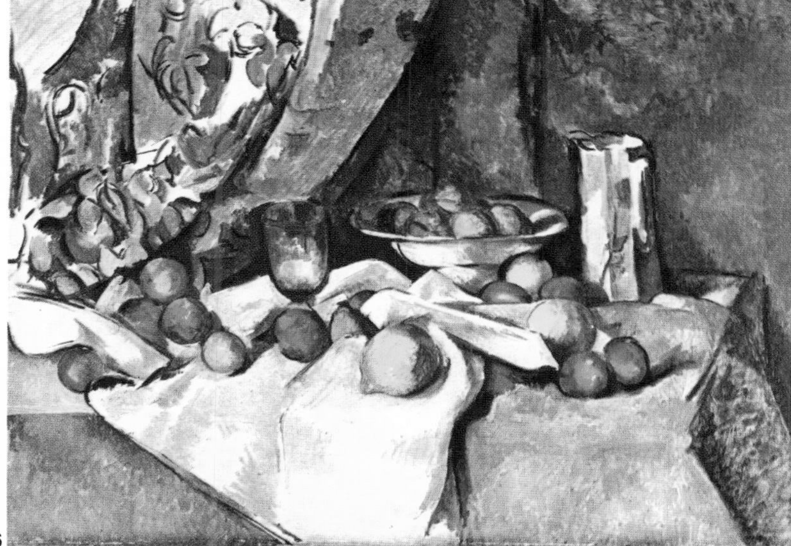
6

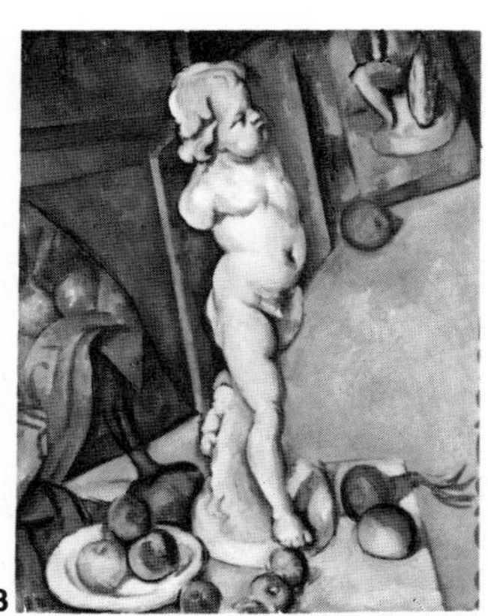
3

Henri Fantin-Latour (1836–1904)
1. *Engagement Still Life* (so called). 1869. Musée de Peinture et de Sculpture, Grenoble

Henri-Marie-Raymond de Toulouse-Lautrec (1864–1901)
2. *Portrait of Hélène Vary.* About 1888. Kunsthalle, Bremen
3. *Jane Avril au Jardin de Paris.* Poster. 1893
4. *A la mie.* 1891. Boston Museum of Fine Arts
5. *Yvette Guilbert taking a Bow.* 1894. Musée Toulouse-Lautrec, Albi
6. *Portrait of G.-H. Manuel.* 1891. Emil G. Bührle Foundation, Zurich
7. *Au salon de la rue des Moulins.* 1894. Musée Toulouse-Lautrec, Albi
8. *Dance at the Moulin Rouge.* 1890. Henry P. McIlhenny Collection, Philadelphia

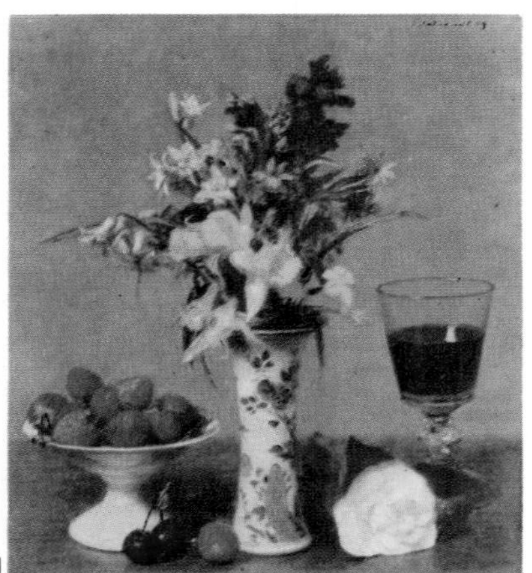
1

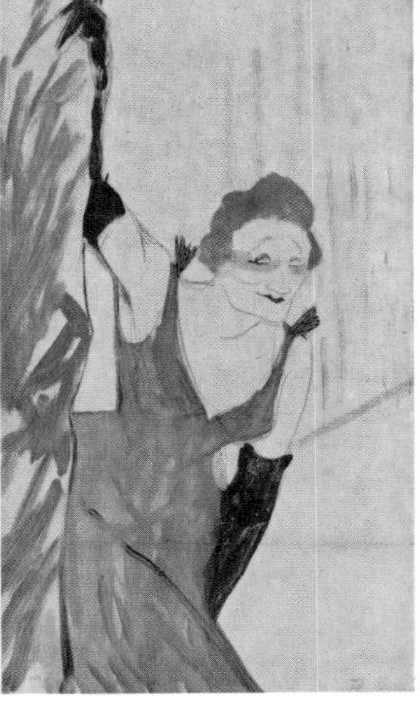
5

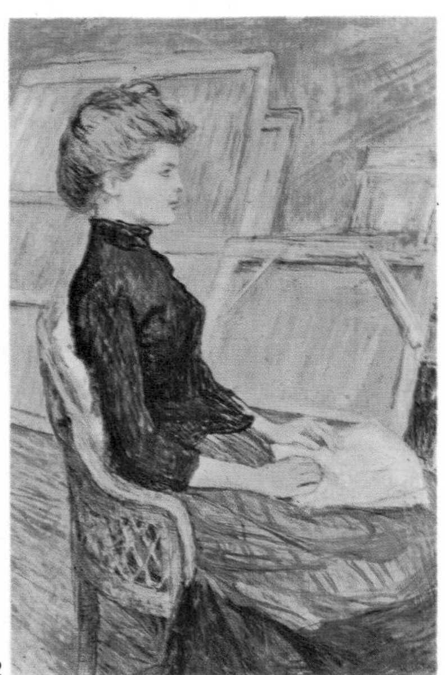
2

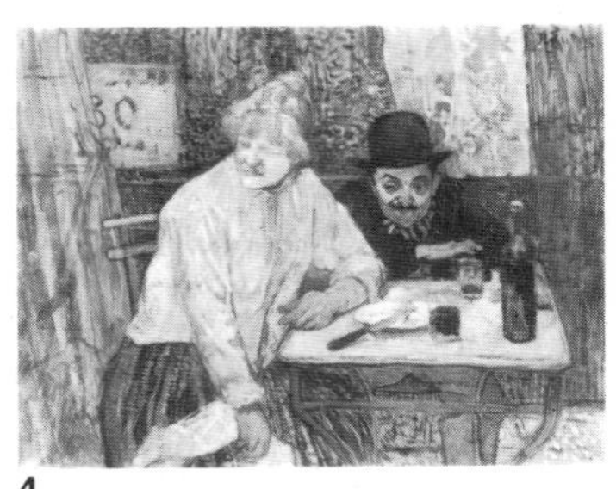
4

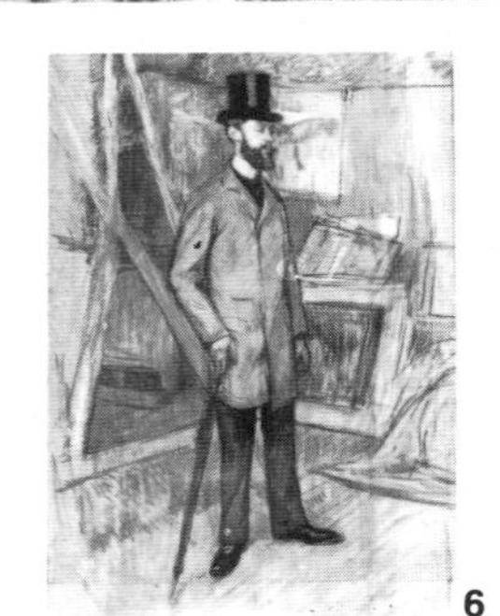
6

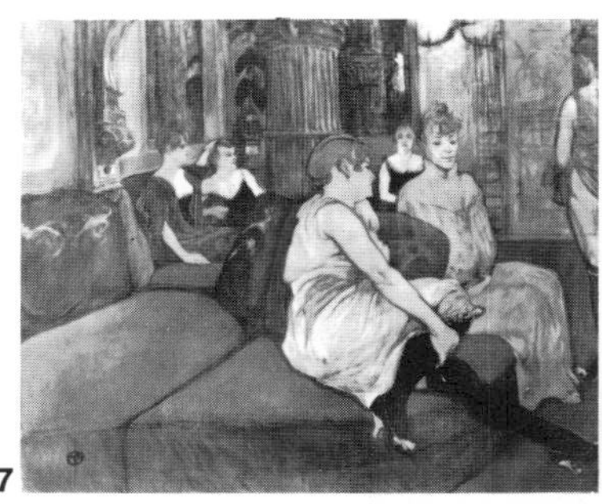
7

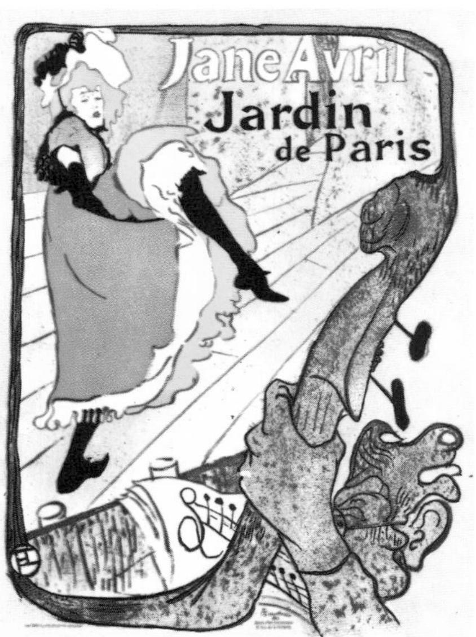

3

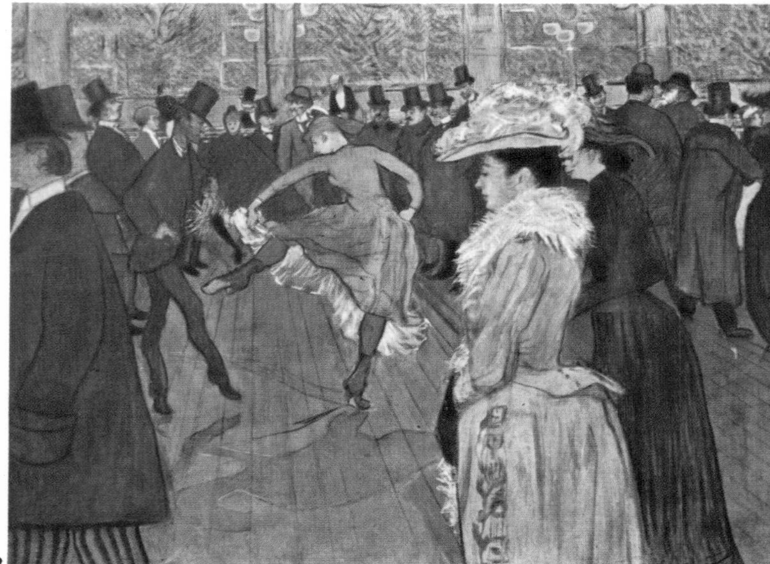
8

Auguste Rodin (1840–1917)

1. Detail from *The Burghers of Calais.* Bronze. 1884–6. Musée Rodin, Paris
2. *A Dancer.* Crayon study. Musée Rodin, Paris
3. *The Gate of Hell.* Detail. Bronze. 1880–1917. Kunsthaus, Zurich
4. *The Head of Sorrow.* Bronze. 1882. Musée Rodin, Paris
5. *The fallen Caryatid carrying its Stone.* Bronze. 1880–1. Musée Rodin, Paris
6. *The Kiss.* Marble. 1886. Musée Rodin, Paris
7. *Study for Balzac.* Final version. Plaster. 1897. Musée Rodin, Paris

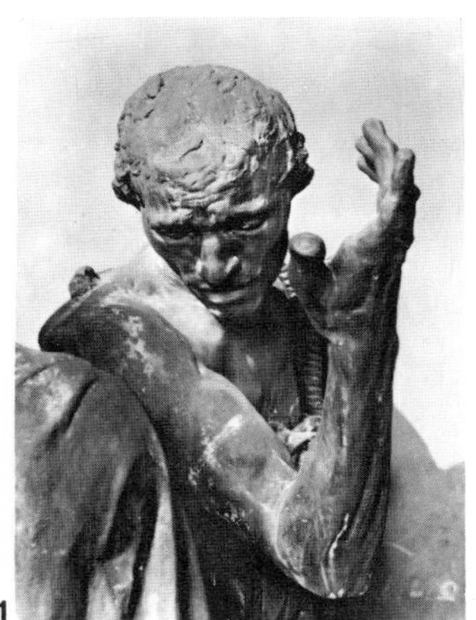

1

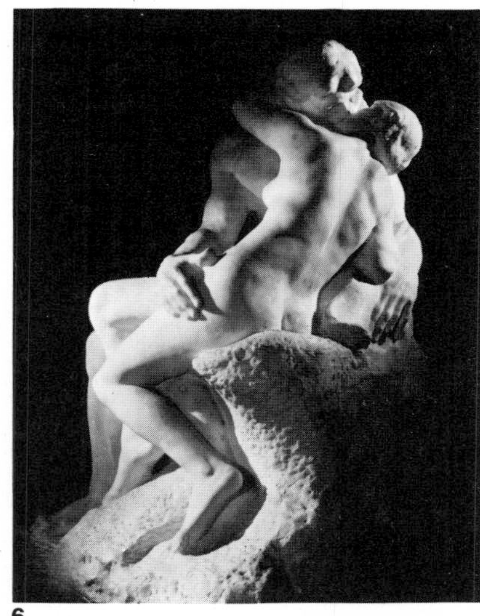

6

2

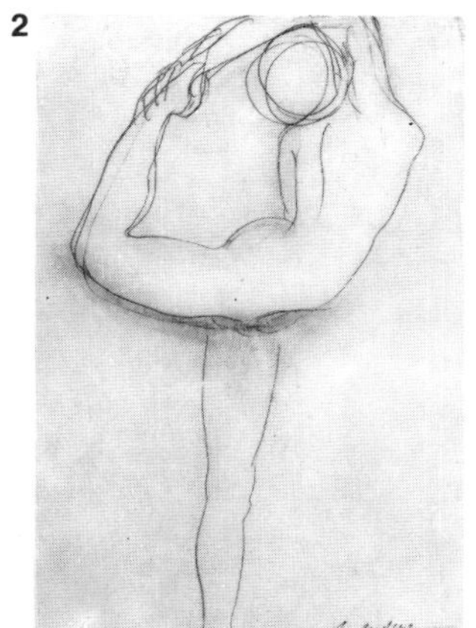

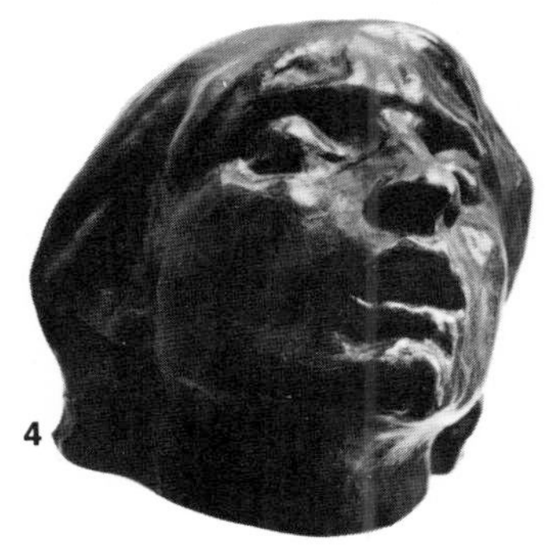

4

7

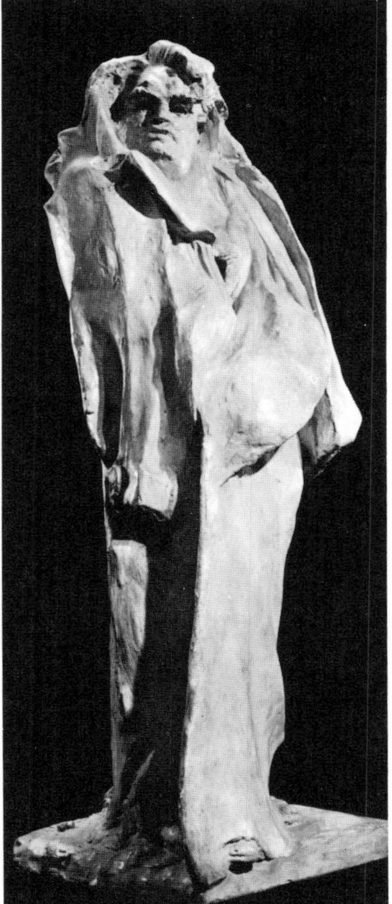

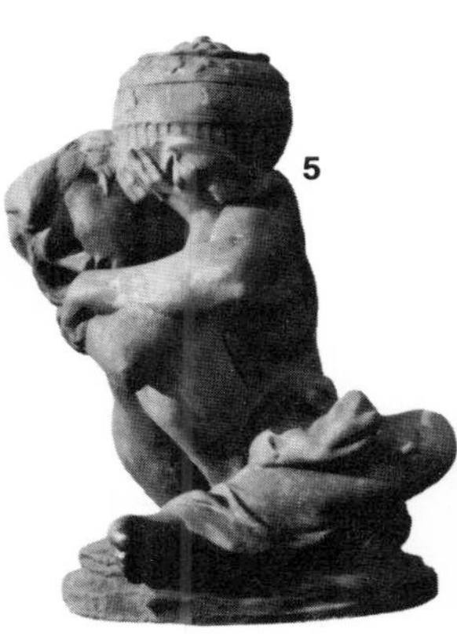

5

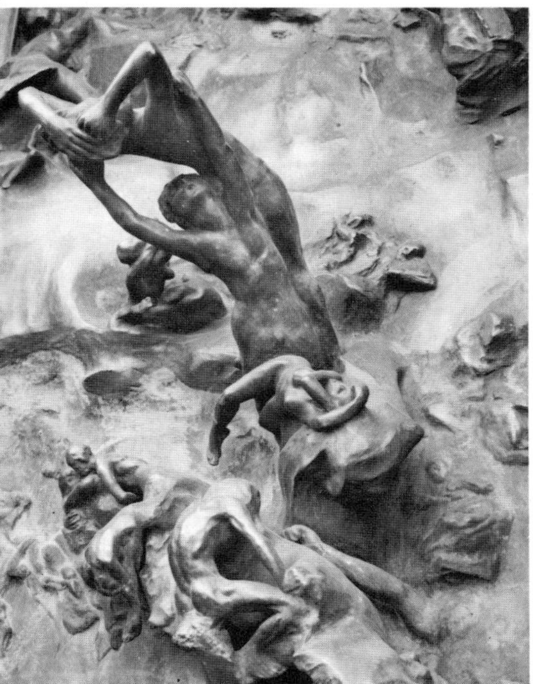

Vincent van Gogh (1853–90)

1. *A Pair of Shoes.* 1886. Vincent van Gogh Museum, Amsterdam
2. *Self-portrait with a severed Ear.* 1889. Private Collection
3. *Sunflowers.* 1888. Tate Gallery, London
4. *The Church at Auvers.* 1890. Louvre, Paris
5. *A Cornfield.* Pen and reed. 1888. Private Collection
6. *Boats at Saintes-Maries-de-la-Mer.* Watercolour. 1888. Private Collection

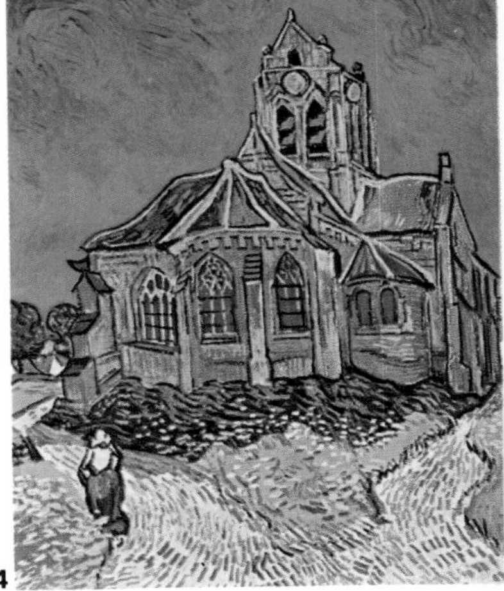

4

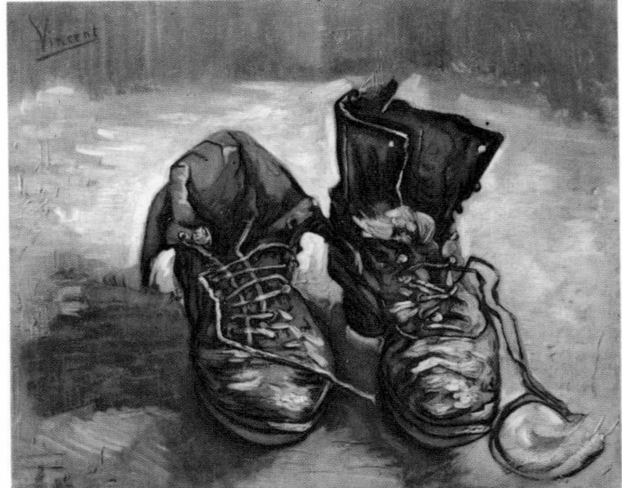

1

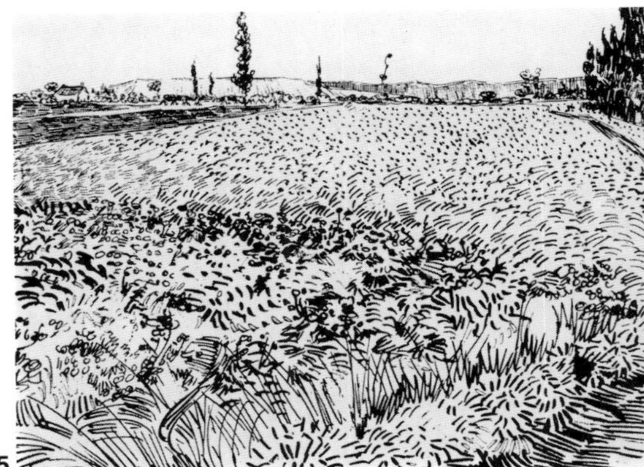

5

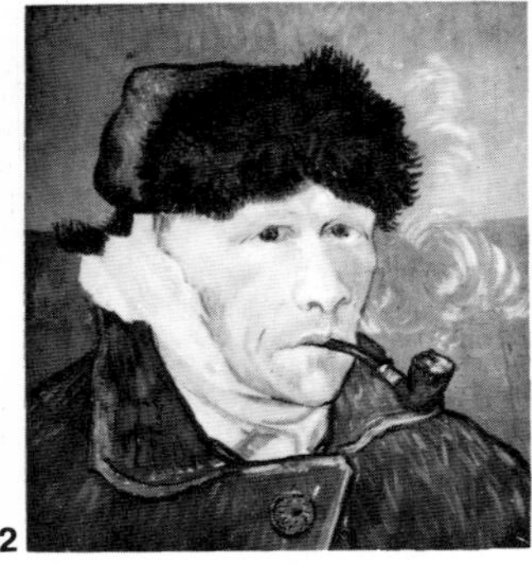

2

3

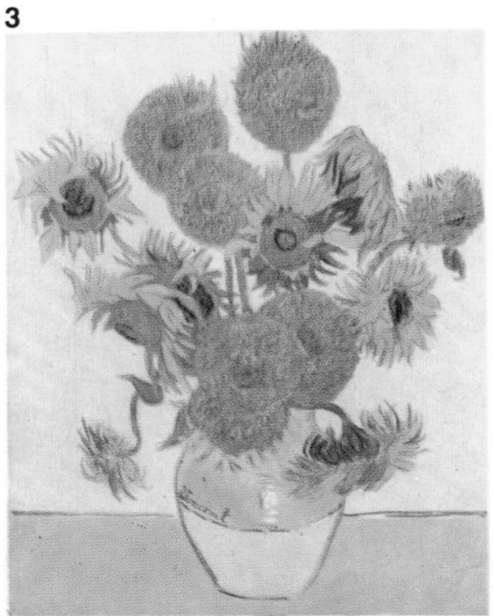

6

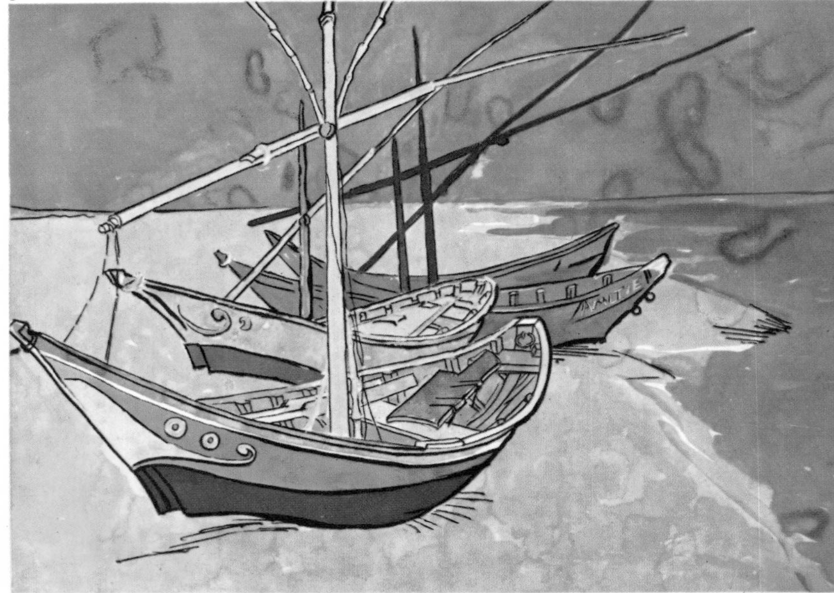

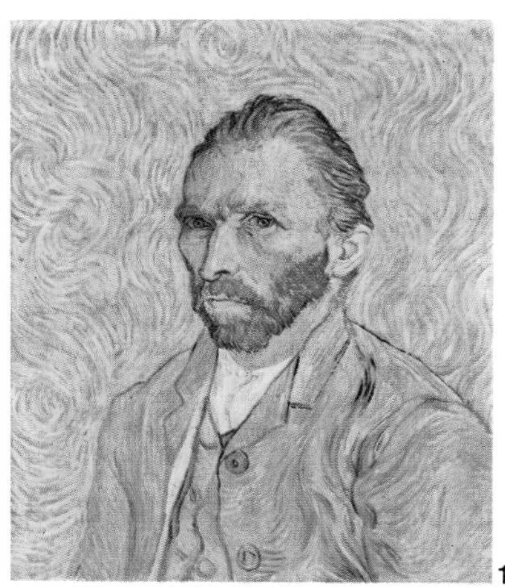
1

Vincent van Gogh (1853–90)

1. *Self-portrait.* 1889. Musée de l'Impressionnisme, Paris
2. *The Painter's Bedroom at Arles.* 1889. Musée de l'Impressionnisme, Paris
3. *Portrait of Armand Roulin.* 1888. Folkwang Museum, Essen
4. *L'Arlésienne* (*Madame Ginoux*). 1888. Metropolitan Museum of Art (Sam A. Lewisohn Collection), New York
5. *Starry Night.* 1889. Museum of Modern Art, New York
6. *At the Foot of the Alpilles.* 1890. Rijksmuseum Kröller-Müller, Otterlo

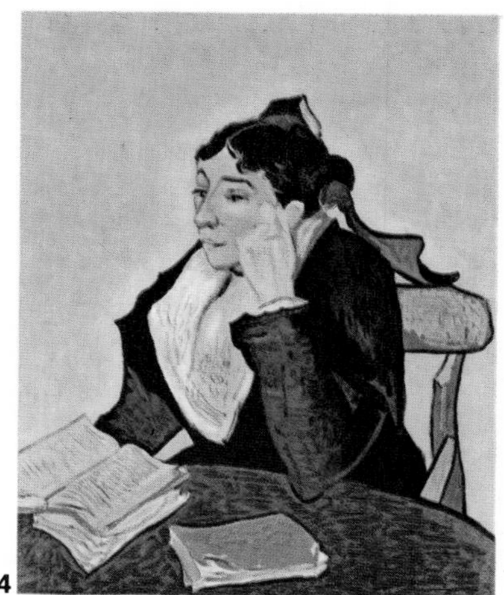
4

2
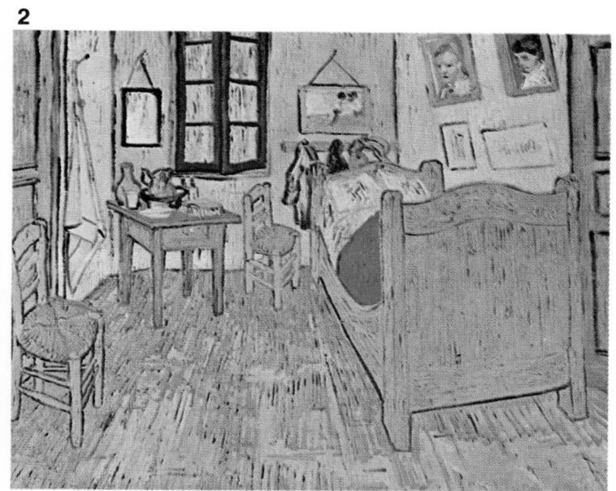

5
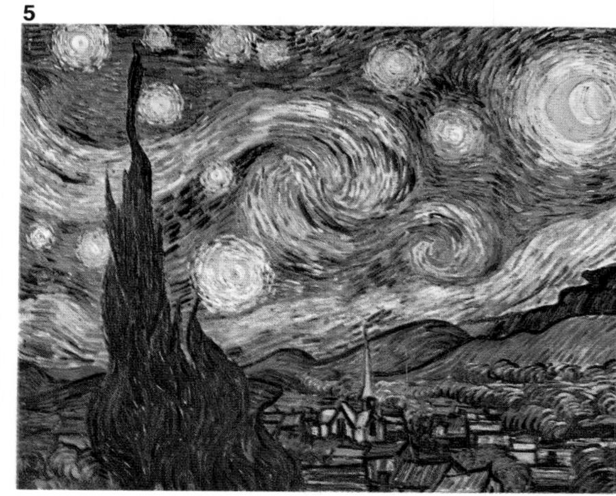

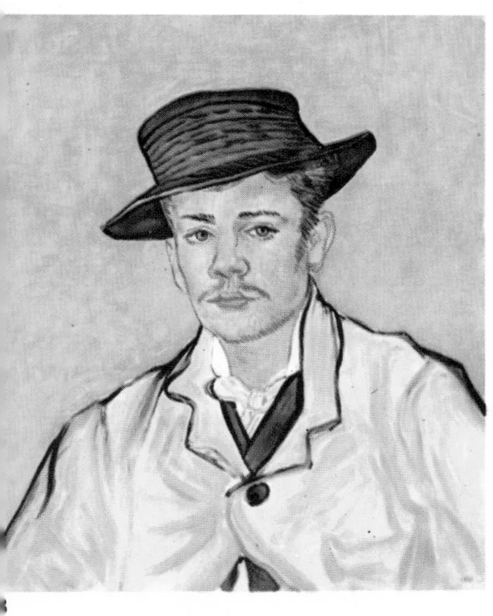

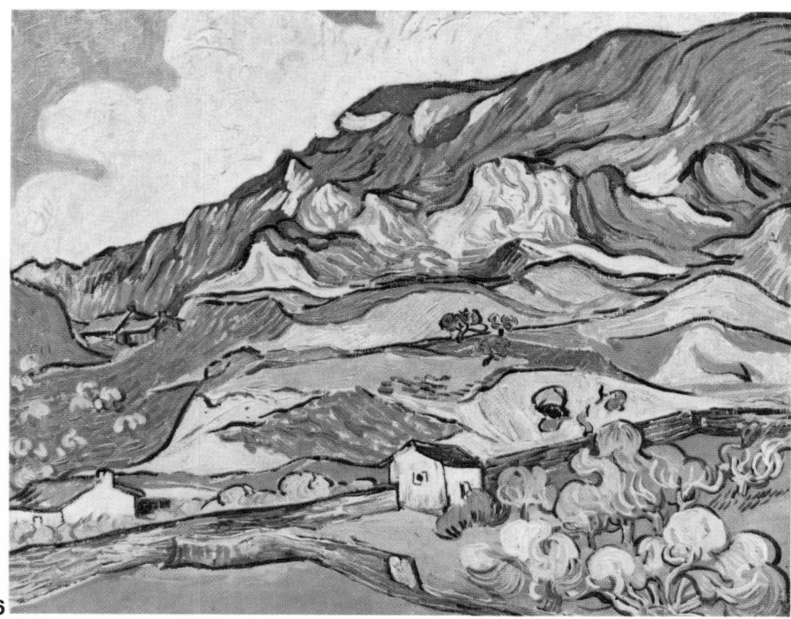
6

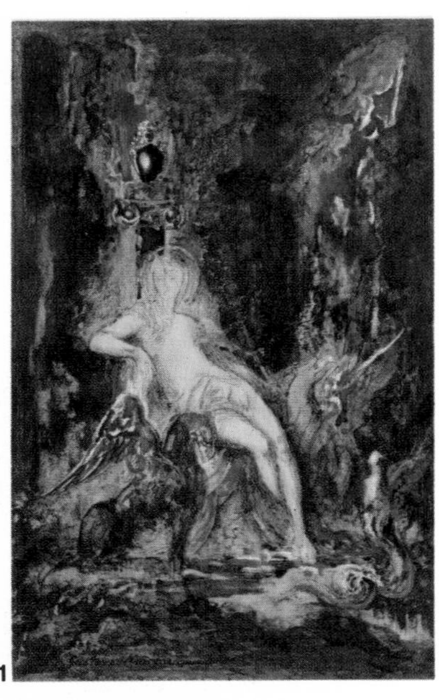

1

1. **Gustave Moreau** (1826–98): *A Fairy with Griffins.* Watercolour. About 1878–80. Private Collection
2. **Gustave Eiffel** (1832–1923): The Eiffel Tower, Paris. 1887–9
3. **Charles Garnier** (1825–98): The Opéra, Paris. 1862–75
4. **Victor Baltard** (1805–74): Church of St-Augustin, Paris. 1860–71
5. **Odilon Redon** (1840–1916): *Anemones.* 1908. Private Collection
6. **Jakob Ignaz Hittorf** (1792–1867): The Gare du Nord, Paris. 1861–5
7. **Charles Garnier** (1825–98): Grand Staircase of the Opéra, Paris. 1862–75

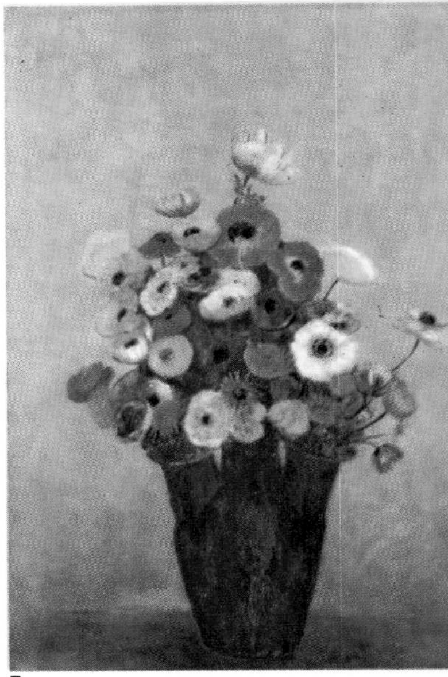

5

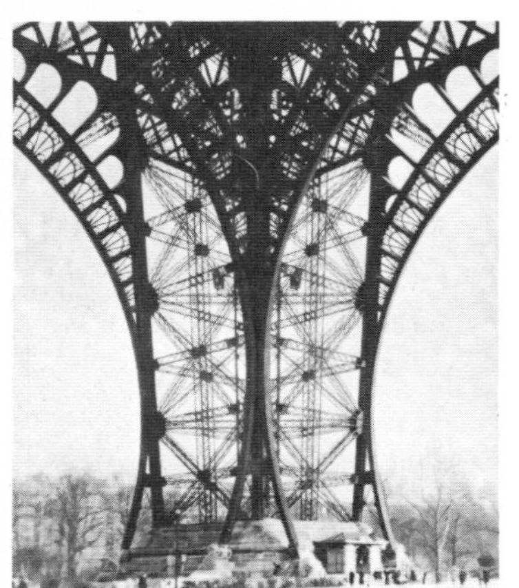

2

4

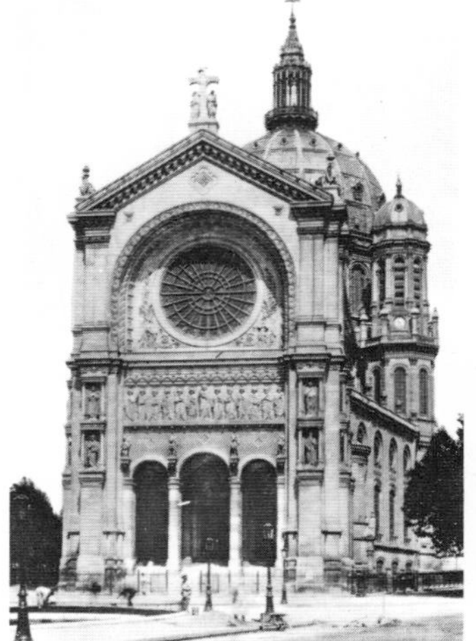

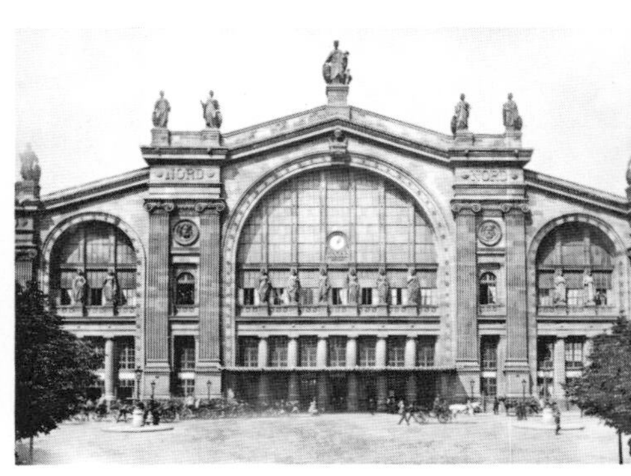

3

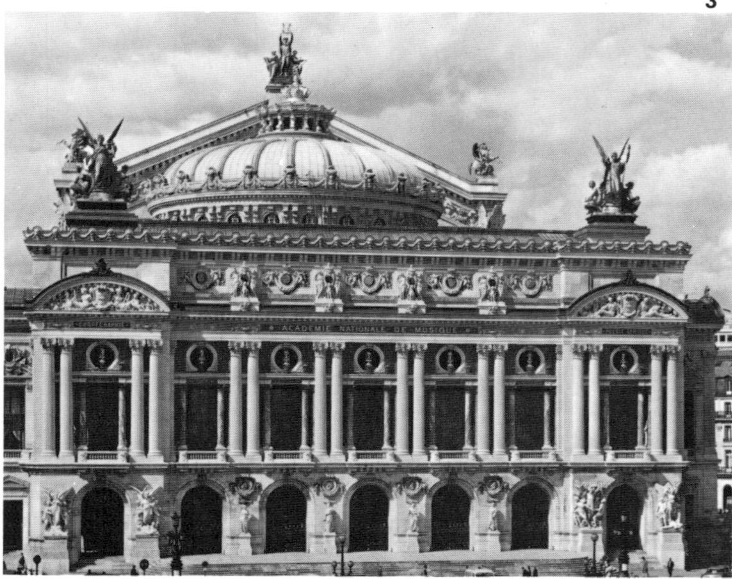

7

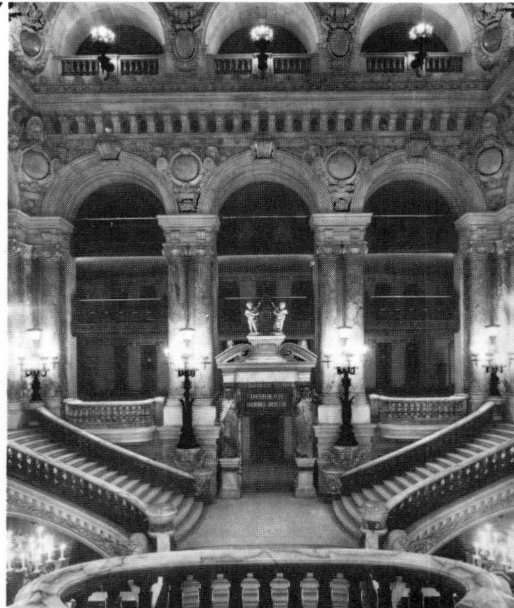

ne arts during the twentieth century have ɜen in a remarkably volatile state. It could be ɪid that they match the tenor of the age. The dical changes that were introduced in quick ɪccession demanded theoretical explanation, ɪd perhaps no previous century, except ɔssibly the seventeenth, has been so ɔncerned with manifestos and apologias. The ɪinters Paul Klee and Wassily Kandinsky, as ell as the architect Le Corbusier, were nongst a host of individuals who published eories about art. As regards painting, the versity of artistic activity may be conveniently ɪbsumed under two general heads, in which ɪmerous separate movements have to be corporated: Expressionist and Abstract. though Paris acted as a catalyst for many of e new developments in twentieth-century t, Austria, Switzerland, Belgium and Holland so contributed before the supremacy of odern art passed to America. Expressionist t includes such groups as the Nabis, the ɪuves, the Symbolists, Dada and ɪrrealism, as well as Pop Art. These various ovements found outlets in, and were ɔmetimes inspired by, painters working ɪtside Paris – *Die Brücke* in Dresden, *Der 'aue Reiter* in Munich and *Die Sezession* imarily in Vienna. The painters who formed ose groups generically entitled Expressionist operated within a private world, the workings their inner minds becoming the subjects of eir pictures. They portrayed the tensions, ntasies and anxieties of their own lives, to which the viewer was invited to read his vn personal predicament. The concern with e human form that had preoccupied ɪropean art for so long, almost since its ception, was now suddenly abandoned and ɪbstitute images were found. In one sense e fantasies of Miró, Ernst, Chagall, Klee, ɪchamp amd Dali may seem to be ɪpenetrable, but in another they are an ktraordinarily vivid visual record of our own ght.

Abstract painting clearly stems from the new ɪderstanding nurtured by the Neo-ɪpressionists and developed further by Cézanne. By the end of the first decade of the twentieth century, Picasso and Braque had formulated Cubism, which was undoubtedly the most influential style evolved during the first half of the century, introducing a totally new concept of space. In Cubism different forms of varying shapes lock together in such a way that a recognizable image finally emerges. The most radical abstract artist was the Hollander Mondrian. His paintings analyse and simplify observed forms, finally reducing them to their essential elements. Op Art is a modern offshoot of abstract art. Abstract painting has a precision and purity akin to mathematics and is diametrically opposed to the almost self-indulgent excesses, but none the less highly skilful renderings, of the Expressionists. Both these movements, however, continue to exist separately in America although, in the action paintings of Jackson Pollock and others, they are perhaps theoretically blended.

The outstanding development in the present century is the use of new materials. Although evident in painting with the introduction of collage, it is in the fields of sculpture and architecture that the greatest expansion has taken place. The same freedom in representing the human figure (Giacometti and Moore), the same concern with symbolism and abstractionism (Brancusi) and the same fertility of mind (Gabo) can be found in sculpture as in painting. While sculptors were busy experimenting with wood, glass, wire and string, architects were trying out not only new materials, but also new techniques. Flexibility and practicability are perhaps the best words to describe the designs of the Bauhaus group in Germany. Both as regards design and decoration, architects partook of the same general artistic principles as in the painting and sculpture of the twentieth century – Expressionism and Abstractionism – and in so doing imposed new attitudes to living. Although these revolutionary ideas in the style of living began in Europe (Germany, Belgium and Holland), it is in America that they have found their true outlet.

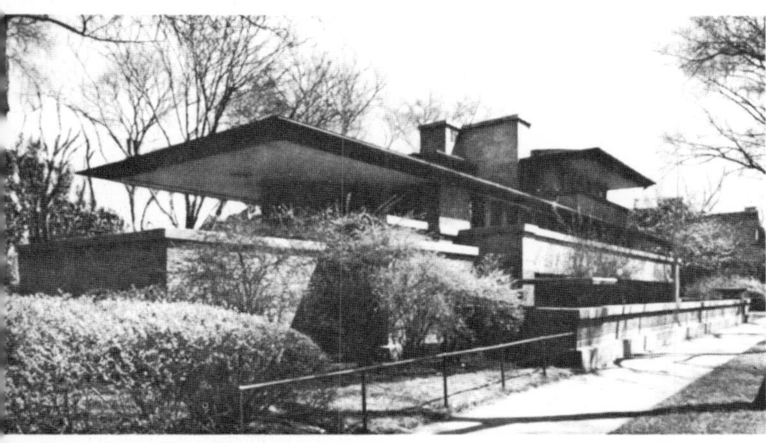

ank Lloyd Wright: Robie House, Chicago. 1909

Part 10

Europe and The Americas since 1900

1. **Pierre Bonnard** (1867–1947): *The Red Bodice.* 1925. Musée National d'Art Moderne, Paris
2. **Pierre Bonnard** (1867–1947): *Nude in front of the Fireplace.* 1917. Musée de l'Annonciade, St-Tropez
3. **Aristide Maillol** (1861–1944): *Desire.* Lead relief. 1903–5. Musée National d'Art Moderne, Paris
4. **Aristide Maillol** (1861–1944): *The Ile-de-France.* Bronze. 1920–5
5. **Pierre Bonnard** (1867–1947): *La Toilette.* About 1922. Musée National d'Art Moderne, Paris
6. **Édouard Vuillard** (1868–1940): *Portrait of Madame Sert.* Private Collection
7. **Édouard Vuillard** (1868–1940): *Annette's Supper.* 1900. Musée de l'Annonciade, St-Tropez

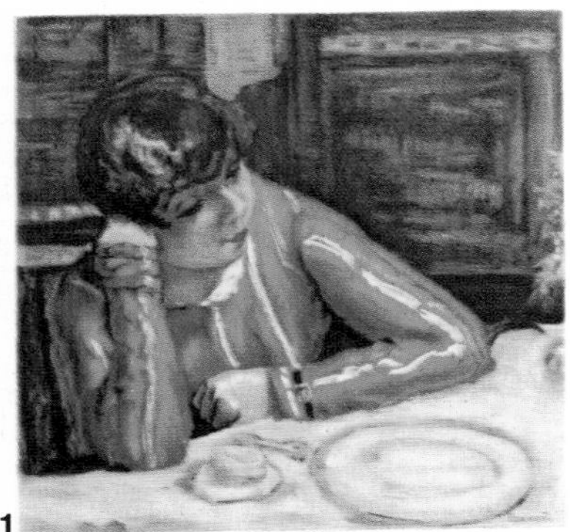
1

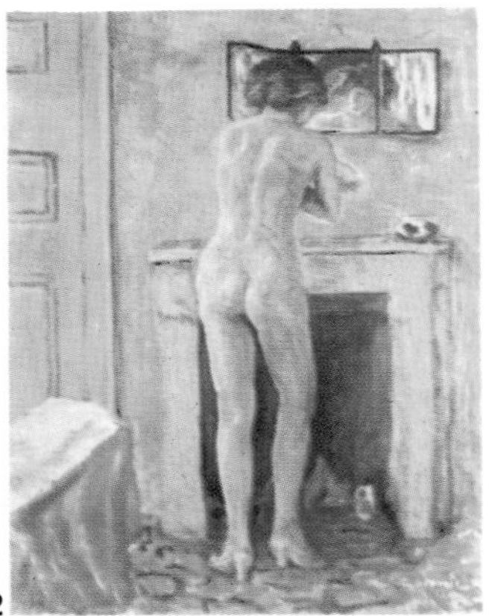
2

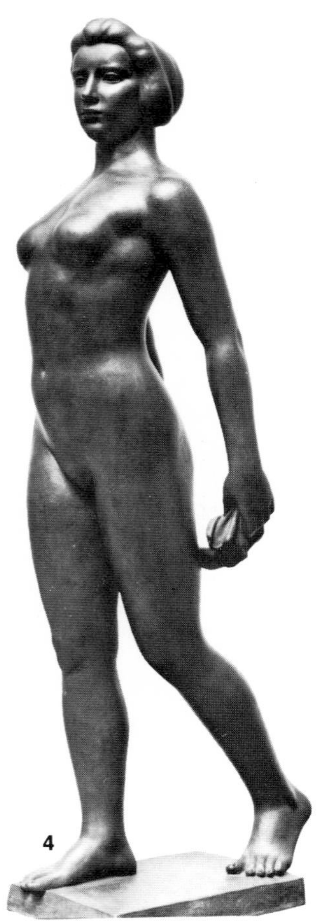
4

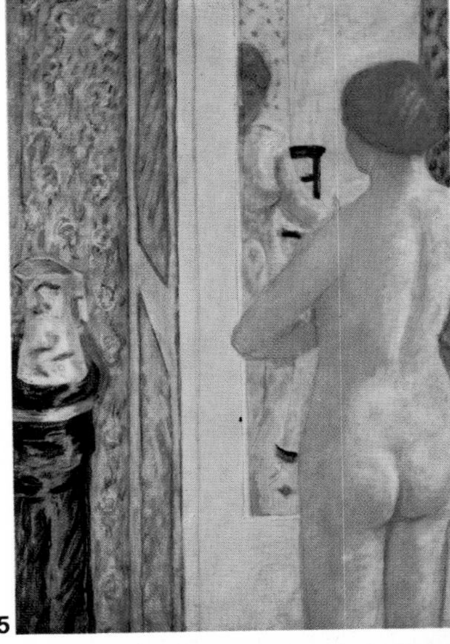
5

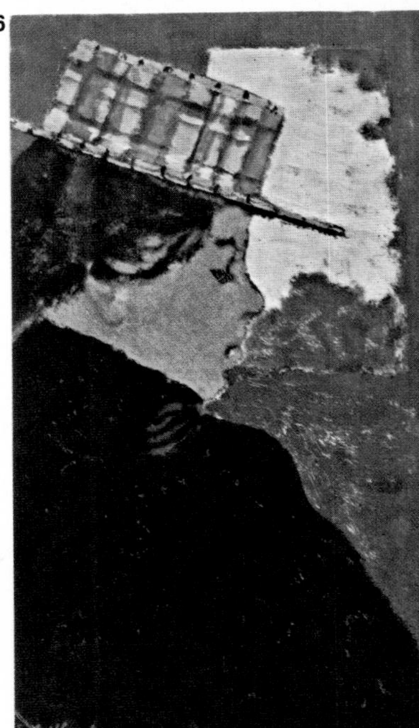
6

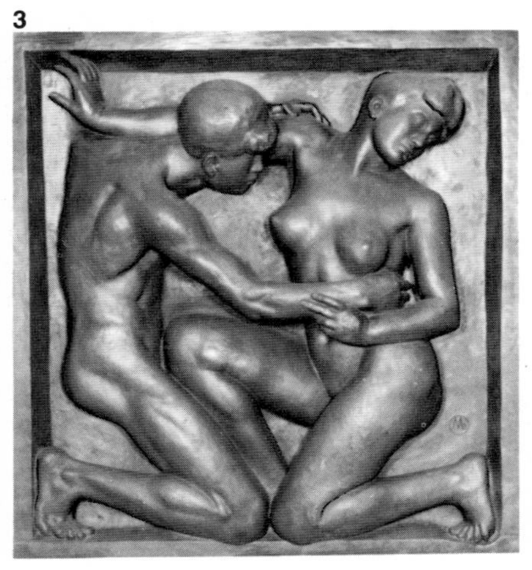
3

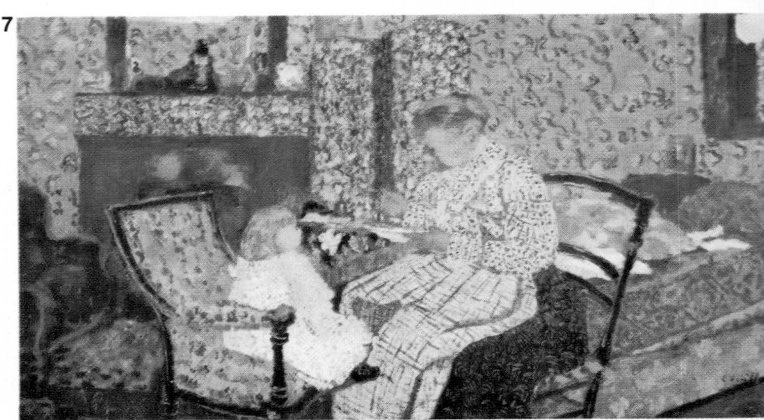
7

1. **Maurice Denis** (1870–1943): *Homage to Cézanne.* 1900. Musée National d'Art Moderne, Paris
2. **Maurice Denis** (1870–1943): *The Muses.* 1893. Musée National d'Art Moderne, Paris
3. **Mané-Katz** (1894–1962): *Rabbis with the Torah.* 1935. Oscar Ghez Modern Art Foundation, Geneva
4. **Nicholas de Staël** (1914–55): *Little Footballers.* 1952. Private Collection
5. **Nicholas de Staël** (1914–55): *Drawing.* Pen and ink. 1947. Private Collection
6. **Nicholas de Staël** (1914–55): *Parc des Princes.* 1952. Private Collection
7. **Jules Pascin** (1885–1930): *Nude with Red Sandals.* 1927. Oscar Ghez Modern Art Foundation, Geneva

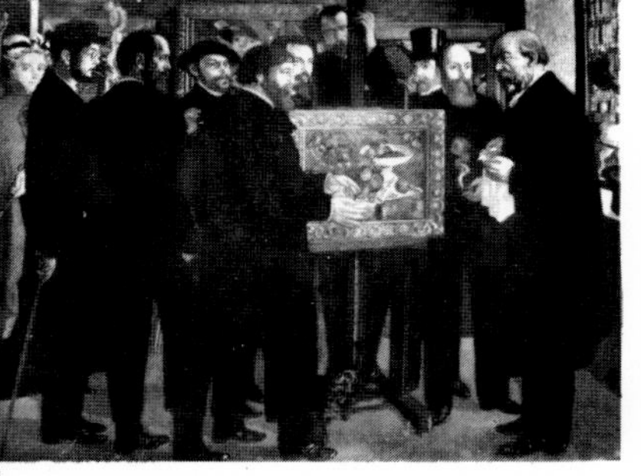

1

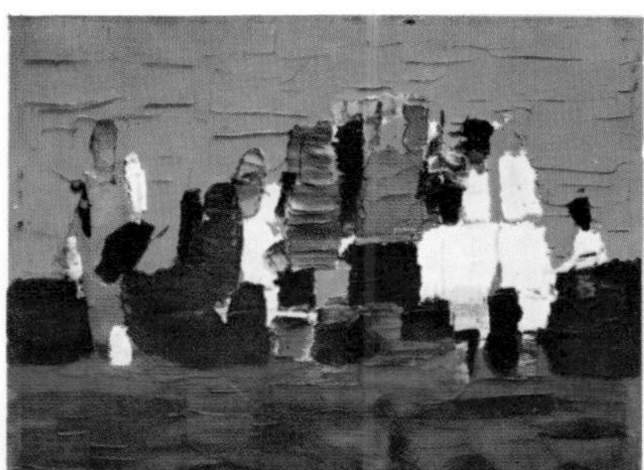

4

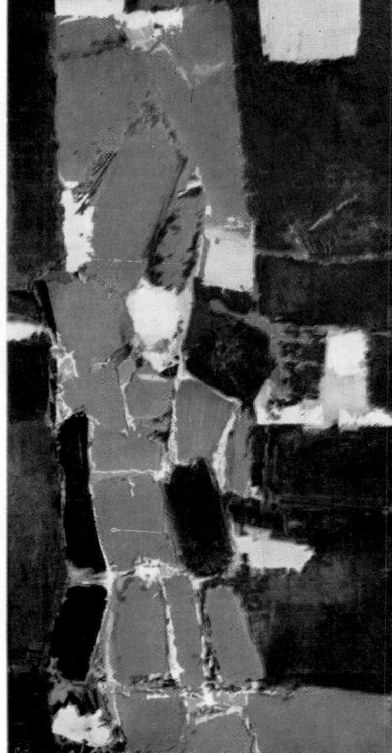

6

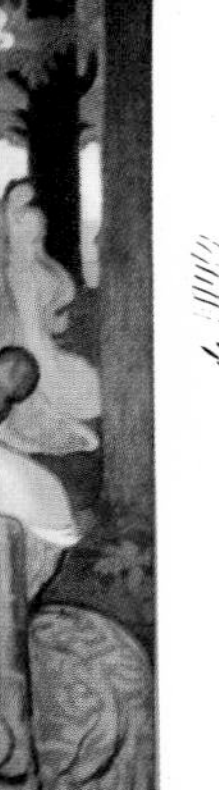

2

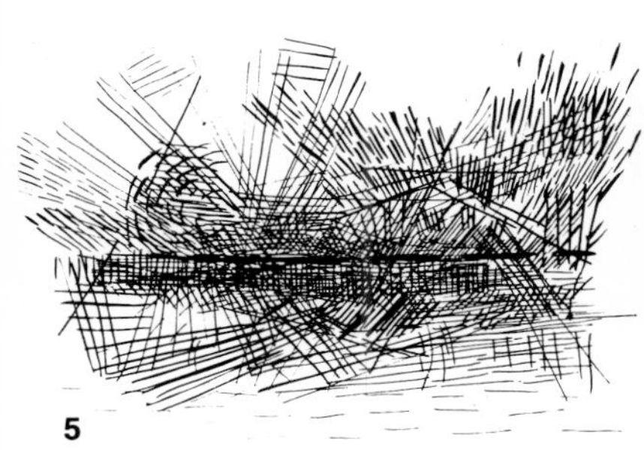

5

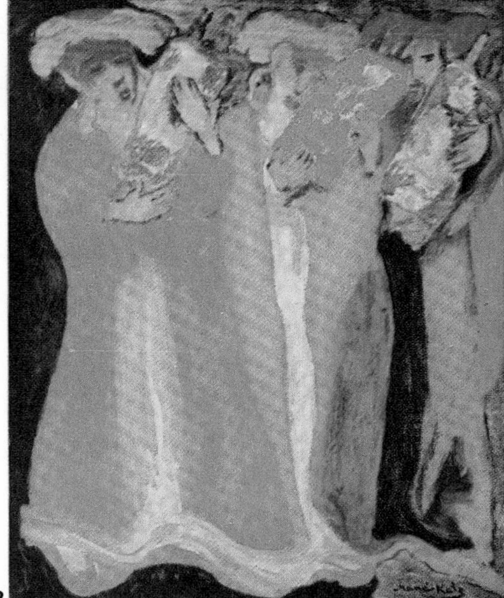

3

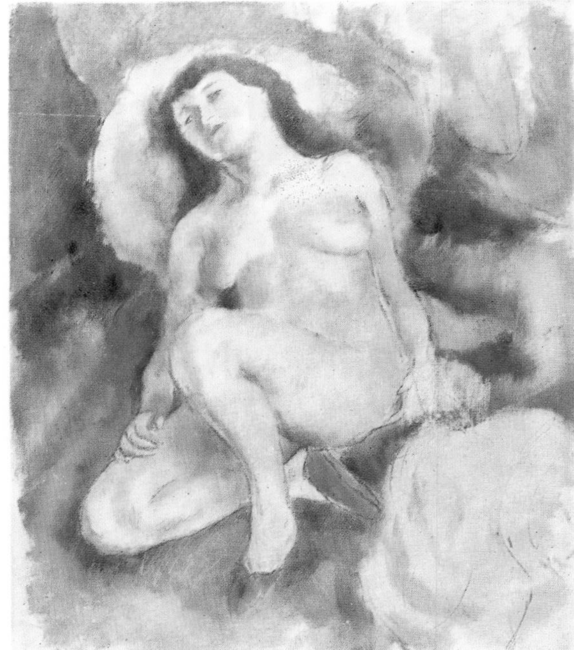

7

1. **Max Pechstein** (1881–1955): *A seated Female Nude.* 1910. Private Collection
2. **Lovis Corinth** (1858–1925): *View of the Walchensee, Bavaria.* 1922. Private Collection
3. **Max Beckmann** (1884–1950): *The Departure.* 1932–3. Museum of Modern Art, New York
4. **Max Liebermann** (1847–1935): *The Courtyard of the Amsterdam Orphanage.* 1882. Städelsches Kunstinstitut, Frankfurt
5. **Max Liebermann** (1847–1935): *Parrots' Walk at the Amsterdam Zoo.* 1902. Kunsthalle, Bremen
6. **Max Beckmann** (1884–1950): *Self-portrait.* 1944. Bayerische Staatsgemäldesammlungen, Munich

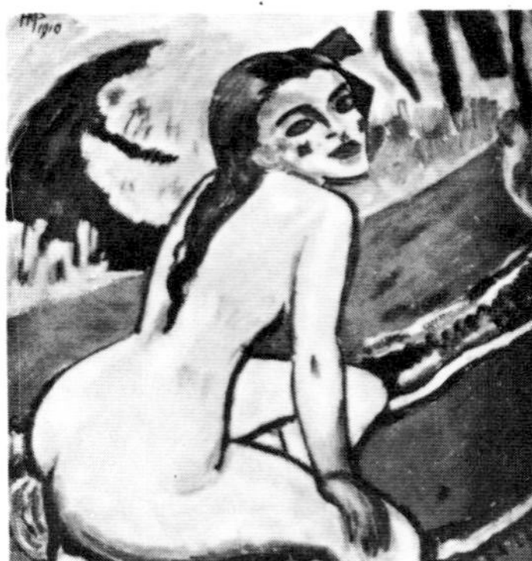
1

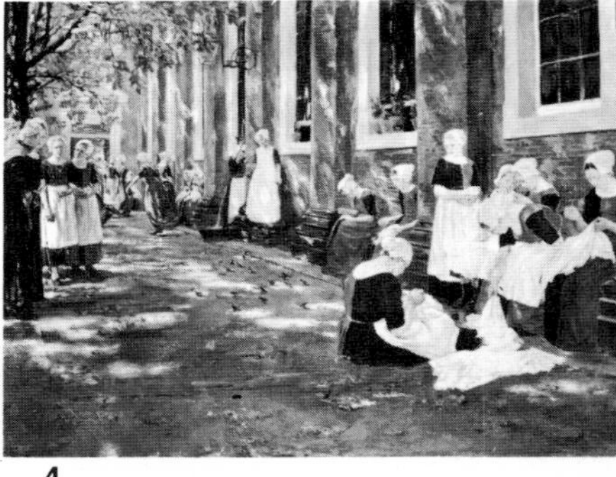
4

2

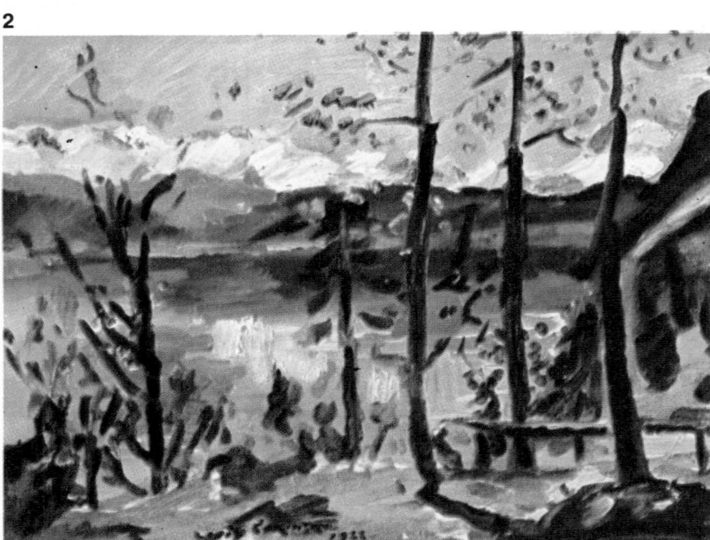

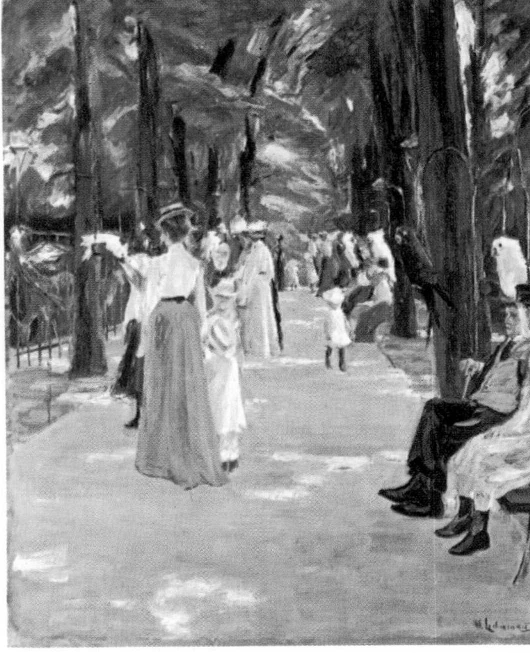

3

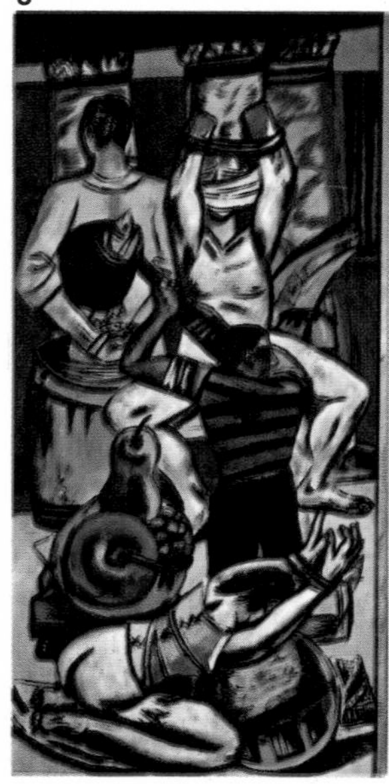

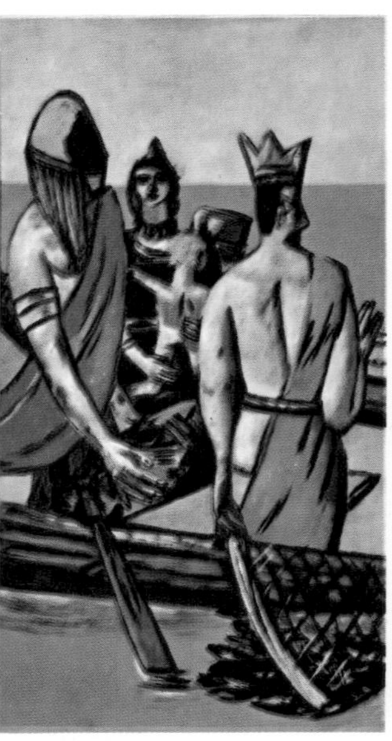

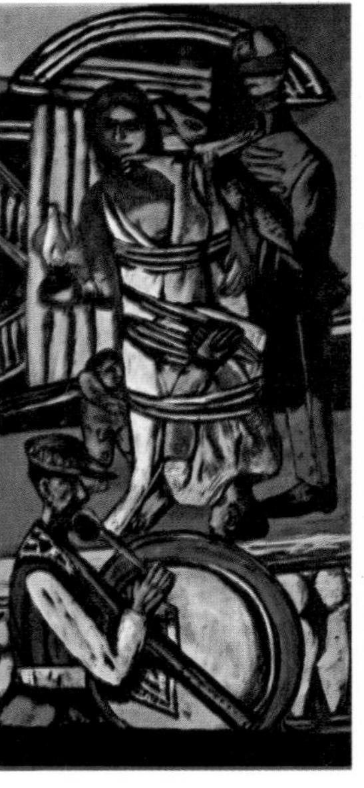

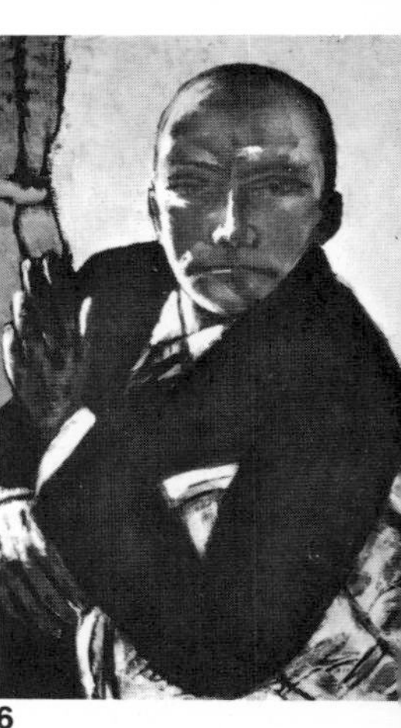
6

Edvard Munch (1863–1944)
1. *Anxiety*. 1894. Munch-museet, Oslo
2. *Girls on a Bridge*. 1901. Nasjonalgalleriet, Oslo
3. *Karl Johans Street, Oslo*. 1892. Private Collection
4. *The Cry*. Lithograph. 1893

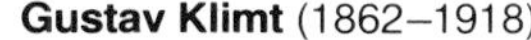

Gustav Klimt (1862–1918)
5. Drawing published in *Ver Sacrum*. Pen and ink. 1900
6. *Judith with the Head of Holofernes*. 1901. Osterreichische Galerie, Vienna
7. *The Kiss*. Cardboard mosaic for the Stoclet House, Brussels. 1909. Musée des Beaux-Arts, Strasbourg

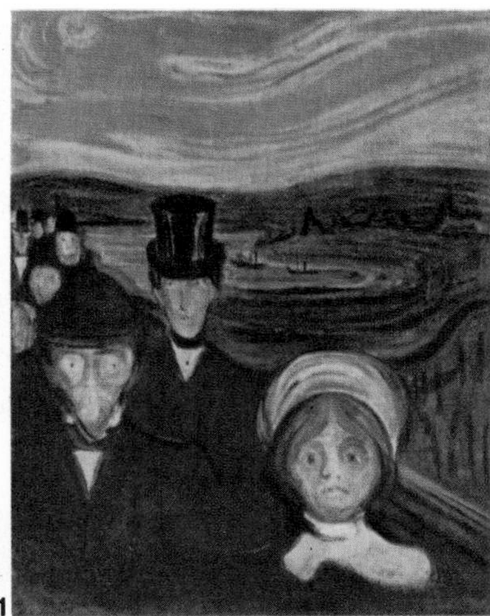

1

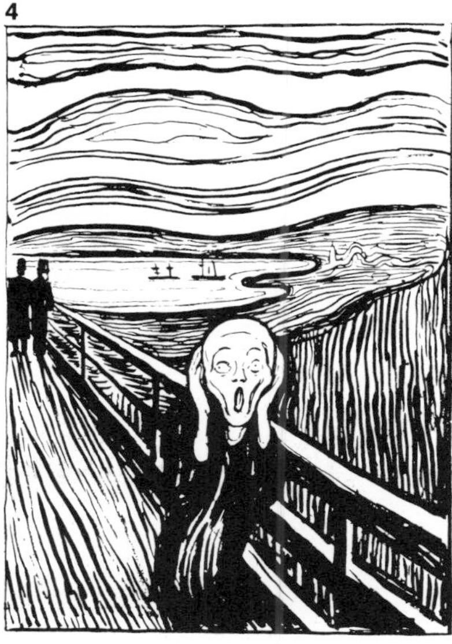

4

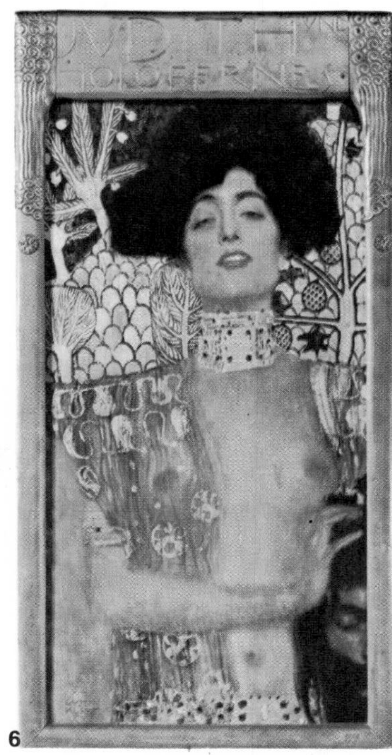

6

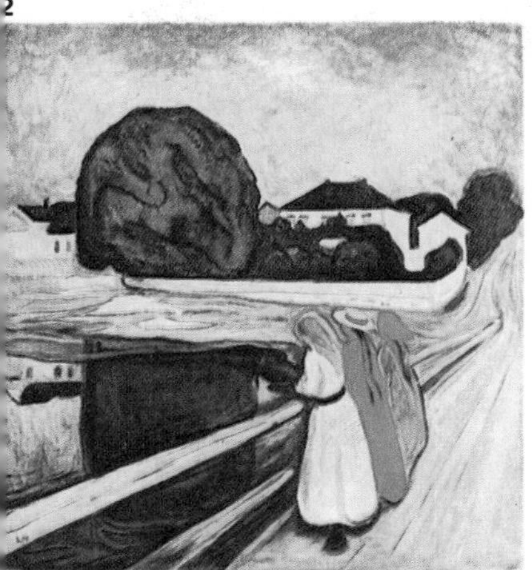

2

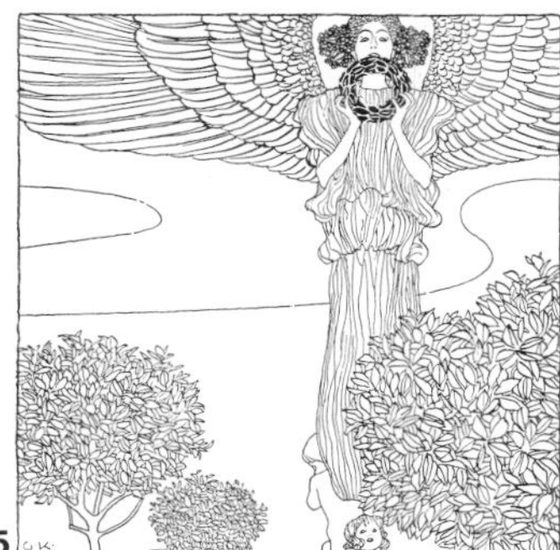

5

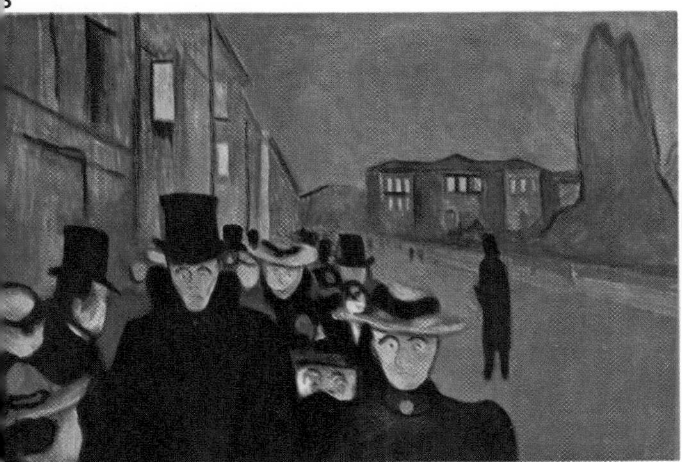

3

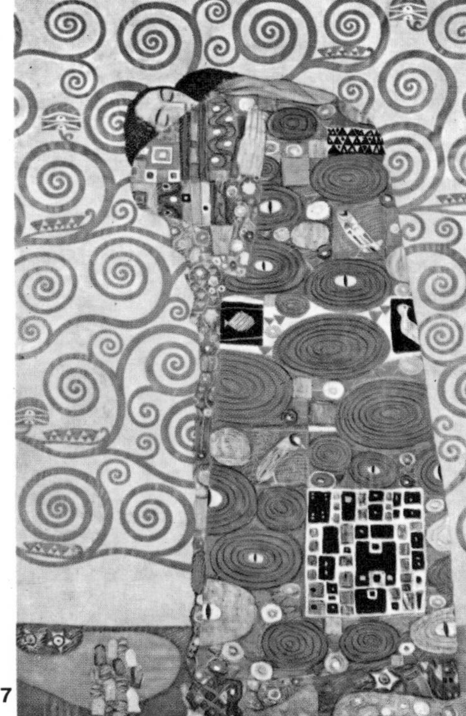

7

Henri Matisse (1869–1954)

1. *Portrait of Madame Matisse with a green Stripe.* 1905. Statens Museum for Kunst, Copenhagen
2. *White Feathers.* 1919. Minneapolis Institute of Arts
3. *The Open Window, Collioure.* 1905. John Hay Whitney Collection, New York
4. *Pink Onions.* 1906. Statens Museum for Kunst, Copenhagen
5. *The Dance.* 1909–10. Hermitage, Leningrad
6. *Zorah standing* or *The Moroccan.* 1912. Pushkin Museum of Fine Arts, Moscow
7. *The Piano Lesson.* 1917. Museum of Modern Art, New York

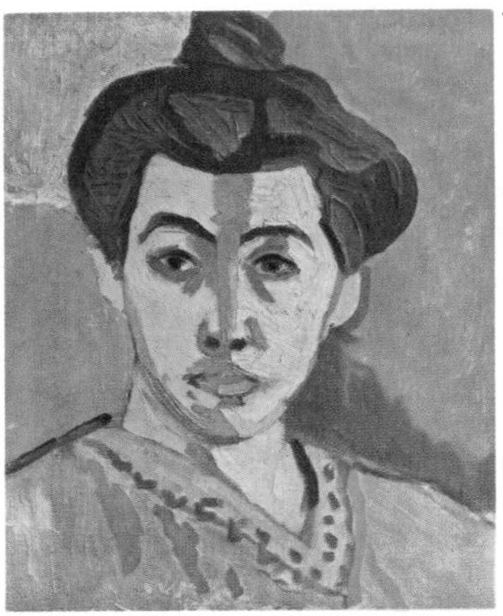
1

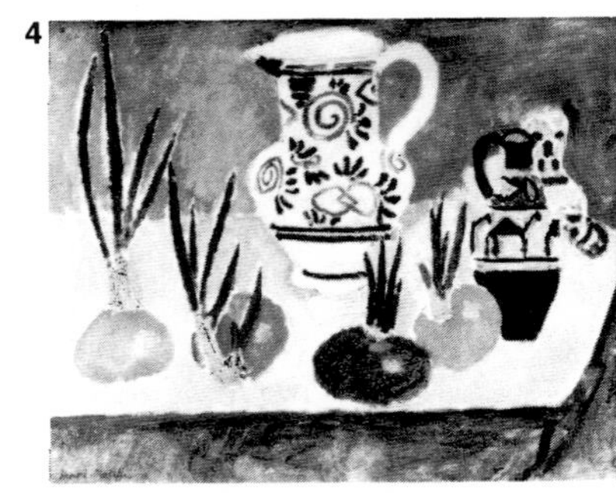
4

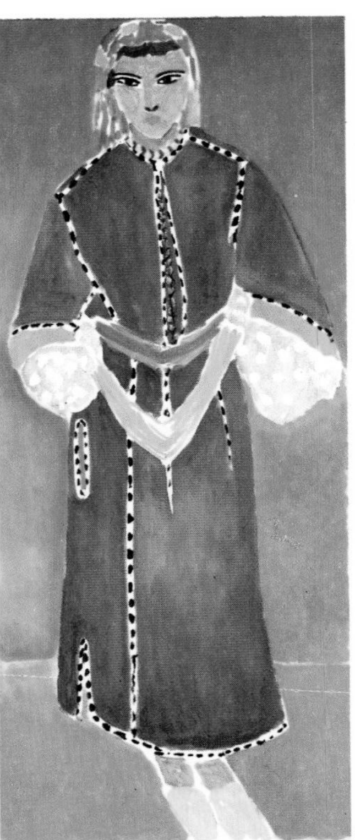
6

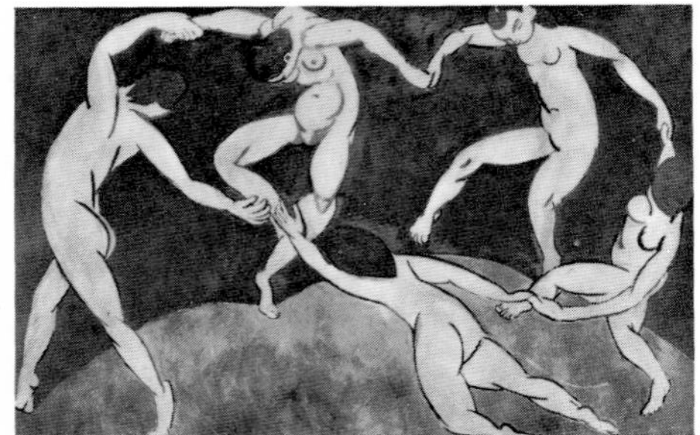
5

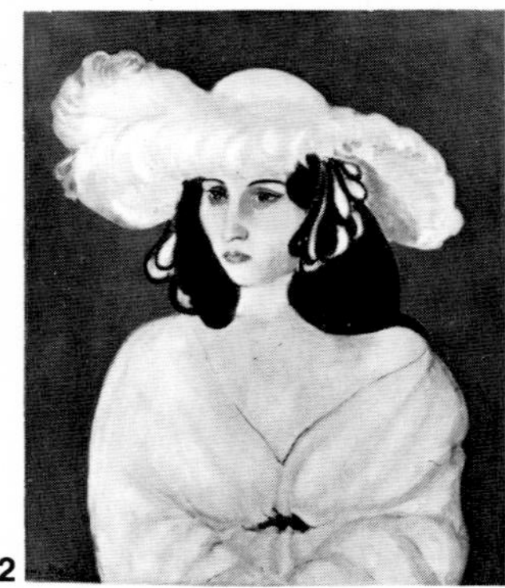
2

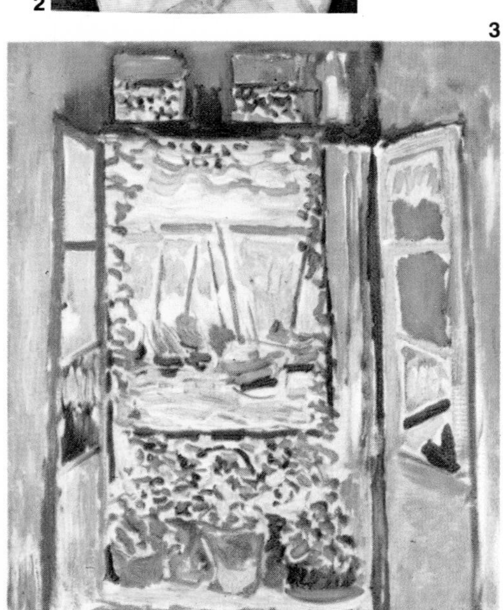
3

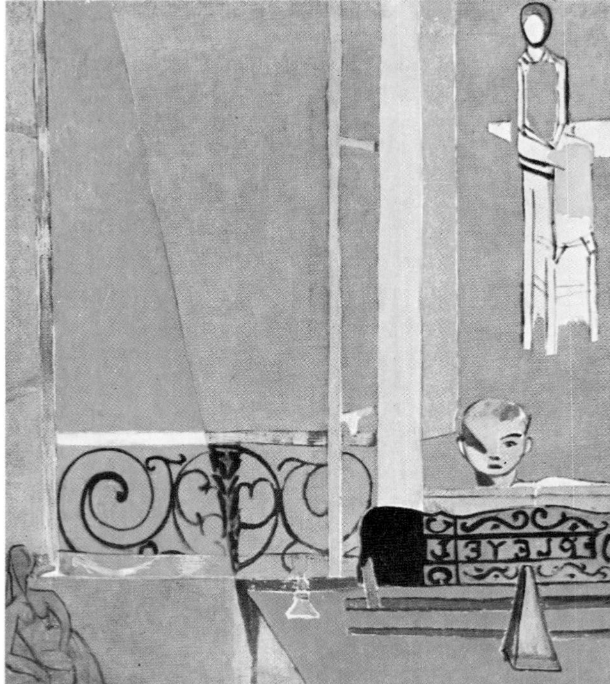
7

Henri Matisse (1869–1954)

1. *The Melancholy of the King.* Gouache and *papier collé.* 1952. Musée National d'Art Moderne, Paris
2. *Still Life.* India ink. 1941
3. *The Green Sideboard.* 1928. Musée National d'Art Moderne, Paris
4. *Le Tiaré.* Bronze. 1930. Ahrenberg Collection, Sweden
5. *Reclining Nude.* India ink. 1935
6. *The Persian Dress.* 1937. Private Collection

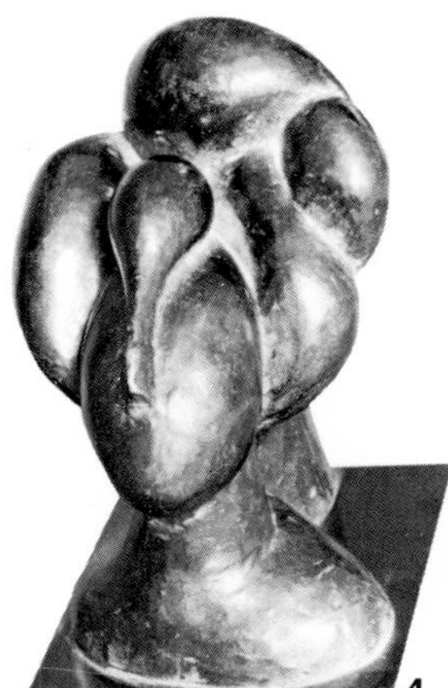

4

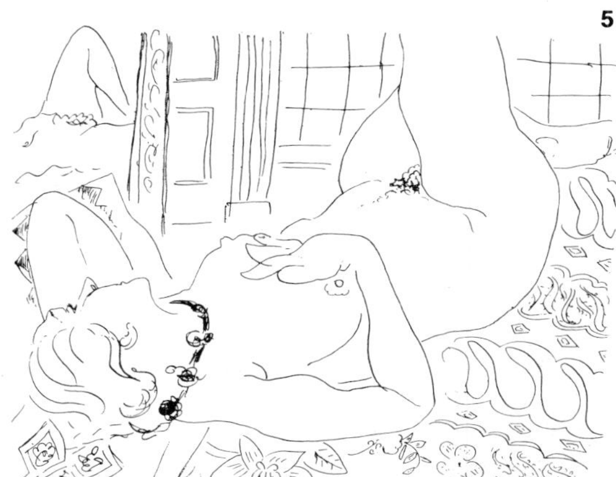

5

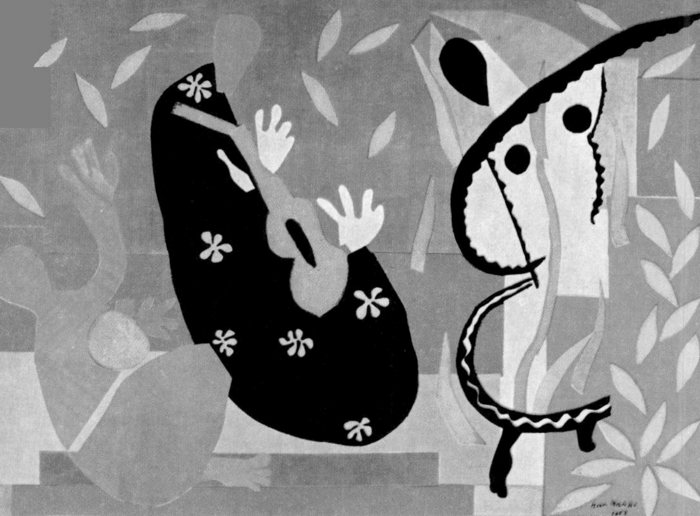

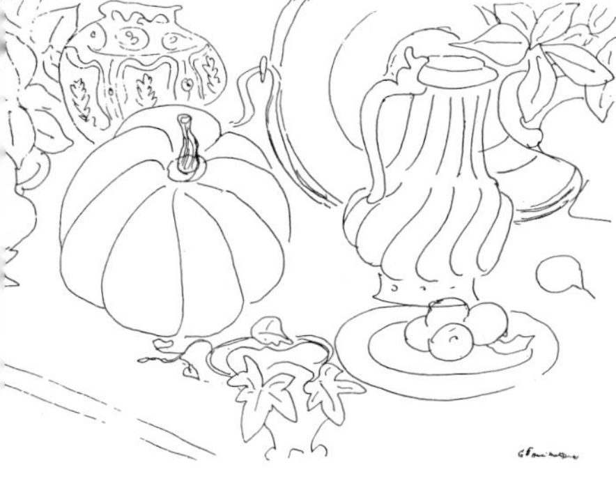

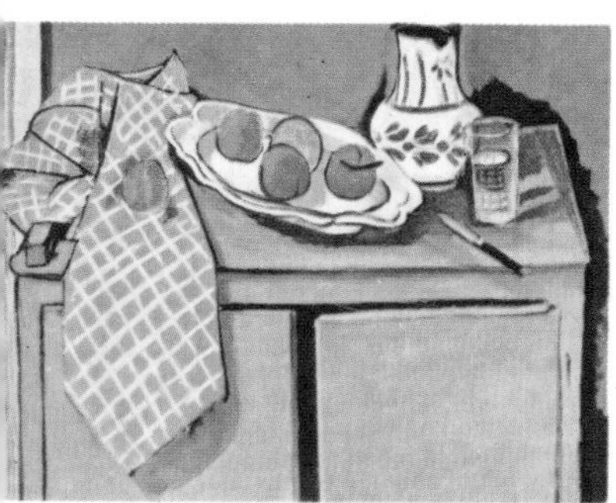

6

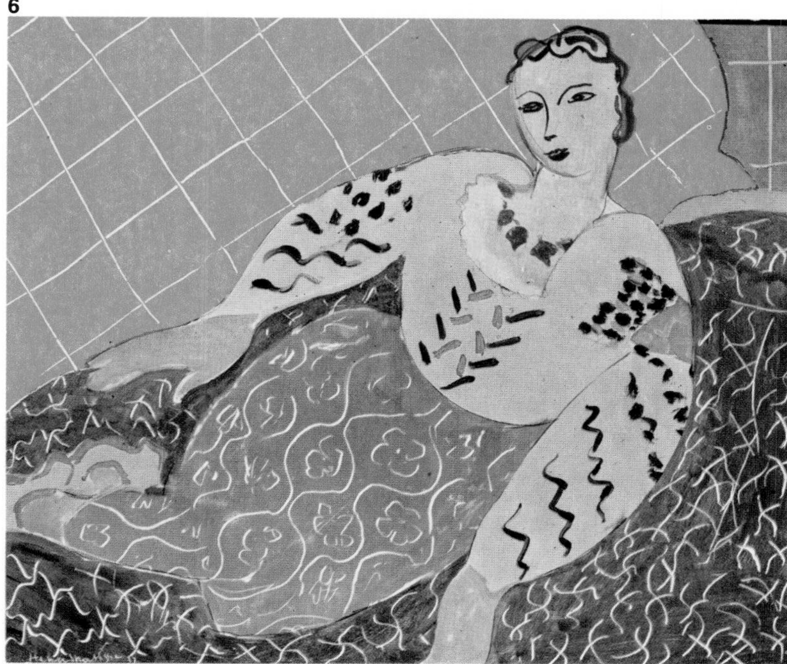

1. **André Derain** (1880–1954): *Nude in front of a green Curtain.* 1923. Musée National d'Art Moderne, Paris
2. **Maurice de Vlaminck** (1876–1958): *The Painter's House at Valmondois* or *The Clapboard House.* 1920. Musée National d'Art Moderne, Paris
3. **Raoul Dufy** (1877–1953): *The Regatta.* 1938. Stedelijk Museum, Amsterdam
4. **André Derain** (1880–1954): *The Dancer.* 1906. Statens Museum for Kunst, Copenhagen
5. **Albert Marquet** (1875–1947): *Portrait of a Sergeant of the Colonial Army.* 1907 Metropolitan Museum of Art (Robert Lehman Collection), New York
6. **Kees van Dongen** (1877–1968): *Anita.* 1905. Formerly collection of the artist

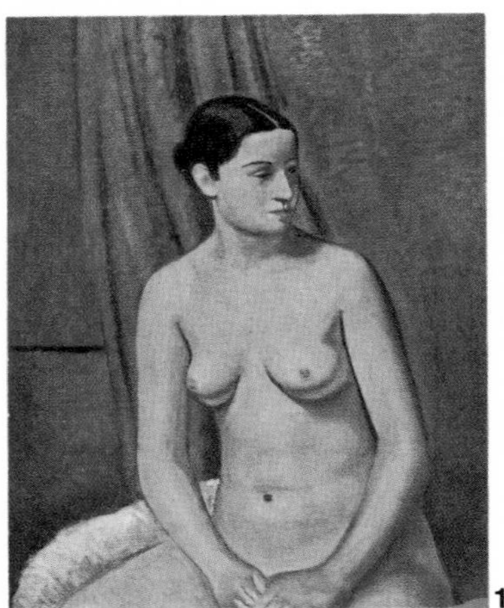
1

4

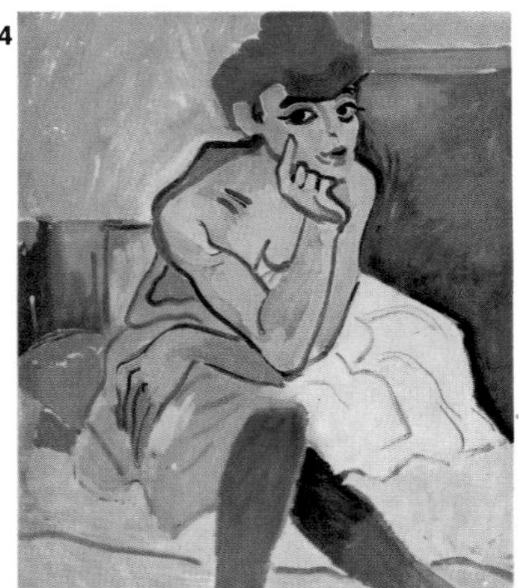

5

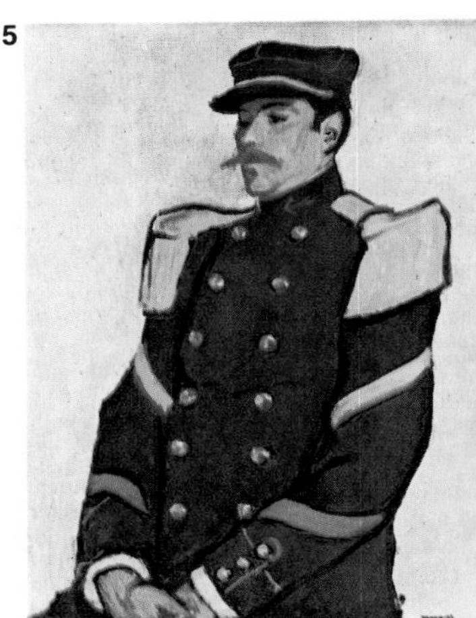

2

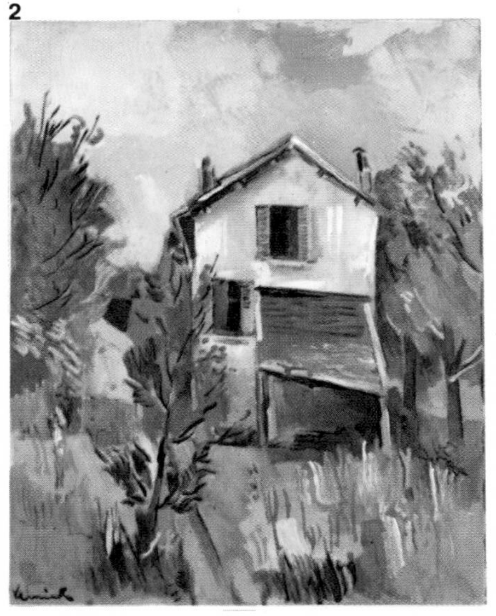

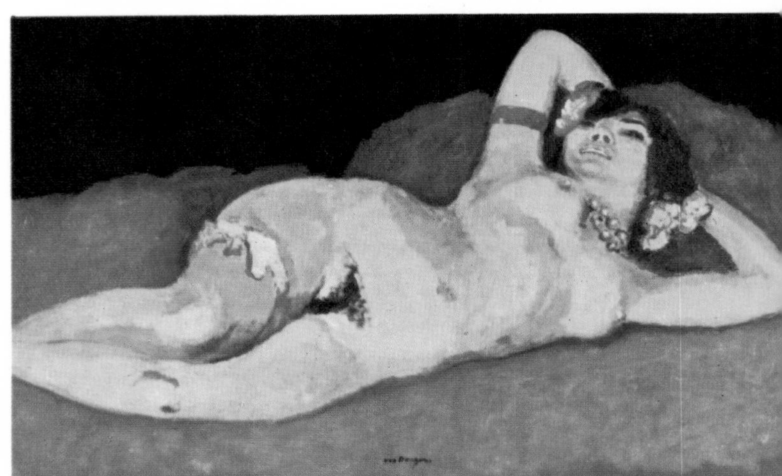

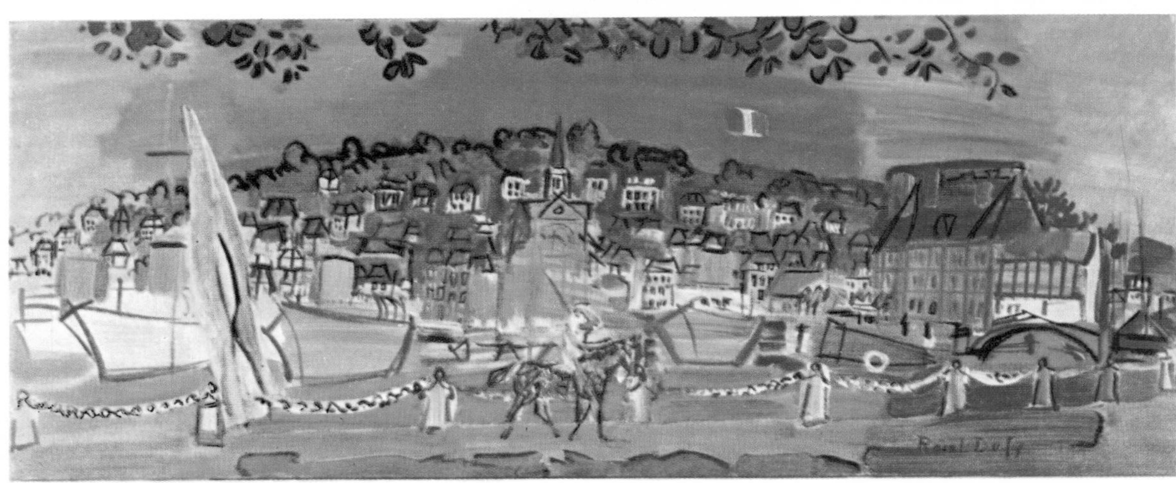

3

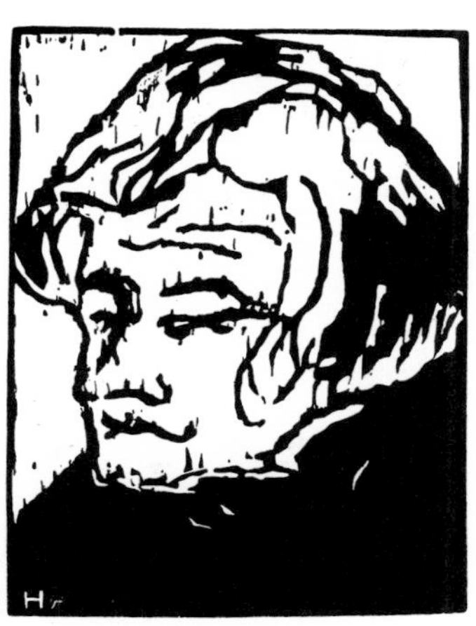
1

1. **Erich Heckel** (1883–1970): *Head of a Violinist.* Woodcut. 1907
2. **Erich Heckel** (1883–1970): *The Model.* Pen and ink. 1911
3. **Ernst Ludwig Kirchner** (1880–1938): *Nude with a Hat.* 1911. Wallraf-Richartz-Museum, Cologne
4. **Ernst Ludwig Kirchner** (1880–1938): *A young Girl on a blue Sofa.* 1907–8. Minneapolis Institute of Arts
5. **Ernst Ludwig Kirchner** (1880–1938): *Girl seated in a Meadow.* 1908. Private Collection
6. **Ernst Ludwig Kirchner** (1880–1938): Poster for an exhibition of the New Secession in Berlin. Wood engraving. 1910
7. **Karl Schmidt-Rottluff** (1884–1976): *Resting in the Studio.* 1910. Kunsthalle, Hamburg

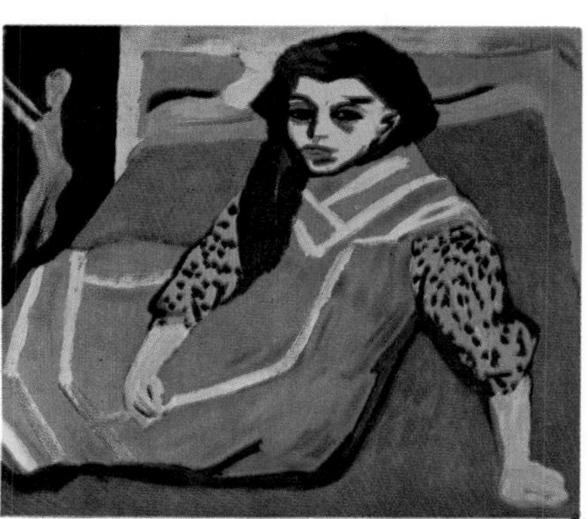
4

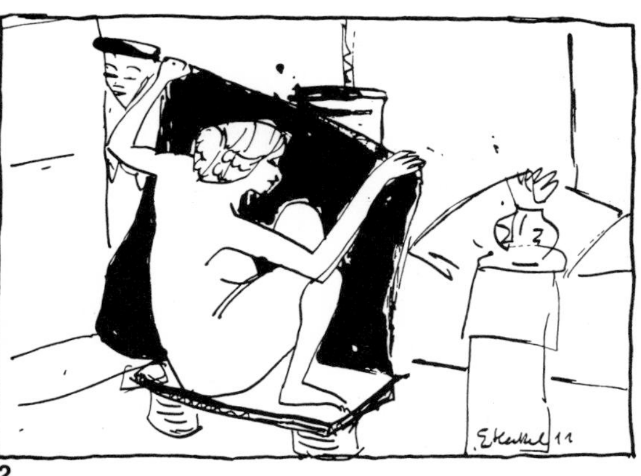
2

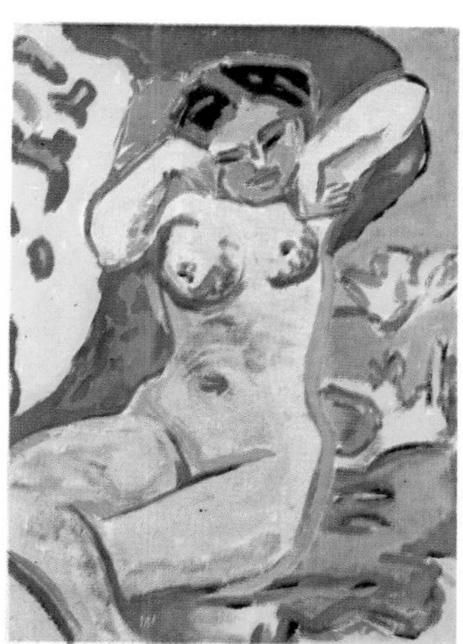
5

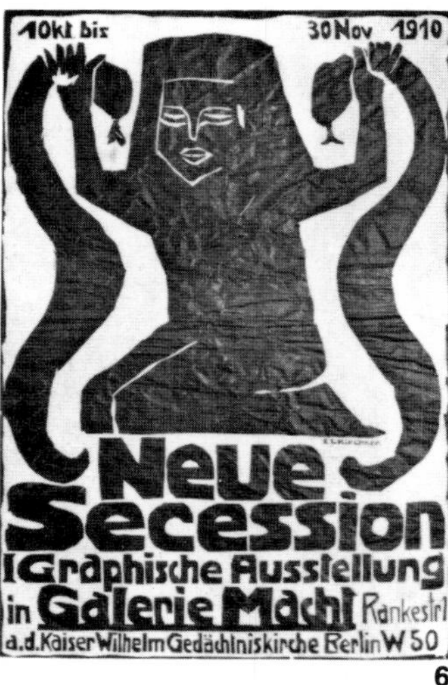

6

3
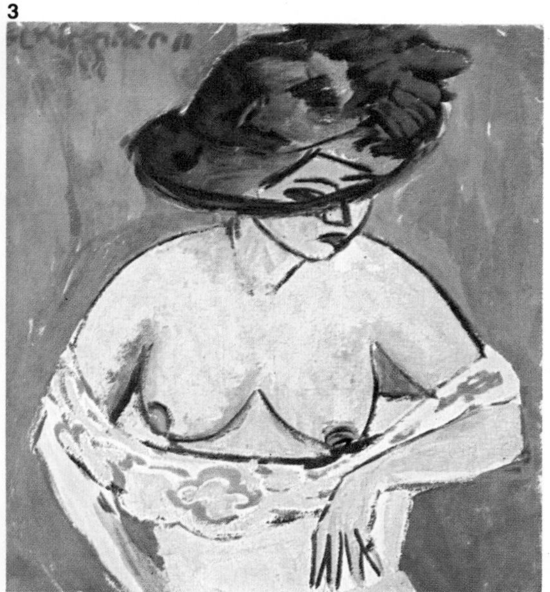

7
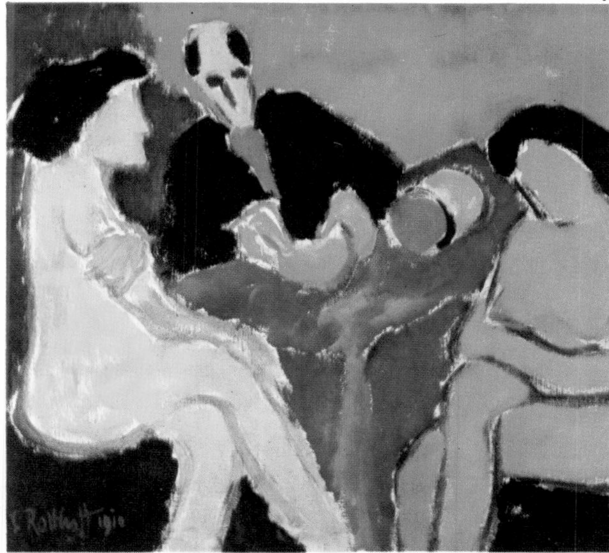

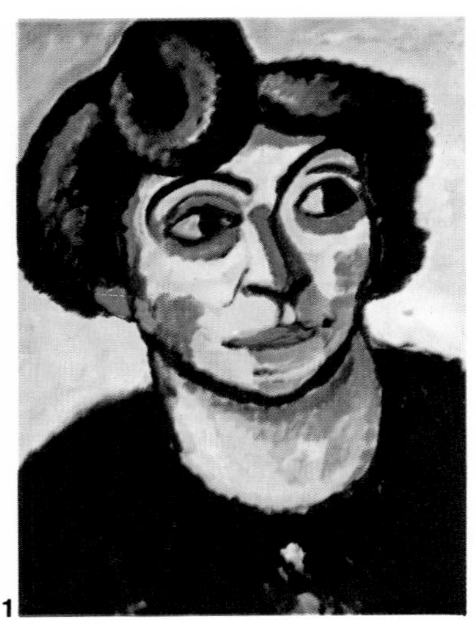
1

Alexej Jawlensky (1864–1941)
1. *Woman with Forelock.* 1913. Städtisches Museum, Wiesbaden
2. *Medusa.* 1923. Musée des Beaux-Arts, Lyons
3. *The Peonies.* 1909. Städtisches Museum, Wuppertal

Wassily Kandinsky (1866–1944)

4. *Shrill-Peaceful Rose Colour.* 1924. Wallraf-Richartz-Museum, Cologne
5. *Improvisation 14.* 1910. Private Collection
6. *Little Dream in Red.* 1925. Private Collection

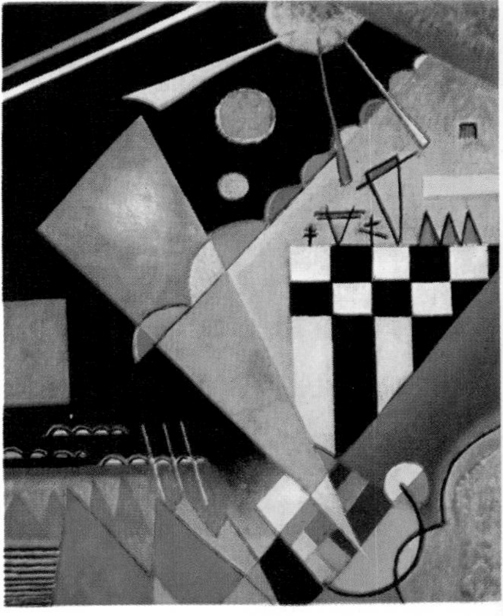
4

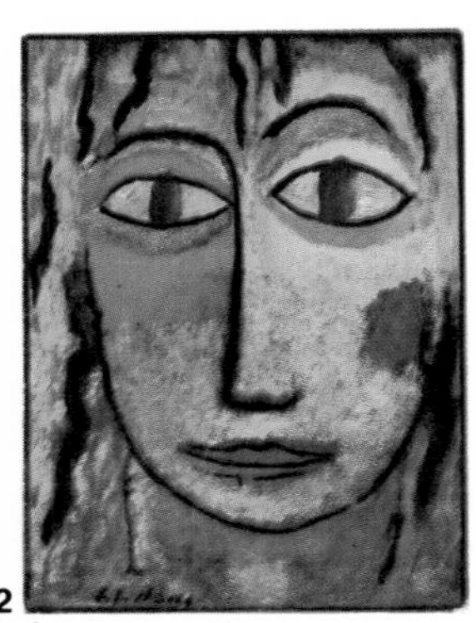
2

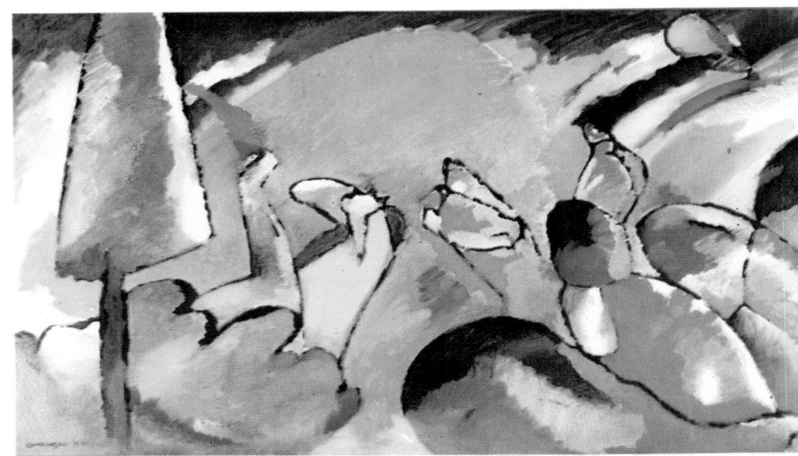
5

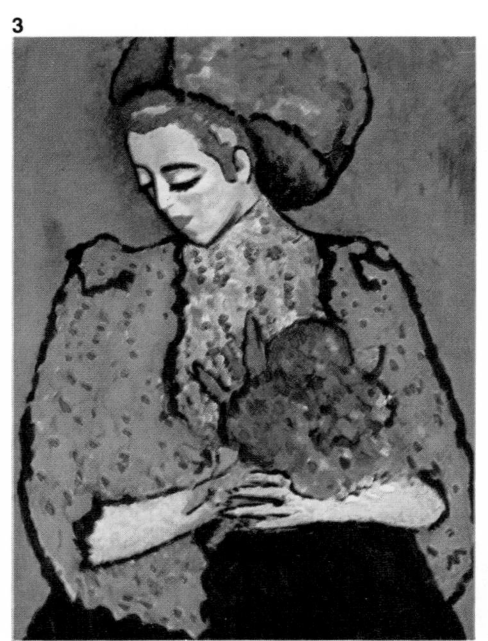
3

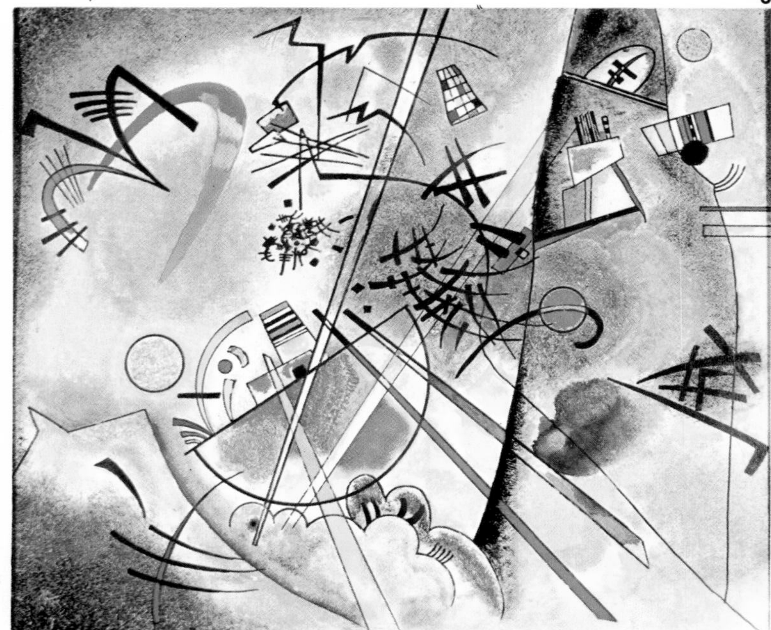
6

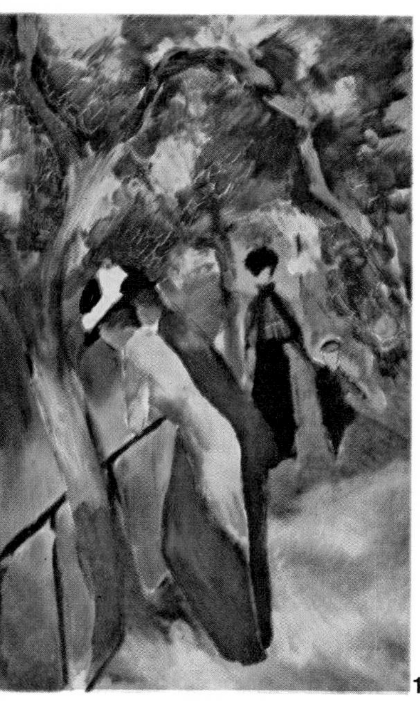

1

1. **August Macke** (1887–1914): *Sunny Path.* 1913. Private Collection
2. **Franz Marc** (1880–1916): *Gazelles.* 1913. Private Collection
3. **Paul Klee** (1879–1940): *Niesen Mountain.* Watercolour. 1915. Private Collection
4. **Franz Marc** (1880–1916): *Blue Horse.* 1911. Private Collection
5. **August Macke** (1887–1914): *Kairouan I.* Watercolour. 1914. Private Collection
6. **Franz Marc** (1880–1916): *Composition of Abstract Forms.* 1914. Private Collection

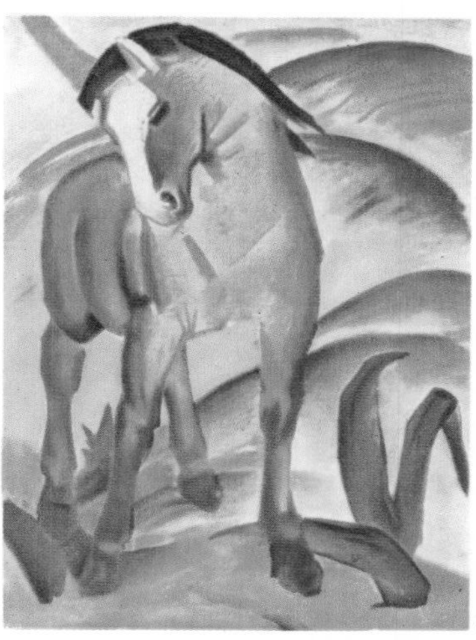

4

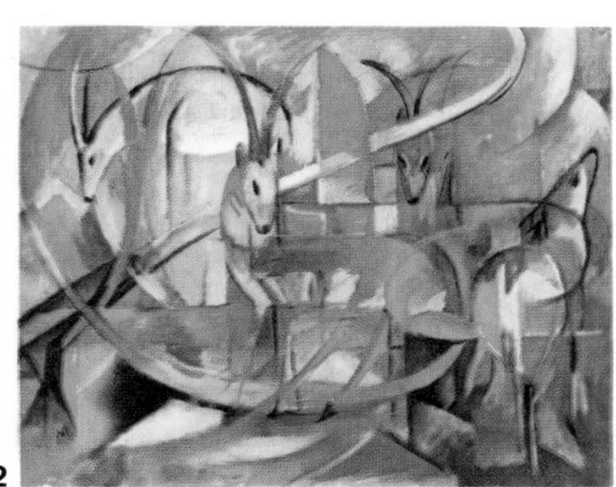

2

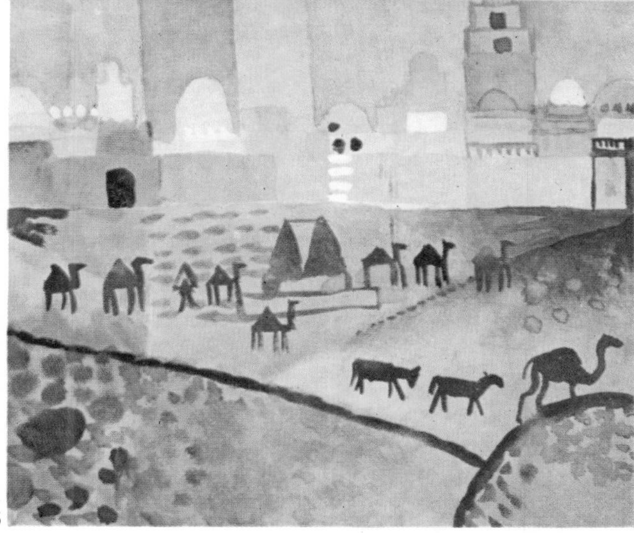

5

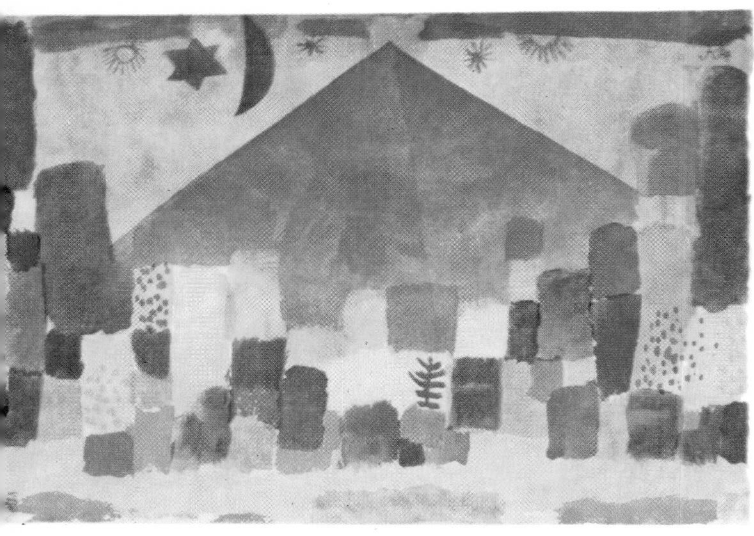

6

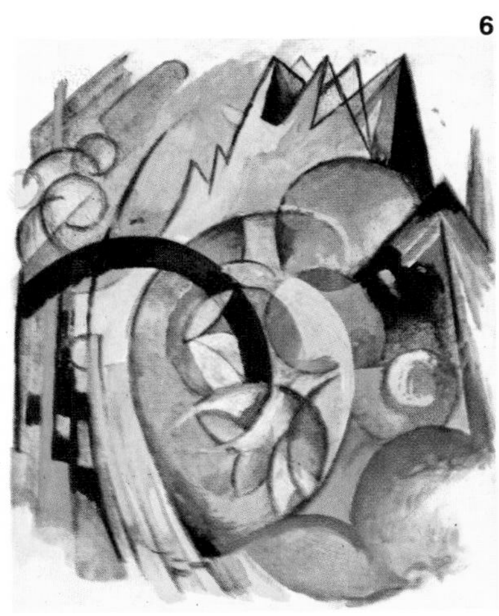

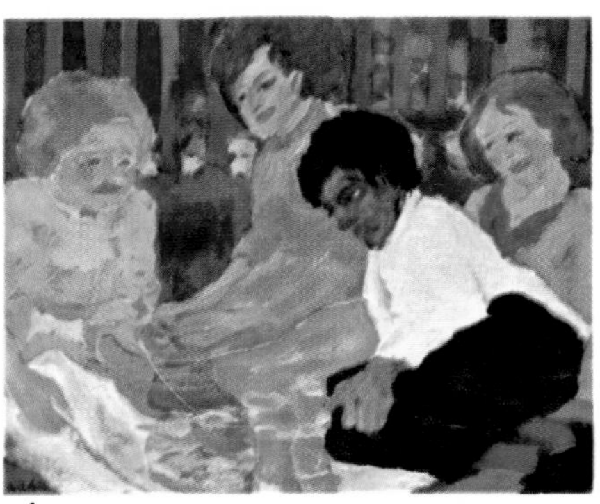

1

1. **Emil Nolde** (1867–1956): *Luncheon Feast.* 1907. Private Collection
2. **James Ensor** (1860–1949): *Ostend Rooftops.* 1898. Private Collection
3. **George Grosz** (1893–1959): *A Berlin Street.* Metropolitan Museum of Art (Hugo Kastor Fund), New York
4. **James Ensor** (1860–1949): *Skeletons warming themselves around a Stove.* 1889. Private Collection
5. **James Ensor** (1860–1949): *Intrigue.* Detail. 1890. Koninklijk Museum voor Schone Kunsten, Antwerp
6. **Emil Nolde** (1867–1956): *Marshy Landscape.* 1916. Kunstmuseum, Basle

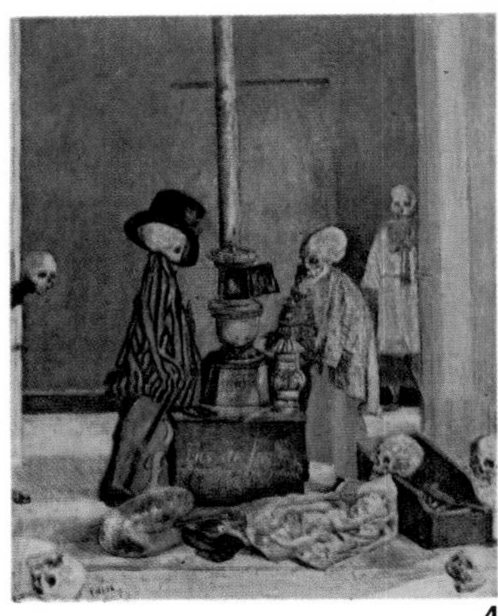

4

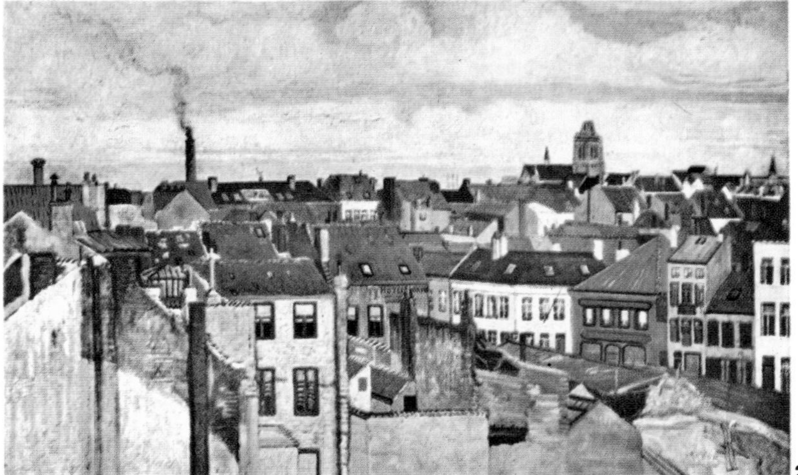

2

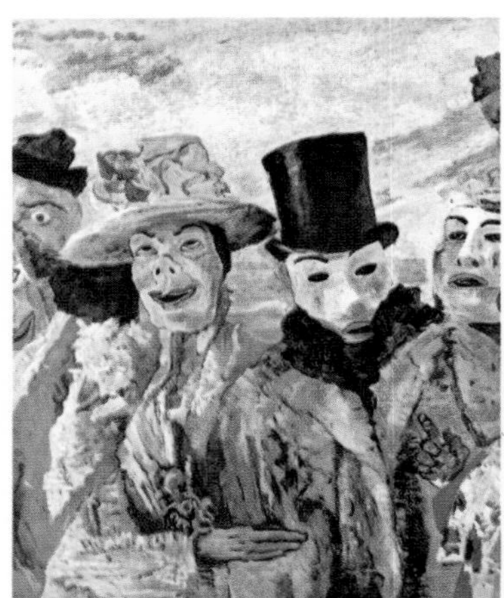

5

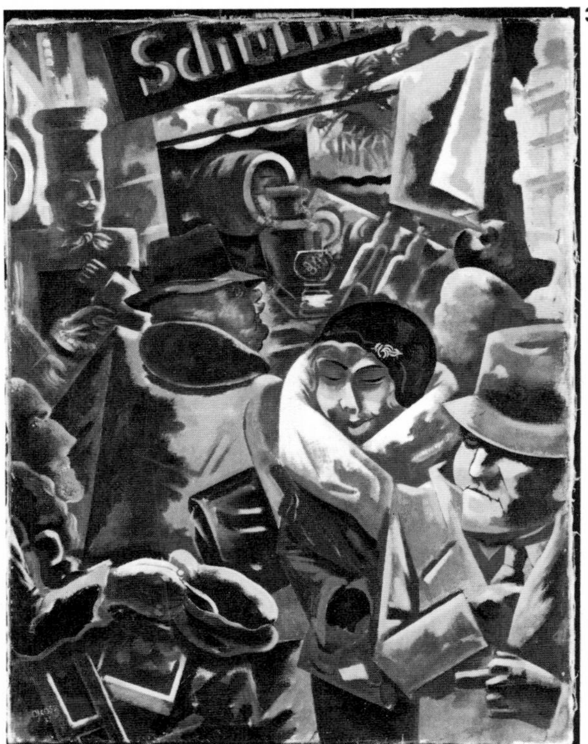

3

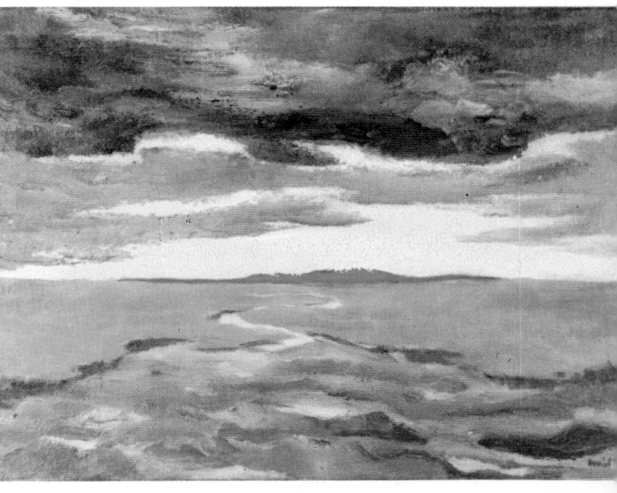

1. **Oskar Kokoschka** (b.1886): *Loving Couple with a Cat.* 1917. Kunsthaus, Zurich
2. **Egon Schiele** (1890–1918): *Self-portrait.* 1911. Private Collection
3. **Otto Wagner** (1841–1918): The Post Office Savings Bank, Vienna. The main hall. 1904–6
4. **Oskar Kokoschka** (b.1886): *Bridges over the River Elbe at Dresden.* 1923. Folkwang Museum, Essen
5. **Oskar Kokoschka** (b.1886): *Portrait of Herwarth Walden.* 1910. Private Collection

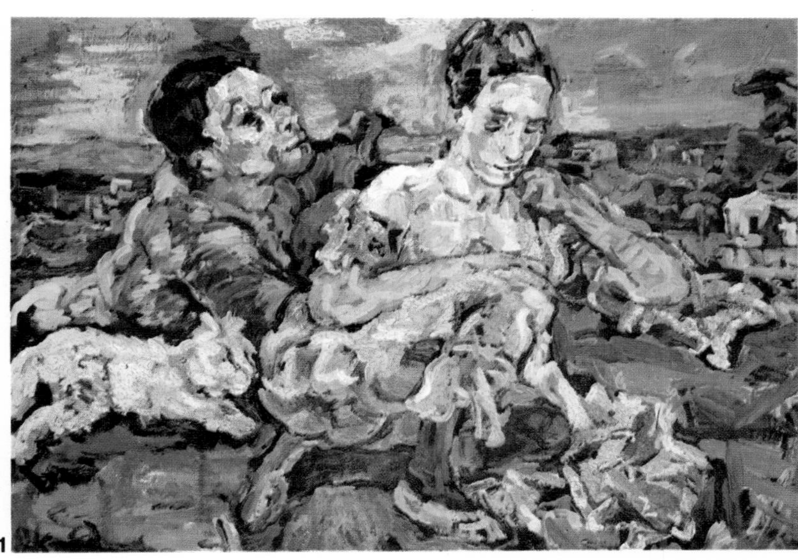

1

4

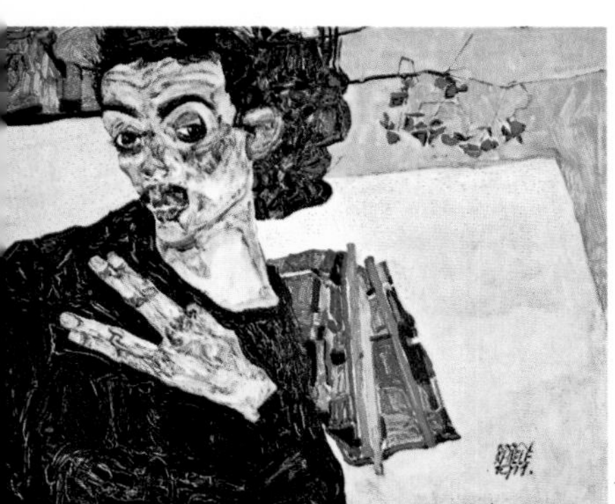

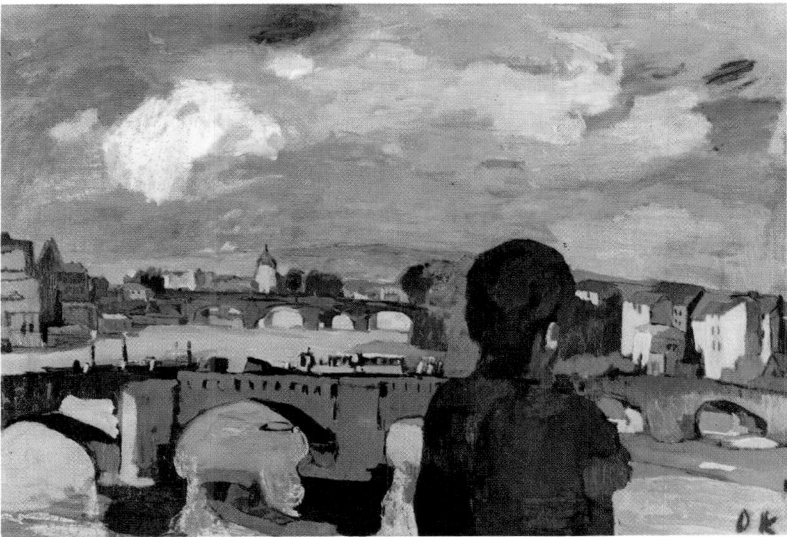

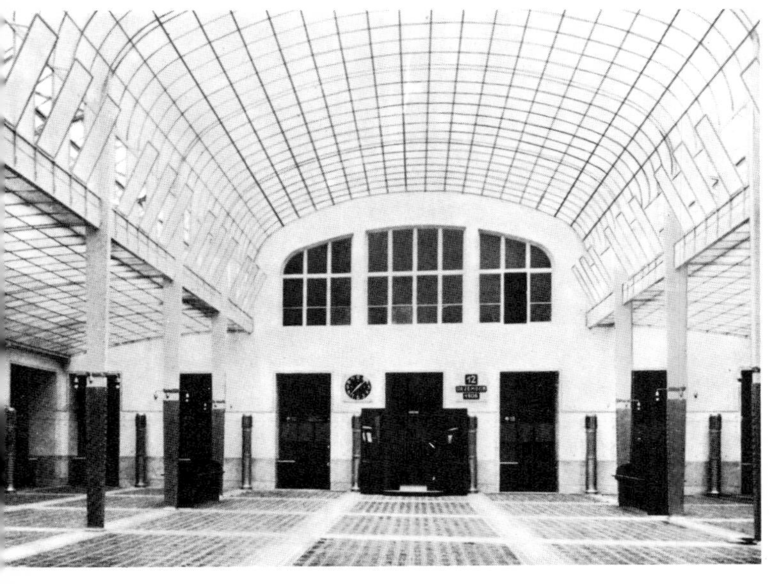

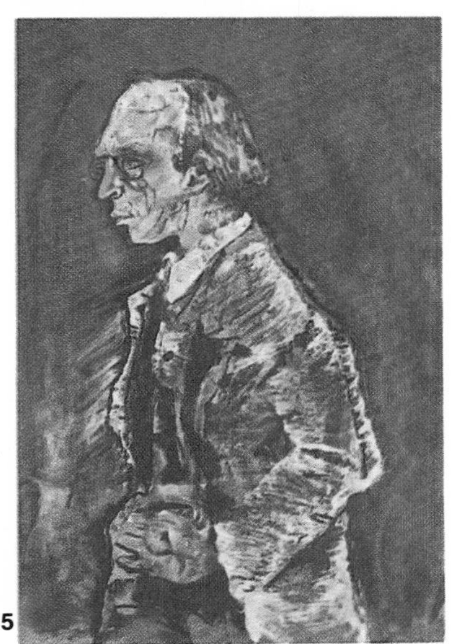

5

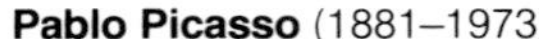

Pablo Picasso (1881–1973)

1. *Frugal Repast.* Watercolour. 1904
2. *Harlequin's Family.* Gouache. 1905. Private Collection
3. *Les Demoiselles d'Avignon.* 1907. Museum of Modern Art, New York
4. *Still Life with Cane Chair.* 1911–12. Formerly collection of the artist
5. *Self-portrait.* 1906. Philadelphia Museum of Art
6. *Nude Women.* 1906. Private Collection
7. *The Aficionado.* 1912. Kunstmuseum, Basle

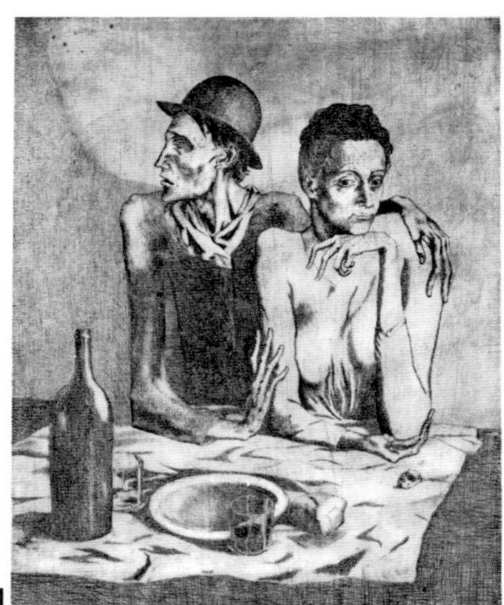

1

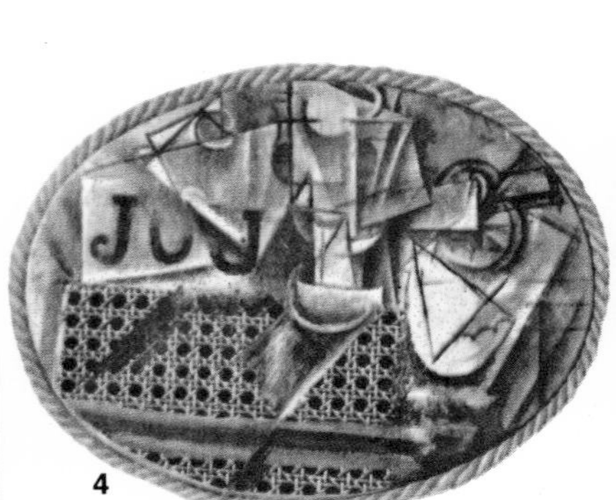

4

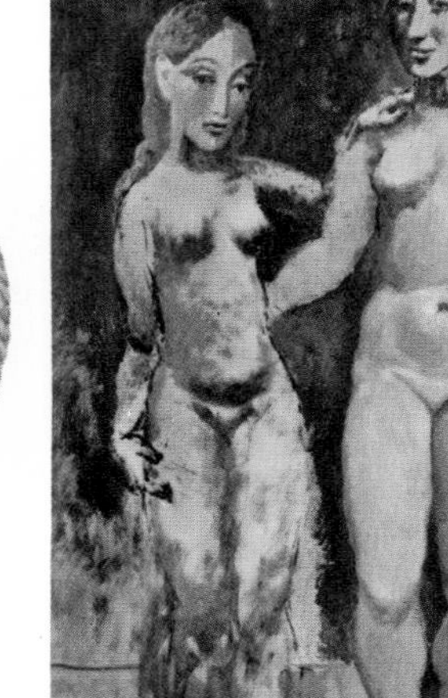

6

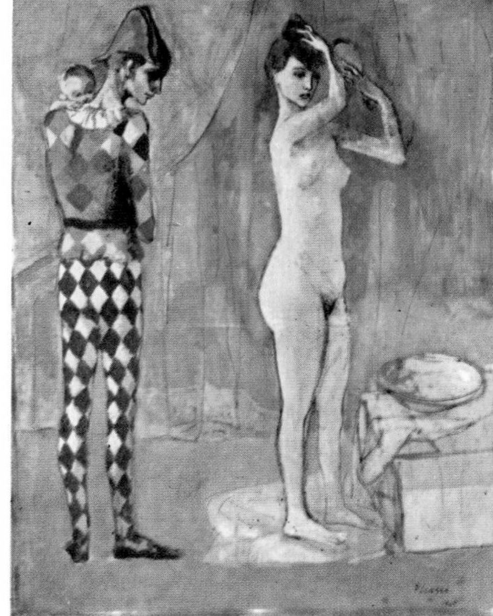

2

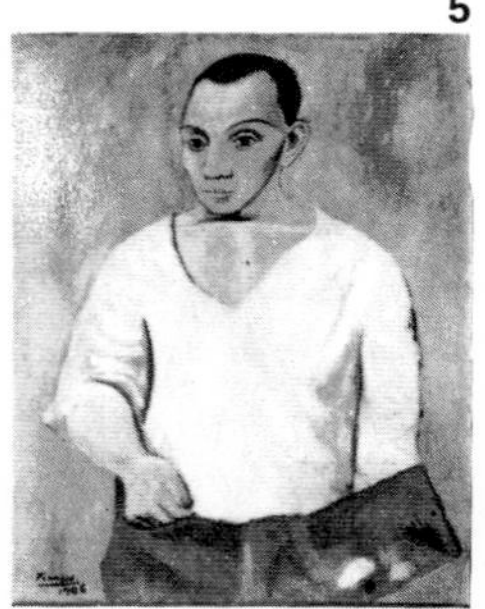

5

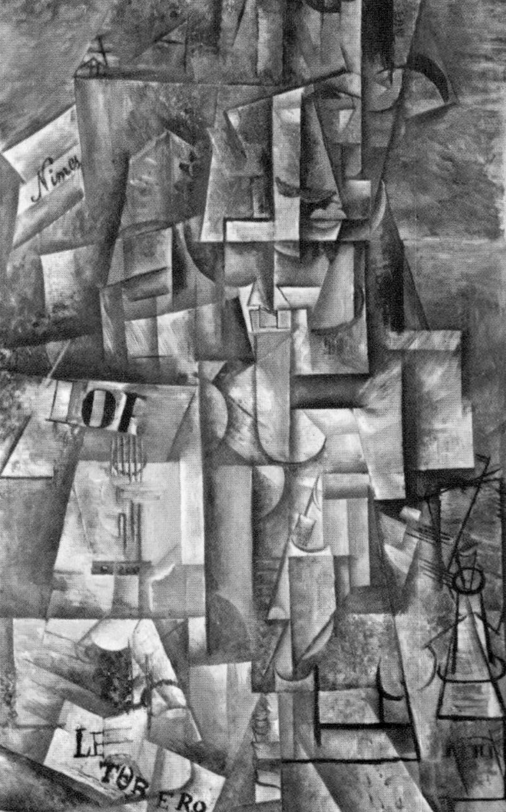

7

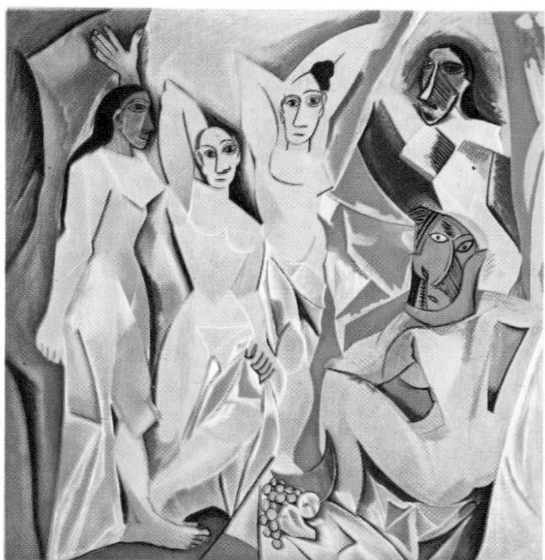

3

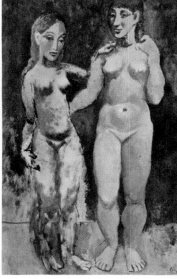

Pablo Picasso (1881–1973)

1. *Head of a Woman.* Pastel. 1921. Worcester Art Museum, Worcester, Massachusetts
2. *Glass, Bottle and Newspaper on a Table. Papier collé* and charcoal. 1914. Private Collection
3. *Artist and Model.* 1936. Private Collection
4. *Three Women at the Fountain.* 1921. Museum of Modern Art, New York
5. *Three Musicians.* 1921. Museum of Modern Art, New York
6. Wire construction. 1930
7. *Head of a Woman.* Gilt bronze. 1931–2

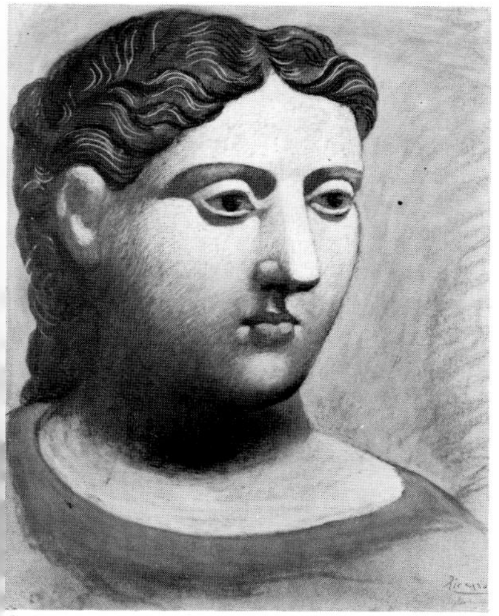

1

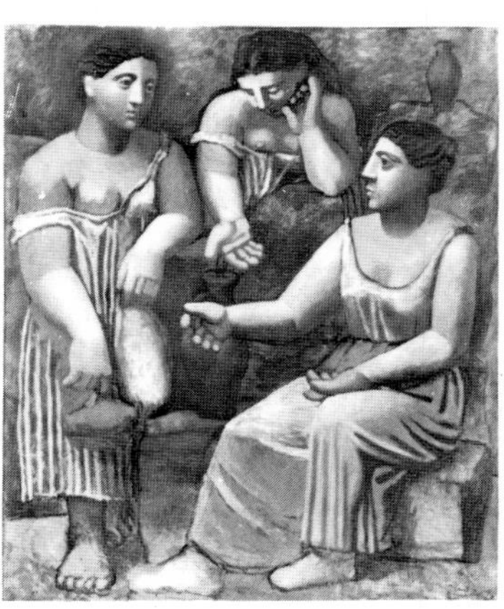

4

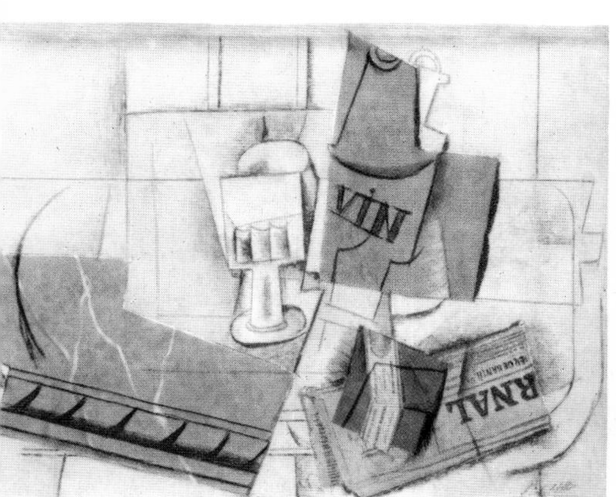

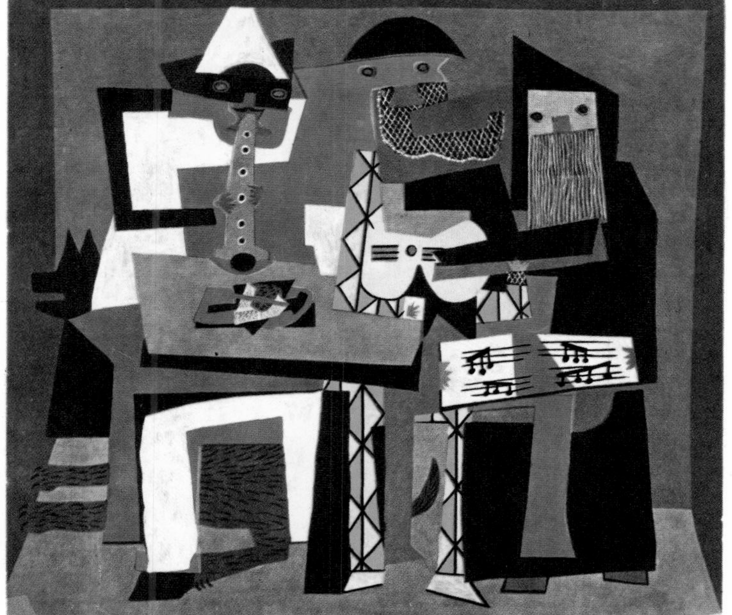

5

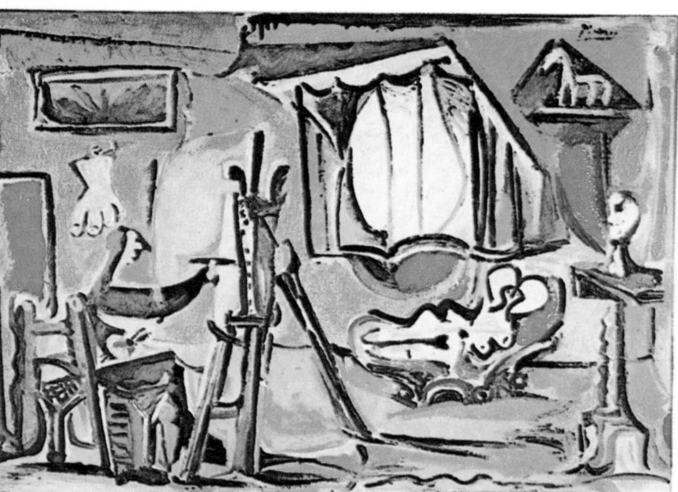

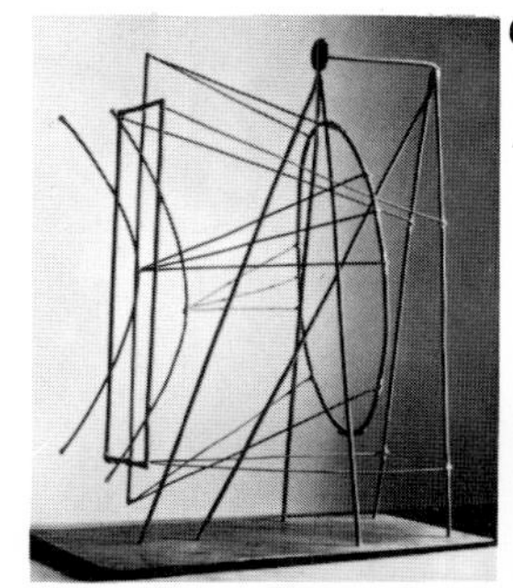

6

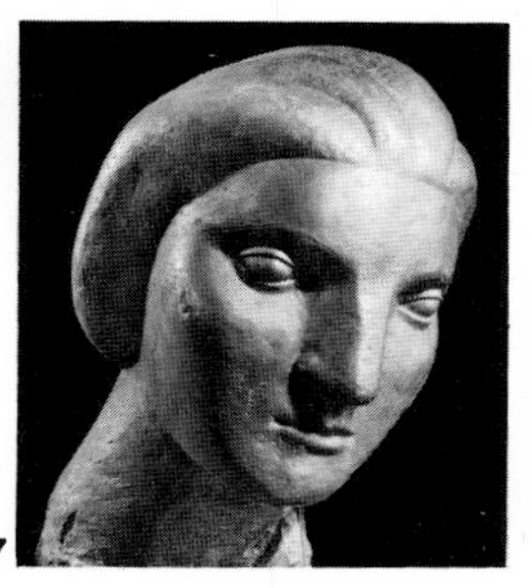

7

Pablo Picasso (1881–1973)

1. *Weeping Woman.* 1937. Private Collection
2. *Faun unveiling a Woman.* Aquatint. 1936
3. *Guernica.* 1937. Museum of Modern Art, New York
4. *A Goat.* Bronze. 1950
5. *A Faun.* 1946. Musée d'Antibes
6. *Woman and Dog.* 1953. Private Collection

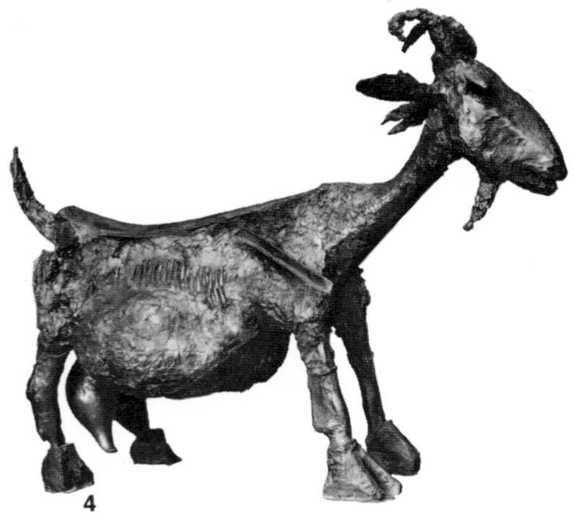

4

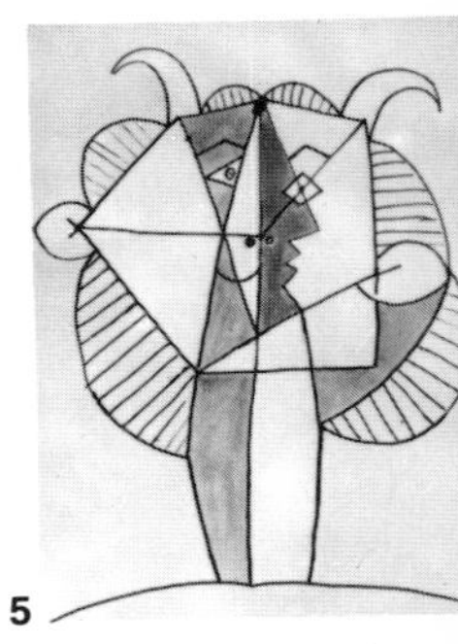

5

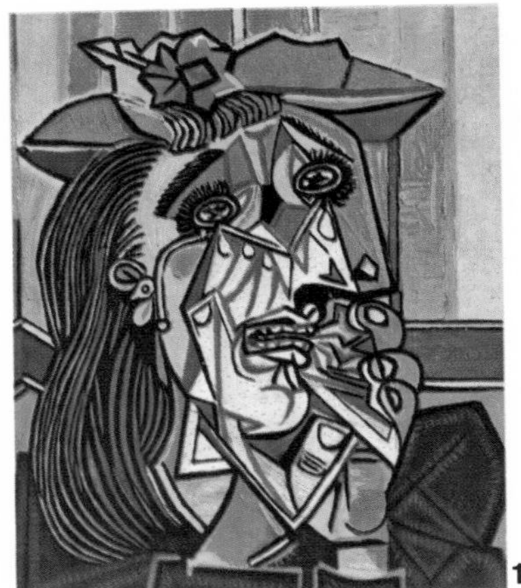

1

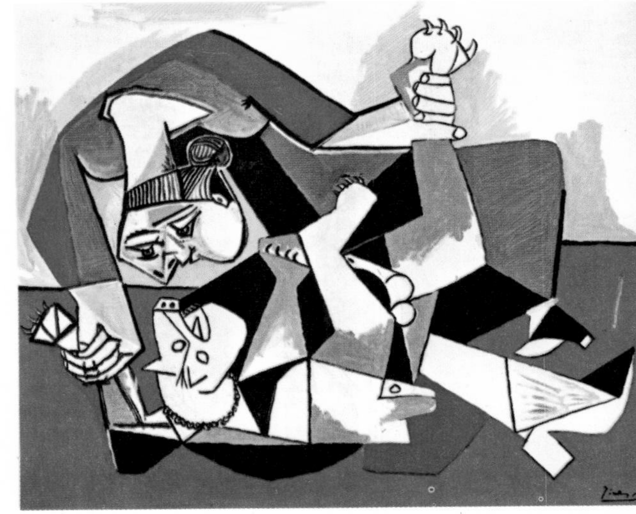

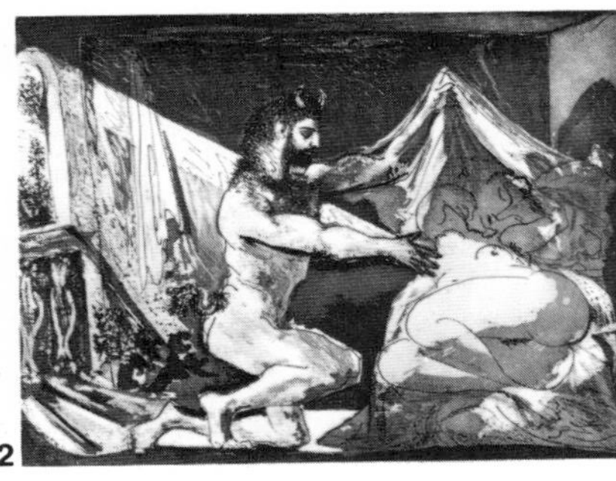

2

3

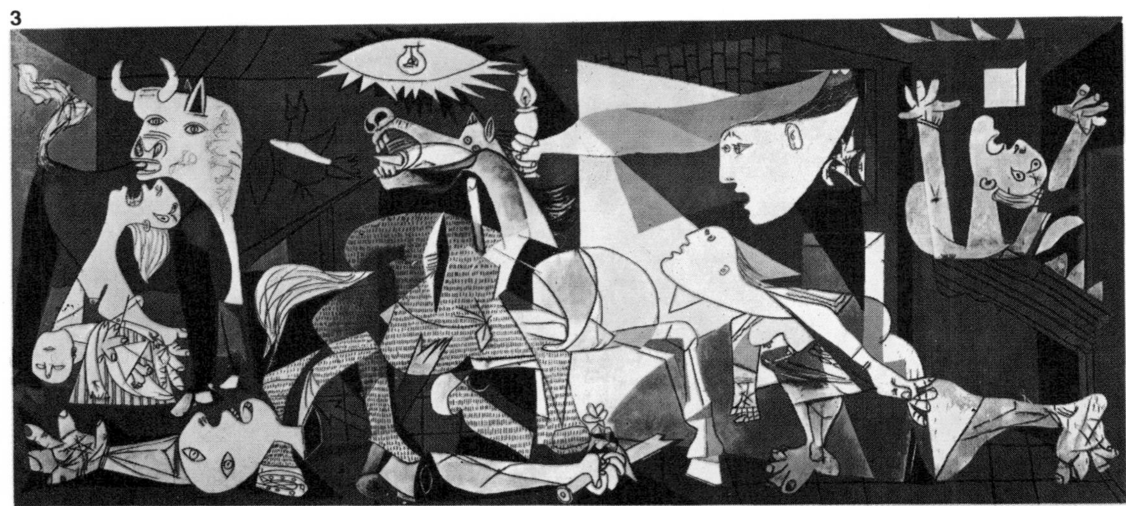

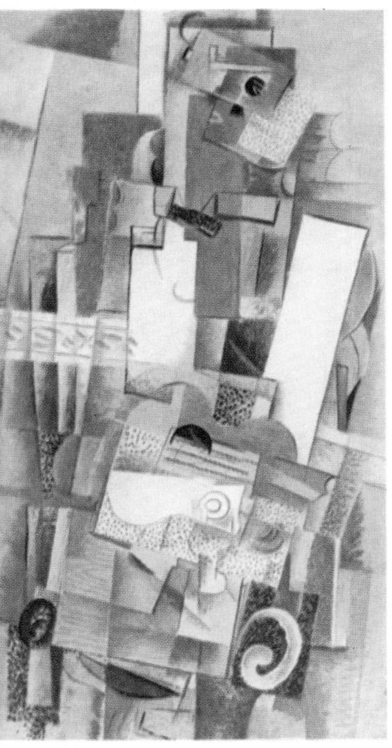

Georges Braque (1882–1963)
1. *The Guitarist.* 1919. Private Collection
2. *Gentian Bottle.* Pen and ink. 1914
3. *Echo.* 1956. Private Collection
4. *Painter and Model.* 1939. Private Collection
5. *Yellow Bouquet.* 1952
6. *Still Life.* 1929. Private Collection
7. *Night Flight.* 1959. Formerly collection of the artist

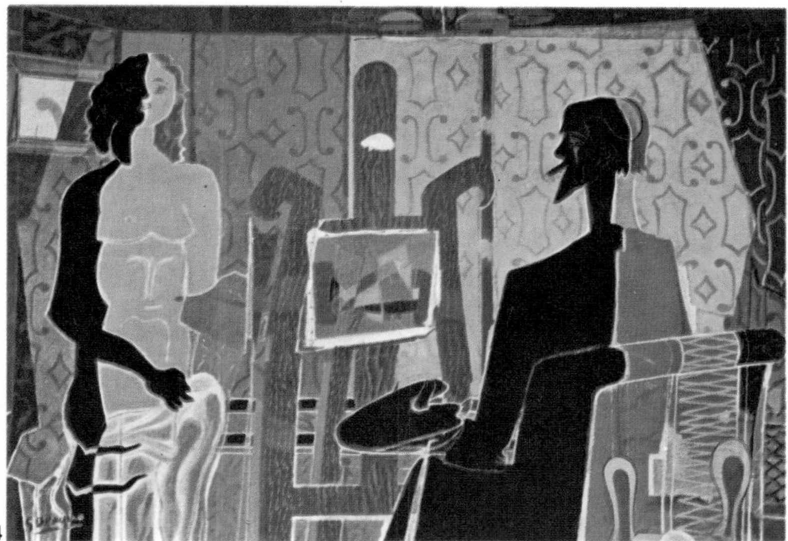

4

2

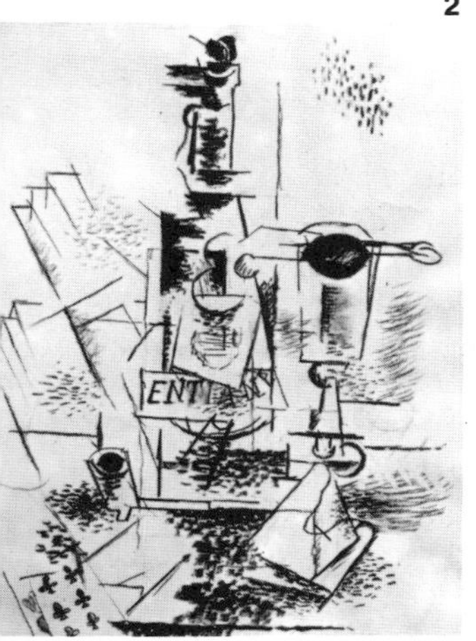

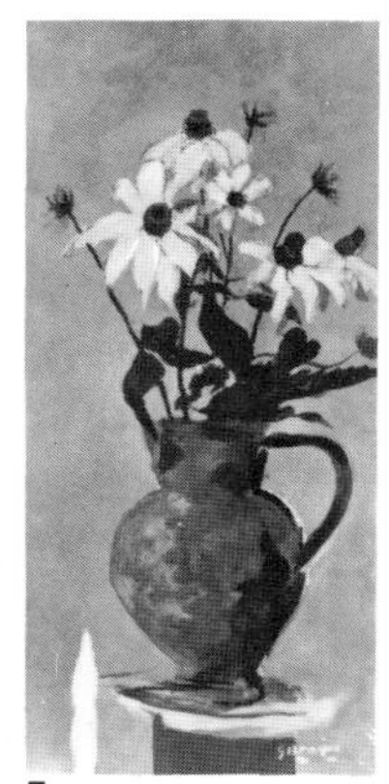

5

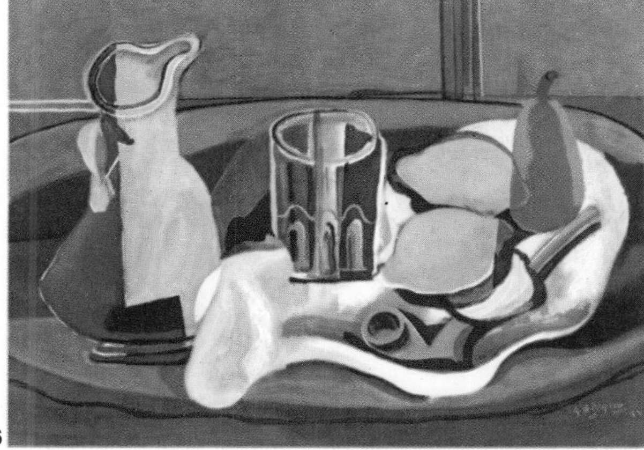

6

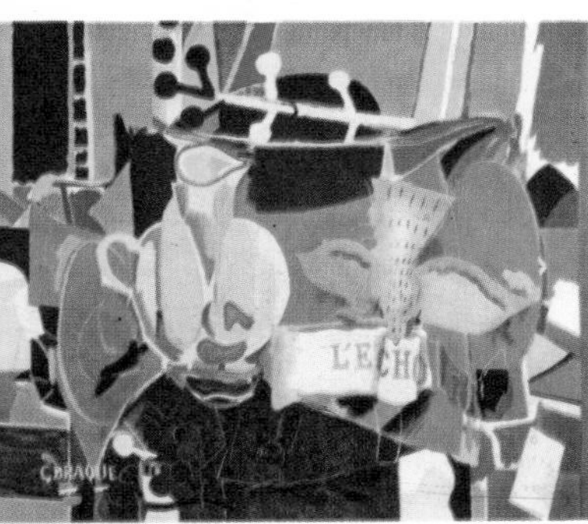

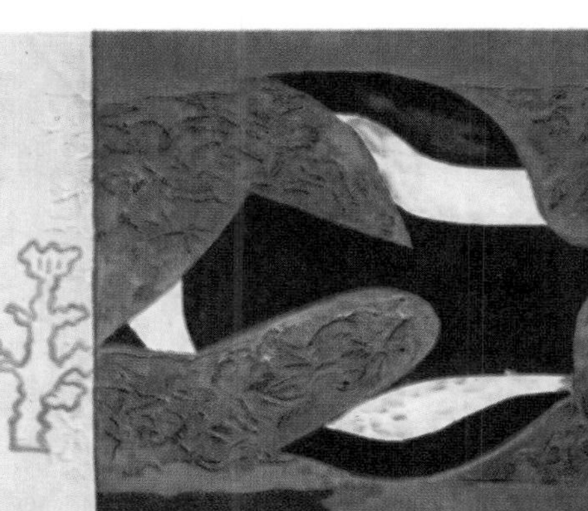

7

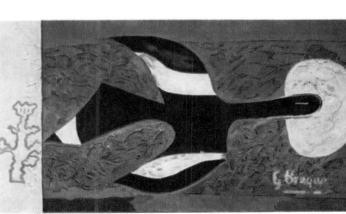

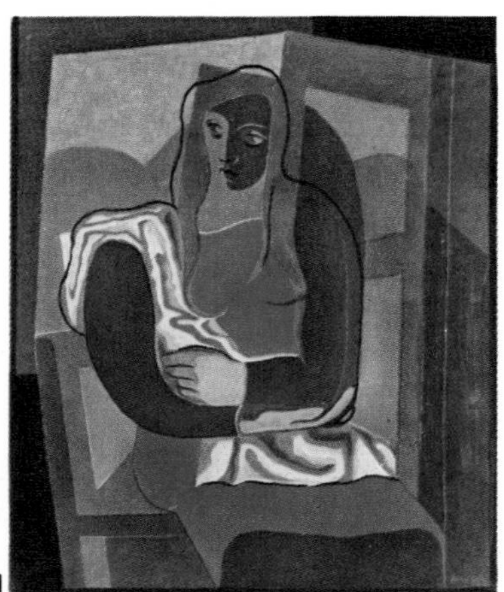
1

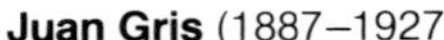

Juan Gris (1887–1927)
1. *Woman at the Window*. 1926. Galerie Louise Leiris, Paris
2. *Still Life with Bottles.* 1912. Rijksmuseum Kröller-Müller, Otterlo
3. *Breakfast.* Collage, crayon and oil. 1914. Museum of Modern Art, New York
4. *Poèmes en prose.* Private Collection
5. *Self-portrait.* Pencil. 1920

Emilio Pettoruti (1892–1971)
6. *Harlequin with Accordion.* 1928
7. *Light-Élan.* 1916. Private Collection

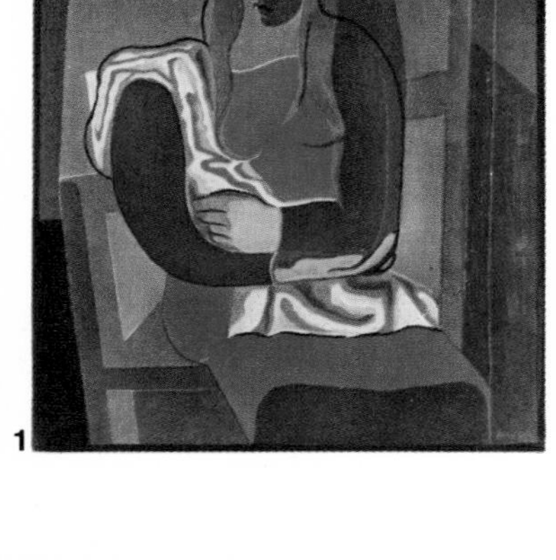

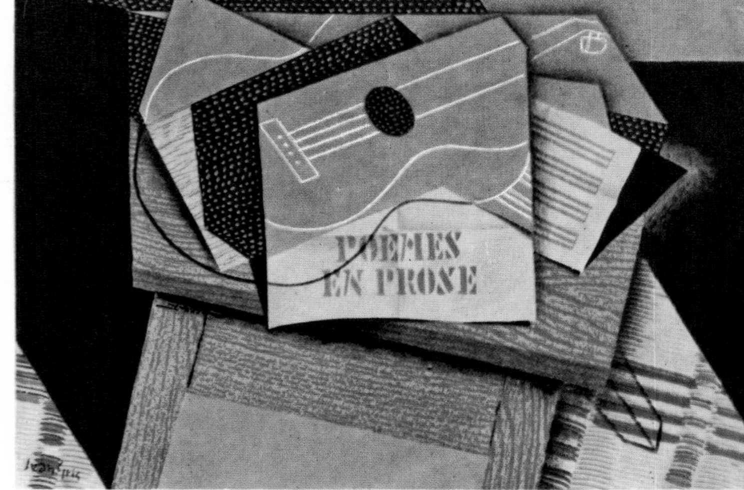

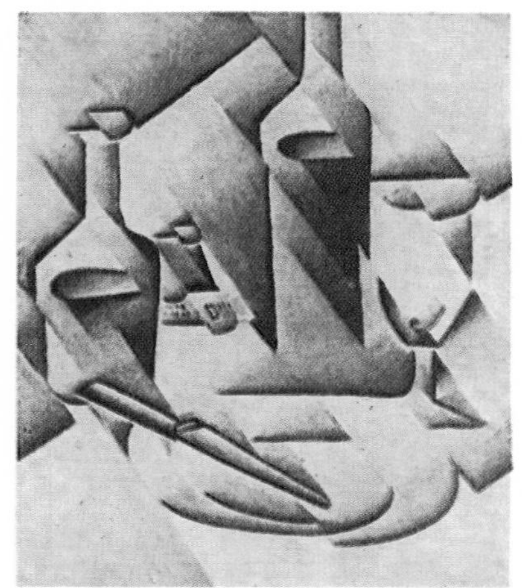
2

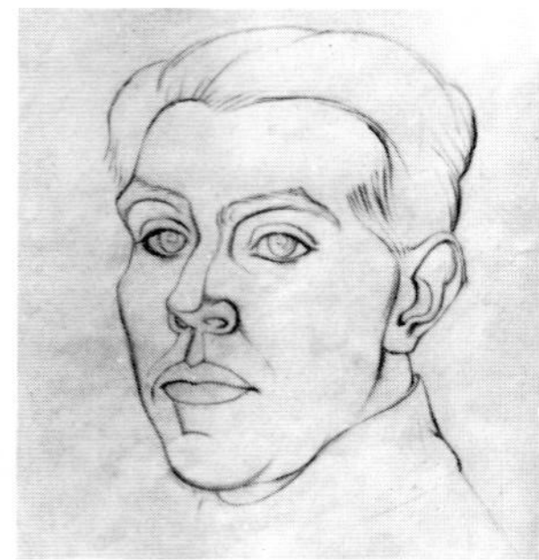

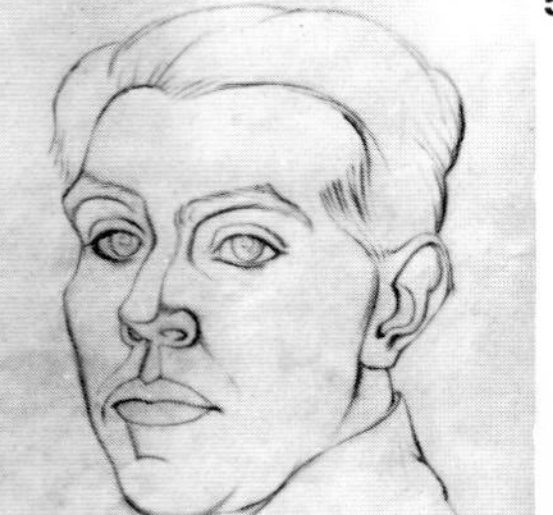
5

3

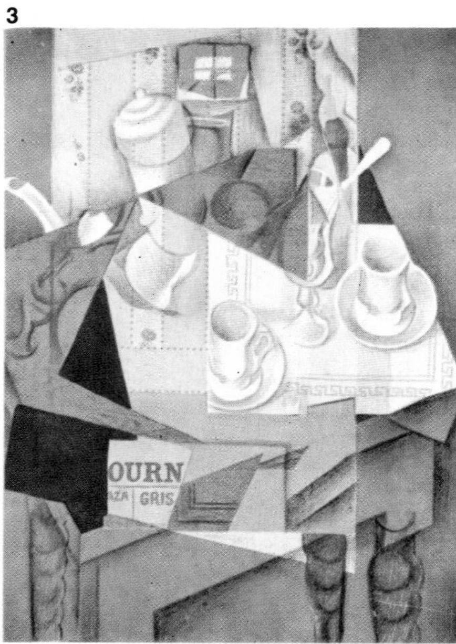

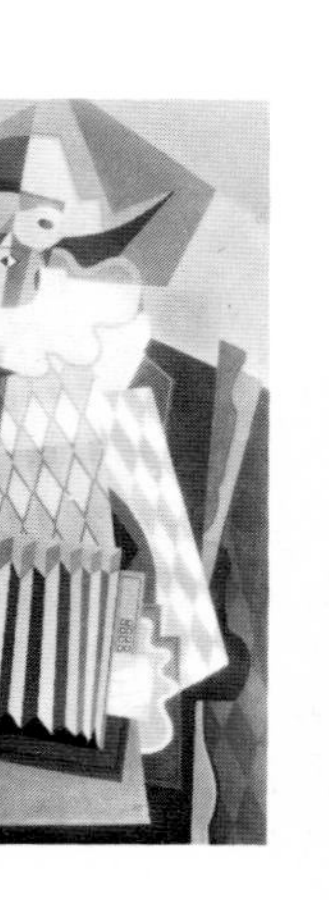

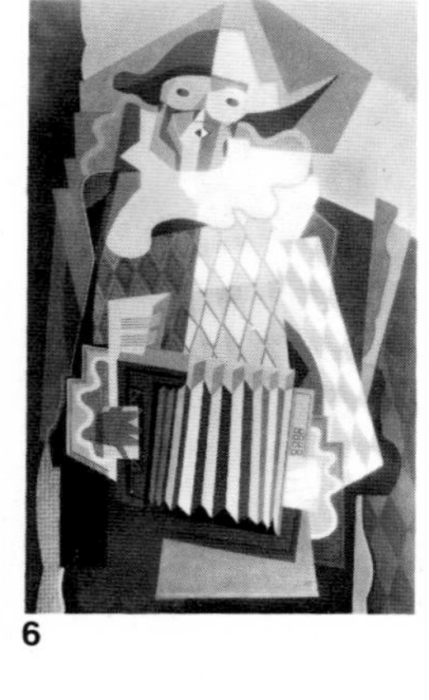
6

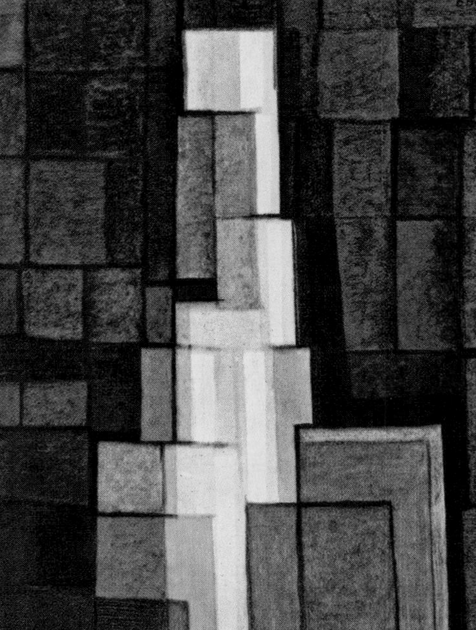
7

Fernand Léger (1881–1955)
1. *Disks and Town.* 1919–20. Galerie Louise Leiris, Paris
2. *La Baigneuse.* 1931. Galerie Louis Carré, Paris
3. *The Fourteenth of July 1914.*
4. *Two Women holding Flowers.* 1954. Tate Gallery, London

Lyonel Feininger (1871–1956)
5. *Gelmeroda.* Woodcut. 1923
6. *Schooner in the Baltic.* 1924. Private Collection

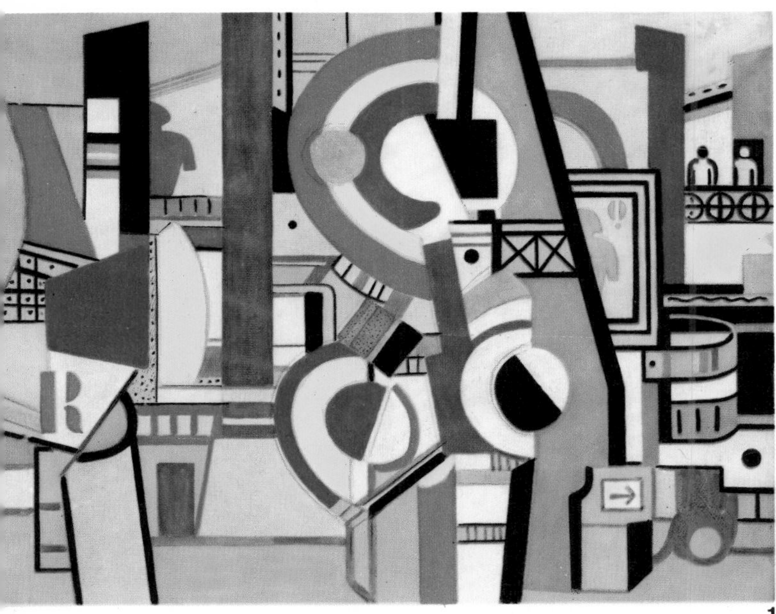
1

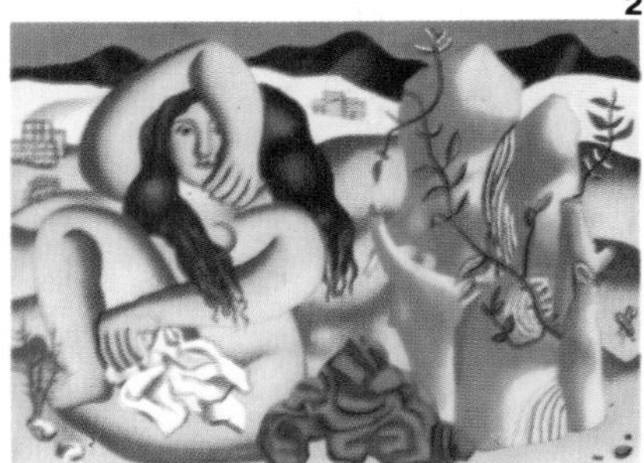
2

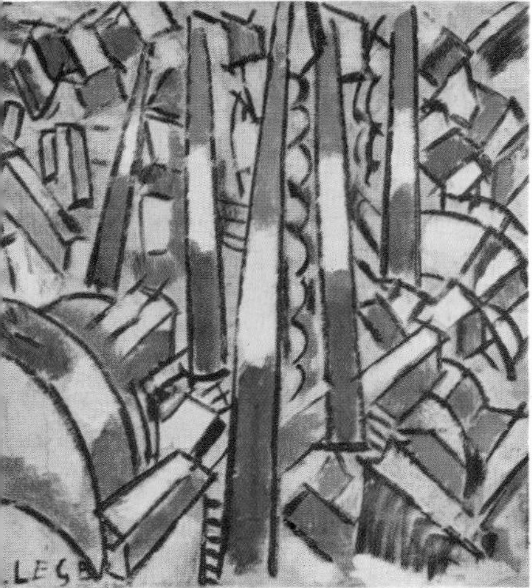

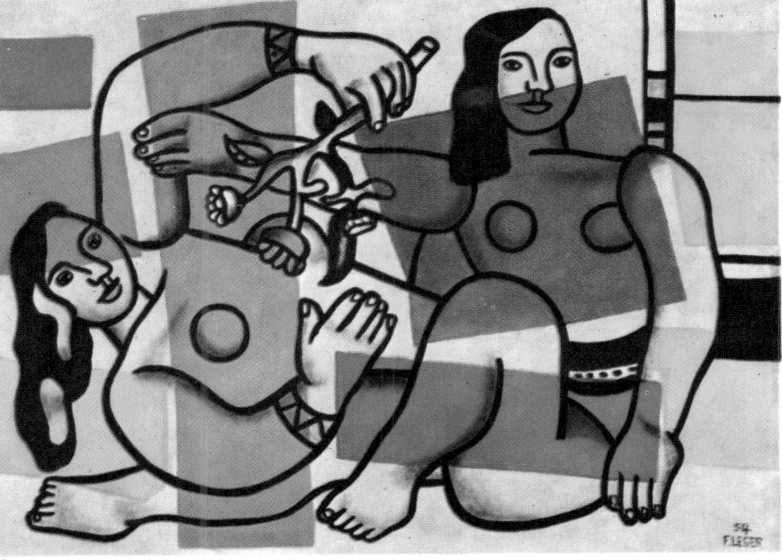
4

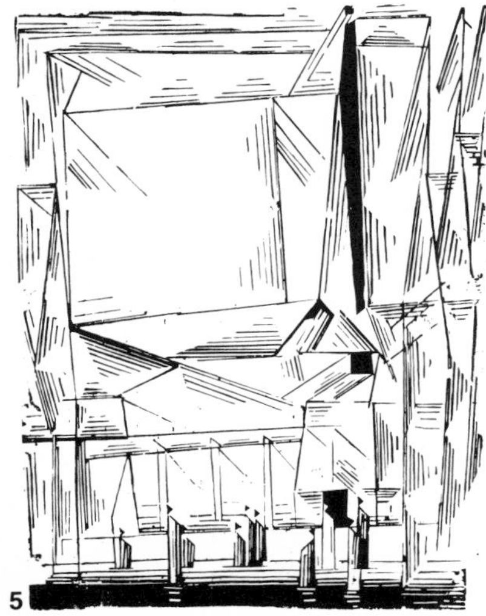
5

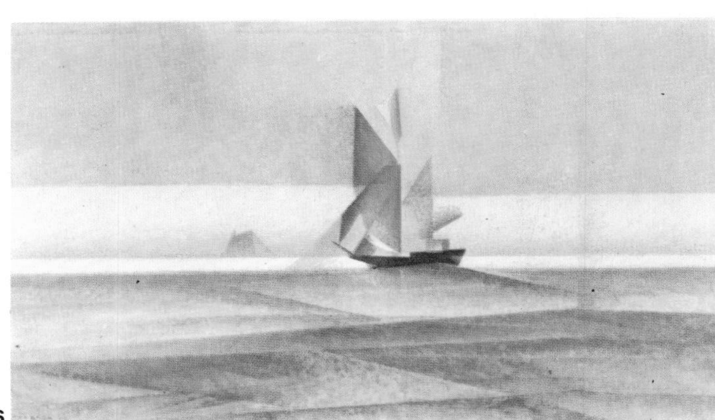
6

1. **Robert Delaunay** (1885–1941): *Window.* 1912. Musée National d'Art Moderne, Paris
2. **Roger de La Fresnaye** (1885–1925): *Still Life.* 1913. Private Collection
3. **Roger de La Fresnaye** (1885–1925): *Portrait of J.L.Gampert.* 1920. Musée National d'Art Moderne, Paris
4. **Roger de La Fresnaye** (1885–1925): *Conquest of the Air.* 1913. Museum of Modern Art, New York
5. **Robert Delaunay** (1885–1941): *Orange Relief.* 1936. Private Collection
6. **Sonia Terk Delaunay** (b.1885): *Composition.* 1952. Private Collection
7. **Chaïm Soutine** (1894–1943): *Landscape.* 1926. Private Collection
8. **Chaïm Soutine** (1894–1943): *Portrait of a Choirboy.* 1928. Private collection

1

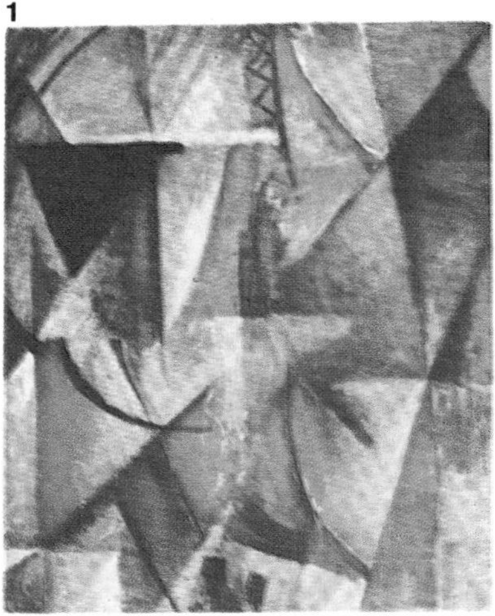

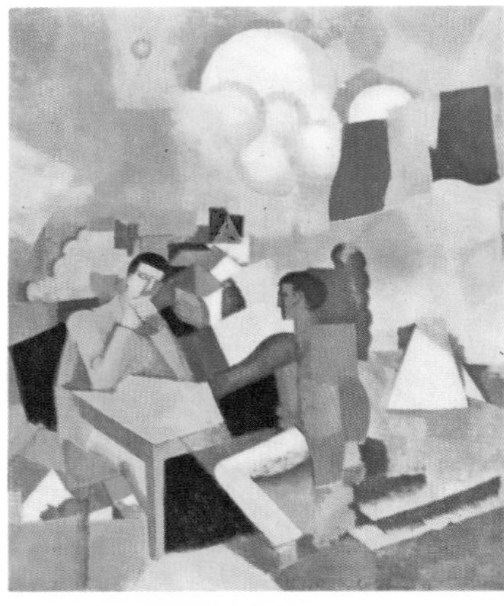

4

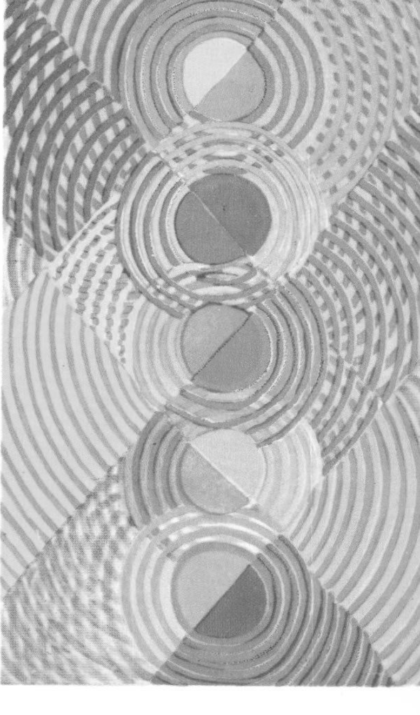

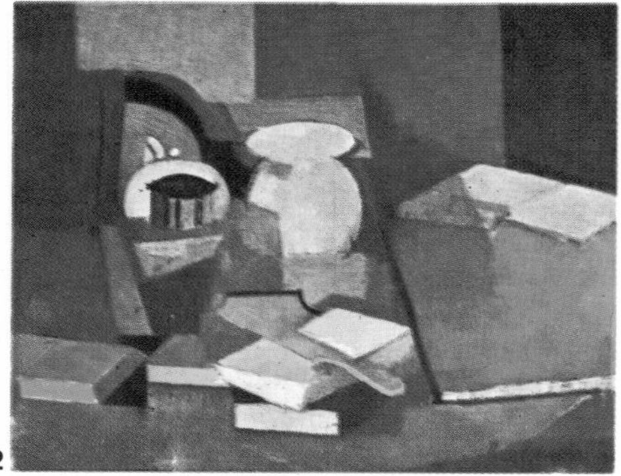

2

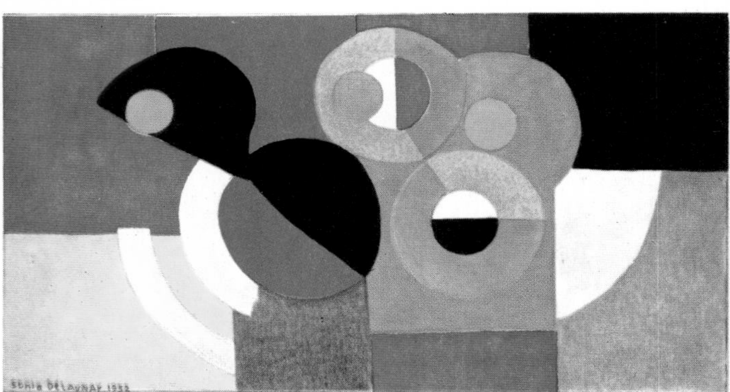

6

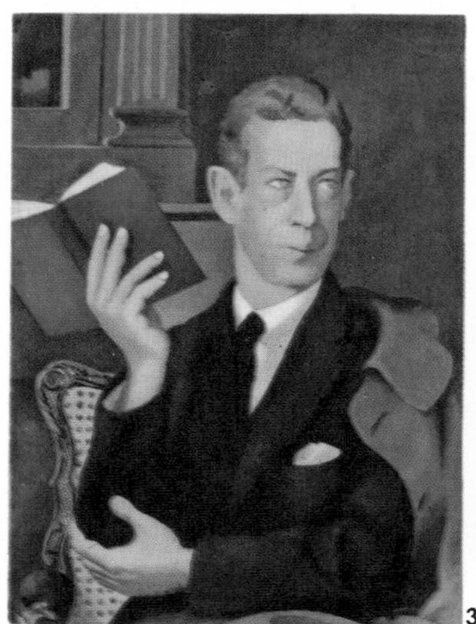

3

7

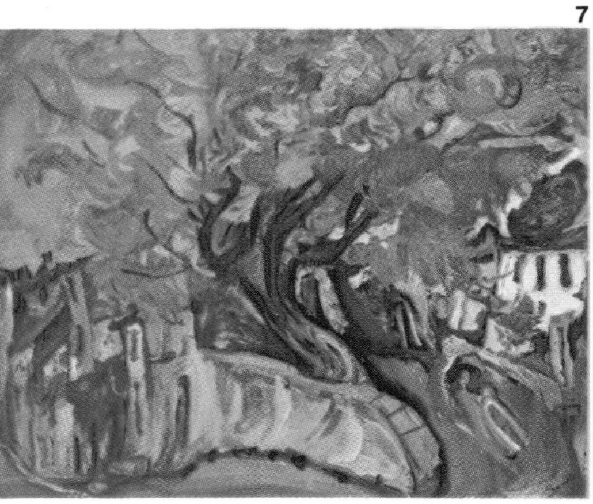

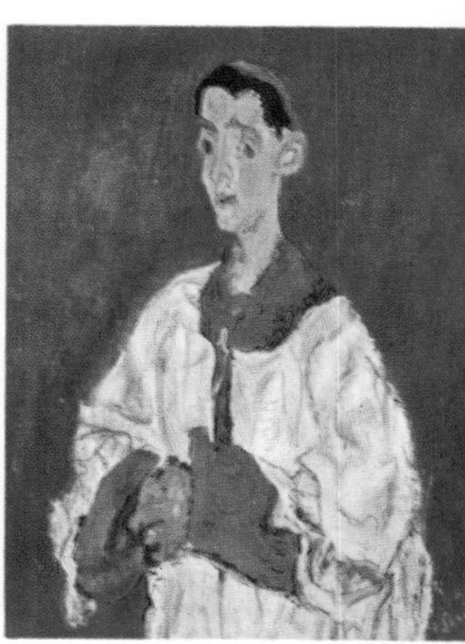

1. **Marc Chagall** (b.1887): *Madonna of the Sleigh*. 1947. Private Collection
2. **Marc Chagall** (b.1887): *Over the Town*. 1917. Tretyakov Gallery, Moscow
3. **Georges Rouault** (1871–1958): *The Little Family*. 1932. Private Collection
4. **Marc Chagall** (b.1887): *Portrait of Bella in Green*. 1934–5. Stedelijk Museum, Amsterdam
5. **Georges Rouault** (1871–1958): *A Prostitute at her Mirror*. 1906. Musée National d'Art Moderne, Paris

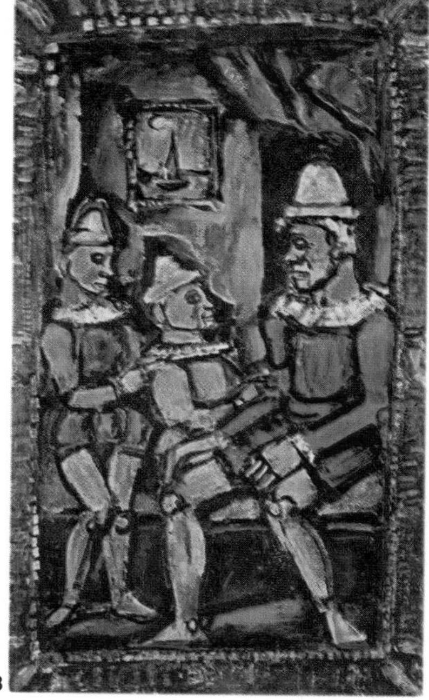

3

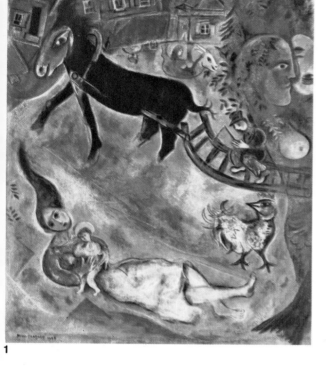

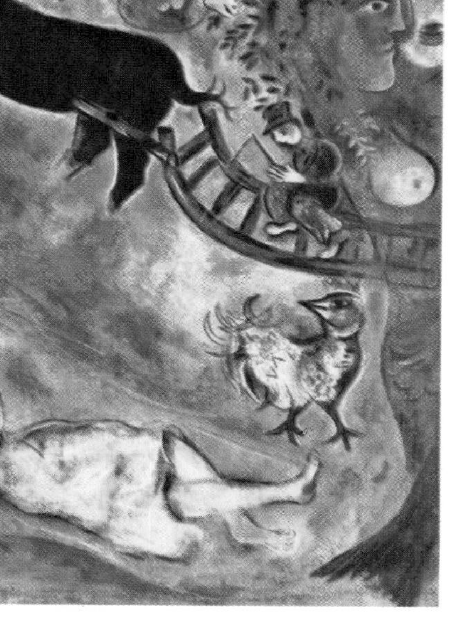

1

4

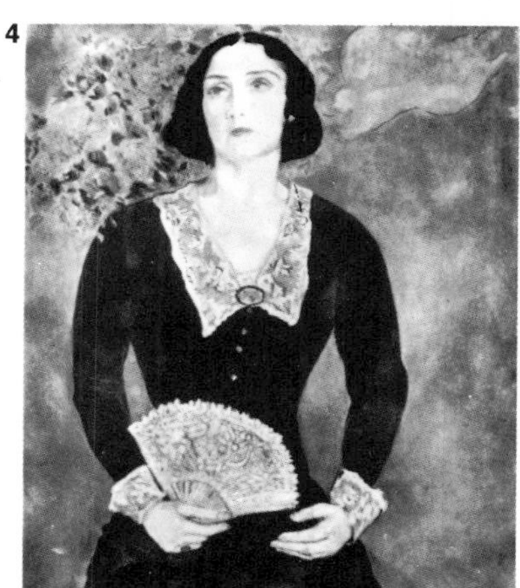

2

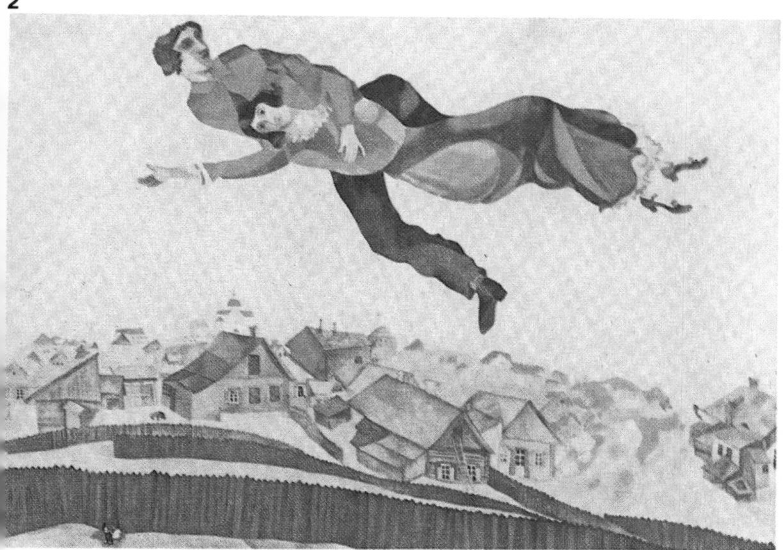

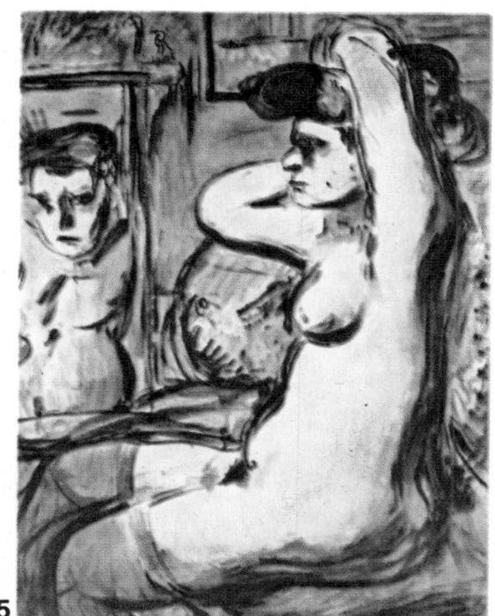

5

1. **Jacques Villon** (1875–1963): *Self-portrait.* 1949. Private Collection, Paris
2. **Maurice Utrillo** (1883–1955): *The Church of Mourning.* 1912. Private Collection
3. **Jacques Villon** (1875–1963): *Racehorse.* 1922. Galerie Louis Carré, Paris
4. **Hans Hartung** (b.1904): Engraving. 1953
5. **Jean (Hans) Arp** (1887–1966): *Painted Wood.* 1917. Formerly collection of the artist
6. **Alfred Manessier** (b.1911): Wash drawing

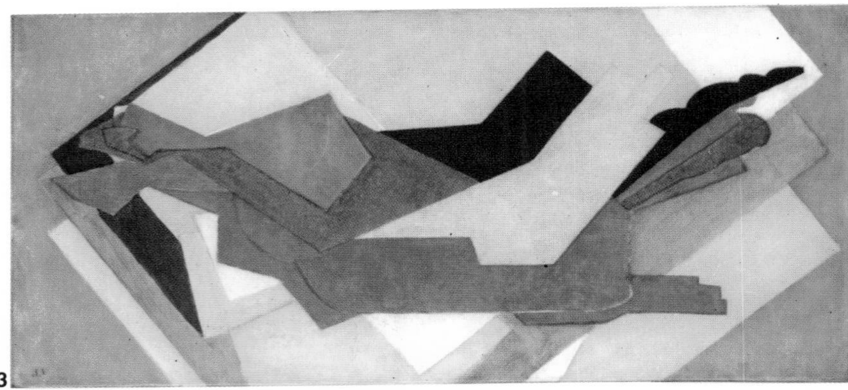

3

1

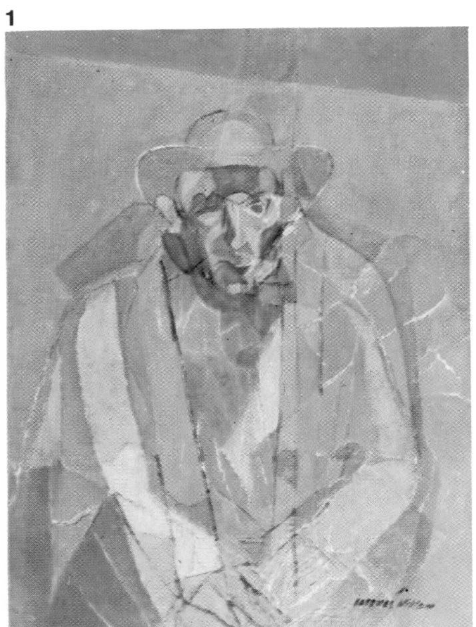

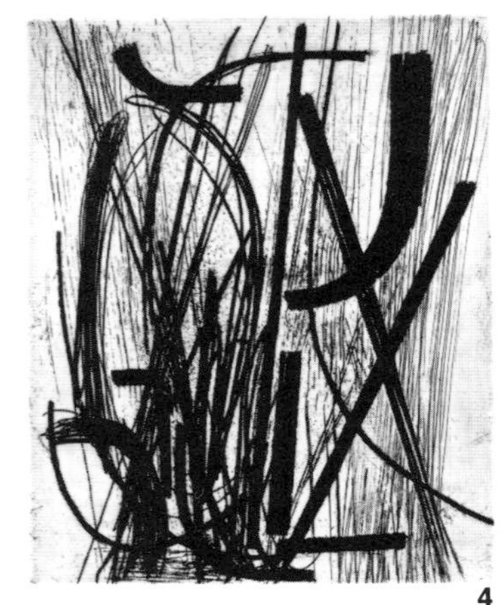

4

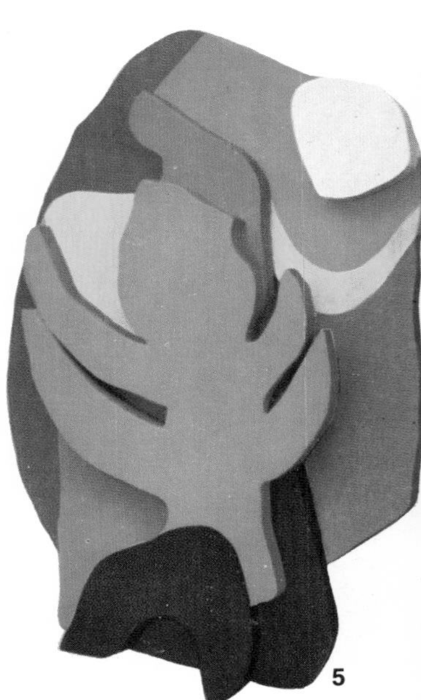

5

2

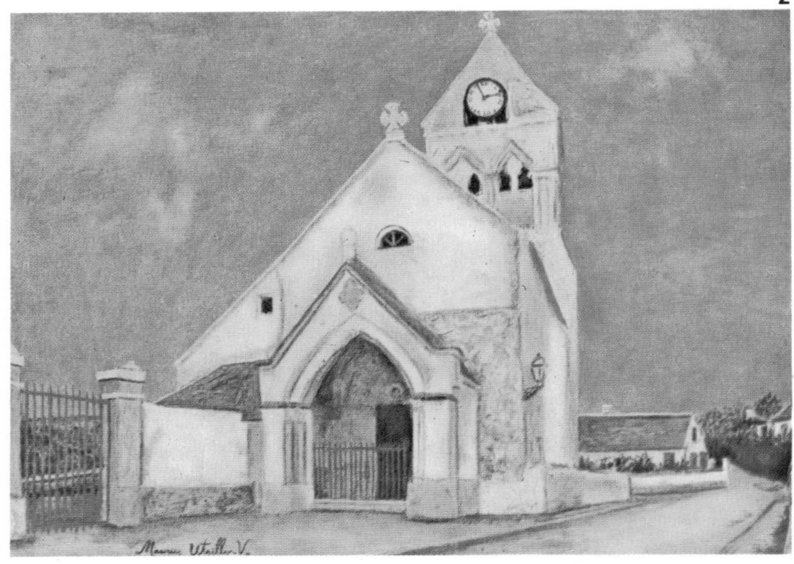

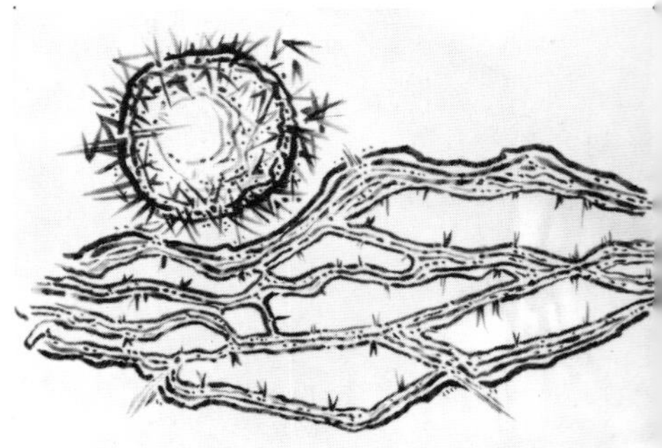

6

1. **José Clemente Orozco** (1883–1949): *Zapatistas.* 1931. Museum of Modern Art, New York
2. **Amedeo Modigliani** (1884–1920): *Seated Nude.* About 1917. Courtauld Institute of Art, London
3. **Amedeo Modigliani** (1884–1920): *Italian Woman.* Metropolitan Museum of Art (Chester Dale Collection), New York
4. **Bernard Buffet** (b.1928): *Canal St-Martin, Paris.* 1956. Private Collection
5. **Bernard Buffet** (b.1928): *An Interior.* 1950. Musée National d'Art Moderne, Paris
6. **Amedeo Modigliani** (1884–1920): *Recumbent Nude.* 1917–18. Private Collection
7. **Amedeo Modigliani** (1884–1920): *Portrait of Chaïm Soutine.* 1917. Staatsgalerie, Stuttgart

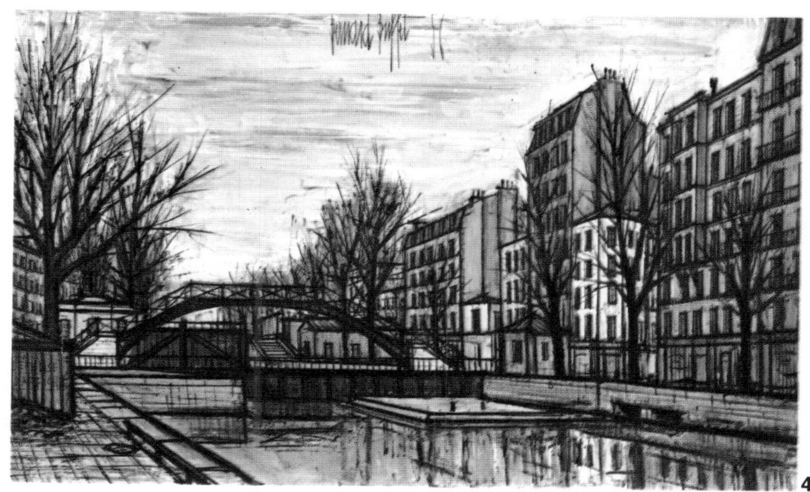

4

1

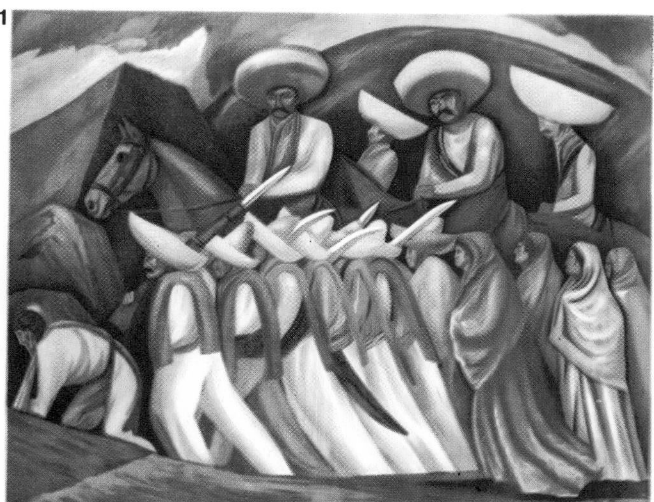

5

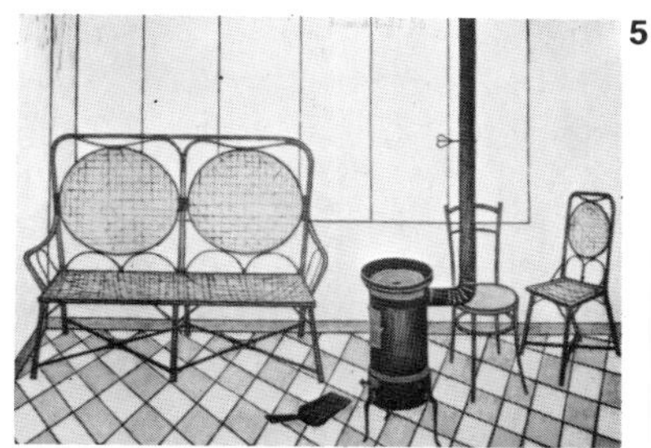

6

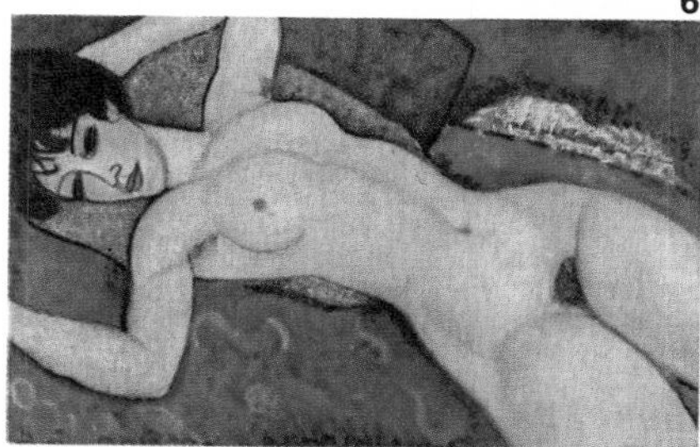

2

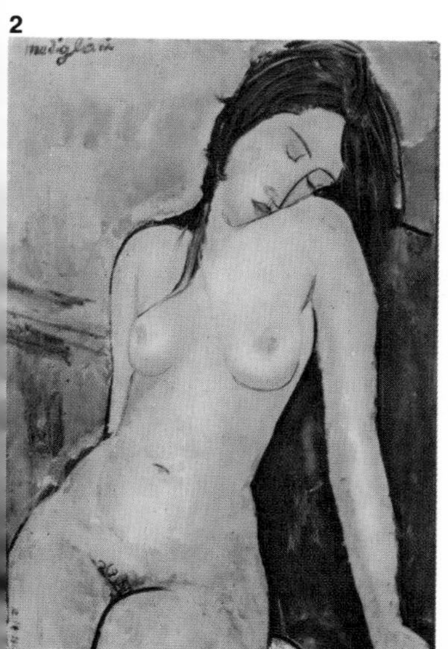

3

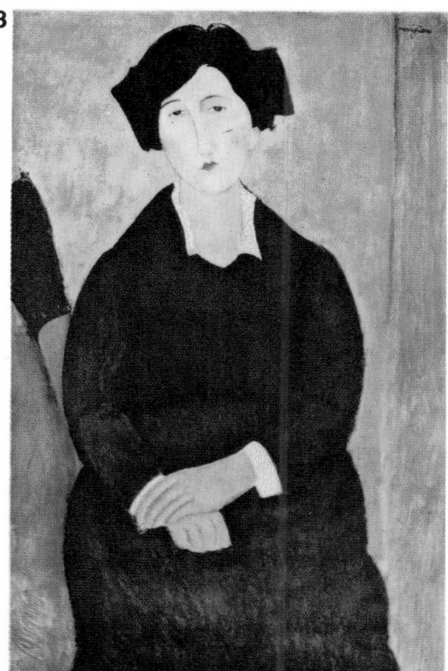

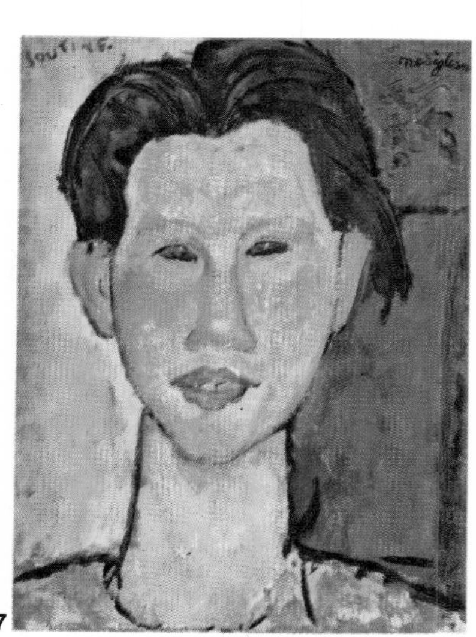

7

1. **Antoine Pevsner** (1886–1962): *Developable Column.* Oxidized bronze
2. **Antoine Pevsner** (1886–1962): *Peace Column.* Oxidized bronze
3. **Naum Gabo** (1890–1978): *Female Head.* Celluloid and metal. 1916. Museum of Modern Art, New York
4. **Antoine Pevsner** (1886–1962): *Spectral Vision.* Oxidized bronze. 1959
5. **Naum Gabo** (1890–1978): *Linear Construction in Space, No. 2.* Plastic and nylon
6. **Vladimir Tatlin** (1885–1953?): *Project for the Monument for the Third International, Moscow.* 1920
7. **Vladimir Tatlin** (1885–1953?): *Counter-relief.* Iron. 1914–15
8. **Antoine Pevsner** (1886–1962): *Portrait of the artist Marcel Duchamp.* Celluloid, zinc and leather. 1926. Yale University Art Gallery, New Haven

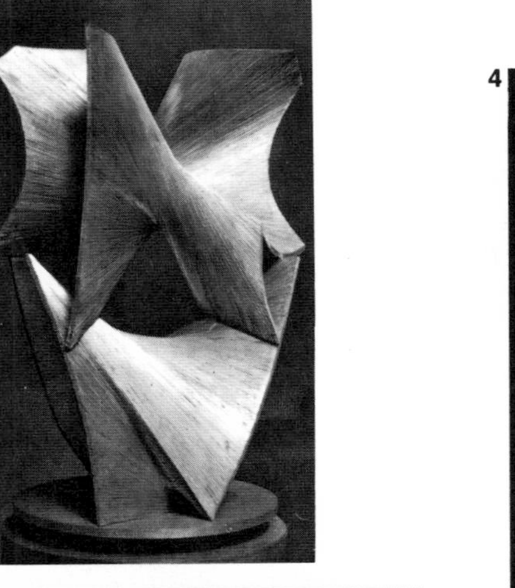
1

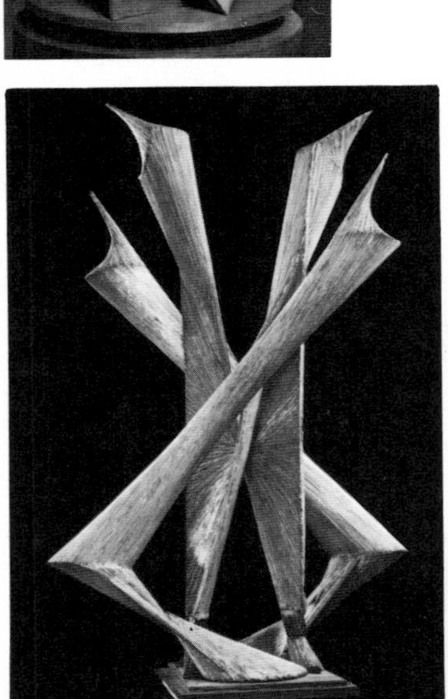
2

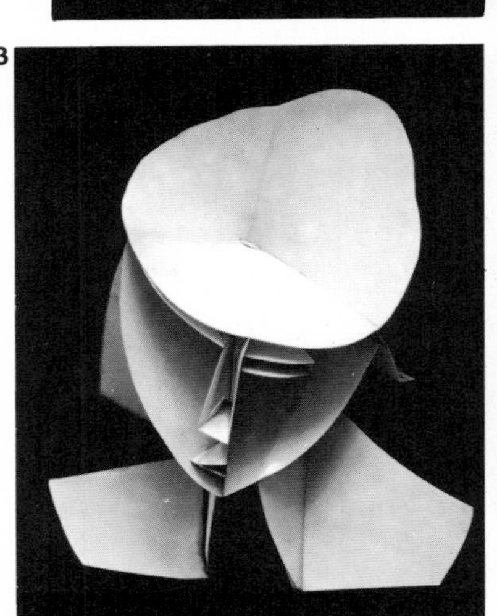
3

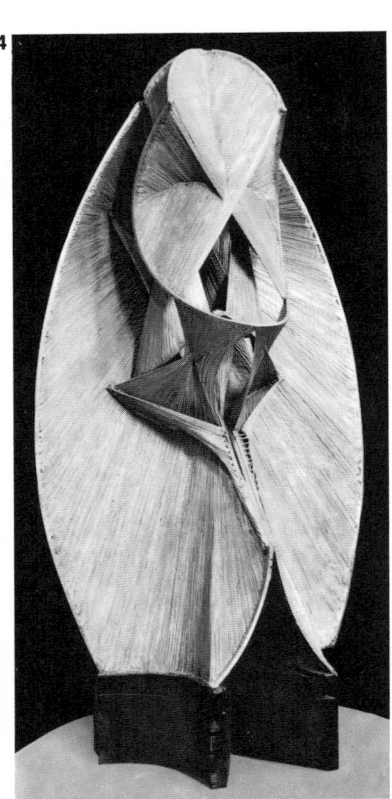
4

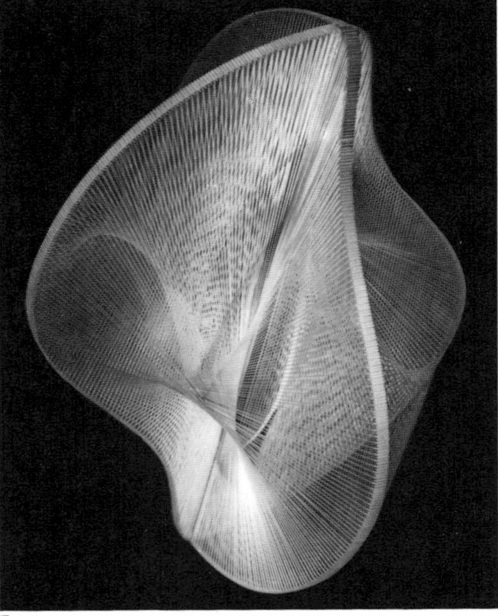
5

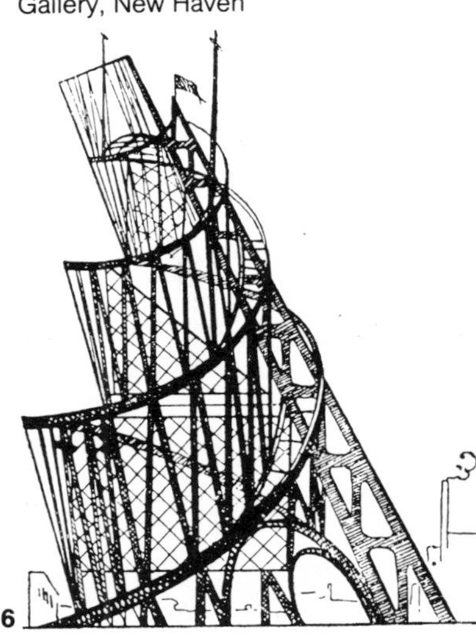
6

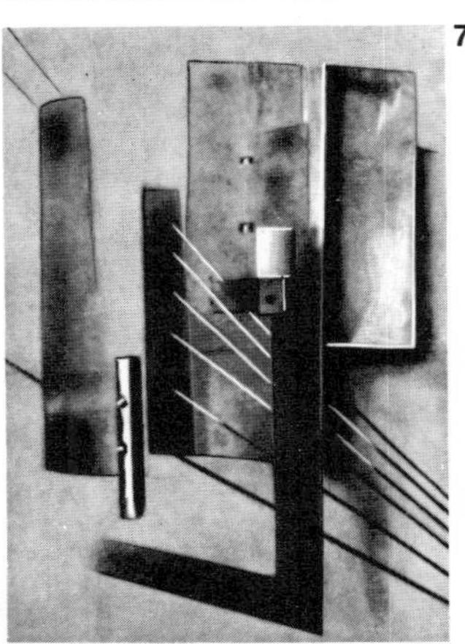
7

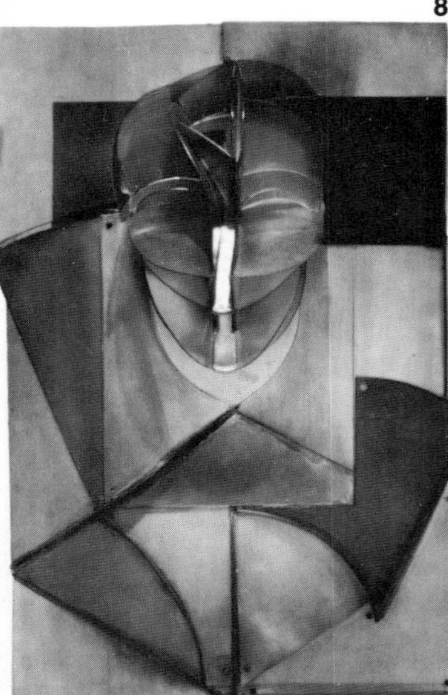
8

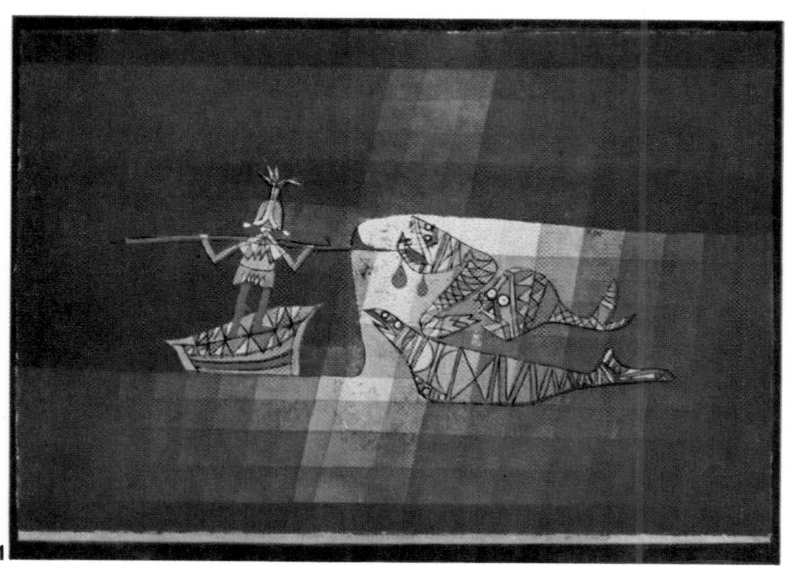

1

1. **Paul Klee** (1879–1940): *Battle Scene from the comic opera 'The Navigator'.* Watercolour and oil on paper. 1923. Private Collection
2. **László Moholy-Nagy** (1895–1946): *Double Loop.* Plexiglass. 1946. Bayerische Staatsgemäldesammlungen, Munich
3. **Walter Gropius** (1883–1969) and the Architects' Collaborative: Apartment block, Berlin. 1957. Built to coincide with the Interbau Exhibition
4. **Paul Klee** (1879–1940): *Death and Fire.* 1940. Paul-Klee-Stiftung, Berne
5. **Walter Gropius** (1883–1969): The Bauhaus at Dessau. 1926

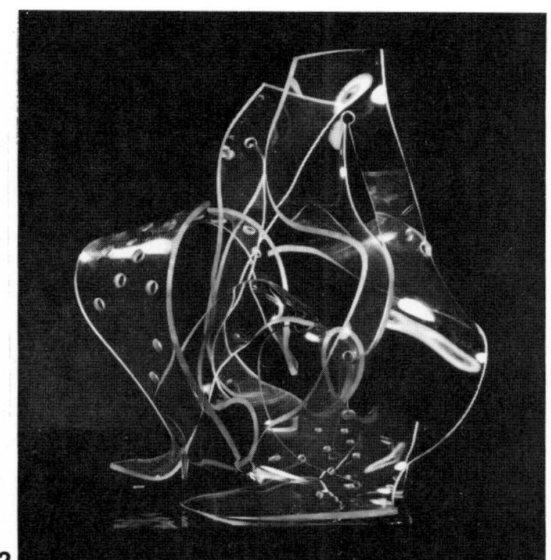

2

4

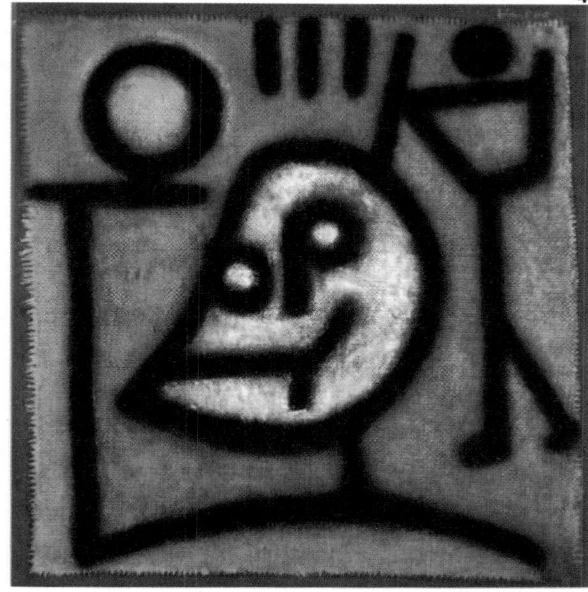

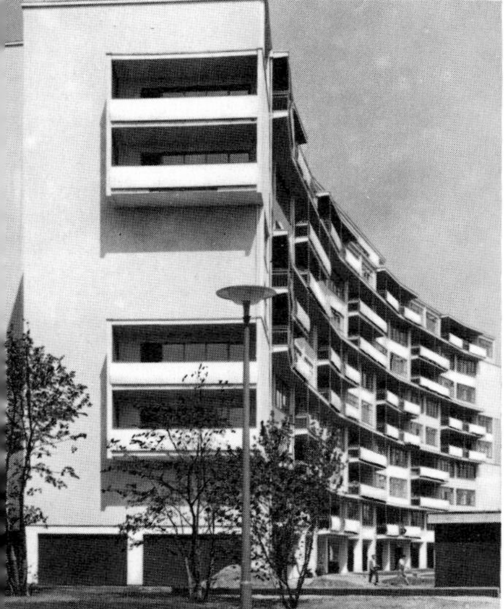

5

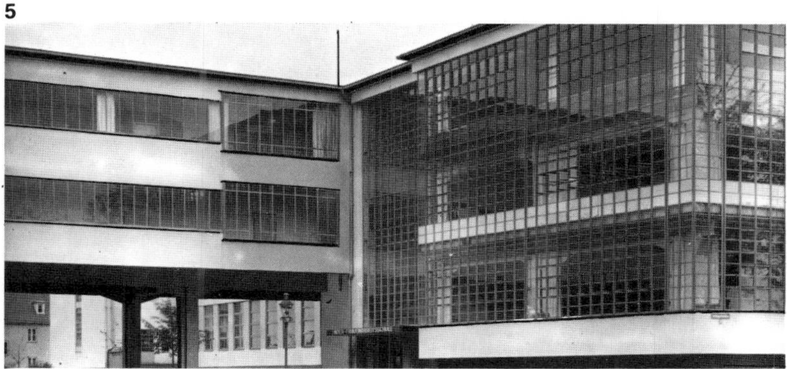

Le Corbusier (1887–1965)

1. Villa Savoye, Poissy. 1929–31
2. The Carpenter Center for the Visual Arts, Harvard University. 1961–4
3. The Chapel of Notre-Dame-du-Haut, Ronchamp. 1950–5
4. Apartment block, Marseilles. 1947–52
5. The Salvation Army Hostel, Paris (model). 1929–33
6. Unité d'Habitation, Marseilles. 1947–52 View of roof terrace and ventilating shaft with kindergarten in the background

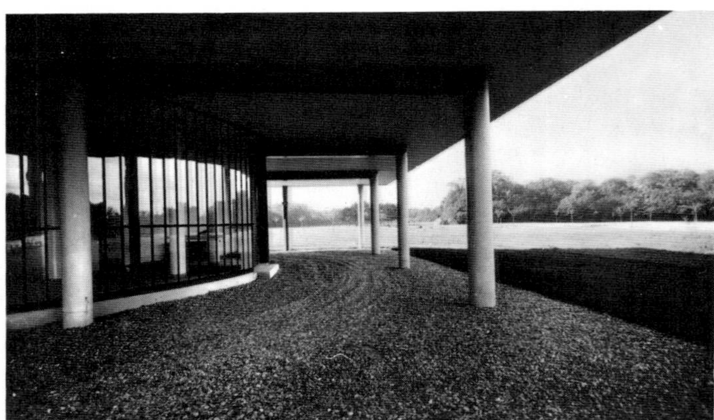

1

4

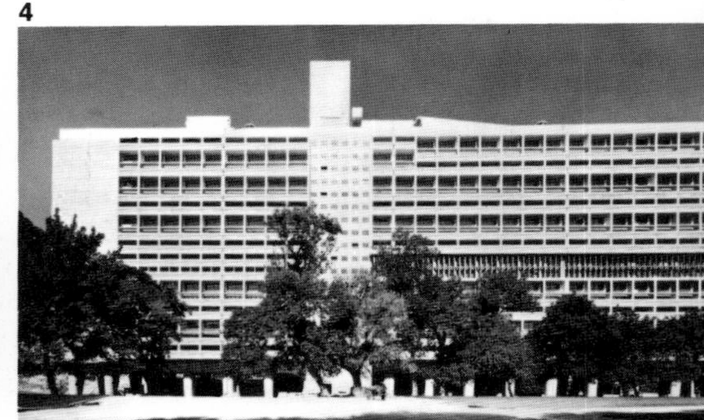

2

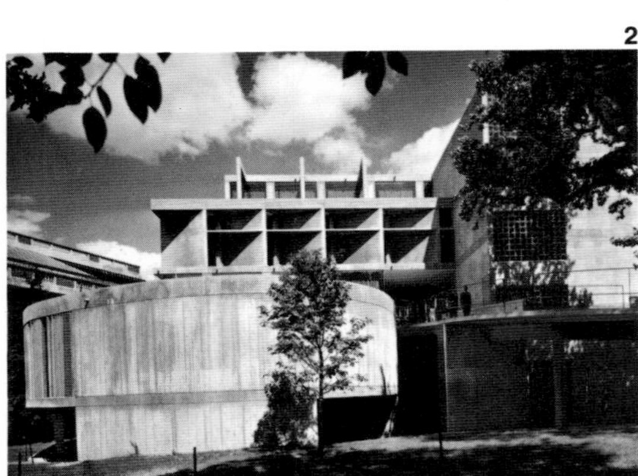

5

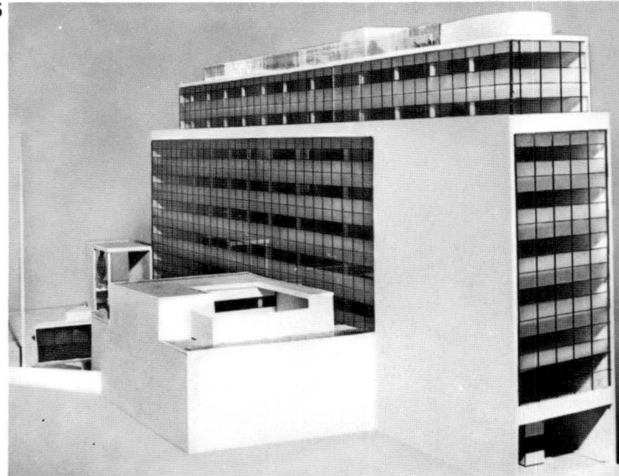

3

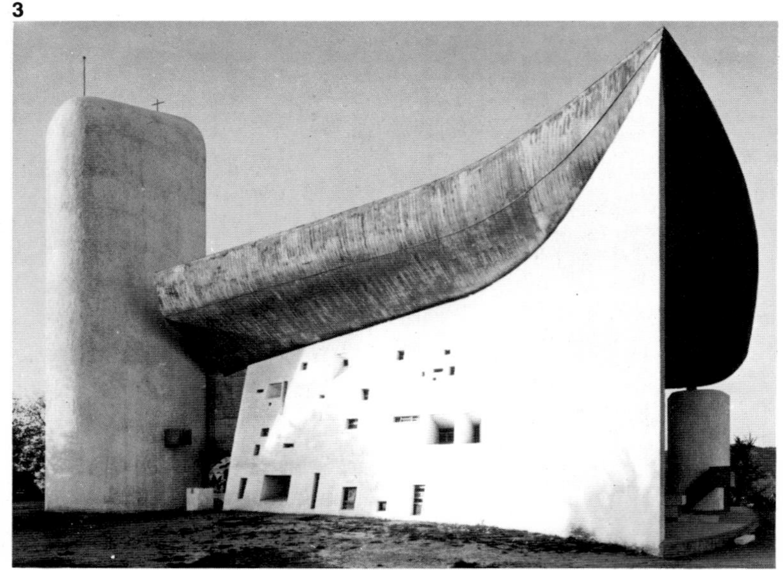

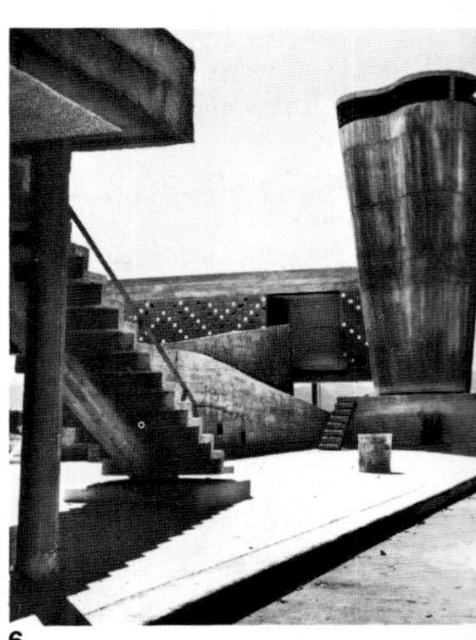

6

Ludwig Mies van der Rohe (1886–1969)

1. The Alumni Memorial Hall, Illinois Institute of Technology, Chicago. Detail of construction. 1946
2. Monument to the memory of Karl Liebknecht and Rosa Luxemburg, Berlin. 1926
3. Crown Hall, Illinois Institute of Technology, Chicago. 1952–6
4. Farnsworth House, Plano, Illinois. 1946–50
5. The Seagram Building, New York. 1956–9

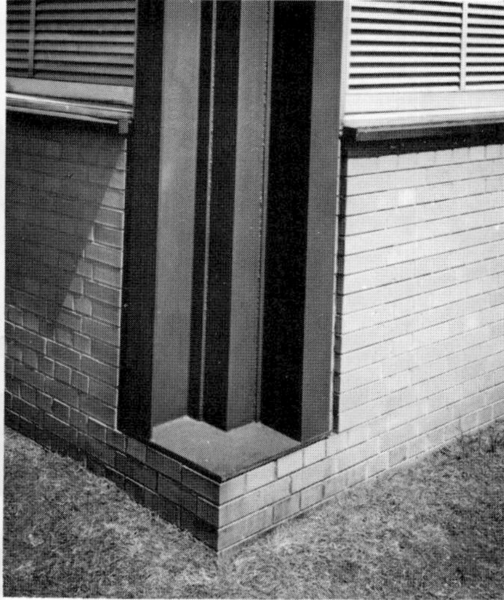

1

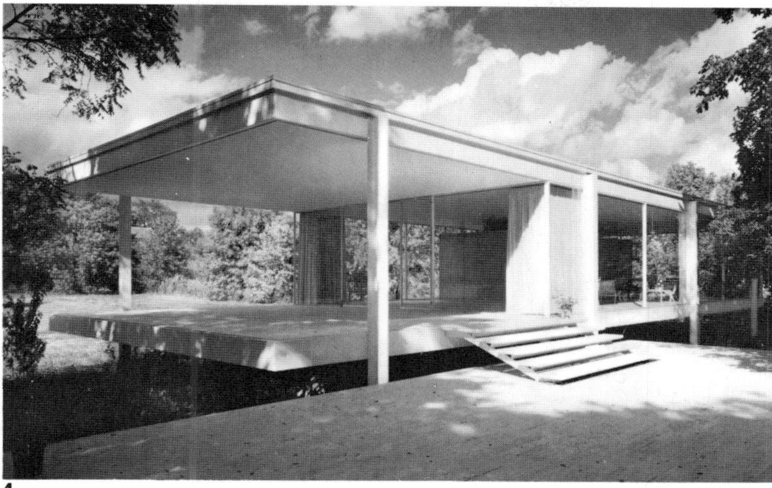

4

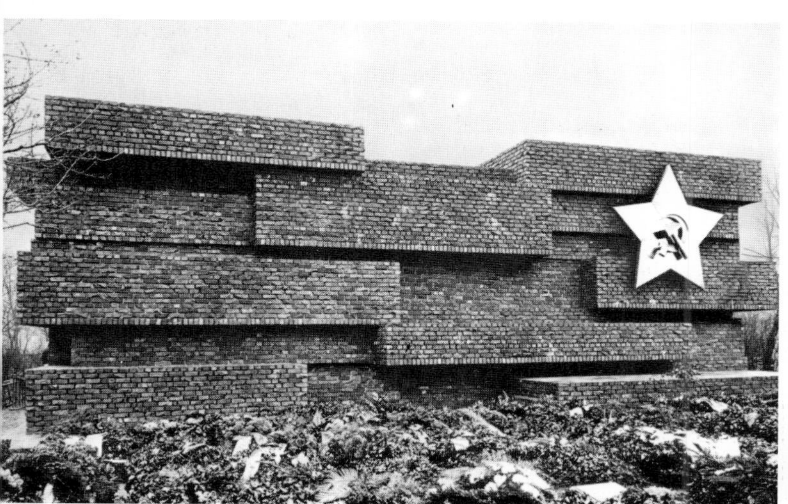

2

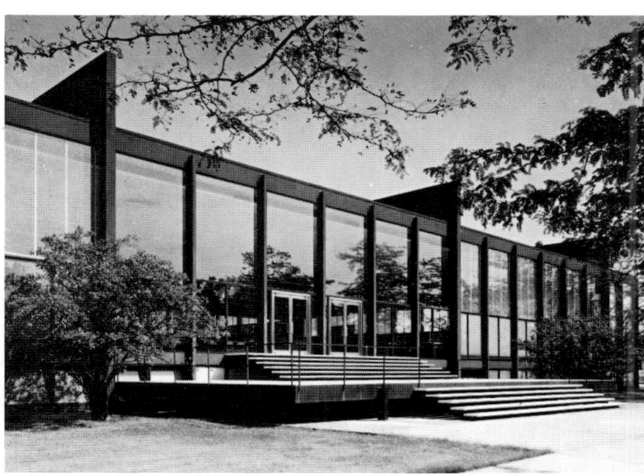

3

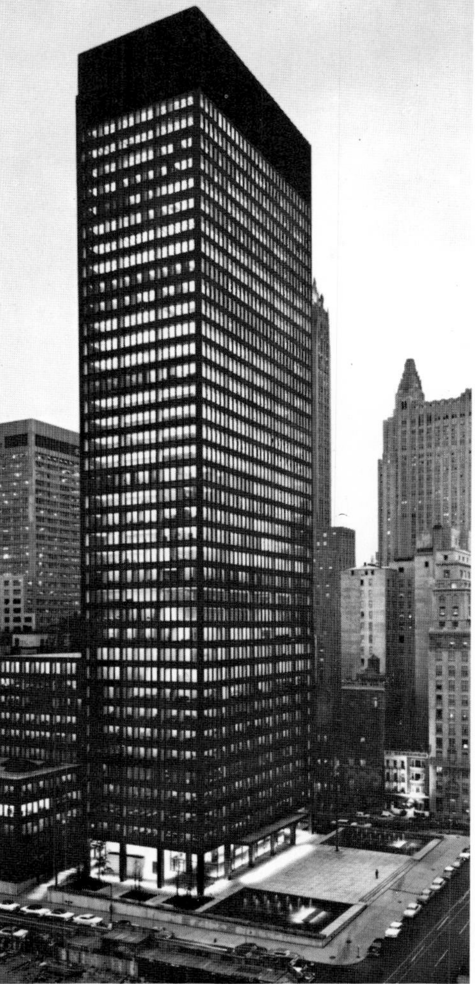

5

1. **Louis Henry Sullivan** (1856–1924) with Dankmar Adler: The Wainwright Building, St Louis, Missouri. 1890–1
2. **Richard Joseph Neutra** (1892–1970): Kaufmann House, Palm Springs, California. 1946–7
3. **Richard Joseph Neutra** (1892–1970): The Lovell Health House, Griffith Park, California. 1927–9
4. **Louis Kahn** (b.1901): The Alfred Newton Richards Medical Research Building, University of Pennsylvania, Philadelphia. 1958–60
5. **Daniel Hudson Burnham** (1846–1912) and **John Wellborn Root** (1850–91): The Reliance Building, Chicago. 1890–4
6. **Edward Durell Stone** (1902–78): The United States Embassy, New Delhi. 1958

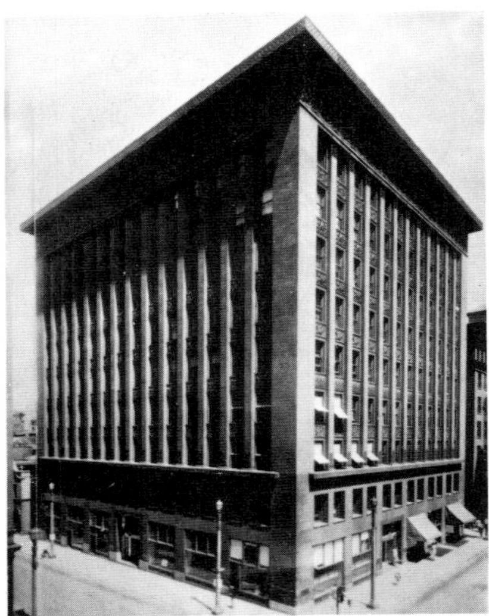
1

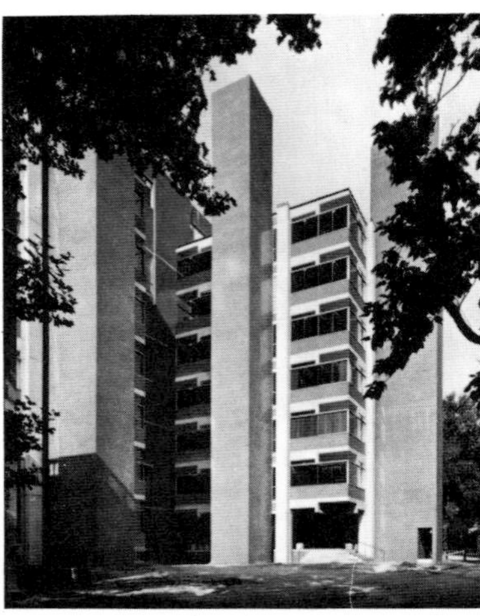
4

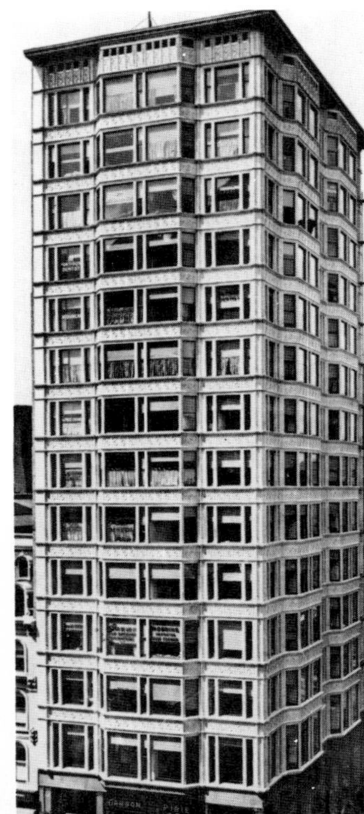
5

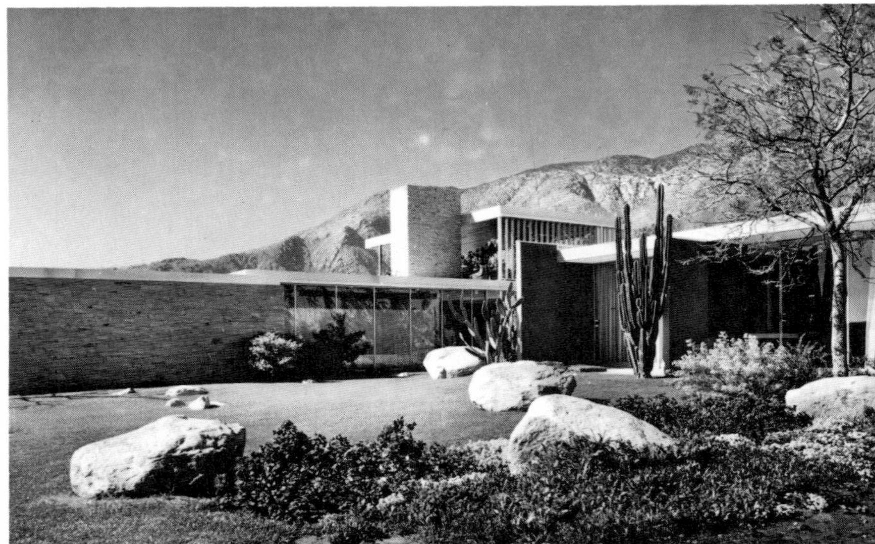
2

6

3

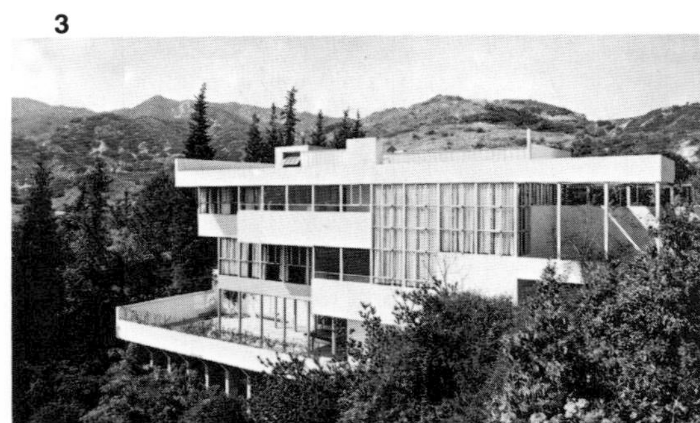

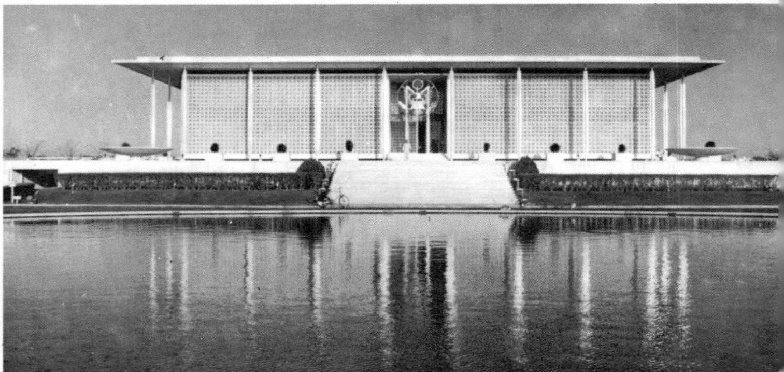

Oscar Niemeyer (b.1907): Brasilia Cathedral (during construction). View of supports. 1959–60
Marcel Breuer (b.1902): The Lecture Hall, New York University, University Heights. 1956–61
Philip C. Johnson (b.1906): The Sheldon Memorial Art Gallery, University of Nebraska, Lincoln. 1962
Oscar Niemeyer (b.1907): The Presidential Palace, or Palace of the Dawn, Brasilia. 1958
Oscar Niemeyer (b.1907): The Yacht Club, Pampulha. 1942
Marcel Breuer (b.1902): Starkey House, Duluth, Minnesota. 1954–5

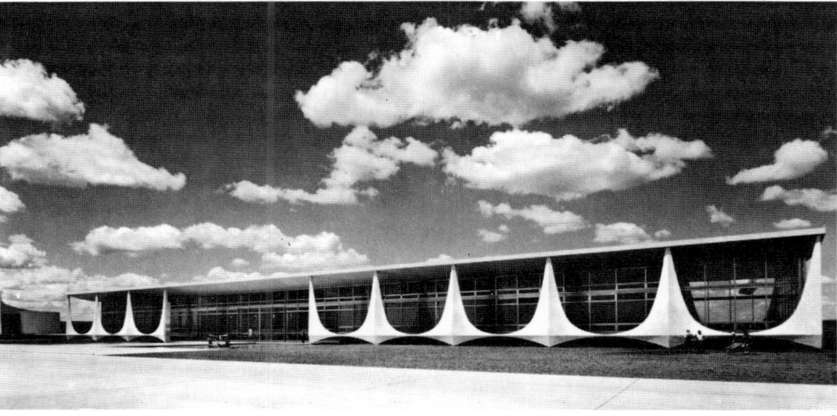

4

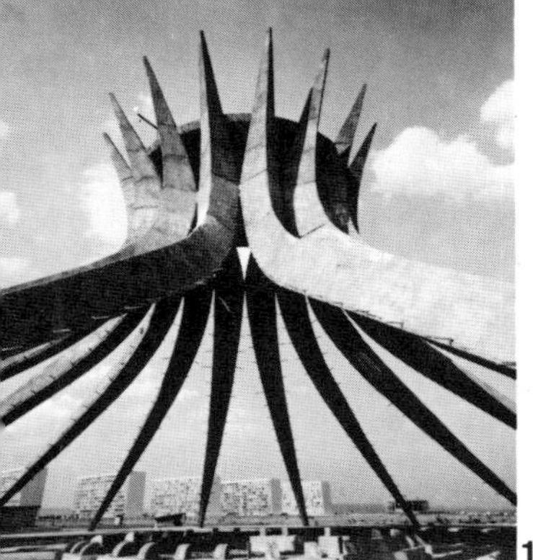

1

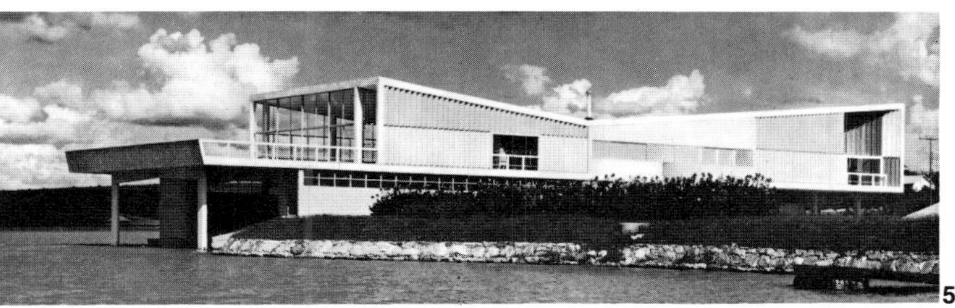

5

2

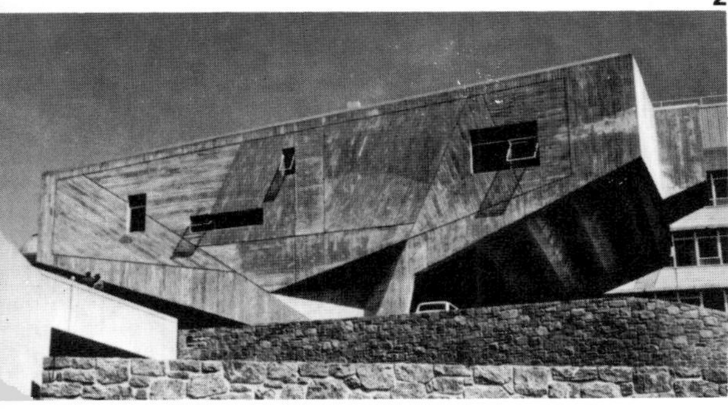

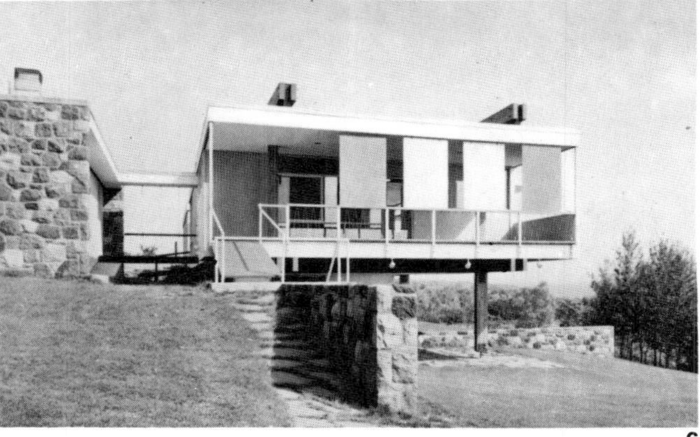

6

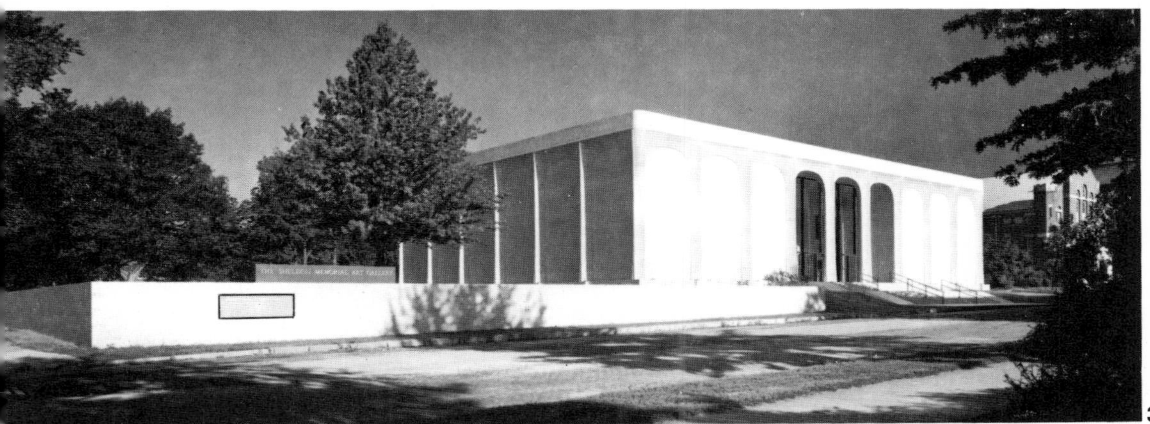

3

1. **Alvar Aalto** (b.1898): Carré House, Bazoches-sur-Guyonne. 1956–9
2. **Sir Edwin Lutyens** (1869–1944): The Viceroy's House, New Delhi. 1920–31
3. **Auguste Perret** (1874–1954): Ponthieu Garage, Paris. 1906
4. **Arne Jacobsen** (1902–71): The SAS Building, Copenhagen. 1959
5. **Pier Luigi Nervi** (1891–1979): The Palazzetto dello Sport, Rome. 1957–9
6. **Erich Mendelsohn** (1887–1953): Synagogue, Cleveland, Ohio. 1946–52

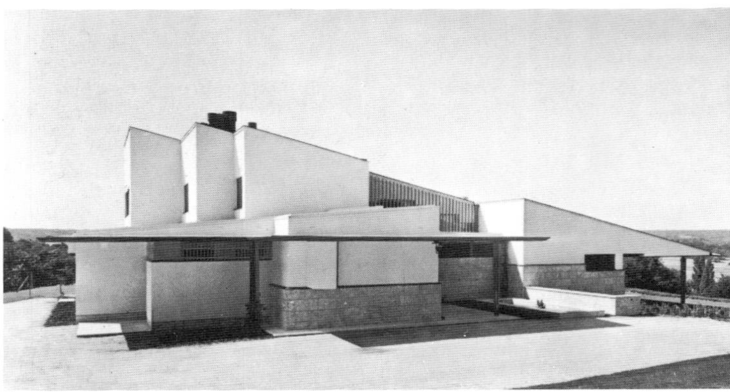

1

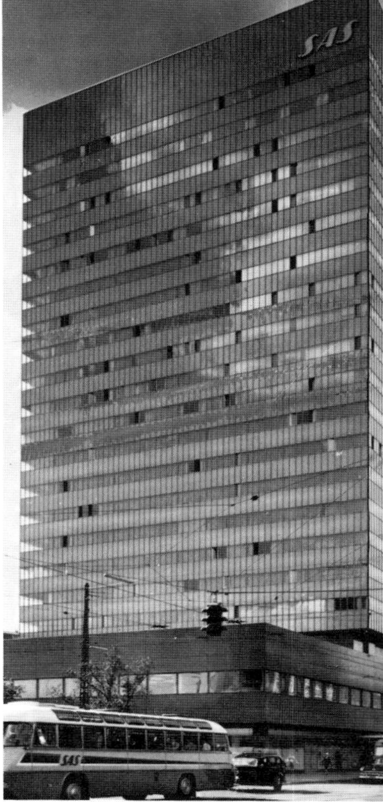

4

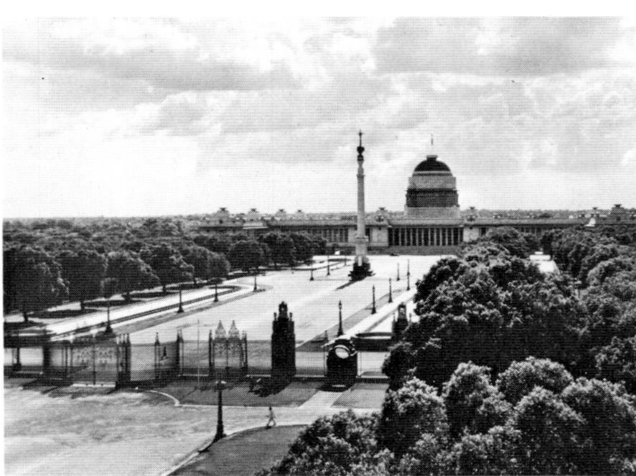

2

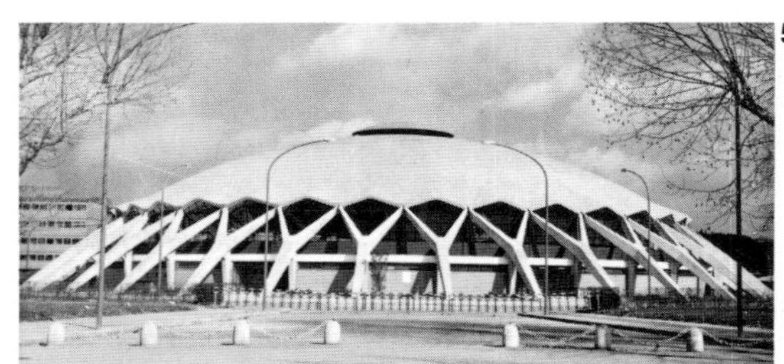

5

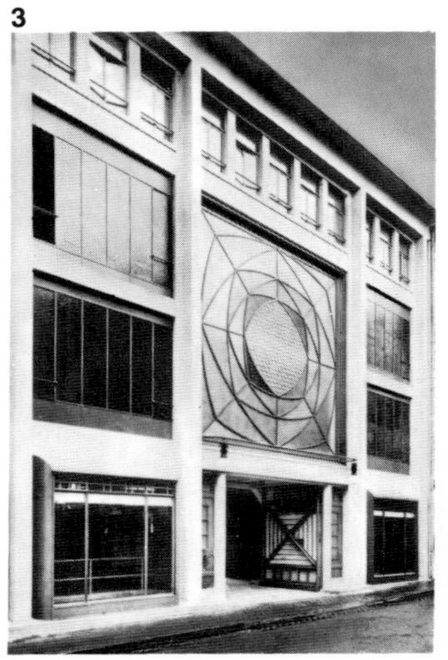

3

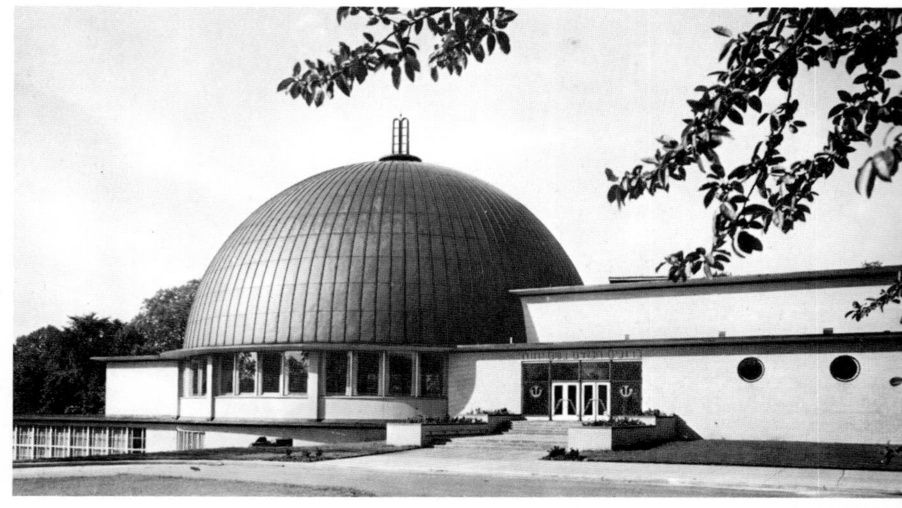

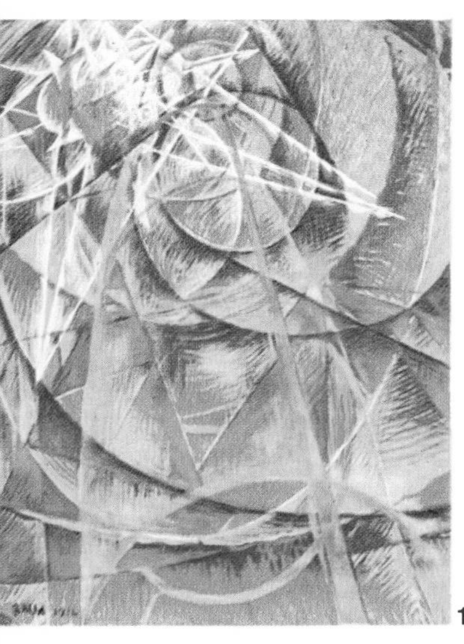

1. **Giacomo Balla** (1871–1958): *Mercury passing before the Sun.* 1914. Private Collection
2. **Gino Severini** (1883–1966): *The Boulevard.* 1910. Private Collection
3. **Umberto Boccioni** (1882–1916): *Elasticity.* 1912. Private Collection
4. **Umberto Boccioni** (1882–1916): *The Artist's Mother* (*Antigrazioso*). 1911. Galleria Nazionale d'Arte Moderna, Rome
5. **Giacomo Balla** (1871–1958): *A Dog on a Leash.* 1912. Museum of Modern Art, New York
6. **Antonio Sant'Elia** (1888–1916): *Project for a Skyscraper.* 1913. Villa Olmo, Como

1

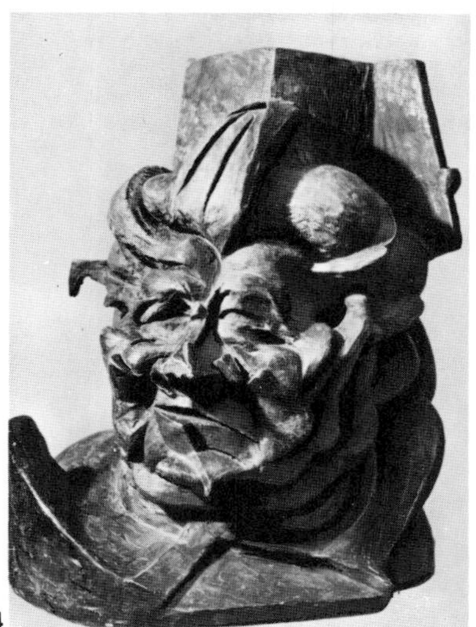

4

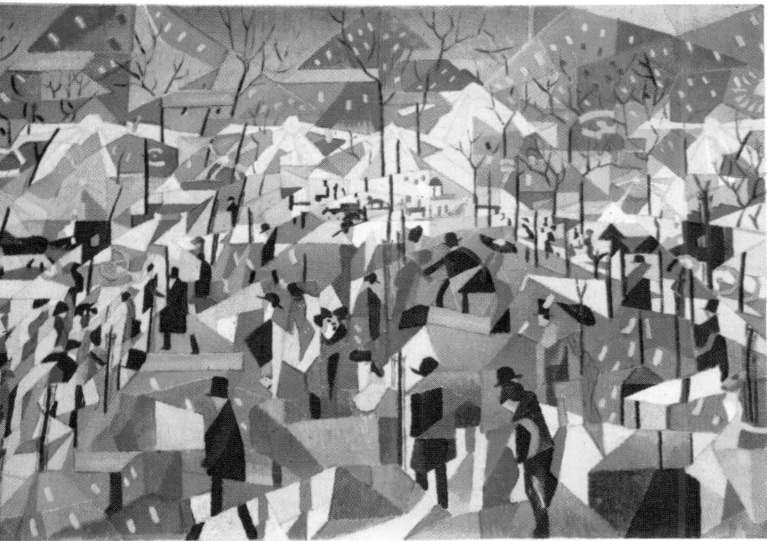

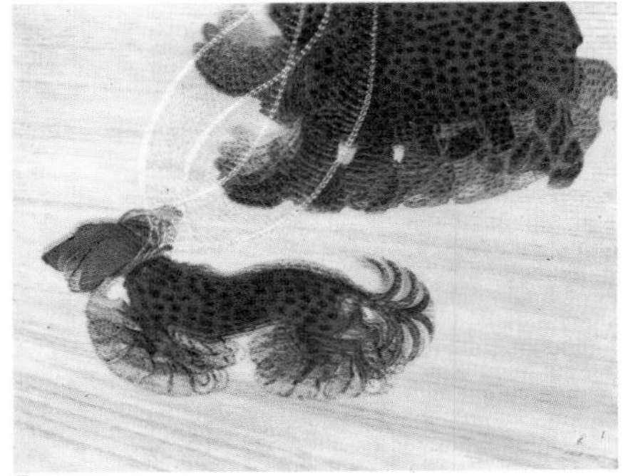

5

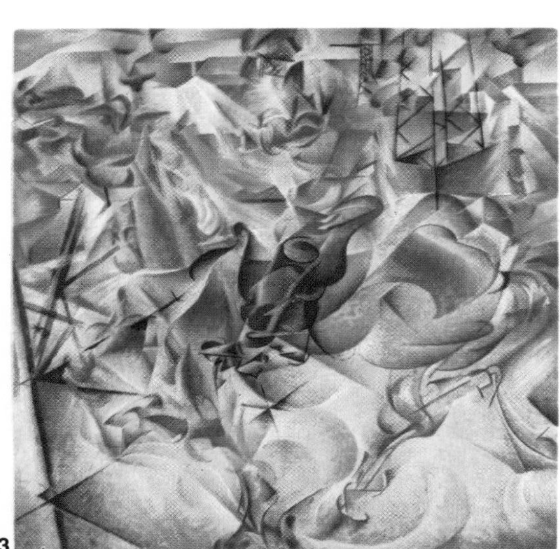

3

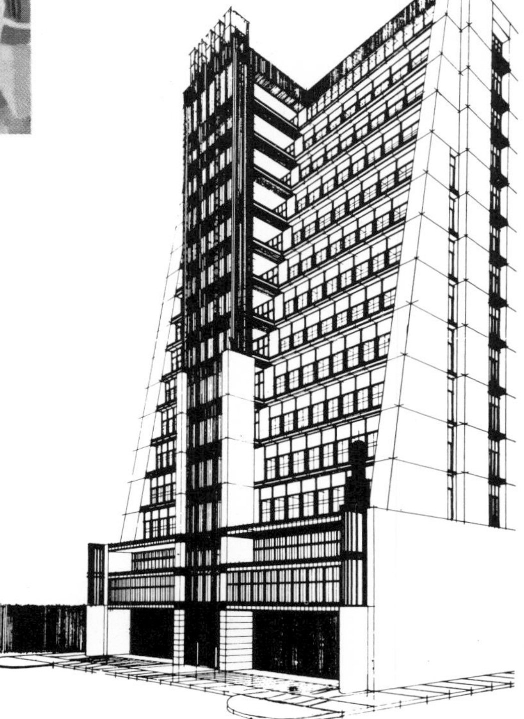

6

1. **Max Ernst** (1891–1976): *Chaste Joseph.* 1928. Private Collection
2. **Max Ernst** (1891–1976): *Oedipus Rex.* 1921. Private Collection
3. **Kurt Schwitters** (1887–1948): *Collage in Blue and White.* 1926. Private Collection
4. **Francis Picabia** (1879–1953): *Optophone.* Watercolour. 1921. Formerly H.-P. Roche Collection
5. **Marcel Duchamp** (1887–1968): *Nude descending a Staircase, No. 2.* 1912. Philadelphia Museum of Art
6. **Francis Picabia** (1879–1953): *Prenez garde à la peinture.* 1917. Private Collection
7. **Marcel Duchamp** (1887–1968): *The Bride stripped bare by her Bachelors, even.* Lower panel. Oil and lead wire on glass. Philadelphia Museum of Art

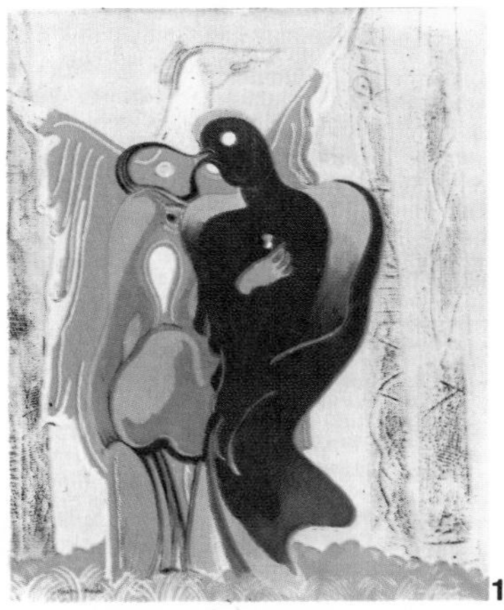
1

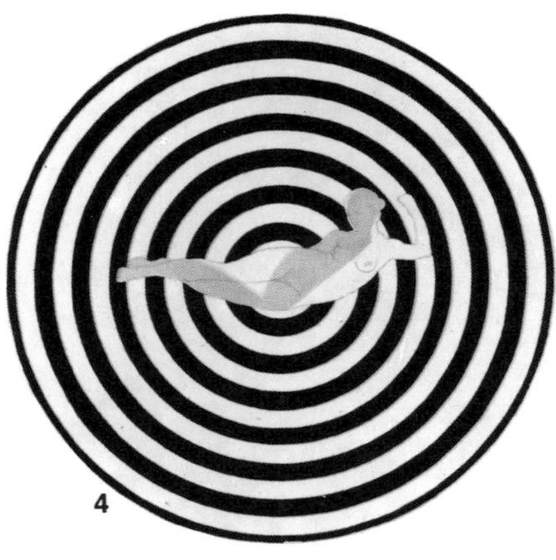
4

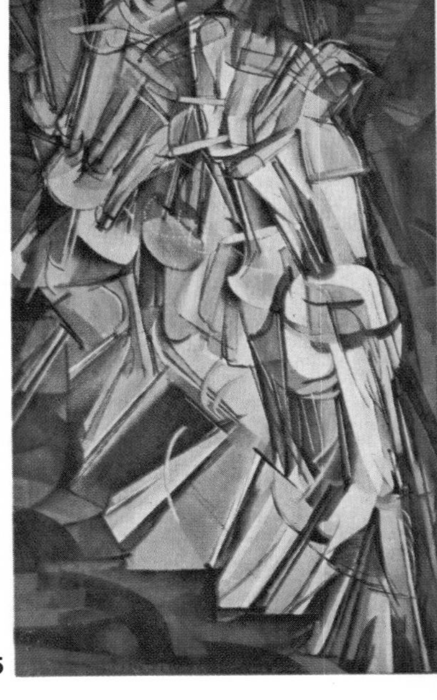
5

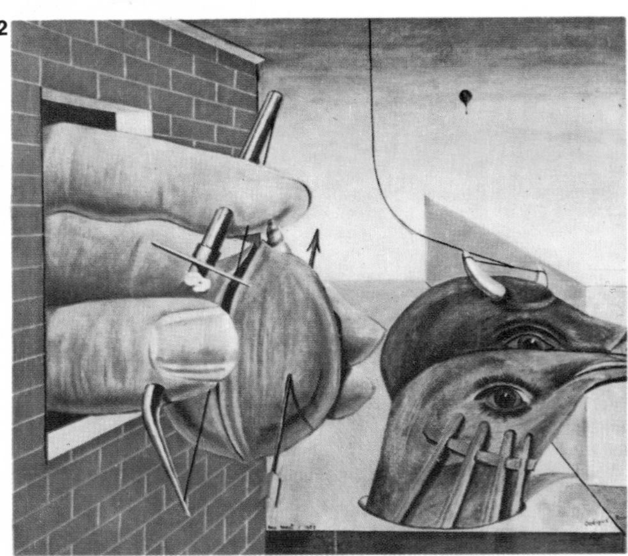
2

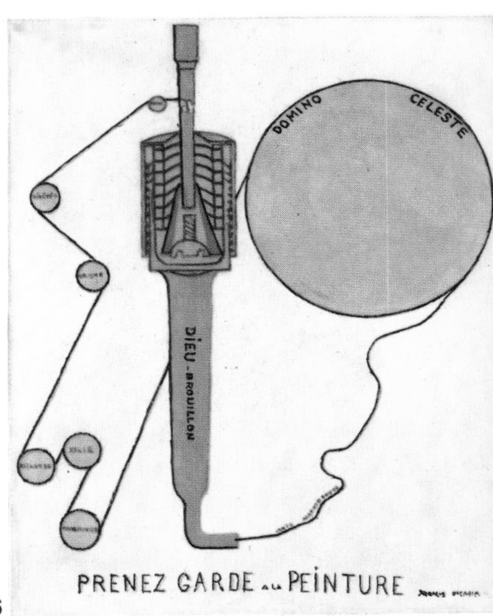

6

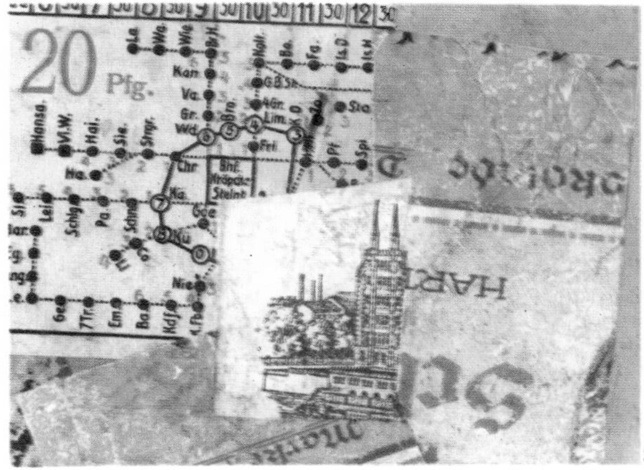

3

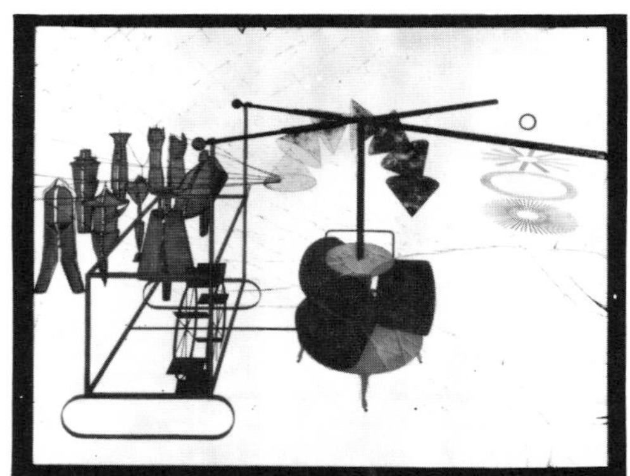
7

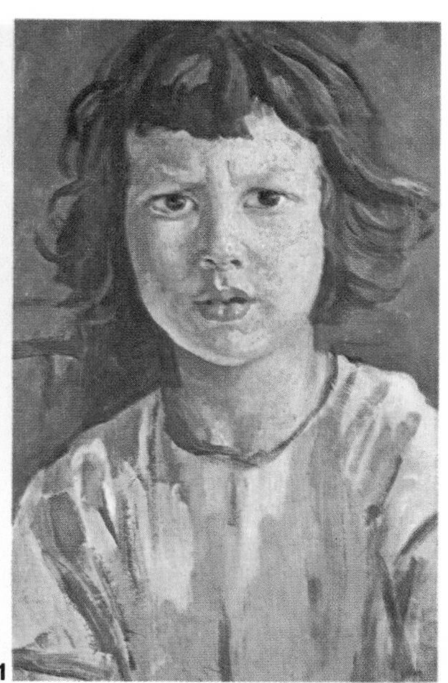

1

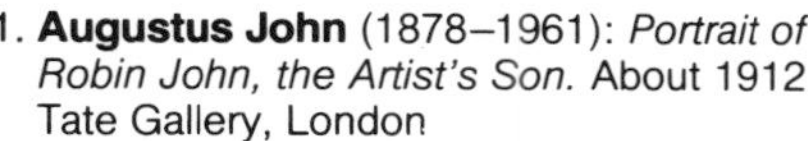

1. **Augustus John** (1878–1961): *Portrait of Robin John, the Artist's Son.* About 1912. Tate Gallery, London
2. **Wyndham Lewis** (1882–1957): *Composition.* 1913. Tate Gallery, London
3. **Augustus John** (1878–1961): *Portrait of Alick Schepeler.* Drawing. Fitzwilliam Museum, Cambridge
4. **Wyndham Lewis** (1882–1957): *The Surrender of Barcelona.* 1934–7. Tate Gallery, London
5. **Henri Gaudier-Brzeska** (1891–1915): *Stags.* Alabaster. 1914. Art Institute of Chicago
6. **Henri Gaudier-Brzeska** (1891–1915): *Standing Birds.* 1914. Museum of Modern Art, New York
7. **Sir Matthew Smith** (1879–1959): *Apples.* 1919–20. Tate Gallery, London

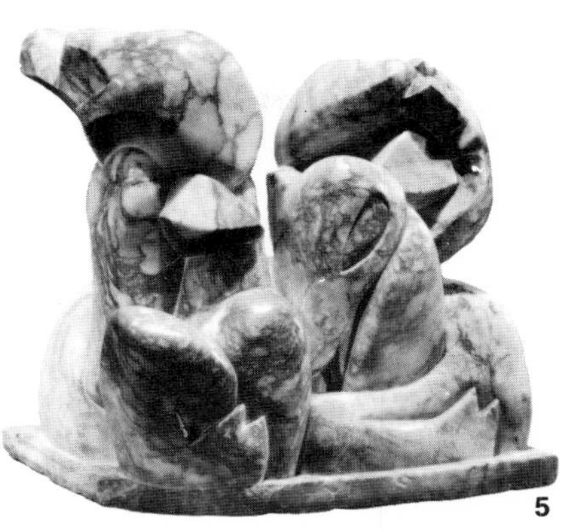

5

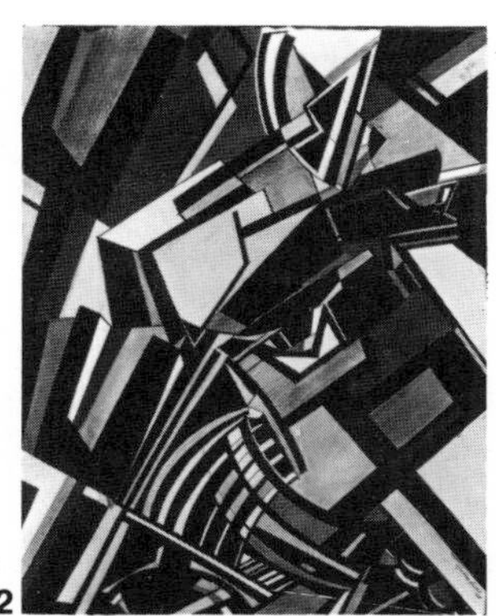

2

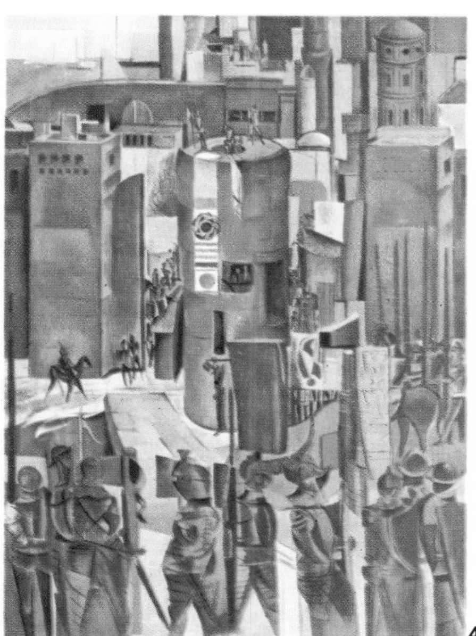

4

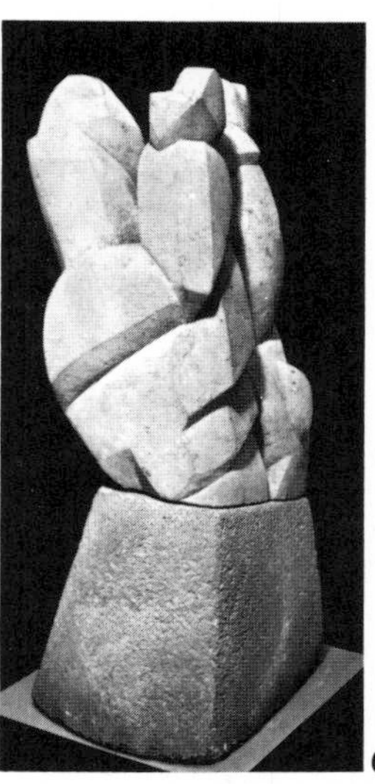

6

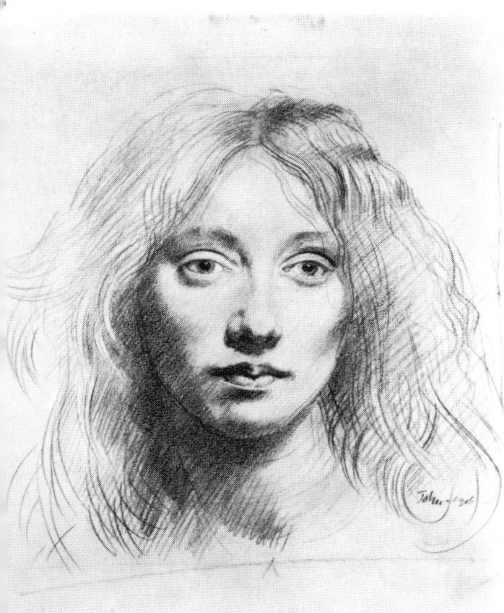

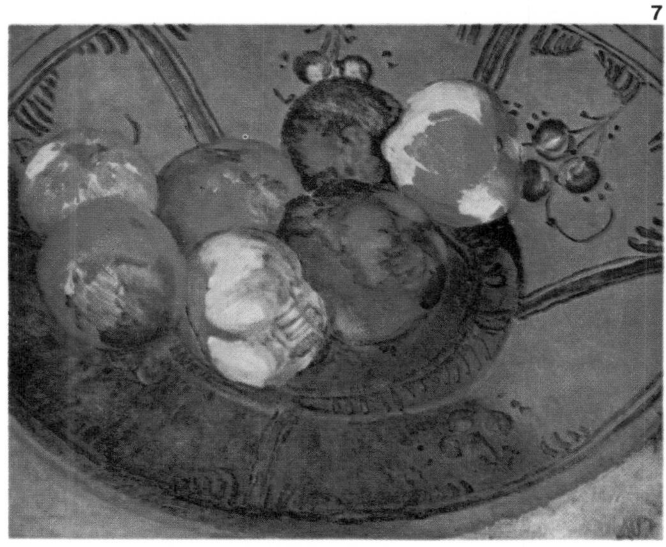

7

Giorgio de Chirico (1888–1978)
1. *The Great Tower.* About 1913. Formerly collection of the artist
2. *The Enigma of Time.* 1911. Private Collection
3. *Premonitory Portrait of Apollinaire.* Wood engraving. 1914

Salvador Dali (b.1904)
4. *Bacchanalia.* 1939. Private Collection
5. *The Persistence of Memory.* 1931. Museum of Modern Art, New York
6. *Mae West.* Gouache on paper. 1936. Art Institute of Chicago
7. *The Crucifixion.* 1951. Glasgow Art Gallery

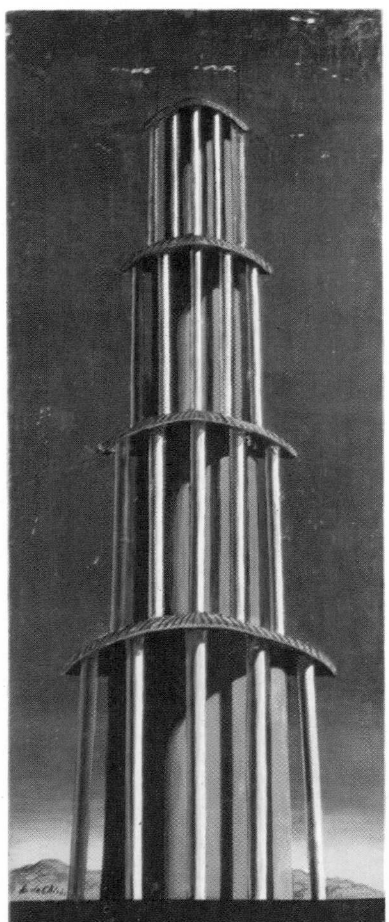
1

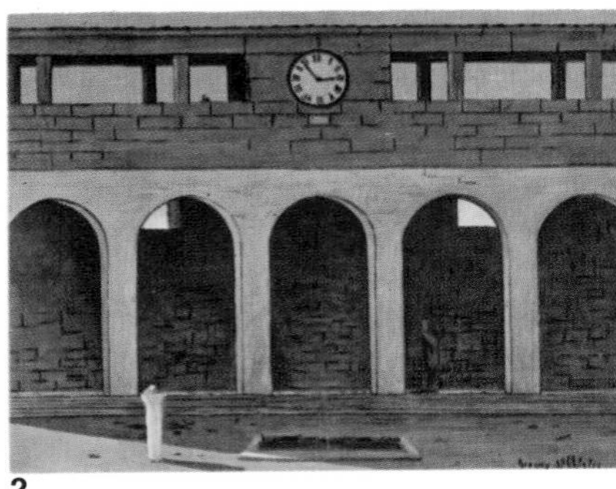
2

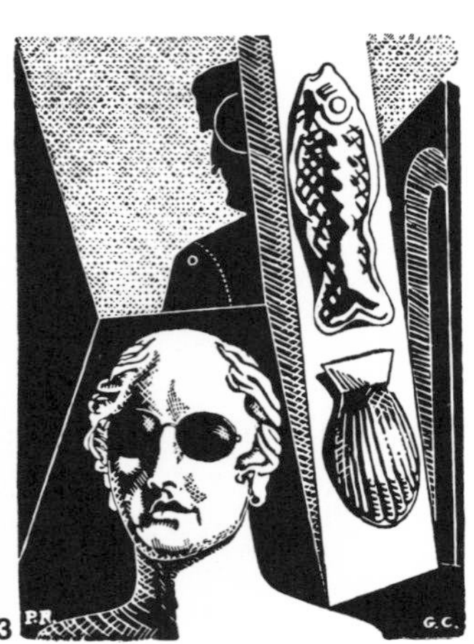

3

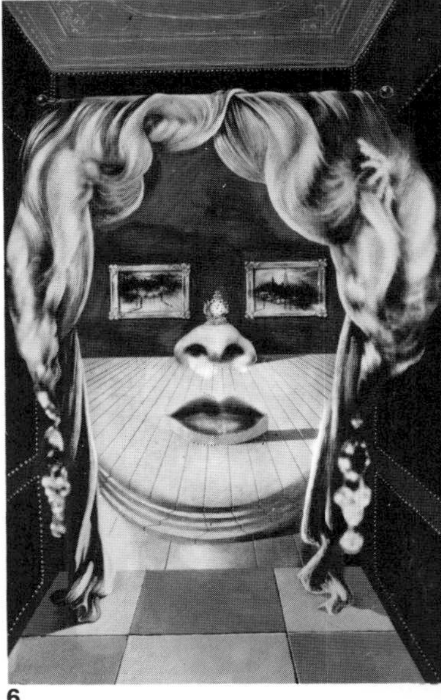
6

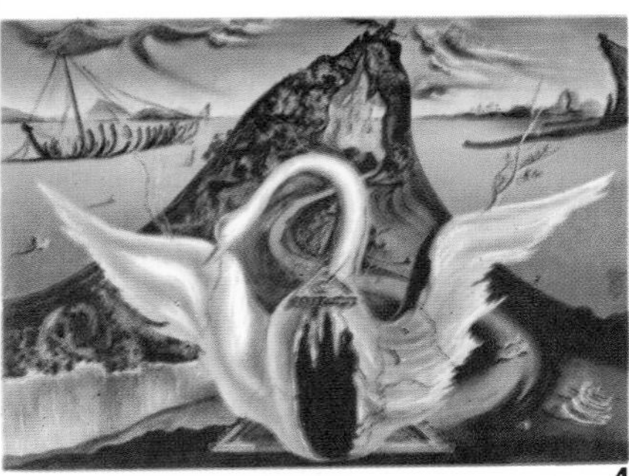
4

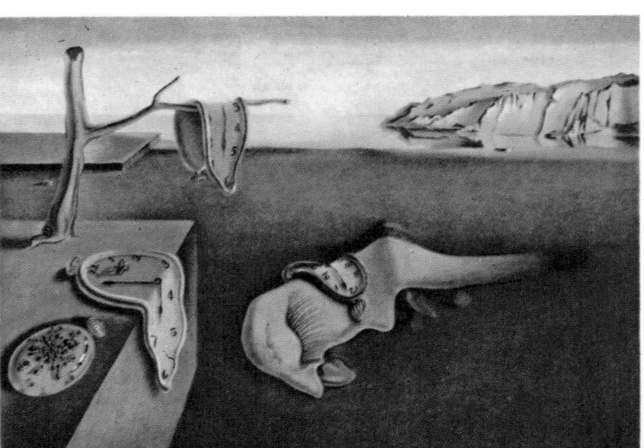
5

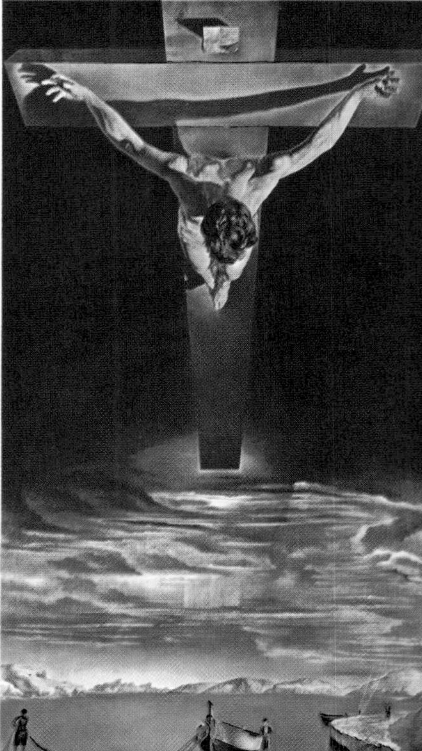
7

. **René Magritte** (1898–1967): *The Childhood of Icarus.* 1960. Private Collection
. **Yves Tanguy** (1900–55): *Divisibilité Indéfinie.* 1942. Albright-Knox Art Gallery, Buffalo, New York
. **René Magritte** (1898–1967): *Le grand Siècle.* Galerie Alexandre Iolas, Paris

4. **René Magritte** (1898–1967): *Rough Crossing.* 1926. Private Collection
5. **Yves Tanguy** (1900–55): *Mummy, Daddy is Injured!* 1927. Museum of Modern Art, New York
6. **Yves Tanguy** (1900–55): *Four Hours of Summer, Hope.* 1929. Private Collection
7. **Paul Délvaux** (b.1897): *Hands.* 1941. Private Collection

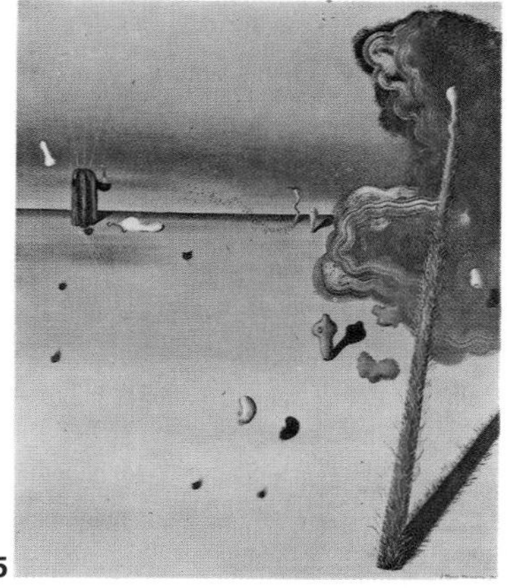

5

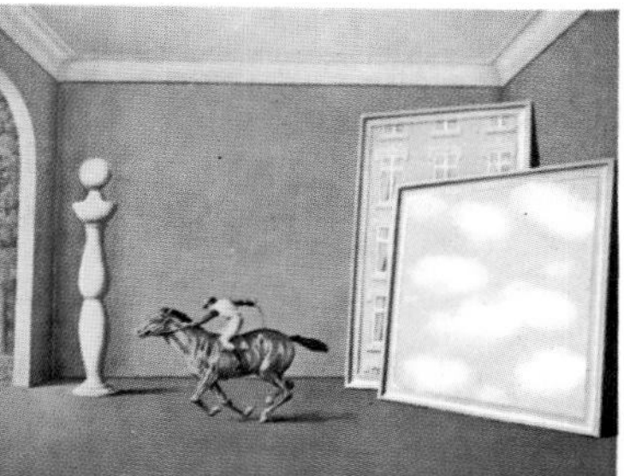

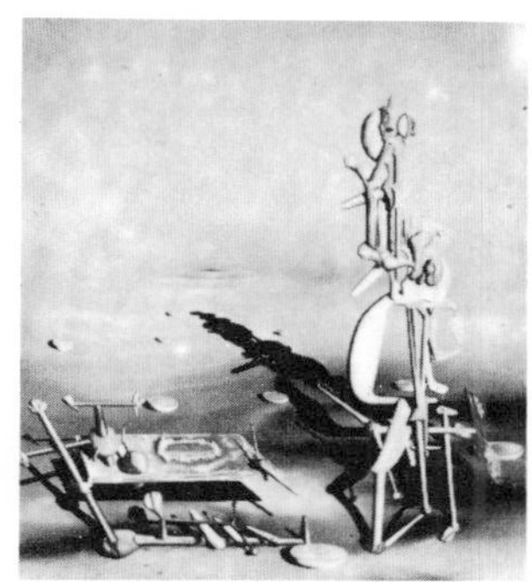

2

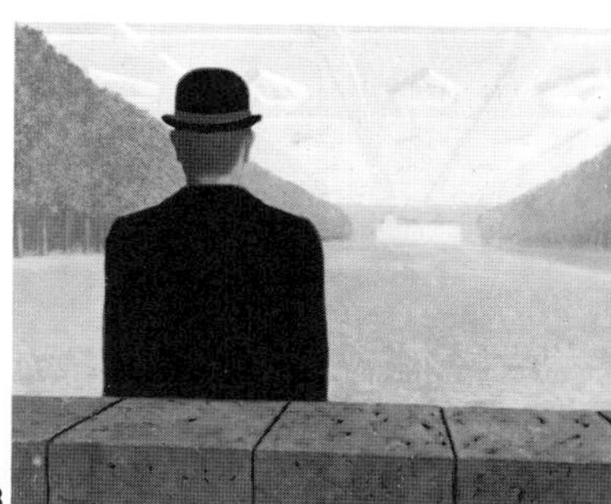

3

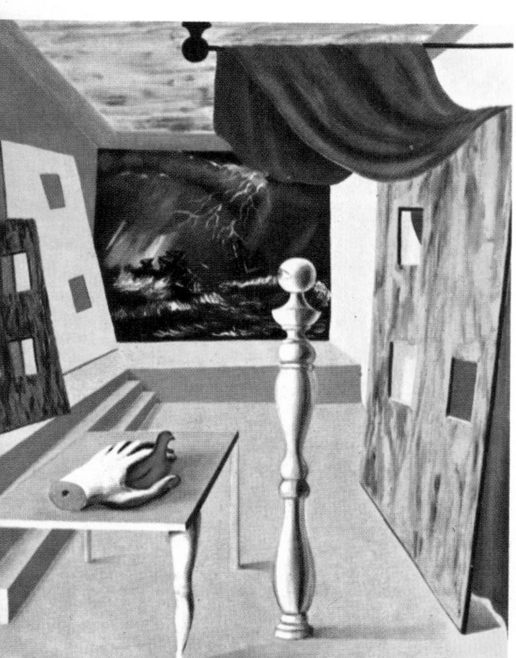

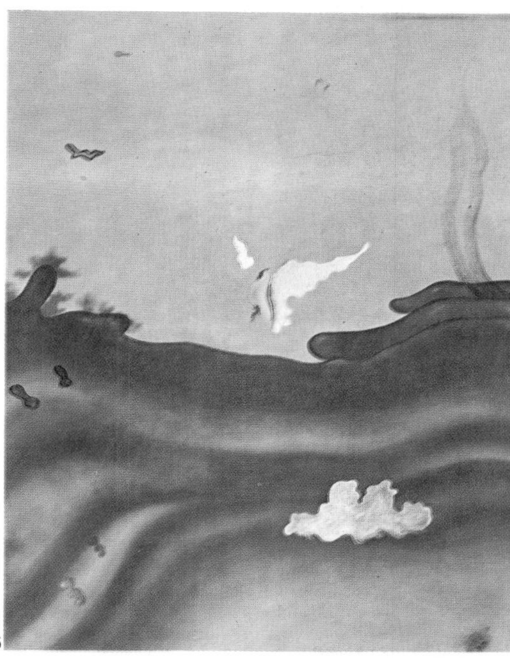

6

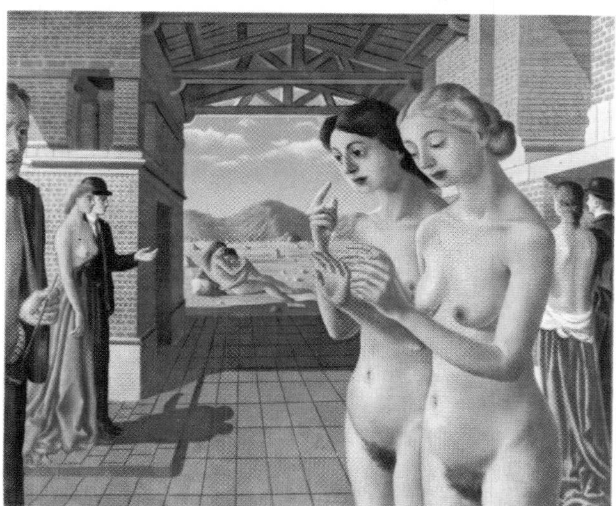

7

1. **André Masson** (b.1896): *A Nude.* 1924–5. Peggy Guggenheim Collection, Venice
2. **Wifredo Lam** (b.1902): *The Tropic of Capricorn.* 1961. Private Collection
3. **André Masson** (b.1896): *Niobe.* 1947. Galerie Louise Leiris, Paris
4. **Wifredo Lam** (b.1902): *We are Waiting.* 1963. Collection of the artist
5. **Hans Bellmer** (b.1902): *A Drawing.* 1965 Private Collection
6. **Joan Miró** (b.1893): *Composition.* 1933. Museum of Modern Art, New York

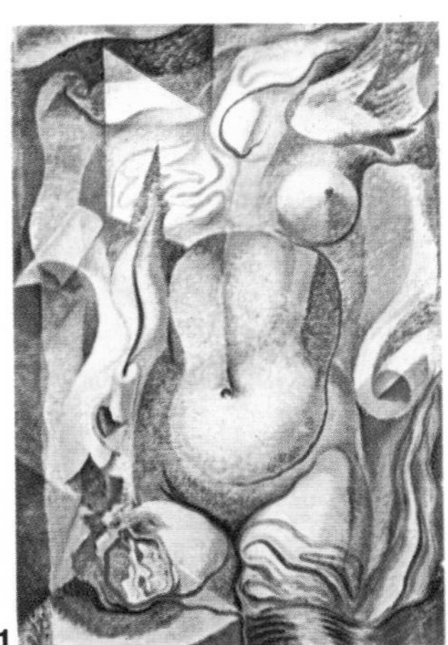
1

2
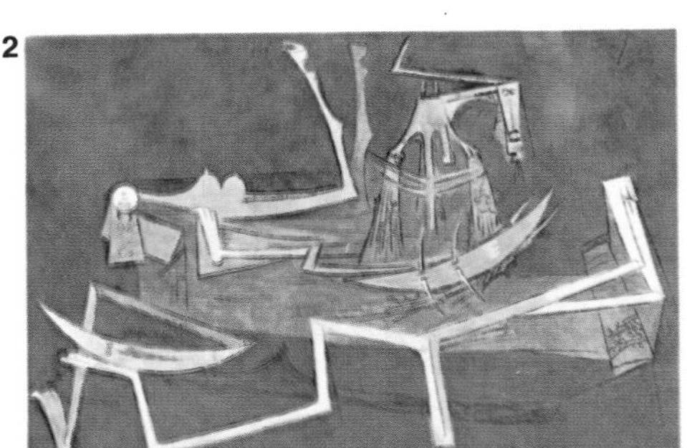

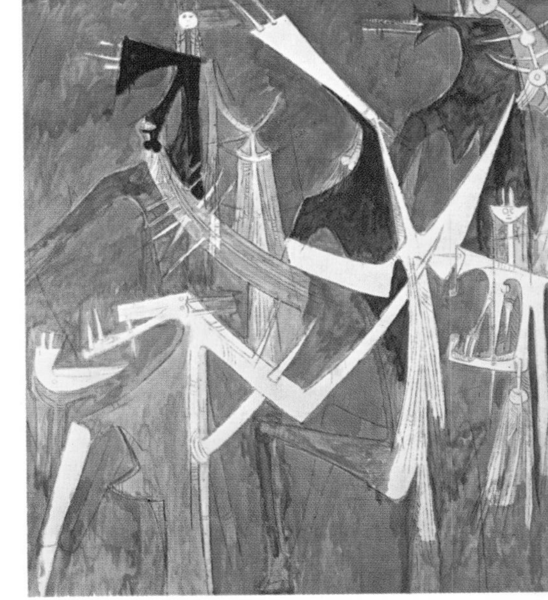
4

3
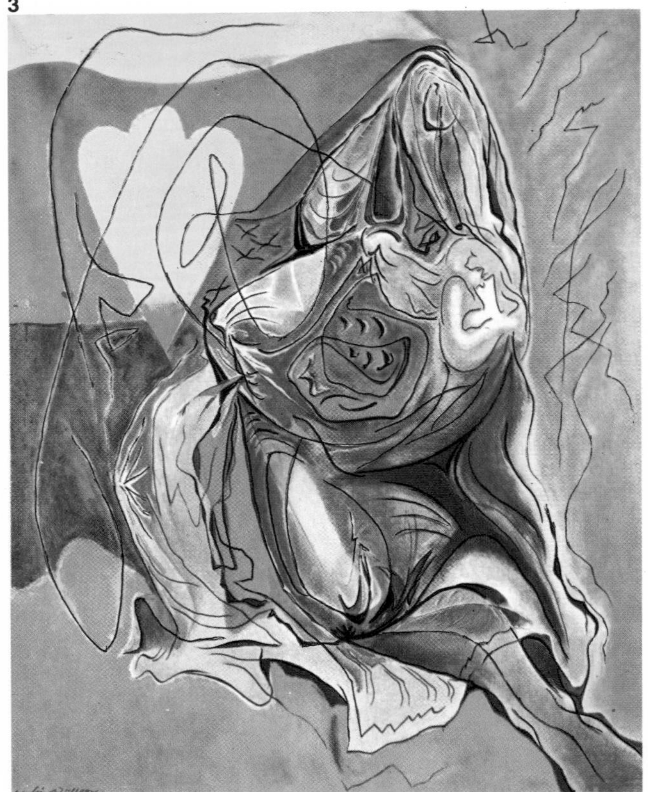

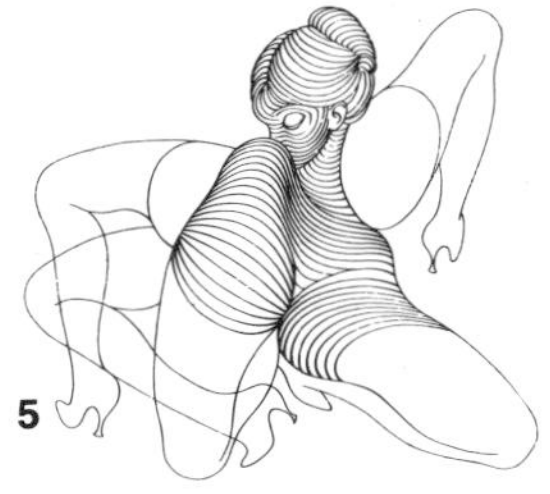
5

6
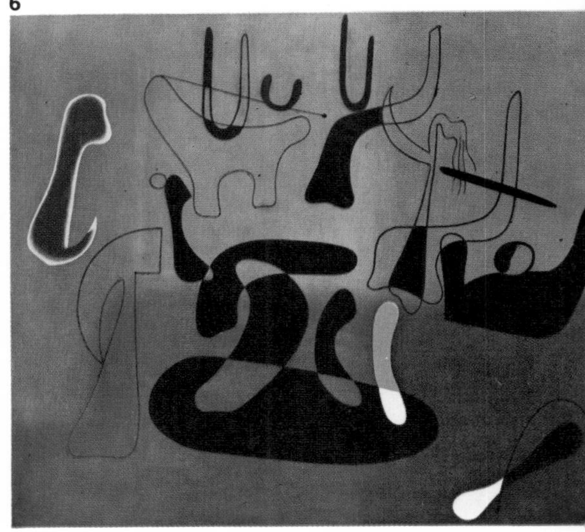

1. **Joan Miró** (b.1893): *White Lady.* 1950. Private Collection
2. **Piet Mondrian** (1872–1944): *Broadway Boogie Woogie.* 1942–3. Museum of Modern Art, New York
3. **Ben Nicholson** (b.1894): *May 1957 (Aegina).* Private Collection
4. **Wassily Kandinsky** (1866–1944): *On White.* 1923. Private Collection
5. **Piet Mondrian** (1872–1944): *A Tree.* About 1911. Munson-Williams-Proctor Institute, Utica, New York
6. **Piet Mondrian** (1872–1944): *Square Composition in Red, Yellow and Blue.* 1926. Private Collection
7. **Joan Miró** (b.1893): *The Princess's Snob Soirée.* 1944. Private Collection

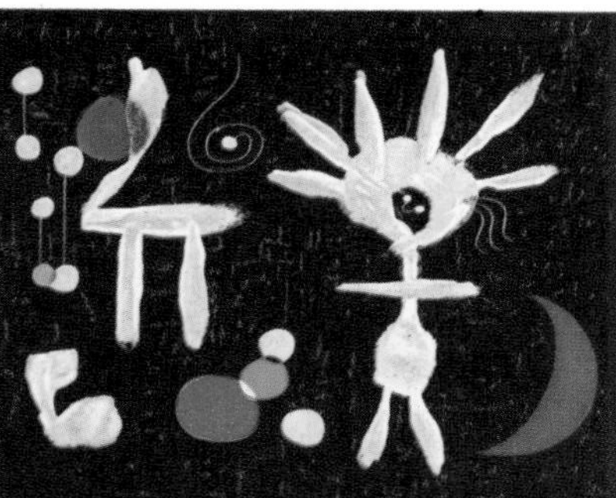
1

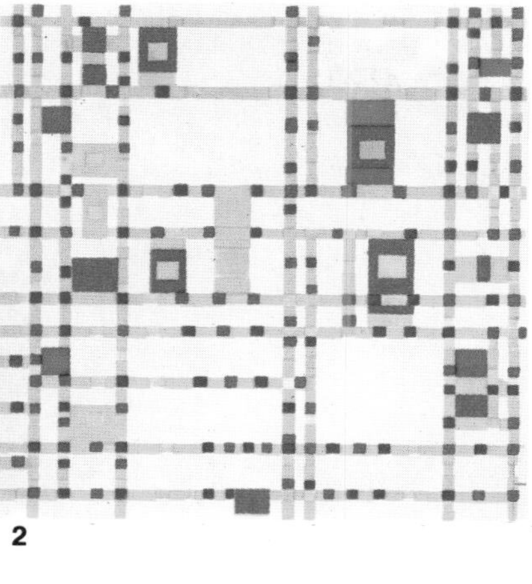
2

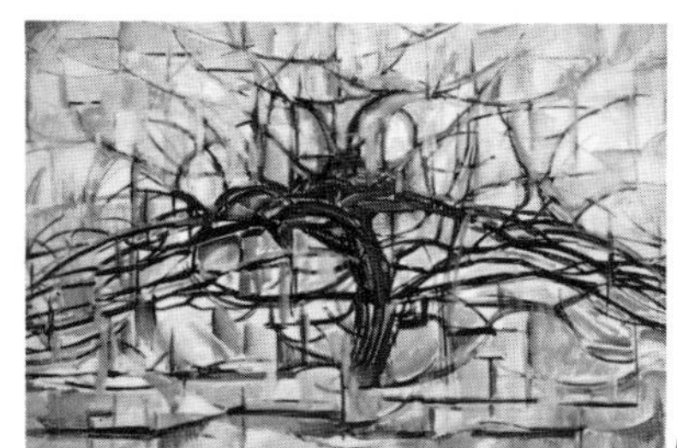
5

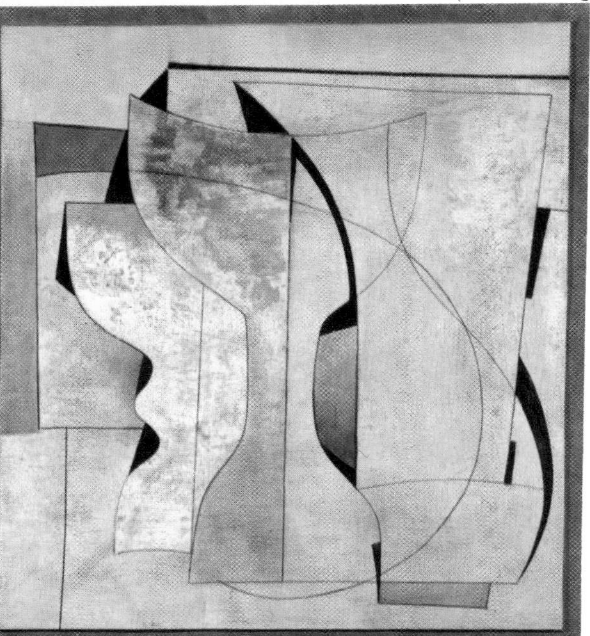
3

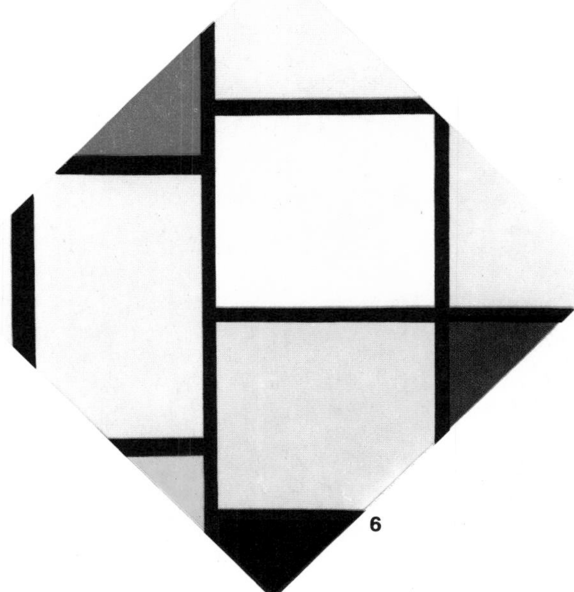
6

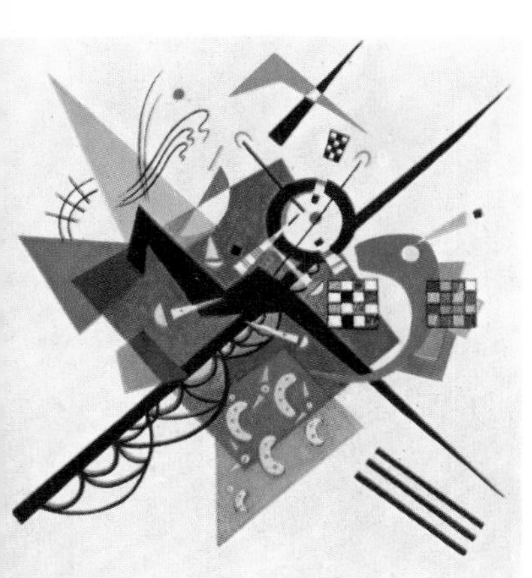

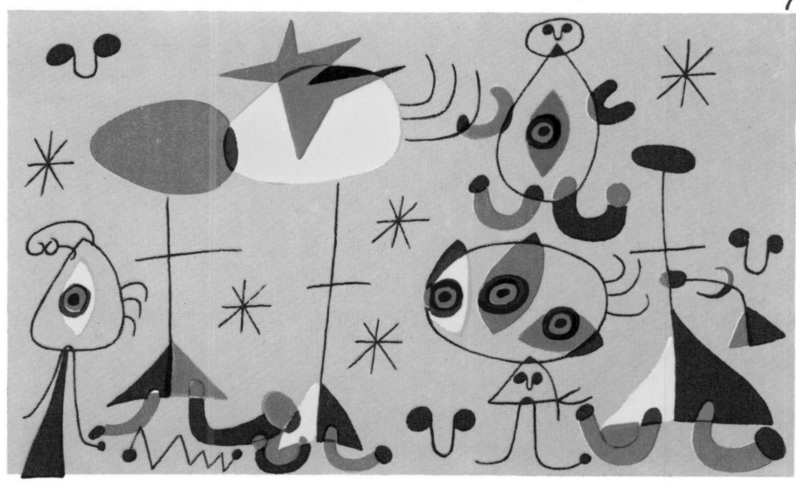
7

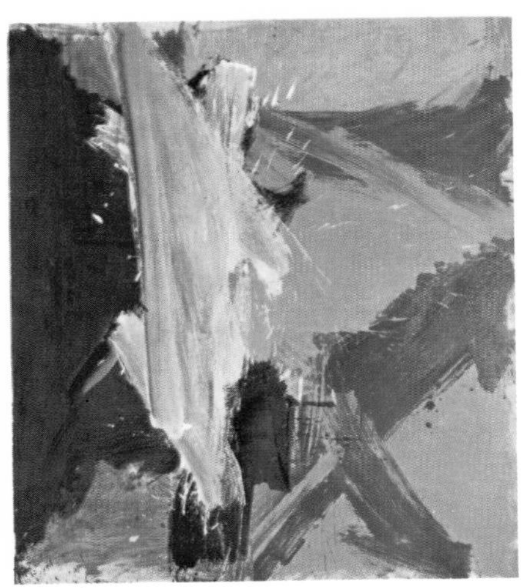
1

1. **Willem de Kooning** (b.1904): *The Merritt Parkway.* 1959. Sidney Janis Gallery, New York
2. **Jackson Pollock** (1912–56): *Number 12, 1952.* Private Collection
3. **Jackson Pollock** (1912–56): *Blue Poles.* 1953. Private Collection
4. **Otto Freundlich** (1878–1943): *Mountain Sculpture.* Plaster. 1934
5. **Kasimir Malevich** (1878–1935): *Suprematist Composition.* 1915. Private Collection
6. **Willem de Kooning** (b.1904): *Woman.* 1961. Sidney Janis Gallery, New York

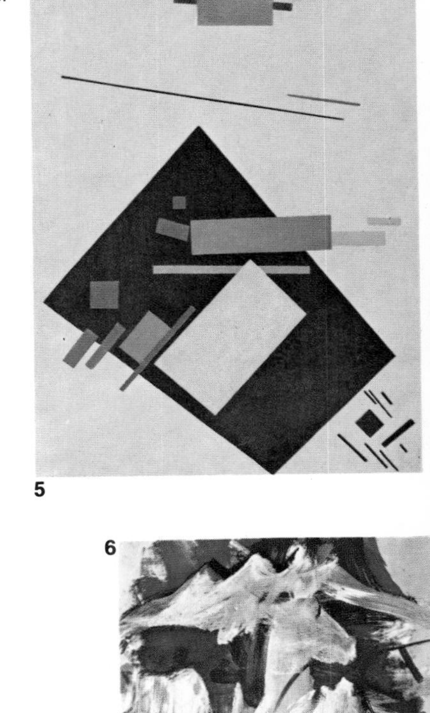
5

2
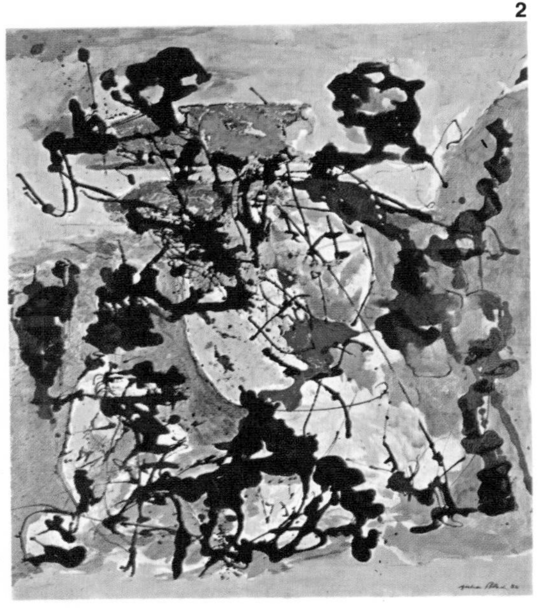

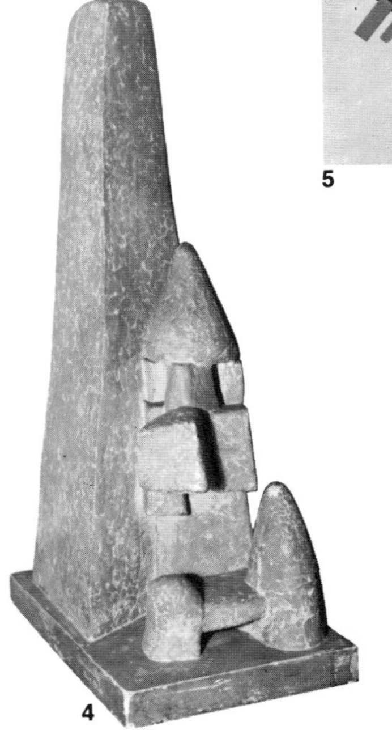
4

6

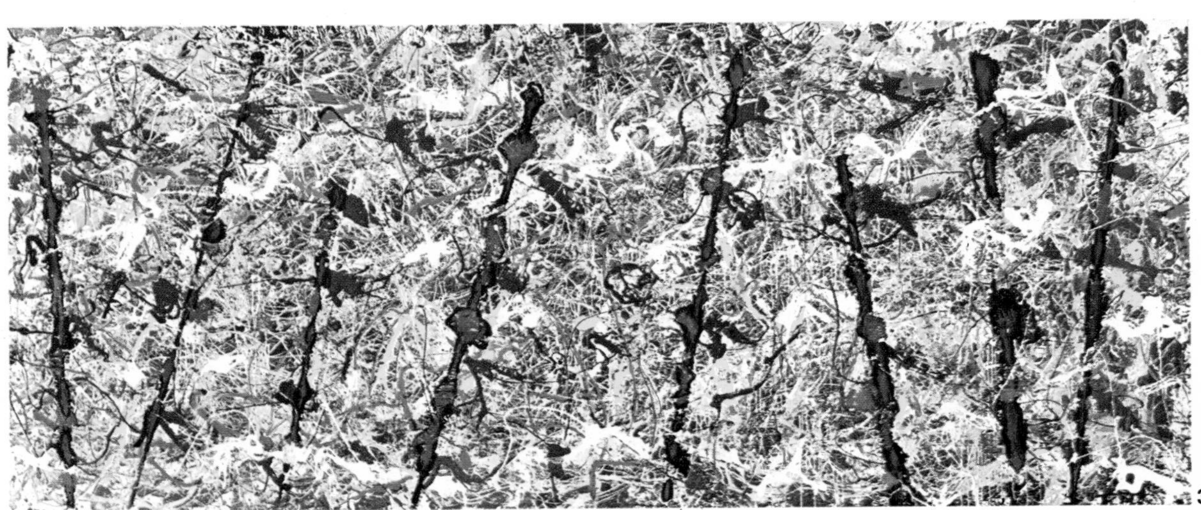
3

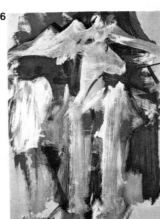

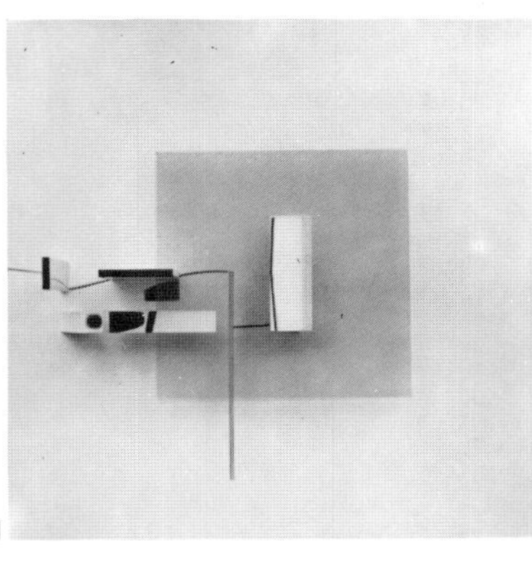
1

1. **Victor Pasmore** (b.1908): *Construction-relief.* Wood and plastic. 1966. Marlborough Fine Art Ltd, London
2. **Victor Pasmore** (b.1908): *Red Abstract No. 5.* 1960. City Art Gallery, Bristol
3. **Wols** (1913–51): *Painting.* Private Collection
4. **František Kupka** (1871–1957): *Philosophic Architecture.* 1913. Galerie Louis Carré, Paris
5. **Alberto Magnelli** (1888–1971): *Painting No. 0530.* 1915. Formerly collection of the artist
6. **Willi Baumeister** (1889–1955): *A Black Rock with Spots of Colour.* 1955. Private Collection

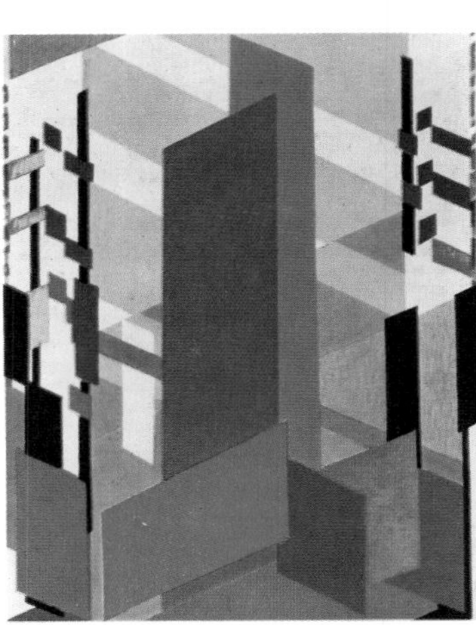
4

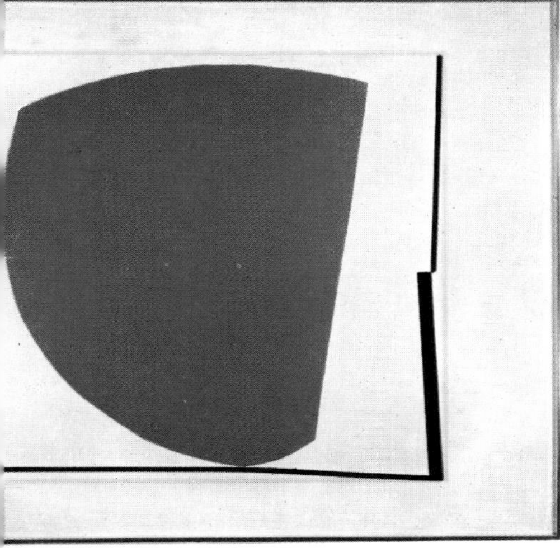
2

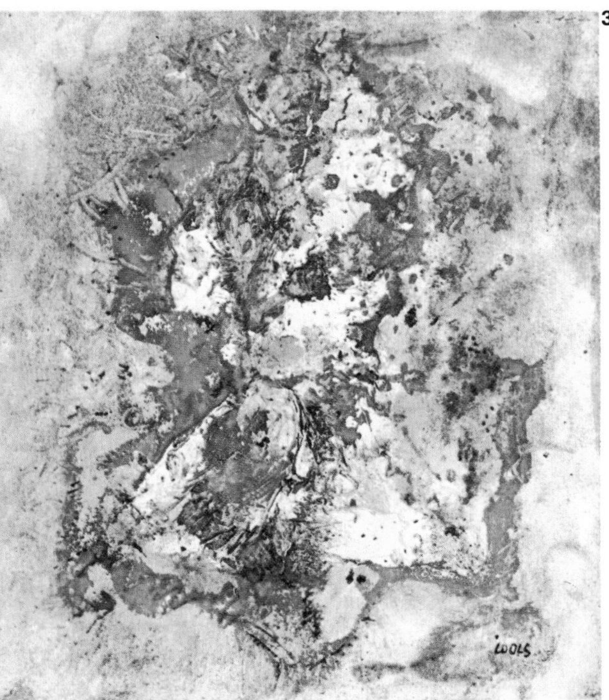
3

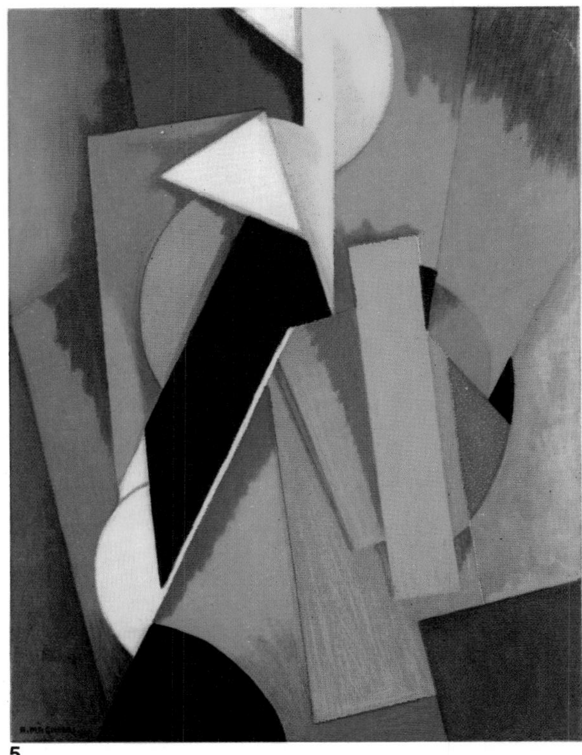
5

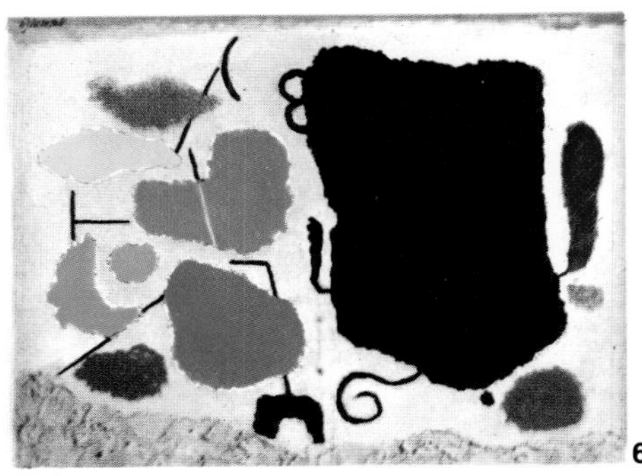
6

1. **Käthe Kollwitz** (1867–1945): *The Father.* Figure from the *Monument to the Dead,* Diksmuide, Belgium. 1924–32
2. **Constantin Brancusi** (1876–1957): *Cock.* Polished bronze. 1941. Musée National d'Art Moderne, Paris
3. **Alberto Giacometti** (1901–66): *Large Head of Diego.* Bronze. 1954
4. **Alberto Giacometti** (1901–66): *Suspended Ball.* Plaster. 1930
5. **Ernst Barlach** (1870–1938): *A Man singing.* 1928–30. Kunsthalle, Hamburg
6. **Alberto Giacometti** (1901–66): *Invisible Object* (*Hands holding the Void*). Bronze. 1934–5
7. **Wilhelm Lehmbruck** (1881–1919): *Kneeling Woman.* Cast stone. 1911. Museum of Modern Art, New York
8. **Constantin Brancusi** (1876–1957): *Mademoiselle Pogany.* Bronze. 1913. Museum of Modern Art (Lillie P. Bliss Collection), New York

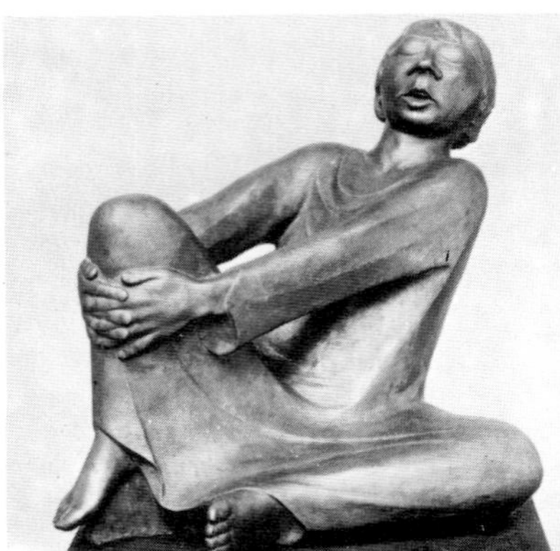
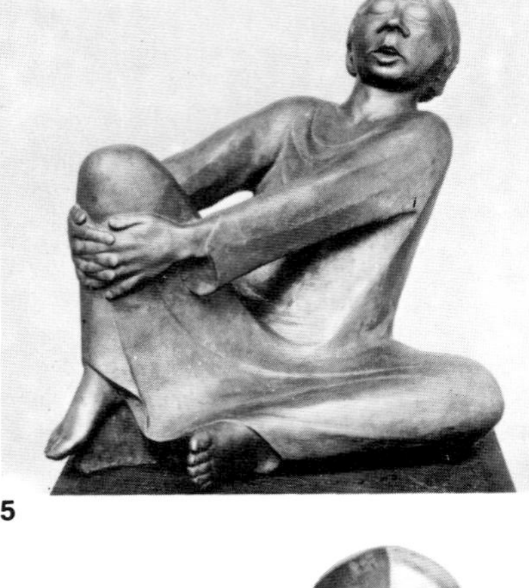
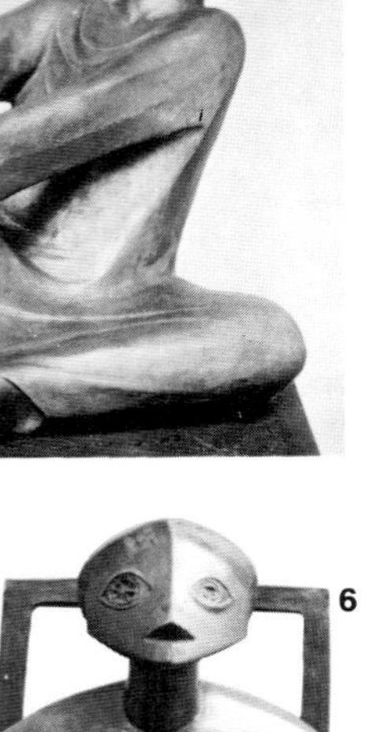

5

1

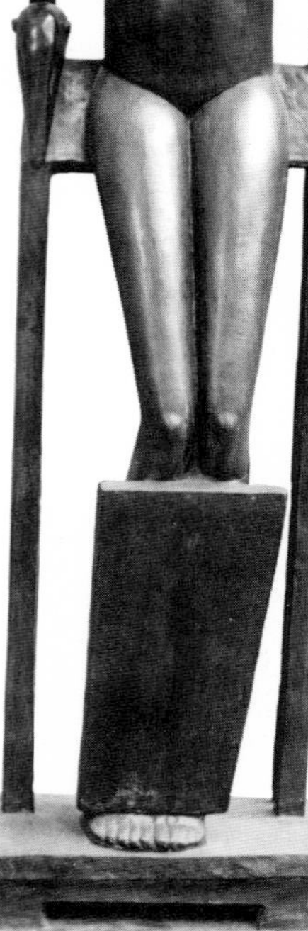

6

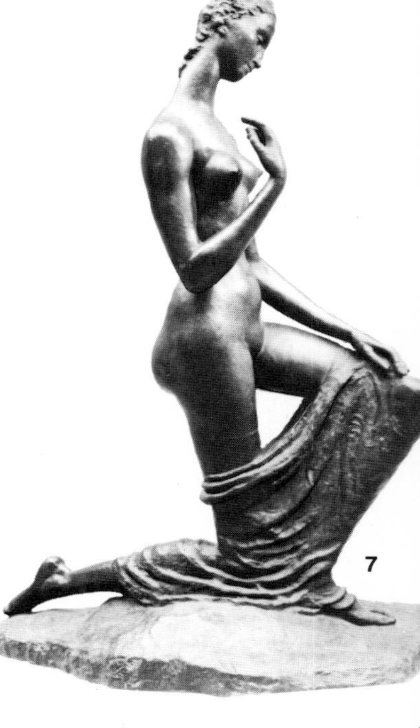

7

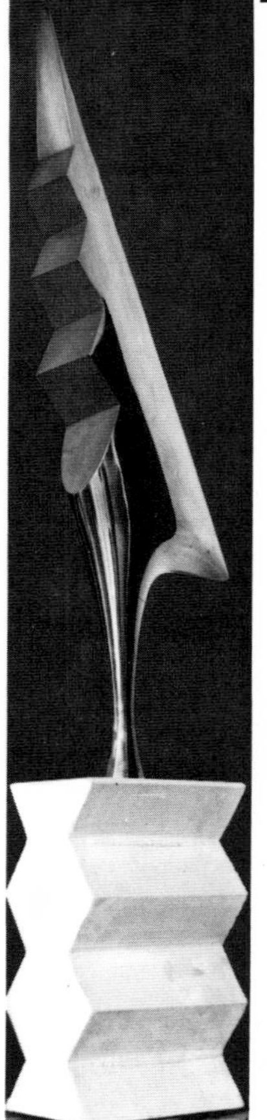

2

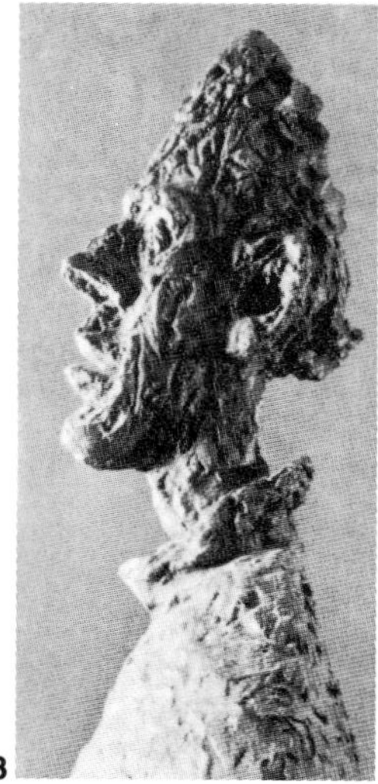

3

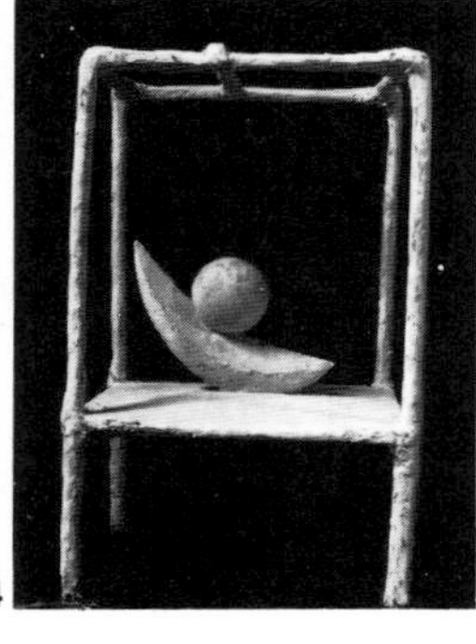

4

8

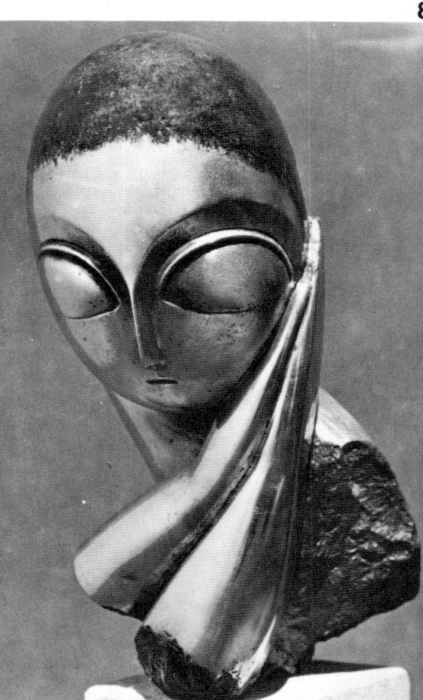

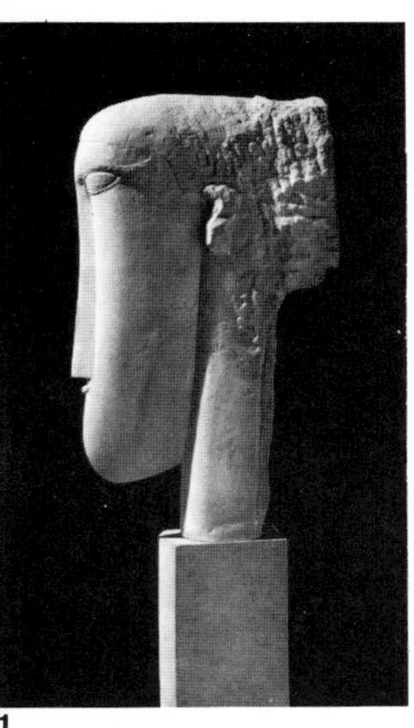
1

1. **Amedeo Modigliani** (1884–1920): *Head.* Stone. About 1912. Tate Gallery, London
2. **Marino Marini** (b.1901): *Horseman.* Bronze. 1952. Walker Art Center, Minneapolis
3. **Alexander Calder** (1898–1976): *Constellation with Diabolo.* Mobile. Wood and metal
4. **Jacques Lipchitz** (1891–1973): *Couple.* Bronze. 1928–9
5. **Jacques Lipchitz** (1891–1973): *Musical Instruments.* Bronze. 1924
6. **Raymond Duchamp-Villon** (1876–1918): *Head of the poet Baudelaire.* 1911. Musée Nationa d'Art Moderne, Paris
7. **Fritz Wotruba** (b.1907): *Standing Figure.* Breccia. 1953–5. Musée National d'Art Moderne, Paris
8. **Marino Marini** (b.1901): *Horse.* Bronze. 1950. Kunstverein (Sprengel Collection), Hanover

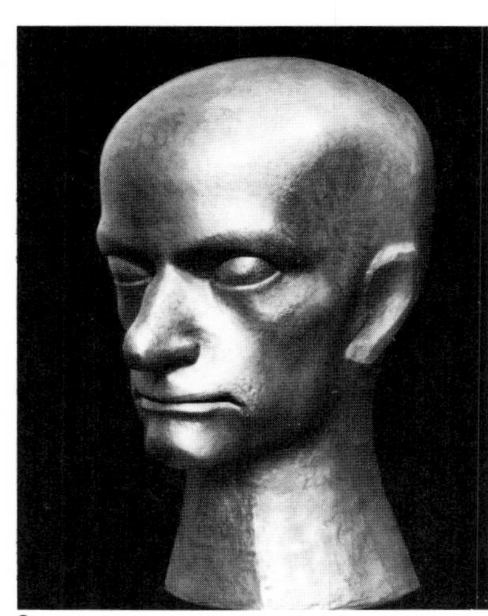
6

2

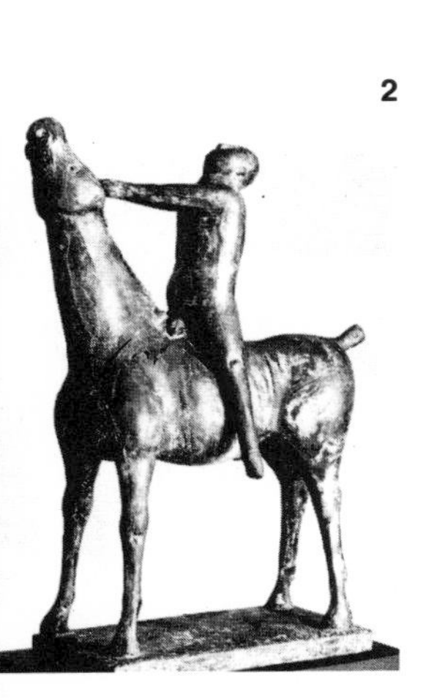

4

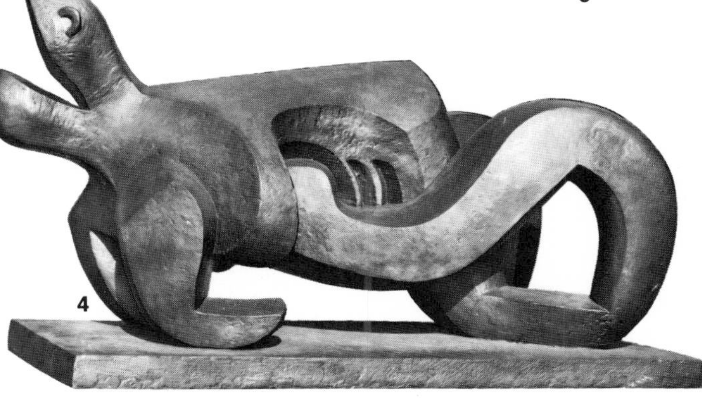

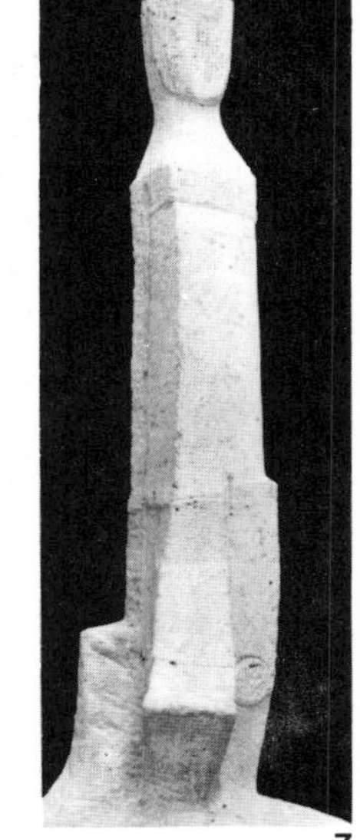

5

7

3

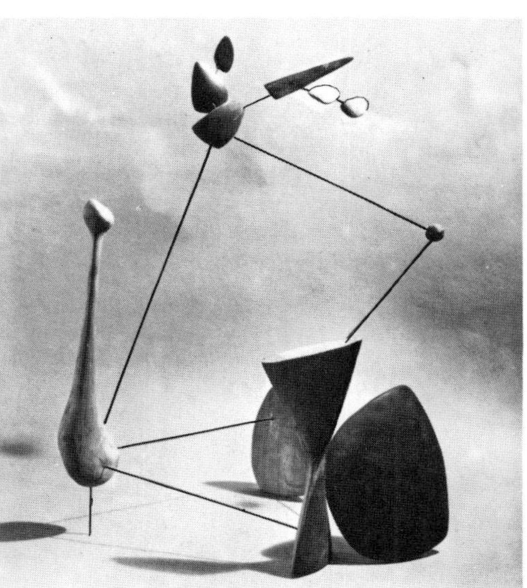

8

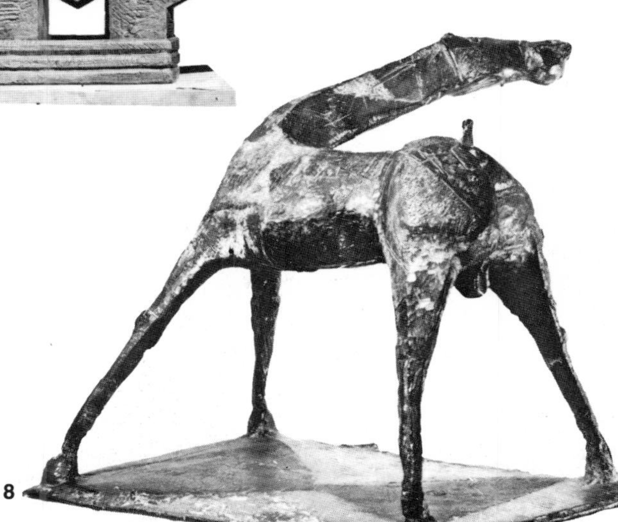

1. **Barbara Hepworth** (1903–75): *Concave Form* (*Wave II*). Bronze and wire. 1959
2. **Henry Moore** (b. 1898): *Reclining Figure.* Marble. 1957–8. UNESCO Building, Paris
3. **Henry Moore** (b.1898): *Reclining Figure.* Bronze. 1951. Private Collection
4. **Henry Moore** (b.1898): *Reclining Figure.* Study for a sculpture in wood. 1940. Private Collection
5. **Barbara Hepworth** (1903–75): *Two Figures* (*Menhirs*). Teakwood. 1954–5. Formerly collection of the artist
6. **Henry Moore** (b.1898): *Mother and Child.* Stone. 1924. City Art Gallery, Manchester
7. **Sir Jacob Epstein** (1880–1959): *The Madonna and Child.* 1950–2. Convent of the Holy Child Jesus, Cavendish Square, London

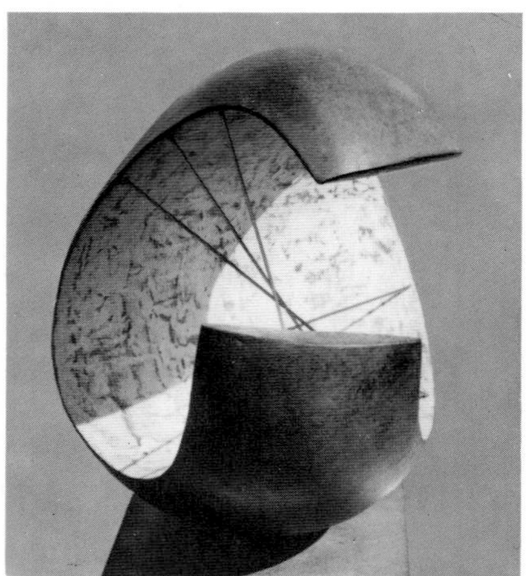

1

2

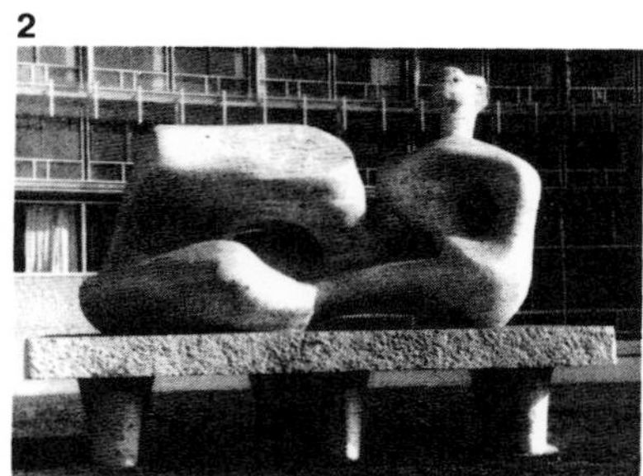

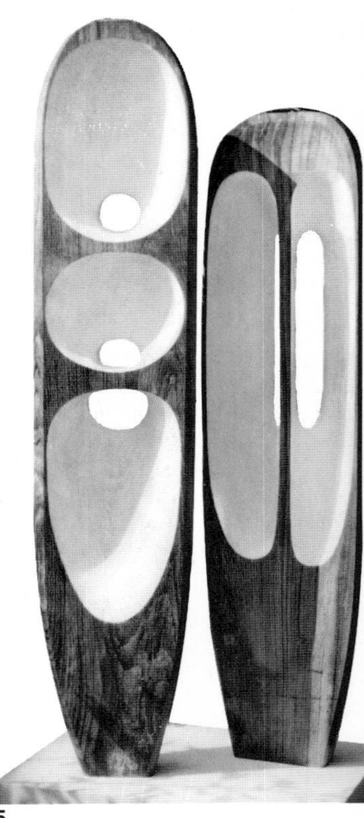

5

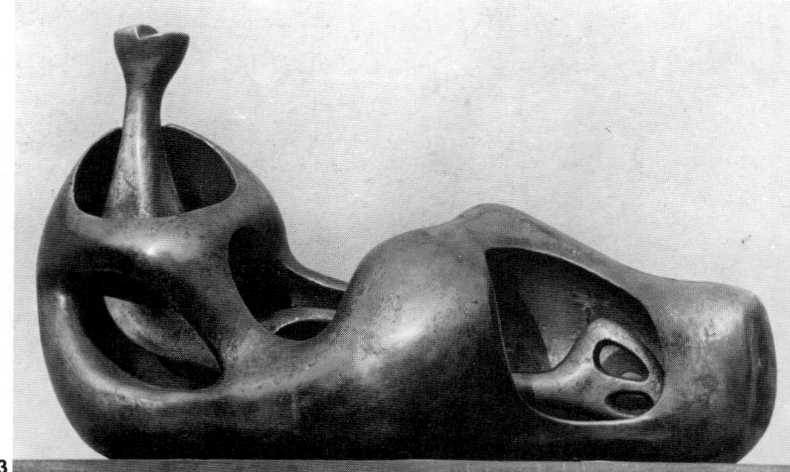

3

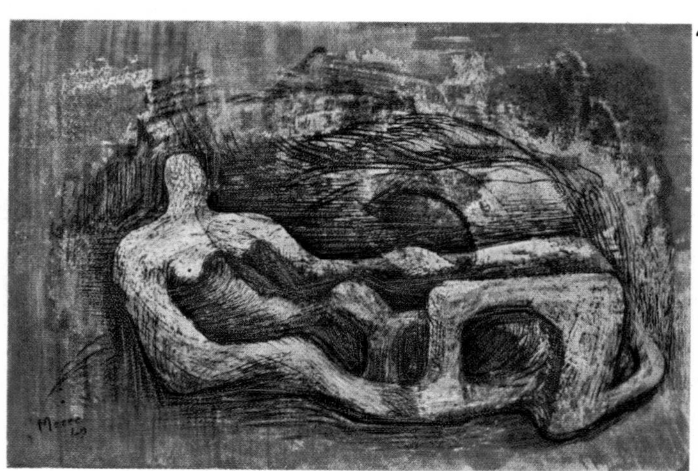

4

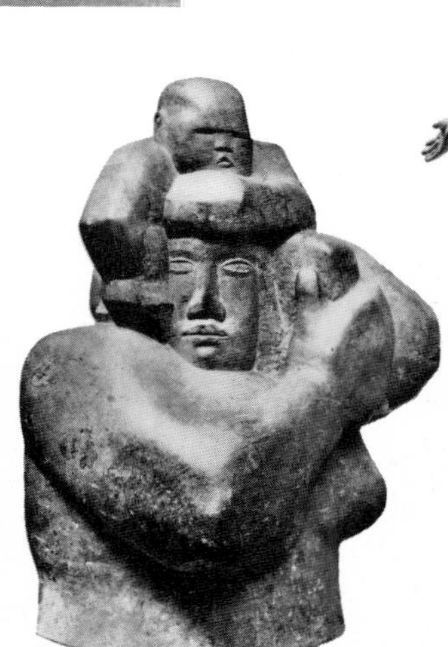

6

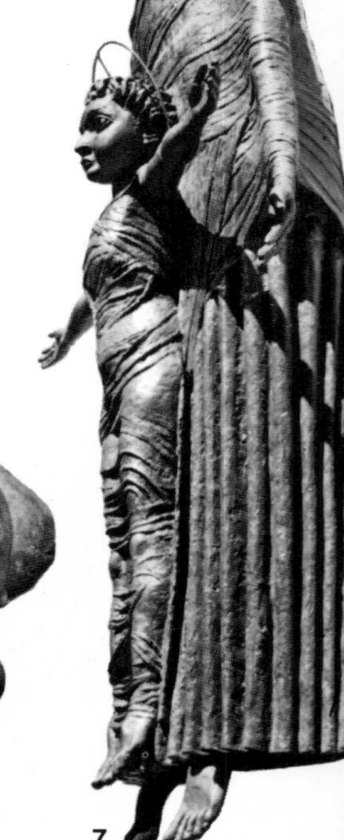

7

1. **Graham Sutherland** (b.1903): *Head of Thorns.* 1946. Private Collection
2. **Ben Nicholson** (b.1894): *Drop curtain for Leonide Massine's ballet 'Seventh Symphony by Beethoven'.* 1934. Private Collection
3. **Paul Nash** (1889–1946): *Pillar and Moon.* 1932–42. Tate Gallery, London
4. **Laurence Stephen Lowry** (1887–1976): *An Accident.* 1926. City Art Gallery, Manchester
5. **John Piper** (b.1903): *Somerset Place, Bath.* Watercolour. 1942. Tate Gallery, London
6. **Francis Bacon** (b.1909): *Man and Child.* 1963. Marlborough Fine Art Ltd, London

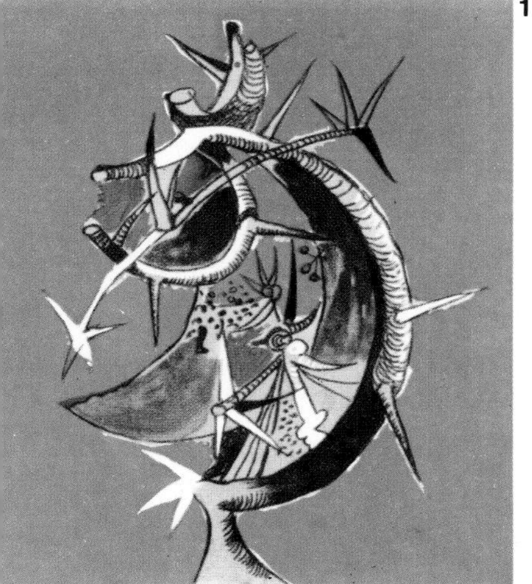

1

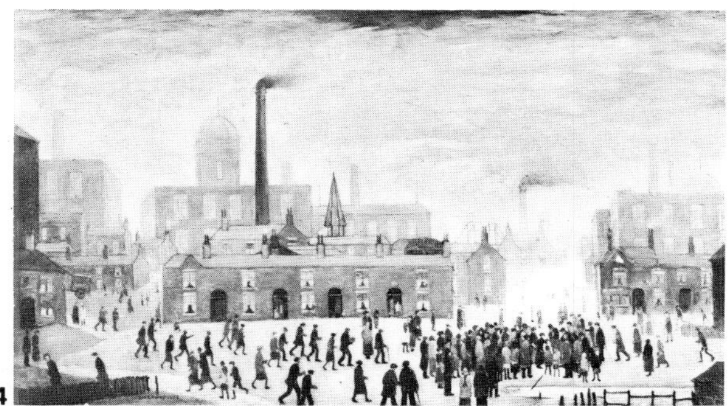

4

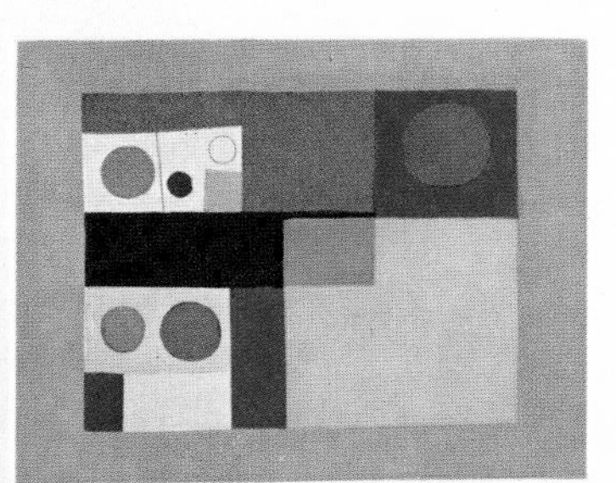

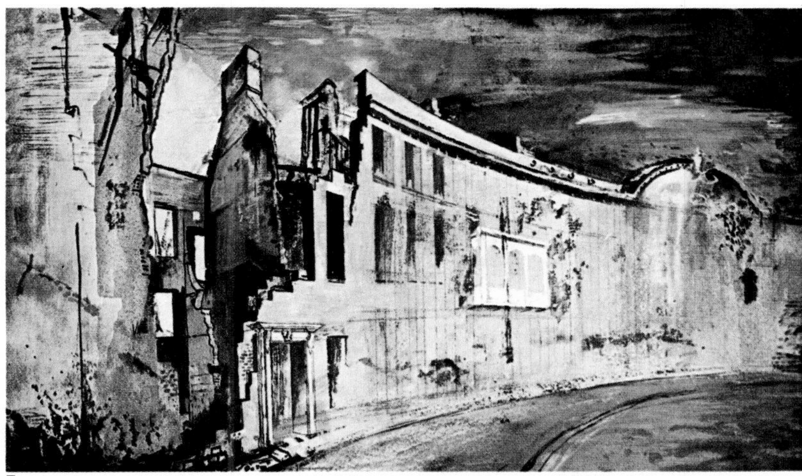

5

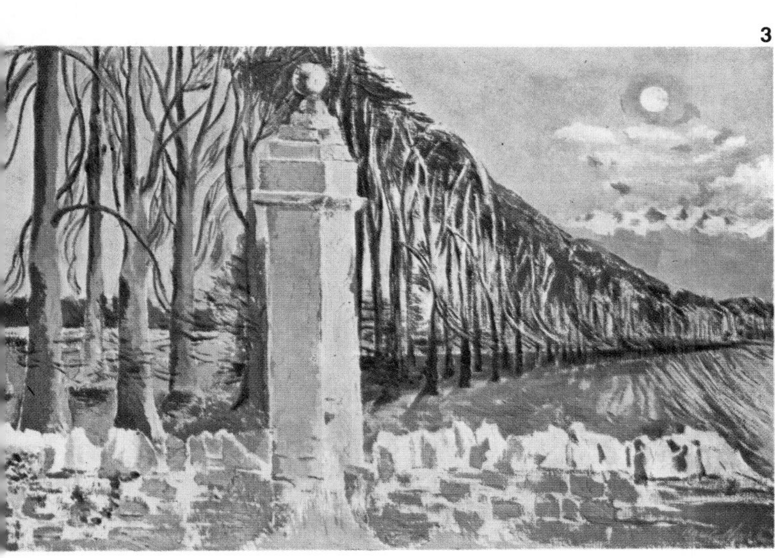

3

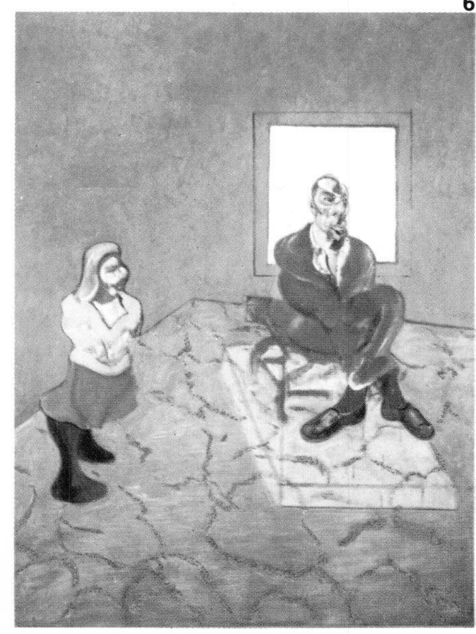

6

Frank Lloyd Wright (1869–1959)

1. Beth Sholem Synagogue, Elkins Park, Pennsylvania. 1957–9
2. Price Tower, Bartlesville, Oklahoma. 1955
3. Administrative buildings of the S.C. Johnson Wax Company, Racine, Wisconsin. 1936 and 1949
4. Solomon R. Guggenheim Museum, New York. 1956–9. Cross section of the main gallery showing the six stories and the ramp rising to the dome
5. The Edgar J. Kaufmann House, called 'Falling Water', Bear Run, Pennsylvania. 1936

3

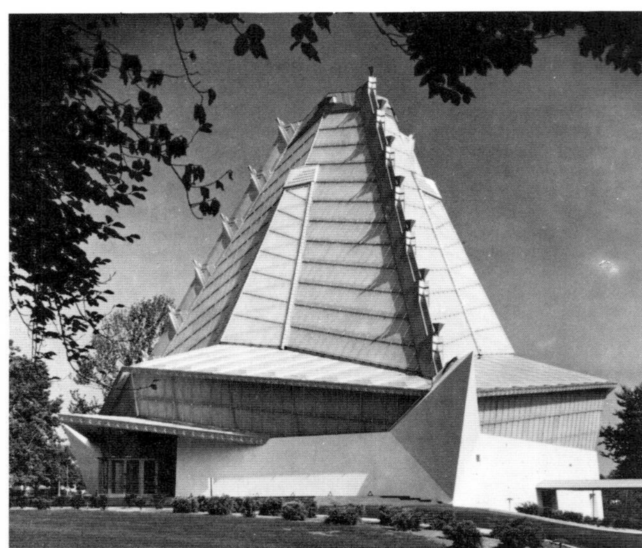

1

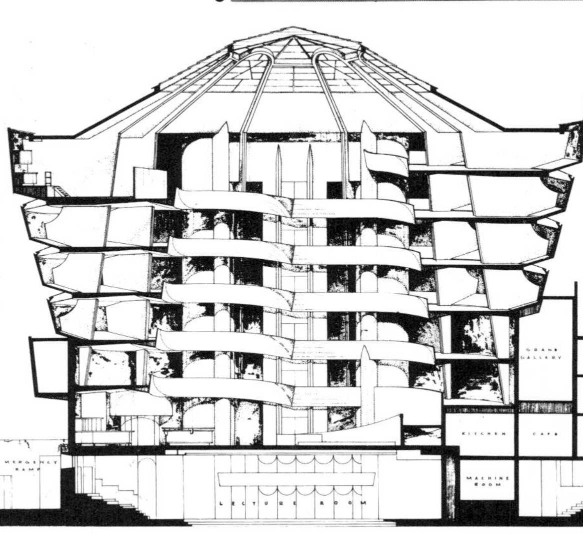

4

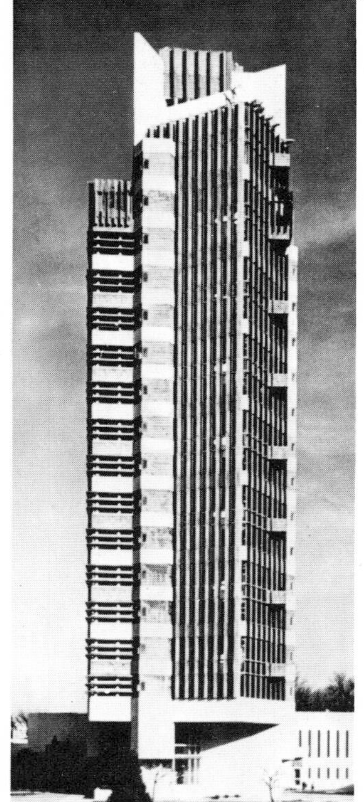

2

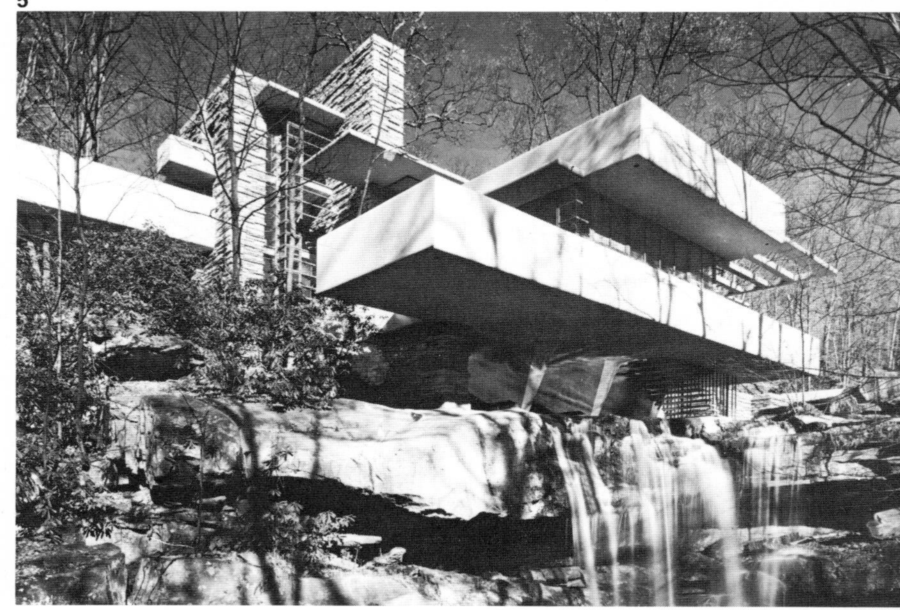

5

1. **Grant Wood** (1892–1942): *American Gothic.* 1930. Art Institute of Chicago
2. **Maurice Prendergast** (1859–1924): *Central Park, New York.* 1901. Whitney Museum of American Art, New York
3. **Ben Shahn** (1898–1969): *Handball.* 1939. Museum of Modern Art, New York
4. **Andrew Wyeth** (b.1917): *Christina's World.* 1949. Museum of Modern Art, New York
5. **Maurice Prendergast** (1859–1924): *Along the Boulevard.* Watercolour. Albright-Knox Art Gallery, Buffalo, New York
6. **Joseph Pickett** (1848–1918): *Manchester Valley.* About 1914–18. Museum of Modern Art, New York

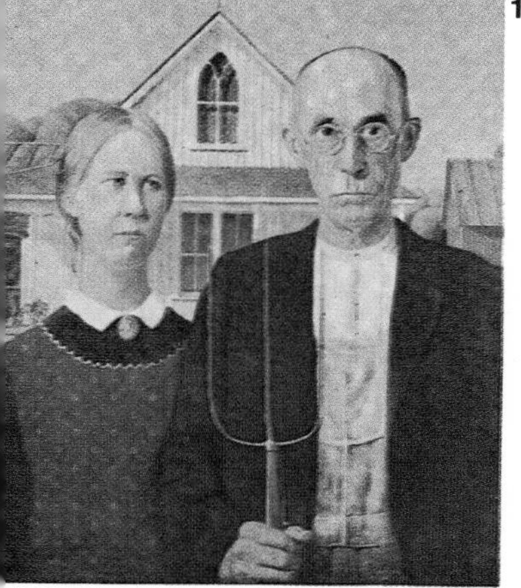
1

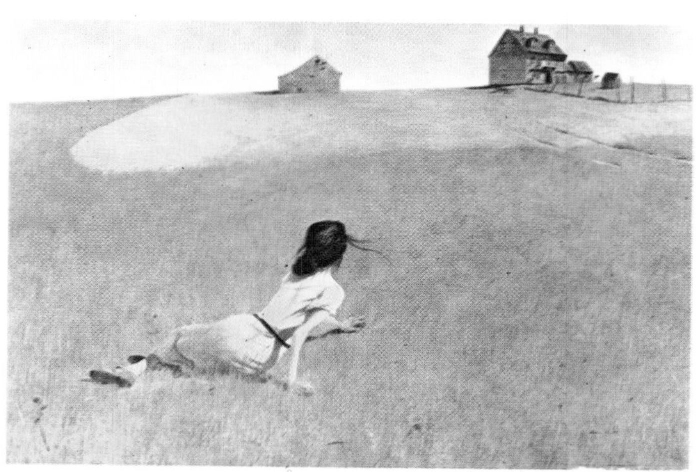
4

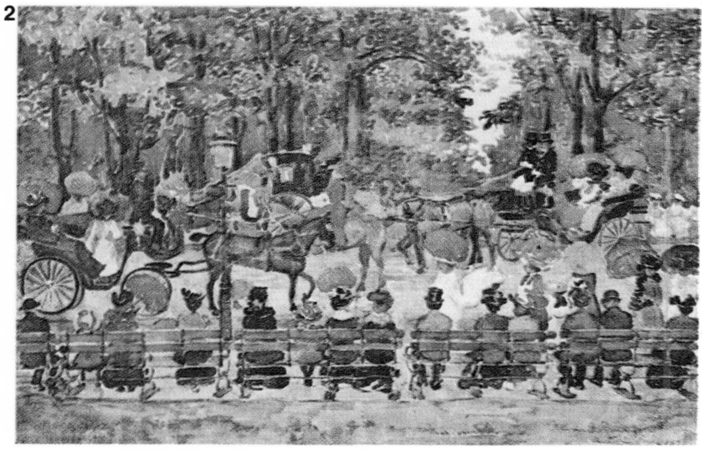
2

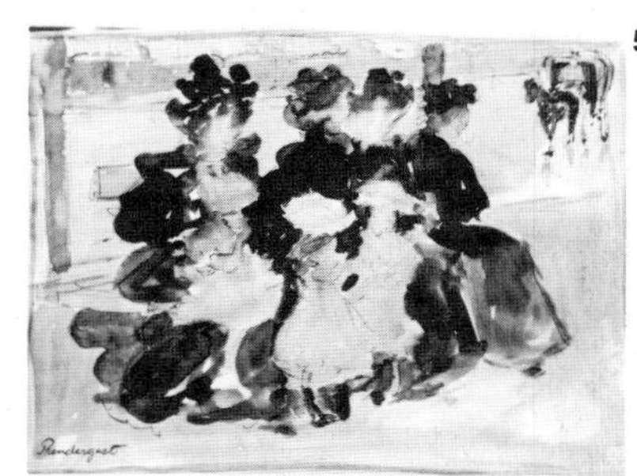

5

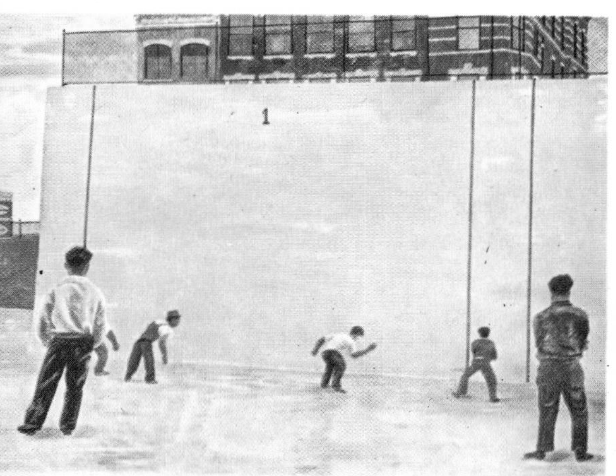

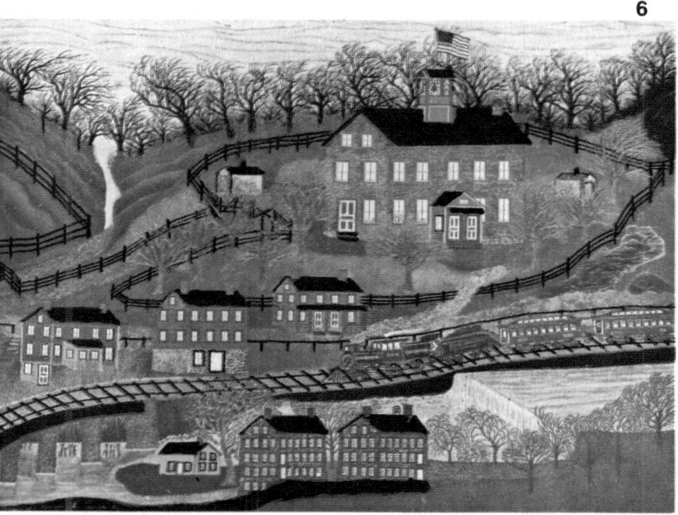
6

1

1. **Mark Rothko** (1903–70): *Sassrom.* 1958. Cardazzo Collection, Venice
2. **Robert Motherwell** (b.1915): *Elegy to the Spanish Republic, 34.* 1954. Albright-Knox Art Gallery, Buffalo, New York
3. **Franz Kline** (1910–62): *High Street.* 1950
4. **Robert Motherwell** (b.1915): *Pancho Villa Dead and Alive.* Gouache and oil, collage on board. 1943. Museum of Modern Art, New York
5. **Mark Rothko** (1903–70): *Number 10.* 1950. Museum of Modern Art, New York
6. **Franz Kline** (1910–62): *Green Vertical.* 1958. Sidney Janis Gallery, New York

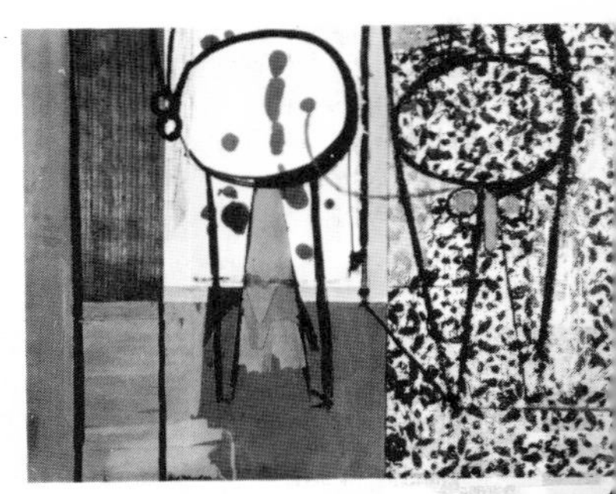

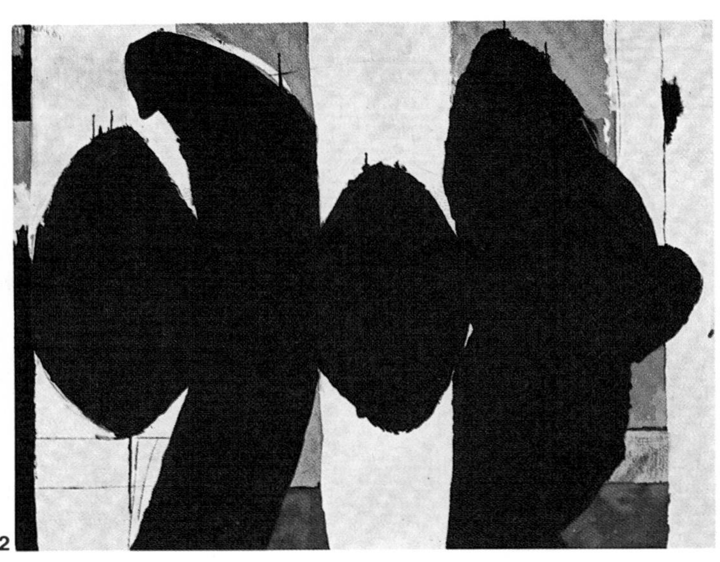

2

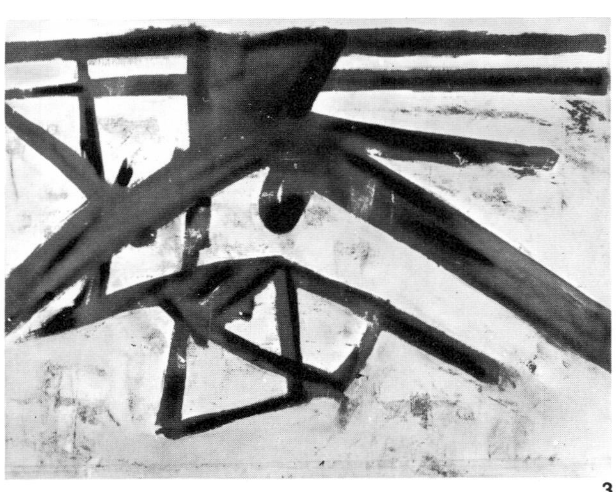

3

6

1. **Josef Albers** (1888–1976): *Fugue.* Engraved and painted frosted glass. 1925. Kunstmuseum, Basle
2. **Victor Vasarély** (b.1908): *Orion.* 1961 Architectonic collage
3. **Victor Vasarély** (b.1908): *'Mach-C'.* 1952–3
4. **Victor Vasarély** (b.1908): *Zebra.* 1935
5. **Bridget Riley** (b.1931): *Fall.* Acrylic on board. 1963. Tate Gallery, London
6. **Josef Albers** (1888–1976): *Study of Movement on a Plane*
7. **Yaacov Agam** (b.1928): *Transformable Movement Painting.* 1954

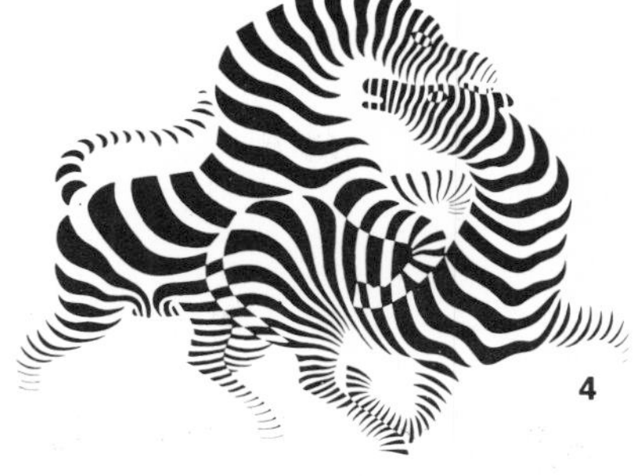

4

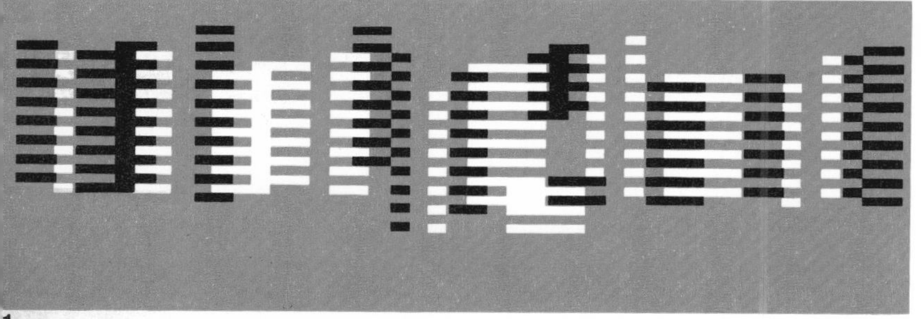

1

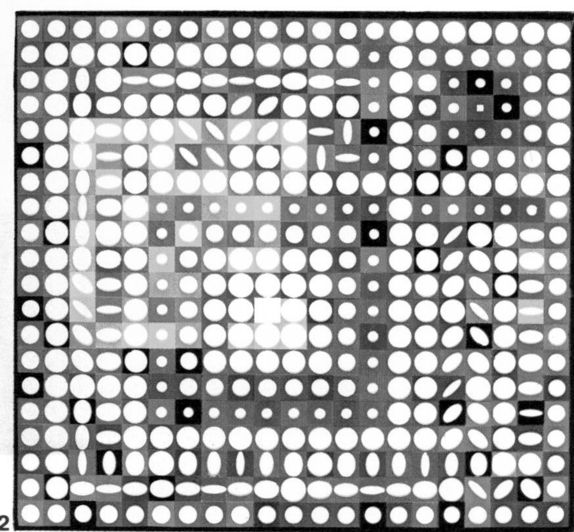

2

5

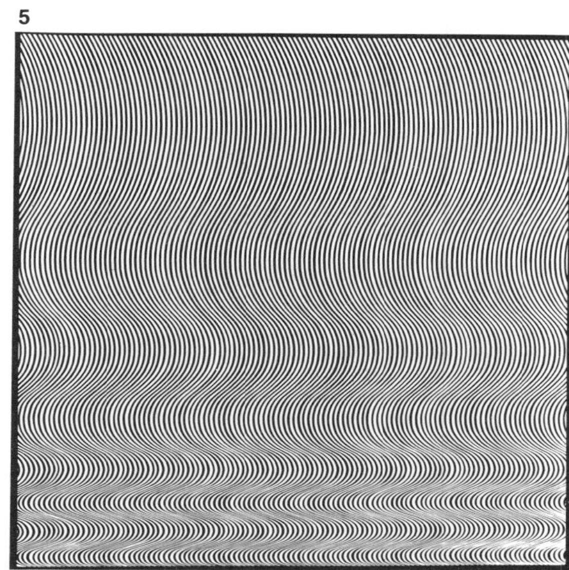

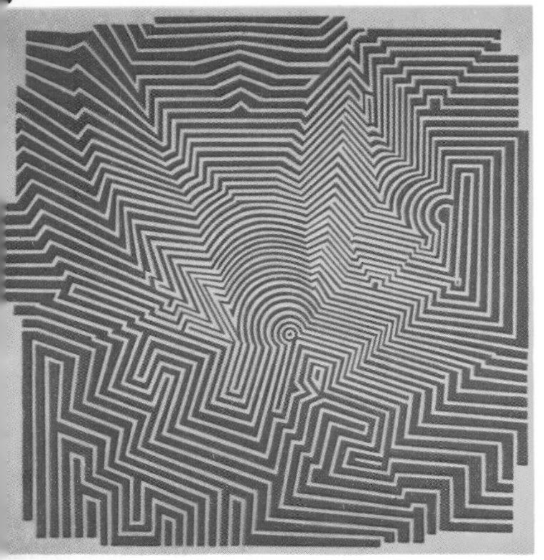

6

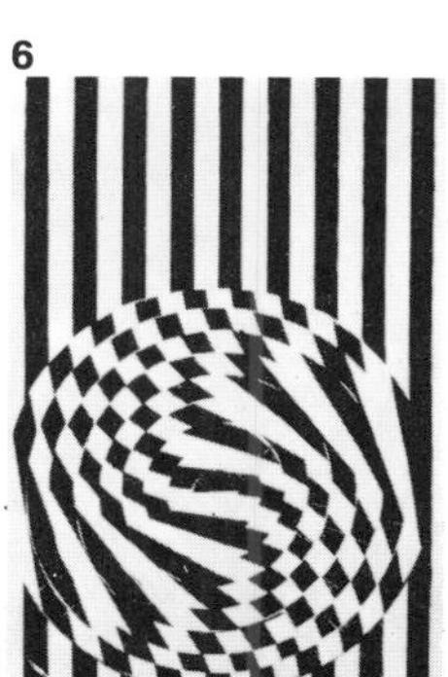

7

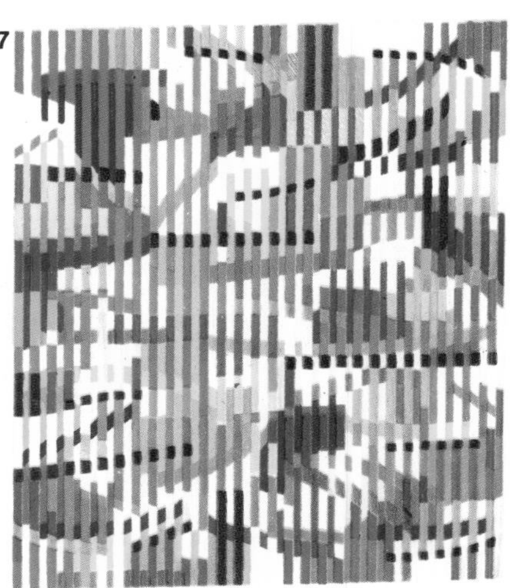

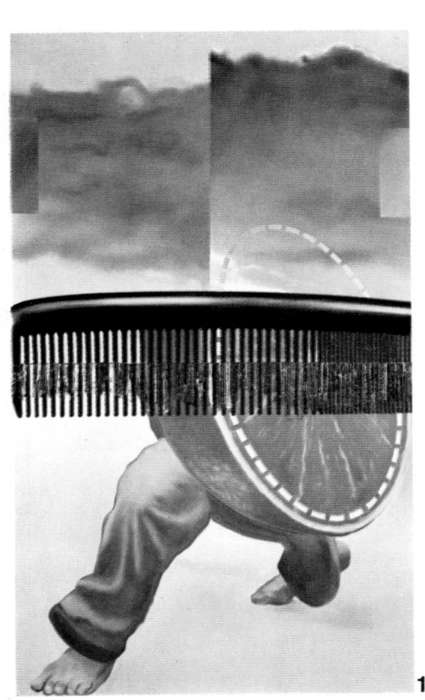

1

1. **James Rosenquist** (b.1933): *Early in the Morning.* 1963. Private Collection
2. **David Hockney** (b.1937): *A bigger Splash.* Acrylic on canvas. 1966–7. Private Collection
3. **Jasper Johns** (b.1930): *Field Painting.* 1963–4
4. **Robert Rauschenberg** (b.1925): *Tracer.* 1963. Private Collection
5. **Andy Warhol** (b.1930): *Marilyn Monroe.* Silkscreened photograph. 1962
6. **Tom Wesselmann** (b.1931): *Bathtub Collage.* Mixed media. 1963

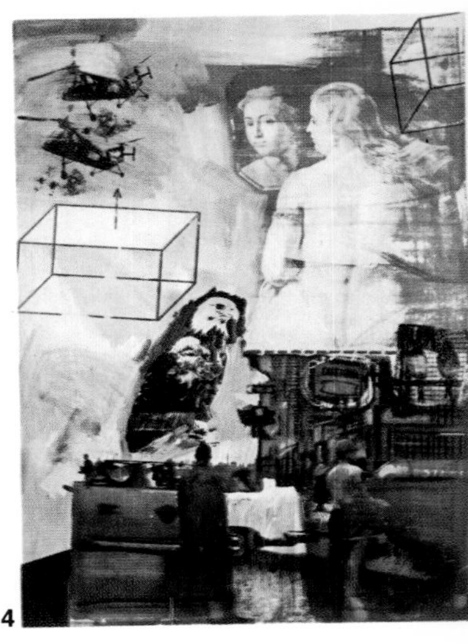

4

5

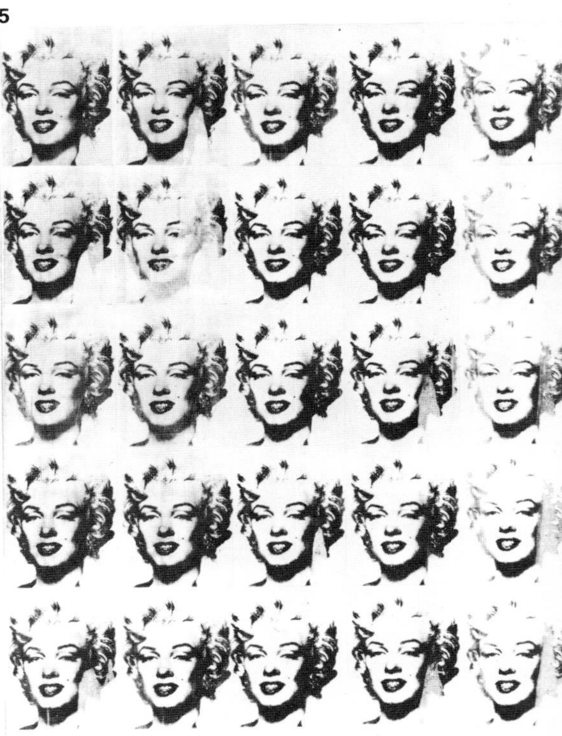

2

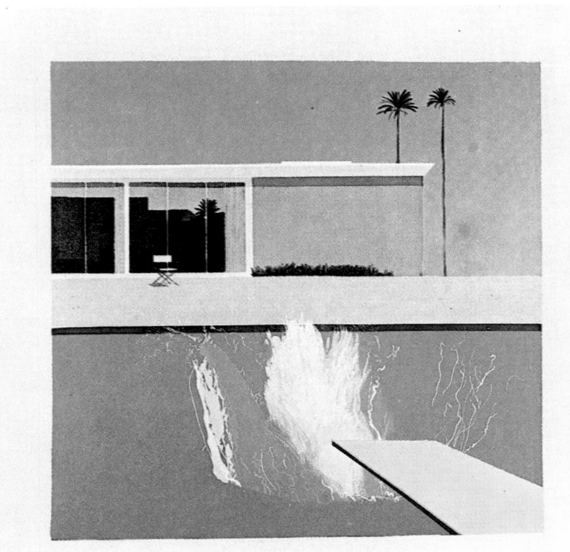

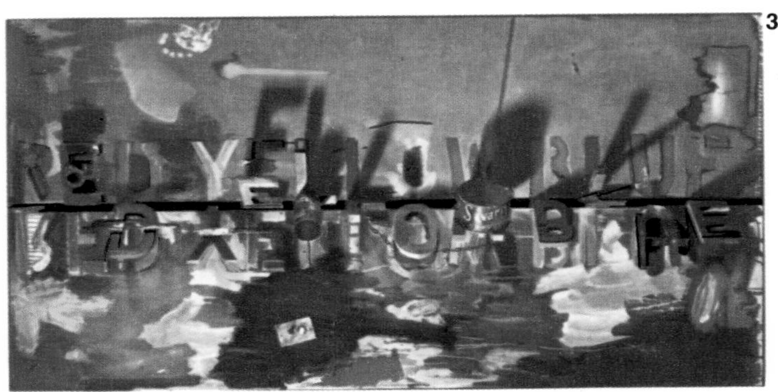

3

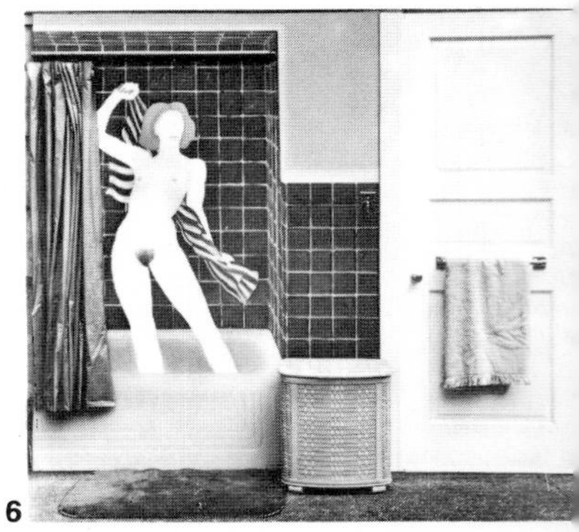

6

Biographical notes

The numbers at the end of the entries refer to pages on which works by that artist can be found.

Aalto, Alvar (*b.*1898 Finland). Finnish architect and one of the foremost European architects. **288**

Adam, Robert (*b.*1728 Kirkcaldy, Scotland, *d.*1792 London). One of the greatest 18th-century British architects; also decorator and furniture designer. Worked frequently with his brothers John and James; their classical style was enormously popular. **215**

Aertsen, Pieter (*b. c.*1507/8 Amsterdam, *d.*1575 Amsterdam). Netherlandish painter of genre and kitchen scenes, still lifes and religious pictures. Active in Antwerp, *c.*1535–55, before returning to Amsterdam. **142**

Agam (*b.*1928 Rishon-le-Zion, Israel). Yaacov Gipstein is an Israeli kinetic and Op artist; most of his works are variable paintings and reliefs. **305**

Albers, Josef (*b.*1888 Bottrop, Germany, *d.*1976 US). Naturalized American designer and painter; Bauhaus pupil and teacher. His dominant theme became the square, seen in his Homage to the Square series begun in 1949. **305**

Alberti, Leon Battista (*b.*1404 Genoa, *d.*1472 Rome). Renaissance man: architect, writer and scholar. His theoretical writings on art include *Della pittura* (1436) and *De re aedificatoria* (begun 1450). **89**

Albertinelli, Mariotto (*b.*1474 Florence, *d.*1515 Florence). Florentine painter; collaborated with Fra Bartolommeo; abandoned painting for inn-keeping. **103**

Altdorfer, Albrecht (*b. c.*1480 Regensburg, Bavaria, *d.*1538 Regensburg). Painter and engraver, he gave new importance to landscape painting. Represents the Danube school. **129, 150**

Andrea del Castagno (*b. c.*1419 Castagno, near Florence, *d.*1457 Florence). Important and influential Florentine painter. Departed from the Masaccio tradition and took up a more dramatic and linear style. **101**

Andrea del Sarto (*b.*1486 Florence, *d.*1530 Florence). Gifted contemporary of Raphael and Michelangelo. Epitome of Renaissance classicism but taught Pontormo and Rosso, leading Mannerists. **103**

Andrea Pisano (*b. c.*1290 Pontedera, near Pisa, *d.*1348 Orvieto). Sculptor, architect and goldsmith, most famous for his bronze door of the Baptistery and the bas-reliefs of the Campanile in Florence. **73**

Angelico, Fra (*b.*1400 Vicchio, Tuscany, *d.*1455 Rome). Fra Giovanni da Fiesole was a Dominican friar and an important painter. Most famous are his frescoes in the Convent of San Marco, Florence. **82**

Antonello da Messina (*b. c.*1430 Messina, Sicily, *d.*1479 Messina). Influenced by Flemish painting, reflected in his style and technique. He in turn influenced Giovanni Bellini and other Venetians. **102**

Apollodorus of Damascus (*fl.* late 2nd century). Syrian architect who worked for the Emperor Trajan in Rome; the Forum of Trajan is his best-known accomplishment. **43**

Arcimboldo, Giuseppe (*b.*1527 Milan, *d.*1593 Milan). Painted fantastic heads composed of flowers, vegetables and other objects. **126**

Arp, Jean (Hans) (*b.*1887 Strasbourg, *d.*1966 Locarno). Painter, sculptor and poet. Exhibited with the *Blaue Reiter,* helped to found Dada, and joined the Surrealists. **280**

Athenodoros (1st century BC). Greek sculptor said to have produced, with Polydoros and Hagesandros, the marble Laocoön group. **36**

Audubon, John James (*b.*1785 Haiti, *d.*1851 New York). American artist and naturalist. Best known for his *Birds of America.* **223**

Avercamp, Hendrick (*b.*1585 Amsterdam, *d.*1634 Kampen). Dutch painter who specialized in outdoor scenes filled with people. **177**

Bacon, Francis (*b.*1909 Dublin). Self-taught British painter, whose works are characterized by their expression of horror and terror. **301**

Baldung Grien, Hans (*b.*1484/5 Gmünd, Swabia, *d.*1545 Strasbourg). Painter, printmaker and designer of stained glass. Probably trained in Dürer's workshop. Spent most of his life in Strasbourg. **150**

Balla, Giacomo (*b.*1871 Turin, *d.*1958 Rome). Member of the Futurist movement during its brief life (1909 until the First World War) and became a leading abstract painter. **289**

Baltard, Victor (*b.*1805 Paris, *d.*1874 Paris). French architect whose most famous work was the central market, Les Halles, in Paris. **258**

Barlach, Ernst (*b.*1870 Wedel, near Hamburg, *d.*1938 Rostock, Mecklenburg). German sculptor, illustrator and dramatist. His most famous works are woodcarvings of figures. **298**

Barry, Sir Charles (*b.*1795 London, *d.*1860 London). Architect who designed, with Augustus Pugin, the Houses of Parliament in London. **227**

Bartolommeo, Fra (*b. c.*1472 Florence, *d.*1517 Florence). Under Savonarola's influence he became a Dominican friar. From 1504 he directed the workshop in the Convent of S. Marco. **103**

Bassano, Jacopo (*b. c.*1510 Bassano, near Venice, *d.*1592 Bassano). Jacopo dal Ponte, whose father and three sons were also painters, belongs to the Venetian school. He favoured rustic genre scenes with religious themes. **127**

Baumeister, Willi (*b.*1889 Stuttgart, *d.*1955 Stuttgart). Constructivist who turned to abstract painting. **297**

Bazille, Frédéric (*b.*1841 Montpellier, *d.*1870 Beaune-la-Rolande, Loiret). On close terms with many Impressionists. He painted mostly outdoor scenes with well-dressed figures. Killed in the Franco-Prussian War. **247**

Beardsley, Aubrey (*b.*1872 Brighton, *d.*1898 Menton). English illustrator who epitomized the Art Nouveau style. **234**

Beckmann, Max (*b.*1884 Leipzig, *d.*1950 New York). A leading German Expressionist painter and graphic artist. His paintings after the First World War reveal his deep pessimism, notably his famous triptychs. **262**

Bellechose, Henri (*b. c.*1380 Brabant, Flanders, *d.*1440/4 Dijon?). Active in Dijon, where he was court painter to the dukes of Burgundy. **132**

Bellini, Gentile (*b. c.*1429 Venice, *d.*1507 Venice). Son of Jacopo and brother of Giovanni Bellini, also painters of the Venetian school. His major work, a cycle of history paintings in the Doges' Palace, was destroyed by fire in 1577. **104**

Bellini, Giovanni (*b. c.*1430 Venice, *d.*1516 Venice). Son of Jacopo and brother of Gentile Bellini. Influenced by Mantegna (his brother-in-law); he in turn influenced Giorgioni, Titian and other younger Venetians. **104, 105**

Bellmer, Hans (*b.*1902 Katowice, Upper Silesia). Polish-French graphic artist, sculptor and painter associated with the Surrealists. The female body is his principal theme. **294**

Bellotto, Bernardo (*b.*1720 Venice, *d.*1780 Warsaw). Italian painter of *vedute* similar to those of his uncle, Canaletto, whose pupil he was. He was court painter in Dresden and Warsaw and produced many views of those cities. **173**

Berckheyde, Gerrit Adriaensz (*b.*1638 Haarlem, *d.*1698 Haarlem). Dutch painter of townscapes, particularly of Haarlem, Amsterdam and The Hague. **186**

Bermejo, Bartolomé (*b. c.*1440 Cordoba, *d. c.*1500). Spanish painter influenced by the Flemish school, evident in his use of oils and in his precise realism. **158**

Bernini, Gian Lorenzo (*b.*1598 Naples, *d.*1680 Rome). Baroque sculptor, architect, decorator and painter. Dominated sculpture and architecture in Rome under Popes Urban VIII and Alexander II. **159, 166, 167**

Berruguete, Alonso de (*b.*1489? Paredes de Nava, near Valladolid, *d.*1561 Toledo). The major Spanish sculptor of the 16th century; son of Pedro; trained first in Spain, then in Italy, where he was influenced by Mannerism. **158**

Berruguete, Pedro de (*b. c.*1450, *d. c.*1503). Spanish Renaissance painter; court painter to Ferdinand and Isabella; probably spent some years in Urbino. **158**

Blake, William (*b.*1757 London, *d.*1827 London). English poet, mystic, engraver and painter who wrote, illustrated, engraved and published a number of his own books and illustrated those of others, notably Dante and the Book of Job. **228**

Boccioni, Umberto (*b.*1882 Reggio Calabria, *d.*1916 Sorte, near Verona). Italian Futurist painter and theorist; also a sculptor; in 1914 he published a book on Futurist painting. **289**

Böcklin, Arnold (*b.*1827 Basle, *d.*1901 San Domenico, near Florence). Swiss Romantic painter; his most famous work is *The Isle of the Dead.* **238**

Boldoni, Giovanni (*b.*1845 Ferrara, *d.*1931 Paris). Italian painter very popular as a portraitist. Visited London before settling in Paris in 1872. **226**

Bologna, Giovanni (*b.*1529 Douai, *d.*1608 Florence). Born Jean Boulogne and also called Giambologna, he was one of the greatest of all Italian sculptors. He was born and trained in Flanders before he settled in Florence. His Mannerist style was imitated throughout Europe. He worked in both bronze and marble. **120**

Bonanno of Pisa (*fl.* 1174–86). Italian sculptor whose principal work, the decoration of the main door of Pisa Cathedral, was destroyed by fire. His Ranieri portal survives. **60, 72**

Bonington, Richard Parkes (*b.*1802 Arnold, near Nottingham, *d.*1828 London). English landscape painter who spent much of his life in France. Died young of consumption. **229**

Bonnard, Pierre (*b.*1867 Fontenay-aux-Roses, near Paris, *d.*1947 Le Cannet). French painter and graphic artist; joined the Nabis, 1890, before taking up a more Impressionist style known as *Intimisme.* **260**

Borch, Gerard ter (*b.*1617 Zwolle, *d.*1681 Deventer). Dutch genre and portrait painter famed for his detail and treatment of textures. **181**

Borromini, Francesco (*b.*1599 Bissone, near Lugano, *d.*1667 Rome). One of the great architects of the Italian High Baroque, he was a contemporary and bitter rival of Bernini. He rejected classicism for a more complex style, full of movement and contrast. **168**

Bosch, Hieronymus (*b. c.*1450 's Hertogenbosch, *d.*1516 's Hertogenbosch). Flemish painter of genius, whose fantasies are extraordinarily inventive and deeply symbolic. **136**

Botticelli, Sandro (*b. c.*1445 Florence, *d.*1510 Florence). One of the great Renaissance painters in Florence, he was probably taught by Fra Filippo Lippi after an early training as a goldsmith. His first works were influenced by Verrocchio and Pollaiuolo. Some of his most famous paintings were commissioned by the Medici. He was deeply affected by Savonarola's teaching. His popularity declined after 1500, as the modern ideas of Leonardo and Michelangelo gained favour. **98, 99**

Bouchardon, Edmé (*b.*1698 Chaumont, *d.*1762 Paris). French sculptor active in Rome and Paris; rejected the fashionable Rococo for a more classical style. **203**

Boucher, François (*b.*1703 Paris, *d.*1770 Paris). Rococo decorator and painter, he was a protégé of Mme de Pompadour and became painter to the king in 1765. He also designed tapestries. **207**

Boudin, Eugène (*b.*1824 Honfleur, *d.*1898 Deauville). On the Normandy coast, where he spent most of his life, he painted seascapes and beach scenes with luminous skies that anticipate Impressionism. **247**

Bouts, Dieric (*b. c.*1415 Haarlem, *d.*1475 Louvain). Netherlandish painter strongly influenced by Rogier van der Weyden. He in turn influenced 15th-century German painting. **134**

Bramante (*b.*1444 near Urbino, *d.*1514 Rome). A major architect of the High Renaissance, he settled in Rome in 1499. His Tempietto in Rome epitomizes the High Renaissance style. **113**

Brancusi, Constantin (*b.*1876 Rumania, *d.*1957 Paris). Outstanding and influential modern sculptor; he spent most of his life in Paris. **298**

Braque, Georges (*b.*1882 Argenteuil, *d.*1963 Paris). Developed Cubism with Picasso and is one of the major artists of the 20th century. **275**

Breuer, Marcel (*b.*1902 Pécs, Hungary). Architect who studied and taught at the Bauhaus and worked closely with Gropius. Settled in America in 1937. **287**

Bril, Paul (*b.*1554 Antwerp, *d.*1626 Rome). Flemish landscape artist who spent most of his life in Rome. He is best known for his small paintings on copper. **177**

Bronzino, Agnolo (*b.*1503 Florence, *d.*1572 Florence). Pupil of Pontormo; leading Mannerist portraitist in Florence. **119**

Brouwer, Adriaen (*b.*1605/6 Oudenaarde, *d.*1638 Antwerp). Brilliant Flemish genre painter of peasant life. **177**

Brown, Ford Madox (*b.*1821 Calais, *d.*1893 London). English painter; associated with the Pre-Raphaelites though not a member; painted literary, historical and genre pictures. **233**

Bruant, Libéral (*b. c.*1635 Paris, *d.*1697 Paris). French architect; he built the Hôtel des Invalides in Paris. **200**

Bruegel, Jan (*b.*1568 Brussels, *d.*1625 Antwerp). Called 'Velvet Bruegel'; son of Pieter Bruegel the Elder; painted flowers and landscapes. **177**

Bruegel, Pieter (*b. c.*1525 Brögel, *d.*1569 Brussels). One of the greatest Netherlandish painters of landscape and daily life. Also a satirist in the tradition of Bosch. Called 'Pieter Bruegel the Elder' to distinguish him from his elder son. **140, 141**

Brugghen, Hendrick ter (*b.*1588 Deventer?, *d.*1629 Utrecht). Painter of the Utrecht school, whose members were strongly influenced by Caravaggio; painted figures and religious pictures. **177**

Brunelleschi, Filippo (*b.*1377 Florence, *d.*1446 Florence). The creator and supreme master of Italian Renaissance architecture, which was inspired by the forms of classical Rome. **86, 87**

Buffet, Bernard (*b.*1928 Paris). French painter and illustrator whose work is characterized by a spiky style and muddy grey colours. **281**

Burghausen, Hans von (*d.*1432 Landshut, near Munich). German mason and architect from Burghausen in Upper Bavaria. He built a number of churches. **68**

Burne-Jones, Sir Edward Coley (*b.*1833 Birmingham, *d.*1898 London). English painter associated with the Pre-Raphaelites; he also designed stained-glass windows and tapestries. **232**

Burnham, Daniel Hudson (*b.*1846 Henderson, NY, *d.*1912 Heidelberg). Leading American architect of the Chicago School; collaborated with Root. **286**

Calder, Alexander (*b.*1898 Philadephia, *d.*1976). American sculptor who had trained and practised as an engineer. His ingenious combining of engineering and sculpture resulted in stabiles and mobiles. **299**

Callicrates (*fl.* mid-5th century BC). Greek architect; collaborated on the Parthenon in Athens; thought to have designed the Temple of Athena Nike, Athens. **33**

Callot, Jacques (*b.*1592/3 Nancy, *d.*1635 Nancy). One of the most important early masters of the art of engraving and etching. **199**

Cameron, Charles (*b. c.*1740 Scotland, *d.*1812 St Petersburg). Scottish architect; all of his works are in Russia, where he lived from about 1779. An admirer and follower of Adam. **224**

Campin, Robert (*b. c.*1378 Valenciennes?, *d.*1444 Tournai). Also called the Master of Flémalle, he is one of the most important painters of the Flemish school. He taught Rogier van der Weyden. **132**

Canaletto (*b.*1697 Venice, *d.*1768 Venice). Born Giovanni Antonio Canal, he specialized in *vedute*, or city views, and enjoyed immense popularity in Italy and in England, where he lived for some years. **172, 173**

Canova, Antonio (*b.*1757 Possagno, *d.*1822 Venice). The most famous Neoclassical sculptor in Italy. **226**

Caravaggio, Michelangelo Merisi da (*b.*1571 Caravaggio, Lombardy, *d.*1610 Port'Ercole, Tuscany). A leading though controversial painter in his day, whose revolutionary ideas of lighting and his harsh realism profoundly influenced successive generations of artists throughout Europe. **160, 161**

Carpaccio, Vittore (*b. c.*1465/7 Venice, *d.*1525/6 Venice). Venetian painter influenced by Gentile and Giovanni Bellini. His best works are his narrative cycles such as *The Legend of St Ursula* (Accademia, Venice). **106**

Carracci, Agostino (*b.*1557 Bologna, *d.*1602 Parma). Elder brother of Annibale, with whom he worked briefly on the Palazzo Farnese decorations. **163**

Carracci, Annibale (*b.*1560 Bologna, *d.*1609 Rome). The greatest of a family of painters; his work is in the classical tradition. Most famous is his monumental ceiling decoration in the Palazzo Farnese in Rome. **159, 163**

Cassatt, Mary (*b.*1845 Pittsburgh, *d.*1926 Mesnil-Beaufresne, Oise). American painter and printmaker; exhibited with the Impressionists and helped to promote them in America. **236**

Cavallini, Pietro (*fl.* 1273–1308). Italian painter; did the frescoes in S. Cecilia in Trastevere, Rome. **73**

Cellini, Benvenuto (*b.*1500 Florence, *d.*1571 Florence). Sculptor and goldsmith, but perhaps most famous for his *Autobiography*. He was influenced by Mannerism and represents the Second School of Fontainebleau. **120**

Cézanne, Paul (*b.*1839 Aix-en-Provence, *d.*1906 Aix-en-Provence). The most important Post-Impressionist, whose innovations influenced all subsequent major art movements. **253**

Chagall, Marc (*b.*1887 Vitebsk, Russia). Childhood memories, Russian folk-tales and, later, religious themes were the main subjects of his imaginative paintings. His fantasies anticipated Surrealism. **279**

Chambers, Sir William (*b.*1723 Göteborg, Sweden, *d.*1796 London). Architect; settled in London in 1755; most of his works are rigidly classical. Founder member of the RA. **214**

Chardin, Jean-Baptiste-Siméon (*b.*1699 Paris, *d.*1779 Paris). The greatest French genre and still-life painter of the 18th century. **204**

Charton, Enguerrand (*b. c.*1410 Laon, *d.*after 1462 Avignon). French painter active mainly around Avignon; famous for two altarpieces. **153**

Chirico, Giorgio de (*b.*1888 Volo, Greece, *d.*1978). Italian painter, writer and stage designer, he founded the Metaphysical school and then joined, briefly, the Surrealists. **292**

Christus, Petrus (*b. c.*1410 near Ghent, *d.*1472/3 Bruges). Netherlandish artist influenced by Van Eyck, Rogier van der Weyden and Bouts. **134**

Cima da Conegliano, Giovanni Battista (*b.*1459/60 Conegliano, *d.*1517/18 Conegliano). Venetian painter much influenced by Giovanni Bellini. **126**

Cimabue (*b.*1240/50 Florence, *d.*1302? Pisa). Florentine painter who combined the Byzantine style with hints of a new naturalism that was to be developed by Giotto. **73**

Civitali, Matteo di Giovanni (*b.*1436 Lucca, *d.*1501 Lucca). Italian sculptor, medalist and architect. **103**

Claude Lorrain (*b.*1600 Champagne, Lorraine, *d.*1682 Rome). Born Claude Gellée, he spent most of his life in Rome, whose countryside was the main subject of his tranquil and romantic landscapes. **197**

Clouet, François (*b. c.*1522 Tours, *d.*1572 Paris). He succeeded his father, Jean Clouet, as court painter in Paris, and became even more famous as a royal portrait painter. **154**

Clouet, Jean (*b. c.*1485, *d. c.*1540 Paris). Of Flemish origin, he became court painter in France and specialized in royal portraits. **154**

Cole, Thomas (*b.*1801 Bolton-le-Moors, Lancs, *d.*1848 Catskill, NY). American landscape painter. **23**

Constable, John (*b.*1776 East Bergholt, Suffolk, *d.*1837 London). One of the greatest English landscape painters, he had considerable influence on art in France, where his genius was recognized much earlier than in his own country. **230**

Cooper, Samuel (*b.*1609 London, *d.*1672 London). Miniaturist who was one of the greatest English portrait painters of the 17th century. **212**

Copley, John Singleton (*b.*1738 Boston, *d.*1815 London). American painter whose early career was as a portraitist. From 1775, when he settled in England, he painted mainly large-scale, modern history pictures. **223**

Corinth, Lovis (*b.*1858 Tapiau, East Prussia, *d.*1925 Zandvoort). Sometimes called a German Impressionist; a member of the Berlin *Sezession* group. After a stroke in 1911, his style became more Expressionistic. **262**

Corot, Jean-Baptiste-Camille (*b.*1796 Paris, *d.*1875 Paris). Important French landscape painter of the 19th century; he profoundly influenced the course of landscape painting in France. **240**

Correggio, Antonio Allegri da (*b.*1489/94 Correggio, Reggio Emilia, *d.*1534 Correggio). Influenced by Leonardo, Michelangelo and Raphael, but he rejected their clarity and classical balance for a more sensual, illusionistic style that was to be taken up a century later by the Baroque artists. **117**

Cosmati artists (*c.*1100–1300 Rome). Skilled decorators in coloured glass, semi-precious stones and gilding; Cosmati work was applied to cloisters, floors, façades, etc. **72**

Cossa, Francesco del (*b. c.*1435 Ferrara, *d. c.*1477 Bologna). Influenced by Mantegna and Piero della Francesca; his best-known works are his frescoes at the Palazzo Schifanoia in Ferrara. **107**

Cotman, John Sell (*b.*1782 Norwich, *d.*1842 London). British landscape watercolourist and leading member of the Norwich school. **229**

Courbet, Gustave (*b.*1819 Ornans, Doubs, *d.*1877 La Tour-de-Peilz, Switzerland). A revolutionary French painter who espoused a realistic, naturalistic approach to art, and vigorously practised it. **241**

Cranach the Elder, Lucas (*b.*1472 Kronach, Franconia, *d.*1553 Weimar). Painter, engraver and designer of woodcuts, he was one of the leading artists of the German Renaissance. His interest in landscape links him to the Danube school. **151**

Cranach the Younger, Lucas (*b.*1515 Wittenberg, *d.*1586 Weimar). Son of Lucas the Elder; he took over his father's thriving workshop in 1553. **151**

Crivelli, Carlo (*b. c.*1435 Venice, *d. c.*1495). Renaissance painter of religious subjects. Though born in Venice, he spent most of his life in the Marches. **107**

Crome, John (*b.*1768 Norwich, *d.*1821 Norwich). Landscape painter of the Norwich school. He was strongly influenced by the 17th-century Dutch landscape painters. **217**

Cuyp, Aelbert (*b.*1620 Dordrecht, *d.*1691 Dordrecht). One of the great Dutch landscape artists, he also painted seascapes, portraits and still lifes. **182**

Daddi, Bernardo (*b. c.*1290 Florence, *d.*1348? Florence). Pupil of Giotto but also influenced by the Sienese school, in particular by Lorenzetti. **77**

Dali, Salvador (*b.*1904 Figueras, Catalonia). Spanish painter; became a Surrealist in 1929. **292**

Daubigny, Charles-François (*b.*1817 Paris, *d.*1878 Paris). French landscape painter strongly influenced by the Barbizon school. **244**

Daumier, Honoré (*b.*1808 Marseilles, *d.*1879 Valmondois). Painter, lithographer and satirical caricaturist. **245**

David, Gerard (*b. c.*1460 Oudewater, *d.*1523 Bruges). The last important representative of the 15th-century Bruges school. **138**

David, Jacques-Louis (*b.*1748 Paris, *d.*1825 Brussels). The leading French painter of the Neoclassical style, and closely involved in the politics of his age, as a revolutionary and later as an ardent Bonapartist. **9, 210**

Degas, Edgar (*b.*1834 Paris *d.*1917 Paris). A great and innovative artist and sculptor; a regular contributor to the Impressionist exhibitions. Most famous are his paintings of dancers. **250**

Delacroix, Eugène (*b.*1798 Charenton-St-Maurice, *d.*1863 Paris). The major French Romantic painter, and rival of the classicist, Ingrés. **243**

Delaunay, Robert (*b.*1885 Paris, *d.*1941 Montpellier). Painter who moved from Neo-Impressionism to Cubism to abstract art, exhibited with the *Blaue Reiter* and invented Orphism. **278**

Delaunay, Sonia Terk (*b.*1885 Ukraine). Russian-born wife of Robert Delaunay; her paintings reflect her preoccupation with colours. **278**

Delvaux, Paul (*b.*1897 Antheit, near Huy). Belgian Surrealist painter. **293**

Denis, Maurice (*b.*1870 Granville, *d.*1943 Paris). French painter; co-founder of the Nabis. **261**

Derain, André (*b.*1880 Chatou, Seine-et-Oise, *d.*1954 Garches, Seine-et-Oise). Fauve painter; also sculptor and designer of woodcuts. **266**

Desiderio da Settignano (*b. c.*1430 Settignano, *d.*1464 Florence). Gifted Florentine sculptor whose style was more delicate than Donatello's. He used the technique of very low relief (*relievo schiacciato*). **92**

Desportes, François (*b.*1661 Champigneulle, Haute-Marne, *d.*1743 Paris). French painter who specialized in animal and still-life pictures. **204**

Devis, Arthur (*b.*1711 Preston, Lancs, *d.*1787 Brighton). English painter of conversation pieces portraying upper-middle-class life. **217**

Domenichino (*b.*1581 Bologna, *d.*1641 Naples). Born Domenico Zampieri, he assisted Carracci in the decorating of the Palazzo Farnese. **165**

Domenico Veneziano (*b. c.*1410 Venice, *d.*1461 Florence). Florentine school though born in Venice. His major known work is the S. Lucia altarpiece now in the Uffizi. **85**

Donatello (*b. c.*1386 Florence, *d.*1466 Florence). One of the major figures of the early Renaissance and the greatest Florentine sculptor of his day. **90, 91**

Dongen, Kees van (*b.*1877 Delfshaven, near Rotterdam, *d.*1968 Monte Carlo). He spent his working life in France and was associated with the Fauves. He become a popular portrait painter. **266**

Dosso Dossi (*fl.* 1512–42 (*d.*) Ferrara). Painted mainly mythological and allegorical pictures. **126**

Dou, Gerrit (*b.*1613 Leiden, *d.*1675 Leiden). Dutch genre and figure painter. Pupil of Rembrandt. **180**

Duccio di Buoninsegna (*b. c.*1255 Siena, *d. c.*1319 Siena). A great Sienese painter, whose masterpiece is the Maestà altarpiece painted for the cathedral in Siena. **76**

Duchamp, Marcel (*b.*1887 Blainville, *d.*1968 Neuilly-sur-Seine). Painter and sculptor; brother of Raymond Duchamp-Villon and Jacques Villon. He anticipated Dada before its invention. He spent most of his life in New York. **290**

Duchamp-Villon, Raymond (*b.*1876 Damville, Eure, *d.*1918 Cannes). Sculptor; brother of Marcel Duchamp and Jacques Villon. **299**

Dufy, Raoul (*b.*1877 Le Havre, *d.*1953 Forcalquier, Basses-Alpes). Painter and designer much influenced by the Fauves, with whom he exhibited. **266**

Dürer, Albrecht (*b.*1471 Nuremberg, *d.*1528 Nuremberg). Painter, draughtsman, printmaker and the greatest German artist. He was deeply affected by the ideas of the Italian Renaissance. **129, 148, 149**

Dyck, Sir Anthony van (*b.*1599 Antwerp, *d.*1641 London). Flemish Baroque portrait painter; assistant of Rubens. He lived in England from 1632 and was court painter to Charles I, was knighted him. **176**

Eakins, Thomas (*b.*1844 Philadelphia, *d.*1916 Philadelphia). American painter; his pictures are realistic. **237**

Eiffel, Gustave (*b.*1832 Dijon, *d.*1923 Paris). French engineer who achieved the feat of using iron to construct the then highest building in the world, the Eiffel Tower. He also built enormous bridges on the same principles. **258**

Ensor, James (*b.*1860 Ostend, *d.*1949 Ostend). Belgian Expressionist painter and engraver. **270**

Epstein, Sir Jacob (*b.*1880 New York, *d.*1959 London). American-born English sculptor; worked in stone and bronze. **300**

Ernst, Max (*b.*1891 Brühl, near Cologne, *d.*1976). Naturalized French painter; introduced Dada to Cologne and became a leading Surrealist. **290**

Exekias (*fl.* late 6th century BC). Greek potter and vase painter whose work dominates the production of black-figure pottery in the late 6th century. **29**

Eyck, Jan van (*b. c.*1390 Maaseik or Maastricht?, *d.*1441 Bruges). One of the most important painters of the Netherlandish school. He painted, probably with his brother **Hubert van Eyck** (*d.*1426), the Ghent altarpiece, a masterpiece. **129, 130, 131**

Fabritius, Carel (*b.*1622 Midden-Beemster, *d.*1654 Delft). The most gifted pupil of Rembrandt and probably teacher of Vermeer. He died in an explosion. **181**

Falconet, Étienne-Maurice (*b.*1716 Paris, *d.*1791 Paris). French sculptor who worked under Jean-Baptiste Lemoyne. **203**

Fantin-Latour, Henri (*b.*1836 Grenoble, *d.*1904 Buré, Orne). French Post-Impressionist painter of group portraits and, particularly, flower pieces. **254**

Fattori, Giovanni (*b.*1825 Leghorn, *d.*1908 Florence). Leading painter of the Macchiaioli, whose rejection of traditional artistic values and emphasis on colour and splahes of paint (blob=*macchia*) were not unlike the French Impressionists. **226**

Feininger, Lyonel (*b.*1871 New York, *d.*1956 New York). Cubist painter; exhibited with the *Blaue Reiter;* taught at the Bauhaus. **277**

Feti, Domenico (*b. c.*1589 Rome, *d.*1624 Venice). Italian painter much influenced by Caravaggio. **165**

Feuchtmayer, Joseph Anton (*b.*1696 Linz, *d.*1770 Mimmenhausen, Lake Constance). German Rococo sculptor and stucco-worker. **187**

Fischer, Johann Michael (*b.*1692 Burglengenfeld, Bavaria, *d.*1766 Munich). German ecclesiastical architect of the Baroque period. **189**

Fischer von Erlach, Johann Bernhard (*b.*1656 Graz, *d.*1723 Vienna). Austrian Baroque architect. **189**

Floris, Frans (*b.*1516 Antwerp, *d.*1570 Antwerp). Flemish painter; a follower of the Italian Mannerist style. **142**

Fontaine, Pierre-François-Léonard (*b.*1762 Pontoise, *d.*1853 Paris). Official architect to Napoleon. **211**

Foppa, Vincenzo (*b.*1427/30 Brescia, *d.*1515/16 Brescia). Leading Milanese painter of the period. **93**

Fouquet, Jean (*b. c.*1420 Tours, *d. c.*1480 Tours). Most important French painter of the 15th century; worked in Italy for some years; painted miniatures and some easel pictures. **152**

Fragonard, Jean-Honoré (*b.*1732 Grasse, *d.*1806 Paris). Taught by Chardin and Boucher, he was a painter of the gallant, Rococo style. **209**

Francesco di Giorgio Martini (*b.*1439 Siena, *d.*1501/2 Siena). Italian architect, engineer, sculptor and painter; also a theorist, whose ideas influenced Leonardo. **116**

Francke, Master (*fl. c.*1405–after 1424 Hamburg). Painter of the Soft Style; best known for the Thomas à Becket altarpiece. **142**

Freundlich, Otto (*b.*1878 Stolp, Pomerania, *d.*1943 near Lublin, Poland). German painter and sculptor; his subjects were in the main abstract. **296**

Friedrich, Caspar David (*b.*1774 Greifswald, *d.*1840 Dresden). The most important German Romantic landscape painter. **238**

Frith, William Powell (*b.*1819 Aldfield, Yorks, *d.*1909 London). English painter of literary, historical and contemporary scenes. RA. **229**

Froment, Nicolas (*b. c.*1425 Uzés, Gard, *d.*1483/6 Avignon). French painter of the Provençal school. **152**

Fuseli, Henry (*b.*1741 Zurich, *d.*1825 London). Born Johann Füssli, he spent much of his life in England. His pictures are full of fantasies and nightmares. **228**

Gabo, Naum (*b.*1890 Briansk, Russia, *d.*1978). Sculptor and Constructivist; born Naum Pevsner, brother of Antoine Pevsner. **282**

Gabriel, Jacques (*b.*1667 Paris, *d.*1742 Fontainebleau). French Rococo architect; built the Musée Rodin in Paris. **201**

Gabriel, Jacques-Ange (*b.*1698 Paris, *d.*1782 Paris). Most important French architect of the 18th century; he designed in the classical tradition. **201**

Gaddi, Taddeo (*b. c.*1300 Florence?, *d.*1366 Florence). Pupil and faithful follower of Giotto. **80**

Gainsborough, Thomas (*b.*1727 Sudbury, Suffolk, *d.*1788 London). One of the major and best-loved English landscape and portrait painters. **221**

Garnier, Charles (*b.*1825 Paris, *d.*1898 Paris). French architect whose most famous work was the Paris Opéra. **258**

Gaudier-Brzeska, Henri (*b.*1891 St-Jean-de-Braye, *d.*1915 Beuville-St-Vaast). Sculptor associated with the Vorticist movement in England, where he lived. Killed in the war. **291**

Gauguin, Paul (*b.*1848 Paris, *d.*1903 Atuana, Dominica). Immensely influential Post-Impressionist painter; he formed the Pont-Aven school, which rejected the naturalistic approach to art and adopted 'Synthetism'. He spent his last years in the South Sea Islands. **10, 225, 252**

Gentile da Fabriano (*b. c.*1370 Fabriano, the Marches, *d.*1427 Rome). A master of the International Gothic style. His masterpiece is *The Adoration of the Magi* (Uffizi). **81**

Gentileschi, Artemisia (*b.*1593 Rome, *d. c.*1652 Naples). Like her father, Orazio Gentileschi, she was a follower of Caravaggio. **162**

Gentileschi, Orazio (*b.*1563 Pisa, *d.*1639 London). A follower of Caravaggio; lived in England from 1626 as court painter. **162**
Gerhaert van Leyden, Nicolaus (*d. c.*1473 Wiener-Neustadt). German Late Gothic sculptor of Dutch origin. **144**
Géricault, Théodore (*b.*1791 Rouen, *d.*1824 Paris). Romantic painter and draughtsman who influenced Delacroix and the French Romantic movement. **242**
Ghiberti, Lorenzo (*b.*1378 Florence, *d.*1455 Florence). Sculptor famous for his bronze doors of the Baptistery in Florence, known as the Doors of Paradise. **88**
Ghirlandaio, Domenico (*b.*1449 Florence, *d.*1494 Florence). A leading fresco painter of the Renaissance. **101**
Giacometti, Alberto (*b.*1901 Stampa, Switzerland, *d.*1966 Chur, Switzerland). Sculptor (also painter and draughtsman) whose most characteristic works are elongated, emaciated figures. **298**
Gibbs, James (*b.*1682 near Aberdeen, *d.*1754 London). Scottish architect. He designed a number of churches in England, mainly in the tradition of Wren. **214**
Gillray, James (*b.*1756 London, *d.*1815 London). English satirical caricaturist. **216**
Giordano, Luca (*b.*1634 Naples, *d.*1705 Naples). A leading painter of the Italian High Baroque. Probably taught by Ribera. Strongly influenced by Pietro da Cortona. Court painter in Madrid, 1692–1702. **169**
Giorgione (*b.*1477/8 Castelfranco Veneto, *d.*1510 Venice). One of the greatest Venetian painters; his work represents the High Renaissance in Venice. **121**
Giotto (*b.*1266?, *d.*1337). Giotto di Bondone is considered to be the founder of modern painting. His figures have a humanity not before seen in art. **74, 75**
Giovanni da Milano (*fl. c.*1346–69). Originally from Como, he worked in Lombardy before settling in Florence, where his greatest works are. **80**
Giovanni di Balduccio (*c.*1300 Pisa, after 1360 Milan?). Italian sculptor active in Pisa and Milan; directed the studio in Milan that produced the shrine of St Peter Martyr. **73**
Giovanni di Paolo (*b. c.*1400 Siena, *d.*1482 Siena). A leading Sienese master of the 15th century. **85**
Giovanni Pisano (*b. c.*1245, *d.*after 1314). Important sculptor and architect; he combined Gothic and classical elements. Son of Nicola Pisano. **72**
Girardon, François (*b.*1628 Troyes, *d.*1715 Paris). French sculptor; the most classical of the sculptors active at Versailles under Louis XIV. **202**
Girodet-Trioson, Anne-Louis (*b.*1767 Mantargis, Loiret, *d.*1824 Paris). French painter; pupil of David but moved away from Neoclassicism to Romanticism. **211**
Girtin, Thomas (*b.*1775 London, *d.*1802 London). English landscapist; he revolutionized the art of watercolour painting. **216**
Gislebertus (12th century). French sculptor of the tympanum figures on the entrance portal of St-Lazare Cathedral, Autun. **56**
Giulio Romano (*b.*1499? Rome, *d.*1546 Mantua). Painter, architect and decorator of the Italian Mannerist style. Pupil of Raphael. **118, 119**
Goes, Hugo van der (*b. c.*1440/5 Ghent, *d.*1482 Rode Klooster, Brussels). Gifted Ghent master, whose most famous work is the Portinari altarpiece (Uffizi). **135**
Gogh, Vincent van (*b.*1853 Groot-Zundert, Holland, *d.*1890 Auvers-sur-Oise, France). A major Post-Impressionist, whose expressive use of colour influenced Expressionism and Fauvism. **225, 256, 257**
Gonçalves, Nuno (*fl.* 1450–80). The major Portuguese painter of the 15th century; court painter from 1450. **158**
Gossaert, Jan (*b.*1470/80 Maubeuge, Hainaut, *d.*1532 Antwerp). Netherlandish painter who introduced Italian elements into his northern style. **137**
Goya y Lucientes, Francisco de (*b.*1746 Fuendetodos, near Saragossa, *d.*1828 Bordeaux). Great Spanish painter and graphic artist, whose work ranges from early Rococo-style paintings to starkly candid portraits and politically motivated scenes to nightmarish fantasies. **194, 195**
Goyen, Jan van (*b.*1596 Leiden, *d.*1656 The Hague). One of the great Dutch landscape and seascape painters of the 17th century. **181**
Gozzoli, Benozzo (*b.*1420 Florence, *d.*1497 Pistoia). His most famous fresco is *The Journey of the Magi*, painted in the chapel of the Palazzo Medici-Riccardi. **95**
Greco, El (*b.*1541 Crete, *d.*1614 Toledo). An outstanding painter of the Mannerist school. His work reflects the Byzantine tradition, the Venetian masters and Michelangelo. Worked mainly in Spain. **156, 157**
Greuze, Jean-Baptiste (*b.*1725 Tournus, Saône-et-Loire, *d.*1805 Paris). Gained early popularity with his genre and gallant pictures and female portraits. **207**
Gris, Juan (*b.*1887 Madrid, *d.*1927 Boulogue-sur-Seine). Cubist and collage artist. Spent his working life in France. **276**
Gropius, Walter (*b.*1883 Berlin, *d.*1969 Boston). Important architect; founder of the Bauhaus. **283**
Gros, Baron Antoine-Jean (*b.*1771 Paris, *d.*1835 Mendon, near Paris). Pupil and admirer of David; he recorded many Napoleonic events; influenced Géricault and Delacroix, both Romantics, though his own style remained basically Neoclassical. **211**
Grosz, George (*b.*1893 Berlin, *d.*1959 Berlin). Satirical draughtsman and Berlin Dada artist. **270**
Grünewald, Matthias (*b. c.*1470 Würzburg, *d.*1528 Halle, Saxony). Matthis Gothardt-Neithardt, called Grünewald, was a contemporary of Dürer but painted in the Late Gothic tradition. His masterpiece is the Isenheim altarpiece. **129, 147**
Guardi, Francesco (*b.*1712 Venice, *d.*1793 Venice). Painted atmospheric *vedute* of Venice. **172, 173**
Guarini, Guarino (*b.*1624 Modena, *d.*1683 Milan). Baroque architect who was a well-known mathematician and philosopher. Influenced by Borromini. His important works survive only in Turin. **169**
Guercino (*b.*1591 Cento, *d.*1666 Bologna). Giovanni Francesco Barbieri was a painter of the High Baroque. Strongly influenced by Carracci. **165**
Günther, Ignaz (*b.*1725 Altmannstein, *d.*1775 Munich). Bavarian Rococo sculptor influenced by Mannerism. **187**
Hagesandros (1st century BC). Greek sculptor said to have produced, with Polydoros and Athenodoros, the marble Laocoön group. **36**
Hals, Frans (*b.*1581/5 Antwerp, *d.*1666 Haarlem). One of the greatest Dutch portrait and genre painters. **184**
Hardouin-Mansart, Jules (*b.*1646 Paris, *d.*1708 near Paris). French Baroque architect under Louis XIV; grand nephew of François Mansart, whose name he took. In charge of Versailles extensions from 1678. **201**
Hartung, Hans (*b.*1904 Leipzig). Abstract painter. Settled in France in 1935. **280**
Hawksmoor, Nicholas (*b.*1661 Ragnall?, Notts, *d.*1736 London). One of the most gifted English architects of the early 18th century. Worked with Wren and Vanbrugh. **214**
Hayez, Francesco (1791 Venice, *d.*1882 Milan). Italian Romantic painter. **226**
Heckel, Erich (*b.*1883 Döbeln, Saxony, *d.*1970). Expressionist painter and graphic artist; one of the founders of the *Brücke*. **267**
Heda, Willem Claesz (*b.*1594 Haarlem, *d.*1680 Haarlem). Dutch still-life painter of food and the laden table. **183**
Hepworth, Barbara (*b.*1903 Wakefield, Yorks, *d.*1975). British abstract sculptor; married to Ben Nicholson. **300**
Heyden, Jan van der (*b.*1637 Gorinchem, *d.*1712 Amsterdam). Dutch townscape, landscape and still-life painter. **183**
Hicks, Edward (*b.*1780 Attleborough, Pa, *d.*1849 Newtown, Pa). American Primitive painter. **236**
Hildebrandt, Johann Lukas von (*b.*1668 Genoa, *d.*1745 Vienna). One of the greatest Austrian Baroque architects. **188**
Hilliard, Nicholas (*b. c.*1547 Exeter, *d.*1619 London). English miniaturist of the Elizabethan age. **212**
Hittorf, Jakob Ignaz (*b.*1792 Cologne, *d.*1867). Architect who spent his working life in France. **258**
Hobbema, Meindert (*b.*1638 Amsterdam, *d.*1709 Amsterdam). Landscape painter taught by Ruisdael. Not appreciated until the 19th century. **182**
Hockney, David (*b.*1937 Bradford, Yorks). British painter and etcher; an early Pop artist, he has moved towards straight representational art. **306**
Hodler, Ferdinand (*b.*1853 Berne, *d.*1918 Geneva). With Böcklin, the greatest 19th-century Swiss painter. **238**
Hogarth, William (*b.*1697 London, *d.*1764 London). A major English painter and engraver, he promoted a native school of painting. Most famous are his moral subjects. **218**
Holbein the Elder, Hans (*b. c.*1465 Augsburg, *d.*1524 Isenheim). Painter and draughtsman in the Late Gothic tradition. **146**
Holbein the Younger, Hans (*b.*1497/8 Augsburg, *d.*1543 London). One of the greatest of all portrait painters; also a draughtsman, illustrator and decorator. He represents the end of the German Renaissance. He worked mainly in Basle and was also court painter to Henry VIII in London. **146**
Homer, Winslow (*b.*1836 Boston, *d.*1910 Prouts Neck, Maine). Influential American painter and illustrator. **236**
Honthorst, Gerrit van (*b.*1590 Utrecht, *d.*1656 Utrecht). Portrait and genre painter strongly influenced by Caravaggio. **180**
Hooch, Pieter de (*b.*1629 Rotterdam, *d.*1684 Amsterdam). One of the greatest Dutch genre painters, he painted primarily interiors and courtyard scenes. **186**
Houdon, Jean-Antoine (*b.*1741 Versailles, *d.*1828 Paris). The foremost French sculptor of the 18th century. **203**
Hughes, Arthur (*b.*1830 London, *d.*1915 Kew Green). Painter and book illustrator closely connected to the Pre-Raphaelites. **233**
Hunt, William Holman (*b.*1827 London, *d.*1910 London). Founder member of the Pre-Raphaelites. **232**
Ingres, Jean-Auguste-Dominique (*b.*1780 Montauban, Tarn-et-Garonne, *d.*1867 Paris). Neoclassical painter and draughtsman; opposed the Romantic movement. **239**
Jacobsen, Arne (*b.*1902 Copenhagen, *d.*1971). Major Danish architect of this century. **288**
Jacopo della Quercia (*b.*1374/5 Siena, *d.*1438 Bologna). Greatest Sienese sculptor of the Renaissance. **81**
Jawlensky, Alexej (*b.*1864 Kuslovo, Russia, *d.*1941 Wiesbaden). Russian Expressionist painter who spent his working life in Germany. Though not a member, he was closely associated with the *Blaue Reiter* group. **268**
Jefferson, Thomas (*b.*1743 Shadwell, Va, *d.*1826 Monticello). American statesman, legislator and Neoclassical architect. **223**
John, Augustus Edwin (*b.*1878 Tenby, Wales, *d.*1961 Fordingbridge, Hants). Painter and draughtsman. **291**
Johns, Jasper (*b.*1930 Allendale, S.C.). American Pop artist. **306**
Johnson, Philip Cortelyou (*b.*1906 Cleveland,

Ohio). Architect; co-author of *The International Style,* which described the architectural style of the 1920s. **287**

Jones, Inigo (*b.*1573 London, *d.*1652 London). Foremost English classical architect of the Palladian style. Also a stage designer. **213**

Joos van Cleve (*b. c.*1480/5 Cleve?, *d.*1540 Antwerp). Probably trained in Bruges; active in Antwerp; portrait painter to Francis I of France. **137**

Jordaens, Jacob (*b.*1593 Antwerp, *d.*1678 Antwerp). Leading Baroque figure painter in Antwerp after Rubens (his teacher) and Van Dyck died. **181**

Kahn, Louis Isadore (*b.*1901 Saare, Estonia). A major American architect. **286**

Kalf, Willem (*b.*1619 Rotterdam, *d.*1693 Rotterdam). Dutch painter of still lifes, usually full of luxurious porcelain, glass, carpets, etc. **182**

Kandinsky, Wassily (*b.*1866 Moscow, *d.*1944 Neuilly-sur-Seine). The first painter of purely abstract pictures; helped to found the *Blaue Reiter* and taught at the Bauhaus. Became a French citizen. **268, 295**

Kent, William (*b.*1685 Bridlington, Yorks, *d.*1748 London). Landscape gardener, decorator and architect. He and Lord Burlington designed several buildings together in the Palladian style. **214**

Kirchner, Ernst Ludwig (*b.*1880 Aschaffenburg, Germany, *d.*1938 Frauenkirche, Switzerland). German Expressionist painter; helped to found the *Brücke* group. **267**

Klee, Paul (*b.*1879 Münchenbuchsee, near Berne, *d.*1940 Muralto, near Locarno). A major painter of the 20th century. Exhibited with the *Blaue Reiter* and taught at the Bauhaus. **269, 283**

Klenze, Leo von (*b.*1784 near Hildesheim, *d.*1864 Munich). German architect whose works are largely in the classical tradition. **235**

Klimt, Gustav (*b.*1862 Vienna, *d.*1918 Vienna). Jugendstil painter and decorator and a founder of the Vienna *Sezession.* **263**

Kline, Franz (*b.*1910 Wilkes Barre, Pa, *d.*1962 New York). A leading American Abstract Expressionist painter. **304**

Kneller, Sir Godfrey (*b.*1646 Lübeck, *d.*1723 London). Foremost portrait painter of his day in England. **216**

Knobelsdorff, Georg Wenzeslaus von (*b.*1699 Kuckädel, Poland, *d.*1753 Berlin). Prussian Baroque architect. **188**

Koch, Joseph Anton (*b.*1768 Obergibeln, Tyrol, *d.*1839 Rome). Austrian landscape painter. **238**

Kokoschka, Oskar (*b.*1886 Pochlarn, Lower Austria). One of the most important Expressionist painters of the 20th century. He left Austria in 1934 for England and later Switzerland. **271**

Kollwitz, Käthe (*b.*1867 Königsberg, East Prussia, *d.*1945 Moritzburg). Sculptor and graphic artist. **298**

Kooning, Willem de (*b.*1904 Rotterdam). A leading modern Expressionist painter; settled in the US in 1926. **296**

Kupka, František (*b.*1871 Opocno, Bohemia, *d.*1957 near Paris). One of the early abstract painters. **297**

La Fresnaye, Roger de (*b.*1885 Le Mans, *d.*1925 Grasse, Alpes–Maritimes). French painter, sculptor and draughtsman; briefly a Cubist. **278**

Lam, Wifredo (*b.*1902 Cuba). Surrealist artist. **294**

Lambert, George (*b.*1700 Kent?, *d.*1765 London). English landscape painter. **219**

Lancret, Nicolas (*b.*1690 Paris, *d.*1743 Paris). Rococo painter of *fêtes galantes.* **206**

Landseer, Sir Edwin Henry (*b.*1802 London, *d.*1873 London). Popular painter of animal subjects. **233**

Lanfranco, Giovanni (*b.*1582 Parma, *d.*1647 Rome). Painter of the High Baroque active mainly in Rome and Naples; follower of the Carracci and worked with Annibale on the decoration of the Palazzo Farnese. **164**

Langhans, Carl Gotthard (*b.*1732 Kamienna Góra, Silesia, *d.*1808 Grüneiche, near Breslau). German Neoclassical architect famous for the Brandenburg Gate in Berlin. **189**

Largillière, Nicolas de (*b.*1656 Paris, *d.*1746 Paris). Portrait painter; spent some years in Antwerp, and then in England as Lely's assistant. **205**

La Tour, Georges de (*b.*1593 Vic-sur-Seille, Alsace-Lorraine, *d.*1652 Lunéville). Painter of religious and genre pictures reminiscent of Caravaggio. **198**

La Tour, Maurice-Quentin de (*b.*1704 St-Quentin, *d.*1788 St-Quentin). Foremost French pastellist of the 18th century. **208**

Lawrence, Sir Thomas (*b.*1769 Bristol, *d.*1830 London). Successful portrait painter who gained a European reputation. **222**

Le Brun, Charles (*b.*1619 Paris, *d.*1690 Paris). Painter and designer; as head of the French Academy, he dictated the trend of the arts under Louis XIV. **199, 201**

Le Corbusier (*b.*1887 La Chaux-de-Fonds, Switzerland, *d.*1965 Roquebrune, Alpes-Maritime). Born Charles-Édouard Jeanneret; one of the major architects of the 20th century and a prime creator of the International Style of the 1920s. **284**

Léger, Fernand (*b.*1881 Argentan, Normandy, *d.*1955 near Paris). A major figure in 20th-century art, his paintings reflect an industrialized world, full of geometric shapes of machinery; an early Cubist. **277**

Lehmbruck, Wilhelm (*b.*1881 Duisburg, *d.*1919 Berlin-Friedenau). German sculptor; his characteristic figures are elongated and sad. **298**

Leighton, Frederic, Lord (*b.*1830 Scarborough, Yorks, *d.*1896 London). Victorian painter who admired the Italian Renaissance and attempted to emulate its style. **233**

Lely, Sir Peter (*b.*1618 Soest, Westphalia, *d.*1680 London). English portrait painter born of Dutch parents. Principal Painter to Charles II and a strong influence on portrait painting in England. **212**

Lemoyne, Jean-Baptiste (*b.*1704 Paris, *d.*1778 Paris). French sculptor best known for his portrait busts; official sculptor to Louis XV. **202**

Le Nain, Louis (*b.*1593 Laon, *d.*1648 Paris). One of three brothers, all painters; they collaborated in their paintings, usually peasant scenes realistically portrayed. **198**

Leonardo da Vinci (*b.*1452 Vinci, near Florence, *d.*1519 Amboise). One of the great Renaissance figures. Not only a gifted painter and draughtsman, he excelled as an architect, sculptor, engineer, inventor and man of science. He worked in Florence, Milan and (briefly) Rome. **108, 109**

Le Sueur, Eustache (*b.*1616 Paris, *d.*1655 Paris). Painter of religious and allegorical subjects; influenced by Poussin. **199**

Le Tavernier, Jean (*fl.* early 15th century). Miniaturist from Oudenaarde, near Ghent. Worked for dukes of Burgundy. **132**

Le Vau, Louis (*b.*1612 Paris, *d.*1670 Paris). The leading Baroque architect in France. **200, 201**

Lewis, Percy Wyndham (*b.*1882 Nova Scotia, *d.*1957 London). English painter, writer, art critic, and founder of Vorticism, a derivative of Cubism and Futurism. **291**

Liebermann, Max (*b.*1847 Berlin, *d.*1935 Berlin). German Impressionist and a member of the Berlin *Sezession.* **262**

Limbourg, Paul, Herman and Jean de (*d.*1416). The three brothers came from the Duchy of Guelders and worked in Dijon. Their most famous work is the illumination of the *Très Riches Heures,* commissioned by the Duc de Berry and a masterpiece of the International Gothic style. **132**

Lipchitz, Jacques (*b.*1891 Lithuania, *d.*1973). Sculptor who lived in France from 1909 to 1941 and thereafter in the United States. Influenced by Cubism. **299**

Lippi, Filippino (*b. c.*1457 Prato, *d.*1504 Florence). Painter; son of Fra Filippo Lippi and pupil in Botticelli's workshop. **94**

Lippi, Fra Filippo (*b. c.*1406 Florence, *d.*1469 Spoleto). Important Florentine painter of the 15th century; also a Carmelite monk. Patronized by the Medici. **85**

Lochner, Stefan (*d.*1451 Cologne). German painter probably trained in the Netherlands. Late representative of the International Gothic style. **143**

Longhena, Baldassare (*b.*1598 Venice, *d.*1682 Venice). Major Venetian Baroque architect; built S. Maria della Salute in Venice. **169**

Longhi, Pietro (*b.*1702 Venice, *d.*1785 Venice). Painter of small genre scenes. **173**

Loo, Carle van (*b.*1705 Nice, *d.*1765 Paris). French decorative painter; appointed painter to the king, 1762. **207**

Lorenzetti, Ambrogio (*fl.*1319–47 Siena). Important Sienese painter; brother of Pietro. Most famous are his frescoes of *Good and Bad Government* in the Palazzo Pubblico, Siena. **8, 78**

Lorenzetti, Pietro (*fl.*1306?–1348). Important Sienese painter; brother of Ambrogio and, like him, influenced by Giotto. **78**

Lorenzo di Credi (*b. c.*1458 Florence, *d.*1537 Florence). Florentine painter taught by Verrocchio. **103**

Lorenzo Monaco (*b. c.*1370 Siena, *d. c.*1422 Florence). Italian painter influenced by the 14th-century Sienese masters and by the Florentine school, particularly Orcagna. **80**

Lorenzo Veneziano (*fl.*1356–72 Venice). Venetian painter influenced by the Byzantine tradition. **79**

Lotto, Lorenzo (*b. c.*1480 Venice, *d.*1556 Loreto). Restless painter who worked in several cities. Influenced by Giovanni Bellini. **127**

Loutherbourg, Philip James de (*b.*1740 Strasbourg, *d.*1812 London). Painter who lived in England from 1771; painted landscapes, religious pictures, battle scenes and coastal views. RA. **219**

Lowry, Laurence Stephen (*b.*1887 Manchester, *d.*1976). Painter of the industrial cities in the Midlands of England. **301**

Lucas van Leyden (*b. c.*1494? Leiden, *d.*1533 Leiden). Dutch Renaissance engraver; also painter. Influenced by Dürer and the northern school and to a lesser degree by the Italian Renaissance. **137**

Lutyens, Sir Edwin Landseer (*b.*1869 London, *d.*1944 London). English architect, most of whose work is in the classical tradition. **288**

Macke, August (*b.*1887 Meschede, North Rhine – Westphalia, *d.*1914 Perthes, Seine-et-Maine). German *Blaue Reiter* painter; his promising career was cut short when he fell early in the war. **269**

Magnelli, Alberto (*b.*1888 Florence, *d.*1971). Abstract painter whose early works were influenced by the Cubists and Futurists; settled in France in 1933. **297**

Magritte, René (*b.*1898 Lessines, Belgium, *d.*1967 Brussels). Belgian Surrealist painter. **293**

Maillol, Aristide (*b.*1861 Banyuls-sur-Mer, Pyrénées-Orientales, *d.*1944 Perpignan). French sculptor of primarily female nudes. Member of the Nabis. **260**

Malevich, Kasimin (*b.*1878 Liev, *d.*1935 Leningrad). Russian abstract painter; founded Suprematism. **10, 296**

Mané-Katz (*b.*1894 Ukraine, *d.*1962 Tel Aviv). French painter and sculptor of Jewish origin. **261**

Manessier, Alfred (*b.*1911 St-Ouen, Somme). French abstract painter, and designer of stained glass; his works reflect his deeply religious feelings. **280**

Manet, Édouard (*b.*1832 Paris, *d.*1883 Rueil-Malmaison). Innovative and important painter of the 19th century who played a decisive role in the course of modern painting. He was strongly influenced by Hals, Velazquez and Goya. **246**

Manfredi, Bartolomeo (*b. c.*1587 Ustiano, near

Mantua, *d.*1620/1 Rome). Follower of Caravaggio; influenced the northern painters working in Rome, particularly the Utrecht school.**162**

Mansart, François (*b.*1598 Paris, *d.*1666 Paris). Architect; an early exponent of the classicist style in French architecture.**200**

Mantegna, Andrea (*b.*1430/1 near Vicenza, *d.*1506 Mantua). One of the most important painters of the Early Renaissance; influenced by Donatello; active in Padua and Mantua; married Jacopo Bellini's daughter.**100**

Marc, Franz (*b.*1880 Munich, *d.*1916 Verdun). German Expressionist painter and a member of the *Blaue Reiter*. He painted animals until his abstract works of 1913/14. Killed at Verdun.**269**

Marini, Marino (*b.*1901 Pistoia, Tuscany). A leading Italian sculptor; also painter and graphic artist.**299**

Marlow, William (*b.*1740 London, *d.*1813 Twickenham, Middlesex). English painter of landscapes and caprices; pupil of Samuel Scott and Richard Wilson; influenced by Canaletto.**217**

Marquet, Albert (*b.*1875 Bordeaux, *d.*1947 Paris). Painter and draughtsman. Exhibited with the Fauves; friend of Matisse. Painted hazy landscapes.**266**

Martin, John (*b.*1789 Haydon Bridge, Northumb, *d.*1854 Isle of Man). Romantic painter and engraver. Called 'Mad Martin'.**228**

Masaccio (*b.*1401 Valdarno, *d. c.*1428 Rome). The first and greatest painter of the Early Renaissance. His role in painting is comparable to Brunelleschi's in architecture and Donatello's in sculpture.**84**

Maso di Banco (*fl.* 1340s Florence). The most important of Giotto's followers.**77**

Masolino (*b. c.*1383 Panicale, *d.* after 1432). Painter of the International Gothic style; worked with Masaccio on the Brancacci Chapel frescoes.**80**

Masson, André (*b.*1896 Balagny, Oise). French painter and graphic artist; associated with Surrealism.**294**

Massys, Jan (*b. c.*1509 Antwerp, *d.*1575 Antwerp). Son of Quinten Massys. Adopted Italian Mannerist style in the late 1550s.**139**

Massys, Quinten (*b.*1465/6 Louvain, *d.*1530 Antwerp). The leading painter in Antwerp of his day.**139**

Master of the Aix-la-Chapelle Altarpiece (*fl. c.*1480–1520 Cologne). German painter whose name comes from the altarpiece on the high altar of Aix-la-Chapelle Cathedral.**144**

Master of the Female Half-lengths (*fl.* early 16th century Antwerp). Flemish painter who takes his name from the *Lady Musicians* (Graf Harrach'sche Gemäldegalerie, Vienna).**139**

Master of the Garden of Paradise (*fl.* early 15th century). German painter of the Rhine region who painted the *Garden of Paradise* (Frankfurt).**145**

Master of the Housebook (*fl.* 1475–90). German painter and engraver named after the *Hausbuch*, a book of drawings.**144**

Master of the Last Judgement of Tahull (*fl.* early 12th century Catalonia). Romanesque painter of frescoes in the church of S. Maria, Tahull.**61**

Master of the Life of the Virgin (*fl. c.*1460–80/90 Cologne). Painter of the Cologne school named after an altarpiece (seven panels in the Alte Pinakothek, one in the National Gallery, London).**145**

Master of Moulins (*fl. c.*1480–99). French painter named after the triptych in Moulins Cathedral, an important work in French art.**153**

Master of Pedret (*fl. c.*1200 Catalonia). Romanesque painter most famous for his frescoes in the church of S. Quirze at Pedret.**61**

Master of the St Bartholomew Altarpiece (*fl.*late 15th century Cologne). German painter of several altarpieces, including one in the Alte Pinakothek from which he takes his name.**143**

Master of St Giles (*fl.* 1490–1510). Painter, probably French, of four panels, two (St Giles) in the National Gallery, London, and two in Washington.**153**

Master of the View of St Gudule (*fl.* 1470–1500 Brussels). Flemish painter whose paintings sometimes have the cathedral of St Gudule in the background.**137**

Master of 1456 (*fl.* mid-15th century). French painter of the famous *Portrait of a Man* (Vaduz).**153**

Matisse, Henri (*b.*1869 Le Cateau, *d.*1954 Vence). Principal Fauve painter; also a draughtsman, lithographer and sculptor. A major figure of 20th-century art.**264, 265**

Melozzo da Forlì (*b.*1438 Forlì, near Bologna, *d.*1494 Forlì). Fresco painter active in Rome, Urbino and Loreto. Pupil of Piero della Francesca.**103**

Memling, Hans (*b. c.*1435 Seligenstadt, near Frankfurt, *d.*1494 Bruges). Active in Bruges and painter of the Netherlandish school. Influenced by Rogier van der Weyden and Bouts.**135**

Memmi, Lippo (*fl.* 1317–47 Siena). Sienese painter; collaborated with his brother-in-law, Simone Martini. **79**

Mendelsohn, Erich (*b.*1887 Allenstein, East Prussia, *d.*1953 San Francisco). Architect who left Germany in 1933 and lived in Brussels and London before settling in the United States (1945).**288**

Mercier, Philippe (*b.*1689 or 1691 Berlin, *d.*1760 London). Born of French parents, he lived in Germany and England; painted in the Rococo style of Watteau.**206**

Metsu, Gabriel (*b.*1629 Leiden, *d.*1667 Amsterdam). Leiden master of figure and genre pictures.**180**

Michelangelo Buonarroti (*b.*1475 Caprese, *d.*1564 Rome). A creative genius and one of the greatest artists of all time, he excelled as sculptor, painter and architect. Pupil in Ghirlandaio's workshop; came into contact with scholars and philosophers while living in Lorenzo de'Medici's palace. He was famous as a sculptor by 1501; painted the Sistine Chapel ceiling in 1508–12. His architectural achievements include the Medici Chapel in S. Lorenzo and the Biblioteca Laurenziana.**110, 111, 112**

Michelozzo di Michelozzi (*b.*1396 Florence, *d.*1472 Florence). Architect; also sculptor and decorator. Designed the Palazzo Medici-Riccardi and the convent of S. Marco in Florence.**88**

Mies van der Rohe, Ludwig (*b.*1886 Aachen, *d.*1969 Chicago). One of the most influential architects of his day; a leader of the International Style and director of the Bauhaus. Also designed furniture. Settled in the United States in 1938.**285**

Millais, Sir John Everett (*b.*1829 Southampton, *d.*1896 London). Popular painter of portraits and genre; a founder of the Pre-Raphaelite Brotherhood. President of the RA.**232**

Millet, Jean-François (*b.*1814 Gruchy, Manche, *d.*1875 Barbizon). French painter of peasant scenes; a leading member of the Barbizon school.**244**

Miró, Joan (*b.*1893 Montroig, Catalonia). A major Spanish Surrealist painter; also potter and sculptor.**294, 295**

Modigliani, Amedeo (*b.*1884 Leghorn, *d.*1920 Paris). One of the greatest Italian painters of the 20th century; also a sculptor and draughtsman.**281, 299**

Moholy-Nagy, László (*b.*1895 Bács-Borsod, Hungary, *d.*1946 Chicago). Hungarian painter, sculptor, teacher, experimental artist; taught at the Bauhaus and was director of the New Bauhaus (Institute of Design) in Chicago.**283**

Mondrian, Piet (*b.*1872 Amersfoort, *d.*1944 New York). Dutch abstract painter; founded the magazine *De Stijl*, which promoted his Neoplasticism.**295**

Monet, Claude (*b.*1840 Paris, *d.*1926 Giierny). A leading Impressionist painter. Latterly his favourite subject was the water lilies in his garden.**249**

Moore, Henry (*b.*1898 Castleford, Yorks). The major British sculptor of the 20th century.**300**

Moreau, Gustave (*b.*1826 Paris, *d.*1898 Paris). Painter and draughtsman of elaborate fantasies.**258**

Morisot, Berthe (*b.*1841 Bourges, *d.*1895 Paris). French Impressionist painter; married Manet's brother.**247**

Morris, William (*b.*1834 Walthamstow, Essex, *d.*1896 Kelmscott, Oxon). Designer, poet, critic, printer and social reformer.**233**

Moser, Lukas (*fl.* first half of 15th century). German painter whose only known work is the Magdalene altarpiece at Tiefenbronn.**143**

Mostaert, Jan (*b. c.*1472/3 Haarlem, *d.*1555/6 Haarlem). Dutch painter about whom little is known.**139**

Motherwell, Robert (*b.*1915). American Abstract Expressionist painter; also art critic.**304**

Munch, Edvard (*b.*1863 Løten, *d.*1944 Ekely, near Oslo). Norwegian painter and graphic artist whose pictures dwell on themes of illness, death and fear.**263**

Murillo, Bartolomé Esteban (*b.*1617 Seville, *d.*1682 Seville). Leading Spanish painter of the late 17th century. Painted chiefly religious pictures. Influenced by Velazquez and Zurbarán.**191**

Myron (*fl.* mid-5th century BC Athens). Greek sculptor of the early Classical period. Most famous work: the *Discobolus*.**31**

Nanni di Banco (*b. c.*1384 Florence, *d.*1421 Florence). Florentine sculptor; his works reflect the ideals of the Early Renaissance that were taken further by Donatello, his contemporary.**80**

Nash, John (*b.*1752 London, *d.*1835 Cowes). The major architect of the Regency period in England.**227**

Nash, Paul (*b.*1889 London, *d.*1946 Boscombe, near Bournemouth). Painter and illustrator; war artist in both world wars. Painted mostly landscapes.**301**

Nattier, Jean-Marc (*b.*1685 Paris, *d.*1766 Paris). Fashionable portrait painter who specialized in ladies at the court of Louis XV.**206**

Nervi, Pier Luigi (*b.*1891 Sondrio, *d.*1979). Leading Italian engineer and architect.**288**

Neumann, Johann Balthasar (*b.*1687 Eger, Bohemia, *d.*1753 Würzburg). One of the major German Baroque architects.**188**

Neutra, Richard Joseph (*b.*1892 Vienna, *d.*1970). American architect; promoted the European style.**2**

Niccolò dell'Abbate (*b. c.*1509 Modena, *d.*1571 Fontainebleau). Italian painter and decorator. Worked with Primaticcio at Fontainebleau and is a representative of the School of Fontainebleau.**154**

Niccolò dell'Arca (*b. c.*1435 Bari, *d.*1494 Bologna). Italian sculptor active mainly in Bologna.**92**

Nicholson, Ben (*b.*1894 Denham, Bucks).British abstract painter; also sculptor.**295, 301**

Nicola Pisano (*fl.* 1258–78). Italian sculptor active in Tuscany; inspired by classical art.**73**

Niemeyer, Oscar (*b.*1907 Rio de Janeiro). Influential Brazilian architect.**287**

Nolde, Emil (*b.*1867 Nolde, Schleswig, *d.*1956 Seebull, Schleswig). German Expressionist painter and graphic artist.**270**

Oliver, Isaac (*b.*Rouen, *d.*1617). Brought to England as a child in 1568, he was trained as a miniaturist by Hilliard, whose rival he became.**212**

Oltos (*fl.* late 6th century BC Athens). Greek red-vase painter.**29**

Onesimos (*fl.* early 5th century BC). Greek cup painter; represents the Severe Style.**30**

Orcagna, Andrea (*fl.* 1344–68 Florence). Major Florentine painter, sculptor and architect. Though influenced by Giotto, his painting is less naturalistic, more hieratic.**77**

Orley, Bernaert van (*b. c.*1492 Brussels, *d.*1541 Brussels). Major Brussels painter of his day; also stained-glass and tapestry designer; influenced by the Italian Renaissance.**142**

Orozco, José Clemente (*b.*1883 Zapotlán, Mexico *d.*1949 Mexico City). Mexican painter; he did many large murals, usually with political overtones.**281**

stade, Adriaen van (*b.*1610 Haarlem, *d.*1685 aarlem). Dutch genre painter; pupil of Frans als. **186**

udry, Jean-Baptiste (*b.*1686 Paris, *d.*1755 eauvais). French painter of animal and still-life ubjects, usually with hunting themes; also designer f tapestries and engraver. **206**

acher, Michael (*fl.* 1465?–1498 Salzburg). Austrian ainter and sculptor of altarpieces. **144**

alladio, Andrea (*b.*1508 Padua, *d.*1580 Vicenza). rchitect inspired by buildings of antiquity that he aw in Rome and elsewhere. His classical style as revived in the 18th century and became the shion all over Europe and the United States. **128**

almer, Samuel (*b.*1805 London, *d.*1881 Reigate). nglish painter of landscapes with a mystical, sionary quality. **229**

anini, Giovanni Paolo (*b.*1691/2 Piacenza, *d.*1765 ome). Painter of *vedute,* also of *capricci,* or naginary views with Roman ruins. **171**

armigianino (*b.*1503 Parma, *d.*1540 Castel aggiore). A leading Italian Mannerist painter, fluenced by Correggio. **118, 119**

ascin, Jules (*b.*1885 Vidin, Bulgaria, *d.*1930 aris). Painter who became an American citizen nough he worked mostly in Paris, where he killed mself. Painted mainly women. **261**

asmore, Victor (*b.*1908 Chesham, Bucks). British ainter, teacher, maker of abstract constructions. ainted landscapes before 1947, when he turned to bstract art. **297**

atenier, Joachim (*b. c.*1480 Dinant, *d. c.*1524 ntwerp). Important Antwerp landscape painter; one f the first painters to specialize in landscape. **138**

ater, Jean-Baptiste (*b.*1695 Valenciennes, *d.*1736 aris). French Rococo painter; pupil and follower of Vatteau. **206**

axton, Joseph (*b.*1803 Milton-Bryant, Beds, *d.*1865 ydenham, London). English architect; he built the amous Crystal Palace, made of iron and glass, with o training as an architect or engineer. **227**

echstein, Max (*b.*1881 Eckersbach, *d.*1955 Berlin). German Expressionist painter; a member of the *rücke* group. **262**

ercier, Charles (*b.*1764 Paris, *d.*1838 Paris). rench architect of the Empire style; collaborated vith Pierre Fontaine. **211**

ermoser, Balthasar (*b.*1651 Kammer, Upper avaria, *d.*1732 Dresden). German Baroque sculptor; ourt sculptor in Dresden. **187**

errault, Claude (*b.*1613 Paris, *d.*1688 Paris). rench architect under Louis XIV; partly responsible or the east front of the Louvre. **201**

erret, Auguste (*b.*1874 Brussels, *d.*1954 Paris). rench architect; strong advocate of concrete as a uilding material. **288**

erronneau, Jean-Baptiste (*b.*1715? Paris, *d.*1783 msterdam). French portrait painter, mainly in astel. **208**

erugino (*b. c.*1445 Città della Pieve, Umbria, .1523 Fontignano, near Perugia). Italian painter; robably a pupil of Verrocchio and Piero della rancesca. Active in Florence and Perugia. **94**

esellino (*b. c.*1422 Florence, *d.*1457 Florence). ainter whose only documented work is part of an ltarpiece (National Gallery, London). **93**

ettoruti, Emilio (*b.*1892 Buenos Aires, *d.*1971). ubist/Futurist painter active in Italy, Argentina and rance. **276**

evsner, Antoine (*b.*1886 Orel, Russia, *d.*1962 aris). Sculptor and painter. A founder, with his rother Gabo, of Constructivism. Lived mainly in aris. **282**

hidias (*b. c.*500 BC, *d. c.*430 BC). Athenian culptor; supervised the Acropolis decoration, thens. **32**

iazzetta, Giovanni Battista (*b.*1683 Venice, .1754 Venice). Venetian painter and draughtsman f the Rococo style that was to be taken further y Tiepolo. **171**

Picabia, Francis (*b.*1879 Paris, *d.*1953 Paris). French painter associated with Cubism, Dada and Surrealism. **290**

Picasso, Pablo Ruiz y (*b.*1881 Malaga, *d.*1973). Spanish painter, sculptor, draughtsman, ceramist, engraver; the most famous and influential artist of the 20th century. With Braque invented Cubism. He lived in France from 1901. **9, 272, 273, 274**

Pickett, Joseph (*b.*1848 New Hope, Pa, *d.*1918 New Hope, Pa). American primitive painter; his works were virtually unknown until after his death. **303**

Piero della Francesca (*b.*1410/20 Borgo S. Sepolcro, Tuscany, *d.*1492 Borgo S. Sepolcro). A major painter of the Renaissance. He worked in various places, including Florence, Urbino, Ferrara and Arezzo. **96, 97**

Piero di Cosimo (*b. c.*1462 Florence, *d. c.*1521 Florence). Florentine painter; pupil of Cosimo Rosselli; painted a number of mythologies. **102**

Pietro da Cortona (*b.*1596 Cortona, *d.*1669 Rome). Painter, architect and decorator of the High Baroque in Rome. His most famous work is the vast ceiling decoration in the Palazzo Barberini, Rome. **164, 165**

Pigalle, Jean-Baptiste (*b.*1714 Paris, *d.*1785 Paris). French sculptor; pupil of Jean-Baptiste Lemoyne. **203**

Pilon, Germain (*b. c.*1531 Paris, *d.*1590). Major French sculptor; influenced by Primaticcio, with whom he worked at Fontainebleau. **153**

Pintoricchio (*b. c.*1454 Perugia, *d.*1513 Siena). Painter active in Perugia, Rome and Siena. Painted frescoes in the Borgia apartments in the Vatican. **94**

Piper, John (*b.*1903 Epsom). Romantic British topographical painter; also illustrator. **301**

Piranesi, Giovanni Battista (*b.*1720 near Venice, *d.*1778 Rome). Famous as an engraver of *vedute* of ancient and modern Rome; also an architect. **171**

Pisanello (*b. c.*1395 Pisa, *d. c.*1455). The major International Gothic painter after Gentile da Fabriano, whose pupil he was; also a medallist. **81**

Pissarro, Camille (*b.*1830 St Thomas, Virgin Islands, 1903 Paris). French Impressionist painter. Pupil of Corot. **9, 247**

Pollaiuolo, Antonio (*b. c.*1432 Florence, *d.*1498 Rome) and **Piero** (*b. c.*1441 Florence, *d.*1496 Rome). Brothers who were painters, sculptors, engravers and goldsmiths. No authenticated painting by Antonio, who was probably mainly a sculptor and goldsmith. **95**

Pollock, Jackson (*b.*1912 Cody, Wyoming, *d.*1956 East Hampton, NY). American Abstract Expressionist painter whose technique of splashing and dripping paint is known as 'action painting'. **296**

Polycletus (*fl. c.*450–420 BC). Greek sculptor, whose harmoniously proportioned figures embody the classical ideal of beauty. **31**

Polycletus the Younger (*fl.* mid-4th century BC). Greek architect thought to have designed the tholos and theatre at Epidauros. **35**

Polydoros (1st century BC). Greek sculptor said to have produced, with Hagesandros and Athenodoros, the famous Laocoön group (Vatican Museums). **36**

Pontormo, Jacopo da (1494 Pontormo, 1557 Florence). A leading Mannerist painter and draughtsman of the Florentine school. Pupil of Andrea del Sarto. **118**

Pöppelmann, Matthäus Daniel (*b.*1662 Herford, Westphalia, *d.*1736 Dresden). One of the great architects of the German Baroque; designed the Zwinger in Dresden. **189**

Poussin, Nicolas (*b.*1594 Villers, Normandy, *d.*1665 Rome). Greatest French exponent of classicism in the 17th century. Lived mainly in Rome. **196**

Pozzo, Andrea (*b.*1642 Trento, *d.*1709 Vienna). A major Italian decorative artist of the Baroque; a master of perspective and illusionism. **169**

Prandtauer, Jakob (*b.*1660 Stanz, Tyrol, *d.*1726 Sankt-Pölten, Lower Austria). Austrian Baroque architect of churches and monasteries; also sculptor. **188**

Praxiteles (1st half of 4th century BC). Greek sculptor; much copied by the Romans. **34**

Predis, Giovanni Ambrogio de (*b. c.*1455 Milan, *d. c.*1517 Milan). Italian painter; worked with Leonardo, whose close follower he was. **93**

Prendergast, Maurice (*b.*1859 St John's, Newfoundland, *d.*1924 New York). American painter of outdoor scenes; influenced by the Nabis. **303**

Primaticcio, Francesco (*b.*1504 Bologna, *d.*1570 Paris). Italian Mannerist painter, sculptor, architect and decorator; head of the First School of Fontainebleau. **155**

Prud'hon, Pierre-Paul (*b.*1758 Cluny, *d.*1823 Paris). French painter; much influenced by Correggio; link between Neoclassicism and Romanticism. **211**

Pucelle, Jean (*fl.* 1320s Paris). Important and innovative French painter; directed an active studio for illumination work in Paris. **64**

Puget, Pierre (*b.*1620 Séon, near Marseilles, *d.*1694 Marseilles). French sculptor who spent much time in Italy; pupil of Pietro da Cortona. **202**

Pugin, Augustus Welby Northmore (*b.*1812 London, *d.*1852 Ramsgate, Kent). British Neo-Gothic architect and writer on architecture. Helped with details on façade, and fitments, of Barry's Houses of Parliament. **227**

Puvis de Chavannes, Pierre (*b.*1824 Lyons, *d.*1898 Paris). French painter of large decorative murals; admired by Neo-Impressionists and Post-Impressionists. **245**

Raeburn, Sir Henry (*b.*1756 near Edinburgh, *d.*1823 Edinburgh). Scottish portrait painter; RA and King's Limner for Scotland. **222**

Ramsay, Allan (*b.*1713 Edinburgh, *d.*1784 Dover). Scottish portrait painter in the Italian Grand Manner; painter to George III. **216**

Raphael (*b.*1483 Urbino, *d.*1520 Rome). Raffaello Santi was one of the great painters of the High Renaissance; he brought classicism in the Renaissance to its height, as seen in his Madonnas, who embody the ideal classical beauty. **114, 115**

Rastrelli, Bartolomeo Francesco (*b.*1700 Paris, *d.*1771 St Petersburg). Baroque architect of Italian descent who spent his working life in St Petersburg; he remodelled most of the royal palaces. **224**

Rauschenberg, Robert (*b.*1925 Port Arthur, Texas). American painter; an early Pop artist. **306**

Redon, Odilon (*b.*1840 Bordeaux, *d.*1916 Paris). One of the principal French Symbolist painters and lithographers. **258**

Rembrandt Harmensz van Rijn (*b.*1606 Leiden, *d.*1669 Amsterdam). The greatest Dutch painter and graphic artist. From 1632 he lived in Amsterdam. He went bankrupt and died in poverty. **9, 178, 179**

Reni, Guido (*b.*1575 Bologna, *d.*1642 Bologna). Baroque painter immensely popular in his time. Influenced by the Carracci. **164**

Renoir, Pierre-Auguste (*b.*1841 Limoges, *d.*1919 Cagnes-sur-Mer). A leading Impressionist painter. Courbet was an early influence. After 1905 progressively crippled by arthritis. **248**

Reynolds, Sir Joshua (*b.*1723 Plympton, Devon, *d.*1792 London). One of the greatest British portrait painters. Studied in Rome and took up the Grand Manner of painting, which he espoused in his *Discourses*. First RA president. **220**

Ribalta, Francisco (*b.*1565 Solsona, *d.*1628 Valencia). Spanish realist painter whose lighting shows probable influence of Caravaggio. **158**

Ribera, Jusepe de (*b.*1591? Játiva, near Valencia, *d.*1652 Naples). Spanish painter who had settled in Naples by 1616 and was known there as 'Lo Spagnoletto'. Brutal realism and Caravaggesque chiaroscuro characterized his works. **190**

Ricci, Marco (*b.*1676 Belluno, *d.*1730 Venice). Venetian painter and etcher of landscapes. Collaborated with his uncle, Sebastiano. **171**

Ricci, Sebastiano (*b.*1659 Belluno, *d.*1734 Venice). Venetian school, but travelled widely. Influenced by Correggio and Veronese among others. **171**

Riemenschneider, Tilman (*b. c.*1460 Osterode, *d.*1531 Würzburg). Important German Late Gothic sculptor. He worked mainly in wood. **145**
Rigaud, Hyacinthe (*b.*1659 Perpignan, *d.*1743 Paris). Principal portraitist under Louis XIV. **204**
Riley, Bridget (*b.*1931 London). British Op artist; influenced by Vasarély. **305**
Rizzo, Antonio (*b. c.*1430 Verona, *d.*1499/1500 Foligno, near Perugia). Sculptor and architect of the Venetian school. **93**
Robbia, Andrea della (*b.*1435, *d.*1525). Nephew and assistant of Luca della Robbia, he carried on his uncle's business of making glazed terracotta works. **87**
Robbia, Luca della (*b.*1399/1400 Florence, *d.*1482 Florence). One of the most innovative sculptors of the 15th century, best known for his glazed terracotta work, usually with white figures against a blue background. **85**
Robert, Hubert (*b.*1733 Paris, *d.*1808 Paris). French painter of views with ruins in the style of Piranesi and Panini. **208**
Roberti, Ercole de' (*b. c.*1450 Ferrara, *d.*1496 Ferrara). Ferrarese painter who also worked in Bologna; pupil and assistant of Francesco del Cossa. **93**
Rodin, Auguste (*b.*1840 Paris, *d.*1917 Mendon). Outstanding French sculptor of the 19th century. **255**
Romney, George (*b.*1734 Dalton-in-Furness, Lancs, *d.*1802 Kendal, Westmorland). English portrait painter; best known are his portraits of Lady Hamilton. **222**
Root, John Wellborn (*b.*1850 Lumpkin, Ga, *d.*1891 Chicago). American architect; collaborated with Burnham. **286**
Rosenquist, James (*b.*1933 Grand Forks, N.D.). American Pop artist; his works are characterized by their use of every-day objects and photographic blow-ups. **306**
Roslin, Alexandre (*b.*1718 Malmö, *d.*1793 Paris). Swedish portrait painter who lived in France from 1752. **208**
Rossellino, Antonio (*b.*1427 Settignano, *d. c.*1479 Florence). Important Renaissance sculptor. **92**
Rossellino, Bernardo (*b.*1409 Settignano, *d.*1464 Florence). Architect and sculptor; assistant to Alberti; teacher of his brother, Antonio, and of Desiderio da Settignano. **89**
Rossetti, Dante Gabriel (*b.*1828 London, *d.*1882 Birchington-on-Sea, Kent). Painter and poet; one of the founders of the Pre-Raphaelite Brotherhood. **232**
Rosso, Giovanni Battista (*b.*1494 Florence, *d.*1540 Paris). Called Rosso Fiorentino, he was a founder of Italian Mannerism, seen in his elongated figures and anti-classical style. **118**
Rothko, Mark (*b.*1903 Dvinsk, Latvia, *d.*1970 New York). American abstract painter whose canvases are usually made up of bands of colour. **304**
Rouault, Georges (*b.*1871 Paris, *d.*1958 Paris). French Expressionist painter and engraver of chiefly religious pictures; pupil of Gustave Moreau and influenced by the Fauves. **279**
Rousseau, Henri (*b.*1844 Laval, Mayenne, *d.*1910 Paris). Called 'Le Douanier' because he was a toll inspector, he is the most important modern primitive painter. **245**
Rousseau, Théodore (*b.*1812 Paris, *d.*1867 Barbizon). Leader of the Barbizon school of landscape painters. **244**
Rowlandson, Thomas (*b.*1756 London, *d.*1827 London). Major British draughtsman and caricaturist of his time; his style was close to French Rococo. **216**
Rubens, Sir Peter Paul (*b.*1577 Siegen, Westphalia, *d.*1640 Antwerp). One of the most important painters of northern Europe. He lived chiefly in Antwerp after 1587 except for some years in Italy and diplomatic missions to several countries, including England. He was deeply influenced by Italian art, and introduced the Baroque style to the north. **174, 175**
Ruisdael, Jacob van (*b.*1628/9 Haarlem, *d.*1682 Amsterdam?). The greatest of the Dutch landscape painters and a strong influence on 19th-century landscape painting. **182**
Runge, Philipp Otto (*b.*1777 Wolgast, Mecklenburg, *d.*1810 Hamburg). A leading German Romantic painter; also a poet. **238**
Ruysdael, Salomon van (*b.*1600/3 Naarden, *d.*1670 Haarlem). Dutch landscape painter; uncle and probably teacher of Jacob van Ruisdael. **183**
Sacchi, Andrea (*b.*1599/1600 Rome or Fermo, *d.*1661 Rome). Italian painter; represented the classical tradition in Roman Baroque painting. **165**
Saenredam, Pieter Jansz (*b.*1597 Assendelft, *d.*1665 Haarlem). Dutch painter of church interiors and topographical views. **180**
Sangallo, Giuliano da (*b.*1445 Florence, *d.*1516 Florence). Architect of the Early Renaissance; follower of Brunelleschi; also sculptor and military engineer; identified the Laocoön group when it was excavated (1506). **116**
Sangallo the Younger, Antonio da (*b.*1485 Florence, *d.*1546 Terni). A leading architect of the High Renaissance in Rome; nephew of Giuliano da Sangallo. **116**
Sansovino, Andrea (*b. c.*1467 Monte S. Savino, near Arezzo, *d.*1529 Monte S. Savino). Italian sculptor; probably a pupil of Antonio Pollaiuolo. **120**
Sansovino, Jacopo (*b.*1486 Florence, *d.*1570 Venice). Sculptor and architect; introduced the High Renaissance to Venice; a pupil of Andrea Sansovino, whose name he took. **116**
Sant'Elia, Antonio (*b.*1888 Como, *d.*1916 Monfalcone, Italy). Italian Futurist architect; killed in action before any of his drawings could be realized. **289**
Sargent, John Singer (*b.*1856 Florence, *d.*1925 London). American painter who lived mainly in England; best known for his portraits. **237**
Sassetta (*b.*1392?, *d.*1450 Siena). A major Sienese painter of the 15th century; he largely continued the Sienese Gothic style of painting. **94**
Scamozzi, Vincenzo (*b.*1552 Vicenza, *d.*1616 Venice). Architect much influenced by Palladio. **128**
Schedoni, Bartolomeo (*b.*1578 Modena, *d.*1615 Parma). Italian painter active mainly in Parma; influenced by Correggio and Caravaggio. **162**
Schiele, Egon (*b.*1890 Tulln, Austria, *d.*1918 Vienna). Austrian Expressionist painter; influenced by Klimt. **271**
Schinkel, Karl Friedrich (*b.*1781 Neuruppin, Prussia, *d.*1841 Berlin). The major German architect of the 19th century; most of his buildings are in a classical Greek style. **235**
Schlüter, Andreas (*b.*1662/9 Danzig or Hamburg, *d.*1760 St Petersburg). A leading German Baroque sculptor and architect. **187**
Schmidt-Rottluff, Karl (*b.*1884 Rottluff, Saxony, *d.*1976). German Expressionist painter and graphic artist; a founder of the *Brücke*. **267**
Schongauer, Martin (*b. c.*1450 Colmar?, *d.*1491 Breisach). German engraver and painter; influenced by Rogier van der Weyden and other Netherlanders. **144**
Schwitters, Kurt (*b.*1887 Hanover, *d.*1948 Ambleside, Westmorland). German painter; on the fringe of Dada, he invented *Merz* pictures, which are collages of discarded items such as rags, paper, bits of wire, etc. **290**
Scorel, Jan van (*b.*1495 Schoorl, *d.*1562 Utrecht). Dutch painter; also architect and engineer. Spent several years in Italy. **138**
Scott, Samuel (*b. c.*1702 London, *d.*1772 Bath). English marine painter in the tradition of the Van de Veldes. **216**
Sebastiano del Piombo (*b. c.*1485 Venice, *d.*1547 Rome). Venetian painter; deeply influenced by Giorgione; from 1511 in Rome, where he was influenced by Raphael and Michelangelo. **126**
Segantini, Giovanni (*b.*1858 Arco, near Trento, *d.*1899 The Engadine). Italian painter; his best works are landscapes of the Swiss Alps. **226**
Seghers, Hercules Pietersz (*b.*1589/90 Haarlem?, *d.*1633/8 The Hague or Amsterdam). Dutch landscape painter and etcher; important figure in the development of Dutch landscape painting. **180**
Semper, Gottfried (*b.*1803 Hamburg, *d.*1879 Rome). A leading German architect of the 19th century; his most famous works are in Dresden. **235**
Seurat, Georges (*b.*1859 Paris, *d.*1891 Paris). The most important of the Neo-Impressionist painters. His theories found expression in the Societé des Artistes Indépendants, founded in 1884. **251**
Severini, Gino (*b.*1883 Cortona, *d.*1966 Paris). Italian painter; an original Futurist, he moved to Cubism; also sculptor and illustrator. **289**
Shahn, Ben (*b.*1898 Kovno, Lithuania, *d.*1969 New York). American painter (emigrated in 1906); most of his works have a social message. **303**
Sickert, Walter Richard (*b.*1860 Munich, *d.*1942 Bathampton, near Bath). English genre and portrait painter. Deeply influenced by Degas; favourite subjects were London music-hall scenes. **234**
Signac, Paul (*b.*1863 Paris, *d.*1935 Paris). Neo-Impressionist and pointillist painter; follower of Seurat, whose Neo-Impressionist ideas he carried on after Seurat's death. **251**
Signorelli, Luca (*b.*1441? Cortona, Tuscany, *d.*1523 Cortona). Important Tuscany painter; his dramatic works influenced Michelangelo. Best known are his frescoes in Orvieto Cathedral. **102**
Simone Martini (*b. c.*1284 Siena, *d.*1344 Avignon). One of the great Sienese masters to follow Duccio, whose pupil he was. Also influenced by Giotto. **79**
Sisley, Alfred (*b.*1839 Paris, *d.*1899 Moret-sur-Loing). French Impressionist landscape painter born of British parents. **247**
Sluter, Claes (*b. c.*1350 Haarlem, *d.*1405/6 Dijon). Realist sculptor whose works were a departure from the Gothic tradition; active chiefly in Burgundy. **134**
Smith, Sir Matthew (*b.*1879 Halifax, Yorks, *d.*1959 London). English painter who lived much in France. Deeply influenced by the Fauves. **291**
Snyders, Frans (*b.*1579 Antwerp, *d.*1657 Antwerp). Painter of animal still lifes and hunting scenes. **180**
Soane, Sir John (*b.*1753 Goring-on-Thames, Oxon, *d.*1837 London). English architect of great originality; his style was basically Neoclassical. **227**
Sodoma (*b.*1477 Vercelli, *d.*1549 Siena). Giovanni Antonio Bazzi, called 'Il Sodoma', was a painter active chiefly in Siena; influenced by Signorelli, Raphael and Leonardo. **126**
Solari, Andrea (*b. c.*1470 Milan, *d.*1524). Painter active mainly in Milan and Venice. Influenced by Leonardo and by the Venetian school. **103**
Solari, Cristoforo (*b. c.*1460 Angera, Lago Maggiore, *d. c.*1527 Milan). Sculptor and architect; brother of Andrea Solari. **102**
Soutine, Chaïm (*b.*1894 near Minsk, *d.*1943 Paris). Russian Lithuanian painter of distorted, morbid works; lived in France from 1911. **278**
Staël, Nicholas de (*b.*1914 St Petersburg, *d.*1955 Antibes). French abstract painter (left Russia in 1919); killed himself. **10, 261**
Steen, Jan (*b.*1625/6 Leiden, *d.*1679 Leiden). One of the greatest Dutch genre painters. **183**
Steer, Philip Wilson (*b.*1860 Birkenhead, Cheshire, *d.*1942 London). English landscape, genre and portrait painter; influenced by Degas and Impressionism. **234**
Stevens, Alfred (*b.*1817 Blandford, Dorset, *d.*1875 London). English sculptor, portrait painter and draughtsman. **229**
Stone, Edward Durell (*b.*1902 Fayetville, Arkansas, *d.*1978). American architect. He designed the Museum of Modern Art in New York. **286**
Stoss, Veit (*b.*1438/47 Horb, Swabia, *d.*1533 Nuremberg). One of the leading German Late Gothic

sculptors; spent some years in Cracow, where he carved his famous high altar. **145**

Stuart, Gilbert (*b.*1755 North Kingstown, R.I., *d.*1828 Boston). American portrait painter. **223**

Stubbs, George (*b.*1724 Liverpool, *d.*1806 London). Gifted animal painter; taught and wrote on anatomy. **218**

Sullivan, Louis Henry (*b.*1856 Boston, *d.*1924 Chicago). American architect; pupil of Frank Lloyd Wright. **286**

Sutherland, Graham (*b.*1903 London). A leading 20th-century British painter; started as etcher and engraver. **301**

Tanguy, Yves (*b.*1900 Paris, *d.*1955 Woodbury, Conn). American Surrealist painter. **293**

Tatlin, Vladimir (*b.*1885 Ukraine, *d.*1953? Novodevichye). Russian painter and sculptor; founded Constructivism. **282**

Teniers the Younger, David (*b.*1610 Antwerp, *d.*1690 Brussels). Genre and landscape painter. Very popular in his day. **186**

Thorvaldsen, Bertel (*b.*1768 Copenhagen, *d.*1844 Copenhagen). Danish Neoclassical sculptor of international acclaim. **225, 235**

Tiepolo, Giovanni Battista (*b.*1696 Venice, *d.*1770 Madrid). Major Venetian decorative painter and exponent of the Rococo. **170**

Tintoretto, Jacopo (*b.*1518 Venice, *d.*1594 Venice). The leading Venetian Mannerist painter, and one of the greatest of Venetian artists. **124**

Titian (*b. c.*1489 Pieve di Cadore, Belluno, *d.*1576 Venice). Tiziano Vecellio was the greatest Venetian painter; Heir of Giorgione. In demand as portraitist from rulers, princes and popes. **122, 123**

Toulouse-Lautrec, Henri-Marie-Raymond de (*b.*1864 Albi, *d.*1901 Malromé, near Bordeaux). French painter, draughtsman and lithographer; actresses, dancers, prostitutes, clowns, café-concerts were principal subjects. **254**

Trumbull, John (*b.*1756 Lebanon, Conn, *d.*1843 New York). American history and portrait painter. **223**

Tura, Cosimo (*b. c.*1430 Ferrara, *d.*1495 Ferrara). First important Ferrarese painter; active at the Este court; influenced by Mantegna. **107**

Turner, Joseph Mallord William (*b.*1775 London, *d.*1851 London). One of the greatest English landscape painters; his works were romantic and dramatic and, in their light effects, anticipated Impressionism. **225, 231**

Uccello, Paolo (*b. c.*1397 Florence, *d.*1475 Florence). Painter and mosaicist; fascinated by geometry and perspective. **83**

Utrillo, Maurice (*b.*1883 Paris, *d.*1955 near Paris). Painter whose principal subjects were town views. **280**

Vanbrugh, Sir John (*b.*1664 London, *d.*1726 London). English Baroque architect who had no formal training; designed Blenheim Palace. **214**

Vasarély, Victor (*b.*1908 Pécs, Hungary). French painter, sculptor and graphic artist; his geometric forms inspired Op art. **305**

Vasari, Giorgio (*b.*1511 Arezzo, *d.*1574 Florence). Mannerist architect and painter, and a theoretician on art. Most famous for his book on the lives of artists (1550, enlarged 1568). **119**

Vassalletti, The (*fl. c.*1150–1250). Family of Cosmati artists; one or more of them decorated the cloister of S. Paolo fuori le Mura, Rome. **72**

Vecchietta (*b. c.*1412 near Siena, *d.*1480 Siena). Sienese sculptor, painter and architect; pupil of Sassetta. **93**

Velázquez, Diego Rodriquez de Silva y (*b.*1599 Seville, *d.*1660 Madrid). Baroque painter and one of the greatest Spanish artists; court painter in Madrid; influenced by Caravaggio and Rubens. **192, 193**

Velde the Younger, Willem van de (*b.*1633 Leiden, *d.*1707 London). Leading Dutch marine painter of the 17th century. Court painter in London. **186**

Vermeer, Johannes (*b.*1632 Delft, *d.*1675 Delft). One of the greatest Dutch painters; most of his small *oeuvre* (fewer than forty paintings) are interior scenes. **185**

Vernet, Claude-Joseph (*b.*1714 Avignon, *d.*1789 Paris). French painter of landscapes. Lived much in Italy. **208**

Veronese, Paolo (*b.*1528? Verona, *d.*1588 Venice). Settled in Venice about 1553 and was a leading Venetian painter and decorator; influenced by Titian. **125**

Verrocchio, Andrea del (*b.*1435 Florence, *d.*1488 Venice). Florentine sculptor, goldsmith and painter. Among his pupils were Leonardo and Perugino. **92**

Vigée-Lebrun, Élisabeth-Louise (*b.*1755 Paris, *d.*1842 Paris). French portrait painter; she painted about 20 portraits of Marie-Antoinette. **208**

Vignon, Pierre-Alexandre (*b.*1763 Paris, *d.*1828 Paris). French architect best known for his church of La Madeleine, Paris. **211**

Villard de Honnecourt (*fl.* 1225–35). French architect and draughtsman. **65**

Villon, Jacques (*b.*1875 Damville, *d.*1963 near Paris). French painter and engraver; brother of Marcel Duchamp and Raymond Duchamp-Villon. **280**

Vischer the Elder, Peter (*b. c.*1460, *d.*1529). Nuremberg sculptor; slight influence of Renaissance ideas seen in his work. His most famous work is the St Sebald shrine in Nuremberg. **147**

Vischer the Younger, Peter (*b.*1487, *d.*1528). Nuremberg sculptor; assisted his father, Peter Vischer the Elder, on the St Sebald shrine. **147**

Vivarini, Bartolomeo (*b. c.*1432 Murano, *d. c.*1499 Murano). Venetian painter; influenced by Mantegna. **83**

Vlaminck, Maurice de (*b.*1876 Paris, *d.*1958 Rueil-la-Gadelière). Fauve painter; influenced by Van Gogh and Cézanne. **266**

Vouet, Simon (*b.*1590 Paris, *d.*1649 Paris). French painter who spent many years in Italy and was a follower of Caravaggio; court painter in Paris; best works are in the classical Baroque style. **162, 199**

Vries, Adriaen de (*b. c.*1560 The Hague, *d.*1626 Prague). Late Mannerist sculptor; pupil of Giovanni Bologna in Italy; worked mainly in Prague. **142**

Vuillard, Édouard (*b.*1868 Cuiseaux, Saône-et-Loire, *d.*1940 La Baule). Intimist painter; a founder, with his close friend Bonnard, of the Nabis. **260**

Wagner, Otto (*b.*1841 near Vienna, *d.*1918 Vienna). Austrian architect; closely associated with the Vienna *Sezession.* **271**

Warhol, Andy (*b.*1930 Philadelphia). American Pop artist; also film-maker. **306**

Watteau, Antoine (*b.*1684 Valenciennes, *d.*1721 Nogent-sur-Marne). French painter of *fêtes galantes.* His style was much imitated. **8, 205**

Watts, George Frederic (*b.*1817 London, *d.*1904 Compton, Surrey). English painter of allegorical history subjects and portraits, and sculptor; RA. **233**

Wesselmann, Tom (*b.*1931 Cincinnati). American Pop artist. **306**

West, Benjamin (*b.*1738 Springfield, Pa, *d.*1820 London). American painter who lived in England from 1763. Best known for his history paintings. RA founder member. **223**

Weyden, Rogier van der (*b.*1399/1400 Tournai, *d.*1464 Brussels). One of the greatest painters of the early Netherlandish school; probably taught by Robert Campin; there are no signed pictures by him. **133**

Wheatley, Francis (*b.*1747 London, *d.*1801 London). English painter of portraits and rural scenes; spent some years in Dublin. RA. **219**

Whistler, James Abbott McNeill (*b.*1834 Lowell, Mass, *d.*1903 London). American painter and etcher who worked mainly in London and Paris; deeply influenced by Japanese art. **237**

Wilson, Richard (*b.*1714 Penegoes, Wales, *d.*1782 Llanberis, Wales). Painter of classical landscapes; influenced by Claude Lorrain; spent some years in Italy; RA founder member. **217**

Witte, Emanuel de (*b.*1616/18 Alkmaar, *d.*1692 Amsterdam). Dutch painter of church interiors, and domestic and market scenes with figures. **183**

Witz, Konrad (*b. c.*1400 Rottweil, Swabia, *d. c.*1445 Basle or Geneva). An important German painter, probably active chiefly in Basle; he rejected the style of International Gothic for one of realism. **143**

Wols (*b.*1913 Berlin, *d.*1951 Paris). Born Wolfgang Schulze, he was an abstract painter; he studied at the Bauhaus before going to Paris in 1933. **297**

Wood, Grant (*b.*1892 Anamosa, Iowa, *d.*1942 Iowa City). American painter; he portrayed Iowa people and places in a meticulous, detailed style derived from early German and Flemish masters, whom he admired. **303**

Wotruba, Fritz (*b.*1907 Vienna). Sculptor; began as engraver; most of his works are human figures, often treated abstractly. **299**

Wren, Sir Christopher (*b.*1632 East Knoyle, Wilts, *d.*1723 Hampton Court, Middlesex). Architect, scientist and mathematician; rebuilt 51 City of London churches and St Paul's Cathedral after the Great Fire in London, 1666; Surveyor-General. **213**

Wright, Frank Lloyd (*b.*1869 Rickland Center, Wis., *d.*1959 Phoenix, Arizona). Probably the greatest American architect. **259, 302**

Wright of Derby, Joseph (*b.*1734 Derby, *d.*1797 Derby). English painter of genre subjects and portraits; interested in light effects and scientific inquiry. **217**

Wyatt, James (*b.*1746 Weeford, Staffs, *d.*1813 Marlborough, Wilts). A successful and fashionable architect; designed in various styles, chiefly classical and Gothic. **215**

Wyeth, Andrew (*b.*1917 Chadds Ford, Pa). American painter; his style is realistic, with precise detail. **303**

Zimmermann, Dominikus (*b.*1685 near Wessobrunn, *d.*1766 Wies, Upper Bavaria). One of the great South German Baroque architects; trained as a stucco-worker. **189**

Zoffany, Johann (*b.*1733 near Frankfurt, *d.*1810 London). German-born English painter of conversation pieces, portraits and theatrical scenes. RA. **219**

Zoppo, Marco (*b. c.*1432 Cento, *d. c.*1478 Venice). Pupil of Squarcione of Padua; thereafter in Venice and Bologna. **83**

Zurbarán, Francisco de (*b.*1598 Fuente de Cantos, Badajoz, *d.*1664 Madrid). Spanish painter active in Seville and Madrid; his austere, realistic style lost popularity with the rise of Murillo's softer style, which he tried, not successfully, to imitate. He died in poverty. **190, 191**

Select bibliography

General

Arnheim, Rudolf, *Art and Visual Perception,* University of California Press, Berkeley, 1974

Baumgart, Fritz, *A History of Architectural Styles,* Praeger, New York, 1970

Clark, Kenneth, *Landscape into Art,* John Murray, London, 1949

———, *The Nude,* Penguin, Harmondsworth and Baltimore, 1970

Elsen, Albert E., *Purposes of Art,* 3rd edn, Holt, Rinehart and Winston, New York, 1972

Gombrich, Ernst H., *Art and Illusion,* 5th edn, Phaidon Press, Oxford, 1977

———, *The Story of Art,* 13th edn, Phaidon Press, Oxford, 1978

Janson, H. W., *A History of Art,* Thames and Hudson, London, 1977

Murray, Peter and Linda, *A Dictionary of Art and Artists,* 4th edn, Penguin Books, Harmondsworth and Baltimore, 1976

The Oxford Companion to Art, ed. H. Osborne, Oxford University Press, 1970

Panofsky, Erwin, *Meaning in the Visual Arts,* Anchor Books, Garden City, 1955

Read, Herbert E., *Art and Society,* 2nd edn, Pantheon Books, New York, 1950

Rosenberg, Harold, *The Anxious Object: Art Today and Its Audience,* Thames and Hudson, London, 1965

Part 1: Prehistoric Art

Childe, Vere Gordon, *The Dawn of European Civilization,* 6th edn, Knopf, New York, 1958

Leroi-Gourhan, André, *Treasures of Prehistoric Art,* Abrams, New York, 1967

Powell, Thomas G. E., *Prehistoric Art,* Thames and Hudson, London, 1966

Sandars, Nancy K., *Prehistoric Art in Europe,* Pelican History of Art, Penguin Books, Harmondsworth and Baltimore, 1968

Aldred, Cyril, *Art of Ancient Egypt,* 3 vols., Transatlantic, New York, 1974

Frankfort, Henri, *The Art and Architecture of the Ancient Orient,* rev. edn, Pelican History of Art, Penguin Books, Harmondsworth and Baltimore, 1971

Lange, Kurt, and Hirmer, Max, *Egypt,* 4th edn, Phaidon Press, London, 1968

Lloyd, Seton, *The Art of the Ancient Near East,* Thames and Hudson, London, 1961

Mellaart, James, *Earliest Civilizations of the Near East,* Thames and Hudson, London, 1965

Michalowski, Kazimierz, *Art of Ancient Egypt,* Thames and Hudson, London, 1969

Moortgat, Anton, *The Art of Ancient Mesopotamia,* Phaidon Press, London and New York, 1969

Poulsen, Vagn, *Egyptian Art,* New York Graphic Society, Greenwich, 1968

Smith, William Stevenson, *The Art and Architecture of Ancient Egypt,* Pelican History of Art, Penguin Books, Harmondsworth and Baltimore, 1965

Part 3: The Greek World

Ashmole, Bernard, *Architect and Sculptor in Classical Greece,* New York University Press, 1972

———, and Yalouris, Nicholas, *Olympia: The Sculptures of the Temple of Zeus,* Phaidon Press, London, 1967

Beazley, John D., and Ashmole, Bernard, *Greek Sculpture and Painting to the End of the Hellenistic Period,* Cambridge University Press, 1966

Boardman, John, *Greek Art,* rev. edn, Thames and Hudson, London, 1973

Brilliant, Richard, *Arts of the Ancient Greeks,* McGraw-Hill, New York, 1973

Charbonneaux, Jean, Martin, Roland, and Villard, François, *Archaic Greek Art,* Thames and Hudson, London, 1971

Demargne, Pierre, *Aegean Art: The Origins of Greek Art,* tr. Stuart Gilbert and James Emmons, Thames and Hudson, London, 1964

Havelock, Christine M., *Hellenistic Art,* New York Graphic Society, Greenwich, 1970, Phaidon Press, London, 1970

Higgins, Reynold, *Minoan and Mycenaean Art,* Thames and Hudson, London, 1967

Lawrence, Arnold W., *Greek Architecture,* 2nd edn, Pelican History of Art, Penguin Books, Harmondsworth and Baltimore, 1967

Marinatos, Spyridon N., and Hirmer, Max, *Crete and Mycenae,* Thames and Hudson, London, 1960

Richter, Gisela M. A., *A Handbook of Greek Art,* 6th edn, Phaidon Press, London, 1969

———, *The Sculpture and Sculptors of the Greeks,* 4th edn, rev., Yale University Press, New Haven, 1970

Robertson, C. M., *History of Greek Art,* 2 vols., Cambridge University Press, 1975

Vermeule, Emily, *Greece in the Bronze Age,* University of Chicago Press, 1972

Part 4: The Roman World and the Early Middle Ages

Beckwith, John, *The Art of Constantinople,* Phaidon Press, London, 1968

———, *Coptic Sculpture, 300–1300,* Tiranti, London, 1963

Brilliant, Richard, *Roman Art,* Phaidon Press, London, 1974

Brown, Frank E., *Roman Architecture,* Braziller, New York, 1961

Charles-Picard, Gilbert, *Roman Painting,* Pallas Library of Art, New York Graphic Society, Greenwich, 1970

Conant, Kenneth J., *Carolingian and Romanesque Architecture, 800–1200,* 3rd edn, Pelican History of Art, Penguin Books, Harmondsworth and Baltimore, 1973

Dodwell, Charles R., *Painting in Europe: 800–1200,* Pelican History of Art, Penguin Books, Harmondsworth and Baltimore, 1971

Grabar, André, *The Beginnings of Christian Art, 200–395,* tr. Stuart Gilbert and James Emmons, Thames and Hudson, London, 1967

Hanfmann, George M. A., *Roman Art,* New York Graphic Society, Greenwich, 1964

Hamilton, George Heard, *Art and Architecture of Russia,* Pelican History of Art, Penguin Books, Harmondsworth and Baltimore, 1954

Krautheimer, Richard, *Early Christian and Byzantine Architecture,* Pelican History of Art, Penguin Books, Harmondsworth and Baltimore, 1965

Lasko, Peter, *Ars Sacra, 800–1200,* Pelican History of Art, Penguin Books, Harmondsworth and Baltimore, 1972

Pevsner, Nikolaus, *An Outline of European Architecture,* 6th edn, Penguin Books, Harmondsworth and Baltimore, 1960

Rice, David Talbot, *Art of the Byzantine Era,* Thames and Hudson, London, 1966

Toynbee, Jocelyn M. C., *The Art of the Romans,* Thames and Hudson, London, 1965

Ward-Perkins, John B., *Roman Architecture,* Abrams, New York, 1977

Zarnecki, George, *Art of the Medieval World,* Abrams, New York, 1976

Part 5: The Late Middle Ages

Dupont, Jacques, and Gnudi, Cesare, *Gothic Painting,* Skira, Geneva, 1954

Evans, Joan, *Art in Medieval France,* Oxford University Press, Oxford, 1969

Focillon, Henri, *The Art of the West in the Middle Ages,* ed. Jean Bony, tr. Donald King, 2 vols., Phaidon Press, London and New York, 1963

Frankl, Paul, *Gothic Architecture,* tr. Dieter Pevsner, Pelican History of Art, Penguin Books, Harmondsworth and Baltimore, 1962

Grodecki, Louis, *Gothic Architecture,* Abrams, New York, 1977

Landolt, Hanspeter, *German Painting: The Late Middle Ages: 1350–1500,* Skira, Geneva, 1968

Male, Emile, *The Gothic Image: Religious Art in France of the Thirteenth Century,* tr. Dora Nussey, Harper, New York, 1958

Martindale, Andrew, *Gothic Art,* Thames and Hudson, London, 1967

Pope-Hennessy, John, *Italian Gothic Sculpture,* 2nd edn, Phaidon Press, London and New York, 1972

Rickert, Margaret, *Painting in Britain in the Middle Ages,* 2nd edn, Pelican History of Art, Penguin Books, Harmondsworth and Baltimore, 1965

Stone, Lawrence, *Sculpture in Britain: The Middle Ages,* 2nd edn, Pelican History of Art, Penguin Books, Harmondsworth and Baltimore, 1972

Timmers, J. J. M., *A Handbook of Romanesque Art,* Macmillan, New York, 1969

Webb, Geoffrey F., *Architecture in Britain: The Middle Ages,* 2nd edn, Pelican History of Art, Penguin Books, Harmondsworth and Baltimore, 1965

Zarnecki, George, *Romanesque Art,* Universe History of Art, Universe Books, New York, 1971

Part 6: The Italian Renaissance 1400–1600

Baxandall, Michael, *Painting and Experience in Fifteenth-Century Italy,* Clarendon Press, Oxford, 1972

Berenson, Bernard, *Italian Painters of the Renaissance,* Phaidon Press, London, 1967

Burckhardt, Jakob, *The Civilization of the Renaissance in Italy,* tr. S. G. C. Middlemore, Phaidon Press, London, 1950

Cellini, Benvenuto, *Autobiography,* ed. John Pope-Hennessy, Phaidon Press, London, 1960

Clark, Kenneth, *Leonardo da Vinci,* rev. edn, Penguin Books, Harmondsworth and Baltimore, 1967

Freedberg, Sydney J., *Painting in Italy, 1500–1600,* Pelican History of Art, Penguin Books, Harmondsworth and Baltimore, 1971

Gilbert, Creighton, *History of Renaissance Art Throughout Europe: Painting, Sculpture, Architecture,* Abrams, New York, 1973

Hartt, Frederick, *History of Italian Renaissance Art,* Thames and Hudson, London, 1971

Hibbard, Howard, *Michelangelo,* Penguin Books, Harmondsworth and Baltimore, 1978 evey, Michael, *High Renaissance, Style and Civilization,* Penguin Books, Harmondsworth and Baltimore, 1975

urray, Peter, *The Architecture of the Italian Renaissance,* Thames and Hudson, London, 1969

aatz, Walter, *The Arts of the Italian Renaissance: Painting, Sculpture, Architecture, Decorative Arts,* Abrams, New York, 1976

ater, Walter, *Renaissance,* Fontana, 1967

ope-Hennessy, John, *Italian High Renaissance and Baroque Sculpture,* Phaidon Press, London and New York, 1971

———, *Italian Renaissance Sculpture,* Phaidon Press, London and New York, 1971

eymour, Charles, Jr., *Sculpture in Italy, 1400–1500,* Pelican History of Art, Penguin Books, Harmondsworth and Baltimore, 1966

hearman, John, *Mannerism, Style and Civilization,* Penguin Books, Harmondsworth and Baltimore, 1967

asari, Giorgio, *The Lives of the Artists,* Penguin Books, Harmondsworth and Baltimore, 1970

/hite, John, *Art and Architecture in Italy, 1250–1400,* Pelican History of Art, Penguin Books, Harmondsworth and Baltimore, 1970

/ittkower, Rudolf, *Architectural Principles in the Age of Humanism,* Random House, New York, 1965

/ölfflin, Heinrich, *Classic Art: An Introduction to the Italian Renaissance,* 3rd edn, Phaidon Press, London and New York, 1968

art 7: The Renaissance outside Italy 1400–1600

enesch, Otto, *The Art of the Renaissance in Northern Europe,* rev. edn, Phaidon Press, London, 1965

lunt, Anthony, *Art and Architecture in France, 1500–1700,* 2nd edn, Pelican History of Art, Penguin Books, Harmondsworth and Baltimore, 1970

avies, Martin, *Rogier van der Weyden,* an Essay with a Critical Catalogue of Paintings, Phaidon Press, London and New York, 1972

riedländer, Max J., *Early Netherlandish Painting,* 14 vols., tr. Heinz Norden, Praeger, New York, 1967–73

)sten, Gert von der, and Vey, Horst, *Painting and Sculpture in Germany and the Netherlands, 1500–1600,* Pelican History of Art, Penguin Books, Harmondsworth and Baltimore, 1969

anofsky, Erwin, *Albrecht Dürer,* 2 vols., 3rd edn, Princeton University Press, 1948

anofsky, Erwin, *Early Netherlandish Painting,* 2 vols., Harvard University Press, Cambridge, 1958

ummerson, John, *Architecture in Britain, 1530–1830,* 4th rev. edn, Pelican History of Art, Harmondsworth and Baltimore, 1969

Vaterhouse, Ellis, *Painting in Britain, 1530–1790,* 3rd edn, Pelican History of Art, Penguin Books, Harmondsworth and Baltimore, 1969

art 8: Europe and America 1600–1800

aunt, William, *The Great Century of British Painting: Hogarth to Turner,* Phaidon Press, London, 1971

romentin, Eugene, *The Masters of Past Time,* Phaidon Press, London, 1948

erson, Horst, and Ter Kuile, E. H., *Art and Architecture in Belgium, 1600–1800,* Pelican History of Art, Penguin Books, Harmondsworth and Baltimore, 1960

leld, Julius, and Posner, Donald, *Seventeenth and Eighteenth Century: Baroque Painting, Sculpture, Architecture,* Abrams, New York, 1971

laskell, Francis, *Patrons and Painters,* Chatto, London, 1963

lerrmann, Luke, *British Landscape Painting of the 18th Century,* Faber, London, 1973

Keutner, Herbert, *Sculpture: Renaissance to Rococo,* Vol. III, *A History of Western Sculpture,* Michael Joseph and Rainbird, 1969

Kubler, George A., and Soria, Martin, *Art and Architecture in Spain and Portugal and their American Dominions, 1500–1800.* Pelican History of Art, Penguin Books, Harmondsworth and Baltimore, 1959

Levey, Michael, *Painting in XVIII Century Venice,* Phaidon Press, 1967

Norberg-Schulz, Christian, *Baroque Architecture,* Abrams, New York, 1972

Rosenberg, Jakob, *Rembrandt, Life and Work,* 3rd edn, Phaidon Press, London, 1968

———, Slive, Seymour, and Ter Kuile, E. H., *Dutch Art and Architecture, 1600–1800,* rev. edn, Pelican History of Art, Penguin Books, Harmondsworth and Baltimore, 1972

Soehner, Halldor, and Schönberger, Arno, *The Rococo Age: Art and Civilization of the 18th Century,* McGraw-Hill, New York, 1960

Waterhouse, Ellis K., *Italian Baroque Painting,* Phaidon Press, Oxford, 1976

Wittkower, Rudolf, *Art and Architecture in Italy, 1600–1750,* 3rd edn, Pelican History of Art, Penguin Books, Harmondsworth and Baltimore, 1973

Part 9: Europe and America 1800–1900

Barker, Virgil, *American Painting, History and Interpretation,* Bonanza, New York, 1960

Clark, Kenneth, *The Gothic Revival,* John Murray, London, 1974

Friedlaender, Walter F., *From David to Delacroix,* Harvard University Press, Cambridge, 1952

Goncourt, Edmond de and Jules de, *French Eighteenth-Century Painters,* Phaidon Press, London, 1948

Hamilton, George Heard, *Nineteenth and Twentieth Century Art: Painting, Sculpture, Architecture,* Abrams, New York, 1970

Hitchcock, Henry-Russell, *Architecture: Nineteenth and Twentieth Centuries,* 2nd edn, Pelican History of Art, Penguin Books, Harmondsworth and Baltimore, 1971

Honour, Hugh, *Neoclassicism, Style and Civilization,* Penguin Books, Harmondsworth and Baltimore, 1968

———, *Romanticism,* Allen Lane, London, 1979

Licht, Fred, *Sculpture, 19th and 20th Century,* New York Graphic Society, Greenwich, 1967

Leslie, C. R., *Memoirs of the Life of John Constable,* Phaidon Press, London, 1971

McCoubrey, John, *American Art, 1700–1960: Sources and Documents,* Prentice-Hall, Englewood Cliffs, 1965

Madsen, Stephan T., *Art Nouveau,* McGraw-Hill, New York, 1967

Muller, Joseph-Emile, *Fauvism,* Praeger, New York, 1967

Nochlin, Linda, *Impressionism and Post Impressionism, 1874–1904: Sources and Documents,* Prentice-Hall, Englewood Cliffs, 1966

———, *Realism and Tradition in Art, 1848–1900: Sources and Documents,* Prentice-Hall, Englewood Cliffs, 1966

Novotny, Fritz, *Painting and Sculpture in Europe, 1780–1880,* Pelican History of Art, Penguin Books, Harmondsworth and Baltimore, 1960

Rewald, John, *The History of Impressionism,* 4th rev. edn, New York Graphic Society, for the Museum of Modern Art, New York, 1973

———, *Post-Impressionism from van Gogh to Gauguin,* 2nd edn, Museum of Modern Art, New York, 1962

Reynolds, Graham, *Victorian Painting,* Studio Vista, London, 1966

Rheims, Maurice, *The Flowering of Art Nouveau,* tr. Patrick Evans, Thames and Hudson, London, 1966

Schmutzler, Robert, *Art Nouveau,* tr. Edouard Roditi, Thames and Hudson, London, 1964

Selz, Peter, and Constantine, Mildred, eds. *Art Nouveau: Art and Design at the Turn of the Century,* Doubleday, Garden City, for the Museum of Modern Art, New York, 1960

Part 10: Europe and The Americas since 1900

Arnason, H. H., *History of Modern Art: Painting, Sculpture, Architecture,* 2nd edn, Thames and Hudson, London, 1977

Barr, Alfred H., Jr., ed., *Cubism and Abstract Art,* reprint of 1936 edn of the Museum of Modern Art, Arno Press, New York, 1966

———, ed., *Fantastic Art, Dada, Surrealism,* reprint of 1936 edn of the Museum of Modern Art, Arno Press, New York, 1969

Bayer, Herbert, *Bauhaus 1919–1928,* New York Graphic Society, for the Museum of Modern Art, New York, 1976

Bowness, Alan, *Modern European Art,* Thames and Hudson, London, 1972

Duthuit, Georges, *The Fauvist Painters,* Wittenborn, Schultz, New York, 1950

Encyclopedia of Modern Architecture, Thames and Hudson, London, 1963

Finch, Christopher, *Pop Art: The Object and the Image,* Dutton, New York, 1968

Fitch, James Marsden, *American Building,* 2nd edn, 2 vols., Houghton, Mifflin, Boston, 1966–72

Fry, Edward F., *Cubism,* Thames and Hudson, London, 1966

Geldzahler, Henry, *American Painting in the Twentieth Century,* Metropolitan Museum of Art, New York, 1965

Golding, John, *Cubism: A History and an Analysis, 1907–1914,* rev. edn, Boston Book and Art Shop, 1968

Goldwater, Robert J., *Primitivism in Modern Art,* rev. edn, Vintage Books, New York, 1967

Gray, Camilla, *The Russian Experiment in Art, 1863–1922,* Thames and Hudson, London, 1971

Gropius, Walter, *Scope of Total Architecture,* Harper, New York, 1954

Haftmann, Werner, *Painting in the Twentieth Century,* expanded edn, 2 vols., Praeger, New York, 1965

Hitchcock, Henry-Russell, *Architecture: Nineteenth and Twentieth Centuries,* Pelican History of Art, Penguin Books, Harmondsworth and Baltimore, 1971

Hunter, Sam, and Jacobus, John, *American Art of the Twentieth Century: Painting, Sculpture, Architecture,* Abrams, New York, 1973

Pevsner, Nikolaus, *The Sources of Modern Architecture and Design,* Thames and Hudson, London, 1968

Phaidon Dictionary of Twentieth-Century Art, Phaidon Press, Oxford, 1977

Roh, Franz, *German Art in the 20th Century,* Thames and Hudson, London, 1968

Rose, Barbara, *American Art Since 1900,* rev. edn, Thames and Hudson, London, 1975

Rosenbaum, Robert, *Cubism and Twentieth-Century Art,* Abrams, New York, 1968

Sandler, Irving, *The Triumph of American Painting: A History of Abstract Expressionism,* Praeger, New York, 1970

Tafuri, Manfredo, *Contemporary Architecture,* Abrams, New York, 1977

Index

Part 1

Part 2

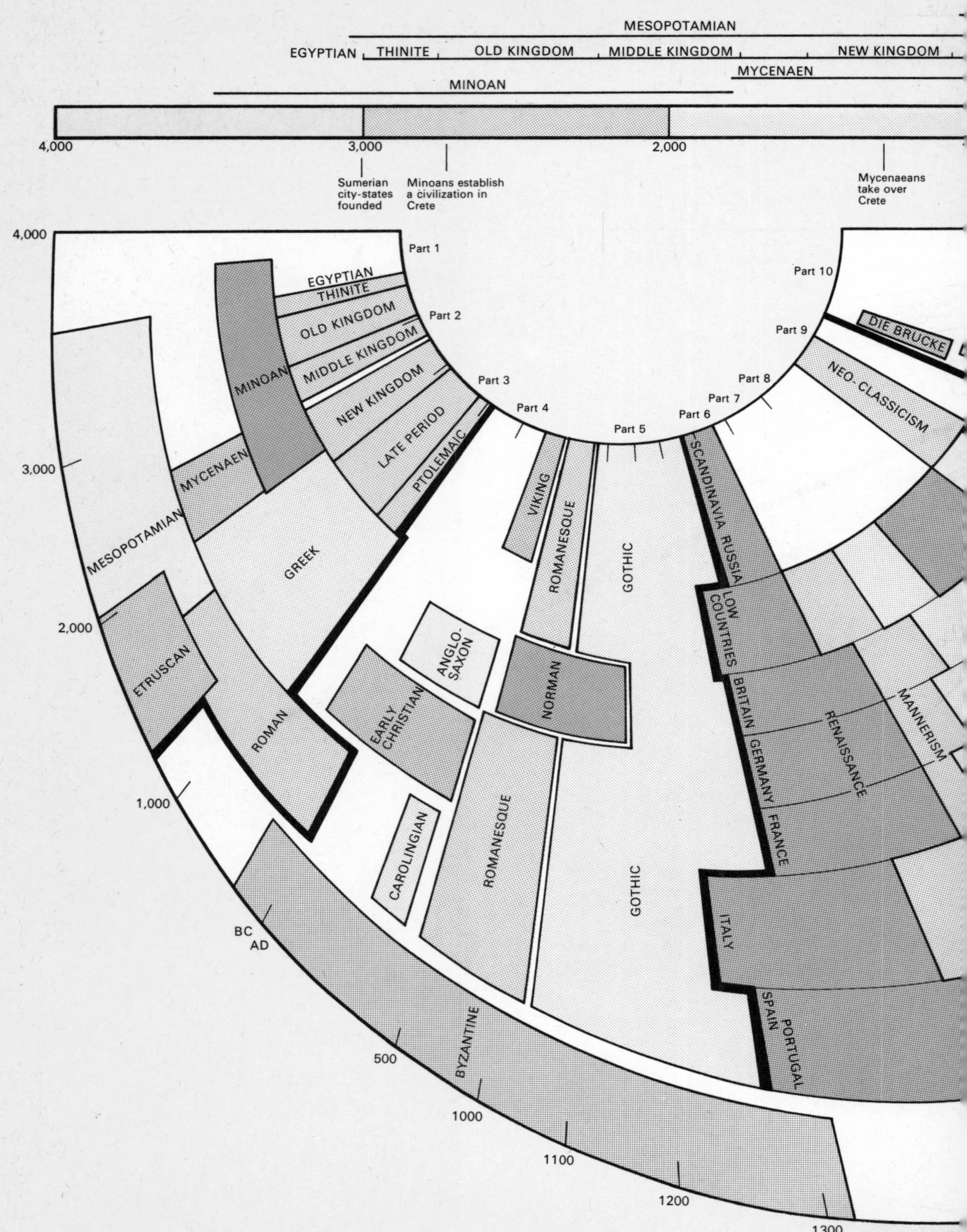

MESOPOTAMIAN
EGYPTIAN
THINITE
OLD KINGDOM
MIDDLE KINGDOM
NEW KINGDOM
MYCENAEN
MINOAN
4,000
3,000
2,000
Sumerian city-states founded
Minoans establish a civilization in Crete
Mycenaeans take over Crete
4,000
Part 1
EGYPTIAN
THINITE
OLD KINGDOM
Part 2
MIDDLE KINGDOM
NEW KINGDOM
LATE PERIOD
PTOLEMAIC
Part 3
Part 4
Part 5
Part 6
Part 7
Part 8
Part 9
Part 10
MINOAN
MYCENAEN
MESOPOTAMIAN
GREEK
ETRUSCAN
ROMAN
3,000
2,000
1,000
VIKING
ROMANESQUE
GOTHIC
ANGLO-SAXON
NORMAN
EARLY CHRISTIAN
CAROLINGIAN
ROMANESQUE
GOTHIC
SCANDINAVIA
RUSSIA
LOW COUNTRIES
BRITAIN
GERMANY
FRANCE
ITALY
SPAIN
PORTUGAL
RENAISSANCE
MANNERISM
NEO-CLASSICISM
DIE BRUCKE
BC
AD
BYZANTINE
500
1000
1100
1200
1300